Dear West Customer:

West Academic Publishing has changed the look of its American Casebook Series®.

In keeping with our efforts to promote sustainability, we have replaced our former covers with book covers that are more environmentally friendly. Our casebooks will now be covered in a 100% renewable natural fiber. In addition, we have migrated to an ink supplier that favors vegetable-based materials, such as soy.

Using soy inks and natural fibers to print our textbooks reduces VOC emissions. Moreover, our primary paper supplier is certified by the Forest Stewardship Council, which is testament to our commitment to conservation and responsible business management.

The new cover design has migrated from the long-standing brown cover to a contemporary charcoal fabric cover with silver-stamped lettering and black accents. Please know that inside the cover, our books continue to provide the same trusted content that you've come to expect from West.

We've retained the ample margins that you have told us you appreciate in our texts while moving to a new, larger font, improving readability. We hope that you will find these books a pleasing addition to your bookshelf.

Another visible change is that you will no longer see the brand name Thomson West on our print products. With the recent merger of Thomson and Reuters, I am pleased to announce that books published under the West Academic Publishing imprint will once again display the West brand.

It will likely be several years before all of our casebooks are published with the new cover and interior design. We ask for your patience as the new covers are rolled out on new and revised books knowing that behind both the new and old covers, you will find the finest in legal education materials for teaching and learning.

Thank you for your continued patronage of the West brand, which is both rooted in history and forward looking towards future innovations in legal education. We invite you to be a part of our next evolution.

Best regards,

Louis H. Higgins
Editor in Chief, West Academic Publishing

West's Law School Advisory Board

JESSE H. CHOPER
Professor of Law,
University of California, Berkeley

JOSHUA DRESSLER
Professor of Law, Michael E. Moritz College of Law,
The Ohio State University

YALE KAMISAR
Professor of Law, University of San Diego
Professor of Law, University of Michigan

MARY KAY KANE
Professor of Law, Chancellor and Dean Emeritus,
University of California,
Hastings College of the Law

LARRY D. KRAMER
Dean and Professor of Law, Stanford Law School

JONATHAN R. MACEY
Professor of Law, Yale Law School

ARTHUR R. MILLER
University Professor, New York University
Professor of Law Emeritus, Harvard University

GRANT S. NELSON
Professor of Law, Pepperdine University
Professor of Law Emeritus, University of California, Los Angeles

A. BENJAMIN SPENCER
Associate Professor of Law,
Washington & Lee University School of Law

JAMES J. WHITE
Professor of Law, University of Michigan

REMEDIES: PUBLIC AND PRIVATE

Fifth Edition

■ ■ ■

By

David I. Levine
*Professor of Law
University of California
Hastings College of the Law*

David J. Jung
*Professor of Law
University of California
Hastings College of the Law*

Tracy A. Thomas
*Professor of Law
The University of Akron
School of Law*

AMERICAN CASEBOOK SERIES®

A Thomson Reuters business

Mat #40635426

Thomson Reuters created this publication to provide you with accurate and authoritative information concerning the subject matter covered. However, this publication was not necessarily prepared by persons licensed to practice law in a particular jurisdiction. Thomson Reuters does not render legal or other professional advice, and this publication is not a substitute for the advice of an attorney. If you require legal or other expert advice, you should seek the services of a competent attorney or other professional.

American Casebook Series is a trademark registered in the U.S. Patent and Trademark Office.

COPYRIGHT © 1990, 1995 WEST PUBLISHING CO.
© West, a Thomson business, 2002, 2006
© 2009 Thomson Reuters

    610 Opperman Drive
    St. Paul, MN 55123
    1–800–313–9378

Printed in the United States of America

ISBN: 978–0–314–18410–8

For David Schoenbrod and Angus Macbeth, who started it all,
and
For Arie, Liora, Carlo and Mira (D.I.L.)
For Grady and Brennan (D.J.J.)
For Steve, Peter, and Caroline (T.A.T.)

*

PREFACE TO THE FIFTH EDITION

Three thousand years ago in *The Illiad*, Homer wrote of remedies. Describing a scene on Achilles' fabulous shield, Homer wrote:

> [A] quarrel had broken out and two men struggled
> over the blood-price for a kinsman just murdered.
> One declaimed in public, vowing payment in full—
> The other spurned him, he would not take a thing—
> so both men pressed for a judge to cut the knot.

A wrong had been done and the choice of a remedy—compensation, exile or execution—was left to judges:

> The crowd cheered on both, they took both sides,
> but heralds held them back as the city elders sat
> on polished stone benches, forming the sacred circle,
> grasping in hand the staffs of clear-voiced heralds,
> and each leapt to his feet to plead the case in turn,
> Two bars of solid gold shone on the ground before them,
> a prize for the judge who'd speak the straightest verdict.

Homer, "The Shield of Achilles," from The Illiad 483–484 (Robert Fagles, trans., 1990).

In a way, the story of the Trojan War is a parable about the price to be paid when remedies for wrongs are uncertain or lacking. Helen's abduction by Paris of Troy was a wrong in the eyes of both the Trojans and the Achaeans. The Trojans, however, were of two minds about whether to pay compensation or to return Helen, and so they provided no remedy at all. Denied a remedy, the Achaeans resorted to self help in the form of a bloody war. Then Agamemnon, the Achaean king, took the mistress of his most powerful warrior, Achilles, who refused to fight. When the sandal was on the other foot, the Achaeans recognized that the failure to remedy a wrong could bring bloody ruin. They offered to return Achilles' mistress and to pay splendid compensation. Achilles returned to the battle, and the Trojans paid the price.

Our purpose in writing this casebook is to help law students become lawyers and judges who "speak the straightest" on remedies. While they may not be able to expect "two bars of solid gold" as their reward, they can have the satisfaction of upholding a system of justice in which those who suffer wrongs have access to a remedy in a court of law. The ways in which we have pursued that purpose are described in the preface to the first edition. We remain committed to providing teachers and students with materials that are coherent, intellectually stimulating, and pedagogically sound. We also remain convinced that studying the way remedies operate in the public law and private law contexts is critical to a full understanding of the subject.

The Supreme Court of the United States has remained active in the remedies field, and those developments are well represented in this edition. Some recent developments the fifth edition includes are new decisions on preliminary and permanent injunctions, the common law and constitutional regulation of punitive damages, and declaratory relief. We have reorganized the chapter on punishment and punitive damages and placed it right behind the chapter on compensatory damages. Otherwise, we have not greatly changed the familiar structure and organization of the casebook. We have substituted new cases for older ones only when they represent important new developments or when experience has proven the replacements to be better teaching tools.

There are many people whom we would like to thank for their contributions to this edition. Our student assistants were invaluable; in particular, for this edition, we would like to acknowledge: Navjot S. Athwal, Elizabeth Davis, Shelley Kennedy, Kristina Melomed, and Brendan O'Brine. As in previous editions, Robert Lehrer, Esq., provided many thoughtful suggestions. We appreciate the research support we received from Akron and Hastings.

DIL
DJJ
TAT

April 2009

The line-up of authors in this edition represents the completion of the change of the guard, which started in 2002. David Schoenbrod and Angus Macbeth originated this book with their own teaching materials over twenty-five years ago. Their willingness to share their work product with a new assistant professor who was a stranger to them led to firm friendships, the creation of this casebook, and an ideal cross-country working relationship. After the publication of the third edition, however, they decided to bow out of the continued maintenance of the casebook; since then, they have contributed valuable suggestions and unwavering support. They, obviously, are not responsible for any errors that may have cropped up in this edition of the casebook. In order to help fill their large roles on this project, we invited Tracy A. Thomas to join the casebook after the publication of the fourth edition. Her knowledge and participation ensure that the casebook will be a mainstay in the field for many more years to come.

DIL
DJJ

PREFACE TO THE FIRST EDITION

We believe a remedies casebook should meet four needs:

First, a remedies book should cover the essential topics of remedies law. Most law schools offer a single remedies course which reviews the damages issues covered piecemeal in first-year courses, such as torts and contracts, and introduces restitution and equitable remedies. Most remedies casebooks cover this material exclusively from the perspective of private law litigation. Our book, as the title suggests, treats remedies in both public and private law cases. Remedies in public law cases are an important topic in practice, important to society, and indeed important to a full understanding of remedies in private law cases. Some existing remedies casebooks do make a bow in the direction of public law remedies, but they usually limit their coverage to the structural injunction, without considering how the full panoply of remedies—damages, injunctions, and restitution—can be applied to public law problems. Moreover, by focusing only on civil rights cases, those books don't do justice to the administrative and regulatory cases that students are far more likely to encounter once they are in practice. Finally, administrative law cases, particularly those enforcing regulatory prohibitions and correcting agency errors, often provide some of the best examples of courts trying to state and apply general remedial principles.

Second, a remedies book should treat the topic in a coherent way. In particular, it must be built around a perspective that the teacher can use to make a whole of the many elements that the remedies course combines. The traditional organization of a remedies book subordinates the remedy to the substantive law, classifying the material in whole or in part by cause of action: remedies for damage to chattel, remedies for damage to land, remedies for breach of contract, etc. We believe that there is more to be learned by adopting a transsubstantive approach to remedies. By organizing the material around the remedy, and not the substantive law, our materials allow the professor and the student to explore the concerns that are common to remedial issues in whatever substantive context they arise.

To offer an example, although the remedial problems in, say, a contracts case, a judicial review of administrative action, and a school desegregation case look quite different on the surface, the courts approaching these cases will share common institutional concerns—concerns about their ability to dictate wisely future conduct and the legitimacy of their doing so. Courts in each of these three kinds of cases are therefore inclined to use tactics designed to, in essence, remand the question of future conduct to the defendant. So the contracts remedy is likely to be damages rather than specific performance, the judicial review remedy is likely to be a remand to the agency, and the school desegregation remedy is likely to be a requirement that the school board design a plan to end the violation. Where such approaches result in harm to important interests, the courts become more intrusive, but usually only in graduated increments designed to minimize the impact on judicial capacity.

Third, a remedies book should offer intellectual stimulation to the students as well as the teacher. The remedies course can be exciting if it addresses the root questions and deadly dull if it does no more than rehearse doctrine. Our book confronts the root questions frontally and from the outset. Chapter one asks: What does it mean to remedy a wrong? How much discretion should a judge have? How should that discretion be exercised? Chapter two presents some of the rare opinions that openly address these questions. This material raises issues of legitimacy, comity, judicial competence and judicial convenience, which go far to explain judicial conduct in all areas of remedies.

We go on to relate these root questions to the material in the balance of the book, emphasizing material that is not usually covered in other remedies casebooks. For example, we have included a chapter which contrasts civil and criminal penalties, including punitive damages. This juxtaposition raises particularly exciting and sometimes disturbing questions about the use of judicial and legislative power to achieve remedial goals.

Fourth, a remedies book should teach well. Our concern with pedagogy is reflected in a number of features of the book.

> —*The book uses text and secondary sources to teach the basics.* The students in the remedies course, having already completed their first year, are entirely familiar with, if not jaded by, the case method and have encountered remedies issues in their first year courses. Using cases to teach them those basics that they can absorb by reading text wastes time better spent on the hard issues.
>
> —*The book uses problems.* We have used one basic fact pattern, styled *Country Lodge v. Miller,* in various problems throughout the casebook. Its recurrence helps to illustrate a variety of issues and encourages a comparison of remedial outcomes in various contexts. We have usually made *Country Lodge* a private law problem to prompt students to find transsubstantive remedial principles in the public law cases that the book frequently features. We have used other fact patterns in problems which did not lend themselves to the *Country Lodge* format, particularly where the problems are based on actual cases.
>
> —*We have resisted the temptation to follow the cases with a profusion of leading questions.* When we have information to convey or an opinion to offer, we make a statement. When we want students to ponder a question, we leave the question unanswered (except for a citation or two to helpful material). We have limited the number of questions so that students can reasonably be expected to read and consider all

of them with care, even though the professor undoubtedly will discuss only some in class.

Although the topic is old and enduring, courts and scholars have far to go in explaining how the law provides remedies. We have enjoyed writing and teaching from these materials because of a sense that we were creating a more coherent way of looking at an important, and all too often jumbled topic. We hope that those who use the book will find that the intellectual stimulation that we have enjoyed will rub off.

We have adopted several standard editorial conventions. In editing the judicial opinions and other material, we have eliminated nonessential citations and footnotes without so specifying. Numbered footnotes retain the original numbering. Author-supplied footnotes are lettered rather than numbered. Other omissions are indicated with a series of asterisks.

In the course of the preparation of these materials, we have had the benefit of the suggestions of many professional colleagues, including Philip P. Frickey, Quintin Johnstone, Mary Kay Kane, and John Sexton. We also wish to recognize the intellectual debt we owe to Dan Dobbs, Owen Fiss and Douglas Laycock. Many students who used these materials in earlier forms provided helpful suggestions. Our student assistants provided indispensable help. In particular, we wish to acknowledge Lara Bierman, John Cusker, Andres Diaz, Judy Ganley, James Gregory, David Hays, Stephanie Irey, Carol Johnston, Alice McGill, Eddie Schrock, Lupe Valencia, Seth Watkins, and Jennifer Ways. The technical assistance of Eric Noble and Linda Haumant was invaluable in preparing the manuscript. Hastings and New York Law School helped us to complete this project on schedule by supporting our research in a number of ways.

DS
New York, New York
AM
Washington, D.C.
DIL
DJJ
San Francisco, California

April, 1990

*

ACKNOWLEDGEMENTS

The authors wish to acknowledge the following permissions to reprint copyrighted material:

Lloyd C. Anderson, "Congressional Compromise Over the Jurisdiction of the Federal Courts: A New Threat to James Madison's Compromise," 39 Brandeis Law Journal 417 (2000–01).

Alexander Bickel, "The Least Dangerous Branch." Copyright © by Yale University Press. Reprinted by permission.

James J. Brown, "Collecting a Judgment," 13 Litigation 31 (1986).

Guido Calabresi & Douglas Melamed, "Property Rules, Liability Rules, and Inalienability: One View of the Cathedral," 85 Harv.L.Rev. 1089 (1972). Copyright © 1972 by the Harvard Law Review Association.

Abram Chayes, "The Role of the Judge in Public Law Litigation," 82 Harv.L.Rev. 1281 (1976). Copyright © 1976 by the Harvard Law Review Association.

Paul Dimond, "*Brown* and the Transformation of the Constitution: Concluding Remarks," 61 Fordham L.Rev. 63, 65–66 (1992).

Dan B. Dobbs, "Contempt of Court: A Survey." Copyright © 1971 by Cornell University and Dan B. Dobbs. All Rights Reserved. This article originally appeared in Volume 56, Number 2 of the Cornell Law Review at page 186.

John F. Dobbyn, "Contempt Power of the Equity Court over Outside Agitators," 8 St.Mary's L.J. 1,7 (1976).

Frank A. Easterbrook, "Civil Rights and Remedies," 14 Harv.J.L. & Pub.Pol. 103, 103–104 (1991).

Lisa W. Foderaro, "Threat of Yonkers Layoffs Jolts Foes of Housing Plan." Copyright © 1989 by New York Times Company. Reprinted by permission.

Daniel Friedmann, "Restitution of Benefits Obtained Through the Appropriation of Property or the Commission of a Wrong." Copyright © 1980 by the Directors of the Columbia Law Review Association, Inc. All Rights Reserved. This article originally appeared at 80 Colum.L.Rev. 504 (1980). Reprinted by permission.

Lon Fuller and William Perdue, "The Reliance Interest in Contract Damages." Reprinted by permission of The Yale Law Journal Company and Fred B. Rothman & Company from The Yale Law Journal, vol. 46, pp. 52–96.

Charles J. Goetz and Robert E. Scott, "Measuring Sellers' Damages: The Lost Profits Puzzle," 31 Stanford L.Rev. 323 (1979). Copyright © 1979 by the Board of Trustees for the Leland Stanford Junior University.

James A. Henderson & Richard A. Pearson, "Implementing Federal Environmental Policies: The Limits of Aspirational Commands." Copyright © 1978 by the Directors of the Columbia Law Review Association, Inc. All Rights Reserved. This article originally appeared at 78 Colum.L.Rev. 1429 (1978). Reprinted by permission.

Timothy S. Jost, "From *Swift* to *Stotts* & Beyond: Modification of Injunctions in the Federal Courts." Published originally in 64 Texas Law Review 1101 (1986). Copyright © 1986 by the Texas Law Review Association. Reprinted by permission.

Douglas Laycock, "Injunctions and the Irreparable Injury Rule." Published originally in 57 Texas Law Review 1065, 1071–72 (1979). Copyright © 1979 by the Texas Law Review Association. Reprinted by permission.

Douglas Laycock, "The Death of the Irreparable Injury Rule," 103 Harv. L.Rev. 687 (1990). Copyright © 1990 by the Harvard Law Review Association.

Douglas Laycock, "The Scope and Significance of Restitution." Published originally in 67 Tex.L.Rev. 1277 (1989). Copyright © 1989 by the Texas Law Review Association. Reprinted by permission.

John Leubsdorf, "The Standard for Preliminary Injunctions," 91 Harv. L.Rev. 525 (1978). Copyright © 1978 by the Harvard Law Review Association.

Murray Levine, Charles P. Ewing & David I. Levine, "The Use of Law for Prevention in the Public Interest," 5 Prevention In Human Services 241 (1987) published by The Haworth Press, Inc., 10 Alice Street, Binghamton, N.Y. 13904.

Michael Lottman, "Enforcement of Judicial Decrees: Now Comes the Hard Part," 1 Mental Disability Law Reporter 69 (1976).

Richard L. Marcus, "*Public Law Litigation* and Legal Scholarship." Reprinted by permission of the University of Michigan Journal of Law Reform from the University of Michigan Journal of Law Reform, Vol. 21, pp. 671–81.

Dale Oesterle, "Deficiencies of the Restitutionary Right to Trace Misappropriated Property in Equity and in UCC § 9–306," 68 Cornell Law Review 172, 198 (1983). Copyright © 1983 by Cornell University; All Rights Reserved.

Richard Posner, *Economic Analysis of Law* (7th ed.2007). Reprinted with permission of Aspen Publishers, Inc.

David R. Rosenberg, "The Causal Connection in Mass Exposure Cases: A Public Law Vision of the Tort System," 97 Harv.L.Rev. 849 (1984).

David Schoenbrod, "The Measure of an Injunction: A Principle to Replace Balancing the Equities and Tailoring the Remedy," 72 Minn. L.Rev. 627 (1988).

Peter H. Schuck, "The Role of Judges in Settling Complex Cases: The Agent Orange Example." Reprinted by permission of the University of Chicago Law Review from The University of Chicago Law Review, vol. 53, pp. 341–48.

Alan Schwartz, "The Case for Specific Performance." Reprinted by permission of The Yale Law Journal Company and Fred B. Rothman & Company from The Yale Law Journal, Vol. 89, pp. 271–306.

Peter Shane, "Rights, Remedies and Restraint." First printed in 64 Chi. Kent L.Rev. 531 (1988).

Peter Shane, "School Desegregation Remedies and the Fair Governance of School." Reprinted by permission of the University of Pennsylvania Law Review and Fred B. Rothman & Company from 132 U.Pa. L.Rev. 1041, 1065–66 (1984).

Justin Sweet, "Liquidated Damages in California." Copyright © 1972 by California Law Review, Inc. Reprinted from California Law Review, Vol. 60, No. 1, January 1972, pp. 84–146, by permission.

Juan Williams, "A Question of Fairness." Atlantic Monthly, February, 1987, at p. 70.

Donald H. Ziegler, "Rights Require Remedies: A New Approach to the Enforcement of Rights in the Federal Courts." Copyright © 1987 Hastings College of Law, reprinted from 38 Hastings L.J. 665 with permission.

"California's Collateral Source Rule and Plaintiffs Receipt of Uninsured Motorist Benefits." Copyright © 1986 Hastings College of Law, reprinted from 37 Hastings L.J. with permission.

"Developments in the Law—Injunctions," 78 Harv.L.Rev. 993 (1965). Copyright © 1965 by the Harvard Law Review Association.

"Interest as Damages in California," 5 UCLA L.Rev. 262 (1958).

Restatement of the Law, 2d, Contracts, copyright © 1981 by the American Law Institute; Restatement of the Law, Restitution, copyright © 1937 by the American Law Institute; Restatement of the Law, 2d, Torts, copyright © 1979 by the American Law Institute. Reprinted with the permission of The American Law Institute.

"Restitution: Concepts and Terms." Copyright © 1986 Hastings College of Law, reprinted from 37 Hastings L.J. 667–695 with permission.

"Special Project—The Remedial Process in Institutional Reform Litigation." Copyright © 1978 by the Directors of the Columbia Law Review Association, Inc. All Rights Reserved. This article originally appeared at 78 Colum.L.Rev. 784 (1978). Reprinted by permission.

"The Wheeling Bridge Exception: Reopening Executory Judgments of Article III Courts." Reprinted by permission of the University of Chicago Law Review from The University of Chicago Law Review, vol. 67, pp. 547, 560.

*

Summary of Contents

	Page
Preface to the Fifth Edition	v
Preface to the First Edition	vii
Acknowledgements	xi
Table of Cases	xxv

Chapter 1. Introduction to the Law of Remedies 1
A. A General Approach to Crafting a Remedy 2
B. Private Law and Public Law 4
C. "Where There's a Right, There's a Remedy"? 10

Chapter 2. The Nature, Availability, and Scope of Injunctions 33
A. The Nature of an Injunction 33
B. The Plaintiff's Rightful Position as the Measure of an Injunction 37
C. The Prerequisites for Injunctive Relief 54
D. Balancing the Equities 90
E. Specific Remedies Other Than Injunctions 182

Chapter 3. Procedures for Formulating, Administering, and Enforcing the Injunction 186
A. Obtaining Preliminary Injunctive Relief 186
B. Formulating and Administering the Injunction 212
C. Enforcement of the Decree 299

Chapter 4. Declaratory Judgment 415

Chapter 5. Damages 441
A. Introduction 441
B. The Basic Issues 456
C. An Overview of Tort Damages 484
D. An Overview of Contract Damages 564
E. Adjustments to the Damage Award 609

Chapter 6. Punishment and Punitive Damages 640
A. Distinguishing Civil and Criminal Punishment 640
B. Punitive Damages at Common Law 661
C. Constitutional Limitations on Punitive Damages 695

Chapter 7. Restitution and Restitutionary Remedies 717
A. Introduction 717
B. Restitution and Unsolicited Benefits 723
C. Restitution and Wrongfully Acquired Benefits 731
D. Restitution and Solicited Benefits 741
E. Equitable Restitutionary Remedies 759

Chapter 8. Collection of Monetary Judgments 787
A. Provisional Relief 787

	Page
B. Post-Judgment Relief	817
Chapter 9. Conduct of the Plaintiff: Bars to Obtaining Relief	**850**
A. Unclean Hands and In Pari Delicto	852
B. Estoppel	870
C. Laches and Statutes of Limitations	880
Chapter 10. Attorney's Fees	**900**
A. The Power of the Court to Award Attorney's Fees	901
B. The Parties That Congress Has Made Eligible for Attorney's Fees	913
C. The Measure of the Fees	930
D. Conflicts of Interest	966
APPENDIX: SELECTED FEDERAL RULES OF CIVIL PROCEDURE	975
INDEX	991

TABLE OF CONTENTS

	Page
PREFACE TO THE FIFTH EDITION	v
PREFACE TO THE FIRST EDITION	vii
ACKNOWLEDGEMENTS	xi
TABLE OF CASES	xxv

Chapter 1. Introduction to the Law of Remedies 1
A. A General Approach to Crafting a Remedy 2
    Problem: Country Lodge v. Miller Remedies in a Traditional Private Case 4
B. Private Law and Public Law 4
    Problem: Country Lodge v. Miller (Reprised) Remedies in a Public Law Case 5
    Abram Chayes, The Role of the Judge in Public Law Litigation 5
    Notes 8
C. "Where There's a Right, There's a Remedy"? 10
    Bivens v. Six Unknown Named Agents of Federal Bureau of Narcotics 12
    Notes 18
    Schweiker v. Chilicky 20
    Notes 26
    A Digression: Remedial Choice in the Statutory Context 28

Chapter 2. The Nature, Availability, and Scope of Injunctions ... 33
A. The Nature of an Injunction 33
    Problem: Country Lodge v. Miller (Reprised) The Choice Between an Injunction and Damages ... 33
B. The Plaintiff's Rightful Position as the Measure of an Injunction 37
    Problem: Country Lodge v. Miller (Reprised) Defining the Rightful Position ... 37
    Mt. Healthy City School District Board of Education v. Doyle 37
    Notes 40
    Note on Rightful Position as Reconsideration or Remand in Administrative Law ... 43
    Problem: The Racially Biased Election 45
    Rizzo v. Goode 46
    Notes 52
    Note on the Microsoft Antitrust Litigation 53
C. The Prerequisites for Injunctive Relief 54
    1. Threat of Harm 54
        Problem: Country Lodge v. Miller (Reprised) The Threat of Harm 54
        Hecht Co. v. Bowles 55
        Notes 59
        Note on Mootness and Ripeness 60
        City of Los Angeles v. Lyons 62
        Notes 71
        Note on Who Is Protected by an Injunction 75
        Note on the Relationship Between Threat of Harm and the Scope of an Injunction ... 76

		Page
C.	The Prerequisites for Injunctive Relief—Continued	
	2. Inadequate Remedy at Law	78
	Problem: Country Lodge v. Miller (Reprised) The Choice Between Legal and Equitable Remedies	78
	Note on the Maxims of Equity	79
	Note on the Declining Importance of the Inadequate Remedy at Law Rule	81
	Douglas Laycock, *The Death of the Irreparable Injury Rule*	82
	Note on Whether to Abandon the Inadequacy Requirement	83
	Alan Schwartz, *The Case for Specific Performance*	85
	Notes	87
	Note on Constitutional and Statutory Variations on the Inadequacy Requirement	88
D.	Balancing the Equities	90
	1. The Rationale for Balancing	90
	Problem: Country Lodge v. Miller (Reprised) Balancing the Equities	90
	Note on When Injunctions are Efficient	92
	eBay Inc. v. MercExchange, L.L.C.	95
	Notes	99
	2. Granting Less Than Plaintiff's Rightful Position	101
	Smith v. Staso Milling Co.	101
	Notes	103
	Brown v. Board of Education (Brown II)	107
	Notes	110
	Note on the Practicality of Enforcement	112
	Tennessee Valley Authority v. Hill	114
	Notes	121
	Weinberger v. Romero–Barcelo	122
	Notes	129
	David Schoenbrod, *The Measure of an Injunction: A Principle to Replace Balancing the Equities and Tailoring the Remedy*	131
	Note on Balancing in Administrative Enforcement	133
	3. Granting More Than Plaintiff's Rightful Position: Prophylaxis and Impossibility	134
	Problem: Country Lodge v. Miller (Reprised) Prophylactic Orders	134
	(A) The Abortion Protest Example	138
	Madsen v. Women's Health Center, Inc.	138
	Notes	152
	(B) The School Desegregation Example	155
	Swann v. Charlotte–Mecklenburg Board of Education	157
	Notes	162
	Missouri v. Jenkins (Jenkins III)	165
	Notes	179
E.	Specific Remedies Other Than Injunctions	182

Chapter 3. Procedures for Formulating, Administering, and Enforcing the Injunction — 186

A.	Obtaining Preliminary Injunctive Relief	186
	1. Types of Injunctions	186
	Problem: Unauthorized Merchants	189
	2. Standards for Granting Preliminary Relief	189
	Winter v. Natural Resources Defense Council	190
	Notes	201
	American Hospital Supply Corp. v. Hospital Products Ltd.	204
	Notes	207
	Problems	210

	Page
A. Obtaining Preliminary Injunctive Relief—Continued	
3. The Security Requirement	210
(A) The Amount of Security	210
(B) Collecting on the Security	212
B. Formulating and Administering the Injunction	212
Problem: Country Lodge v. Miller (Reprised) Drafting and Administering an Injunction	212
1. Drafting the Injunction	213
Portland Feminist Women's Health Center v. Advocates for Life, Inc.	213
Notes	216
2. Administering the Injunction	220
Problem: Country Lodge v. Miller (Reprised) Determining Compliance With an Injunction	220
James A. Henderson, Jr. & Richard A. Pearson, *Implementing Federal Environmental Policies: The Limits of Aspirational Commands*	221
Notes	224
Special Project—*The Remedial Process in Institutional Reform Litigation*	225
Notes	228
Illinois v. Costle	230
Notes	232
Murray Levine, Charles P. Ewing & David I. Levine, *The Use of Law for Prevention in the Public Interest*	233
Notes	238
Michael S. Lottman, *Enforcing Judicial Decrees: Now Comes the Hard Part*	239
Problems	240
3. Accommodating Changing Circumstances: Interpretation and Modification of the Decree	240
Timothy S. Jost, *From Swift to Stotts and Beyond: Modification of Injunctions in the Federal Courts*	241
Note on Interpretation and Modification of a Decree	243
Problems	244
Firefighters Local Union No. 1784 v. Stotts	245
Notes	254
Rufo v. Inmates of Suffolk County Jail	254
Notes	267
Note on Binding Successors in Office with a Consent Decree	269
4. Retaining and Closing a Case	271
(A) Judicial Direction to Terminate Jurisdiction	271
Problem: Country Lodge v. Miller (Reprised) Obtaining Release From an Injunction	271
Board of Education of Oklahoma City Public Schools v. Dowell	273
Notes	278
(B) Legislative Direction to Terminate Jurisdiction	281
Miller v. French	283
Notes	296
C. Enforcement of the Decree	299
1. The Contempt Power	301
Problem: Country Lodge v. Miller (Reprised) Civil or Criminal Contempt	301
Hicks on Behalf of Feiock v. Feiock	302
Notes on In Personam Versus In Rem Enforcement	309
Notes on the Classification of Contempt Proceedings	309
United Mine Workers v. Bagwell	311
More Notes on the Classification of Contempt Proceedings	322
Notes on the Elements of Contempt	323
Notes on Sanctions	325
Notes on Procedures	327

	Page
C. Enforcement of the Decree—Continued	
2. When Are Parties Bound?	328
Problem: Country Lodge v. Miller (Reprised) Violating an Anticipated Order	328
Griffin v. County School Board of Prince Edward County	329
Notes on Getting Tricky With a Court	333
3. The Collateral Bar Rule	336
Problem: Country Lodge v. Miller (Reprised) The Collateral Bar Rule	336
In re Providence Journal Co.	336
Notes on the Collateral Bar Rule	342
4. Who Is Bound?	346
Problem: Country Lodge v. Miller (Reprised) Injunctions That Coerce Persons Who Are Not Parties	346
State University of New York v. Denton	347
United States v. Hall	349
Notes on Injunctions Against Nonparties	353
Note on Washington v. Washington State Commercial Passenger Fishing Vessel Association	357
Note on Notice	358
Problem: Country Lodge v. Miller (Reprised) Injunctions That Harm Persons Who Are Not Proven Violators	359
Note on Non–Violators	359
Problem: Country Lodge v. Miller (Reprised) Injunctions That Harm Persons Who Are Not Proven Violators and Are Not Parties	361
Note on Martin v. Wilks	361
5. Enforcement Against the Government	364
Problem: Country Lodge v. Miller (Reprised) Injunctions That Require the Cooperation of Public Officials	364
Note on How Politics Complicates Enforcement	366
Note on How Immunity Complicates Enforcement	369
Missouri v. Jenkins (Jenkins II)	376
Notes	384
United States v. City of Yonkers	386
Spallone v. United States	394
Notes on Tactics to Override Legislative Decisions	402
Alexander Bickel, The Least Dangerous Branch	408
Notes	412
Chapter 4. Declaratory Judgment	**415**
Problem: Country Lodge v. Miller (Reprised) Declaratory Judgment	417
Medimmune, Inc. v. Genentech, Inc.	418
Notes	424
Morrison v. Parker	428
Notes	433
Note on Jurisdiction Over Declaratory Judgment Actions in Federal Court	436
Note on Reformation	439
Chapter 5. Damages	**441**
A. Introduction	441
Memphis Community School District v. Stachura	442
Notes	448
Note on Nominal Damages	450
Note on Monetary Relief in Law and Equity	452
Note on the Right to a Jury Trial	455
B. The Basic Issues	456
Problem: Country Lodge v. Miller (Reprised) The Damages Option	456
1. A Roadmap to Damages	457

	Page
B. The Basic Issues—Continued	
Charles McCormick, Handbook on the Law of Damages	457
Notes	458
Note on Election of Remedies	464
2. Value	466
Problems: Valuing the Plaintiff's Loss	467
State v. Bishop	467
Notes	470
Ohio v. Department of the Interior	472
Notes	481
C. An Overview of Tort Damages	484
Ayers v. Jackson Township	486
Notes	498
1. Elements of the Award	506
Bell v. City of Milwaukee	506
Notes	511
2. Measuring the Damages	515
Tullis v. Townley Engineering & Manufacturing Co.	516
Notes	519
Arpin v. United States	520
Notes	523
Walker v. Ritchie	528
Notes	531
3. Limits on Recovery: Foreseeable, Certain and Unavoidable	536
Steinhauser v. Hertz Corp.	536
Dillon v. Evanston Hospital	538
Notes	541
Munn v. Southern Health Plan, Inc.	543
Notes	548
4. Managing Damages Actions: The New Public Law Litigation?	552
Peter H. Schuck, The Role of Judges in Settling Complex Cases: The Agent Orange Example	553
Notes	557
Abram Chayes, The Role of the Judge in Public Law Litigation	557
Richard L. Marcus, Public Law Litigation and Legal Scholarship	557
Notes	561
D. An Overview of Contract Damages	564
1. The Basic Rules	564
Great American Music Machine, Inc. v. Mid–South Record Pressing Co.	564
Notes	571
Charles J. Goetz & Robert E. Scott, Measuring Sellers' Damages: The Lost Profits Puzzle	580
Justin Sweet, Liquidated Damages in California	582
Notes	585
2. Contract or Tort? The Uncertain Boundary	585
Freeman & Mills, Inc. v. Belcher Oil Co.	585
Notes	596
Evra Corp. v. Swiss Bank Corp.	600
Notes	607
E. Adjustments to the Damage Award	609
1. Time and Value: Prejudgment Interest	609
Problem: Country Lodge v. Miller (Reprised) Prejudgment Interest	609
Kansas v. Colorado	610
Notes	616
2. Time and Money: Discounting to Present Value	619
Jones & Laughlin Steel Corporation v. Pfeifer	619

	Page
E. Adjustments to the Damage Award—Continued	
Notes	627
Energy Capital Corp. v. United States	628
Notes	631
3. Taxation of Damage Awards	631
Commissioner of Internal Revenue v. Banks	631
Notes	636

Chapter 6. Punishment and Punitive Damages — 640

A. Distinguishing Civil and Criminal Punishment	640
Hudson v. United States	642
Notes	647
Notes on Differences Between Civil and Criminal Proceedings	648
United States v. Bajakajian	651
Notes	659
B. Punitive Damages at Common Law	661
Grimshaw v. Ford Motor Co.	663
Notes	672
Exxon Shipping Co. v. Baker	673
Notes	688
Notes on Tort Reform	689
Arbino v. Johnson & Johnson	691
C. Constitutional Limitations on Punitive Damages	695
State Farm Mutual Automobile Insurance Co. v. Campbell	696
Notes	707
Mathias v. Accor Economy Lodging, Inc.	711
Notes	716

Chapter 7. Restitution and Restitutionary Remedies — 717

A. Introduction	717
Restatement of Restitution	717
Douglas Laycock, The Scope and Significance of Restitution	717
Note on Approaching Restitution Cases	719
B. Restitution and Unsolicited Benefits	723
Problem: Country Lodge v. Miller (Reprised) Restitution for Benefits Conferred	723
Kossian v. American National Insurance Co.	723
Notes	726
C. Restitution and Wrongfully Acquired Benefits	731
Problem: Country Lodge v. Miller (Reprised) A Restitution Option?	731
Olwell v. Nye & Nissen	732
Notes	734
D. Restitution and Solicited Benefits	741
Hutchison v. Pyburn	741
Notes	743
EarthInfo, Inc. v. Hydrosphere Resource Consultants, Inc.	748
Notes	754
E. Equitable Restitutionary Remedies	759
Problem: Moore v. Regents of the University of California	759
Latham v. Father Divine	759
Snepp v. United States	760
Notes	765
Torres v. Eastlick (In Re North American Coin & Currency, Ltd.)	769
Notes	771
The Corporation of the President of the Church of Jesus Christ of Latter-Day Saints v. Jolley	774
Notes	775

	Page
E. Equitable Restitutionary Remedies—Continued	
In re Mushroom Transportation Co.	779
Notes	784
A Tracing Problem	786

Chapter 8. Collection of Monetary Judgments — 787

A. Provisional Relief — 787
    Connecticut v. Doehr — 788
    Notes — 799
    United States v. James Daniel Good Real Property — 803
    Notes — 816
B. Post-Judgment Relief — 817
    1. Basic Collection Strategy — 817
        James J. Brown, Collecting a Judgment — 817
        Notes — 820
        Kahn v. Berman — 823
        Notes — 828
    2. Exempt Property — 829
        Gutterman v. First National Bank of Anchorage — 829
        Notes — 834
        Laws v. Laws — 836
        Notes — 839
    3. Foreclosure Sales — 841
        Griggs v. Miller — 841
        Notes — 843
    4. Body Execution — 845
        Landrigan v. McElroy — 845
        Notes — 848

Chapter 9. Conduct of the Plaintiff: Bars to Obtaining Relief — 850

Problem: Country Lodge v. Miller (Reprised) Plaintiff's Conduct — 851
A. Unclean Hands and In Pari Delicto — 852
    Keystone Driller Co. v. General Excavator Co. — 853
    Notes — 856
    Clinton E. Worden & Co. v. California Fig Syrup Co. — 858
    Notes — 860
    Bateman Eichler, Hill Richards, Inc. v. Berner — 861
    Notes — 868
B. Estoppel — 870
    Johnson v. Williford — 870
    Notes — 874
    Note on the Government as Plaintiff — 878
C. Laches and Statutes of Limitations — 880
    TRW Inc. v. Andrews — 881
    Notes — 888
    Pro-Football, Inc. v. Harjo — 892
    Notes — 897

Chapter 10. Attorney's Fees — 900

A. The Power of the Court to Award Attorney's Fees — 901
    Problem: Country Lodge v. Miller (Reprised) Paying the Attorneys — 901
    Bernhard v. Farmers Insurance Exchange — 904
    Notes — 911
B. The Parties That Congress Has Made Eligible for Attorney's Fees — 913
    Buckhannon Board and Care Home, Inc. v. West Virginia Department of Health and Human Resources — 914
    Notes — 924

	Page
C. The Measure of the Fees	930
1. What Work Is Compensable?	931
Sullivan v. Hudson	931
Notes	938
2. The Rate of Compensation	941
(A) Superior Performance	942
(B) Risk of Loss Contingency	943
(C) Contingency Fee Contract	944
Notes	946
3. Applying the Lodestar Method	948
Gratz v. Bollinger	948
Notes	963
D. Conflicts of Interest	966
Evans v. Jeff D.	966
Notes	972
APPENDIX: SELECTED FEDERAL RULES OF CIVIL PROCEDURE	975
INDEX	991

TABLE OF CASES

The principal cases are in bold type. Cases cited or discussed in the text are in roman type. References are to pages. Cases cited in principal cases and within other quoted materials are not included.

Aacen v. San Juan County Sheriff's Dept., 944 F.2d 691 (10th Cir.1991), 836

Abbott v. Burke, 119 N.J. 287, 575 A.2d 359 (N.J.1990), 45

Abbott v. Burke, 100 N.J. 269, 495 A.2d 376 (N.J.1985), 374

Abbott Laboratories v. Gardner, 387 U.S. 136, 87 S.Ct. 1507, 18 L.Ed.2d 681 (1967), 428

A.B. Dick Co. v. Burroughs Corp., 798 F.2d 1392 (Fed.Cir.1986), 857

Ace v. Aetna Life Ins. Co., 139 F.3d 1241 (9th Cir.1998), 709

Acuna, People ex rel. Gallo v., 60 Cal.Rptr.2d 277, 929 P.2d 596 (Cal.1997), 153

Adarand Constructors, Inc. v. Peña, 515 U.S. 200, 115 S.Ct. 2097, 132 L.Ed.2d 158 (1995), 72, 181

Adarand Constructors, Inc. v. Slater, 528 U.S. 216, 120 S.Ct. 722, 145 L.Ed.2d 650 (2000), 72

Administrative Enterprises, United States v., 46 F.3d 670 (7th Cir.1995), 899

Aetna Life Ins. Co. v. Haworth, 300 U.S. 227, 57 S.Ct. 461, 81 L.Ed. 617 (1937), 425

Aetna Life Ins. Co. v. Haworth, 84 F.2d 695 (8th Cir.1936), 434

African–American Slave Descendants Litigation, In re, 471 F.3d 754 (7th Cir.2006), 777

Agee v. Central Intelligence Agency, 500 F.Supp. 506 (D.D.C.1980), 768

Agostini v. Felton, 521 U.S. 203, 117 S.Ct. 1997, 138 L.Ed.2d 391 (1997), 268

Air Crash At Little Rock, Arkansas, June 1, 1999, In re, 170 F.Supp.2d 861 (E.D.Ark. 2001), 524

Alabama v. Pugh, 438 U.S. 781, 98 S.Ct. 3057, 57 L.Ed.2d 1114 (1978), 372

Alabama Power Co. v. Costle, 636 F.2d 323 (D.C.Cir.1979), 134

Alcorn County, Miss. v. United States Interstate Supplies, Inc., 731 F.2d 1160 (5th Cir.1984), 748

Alden v. Maine, 527 U.S. 706, 119 S.Ct. 2240, 144 L.Ed.2d 636 (1999), 11

Alemite Mfg. v. Staff, 42 F.2d 832 (2nd Cir. 1930), 354

Alexander v. Riga, 208 F.3d 419 (3rd Cir.2000), 452

Alexander v. Sandoval, 532 U.S. 275, 121 S.Ct. 1511, 149 L.Ed.2d 517 (2001), 29

Alexander v. Scheid, 726 N.E.2d 272 (Ind. 2000), 515, 541

All Funds, United States v., 832 F.Supp. 542 (E.D.N.Y.1993), 786

Alliance to End Repression v. City of Chicago, 66 F.Supp.2d 899 (N.D.Ill.1999), 279

Alyeska Pipeline Service Co. v. Wilderness Society, 421 U.S. 240, 95 S.Ct. 1612, 44 L.Ed.2d 141 (1975), 903

Amchem Products, Inc. v. Windsor, 521 U.S. 591, 117 S.Ct. 2231, 138 L.Ed.2d 689 (1997), 562

American Airlines, Inc. v. Allied Pilots Ass'n, 228 F.3d 574 (5th Cir.2000), 325

American Civil Liberties Union v. National Sec. Agency, 493 F.3d 644 (6th Cir.2007), 72

American Cyanamid v. EPA, 810 F.2d 493 (5th Cir.1987), 224, 879

American Hosp. Supply Corp. v. Hospital Products Ltd., 780 F.2d 589 (7th Cir. 1986), **204**

American States Ins. Co. v. Bailey, 133 F.3d 363 (5th Cir.1998), 426, 434

American Tobacco Co., United States v., 221 U.S. 106, 31 S.Ct. 632, 55 L.Ed. 663 (1911), 229

A&M Records, Inc. v. Napster, Inc., 239 F.3d 1004 (9th Cir.2001), 188

Anchorage Asphalt Paving Co. v. Lewis, 629 P.2d 65 (Alaska 1981), 618

Anderson v. Dunn, 19 U.S. 204, 5 L.Ed. 242 (1821), 326

Anglin v. Department of Corrections, 160 Or. App. 463, 982 P.2d 547 (Or.App.1999), 913

Anzalone v. Kragness, 356 Ill.App.3d 365, 292 Ill.Dec. 331, 826 N.E.2d 472 (Ill.App. 1 Dist. 2005), 471

A.O. Smith Corp. v. F.T.C., 530 F.2d 515 (3rd Cir.1976), 428

Aptix Corp. v. Quickturn Design Systems, Inc., 269 F.3d 1369 (Fed.Cir.2001), 857

Arbino v. Johnson & Johnson, 116 Ohio St.3d 468, 880 N.E.2d 420 (Ohio 2007), 504, **691**

Arcambel v. Wiseman, 3 U.S. 306, 3 Dall. 306, 1 L.Ed. 613 (1796), 901

Ardestani v. I.N.S., 502 U.S. 129, 112 S.Ct. 515, 116 L.Ed.2d 496 (1991), 939

Arlington Cent. School Dist. Bd. of Educ. v. Murphy, 548 U.S. 291, 126 S.Ct. 2455, 165 L.Ed.2d 526 (2006), 942

Armour & Co., United States v., 402 U.S. 673, 91 S.Ct. 1752, 29 L.Ed.2d 256 (1971), 243

Arpin v. United States, 521 F.3d 769 (7th Cir.2008), **520**

Atlantic Sounding Co. v. Townsend, 496 F.3d 1282 (11th Cir.2007), 688

Atlantic States Legal Foundation v. Al Tech Specialty Steel Corp., 635 F.Supp. 284 (N.D.N.Y.1986), 891

Atlas Food Systems and Services, Inc. v. Crane Nat. Vendors, Inc., 99 F.3d 587 (4th Cir. 1996), 710

A.V. by Versace, Inc. v. Gianni Versace S.p.A., 87 F.Supp.2d 281 (S.D.N.Y.2000), 326

Ayers v. Jackson Tp., 106 N.J. 557, 525 A.2d 287 (N.J.1987), **486**

Ayers v. Robinson, 887 F.Supp. 1049 (N.D.Ill. 1995), 526

Aynes v. Space Guard Products, Inc., 201 F.R.D. 445 (S.D.Ind.2001), 925

Ayotte v. Planned Parenthood, 546 U.S. 320, 126 S.Ct. 961, 163 L.Ed.2d 812 (2006), 91

Badgley v. Santacroce, 800 F.2d 33 (2nd Cir. 1986), 402

Bajakajian, United States v., 524 U.S. 321, 118 S.Ct. 2028, 141 L.Ed.2d 314 (1998), 648, **651**

Baker v. General Motors Corp., 522 U.S. 222, 118 S.Ct. 657, 139 L.Ed.2d 580 (1998), 114, 363

Baker v. State, 170 Vt. 194, 744 A.2d 864 (Vt.1999), 372

Baker, United States v., 641 F.2d 1311 (9th Cir.1981), 359

Balance Dynamics Corp. v. Schmitt Industries, Inc., 204 F.3d 683 (6th Cir.2000), 738

Balboa Island Village Inn v. Lemen, 57 Cal. Rptr.3d 320, 156 P.3d 339 (Cal.2007), 155

Ballek, United States v., 170 F.3d 871 (9th Cir.1999), 849

Banco Cafetero Panama, United States v., 797 F.2d 1154 (2nd Cir.1986), 767, 786

Bank of Alex Brown v. Goldberg, 158 B.R. 188 (Bkrtcy.E.D.Cal.1993), 786

Banks, Commissioner v., 543 U.S. 426, 2005-15 I.R.B. 850, 125 S.Ct. 826, 160 L.Ed.2d 859 (2005), **631, **947

Barnes v. Gorman, 536 U.S. 181, 122 S.Ct. 2097, 153 L.Ed.2d 230 (2002), 672

BASF Corp. v. Symington, 50 F.3d 555 (8th Cir.1995), 434

Bateman Eichler, Hill Richards, Inc. v. Berner, 472 U.S. 299, 105 S.Ct. 2622, 86 L.Ed.2d 215 (1985), **861**

Baur v. Veneman, 352 F.3d 625 (2nd Cir.2003), 73

Bay Mills Indian Community, United States v., 692 F.Supp. 777 (W.D.Mich.1988), 80

Beacon Theatres, Inc. v. Westover, 359 U.S. 500, 79 S.Ct. 948, 3 L.Ed.2d 988 (1959), 417

Bearden v. Georgia, 461 U.S. 660, 103 S.Ct. 2064, 76 L.Ed.2d 221 (1983), 848

Bear Kaufman Realty, Inc. v. Spec Development, Inc., 268 Ill.App.3d 898, 206 Ill.Dec. 239, 645 N.E.2d 244 (Ill.App. 1 Dist.1994), 766

Bell v. City of Milwaukee, 746 F.2d 1205 (7th Cir.1984), **506**

Bell v. Southwell, 376 F.2d 659 (5th Cir.1967), 45

Bellis v. United States, 417 U.S. 85, 94 S.Ct. 2179, 40 L.Ed.2d 678 (1974), 650

Benjamin v. Jacobson, 172 F.3d 144 (2nd Cir. 1999), 298

Benjamin v. Malcolm, 156 F.R.D. 561 (S.D.N.Y. 1994), 269, 414

Bent v. Commissioner, 835 F.2d 67 (3rd Cir. 1987), 638

Bernhard v. Farmers Ins. Exchange, 915 P.2d 1285 (Colo.1996), **904**

Bernhardt v. Los Angeles County, 339 F.3d 920 (9th Cir.2003), 973

Berry v. Barbour, 279 P.2d 335 (Okla.1954), 729

BFP v. Resolution Trust Corp., 511 U.S. 531, 114 S.Ct. 1757, 128 L.Ed.2d 556 (1994), 844

Biegler v. American Family Mut. Ins. Co., 621 N.W.2d 592 (S.D.2001), 912

Birmingham Reverse Discrimination Employment Litigation, In re, 20 F.3d 1525 (11th Cir.1994), 363

Bishop, State v., 800 N.E.2d 918 (Ind.2003), **467**

Bivens v. Six Unknown Named Agents of Federal Bureau of Narcotics, 403 U.S. 388, 91 S.Ct. 1999, 29 L.Ed.2d 619 (1971), **12**

Blanchard v. Bergeron, 489 U.S. 87, 109 S.Ct. 939, 103 L.Ed.2d 67 (1989), 944

Blim v. Western Elec. Co., 731 F.2d 1473 (10th Cir.1984), 89

Blum v. Stenson, 465 U.S. 886, 104 S.Ct. 1541, 79 L.Ed.2d 891 (1984), 941

Blunt v. Little, 3 F.Cas. 760 (C.C.D.Mass. 1822), 709

B & M Homes v. Hogan, 376 So.2d 667 (Ala. 1979), 609

BMW of North America, Inc. v. Gore, 517 U.S. 559, 116 S.Ct. 1589, 134 L.Ed.2d 809 (1996), 707

Boardman v. Phipps, [1967] 2 A.C. 46 (House of Lords 1966), 739, 767

Board of Education v. Dowell, 498 U.S. 237, 111 S.Ct. 630, 112 L.Ed.2d 715 (1991), 163, **273**

Bodenhamer v. Patterson, 278 Or. 367, 563 P.2d 1212 (Or.1977), 748

Boehner v. McDermott, 541 F.Supp.2d 310 (D.D.C.2008), 948

Boerne, City of v. Flores, 521 U.S. 507, 117 S.Ct. 2157, 138 L.Ed.2d 624 (1997), 550

Bogan v. Scott–Harris, 523 U.S. 44, 118 S.Ct. 966, 140 L.Ed.2d 79 (1998), 406

Boomer v. Atlantic Cement Co., 26 N.Y.2d 219, 309 N.Y.S.2d 312, 257 N.E.2d 870 (N.Y. 1970), 104

Booth v. Churner, 532 U.S. 731, 121 S.Ct. 1819, 149 L.Ed.2d 958 (2001), 90

Borland By and Through Utah State Dept. of Social Services v. Chandler, 733 P.2d 144 (Utah 1987), 880

Bourdais v. New Orleans 485 F.3d 294 (5th Cir.2007), 41

Bowen v. City of New York, 476 U.S. 467, 106 S.Ct. 2022, 90 L.Ed.2d 462 (1986), 899

Bowen v. Massachusetts, 487 U.S. 879, 108 S.Ct. 2722, 101 L.Ed.2d 749 (1988), 89, 309

Bowers, United States v., 828 F.2d 1169 (6th Cir.1987), 366

Boyce's Ex'rs v. Grundy, 28 U.S. 210, 3 Pet. 210, 7 L.Ed. 655 (1830), 79

Brabson v. United States, 73 F.3d 1040 (10th Cir.1996), 639

Bradley v. University of Texas M.D. Anderson Cancer Center, 3 F.3d 922 (5th Cir.1993), 204

Brady v. Maryland, 373 U.S. 83, 83 S.Ct. 1194, 10 L.Ed.2d 215 (1963), 650

Brandau v. Kansas, 168 F.3d 1179 (10th Cir. 1999), 451

Brandt v. Superior Court, 210 Cal.Rptr. 211, 693 P.2d 796 (Cal.1985), 911

Bray v. Safeway Stores, 392 F.Supp. 851 (N.D.Cal.1975), 112

Brickwood Contractors, Inc. v. United States, 288 F.3d 1371 (Fed.Cir.2002), 926

Brinn v. Tidewater Transp. Dist. Com'n, 242 F.3d 227 (4th Cir.2001), 374

British Intern. Ins. Co. Ltd. v. Seguros La Republica, S.A., 212 F.3d 138 (2nd Cir. 2000), 802

Brockum Intern. v. Various John Does, 551 F.Supp. 1054 (E.D.Wis.1982), 189

Brooks v. Cook, 938 F.2d 1048 (9th Cir.1991), 928

Brown v. Board of Educ. (Brown II), 349 U.S. 294, 75 S.Ct. 753, 99 L.Ed. 1083 (1955), **107**

Brown v. Board of Educ. of Topeka, Shawnee County, Kan., 978 F.2d 585 (10th Cir.1992), 110

Brown v. Unified School Dist. No. 501, 56 F.Supp.2d 1212 (D.Kan.1999), 110, 112

Browning–Ferris Industries of Vermont, Inc. v. Kelco Disposal, Inc., 492 U.S. 257, 109 S.Ct. 2909, 106 L.Ed.2d 219 (1989), 659

Brunswick Corp. v. Jones, 784 F.2d 271 (7th Cir.1986), 208

Bryant, People v., 94 P.3d 624 (Colo.2004), 345

Buchwald v. Paramount Pictures Corp., 13 U.S.P.Q.2d 1497 (Cal.Super.Ct.1990), 739

Buckhannon Bd. and Care Home, Inc. v. West Virginia Dept. of Health and Human Resources, 532 U.S. 598, 121 S.Ct. 1835, 149 L.Ed.2d 855 (2001), **914**

Burke, United States v., 504 U.S. 229, 112 S.Ct. 1867, 119 L.Ed.2d 34 (1992), 638

Burlington, City of v. Dague, 505 U.S. 557, 112 S.Ct. 2638, 120 L.Ed.2d 449 (1992), 943

Bush v. Gore, 531 U.S. 98, 121 S.Ct. 525, 148 L.Ed.2d 388 (2000), 46, 203

Bussell v. DeWalt Products Corp., 105 N.J. 223, 519 A.2d 1379 (N.J.1987), 638

Bustop v. Superior Court, 69 Cal.App.3d 66, 137 Cal.Rptr. 793 (Cal.App. 2 Dist.1977), 219

Busy Beaver Bldg. Centers, In re, 19 F.3d 833 (3rd Cir.1994), 965

Butz v. Glover Livestock Commission Co., 411 U.S. 182, 93 S.Ct. 1455, 36 L.Ed.2d 142 (1973), 651

Cabletron Systems Securities Litigation, In re, 239 F.R.D. 30 (D.N.H.2006), 965

California v. American Stores Co., 495 U.S. 271, 110 S.Ct. 1853, 109 L.Ed.2d 240 (1990), 61

California v. Sierra Club, 451 U.S. 287, 101 S.Ct. 1775, 68 L.Ed.2d 101 (1981), 29

California Ins. Guarantee Assn. v. Superior Court, 231 Cal.App.3d 1617, 283 Cal.Rptr. 104 (Cal.App. 2 Dist.1991), 426

Calva–Cerqueira v. United States, 281 F.Supp.2d 279 (D.D.C.2003), 627

Campbell v. State Farm Mut. Auto. Ins. Co., 98 P.3d 409 (Utah 2004), 707

Campbell v. State Farm Mut. Auto. Ins. Co., 65 P.3d 1134 (Utah 2001), 912

Canell v. Lightner, 143 F.3d 1210 (9th Cir. 1998), 449

Capacchione v. Charlotte–Mecklenburg Schools, 57 F.Supp.2d 228 (W.D.N.C.1999), 164

Carlson v. Green, 446 U.S. 14, 100 S.Ct. 1468, 64 L.Ed.2d 15 (1980), 27

Carol J. v. William J., 119 Misc.2d 739, 464 N.Y.S.2d 635 (N.Y.Fam.Ct.1983), 838

Caron v. United States, 410 F.Supp. 378 (D.R.I.1975), 532

Carr v. Carr, 120 N.J. 336, 576 A.2d 872 (N.J. 1990), 772

Carroll v. President & Com'rs of Princess Anne, 393 U.S. 175, 89 S.Ct. 347, 21 L.Ed.2d 325 (1968), 187

Castellani v. Bailey, 218 Wis.2d 245, 578 N.W.2d 166 (Wis.1998), 892

Castle Rock, Town of v. Gonzales, 545 U.S. 748, 125 S.Ct. 2796, 162 L.Ed.2d 658 (2005), 370

Catanzano v. Dowling, 847 F.Supp. 1070 (W.D.N.Y.1994), 75

Cavalier ex rel. Cavalier v. Caddo Parish School Bd., 403 F.3d 246 (5th Cir.2005), 281

Cavel Intern., Inc. v. Madigan, 500 F.3d 544 (7th Cir.2007), 208

Cayuga Indian Nation of N.Y. v. Pataki, 413 F.3d 266 (2nd Cir.2005), 616, 899

Cayuga Indian Nation of N.Y. v. Pataki, 165 F.Supp.2d 266 (N.D.N.Y.2001), 616

CBS Broadcasting, Inc. v. EchoStar Communications, 450 F.3d 505 (11th Cir.2006), 59

Cendant Corp. Litigation, In re, 264 F.3d 201 (3rd Cir.2001), 964
Central Bank and Trust Co. v. General Finance Corp., 297 F.2d 126 (5th Cir.1961), 870
Chadwick v. Hill, 2008 WL 1886128 (E.D.Pa. 2008), 326
Chalk v. United States Dist. Court, 840 F.2d 701 (9th Cir.1988), 203
Chambers v. NASCO, Inc., 501 U.S. 32, 111 S.Ct. 2123, 115 L.Ed.2d 27 (1991), 903
Chandler v. Roudebush, 425 U.S. 840, 96 S.Ct. 1949, 48 L.Ed.2d 416 (1976), 45
Chauffeurs, Teamsters and Helpers, Local No. 391 v. Terry, 494 U.S. 558, 110 S.Ct. 1339, 108 L.Ed.2d 519 (1990), 455
Chavez v. Illinois State Police, 251 F.3d 612 (7th Cir.2001), 73
Cheff v. Schnackenberg, 384 U.S. 373, 86 S.Ct. 1523, 16 L.Ed.2d 629 (1966), 328
Chicago, City of v. Cecola, 75 Ill.2d 423, 27 Ill.Dec. 462, 389 N.E.2d 526 (Ill.1979), 80
Chicago, City of v. Morales, 527 U.S. 41, 119 S.Ct. 1849, 144 L.Ed.2d 67 (1999), 154
Chicago, City of v. Roppolo, 113 Ill.App.3d 602, 69 Ill.Dec. 435, 447 N.E.2d 870 (Ill.App. 1 Dist.1983), 740
Choctaw Maid Farms, Inc. v. Hailey, 822 So.2d 911 (Miss.2002), 511
Christiansburg Garment Co. v. EEOC, 434 U.S. 412, 98 S.Ct. 694, 54 L.Ed.2d 648 (1978), 927
Cisarik v. Palos Community Hosp., 144 Ill.2d 339, 162 Ill.Dec. 59, 579 N.E.2d 873 (Ill. 1991), 519
Citibank, N.A. v. Baer, 651 F.2d 1341 (10th Cir.1980), 467
Citizens Federal Bank v. Cardian Mortgage Corp., 122 B.R. 255 (Bkrtcy.E.D.Va.1990), 772
City of (see name of city)
Clarke v. United States, 886 F.2d 404 (D.C.Cir. 1989), 405
Clearfield Trust Co. v. United States, 318 U.S. 363, 318 U.S. 744, 63 S.Ct. 573, 87 L.Ed. 838 (1943), 898
Clinton E. Worden & Co. v. California Fig Syrup Co., 187 U.S. 516, 23 S.Ct. 161, 47 L.Ed. 282 (1903), **858**
Clymore, United States v., 245 F.3d 1195 (10th Cir.2001), 899
CNN, United States v., 865 F.Supp. 1549 (S.D.Fla.1994), 345
Cobell v. Norton, 283 F.Supp.2d 66 (D.D.C. 2003), 238
Cobell v. Norton, 334 F.3d 1128 (D.C.Cir.2003), 238, 356
Cochran v. Tory, 2003 WL 22451378 (Cal.App. 2 Dist.2003), 155
Codispoti v. Pennsylvania, 418 U.S. 506, 94 S.Ct. 2687, 41 L.Ed.2d 912 (1974), 327
Coetzee v. South Africa, CCT 19–94 (1995), 848
Coho Resources v. McCarthy, 829 So.2d 1 (Miss.2002), 617

Colorado River Water Conservation Dist. v. United States, 424 U.S. 800, 96 S.Ct. 1236, 47 L.Ed.2d 483 (1976), 435
Commodity Futures Trading Com'n v. Frankwell Bullion Ltd., 99 F.3d 299 (9th Cir. 1996), 228
Commonwealth of (see name of Commonwealth)
Conkey v. Reno, 885 F.Supp. 1389 (D.Nev. 1995), 817
Connecticut v. Doehr, 501 U.S. 1, 111 S.Ct. 2105, 115 L.Ed.2d 1 (1991), **788**
Connecticut Dept. of Public Safety v. Doe, 538 U.S. 1, 123 S.Ct. 1160, 155 L.Ed.2d 98 (2003), 648
Consumer Advisory Bd. v. Glover, 989 F.2d 65 (1st Cir.1993), 238
Consumer Advisory Bd. v. Harvey, 2008 WL 4594353 (D.Me.2008), 238
Continental Illinois Securities Litigation, In re, 750 F.Supp. 868 (N.D.Ill.1990), 963
Continental Illinois Securities Litigation, In re, 572 F.Supp. 931 (N.D.Ill.1983), 963
Continuum Co. v. Incepts, Inc., 873 F.2d 801 (5th Cir.1989), 211
Cook v. Niedert, 142 F.3d 1004 (7th Cir.1998), 946
Cook County, Ill. v. United States ex rel. Chandler, 538 U.S. 119, 123 S.Ct. 1239, 155 L.Ed.2d 247 (2003), 673
Cooper Industries, Inc. v. Leatherman Tool Group, Inc., 532 U.S. 424, 121 S.Ct. 1678, 149 L.Ed.2d 674 (2001), 709
Corbello v. Iowa Production, 850 So.2d 686 (La.2003), 484
Corporation of President of Church of Jesus Christ of Latter–Day Saints v. Jolley, 24 Utah 2d 187, 467 P.2d 984 (Utah 1970), **774**
Correctional Services Corp. v. Malesko, 534 U.S. 61, 122 S.Ct. 515, 151 L.Ed.2d 456 (2001), 27
Cort v. Ash, 422 U.S. 66, 95 S.Ct. 2080, 45 L.Ed.2d 26 (1975), 29
Costello v. United States, 365 U.S. 265, 81 S.Ct. 534, 5 L.Ed.2d 551 (1961), 898
Crawford Fitting Co. v. J.T. Gibbons, Inc., 482 U.S. 437, 107 S.Ct. 2494, 96 L.Ed.2d 385 (1987), 942
Cronin v. Browner, 90 F.Supp.2d 364 (S.D.N.Y. 2000), 269
Cutter v. Wilkinson, 544 U.S. 709, 125 S.Ct. 2113, 161 L.Ed.2d 1020 (2005), 550

Daccarett, United States v., 6 F.3d 37 (2nd Cir.1993), 816
Dardinger v. Anthem Blue Cross & Blue Shield, 98 Ohio St.3d 77, 781 N.E.2d 121 (Ohio 2002), 690
Davis v. Passman, 442 U.S. 228, 99 S.Ct. 2264, 60 L.Ed.2d 846 (1979), 27, 28
DCB Const. Co., Inc. v. Central City Development Co., 965 P.2d 115 (Colo.1998), 730
Dean v. Riser, 240 F.3d 505 (5th Cir.2001), 925
Deibler v. Atlantic Properties Group, Inc., 652 A.2d 553 (Del.Supr.1995), 843

Delaney v. Cade, 255 Kan. 199, 873 P.2d 175 (Kan.1994), 541
Delaware Valley Citizens' Council for Clean Air v. Pennsylvania, 755 F.2d 38 (3rd Cir. 1985), 402
Delaware Valley Citizens' Council for Clean Air v. Pennsylvania, 678 F.2d 470 (3rd Cir. 1982), 402
DelCostello v. International Broth. of Teamsters, 462 U.S. 151, 103 S.Ct. 2281, 76 L.Ed.2d 476 (1983), 890
DeLonga v. Diocese of Sioux Falls, 329 F.Supp.2d 1092 (D.S.D.2004), 892
Delta Air Lines, Inc. v. Air Line Pilots Ass'n, 238 F.3d 1300 (11th Cir.2001), 204
Department of Environmental Protection v. Department of Environmental Conservation, 70 N.Y.2d 233, 519 N.Y.S.2d 539, 513 N.E.2d 706 (N.Y.1987), 325
Department of Revenue v. Kurth Ranch, 511 U.S. 767, 114 S.Ct. 1937, 128 L.Ed.2d 767 (1994), 648
DePass v. United States, 721 F.2d 203 (7th Cir.1983), 542
Desert Palace, Inc. v. Costa, 539 U.S. 90, 123 S.Ct. 2148, 156 L.Ed.2d 84 (2003), 42
Diamond v. Oreamuno, 24 N.Y.2d 494, 301 N.Y.S.2d 78, 248 N.E.2d 910 (N.Y.1969), 766
Dillon v. Evanston Hosp., 199 Ill.2d 483, 264 Ill.Dec. 653, 771 N.E.2d 357 (Ill.2002), 501, **538**
Dimick v. Schiedt, 293 U.S. 474, 55 S.Ct. 296, 79 L.Ed. 603 (1935), 462, 709
Doctor's Associates, Inc. v. Reinert & Duree, P.C., 191 F.3d 297 (2nd Cir.1999), 353, 355
Doe v. Dunbar, 320 F.Supp. 1297 (D.Colo. 1970), 428
Doehr v. DiGiovanni, 1997 WL 835067 (D.Conn.1997), 799
Dorn v. Burlington Northern Santa Fe Railroad Co., 397 F.3d 1183 (9th Cir.2005), 526
Dowell v. Board of Educ. of Oklahoma City Public Schools, 8 F.3d 1501 (10th Cir.1993), 278
Downie v. United States Lines Co., 359 F.2d 344 (3rd Cir.1966), 515
Doyle v. Mt. Healthy, 670 F.2d 59 (6th Cir. 1982), 41
Duarte v. Zachariah, 28 Cal.Rptr.2d 88 (Cal. App. 3 Dist.1994), 542
Duffy v. Longo, 207 A.D.2d 860, 616 N.Y.S.2d 760 (N.Y.A.D. 2 Dept.1994), 407
Duke Power Co. v. City of High Point, 69 N.C.App. 335, 317 S.E.2d 699 (N.C.App. 1984), 83
Dumas v. Cooney, 235 Cal.App.3d 1593, 1 Cal. Rptr.2d 584 (Cal.App. 6 Dist.1991), 542
Dunn v. HOVIC, 1 F.3d 1371 (3rd Cir.1993), 663
Dupuy v. Samuels, 465 F.3d 757 (7th Cir. 2006), 217
Duquesne Light Co. v. E.P.A., 698 F.2d 456 (D.C.Cir.1983), 879
Dusenbery v. United States, 534 U.S. 161, 122 S.Ct. 694, 151 L.Ed.2d 597 (2002), 817

Dyer, In re, 322 F.3d 1178 (9th Cir.2003), 328
EarthInfo, Inc. v. Hydrosphere Resource Consultants, Inc., 900 P.2d 113 (Colo. 1995), **748**
Eastman Kodak Co., United States v., 63 F.3d 95 (2nd Cir.1995), 268
Easyriders Freedom F.I.G.H.T. v. Hannigan, 92 F.3d 1486 (9th Cir.1996), 76
eBay Inc. v. MercExchange, L.L.C., 547 U.S. 388, 126 S.Ct. 1837, 164 L.Ed.2d 641 (2006), **95**
EC Term of Years Trust v. United States, 550 U.S. 429, 2007-46 I.R.B. 986, 127 S.Ct. 1763, 167 L.Ed.2d 729 (2007), 890
Edelman v. Jordan, 415 U.S. 651, 94 S.Ct. 1347, 39 L.Ed.2d 662 (1974), 371
Eden Elec., Ltd. v. Amana Co., 370 F.3d 824 (8th Cir.2004), 716
Edgar v. MITE Corp., 457 U.S. 624, 102 S.Ct. 2629, 73 L.Ed.2d 269 (1982), 346
Edgar, People ex rel. v. Miller, 110 Ill.App.3d 264, 65 Ill.Dec. 814, 441 N.E.2d 1328 (Ill. App. 4 Dist.1982), 89
Edwards v. Lee's Adm'r, 265 Ky. 418, 96 S.W.2d 1028 (Ky.1936), 740
Employment Div., Dept. of Human Resources v. Smith, 494 U.S. 872, 110 S.Ct. 1595, 108 L.Ed.2d 876 (1990), 550
Energy Capital Corp. v. United States, 302 F.3d 1314 (Fed.Cir.2002), **628**
Engle v. Liggett Group, Inc., 945 So.2d 1246 (Fla.2006), 708
Ensley Branch v. Seibels, 31 F.3d 1548 (11th Cir.1994), 363
Environmental Defense Fund, Inc. v. Alexander, 614 F.2d 474 (5th Cir.1980), 897
Epperson v. Arkansas, 393 U.S. 97, 89 S.Ct. 266, 21 L.Ed.2d 228 (1968), 427
Epping v. Commonwealth Edison Co., 315 Ill. App.3d 1069, 248 Ill.Dec. 625, 734 N.E.2d 916 (Ill.App. 1 Dist.2000), 527
Epstein v. Gluckin, 233 N.Y. 490, 135 N.E. 861 (N.Y.1922), 183
Erie R. Co. v. Tompkins, 304 U.S. 64, 58 S.Ct. 817, 82 L.Ed. 1188 (1938), 462
Erlich v. Menezes, 87 Cal.Rptr.2d 886, 981 P.2d 978 (Cal.1999), 609
E.R. Squibb & Sons, Inc. v. Lloyd's & Companies, 241 F.3d 154 (2nd Cir.2001), 426
Estevez v. United States, 72 F.Supp.2d 205 (S.D.N.Y.1999), 637
Evans v. City of Chicago, 10 F.3d 474 (7th Cir.1993), 269
Evans v. Jeff D., 475 U.S. 717, 106 S.Ct. 1531, 89 L.Ed.2d 747 (1986), **966**
Evans v. Williams, 206 F.3d 1292 (D.C.Cir. 2000), 268, 323, 345
Evcco Leasing Corp. v. Ace Trucking Co., 828 F.2d 188 (3rd Cir.1987), 843
Evergreen Amusement Corp. v. Milstead, 206 Md. 610, 112 A.2d 901 (Md.1955), 578
Evra Corp. v. Swiss Bank Corp., 673 F.2d 951 (7th Cir.1982), **600**
Ewing v. California, 538 U.S. 11, 123 S.Ct. 1179, 155 L.Ed.2d 108 (2003), 660

Ex parte (see name of party)
Exxon Shipping Co. v. Baker, 554 U.S. ___, 128 S.Ct. 2605, 171 L.Ed.2d 570 (2008), **673**
Exxon Valdez, In re, 270 F.3d 1215 (9th Cir. 2001), 688

Fabry v. Commissioner, 223 F.3d 1261 (11th Cir.2000), 638
Farrar v. Hobby, 506 U.S. 103, 113 S.Ct. 566, 121 L.Ed.2d 494 (1992), 451, 925, 928, 946
FDL Technologies, Inc. v. United States, 967 F.2d 1578 (Fed.Cir.1992), 947
Federated Dept. Stores, Inc. v. Moitie, 452 U.S. 394, 101 S.Ct. 2424, 69 L.Ed.2d 103 (1981), 241
Feiock, In re, 215 Cal.App.3d 141, 263 Cal. Rptr. 437 (Cal.App. 4 Dist.1989), 310
Feltner v. Columbia Pictures Television, Inc., 523 U.S. 340, 118 S.Ct. 1279, 140 L.Ed.2d 438 (1998), 455
Fennell v. Southern Maryland Hosp. Center, Inc., 320 Md. 776, 580 A.2d 206 (Md.1990), 542
Ferdon ex rel. Petrucelli v. Wisconsin Patients Compensation Fund, 284 Wis.2d 573, 701 N.W.2d 440 (Wis.2005), 524, 525
Fina Oil & Chemical Co. v. Ewen, 123 F.3d 1466 (Fed.Cir.1997), 437
Fine Paper Antitrust Litigation, In re, 98 F.R.D. 48 (E.D.Pa.1983), 963
Firefighters Local Union No. 1784 v. Stotts, 467 U.S. 561, 104 S.Ct. 2576, 81 L.Ed.2d 483 (1984), **245,** 278
First Capital Holdings Corp., In re, 33 F.3d 29 (9th Cir.1994), 965
Fitzgerald v. Barnstable School Committee, 555 U.S. ___, 129 S.Ct. 788, 172 L.Ed.2d ___ (2009), 31
Fitzgerald v. O'Connell, 120 R.I. 240, 386 A.2d 1384 (R.I.1978), 898
F.J. Hanshaw Enterprises, Inc. v. Emerald River Development, Inc., 244 F.3d 1128 (9th Cir.2001), 323
Flagg Bros., Inc. v. Brooks, 436 U.S. 149, 98 S.Ct. 1729, 56 L.Ed.2d 185 (1978), 801
Fleischmann Distilling Corp. v. Maier Brewing Co., 386 U.S. 714, 87 S.Ct. 1404, 18 L.Ed.2d 475 (1967), 902
Fleming v. Quigley, 2003 Guam 4, 2003 WL 554665 (Guam Terr. 2003), 912
Fletcher v Bealey, 1885 WL 17202 (Ch D 1885), 61
Florida v. White, 526 U.S. 559, 119 S.Ct. 1555, 143 L.Ed.2d 748 (1999), 800
Fogerty v. Fantasy, Inc., 510 U.S. 517, 114 S.Ct. 1023, 127 L.Ed.2d 455 (1994), 927
Fontana, United States v., 528 F.Supp. 137 (S.D.N.Y.1981), 772
Fordice, United States v., 505 U.S. 717, 112 S.Ct. 2727, 120 L.Ed.2d 575 (1992), 111
Ford & Vlahos v. ITT Commercial Finance Corp., 36 Cal.Rptr.2d 464, 885 P.2d 877 (Cal.1994), 843
47 West 644 Route 38, Maple Park, Ill., United States v., 190 F.3d 781 (7th Cir.1999), 817
Franchise Tax Bd. v. Construction Laborers Vacation Trust, 463 U.S. 1, 103 S.Ct. 2841, 77 L.Ed.2d 420 (1983), 438
Francis v. Evans, 69 Wis. 115, 33 N.W. 93 (Wis.1887), 777
Francisco v. United States, 267 F.3d 303 (3rd Cir.2001), 639
Franks v. Bowman Transp. Co., Inc., 424 U.S. 747, 96 S.Ct. 1251, 47 L.Ed.2d 444 (1976), 360
Frazar v. Ladd, 457 F.3d 432 (5th Cir.2006), 271
Freeman v. Pitts, 503 U.S. 467, 112 S.Ct. 1430, 118 L.Ed.2d 108 (1992), 163, 279
Freeman & Mills, Inc. v. Belcher Oil Co., 44 Cal.Rptr.2d 420, 900 P.2d 669 (Cal. 1995), **585**
Frew v. Hawkins, 540 U.S. 431, 124 S.Ct. 899, 157 L.Ed.2d 855 (2004), 270, 371
Friends of the Earth v. Laidlaw Environmental Services (TOC), Inc., 528 U.S. 167, 120 S.Ct. 693, 145 L.Ed.2d 610 (2000), 71
F.T.C. v. Kuykendall, 371 F.3d 745 (10th Cir. 2004), 324
F.T.C. v. National Lead Co., 352 U.S. 419, 77 S.Ct. 502, 1 L.Ed.2d 438 (1957), 137
F.T.C. v. Verity Intern., Ltd., 443 F.3d 48 (2nd Cir.2006), 738

Gail v. United States, 58 F.3d 580 (10th Cir. 1995), 636
Gallo, People ex rel. v. Acuna, 60 Cal.Rptr.2d 277, 929 P.2d 596 (Cal.1997), 153
Gardner v. United States, 211 F.3d 1305 (D.C.Cir.2000), 89
Gasperini v. Center for Humanities, Inc., 518 U.S. 415, 116 S.Ct. 2211, 135 L.Ed.2d 659 (1996), 462
Gates v. Collier, 616 F.2d 1268 (5th Cir.1980), 373
Gautreaux v. Chicago Housing Authority, 491 F.3d 649 (7th Cir.2007), 182
Gautreaux v. Romney, 457 F.2d 124 (7th Cir. 1972), 376
Gedraitis, United States v., 520 F.Supp. 84 (E.D.Pa.1981), 359
General Bldg. Contractors Ass'n v. Pennsylvania, 458 U.S. 375, 102 S.Ct. 3141, 73 L.Ed.2d 835 (1982), 359
General Contractors v. Jacksonville, 508 U.S. 656, 113 S.Ct. 2297, 124 L.Ed.2d 586 (1993), 73
General Motors Corp. v. E.P.A., 871 F.2d 495 (5th Cir.1989), 879
General Motors Corp. v. United States, 496 U.S. 530, 110 S.Ct. 2528, 110 L.Ed.2d 480 (1990), 224, 879
General Motors Corp., United States v., 876 F.2d 1060 (1st Cir.1989), 879
General Tel. Co. v. EEOC, 446 U.S. 318, 100 S.Ct. 1698, 64 L.Ed.2d 319 (1980), 75
Gen–Probe Inc. v. Vysis, Inc., 359 F.3d 1376 (Fed.Cir.2004), 424
Georgia, United States v., 546 U.S. 151, 126 S.Ct. 877, 163 L.Ed.2d 650 (2006), 370

Germantown Sav. Bank v. City of Philadelphia, 98 Pa.Cmwlth. 508, 512 A.2d 756 (Pa. Cmwlth.1986), 503

Gertz v. Robert Welch, Inc., 418 U.S. 323, 94 S.Ct. 2997, 41 L.Ed.2d 789 (1974), 661

Giampapa v. American Family Mut. Ins. Co., 64 P.3d 230 (Colo.2003), 599, 662

Gillette Motor Transport, Inc., Commissioner v., 364 U.S. 130, 80 S.Ct. 1497, 4 L.Ed.2d 1617 (1960), 636

Gilmore v. California, 220 F.3d 987 (9th Cir. 2000), 298

Goldberger v. Integrated Resources, Inc., 209 F.3d 43 (2nd Cir.2000), 965

Golden Eagle Archery v. Jackson, 116 S.W.3d 757 (Tex.2003), 515

Golden State Bottling Co., Inc. v. NLRB, 414 U.S. 168, 94 S.Ct. 414, 38 L.Ed.2d 388 (1973), 356

Goldman v. Simpson, 72 Cal.Rptr.3d 729 (Cal. App. 2 Dist.2008), 822

Gonzaga University v. Doe, 536 U.S. 273, 122 S.Ct. 2268, 153 L.Ed.2d 309 (2002), 30

Gonzales v. Thomas, 547 U.S. 183, 126 S.Ct. 1613, 164 L.Ed.2d 358 (2006), 44

Gonzalez, People v., 50 Cal.Rptr.2d 74, 910 P.2d 1366 (Cal.1996), 343

Goodwin v. Dick, 220 Mass. 556, 107 N.E. 925 (Mass.1915), 743

Gore v. Harris, 773 So.2d 524 (Fla.2000), 46

Gore v. Harris, 772 So.2d 1243 (Fla.2000), 46

Gould, Inc. v. A & M Battery and Tire Service, 950 F.Supp. 653 (M.D.Pa.1997), 356

Goyzueta v. State, 266 S.W.3d 126 (Tex.App.-Fort Worth 2008), 155

Graham v. DaimlerChrysler Corp., 21 Cal. Rptr.3d 331, 101 P.3d 140 (Cal.2004), 926

Graham County Soil & Water Conservation Dist. v. United States ex rel. Wilson, 545 U.S. 409, 125 S.Ct. 2444, 162 L.Ed.2d 390 (2005), 890

Granfinanciera, S.A. v. Nordberg, 492 U.S. 33, 109 S.Ct. 2782, 106 L.Ed.2d 26 (1989), 455

Gratz v. Bollinger, 353 F.Supp.2d 929 (E.D.Mich.2005), **948**

Gratz v. Bollinger, 539 U.S. 244, 123 S.Ct. 2411, 156 L.Ed.2d 257 (2003), 74

Great Am. Music Mach., Inc. v. Mid–South Record Pressing Co., 393 F.Supp. 877 (M.D.Tenn.1975), **564**

Great Lakes Dredge & Dock Co. v. Huffman, 319 U.S. 293, 63 S.Ct. 1070, 87 L.Ed. 1407 (1943), 436

Green v. Christiansen, 732 F.2d 1397 (9th Cir. 1984), 877

Green v. Mansour, 474 U.S. 64, 106 S.Ct. 423, 88 L.Ed.2d 371 (1985), 436

Green v. School Bd. of New Kent County, 391 U.S. 430, 88 S.Ct. 1689, 20 L.Ed.2d 716 (1968), 155

Greer v. United States, 207 F.3d 322 (6th Cir.2000), 638

Gregg, United States v., 226 F.3d 253 (3rd Cir.2000), 153

Greyhound Lines, Inc. v. Sutton, 765 So.2d 1269 (Miss.2000), 533

Griffin v. California, 380 U.S. 609, 85 S.Ct. 1229, 14 L.Ed.2d 106 (1965), 650

Griffin v. County School Bd., 363 F.2d 206 (4th Cir.1966), **329**

Griffin v. County School Bd. of Prince Edward County, 377 U.S. 218, 84 S.Ct. 1226, 12 L.Ed.2d 256 (1964), 373

Griffin v. Tri–County Metropolitan Transp. Dist., 318 Or. 500, 870 P.2d 808 (Or.1994), 913

Griffith v. Kentucky, 479 U.S. 314, 107 S.Ct. 708, 93 L.Ed.2d 649 (1987), 112

Griggs v. Miller, 374 S.W.2d 119 (Mo.1963), **841**

Grimshaw v. Ford Motor Co., 119 Cal. App.3d 757, 174 Cal.Rptr. 348 (Cal.App. 4 Dist.1981), **663**

Griswold v. Connecticut, 381 U.S. 479, 85 S.Ct. 1678, 14 L.Ed.2d 510 (1965), 427

Groves v. John Wunder Co., 205 Minn. 163, 286 N.W. 235 (Minn.1939), 483

Grupo Mexicano de Desarrollo S.A. v. Alliance Bond Fund, Inc., 527 U.S. 308, 119 S.Ct. 1961, 144 L.Ed.2d 319 (1999), 204, 787

Grutter v. Bollinger, 539 U.S. 306, 123 S.Ct. 2325, 156 L.Ed.2d 304 (2003), 41

Guam Society of Obstetricians & Gynecologists v. Ada, 100 F.3d 691 (9th Cir.1996), 946

Guaranty Trust Co. v. United States, 304 U.S. 126, 58 S.Ct. 785, 82 L.Ed. 1224 (1938), 891

Guardian Loan Co. v. Early, 47 N.Y.2d 515, 419 N.Y.S.2d 56, 392 N.E.2d 1240 (N.Y. 1979), 843

Guidry v. Sheet Metal Workers Nat. Pension Fund, 39 F.3d 1078 (10th Cir.1994), 840

Gutterman v. First Nat. Bank of Anchorage, 597 P.2d 969 (Alaska 1979), **829,** 840

Hadley v. Baxendale, 156 Eng. Rep. 145 (Ex. 1854), 500, 576

Halderman v. Pennhurst State School and Hospital, 533 F.Supp. 631 (E.D.Pa.1981), 372

Halderman v. Pennhurst State School & Hosp., 49 F.3d 939 (3rd Cir.1995), 940

Hall, United States v., 472 F.2d 261 (5th Cir.1972), **349**

Halper, United States v., 490 U.S. 435, 109 S.Ct. 1892, 104 L.Ed.2d 487 (1989), 643

Hampton v. United States, 425 U.S. 484, 96 S.Ct. 1646, 48 L.Ed.2d 113 (1976), 861

Hans v. Louisiana, 134 U.S. 1, 10 S.Ct. 504, 33 L.Ed. 842 (1890), 370

Hansford v. Maplewood Station Business Park, 621 N.E.2d 347 (Ind.App. 5 Dist.1993), 229

Harper v. Virginia Dept. of Taxation, 509 U.S. 86, 113 S.Ct. 2510, 125 L.Ed.2d 74 (1993), 112

Harris v. City of Philadelphia, 47 F.3d 1311 (3rd Cir.1995), 322

Harris v. Garner, 216 F.3d 970 (11th Cir.2000), 449

Hart v. E.P. Dutton & Co., 197 Misc. 274, 93 N.Y.S.2d 871 (N.Y.Sup.1949), 735

Hazen ex rel. LeGear v. Reagen, 208 F.3d 697 (8th Cir.2000), 299

Hearst Newspapers Partnership, L.P., In re, 241 S.W.3d 190 (Tex.App.-Hous. (1 Dist.) 2007), 357
Hecht Co. v. Bowles, 321 U.S. 321, 64 S.Ct. 587, 88 L.Ed. 754 (1944), **55**
Heckler v. Community Health Services of Crawford County, Inc., 467 U.S. 51, 104 S.Ct. 2218, 81 L.Ed.2d 42 (1984), 874
Heckler v. Day, 467 U.S. 104, 104 S.Ct. 2249, 81 L.Ed.2d 88 (1984), 232
Helfend v. Southern Cal. Rapid Transit Dist., 84 Cal.Rptr. 173, 465 P.2d 61 (Cal.1970), 503
Henry v. Dow Chemical Co., 473 Mich. 63, 701 N.W.2d 684 (Mich.2005), 499
Hensley v. Eckerhart, 461 U.S. 424, 103 S.Ct. 1933, 76 L.Ed.2d 40 (1983), 952
Herrington v. County of Sonoma, 883 F.2d 739 (9th Cir.1989), 927
Hetzel v. Prince William County, 523 U.S. 208, 118 S.Ct. 1210, 140 L.Ed.2d 336 (1998), 709
Hewitt v. Helms, 482 U.S. 755, 107 S.Ct. 2672, 96 L.Ed.2d 654 (1987), 925
Hewlett v. Barge Bertie, 418 F.2d 654 (4th Cir.1969), 482
Hibschman Pontiac, Inc. v. Batchelor, 266 Ind. 310, 362 N.E.2d 845 (Ind.1977), 599
Hicks on Behalf of Feiock v. Feiock, 485 U.S. 624, 108 S.Ct. 1423, 99 L.Ed.2d 721 (1988), **302**, 848
Highway Equipment Co. v. FECO, Ltd., 469 F.3d 1027 (Fed.Cir.2006), 925
Hilao v. Estate of Marcos, 103 F.3d 767 (9th Cir.1996), 688
Hill v. Colorado, 530 U.S. 703, 120 S.Ct. 2480, 147 L.Ed.2d 597 (2000), 153
H.K. Porter Co. v. National Friction Products Corp., 568 F.2d 24 (7th Cir.1977), 334
H.K. Porter Co. v. NLRB, 397 U.S. 99, 90 S.Ct. 821, 25 L.Ed.2d 146 (1970), 138
Hodgers-Durgin v. de la Vina, 199 F.3d 1037 (9th Cir.1999), 73
Hodgson v. Corning Glass Works, 474 F.2d 226 (2nd Cir.1973), 76
Holston v. Sisters of The Third Order of St. Francis, 247 Ill.App.3d 985, 187 Ill.Dec. 743, 618 N.E.2d 334 (Ill.App. 1 Dist.1993), 511
Honda Motor Co., Ltd. v. Oberg, 512 U.S. 415, 114 S.Ct. 2331, 129 L.Ed.2d 336 (1994), 709
Honeywell Intern. Inc. v. E.P.A., 393 F.3d 1315 (D.C.Cir.2005), 44
Honeywell Intern. Inc. v. E.P.A., 374 F.3d 1363 (D.C.Cir.2004), 44
Hook v. Arizona, 907 F.Supp. 1326 (D.Ariz. 1995), 404
Hooker Chemicals & Plastics Corp., United States v., 748 F.Supp. 67 (W.D.N.Y.1990), 672
Hopkins v. Price Waterhouse, 737 F.Supp. 1202 (D.D.C.1990), 42
Hopwood v. Texas, 78 F.3d 932 (5th Cir.1996), 41
Hoskins v. Business Men's Assur., 79 S.W.3d 901 (Mo.2002), 689

Household Bank v. JFS Group, 320 F.3d 1249 (11th Cir.2003), 437, 438
Howard v. Mail–Well Envelope Co., 150 F.3d 1227 (10th Cir.1998), 947
Hudson v. United States, 522 U.S. 93, 118 S.Ct. 488, 139 L.Ed.2d 450 (1997), **642**
Hutchison v. Pyburn, 567 S.W.2d 762 (Tenn. Ct.App.1977), **741**
Hutto v. Finney, 437 U.S. 678, 98 S.Ct. 2565, 57 L.Ed.2d 522 (1978), 136, 374, 929

Idaho Schools For Equal Educational Opportunity v. State, 140 Idaho 586, 97 P.3d 453 (Idaho 2004), 385
Ihler v. Chisholm, 298 Mont. 254, 995 P.2d 439 (Mont.2000), 946
Illinois v. Costle, 12 Env't Rep.Cas. (B.N.A.) 1597 (D.D.C.1979), **230**
Imprisoned Citizens Union v. Ridge, 169 F.3d 178 (3rd Cir.1999), 298
Independent Federation of Flight Attendants v. Zipes, 491 U.S. 754, 109 S.Ct. 2732, 105 L.Ed.2d 639 (1989), 927
Inmates of Suffolk County Jail v. Rouse, 129 F.3d 649 (1st Cir.1997), 298
Inmates of Suffolk County Jail v. Rufo, 148 F.R.D. 14 (D.Mass.1993), 267
In re (see name of party)
International Broth. of Teamsters v. United States, 431 U.S. 324, 97 S.Ct. 1843, 52 L.Ed.2d 396 (1977), 45, 361

J'Aire Corp. v. Gregory, 157 Cal.Rptr. 407, 598 P.2d 60 (Cal.1979), 607
James B. Beam Distilling Co. v. Georgia, 501 U.S. 529, 111 S.Ct. 2439, 115 L.Ed.2d 481 (1991), 112
James Daniel Good Real Property, United States v., 510 U.S. 43, 114 S.Ct. 492, 126 L.Ed.2d 490 (1993), **803**
Jarrell v. Petoseed Co., 331 S.C. 207, 500 S.E.2d 793 (S.C.App.1998), 326
Jean, Commissioner v., 496 U.S. 154, 110 S.Ct. 2316, 110 L.Ed.2d 134 (1990), 940
Jeff D. v. Kempthorne, 2007 WL 3256620 (D.Idaho 2007), 974
Jeff D. v. Kempthorne, 365 F.3d 844 (9th Cir. 2004), 268
Jefferson County, United States v., 720 F.2d 1511 (11th Cir.1983), 363
Jenkins v. Missouri, 959 F.Supp. 1151 (W.D.Mo.1997), 385
Jenkins v. Missouri, 127 F.3d 709 (8th Cir. 1997), 926
Jinks v. Richland County, 538 U.S. 456, 123 S.Ct. 1667, 155 L.Ed.2d 631 (2003), 892
Joel v. Various John Does, 499 F.Supp. 791 (E.D.Wis.1980), 189
Johansen v. Combustion Engineering, Inc., 170 F.3d 1320 (11th Cir.1999), 709
Johansen v. State, 491 P.2d 759 (Alaska 1971), 841
Johnson v. City of Tulsa, 489 F.3d 1089 (10th Cir.2007), 940
Johnson v. District of Columbia, 190 F.Supp.2d 34 (D.D.C.2002), 973

Johnson v. Ford Motor Co., 29 Cal.Rptr.3d 401, 113 P.3d 82 (Cal.2005), 708

Johnson v. Williford, 682 F.2d 868 (9th Cir. 1982), **870**

Johnson v. Women's Health Center, Inc., 714 So.2d 580 (Fla.App. 5 Dist.1998), 153

Joint Anti–Fascist Refugee Committee v. McGrath, 341 U.S. 123, 71 S.Ct. 624, 95 L.Ed. 817 (1951), 370

Joint School Dist. No. 1 v. Wisconsin Rapids Educ. Ass'n, 70 Wis.2d 292, 234 N.W.2d 289 (Wis.1975), 359

Jones v. City of Los Angeles, 24 Cal.Rptr.2d 528 (Cal.App. 2 Dist.1993), 519

Jones v. Clinton, 57 F.Supp.2d 719 (E.D.Ark. 1999), 327

Jones v. Flowers, 547 U.S. 220, 126 S.Ct. 1708, 164 L.Ed.2d 415 (2006), 817

Jones v. R.R. Donnelley & Sons Co., 541 U.S. 369, 124 S.Ct. 1836, 158 L.Ed.2d 645 (2004), 890

Jones v. Wilkinson, 800 F.2d 989 (10th Cir. 1986), 927

Jones & Laughlin Steel Corp. v. Pfeifer, 462 U.S. 523, 103 S.Ct. 2541, 76 L.Ed.2d 768 (1983), 618, **619,** 637

Joyce v. City and County of San Francisco, 846 F.Supp. 843 (N.D.Cal.1994), 112

Judd v. Drezga, 103 P.3d 135 (Utah 2004), 525

Jutzi–Johnson v. United States, 263 F.3d 753 (7th Cir.2001), 526, 528

Kaczkowski v. Bolubasz, 491 Pa. 561, 421 A.2d 1027 (Pa.1980), 627

Kadonsky v. United States, 216 F.3d 499 (5th Cir.2000), 817

Kahn v. Berman, 198 Cal.App.3d 1499, 244 Cal.Rptr. 575 (Cal.App. 1 Dist.1988), **823**

Kansas v. Colorado, 543 U.S. 86, 125 S.Ct. 526, 160 L.Ed.2d 418 (2004), 616

Kansas v. Colorado, 533 U.S. 1, 121 S.Ct. 2023, 150 L.Ed.2d 72 (2001), **610**

Kansas City Southern Ry. Co. v. Guardian Trust Co., 281 U.S. 1, 50 S.Ct. 194, 74 L.Ed. 659 (1930), 902

Kansas City Southern Ry. Co. v. Johnson, 798 So.2d 374 (Miss.2001), 526

Kansas Health Care Ass'n, Inc. v. Kansas Dept. of Social & Rehabilitation Services, 31 F.3d 1536 (10th Cir.1994), 75

Katz v. Van Der Noord, 546 So.2d 1047 (Fla. 1989), 748

Kay v. Ehrler, 499 U.S. 432, 111 S.Ct. 1435, 113 L.Ed.2d 486 (1991), 927

Kelley v. Metropolitan County Bd. of Educ., 836 F.2d 986 (6th Cir.1987), 371

Kelo v. City of New London, 545 U.S. 469, 125 S.Ct. 2655, 162 L.Ed.2d 439 (2005), 88

Kemp v. American Tel. & Tel. Co., 393 F.3d 1354 (11th Cir.2004), 716

Keystone Driller Co. v. General Excavator Co., 290 U.S. 240, 54 S.Ct. 146, 78 L.Ed. 293 (1933), **853**

Key Tronic Corp. v. United States, 511 U.S. 809, 114 S.Ct. 1960, 128 L.Ed.2d 797 (1994), 912

Kimel v. Florida Bd. of Regents, 528 U.S. 62, 120 S.Ct. 631, 145 L.Ed.2d 522 (2000), 31

Kinsey v. Preeson, 746 P.2d 542 (Colo.1987), 848

Kinsman Transit Co., Petition of, 338 F.2d 708 (2nd Cir.1964), 607

Kirk v. Denver Pub. Co., 818 P.2d 262 (Colo. 1991), 689

Kleiner v. First Nat. Bank, 751 F.2d 1193 (11th Cir.1985), 335

Knatchbull v. Hallett, 13 Ch.Div. 356 (1879), 784

Kokkonen v. Guardian Life Ins. Co., 511 U.S. 375, 114 S.Ct. 1673, 128 L.Ed.2d 391 (1994), 323

Kolender v. Lawson, 461 U.S. 352, 103 S.Ct. 1855, 75 L.Ed.2d 903 (1983), 154

Kolstad v. American Dental Ass'n, 527 U.S. 526, 119 S.Ct. 2118, 144 L.Ed.2d 494 (1999), 688

Kossian v. American Nat. Ins. Co., 254 Cal.App.2d 647, 62 Cal.Rptr. 225 (Cal.App. 5 Dist.1967), **723**

Kovacs v. Commissioner, 100 T.C. 124 (U.S.Tax Ct.1993), 639

Krouse v. Graham, 137 Cal.Rptr. 863, 562 P.2d 1022 (Cal.1977), 515

Kush v. Lloyd, 616 So.2d 415 (Fla.1992), 505

Laaman v. Warden, New Hampshire State Prison, 238 F.3d 14 (1st Cir.2001), 282

Landgraf v. USI Film Products, 511 U.S. 244, 114 S.Ct. 1483, 128 L.Ed.2d 229 (1994), 450

Landrigan v. McElroy, 457 A.2d 1056 (R.I. 1983), **845**

Lankford v. Gelston, 364 F.2d 197 (4th Cir. 1966), 72

La Plante v. American Honda Motor Co., 27 F.3d 731 (1st Cir.1994), 619

Latham v. Father Divine, 299 N.Y. 22, 85 N.E.2d 168 (N.Y.1949), **759**

Laws v. Laws, 758 A.2d 1226 (Pa.Super.2000), **836**

Ledbetter v. Goodyear Tire & Rubber Co., 550 U.S. 618, 127 S.Ct. 2162, 167 L.Ed.2d 982 (2007), 889

Lennon, In re, 166 U.S. 548, 17 S.Ct. 658, 41 L.Ed. 1110 (1897), 353

Lepak v. McClain, 844 P.2d 852 (Okla.1992), 849

Levine v. Comcoa Ltd., 70 F.3d 1191 (11th Cir.1995), 188

Lewis v. Casey, 518 U.S. 343, 116 S.Ct. 2174, 135 L.Ed.2d 606 (1996), 77

Lewis v. United States, 518 U.S. 322, 116 S.Ct. 2163, 135 L.Ed.2d 590 (1996), 327

Library of Congress v. Shaw, 478 U.S. 310, 106 S.Ct. 2957, 92 L.Ed.2d 250 (1986), 616

Lincoln, City of v. Realty Trust Group, 270 Neb. 587, 705 N.W.2d 432 (Neb.2005), 471

Local No. 93 v. City of Cleveland, 478 U.S. 501, 106 S.Ct. 3063, 92 L.Ed.2d 405 (1986), 254

Lockhart v. United States, 546 U.S. 142, 126 S.Ct. 699, 163 L.Ed.2d 557 (2005), 840

Los Angeles, City of v. David, 538 U.S. 715, 123 S.Ct. 1895, 155 L.Ed.2d 946 (2003), 800

Los Angeles, City of v. Lyons, 461 U.S. 95, 103 S.Ct. 1660, 75 L.Ed.2d 675 (1983), **62**
Los Angeles, City of v. Manhart, 435 U.S. 702, 98 S.Ct. 1370, 55 L.Ed.2d 657 (1978), 130, 361
Louisiana ACORN Fair Housing v. LeBlanc, 211 F.3d 298 (5th Cir.2000), 452
Love v. City of Monterey, 43 Cal.Rptr.2d 911 (Cal.App. 6 Dist.1995), 817
Lugar v. Edmondson Oil Co., 457 U.S. 922, 102 S.Ct. 2744, 73 L.Ed.2d 482 (1982), 801
Lujan v. G & G Fire Sprinklers, Inc., 532 U.S. 189, 121 S.Ct. 1446, 149 L.Ed.2d 391 (2001), 816
Lujan v. National Wildlife Federation, 497 U.S. 871, 110 S.Ct. 3177, 111 L.Ed.2d 695 (1990), 77
Lumley v. Wagner, 42 Eng.Rep. 687 (Q.B. 1852), 183

Mack v. Suffolk County, 191 F.R.D. 16 (D.Mass.2000), 75
Mackby, United States v., 261 F.3d 821 (9th Cir.2001), 647
Madison Guar. Sav. & Loan, (Clinton Fee Application), In re, 334 F.3d 1119 (D.C.Cir. 2003), 939
Madrid v. Marquez, 131 N.M. 132, 33 P.3d 683 (N.M.App.2001), 748
Madsen v. Women's Health Center, Inc., 512 U.S. 753, 114 S.Ct. 2516, 129 L.Ed.2d 593 (1994), **138,** 323
Maggio v. Zeitz, 333 U.S. 56, 68 S.Ct. 401, 92 L.Ed. 476 (1948), 324
Marbury v. Madison, 5 U.S. 137, 2 L.Ed. 60 (1803), 11
Marek v. Chesny, 473 U.S. 1, 105 S.Ct. 3012, 87 L.Ed.2d 1 (1985), 973
Marks v. Stinson, 19 F.3d 873 (3rd Cir.1994), 45
Marquardo, United States v., 149 F.3d 36 (1st Cir.1998), 322
Marriage of (see name of party)
Marsh v. Green, 782 So.2d 223 (Ala.2000), 503
Martin v. Atlantic Coast Line R. R., 268 F.2d 397 (5th Cir.1959), 515
Martin v. Ellandson, 122 F.Supp.2d 1017 (S.D.Iowa 2000), 299
Martin v. Franklin Capital Corp., 546 U.S. 132, 126 S.Ct. 704, 163 L.Ed.2d 547 (2005), 929
Martin v. Hadix, 527 U.S. 343, 119 S.Ct. 1998, 144 L.Ed.2d 347 (1999), 930
Martin v. Wilks, 490 U.S. 755, 109 S.Ct. 2180, 104 L.Ed.2d 835 (1989), 219, 254, 362
Martin, State v., 151 N.H. 107, 849 A.2d 138 (N.H.2004), 892
Maryland Cas. Co. v. Pacific Coal & Oil Co., 312 U.S. 270, 61 S.Ct. 510, 85 L.Ed. 826 (1941), 425
Maryland Dept. of Human Resources v. United States Dept. of Agriculture, 976 F.2d 1462 (4th Cir.1992), 211
Mascenic v. Anderson, 53 Ill.App.3d 971, 11 Ill.Dec. 718, 369 N.E.2d 172 (Ill.App. 1 Dist. 1977), 869

Mason v. City of Hoboken, 196 N.J. 51, 951 A.2d 1017 (N.J.2008), 924
Massachusetts v. Microsoft Corp., 373 F.3d 1199 (D.C.Cir.2004), 54
Mathias v. Accor Economy Lodging, Inc., 347 F.3d 672 (7th Cir.2003), **711**
Matter of (see name of party)
Matthew V. ex rel. Craig V. v. Dekalb County School Sys tem, 244 F.Supp.2d 1331 (N.D.Ga.2003), 928
McCahill v. New York Transp. Co., 201 N.Y. 221, 94 N.E. 616 (N.Y.1911), 501
McCarthy v. Briscoe, 429 U.S. 1317, 97 S.Ct. 10, 50 L.Ed.2d 49 (1976), 137, 373
McComb v. Jacksonville Paper Co., 336 U.S. 187, 69 S.Ct. 497, 93 L.Ed. 599 (1949), 216
McDermott, United States v., 507 U.S. 447, 113 S.Ct. 1526, 123 L.Ed.2d 128 (1993), 828
McDougald v. Garber, 73 N.Y.2d 246, 538 N.Y.S.2d 937, 536 N.E.2d 372 (N.Y.1989), 511
McDuffy v. Secretary of Educ., 415 Mass. 545, 615 N.E.2d 516 (Mass.1993), 111
McGowan v. Estate of Wright, 524 So.2d 308 (Miss.1988), 511
McGraw–Hill Companies v. Procter & Gamble Co., 515 U.S. 1309, 116 S.Ct. 6, 132 L.Ed.2d 892 (1995), 345
McIntosh v. Melroe Co., 729 N.E.2d 972 (Ind. 2000), 892
McKennon v. Nashville Banner Pub. Co., 513 U.S. 352, 115 S.Ct. 879, 130 L.Ed.2d 852 (1995), 42, 861
McMillan v. City of New York, 253 F.R.D. 247 (E.D.N.Y.2008), 534
McMillan v. Pennsylvania, 477 U.S. 79, 106 S.Ct. 2411, 91 L.Ed.2d 67 (1986), 650
MedImmune, Inc. v. Genentech, Inc., 549 U.S. 118, 127 S.Ct. 764, 166 L.Ed.2d 604 (2007), **418**
MedPointe Healthcare Inc. v. Hi–Tech Pharmacal Co., 380 F.Supp.2d 457 (D.N.J.2005), 857
Meinhold v. United States Dept. of Defense, 1993 WL 513209 (C.D.Cal.1993), 76
Meinhold v. United States Dept. of Defense, 808 F.Supp. 1455 (C.D.Cal.1993), 76
Melkonyan v. Sullivan, 501 U.S. 89, 111 S.Ct. 2157, 115 L.Ed.2d 78 (1991), 940
Memphis Community School Dist. v. Stachura, 477 U.S. 299, 106 S.Ct. 2537, 91 L.Ed.2d 249 (1986), **442**
Mendoza v. United States, 623 F.2d 1338 (9th Cir.1980), 968
Mercado v. Ahmed, 974 F.2d 863 (7th Cir. 1992), 526
Mercer v. Duke University, 401 F.3d 199 (4th Cir.2005), 946
Mertens v. Hewitt Associates, 508 U.S. 248, 113 S.Ct. 2063, 124 L.Ed.2d 161 (1993), 453
Metro–North Commuter Railroad Co. v. Buckley, 521 U.S. 424, 117 S.Ct. 2113, 138 L.Ed.2d 560 (1997), 505
Metropolitan Opera Ass'n v. Local 100, Hotel Employees and Restaurant Employees In-

tern. Union, 239 F.3d 172 (2nd Cir.2001), 216
Microsoft, United States v., 231 F.Supp.2d 144 (D.D.C.2002), 53
Microsoft Corp., United States v., 97 F.Supp.2d 59 (D.D.C.2000), 53
Microsoft Corp., United States v., 87 F.Supp.2d 30 (D.D.C.2000), 53
Microsoft Corp., United States v., 84 F.Supp.2d 9 (D.D.C.1999), 53
Microsoft Corp., United States v., 147 F.3d 935 (D.C.Cir.1998), 90, 188, 219
Microsoft Corp., United States v., 56 F.3d 1448 (D.C.Cir.1995), 220
Miller v. French, 530 U.S. 327, 120 S.Ct. 2246, 147 L.Ed.2d 326 (2000), 59, **283**
Miller v. Johnson, 515 U.S. 900, 115 S.Ct. 2475, 132 L.Ed.2d 762 (1995), 181
Miller v. Town of Hull, 878 F.2d 523 (1st Cir.1989), 405
Miller, People ex rel. Edgar v., 110 Ill.App.3d 264, 65 Ill.Dec. 814, 441 N.E.2d 1328 (Ill. App. 4 Dist.1982), 89
Milliken v. Bradley, 433 U.S. 267, 97 S.Ct. 2749, 53 L.Ed.2d 745 (1977), 366, 371
Milliken v. Bradley, 418 U.S. 717, 94 S.Ct. 3112, 41 L.Ed.2d 1069 (1974), 169
Mills v. Electric Auto-Lite Co., 396 U.S. 375, 90 S.Ct. 616, 24 L.Ed.2d 593 (1970), 903
Mills v. Freeman, 942 F.Supp. 1449 (N.D.Ga. 1996), 281
Milwaukee, City of v. Activated Sludge, 69 F.2d 577 (7th Cir.1934), 101
Milwaukee, City of v. National Gypsum Co., 515 U.S. 189, 115 S.Ct. 2091, 132 L.Ed.2d 148 (1995), 613
Missouri v. Jenkins (Jenkins III), 515 U.S. 70, 115 S.Ct. 2038, 132 L.Ed.2d 63 (1995), 163, **165**
Missouri v. Jenkins (Jenkins II), 495 U.S. 33, 110 S.Ct. 1651, 109 L.Ed.2d 31 (1990), 373, **376**
Missouri v. Jenkins (Jenkins I), 491 U.S. 274, 109 S.Ct. 2463, 105 L.Ed.2d 229 (1989), 929, 942
Mitchell v. Dunn, 211 Cal. 129, 294 P. 386 (Cal.1930), 785
Mitchell v. Robert DeMario Jewelry, Inc., 361 U.S. 288, 80 S.Ct. 332, 4 L.Ed.2d 323 (1960), 454
Mitsui Manufacturers Bank v. Unicom Computer Corp., 13 F.3d 321 (9th Cir.1994), 773
Mobil Oil Exploration and Producing Southeast, Inc. v. United States, 530 U.S. 604, 120 S.Ct. 2423, 147 L.Ed.2d 528 (2000), 755
Moffer v. Watt, 690 F.2d 1037 (D.C.Cir.1982), 651
Monterey, City of v. Del Monte Dunes at Monterey, Ltd., 526 U.S. 687, 119 S.Ct. 1624, 143 L.Ed.2d 882 (1999), 456
Montgomery Ward & Co. v. NLRB, 904 F.2d 1156 (7th Cir.1990), 138
Moore v. Regents of University of California, 271 Cal.Rptr. 146, 793 P.2d 479 (Cal.1990), 759
Morgan v. Foretich, 564 A.2d 1 (D.C.1989), 327

Morgan v. McDonough, 540 F.2d 527 (1st Cir. 1976), 366
Morrison v. Parker, 90 F.Supp.2d 876 (W.D.Mich.2000), **428**
Moser v. United States, 341 U.S. 41, 71 S.Ct. 553, 95 L.Ed. 729 (1951), 872
Moses v. Macferlan, 2 Burr. 1005, 97 Eng.Rep. 676 (K.B.1760), 721
Moss v. Superior Court, 71 Cal.Rptr.2d 215, 950 P.2d 59 (Cal.1998), 310, 841
Mosser v. Darrow, 341 U.S. 267, 71 S.Ct. 680, 95 L.Ed. 927 (1951), 766
Motorola Credit Corp. v. Uzan, 509 F.3d 74 (2nd Cir.2007), 688
Mt. Healthy City School Dist. Bd. of Educ. v. Doyle, 429 U.S. 274, 97 S.Ct. 568, 50 L.Ed.2d 471 (1977), **37**
Muniz v. Hoffman, 422 U.S. 454, 95 S.Ct. 2178, 45 L.Ed.2d 319 (1975), 328
Munn v. Algee, 924 F.2d 568 (5th Cir.1991), 550
Munn v. Southern Health Plan, Inc., 719 F.Supp. 525 (N.D.Miss.1989), **543**
Murphy v. IRS, 460 F.3d 79 (D.C.Cir.2006), 637
Mushroom Transp. Co., In re, 227 B.R. 244 (Bkrtcy.E.D.Pa.1998), **779**

Nappe v. Anschelewitz, Barr, Ansell & Bonello, 97 N.J. 37, 477 A.2d 1224 (N.J.1984), 451
National Ass'n of Home Builders v. Defenders of Wildlife, 551 U.S. 644, 127 S.Ct. 2518, 168 L.Ed.2d 467 (2007), 121
National Council of La Raza v. Mukasey, 283 Fed.Appx. 848 (2nd Cir.2008), 72
National Private Truck Council, Inc. v. Oklahoma Tax Com'n, 515 U.S. 582, 115 S.Ct. 2351, 132 L.Ed.2d 509 (1995), 89
Natural Resources Defense Council, Inc. v. Morton, 337 F.Supp. 167 (D.D.C.1971), 211
Naylor v. Hall, 201 Mont. 59, 651 P.2d 1010 (Mont.1982), 183
Nesmith v. Texaco, 727 F.2d 497 (5th Cir. 1984), 627
Network Intern. L.C. v. Worldcom Technologies, Inc., 133 F.Supp.2d 713 (D.Md.2001), 212
Neulander, State v., 173 N.J. 193, 801 A.2d 255 (N.J.2002), 357
Newark Coalition For Low Income Housing v. Newark Redevelopment and Housing Authority, 524 F.Supp.2d 559 (D.N.J.2007), 268
New Destiny Development Corp. v. Piccione, 802 F.Supp. 692 (D.Conn.1992), 800
New Hampshire v. Maine, 532 U.S. 742, 121 S.Ct. 1808, 149 L.Ed.2d 968 (2001), 870
Newhouse v. McCormick & Co., 110 F.3d 635 (8th Cir.1997), 946
New Jersey, United States v., 194 F.3d 426 (3rd Cir.1999), 243
Newman v. Piggie Park Enterprises, Inc., 390 U.S. 400, 88 S.Ct. 964, 19 L.Ed.2d 1263 (1968), 927
Newport v. Fact Concerts, Inc., 453 U.S. 247, 101 S.Ct. 2748, 69 L.Ed.2d 616 (1981), 673

Newton v. Cox, 878 S.W.2d 105 (Tenn.1994), 947

New York ex. rel. People, City of v. Taliaferrow, 144 Misc.2d 649, 544 N.Y.S.2d 273 (N.Y.Sup.1989), 672

New York Gaslight Club, Inc. v. Carey, 447 U.S. 54, 100 S.Ct. 2024, 64 L.Ed.2d 723 (1980), 938

New York Rayon Importing Co., United States v., 329 U.S. 654, 67 S.Ct. 601, 91 L.Ed. 577 (1947), 619

New York State Ass'n for Retarded Children, Inc. v. Carey, 631 F.2d 162 (2nd Cir.1980), 372, 375

New York State Federation of Taxi Drivers, Inc. v. Westchester County Taxi and Limousine Com'n, 272 F.3d 154 (2nd Cir.2001), 926

New York State Nat. Organization for Women v. Terry, 159 F.3d 86 (2nd Cir.1998), 322

New York Times Co. v. United States, 403 U.S. 713, 91 S.Ct. 2140, 29 L.Ed.2d 822 (1971), 89

Niles, In re, 176 N.J. 282, 823 A.2d 1 (N.J. 2003), 912

Niner v. Hanson, 217 Md. 298, 142 A.2d 798 (Md.1958), 857

NLRB v. American Geri–Care, Inc., 697 F.2d 56 (2nd Cir.1982), 44

NLRB v. Gissel Packing Co., 395 U.S. 575, 89 S.Ct. 1918, 23 L.Ed.2d 547 (1969), 138

NLRB v. Wyman–Gordon Co., 394 U.S. 759, 89 S.Ct. 1426, 22 L.Ed.2d 709 (1969), 44

Nordic Village Inc., United States v., 503 U.S. 30, 112 S.Ct. 1011, 117 L.Ed.2d 181 (1992), 370

Norfolk & Western Ry. Co. v. Ayers, 538 U.S. 135, 123 S.Ct. 1210, 155 L.Ed.2d 261 (2003), 499

Norfolk & Western Ry. Co. v. Liepelt, 444 U.S. 490, 100 S.Ct. 755, 62 L.Ed.2d 689 (1980), 637

Noriega, United States v., 752 F.Supp. 1032 (S.D.Fla.1990), 345

North Carolina Dept. of Transp. v. Crest Street Community Council, Inc., 479 U.S. 6, 107 S.Ct. 336, 93 L.Ed.2d 188 (1986), 938

North Carolina State Bd. of Ed. v. Swann, 402 U.S. 43, 91 S.Ct. 1284, 28 L.Ed.2d 586 (1971), 373

Northern Ins. Co. v. Chatham County, 547 U.S. 189, 126 S.Ct. 1689, 164 L.Ed.2d 367 (2006), 370

Northern Utilities, Inc. v. Lewiston Radiator Works, Inc., 2005 WL 758466 (D.Me.2005), 428

Northwest Airlines, Inc. v. Transport Workers Union of America, AFL–CIO, 451 U.S. 77, 101 S.Ct. 1571, 67 L.Ed.2d 750 (1981), 869

Norton v. Ashcroft, 298 F.3d 547 (6th Cir. 2002), 153

NOW v. Operation Rescue, 37 F.3d 646 (D.C.Cir.1994), 322

Oatway, In re (Hertslet v. Oatway), [1903] 2 Ch.Div. 356 (Ch.D. 1903), 785

Ober v. Whitman, 243 F.3d 1190 (9th Cir. 2001), 134

O Centro Espirita Beneficiente Uniao Do Vegetal v. Ashcroft, 389 F.3d 973 (10th Cir. 2004), 202

Oelrichs v. Spain, 82 U.S. 211, 21 L.Ed. 43 (1872), 902

Office of Personnel Management v. Richmond, 496 U.S. 414, 110 S.Ct. 2465, 110 L.Ed.2d 387 (1990), 876

Ogden v. J.M. Steel Erecting, Inc., 201 Ariz. 32, 31 P.3d 806 (Ariz.App. Div. 1 2001), 515

Ohio v. Department of the Interior, 880 F.2d 432 (D.C.Cir.1989), **472**

Olwell v. Nye & Nissen Co., 26 Wash.2d 282, 173 P.2d 652 (Wash.1946), **732**

Oncology Associates, United States ex rel. Rahman v., 198 F.3d 489 (4th Cir.1999), 788

Onishea v. Hopper, 171 F.3d 1289 (11th Cir. 1999), 204

Opinion of the Justices, 624 So.2d 107 (Ala. 1993), 414

Oracle Securities Litigation, In re, 852 F.Supp. 1437 (N.D.Cal.1994), 964

Oracle Securities Litigation, In re, 136 F.R.D. 639 (N.D.Cal.1991), 964

Oracle Securities Litigation, In re, 132 F.R.D. 538 (N.D.Cal.1990), 964

Ortiz v. Fibreboard Corp., 527 U.S. 815, 119 S.Ct. 2295, 144 L.Ed.2d 715 (1999), 563

O'Sullivan v. City of Chicago, 396 F.3d 843 (7th Cir.2005), 271

Owner Operator Independent Drivers Ass'n, Inc. v. Swift Transp. Co., 367 F.3d 1108 (9th Cir.2004), 130

PacifiCare Health Systems, Inc. v. Book, 538 U.S. 401, 123 S.Ct. 1531, 155 L.Ed.2d 578 (2003), 641

Pacific Mut. Life Ins. Co. v. Haslip, 499 U.S. 1, 111 S.Ct. 1032, 113 L.Ed.2d 1 (1991), 702, 708

Palmigiano v. Garrahy, 448 F.Supp. 659 (D.R.I. 1978), 365

Pan–American Petroleum & Transport Co. v. United States, 273 U.S. 456, 47 S.Ct. 416, 71 L.Ed. 734 (1927), 879

Panola Land Buying Ass'n v. Clark, 844 F.2d 1506 (11th Cir.1988), 973

Paramount Pictures Corp. v. Davis, 228 Cal. App.2d 827, 39 Cal.Rptr. 791 (Cal.App. 2 Dist.1964), 135

Parcel of Property, United States v., 337 F.3d 225 (2nd Cir.2003), 817

Pardini v. Allegheny Intermediate Unit, 524 F.3d 419 (3rd Cir.2008), 928

Parents Involved in Community Schools v. Seattle School Dist. No. 1, 551 U.S. 701, 127 S.Ct. 2738, 168 L.Ed.2d 508 (2007), 164

Parev Products Co. v. I. Rokeach, 124 F.2d 147 (2nd Cir.1941), 241

Park v. Forest Service, 205 F.3d 1034 (8th Cir.2000), 74

Parkview Associates v. City of New York, 71 N.Y.2d 274, 525 N.Y.S.2d 176, 519 N.E.2d 1372 (N.Y.1988), 130

Parrotte v. Sensenich, 22 F.3d 472 (2nd Cir. 1994), 835
Parsons v. Bedford, 28 U.S. 433, 3 Pet. 433, 7 L.Ed. 732 (1830), 455
Patterson v. Cronin, 650 P.2d 531 (Colo.1982), 800
Peevyhouse v. Garland Coal & Min. Co., 382 P.2d 109 (Okla.1962), 483
Pennsylvania v. Delaware Valley Citizens' Council for Clean Air, 478 U.S. 546, 106 S.Ct. 3088, 92 L.Ed.2d 439 (1986), 942
Pennsylvania v. Muniz, 496 U.S. 582, 110 S.Ct. 2638, 110 L.Ed.2d 528 (1990), 649
Pennsylvania, Commonwealth of v. Porter, 659 F.2d 306 (3rd Cir.1981), 53
Pennsylvania Environmental Defense Foundation v. Canon–McMillan School Dist., 152 F.3d 228 (3rd Cir.1998), 964
People v. _____ (see opposing party)
People Against Police Violence v. City of Pittsburgh, 520 F.3d 226 (3rd Cir.2008), 926
People ex rel. v. _____(see opposing party and relator)
People Who Care v. Rockford Bd. of Educ., 246 F.3d 1073 (7th Cir.2001), 281
People Who Care v. Rockford Bd. of Educ., 111 F.3d 528 (7th Cir.1997), 135
PepsiCo v. Redmond, 54 F.3d 1262 (7th Cir. 1995), 164
Perma Life Mufflers, Inc. v. International Parts Corp., 392 U.S. 134, 88 S.Ct. 1981, 20 L.Ed.2d 982 (1968), 863
Petition of (see name of party)
Pharmaceutical Soc. of State of New York v. New York State Dept. of Social Services, 50 F.3d 1168 (2nd Cir.1995), 212
Philadelphia, City of, United States v., 644 F.2d 187 (3rd Cir.1980), 53
Philip Morris USA v. Williams, 553 U.S. ___, 128 S.Ct. 2904, 171 L.Ed.2d 840 (2008), 711
Philip Morris USA v. Williams, 549 U.S. 346, 127 S.Ct. 1057, 166 L.Ed.2d 940 (2007), 711
Pierce v. Douglas School Dist. No. 4, 297 Or. 363, 686 P.2d 332 (Or.1984), 183
Pierce v. Underwood, 487 U.S. 552, 108 S.Ct. 2541, 101 L.Ed.2d 490 (1988), 928
Pinsky v. Duncan, 79 F.3d 306 (2nd Cir.1996), 799
Pinter v. Dahl, 486 U.S. 622, 108 S.Ct. 2063, 100 L.Ed.2d 658 (1988), 868
Planned Parenthood of Houston and Southeast Texas v. Sanchez, 480 F.3d 734 (5th Cir. 2007), 926
Plant v. Doe, 19 F.Supp.2d 1316 (S.D.Fla. 1998), 189
Plata v. Schwarzenegger, 2005 WL 2932253 (N.D.Cal.2005), 229
P.N. v. Seattle School Dist., 474 F.3d 1165 (9th Cir.2007), 925
Poe v. Ullman, 367 U.S. 497, 81 S.Ct. 1752, 6 L.Ed.2d 989 (1961), 427
Pollard v. E.I. du Pont de Nemours & Co., 532 U.S. 843, 121 S.Ct. 1946, 150 L.Ed.2d 62 (2001), 454
Polselli v. Nationwide Mut. Fire Ins. Co., 126 F.3d 524 (3rd Cir.1997), 912

Porter v. Warner Holding Co., 328 U.S. 395, 66 S.Ct. 1086, 90 L.Ed. 1332 (1946), 454
Portland Feminist Women's Health Center v. Advocates for Life, Inc., 859 F.2d 681 (9th Cir.1988), **213**
Pounders v. Watson, 521 U.S. 982, 117 S.Ct. 2359, 138 L.Ed.2d 976 (1997), 328
Powers v. Eichen, 229 F.3d 1249 (9th Cir. 2000), 965
Prandini v. National Tea Co., 557 F.2d 1015 (3rd Cir.1977), 968
Prasco, LLC v. Medicis Pharmaceutical Corp., 537 F.3d 1329 (Fed.Cir.2008), 425
Pratt v. Shell Petroleum Corp., 100 F.2d 833 (10th Cir.1938), 766
Precision Instrument Mfg. Co. v. Automotive Maintenance Machinery Co., 324 U.S. 806, 65 S.Ct. 993, 89 L.Ed. 1381 (1945), 856
Pretre v. United States, 531 F.Supp. 931 (E.D.Mo.1981), 241, 531
Price v. Austin Independent School Dist., 945 F.2d 1307 (5th Cir.1991), 278
Price Waterhouse v. Hopkins, 490 U.S. 228, 109 S.Ct. 1775, 104 L.Ed.2d 268 (1989), 41
Pro–Football, Inc. v. Harjo, 567 F.Supp.2d 46 (D.D.C.2008), 897
Pro–Football, Inc. v. Harjo, 415 F.3d 44 (D.C.Cir.2005), **892**
Pro–Football, Inc. v. Harjo, 284 F.Supp.2d 96 (D.D.C.2003), 897
Providence Journal Co., In re, 820 F.2d 1354 (1st Cir.1987), **336**
Providence Journal Co., In re, 820 F.2d 1342 (1st Cir.1986), **336**
Public Interest Research Group of New Jersey, Inc. v. Windall, 51 F.3d 1179 (3rd Cir.1995), 938
Puget Sound Gillnetters Ass'n v. United States Dist. Court, 573 F.2d 1123 (9th Cir.1978), 356
Pulliam v. Allen, 466 U.S. 522, 104 S.Ct. 1970, 80 L.Ed.2d 565 (1984), 929
Purdue Pharma L.P. v. Endo Pharmaceuticals Inc., 438 F.3d 1123 (Fed.Cir.2006), 856
Pyeatte v. Pyeatte, 135 Ariz. 346, 661 P.2d 196 (Ariz.App. Div. 1 1982), 745

Quern v. Jordan, 440 U.S. 332, 99 S.Ct. 1139, 59 L.Ed.2d 358 (1979), 371
Quick v. Samp, 697 N.W.2d 741 (S.D.2005), 869

Rahman, United States ex rel. v. Oncology Associates, 198 F.3d 489 (4th Cir.1999), 788
Rajender v. University of Minnesota, 730 F.2d 1110 (8th Cir.1984), 244
Ramirez de Arellano v. Weinberger, 724 F.2d 143 (D.C.Cir.1983), 113
Rancho Palos Verdes, City of v. Abrams, 544 U.S. 113, 125 S.Ct. 1453, 161 L.Ed.2d 316 (2005), 31
Raygor v. Regents of University of Minnesota, 534 U.S. 533, 122 S.Ct. 999, 152 L.Ed.2d 27 (2002), 892
Redevelopment Agency v. Gilmore, 214 Cal. Rptr. 904, 700 P.2d 794 (Cal.1985), 618

Red Owl Stores, Inc., State v., 253 Minn. 236, 92 N.W.2d 103 (Minn.1958), 80
Reebok Intern. Ltd. v. McLaughlin, 49 F.3d 1387 (9th Cir.1995), 355
Regan, United States v., 232 U.S. 37, 34 S.Ct. 213, 58 L.Ed. 494 (1914), 650
Reich v. Cambridgeport Air Systems, 26 F.3d 1187 (1st Cir.1994), 672
Reich v. Sea Sprite Boat Co., Inc., 50 F.3d 413 (7th Cir.1995), 322
Reisenfeld & Co. v. Network Group, Inc., 277 F.3d 856 (6th Cir.2002), 731
Rendine v. Pantzer, 141 N.J. 292, 661 A.2d 1202 (N.J.1995), 946
Renger Memorial Hosp. v. State, 674 S.W.2d 828 (Tex.App.-Austin 1984), 821
Republic Nat. Bank v. United States, 506 U.S. 80, 113 S.Ct. 554, 121 L.Ed.2d 474 (1992), 828
Republic Supply Co. v. Richfield Oil Co., 79 F.2d 375 (9th Cir.1935), 785
Reynolds v. Roberts, 251 F.3d 1350 (11th Cir. 2001), 243
Rhodes v. Stewart, 488 U.S. 1, 109 S.Ct. 202, 102 L.Ed.2d 1 (1988), 925
Richlin Sec. Service Co. v. Chertoff, 553 U.S. ___, 128 S.Ct. 2007, 170 L.Ed.2d 960 (2008), 942
Richmond, City of v. J.A. Croson Co., 488 U.S. 469, 109 S.Ct. 706, 102 L.Ed.2d 854 (1989), 181, 362
Right v. Breen, 277 Conn. 364, 890 A.2d 1287 (Conn.2006), 450, 462
Riley v. Kurtz, 194 F.3d 1313 (6th Cir.1999), 709
Rivera v. Horton, 7 F.Supp.2d 147 (N.D.N.Y. 1998), 451
Riverside, City of v. Rivera, 477 U.S. 561, 106 S.Ct. 2686, 91 L.Ed.2d 466 (1986), 946
Rizzo v. Goode, 423 U.S. 362, 96 S.Ct. 598, 46 L.Ed.2d 561 (1976), **46**
Robbins v. DeBuono, 218 F.3d 197 (2nd Cir. 2000), 840
Robert R. Wisdom Oil Co. v. Gatewood, 682 S.W.2d 882 (Mo.App. S.D.1984), 844
Roberts v. Ohio Permanente Med. Group, Inc., 76 Ohio St.3d 483, 668 N.E.2d 480 (Ohio 1996), 541
Robinson v. Cahill, 69 N.J. 449, 355 A.2d 129 (N.J.1976), 374, 376
Roe v. Operation Rescue, 54 F.3d 133 (3rd Cir.1995), 353
Roginsky v. Richardson–Merrell, Inc., 378 F.2d 832 (2nd Cir.1967), 662
Rohm & Haas v. Crystal Chemical Co., 722 F.2d 1556 (Fed.Cir.1983), 857
Rolf v. Tri State Motor Transit Co., 91 Ohio St.3d 380, 745 N.E.2d 424 (Ohio 2001), 523
Romberg v. Nichols, 48 F.3d 453 (9th Cir. 1995), 928
Rosado v. Wyman, 397 U.S. 397, 90 S.Ct. 1207, 25 L.Ed.2d 442 (1970), 43
Rosen, People v., 11 Cal.2d 147, 78 P.2d 727 (Cal.1938), 869

Rosener v. Sears, Roebuck & Co., 110 Cal. App.3d 740, 168 Cal.Rptr. 237 (Cal.App. 1 Dist.1980), 599
Rosewell v. LaSalle Nat. Bank, 450 U.S. 503, 101 S.Ct. 1221, 67 L.Ed.2d 464 (1981), 89
Ross v. Kansas City Power & Light Co., 293 F.3d 1041 (8th Cir.2002), 709
Rousey v. Jacoway, 544 U.S. 320, 2006-13 I.R.B. 656, 125 S.Ct. 1561, 161 L.Ed.2d 563 (2005), 840
Royal v. Kautzky, 375 F.3d 720 (8th Cir.2004), 449
Rozpad v. Commissioner, 154 F.3d 1 (1st Cir. 1998), 638
Ruff v. Weintraub, 105 N.J. 233, 519 A.2d 1384 (N.J.1987), 619
Rufo v. Inmates of Suffolk County Jail, 502 U.S. 367, 112 S.Ct. 748, 116 L.Ed.2d 867 (1992), **254**
Rufo v. Simpson, 103 Cal.Rptr.2d 492 (Cal.App. 2 Dist.2001), 514, 523, 527
Ruiz v. Estelle, 161 F.3d 814 (5th Cir.1998), 299
Ruiz v. Johnson, 154 F.Supp.2d 975 (S.D.Tex. 2001), 299
Ruiz v. United States, 243 F.3d 941 (5th Cir. 2001), 297
Russell, United States v., 411 U.S. 423, 93 S.Ct. 1637, 36 L.Ed.2d 366 (1973), 861

Samsung Electronics Co. v. ON Semiconductor Corp., 541 F.Supp.2d 645 (D.Del.2008), 425
Samuels v. Mackell, 401 U.S. 66, 91 S.Ct. 764, 27 L.Ed.2d 688 (1971), 435, 436
Sanchez–Lopez v. Fuentes–Pujols, 375 F.3d 121 (1st Cir.2004), 41
Sancho v. United States Dept. of Energy, 578 F.Supp.2d 1258 (D.Hawai'i 2008), 210
Sanders v. Dooly County, 245 F.3d 1289 (11th Cir.2001), 898
Sasso, United States v., 215 F.3d 283 (2nd Cir.2000), 229
Saunders v. Branch Banking & Trust Co., 526 F.3d 142 (4th Cir.2008), 716
Scafidi v. Seiler, 119 N.J. 93, 574 A.2d 398 (N.J.1990), 542
Schaerrer v. Westman Com'n Co., 769 P.2d 1058 (Colo.1989), 840
Schefke v. Reliable Collection Agency, Ltd., 32 P.3d 52 (Hawai'i 2001), 946
Scheiber v. Dolby Laboratories, Inc., 293 F.3d 1014 (7th Cir.2002), 80, 852
Schenck v. Pro–Choice Network Of Western New York, 519 U.S. 357, 117 S.Ct. 855, 137 L.Ed.2d 1 (1997), 153
Schiavo ex rel. Schindler v. Schiavo, 403 F.3d 1223 (11th Cir.2005), 188
Schleier, Commissioner v., 515 U.S. 323, 115 S.Ct. 2159, 132 L.Ed.2d 294 (1995), 638
Schmerber v. California, 384 U.S. 757, 86 S.Ct. 1826, 16 L.Ed.2d 908 (1966), 649
School Committee of Burlington v. Department of Educ. of Mass., 471 U.S. 359, 105 S.Ct. 1996, 85 L.Ed.2d 385 (1985), 454
Schultz v. Hembree, 975 F.2d 572 (9th Cir. 1992), 940

Schweiker v. Chilicky, 487 U.S. 412, 108 S.Ct. 2460, 101 L.Ed.2d 370 (1988), **20**
Scotts Co. v. United Industries Corp., 315 F.3d 264 (4th Cir.2002), 208
Sealy Connecticut, Inc. v. Litton Industries, Inc., 93 F.Supp.2d 177 (D.Conn.2000), 912
Searles v. Van Bebber, 251 F.3d 869 (10th Cir.2001), 452
S.E.C. v. Homa, 514 F.3d 661 (7th Cir.2008), 355
S.E.C. v. Rind, 991 F.2d 1486 (9th Cir.1993), 891
S.E.C. v. Smyth, 420 F.3d 1225 (11th Cir. 2005), 217
Serawop, United States v., 505 F.3d 1112 (10th Cir.2007), 532
Serrano v. Priest, 141 Cal.Rptr. 315, 569 P.2d 1303 (Cal.1977), 904
Shaheed–Muhammad v. Dipaolo, 393 F.Supp.2d 80 (D.Mass.2005), 449
Shalala v. Schaefer, 509 U.S. 292, 113 S.Ct. 2625, 125 L.Ed.2d 239 (1993), 941
Sharon v. Tucker, 144 U.S. 533, 12 S.Ct. 720, 36 L.Ed. 532 (1892), 416
Shaumyan v. O'Neill, 987 F.2d 122 (2nd Cir. 1993), 800
Shaw v. Delta Air Lines, Inc., 463 U.S. 85, 103 S.Ct. 2890, 77 L.Ed.2d 490 (1983), 436
Sheldon v. Metro–Goldwyn Pictures Corporation, 309 U.S. 390, 60 S.Ct. 681, 84 L.Ed. 825 (1940), 739
Sherrill, City of v. Oneida Indian Nation of New York, 544 U.S. 197, 125 S.Ct. 1478, 161 L.Ed.2d 386 (2005), 898
Sheshtawy, In re, 154 S.W.3d 114 (Tex.2004), 343
Shipp, United States v., 214 U.S. 386, 29 S.Ct. 637, 53 L.Ed. 1041 (1909), 343
Shuttlesworth v. City of Birmingham, 394 U.S. 147, 89 S.Ct. 935, 22 L.Ed.2d 162 (1969), 343
Sierra Club v. E.P.A., 322 F.3d 718 (D.C.Cir. 2003), 926
Sierra Club v. Morton, 405 U.S. 727, 92 S.Ct. 1361, 31 L.Ed.2d 636 (1972), 107
Simon v. San Paolo United States Holding Co., Inc., 29 Cal.Rptr.3d 379, 113 P.3d 63 (Cal. 2005), 708
Simon and Schuster, Inc. v. Members of New York State Crime Victims Bd., 502 U.S. 105, 112 S.Ct. 501, 116 L.Ed.2d 476 (1991), 768
Simpson, In re Marriage of, 14 Cal.Rptr.2d 411, 841 P.2d 931 (Cal.1992), 841
Sims v. Stuart, 291 F. 707 (S.D.N.Y.1922), 204
SizeWise Rentals, Inc. v. Mediq/PRN Life Support Services, Inc., 216 F.3d 1088 (10th Cir.2000), 211
Skelly Oil Co. v. Phillips Petroleum Co., 339 U.S. 667, 70 S.Ct. 876, 94 L.Ed. 1194 (1950), 436
SKS Merch, LLC v. Barry, 233 F.Supp.2d 841 (E.D.Ky.2002), 189
Skwira v. United States, 344 F.3d 64 (1st Cir. 2003), 890

Slater v. Oriental Mills, 18 R.I. 352, 27 A. 443 (R.I.1893), 778
Slater v. Skyhawk Transp., Inc., 77 F.Supp.2d 580 (D.N.J.1999), 637
Small v. Combustion Engineering, 209 Mont. 387, 681 P.2d 1081 (Mont.1984), 548
Smith v. Doe, 538 U.S. 84, 123 S.Ct. 1140, 155 L.Ed.2d 164 (2003), 648
Smith v. Fitchburg Public Schools, 401 F.3d 16 (1st Cir.2005), 926
Smith v. Staso Milling Co., 18 F.2d 736 (2nd Cir.1927), **101**, 850
Smith v. Wade, 461 U.S. 30, 103 S.Ct. 1625, 75 L.Ed.2d 632 (1983), 672
Smith, United States v., 47 F.3d 681 (4th Cir. 1995), 840
Snepp v. United States, 444 U.S. 507, 100 S.Ct. 763, 62 L.Ed.2d 704 (1980), **760**
Snow v. Villacci, 754 A.2d 360 (Me.2000), 532
Snow, Nuffer, Engstrom & Drake v. Tanasse, 980 P.2d 208 (Utah 1999), 821
Softsolutions, Inc. v. Brigham Young University, 1 P.3d 1095 (Utah 2000), 946
Soldal v. Cook County, Ill., 506 U.S. 56, 113 S.Ct. 538, 121 L.Ed.2d 450 (1992), 803
Sole v. Wyner, 551 U.S. 74, 127 S.Ct. 2188, 167 L.Ed.2d 1069 (2007), 926
Sommer v. Sommer, 947 P.2d 512 (Okla.1997), 849
Sorrell v. Thevenir, 69 Ohio St.3d 415, 633 N.E.2d 504 (Ohio 1994), 503
Southwest Voter Registration Educ. Project v. Shelley, 278 F.Supp.2d 1131 (C.D.Cal.2003), 203
Spallone v. United States, 493 U.S. 265, 110 S.Ct. 625, 107 L.Ed.2d 644 (1990), **394**
Spomer v. Littleton, 414 U.S. 514, 94 S.Ct. 685, 38 L.Ed.2d 694 (1974), 76
Spur Industries v. Del E. Webb Development Co., 108 Ariz. 178, 494 P.2d 700 (Ariz. 1972), 106
State v. _____(see opposing party)
State Farm Mut. Auto. Ins. Co. v. Campbell, 538 U.S. 408, 123 S.Ct. 1513, 155 L.Ed.2d 585 (2003), **696**
State of (see name of state)
State University of New York v. Denton, 35 A.D.2d 176, 316 N.Y.S.2d 297 (N.Y.A.D. 4 Dept.1970), **347**
Steffel v. Thompson, 415 U.S. 452, 94 S.Ct. 1209, 39 L.Ed.2d 505 (1974), 435
Steinhauser v. Hertz Corp., 421 F.2d 1169 (2nd Cir.1970), **536**
Sterling v. Velsicol Chemical Corp., 855 F.2d 1188 (6th Cir.1988), 542
Sterling Drug, Inc. v. Bayer AG, 14 F.3d 733 (2nd Cir.1994), 179
Stogner v. California, 539 U.S. 607, 123 S.Ct. 2446, 156 L.Ed.2d 544 (2003), 891
Stover v. Lakeland Square Owners Ass'n, 434 N.W.2d 866 (Iowa 1989), 637
Sulit v. Schiltgen, 213 F.3d 449 (9th Cir.2000), 877
Sullivan v. Hudson, 490 U.S. 877, 109 S.Ct. 2248, 104 L.Ed.2d 941 (1989), **931**

Summerlin, United States v., 310 U.S. 414, 60 S.Ct. 1019, 84 L.Ed. 1283 (1940), 891, 898

Supreme Court of Virginia v. Consumers Union, 446 U.S. 719, 100 S.Ct. 1967, 64 L.Ed.2d 641 (1980), 929

Swan v. Clinton, 100 F.3d 973 (D.C.Cir.1996), 184

Swann v. Charlotte–Mecklenburg Bd. of Ed., 402 U.S. 1, 91 S.Ct. 1267, 28 L.Ed.2d 554 (1971), **157,** 163

Sweeton v. Brown, 27 F.3d 1162 (6th Cir. 1994), 268

Swift & Co., United States v., 1982–1 Trade Cases (CCH) ¶ 64,464 (N.D.Ill.1981), 244

Swift & Co., United States v., 286 U.S. 106, 52 S.Ct. 460, 76 L.Ed. 999 (1932), 243

Sylvan Lake Golf & Tennis Club Ltd. v. Performance Industries Ltd., [2002] 209 D.L.R. (4th) 318 (S.C.C.2002), 597

Synthroid Marketing Litigation, In re, 325 F.3d 974 (7th Cir.2003), 965

Synthroid Marketing Litigation, In re, 264 F.3d 712 (7th Cir.2001), 965

System Federation No. 91 v. Wright, 364 U.S. 642, 81 S.Ct. 368, 5 L.Ed.2d 349 (1961), 244

Talbot v. Quaker–State Oil Refining Co., 104 F.2d 967 (3rd Cir.1939), 436

Taylor v. Diamant, 178 B.R. 480 (9th Cir. 1995), 772

Taylor v. Meirick, 712 F.2d 1112 (7th Cir. 1983), 738

Telecommunications Research & Action Center v. Federal Communications Commission, 750 F.2d 70 (D.C.Cir.1984), 232

Telesphere Intern. Securities Litigation, In re, 753 F.Supp. 716 (N.D.Ill.1990), 948

Tennessee Valley Authority v. Hill, 437 U.S. 153, 98 S.Ct. 2279, 57 L.Ed.2d 117 (1978), **114**

Terry, United States v., 17 F.3d 575 (2nd Cir. 1994), 344

Texas v. Lesage, 528 U.S. 18, 120 S.Ct. 467, 145 L.Ed.2d 347 (1999), 74

Texas Industries, Inc. v. Radcliff Materials, Inc., 451 U.S. 630, 101 S.Ct. 2061, 68 L.Ed.2d 500 (1981), 869

Texas State Teachers Ass'n v. Garland Independent School Dist., 489 U.S. 782, 109 S.Ct. 1486, 103 L.Ed.2d 866 (1989), 925

Textron v. United Automobile Workers, 523 U.S. 653, 118 S.Ct. 1626, 140 L.Ed.2d 863 (1998), 437

31 Foster Children v. Bush, 329 F.3d 1255 (11th Cir.2003), 75

Thomas v. Collins, 323 U.S. 516, 65 S.Ct. 315, 89 L.Ed. 430 (1945), 341

Thomas v. Oregon Fruit Products Co., 228 F.3d 991 (9th Cir.2000), 456

Thompson v. Gomez, 45 F.3d 1365 (9th Cir. 1995), 940

Thompson v. KFB Ins. Co., 252 Kan. 1010, 850 P.2d 773 (Kan.1993), 503

Thompson v. Thompson, 484 U.S. 174, 108 S.Ct. 513, 98 L.Ed.2d 512 (1988), 29

3M Co. v. Browner, 17 F.3d 1453 (D.C.Cir. 1994), 891

Tilcon Minerals, Inc. v. Orange & Rockland Utilities, Inc., 851 F.Supp. 529 (S.D.N.Y. 1994), 435

Tillamook Country Smoker, Inc. v. Tillamook County Creamery Ass'n, 465 F.3d 1102 (9th Cir.2006), 897

Time Warner Entertainment v. Six Flags Over Georgia, 254 Ga.App. 598, 563 S.E.2d 178 (Ga.App.2002), 688

Timm v. Progressive Steel Treating, Inc., 137 F.3d 1008 (7th Cir.1998), 716

Toilet Goods Ass'n, Inc. v. Gardner, 387 U.S. 167, 87 S.Ct. 1530, 18 L.Ed.2d 704 (1967), 428

Toilet Goods Ass'n, Inc. v. Gardner, 387 U.S. 158, 87 S.Ct. 1520, 18 L.Ed.2d 697 (1967), 428

Torres v. Eastlick (In re North American Coin & Currency, Ltd.), 767 F.2d 1573 (9th Cir.1985), **769**

Town of (see name of town)

Transportation Ins. Co. v. Moriel, 879 S.W.2d 10 (Tex.1994), 690

Travelers Cas. & Sur. Co. v. Pacific Gas & Elec. Co., 549 U.S. 443, 127 S.Ct. 1199, 167 L.Ed.2d 178 (2007), 903

Travelhost, Inc. v. Blandford, 68 F.3d 958 (5th Cir.1995), 356

Trustees v. Greenough, 105 U.S. 527, 15 Otto 527, 26 L.Ed. 1157 (1881), 903

TRW Inc. v. Andrews, 534 U.S. 19, 122 S.Ct. 441, 151 L.Ed.2d 339 (2001), **881**

Tucker, United States v., 28 F.3d 1420 (6th Cir.1994), 861

Tull v. United States, 481 U.S. 412, 107 S.Ct. 1831, 95 L.Ed.2d 365 (1987), 455

Tullis v. Townley Engineering & Mfg. Co., 243 F.3d 1058 (7th Cir.2001), **516**

Turner v. Guy, 2 Mass.App.Ct. 343, 311 N.E.2d 921 (Mass.App.Ct.1974), 880

Twentieth Century Fox Film Corp., United States v., 882 F.2d 656 (2nd Cir.1989), 328

TXO Production Corp. v. Alliance Resources Corp., 509 U.S. 443, 113 S.Ct. 2711, 125 L.Ed.2d 366 (1993), 708

Tynes v. Bankers Life Co., 224 Mont. 350, 730 P.2d 1115 (Mont.1986), 912

Union Carbide Corp. v. UGI Corp., 731 F.2d 1186 (5th Cir.1984), 55

United Mine Workers v. Bagwell, 512 U.S. 821, 114 S.Ct. 2552, 129 L.Ed.2d 642 (1994), **311**

United Mine Workers, United States v., 330 U.S. 258, 67 S.Ct. 677, 91 L.Ed. 884 (1947), 301, 324

United Shoe Machinery Corp., United States v., 391 U.S. 244, 88 S.Ct. 1496, 20 L.Ed.2d 562 (1968), 53, 244

United States v. _____ (see opposing party)

United States Catholic Conference v. Abortion Rights Mobilization, Inc., 487 U.S. 72, 108 S.Ct. 2268, 101 L.Ed.2d 69 (1988), 344

United States ex rel. v. _____ (see opposing party and relator)
United Steelworkers of America v. Weber, 443 U.S. 193, 99 S.Ct. 2721, 61 L.Ed.2d 480 (1979), 362
Utemark v. Samuel, 118 Cal.App.2d 313, 257 P.2d 656 (Cal.App. 2 Dist.1953), 747

Venegas v. Mitchell, 495 U.S. 82, 110 S.Ct. 1679, 109 L.Ed.2d 74 (1990), 947
Ventura v. Titan Sports, Inc., 65 F.3d 725 (8th Cir.1995), 471, 617
Verizon Maryland, Inc. v. Public Service Com'n, 535 U.S. 635, 122 S.Ct. 1753, 152 L.Ed.2d 871 (2002), 436
Vernon, City of v. Superior Court, 38 Cal.2d 509, 241 P.2d 243 (Cal.1952), 369
Virginia v. American Booksellers Ass'n, 484 U.S. 383, 108 S.Ct. 636, 98 L.Ed.2d 782 (1988), 427
Virginia v. West Virginia, 246 U.S. 565, 38 S.Ct. 400, 59 L.Ed. 1272 (1918), 367
Volk v. Gonzalez, 262 F.3d 528 (5th Cir.2001), 940
V&V Food Products, Inc. v. Cacique Cheese Co., 2003 WL 255235 (N.D.Ill.2003), 269

Waffenschmidt v. MacKay, 763 F.2d 711 (5th Cir.1985), 355
Waiste v. State, 10 P.3d 1141 (Alaska 2000), 816
Walgreen Co. v. Sara Creek Property Co., 966 F.2d 273 (7th Cir.1992), 105
Walker v. Bain, 257 F.3d 660 (6th Cir.2001), 930
Walker v. Farmers Ins. Exchange, 63 Cal. Rptr.3d 507 (Cal.App. 2 Dist.2007), 707
Walker v. Ritchie, 197 O.A.C. 81 (Ont. C.A. 2005), **528**
Wallis v. Superior Court, 160 Cal.App.3d 1109, 207 Cal.Rptr. 123 (Cal.App. 4 Dist.1984), 599
Ward v. Rock Against Racism, 491 U.S. 781, 109 S.Ct. 2746, 105 L.Ed.2d 661 (1989), 153
Watkins v. United States Army, 875 F.2d 699 (9th Cir.1989), 877
Webb v. Dyer County Board of Educ., 471 U.S. 234, 105 S.Ct. 1923, 85 L.Ed.2d 233 (1985), 938
Webster v. Doe, 486 U.S. 592, 108 S.Ct. 2047, 100 L.Ed.2d 632 (1988), 28
Wehringer v. Powers & Hall, 874 F.Supp. 425 (D.Mass.1995), 609
Weinberger v. Romero–Barcelo, 456 U.S. 305, 102 S.Ct. 1798, 72 L.Ed.2d 91 (1982), **122**
Welsch v. Likins, 550 F.2d 1122 (8th Cir.1977), 374
West Covina v. Perkins, 525 U.S. 234, 119 S.Ct. 678, 142 L.Ed.2d 636 (1999), 817
West Virginia University Hospitals, Inc. v. Casey, 499 U.S. 83, 111 S.Ct. 1138, 113 L.Ed.2d 68 (1991), 942
Whalen v. Union Bag & Paper Co., 208 N.Y. 1, 101 N.E. 805 (N.Y.1913), 104

Wheeler Tarpeh–Doe v. United States, 771 F.Supp. 427 (D.D.C.1991), 533
Whiten v. Pilot Insurance Co., [2002] 209 D.L.R. (4th) 257 (S.C.C.2002), 597
Wickham Contracting v. Local Union No. 3, IBEW, 955 F.2d 831 (2nd Cir.1992), 617
Wilkie v. Robbins, 551 U.S. 537, 127 S.Ct. 2588, 168 L.Ed.2d 389 (2007), 26
Will v. United States, 389 U.S. 90, 88 S.Ct. 269, 19 L.Ed.2d 305 (1967), 184
Willard v. City of Los Angeles, 803 F.2d 526 (9th Cir.1986), 973
Williams v. Bright, 230 A.D.2d 548, 658 N.Y.S.2d 910 (N.Y.A.D. 1 Dept.1997), 551
Williams v. Bright, 167 Misc.2d 312, 632 N.Y.S.2d 760 (N.Y.Sup.1995), 550
Williams v. Herring, 183 Iowa 127, 165 N.W. 342 (Iowa 1917), 766
Williams v. New York, 337 U.S. 241, 69 S.Ct. 1079, 93 L.Ed. 1337 (1949), 650
Williams v. Philip Morris Inc., 344 Or. 45, 176 P.3d 1255 (Or.2008), 710
Willy v. Coastal Corp., 503 U.S. 131, 112 S.Ct. 1076, 117 L.Ed.2d 280 (1992), 903
Wilson v. Garcia, 471 U.S. 261, 105 S.Ct. 1938, 85 L.Ed.2d 254 (1985), 890
Wilton v. Seven Falls Co., 515 U.S. 277, 115 S.Ct. 2137, 132 L.Ed.2d 214 (1995), 434
Wimberly v. Gatch, 635 So.2d 206 (La.1994), 891
Windeler v. Scheers Jewelers, 8 Cal.App.3d 844, 88 Cal.Rptr. 39 (Cal.App. 1 Dist.1970), 501
Winkelman v. Parma City School Dist., 550 U.S. 516, 127 S.Ct. 1994, 167 L.Ed.2d 904 (2007), 928
Winter v. Natural Resources Defense Council, 555 U.S. ___, 129 S.Ct. 365, 172 L.Ed.2d 249 (2008), **190**
W.L. Gore & Associates, Inc. v. C.R. Bard, Inc., 977 F.2d 558 (Fed.Cir.1992), 268
Women Prisoners v. District of Columbia, 877 F.Supp. 634 (D.D.C.1994), 136
W.R. Grace & Company v. Waters, 638 So.2d 502 (Fla.1994), 690
W.T. Grant Co., United States v., 345 U.S. 629, 73 S.Ct. 894, 97 L.Ed. 1303 (1953), 60
Wyatt v. Aderholt, 503 F.2d 1305 (5th Cir. 1974), 375
Wyatt v. Cole, 994 F.2d 1113 (5th Cir.1993), 803
Wyatt v. Cole, 504 U.S. 158, 112 S.Ct. 1827, 118 L.Ed.2d 504 (1992), 803
Wyatt v. Stickney, 325 F.Supp. 781 (M.D.Ala. 1971), 8
Wyatt v. Sawyer, 219 F.R.D. 529 (M.D.Ala. 2004), 8

Yonkers, City of, United States v., 856 F.2d 444 (2nd Cir.1988), **386**
Young v. United States ex rel. Vuitton et Fils S.A., 481 U.S. 787, 107 S.Ct. 2124, 95 L.Ed.2d 740 (1987), 301
Young, Ex parte, 209 U.S. 123, 28 S.Ct. 441, 52 L.Ed. 714 (1908), 370

Younger v. Harris, 401 U.S. 37, 91 S.Ct. 756, 27 L.Ed.2d 669 (1971), 435
Youngs v. Old Ben Coal Co., 243 F.3d 387 (7th Cir.2001), 484
Yowell v. Piper Aircraft, 703 S.W.2d 630 (Tex. 1986), 515

Zehner v. Trigg, 133 F.3d 459 (7th Cir.1997), 27

REMEDIES: PUBLIC AND PRIVATE
Fifth Edition

*

CHAPTER 1

INTRODUCTION TO THE LAW OF REMEDIES

■ ■ ■

In law school, it is easy to fall into the habit of equating law and liability. Liability—the determination that a defendant is legally responsible for some harm to the plaintiff—is only half the story, however. The other half is the remedy—the action to be taken in response to the harm. For clients, the remedy may be the more important half, because it is with the remedy that the court acts for them or against them.

Perhaps the remedies half of the equation is neglected because it is tempting to think of remedies as mechanically derived from the legal harm and therefore obvious. That is what the Babylonian King Hammurabi suggested 4000 years ago by displaying to his subjects large stone tablets that listed specific remedies for specific wrongs:

> Rule 195. If a son has struck his father, one shall cut off his hands.
>
> Rule 196. If one destroys the eye of a free born man, his eye one shall destroy. * * *
>
> Rule 198. If the eye of a nobleman he has destroyed, * * * one mina of silver he shall pay.
>
> Rule 199. If he has destroyed the eye of the slave of a free born man * * *, he shall pay half of [the slave's] price. * * *
>
> Rule 206. If a man has struck another in a quarrel, and has wounded him and that man shall swear, "I did not strike him wittingly," he shall pay the doctor.
>
> Rule 207. If he dies of the blows, he shall swear again, and if it was a free born man, he shall pay one half mina of silver.
>
> Rule 208. If it was a freedman, he shall pay one third a mina of silver.

The Code of Hammurabi, quoted in Howard L. Oleck, Damages to Persons and Property § 2 at 3–4 (1961 rev.ed.).

Remedies, however, cannot be carved in stone. A mechanical approach to determining the appropriate remedy is ultimately impractical because no list can include all harms or take account of the variations in circumstance that could make a given remedy inappropriate. Indeed, Babylonian court records show that courts did not follow the Code of Hammurabi mechanically, but rather took a common law approach to shaping the remedy. The "code" apparently was in fact a systematic presentation of decided cases and related hypotheticals, aimed as much at the public as at the judges—a political ad claiming, "the rule of law applied here."

The polar opposite of the mechanical approach is to let each judge select whatever remedy does justice in the case at hand. This is what the Ten Commandments seem to do in establishing a law of liability while saying nothing about remedy, as in "Thou shalt not kill." Exodus 20:2–17. But this approach also has its problems. A judge with unfettered discretion over the remedy can effectively nullify the provisions of constitutions, statutes, and cases. Indeed, Hebrew judges apparently did not have such discretion; the Ten Commandments are followed immediately by what are known as "specific judicial rulings" (*Mishpatim*), which speak to remedies for various civil and criminal offenses in terms remarkably similar to the Code of Hammurabi. Exodus 21:1–22:16.

Staking out a middle ground between a mechanical and a wholly discretionary approach to remedies raises important theoretical and political questions. For example,

- To what extent should judges in individual cases have discretion or be constrained in formulating a remedy?
- Are there general principles of remedies that can cabin the courts' discretion?
- Should institutional concerns about the role of courts in society limit the courts' authority, even if it means an injured person will go without a remedy?

Remedies is often called a capstone course, because it provides you with the opportunity to bring together all you have learned in your courses on substantive and procedural law in service of the intensely practical question, "What can be done about it?" While the subject arms you with the tools you will need to accomplish your clients' goals, it also provides the opportunity to reflect on basic questions about the role of law and the role of courts that you have touched on throughout your study of the legal system.

A. A GENERAL APPROACH TO CRAFTING A REMEDY

Despite its practical importance, the law of remedies has evolved piecemeal. Rather than developing general principles that cut across areas of substantive law—transsubstantive principles, if you will—courts have tended (like Hammurabi?) to pair remedies with specific rights: remedies for trespass, remedies for breach of an agreement to sell goods, remedies for violations of civil rights, etc. Thus, while some attention may be paid to remedies in the torts class, the contracts class and so on, transsubstantive principles are ignored.

This cookbook approach sometimes makes it difficult for lawyers to locate or apply the law that they need to help their clients. They may be unable, for instance, to deal with a novel remedies question by drawing appropriate analogies to remedies from other substantive areas of law. One of this casebook's themes is to encourage you to think about remedial principles that reach beyond specific causes of action, empowering you to think creatively about remedies.

As a first step toward transsubstantive remedial principles, here are some critical choices in identifying the appropriate remedy:

The first critical choice is to identify the remedy's goal. There are many possibilities. One goal might simply be to *declare* the parties' rights, to establish as a matter of principle who was right and who was wrong. Another might be to restore the plaintiff to the *plaintiff's rightful position*, that is, to the position the plaintiff would have occupied if the defendant had never violated the law. Or, its goal might be to restore the defendant to the *defendant's rightful position*, that is, the position that the defendant would have occupied absent the violation. A fourth goal might be to *punish* the defendant for doing wrong.

Are there other possibilities? If the various possible goals lead to quite different results, what principles or policies might guide the choice between them?

The second choice in defining an appropriate remedy is the choice between a *specific* and a *substitutionary* remedy. Specific remedies achieve the remedy's goal in kind, by giving the plaintiff the exact thing to which he or she is entitled. For example, if the goal of the remedy in a nuisance case is to restore the plaintiff to his or her rightful position, a specific remedy would order the defendant to stop the nuisance.

Substitutionary remedies operate by giving the plaintiff a substitute—typically, an award of money—equal to the value of the plaintiff's entitlement. Again, for example, in a nuisance case, a substitutionary remedy might be to give the plaintiff the difference between the value of his land before the nuisance occurred and the value of his land after the nuisance began. What principles should guide the choice between a specific and a substitutionary remedy?

The third choice has to do with how to implement the first two choices in crafting the remedy. If the goal is returning the plaintiff to his or her rightful position, how does the court go about deciding what the rightful position is in a particular case? And, if the remedy is to be substitutionary, how does the court decide how much money is an adequate substitute?

The fourth choice is how to enforce the remedy. If the defendant does not cooperate, what can and should be done?

These questions arise when you reach the remedy stage in any substantive area of the law, whether torts or contracts, admiralty or antitrust. Moreover, they are not questions only for courts. Legislatures face the same questions when they craft a statute that creates substantive rights. Although the particular substantive law affects how remedies issues are resolved, the issues themselves are universal. Thus, after a right is declared, whether by legislative enactment or judicial decision, these questions, and the principles that emerge from their study, can be used to craft the remedy.

Accordingly, our focus is transsubstantive. These materials are organized by types of remedies (injunctions, declaratory judgments, punitive damages and other sanctions, compensatory damages, restitution, and attorney's fees), rather than canvassing the remedies for particular harms (remedies for property damage, remedies for breach of contract, etc.). By studying each remedy across a variety of cases, from administrative law to breach of contract to civil rights, you should be able to see remedies not as a list of responses to specific harms, but as a set of principles exemplified in particular cases and extending beyond them.

In this spirit, consider the following problem, which will probably remind you of your torts and property courses:

PROBLEM: COUNTRY LODGE v. MILLER
REMEDIES IN A TRADITIONAL PRIVATE CASE

Miller owns an apple orchard where she recently built a plant to press and bottle apple cider. The cider press produces apple mash as waste. Last fall, in her first season of operation, she disposed of the waste by putting it into a pipe that empties into the Rural River. This cost her nothing while the cheapest alternative means of disposal would have cost $20,000 per year. The guests at the nearby, long-established Country Lodge disliked the sight of the apple mash in the water. As a result, Country Lodge lost $10,000 in profits that fall. In a suit Country Lodge brought against Miller, the judge found Miller's operation to be a nuisance, because her conduct was unreasonable and resulted in substantial harm to Country Lodge.

Consider the remedies that should be available to Country Lodge. Do not be constrained by what you think you know of the applicable precedent. What purpose does each remedy serve? Do you see any problem in achieving that purpose?

B. PRIVATE LAW AND PUBLIC LAW

In a classic law review article, excerpted below, Professor Abram Chayes argued that a new model of civil litigation was emerging. Looking at the challenges that faced courts in enforcing students' rights to attend desegregated schools, prisoners' rights to be free from cruel and unusual punishment, and confined mental patients' right to treatment, Professor Chayes concluded that courts had assumed a new role. Part of what made that role new was the nature of the rights the courts were enforcing. Equally new were the kinds of remedies the courts used.

After you have read the excerpt from Professor Chayes' article, consider this variation on the Country Lodge problem, which has been modified to suggest some of the same issues:

PROBLEM: COUNTRY LODGE v. MILLER (REPRISED)[a]
REMEDIES IN A PUBLIC LAW CASE

How would your answer in *Country Lodge v. Miller* change if:

(a) Miller's pollution hurts people beyond Country Lodge?

(b) putting the apple mash in the river is not a common law nuisance but does violate a federal environmental statute?

(c) the violator of the statute is not Miller but rather a municipality that puts untreated municipal waste into the river?

(d) the court orders the municipality to build a sewage treatment plant and have it in operation in three years, but the city council does not appropriate the necessary funds?

(e) the city council appropriates the necessary funds, but makes them available on a schedule that would mean that the plant will not be operational for five years?

ABRAM CHAYES, THE ROLE OF THE JUDGE IN PUBLIC LAW LITIGATION

89 Harv.L.Rev. 1281, 1282–84, 1292–95, 1298 (1976)

* * * We are witnessing the emergence of a new model of civil litigation and, I believe, our traditional conception of adjudication and the assumptions upon which it is based provide an increasingly unhelpful, indeed misleading framework for assessing either the workability or the legitimacy of the roles of judge and court within this model.

In our received tradition, the lawsuit is a vehicle for settling disputes between private parties about private rights. The defining features of this conception of civil adjudication are:

(1) The lawsuit is *bipolar*. Litigation is organized as a contest between two individuals or at least two unitary interests, diametrically opposed, to be decided on a winner-takes-all basis.

(2) Litigation is *retrospective*. The controversy is about an identified set of completed events: whether they occurred, and if so, with what consequences for the legal relations of the parties.

---

a. This problem is the first of many reprises of the *Country Lodge v. Miller* problem. Each reprise varies the initial fact pattern to illustrate particular aspects of the law of remedies.

(3) *Right and remedy are interdependent.* The scope of the relief is derived more or less logically from the substantive violation under the general theory that the plaintiff will get compensation measured by the harm caused by the defendant's breach of duty—in contract by giving plaintiff the money he would have had absent the breach; in tort by paying the value of the damage caused.

(4) The lawsuit is a *self-contained* episode. The impact of the judgment is confined to the parties. If plaintiff prevails there is a simple compensatory transfer, usually of money, but occasionally the return of a thing or the performance of a definite act. If defendant prevails, a loss lies where it has fallen. In either case, entry of judgment ends the court's involvement.

(5) The process is *party-initiated* and *party-controlled*. The case is organized and the issues defined by exchanges between the parties. Responsibility for fact development is theirs. The trial judge is a neutral arbiter of their interactions who decides questions of law only if they are put in issue by an appropriate move of a party.

This capsule description of what I have called the traditional conception of adjudication is no doubt overdrawn. It was not often, if ever, expressed so severely; indeed, because it was so thoroughly taken for granted, there was little occasion to do so. Although I do not contend that the traditional conception ever conformed fully to what judges were doing in fact, I believe it has been central to our understanding and our analysis of the legal system.

Whatever its historical validity, the traditional model is clearly invalid as a description of much current civil litigation in the federal district courts. Perhaps the dominating characteristic of modern federal litigation is that lawsuits do not arise out of disputes between private parties about private rights. Instead, the object of litigation is the vindication of constitutional or statutory policies. The shift in the legal basis of the lawsuit explains many, but not all, facets of what is going on "in fact" in federal trial courts. For this reason, although the label is not wholly satisfactory, I shall call the emerging model "public law litigation."

The characteristic features of the public law model are very different from those of the traditional model. The party structure is sprawling and amorphous, subject to change over the course of the litigation. The traditional adversary relationship is suffused and intermixed with negotiating and mediating processes at every point. The judge is the dominant figure in organizing and guiding the case, and he draws for support not only on the parties and their counsel, but on a wide range of outsiders—masters, experts, and oversight personnel. Most important, the trial judge has increasingly become the creator and manager of complex forms of ongoing relief, which have widespread effects on persons not before the court and require the judge's continuing involvement in administration and implementation. School desegregation, employment discrimination, and prisoners' or inmates' rights cases come readily to mind as avatars of this new form of litigation. But it would be mistaken to suppose that it is confined to these areas. Antitrust, securities fraud and other aspects of the conduct of corporate business, bankruptcy and reorganizations, union governance, consumer fraud, housing discrimination, electoral reapportionment, environmental management—cases in all these fields display in varying degrees the features of public law litigation. * * *

One of the most striking procedural developments of this century is the increasing importance of equitable relief. It is perhaps too soon to reverse the traditional maxim to read that money damages will be awarded only when no suitable form of specific relief can be devised. But surely, the old sense of equitable remedies as "extraordinary" has faded.

I am not concerned here with specific performance—the compelled transfer of a piece of land or a unique thing. This remedy is structurally little different from traditional money-damages. It is a one-time, one-way transfer requiring for its enforcement no continuing involvement of the court. Injunctive relief, however, is different in kind, even when it takes the form of a simple negative order. Such an order is a presently operative prohibition, enforceable by contempt, and it is a much greater constraint on activity than the risk of future liability implicit in the damage remedy. Moreover, the injunction is continuing. Over time, the parties may resort to the court for enforcement or modification of the original order in light of changing circumstances. Finally, by issuing the injunction, the court takes public responsibility for any consequences of its decree that may adversely affect strangers to the action.

Beyond these differences, the prospective character of the relief introduces large elements of contingency and prediction into the proceedings. Instead of a dispute retrospectively oriented toward the consequences of a closed set of events, the court has a controversy about future probabilities. Equitable doctrine, naturally enough, given the intrusiveness of the injunction and the contingent nature of the harm, calls for a balancing of the interests of the parties. And if the immediate parties' interests were to be weighed and evaluated, it was not too difficult to proceed to a consideration of other interests that might be affected by the order.

The comparative evaluation of the competing interests of plaintiff and defendant required by the remedial approach of equity often discloses alternatives to a winner-takes-all decision. An arrangement might be fashioned that could safeguard at least partially the interests of both parties, and perhaps even of others as well. And to the extent such an arrangement is possible, equity seems to require it. Negative orders directed to one of the parties—even though pregnant with affirmative implications—are often not adequate to this end. And so the historic power of equity to order affirmative action gradually freed itself from the encrustation of nineteenth century restraints. The result has often been a decree embodying an affirmative regime to govern the range of activities in litigation and having the force of law for those represented before the court.

At this point, right and remedy are pretty thoroughly disconnected. The form of relief does not flow ineluctably from the liability determination, but is fashioned ad hoc. In the process, moreover, right and remedy have been to some extent transmuted. The liability determination is not simply a pronouncement of the legal consequences of past events, but to some extent a prediction of what is likely to be in the future. And relief is not a terminal, compensatory transfer, but an effort to devise a program to contain future consequences in a way that accommodates the range of interests involved. * * * If a mental patient complains that he has been denied a right to treatment, it will not do to order the superintendent to "cease to deny" it. So with segregation in education, discrimination in hiring, apportionment of legislative districts, environmental management. And the list could be extended. * * *

The centerpiece of the emerging public law model is the decree. It differs in almost every relevant characteristic from relief in the traditional model of adjudication, not the least in that it is the centerpiece. The decree seeks to adjust future behavior, not to compensate for past wrong. It is deliberately fashioned rather than logically deduced from the nature of the legal harm suffered. It provides for a complex, on-going regime of performance rather than a simple, one-shot, one-way transfer. Finally, it prolongs and deepens, rather than terminates, the court's involvement with the dispute. * * *

Notes

1. For an example of public law litigation, consider Wyatt v. Stickney, 325 F.Supp. 781 (M.D.Ala.1971), enforced, 344 F.Supp. 373, 387 (M.D.Ala. 1972), modified, 503 F.2d 1305 (5th Cir.1974). *Wyatt* began in 1970 as a class action on behalf of mental patients and employees at a mental hospital against state officials, including the governor, alleging violations of an asserted right of the involuntarily confined to treatment and decent living conditions. The class of plaintiffs grew to include mental patients at other hospitals, geriatric patients, and mentally retarded patients. Judge Frank Johnson issued orders that imposed detailed guidelines on the institutions' operations and tried to prompt the state to provide the funds to implement his orders. Judge Johnson also involved the United States government and established various entities to oversee implementation of his orders. See, e.g., Note, The *Wyatt* Case: Implementation of a Judicial Decree Ordering Institutional Change, 84 Yale L.J. 1338 (1975). After thirty years of litigation and judicial supervision, involving more than fifty published opinions, the district court finally dismissed the lawsuit in 2004. Wyatt v. Sawyer, 219 F.R.D. 529 (M.D.Ala.2004). Finding the final settlement and dismissal to be in the class's interest, Judge Myron Thompson wrote:

> [T]his case illustrates why, despite the difficulties inherent in structural reform litigation, such cases are, finally, so important and worthwhile. While this case has followed a "long, winding, and often quite bumpy" road, the enormity of what this case has accomplished cannot be overstated. The principles of humane treatment of people with mental illness

and mental retardation embodied in this litigation have become part of the fabric of law in this country and, indeed, international law.

* * * The *Wyatt* standards have had a reverberating impact on state and national law, and, perhaps even more importantly, on public consciousness about mental illness. The standards have been incorporated into state and federal mental-health codes and regulations. The concept of treatment in the "least restrictive setting" contained in the *Wyatt* standards was "echoed" in the Americans with Disabilities Act of 1990. The nationwide Protection and Advocacy system is a "direct descendant" of the Human Rights Committees Judge Johnson appointed in the *Wyatt* case. Part of Judge Johnson's March 1972 opinion enumerating rights due the plaintiff class, such as the right to privacy, the right to be treated with dignity, and the right to be free of unnecessary medication and physical restraint, has come to be known among mental-health professionals as a "bill of rights for patients."

* * * Finally, *Wyatt* heightened public awareness of the needs of institutionalized people and people with mental illness and mental retardation. Today, as a result, any judge, legislator, or executive official who would seek to reverse the everyday involvement and oversight of state and local advocacy groups, friends and family members of people with mental disabilities, and self-advocacy by consumers of mental-health care, would face universal condemnation. This legacy of this litigation cannot be terminated by any court.

219 F.R.D. at 533. Litigation over unconstitutional conditions in America's prisons provides another excellent example. See Malcolm M. Feeley & Edward L. Rubin, Judicial Policy Making and the Modern State: How the Courts Reformed America's Prisons (1998).

2. While Judge Thompson and some others applaud the role public law litigation played in the evolution of disability law, critics find it troubling that crafting the remedy in a public law case can cast the judge as "a legislator in robes." Thus, public law litigation—or institutional reform litigation—has been a prime focus of calls for courts to abandon what some call "judicial activism." For example, in the area of prison reform litigation, Congress has responded. The Prison Litigation Reform Act (PLRA), 18 U.S.C. § 3626, sharply limits the remedies courts can order in lawsuits over unconstitutional conditions of confinement in American prisons. See Chapter 3(B)(4)(b).

3. Law, of course, is a moving target. There is considerable debate over whether the structural injunction is a relic of the past. For a discussion of the issue, see Margo Schlanger, Civil Rights Injunctions Over Time: A Case Study of Jail and Prison Court Orders, 81 N.Y.U.L.Rev. 550 (2006). Professor Schlanger concludes that as far as prison reform is concerned, arguments that institutional reform litigation is "something that is over and done with" are simply wrong. Rather, prison litigation continued at a stable rate up to the passage of the Prison Litigation Reform Act. See also Myriam Gilles, An Autopsy of the Structural Reform Injunction: Oops . . . It's Still Moving!, 58 U. Miami L. Rev. 143 (2003).

Professor Schlanger suggests, however, that while the rate of litigation did not change, the kind of injunctions courts entered did. Courts moved away from the kind of broad injunctive relief that Chayes saw as characterizing public law litigation, and toward more focused and precise remedies. Similarly, others have argued that public law litigation "has moved away from remedial intervention modeled on command-and-control bureaucracy toward a kind of intervention that can be called 'experimentalist.'" Charles F. Sabel & William Simon, Destabilization Rights: How Public Law Litigation Succeeds, 117 Harv.L.Rev. 1015 (2004). The authors claim that this alternative model for public law litigation may answer doctrinal and jurisprudential objections to the Chayes model of public law litigation. Again, these are claims to which we will return.

4. Public law litigation and private law litigation are not separated by a bright line, of course. Remedies in some forms of traditional, private litigation like bankruptcy, probate and trusts have always exhibited many of the characteristics of public law litigation, and the remedial and procedural changes Professor Chayes first observed in public law cases have since migrated to private law. See Theodore Eisenberg & Stephen Yeasell, The Ordinary and the Extraordinary in Institutional Litigation, 93 Harv.L.Rev. 465, 481–86 (1980); Richard L. Marcus, Public Law Litigation and Legal Scholarship, 21 Mich.J.L.Reform 47, 668–82 (1988). Private law litigation and public law litigation are better understood as poles of a continuum. The lessons learned in high profile public law cases about the way judges think about remedies provide critical insights into private law cases as well. That, along with the intrinsic importance of public law, is the reason for this casebook's unique focus on public and private law.

C. "WHERE THERE'S A RIGHT, THERE'S A REMEDY"?

Accusations of judicial activism await courts that interpret the constitution, apply a statute, or construe the common law to recognize a new right. Thus, before judges declare a right, they think carefully not simply about the justice of the party's cause, but also about the limits of a court's power.

Once a right has been established, however, the power of the court to declare a remedy has been much less controversial, and as a result, less scrutinized. Ask where the power to shape a remedy is derived, and the answer is likely to be that it is an inherent power, existing because *ubi ius, ibi remedium*: "Where there's a right, there's a remedy."

Some would even say that a right without a remedy is not a right at all:

> To begin, a right without a remedy is not a legal right; it is merely a hope or a wish. This follows from the definition of a legal right. * * * [By definition], a right entails a correlative duty to act or refrain from acting for the benefit of another person. Unless a duty can be enforced, it is not really a duty; it is only a voluntary obligation that a person can fulfill or not at his whim. In such circumstances, the holder of the correlative "right" can only hope that the act or

forbearance will occur. Thus, a right without a remedy is simply not a legal right.

To understand why it is important for legal claims to be enforceable to be *rights*—rather than mere requests for favors—it is necessary to explore the purposes of rights. Rights define social relations. They serve as means to very important ends. Rights promote well-being in the broadest sense. They secure the dignity and the integrity of human beings. They enable people to grow, to develop, to fulfill their aspirations, and to accumulate necessary material goods. Rights give people control over their lives and are essential to self-respect. Theories of rights often are considered to conflict with social utility because recognizing rights is sometimes inefficient. Nonetheless, legal rights plainly serve some utilitarian purposes. They assist society in treating people equally. They also promote order and predictability, thus enabling people to act upon reasonable expectations in managing their affairs.

Having described the purposes of rights, it is relatively easy to envision the consequences of their inadequate enforcement. The dignity of the individual is diminished and people are less able to achieve their goals. People feel insecure and lose their self-respect. If the legal system tells a person that it is acceptable for his rights to be violated, the implicit message is that the person lacks worth. And, when the system vindicates another person's rights in similar circumstances, the message is that the other person has greater worth. When denial of rights occurs systematically over time, the result is alienation, isolation, anger, and fear. In extreme cases, the result is totalitarianism or chaos.

Donald H. Zeigler, Rights Require Remedies: A New Approach to the Enforcement of Rights in the Federal Courts, 38 Hastings L.J. 665, 678–79 (1987).

That there must be a remedy for every violation of a right is a powerful idea; Justice Marshall called it "[t]he very essence of civil liberty." Marbury v. Madison, 5 U.S. (1 Cranch) 137, 163, 2 L.Ed. 60 (1803). There is evidence that the concept was considered well grounded in eighteenth-century jurisprudence or earlier. Alden v. Maine, 527 U.S. 706, 769, 119 S.Ct. 2240, 2274, 144 L.Ed.2d 636 (1999) (Souter, J., dissenting). See John C.P. Goldberg, The Constitutional Status of Tort Law, 115 Yale L.J. 524 (2005) (arguing a right to redress for wrongs can be traced to the unwritten English constitution and to the writings of Locke and Blackstone). Some have even argued that the right to a remedy is a fundamental right protected by the due process clause. See id.; Tracy A. Thomas, Ubi Jus, Ibi Remedium: The Fundamental Right to a Remedy Under Due Process, 41 San Diego L.Rev. 1633 (2004).

Yet, if rights "require" remedies, remedies should be an easy subject. As Professor Chayes explains in the excerpt in part B of this chapter, if rights and remedies were so closely linked, judges would be able simply to deduce the proper remedy from the right that was violated. If there were such a close nexus between rights and remedies, there would be no need to look for a source for the courts' remedial power, because deciding on the proper remedy would not be an exercise of power at all, but a formal process of mechanical, logical deduction.

Professor Chayes, however, contends that at least in the context of public law litigation, designing a remedy is far from a mechanical process. Rather, the design of a remedy is an exercise of power independent of the declaration of a right, and so requires its own justification. The remedies course should convince you that public law cases are not unique in this regard. Defining the remedy for any particular wrong is an exercise in judgment and discretion—an exercise of power—no different in kind from the decision to declare a right in the first instance.

Thus, if there is one thing to be learned from a course in remedies, it is that "Where there's a right, there's a remedy" is a singularly unhelpful maxim. Providing a complete remedy for every violation of right is an important, well-accepted goal, but it is not the only goal the law serves. Further, in any particular situation, any number of remedies may be available. In that event, who is to decide which remedy is available to whom, and how is that to be decided?

Questions such as these are rarely discussed plainly in the cases. After all, the nature and source of a court's power are abstract concerns, while adjudication is a pragmatic, concrete business. So, despite its being with the declaration of a remedy that the court's power is truly exercised (or perhaps because this is where the power is truly exercised), the nature of a court's remedial authority goes largely undiscussed.

Sometimes, however, courts cannot veil the exercise of judgment in the design of a remedy. For example, where a right unquestionably exists and the only question is what remedy is appropriate, a court may be forced to explore the whys and wherefores of its remedial power in plain terms. The following case presents such a situation.

BIVENS v. SIX UNKNOWN NAMED AGENTS OF FEDERAL BUREAU OF NARCOTICS

Supreme Court of the United States, 1971
403 U.S. 388, 91 S.Ct. 1999, 29 L.Ed.2d 619

MR. JUSTICE BRENNAN delivered the opinion of the Court.

The Fourth Amendment provides that:

"The right of the people to be secure in their persons, houses, papers, and effects, against unreasonable searches and seizures, shall not be violated...."

In Bell v. Hood, 327 U.S. 678, 66 S.Ct. 773, 90 L.Ed. 939 (1946), we reserved the question whether violation of that command by a federal agent acting under color of his authority gives rise to a cause of action for damages consequent upon his unconstitutional conduct. Today we hold that it does.

This case has its origin in an arrest and search carried out on the morning of November 26, 1965. Petitioner's complaint alleged that on that day respondents, agents of the Federal Bureau of Narcotics acting under claim of federal authority, entered his apartment and arrested him for alleged narcotics violations. The agents manacled petitioner in front of his wife and children, and threatened to arrest the entire family. They searched the apartment from stem to stern. Thereafter, petitioner was taken to the federal courthouse in Brooklyn, where he was interrogated, booked, and subjected to a visual strip search.

On July 7, 1967, petitioner brought suit in Federal District Court. In addition to the allegations above, his complaint asserted that the arrest and search were effected without a warrant, and that unreasonable force was employed in making the arrest; fairly read, it alleges as well that the arrest was made without probable cause. Petitioner claimed to have suffered great humiliation, embarrassment, and mental suffering as a result of the agents' unlawful conduct, and sought $15,000 damages from each of them. The District Court, on respondents' motion, dismissed the complaint on the ground, *inter alia*, that it failed to state a cause of action. The Court of Appeals, one judge concurring specially, affirmed on that basis. * * * We reverse.

I

Respondents do not argue that petitioner should be entirely without remedy for an unconstitutional invasion of his rights by federal agents. In respondents' view, however, the rights that petitioner asserts—primarily rights of privacy—are creations of state and not of federal law. Accordingly, they argue, petitioner may obtain money damages to redress invasion of these rights only by an action in tort, under state law, in the state courts. In this scheme the Fourth Amendment would serve merely to limit the extent to which the agents could defend the state law tort suit by asserting that their actions were a valid exercise of federal power: if the agents were shown to have violated the Fourth Amendment, such a defense would be lost to them and they would stand before the state law merely as private individuals. * * *

We think that respondents' thesis rests upon an unduly restrictive view of the Fourth Amendment's protection against unreasonable searches and seizures by federal agents, a view that has consistently been rejected by this Court. Respondents seek to treat the relationship between a citizen and a federal agent unconstitutionally exercising his authority as no different from the relationship between two private citizens. In so doing, they ignore the fact that power, once granted, does not disappear like a magic gift when it is wrongly used. An agent acting—albeit unconstitutionally—in the name of the United States possesses a far greater capacity for harm than an individual trespasser exercising no authority other than his own. Accordingly, as our cases make clear, the

Fourth Amendment operates as a limitation upon the exercise of federal power regardless of whether the State in whose jurisdiction that power is exercised would prohibit or penalize the identical act if engaged in by a private citizen. * * *

That damages may be obtained for injuries consequent upon a violation of the Fourth Amendment by federal officials should hardly seem a surprising proposition. Historically, damages have been regarded as the ordinary remedy for an invasion of personal interests in liberty. Of course, the Fourth Amendment does not in so many words provide for its enforcement by an award of money damages for the consequences of its violation. But "it is * * * well settled that where legal rights have been invaded, and a federal statute provides for a general right to sue for such invasion, federal courts may use any available remedy to make good the wrong done." The present case involves no special factors counseling hesitation in the absence of affirmative action by Congress. We are not dealing with a question of "federal fiscal policy," as in United States v. Standard Oil Co., 332 U.S. 301, 311, 67 S.Ct. 1604, 1609–1610, 91 L.Ed. 2067 (1947). In that case we refused to infer from the Government-soldier relationship that the United States could recover damages from one who negligently injured a soldier and thereby caused the Government to pay his medical expenses and lose his services during the course of his hospitalization. Noting that Congress was normally quite solicitous where the federal purse was involved, we pointed out that "the United States [was] the party plaintiff to the suit. And the United States has power at any time to create the liability." Nor are we asked in this case to impose liability upon a congressional employee for actions contrary to no constitutional prohibition, but merely said to be in excess of the authority delegated to him by the Congress. Finally, we cannot accept respondents' formulation of the question as whether the availability of money damages is necessary to enforce the Fourth Amendment. For we have here no explicit congressional declaration that persons injured by a federal officer's violation of the Fourth Amendment may not recover money damages from the agents, but must instead be remitted to another remedy, equally effective in the view of Congress. The question is merely whether petitioner, if he can demonstrate an injury consequent upon the violation by federal agents of his Fourth Amendment rights, is entitled to redress his injury through a particular remedial mechanism normally available in the federal courts. "The very essence of civil liberty certainly consists in the right of every individual to claim the protection of the laws, whenever he receives an injury." Marbury v. Madison, 1 Cranch 137, 163, 2 L.Ed. 60 (1803). Having concluded that petitioner's complaint states a cause of action under the Fourth Amendment, * * * we hold that petitioner is entitled to recover money damages for any injuries he has suffered as a result of the agents' violation of the Amendment.

II

In addition to holding that petitioner's complaint had failed to state facts making out a cause of action, the District Court ruled that in any event respondents were immune from liability by virtue of their official position. This question was not passed upon by the Court of Appeals, and accordingly we do not consider it here. The judgment of the Court of Appeals is reversed and the case is remanded for further proceedings consistent with this opinion.

So ordered.

Mr. Justice Harlan, concurring in the judgment.

* * * For the reasons set forth below, I am of the opinion that federal courts do have the power to award damages for violation of "constitutionally protected interests" and I agree with the Court that a traditional judicial remedy such as damages is appropriate to the vindication of the personal interests protected by the Fourth Amendment.

I

I turn first to the contention that the constitutional power of federal courts to accord Bivens damages for his claim depends on the passage of a statute creating a "federal cause of action." Although the point is not entirely free of ambiguity, I do not understand either the Government or my dissenting Brothers to maintain that Bivens' contention that he is entitled to be free from the type of official conduct prohibited by the Fourth Amendment depends on a decision by the State in which he resides to accord him a remedy. * * * [T]he interest which Bivens claims—to be free from official conduct in contravention of the Fourth Amendment—is a federally protected interest. Therefore, the question of judicial *power* to grant Bivens damages is not a problem of the "source" of the "right"; instead, the question is whether the power to authorize damages as a judicial remedy for the vindication of a federal constitutional right is placed by the Constitution itself exclusively in Congress' hands.

II

The contention that the federal courts are powerless to accord a litigant damages for a claimed invasion of his federal constitutional rights until Congress explicitly authorizes the remedy cannot rest on the notion that the decision to grant compensatory relief involves a resolution of policy considerations not susceptible of judicial discernment. Thus, in suits for damages based on violations of federal statutes lacking any express authorization of a damage remedy, this Court has authorized such relief where, in its view, damages are necessary to effectuate the congressional policy underpinning the substantive provisions of the statute.

If it is not the nature of the remedy which is thought to render a judgment as to the appropriateness of damages inherently "legislative," then it must be the nature of the legal interest offered as an occasion for invoking otherwise appropriate judicial relief. But I do not think that the fact that the interest is protected by the Constitution rather than statute or common law justifies the assertion that federal courts are powerless to grant damages in the absence of explicit congressional action authorizing the remedy. Initially, I note that it would be at least anomalous to conclude that the federal judiciary—while competent to choose among the range of traditional judicial remedies to implement statutory and common-law policies, and even to generate substantive rules governing primary behavior in furtherance of broadly formulated policies articulated by statute or Constitution—is powerless to accord a damages remedy to vindicate social policies which, by virtue of their inclusion in the Constitution, are aimed predominantly at restraining the Government as an instrument of the popular will.

More importantly, the presumed availability of federal equitable relief against threatened invasions of constitutional interests appears entirely to negate the contention that the status of an interest as constitutionally protected divests federal courts of the power to grant damages absent express congressional authorization. * * *

If explicit congressional authorization is an absolute prerequisite to the power of a federal court to accord compensatory relief regardless of the necessity or appropriateness of damages as a remedy simply because of the status of a legal interest as constitutionally protected, then it seems to me that explicit congressional authorization is similarly prerequisite to the exercise of equitable remedial discretion in favor of constitutionally protected interests. Conversely, if a general grant of jurisdiction to the federal courts by Congress is thought adequate to empower a federal court to grant equitable relief for all areas of subject-matter jurisdiction enumerated therein, see 28 U.S.C. § 1331(a), then it seems to me that the same statute is sufficient to empower a federal court to grant a traditional remedy at law. Of course, the special historical traditions governing the federal equity system might still bear on the comparative appropriateness of granting equitable relief as opposed to money damages. That possibility, however, relates, not to whether the federal courts have the power to afford one type of remedy as opposed to the other, but rather to the criteria which should govern the exercise of our power. To that question, I now pass.

III

The major thrust of the Government's position is that, where Congress has not expressly authorized a particular remedy, a federal court should exercise its power to accord a traditional form of judicial relief at the behest of a litigant, who claims a constitutionally protected interest has been invaded, only where the remedy is "essential," or "indispensable for vindicating constitutional rights." * * * It is argued that historically the Court has rarely exercised the power to accord such relief in the absence of an express congressional authorization and that "[i]f Congress had thought that federal officers should be subject to a law different than state law, it would have had no difficulty in saying so, as it did with respect to state officers * * *" 42 U.S.C. § 1983. Although conceding that the standard of determining whether a damage remedy should be utilized to effectuate statutory policies is one of "necessity" or "appropriateness," the Government contends that questions concerning congressional discretion to modify judicial remedies relating to constitutionally protected interests warrant a more stringent constraint on the exercise of judicial power with respect to this class of legally protected interests.

These arguments for a more stringent test to govern the grant of damages in constitutional cases seem to be adequately answered by the point that the judiciary has a particular responsibility to assure the vindication of constitutional interests such as those embraced by the Fourth Amendment. To be sure, "it must be remembered that legislatures are ultimate guardians of the liberties and welfare of the people in quite as great a degree as the courts." But it must also be recognized that the Bill of Rights is particularly intended to vindicate the interests of the individual in the face of the popular will as expressed in legislative majorities; at the very least, it strikes me as no more appropriate to await express congressional authorization of traditional judicial relief with regard to these legal interests than with respect to interests protected by federal statutes.

The question then, is, as I see it, whether compensatory relief is "necessary" or "appropriate" to the vindication of the interest asserted. In resolving that question, it seems to me that the range of policy considerations we may take into account is at least as broad as the range of those a legislature would consider with respect to an express statutory authorization of a traditional remedy. In this regard I agree with the Court that the appropriateness of according Bivens compensatory relief does not turn simply on the deterrent effect liability will have on federal official conduct. Damages as a traditional form of compensation for invasion of a legally protected interest may be entirely appropriate even if no substantial deterrent effects on future official lawlessness might be thought to result. * * *

And I think it is clear that Bivens advances a claim of the sort that, if proved, would be properly compensable in damages. The personal interests protected by the Fourth Amendment are those we attempt to capture by the notion of "privacy"; while the Court today properly points out that the type of harm which officials can inflict when they invade protected zones of an individual's life are different from the types of harm private citizens inflict on one another, the experience of judges in dealing with private trespass and false imprisonment claims supports the conclusion that courts of law are capable of making the types of judgment concerning causation and magnitude of injury necessary to accord meaningful compensation for invasion of Fourth Amendment rights.

* * * [I]t is apparent that some form of damages is the only possible remedy for someone in Bivens' alleged position. It will be a rare case indeed in which an individual in Bivens' position will be able to obviate the harm by securing injunctive relief from any court. However desirable a direct remedy against the Government might be as a substitute for individual official liability, the sovereign still remains immune to suit.

Finally, assuming Bivens' innocence of the crime charged, the "exclusionary rule" is simply irrelevant. For people in Bivens' shoes, it is damages or nothing.

The only substantial policy consideration advanced against recognition of a federal cause of action for violation of Fourth Amendment rights by federal officials is the incremental expenditure of judicial resources that will be necessitated by this class of litigation. * * * I simply cannot agree with my Brother Black that the possibility of "frivolous" claims—if defined simply as claims with no legal merit—warrants closing the courthouse doors to people in Bivens' situation. There are other ways, short of that, of coping with frivolous lawsuits.

* * * Judicial resources, I am well aware, are increasingly scarce these days. Nonetheless, when we automatically close the courthouse door solely on this basis, we implicitly express a value judgment on the comparative importance of classes of legally protected interests. And current limitations upon the effective functioning of the courts arising from budgetary inadequacies should not be permitted to stand in the way of the recognition of otherwise sound constitutional principles. * * *

[The dissenting opinions of CHIEF JUSTICE BURGER, JUSTICE BLACK, and JUSTICE BLACKMUN have been omitted.]

NOTES

1. Did the *Bivens* court usurp a power belonging to Congress? Chief Justice Burger, Justice Blackmun, and Justice Black each dissented in *Bivens*. Although each wrote separately, all agreed that creating a remedy for violations of the Fourth Amendment was a power reserved to Congress under the Constitution:

> Although Congress has created such a federal cause of action against *state* officials acting under color of state law [42 U.S.C. § 1983], it has never created such a cause of action against federal officials. If it wanted to do so, Congress could, of course, create a remedy against federal officials who violate the Fourth Amendment in the performance of their duties. But the point of this case and the fatal weakness in the Court's judgment is that neither Congress nor the State of New York has enacted legislation creating such a right of action. For us to do so is, in my judgment, an exercise of power that the Constitution does not give us.

403 U.S. at 427–28, 91 S.Ct. at 2020–21 (Black, J. dissenting).

The dissenters contended that the Court cannot provide a remedy for a violation of some constitutional rights unless the remedy is authorized by Congress or by the Constitution itself. The majority seemed to say that the Court is free to use any traditional remedy to vindicate the plaintiff's rights, unless Congress has withdrawn that authority. Who has the better of the argument?

As Justice Harlan points out, it has always been presumed that the court has the power to issue an injunction at an individual's behest to stop a federal officer from violating the Constitution, even without an express congressional enactment authorizing that remedy. Would the dissenters deny the court the authority to grant an injunction to prevent a threatened violation of the Constitution? What is the difference between enjoining a future violation and awarding damages for a past violation? See John C. Jeffries, The Right–Remedy Gap in Constitutional Law, 109 Yale L.J. 87, 90 (1999) (arguing that by limiting the damages remedy while affording complete injunctive relief, courts shift the emphasis of constitutional litigation from "reparation toward reform" and thus "facilitate constitutional change by reducing the costs of innovation").

2. Where does the majority locate the authority it is exercising in *Bivens?* Is it conferred by the text of the Constitution, perhaps by article III, section 2, which extends the judicial power "to all cases * * * arising under this Constitution"? Or is it by the grant of jurisdiction contained in 28 U.S.C. § 1331(a), which provides, "the district courts shall have original jurisdiction of all civil actions arising under the Constitution, laws, or treaties of the United States"? Sometimes it is suggested that a mandate can be found in the due process clause of the fifth amendment, see Richard H. Fallon, Of Legislative Courts, Administrative Agencies, and Article III, 101 Harv.L.Rev. 916, 955 n.223 (1988), or that the amendments themselves carry "a self-executing force that not only permits but requires the courts to recognize remedies appropriate for their violation." Walter E. Dellinger, Of Rights and Remedies: The Constitution as a Sword, 85 Harv.L.Rev. 1532 (1972). Does the source of the court's authority matter?

3. Once the Supreme Court decided that it did not need express congressional authorization to allow Bivens to sue for damages, it still had to decide whether damages were appropriate. What is it that convinces the Court that an award of damages is an appropriate remedy for a violation of the fourth amendment? After all, Bivens already had a number of remedies at his disposal. He could have sued to enjoin future violations of his rights. If he had been arrested, he could have invoked the exclusionary rule to prevent the use of the evidence in a criminal proceeding. See William C. Hefferman, Foreward: The Fourth Amendment Exclusionary Rule as a Constitutional Remedy, 88 Geo.L.J. 799 (2000). Bivens could have sued the federal officers in state court for a number of torts, including trespass, assault, battery, false arrest, defamation and intentional infliction of emotional distress. With all of these remedies available, why does the Court allow a suit for damages for violation of Bivens's constitutional rights?

If a damages remedy is appropriate when the fourth amendment is violated, does it necessarily follow that a damages remedy is equally appropriate for all constitutional violations? Justice Harlan's concurrence suggests not. After noting that the personal interests the fourth amendment protects are very closely analogous to such torts as false imprisonment and trespass, providing judges a background of experience for handling compensation claims, Justice Harlan noted, "The same, of course, may not be true with respect to other types of constitutionally protected interests, and therefore the appropriateness of money damages may well vary with the nature of the personal interest asserted." 403 U.S. at 409 n.9, 91 S.Ct. at 2011 n.9.

4. After *Bivens,* what exactly is the relationship between rights and remedies, and between Congress and the Court? Is it that:

a. The Constitution implicitly requires courts to award damages whenever an individual's constitutional rights are violated?

b. The Court has the authority to ensure that an adequate remedy is available whenever the Constitution is violated?

c. Both the Court and Congress may create remedies for constitutional violations, but if Congress has spoken clearly, the Court must defer to Congress's judgment?

d. The ultimate authority lies with Congress, but the Court will allow a damages action to proceed if it can infer that Congress would agree?

e. The ultimate authority lies with Congress, and Congress must expressly authorize the Court to act?

See if the following case causes you to reevaluate your response.

SCHWEIKER v. CHILICKY

Supreme Court of the United States, 1988
487 U.S. 412, 108 S.Ct. 2460, 101 L.Ed.2d 370

JUSTICE O'CONNOR delivered the opinion of the Court.

This case requires us to decide whether the improper denial of Social Security disability benefits, allegedly resulting from violations of due process by government officials who administered the Federal Social Security program, may give rise to a cause of action for money damages against those officials. We conclude that such a remedy, not having been included in the elaborate remedial scheme devised by Congress, is unavailable.

I

A

[In 1980, Congress passed legislation requiring States to review the disability determinations of persons receiving disability benefits under Title II of the Social Security Act at least every three years. Claimants whose benefits were denied under this continuing disability review (CDR) program could appeal, but the administrative appeals process typically took nine to eighteen months, and during that period claimants received no benefits (although if the termination was later reversed, benefits could be awarded retroactively).

Finding that benefits were too often being improperly terminated by state agencies, only to be reinstated by a federal administrative law judge (ALJ), Congress enacted the Social Security Disability Benefits Reform Act of 1984. The 1984 Reform Act required a more careful review before benefits could be terminated, and provided that benefits would continue through the penultimate stage of the appeals process, which was an appeal to a federal ALJ.]

The problems to which Congress responded so emphatically were widespread. One of the cosponsors of the 1984 Reform Act, who had conducted hearings on the administration of CDR, summarized evidence from the General Accounting Office as follows:

"[T]he message perceived by the State agencies, swamped with cases, was to deny, deny, deny, and, I might add, to process cases faster and faster and faster. In the name of efficiency, we have scanned our computer terminals, rounded up the disabled workers in the country, pushed the discharge button, and let them go into a free [f]all toward economic chaos." (Sen. Cohen).

* * * The Social Security Administration itself apparently reported that about 200,000 persons were wrongfully terminated, and then reinstated, between March 1981 and April 1984. * * *

Congress was also made aware of the terrible effects on individual lives that CDR had produced. The Chairman of the Senate's Special Committee on Aging pointed out that "[t]he human dimension of this crisis—the unnecessary suffering, anxiety, and turmoil—has been graphically exposed by dozens of congressional hearings and in newspaper articles all across the country." * * *

B

[Respondents James Chilicky, Spencer Harris and Dora Adelerte had their Social Security disability benefits terminated under the CDR program. Harris and Adelerte pursued administrative appeals, and their benefits were reinstated, retroactively. Chilicky filed a new application for benefits, which was granted. He also received a retroactive award.

Chilicky, Harris and Adelerte then sued to recover damages for the harm caused by months-long delay in the restoration of their benefits, including loss of food, shelter, and other necessities, as well as emotional distress. They alleged that state and federal officials had violated their due process rights by adopting illegal policies that terminated their benefits. The District Court dismissed their complaint, but the Court of Appeals reversed and remanded, concluding that respondents had stated a claim under *Bivens*.] * * *

The petition for certiorari presented one question: "Whether a *Bivens* remedy should be implied for alleged due process violations in the denial of social security disability benefits." We granted the petition, and now reverse.

II

A

* * * Our more recent decisions have responded cautiously to suggestions that *Bivens* remedies be extended into new contexts. The absence of statutory relief for a constitutional violation, for example, does not by any means necessarily imply that courts should award money damages against the officers responsible for the violation. Thus, in Chappell v. Wallace, 462 U.S. 296, 103 S.Ct. 2362, 76 L.Ed.2d 586 (1983), we refused—unanimously—to create a *Bivens* action for enlisted military personnel who alleged that they had been injured by the unconstitutional actions of their superior officers and who had no remedy against the Government itself:

> "The special nature of military life—the need for unhesitating and decisive action by military officers and equally disciplined responses by enlisted personnel—would be undermined by a judicially created remedy exposing officers to personal liability at the hands of those they are charged to command. . . .
>
> "Also, Congress, the constitutionally authorized source of authority over the military system of justice, has not provided a damages remedy for claims by military personnel that constitutional rights have been violated by superior officers. *Any action to provide a judicial response by way of such a remedy would be plainly inconsistent with Congress' authority in this field.*
>
> "Taken together, the unique disciplinary structure of the Military Establishment and Congress' activity in the field constitute 'special factors' which dictate that it would be inappropriate to provide enlisted military personnel a *Bivens*-type remedy against their superior officers."

* * * Similarly, we refused—again unanimously—to create a *Bivens* remedy for a First Amendment violation "aris[ing] out of an employment relationship that is governed by comprehensive procedural and substantive provisions giving meaningful remedies against the United States." Bush v. Lucas, 462 U.S. 367, 368, 103 S.Ct. 2404, 2406, 76 L.Ed.2d 648 (1983). In that case, a federal employee was demoted, allegedly in violation of the First Amendment, for making public statements critical of the agency for which he worked. He was reinstated through the administrative process, with retroactive seniority and full back pay, but he was not permitted to recover for any loss due to emotional distress or mental anguish, or for attorney's fees. Concluding that the administrative system created by Congress "provides meaningful remedies for employees who may have been unfairly disciplined for making critical comments about their agencies," the Court refused to create a *Bivens* action even though it assumed a First Amendment violation and acknowledged that "existing remedies do not provide complete relief for the plaintiff." The Court stressed that the case involved policy questions in an area that had received careful attention from Congress. Noting that the Legislature is far more competent than the Judiciary to carry out the necessary "balancing [of] governmental efficiency and the rights of employees," we refused to "decide whether or not it would be good policy to permit a federal employee to recover damages from a supervisor who has improperly disciplined him for exercising his First Amendment rights."

In sum, the concept of "special factors counseling hesitation in the absence of affirmative action by Congress" has proved to include an appropriate judicial deference to indications that congressional action has not been inadvertent. When the design of a government program suggests that Congress has provided what it considers adequate remedial mechanisms for constitutional violations that may occur in the course of its administration, we have not created additional *Bivens* remedies.

[Deferential POV]

B

* * * The case before us cannot reasonably be distinguished from *Bush v. Lucas*. Here, exactly as in *Bush*, Congress has failed to provide for "complete relief": respondents have not been given a remedy in damages for emotional distress or for other hardships suffered because of delays in their receipt of Social Security benefits. The creation of a *Bivens* remedy would obviously offer the prospect of relief for injuries that must now go unredressed. Congress, however, has not failed to provide meaningful safeguards or remedies for the rights of persons situated as respondents were. Indeed, the system for protecting their rights is, if anything, considerably more elaborate than the civil service system considered in *Bush*. The prospect of personal liability for official acts, moreover, would undoubtedly lead to new difficulties and expense in recruiting administrators for the programs Congress has established. Congressional competence at "balancing governmental efficiency and the rights of [individuals]," is no more questionable in the social welfare context than it is in the civil service context.

Congressional attention to problems that have arisen in the administration of CDR (including the very problems that gave rise to this case) has, moreover, been frequent and intense. * * * At each step, Congress chose specific forms and levels of protection for the rights of persons affected by incorrect eligibility determinations under CDR. At no point did Congress choose to extend to any person the kind of remedies that respondents seek in this lawsuit. Thus, congressional unwillingness to provide consequential damages for unconstitutional deprivations of a statutory right is at least as clear in the context of this case as it was in *Bush*.

Respondents nonetheless contend that *Bush* should be confined to its facts, arguing that it applies only in the context of what they call "the special nature of federal employee relations." Noting that the parties to this case did "not share the sort of close, collaborative, continuing juridical relationship found in the federal civil service," respondents suggest that the availability of *Bivens* remedies would create less "inconvenience" to the Social Security system than it would in the context of the civil service. The Solicitor General is less sanguine, arguing that the creation of *Bivens* remedy in this context would lead to "a complete disruption of [a] carefully crafted and constantly monitored congressional scheme."

[irrelevant]

We need not choose between these competing predictions, which have little bearing on the applicability of *Bush* to this case. The decision in *Bush* did not rest on this Court's belief that *Bivens* actions would be more disruptive of the civil service than they are in other contexts where they have been allowed, such as federal law enforcement agencies (*Bivens* itself) or the federal prisons (Carlson v. Green, 446 U.S. 14, 100 S.Ct. 1468, 64 L.Ed.2d 15 (1980)). Rather, we declined in *Bush* " 'to create a new substantive legal liability ...' because we are convinced that Congress is in a better position to decide whether or not the public interest would be served by creating it." * * *

In the end, respondents' various arguments are rooted in their insistent and vigorous contention that they simply have not been adequately recompensed for their injuries. * * *

We agree that suffering months of delay in receiving the income on which one has depended for the very necessities of life cannot be fully remedied by the "belated restoration of back benefits." The trauma to respondents, and thousands of others like them, must surely have gone beyond what anyone of normal sensibilities would wish to see imposed on innocent disabled citizens. Nor would we care to "trivialize" the nature of the wrongs alleged in this case. Congress, however, has addressed the problems created by state agencies' wrongful termination of disability benefits. Whether or not we believe that its response was the best response, Congress is the body charged with making the inevitable compromises required in the design of a massive and complex welfare benefits program. * * *

JUSTICE STEVENS, concurring in part and concurring in the judgment. [omitted]

JUSTICE BRENNAN, with whom JUSTICE MARSHALL and JUSTICE BLACKMUN join, dissenting. * * *

A

* * * In *Chappell* and *Bush,* we dealt with elaborate administrative systems in which Congress anticipated that federal officials might engage in unconstitutional conduct, and in which it accordingly sought to afford injured persons a form of redress as complete as the Government's institutional concerns would allow. * * *

Here, as the legislative history of the 1984 Reform Act makes abundantly clear, Congress did not attempt to achieve a delicate balance between the constitutional rights of Title II beneficiaries on the one hand, and administrative concerns on the other. * * * Congress confronted a paralyzing breakdown in a vital social program, which it sought to rescue from near-total anarchy. Although the legislative debate surrounding the 1984 Reform Act is littered with references to "arbitrary," "capricious," and "wrongful" terminations of benefits, it is clear that neither Congress nor anyone else identified unconstitutional conduct by state agencies as the cause of this paralysis. Rather, Congress blamed the systemic problems it faced in 1984 on SSA's determination to control the cost of the disability insurance program by accelerating the CDR process and mandating more restrictive reviews. * * *

At no point during the lengthy legislative debate * * * did any Member of Congress so much as hint that the substantive eligibility criteria, notice requirements, and interim payment provisions that would govern *future* disability reviews adequately redressed the harms that beneficiaries may have suffered as a result of the unconstitutional actions of individual state and federal officials in *past* proceedings, or that the constitutional rights of those unjustly deprived of benefits in the past had to be sacrificed in the name of administrative efficiency or any other governmental interest. The Court today identifies no legislative compromise, "inevitable" or otherwise, in which lawmakers expressly declined to afford a remedy for such past wrongs. * * *

The mere fact, that Congress was aware of the prior injustices and failed to provide a form of redress for them, standing alone, is simply not a "special factor counseling hesitation" in the judicial recognition of a remedy. Inaction, we have repeatedly stated, is a notoriously poor indication of congressional intent, all the more so where Congress is legislating in the face of a massive breakdown calling for prompt and sweeping corrective measures. * * *

B

Our decisions in *Chappell* and *Bush* reveal yet another flaw in the "special factors" analysis the Court employs today. In both those cases, we declined to legislate in areas in which Congress enjoys a special expertise that the judiciary clearly lacks. * * *

Ignoring the unique characteristics of the military and civil service contexts that made judicial recognition of a *Bivens* action inappropriate in those cases, the Court today observes that "[c]ongressional competence at 'balancing governmental efficiency and the rights of [individuals]' is no more questionable in the social welfare context than it is in the civil service context." This observation, however, avails the Court nothing, for in *Bush* we declined to create a *Bivens* action for aggrieved federal employees not because Congress is simply competent to legislate in the area of federal employment relations, but because Congress is far more capable of addressing the special problems that arise in those relations than are the courts. * * *

Congress, of course, created the disability insurance program and obviously may legislate with respect to it. But unlike the military setting, where Congress' authority is plenary and entitled to considerable judicial deference, or the federal employment context, where Congress enjoys special expertise, social welfare is hardly an area in which the courts are largely incompetent to act. The disability insurance program is concededly large, but it does not involve necessarily unique relationships like those between enlisted military personnel and their superior officers, or Government workers and their federal employers. Rather, like the federal law enforcement and penal systems that gave rise to the constitutional claims in *Bivens* and *Carlson, supra,* the constitutional issues that surface in the social welfare system turn on the relationship of the Government and those it governs—the relationship that lies at the heart of constitutional adjudication. Moreover, courts do not lack familiarity or expertise in determining what the dictates of the Due Process Clause are. In short, the social welfare context does not give rise to the types of concerns that make it an area where courts should refrain from creating a damages action even in the absence of congressional action. * * *

Because I am convinced that Congress did not intend to preclude judicial recognition of a cause of action for such injuries, and because I believe there are no special factors militating against the creation of such a remedy here, I dissent.

NOTES

1. In Note 4 following *Bivens* at p. 20, five possible ways of accommodating the power of the courts and the power of Congress to declare a remedy are suggested. After *Chilicky*, which is correct? Have *Chilicky* and *Bush* made congressional intent dispositive by treating Congress's omission of a private cause of action as a "special factor counseling hesitation"?

2. The availability of an alternative remedial scheme is not the only "special factor" that may counsel hesitation. In Wilkie v. Robbins, 551 U.S. 537, 127 S.Ct. 2588, 168 L.Ed.2d 389 (2007), Robbins alleged that federal agents had engaged in a series of vindictive and extortionate acts in an attempt to force him to convey an easement across his land. The Court acknowledged that federal law did not provide the plaintiff with any alternative to a *Bivens* action, but still refused to create a cause of action:

> [O]ur consideration of a *Bivens* request follows a familiar sequence, and on the assumption that a constitutionally recognized interest is adversely affected by the actions of federal employees, the decision whether to recognize a *Bivens* remedy may require two steps. In the first place, there is the question whether any alternative, existing process for protecting the interest amounts to a convincing reason for the Judicial Branch to refrain from providing a new and freestanding remedy in damages. But even in the absence of an alternative, a *Bivens* remedy is a subject of judgment: "the federal courts must make the kind of remedial determination that is appropriate for a common-law tribunal, paying particular heed, however, to any special factors counselling [sic] hesitation before authorizing a new kind of federal litigation."

The line-drawing problems that would result from recognizing a cause of action when government agents "demanded too much and went too far" counseled against recognizing a cause of action:

> A judicial standard to identify illegitimate pressure going beyond legitimately hard bargaining would be endlessly knotty to work out, and a general provision for tortlike liability when Government employees are unduly zealous in pressing a governmental interest affecting property would invite an onslaught of *Bivens* actions.

127 S.Ct. at 2604.

3. When plaintiffs invoke *Bivens* to challenge a pervasive government policy, as in *Chilicky*, they are engaging in a form of public law litigation. Yet, in denying a damages remedy for alleged governmental wrongdoing,

> *Wilkie* is representative. * * * [I]n most cases, *Bivens* claims go nowhere. The Supreme Court did not find for a *Bivens* plaintiff between 1980 and 2004. By 1996, the D.C. Circuit located evidence that the government had only paid four *Bivens* claims

David Zaring, Three Models of Constitutional Torts, 2 J. Tort L. 3, 8 (2008). Since *Bivens* itself, the Supreme Court has endorsed a *Bivens* action in only two other cases, Davis v. Passman, 442 U.S. 228, 99 S.Ct. 2264, 60 L.Ed.2d 846 (1979) (due process clause of the fifth amendment), and Carlson v. Green, 446 U.S. 14, 100 S.Ct. 1468, 64 L.Ed.2d 15 (1980) (eighth amendment's cruel and unusual punishment clause).

Justice Scalia, for one, has made his position clear on why this should be so:

> *Bivens* is a relic of the heady days in which this Court assumed common-law powers to create causes of action—decreeing them to be "implied" by the mere existence of a statutory or constitutional prohibition. As the Court points out, * * * we have abandoned that power to invent "implications" in the statutory field. There is even greater reason to abandon it in the constitutional field, since an "implication" imagined in the Constitution can presumably not even be repudiated by Congress. I would limit *Bivens* and its two follow-on cases [*Davis* and *Carlson*] to the precise circumstances that they involved.

Correctional Services Corp. v. Malesko, 534 U.S. 61, 75, 122 S.Ct. 515, 524, 151 L.Ed.2d 456, 469 (2001). In the final analysis, have the *Bivens* dissenters prevailed? See George D. Brown, Letting Statutory Tails Wag Constitutional Dogs—Have the *Bivens* Dissenters Prevailed?, 64 Ind.L.J. 263 (1989).

4. If the violations that plagued the CDR process (described in *Chilicky*) had continued, could the plaintiffs have sought injunctive relief to prevent further unconstitutional denials of benefits? Despite what appears to be a retreat from *Bivens* as far as damages actions are concerned, no member of the Court has challenged the received wisdom that the federal courts can enjoin continuing violations of the Constitution even though Congress has never specifically authorized them to do so. Isn't this a fatal inconsistency? If the courts have the authority to enjoin violations, don't they also have the authority to award damages to individual victims? If the concern in *Chilicky* is with disturbing the operation of Congress's remedial scheme, wouldn't injunctions, which could bring the entire process to a halt, pose a greater threat than isolated damage awards? What explains the Court's hostility to allowing plaintiffs allegedly injured by unconstitutional acts to recover damages?

5. Can Congress prohibit the federal courts from granting a remedy for constitutional violations? In the Prison Litigation Reform Act (PLRA), 18 U.S.C. § 362, Congress prohibited prisoners from bringing a federal civil action for mental or emotional injury suffered while in custody without a showing of prior physical injury. In Zehner v. Trigg, 133 F.3d 459 (7th Cir.1997), the court relied on this section to deny damages for mental distress

to prisoners who had been exposed to asbestos, but who had not suffered a physical injury. As for the prisoners' claim that this section of the PLRA was an unconstitutional attempt by Congress to strip the federal courts of their power to remedy constitutional violations, the court said:

> But the legal point remains: the Constitution does not demand an individually effective remedy for every constitutional violation. * * * If other prisoners are currently being exposed to asbestos within the Indiana prison system, they may seek injunctive relief for the violation. If the plaintiffs in this case develop asbestos-related illnesses, they themselves will be able to sue for damages. Because these remedies remain, Congress' decision to restrict the availability of damages is constitutional as applied in this case.

133 F.3d at 462. What about the observation in *Bivens* that for certain plaintiffs, it is "damages, or nothing"?

Could Congress eliminate the federal courts' power to grant injunctive relief? The Supreme Court has never directly addressed the issue. In Webster v. Doe, 486 U.S. 592, 108 S.Ct. 2047, 100 L.Ed.2d 632 (1988), however, the Court refused to interpret a statute to preclude all claims for injunctive relief for violations of constitutional rights, because "serious constitutional questions would arise if a federal statute were construed to deny any judicial forum for a colorable constitutional claim." Justice Scalia dissented: "[I]t is simply untenable that there must be a judicial remedy for every constitutional violation." 486 U.S. at 613, 108 S.Ct. at 2059.

A DIGRESSION: REMEDIAL CHOICE IN THE STATUTORY CONTEXT

In Davis v. Passman, 442 U.S. 228, 99 S.Ct. 2264, 60 L.Ed.2d 846 (1979), Justice Brennan defined some basic terms:

> *[J]urisdiction* is a question of whether a federal court has the power, under the constitution or laws of the United States, to hear a case; *standing* is a question of whether a plaintiff is sufficiently adversary to a defendant to create an Art. III case or controversy, or at least to overcome prudential limitations on federal court jurisdiction; *cause of action* is a question of whether a particular plaintiff is a member of the class of litigants that may, as a matter of law, appropriately invoke the power of the court; and *relief* is a question of the various remedies a federal court may make available.

442 U.S. at 239 n.18, 99 S.Ct. at 2274 n.18. *Bivens* addressed the last two of these inquiries, asking, does a cause of action for damages exist when the fourth amendment is violated?

Just as the Constitution often confers rights without mentioning remedies, Congress occasionally enacts a statute without expressly indicating whether individuals harmed by a violation of the statute can sue. For example, Congress may pass legislation making conduct a crime, but say nothing about whether those whom the conduct injures may sue for damages, injunctive relief, or any other remedy. In such a case, should the courts recognize a private cause of action if they believe it is "necessary and appropriate" to effectuate the statutory scheme, as Justice Harlan's concurrence in *Bivens* suggests? If a cause of action is recognized, what remedies should be available?

The Supreme Court addressed this issue in Cort v. Ash, 422 U.S. 66, 95 S.Ct. 2080, 45 L.Ed.2d 26 (1975). In *Cort*, Congress had made it a crime punishable by a fine of $5000 for a corporation to contribute to a Presidential campaign. (The statute was later repealed, although it has been replaced by similar provisions. See 2 U.S.C. § 441(b).) Cort sued on behalf of a corporation in which he held stock, alleging that the corporation's directors had violated the statute, and seeking damages.

Writing for the majority, Justice Brennan withdrew considerably from the position that a private cause of action will be made available any time a court views it as "necessary or appropriate" to effectuate the statutory scheme. Rather, to infer that a private cause of action exists, a court must examine four factors:

- Was the statute enacted to benefit a class, of which the plaintiff is a member?
- Did the legislature intend to create a private right of action?
- Is implication of a private right consistent with the legislative scheme?
- Is this an area of law traditionally left to state control?

Applying this test, Justice Brennan concluded that the statute was not intended to protect shareholders from the fiscal consequences of campaign contributions, and that therefore it would be inappropriate to allow shareholders a private cause of action for damages.

Some members of the Court believe that the courts' role in deciding that a private cause of action should exist for statutory violations should be even more limited. According to Justice Scalia, for example, the focus should be exclusively on legislative intent. Further, in order to promote certainty in the law, Congress should be on notice that it must speak explicitly if it wishes to create a remedy, and therefore "a flat rule that private rights of action will not be implied in statutes hereafter enacted" should be followed. Thompson v. Thompson, 484 U.S. 174, 192, 108 S.Ct. 513, 523, 98 L.Ed.2d 512 (1988) (Scalia, J. concurring). The Court, however, generally remains committed to the *Cort* test, although it has indicated that evidence of congressional intent is clearly the critical factor. See California v. Sierra Club, 451 U.S. 287, 297, 101 S.Ct. 1775, 68 L.Ed.2d 101 (1981) (third and fourth *Cort* factors need not be considered if congressional intent is clear); Alexander v. Sandoval, 532 U.S. 275, 286, 121 S.Ct. 1511, 149 L.Ed.2d 517 (2001) (inquiry "begins and ends with the text and structure of the statute").

Which is the better position? Should federal courts be allowed to use any remedy that is effective in pursuing the goals of a law, unless Congress has expressly indicated that the remedial scheme it developed is to be exclusive? Or should courts limit the available remedies to those expressly authorized by Congress, unless evidence exists from which a court can infer that Congress intended other remedies to exist? To the extent that the Court has retreated from its earlier, more expansive view of judicial power, should *Bivens* itself be rethought? Or are constitutional violations different? What about rights created by treaty, if the treaty is silent as to remedies? See John Quigley, Must Treaty Violations be Remedied?: A Critique of Sanchez–Llamas v. Oregon, 36 Ga.J. Int'l & Comp.L. 355 (2008).

When a state actor violates a federal statute or the U.S. Constitution, another federal statute, 42 U.S.C. § 1983, can come into play. Section 1983, to which you have already seen several references, is an important vehicle for the protection of federal rights and provides the statutory foundation for many public law cases. It reads:

> Every person who, under color of [state law], subjects or causes to be subjected, any citizen of the United States or other person within the jurisdiction thereof to the deprivation of any rights, privileges or immunities secured by the Constitution *and laws*, shall be liable to the party injured in an action at law, suit in equity or other proper proceeding for redress.

42 U.S.C. § 1983 (emphasis added). In Gonzaga University v. Doe, 536 U.S. 273, 122 S.Ct. 2268, 153 L.Ed.2d 309 (2002), Chief Justice Rehnquist explained the distinction between a claim made under section 1983 and an implied cause of action for violation of a federal law:

> Plaintiffs suing under § 1983 do not have the burden of showing an intent to create a private remedy because § 1983 generally supplies a remedy for the vindication of rights secured by federal statutes. Once a plaintiff demonstrates that a statute confers an individual right, the right is presumptively enforceable by § 1983.

Not every federal law, however, confers individual rights. Chief Justice Rehnquist continued:

> But the initial inquiry—determining whether a statute confers any right at all—is no different from the initial inquiry in an implied right of action case, the express purpose of which is to determine whether or not a statute "confers rights on a particular class of persons."
>
> * * * Accordingly, where the text and structure of a statute provide no indication that Congress intends to create new individual rights, there is no basis for a private suit, whether under § 1983 or under an implied right of action.

536 U.S. at 284–285, 122 S.Ct. at 2276. Thus, Chief Justice Rehnquist concluded that a student who was harmed when his school records were wrongly disclosed had no cause of action under the Family Educational Rights and Privacy Act, because Congress did not intend to create individually enforceable rights when it enacted the law. Similarly, no section 1983 cause of action is available if Congress expressly or implicitly

indicates that a statute's enforcement scheme is to be the exclusive remedy for a violation. Compare Fitzgerald v. Barnstable School Committee, 555 U.S. ___, 129 S.Ct. 788, 172 L.Ed.2d ___ (2009) (Congress did not intend Title IX to preclude a section 1983 action for unconstitutional gender discrimination in the schools) with City of Rancho Palos Verdes v. Abrams, 544 U.S. 113, 125 S.Ct. 1453, 161 L.Ed.2d 316 (2005) (no cause of action under section 1983 for violation of the Telecommunication Act of 1996).

"Where there's a right, there's a remedy"

The idea that there must be a remedy for every violation of a right is a powerful one. It has been used, as in *Bivens*, to justify the creation of a cause of action without express constitutional or statutory warrant. It has also been invoked by state courts to check legislative action that limits the remedies available to injured plaintiffs. See Thomas A. Phillips, The Constitutional Right to a Remedy, 78 N.Y.U.L.Rev. 1309 (2003) (discussing cases relying on "right to a remedy" or "open courts" guarantees in state constitutions to strike down a variety of tort reform measures). See also John C.P. Goldberg, The Constitutional Status of Tort Law, 115 Yale L.J. 524 (2005) (providing remedies for private wrongs is a fundamental element of the American legal system that is embodied in the constitution and limits the power of states to enact tort reform legislation).

Yet as this chapter makes clear, the commitment to this principle is hardly total. Not every violation of a law violates an individual's rights; not every violation of a right gives rise to a cause of action in federal or state court. As one scholar has argued, "modern doctrine clearly refutes the notion that there is a constitutional right to a remedy for every constitutional violation." Richard H. Fallon, Jr., Some Confusions About Due Process, Judicial Review, and Constitutional Remedies, 93 Colum.L.Rev. 309 (1993). Even in *Bivens*, after all, Justice Brennan made allowance for "special factors counseling hesitation"—concerns, that is, that are allowed to undercut the goal of a complete remedy. Concern for federalism, separation of powers, and a proper accommodation of the interests of the plaintiff and the defendant all factor into the search for the proper remedy.

Questions about the exact nature of the relationship between right and remedy have taken on increased importance as Congress—in the Prison Litigation Reform Act, for example—has attempted to reign in the courts' remedial authority, or as the Supreme Court has attempted to reign in Congress's assertions of its remedial authority under section five of the fourteenth amendment. See, e.g., Kimel v. Florida Board of Regents, 528 U.S. 62, 120 S.Ct. 631, 145 L.Ed.2d 522 (2000) (legislation purporting to abrogate the states' sovereign immunity in age discrimination lawsuits was "so out of proportion to a supposed remedial or preventive object" that it could not be justified as an exercise of Congress's power to remedy violations of the equal protection clause). One result has been a vigorous debate in the law reviews over *whether* "where there's a right, there's a remedy." See, e.g., Judith Resnik, Constricting Remedies: The Rehnquist Judiciary, Congress and Federal Power, 78 Ind.L.J. 223 (2003); Tracy A.

Thomas, Congress' Section 5 Power and Remedial Rights, 34 U.C. Davis L.Rev. 673 (2001); Ashutosh Bhagwat, Hard Cases and the (D)Evolution of Constitutional Doctrine, 30 Conn.L.Rev. 961 (1998).

On balance, it is probably more accurate to say that where there's a right, there may be many remedies, or none. If so, who should choose, and how? Professor Fallon contends that what is constitutionally indispensable is a "scheme of constitutional remedies sufficient to keep government tolerably within the bounds of law." 93 Colum.L.Rev. at 338. What criteria would you use to determine whether a particular scheme is "sufficient"? For example, would you agree that "an adequate remedy must be one that provides individualized redress to the plaintiff," as Professor Thomas contends? 34 U.C. Davis L.Rev. at 761. Should the range of available remedies be determined by a court, or by a legislature? Whichever body will make the decision, how is it to decide? If more than one remedy is available, how is a lawyer to decide which of the available remedies best serves the client's interests?

These are the questions that occupy the remedies course. Whether it is a legislature, a court, or counsel deciding, the key to choosing among remedies lies in understanding the nature and characteristics of each remedy: how it works, how much it costs, when it works well, and what its limits are. To these issues we now turn.

Chapter 2

The Nature, Availability, and Scope of Injunctions

■ ■ ■

A. THE NATURE OF AN INJUNCTION

Problem: Country Lodge v. Miller (Reprised)
The Choice Between an Injunction and Damages

Country Lodge has requested an injunction: (a) requiring Miller to clean up the apple mash that washed ashore on its property last fall; and (b) prohibiting Miller from committing future nuisances. Miller urges the court to deny injunctive relief and instead give Country Lodge compensatory damages for both past and future harms. What should the court do?

The choice between injunctions and compensatory damages is of real consequence to the parties and the court. An injunction, an equitable remedy, is an order that directs a person to act or refrain from acting in a specified way. In contrast, a money judgment, a legal remedy, is not a direct order from the court addressed to a specific person demanding action. As a result, the regimes for enforcement are very different.

[C]oercive remedies in equity are variants of the injunction. The injunction is a personal order to the defendant. It is not merely a judgment such as the law courts might issue. It did not merely declare the defendant's debt or obligation, but instead commanded the defendant to do or refrain from a specified act. * * * The essence of the remedy in most instances * * * is the *in personam* order, enforced by the distinctive power of contempt. * * *

The old separate law courts did not issue injunctive orders; they rendered judgments instead. The law courts did not seek to enforce their orders by contempt powers, but by seizure of property.

Dan B. Dobbs, The Law of Remedies § 2.1(1) (2d ed.1993).

Violation of an injunction, as an order of the court, is contempt of court and punishable under the courts' contempt power. Chapter 3 treats the contempt power in detail, but it is useful to go over some basics now.

If the injunction is violated, the court may award monetary compensation to the plaintiff. This is known as *compensatory civil contempt*. It differs from an ordinary action for compensatory damages in that the contemnor does not have a right to a jury trial and the court generally has authority to award the plaintiff attorney's fees.

If compensatory civil contempt were the only remedy for contempt, an injunction would, in essence, be a substitutionary rather than a specific remedy. In order to enforce its orders specifically, the court has two additional weapons. First, the court may coerce the contemnor into obeying the order by jailing or fining her so long as the disobedience continues. This is known as *coercive civil contempt*. The measure of the duress is what is needed to make the contemnor comply with the specific court order, not the plaintiff's ultimate rightful position in the action. Second, if the violation of the injunction is willful, the court may adjudge the contemnor guilty of a crime and impose a sentence. This is known as *criminal contempt*.

Coercive civil contempt and criminal contempt take away from the defendant the option of paying damages to the plaintiff instead of obeying the injunction. This leads to important differences between injunctive and damage relief noted by Judge Guido Calabresi and Mr. Douglas Melamed:

> An entitlement [i.e., a right] is protected by a property rule [e.g., an injunction] to the extent that someone who wishes to remove the entitlement from its holder must buy it from him in a voluntary transaction in which the value of the entitlement is agreed upon by the seller. It is the form of entitlement which gives rise to the least amount of state intervention: once the original entitlement is decided upon, the state does not try to decide its value. It lets each of the parties say how much the entitlement is worth to him, and gives the seller a veto if the buyer does not offer enough. Property rules involve a collective decision as to whom is to be given an initial entitlement but not as to the value of the entitlement.
>
> Whenever someone may destroy the initial entitlement if he is willing to pay an objectively determined value for it, an entitlement is protected by a liability rule [e.g., compensatory damages]. This value may be what it is thought the original holder of the entitlement would have sold it for. But the holder's complaint that he would have demanded more will not avail him once the objectively determined value is set. Obviously, liability rules involve an additional stage of state intervention: not only are entitlements protected, but their transfer or destruction is allowed on the basis of a value determined by some organ of the state rather than by the parties themselves.

Guido Calabresi & A. Douglas Melamed, Property Rules, Liability Rules, and Inalienability: One View of the Cathedral, 85 Harv.L.Rev. 1089, 1092 (1972). The term "property rule" is used because the law tends to protect property entitlements with injunctive relief and/or criminal sanctions, as in cases of trespass or theft.

So, for example, denying Country Lodge an injunction against future nuisances means that Miller may override Country Lodge's entitlement to be free from the nuisance by merely paying damages. Suppose that the court sets the damages at $10,000 annually, based upon an estimate of lost profits. Miller would obviously prefer this outcome to an injunction because it would cost her $20,000 annually to dispose of the waste without making a nuisance.

There are many reasons why Country Lodge may prefer an injunction. First, and most basically, Miller is taking Country Lodge's entitlement by paying compensation. In contrast, the Constitution's fifth and fourteenth amendments prohibit the taking of private property for *private* purposes, even if compensation is paid. Second, Country Lodge may believe that $10,000 annually underestimates its lost profits. Third, Country Lodge's owners may place a subjective value on a clean river that is not recoverable as damages.

Fourth, and finally, if Country Lodge gets an injunction, it might make a deal with Miller to trade the injunction for more than $10,000 annually. Miller would be better off paying any amount up to $20,000, and Country Lodge would be better taking any amount more than the value to it of a clean river. If that amount is less than $20,000, there is room for a deal. If a deal is made, the price that Miller will pay to Country Lodge will depend upon their respective negotiating skills and bargaining positions. Economists call the difference between what a seller (Country Lodge) and a buyer (Miller) each place on a right "gains from trade." Relegating Country Lodge to damages gives all of the gains from trade to Miller. Issuing an injunction gives Country Lodge some of these gains, if they make a deal. Country Lodge may think this only fair. On the other hand, Miller may view Country Lodge's demanding more than its subjective loss as extortion.

Miller has other reasons to prefer paying damages to an injunction. First, Miller may fail to get Country Lodge to agree to sell its entitlement. Second, Miller would be the target of what is, in essence, a mini-criminal statute aimed exclusively at her. Third, the court may draft an injunction that is quite broad, prohibiting her from otherwise legal activity. Fourth, should she happen to violate the injunction, Miller will have to pay Country Lodge's attorney's fees and will not have the option to have a jury, as she would in an ordinary civil suit for damages.

The court also has a stake in the choice of remedy. Setting damages and collecting them can be burdensome, but so can be drafting an injunction and enforcing it.

To get an injunction, the plaintiff must establish that it meets a number of prerequisites for injunctive relief. The plaintiff must show that there is a *threat of harm* from the defendant. For instance, Country Lodge could not get an injunction unless Miller seems likely to repeat the nuisance.

The plaintiff must also, according to black letter law, show that there is *no adequate remedy at law,* such as compensatory damages. One way to show that the remedy at law is inadequate is to demonstrate that the plaintiff could not replace what the defendant has taken with compensatory damages—that is, to demonstrate *irreparable injury.* Country Lodge could demonstrate irreparable injury from future nuisances because, apart from Miller, no one can sell it a clean river in front of its property and courts usually treat each piece of real estate as unique. Country Lodge might, however, have a tougher time getting an injunction requiring Miller to clean up the mess from the past nuisance because it could use compensatory damages to hire a contractor to do the job. Indeed, Country Lodge would prefer compensatory damages if it wanted the clean up done before adjudication or the right to choose who did the clean up. But if Country Lodge nonetheless sought an injunction to clean up past wrongs, the court probably would find damages to be an inadequate remedy so that the plaintiff would not have to bear the risk that compensatory damages will fall short of the actual costs or suffer the aggravation of correcting the defendant's intentional wrongdoing. Douglas Laycock, The Death of the Irreparable Injury Rule, 103 Harv.L.Rev. 688, 710–14 (1990).

These prerequisites are only part of the inquiry. Under the rubric of *balancing the equities,* courts grant injunctions that fall short of the plaintiff's rightful position or even deny injunctive relief altogether. For example, a court might conclude that issuing an injunction would impose an undue hardship or would otherwise be unfair to the defendant. A court might also deny an injunction if it believes that it would not be practical to enforce the order without unduly burdening the court. Even if a court takes these matters into consideration, the plaintiff can still get damages for any harm the injunction fails to prevent. For example, Miller might avoid an injunction prohibiting future nuisances on the ground that this would put her out of business, but she would nonetheless have to pay damages for any future harm.

A court usually does not aim to give the plaintiff more than its rightful position. Nonetheless, it can issue injunctions that achieve more than the plaintiff's rightful position for prophylactic purposes when an injunction precisely targeted at the plaintiff's rightful position would be difficult to enforce.

Section B of this chapter considers problems in determining the plaintiff's rightful position. Section C considers the major prerequisites to injunctive relief—threat of harm and no adequate remedy at law. Section D considers the rationale for balancing the equities and when it is appropriate to grant less or more than the plaintiff's rightful position. Section E considers coercive remedies other than injunctions. These include specific performance of contracts, some judicial orders to correct administrative errors, and administrative orders to enforce regulatory statutes. While these coercive orders do not go by the name "injunction" and are subject to special doctrines, as discussed in Section E, they serve a function like that of injunctions and are, in general, controlled by the

B. THE PLAINTIFF'S RIGHTFUL POSITION AS THE MEASURE OF AN INJUNCTION

An injunction's primary mission must be to protect the plaintiff's rightful position. This phrase encompasses preventing future wrongdoing and, if the wrong has already occurred, repairing the harm done to the plaintiff.

In many cases, what an injunction should do to protect the plaintiff's rightful position is evident from the law of liability. When the defendant fails to make deliveries under a contract, an injunction to protect the plaintiff's rightful position would require the defendant to make the deliveries. Or, when the defendant trespasses, an injunction to protect the plaintiff's rightful position would forbid future trespasses.

Sometimes, however, what an injunction should do to protect the plaintiff's rightful position is not so evident.

PROBLEM: COUNTRY LODGE V. MILLER (REPRISED)
DEFINING THE RIGHTFUL POSITION

Suppose the court found Miller liable because it is a private nuisance to put enough debris in the river to be visible.

(a) Country Lodge has asked for an injunction permanently barring Miller from placing any effluent into the river. Should the court grant such an injunction?

(b) Would your answer change if the basis of liability was, instead of the common law of nuisance, a statute prohibiting placing effluent into a river without a permit?

(c) Can the court include in the injunction an order for Miller to attend a two-hour course at the local community college on environmental values?

MT. HEALTHY CITY SCHOOL DISTRICT BOARD OF EDUCATION v. DOYLE

Supreme Court of the United States, 1977
429 U.S. 274, 97 S.Ct. 568, 50 L.Ed.2d 471

MR. JUSTICE REHNQUIST delivered the opinion of the Court.

Respondent Doyle sued petitioner Mt. Healthy Board of Education in the United States District Court for the Southern District of Ohio. Doyle claimed that the Board's refusal to renew his contract in 1971 violated his rights under the First and Fourteenth Amendments to the United States Constitution. After a bench trial the District Court held that Doyle was entitled to reinstatement with backpay. The Court of Appeals for the Sixth Circuit affirmed the judgment, and we granted the Board's petition for certiorari * * *.

Doyle was first employed by the Board in 1966. He worked under one-year contracts for the first three years, and under a two-year contract from 1969 to 1971. In 1969 he was elected president of the Teachers' Association * * *. During Doyle's one-year term as president of the Association, and during the succeeding year when he served on its executive committee, there was apparently some tension in relations between the Board and the Association.

Beginning early in 1970, Doyle was involved in several incidents not directly connected with his role in the Teachers' Association. In one instance, he engaged in an argument with another teacher which culminated in the other teacher's slapping him. Doyle subsequently refused to accept an apology and insisted upon some punishment for the other teacher. His persistence in the matter resulted in the suspension of both teachers for one day, which was followed by a walkout by a number of other teachers, which in turn resulted in the lifting of the suspensions.

On other occasions, Doyle got into an argument with employees of the school cafeteria over the amount of spaghetti which had been served him; referred to students, in connection with a disciplinary complaint, as "sons of bitches"; and made an obscene gesture to two girls in connection with their failure to obey commands made in his capacity as cafeteria supervisor. Chronologically the last in the series of incidents which respondent was involved in during his employment by the Board was a telephone call by him to a local radio station. It was the Board's consideration of this incident which the court below found to be a violation of the First and Fourteenth Amendments.

In February 1971, the principal circulated to various teachers a memorandum relating to teacher dress and appearance, which was apparently prompted by the view of some in the administration that there was a relationship between teacher appearance and public support for bond issues. Doyle's response to the receipt of the memorandum on a subject which he apparently understood was to be settled by joint teacher-administration action was to convey the substance of the memorandum to a disc jockey at WSAI, a Cincinnati radio station, who promptly announced the adoption of the dress code as a news item. Doyle subsequently apologized to the principal, conceding that he should have made some prior communication of his criticism to the school administration.

Approximately one month later the superintendent made his customary annual recommendations to the Board as to the rehiring of nontenured teachers. He recommended that Doyle not be rehired. The same recommendation was made with respect to nine other teachers in the district, and in all instances, including Doyle's, the recommendation was adopted by the Board. Shortly after being notified of this decision, respondent requested a statement of reasons for the Board's actions. He received a statement citing "a notable lack of tact in handling professional matters which leaves much doubt as to your sincerity in establishing good school relationships." That general statement was followed by references to the radio station incident and to the obscene-gesture incident.

The District Court found that all of these incidents had in fact occurred. It concluded that respondent Doyle's telephone call to the radio station was "clearly protected by the First Amendment," and that because it had played a "substantial part" in the decision of the Board not to renew Doyle's employment, he was entitled to reinstatement with backpay. * * *

Doyle's claims under the First and Fourteenth Amendments are not defeated by the fact that he did not have tenure. Even though he could have been discharged for no reason whatever, and had no constitutional right to a hearing prior to the decision not to rehire him, he may nonetheless establish a claim to reinstatement if the decision not to rehire him was made by reason of his exercise of constitutionally protected First Amendment freedoms.

* * * We * * * accept the District Court's finding that the communication was protected by the First and Fourteenth Amendments. We are not, however, entirely in agreement with that court's manner of reasoning from this finding to the conclusion that Doyle is entitled to reinstatement with backpay.

The District Court made the following "conclusions" on this aspect of the case:

> "1) If a non-permissible reason, e.g., exercise of First Amendment rights, played a substantial part in the decision not to renew even in the face of other permissible grounds—the decision may not stand (citations omitted).
>
> "2) A non-permissible reason did play a substantial part. That is clear from the letter of the Superintendent immediately following the Board's decision, which stated two reasons—the one, the conversation with the radio station, clearly protected by the First Amendment. A court may not engage in any limitation of First Amendment rights based on 'tact'—that is not to say that the 'tactfulness' is irrelevant to other issues in this case."

At the same time, though, it stated that "(i)n fact, as this Court sees it and finds, both the Board and the Superintendent were faced with a situation in which there did exist in fact reason * * * independent of any First Amendment rights or exercise thereof, to not extend tenure."

Since respondent Doyle had no tenure, and there was therefore not even a state-law requirement of "cause" or "reason" before a decision could be made not to renew his employment, it is not clear what the District Court meant by this latter statement. Clearly the Board legally could have dismissed respondent had the radio station incident never come to its attention. One plausible meaning of the court's statement is that the Board and the Superintendent not only could, but in fact would have reached that decision had not the constitutionally protected incident of the telephone call to the radio station occurred. We are thus brought to the issue whether, even if that were the case, the fact that the protected conduct played a "substantial part" in the actual decision not to renew would necessarily amount to a constitutional violation justifying remedial action. We think that it would not.

A rule of causation which focuses solely on whether protected conduct played a part, "substantial" or otherwise, in a decision not to rehire, could place an employee in a better position as a result of the exercise of constitutionally protected conduct than he would have occupied had he done nothing. The difficulty with the rule enunciated by the District Court is that it would require reinstatement in cases where a dramatic and perhaps abrasive incident is inevitably on the minds of those responsible for the decision to rehire, and does indeed play a part in that decision even if the same decision would have been reached had the incident not occurred. The constitutional principle at stake is sufficiently vindicated if such an employee is placed in no worse a position than if he had not engaged in the conduct. A borderline or marginal candidate should not have the employment question resolved against him because of constitutionally protected conduct. But that same candidate ought not to be able, by engaging in such conduct, to prevent his employer from assessing his performance record and reaching a decision not to rehire on the basis of that record, simply because the protected conduct makes the employer more certain of the correctness of its decision.

This is especially true where, as the District Court observed was the case here, the current decision to rehire will accord "tenure." * * *

Initially, in this case, the burden was properly placed upon respondent to show that his conduct was constitutionally protected, and that this conduct was a "substantial factor" * * * in the Board's decision not to rehire him. Respondent having carried that burden, however, the District Court should have gone on to determine whether the Board had shown by a preponderance of the evidence that it would have reached the same decision as to respondent's reemployment even in the absence of the protected conduct.

We cannot tell from the District Court opinion and conclusions, nor from the opinion of the Court of Appeals affirming the judgment of the District Court, what conclusion those courts would have reached had they applied this test. The judgment of the Court of Appeals is therefore vacated, and the case remanded for further proceedings consistent with this opinion.

Notes

1. *Plaintiff's rightful position is not necessarily what the plaintiff wants.* On remand in *Mt. Healthy,* the district court determined that the original

record established, by a preponderance of the evidence, that Doyle would not have been rehired for reasons quite apart from his constitutionally protected speech, and the Court of Appeals affirmed. Doyle v. Mt. Healthy, 670 F.2d 59 (6th Cir.1982). Should Doyle have gotten his job back anyway? See Symposium, The Burgeoning *Mt. Healthy* Mixed–Motive Defense to Civil Rights and Employment Discrimination Claims, 51 Mercer L.Rev. 583 (2000).

In Hopwood v. Texas, 78 F.3d 932 (5th Cir.), cert. denied, 518 U.S. 1033, 116 S.Ct. 2580, 135 L.Ed.2d 1094 (1996), non-minority applicants who were rejected by a state university law school gained a judgment that the school's race-conscious affirmative action admissions programs violated equal protection. Citing *Mt. Healthy*, the court of appeals held that the plaintiffs were not entitled to an injunction requiring their admittance. Instead, the court ordered a further proceeding in which the law school had to shoulder the burden of showing by a preponderance of the evidence that the plaintiffs would not have been admitted in the absence of the violations. 78 F.3d at 956. The law school was able to demonstrate that the plaintiffs would have had no reasonable chance of being admitted to the program under a race-blind admission system. 236 F.3d 256 (5th Cir.2000), cert. denied, 533 U.S. 929, 121 S.Ct. 2550, 150 L.Ed.2d 717 (2001). The Fifth Circuit has assumed that its adoption of the *Mt. Healthy* burden-shifting methodology continues to apply to racial preference cases even though *Hopwood* was abrogated on other grounds by the U.S. Supreme Court's decision in Grutter v. Bollinger, 539 U.S. 306, 123 S.Ct. 2325, 156 L.Ed.2d 304 (2003). Bourdais v. New Orleans, 485 F.3d 294, 300 n.7 (5th Cir.2007).

2. *The court cannot always reproduce the plaintiff's rightful position exactly*. *Mt. Healthy* states that "[t]he constitutional principle at stake is sufficiently vindicated if such an employee is placed in no worse a position than if he had not engaged in the conduct." However, the Court's remedy puts Doyle in a better than rightful position. If Doyle had never contacted the radio station, the school board could have dismissed him without giving any reason; but, having violated his rights, the board must reinstate him unless it can convince the district court that there is good reason not to rehire him. Is there any remedy that would put Doyle in the rightful position exactly? When there is no remedy that will achieve the rightful position exactly, the injunction's *terms* may overreach the rightful position so long as the injunction's *aim* is to achieve no more than the rightful position.

3. *Plaintiff's rightful position and questions of causation*. The factual question in *Mt. Healthy* was whether the board would have rehired Doyle but for its reaction to his first amendment activities. Is that a question of remedy or a question of liability? See Sanchez–Lopez v. Fuentes–Pujols, 375 F.3d 121 (1st Cir.2004) (discussing proper jury instructions when *Mt. Healthy* defense is raised). In thinking about this question, suppose that the board rehired Doyle, but gave his call to the radio station as one reason to deny him a pay raise, even though they would have denied him a pay raise even if he had not called the radio station. Could Doyle get an injunction against the board's penalizing his first amendment activities in the future?

Cause-in-fact can be relevant to liability, as in torts. Price Waterhouse v. Hopkins, 490 U.S. 228, 109 S.Ct. 1775, 104 L.Ed.2d 268 (1989), presents a factual issue similar to that in *Mt. Healthy.* but in the liability context. Price Waterhouse decided not to promote Ann Hopkins, partly because of her gender and partly because of legitimate reasons. Hopkins sued under Title VII of the Civil Rights Act of 1964, 42 U.S.C. § 2000e et seq., which, inter alia, forbids adverse employment actions "because of" gender. Price Waterhouse claimed that the legitimate reasons were sufficient to block her promotion. All members of the Court agreed that, given the wording of Title VII, liability requires that the impermissible motive must have caused the unfavorable employment decision. At the same time, however, a majority of the Court decided that once the employer had purposely taken her gender into account, the burden shifted to it to show that she would not have been promoted for legitimate reasons. On remand in *Price Waterhouse*, the district court held that the firm failed to prove that it would have deferred Hopkins's promotion but for her gender and ordered that she be made a partner. Hopkins v. Price Waterhouse, 737 F.Supp. 1202 (D.D.C.), aff'd, 920 F.2d 967 (D.C.Cir.1990). Hopkins has discussed her experiences in the case, including what happened after she returned to the accounting firm at the court's direction. Ann B. Hopkins, Price Waterhouse v. Hopkins: A Personal Account of a Sexual Discrimination Plaintiff, 22 Hofstra Lab. & Employ. L.J. 357 (2005).

The Civil Rights Act of 1991 altered *Price Waterhouse* by providing that "an unlawful practice is established when the complaining party demonstrates that race, color, religion, sex, or national origin was a motivating factor for any employment practice, even though other factors also motivated the practice." The Supreme Court unanimously held that under the 1991 Act, a plaintiff could use either circumstantial or direct evidence to prove that an impermissible consideration was a "motivating factor" in an adverse employment action. Desert Palace, Inc. v. Costa, 539 U.S. 90, 123 S.Ct. 2148, 156 L.Ed.2d 84 (2003). The 1991 Act, however, limits the remedy to injunctive and declaratory relief and attorney's fees and costs where the defendant proves that it would have acted in the same way towards the employee even if the impermissible factor had not been considered. 42 U.S.C. §§ 2000e–2(m) & 2000e–5(g).

4. *The "after-acquired evidence" cases.* In McKennon v. Nashville Banner Publishing Co., 513 U.S. 352, 115 S.Ct. 879, 130 L.Ed.2d 852 (1995), Christine McKennon alleged that the company fired her on account of her age in violation of the Age Discrimination in Employment Act of 1967. In discovery, she admitted that she had taken home confidential documents, claiming that she wanted them to defend herself should she be illegally fired. Citing *Mt. Healthy*, the lower courts dismissed McKennon's suit on the theory that this evidence acquired after her supposedly illegal firing provided a supervening legal reason to fire her. A unanimous Supreme Court reversed. It distinguished *Mt. Healthy* because there the employer had two motives at the time of firing, one lawful, the other unlawful. But, McKennon "comes to us on the express assumption that an unlawful motive was the sole basis for the firing," the lawful motive for firing coming to light only later. Nonetheless, the after-acquired evidence is relevant to the remedy:

> It would be both inequitable and pointless to order the reinstatement of someone the employer would have terminated, and will terminate, in any event and upon lawful grounds. [As to backpay,] [t]he object of

compensation is to restore the employee to the position he or she would have been in absent the discrimination, but that principle is difficult to apply with precision where there is after-acquired evidence of wrongdoing that would have led to termination on legitimate grounds had the employer known about it. * * * The beginning point in the trial court's formulation of a remedy should be calculation of backpay from the date of the unlawful discharge to the date the new information was discovered.

513 U.S. at 362. Has the Court put McKennon in her rightful position?

NOTE ON RIGHTFUL POSITION AS RECONSIDERATION OR REMAND IN ADMINISTRATIVE LAW

The most important lesson from *Mt. Healthy* is that the plaintiff's rightful position and therefore the aim of the injunction depend upon a clear understanding of the plaintiff's right. *The framing of an injunction must begin with a careful definition of the plaintiff's right.* In *Mt. Healthy*, Doyle did not have a right to a government job but rather a right not to be fired for his speech. Given this right, Doyle gets consideration of whether he would have kept his job apart from the violation of his free speech rights rather than the job itself.

Mt. Healthy is but one example of a broad range of cases where the plaintiff has no absolute right to an ultimate objective but rather a right not to be denied that objective for the wrong reason or in the wrong way. If Doyle had been fired because of accusations to which he was denied an opportunity to respond in violation of due process or in violation of a civil service statute, the injunction would not restore his job but would give him an appropriate hearing to consider the charges. Or, if Doyle was about to lose his job because the school was to be torn down to make way for a highway whose funding was approved without statutorily required environmental analysis, the injunction would not permanently bar the highway but would bar it unless and until the statutorily required analysis was performed to consider whether to approve or disapprove the highway. Or, if Doyle's school received a state or federal grant one of whose conditions was that teachers be paid more, the injunction would not require that Doyle be paid more but that the school not receive the grant unless the teachers were paid more. The school would then have to consider whether to forego the grant or pay more. Rosado v. Wyman, 397 U.S. 397, 420, 90 S.Ct. 1207, 1221–22, 25 L.Ed.2d 442, 460 (1970). See also Lisa E. Key, Private Enforcement of Federal Funding Conditions Under § 1983: The Supreme Court's Failure to Adhere to the Doctrine of Separation of Powers, 29 U.C. Davis L.Rev. 283 (1996) (criticizing the Supreme Court for making it harder to obtain such orders).

Reconsideration relief is common in the administrative law context. For example, when an administrative agency denies an application for a permit and in so doing considers a factor that is improper under the governing statute, the court sitting in review of the agency ordinarily will not order the agency to grant the permit. To do so may put the applicant in a better than rightful position because the agency might have denied the permit for a statutorily proper reason.

Quite apart from whether the relief shall be reconsideration is the question of *who* should do the reconsidering. In *Mt. Healthy,* the Supreme Court required the reconsideration to be performed by the district court rather than by the school board. Remanding to the board probably would not have been a reliable way to put Doyle in his rightful position because the board might have continued to punish Doyle for his privileged activities while pretending to fire him for some other reason. Transferring the decision whether to reinstate Doyle from the board to the district court is another instance where the aim of putting the plaintiff in his rightful position resulted in his ending up in a better position.

In judicial review of agency action, a court's determination that the agency has committed an error is like a judgment of liability in a civil suit. The error may be, for instance, consideration of an improper factor, failing to follow the requisite procedures, or arbitrary reasoning. The agency action may be, for example, the issuance of regulations, the grant of a permit, the issuance of a license, or a decision not to take such actions. What the court does in response to that error is a decision about a remedy. The ordinary remedy is a remand to the agency for a proper reconsideration. Gonzales v. Thomas, 547 U.S. 183, 126 S.Ct. 1613, 164 L.Ed.2d 358 (2006). But other remedies are possible. If the court is sure that the agency would, for example, have granted the permit that the petitioner had sought, then the court will reverse the agency, ordering it to grant the permit. NLRB v. Wyman–Gordon Co., 394 U.S. 759, 766 n. 6, 89 S.Ct. 1426, 1430 n. 6, 22 L.Ed.2d 709, 715 n. 6 (1969). Or, if the agency had granted the permit and the court is sure that it would not have but for the error, the court could reverse the agency and vacate the permit. However, if the court is sure that agency would have reached the same result even if it had not made the error, the court will say there is no reversible error and will affirm the agency action. NLRB v. American Geri–Care Inc., 697 F.2d 56, 64 (2d Cir.1982), cert. denied, 461 U.S. 906, 103 S.Ct. 1876, 76 L.Ed.2d 807 (1983). But, when in doubt, the court remands. See Honeywell International, Inc. v. E.P.A., 374 F.3d 1363 (D.C.Cir. 2004), 393 F.3d 1315 (D.C.Cir.2005) (concurring and dissenting opinions discussing question of propriety of remand or vacatur as proper remedy for agency error); Ronald Mark Levin, "Vacation" at Sea: Judicial Remedies and Equitable Discretion in Administrative Law, 53 Duke L.J. 291 (2003) (criticizing the judicial practice of ordering a "remand without vacation," which allows an agency action to remain in place during what might constitute lengthy proceedings on remand).

The remand remedy differs from a simple reversal in two respects. First, as a matter of substance, the successful complainant will not necessarily get what it ultimately wants but rather a reconsideration, theoretically free from error. Second, as a matter of procedure, doubtful cases are to be decided by the governmental entity originally charged with making the decision rather than by the court. Do you see why both these differences are compelled by the rightful position concept?

It may seem bizarre to remand a matter back to the very agency that has reached a flawed result. However, the defendants in these administrative law cases are coordinate branches of government. Courts generally presume that such coordinate branches will act properly once they have a clear understanding of the law, just as appellate courts usually presume that lower courts will act as instructed when a case is remanded. Should the agency repeat its error on remand, the petitioner can once again get the reviewing court to intervene, if petitioner has the money for legal fees and the time to wait and if the agency has not successfully camouflaged its error with pretexts.

In light of *Mt. Healthy,* it should come as no surprise that Congress, in enacting Title VII, the federal statute forbidding employment discrimination, 42 U.S.C. § 2000e et seq., specified that the remedy should be neither reversal of the employer's decision nor a remand to the employer but rather de novo reconsideration by a court. Under this statute, the Supreme Court has specified in some detail how the district court should try to mimic how a non-discriminatory employer would have acted. International Brotherhood of Teamsters v. United States, 431 U.S. 324, 371–72, 97 S.Ct. 1843, 1873, 52 L.Ed.2d 396, 437–38 (1977). When the discriminating employer is a federal agency, the tradition of remand in administrative law could well have resulted in a remand to the agency, but the Supreme Court has read Title VII to require de novo judicial reconsideration. Chandler v. Roudebush, 425 U.S. 840, 862, 96 S.Ct. 1949, 1960, 48 L.Ed.2d 416, 431–32 (1976).

Courts sometimes remand to legislatures to rewrite invalid laws just as they sometimes remand to agencies to reconsider invalid administrative decisions. So, for example, after holding that the state's educational finance statute failed to comply with the state constitution, the New Jersey Supreme Court requested the legislature to rewrite the statute. Abbott v. Burke, 119 N.J. 287, 575 A.2d 359 (1990).

PROBLEM: THE RACIALLY BIASED ELECTION

Where the plaintiff is a losing candidate who proves that the election was flawed because votes were counted that should not have been or votes that should have been counted were not, the court will not declare the plaintiff the winner. At most the court will order a new election be held—in essence remanding the case to the electoral process—but only if the plaintiff proves that more votes were affected than the margin of victory. If that burden cannot be carried, the plaintiff's rightful position is as an electoral loser. See, e.g., Marks v. Stinson, 19 F.3d 873 (3d Cir.1994). Suppose, rather than work-a-day fraud, the problem with the election was unconstitutional exclusion of almost all African–American voters in an election between a white and an African–American candidate and that the margin of victory for the white candidate was several times larger than the number of voters excluded. Would the plaintiffs—the African–American candidate and the excluded voters—be in their rightful position if the election is affirmed? On such facts, Bell v. Southwell, 376 F.2d 659 (5th Cir.1967), ordered a new election on the theory that it could not be presumed that the African–American candidate would have lost an election untainted by racial discrimination, which may have created a racially charged atmosphere that dissuaded white voters from voting for her. Given southern politics in the 1960's, does this seem realistic? The court offered an additional argument that "state-imposed racial discrimination cannot be tolerated and to eliminate the practice or the temptation toward it, the law must extinguish the judgment wrought by such a procedure." Id. at 663. Does this rationale satisfy the rightful position principle? In connection with another issue in the case, the court stated:

> Mrs. Bell as a former candidate did not seek to be selected over Southwell or any other opponent. What, and all, she and [the other plaintiffs, who were frustrated voters,] sought was an election conducted free of such indefensible, racial distinctions. That being so, it was not the usual case of counting votes and denying relief for want of affirmative proof of a different result.

Id. at 664–65. Does this observation provide a stronger justification for ordering a new election?

In contrast, the courts did not order a new election in the dispute arising out of the 2000 U.S. presidential race between George W. Bush and Albert Gore. The Supreme Court of Florida ordered a manual recount for several counties to rectify the failure to count a number of legal votes "sufficient to change or place in doubt the result of the election" in those counties because of defective voting machines and problematic ballots. Gore v. Harris, 772 So.2d 1243 (Fla.2000). The U.S. Supreme Court struck down the state recount remedy, finding that its arbitrary recount standards created unequal treatment of voters in violation of the Equal Protection Clause. Bush v. Gore, 531 U.S. 98, 121 S.Ct. 525, 148 L.Ed.2d 388 (2000) (per curiam). The Court instead ordered that any recount would need to have additional precautions and safeguards to be constitutionally valid; there was insufficient time to actually implement these steps. Gore v. Harris, 773 So.2d 524 (Fla.2000). See Tracy A. Thomas, Understanding Prophylactic Remedies Through the Looking Glass of *Bush v. Gore*, 11 Wm. & M. Bill Rts. J. 343 (2002) (suggesting that the Supreme Court overreached its equitable discretion by ordering prophylactic relief that was not designed to remedy the underlying denial of votes). Remedies for election wrongs have been difficult to achieve. See Richard L. Hasen, The Untimely Death of *Bush v. Gore*, 60 Stan.L.Rev. 1 (2007) (discussing the courts' failure to create meaningful election reforms); Steven F. Huefner, Remedying Election Wrongs, 44 Harv.J.Leg. 265 (2007) (recommending the use of non-judicial forums like administrative or legislative tribunals to issue appropriate remedies for election wrongs).

RIZZO v. GOODE

Supreme Court of the United States, 1976
423 U.S. 362, 96 S.Ct. 598, 46 L.Ed.2d 561

Mr. Justice Rehnquist delivered the opinion of the Court.

The District Court for the Eastern District of Pennsylvania, after parallel trials of separate actions filed in 1970, entered an order in 1973 requiring petitioners "to submit to [the District] Court for its approval a comprehensive program for improving the handling of citizen complaints alleging police misconduct" in accordance with a comprehensive opinion filed together with the order. The proposed program, negotiated between petitioners and respondents for the purpose of complying with the order, was incorporated six months later into a final judgment. Petitioner City Police Commissioner was thereby required, inter alia, to put into force a directive governing the manner by which citizens' complaints against police officers should henceforth be handled by the department. The Court of Appeals for the Third Circuit, upholding the District Court's finding that the existing procedures for handling citizen complaints were "inadequate," affirmed the District Court's choice of equitable relief: "The revisions were ... ordered because they appeared to have the potential for prevention of future police misconduct." We granted certiorari to consider petitioners' claims that the judgment of the District Court represents an unwarranted intrusion by the federal judiciary into the discretionary authority committed to them by state and local law to perform their official functions. We find ourselves substantially in agreement with these claims, and we therefore reverse the judgment of the Court of Appeals.

I

The central thrust of respondents' efforts in the two trials was to lay a foundation for equitable intervention, in one degree or another, because of an assertedly pervasive pattern of illegal and unconstitutional mistreatment by police officers. This mistreatment was said to have been directed against minority citizens in particular and against all Philadelphia residents in general. The named individual and group respondents were certified to represent these two classes. The principal petitioners here—the Mayor, the City Managing Director, and the Police Commissioner—were charged with conduct ranging from express authorization or encouragement of this mistreatment to failure to act in a manner so as to assure that it would not recur in the future.

Hearing some 250 witnesses during 21 days of hearings, the District Court was faced with a staggering amount of evidence; each of the 40-odd incidents might alone have been the *piece de resistance* of a short, separate trial. * * *

The District Court made a number of conclusions of law, not all of which are relevant to our analysis. It found that the evidence did not establish the existence of any policy on the part of the named petitioners to violate the legal and constitutional rights of the plaintiff classes, but it did find that evidence of departmental procedure indicated a tendency to discourage the filing of civilian complaints and to minimize the consequences of police misconduct. It found that as to the larger plaintiff class, the residents of Philadelphia, only a small percentage of policemen commit violations of their legal and constitutional rights, but that the frequency with which such violations occur is such that "they cannot be dismissed as rare, isolated instances." * * *

The District Court concluded by directing petitioners to draft, for the court's approval, "a comprehensive program for dealing adequately with civilian complaints", to be formulated along * * * "guidelines" suggested by the court * * *.

While noting that the "guidelines" were consistent with "generally recognized minimum standards" and imposed "no substantial burdens" on the police department, the District Court emphasized that respondents had no constitutional *right* to improved police procedures for handling civilian complaints. But given that violations of constitutional rights of citizens occur in "unacceptably" high numbers, and are likely to continue to occur, the court-mandated revision was a "necessary first step" in attempting to prevent future abuses. * * *

II

A

These actions were brought, and the affirmative equitable relief fashioned, under the Civil Rights Act of 1871, 42 U.S.C. § 1983. It provides that "[e]very person who, under color of [law] subjects, or causes to be subjected, any ... person within the jurisdiction [of the United States] to the deprivation of any rights ... secured by the Constitution and laws, shall be liable to the party injured in an action at law [or] suit in equity...." * * *

The findings of fact made by the District Court at the conclusion of these two parallel trials—in sharp contrast to that which respondents sought to prove with respect to petitioners—disclose a central paradox which permeates that court's legal conclusions. Individual police officers *not named as parties* to the action were found to have violated the constitutional rights of particular individuals, only a few of whom were parties plaintiff. As the facts developed, there was no affirmative link between the occurrence of the various incidents of police misconduct and the adoption of any plan or policy by petitioners—express or otherwise—showing their authorization or approval of such misconduct. Instead, the *sole* causal connection found by the District Court between petitioners and the individual respondents was that in the absence of a change in police disciplinary procedures, the incidents were likely to continue to occur, *not* with respect to them, but as to the members of the classes they represented. In sum, the genesis of this lawsuit—a heated dispute between individual citizens and certain policemen—has evolved into an attempt by the federal judiciary to resolve a "controversy" between the entire citizenry of Philadelphia and the petitioning elected and appointed officials over what steps might, in the Court of Appeals' words, "[appear] to have the potential for prevention of future police misconduct." * * *

B

Nothing in Hague v. CIO, 307 U.S. 496, 59 S.Ct. 954, 83 L.Ed. 1423 (1939), the only decision of this Court cited by the District Court, or any other case from this Court, supports such an open-ended construction of § 1983. In *Hague*, the pattern of police misconduct upon which liability and injunctive relief were grounded was the adoption and enforcement of deliberate policies by the defendants there (including the Mayor and the Chief of Police) of excluding and removing the plaintiff's labor organizers and forbidding peaceful communication of their views to the citizens of Jersey City. These policies were implemented "by force and violence" on the part of individual policemen. There was no mistaking that the defendants proposed to continue their unconstitutional policies against the members of this discrete group. * * *

Respondents stress that the District Court not only found an "unacceptably high" number of incidents but held, as did the Court of Appeals, that "when a *pattern* of frequent police violations of rights is shown, the law is clear that injunctive relief may be granted." However, there was no showing that the behavior of the Philadelphia police was different in kind or degree from that which exists elsewhere; indeed, the District Court found "that the problems disclosed by the record * * * are fairly typical of [those] afflicting police departments in major urban areas." Thus, invocation of the word "pattern" in a case where, unlike *Hague* * * *, the defendants are not causally linked to it, is but a distant echo of the findings in those cases. The focus in *Hague* * * * was not simply on the number of violations which occurred but on the common thread running through them: a "pervasive pattern of intimidation" flowing from a deliberate plan by the *named* defendants to crush the nascent labor organizations. The District Court's unadorned finding of a statistical pattern is quite dissimilar to the factual settings of these two cases.

The theory of liability underlying the District Court's opinion, and urged upon us by respondents, is that even without a showing of direct responsibility for the actions of a small percentage of the police force, petitioners' *failure* to act in the face of a statistical pattern is indistinguishable from the active conduct enjoined in *Hague* * * *. Respondents posit a constitutional "duty" on the part of petitioners (and a corresponding "right" of the citizens of Philadelphia) to "eliminate" future police misconduct; a "default" of that affirmative duty being shown by the statistical pattern, the District Court is empowered to act in petitioners' stead and take whatever preventive measures are necessary, within its discretion, to secure the "right" at issue. Such reasoning, however, blurs accepted usages and meanings in the English language in a way which would be quite inconsistent with the words Congress chose in § 1983. We have never subscribed to these amorphous propositions, and we decline to do so now.

Respondents claim that the theory of liability embodied in the District Court's opinion is supported by desegregation cases such as Swann v. Charlotte–Mecklenburg Board of Education, 402 U.S. 1, 91 S.Ct. 1267, 28 L.Ed.2d 554 (1971). * * *

Respondents, in their effort to bring themselves within the language of *Swann,* ignore a critical factual distinction between their case and the desegregation cases decided by this Court. In the latter, segregation imposed by law had been implemented by state authorities for varying periods of time, whereas in the instant case the District Court found that the responsible authorities had played no affirmative part in depriving any members of the two respondent classes of any constitutional rights. Those against whom injunctive relief was directed in cases such as *Swann* and

Brown were not administrators and school board members who had in their employ a small number of individuals, which latter on their own deprived Afro–American students of their constitutional rights to a unitary school system. They were administrators and school board members who were found by their *own* conduct in the administration of the school system to have denied those rights. Here, the District Court found that none of the petitioners had deprived the respondent classes of any rights secured under the Constitution. Under the well-established rule that federal "judicial powers may be exercised only on the basis of a constitutional violation," *Swann*, this case presented no occasion for the District Court to grant equitable relief against petitioners.

C

Going beyond considerations concerning the existence of a live controversy and threshold statutory liability, we must address an additional and novel claim advanced by respondent classes. They assert that given the citizenry's "right" to be protected from unconstitutional exercises of police power, and the "need for protection from such abuses," respondents have a right to mandatory equitable relief in some form when those in supervisory positions do not institute steps to reduce the incidence of unconstitutional police misconduct. The scope of federal equity power, it is proposed, should be extended to the fashioning of prophylactic procedures for a state agency designed to minimize this kind of misconduct on the part of a handful of its employees. However, on the facts of this case, not only is this novel claim quite at odds with the settled rule that in federal equity cases "the nature of the violation determines the scope of the remedy," but important considerations of federalism are additional factors weighing against it. Where, as here, the exercise of authority by state officials is attacked, federal courts must be constantly mindful of the "special delicacy of the adjustment to be preserved between federal equitable power and State administration of its own law." Section 1983 by its terms confers authority to grant equitable relief as well as damages, but its words "allow a suit in equity only when that is the proper proceeding for redress, and they refer to existing standards to determine what is a proper proceeding." * * * When a plaintiff seeks to enjoin the activity of a government agency, even within a unitary court system, his case must contend with "the well-established rule that the Government has traditionally been granted the widest latitude in the 'dispatch of its own internal affairs.'" The District Court's injunctive order here, significantly revising the internal procedures of the Philadelphia police department, was indisputably a sharp limitation on the department's "latitude in the 'dispatch of its own internal affairs'."

When the frame of reference moves from a unitary court system, governed by the principles just stated, to a system of federal courts representing the Nation, subsisting side by side with 50 state judicial, legislative, and executive branches, appropriate consideration must be given to principles of federalism in determining the availability and scope of equitable relief. * * *

Contrary to the District Court's flat pronouncement that a federal court's legal power to "supervise the functioning of the police department ... is firmly established," it is the foregoing cases and principles that must govern consideration of the type of injunctive relief granted here. When it injected itself by injunctive decree into the internal disciplinary affairs of this state agency, the District Court departed from these precepts. * * *

MR. JUSTICE STEVENS took no part in the consideration or decision of this case.

MR. JUSTICE BLACKMUN with whom MR. JUSTICE BRENNAN and MR. JUSTICE MARSHALL join, dissenting.

* * * To be sure, federal-court intervention in the daily operation of a large city's police department, as the Court intimates, is undesirable and to be avoided if at all possible. The Court appropriately observes, however, that what the Federal District Court did here was to engage in a careful and conscientious resolution of often sharply conflicting testimony and to make detailed findings of fact, now accepted by both sides, that attack the problem that is the subject of the respondents' complaint. The remedy was one evolved with the defendant officials' assent, reluctant though that assent may have been, and it was one that the police department concededly could live with. Indeed, the District Court * * * stated that "the resolution of all the disputed items was more nearly in accord with the defendants' position than with the plaintiffs' position," and that the relief * * * "did not go beyond what the defendants had always been willing to accept." No one, not even this Court's majority, disputes the apparent efficacy of the relief or the fact that it effectuated a betterment in the system and should serve to lessen the number of instances of deprival of constitutional rights of members of the respondent classes. What is worrisome to the Court is abstract principle, and, of course, the Court has a right to be concerned with abstract principle that, when extended to the limits of logic, may produce untoward results in other circumstances on a future day.

But the District Court here, with detailed, careful, and sympathetic findings, ascertained the existence of violations of citizens' *constitutional* rights, of a *pattern* of that type of activity, of its likely continuance and recurrence, and of an official indifference as to doing anything about it. * * * There must be federal relief available against persistent deprival of federal constitutional rights even by (or, perhaps I should say, particularly by) constituted authority on the state side. * * *

I would regard what was accomplished in this case as one of those rightly rare but nevertheless justified instances * * * of federal-court "intervention" in a state or municipal executive area. The facts, the deprival of constitutional rights, and the pattern are all proved in sufficient degree. And the remedy is carefully delineated, worked out within the administrative structure rather then superimposed by edict upon it, and essentially, and concededly, "livable." In the City of Brotherly Love—or in any other American city—no less should be expected. It is a matter of regret that the Court sees fit to nullify what so meticulously and thoughtfully has been evolved to satisfy an existing need relating to constitutional rights that we cherish and hold dear. * * *

Notes

1. The majority concludes that the plaintiffs' rights were violated by individual police officers, but not by the city or its top officials. What sort of a factual showing would have satisfied the majority that the city and its top officials were liable? The majority's reading of the law of liability itself is controversial; but, because our focus is the law of remedies, the important point is that the majority goes on to argue that the scope of the remedy must be tailored so that it is limited to forcing only those adjudged to have violated the plaintiffs' rights to restore them to their rightful position. In other words, where there is no right against a defendant that has been or will be violated by that defendant, there is no remedy against that defendant.

2. Why didn't the plaintiffs side-step the majority's argument by seeking damages from the individual police officers who brutalized them instead of an injunction against the city and its top officials?

3. The plaintiffs, as well as the lower courts, thought that the injunction requiring a civilian complaint review process was the best way to prevent brutality in the future. Although the defendants opposed the review process in concept and participated in its design only under duress, they were able to reach agreement on the specifics. What then does the majority find objectionable about an injunction mandating the complaint review scheme, in these circumstances? After all, Professor Chayes (in the excerpt in Chapter 1) sees injunctions in public law litigation as judicial policy making rather than as "logically deduced from the nature of the legal harm suffered."

4. *Preventive, reparative, and structural injunctions.* Professor Owen M. Fiss applies the label "preventive" to injunctions that prevent wrongs, such as future trespasses, and the label "reparative" to injunctions that "seek to eliminate the effects of a past wrong." Owen M. Fiss, The Civil Rights Injunction 10 (1978). An injunction sometimes contains both preventive and reparative orders. Professor Fiss also writes of "structural" injunctions, which restructure or change how social institutions such as jails or schools work in order to ensure that preventive or reparative aims are in fact achieved. Id. at 9–11. Which type of injunction are the plaintiffs in *Rizzo* seeking?

5. The *Rizzo* case was but one aspect of an extended controversy over police brutality in Philadelphia going back to 1952. Phillip J. Cooper, Hard Judicial Choices 297–327 (1988)(detailing background of case). From mid–1976 to mid–1977, 110 lawsuits seeking compensatory and punitive damages for police brutality were filed. Newsweek, Roundhouse Punches, July 4, 1977. After *Rizzo*, a federal investigation brought to light evidence that the City did promote police brutality and an injunction against the chief of police and the

mayor was finally granted. United States v. City of Philadelphia, 644 F.2d 187 (3d Cir.1980)(injunction denied); Commonwealth of Pennsylvania v. Porter, 659 F.2d 306 (3d Cir.1981) (injunction granted). While this litigation was pending, Philadelphia voters rejected by a 2 to 1 margin a city charter amendment that would have allowed Mayor Rizzo to seek a third term. Both major party candidates for mayor vowed to reform police practices. All's well that ends well?

Note on the Microsoft Antitrust Litigation

The concept of rightful position casts an interesting perspective on the Microsoft antitrust litigation. The United States and many state governments brought civil actions against the huge software company, charging it with violating federal antitrust laws by using unlawful methods to defend its monopoly in the operating systems market and attempting to extend it to the browser market. The district court held for the plaintiffs and ordered, inter alia, that Microsoft submit a plan to separate by divestiture the operating systems business from the applications business, and to establish a compliance committee to be supervised by a newly hired chief compliance officer responsible for development and supervision of Microsoft's internal programs. United States v. Microsoft Corp., 84 F.Supp.2d 9 (D.D.C.1999) (findings of fact); 87 F.Supp.2d 30 (D.D.C.2000) (conclusions of law); 97 F.Supp.2d 59 (D.D.C.2000) (imposing remedy). On appeal, the D.C. Circuit en banc unanimously affirmed the findings of liability in part, reversed them in part, and vacated the remedy. United States v. Microsoft, 253 F.3d 34 (D.C.Cir.), cert. denied, 534 U.S. 952, 122 S.Ct. 350, 151 L.Ed.2d 264 (2001). It vacated the remedy in large measure because the district court had failed to explain the remedy in terms of rightful position. The court of appeals, quoting the Supreme Court's application of the rightful position concept to monopolization cases, United States v. United Shoe Machinery Corp., 391 U.S. 244, 250, 88 S.Ct. 1496, 20 L.Ed.2d 562 (1968), held that the remedy should seek to "terminate the illegal monopoly, deny to the defendant the fruits of its statutory violation, and ensure that there remain no practices likely to result in monopolization in the future." The court of appeals held that "[n]owhere did the District Court discuss the objectives the Supreme Court deems relevant." 253 F.3d at 103.

At the circuit court's direction, the case was reassigned to another district court judge. She ordered the parties to try to settle the matter in light of the circuit's opinion. The United States and several states entered into a consent decree, which the district court approved. After a lengthy hearing and considering competing remedial proposals from the non-settling states, the district court entered an injunction closely paralleling the negotiated consent decree. The district court's injunction contained preventive measures enjoining the exact conduct found to violate the antitrust laws, prophylactic measures to facilitate future software competition, and monitoring to ensure compliance with the order. United States v. Microsoft Corp., 231 F.Supp.2d 144 (D.D.C.2002). Among the original plaintiffs, only Massachusetts appealed the result. In affirming, the circuit court enthusiastically approved of the injunction: "Far from abusing its discretion, therefore, the district court, by remedying the anticompetitive effect of commingling, went to the heart of the problem Microsoft had created, and it did so without intruding itself into the design and engineering of the Windows operating system. We say, Well done!" Massachusetts v. Microsoft Corp., 373 F.3d 1199, 1210 (D.C.Cir. en banc 2004). "The district court certainly did not abuse its discretion by adopting a remedy that denies Microsoft the ability to take the same or similar actions to limit competition in the future rather than a remedy aimed narrowly at redressing the harm suffered by specific competitors in the past. This distinction underlies the difference between a case brought in equity by the Government and a damage action brought by a private plaintiff." Id. at 1233.

Despite the broad injunctive remedy, Microsoft still seemed to win the "browser wars." Its key browser competitor, Netscape, was discontinued as of March 2008. Netscape's earlier success triggered Microsoft's exclusionary practices that resulted in the monopolization litigation. Netscape's technological spinoff, Mozilla's Firefox, obtained almost 18 percent of the browser market as of May 2008, but Microsoft's Internet Explorer still retained more than 90 percent of the desktop operating system market, the market that the district court judge found in 2000 it had illegally monopolized. See Harry First, Netscape is Dead: Remedy Lessons from the Microsoft Litigation, www.ssrn.com/abstract=1260803 (highlighting the problem of remedy in monopolization cases and arguing that enforcers need to better evaluate potential remedies, monitor achievement of those remedies, and consider broader remedies such as restructuring and fines). It may be that "[a]fter a decade of global antitrust enforcement against Microsoft we seem to be back to where we started," worried about the same products and Microsoft's monopoly position in the operating system market. Id. at *3.

C. THE PREREQUISITES FOR INJUNCTIVE RELIEF

1. THREAT OF HARM

Problem: Country Lodge v. Miller (Reprised)
The Threat of Harm

Should the court refuse to grant Country Lodge an injunction prohibiting future nuisances if:

(a) Miller was just beginning to build her cider press and has not indicated how she will dispose of the apple mash?

(b) Miller has put mash in the river, was found in violation, and then wrote Country Lodge a letter promising never again to put waste in the river?

(c) Miller wrote such a letter and dismantled her cider press?

(d) Miller made no promises but last fall's discharge of waste would not have caused any harm to Country Lodge except for unusual river conditions—conditions which occur only one year in a hundred?

An injunction to prevent future violations will issue only if the plaintiff faces a threat of being harmed by the defendant. For example, the plaintiff, the owner of Blackacre, will not get an injunction against the defendant entering Blackacre and thus interfering with the plaintiff's rightful position, unless there is reason to fear that the defendant will trespass. To help understand why, recall the attributes of an injunction summarized in Section A of this chapter, which make it, in essence, a criminal statute applicable only to the persons to whom it is addressed.

The plaintiff can easily show threat of harm if the defendant has made an explicit threat, such as "I'm coming on Blackacre whether you like it or not." If the defendant is not so accommodating, but has trespassed on Blackacre in the past or, clearer still, is engaged in a continuing trespass, the plaintiff can argue that future violations are likely. But past violations are not essential; they are only one kind of evidence of a threat of future harm. For example, in Union Carbide v. UGI Corp., 731 F.2d 1186, 1191–92 (5th Cir.1984), the court enjoined a former Union Carbide employee who knew its trade secrets from working in certain positions at UGI, where the trade secrets would be useful, even in the absence of conclusive proof that the employee had divulged any secrets. The court was influenced by UGI's failure to exclude the employee from situations where disclosure of confidential information would be difficult to avoid.

On the other hand, a court may find no threat of future harm despite past violations.

HECHT CO. v. BOWLES

Supreme Court of the United States, 1944
321 U.S. 321, 64 S.Ct. 587, 88 L.Ed. 754

Mr. Justice Douglas delivered the opinion of the Court.

Sec. 205(a) of the Emergency Price Control Act of 1942 provides:

"Whenever in the judgment of the Administrator any person has engaged or is about to engage in any acts or practices which constitute or will constitute a violation of any provision of section 4 of this Act, he may make application to the appropriate court for an order enjoining such acts or practices, or for an order enforcing compliance with such provision, and upon a showing by the Administrator that such person has engaged or is about to engage in any such acts or practices a permanent or temporary injunction, restraining order, or other order shall be granted without bond."

The question in this case is whether the Administrator, having established that a defendant has engaged in acts or practices violative of § 4 of the Act is entitled as of right to an injunction restraining the defendant from engaging in such acts or practices or whether the court has some discretion to grant or withhold such relief.

Sec. 4(a) of the Act makes it unlawful for a person to sell or deliver any commodity in violation of specified orders or regulations of the Administrator. A regulation issued under § 2 of the Act and effective in May, 1942 provided that no person should sell or deliver any commodity at a price higher than the authorized maximum price as fixed and determined by the regulation. Since maximum prices were fixed with reference to earlier base periods, the regulation also provided for the preservation and examination of existing records. And provision was likewise made for the keeping of current records reflecting sales made under the regulation and for the filing of maximum prices with the Administrator.

There is no substantial controversy over the facts. Petitioner operates a large department store in Washington, D.C. and did a business of about $20,000,000 in 1942. There are 107 departments in the store and each sells a separate line of merchandise. In the fall of 1942 the Administrator started an investigation to determine whether petitioner was complying with the Act and the regulation. The investigation was a "spot check", confined to seven departments. In each of the seven departments violations were disclosed. As a result of this suit was brought. The complaint charged violations of the maximum price provisions of the regulation and violations of the regulations governing the keeping of records and reporting to the Administrator. The Administrator prayed for an injunction enjoining petitioner from selling, delivering or offering for sale or delivery any commodity in violation of the regulation and from failing to keep complete and accurate records as required by the regulation. In its answer petitioner pleaded among other things that any failure or neglect to comply with the regulation was involuntary and was corrected as soon as discovered.

Numerous violations both as respects prices and records were discovered. Thus in six of the seven departments investigated there had occurred between May and October, 1942 some 3700 sales in excess of the maximum prices with overcharges of some $4600. The statements filed with the Administrator were deficient, some 400 items of merchandise being omitted. And there were over 300 items with respect to which no records were kept showing how the maximum prices had been determined.

There is no doubt, however, of petitioner's good faith and diligence. The District Court found that the manager of the store had offered it as a laboratory in which the Administrator might experiment with any regulation which might be issued. Prior to the promulgation of the regulation the petitioner had created a new section known as the price control office. That office undertook to bring petitioner into compliance with the requirements of the regulation in advance of its effective date. The head of that office together with seven assistants devoted full time to that endeavor. But the store had about 2,000 employees and over one million two hundred thousand articles of merchandise. In the furniture departments alone there were over fifty-four thousand transactions in the first ten months of 1942. Difficulties were encountered in interpreting the regulation, in determining the exact nature of an article and whether it had been previously sold and at what price, etc. The absence of adequate records made it difficult to ascertain prices during the earlier base-period. Misunderstanding of the regulation, confusion on the part of employees not trained in such problems of interpretation and administration, the complexity of the problem, and the fallibility of humans all combined to produce numerous errors. But the District Court concluded that the "mistakes in pricing and listing were all made in good faith and without intent to violate the regulations."

The District Court also found that the mistakes brought to light "were at once corrected, and vigorous steps were taken by The Hecht Company to prevent recurrence of these mistakes or further mistakes in the future." The company increased its price control office to twenty-eight employees. New methods of internal control were instituted early in November, 1942 with the view of avoiding future violations. That new system of control "greatly improved" the situation. Petitioner undertook to make repayment of all overcharges brought to light by the investigation in case of customers who could be identified. It proposed to contribute the remaining amount of such overcharges to some local charity. The District Court concluded that the issuance of an injunction would have "no effect by way of insuring better compliance in the future" and would be "unjust" to petitioner and not "in the public interest". It accordingly dismissed the complaint. On appeal the Court of Appeals for the District of Columbia reversed that judgment * * * [on the basis that § 205(a) mandated the issuance of an injunction or other order once a violation was found].

Respondent insists that the mandatory character of § 205(a) is clear from its language, history and purpose. He argues that "shall be granted" is not permissive, that since the same section provides that the Administrator "may" apply for an injunction and that, if so, the injunction "shall" be granted, "may" and "shall" are each used in the ordinary sense. It is pointed out that when the bill (for which the Act in its final form was substituted) passed the House, § 205(a) provided that "upon a proper showing" an injunction or other order "shall be granted without bond." The words "upon a proper showing" were stricken in the Senate and were replaced by the words "upon a showing by the Administrator that such person has engaged or is about to engage in any such acts or practices." * * *

We agree that the cessation of violations, whether before or after the institution of a suit by the Administrator, is no bar to the issuance of an injunction under § 205(a). But we do not think that under all circumstances the court must issue the injunction or other order which the Administrator seeks.

It seems apparent on the face of § 205(a) that there is some room for the exercise of discretion on the part of the court. For the requirement is that a "permanent or temporary injunction, restraining order, or other order" be granted. Though the Administrator asks for an injunction, some "other order" might be more appropriate, or at least so appear to the court. Thus in the present case one judge in the Court of Appeals felt that the District Court should not have dismissed the complaint but should have entered an order retaining the case on the docket with the right of the Administrator, on notice, to renew his application for injunctive relief if violations recurred. It is indeed not difficult to imagine that in some situations that might be the fairest course to follow and one which would be as practically effective as the issuance of an injunction. Such an order, moreover, would seem to be a type of "other order" which a faithful reading of § 205(a) would permit a court to issue in a compliance proceeding. However that may be, it would seem clear that the court might deem some "other order" more appropriate for the evil at hand than the one which was sought. We cannot say that it lacks the power to make that choice. Thus it seems that § 205(a) falls short of making mandatory the issuance of an injunction merely because the Administrator asks it.

There is, moreover, support in the legislative history of § 205(a) for the view that "shall be granted" is less mandatory than a literal reading might suggest. [The Senate Report states that] " * * * courts are given jurisdiction to issue whatever order to enforce compliance is proper in the circumstances of each particular case." A grant of jurisdiction to issue compliance orders hardly suggests an absolute duty to do so under any and all circumstances. We cannot but think that if Congress had intended to make such a drastic departure from the traditions of equity practice, an unequivocal statement of its purpose would have been made.

We do not stop to compare the provisions of § 205(a) with the requirements of other federal statutes governing administrative agencies which, it is said, make it mandatory that those agencies take action when certain facts are shown to exist. We are dealing here with the requirements of equity practice with a background of several hundred years of history. Only the other day we stated that "An appeal to the equity jurisdiction conferred on federal district courts is an appeal to the sound discretion which guides the determinations of courts of equity." The historic injunctive process was designed to deter, not to punish. The essence of equity jurisdiction has been the power of the Chancellor to do equity and to mould each decree to the necessities of the particular case. Flexibility rather than rigidity has distinguished it. The qualities of mercy and practicality have made equity the instrument for nice adjustment and reconciliation between the public interest and private needs as well as between competing private claims. We do not believe that such a major departure from that long tradition as is here proposed should be lightly implied. We do not think the history or language of § 205(a) compel it. It should be noted, moreover, that § 205(a) governs the procedure in both federal and state courts. For § 205(c) gives the state courts concurrent jurisdiction with federal district courts of civil enforcement proceedings. It is therefore even more compelling to conclude that, if Congress desired to make such an abrupt departure from traditional equity practice as is suggested, it would have made its desire plain. Hence we resolve the ambiguities of § 205(a) in favor of that interpretation which affords a full opportunity for equity courts to treat enforcement proceedings under this emergency legislation in accordance with their traditional practices, as conditioned by the necessities of the public interest which Congress has sought to protect.

We do not mean to imply that courts should administer § 205(a) grudgingly. * * * [T]heir discretion under § 205(a) must be exercised in light of the large objectives of the Act. For the standards of the public interest, not the requirements of private litigation measure the propriety and need for injunctive relief in these cases. That discretion should reflect an acute awareness of the Congressional admonition that "of all the consequences of war, except human slaughter, inflation is the most destructive" and that delay or indifference may be fatal. Whether the District Court abused its discretion in dismissing the complaint is a question which we do not reach. The judgment must be reversed and the cause remanded to the Court of Appeals for that determination. * * *

MR. JUSTICE FRANKFURTER agrees that § 205(a) of the Emergency Price Control Act, apart from dispensing with any requirement for a bond, does not change the historic conditions for the exercise by courts of equity of their power to issue injunctions, according to which the Court of Appeals should now dispose of this cause.

MR. JUSTICE ROBERTS is of opinion that the judgment of the Court of Appeals should be reversed and that of the District Court affirmed.

NOTES

1. *Hecht* makes a number of points with import far beyond threat of harm as a prerequisite to injunctive relief. The case is much cited for its statements that courts have great flexibility in framing injunctions, as you will see in Section D of this chapter. *Hecht* also states an important canon of statutory construction—that courts should not read statutes to limit traditional equity practices unless the legislature clearly states that it intends to do so. See also Miller v. French, 530 U.S. 327, 120 S.Ct. 2246, 147 L.Ed.2d 326 (2000) (reiterating canon). *Hecht* applies this canon in refusing to read the Emergency Price Control Act to transfer from the courts to the administrator the power to determine whether an injunction is warranted.

In CBS Broadcasting, Inc. v. EchoStar Communications, 450 F.3d 505 (11th Cir.2006), cert. denied, 549 U.S. 1113, 127 S.Ct. 945, 166 L.Ed.2d 705 (2007), the Eleventh Circuit found that statutory language in the Satellite Home Viewer Act providing that a "court shall order a permanent injunction barring the secondary transmission by the satellite carrier" was mandatory and did intend to depart from traditional equitable practice. The appellate court distinguished *Hecht*, finding that there was no ambiguous history or legislative history indicating that the statutory language was discretionary and that the statute represented an unequivocal statement of purpose to restrict the courts' traditional equitable authority for injunctions. On remand, the district court refused to accept the parties' settlement agreement providing for narrower relief, finding that the remand order and the statute required the issuance of a permanent injunction. 472 F.Supp.2d 1367 (S.D.Fla.2006).

2. Did *Hecht* hold that there was no threat of future violations? That an injunction would do no good? The majority says that issuing an injunction would not be "just" to the Hecht Co. Had not the Hecht Co. earned the disadvantages of an injunction through its violations?

3. If there have been past violations, which party should have the burden of showing the probability (or nonprobability) of a future violation?

NOTE ON MOOTNESS AND RIPENESS

Hecht invoked the doctrine of *equitable discretion* to give effect to its finding that the Hecht Co. posed little threat. Threat of harm finds expression in a variety of overlapping doctrines, another one of which is *mootness,* a constitutional doctrine under which the defendant can get the case dismissed as a matter of right rather than discretion. Suppose that Hecht Co. neither admitted nor denied that its conduct was illegal but stated that it would comply with the regulations. It could not get the case dismissed as moot; United States v. W.T. Grant Co., 345 U.S. 629, 632–33, 73 S.Ct. 894, 897, 97 L.Ed. 1303, 1309 (1953) explains why:

> Both sides agree to the abstract proposition that voluntary cessation of allegedly illegal conduct does not deprive the tribunal of power to hear and determine the case, i.e., does not make the case moot. A controversy may remain to be settled in such circumstances, e.g., a dispute over the legality of the challenged practices. The defendant is free to return to his old ways. This, together with a public interest in having the legality of the practices settled, militates against a mootness conclusion. For to say that the case has become moot means that the defendant is entitled to dismissal as a matter of right. The courts have rightly refused to grant defendants such a powerful weapon against public law enforcement.
>
> The case may nevertheless be moot if the defendant can demonstrate that "there is no reasonable expectation that the wrong will be repeated." The burden is a heavy one. Here the defendants told the court that the [allegedly illegal practices] no longer existed and disclaimed any intention to revive them. Such a profession does not suffice to make a case moot although it is one of the factors to be considered in determining the appropriateness of granting an injunction against the now-discontinued acts.

If Congress repealed the statute that Hecht Co. had violated, the case would certainly be moot because the threat of future violations would have ended.

Hecht dealt with a case in which the issue was whether the violation would recur. It is the small or non-existent probability of *recurrence* that leads to the exercise of equitable discretion or finding of mootness. If, however, no violation had ever taken place and there was no showing a future violation was threatened, a court might say that the harm was not *imminent* or that the case was not *ripe*. The word "imminent," as used by courts in this context, means that a violation is likely to occur, not that it will occur soon. A court can find that the threat is not imminent (or the case not ripe) because the plaintiff lacks proof that the defendant will commit the violation.

As a variant on this theme, Professor Gene Shreve notes that "a court may deny a request for an injunction to a plaintiff in imminent danger of being wronged by a defendant because the wrong is not substantial." Gene R. Shreve, Federal Injunctions and the Public Interest, 51 Geo.Wash.L.Rev. 382, 392 (1983). For example, in Fletcher v. Bealey, 28 Ch.D. 688 (1885), the court denied an injunction against the defendant's storing chemical wastes on the basis, inter alia, that even if the wastes were released, there was insufficient proof that the wastes would harm the plaintiff's business. To be "substantial" a harm does not have to bulk large in monetary terms. For instance, a trespass would be a substantial harm even though the plaintiff cannot show that the trespasser will do monetarily significant damage because the law of trespass puts a paramount value on the owner's right to exclude. By contrast, *Fletcher v. Bealey* arose under nuisance law, which balances the competing interests of neighbors.

Legislatures sometimes borrow the phrase "imminent and substantial," but its meaning may differ from that in traditional equity cases. For example, a federal environmental law empowers courts to order persons responsible for threatened releases of toxic substances to abate the release if "there may be an imminent and substantial endangerment to the public health or welfare or environment," 42 U.S.C. § 9606(a), but Congress intended "imminent and substantial" to mean that injunctions would issue only if there were an emergency with which the Environmental Protection Agency could not cope through ordinary administrative mechanisms in the statute. H.R.Rep. No. 1185, 93d Cong., 2d Sess. 35–36 (1974).

Like recurrence, imminence/ripeness can give rise to the invocation of an equitable, discretionary doctrine (sometimes called *remedial ripeness*) as well as a constitutional, jurisdictional one (sometimes called *constitutional ripeness*) because, when there is no chance of harm, there is no "case or controversy," as required under Article III of the U.S. Constitution. Professor Richard Fallon has argued that the Court's concern for the appropriateness of certain remedies frequently influences it to make adjustments through one of the justiciability doctrines of standing, mootness, ripeness, or political question. Richard H. Fallon, Jr., The Linkage Between Justiciability and Remedies—and Their Connections to Substantive Rights, 92 Va.L.Rev. 633 (2006). For example, suppose that the Hecht Company had never violated the regulations because it was just setting up its business and the government sought an injunction out of concern that the new company would violate the regulations. If the company claimed that the regulations were invalid but that it would not violate them until their invalidity was judicially determined and the government had no proof to the contrary, a court might well decide that the plea for an injunction was not ripe.

The focus so far has been on whether the defendant threatens to violate the law in the future. Even if the defendant surely will do so, the plaintiff would not satisfy the threat of harm prerequisite unless the court can conclude that the violation will harm the plaintiff. California v. American Stores, 495 U.S. 271, 296, 110 S.Ct. 1853, 1867, 109 L.Ed.2d 240 (1990) ("A private litigant [under a statute authorizing divestiture as a remedy for anti-competitive mergers] * * * must prove 'threatened loss or damage' to his own interests in order to obtain relief"). Suppose that Bowles was not the public official in charge of enforcing price controls but rather a resident of Boise, Idaho who was visiting Washington, D.C., where the Hecht Company had overcharged him. If the Hecht Company will continue to violate the law, but Bowles has no plans for another visit to our nation's capital, is there an enjoinable threat of harm? See the following case.

CITY OF LOS ANGELES v. LYONS

Supreme Court of the United States, 1983
461 U.S. 95, 103 S.Ct. 1660, 75 L.Ed.2d 675

JUSTICE WHITE delivered the opinion of the Court.

The issue here is whether respondent Lyons satisfied the prerequisites for seeking injunctive relief in the Federal District Court.

I

This case began on February 7, 1977, when respondent, Adolph Lyons, filed a complaint for damages, injunction, and declaratory relief in the United States District Court for the Central District of California. The defendants were the City of Los Angeles and four of its police officers. The complaint alleged that on October 6, 1976, at 2 a.m., Lyons was stopped by the defendant officers for a traffic or vehicle code violation and that although Lyons offered no resistance or threat whatsoever, the officers, without provocation or justification, seized Lyons and applied a "chokehold"—either the "bar arm control" hold or the "carotid-artery control" hold or both—rendering him unconscious and causing damage to his larynx. Counts I through IV of the complaint sought damages against the officers and the City. Count V, with which we are principally concerned here, sought a preliminary and permanent injunction against the City barring the use of the control holds. That count alleged that the city's police officers, "pursuant to the authorization, instruction and encouragement of defendant City of Los Angeles, regularly and routinely apply these chokeholds in innumerable situations where they are not threatened by the use of any deadly force whatsoever," that numerous persons have been injured as the result of the application of the chokeholds, that Lyons and others similarly situated are threatened with irreparable injury in the form of bodily injury and loss of life, and that Lyons "justifiably fears that any contact he has with Los Angeles police officers may result in his being choked and strangled to death without provocation, justification or other legal excuse." Lyons alleged the threatened impairment of rights protected by the First, Fourth, Eighth, and Fourteenth Amendments. Injunctive relief was sought against the use of the control holds "except in situations where the proposed victim of said control reasonably appears to be threatening the immediate use of deadly force." Count VI sought declaratory relief against the City, i.e., a judgment that use of the chokeholds absent the threat of immediate use of deadly force is a *per se* violation of various constitutional rights.

The District Court, by order, granted the City's motion for partial judgment on the pleadings and entered judgment for the City on Count V and VI. The Court of Appeals reversed the judgment for the City on Count V and VI, holding over the City's objection that despite our decisions in O'Shea v. Littleton, 414 U.S. 488, 94 S.Ct. 669, 38 L.Ed.2d 674 (1974), and Rizzo v. Goode, 423 U.S. 362, 96 S.Ct. 598, 46 L.Ed.2d 561 (1976), Lyons had standing to seek relief against the application of the chokeholds. The Court of Appeals held that there was a sufficient likelihood that Lyons would again be stopped and subjected to the unlawful use of force to constitute a case or controversy and to warrant the issuance of an injunction, if the injunction was otherwise authorized. We denied certiorari.

On remand, Lyons applied for a preliminary injunction. Lyons pressed only the Count V claim at this point. The motion was heard on affidavits, depositions and government records. The District Court found that Lyons had been stopped for a traffic infringement and that without provocation or legal justification the officers involved had applied a "Department-authorized chokehold which resulted in injuries to the plaintiff." The court further found that the department authorizes the use of the holds in situations where no one is threatened by death or grievous bodily harm, that officers are insufficiently trained, that the use of the holds involves a high risk of injury or death as then employed, and that their continued use in situations where neither death nor serious bodily injury is threatened "is unconscionable in a civilized society." The court concluded that such use violated Lyons' substantive due process rights under the Fourteenth Amendment. A preliminary injunction was entered enjoining "the use of both the carotid-artery and bar arm holds under circumstances which do not threaten death or serious bodily injury." An improved training program and regular reporting and recordkeeping were also ordered. The Court of Appeals affirmed * * *. We granted certiorari and now reverse.

II

Since our grant of certiorari, circumstances pertinent to the case have changed. Originally, Lyons' complaint alleged that at least two deaths had occurred as a result of the application of chokeholds by the police. His first amended complaint alleged that 10 chokehold-related deaths had occurred. By May 1982, there had been five more such deaths. On May 6, 1982, the Chief of Police in Los Angeles prohibited the use of the bar-arm chokehold in any circumstances. A few days later, on May 12, 1982, the Board of Police Commissioners imposed a six-month moratorium on the use of the carotid-artery chokehold except under circumstances where deadly force is authorized.

[Lyons contended that these developments mooted the case because he is no longer subject to a threat of injury so that the preliminary injunction should be vacated.] The City, on the other hand, while acknowledging that subsequent events have significantly changed the posture of this case, again asserts that the case is not moot because the moratorium is not permanent and may be lifted at any time.

We agree with the City that the case is not moot, since the moratorium by its terms is not permanent. * * *

III

It goes without saying that those who seek to invoke the jurisdiction of the federal courts must satisfy the threshold requirement imposed by Art. III of the Constitution by alleging an actual case or controversy. Plaintiffs must demonstrate a "personal stake in the outcome" in order to "assure that concrete adverseness which sharpens the presentation of issues" necessary for the proper resolution of constitutional questions. Baker v. Carr, 369 U.S. 186, 204, 82 S.Ct. 691, 703, 7 L.Ed.2d 663 (1962). Abstract injury is not enough. The plaintiff must show that he "has sustained or is immediately in danger of sustaining some direct injury" as the result of the challenged official conduct and the injury or threat of injury must be both "real and immediate," not "conjectural" or "hypothetical."

In O'Shea v. Littleton, 414 U.S. 488, 94 S.Ct. 669, 38 L.Ed.2d 674 (1974), we dealt with a case brought by a class of plaintiffs claiming that they had been subjected to discriminatory enforcement of the criminal law. Among other things, a county magistrate and judge were accused of discriminatory conduct in various respects, such as sentencing members of plaintiff's class more harshly than other defendants. * * *

Although it was claimed in that case that particular members of the plaintiff class had actually suffered from the alleged unconstitutional practices, we observed that "[p]ast exposure to illegal conduct does not in itself show a present case or controversy regarding injunctive relief * * * if unaccompanied by any continuing, present adverse effects." Past wrongs were evidence bearing on "whether there is a real and immediate threat of repeated injury." But the prospect of future injury rested "on the likelihood that [plaintiffs] will again be arrested for and charged with violations of the criminal law and will again be subjected to bond proceedings, trial, or sentencing before petitioners." The most that could be said for plaintiffs' standing was "that *if* [plaintiffs] proceed to violate an unchallenged law and *if* they are charged, held to answer, and tried in any proceedings before petitioners, they will be subjected to the discriminatory practices that petitioners are alleged to have followed." We could not find a case or controversy in those circumstances: the threat to the plaintiffs was not "sufficiently real and immediate to show an existing controversy simply because they anticipate violating lawful criminal statutes and being tried for their offenses * * *." It was to be assumed "that [plaintiffs] will conduct their activities within the law and so avoid prosecution and conviction as well as exposure to the challenged course of conduct said to be followed by petitioners."

We further observed that case or controversy considerations "obviously shade into those determining whether the complaint states a sound basis for equitable relief," and went on to hold that even if the complaint presented an existing case or controversy, an adequate basis for equitable relief against petitioners had not been demonstrated [because of, inter alia, insufficient threat of harm.]

Another relevant decision for present purposes is *Rizzo v. Goode* [reproduced at page 46] * * *. The claim of injury rested upon "what one of a small, unnamed minority of policemen might do to [plaintiffs] in the future because of that unknown policeman's perception of departmental procedures." This hypothesis was "even more attenuated than those allegations of future injury found insufficient in *O'Shea* to warrant [the] invocation of federal jurisdiction."

IV

No extension of *O'Shea* and *Rizzo* is necessary to hold that respondent Lyons has failed to demonstrate a case or controversy with the City that would justify the equitable relief sought.[6] Lyons' standing to seek the injunction requested depended on whether he was likely to suffer future injury from the use of the chokeholds by police officers. * * * That Lyons may have been illegally choked by the police on October 6, 1976, while presumably affording Lyons standing to claim damages against the individual officers and perhaps against the City, does nothing to establish a real and immediate threat that he would again be stopped for a traffic violation, or for any other offense, by an officer or officers who would illegally choke him into unconsciousness without any provocation or resistance on his part. The additional allegation in the complaint that the police in Los Angeles routinely apply chokeholds in situations where they are not threatened by the use of deadly force falls far short of the allegations that would be necessary to establish a case or controversy between these parties.

In order to establish an actual controversy in this case, Lyons would have had not only to allege that he would have another encounter with the police but also to make the incredible assertion either, (1) that *all* police officers in Los Angeles *always* choke any citizen with whom they happen to have an encounter, whether for the purpose of arrest, issuing a citation or for questioning or, (2) that the City ordered or authorized police officers to act in such manner. Although Count V alleged that the City authorized the use of the control holds in situations where deadly force was not threatened, it did not indicate why Lyons might be realistically threatened by police officers who acted within the strictures of the City's policy. If, for example, chokeholds were authorized to be used only to counter resistance to an arrest by a suspect, or to thwart an effort to escape, any future

---

6. The City states in its brief that on remand from the Court of Appeals' first judgment "[t]he parties agreed and advised the district court that the respondent's damages claim could be severed from his effort to obtain equitable relief." Respondent does not suggest otherwise. This case, therefore, as it came to us, is on all fours with *O'Shea* and should be judged as such.

threat to Lyons from the City's policy or from the conduct of police officers would be no more real than the possibility that he would again have an encounter with the police and that either he would illegally resist arrest or detention or the officers would disobey their instructions and again render him unconscious without any provocation.[7]

Under *O'Shea* and *Rizzo,* these allegations were an insufficient basis to provide a federal court with jurisdiction to entertain Count V of the complaint.[8] * * * For several reasons—each of them infirm, in our view—the Court of Appeals thought reliance on *O'Shea* and *Rizzo* was misplaced and reversed the District Court.

First, the Court of Appeals thought that Lyons was more immediately threatened than the plaintiffs in those cases since, according to the Court of Appeals, Lyons need only be stopped for a minor traffic violation to be subject to the strangleholds. * * * We cannot agree that the "odds" that Lyons would not only again be stopped for a traffic violation but would also be subjected to a chokehold without any provocation whatsoever are sufficient to make out a federal case for equitable relief. We note that five months elapsed between October 6, 1976, and the filing of the complaint, yet there was no allegation of further unfortunate encounters between Lyons and the police.

Of course, it may be that among the countless encounters between the police and the citizens of a great city such as Los Angeles, there will be

---

7. The centerpiece of Justice Marshall's dissent is that Lyons had standing to challenge the City's policy because to recover damages he would have to prove that what allegedly occurred on October 6, 1976, was pursuant to City authorization. We agree completely that for Lyons to succeed in his damages action, it would be necessary to prove that what happened to him—that is, as alleged, he was choked without any provocation or legal excuse whatsoever—was pursuant to a City policy. For several reasons, however, it does not follow that Lyons had standing to seek the injunction prayed for in Count V.

First, [the complaint describes the city's policy] as authorizing the use of chokeholds "in situations where [the officers] are threatened by far less than deadly force." This is not equivalent to the unbelievable assertion that the City either orders or authorizes application of the chokeholds where there is no resistance or other provocation.

Second, even if such an allegation is thought to be contained in the complaint, it is belied by the record made on the application for preliminary injunction.

Third, even if the complaint must be read as containing an allegation that officers are authorized to apply the chokeholds where there is no resistance or other provocation, it does not follow that Lyons has standing to seek an injunction against the application of the restraint holds in situations that he has not experienced, as for example, where the suspect resists arrest or tries to escape but does not threaten the use of deadly force. Yet that is precisely the scope of the injunction that Lyons prayed for in Count V.

Fourth, and in any event, to have a case or controversy with the City that could sustain Count V, Lyons would have to credibly allege that he faced a realistic threat from the future application of the City's policy. Justice Marshall nowhere confronts this requirement—the necessity that Lyons demonstrate that he, himself, will not only again be stopped by the police but will be choked without any provocation or legal excuse. Justice Marshall plainly does not agree with that requirement, and he was in dissent in *O'Shea v. Littleton.* We are at issue in that respect.

8. * * * Lyons alleged that he feared he would be choked in any future encounter with the police. The reasonableness of Lyons' fear is dependent upon the likelihood of a recurrence of the allegedly unlawful conduct. It is the *reality* of the threat of repeated injury that is relevant to the standing inquiry, not the plaintiff's subjective apprehensions. The emotional consequences of a prior act simply are not a sufficient basis for an injunction absent a real and immediate threat of future injury by the defendant. Of course, emotional upset is a relevant consideration in a damages action.

certain instances in which strangleholds will be illegally applied and injury and death unconstitutionally inflicted on the victim. * * * [I]t is surely no more than speculation to assert either that Lyons himself will again be involved in one of those unfortunate instances, or that he will be arrested in the future and provoke the use of a chokehold by resisting arrest, attempting to escape, or threatening deadly force or serious bodily injury.

Second, the Court of Appeals viewed *O'Shea* and *Rizzo* as cases in which the plaintiffs sought "massive structural" relief against the local law enforcement systems * * *. *O'Shea* and *Rizzo,* however, cannot be so easily confined to their facts. If Lyons has made no showing that he is realistically threatened by a repetition of his experience of October, 1976, then he has not met the requirements for seeking an injunction in a federal court, whether the injunction contemplates intrusive structural relief or the cessation of a discrete practice.

The Court of Appeals also asserted that Lyons "had a live and active claim" against the City "if only for a period of a few seconds" while the stranglehold was being applied to him [so that] the claim had not become moot * * *. [T]he issue here is not whether that claim has become moot but whether Lyons meets the preconditions for asserting an injunctive claim in a federal forum. The equitable doctrine that cessation of the challenged conduct does not bar an injunction is of little help in this respect, for Lyons' lack of standing does not rest on the termination of the police practice but on the speculative nature of his claim that he will again experience injury as the result of that practice even if continued.

* * * The record and findings made on remand do not improve Lyons' position with respect to standing. * * * The City's policy was described [by the district court] as authorizing the use of the strangleholds "under circumstances where no one is threatened with death or grievous bodily harm." That policy was not further described, but the record before the court contained the department's existing policy * * *.[9] * * * [P]olice officers were instructed to use chokeholds only when lesser degrees of force do not suffice and then only "to gain control of a suspect who is violently resisting the officer or trying to escape."

Our conclusion is that the Court of Appeals failed to heed *O'Shea*, *Rizzo*, and other relevant authority, and that the District Court was quite right in dismissing Count V.

V
* * *

Absent a sufficient likelihood that he will again be wronged in a similar way, Lyons is no more entitled to an injunction than any other

---

9. The dissent notes that a LAPD training officer stated that the police are authorized to employ the control holds whenever an officer "feels" that there is about to be a bodily attack. The dissent's emphasis on the word "feels" apparently is intended to suggest that LAPD officers are authorized to apply the holds whenever they "feel" like it. If there is a distinction between permitting the use of the holds when there is a "threat" of serious bodily harm, and when the officer "feels" or believes there is about to be a bodily attack, the dissent has failed to make it clear. * * *

citizen of Los Angeles; and a federal court may not entertain a claim by any or all citizens who no more than assert that certain practices of law enforcement officers are unconstitutional. This is not to suggest that such undifferentiated claims should not be taken seriously by local authorities. Indeed, the interest of an alert and interested citizen is an essential element of an effective and fair government, whether on the local, state, or national level.[10] A federal court, however, is not the proper forum to press such claims unless the requirements for entry and the prerequisites for injunctive relief are satisfied.

We decline the invitation to slight the preconditions for equitable relief; for as we have held, recognition of the need for a proper balance between state and federal authority counsels restraint in the issuance of injunctions against state officers engaged in the administration of the states' criminal laws in the absence of irreparable injury which is both great and immediate. *O'Shea;* Younger v. Harris, 401 U.S. 37, 46, 91 S.Ct. 746, 751, 27 L.Ed.2d 669 (1971). * * *

As we noted in *O'Shea,* withholding injunctive relief does not mean that the "federal law will exercise no deterrent effect in these circumstances." If Lyons has suffered an injury barred by the Federal Constitution, he has a remedy for damages under § 1983. Furthermore, those who deliberately deprive a citizen of his constitutional rights risk conviction under the federal criminal laws.

Beyond these considerations the state courts need not impose the same standing or remedial requirements that govern federal court proceedings. The individual states may permit their courts to use injunctions to oversee the conduct of law enforcement authorities on a continuing basis. But this is not the role of a federal court absent far more justification than Lyons has proffered in this case. * * *

JUSTICE MARSHALL, with whom JUSTICE BRENNAN, JUSTICE BLACKMUN and JUSTICE STEVENS join, dissenting.

* * * There is plainly a "case or controversy" concerning the constitutionality of the city's chokehold policy. The constitutionality of that policy is directly implicated by Lyons' claim for damages against the city. The complaint clearly alleges that the officer who choked Lyons was carrying out an official policy, and a municipality is liable under 42 U.S.C. § 1983 for the conduct of its employees only if they acted pursuant to such a policy. Monell v. New York City Dept. of Social Services, 436 U.S. 658, 694, 98 S.Ct. 2018, 2037, 56 L.Ed.2d 611 (1978). Lyons therefore has standing to challenge the city's chokehold policy and to obtain whatever relief a court may ultimately deem appropriate. None of our prior deci-

---

10. The City's memorandum suggesting a question of mootness informed the Court that the use of the control holds had become "a major civic controversy" and that in April and May of 1982 "a spirited, vigorous, and at times emotional debate" on the issue took place. The result was the current moratorium on the use of the holds.

sions suggests that his requests for particular forms of relief raise any additional issues concerning his standing. * * *

II

At the outset it is important to emphasize that Lyons' entitlement to injunctive relief and his entitlement to an award of damages both depend upon whether he can show that the city's chokehold policy violates the Constitution. An indispensable prerequisite of municipal liability under 42 U.S.C. § 1983 is proof that the conduct complained of is attributable to an unconstitutional official policy or custom. * * *

The Court apparently finds Lyons' complaint wanting because, although it alleges that he was choked without provocation and that the officers acted pursuant to an official policy, it fails to allege *in haec verba* that the city's policy authorizes the choking of suspects without provocation. I am aware of no case decided since the abolition of the old common law forms of action, and the Court cites none, that in any way supports this crabbed construction of the complaint. A federal court is capable of concluding for itself that two plus two equals four.

* * * In sum, it's absolutely clear that Lyons' requests for damages and for injunctive relief call into question the constitutionality of the city's policy concerning the use of chokeholds. If he does not show that policy is unconstitutional, he will be no more entitled to damages than to an injunction.

III

Since Lyons' claim for damages plainly gives him standing, and since the success of that claim depends upon a demonstration that the city's chokehold policy is unconstitutional, it is beyond dispute that Lyons has properly invoked the District Court's authority to adjudicate the constitutionality of the city's chokehold policy. The dispute concerning the constitutionality of that policy plainly presents a "case or controversy" under Art. III. The Court nevertheless holds that a federal court has no power under Art. III to adjudicate Lyons' request, in the same lawsuit, for injunctive relief with respect to that very policy. This anomalous result is not supported either by precedent or by the fundamental concern underlying the standing requirement. Moreover, by fragmenting a single claim into multiple claims for particular types of relief and requiring a separate showing of standing for each form of relief, the decision today departs from this Court's traditional conception of standing and of the remedial powers of the federal courts.

A

It is simply disingenuous for the Court to assert that its decision requires "[n]o extension" of *O'Shea* and *Rizzo*. In contrast to this case *O'Shea* and *Rizzo* involved disputes focusing solely on the threat of future injury which the plaintiffs in those cases alleged they faced. * * *

In addition to the risk that he will be subjected to a chokehold in the future, Lyons has suffered past injury.[15] Because he has a live claim for damages, he need not rely solely on the threat of future injury to establish his personal stake in the outcome of the controversy. In the cases relied on by the majority, the Court simply had no occasion to decide whether a plaintiff who has standing to litigate a dispute must clear a separate standing hurdle with respect to each form of relief sought.

B

The Court's decision likewise finds no support in the fundamental policy underlying the Art. III standing requirement—the concern that a federal court not decide a legal issue if the plaintiff lacks a sufficient "personal stake in the outcome of the controversy as to assure that concrete adverseness which sharpens the presentation of issues upon which the court so largely depends for illumination of difficult ... questions." Baker v. Carr, 369 U.S. 186, 204, 82 S.Ct. 691, 703, 7 L.Ed.2d 663 (1962). * * *

Because Lyons has a claim for damages against the city, and because he cannot prevail on that claim unless he demonstrates that the city's chokehold policy violates the Constitution, his personal stake in the outcome of the controversy adequately assures an adversary presentation of his challenge to the constitutionality of the policy. Moreover, the resolution of this challenge will be largely dispositive of his requests for declaratory and injunctive relief. No doubt the requests for injunctive relief may raise additional questions. But these questions involve familiar issues relating to the appropriateness of particular forms of relief, and have never been thought to implicate a litigant's standing to sue. The denial of standing separately to seek injunctive relief therefore cannot be justified by the basic concern underlying the Art. III standing requirement.

C

* * *

The Court's fragmentation of the standing inquiry is also inconsistent with the way the federal courts have treated remedial issues since the merger of law and equity. The federal practice has been to reserve consideration of the appropriate relief until after a determination of the merits, not to foreclose certain forms of relief by a ruling on the pleadings. * * *

---

15. In Lankford v. Gelston, 364 F.2d 197 (C.A.4 1966)(en banc), which we cited with approval in Allee v. Medrano, 416 U.S. 802, 816, n. 9, 94 S.Ct. 2191, 2200, n. 9, 40 L.Ed.2d 566 (1974), the Fourth Circuit found standing on facts indistinguishable from this case. In *Lankford,* the Court of Appeals held that four Negro families who had been subjected to an illegal house search were entitled to seek injunctive relief against the Baltimore Police Department's policy of conducting wholesale searches based only on uncorroborated anonymous tips, even though the plaintiffs there did not claim that they were more likely than other Negro residents of the city to be subjected to an illegal search in the future.

Rule 54(c) of the Federal Rules of Civil Procedure specifically provides that "every final judgment shall grant the relief to which the party in whose favor it is rendered is entitled, even if the party has not demanded such relief in his pleadings." * * *

VI

The Court's decision removes an entire class of constitutional violations from the equitable powers of a federal court. It immunizes from prospective equitable relief any policy that authorizes persistent deprivations of constitutional rights as long as no individual can establish with substantial certainty that he will be injured, or injured again, in the future. [Chief Justice Burger] asked in Bivens v. Six Unknown Fed. Narcotics Agents, 403 U.S. 388, 419, 91 S.Ct. 1999, 2016, 29 L.Ed.2d 619 (1971)(dissenting opinion), "what would be the judicial response to a police order authorizing 'shoot to kill' with respect to every fugitive?" His answer was that it would be "easy to predict our collective wrath and outrage." We now learn that wrath and outrage cannot be translated into an order to cease the unconstitutional practice, but only an award of damages to those who are victimized by the practice and live to sue and to the survivors of those who are not so fortunate. Under the view expressed by the majority today, if the police adopt a policy of "shoot to kill," or a policy of shooting one out of ten suspects, the federal courts will be powerless to enjoin its continuation. The federal judicial power is now limited to levying a toll for such a systematic constitutional violation. * * *

NOTES

1. *Lyons* mentions four of the doctrines discussed in the text preceding the case. First, the majority rules that the controversy was not moot. (Why, by the way, did Lyons argue that the case was moot?) Second, the majority rules that Lyons did not present a case or controversy in his claim for injunctive relief on the theory that there is only a small probability of recurrence. Third, the majority rules that an injunction should be withheld on the basis of equitable discretion on the theory that there is only a small probability of recurrence. (It is over these second and third doctrines that the majority and the dissent clash.) Fourth, the majority mentions that the threatened harm must be substantial, which it undoubtedly would have found it was, if it had reached the question.

The Supreme Court has spoken of the difference between standing and mootness in two cases decided well after *Lyons*. In Friends of the Earth v. Laidlaw Environmental Services, Inc., 528 U.S. 167, 120 S.Ct. 693, 145 L.Ed.2d 610 (2000), an environmental group sought a civil penalty from a company that had been in violation of the Clean Water Act but had ceased the violation during the litigation. The Court held the case was not moot even though the company was now in substantial compliance, because a finding of mootness would leave the company free to return to its old ways. Whether the environmental group had standing was a separate question. See Symposium,

Citizen Suits and the Future of Standing in the 21st Century: From Lujan to Laidlaw and Beyond, 11 Duke Envt'l L. & Pol'y F. 193; 12 Duke Envt'l L. & Pol'y F. 1 (2001).

In the companion case of Adarand Constructors, Inc. v. Slater, 528 U.S. 216, 120 S.Ct. 722, 145 L.Ed.2d 650 (2000), Adarand Constructors had challenged preferences given in government contracting to companies certified as being disadvantaged business enterprises. The Supreme Court found that Adarand's being so certified, and so receiving the preferences itself, did not moot the suit:

> * * * the Tenth Circuit 'confused mootness with standing,' and as a result placed the burden of proof on the wrong party. * * * [T]he heavy burden of persuad[ing] the court that the challenged conduct cannot reasonably be expected to start up again lies with the party asserting mootness [quoting *Friends of the Earth*].

Id. at 221, 120 S.Ct. at 725.

2. The majority in *Lyons* relies upon the proposition that the plaintiff seeking an injunction must show a significant threat of harm to himself. It discusses this proposition in terms of the threat of harm doctrine and the standing doctrine. How probable is it that Lyons will be subjected in the future to an illegal chokehold? Do you agree with the majority's analysis of that question? The dissent's? If the availability of an injunction depends upon the probability of harm, who should bear the burden of persuasion on probability?

The Sixth Circuit, in American Civil Liberties Union v. National Security Agency, 493 F.3d 644 (6th Cir.2007), cert. denied, 552 U.S. ___, 128 S.Ct. 1334, 170 L.Ed.2d 59 (2008), rejected standing for a group of plaintiffs challenging the federal wiretapping statute, finding that none could show they were the targets of wiretapping. The Catch–22, however, is that in the absence of government disclosure, the plaintiffs are unable to establish that they were targets, and thus can never show the requisite injury. In National Council of La Raza v. Mukasey, 283 Fed.Appx. 848 (2d Cir.2008), the court denied standing to a group seeking to enjoin the Department of Homeland Security's profiling practices of disseminating immigration information to state law enforcement offices, finding that the alleged loss of privacy, diminished public safety, and heightened risk of arrest were inadequate to demonstrate the injury necessary to sue.

3. What can a plaintiff in a case like *Lyons* do to satisfy the threat of harm requirement? Consider the following possibilities:

(a) *Bring a class action*. Would it have been easier for Lyons to show a threat of harm if the case were a class action? *Lyons* was never certified as a class action. Lankford v. Gelston, 364 F.2d 197 (4th Cir.1966), which Justice Marshall argues is indistinguishable, was a class action.

(b) *Provide specific statistics showing a threat of harm*. In an earlier case brought by Adarand, Adarand Constructors, Inc. v. Peña, 515 U.S. 200, 115 S.Ct. 2097, 132 L.Ed.2d 158 (1995), the Supreme Court found that the plaintiff showed the imminent threat of harm required to seek injunctive relief. The harm that Adarand Constructors alleged was that unjustified race-based preferences, as part of an affirmative action program in federal highway contracting, denied it equal protection of the laws. Adarand showed the likelihood of this harm by proving that the kind of contracts upon which it routinely bid were put out for bid with provisions for race-based preferences at an average rate of one and a half per year for the past seven years and that Adarand usually faced competition from firms eligible for race-based preference. See also Baur v. Veneman, 352 F.3d 625 (2d Cir. 2003)(even small—but "present and immediate"—statistical risk of contracting mad cow disease supports standing for party seeking injunction requiring ban on slaughter of "downed" cattle—i.e., cattle exhibiting possible disease symptoms just prior to slaughter).

The plaintiff in a *Lyons*-like case would be well advised to frame the allegations in the complaint so that the odds of harm are high. For example, might a court agree that the odds of a young African–American male driver being subject to a chokehold while driving after midnight in a rich and largely white precinct are likely to be much higher than the odds calculated for all drivers in all neighborhoods?

Such statistical information may be easier to come by in the future. See Floyd Weatherspoon, Ending Racial Profiling of African–Americans in the Selective Enforcement of Laws: In Search of Viable Remedies, 65 U.Pitt.L.Rev. 721 (2004) (surveying efforts at all levels of government to address issue). For an argument that the equal protection cases support standing to challenge racial profiling, see Note, Standing While Black: Distinguishing Lyons in Racial Profiling Cases, 100 Colum.L.Rev. 1815 (2000).

What is not clear is whether these data will assist plaintiffs who want to bring lawsuits to stop these practices. For example, the Ninth Circuit rejected a class action suit where the named plaintiffs used Border Patrol data to allege a pattern and practice by Border Patrol agents of stopping people who merely looked Latino and were driving near Arizona's border with Mexico. The en banc court held that: (1) standing to seek damages does not alone serve as a basis for standing to seek equitable relief against the alleged practice; (2) the motorists named as class representatives, having been stopped only once each in ten years, did not establish a sufficient likelihood of future injury to warrant equitable relief under *Lyons*; and (3) relief could not be based on alleged injury to unnamed class members. Hodgers–Durgin v. de la Vina, 199 F.3d 1037 (9th Cir. en banc 1999). Accord, Chavez v. Illinois State Police, 251 F.3d 612 (7th Cir.2001) (named plaintiffs lacked standing; also, statistics relied on were inadequate to show discriminatory intent or effect). See also Symposium, Race, Crime, and the Constitution, 3 U.Pa. J.Const.L. 1 (2001).

(c) *Allege unequal treatment*. Adarand Constructors was not required to show that it would submit the winning bid but for the racial preference because the "injury in cases of this kind is that a 'discriminatory classification prevent[s] the plaintiff from competing on an equal footing.' " *Adarand Constructors*, 115 S.Ct. at 2105 (quoting General Contractors v. Jacksonville, 508 U.S. 656, 113 S.Ct. 2297, 2304, 124 L.Ed.2d 586 (1993)). Would Lyons have prevailed if he alleged that the police decided whom to choke partly on the basis of the color of their skin?

In Texas v. Lesage, 528 U.S. 18, 120 S.Ct. 467, 145 L.Ed.2d 347 (1999), the Supreme Court spoke to the relationship between *Adarand* and *Mt. Healthy*. The plaintiff claimed that the defendant university unconstitutionally considered his race in rejecting his application for admission, but the university showed that the plaintiff would not have been admitted anyway. The Supreme Court stated:

> * * * where a plaintiff challenges a discrete governmental decision as being based on an impermissible criterion and it is undisputed that the government would have made the same decision regardless, there is no cognizable injury warranting relief under § 1983. * * * Of course, a plaintiff who challenges an ongoing race-conscious program and seeks forward-looking relief need not affirmatively establish that he would receive the benefit in question if race were not considered. The relevant injury in such cases is 'the inability to compete on an equal footing.' See also Adarand Constructors, Inc. v. Peña, 515 U.S. 200, 211, 115 S.Ct. 2097, 132 L.Ed.2d 158 (1995). But where there is no allegation of an ongoing or imminent constitutional violation to support a claim for forward-looking relief, the government's conclusive demonstration that it would have made the same decision absent the alleged discrimination precludes any finding of liability.

120 S.Ct. at 468–69.

The Supreme Court has continued to be rather indulgent in allowing standing in similar cases. For example, in Gratz v. Bollinger, 539 U.S. 244, 123 S.Ct. 2411, 156 L.Ed.2d 257 (2003), the Court majority rejected the claim of two dissenting justices that the named plaintiffs challenging the race-based undergraduate admissions policies at the University of Michigan lacked standing to seek prospective relief. The dissenters noted that the named plaintiffs had gone on to graduate from other institutions, that one plaintiff had not even applied as a transfer student to Michigan, and that someone seeking to enter the university as a transfer student could not represent those who sought to be admitted to the first-year class. The majority held that the plaintiffs' stated intent to apply for admission or transfer should the university be forced to change its race-based policy was sufficient for standing purposes.

(d) Allege illegal conduct in the relevant time period. In Park v. Forest Service, 205 F.3d 1034 (8th Cir.2000), a member of the "Rainbow Family" sought injunctive relief against the Forest Service for employing auto checkpoints targeting association members. The court held the plaintiff failed to show any ongoing threat of unconstitutional conduct. The court stated:

> We do not think, however, that the actual use of checkpoints in 1997, 1998, and 1999 is relevant on the issue of standing because all of these events occurred after Ms. Park filed her original complaint. We believe that it is Ms. Park's burden to show that, at the time she filed her suit in 1996, there was a real and immediate threat that she would again be subjected by the Forest Service to an unconstitutional checkpoint. We do not think that she may use evidence of what happened after the commencement of the suit to make this showing. * * *

It is possible that Ms. Park would have standing to seek injunctive relief in an action commenced today, if these more recent checkpoints establish a pattern of wrongdoing by the Forest Service. It is our hope, however, that Ms. Park will not have to resort to legal action again to be free from future violations of her constitutional rights, and that the administrators of the Forest Service will ensure that the inappropriate conduct of 1996 is not repeated.

205 F.3d at 1037, 1040.

(e) Plead and prove an "iron-clad" policy. In Mack v. Suffolk County, 191 F.R.D. 16 (D.Mass.2000), the court found that strip-searching of all female pre-arraignment detainees was an "iron clad" policy. In *Mack*, unlike *Lyons*, where the plaintiff did not meet his burden to show it was more likely than not that the illegal behavior would recur, the court could predict with certainty that the women would be strip-searched. See also 31 Foster Children v. Bush, 329 F.3d 1255 (11th Cir.), cert. denied, 540 U.S. 984, 124 S.Ct. 483, 157 L.Ed.2d 376 (2003) (alleged pattern and practice of abuse establishes standing to pursue prospective injunction on behalf of foster care children in Florida's custody).

4. Justice Marshall argues that the majority is wrong to test standing for each claim for relief rather than testing standing as to the central factual controversy. Is the majority's approach necessary to serve the purposes behind standing or remedial ripeness? From Justice Marshall's perspective, should the plaintiff in *Bivens* be entitled to an injunction against future searches no matter how low the probability of his home being searched again?

5. Would *Lyons* have come out the same way if Los Angeles had left its original chokehold policy in effect?

NOTE ON WHO IS PROTECTED BY AN INJUNCTION

Assuming that Lyons could show sufficient probability of harm to get an injunction, should the injunction limit the use of the chokehold against just him or also against similarly situated persons who are not parties? The question, which arises chiefly in cases against governmental defendants, is answered along two lines: (1) an injunction can protect nonparties where the defendant explicitly or implicitly consents to a decree that protects nonparties, e.g., Catanzano v. Dowling, 847 F.Supp. 1070 (W.D.N.Y.1994); and (2) an injunction can protect only the plaintiffs., e.g., Kansas Health Care Association, Inc. v. Kansas Department of Social & Rehabilitation Services, 31 F.3d 1536 (10th Cir.1994). The group of plaintiffs can, however, be quite large where the court certifies the case as a class action. In addition, Congress has the power to authorize government agencies to get injunctive relief to protect the public, and agencies may sue in this representative capacity without getting class certification. General Telephone Co. v. EEOC, 446 U.S. 318, 320, 100 S.Ct. 1698, 64 L.Ed.2d 319 (1980).

Even an injunction protecting an individual plaintiff may have the practical effect of protecting others similarly situated. For example, if Country Lodge gets an injunction barring Miller from polluting, compliance will protect those situated similarly to Country Lodge. In contrast, the Los

Angeles Police Department could conceivably comply with an injunction against applying the chokehold to Lyons, but still have the right to apply the chokehold to others. But see Easyriders Freedom F.I.G.H.T. v. Hannigan, 92 F.3d 1486, 1502 (9th Cir.1996) (granting statewide injunction against illegal enforcement policy of motorcycle helmet law so fourteen plaintiffs could obtain the complete relief to which they were entitled). When an injunction would have the practical effect of protecting everyone similarly situated, courts following the second approach sometimes decline to certify a class action. Which approach is appropriate? See George Rutherglen, Notice, Scope, and Preclusion in Title VII Class Actions, 69 Va.L.Rev. 11, 17–21 (1983).

An example of the second, and more common approach, is a case brought by a single individual challenging the constitutionality of the military's policy of discharging avowed homosexuals. The district court judge ordered that "[t]he Department of Defense is permanently enjoined from discharging or denying enlistment to *any* person based on sexual orientation in the absence of sexual conduct which interferes with the military mission of the armed forces * * *." Meinhold v. U.S. Department of Defense, 808 F.Supp. 1455, 1459 (C.D.Cal.1993)(emphasis added). The Ninth Circuit denied a stay pending appeal because, although it noted a legitimate issue about whether the injunction should protect anyone but Meinhold, it found that the department would not suffer irreparable injury in view of the presidential directive on homosexuals in the military. 61 Empl.Prac.Dec. (CCH) ¶ 42,197 (9th Cir. 1993). In a subsequent contempt proceeding brought by Meinhold, the district court amended the injunction, further restraining the Department of Defense from "creating or maintaining files based on sexual orientation and from taking any action against gay or lesbian servicemembers based on their sexual orientation." Meinhold v. U.S. Department of Defense, 1993 WL 513209, 62 Empl.Prac.Dec. (CCH) ¶ 42,619 (C.D.Cal.1993). The Supreme Court granted a stay of the amended injunction to the extent that it applied to persons other than Meinhold. 510 U.S. 939, 114 S.Ct. 374, 126 L.Ed.2d 324 (1993). The Ninth Circuit then held that the district court erred in granting an injunction protecting anyone but Meinhold. 34 F.3d 1469 (9th Cir.1994).

NOTE ON THE RELATIONSHIP BETWEEN THREAT OF HARM AND THE SCOPE OF AN INJUNCTION

In Hodgson v. Corning Glass Works, 474 F.2d 226 (2d Cir.1973), aff'd, 417 U.S. 188, 94 S.Ct. 2223, 41 L.Ed.2d 1 (1974), Secretary of Labor James Hodgson brought an action against Corning Glass Works alleging a violation of the Equal Pay Act of 1963. The court found a violation of the Act only with respect to one class of employees at the defendant's three plants in Corning, New York and there was no evidence of widespread violations of the Act at its twenty-six branch plants nationwide. The district court had enjoined violations at virtually all of the plants, but the Court of Appeals confined the injunction, because "absent a showing of a policy of discrimination which extends beyond the plants at issue * * * there is no basis for a nationwide injunction." Id. at 236. What relief if Corning Glass Works dismisses those responsible for the discrimination at its plants in Corning? See Spomer v. Littleton, 414 U.S. 514, 94 S.Ct. 685, 38 L.Ed.2d 694 (1974).

Lujan v. National Wildlife Federation, 497 U.S. 871, 110 S.Ct. 3177, 111 L.Ed.2d 695 (1990), held in a five-to-four decision that the National Wildlife Federation (NWF) lacked standing to challenge certain government land management practices, but all the justices appeared to agree that the scope of standing can affect the scope of injunctive relief. In the majority's view, the NWF lacked standing because the challenged practices were general policies and the NWF failed to allege with sufficient specificity that the application of those practices to particular tracts of land injured any of its members. The Court also suggested that if the NWF had made sufficient allegations about a particular tract, injunctive relief would be limited to that tract. 497 U.S. at 889–94, 110 S.Ct. at 3189–91, 111 L.Ed.2d at 717–20. On this point, the dissent, by Justice Blackmun, appeared to agree. 497 U.S. at 913–15, 110 S.Ct. at 3201, 111 L.Ed.2d at 731.

In Lewis v. Casey, 518 U.S. 343, 116 S.Ct. 2174, 135 L.Ed.2d 606 (1996), inmates in various prisons in Arizona brought a class action alleging the state failed in its constitutional duty to provide law libraries or persons adequately trained in the law to help prisoners file meaningful legal papers. The Supreme Court rejected the systemwide injunction ordered by the district court. The remedy had to be limited to redressing the inadequacy that produced an injury in fact that the plaintiffs with standing had proven; suing on behalf of a group of prisoners did not help without such proof. As Justice Scalia put it, writing for the majority:

> It is for the courts to remedy past or imminent official interference with individual inmates' presentation of claims to the courts; it is for the political branches of the State and Federal Governments to manage prisons in such fashion that official interference with the presentation of claims will not occur. * * * [T]he distinction between the two roles would be obliterated if, to invoke intervention of the courts, no actual or imminent harm were needed, but merely the status of being subject to a governmental institution that was not organized or managed properly.

Id. at 350, 116 S.Ct. at 2179. Justices Souter, Ginsburg and Breyer concurred, with the understanding that the impropriety of the order of systemic relief did not turn on the standing of class members but on the failure of the plaintiffs to prove that past or imminent denials of access to illiterate prisoners pervaded the State's prison system. Id. at 396, 116 S.Ct. at 2202. Even Justice Stevens, dissenting because he thought the majority reached a number of issues unnecessarily, agreed that the relief ordered by the district court was broader than necessary to redress the proven constitutional violations. Id. at 409, 116 S.Ct. at 2208.

Some have explained such overreaching on the part of lower courts as the evolution of early prison cases in which judges were not content with correcting the constitutional violations, but rather, had the broader agenda of making the prisons into moral institutions run on bureaucratic lines. See Malcolm M. Feeley & Edward L. Rubin, Judicial Policy Making and the Modern State: How the Courts Reformed America's Prisons 162–163 (1998). More recently, courts handling prison cases have seemed to correct for this overreaching by narrowing the target and scope of their relief as they continue to actively award structural injunctions as valuable and effective remedies. Margo Schlanger, Civil Rights Injunctions Over Time: A Case Study of Jail and Prison Court Orders, 81 N.Y.U.L. Rev. 550, 554 (2006).

2. INADEQUATE REMEDY AT LAW

PROBLEM: COUNTRY LODGE V. MILLER (REPRISED)
THE CHOICE BETWEEN LEGAL AND EQUITABLE REMEDIES

(a) Is Country Lodge barred from obtaining an injunction to prevent future water pollution because it might instead get a money judgment for compensatory damages?

(b) Is Country Lodge barred from obtaining an injunction to require Miller to clean up the waste because it might get a money judgment for compensatory damages?

(c) If Miller's pollution is a crime, could the prosecutor get an injunction against its repetition? Would it make a difference if the criminal penalty were a $50 fine or a $50,000 fine?

(d) Suppose that Country Lodge contracts with Eco-cleaners, Inc., for removal of the apple mash from the river bank. The contract specifies that Eco-cleaners will reduce the concentration of apple mash on the bank to less than one part per ten thousand. After Eco-cleaners applies the usual clean-up techniques that it thought would do the job, the concentration is reduced, but still twice that specified in the contract. Eco-cleaners does not want to take any additional steps because the present concentration is neither visible nor attracts insects, and meeting the specifications would result in Eco-cleaners incurring a considerable loss on the contract. Country Lodge wants the contract carried out to the letter. Should Country Lodge's request for specific performance be granted by the court?

Your civil procedure course may have covered the development of separate courts of law and equity in England and, subsequently, in the United States. (For a refresher, see William Q. De Funiak, Handbook of Modern Equity 1–10 (1956).) The part of that story relevant here is that the courts of law would hear no suit to prevent an injury to property or to compel performance of a contract. Instead they offered damages after the injury was done. In contrast, the equity courts offered injunctive relief. But, the law courts' jealous protection of their own jurisdiction forced the equity courts to limit access to those who could show that the law courts provided them with no adequate remedy.

The eventual merger of law and equity courts in this country did away with the jealousy between rival judicial systems, but the merged courts continued to insist on the old maxim that equitable remedies are available only if the remedy at law is inadequate. A traditional test of inadequacy is that the remedy at law is not "as practical and as efficient to the ends of justice and its prompt administration, as the remedy in equity." Boyce's Ex'rs v. Grundy, 28 U.S. (3 Pet.) 210, 215, 7 L.Ed. 655, 657 (1830).

Under this test any one of many different considerations can lead to a finding that the remedy at law is inadequate:

1. the defendant is judgment-proof;

2. the defendant is immune from damages, as may be the case with defendants who are officials or governments;

3. damages are difficult to estimate because the size of monetary loss is hard to estimate, as in the case of lost profits from a new business, or because the plaintiff is likely to put a money value on the property higher than the market value, as in the case of an heirloom;

4. damages cannot be used to put the plaintiff in its rightful position because what is lost is not available in the market place, as in the cases involving a unique item of property, civil rights, or environmental quality;

5. complete recovery would require a multiplicity of suits, as where the plaintiff seeks an injunction against an ongoing nuisance and the jurisdiction does not allow the recovery of all future damages in one action; or

6. allowing the injury to take place would be morally repugnant even if it can be repaired, as in the case of intentional injury to the plaintiff's property.

See, e.g., Dan B. Dobbs, Law of Remedies § 2.5 (2d ed.1993); Developments in the Law—Injunctions, 78 Harv.L.Rev. 994, 997–1021 (1965). Courts presume that there is no adequate remedy at law when real estate is at stake. This presumption is justified in most but not all cases by sentimental attachments, difficulty in ascertaining the monetary value to the plaintiff, or difficulty finding another parcel with exactly the same attributes.

NOTE ON THE MAXIMS OF EQUITY

The inadequate remedy at law rule is one of many so-called "maxims" of equity. Some of the other maxims are closely related to the inadequacy maxim.

One maxim is that equity will not act unless there is "irreparable injury"—meaning that the plaintiff would suffer an injury that a legal remedy cannot repair. By this courts mean some or all of the considerations listed above. See, e.g., Gene R. Shreve, Federal Injunctions and the Public Interest, 51 Geo.Wash.L.Rev. 382, 392–94 (1983).

Another maxim is that "Equity protects property rights, not personal rights." To the extent this maxim means that legal remedies are never an adequate response to trespass, it simply affirms one aspect of the inadequacy doctrine. To the extent that it means legal remedies are always adequate to protect other rights, it erroneously simplifies and generalizes from the traditional tendency to protect contract as opposed to property rights with compensatory damages. The maxim was riddled with exceptions from the beginning and these exceptions grew larger with the growing importance of constitutional rights and statutory rights other than property-related rights and the grant of injunctions to protect them. The maxim is today not a meaningful limitation on the grant of injunctions.

Still another maxim related to the inadequate remedy at law rule is "Equity will not enjoin a crime." Since criminal prosecutions were brought in the courts of law, enjoining a crime deprives the defendants of the procedural rights that the criminal law affords, which include not only a jury trial, but also the proof beyond a reasonable doubt standard and more. Nonetheless, the maxim has long been full of exceptions, although there is more left to it than the maxim that equity protects only property rights. Private parties can get injunctions against crimes that are also torts. The government can get an injunction against a crime when it is a public nuisance or creates a national emergency, or a statute specifically grants power to do so. See, e.g., United States v. Bay Mills Indian Community, 692 F.Supp. 777, 779 (W.D.Mich. 1988), vacated on joint motion of parties, 727 F.Supp. 1110 (W.D.Mich.1989). Courts will also enjoin crimes where criminal sanctions have failed to stop repetitions of the crime or are unlikely to stop future crimes. State v. Red Owl Stores, Inc., 253 Minn. 236, 92 N.W.2d 103 (1958) (prosecution unlikely to be effective because supermarket chains planned store-by-store defense against prosecution for selling over-the-counter drugs without a pharmacy license and fine for violating statute in question was small); City of Chicago v. Cecola, 75 Ill.2d 423, 27 Ill.Dec. 462, 389 N.E.2d 526 (1979) (prosecution unlikely to be effective because $200 fine per day will not put "massage parlor" out of business). Coercive civil contempt or criminal contempt allows the judge to impose sanctions in excess of the statutory penalty for the crime and to avoid jury nullification. A private plaintiff who would otherwise suffer irreparable injury can get an injunction against a crime when the prosecutor will not bring charges. Is it appropriate for a judge to use the contempt power to impose a sanction harsher than the legislature established for the crime? To circumvent jury nullification?

Maxims of equity provide the illusory comfort of absolute answers. Perhaps that is why there are so many of them. Most are unrelated to the inadequacy of legal remedy rule (such as, "Equality is equity"). A large number of such maxims are collected in John McGhee, Snell's Equity ch. 3 (31st rev.ed.2008); and Howard W. Brill, The Maxims of Equity, 1993 Ark. L.Notes 29 (1993). Like the examples discussed above, these maxims are usually so exception-riddled or so vague as to have little meaning. As the Seventh Circuit has said, "whenever some maxim of equity (such as that to get equitable relief you must have 'clean hands') collides with the objectives of the antitrust laws, the equity maxim must give way." Scheiber v. Dolby Laboratories, Inc., 293 F.3d 1014, 1022 (7th Cir.2002), cert. denied, 537 U.S. 1109, 123 S.Ct. 853, 154 L.Ed.2d 781 (2003). In essence, maxims are merely a style of discussing equity, and fortunately an increasingly outmoded one.

The maxims' oversimplification and vagueness are understandable because it is hard to capsulize complex doctrine. Maxims pack a rhetorical zing that erroneously suggests that they are the end rather than the beginning of proper analysis. Professor Douglas Laycock has neatly punctured the puffery in the inadequate remedy at law maxim:

> [T]he full statement of the traditional rule is as follows:
>
> 1. Equity will not act if there is an adequate remedy at law.
>
> 2. "Adequate remedy" means a remedy as complete, practical, and efficient as the equitable remedy.
>
> This rule could be reformulated as follows:
>
> 1. Plaintiff is entitled in all cases to the most complete, practical, and efficient remedy.
>
> 2. If a legal and an equitable remedy are equally complete, practical, and efficient, the legal remedy shall be used.
>
> Although the two formulations are logically equivalent, they are not rhetorically equivalent, especially if one assumes that under either formulation the broader first rule of the pair will be more widely known than the narrower second rule. The second formulation would make clear that the irreparable injury rule is simply a tie-breaker, and that the plaintiff is not to be disadvantaged because of it. The first formulation suggests a stronger prejudice against equity; it is responsible for judicial statements that injunctions are an extraordinary remedy.

Douglas Laycock, Injunctions and the Irreparable Injury Rule (Book Review), 57 Tex.L.Rev. 1065, 1071–72 (1979).

NOTE ON THE DECLINING IMPORTANCE OF THE INADEQUATE REMEDY AT LAW RULE

The rhetoric of the rule does not fool most modern courts. Rather they weigh the practical merits of equitable and legal relief. As a result, if the plaintiff has a good reason for preferring an injunction to damages, that reason is usually good enough to persuade a court to grant injunctive relief, except where there is some special reason for avoiding injunctive relief, such as concern for placing a prior restraint on speech. This does not mean that plaintiffs will always have a good reason, but it does mean that the inadequate remedy at law rule lacks the generalized importance that the maxim suggests.

Professor Laycock has tested this suggestion by systematically surveying modern cases. The Death of the Irreparable Injury Rule, 103 Harv.L.Rev. 687 (1990). See also The Death of the Irreparable Injury Rule (1991) (book version of article containing additional analysis). He notes that plaintiffs seek compensatory damages more often than injunctions for a variety of reasons: specific relief may be impossible after the breach; plaintiffs may prefer damages to coerced performance by unwilling defendants; or, compensatory damages may be equivalent to specific performance, as when the promised performance is the payment of money. That plaintiffs seek damages more often than injunctions does not mean that courts usually say "no" to those plaintiffs who do seek injunctions.

Professor Laycock surveyed more than 1400 recent cases in which the plaintiffs sought specific relief and the courts discussed the irreparable injury rule or its analogues. In the vast majority of cases, the courts found that the irreparable injury rule was no bar to specific relief for the reasons outlined above. Relatively few cases held the legal remedies adequate. Most of these he attributes to reasons other than a generalized preference for legal remedies, such as preventing the plaintiff from getting an advantage over other creditors of the defendant.

DOUGLAS LAYCOCK, THE DEATH OF THE IRREPARABLE INJURY RULE

103 Harv.L.Rev. 687, 722–724 (1990)

* * * There are very few cases not subject to at least one of these doctrines for finding legal remedies inadequate or inapplicable. If plaintiff has any plausible need for specific relief, she can describe that need as irreparable injury and find ample precedent to support her claim. Yet there are still some cases denying specific relief and invoking the irreparable injury rule to support their decision. The results in the great bulk of these cases have nothing to do with a preference for legal remedies and can be explained on other grounds. * * *

There remain a handful of cases that can be explained on no ground other than the traditional understanding of the irreparable injury rule. These are cases in which plaintiff seeks some equitable remedy, and is remitted to a legal remedy instead, on the ground that the legal remedy would be adequate. These opinions do not reveal any special difficulty with the equitable remedy or any judicial hostility to the merits of plaintiff's case. There are remarkably few of these cases—fewer than I expected to find when I began this research—but they do occur. These remnants of the irreparable injury rule do not make a persuasive case for retaining the rule.

In a few of these cases, plaintiff is remitted to some legal form of specific relief, such as replevin, that will accomplish exactly what equity could have accomplished. The remedies may differ in means of enforcement, and sometimes these differences are important. But these cases do not present a choice between specific and substitutionary relief—plaintiff gets specific relief either way.

Most of the remaining cases refuse specific performance of contracts to sell goods. In some, it appears that the goods are fungible and the market is orderly; so far as the opinion reveals, plaintiff can easily and immediately exchange money damages for identical goods. Where that is true, the distinction between specific and substitutionary relief disappears. Unless the opinions are omitting critical facts, it is hard to see why plaintiff seeks specific performance in such a case, why defendant resists it, or why we have a rule that encourages the parties to litigate it.

In these cases, the legal remedy really is as effective as the equitable remedy. Either way, plaintiff gets identical goods, with damages for any difference in price, he gets the goods at the same effective cost. If he measures damages by the difference between the contract price and the cover price, the amount of damages does not even depend on anyone's estimate of value. These cases arise either from bad lawyering or from critical undisclosed facts. If critical facts that drive the litigation are omitted from the opinion, it can only be because the irreparable injury rule has diverted the court's attention from the real issue.

These cases shade into those where the goods are replaceable only with difficulty, or only with similar but not identical goods. Plaintiff argues that cover is difficult or impossible; the court finds that cover is possible and damages are adequate. Where cover is difficult, a majority of cases grant specific relief, but a substantial minority do not. So long as the rule persists that damages are an adequate remedy for breach of a contract to sell goods that are available elsewhere, some cases will fall near the line and some of these cases will be decided each way. We can argue whether this line is worth drawing and litigating over, but for now it survives. It is the principal remnant of the irreparable injury rule.

In the very few cases remaining, damages are plainly not as good for plaintiff as specific relief, but the court fails to recognize the inadequacy or considers it insufficient to satisfy the rule. Plaintiff is worse off for being remitted to damages, and the opinion does not indicate any way in which defendant or the judicial system is better off. Unless there are countervailing considerations that do not appear in the opinions, the irreparable injury rule leads the court to a bad result in these cases. Remarkably, I have found only three modern cases of this sort [out of the sample of 1400 cases]. * * *

Justice Holmes wrote that "[t]he duty to keep a contract at common law means a prediction that you must pay damages if you do not keep it,— and nothing else." Oliver W. Holmes, The Path of the Law, 10 Harv. L.Rev. 457, 462 (1897). Is that still true?

NOTE ON WHETHER TO ABANDON THE INADEQUACY REQUIREMENT

Professor Laycock views the rule as a source of confusion and litigation costs. Professor Dobbs believes that defendants raise it as a dilatory tactic rather than out of a preference for the legal remedy. Dan B. Dobbs, Law of Remedies § 2.5(3) (2d ed.1993). So why not get rid of it?

The rule's original purpose having vanished with the merger of law and equity, several additional purposes have been suggested. One purpose is to preserve the defendant's option in cases at law to have issues of fact heard by a jury. But, the availability of a jury at law does not so much explain the rule as throw into question the lack of a jury in equity. Moreover, the few jurisdictions that provide a jury in equity still pay homage to the inadequacy rule. E.g., Duke Power Co. v. City of High Point, 69 N.C.App. 335, 337, 317 S.E.2d 699, 700 (1984). The preference for law makes more sense where the alternative to an injunction is a criminal prosecution with not only a jury trial but also the many other protections of the criminal process. This purpose does not explain the supposed preference for civil remedies at law.

Another explanation for the irreparable injury rule is that injunctions pose problems for the court in both drafting and enforcement. E.g., Doug Rendleman, The Inadequate Remedy at Law Prerequisite to an Injunction, 33 U.Fla.L.Rev. 346, 353–58 (1981). This is sometimes true, as will be seen in Chapter 3. But, as the following section will show, there are doctrines that deny injunctive relief where it would unduly burden the court. Moreover, calculating and collecting damages can burden the court, as will be seen in Chapters 5 and 8. Whether the equitable or the legal remedy is more burdensome will vary with the case so that burden on the court cannot explain a systematic preference for remedies at law.

Another possible purpose of the rule is to avoid the injunction's intrusion on the defendant's liberty. For example, Miller may choose to keep dumping the waste and paying damages to Country Lodge if no injunction issues but, if one does issue, she has lost that choice. On the other hand, preferring the legal remedy takes away Country Lodge's ability to choose between preventing the wrong or collecting damages. So the cost of protecting the wrongdoer's liberty is infringing on the victim's liberty. Conceivably the defendant's liberty interest may be greater, but there is no reason to suppose that it is so in general. See, e.g., Doug Rendleman, Irreparability Resurrected? Does a Recalibrated Irreparable Injury Rule Threaten the Warren Court's Establishment Clause Legacy? 59 Wash. & Lee L.Rev. 1343 (2002).

A final explanation for the inadequate remedy at law rule is that it promotes efficient allocation of resources. Efficiency is "the relationship between the aggregate benefits of a situation and the aggregate costs of the situation * * *. In other words, efficiency corresponds to the 'size of the pie' [as opposed to] how it is sliced." A. Mitchell Polinsky, An Introduction to Law and Economics 7 (3d ed.2003). For instance, in the Country Lodge problem at the beginning of the chapter, an injunction prohibiting future nuisances might be inefficient because, as discussed, it might impose costs on Miller higher than its benefits to Country Lodge. But, as also seen, courts would regard Country Lodge's damage remedy as inadequate for many reasons. Even in cases where courts find the legal remedy inadequate, concerns about efficiency sometimes lead to denial of injunctive relief under the doctrine of balancing the equities, to be discussed in section D of this chapter. The present question is whether the concept of efficiency can justify the inadequate remedy at law rule where it still holds sway—contracts to deliver goods that are fungible or at least "reasonably" so and where cover is easy or at least "reasonably" so.

Suppose that A contracts to deliver a quantity of widgets to B for $18,000, but then C offers A $20,000 for the same widgets. As a naive form of the efficiency argument goes, specific performance might put the widgets into the hands of B, who values them less highly than C, while the damage remedy would ensure an efficient outcome. This is so, as the argument goes, because A would not breach unless the widgets were worth more to C than B because A would not sell to C unless the price was high enough to cover the cost of delivering the goods to C plus paying damages sufficient to make B whole.

However, this argument assumes that damages fully compensate B. Professor Alan Schwartz questions that assumption.

ALAN SCHWARTZ, THE CASE FOR SPECIFIC PERFORMANCE
89 Yale L.J. 271, 274–278 (1979)

* * *

II. Contract Remedies and the Compensation Goal

Specific performance is the most accurate method of achieving the compensation goal of contract remedies because it gives the promisee the precise performance that he purchased. The natural question, then, is why specific performance is not routinely available. Three explanations of the law's restrictions on specific performance are possible. First, the law's commitment to the compensation goal may be less than complete; restricting specific performance may reflect an inarticulate reluctance to pursue the compensation goal fully. Second, damages may generally be fully compensatory. In that event, expanding the availability of specific performance would create opportunities for promisees to exploit promisors by threatening to compel, or actually compelling, performance, without furthering the compensation goal. The third explanation is that concerns of efficiency or liberty may justify restricting specific performance, despite its greater accuracy; specific performance might generate higher transaction costs than the damage remedy, or interfere more with the liberty interests of promisors. The first justification is beyond the scope of the analysis here. The second and third explanations will be examined in detail. * * *

It is useful to begin by examining the paradigm case for granting specific performance under current law, the case of unique goods. When a promisor breaches and the promisee can make a transaction that substitutes for the performance the promisor failed to render, the promisee will be fully compensated if he receives the additional amount necessary to purchase the substitute plus the costs of making a second transaction. In some cases, however, such as those involving works of art, courts cannot identify which transactions the promisee would regard as substitutes because that information often is in the exclusive possession of the promisee. Moreover, it is difficult for a court to assess the accuracy of a promisee's claim. For example, if the promisor breaches a contract to sell a rare emerald, the promisee may claim that only the Hope Diamond would give him equal satisfaction, and thus may sue for the price difference between the emerald and the diamond. It would be difficult for a court to know whether this claim is true. If the court seeks to award money damages, it has three choices: granting the price differential, which may overcompensate the promisee; granting the dollar value of the promisee's foregone satisfaction as estimated by the court, which may overcompensate or undercompensate; or granting restitution of any sums paid, which undercompensates the promisee. The promisee is fully compensated without risk of overcompensation or undercompensation if the remedy of specific performance is available to him and its use encouraged by the doctrine that damages must be foreseeable and certain.

If specific performance is the appropriate remedy in such cases, there are three reasons why it should be routinely available. The first reason is that in many cases damages actually are undercompensatory. Although promisees are entitled to incidental damages, such damages are difficult to monetize. They consist primarily of the costs of finding and making a second deal, which generally involve the expenditure of time rather than cash; attaching a dollar value to such opportunity costs is quite difficult. Breach can also cause frustration and anger, especially in a consumer context, but these costs also are not recoverable.

Substitution damages, the court's estimate of the amount the promisee needs to purchase an adequate substitute, also may be inaccurate in many cases less dramatic than the emerald hypothetical discussed above. This is largely because of product differentiation and early obsolescence. As product differentiation becomes more common, the supply of products that will substitute precisely for the promisor's performance is reduced. For example, even during the period when there is an abundant supply of new [Nissans] for sale, two-door, two-tone [Nissans] with mag wheels, stereo, and air conditioning may be scarce in some local markets. * * * [A] damage award meant to enable a promisee to purchase "another car" could be undercompensatory.

In addition, problems of prediction often make it difficult to put a promisee in the position where he would have been had his promisor performed. If a breach by a contractor would significantly delay or prevent completion of a construction project and the project differs in important respects from other projects—for example, a department store in a different location than previous stores—courts may be reluctant to award "speculative" lost profits attributable to the breach.

Second, promisees have economic incentives to sue for damages when damages are likely to be fully compensatory. A breaching promisor is reluctant to perform and may be hostile. [Especially when the performance is complex and takes place over time, it may well be costly and time consuming if not impossible to hold the promisor to performing satisfactorily.] * * * The very fact that a promisee requests specific performance thus implies that damages are an inadequate remedy.

The third reason why courts should permit promisees to elect routinely the remedy of specific performance is that promisees possess better information than courts as to both the adequacy of damages and the difficulties of coercing performance. Promisees know better than courts whether the damages a court is likely to award would be adequate because promisees are more familiar with the costs that breach imposes on them. In addition, promisees generally know more about their promisors than do courts. * * *

In sum, restrictions on the availability of specific performance cannot be justified on the basis that damage awards are usually compensatory. On the contrary, the compensation goal implies that specific performance should be routinely available. This is because damage awards actually are undercompensatory in more cases than is commonly supposed; the fact of a specific performance request is itself good evidence that damages would be inadequate; and courts should delegate to promisees the decision of which remedy best satisfies the compensation goal. Further, expanding the availability of specific performance would not result in greater exploitation of promisors. Promisees would seldom abuse the power to determine when specific performance should be awarded because of the strong incentives that promisees face to seek damages when these would be even approximately compensatory.

III. Specific Performance and Efficiency

[S]uppose that the [compensation] goal rests on * * * an assumption that compensating disappointed promisees fully is less costly than not compensating them fully. If the broader availability of specific performance would generate transaction costs that exceed the costs of undercompensation the equitable remedy would avoid, then current restrictions on specific performance would be justified. On the other hand, if the compensation goal rests on a moral notion that promises should be kept, * * * then specific performance is a preferable remedy to damages even though it might generate higher costs. * * *

Both possible bases of the compensation goal thus would support the routine availability of specific performance unless specific performance is a more costly remedy than damages. * * *

Notes

1. How successful is Professor Schwartz in dealing with the contention that promisees will exploit specific performance to get payments that go beyond compensation? Would that be extortion? If A had stolen the goods from B rather than failed to deliver them so that liability is in conversion rather than contract and B then secures an injunction requiring A to return the goods, would it be morally repugnant for B to offer to give up the injunction in return for a payment that exceeds compensation? Courts would not hesitate to enjoin conversion because it is viewed as morally repugnant. Why not view breach of contract the same way?

2. Professor Yorio has argued that the appropriate response to damages being undercompensatory is to change the measure of damages to make them fully compensatory rather than to grant specific performance. Edward Yorio, In Defense of Money Damages for Breach of Contract, 82 Colum.L.Rev. 1365, 1367–70 (1982). He also argues that specific performance is far less flexible about the measure of relief than monetary relief is so that damages can be adjusted to take account of a wide variety of circumstances. Edward Yorio, A Defense of Equitable Defenses, 51 Ohio St.L.J. 1201 (1990).

Professor Schwartz does not evaluate the issue of whether the law should be dedicated to complete compensation. Should it? See Jeffrey Standen, The Fallacy of Full Compensation, 73 Wash.U.L.Q. 145 (1995).

3. Even if compensatory damages are undercompensatory, they may provide a more efficient remedy than specific performance if the new buyer, C, still values the goods more than the contract buyer, B. But if C truly values the widgets more than B, wouldn't C make B an offer for the widgets that B would accept, thereby achieving an efficient outcome? After all, the difference between the values that B and C place on the widgets are potential gains of trade. Similarly, A could pay B for the right to deliver the widgets to C.

Judge Posner asserts that "the seller [A] can always pay the buyer [B] to surrender the right of specific performance and presumably will do so if a substitute transfer [to C] would yield a higher price. But the additional negotiation will not be costless." Richard A. Posner, Economic Analysis of Law § 4.12 at 131 (7th ed.2007). "Transaction costs" include the costs of identifying those with whom one needs to bargain, getting together with them, bargaining with them, and enforcing the bargain. Judge Posner's point is that specific performance generates two bargains—one between A and B to terminate B's right to specific performance and another between A and C to sell the widgets. In contrast, the damage remedy requires only one bargain—between A and C.

Professor Schwartz responds, in a portion of the article not included above, that there are other factors to consider. Alan Schwartz, 89 Yale L.J. at 284–291. If A has to deliver to B, then B could sell the widgets to C, which would mean only one bargain. Or A could deliver to B and then still sell to C by buying substitute goods in the market, just as B would have had to do if relegated to a damage remedy. It would be harder for A to buy substitute goods where there is no smoothly functioning market, but those are precisely the cases where courts are most likely to grant specific performance. Moreover, under the damage remedy, B would have to take A to court to get the damages or else they would have to settle the suit, another bargain, but either would result in transaction costs. So which remedy yields lower transaction costs? If the damage remedy yields lower transaction costs, are they low enough to offset the effects of undercompensatory damages? Many scholars have joined the debate on whether specific performance or damages is the more efficient remedy. See Jeffrey Standen, The Fallacy of Full Compensation, 73 Wash.U.L.Q. 145, 146 n.5 (1995).

Note on Constitutional and Statutory Variations on the Inadequacy Requirement

Constitutions sometimes dictate the choice between injunctive and legal relief. For example, by permitting the taking of property for a public use through the payment of compensation, the fifth amendment effectively denies the property owner injunctive relief. See U.S. Const. amend. V; Kelo v. City of New London, 545 U.S. 469, 125 S.Ct. 2655, 162 L.Ed.2d 439 (2005). For another example, the first amendment's prior restraint doctrine makes it much more difficult to enjoin speech than to rectify the harm done after the fact through an action for damages. New York Times Co. v. United States, 403 U.S. 713, 91 S.Ct. 2140, 29 L.Ed.2d 822 (1971).

Statutes sometimes alter the inadequate remedy at law rule. Thus, the Tax Injunction Act provides that "the district courts shall not enjoin, suspend or restrain the assessment, levy or collection of any tax under State law where a plain, speedy and efficient remedy may be had in the courts of such State." 28 U.S.C. § 1341. Where the only state remedy to overassessment of a tax is to pay the tax and seek a refund, the denial of a federal injunction in effect relegates the taxpayer to a remedy at law. While the Tax Injunction Act makes federal injunctions available in terms that parallel the traditional formulation of the inadequacy rule, federal courts construe the statute more strictly than the inadequacy rule. Compare Rosewell v. LaSalle Nat. Bank, 450 U.S. 503, 101 S.Ct. 1221, 67 L.Ed.2d 464 (1981)(denying injunctive relief against state tax overassessment although state remedy requires two years to get a refund and denies interest on the refund) and National Private Truck Council, Inc. v. Oklahoma Tax Commission, 515 U.S. 582, 115 S.Ct. 2351, 132 L.Ed.2d 509 (1995) (denying both injunctive relief and declaratory judgments when a tax refund, an adequate remedy at law, is available) with Bowen v. Massachusetts, 487 U.S. 879, 108 S.Ct. 2722, 101 L.Ed.2d 749 (1988)(approving injunction against federal withholding of grant on basis that remedy at law would take several years, thereby creating uncertainty). Perhaps the outcomes differ because the Tax Injunction Act has purposes that differ from the inadequacy rule—to protect state sovereignty and the fiscal stability of state and local governments. See also, e.g., 28 U.S.C. § 1342 (limiting injunctions against administrative decisions affecting utility rates); Norris–LaGuardia Act, 29 U.S.C. §§ 101–115 (barring injunctions against peaceful conduct arising out of labor disputes).

The D.C. Circuit has held that, despite the Anti–Injunction Act, a taxpayer was not required to plead irreparable injury or lack of an adequate remedy at law in order to seek an injunction to prevent the Internal Revenue Service from levying his bank account to assess an alleged deficiency. The taxpayer alleged that the IRS had levied his bank account without first mailing him a notice of deficiency, as required by statute. In so doing, the D.C. Circuit rejected the reasoning of three other circuits, which had held that Congress had not intended to disturb the traditional prerequisites for equitable relief. Gardner v. United States, 211 F.3d 1305 (D.C.Cir.2000), cert. denied, 531 U.S. 1114, 121 S.Ct. 860, 148 L.Ed.2d 773 (2001).

Legislatures sometimes provide that courts should grant injunctions without regard to the inadequacy rule. E.g., Cal.Water Code § 13361(c) ("it shall not be necessary to allege or prove * * * that the remedy at law is inadequate"); Cal.Civil Code § 3387 ("[i]t is to be presumed that the breach of an agreement to transfer real property cannot be adequately relieved by pecuniary compensation"). Courts have interpreted some statutes that do not explicitly set aside the inadequacy rule as implicitly doing so. Courts reason that the legislature presumed any violation of the statute would cause irreparable injury (e.g., People ex rel. Edgar v. Miller, 110 Ill.App.3d 264, 65 Ill.Dec. 814, 441 N.E.2d 1328, 1331 (1982)) or that there is inherent judicial power to enforce legislative policy (e.g., Blim v. Western Electric Co., 731 F.2d 1473, 1478 (10th Cir.), cert. denied, 469 U.S. 874, 105 S.Ct. 233, 83 L.Ed.2d

161 (1984)). How does this claim of inherent judicial power square with the cases in Chapter 1(B)?

Finally, a statute may provide that equitable doctrines, such as the inadequacy rule, shall apply. For a very important instance, the Administrative Procedure Act states that "[n]othing herein * * * affects * * * the power or duty of the court to * * * deny relief on any other appropriate legal or equitable ground * * *." 5 U.S.C. § 702(1).

Analogously to the inadequacy doctrine, the statute governing clean up of toxic waste bars courts from considering most challenges to EPA clean-up actions or administrative orders to clean up except after the fact, by which time the relief is substitutionary or penal rather than specific. Comprehensive Environmental Response, Compensation, and Liability Act, 42 U.S.C. § 9613. The statute opts for after-the-fact review, even though it often is not fully adequate to protect the challenger's rightful position, in order to avoid litigation delays in clean ups. For another analogy, consider the exhaustion of administrative remedies doctrine that requires courts to deny relief if the plaintiff has an adequate administrative remedy. E.g., Booth v. Churner, 532 U.S. 731, 121 S.Ct. 1819, 149 L.Ed.2d 958 (2001) (Prison Litigation Reform Act requires administrative exhaustion even where grievance process does not permit award of money damages and prisoner seeks only money damages, as long as grievance tribunal has authority to take some responsive action).

United States v. Microsoft Corp., 147 F.3d 935 (D.C.Cir.1998), in reversing the grant of preliminary injunction for lack of notice, discussed the United States' assertion that a court should presume irreparable injury when a statute is violated. The court held, in the spirit of *Hecht v. Bowles*, and relying on a line of cases that can be traced back to it, that courts should presume that a legislature intended to change the normal rules of equity only when the statute clearly manifests such an intention.

D. BALANCING THE EQUITIES

1. THE RATIONALE FOR BALANCING

PROBLEM: COUNTRY LODGE V. MILLER (REPRISED)
BALANCING THE EQUITIES

Recall that Miller set up her cider press to dump waste apple mash into the river in order to save $20,000 a year. Suppose that Country Lodge has satisfied all the prerequisites for injunctive relief. Miller asks the court to award damages rather than grant an injunction on the ground that the cost to her of complying is greater than the benefit that Country Lodge would derive from the injunction.

(a) What result if the action is brought before the cider press is built (the action being ripe because Miller's intentions are clear)?

(b) What result if compliance would cost Miller no more now than when she built the press and it generates sufficient profits to pay that cost?

(c) What result if compliance would cost Miller not only $20,000 a year, but also an additional one-time expenditure of $50,000 to retrofit the cider press plant, which would have been unnecessary if she had built the press to avoid discharging effluent into the river in the first place? If these retrofit costs were $1,000,000? If these retrofit costs would put her out of business? Should the judge postpone the effective date of the injunctive relief by a month if doing so would reduce the retrofit cost from $50,000 to $5,000?

(d) Should the court refuse to listen to Miller's claim of undue hardship if she had promised Country Lodge that there would be no nuisance? If she knew her planned conduct would be illegal?

(e) Should the court be more likely to deny an injunction on the grounds of undue hardship if Country Lodge knew that Miller's operation would create a nuisance but did not try to prevent it before Miller began to build her cider press?

(f) Should Miller be able to claim undue hardship if liability arises from her building the press on Country Lodge's land rather than creating a nuisance in the river? If liability arises from a contract to supply cider?

(g) In deciding whether a hardship is undue, should the court consider the benefit to nonparties of stopping the pollution?

(h) Should the court refuse to listen to Miller's claim of undue hardship if her liability arises from a constitutional prohibition instead of common law nuisance? From a statutory prohibition?

Balancing the equities is the next part of the equitable process by which a court weighs the impact of issuing the injunction. The court considers the specific equities of the parties and the injunction's practical effect in deciding whether to issue an injunction and determine its proper scope. Rules of proportionality provide that the courts should issue balanced injunctions that match the scope of the threatened harm. However, proportionality is colored by the equities of the case. The Supreme Court has at times depicted the litigants in injunctive cases as the good, the bad, and the ugly: defendants are good, well-meaning public institutions; plaintiffs are bad, greedy, overreaching parties seeking windfall gains; and courts are ugly and overzealous in their abuse of equitable power. Tracy A. Thomas, Proportionality and the Supreme Court's Jurisprudence of Remedies, 59 Hastings L.J. 73 (2007). The Supreme Court has used remedial proportionality as a strict standard of judicial review that often gives plaintiffs less than their expected rightful position.

For example, in Ayotte v. Planned Parenthood, 546 U.S. 320, 126 S.Ct. 961, 163 L.Ed.2d 812 (2006), the Supreme Court vacated an injunction invalidating New Hampshire's parental notification abortion statute, finding that "invalidating a statute entirely is not always necessary or justified, for lower courts may be able to render narrow declaratory and injunctive relief." Id. at 323. The Court was concerned with the federalism implications of its remedy for the defendant, the New Hampshire legislature. It found that it should not use its equitable discretion to devise a remedy that would rewrite state law and frustrate the intent of the legislature as elected representatives of the people.

Balancing the equities allows a judge to withhold injunctive relief altogether or to issue an injunction that stops short of fully achieving the plaintiff's rightful position because of undue hardship or unfairness to the defendant, even when the plaintiff's remedies at law are inadequate. This section considers what might justify the court's power to compromise the plaintiff's rightful position, the limits on this power, and whether it undercuts the goals that the common law, constitutions, or statutes seek to achieve.

Professor Douglas Laycock suggests the following black letter rule for balancing the equities:

A court should deny permanent specific relief if:

(a) the relief would impose hardship on defendant, and

(b) that hardship is substantially disproportionate to the disadvantage to plaintiff of receiving only substitutionary relief.

In balancing the interests, a court should consider the relative fault of each litigant.

Douglas Laycock, The Death of the Irreparable Injury Rule, 103 Harv. L.Rev. 688, 749–50 (1990). This formulation suggests that the court does not simply balance the injunction's advantages to the plaintiff against the burden on the defendant but instead balances the advantage to the plaintiff of specific rather than substitutionary relief against the disadvantage to the defendant of specific rather than substitutionary relief.

NOTE ON WHEN INJUNCTIONS ARE EFFICIENT

As balancing the equities seeks in part (but only in part) to avoid issuing injunctions that result in inefficiency, it is useful to consider when an injunction will lead to inefficiency. Suppose that the cost to Miller of complying with an injunction to stop the nuisance is $20,000 a year or more and the benefit to Country Lodge is $10,000 a year or more. If the court does not know how much more than those dollar amounts for each party, then it cannot know whether implementing the injunction would be efficient. After all, if implementation would cost Miller $1,000,000 to retrofit her operation plus $20,000 a year in added operating expenses and all that Country Lodge loses is $10,000 a year in profits, then the injunction is grossly inefficient. But so would be failing to grant an injunction if complying with it involves no retrofit costs for Miller but Country Lodge's owners have an aesthetic attachment to an unspoiled view of the river, which they value at $100,000 a year. In addition to these two extreme possibilities, there are a host of intermediate ones.

Inefficiency is not a problem for the court if it can be confident that the parties will bargain to reach an efficient result. If the court grants an injunction when Miller's cost to stop the pollution is $20,000 and Country Lodge's benefit is $10,000, they both can gain from a deal in which Miller pays something more than $10,000, but less than $20,000 in return for Country Lodge giving up the injunction. Similarly, if the court fails to grant an injunction when Miller's cost is $20,000 but Country Lodge's benefit is $100,000, they both can gain if Country Lodge agrees to pay Miller something more than $20,000, but less than $100,000 to stop polluting. The size of the payment within these ranges depends upon their bargaining positions and tactics. Whether they actually strike a deal depends upon what economists call "transaction costs." Transaction costs include the time spent bargaining and attorney fees. If the transaction costs are zero, then by definition the parties will bargain to achieve an efficient outcome regardless of whether the remedy is an injunction or compensatory damages or even if Miller is held not liable so that no relief is granted. In Judge Calabresi and Mr. Melamed's terminology (reread the passage at p. 34), the law's choice of entitlements and whether to back them up with a property rule or a liability rule matters to the distribution of income, but not to efficiency.

Suppose, however, that the transaction costs are sufficiently high that the parties cannot bargain to an outcome different from the one that the court decrees. If the court knows the real stakes for the parties, then it can achieve efficiency by issuing an injunction if and only if the costs of the pollution exceeded the costs of its abatement. But, the court will often have trouble determining the true stakes for the parties because the stakes are often subjective or difficult for outsiders to estimate and each party has a reason to exaggerate.

If the court does not know the costs of abatement, but does know the real costs of the pollution to Country Lodge, it can still ensure an efficient outcome by using a damage remedy because Miller would still abate the pollution if the costs of pollution exceed the costs of abatement. Similarly, if the court does not know the real costs of the pollution to Country Lodge, but does know the costs of abatement, it could grant Country Lodge an injunction but require it to pay Miller for the costs of its implementation. This would force Country Lodge's owners to put their money where their mouths are as to the real worth to them of stopping the pollution, but would be unfair because Miller is the one at fault.

The court has a number of other ways to deal with uncertainty about the stakes to the parties, none of them wholly satisfactory. It could estimate the costs of pollution and the costs of abatement and act as if the estimates are accurate, but this course may well lead to inefficiency. Perhaps in part to safeguard plaintiffs from this danger, courts usually require defendants to show that their hardship is not just greater, but much greater than the benefit of granting an injunction. The court could also grant Country Lodge an injunction on the theory that the barriers to efficiency posed by transaction costs are less important than the barriers to efficiency posed by the errors that the court could make in assessing the real costs to the parties.

This final alternative makes it important to consider when transaction costs are likely to be high or low. In the case of Country Lodge and Miller, the time and costs are likely to be small relative to the large monetary stakes because only two parties need to bargain and each knows with whom to do so. But transaction costs can include more than time and costs. Country Lodge and Miller may engage in "strategic bargaining." If Miller knows that Country Lodge would prefer to receive any payment more than $10,000 to an injunction and Country Lodge knows that Miller would prefer to make any payment less than $50,000 to an injunction, Country Lodge may hold out for a payment close to $50,000 while Miller may hold out for a payment close to $10,000. The upshot could be stalemate.

There is potential for such strategic bargaining when there is a "bilateral monopoly." Country Lodge and Miller are both monopolists with respect to the subject of their bargaining—Country Lodge's right under the injunction to stop Miller from committing the nuisance—because Miller is the only one who would want to pay Country Lodge to forego the injunction and Country Lodge is the only one who can sell it. (Does an order requiring specific performance of a contract create a bilateral monopoly and thereby the risk of strategic bargaining?)

Transaction costs can also be high if there are many potential plaintiffs. Suppose that there are 1000 Country Lodges, each damaged $10 a year by Miller's nuisance so that the total harm done by the nuisance is $10,000 a year. Here, transaction costs would prevent bargaining to a more efficient result. (The class action device can sometimes reduce some of these transaction costs.) If any plaintiff can get an injunction as of right, Miller must make a deal with each or risk wasting its payments. The transaction costs include tracking down and reaching agreement with all the plaintiffs, a time-consuming and expensive undertaking. Some plaintiffs probably could not be found or would refuse to make a deal. Other plaintiffs may insist on more than their fair share of the payment so that disputes among the plaintiffs are likely to arise. Nuisance cases are more likely than trespass cases to have many potential plaintiffs because a trespass typically injures only one property while a nuisance typically injures many. However, simulations suggest that when potential plaintiffs number a few dozen or so, they bargain cooperatively and that strategic bargaining would not block efficient bargains. See, e.g., Elizabeth Hoffman & Matthew L. Spitzer, Experimental Law and Economics: An Introduction, 85 Colum.L.Rev. 991, 1009–13 (1985); Mark Kelman, Comment on Hoffman and Spitzer's Experimental Law and Economics, 85 Colum.L.Rev. 1037 (1985).

==Judge Calabresi and Mr. Melamed conclude that the courts are being efficient in routinely granting injunctions in trespass cases because, in them, transaction costs are unlikely to prevent the parties from bargaining to an efficient outcome.== Guido Calabresi & A. Douglas Melamed, Property Rules, Liability Rules, and Inalienability: One View of the Cathedral, 85 Harv.L.Rev. 1089, 1124–27 (1972). If Miller wants to put a store on Country Lodge's property and that is worth more to Miller than the detriment to Country Lodge, transaction costs are unlikely to stand in the way of a deal. Even if Country Lodge has an injunction against Miller's erecting a store on its property, there is no bilateral monopoly because Miller could buy land from some other neighbor and Country Lodge could sell the right to use its property to someone other than Miller. Moreover, it takes only two parties to make this bargain. Judge Calabresi and Mr. Melamed argue that a court should grant an injunction if the transaction costs of avoiding it are low because the court thereby avoids the risk of misjudging the parties' costs. For further general reading on the efficiency of injunctions, see A. Mitchell Polinsky, An Introduction to Law and Economics 13–27 (3d ed.2003).

As noted in Section C(2) of this chapter, the fifth amendment allows takings of property for a public use if "just compensation" is paid. In Judge Calabresi and Mr. Melamed's terms, the amendment allows the government to convert a property owner's entitlement protected by a property rule (an injunction) into an entitlement protected by a liability rule (compensatory damages). Is that efficient? Is it fair to give the government all the gains of trade? See Kelo v. City of New London, 545 U.S. 469, 125 S.Ct. 2655, 162 L.Ed.2d 439 (2005) (city's exercise of eminent domain power in furtherance of economic development plan satisfied constitutional "public use" requirement). Should Miller be able to take Country Lodge's entitlement against nuisances merely by paying just compensation, as the government could do? Or is Country Lodge's getting an injunction and then selling it to Miller in excess of the real costs of pollution nothing but extortion?

eBAY INC. v. MERCEXCHANGE, L.L.C.

Supreme Court of the United States, 2006
547 U.S. 388, 126 S.Ct. 1837, 164 L.Ed.2d 641

JUSTICE THOMAS delivered the opinion of the Court.

Ordinarily, a federal court considering whether to award permanent injunctive relief to a prevailing plaintiff applies the four-factor test historically employed by courts of equity. Petitioners eBay Inc. and Half.com, Inc., argue that this traditional test applies to disputes arising under the Patent Act. We agree and, accordingly, vacate the judgment of the Court of Appeals.

I

Petitioner eBay operates a popular Internet Web site that allows private sellers to list goods they wish to sell, either through an auction or at a fixed price. Petitioner Half.com, now a wholly owned subsidiary of eBay, operates a similar Web site. Respondent MercExchange, L.L.C., holds a number of patents, including a business method patent for an electronic market designed to facilitate the sale of goods between private individuals by establishing a central authority to promote trust among participants. See U.S. Patent No. 5,845,265. MercExchange sought to license its patent to eBay and Half.com, as it had previously done with other companies, but the parties failed to reach an agreement. MercExchange subsequently filed a patent infringement suit against eBay and Half.com in the United States District Court for the Eastern District of Virginia. A jury found that MercExchange's patent was valid, that eBay and Half.com had infringed that patent, and that an award of damages was appropriate.

Following the jury verdict, the District Court denied MercExchange's motion for permanent injunctive relief. The Court of Appeals for the

Federal Circuit reversed, applying its general rule that courts will issue permanent injunctions against patent infringement absent exceptional circumstances. We granted certiorari to determine the appropriateness of this general rule.

II

According to well-established principles of equity, a plaintiff seeking a permanent injunction must satisfy a four-factor test before a court may grant such relief. A plaintiff must demonstrate: (1) that it has suffered an irreparable injury; (2) that remedies available at law, such as monetary damages, are inadequate to compensate for that injury; (3) that, considering the balance of hardships between the plaintiff and defendant, a remedy in equity is warranted; and (4) that the public interest would not be disserved by a permanent injunction. See, e.g., Weinberger v. Romero–Barcelo, 456 U.S. 305, 311–313, 102 S.Ct. 1798, 72 L.Ed.2d 91 (1982); Amoco Production Co. v. Gambell, 480 U.S. 531, 542, 107 S.Ct. 1396, 94 L.Ed.2d 542 (1987). The decision to grant or deny permanent injunctive relief is an act of equitable discretion by the district court, reviewable on appeal for abuse of discretion. See, e.g., *Romero-Barcelo*, 456 U.S., at 320, 102 S.Ct. 1798.

These familiar principles apply with equal force to disputes arising under the Patent Act. As this Court has long recognized, a major departure from the long tradition of equity practice should not be lightly implied. Ibid.; see also *Amoco*, supra, at 542, 107 S.Ct. 1396. Nothing in the Patent Act indicates that Congress intended such a departure. To the contrary, the Patent Act expressly provides that injunctions may issue in accordance with the principles of equity. 35 U.S.C. § 283.

To be sure, the Patent Act also declares that patents shall have the attributes of personal property, § 261, including the right to exclude others from making, using, offering for sale, or selling the invention, § 154(a)(1). According to the Court of Appeals, this statutory right to exclude alone justifies its general rule in favor of permanent injunctive relief. But the creation of a right is distinct from the provision of remedies for violations of that right. Indeed, the Patent Act itself indicates that patents shall have the attributes of personal property [s]ubject to the provisions of this title, 35 U.S.C. § 261, including, presumably, the provision that injunctive relief may issue only in accordance with the principles of equity, § 283.

This approach is consistent with our treatment of injunctions under the Copyright Act. Like a patent owner, a copyright holder possesses the right to exclude others from using his property. Fox Film Corp. v. Doyal, 286 U.S. 123, 127, 52 S.Ct. 546, 76 L.Ed. 1010 (1932); see also id., at 127–128, 52 S.Ct. 546 (A copyright, like a patent, is at once the equivalent given by the public for benefits bestowed by the genius and meditations and skill of individuals, and the incentive to further efforts for the same important objects (internal quotation marks omitted)). Like the Patent Act, the Copyright Act provides that courts may grant injunctive relief on such terms as it may deem reasonable to prevent or restrain infringement of a copyright. 17 U.S.C. § 502(a). And as in our decision today, this Court has consistently rejected invitations to replace traditional equitable considerations with a rule that an injunction automatically follows a determination that a copyright has been infringed. See, e.g., New York Times Co. v. Tasini, 533 U.S. 483, 505, 121 S.Ct. 2381, 150 L.Ed.2d 500 (2001).

Neither the District Court nor the Court of Appeals below fairly applied these traditional equitable principles in deciding respondent's motion for a permanent injunction. Although the District Court recited the traditional four-factor test, it appeared to adopt certain expansive principles suggesting that injunctive relief could not issue in a broad swath of cases. Most notably, it concluded that a plaintiff's willingness to license its patents and its lack of commercial activity in practicing the patents would be sufficient to establish that the patent holder would not suffer irreparable harm if an injunction did not issue. But traditional equitable principles do not permit such broad classifications. For example, some patent holders, such as university researchers or self-made inventors, might reasonably prefer to license their patents, rather than undertake efforts to secure the financing necessary to bring their works to market themselves. Such patent holders may be able to satisfy the traditional four-factor test, and we see no basis for categorically denying them the opportunity to do so. To the extent that the District Court adopted such a categorical rule, then, its analysis cannot be squared with the principles of equity adopted by Congress. The court's categorical rule is also in tension with Continental Paper Bag Co. v. Eastern Paper Bag Co., 210 U.S. 405, 422–430, 28 S.Ct. 748, 52 L.Ed. 1122 (1908), which rejected the contention that a court of equity has no jurisdiction to grant injunctive relief to a patent holder who has unreasonably declined to use the patent.

In reversing the District Court, the Court of Appeals departed in the opposite direction from the four-factor test. The court articulated a general rule, unique to patent disputes, that a permanent injunction will issue once infringement and validity have been adjudged. The court further indicated that injunctions should be denied only in the unusual case, under exceptional circumstances and in rare instances ... to protect the public interest. Just as the District Court erred in its categorical denial of injunctive relief, the Court of Appeals erred in its categorical grant of such relief. Cf. Roche Products v. Bolar Pharmaceutical Co., 733 F.2d 858, 865 (C.A.Fed.1984) (recognizing the considerable discretion district courts have in determining whether the facts of a situation require it to issue an injunction).

Because we conclude that neither court below correctly applied the traditional four-factor framework that governs the award of injunctive relief, we vacate the judgment of the Court of Appeals, so that the District Court may apply that framework in the first instance. In doing so, we take no position on whether permanent injunctive relief should or should not issue in this particular case, or indeed in any number of other disputes arising under the Patent Act. We hold only that the decision whether to grant or deny injunctive relief rests within the equitable discretion of the district courts, and that such discretion must be exercised consistent with traditional principles of equity, in patent disputes no less than in other cases governed by such standards.

Accordingly, we vacate the judgment of the Court of Appeals, and remand for further proceedings consistent with this opinion.

CHIEF JUSTICE ROBERTS, with whom JUSTICE SCALIA and JUSTICE GINSBURG join, concurring.

I agree with the Court's holding that the decision whether to grant or deny injunctive relief rests within the equitable discretion of the district courts, and that such discretion must be exercised consistent with traditional principles of equity, in patent disputes no less than in other cases governed by such standards, and I join the opinion of the Court. That opinion rightly rests on the proposition that a major departure from the long tradition of equity practice should not be lightly implied. Weinberger v. Romero–Barcelo, 456 U.S. 305, 320, 102 S.Ct. 1798, 72 L.Ed.2d 91 (1982).

From at least the early 19th century, courts have granted injunctive relief upon a finding of infringement in the vast majority of patent cases. This long tradition of equity practice is not surprising, given the difficulty of protecting a right to *exclude* through monetary remedies that allow an infringer to *use* an invention against the patentee's wishes—a difficulty that often implicates the first two factors of the traditional four-factor test. This historical practice, as the Court holds, does not *entitle* a patentee to a permanent injunction or justify a *general rule* that such injunctions should issue. The Federal Circuit itself so recognized in Roche Products, Inc. v. Bolar Pharmaceutical Co., 733 F.2d 858, 865–867 (1984). At the same time, there is a difference between exercising equitable discretion pursuant to the established four-factor test and writing on an entirely clean slate. Discretion is not whim, and limiting discretion according to legal standards helps promote the basic principle of justice that like cases should be decided alike. Martin v. Franklin Capital Corp., 546 U.S. 132, 139, 126 S.Ct. 704, 710, 163 L.Ed.2d 547 (2005). When it comes to discerning and applying those standards, in this area as others, a page of history is worth a volume of logic. New York Trust Co. v. Eisner, 256 U.S. 345, 349, 41 S.Ct. 506, 65 L.Ed. 963 (1921) (opinion for the Court by Holmes, J.).

JUSTICE KENNEDY, with whom JUSTICE STEVENS, JUSTICE SOUTER, and JUSTICE BREYER join, concurring.

The Court is correct, in my view, to hold that courts should apply the well-established, four-factor test—without resort to categorical rules—in deciding whether to grant injunctive relief in patent cases. The Chief Justice is also correct that history may be instructive in applying this test. The traditional practice of issuing injunctions against patent infringers, however, does not seem to rest on the difficulty of protecting a right to *exclude* through monetary remedies that allow an infringer to *use* an invention against the patentee's wishes. (Roberts, C.J., concurring). Both the terms of the Patent Act and the traditional view of injunctive relief accept that the existence of a right to exclude does not dictate the remedy for a violation of that right. To the extent earlier cases establish a pattern of granting an injunction against patent infringers almost as a matter of course, this pattern simply illustrates the result of the four-factor test in the contexts then prevalent. The lesson of the historical practice, therefore, is most helpful and instructive when the circumstances of a case bear substantial parallels to litigation the courts have confronted before.

In cases now arising trial courts should bear in mind that in many instances the nature of the patent being enforced and the economic function of the patent holder present considerations quite unlike earlier cases. An industry has developed in which firms use patents not as a basis for producing and selling goods but, instead, primarily for obtaining licensing fees. See FTC, To Promote Innovation: The Proper Balance of Competition and Patent Law and Policy, ch. 3, pp. 38–39 (Oct.2003), available at http://www.ftc.gov/os/2003/ 10/innovationrpt.pdf (as visited May 11, 2006, and available in Clerk of Court's case file). For these firms, an injunction, and the potentially serious sanctions arising from its violation, can be employed as a bargaining tool to charge exorbitant fees to companies that seek to buy licenses to practice the patent. When the patented invention is but a small component of the product the companies seek to produce and the threat of an injunction is employed simply for undue leverage in negotiations, legal damages may well be sufficient to compensate for the infringement and an injunction may not serve the public interest. In addition injunctive relief may have different consequences for the burgeoning number of patents over business methods, which were not of much economic and legal significance in earlier times. The potential vagueness and suspect validity of some of these patents may affect the calculus under the four-factor test.

The equitable discretion over injunctions, granted by the Patent Act, is well suited to allow courts to adapt to the rapid technological and legal developments in the patent system. For these reasons it should be recognized that district courts must determine whether past practice fits the circumstances of the cases before them. With these observations, I join the opinion of the Court.

Notes

1. The crux of the problem in *eBay* was the lower courts' use of presumptions (either for or against) to determine injunctive relief rather than the flexible considerations of equitable discretion. Tracy A. Thomas, eBay Rx, 2 Akron IP L.J.187 (2008). The Court unanimously reaffirmed that the decision to grant or deny a permanent injunction "rests within the equitable discretion of the district courts, and that such discretion must be exercised consistent with traditional principles of equity, in patent disputes no less than

in other cases." The defect in the prior decisions was the failure to apply the traditional test. How would the concurring Justices have applied that traditional test of equitable discretion in this case?

2. Would an injunction enjoining eBay from infringing the patents be efficient?

3. On remand in *eBay*, the district court denied the injunction, finding that money damages were adequate, and thus a necessary prerequisite to injunctive relief was not met. 500 F.Supp.2d 556 (E.D.Va.2007). The parties subsequently settled their patent dispute when eBay purchased the patents it was accused of infringing. EBay Settles Dispute Over "Buy It Now" Feature, N.Y. Times, C3, Feb. 29, 2008. For some of the voluminous scholarship on the *eBay* case focusing on the remedial issues, see *eBay* Symposium, 2 Akron IP Law J. 1–199 (2008); James M. Fischer, The "Right" to Injunctive Relief for Patent Infringement, 24 Santa Clara Comp. & High Tech. L.J. 1 (2007); Doug Rendleman, The Trial Judge's Discretion After eBay v. MercExchange, 27 Rev.Lit. 63 (2007). See also H. Tomás Gómez–Arostegui, What History Teaches Us About Copyright Injunctions and the Inadequate–Remedy–at–Law Requirement, 81 S.Cal.L.Rev. 1197 (2008) (concluding based upon a comprehensive review of Court of Chancery cases from 1660 to 1800 that in *eBay* the Supreme Court incorrectly extended its balancing test to copyright cases because historically the courts did in fact categorically award injunctive relief in these cases).

4. Remedies scholars had "never heard of the four-part test" for permanent injunctions announced in *eBay*. Rendleman, supra, at 76 n.71. The test comes from the preliminary injunction context, as evidenced by the Court's citation to the *Amoco* case on preliminary injunctions as support for the test. As will be discussed in Chapter 3(A), preliminary injunctions are different because they are issued before a final decision on the merits. Plaintiffs must first establish some threatened injury and probability of success on the merits of a legal claim, before making the separate showing of inadequacy of damages for that injury. The Court's terminology in *eBay* adds unnecessary confusion because factor 2, no adequate remedy at law, and factor 1, irreparable injury, are two ways of saying the same thing: irreparability is defined as the inadequacy of legal remedies like damages. The Court fell into the trap of using the shorthand of "irreparability" to stand for the threat of individualized legal harm that is a necessary prerequisite to permanent relief, as discussed in Section C(1). Dan B. Dobbs, Law of Remedies 87 (2d ed.1993). Thus, the four-part *eBay* test might be better thought of as requiring: (1) threat of a legal harm necessitating court action; (2) irreparable injury because damages are inadequate; (3) balance of the hardships; and (4) furtherance of the public interest.

5. The "public interest" part of the test for injunctive relief allows courts to consider the public policy implications and interests of third parties impacted by the issuance of the injunction. See Restatement (Second) of Torts 951, comment *a* (1979) (stating that a countervailing public interest may support denial of an otherwise proper award of injunctive relief). Concerns about the practicality of enforcement, such as those involved with personal service contracts, discussed in Section D(2), may also be weighed in here. It is

rare, however, that the public interest operates to deny the relief entirely. E.g., City of Milwaukee v. Activated Sludge, 69 F.2d 577 (7th Cir.)(denying injunction to shut down sewage treatment plant because of patent infringement due to public health endangerment caused by untreated sewage), cert. denied, 293 U.S. 576, 55 S.Ct. 87, 79 L.Ed. 673 (1934).

2. GRANTING LESS THAN PLAINTIFF'S RIGHTFUL POSITION

SMITH v. STASO MILLING CO.
United States Court of Appeals, Second Circuit, 1927
18 F.2d 736

Appeal from a decree of the District Court of Vermont enjoining the defendant from polluting with slate dust a brook running through the plaintiff's premises, from similarly polluting the air, and from jarring his dwelling house by blasting, and awarding plaintiff judgment in the sum of ten thousand dollars for past damages.

The plaintiff is the owner of a summer residence in the town of Castleton, Vermont, something less than a mile distant from the defendant's crushing mill. This residence he occupied in substantially unchanged form at the time the defendant bought its land and before it put up its mill. The defendant blasts slate rock upon its premises, which it crushes, and makes from the product ground slate roofing material. The grinding creates clouds of dust, part of which, when the wind is in the right direction, is carried over to the plaintiff's premises, which it covers with pulverized dust. This is one grievance.

In the defendant's process of manufacture there are waste products which it puts upon a dump by a belt conveyor. Through the conveyor streams of water are run from driven wells, and the thin, muddy or plastic mass flows out into the first of three settling ponds, the overflow from which passes into a second, and so to a third, the three being together designed to retain all the waste. During heavy rains these ponds become filled with water and carry off through the sluices quantities of the sludge or mud, which the defendant has deposited in them. The last of these empties into a brook which runs through the premises of both parties, and on such occasions quantities of the muddy slate reach the plaintiff's land and leave a sediment upon it. He uses the brook for part of his domestic water supply, and the sludge or silt fills his reservoirs and otherwise interferes with his enjoyment of the premises. This is another and more important grievance.

* * * After the defendant had purchased the land, but before it had put up the plant, the plaintiff wrote, calling attention to the brook which flowed through both premises, advising it that its continued purity was a valuable asset to him, and protesting against any pollution or interference with its flow. The defendant's superintendent called upon him, assured him that there was no danger, because the proposed system of filters and settling basins would prevent any such possibility. The assurance was several times repeated. After the erection of the mill the defendant again assured the plaintiff more than once that the trouble had been in management of the settling ponds.

The defendant has installed dust arresters which are rated to stop 99 per cent of the dust which is produced. It has invested about $1,000,000 altogether in the plant, employs between 125 and 200 men, and its monthly pay roll is between $25,000 and $40,000.

The plaintiff valued his premises at $40,000, though it cost in all less than $30,000 * * *.

The District Judge on conflicting evidence found for the plaintiff on all the questions of fact involved, and absolutely enjoined the activities complained of. * * * The defendant appealed.

LEARNED HAND, Circuit Judge (after stating the facts as above). * * *

The defendant, not arguing that the facts justify no relief, insists that no injunction should go, because of the disastrous effect upon his crushing mill, which must stop its operation if enjoined. We are not satisfied that this must be the consequence, but we are content so to assume. The plaintiff argues that those cases in which such considerations have prevailed, do not represent the law of Vermont, which have never balanced the comparative hardships of the continued wrong and the injunction, when the plaintiff's right is substantial and clear. While we agree that with [a] possible exception [citation omitted], no decision of that state has actually turned upon the doctrine, it appears to us to have had so much recognition in the decisions of its highest court as to be certainly a part of its jurisprudence, at least until we are authoritatively advised to the contrary. * * *

Assuming that the doctrine is not fixed in the law of Vermont, we think that it is as matter of principle a reasonable one. The very right on which the injured party stands in such cases is a quantitative compromise between two conflicting interests. What may be an entirely tolerable adjustment, when the result is only to award damages for the injury done, may become no better than a means of extortion if the result is absolutely to curtail the defendant's enjoyment of his land. Even though the defendant has no power to condemn, at times it may be proper to require of him no more than to make good the whole injury once and for all. If the writ went as of course, we should have no option. Notoriously it * * * is discretionary if any is. To say that whenever an injured party can show that he could recover damages, he has only in addition to prove that the tort will be repeated, appears to us to ignore the substance of the situation in the interest of any apocryphal consistency. Where we are not bound by the local law, we decline to adopt so rigid a canon.

Nevertheless, so far as concerns the pollution of the stream, we think that the injury is so substantial and the wrong so deliberate, that we ought to impose upon the defendant the peril of any failure successfully to avoid it. * * * In the case at bar not only did the defendant have the most explicit warning from the plaintiff, but it gave an equally explicit assurance that it could avoid defiling the brook. It has several times repeated that assurance after occasional overflows. If the plaintiff had filed his bill before the mill was built, the balance of convenience would have been different, and we should not have hesitated to stop what as yet remained only a project. Whether the assurances in fact determined his inaction we need not say; he has shown himself pertinacious, though forbearing, and the chances are that they did. Even if not, these preliminary negotiations seem to us enough absolutely to impose upon the defendant the execution of what it promised. As respects the pollution of the stream, we therefore think that the injunction should remain absolute, and that the defendant must find some way to avoid further injury, or make its peace with the plaintiff as best it can.

As regards the dust the facts are different. True, it is equally a tort so to defile the air. But the injury is less oppressive, and neither the plaintiff's original protest, nor the defendant's promise, covered it. We are not prepared in such a situation to say that, if the defendant cannot by the best known methods arrest all the dust which it emits, it must shut down its mill. The record shows that it has installed arresters which are designed to stop all but one per cent. of the dust, and apparently do so. Yet that which escapes is still enough to affect the plaintiff's enjoyment, and the record does not show beyond question that the defendant cannot prevent it. The best disposition of the case is to affirm the injunction as it stands, but to give leave to the defendant to apply at the foot of the decree for relief upon showing there are no better arresters extant, that it operates those it has at maximum efficiency, that it is theretofore impossible further to reduce the dust, and that if the injunction continues it has no alternative but to stop operation. If that be proved to the satisfaction of the District Judge the injunction should be modified so as merely to limit the dust to that which will escape the arresters now in use. * * *

[The court went on to modify the award of damages.]

NOTES

1. *Factors not reflected in the law of liability.* The court holds that Staso Milling's air pollution wrongs Smith and does not hold that the wrong could be repaired by compensatory damages. Nonetheless, the court refuses to enjoin this wrong, which means that it is not putting Smith in his rightful position. Are the decisions on liability and injunctive relief consistent? The standard of liability in nuisance is whether the interference with the plaintiff's land use is substantial and unreasonable, and as such "would interfere with the normal use and enjoyment of a normal person." Dan B. Dobbs, The Law of Torts § 463 (2000). A land use that would be illegal under this standard does not become legal after it begins. The defendant's expenditure or the reliance of its employees on their jobs ought not to affect liability. However, these factors are relevant to the remedy. Therefore, the remedy question may involve factors not reflected in the law of liability.

What result if Smith sought an injunction prior to the construction of the plant? Was the decision to grant injunctive relief against the water pollution consistent with its decision to deny such relief against the air pollution?

2. *The goals of the law of liability.* While it is possible to distinguish the decisions on liability, injunctive relief for the air pollution, and injunctive relief for water pollution, should those distinctions make a difference? Suppose that Staso Milling were liable not for nuisance but for breaching a contract that promised that no air pollution would be emitted. Should the court enjoin the air pollution? Professor Frederic Maitland wrote: "When a man has definitely contracted not to do a certain thing, it is not for him to say that it will be greatly to his convenience, and not much to the inconvenience of the other party, that he should be allowed to do it." Equity 327–28 (Alfred H. Chaytor & William J. Whittaker rev. 2d ed.1947). What does this suggest about the goals of the law of contract?

Suppose that Staso Milling was liable for an intentional trespass, such as placing part of its factory on Smith's land. Judge Hand probably would not have balanced the equities to allow the trespass to continue because, as he explains it, the goals of nuisance law themselves balance the competing interests of neighbors. In contrast, the goals of trespass law emphasize the owner's right to prevent intentional physical invasions. But even the goals of trespass law are not absolute; many courts will balance the equities in the case of unintentional trespasses that cause little harm to the plaintiff. For instance, where someone inadvertently erects a building that encroaches slightly on a neighbors' land, the victim of the trespass will ordinarily be relegated to a damage remedy. But if the encroachment is intentional, an injunction will issue regardless of the relative hardships of the parties.

As *Staso* indicates, state courts were split in their willingness to balance the equities in nuisance cases. In a portion of the opinion that is deleted, Judge Hand cites Whalen v. Union Bag & Paper Co., 208 N.Y. 1, 5, 101 N.E. 805, 806 (1913), which held that balancing the equities cannot justify failing to issue an injunction to halt a nuisance that causes more than slight harm because otherwise balancing "would deprive the poor litigant of his little property by giving it to those already rich." Judge Hand seems to disagree: "[e]ven though the defendant has no power to condemn, at times it may be proper to require of him no more than to make good the whole injury once and for all." But doesn't balancing the equities tend to give rich nuisance makers the power to condemn their neighbors' property?

Reflecting a national trend towards balancing the equities in nuisance cases, the New York Court of Appeals overruled *Whalen* in Boomer v. Atlantic Cement Co., 26 N.Y.2d 219, 309 N.Y.S.2d 312, 257 N.E.2d 870 (1970). While the *Whalen* court emphasized that the defendant there should have known that its conduct infringed upon the plaintiff's rights, *Boomer* was decided more than a half century later in a more industrialized age, in which reciprocal interference between adjacent landowners has become routine. Indeed, Whalen was a farmer while the Boomers operated a junk yard. Daniel A. Farber, Reassessing *Boomer*: Justice, Efficiency, and Nuisance Law, in Property Law and Legal Education: Essays in Honor of John E. Cribbet 9 (Peter Hay & Michael H. Hoeflich eds. 1988). This change in interaction between adjacent landowners makes Judge Hand's view of nuisance law as a balancing of the competing interests particularly apt.

Boomer was distinguished in Walgreen Co. v. Sara Creek Property Co., 966 F.2d 273 (7th Cir.1992), which affirmed an injunction against the defendant-landlord breaching a lease clause giving the tenant-plaintiff the right to be the only pharmacy in a shopping center. In comparing the pros and cons of damages and injunctive relief, Judge Richard Posner expressed concern that damages would be difficult to calculate and, if too small, could lead to an inefficient breach of the lease clause. He thought that the parties could do a better job than the court of determining the impact upon themselves. At the same time, he expressed concern that an injunction might prove inefficient— that is, that having a second pharmacy in the center might be worth more to the landlord than it cost the tenant, yet the parties might nonetheless be unable to strike a bargain to get rid of it. However, he decided to affirm because the risk of such a failure in negotiations was much smaller than in *Boomer*. Negotiations may fail to get rid of an inefficient injunction because of the more "subtle cost" of the "bilateral monopoly" created by the injunction. Id. at 275. Judge Posner reasoned that the risk from strategic bargaining was much larger in a case like *Boomer*. There, the bargaining range was huge (the damages to the plaintiffs were supposedly a few hundred thousand dollars while an injunction would shut down a factory worth $45 million) while in *Walgreen* the bargaining range was far smaller. The bargaining range is apt to be large in just those cases when the defendant can point to an undue hardship.

3. *Balancing the equities.* Professor Chayes, in the article excerpted in Chapter 1, views balancing the equities as giving the trial judge wide-ranging discretion to decree what seems sensible, whether that is more than, less than, or the same as the plaintiff's rightful position. The polar opposite to Professor Chayes' approach would be to deny the judge discretion and require that the decree order the defendant to achieve the plaintiff's rightful position exactly. Professor Schoenbrod has proposed a middle ground in which the judge has discretion, but it is limited by the following principle:

> The injunction should require the defendant to achieve the plaintiff's rightful position unless (a) different relief is consistent with the goals of the violated rule and (b) the case involves a factor justifying departure from the rule that was not reflected in its formulation, but the injunction may never aim to achieve more than the plaintiff's rightful position.

David Schoenbrod, The Measure of An Injunction: A Principle to Replace Balancing the Equities and Tailoring the Remedy, 72 Minn.L.Rev. 627, 664 (1988).

4. *Efficiency and fairness.* Balancing the equities also goes under the names "undue hardship," "the balance of convenience" and "balancing equities and hardships." *Staso* considers hardship/convenience and equities— in other words, efficiency and fairness. Efficiency and fairness are also the chief concerns of the law of nuisance. The gist of the decision on air pollution in *Staso* is that it is efficient to let it continue, should controlling the emissions be impracticable, but unfair to Smith. An award of damages would then provide some recompense for the unfairness. As to the water pollution,

the court decides in essence that it would be unfair to take account of the hardship on Staso Milling so that considerations of fairness override considerations of efficiency. In contrast, if the wrong is both unfair and inefficient, the court would readily grant an injunction.

We have so far identified three possible outcomes in nuisance cases: (1) no relief, (2) damages to the party injured by the nuisance, and (3) an injunction stopping the nuisance. Scholars have identified a fourth and fifth possibility. As a fourth possibility, a court could enjoin the nuisance but make the victim of the nuisance pay damages to the party enjoined. Such an outcome might make sense when it is efficient to stop the nuisance, but unfair to make the defendant pay the cost. Furthermore, requiring the victim to pay ensures that stopping the nuisance is truly efficient. However, apparently only one court has issued such a compensated injunction. Spur Industries v. Del E. Webb Development Co., 108 Ariz. 178, 494 P.2d 700 (1972). In that case, Del Webb established a large subdivision near Spur's smelly feedlot and sold building lots to the public. Keeping the feedlot open was probably inefficient given the harm to many homeowners relative to the cost of moving the feedlot. Yet, it was fair to put the cost on Webb rather than Spur because Webb had, in essence, come to the nuisance. Should Webb have gotten an injunction if it had not yet sold any lots? If the city rather than Webb had sought the injunction, should the injunction have been granted without requiring compensation to Spur? Would you advise a developer similarly situated to Webb to bring a suit to close down the nuisance?

Professor Farber, at p. 104, offers a fifth possibility. Where it would be highly inefficient to stop the nuisance, but the nuisance is egregious, he would deny an injunction but set damages based not on the harm to the plaintiff, but rather on what it would have cost the defendant to have purchased the right to make the nuisance if it had sought to do so before building its factory. In essence, Farber's proposal is that damages be geared to the defendant's rightful position rather than the plaintiff's. For Farber, ordinary compensatory damages are inadequate because they give all the gains from trade to the defendant and therefore reward the defendant's egregious taking of the plaintiff's rights. Do you agree with his proposal? How would the court apply his measure of damages in *Staso?* Should this proposal be applied to intentional breaches of contracts?

5. *Impact on the public.* Notice that *Staso* weighs the hardship from an injunction on the defendant and the public (Staso's employees) on one side of the balance and the benefits from an injunction to the plaintiff on the other. So the court considers the detriments to the public but not the benefits. *Boomer,* which also considered the impact on the public in the same one-sided way, offered the following explanation:

> The public concern with air pollution arising from many sources in industry and in transportation is currently accorded ever wider recognition accompanied by a growing sense of responsibility in State and Federal Governments to control it. * * *
>
> But there is now before the court private litigation in which individual property owners have sought specific relief from a single plant operation. The threshold question raised by the division of view on this appeal

is whether the court should resolve the litigation between the parties now before it as equitably as seems possible; or whether, seeking promotion of the general public welfare, it should channel private litigation into broad public objectives.

A court performs its essential function when it decides the rights of parties before it. Its decision of private controversies may sometimes greatly affect public issues. Large questions of law are often resolved by the manner in which private litigation is decided. But this is normally an incident to the court's main function to settle controversy. It is a rare exercise of judicial power to use a decision in private litigation as a purposeful mechanism to achieve direct public objectives greatly beyond the rights and interests before the court.

Effective control of air pollution is a problem presently far from solution even with the full public and financial powers of government. In large measure adequate technical procedures are yet to be developed and some that appear possible may be economically impracticable.

It seems apparent that the amelioration of air pollution will depend on technical research in great depth; on a carefully balanced consideration of the economic impact of close regulation; and of the actual effect on public health. It is likely to require massive public expenditure and to demand more than any local community can accomplish and to depend on regional and interstate controls.

A court should not try to do this on its own as a by-product of private litigation and it seems manifest that the judicial establishment is neither equipped in the limited nature of any judgment it can pronounce nor prepared to lay down and implement an effective policy for the elimination of air pollution. This is an area beyond the circumference of one private lawsuit. It is a direct responsibility for government and should not thus be undertaken as an incident to solving a dispute between property owners and a single cement plant—one of many—in the Hudson River valley.

26 N.Y.2d at 222–23, 309 N.Y.S.2d at 314–15, 257 N.E.2d at 871. Are you convinced?

Compare the dictum in Sierra Club v. Morton, 405 U.S. 727, 740 n. 15, 92 S.Ct. 1361, 1369 n. 15, 31 L.Ed.2d 636 (1972)("Once this standing is established, the party may assert the interests of the general public in support of his claims for equitable relief.").

BROWN v. BOARD OF EDUCATION (*BROWN II*)

Supreme Court of the United States, 1955
349 U.S. 294, 75 S.Ct. 753, 99 L.Ed. 1083

MR. CHIEF JUSTICE WARREN delivered the opinion of the Court.

These cases were decided on May 17, 1954. The opinions of that date,[1] declaring the fundamental principle that racial discrimination in public

---

1. 347 U.S. 483, 74 S.Ct. 686, 98 L.Ed. 873 [*Brown I*]. 347 U.S. 497, 74 S.Ct. 693, 98 L.Ed. 884 [*Bolling v. Sharpe*].

education is unconstitutional, are incorporated herein by reference. All provisions of federal, state, or local law requiring or permitting such discrimination must yield to this principle. There remains for consideration the manner in which relief is to be accorded.

Because these cases arose under different local conditions and their disposition will involve a variety of local problems, we requested further argument on the question of relief.[2] In view of the nationwide importance of the decision, we invited the Attorney General of the United States and the Attorneys General of all states requiring or permitting racial discrimination in public education to present their views on that question. The parties, the United States, and the States of Florida, North Carolina, Arkansas, Oklahoma, Maryland, and Texas filed briefs and participated in the oral argument.

These presentations were informative and helpful to the Court in its consideration of the complexities arising from the transition to a system of public education freed of racial discrimination. The presentations also demonstrated that substantial steps to eliminate racial discrimination in public schools have already been taken, not only in some of the communities in which these cases arose, but in some of the states appearing as amici curiae, and in other states as well. Substantial progress has been made in the District of Columbia and in the communities in Kansas and Delaware involved in this litigation. The defendants in the cases coming to us from South Carolina and Virginia are awaiting the decision of this Court concerning relief.

Full implementation of these constitutional principles may require solution of varied local school problems. School authorities have the primary responsibility for elucidating, assessing, and solving these problems; courts will have to consider whether the action of school authorities constitutes good faith implementation of the governing constitutional principles. Because of their proximity to local conditions and the possible

---

2. Further argument was requested on the following questions, 347 U.S. 483, 495–496, note 13, 74 S.Ct. 686, 692, 98 L.Ed. 873, previously propounded by the Court:

"4. Assuming it is decided that segregation in public schools violates the Fourteenth Amendment

"(a) would a decree necessarily follow providing that, within the limits set by normal geographic school districting, Negro children should forthwith be admitted to schools of their choice, or

"(b) may this Court, in the exercise of its equity powers, permit an effective gradual adjustment to be brought about from existing segregated systems to a system not based on color distinctions?

"5. On the assumption on which questions 4(a) and (b) are based, and assuming further that this Court will exercise its equity powers to the end described in question 4(b),

"(a) should this Court formulate detailed decrees in these cases;

"(b) if so, what specific issues should the decrees reach;

"(c) should this Court appoint a special master to hear evidence with a view to recommending specific terms for such decrees;

"(d) should this Court remand to the courts of first instance with directions to frame decrees in these cases, and if so what general directions should the decrees of this Court include and what procedures should the courts of first instance follow in arriving at the specific terms of more detailed decrees?"

need for further hearings, the courts which originally heard these cases can best perform this judicial appraisal. Accordingly, we believe it appropriate to remand the cases to those courts.

In fashioning and effectuating the decrees, the courts will be guided by equitable principles. Traditionally, equity has been characterized by a practical flexibility in shaping its remedies and by a facility for adjusting and reconciling public and private needs.[5] These cases call for the exercise of these traditional attributes of equity power. At stake is the personal interest of the plaintiffs in admission to public schools as soon as practicable on a nondiscriminatory basis. To effectuate this interest may call for elimination of a variety of obstacles in making the transition to school systems operated in accordance with the constitutional principles set forth in our May 17, 1954, decision. Courts of equity may properly take into account the public interest in the elimination of such obstacles in a systematic and effective manner. But it should go without saying that the vitality of these constitutional principles cannot be allowed to yield simply because of disagreement with them.

While giving weight to these public and private considerations, the courts will require that the defendants make a prompt and reasonable start toward full compliance with our May 17, 1954, ruling. Once such a start has been made, the courts may find that additional time is necessary to carry out the ruling in an effective manner. The burden rests upon the defendants to establish that such time is necessary in the public interest and is consistent with good faith compliance at the earliest practicable date. To that end, the courts may consider problems related to administration, arising from the physical condition of the school plant, the school transportation system, personnel, revision of school districts and attendance areas into compact units to achieve a system of determining admission to the public schools on a nonracial basis, and revision of local laws and regulations which may be necessary in solving the foregoing problems. They will also consider the adequacy of any plans the defendants may propose to meet these problems and to effectuate a transition to a racially nondiscriminatory school system. During this period of transition, the courts will retain jurisdiction of these cases.

The judgments below, except that in the Delaware case, are accordingly reversed and the cases are remanded to the District Courts to take such proceedings and enter such orders and decrees consistent with this opinion as are necessary and proper to admit to public schools on a racially nondiscriminatory basis with all deliberate speed the parties to these cases. The judgment in the Delaware case—ordering the immediate admission of the plaintiffs to schools previously attended only by white children—is affirmed on the basis of the principles stated in our May 17, 1954, opinion, but the case is remanded to the Supreme Court of Delaware for such further proceedings as that Court may deem necessary in light of this opinion.

---

5. See Hecht Co. v. Bowles, 321 U.S. 321, 329–330, 64 S.Ct. 587, 591, 592, 88 L.Ed. 754.

NOTES

1. The Topeka schools were not declared unitary until nearly forty-five years later. After the Tenth Circuit ruled that the plaintiffs in *Brown* had yet to be restored fully to their rightful position as of 1992, Brown v. Board of Education, 978 F.2d 585 (10th Cir.1992), cert. denied, 503 U.S. 978, 112 S.Ct. 1657, 118 L.Ed.2d 381 (1992), the school district implemented further plans concerning student, staff and faculty assignments. The district court dismissed the case after a period of successful implementation. Brown v. Unified School Dist. No. 501, 56 F.Supp.2d 1212 (D.Kan.1999). Such is "deliberate speed." What the rightful position entails is controversial, however, as the next section and Chapter 3(B) will show.

2. However the plaintiffs' rightful position is defined, what justification, if any, can there be for failing to grant the plaintiffs their rightful position forthwith in any constitutional case, let alone a case with the importance of *Brown*? Professor Peter Shane writes:

> In some cases, a court may defend remedial delay (rightly or wrongly) as necessary for the maximum vindication of right—because the maximum vindication of right cannot be accomplished without remedial steps that require planning, review, and staged implementation. In some cases, however, such a justification for delay is not available. A pointed example occurs in prisoners' "conditions of confinement" suits. A violation of the constitutional right to freedom from cruel and unusual punishment may be maximally protected by immediate release. While the threat of release is often used to induce state authorities to correct unconstitutional conditions, release is never the remedy of first resort. This can only be because courts recognize a proper place in the remedial process for balancing remedial interests against other legitimate social concerns. Yet, what these concerns comprise and the weight they should enjoy are notably discretionary decisions.

Peter M. Shane, Rights, Remedies, and Restraint, 64 Chi.–Kent L.Rev. 531, 557 (1988). Professor Shane builds upon Professor Paul Gewirtz's thoughtful analysis of *Brown II*. Paul Gewirtz, Remedies and Resistance, 92 Yale L.J. 585 (1983).

3. *Brown II* stated that "it should go without saying that the vitality of these constitutional principles cannot be allowed to yield simply because of disagreement with them." Did the Court really mean this or was it just striking an attractive pose because it did not have the power to implement these principles anyway, no matter how it phrased its mandate in *Brown II*? See Gerald N. Rosenberg, Tilting at Windmills: Brown II and the Hopeless Quest to Resolve Deep–Seated Social Conflict Through Litigation, 24 Law & Ineq. 31, 35 (2006) ("Political and social forces (both local and national) did not support desegregation, providing no pressure for compliance.").

4. Is *Brown II* consistent with Professor Schoenbrod's principle quoted at p. 105?

5. Note that the Supreme Court, in remanding to the lower courts, instructs them to give the defendant school boards a substantial role in

formulating the remedy. In essence, the matters are remanded to the defendants, although with close judicial supervision. See Wendy Parker, The Decline of Judicial Decisionmaking: School Desegregation and District Court Judges, 81 N.C.L.Rev. 1623 (2003) (examining pattern of deference from district court judges to defendants in school desegregation cases). What could justify giving the defendants who had fought desegregation tooth and nail any role in implementing the remedy?

Professor Paul R. Dimond argues that *Brown II* is a great victory precisely because its strategy of giving the political branches the lead in determining the scope, pace, and design of the remedy left the Supreme Court free to identify the wrong in unstinting terms. He argues that because of the limits on the courts in exercising their countermajoritarian powers:

> We should concede that the more massive and entrenched the wrong of discrimination, the more important it is for the courts to declare the full extent of that wrong. The courts must also permit the ultimate remedy to be worked out in a political process in which those who are aggrieved will at least have a continuing claim that the declared wrong cannot be remedied in the courts alone.

Paul R. Dimond, *Brown* and the Transformation of the Constitution: Concluding Remarks, 61 Fordham L.Rev. 63, 65–66 (1992). Do you agree? An example of Professor Dimond's approach is McDuffy v. Secretary of Education, 415 Mass. 545, 615 N.E.2d 516, 555–56 (1993). After the Massachusetts high court declared that the legislators and executives of the Commonwealth and its local governments had violated an enforceable provision of the state constitution requiring them to provide an adequate education, it left those officials "to define the precise nature of the task which they face in fulfilling their constitutional duty" and provided no judicial remedy other than that the trial court have the discretion to retain jurisdiction to determine whether "within a reasonable time, appropriate legislative action has been taken."

6. Whether *Brown II* went as far as it should have, make no mistake that it continues to have a huge impact on how schools and other institutions are operated. United States v. Fordice, 505 U.S. 717, 112 S.Ct. 2727, 120 L.Ed.2d 575 (1992)(establishing criteria for desegregation in Mississippi's public university system). Moreover, Professor Owen M. Fiss in The Civil Rights Injunction (1978) argues that *Brown II* reshaped the law of remedies. Previously, injunctions were the remedies of last resort both because of the inadequate remedy at law rule and the suspicion of injunctions generated by injunctions against strikes in the early days of the union movement. After *Brown II*, the injunction was the remedy of choice for constitutional violations. See Doug Rendleman, Brown II's "All Deliberate Speed" at Fifty: A Golden Anniversary or a Mid-life Crisis for the Constitutional Injunction as a School Desegregation Remedy?, 41 San Diego L.Rev. 1575 (2004)(examining injunction remedies to vindicate the plaintiffs' rights under *Brown*).

7. The Supreme Court sometimes decides that courts should deny redress for past violations when the claim for relief rests on new constitutional doctrines. It is then said that the new doctrine has only "prospective" effect, which suggests that the new law of liability applies only to future cases. But Professors Richard H. Fallon, Jr. and Daniel J. Meltzer argue that these

decisions are best understood as applications of traditional remedial principles, such as avoiding undue hardship caused by reasonable reliance on the old doctrine. Richard H. Fallon, Jr. & Daniel J. Meltzer, New Law, Non–Retroactivity, and Constitutional Remedies, 104 Harv.L.Rev. 1733 (1991). However, denying retrospective application of a new constitutional interpretation raises concerns that the Supreme Court is making it too easy to overrule precedent and is not being evenhanded. In James B. Beam Distilling Co. v. Georgia, 501 U.S. 529, 111 S.Ct. 2439, 115 L.Ed.2d 481 (1991), six members of the Court held that once it gives retroactive application to a new constitutional interpretation in a civil case, it must be given retroactive application in all cases. In Harper v. Virginia Department of Taxation, 509 U.S. 86, 113 S.Ct. 2510, 125 L.Ed.2d 74 (1993), which applied *Beam*, five justices intimated that denying retroactive effect in any civil case might be improper and four others disagreed. The *Harper* majority relied upon Griffith v. Kentucky, 479 U.S. 314, 322–23, 107 S.Ct. 708, 713, 93 L.Ed.2d 649, 658 (1987), which required, henceforth, that in criminal cases all new constitutional interpretations must be applied to all cases on direct appeal.

NOTE ON THE PRACTICALITY OF ENFORCEMENT

"It has long been settled that a court shall not issue an injunction that would be inconvenient or inefficient to administer." Bray v. Safeway Stores, 392 F.Supp. 851, 868 (N.D.Cal.1975). This statement, like many maxims of equity, sacrifices accuracy in describing what courts actually do for the thrill of sounding really decisive.

There is an element of truth in the statement. Concerns about difficulty of enforcement lead to the denial of specific relief of some contracts, particularly personal service or construction contracts where enforcement could involve ongoing monitoring and subjective evaluations of the quality of work. On the other hand, courts often grant injunctions where enforcement will be onerous. Enforcement problems are especially serious in many civil rights and regulatory cases. Indeed, the judicial effort to desegregate the schools of the lead defendant in *Brown v. Board of Education* lasted for nearly 45 years. Brown v. Unified School District No. 501, 56 F.Supp.2d 1212 (D.Kan.1999) (declaring unitary status). Outside of contract cases, injunctions are so rarely denied because of burdens of supervision that the opinions only infrequently even mention the issue. On the other hand, in Joyce v. City and County of San Francisco, 846 F.Supp. 843 (N.D.Cal.1994), the court refused to grant a preliminary injunction barring the police from enforcing the homeless statutes or ordinances prohibiting "life-sustaining" activities in public places. The court was concerned that uncertainty about who is homeless on any particular night and what is a "life-sustaining" activity would create enforcement problems.

The principle does not direct courts to deny specific relief simply because of difficulty of supervision, but only if the "burdens * * * are disproportionate to the advantages to be gained from enforcement and to the harm to be suffered by its denial." Restatement (Second) of Contracts § 366 (1981). Courts generally place a higher value on constitutional, statutory, and common law property rights than they do on enforcement of commercial promises, or at least see compensatory damages as less inadequate in the case of commercial promises. In the rare modern case outside the contract area where the burden of supervision is cited as a reason for denying an injunction, other factors help to explain the outcome. For example, in *Joyce*, the district court was probably more concerned about whether the plaintiffs were correct on the merits.

Ramirez de Arellano v. Weinberger, 724 F.2d 143 (D.C.Cir.1983), vacated, 745 F.2d 1500 (D.C.Cir. en banc 1984), nicely illustrates both how judges' policy priorities can affect the treatment of the supervision issue and clashing judicial attitudes about the supervision issue. The plaintiffs sought an injunction against trespasses on their land in Honduras by United States military forces. Judge Scalia, writing for the panel, expressed concern about supervising a decree that would involve ongoing disputes as to conduct in a foreign land. 724 F.2d at 148. Nonetheless, he questioned whether the burden of supervision could justify dismissing the claim for relief except when combined with other problems that he saw in the claim, such as interfering with the President's exercise of his foreign affairs and military powers in the context of the various wars in Central America. Writing for a divided court, en banc, Judge Wilkey termed concerns about supervision "wild speculation":

> It must be presumed that the defendants, all officials of the United States government present in Washington, D.C., will obey an order of the district court. Furthermore, there is simply no factual basis * * * for concluding that an equitable decree would involve this court in numerous or even any monitoring problems. Courts do not monitor compliance with decrees by personal, on-site inspections. Even if the alleged violations were occurring in the corridors of the Pentagon instead of in Honduras, the district court would not monitor its decree by personally inspecting the affected area. If a dispute arises over compliance with any remedial decree, the parties can introduce evidence in the district court to establish whether a violation in fact has occurred. * * * It is absurd to suggest on the basis of plaintiffs' complaint that judicial monitoring of relief would be so problematic that adjudication of the plaintiffs' constitutional claims is barred.

745 F.2d at 1531–32.

This passage reflects a growing willingness to grant the relief first and worry about the problems of supervision if and when they arise. Of equal import, the passage reflects a willingness to look at enforcement as a problem of proof for the plaintiffs rather than a problem of minimizing the risk that the court will look ineffectual. Courts never refrain from issuing money judgments because the plaintiff will not be able to collect or because the plaintiff's collection efforts may take up the court's time. Should courts treat injunctions any differently? See Dan B. Dobbs, Law of Remedies §§ 2.8(3), 12.19(3) (2d ed.1993).

Practicality of enforcement comprehends not only the burdens of supervising compliance but also impediments to punishing contempt of an order. Courts traditionally hesitate to grant an injunction against out-of-state activity by a non-resident because the defendant might violate the order yet escape punishment. In contrast, judges do not hesitate to issue money judgments against defendants who reside and have their assets outside the geographic limits of the court. The explanation for the difference lies partly in ensuring that court orders are obeyed and partly in the operation of the full faith and credit clause of the United States Constitution. Art. IV, § 1. Although the clause requires the courts of one state to give full faith and credit to "judicial proceedings" of other states, courts have interpreted the clause to require enforcement of money judgments but not injunctions. Restatement (Second) of Conflict of Laws § 102 comment *c* (1971). As matters now stand, a court may enjoin out-of-state activity (id. at § 53) and the court of a sister state might choose—but is not obligated—to enforce the injunction as part of its own proceedings. Even if the injunction from the first state is not enforced directly elsewhere, the sister state will give the findings necessary to the original injunction preclusive effect so that the plaintiff might be entitled to obtain a new order from the sister state. See Baker v. General Motors Corp., 522 U.S. 222, 118 S.Ct. 657, 139 L.Ed.2d 580 (1998). It is also possible that the enjoined defendant will comply voluntarily because he or she does not want to risk being found in contempt by the court issuing the injunction, or the defendant's assets might be found in the original jurisdiction.[a] In any event, "the sky will not fall in if the defendant is successful in flouting the decree." Dan B. Dobbs, Handbook of the Law of Remedies at 64 (1973).

The courts balanced the equities in *Staso,* a common law case, and *Brown II,* a constitutional case. The next question is whether they may balance the equities to allow statutory violations to continue. Professor Zygmunt Plater, who represented the plaintiffs in the following case, later wrote that his clients "made the 'conservative' argument that courts should not be activist but rather should follow the dictates of the words of the statutes before them." Zygmunt Plater, In the Wake of the Snail Darter: An Environmental Law Paradigm and Its Consequences, 19 Mich. J.L. Reform 805, 834 (1986).

TENNESSEE VALLEY AUTHORITY v. HILL

Supreme Court of the United States, 1978
437 U.S. 153, 98 S.Ct. 2279, 57 L.Ed.2d 117

Mr. Chief Justice Burger delivered the opinion of the Court.

The questions presented in this case are (a) whether the Endangered Species Act of 1973 requires a court to enjoin the operation of a virtually completed federal dam—which had been authorized prior to 1973—when, pursuant to authority vested in him by Congress, the Secretary of the Interior has determined that operation of the dam would eradicate an endangered species; and (b) whether continued congressional appropria-

---

a. Courts hesitate to enjoin out of state activity for a reason distinct from practicality of enforcement—that the injunction may interfere with the policies and prerogatives of the sister state. See Restatement (Second) of Conflict of Laws § 53 comments c, d (1971); *Ramirez de Arellano,* 745 F.2d at 1529–30 and 1563 (Scalia, J., dissenting opinion).

tions for the dam after 1973 constituted an implied repeal of the Endangered Species Act, at least as to the particular dam.

I

The Little Tennessee River originates in the mountains of northern Georgia and flows through the national forest lands of North Carolina into Tennessee, where it converges with the Big Tennessee River near Knoxville. The lower 33 miles of the Little Tennessee takes the river's clear, free-flowing waters through an area of great natural beauty. * * * Considerable historical importance attaches to the areas immediately adjacent * * *.

In this area of the Little Tennessee River the Tennessee Valley Authority, a wholly owned public corporation of the United States, began constructing the Tellico Dam and Reservoir Project in 1967, shortly after Congress appropriated initial funds for its development. Tellico is a multipurpose regional development project designed principally to stimulate shoreline development, generate sufficient electric current to heat 20,000 homes, and provide flatwater recreation and flood control, as well as improve economic conditions in "an area characterized by underutilization of human resources and outmigration of young people." Of particular relevance to this case is one aspect of the project, a dam which TVA determined to place on the Little Tennessee, a short distance from where the river's waters meet with the Big Tennessee. When fully operational, the dam would impound water covering some 16,500 acres—much of which represents valuable and productive farmland—thereby converting the river's shallow, fast-flowing waters into a deep reservoir over 30 miles in length.

[The Court describes how litigation under statutes other than the Endangered Species Act slowed and sometimes enjoined the dam's completion. After these efforts to halt the dam had failed and just when the dam was about to go into operation,] a discovery was made in the waters of the Little Tennessee which would profoundly affect the Tellico Project. Exploring the area around Coytee Springs, which is about seven miles from the mouth of the river, a University of Tennessee ichthyologist, Dr. David A. Etnier, found a previously unknown species of perch, the snail darter, or Percina (Imostoma) tanasi. This three-inch, tannish-colored fish, whose numbers are estimated to be in the range of 10,000 to 15,000, would soon engage the attention of environmentalists, the TVA, the Department of the Interior, the Congress of the United States, and ultimately the federal courts, as a new and additional basis to halt construction of the dam.

Until recently the finding of a new species of animal life would hardly generate a cause celebre. This is particularly so in the case of darters, of which there are approximately 130 known species, 8 to 10 of these having been identified only in the last five years. The moving force behind the snail darter's sudden fame came some four months after its discovery, when the Congress passed the Endangered Species Act of 1973 (Act), 87 Stat. 884, 16 U.S.C. § 1531 et seq. (1976 ed.). This legislation, among other things, authorizes the Secretary of the Interior to declare species of animal life "endangered" and to identify the "critical habitat" of these creatures. When a species or its habitat is so listed, the following portion of the Act—relevant here—becomes effective:

> " * * * Federal departments and agencies shall * * * utilize their authorities in furtherance of the purposes of this chapter by carrying out programs for the conservation of endangered species * * * listed pursuant to section 1533 of this title and *by taking such action necessary to insure that actions authorized, funded, or carried out by them do not jeopardize the continued existence of such endangered species * * * or result in the destruction or modification of habitat of such species* which is determined by the Secretary * * * to be critical." 16 U.S.C. § 1536 (emphasis added).

In January 1975, the respondents in this case[10] and others petitioned the Secretary of the Interior to list the snail darter as an endangered species. * * * [T]he Secretary formally listed the snail darter as an endangered species on October 8, 1975. * * * [T]he Secretary determined that the snail darter apparently lives only in that portion of the Little Tennessee River which would be completely inundated by the reservoir created as a consequence of the Tellico Dam's completion. The Secretary went on to explain the significance of the dam to the habitat of the snail darter:

> "[T]he snail darter occurs only in the swifter portions of shoals over clean gravel substrate in cool, low-turbidity water. Food of the snail darter is almost exclusively snails which require a clean gravel substrate for their survival. *The proposed impoundment of water behind the proposed Tellico Dam would result in total destruction of the snail darter's habitat.*" (Emphasis added).

Subsequent to this determination, the Secretary declared the area of the Little Tennessee which would be affected by the Tellico Dam to be the "critical habitat" of the snail darter. Using these determinations as a predicate, and notwithstanding the near completion of the dam, the Secretary declared that pursuant to § 7 of the Act, "all Federal agencies must take such action as is necessary to insure that actions authorized, funded, or carried out by them do not result in the destruction or modification of this critical habitat area." This notice, of course, was pointedly directed at TVA and clearly aimed at halting completion or operation of the dam.

* * * In February 1976, pursuant to § 11(g) of the Endangered Species Act, 16 U.S.C. § 1540(g), respondents filed the case now under review, seeking to enjoin completion of the dam and impoundment of the reservoir on the ground that those actions would violate the Act by directly causing the extinction of the species *Percina (Imostoma) tanasi*.

---

10. Respondents are a regional association of biological scientists, a Tennessee conservation group, and individuals who are citizens or users of the Little Tennessee Valley Area which would be affected by the Tellico Project.

* * * [T]he court entered its memorandum opinion and order denying respondents their requested relief and dismissing the complaint. The District Court found that closure of the dam and the consequent impoundment of the reservoir would "result in the adverse modification, if not complete destruction, of the snail darter's critical habitat," making it "highly probable" that "the continued existence of the snail darter" would be "jeopardize[d]." Despite these findings, the District Court declined to embrace the plaintiffs' position on the merits: that once a federal project was shown to jeopardize an endangered species, a court of equity is compelled to issue an injunction restraining violation of the Endangered Species Act.

In reaching this result, the District Court stressed that the entire project was then about 80% complete and, based on available evidence, "there [were] no alternatives to impoundment of the reservoir, short of scrapping the entire project." The District Court also found that if the Tellico Project was permanently enjoined, "[s]ome $53 million would be lost in nonrecoverable obligations," meaning that a large portion of the $78 million already expended would be wasted. The court also noted that the Endangered Species Act of 1973 was passed some seven years after construction on the dam commenced and that Congress had continued appropriations for Tellico, with full awareness of the snail darter problem. Assessing these various factors, the District Court concluded:

> "At some point in time a federal project becomes so near completion and so incapable of modification that a court of equity should not apply a statute enacted long after inception of the project to produce an unreasonable result. * * * Where there has been an irreversible and irretrievable commitment of resources by Congress to a project over a span of almost a decade, the Court should proceed with a great deal of circumspection." * * *

Thereafter, in the Court of Appeals, respondents argued that the District Court had abused its discretion by not issuing an injunction in the face of "a blatant statutory violation." The Court of Appeals agreed, and on January 31, 1977, it reversed, remanding "with instructions that a permanent injunction issue halting all activities incident to the Tellico Project which may destroy or modify the critical habitat of the snail darter." * * *

II

* * *

[T]wo questions are presented: (a) Would TVA be in violation of the Act if it completed and operated the Tellico Dam as planned? (b) If TVA's actions would offend the Act, is an injunction the appropriate remedy for the violation? For the reasons stated hereinafter, we hold that both questions must be answered in the affirmative.

A

It may seem curious to some that the survival of a relatively small number of three-inch fish among all the countless millions of species extant would require the permanent halting of a virtually completed dam for which Congress has expended more than $100 million. The paradox is not minimized by the fact that Congress continued to appropriate large sums of public money for the project, even after congressional Appropriations Committees were apprised of its apparent impact upon the survival of the snail darter. We conclude, however, that the explicit provisions of the Endangered Species Act require precisely that result.

One would be hard pressed to find a statutory provision whose terms were any plainer than those in § 7 of the Endangered Species Act. Its very words affirmatively command all federal agencies "to *insure* that actions *authorized, funded,* or *carried out* by them do not *jeopardize* the continued existence" of an endangered species or "*result* in the destruction or modification of habitat of such species * * *." 16 U.S.C. § 1536. (Emphasis added.) This language admits of no exception. Nonetheless, petitioner urges, as do the dissenters, that the Act cannot reasonably be interpreted as applying to a federal project which was well under way when Congress passed the Endangered Species Act of 1973. [The Court rejects this argument.] * * *

Concededly, this view of the Act will produce results requiring the sacrifice of the anticipated benefits of the project and of many millions of dollars in public funds. But examination of the language, history, and structure of the legislation under review here indicates beyond doubt that Congress intended endangered species to be afforded the highest of priorities.

* * * [T]he legislative history undergirding § 7 reveals an explicit congressional decision to require agencies to afford first priority to the declared national policy of saving endangered species. The pointed omission of the type of qualifying language previously included in endangered species legislation reveals a conscious decision by Congress to give endangered species priority over the "primary missions" of federal agencies.

* * * One might * * * [argue] that in this case the burden on the public through the loss of millions of unrecoverable dollars would greatly outweigh the loss of the snail darter. But neither the Endangered Species Act nor Art. III of the Constitution provides federal courts with authority to make such fine utilitarian calculations. On the contrary, the plain language of the Act, buttressed by its legislative history, shows clearly that Congress viewed the value of endangered species as "incalculable." Quite obviously, it would be difficult for a court to balance the loss of a sum certain—even $100 million—against a congressionally declared "incalculable" value, even assuming we had the power to engage in such a weighing process, which we emphatically do not.

In passing the Endangered Species Act of 1973, Congress was also aware of certain instances in which exceptions to the statute's broad sweep would be necessary. Thus, § 10, 16 U.S.C. § 1539 (1976 ed.), creates a number of limited "hardship exemptions," none of which would even remotely apply to the Tellico Project. In fact, there are no exemptions in the Endangered Species Act for federal agencies, meaning that under the maxim *expressio unius est exclusio alterius* [the expression of one thing implies the exclusion of the other], we must presume that these were the only "hardship cases" Congress intended to exempt.

* * * [W]e are urged to find that the continuing appropriations for Tellico Dam constitute an implied repeal of the 1973 Act, at least insofar as it applies to the Tellico Project. In support of this view, TVA points to the statements found in various House and Senate Appropriations Committees' Reports; those Reports generally reflected the attitude of the Committees either that the Act did not apply to Tellico or that the dam should be completed regardless of the provisions of the Act. Since we are unwilling to assume that these latter Committee statements constituted advice to ignore the provisions of a duly enacted law, we assume that these Committees believed that the Act simply was not applicable in this situation. But even under this interpretation of the Committees' actions, we are unable to conclude that the Act has been in any respect amended or repealed. * * *

B

Having determined that there is an irreconcilable conflict between operation of the Tellico Dam and the explicit provisions of § 7 of the Endangered Species Act, we must now consider what remedy, if any, is appropriate. It is correct, of course, that a federal judge sitting as a chancellor is not mechanically obligated to grant an injunction for every violation of law. This Court made plain in Hecht Co. v. Bowles, 321 U.S. 321, 329, 64 S.Ct. 587, 591, 88 L.Ed. 754 (1944), that "[a] grant of jurisdiction to issue compliance orders hardly suggests an absolute duty to do so under any and all circumstances." As a general matter it may be said that "[s]ince all or almost all equitable remedies are discretionary, the balancing of equities and hardships is appropriate in almost any case as a guide to the chancellor's discretion." D. Dobbs, Remedies 52 (1973). Thus, in *Hecht Co.* the Court refused to grant an injunction when it appeared from the District Court findings that "the issuance of an injunction would have 'no effect by way of insuring better compliance in the future' and would [have been] 'unjust' to [the] petitioner and not 'in the public interest.'"

But these principles take a court only so far. Our system of government is, after all, a tripartite one, with each branch having certain defined functions delegated to it by the Constitution. While "[i]t is emphatically the province and duty of the judicial department to say what the law is," Marbury v. Madison, 1 Cranch 137, 177, 2 L.Ed. 60 (1803), it is equally—and emphatically—the exclusive province of the Congress not only to formulate legislative policies and mandate programs and projects, but also to establish their relative priority for the Nation. Once Congress, exercising its delegated powers, has decided the order of priorities in a given area, it is for the Executive to administer the laws and for the courts to enforce them when enforcement is sought.

Here we are urged to view the Endangered Species Act "reasonably," and hence shape a remedy "that accords with some modicum of common sense and the public weal." But is that our function? We have no expert knowledge on the subject of endangered species, much less do we have a mandate from the people to strike a balance of equities on the side of the Tellico Dam. Congress has spoken in the plainest of words, making it abundantly clear that the balance has been struck in favor of affording endangered species the highest of priorities, thereby adopting a policy which it described as "institutionalized caution."

Our individual appraisal of the wisdom or unwisdom of a particular course consciously selected by the Congress is to be put aside in the process of interpreting a statute. Once the meaning of an enactment is discerned and its constitutionality determined, the judicial process comes to an end. We do not sit as a committee of review, nor are we vested with the power of veto. The lines ascribed to Sir Thomas More by Robert Bolt are not without relevance here:

> "The law, Roper, the law. I know what's legal, not what's right. And I'll stick to what's legal.... I'm not God. The currents and eddies of right and wrong, which you find such plain-sailing, I can't navigate, I'm no voyager. But in the thickets of the law, oh there I'm a forester.... What would you do? Cut a great road through the law to get after the Devil? ... And when the last law was down, and the Devil turned round on you—where would you hide, Roper, the laws all being flat? ... This country's planted thick with laws from coast to coast—Man's laws, not God's—and if you cut them down ... d'you really think you could stand upright in the winds that would blow them? ... Yes, I'd give the Devil benefit of law, for my own safety's sake." R. Bolt, A Man for All Seasons, Act I, p. 147 (Three Plays, Heinemann ed. 1967).

We agree with the Court of Appeals that in our constitutional system the commitment to the separation of powers is too fundamental for us to pre-empt congressional action by judicially decreeing what accords with "common sense and the public weal." Our Constitution vests such responsibilities in the political branches.

Affirmed.

Mr. Justice Powell, with whom Mr. Justice Blackmun joins, dissenting.

[Justice Powell's opinion took issue with the majority's conclusion as to liability.]

Mr. Justice Rehnquist, dissenting.

In the light of my Brother Powell's dissenting opinion, I am far less convinced than is the Court that the Endangered Species Act of 1973 was intended to prohibit the completion of the Tellico Dam. But the very difficulty and doubtfulness of the correct answer to this legal question convinces me that the Act did not prohibit the District Court from refusing, in the exercise of its traditional equitable powers, to enjoin petitioner from completing the Dam. * * *

This Court had occasion in Hecht Co. v. Bowles, 321 U.S. 321, 64 S.Ct. 587, 88 L.Ed. 754 (1944), to construe language in an Act of Congress that lent far greater support to a conclusion that Congress intended an injunction to issue as a matter of right than does the language just quoted. * * *

I choose to adhere to *Hecht Co.'s* teaching:

> "[A] grant of jurisdiction to issue compliance orders hardly suggests an absolute duty to do so under any and all circumstances. We cannot but think that if Congress had intended to make such a drastic departure from the traditions of equity practice, an unequivocal statement of its purpose would have been made." 321 U.S., at 329, 64 S.Ct., at 591.

Since the District Court possessed discretion to refuse injunctive relief even though it had found a violation of the Act, the only remaining question is whether this discretion was abused in denying respondents' prayer for an injunction. The District Court denied respondents injunctive relief because of the significant public and social harms that would flow from such relief and because of the demonstrated good faith of petitioner. * * *

NOTES

1. Consider three possible interpretations of *TVA v. Hill*: (a) equitable discretion may never be used to allow a statutory violation to continue, (b) equitable discretion may in general be so used, but that the Endangered Species Act prohibited balancing in cases arising under it, or (c) equitable discretion may be so used and the Act does not forbid balancing, but that the balancing in this case came out in favor of the snail darters. Which of these three interpretations best fits the Court's opinion? Assuming that balancing is permissible in the context of the Endangered Species Act, do the equities compel the issuance of the injunction? Would your answer change if scientists agreed that the snail darter could survive and flourish if relocated to another habitat? Would your answer change if the scientists so agreed and TVA knew, before building the dam, that a critical habitat of an endangered species would be destroyed?

2. Subsequently, the Court in National Association of Home Builders v. Defenders of Wildlife, 551 U.S. 644, 127 S.Ct. 2518, 168 L.Ed.2d 467 (2007), interpreted *TVA v. Hill* as standing for the proposition that the Endangered Species Act's "no-jeopardy mandate applies to every *discretionary* agency action—regardless of the burden or expense its application might impose." It distinguished *Home Builders* based upon the mandatory nature of the agency action at issue.

3. American and Russian health agencies, which hold what was thought to be the last known stocks of smallpox virus in liquid nitrogen freezers in Atlanta and Moscow, had agreed to destroy them at the end of 1993, reasoning that the danger posed by release through accident or sabotage was greater than any benefit of keeping them intact. When, however, reports reached Washington that the Russian government was stockpiling smallpox for possible use in germ warfare, the United States prompted a committee of the World Health Organization (WHO) to postpone the destruction of the virus. New York Times, May 22, 1999, at A3. After the attacks on the United States on September 11, 2001, and the subsequent anthrax cases, public health experts expressed concern that smallpox virus may also be in the hands of terrorists. If the United States were ever to decide to destroy the smallpox samples, would a court have to enjoin the destruction?

4. *After the case was over.* Congress eventually enacted legislation that authorized putting the dam into operation although a cost-benefit analysis concluded that, even not counting the money already spent to build the dam, the additional costs of putting it into operation—such as submerging large amounts of farm land—would outweigh the benefits. Zygmunt J.B. Plater, Endangered Species Act Lessons Over 30 Years, and the Legacy of the Snail Darter, a Small Fish in a Pork Barrel, 34 Envt'l L. 289 (2004) (article cites Plater's other writings concerning his experiences with the case). For further information on the environmental and administrative significance of *TVA v. Hill*, see Kenneth M. Murchison, The Snail Darter Case: TVA Versus the Endangered Species Act (2007). Snail darters were discovered ultimately in many other habitats. Those who want to develop a listed habitat now hire consultants who will search out unknown habitats of endangered species. See also David Schoenbrod, Saving Our Environment From Washington: How Congress Grabs Power, Shirks Responsibility, and Shortchanges the People (2005).

WEINBERGER v. ROMERO–BARCELO

Supreme Court of the United States, 1982
456 U.S. 305, 102 S.Ct. 1798, 72 L.Ed.2d 91

JUSTICE WHITE delivered the opinion of the Court.

The issue in this case is whether the Federal Water Pollution Control Act (FWPCA or Act), 86 Stat. 816, as amended, 33 U.S.C. § 1251 et seq. (1976 ed. and Supp. IV), requires a district court to enjoin immediately all discharges of pollutants that do not comply with the Act's permit requirements or whether the district court retains discretion to order other relief to achieve compliance. The Court of Appeals for the First Circuit held that the Act withdrew the courts' equitable discretion. We reverse.

I

For many years, the Navy has used Vieques Island, a small island off the Puerto Rico coast, for weapons training. * * * During air-to-ground training, however, pilots sometimes miss land-based targets, and ordnance falls into the sea. That is, accidental bombings of the navigable waters and, occasionally, intentional bombings of water targets occur. The District Court found that these discharges have not harmed the quality of the water.

In 1978, respondents, who include the Governor of Puerto Rico and residents of the island, sued to enjoin the Navy's operations on the island. * * * After an extensive hearing, the District Court found that under the explicit terms of the Act, the Navy had violated the Act by discharging ordnance into the waters surrounding the island without first obtaining a permit from the Environmental Protection Agency (EPA). [The Navy had contended that no permit was required.]

Under the FWPCA, the "discharge of any pollutant" requires a National Pollutant Discharge Elimination System (NPDES) permit. 33 U.S.C. §§ 1311(a), 1323(a). * * *

As the District Court construed the FWPCA, the release of ordnance from aircraft or from ships into navigable waters is a discharge of pollutants, even though the EPA, which administers the Act, had not promulgated any regulations setting effluent levels or providing for the issuance of an NPDES permit for this category of pollutants. Recognizing that violations of the Act "must be cured," the District Court ordered the Navy to apply for an NPDES permit. It refused, however, to enjoin Navy operations pending consideration of the permit application. It explained that the Navy's "technical violations" were not causing any "appreciable harm" to the environment.[4] Moreover, because of the importance of the island as a training center, "the granting of the injunctive relief sought would cause grievous, and perhaps irreparable harm, not only to Defendant Navy, but to the general welfare of this Nation."[5] The District Court concluded that an injunction was not necessary to ensure suitably prompt compliance by the Navy. To support this conclusion, it emphasized an equity court's traditionally broad discretion in deciding appropriate relief and quoted from the classic description of injunctive relief in Hecht Co. v. Bowles, 321 U.S. 321, 329–330, 64 S.Ct. 587, 591–592, 88 L.Ed. 754 (1944): "The historic injunctive process was designed to deter, not to punish."

The Court of Appeals for the First Circuit vacated the District Court's order and remanded with instructions that the court order the Navy to cease the violation until it obtained a permit. Relying on *TVA v. Hill*, * * * the Court of Appeals concluded that the District Court erred in undertaking a traditional balancing of the parties' competing interests.

---

4. The District Court wrote:

"In fact, if anything, these waters are as aesthetically acceptable as any to be found anywhere, and Plaintiff's witnesses unanimously testified as to their being the best fishing grounds in Vieques." "[I]f the truth be said, the control of large areas of Vieques [by the Navy] probably constitutes a positive factor in its over all ecology. The very fact that there are in the Navy zones modest numbers of various marine species which are practically nonexistent in the civilian sector of Vieques or in the main island of Puerto Rico, is an eloquent example of res ipsa loquitur."

5. The District Court also took into consideration the delay by plaintiffs in asserting their claims. It concluded that although laches should not totally bar the claims, it did strongly militate against the granting of injunctive relief.

"Whether or not the Navy's activities in fact harm the coastal waters, it has an absolute statutory obligation to stop any discharges of pollutants until the permit procedure has been followed and the Administrator of the Environmental Protection Agency, upon review of the evidence, has granted a permit." The court suggested that if the order would interfere significantly with military preparedness, the Navy should request that the President grant it an exemption from the requirements "in the interest of national security."[6]

* * * We now reverse.

II

* * * Where plaintiff and defendant present competing claims of injury, the traditional function of equity has been to arrive at a "nice adjustment and reconciliation" between the competing claims, *Hecht Co. v. Bowles*. In such cases, the court "balances the conveniences of the parties and possible injuries to them according as they may be affected by the granting or withholding of the injunction." Yakus v. United States, 321 U.S. 414, 440, 64 S.Ct. 660, 675, 88 L.Ed. 834 (1944). * * *

In exercising their sound discretion, courts of equity should pay particular regard for the public consequences in employing the extraordinary remedy of injunction. * * * The grant of jurisdiction to ensure compliance with a statute hardly suggests an absolute duty to do so under any and all circumstances, and a federal judge sitting as chancellor is not mechanically obligated to grant an injunction for every violation of law. *TVA v. Hill; Hecht Co. v. Bowles.*

These commonplace considerations applicable to cases in which injunctions are sought in the federal courts reflect a "practice with a background of several hundred years of history," *Hecht Co. v. Bowles*, a practice of which Congress is assuredly well aware. Of course, Congress may intervene and guide or control the exercise of the courts' discretion, but we do not lightly assume that Congress has intended to depart from established principles. *Hecht Co. v. Bowles*. As the Court said in Porter v. Warner Holding Co., 328 U.S. 395, 398, 66 S.Ct. 1086, 1089, 90 L.Ed. 1332 (1946):

> "Moreover, the comprehensiveness of this equitable jurisdiction is not to be denied or limited in the absence of a clear and valid legislative command. Unless a statute in so many words, or by a necessary and inescapable inference, restricts the court's jurisdiction in equity, the full scope of that jurisdiction is to be recognized and applied. 'The great principles of equity, securing complete justice, should not be yielded to light inferences, or doubtful construction.' Brown v. Swann, 10 Pet. 497, 503 [9 L.Ed. 508] . . ."

---

6. Title 33 U.S.C. § 1323(a)(1976) ed., Supp. IV, provides, in relevant part:

"The President may exempt any effluent source of any department, agency, or instrumentality in the executive branch from compliance with any such a requirement if he determines it to be in the paramount interest of the United States to do so.... * * *."

In *TVA v. Hill,* we held that Congress had foreclosed the exercise of the usual discretion possessed by a court of equity. There, we thought that "[o]ne would be hard pressed to find a statutory provision whose terms were any plainer" than that before us. * * * The purpose and language of the statute under consideration in *Hill,* not the bare fact of a statutory violation, compelled that conclusion. * * *

The purpose and language of the statute limited the remedies available to the District Court; only an injunction could vindicate the objectives of the Act.

That is not the case here. An injunction is not the only means of ensuring compliance. The FWPCA itself, for example, provides for fines and criminal penalties. 33 U.S.C. §§ 1319(c) and (d). Respondents suggest that failure to enjoin the Navy will undermine the integrity of the permit process by allowing the statutory violation to continue. The integrity of the Nation's waters, however, not the permit process, is the purpose of the FWPCA.[7] * * *

This purpose is to be achieved by compliance with the Act, including compliance with the permit requirements. Here, however, the discharge of ordnance had not polluted the waters, and, although the District Court declined to enjoin the discharges, it neither ignored the statutory violation nor undercut the purpose and function of the permit system. The court ordered the Navy to apply for a permit. It temporarily, not permanently, allowed the Navy to continue its activities without a permit.

In *Hill,* we also noted that none of the limited "hardship exemptions" of the Endangered Species Act would "even remotely apply to the Tellico Project." The prohibition of the FWPCA against discharge of pollutants, in contrast, can be overcome by the very permit the Navy was ordered to seek. The Senate Report to the 1972 Amendments explains that the permit program would be enacted because "the Committee recognizes the impracticality of any effort to halt all pollution immediately." S.Rep. No. 92–414, p. 43 (1971), U.S.Code Cong. & Admin.News 1972, p. 3709. That the scheme as a whole contemplates the exercise of discretion and balancing of equities militates against the conclusion that Congress intended to deny courts their traditional equitable discretion in enforcing the statute.

Other aspects of the statutory scheme also suggest that Congress did not intend to deny courts the discretion to rely on remedies other than an immediate prohibitory injunction. Although the ultimate objective of the FWPCA is to eliminate all discharges of pollutants into the navigable waters by 1985, the statute sets forth a scheme of phased compliance. * * * This scheme of phased compliance further suggests that this is a statute in which Congress envisioned, rather than curtailed, the exercise of discretion.

---

7. The objective of this statute is in some respects similar to that sought in nuisance suits, where courts have fully exercised their equitable discretion and ingenuity in ordering remedies. E.g., Spur Industries, Inc. v. Del E. Webb Development Co., 108 Ariz. 178, 494 P.2d 700 (1972); Boomer v. Atlantic Cement Co., 26 N.Y.2d 219, 309 N.Y.S.2d 312, 257 N.E.2d 870 (1970).

The FWPCA directs the Administrator of the EPA to seek an injunction to restrain immediately discharges of pollutants he finds to be presenting "an imminent and substantial endangerment to the health of persons or to the welfare of persons." 33 U.S.C. § 1364(a). This rule of immediate cessation, however, is limited to the indicated class of violations. For other kinds of violations, the FWPCA authorizes the Administrator of the EPA "to commence a civil action for appropriate relief, including a permanent or temporary injunction, for any violation for which he is authorized to issue a compliance order * * *." 33 U.S.C. § 1319(b). The provision makes clear that Congress did not anticipate that all discharges would be immediately enjoined. Consistent with this view, the administrative practice has not been to request immediate cessation orders. * * *

Both the Court of Appeals and respondents attach particular weight to the provision of the FWPCA permitting the President to exempt federal facilities from compliance with the permit requirements. 33 U.S.C. § 1323(a). They suggest that this provision indicates congressional intent to limit the court's discretion. According to respondents, the exemption provision evidences Congress' determination that only paramount national interests justify failure to comply and that only the President should make this judgment.

We do not construe the provision so broadly. We read the FWPCA as permitting the exercise of a court's equitable discretion, whether the source of pollution is a private party or a federal agency, to order relief that will achieve compliance with the Act. The exemption serves a different and complementary purpose, that of permitting noncompliance by federal agencies in extraordinary circumstances. * * *

Should the Navy receive a permit here, there would be no need to invoke the machinery of the Presidential exemption. If not, this course remains open. The exemption provision would enable the President, believing paramount national interests so require, to authorize discharges which the District Court has enjoined. Reading the statute to permit the exercise of a court's equitable discretion in no way eliminates the role of the exemption provision in the statutory scheme. * * *

III

* * *

The District Court did not face a situation in which a permit would very likely not issue, and the requirements and objective of the statute could therefore not be vindicated if discharges were permitted to continue. Should it become clear that no permit will be issued and that compliance with the FWPCA will not be forthcoming, the statutory scheme and purpose would require the court to reconsider the balance it has struck.

Because Congress, in enacting the FWPCA, has not foreclosed the exercise of equitable discretion, the proper standard for appellate review is whether the District Court abused its discretion in denying an immediate cessation order while the Navy applied for a permit. We reverse and remand to the Court of Appeals for proceedings consistent with this opinion. * * *

JUSTICE POWELL, concurring. [Opinion omitted.]

JUSTICE STEVENS, dissenting.

The appropriate remedy for the violation of a federal statute depends primarily on the terms of the statute and the character of the violation. Unless Congress specifically commands a particular form of relief, the question of remedy remains subject to a court's equitable discretion. Because the Federal Water Pollution Control Act does not specifically command the federal courts to issue an injunction every time an unpermitted discharge of a pollutant occurs, the Court today is obviously correct in asserting that such injunctions should not issue "automatically" or "mechanically" in every case. It is nevertheless equally clear that by enacting the 1972 Amendments to the FWPCA Congress channeled the discretion of the federal judiciary much more narrowly than the Court's rather glib opinion suggests. Indeed, although there may well be situations in which the failure to obtain an NPDES permit would not require immediate cessation of all discharges, I am convinced that Congress has circumscribed the district courts' discretion on the question of remedy so narrowly that a general rule of immediate cessation must be applied in all but a narrow category of cases. The Court of Appeals was quite correct in holding that this case does not present the kind of exceptional situation that justifies a departure from the general rule.

* * * [T]he Court's opinion grants an open-ended license to federal judges to carve gaping holes in a reticulated statutory scheme designed by Congress to protect a precious natural resource from the consequences of ad hoc judgments about specific discharges of pollutants.

I

Contrary to the impression created by the Court's opinion, * * * [t]he Court of Appeals did not hold that the District Court had no discretion in formulating remedies for statutory violations. It merely "conclude[d] that the district court erred in undertaking a traditional balancing of the parties' competing interests." The District Court was not free to disregard the "congressional ordering of priorities" and "the judiciary's 'responsibility to protect the integrity of the ... process mandated by Congress.'" The Court of Appeals distinguished a statutory violation that could be deemed merely "technical" from the Navy's "[utter disregard of] the statutory mandate." It then pointed out that an order prohibiting any discharge of ordnance into the coastal waters off Vieques until an NPDES permit was obtained would not significantly affect the Navy's training operations because most, if not all, of the Navy's targets were land-based. Finally, it noted that the statute authorized the Navy to obtain an exemption from the President if an injunction would have a significant effect on national security.

Under these circumstances—the statutory violation is blatant and not merely technical, and the Navy's predicament was foreseen and accommodated by Congress—the Court of Appeals essentially held that the District Court retained no discretion to deny an injunction. The discretion exercised by the District Court in this case was wholly at odds with the intent of Congress in enacting the FWPCA. In essence, the District Court's remedy was a judicial permit exempting the Navy's operations in Vieques from the statute until such time as it could obtain a permit from the Environmental Protection Agency or a statutory exemption from the President. The two principal bases for the temporary judicial permit were matters that Congress did not commit to judicial discretion. First, the District Court was persuaded that the pollution was not harming the quality of the coastal waters, and second, the court was concerned that compliance with the Act might adversely affect national security. The Court of Appeals correctly noted that the first consideration is the business of the EPA and the second is the business of the President. * * *

II
* * *

The Court cites no precedent for its holding that an ongoing deliberate violation of a federal statute should be treated like any garden-variety private nuisance action in which the chancellor has the widest discretion in fashioning relief.[9]

Our prior cases involving the appropriate remedy for an ongoing violation of federal law establish a much more stringent test than the Court applies today. * * *

In Albemarle Paper Co. v. Moody, 422 U.S. 405, 95 S.Ct. 2362, 45 L.Ed.2d 280, the Court plainly stated that an equitable remedy for the violation of a federal statute was neither automatic on the one hand, nor simply a matter of balancing the equities on the other. *Albemarle* holds that the district court's remedial decision must be measured against the purposes that inform the Act of Congress that has been violated.

III
* * *

It is true that in *TVA v. Hill* there was no room for compromise between the federal project and the statutory objective to preserve the endangered species; either the snail darter or the completion of the Tellico Dam had to be sacrificed. In the FWPCA, the Court tells us, the congressional objective is to protect the integrity of the Nation's waters, not to protect the integrity of the permit process. Therefore, the Court continues, a federal court may compromise the process chosen by Congress to protect our waters as long as the court is content that the waters are not actually being harmed by the particular discharge of pollutants.

---

9. Indeed, I am unaware of any case in which the Court has permitted a statutory violation to continue.

On analysis, however, this reasoning does not distinguish the two cases. Courts are in no better position to decide whether the permit process is necessary to achieve the objectives of the FWPCA than they are to decide whether the destruction of the snail darter is an acceptable cost of completing the Tellico Dam. Congress has made both decisions, and there is nothing in the respective statutes or legislative histories to suggest that Congress invited the federal courts to second-guess the former decision any more than the latter. * * *

IV

The decision in *TVA v. Hill* did not depend on any peculiar or unique statutory language. Nor did it rest on any special interest in snail darters. The decision reflected a profound respect for the law and the proper allocation of lawmaking responsibilities in our Government. There we refused to sit as a committee of review. Today the Court authorizes free-thinking federal judges to do just that. Instead of requiring adherence to carefully integrated statutory procedures that assign to nonjudicial decision makers the responsibilities for evaluating potential harm to our water supply as well as potential harm to our national security, the Court unnecessarily and casually substitutes the chancellor's clumsy foot for the rule of law. * * *

NOTES

1. *Goals and factors.* In considering whether *Weinberger* is consistent with *Hill*, recall the three proposed readings of *Hill* in note 1 to that case (p. 121). None of the opinions in *Weinberger* embraces the first of those readings—that equitable discretion may never be used to allow a statutory violation to continue. But, all concede that the statute in question affects how the equities are balanced. In particular, the opinions are concerned with the goals of the Federal Water Pollution Control Act and the factors that Congress considered in enacting it.

(a) *The statutory goals.* How do the majority and dissent view the goals of the statute? Whose view is most plausible? Is that view consistent with giving the Navy time to apply for a permit?

(b) *Factors that Congress considered.* Justice Stevens' dissent argues that the absence of harm to water quality cannot be the basis for allowing the violation to continue because Congress required all sources to get permits regardless of harmfulness. He also argues that national security cannot be the basis because Congress created presidential exemptions to deal with national security. If neither lack of harmfulness nor national security alone is sufficient to allow a violation to continue, might they still be weighed in the balance if the case presents some other factor that Congress did not take into account?

Does *Weinberger* mean that polluters can safely wait until a judgment of liability is entered against them before applying for a permit? Suppose, for example, that the defendant was not the United States Navy but a privately owned factory discharging some harmless liquid into a stream, that the factory would have to close down if it could not discharge while its permit application was pending, and it had not applied for a permit before litigation began because it was unaware that the FWPCA applied to it. Should the courts allow the violation to continue pending a permit application? See David Schoenbrod, The Measure of An Injunction: A Principle to Replace Balancing the Equities and Tailoring the Remedy, 72 Minn.L.Rev. 627, 650–651 (1988).

If you think that the violation can continue in this first hypo, should the result be any different if the defendant was aware of the plaintiff's contention that the FWPCA applied, but believed the plaintiff to be wrong? In City of Los Angeles v. Manhart, 435 U.S. 702, 720, 98 S.Ct. 1370, 1381, 55 L.Ed.2d 657, 672 (1978), the Court balanced the equities in the defendants' favor in part because they, not having "the benefit of the extensive briefs and arguments presented to us, may well have assumed that a program like [theirs] was entirely lawful. The courts had been silent on the question, and the administrative agencies had conflicting views."

Should it make any difference if the factory is federally owned but has nothing to do with national security?

Is the Navy's case distinguishable from the previous hypo? A possible distinction is that the Navy did not believe in good faith that it was not liable, but rather used litigation to stall for time. Courts, however, usually feel impelled to assume that coordinate branches of government operate in good faith unless that assumption is demonstrably wrong. But once a court thinks that a defendant is gaming the process, that defendant gets little sympathy. For example, a court enjoined a builder to remove the top twelve floors of a New York City skyscraper. The court found that the builder should have known that the building was taller than was permitted. Parkview Associates v. City of New York, 71 N.Y.2d 274, 525 N.Y.S.2d 176, 519 N.E.2d 1372 (1988). Moreover, once the violation became an issue, the developer rushed to finish the upper floors. Andrew Maykuth, 12 Floors Falling to a Zoning Law: New York Skyscraper Knocked Down to Size, Philadelphia Inquirer, Feb. 22, 1993 at 1.

For analysis showing how the goals and structure of other statutes affect the balancing of the equities, see Owner Operator Independent Drivers Association, Inc. v. Swift Transportation Co., 367 F.3d 1108 (9th Cir.2004) (discusses *Hecht*, *TVA* and *Weinberger* while rejecting the contention that Congress has directed the federal courts to apply reasonable cause test rather than traditional equitable principles for injunctive enforcement of the Truth-in-Leasing regulations); Note, Injunctions for NEPA Violations: Balancing the Equities, 59 U.Chi.L.Rev. 1263 (1992).

2. *Statutory interpretation.* Professor Plater argued, in an article made available to the Court while *Weinberger* was under consideration, that balancing the equities to allow statutory violations to continue is never permissible unless the legislature explicitly permits it. Zygmunt Plater, Statutory Violations and Equitable Discretion, 70 Calif.L.Rev. 524 (1982). Professor Plater's canon of statutory construction is precisely opposite to that in *Hecht*, which states in essence that courts have the power to balance unless the legislature explicitly denies it. How the courts approach this question of statutory interpretation is usually decisive because legislatures hardly ever speak explic-

itly to what discretion courts should have in issuing injunctions. Is Professor Dobbs correct in saying the "Schoenbrod principle" is "a good guide to the construction of statutes"? Dan B. Dobbs, Law of Remedies § 2.10 at 181 (2d ed.1993). Which approach is more likely to reflect what legislators assume about the enforcement of statutes that they enact?

3. *The role of judges.* Is legislative intent the issue here or is it instead the appropriate role for judges? Recall that Justice Harlan, in suggesting in *Bivens* that courts should have power to create remedies where a statute does not explicitly deny that power, showed no concern with legislative intent and much concern with what judges ought to have the power to do. Professor Chayes' article on the role of the judge in public law litigation argues that judges should have broad discretion to balance the equities; Professor Plater argues that judges should have no discretion in statutory cases; Professor Schoenbrod argues for a middle ground. Which position is most compatible with the role of judges in our governmental system? Justice Stevens in *Weinberger* argues that "[c]ourts are in no better position to decide whether the permit process is necessary to achieve the objectives of the FWPCA than they are to decide whether the destruction of the snail darter is an acceptable cost of completing the Tellico Dam." Does balancing put a district court judge in an untenable position? Would the lack of power to balance put a district court judge in an untenable position?

DAVID SCHOENBROD, THE MEASURE OF AN INJUNCTION: A PRINCIPLE TO REPLACE BALANCING THE EQUITIES AND TAILORING THE REMEDY

72 Minn.L.Rev. 627, 654–57, 664–66 (1988)

* * * In determining liability, the judge decides only whether the elements of the violation are present, whereas in balancing the equities when fashioning a remedy, the judge also considers whether there are factors that make it unfair to order the defendant to stop the violation immediately. For instance, if the defendant builds a structure that violates the setback requirements of the local zoning ordinance, that is the beginning and end of the question of liability. If the plaintiff wants the violation enjoined, however, the judge will want to know whether the defendant encroached intentionally or recklessly, the cost to defendant of removing the encroachment, whether removing the encroachment will harm innocent third parties, the importance to the plaintiff of having the encroachment removed, and so on. Courts make this broader inquiry at the remedial stage primarily because granting an injunction rather than damages presents a greater threat of gross inefficiency.

Consequently, equity introduces flexibility into the cold enforcement of law to address the inefficiencies associated with injunctive relief. This flexibility is justified because the judicial process in cases that seek remedies at law has sources of flexibility not available in cases that seek equitable relief. In suits for damages, much of what goes into balancing the equities in injunction cases gets reflected in jury nullification, the determination of the amount of compensatory or punitive damages, limits on garnishment and execution designed to avoid severe hardship, and sometimes a kind of balancing of the equities in the damage context itself. Moreover, criminal actions involve flexibility in prosecutorial discretion, jury nullification, and sentencing judgment. Thus, a suit for an injunction without balancing the equities would present a rare instance of the judicial process without a safety valve.

Although Plater claims that judges should not balance the equities in statutory cases and should apply statutory rules strictly, the reasons for balancing in nonstatutory cases apply fully to statutory cases. In nonstatutory cases, courts balance the equities because injunctive enforcement of a rule of liability that is fair and efficient in general may be unfair or inefficient in a particular context. In formulating statutory rules, legislatures can rarely confine statutory definitions of violations to instances in which enjoining them would invariably be fair and efficient. Judges need the kind of flexibility that they have in nonstatutory cases to act as a safety valve to prevent unfair and inefficient application of a statutory rule. Plater argues that legislative relief, not balancing the equities, provides the appropriate safety valve in statutory cases. That safety valve, however, is available only in extraordinary cases that get priority on the legislative agenda, such as *TVA v. Hill,* not in garden variety cases. The proposed principle provides a safety valve for all statutory cases by giving judges the flexibility necessary, but in a way that restrains judges' discretion, forcing them to honor the choices that the legislature did make.

Moreover, both Plater's and Chayes's approaches would put the judge in a difficult personal position. The judge in street clothes is in principle an equal of the parties. What justifies the power of the judge in robes is that the judge speaks the law. Regarding findings of liability, judges can readily respond to a defendant's rebuke "how dare you find me liable," with "the law made you liable." This answer is inadequate, however, when the defendant challenges the judge's authority to issue an injunction because the judge must exercise discretion in shaping the injunction to fit the case.[138] Relative to the finding of liability, the injunction therefore looks more like personal opinion than impersonal law. By requiring the judge to end the statutory violation regardless of the consequences, Plater's approach would subject the judge to personal criticism by taking away the judge's flexibility to mitigate the consequences. Similarly, by turning the judge into a policy maker, Chayes's approach fails to offer constraints to both legitimate the exercise of equitable discretion and allow the judge to cast at least some of the blame for the injunction's consequences onto the law. * * *

Plater [attempts] to justify permitting broad discretion to grant injunctions in constitutional and common law cases while denying it in statutory cases on the basis that constitutions and the common law

---

138. Even if the judge decides that the violation must end, the injunction will have to state the terms on which this will happen.

provide rules of liability in terms more open textured than do statutory rules of liability. Plater argues that because judges have more discretion in determining the scope of liability in constitutional and common law cases than in statutory cases, they should similarly have more freedom in fashioning injunctive relief in such cases. In determining liability under statutes, common law, and constitutions, however, Professor Ronald Dworkin asserts that judges should interpret the law rather than make policy decisions. As a result, liability in those cases arguably is not a product of discretion, and therefore there is no discretion in determining liability to independently justify discretion in fashioning relief.

If judges disagree with Dworkin and believe that they should make policy decisions in constitutional and common law cases, judges should nevertheless apply the proposed principle to guide the exercise of that discretion in formulating relief. There is no persuasive reason to use different standards when the relevant authority controlling liability is statutory as opposed to case law. If precedent—constitutional or common law—controls the liability decision in the case at hand, the judge's attitude toward that precedent in formulating relief should be just as respectful as it would be toward a controlling statute. As Professors Owen Fiss and Doug Rendleman suggest, it would be bizarre if judges had more freedom to undercut constitutional rights than statutory rights through remedial discretion.

Even when precedent does not directly control the judge's liability decision and the judge can base the decision upon policy, the proposed principle should still apply at the remedy stage because it legitimates the judge's exercise of discretion by providing articulated limits. After fixing the rule of liability, the judge may still not want to grant an injunction that achieves the plaintiff's rightful position. The proposed principle would justify such a result if a remedy less than the plaintiff's rightful position does not conflict with the goals of the rule of liability created by the judge and the case involves a factor not reflected in that rule. If these requirements are not met and the judge denies full injunctive relief, the judge's decision ignores the policy concerns underlying the judge's own rule of liability. Candor as well as giving the public and the bar fair notice of the law's practical impact should compel the judge to restate the rule of liability based on an appropriate policy rationale rather than to grant relief contrary to the spirit of the judge's own rule of liability. * * *

NOTE ON BALANCING IN ADMINISTRATIVE ENFORCEMENT

Statutes frequently authorize administrative agencies to issue orders against violations of prohibitions in statutes or in agency-promulgated regulations. Unless the statute explicitly directs otherwise, the agencies usually do not take this authorization as a command to order the cessation of all violations forthwith, but rather exercise discretion to allow violations to continue in particular cases for reasons analogous to balancing the equities in the judicial sphere. See Alfred C. Aman, Jr., Administrative Equity: An

Analysis of Exceptions to Administrative Rules, 1982 Duke L.J. 277. Closely related to such administrative balancing the equities is the power to grant variances. Zoning ordinances and other legislation sometimes grant administrators the power to permit exceptions to broadly applicable rules of conduct when strict application of the rule would create hardship incommensurate with the public interest.

Instead of allowing violations to continue on a case-by-case basis, can an agency issue a regulation that allows a whole category of violations of a statute to continue on the basis of "equity"?

> Certain limited grounds for the creation of exemptions are inherent in the administrative process, and their unavailability under a statutory scheme should not be presumed, save in the face of the most unambiguous demonstration of congressional intent to foreclose them. But there exists no general administrative power to create exemptions to statutory requirements based upon the agency's perception of costs and benefits.

Alabama Power Co. v. Costle, 636 F.2d 323, 357 (D.C.Cir. 1979)(recognizing inherent power to grant categorical exemptions based upon administrative necessity and de minimis harm). But an agency's decision to create a de minimis exception is subject to review. E.g., Ober v. Whitman, 243 F.3d 1190 (9th Cir.2001).

3. GRANTING MORE THAN PLAINTIFF'S RIGHTFUL POSITION: PROPHYLAXIS AND IMPOSSIBILITY

PROBLEM: COUNTRY LODGE V. MILLER (REPRISED)
PROPHYLACTIC ORDERS

Suppose that Country Lodge's rightful position is that Miller put into the river no more than 50 pounds of waste per week. Country Lodge asks that Miller be enjoined from putting any apple mash in the river on the grounds that it does not know how much is going into the river. Miller objects that she will then have to cart away not only the mash, at a cost of $20,000 per year, but also the water used to clean the cider press at an additional cost of $30,000 per year. Should the court grant Country Lodge's request?

Deciding whether to issue an injunction that grants more than the plaintiff's rightful position, like deciding whether to issue an injunction that grants less, involves balancing. See David Schoenbrod, The Measure of an Injunction: A Principle to Replace Balancing the Equities and Tailoring the Remedy, 72 Minn.L.Rev. 627, 633–34 & nn. 20–23, 636–37 & nn. 41–48 (1988). There are interesting differences and similarities in how the balancing is done. To get an injunction that grants less, the defendant must justify that result through a factor not reflected in the law of liability—a "hardship." To get an injunction that grants more, the plaintiff also must justify the result through a factor not reflected in the law of liability—the difficulty of supervising a resistant defendant or the impossibility of precisely recreating the plaintiff's rightful position. The defendant must show that the hardship outweighs the plaintiff's interest in getting specific rather than substitutionary relief. The plaintiff must show that the threat to its rightful position from a narrower injunction outweighs the harm to the defendant from an injunction going beyond the plaintiff's rightful position. We have seen that in balancing claims of hardship, the courts take account of the respective faults of the parties and the goals of the law of liability. The same is true in balancing plaintiffs' request for broader relief. The degree of the defendant's culpability in violating either the plaintiff's rights or an earlier injunction counts against the defendant.

A good example in the context of a private contract is Paramount Pictures v. Davis, 228 Cal.App.2d 827, 39 Cal.Rptr. 791 (1964). The actor Bette Davis had signed a contract that required her to work exclusively for Paramount on "Where Love Has Gone" for a certain period and thereafter to help finish the film on a nonexclusive basis. Davis honored the contract during the exclusive period but violated it by failing to cooperate on scheduling thereafter. The court prohibited her from working for anyone but Paramount until she completed her role. Paramount got her exclusive services for a longer period than specified in the contract (more than its rightful position), but only for the purpose of ensuring that she honor her commitment to finish the film (part of its rightful position). Ordering her not to work for anyone else gave the studio the upper hand in negotiating a work schedule. However, Davis' prior behavior gave grounds for suspicion that she would take advantage of an order that merely instructed her to complete her contractual obligations, especially after "the love has gone."

Courts may provide more injunctive relief than is necessary to ensure that the plaintiff will actually achieve her rightful position. This type of injunctive relief, often called a "prophylactic" injunction, addresses ancillary conduct with a sufficient causal nexus to the demonstrated harm that facilitates continued violations of the law. "The discretionary power of a district court to formulate an equitable remedy for an adjudicated violation of law is broad. Where necessary for the elimination of the violation, the decree can properly fence the defendant in by forbidding conduct not unlawful in itself." People Who Care v. Rockford Board of Education, 111 F.3d 528 (7th Cir.1997). Like prophylactic measures in medicine, the additional safeguards are taken to avoid future harm, such as a vaccination given to prevent a more serious disease. See Tracy A. Thomas, The Prophylactic Remedy: Normative Principles and Definitional Parameters of Broad Injunctive Relief, 52 Buff.L.Rev. 301 (2004).

A court might order a prophylactic injunction to ensure compliance with an injunction. For example, an injunction whose terms are geared precisely to the plaintiff's rightful position (e.g., "Miller shall discharge no more than 50 pounds of waste per week") may fail to achieve the plaintiff's rightful position if the defendant can disobey the order without being detected. When the threat of such harm is large enough, courts can hold the defendant to a more readily enforceable standard even though it exceeds the plaintiff's rightful position (e.g., "Miller shall discharge nothing" or "Miller shall additionally install a system to measure the amount of waste discharged"). The court still *aims* for the plaintiff's rightful position, but the *terms* of the injunction go beyond that position as prophylaxis against falling short of it. Thomas, Prophylactic Remedy, supra.

Prophylaxis developed in institutional reform cases involving schools, prisons, and other public institutions. For example, in the case of Women Prisoners v. District of Columbia, 877 F.Supp. 634 (D.D.C.1994), modified, 899 F.Supp. 659 (D.D.C.1995), vacated in part, 93 F.3d 910 (D.C.Cir.1996) (invalidating the appointment of a special monitor), the district court crafted a detailed prophylactic injunction addressing the proven constitutional and tort violations stemming from sexual harassment and assault of the women inmates by staff members. The defendant's history of similar violations and the egregious nature of the harms weighed in favor of practical alternatives and precautions that could effectively eliminate the opportunity for the behavior to continue. The district court believed further measures were necessary to address the contributing causes of the harm in order to better prevent future incidents. The prophylactic measures ordered included a complaint hotline, a formal grievance system, reporting mechanisms, employee sanctions, expert consultation, and staff training.

Hutto v. Finney, 437 U.S. 678, 98 S.Ct. 2565, 57 L.Ed.2d 522 (1978), is another instance of an injunction that went beyond the plaintiff's rightful position for prophylactic purposes. There, the district court had found that punitive isolation for longer than 30 days was not in itself cruel and unusual punishment but was so in combination with the terrible conditions in Arkansas's punitive isolation cells. The district court enjoined punitive isolation for longer than 30 days and the Supreme Court affirmed:

> In fashioning a remedy, the District Court had ample authority to go beyond earlier orders and to address each element contributing to the violation. The District Court had given the Department repeated opportunities to remedy the cruel and unusual conditions in the isolation cells. If petitioners had fully complied with the court's earlier orders, the present time limit might well have been unnecessary. But taking the long and unhappy history of the litigation into account, the court was justified in entering a comprehensive order to insure against the risk of inadequate compliance.

437 U.S. at 687, 98 S.Ct. at 2572, 57 L.Ed.2d at 532. *Hutto* suggests that injunctions that go beyond the plaintiffs' rightful position require a demonstrated risk that the defendants would not comply with a narrower order. Such a requirement parallels the requirement of showing a threat of harm to plaintiff's rightful position as a prerequisite to the issuance of any injunction. See section C(1) of this chapter.

Prophylactic orders are also common in enforcement of regulatory statutes. For example, after finding a violation of the securities laws, courts sometimes not only enjoin future violations but also ensure that they do not recur by prohibiting the violator from participating as an officer of any public company, imposing reporting requirements in addition to those in the securities laws, or appointing an independent majority on the violator's board of directors, a receiver, or "special professionals" to ensure compliance. George W. Dent Jr., Ancillary Relief in Federal Securities Law: A Study in Federal Remedies, 67 Minn.L.Rev. 865 (1983). See also FTC v. National Lead Co., 352 U.S. 419, 431, 77 S.Ct. 502, 510, 1 L.Ed.2d 438 (1957) ("[R]espondents must remember that those caught violating the Act must expect some fencing in").

Prophylactic relief, like structural injunctions, has been accused of constituting judicial activism that improperly extends "beyond the right." Certainly not all prophylactic injunctions are valid. *Rizzo*, discussed at pp. 46–52, is an example where the court failed to aim its injunction at a proven legal violation, and instead targeted secondary lawful conduct without any connection to an established wrong by the police department. Professor Tracy Thomas has argued that even the Supreme Court went too far its in establishment of "constitutionally required" prophylactic measures in *Bush v. Gore* that abridged, rather than supported, the voters' legal rights, thereby threatening the proper use and legitimacy of prophylaxis as a remedy. Understanding Prophylactic Remedies Through the Looking Glass of *Bush v. Gore*, 11 Wm. & M. Bill Rts J. 343 (2002). Courts, however, continue to use broad, prophylactic injunctions as an effective and necessary component of the remediation of complex cases. See Tracy A. Thomas, The Continued Vitality of Prophylactic Relief, 27 Rev.Lit. 99 (2007).

Courts issue orders that achieve more than the plaintiff's rightful position for a second reason—because it is impossible to achieve the plaintiff's rightful position precisely, even if the defendant cooperates. In McCarthy v. Briscoe, 429 U.S. 1317, 97 S.Ct. 10, 50 L.Ed.2d 49 (1976), Eugene McCarthy, a former senator, sought the Democratic Party nomination for president and lost. McCarthy then sought to run as an independent, but Texas enacted a statute forbidding independents to appear on the ballot if they had lost a bid for the nomination of a party. McCarthy succeeded in having the statute struck down as unconstitutional just weeks before the general election. Under Texas law, independents need a large number of petition signatures to appear on the ballot, a requirement that is, itself, constitutional. McCarthy had no way of meeting this requirement in the time remaining. His rightful position was to have an opportunity to gather the petition signatures unimpeded by the unconstitutional prohibition on his appearing on the ballot in the general election. Because the court could not recreate his rightful position, it gave him something better—the opportunity to appear on the ballot without any petition signatures.

For another example of an injunction that grants more than the plaintiff's rightful position because achieving it precisely is impossible, consider how the National Labor Relations Board (NLRB) responds to unfair labor practices by employers seeking to prevent their employees from voting to make a union their bargaining agent. The traditional remedy, which puts the employees in their rightful position, is for the NLRB to order that the violations cease and the election be held. When the violations make a fair election impossible and employee sentiment previously expressed through petitioning for an election suggests that the union would have won the election, the NLRB may make the union the exclusive bargaining agent without an election. NLRB v. Gissel Packing Co., 395 U.S. 575, 89 S.Ct. 1918, 23 L.Ed.2d 547 (1969). With impossibility, as with prophylaxis, courts look carefully to consider whether it is really necessary to grant an injunction that goes beyond the plaintiff's rightful position. In Montgomery Ward & Co. v. National Labor Relations Board, 904 F.2d 1156 (7th Cir.1990), the employer had engaged in violations sufficiently severe for the Board to make the union the bargaining agent without an election, but eight years elapsed before the NLRB issued such an order. The court remanded it for the NLRB to consider whether the passage of time and the accompanying large turnover of both employees and supervisory staff might make it possible to hold a fair election now. In addition, the injunction may not grant more than the rightful position if that conflicts with the law's goals. For example, in H.K. Porter Co. v. NLRB, 397 U.S. 99, 107–08, 90 S.Ct. 821, 825–26, 25 L.Ed.2d 146, 153 (1970), the Supreme Court struck down an order that an employer accede to the union's position because, even though the employer had violated a statutory requirement and a previous order to bargain in good faith, the goal of the statute was to make private bargaining the means to settle labor disputes.

In deciding whether an injunction should grant more than the plaintiff's rightful position, constitutional interests are at stake—liberty or property when the addressee of the injunction is a private person and separation of powers or federalism when the addressee is a governmental institution. When, as in the following case, the injunction allegedly violates first amendment rights, the constitutional issue gets heightened scrutiny. In reading the case, consider not just how courts should scrutinize injunctions that assertedly violate the first amendment but also any injunction that intrudes on the liberty or property interests of a private defendant.

(A) THE ABORTION PROTEST EXAMPLE

MADSEN v. WOMEN'S HEALTH CENTER, INC.
Supreme Court of the United States, 1994
512 U.S. 753, 114 S.Ct. 2516, 129 L.Ed.2d 593

CHIEF JUSTICE REHNQUIST delivered the opinion of the Court.

Petitioners challenge the constitutionality of an injunction entered by a Florida state court which prohibits antiabortion protesters from demonstrating in certain places and in various ways outside of a health clinic that performs abortions. We hold that the establishment of a 36–foot buffer zone on a public street from which demonstrators are excluded passes muster under the First Amendment, but that several other provisions of the injunction do not.

I

Respondents operate abortion clinics throughout central Florida. Petitioners and other groups and individuals are engaged in activities near the site of one such clinic in Melbourne, Florida. They picketed and demonstrated where the public street gives access to the clinic. In September 1992, a Florida state court permanently enjoined petitioners from blocking or interfering with public access to the clinic, and from physically abusing persons entering or leaving the clinic. Six months later, respondents sought to broaden the injunction, complaining that access to the clinic was still impeded by petitioners' activities and that such activities had also discouraged some potential patients from entering the clinic, and had deleterious physical effects on others. The trial court thereupon issued a broader injunction, which is challenged here.

The court found that, despite the initial injunction, protesters continued to impede access to the clinic by congregating on the paved portion of the street—Dixie Way—leading up to the clinic, and by marching in front of the clinic's driveways. It found that as vehicles heading toward the clinic slowed to allow the protesters to move out of the way, "sidewalk counselors" would approach and attempt to give the vehicle's occupants antiabortion literature. The number of people congregating varied from a handful to 400, and the noise varied from singing and chanting to the use of loudspeakers and bullhorns.

The protests, the court found, took their toll on the clinic's patients. A clinic doctor testified that, as a result of having to run such a gauntlet to enter the clinic, the patients "manifested a higher level of anxiety and hypertension causing those patients to need a higher level of sedation to undergo the surgical procedures, thereby increasing the risk associated with such procedures." The noise produced by the protestors could be heard within the clinic, causing stress in the patients both during surgical procedures and while recuperating in the recovery rooms. And those patients who turned away because of the crowd to return at a later date, the doctor testified, increased their health risks by reason of the delay.

Doctors and clinic workers, in turn, were not immune even in their homes. Petitioners picketed in front of clinic employees' residences; shouted at passersby; rang the doorbells of neighbors and provided literature identifying the particular clinic employee as a "baby killer." Occasionally, the protestors would confront minor children of clinic employees who were home alone.

This and similar testimony led the state court to conclude that its original injunction had proved insufficient "to protect the health, safety and rights of women in Brevard and Seminole County, Florida, and surrounding counties seeking access to [medical and counseling] services." The state court therefore amended its prior order, enjoining a broader array of activities. The amended injunction prohibits petitioners[1] from engaging in the following acts:

(1) * * * entering the * * * property of the Aware Woman Center for Choice [the Melbourne clinic]....

(2) * * * obstructing * * * access to * * * the Clinic.

(3) * * * entering * * * within [36] feet of the property line of the Clinic.... [There are exceptions: petitioners may come within 5 feet of the Clinic's east line and owners of property adjacent to the Clinic and their invitees may use their property within the buffer zone.]

(4) During the hours of 7:30 a.m. through noon, on Mondays through Saturdays, during surgical procedures and recovery periods, from singing, * * *, shouting, * * *, use of bullhorns, * * * or other sounds or images observable to or within earshot of the patients inside the Clinic.

(5) * * * in an area within [300] feet of the Clinic, from physically approaching any person seeking the services of the Clinic unless such person indicates a desire to communicate by approaching or by inquiring of the [petitioners]....

(6) * * * from approaching * * * within [300] feet of the residence of any of the [respondents'] employees * * * or blocking * * * the entrances * * * of [their] residences * * *

(7) * * * from physically abusing, grabbing, intimidating, harassing, touching, pushing, shoving, crowding or assaulting persons entering or leaving, working at or using services at the [respondents'] Clinic or trying to gain access to, or leave, any of the homes of owners, staff or patients of the Clinic.

(8) * * * from harassing, intimidating or physically abusing, assaulting or threatening any present or former * * * employee or volunteer who assists in providing services at the [respondents'] Clinic.

(9) * * * from encouraging, inciting, or securing other persons to commit any of the prohibited acts listed herein.

The Florida Supreme Court upheld the constitutionality of the trial court's amended injunction. * * *

* * * [T]he United States Court of Appeals for the Eleventh Circuit heard a separate challenge to the same injunction. [It] struck down the injunction, characterizing the dispute as a clash "between an actual prohibition of speech and a potential hindrance to the free exercise of

---

1. In addition to petitioners, the state court's order was directed at "Operation Rescue * * * and all persons acting in concert or participation with them, or on their behalf."

abortion rights." It stated that the asserted interests in public safety and order were already protected by other applicable laws and that these interests could be protected adequately without infringing upon the First Amendment rights of others. * * * We granted certiorari to resolve the conflict between the Florida Supreme Court and the Court of Appeals * * *.

II

We begin by addressing petitioners' contention that the state court's order, because it is an injunction that restricts only the speech of antiabortion protesters, is necessarily content or viewpoint based. Accordingly, they argue, we should examine the entire injunction under the strictest standard of scrutiny. See Perry Education Association v. Perry Local Educators' Association, 460 U.S. 37 (1983). We disagree. To accept petitioners' claim would be to classify virtually every injunction as content or viewpoint based. An injunction, by its very nature, applies only to a particular group (or individuals) and regulates the activities, and perhaps the speech, of that group. It does so, however, because of the group's past actions in the context of a specific dispute between real parties. The parties seeking the injunction assert a violation of their rights; the court hearing the action is charged with fashioning a remedy for a specific deprivation, not with the drafting of a statute addressed to the general public.

The fact that the injunction in the present case did not prohibit activities of those demonstrating in favor of abortion is justly attributable to the lack of any similar demonstrations by those in favor of abortion, and of any consequent request that their demonstrations be regulated by injunction. There is no suggestion in this record that Florida law would not equally restrain similar conduct directed at a target having nothing to do with abortion; none of the restrictions imposed by the court were directed at the contents of petitioner's message.

Our principal inquiry in determining content neutrality is whether the government has adopted a regulation of speech "without reference to the content of the regulated speech" * * *. We thus look to the government's purpose as the threshold consideration. Here, the state court imposed restrictions on petitioners incidental to their antiabortion message because they repeatedly violated the court's original order. That petitioners all share the same viewpoint regarding abortion does not in itself demonstrate that some invidious content or viewpoint-based purpose motivated the issuance of the order. It suggests only that those in the group *whose conduct* violated the court's order happen to share the same opinion regarding abortions being performed at the clinic. * * * Accordingly, the injunction issued in this case does not demand the level of heightened scrutiny set forth in *Perry Education Assn*. And we proceed to discuss the standard which does govern.

III

If this were a content-neutral, generally applicable statute, instead of an injunctive order, its constitutionality would be assessed under the standard set forth in Ward v. Rock Against Racism, 491 U.S. 781 (1989), and similar cases. Given that the forum around the clinic is a traditional public forum, we would determine whether the time, place, and manner regulations were "narrowly tailored to serve a significant governmental interest."

There are obvious differences, however, between an injunction and a generally applicable ordinance. Ordinances represent a legislative choice regarding the promotion of particular societal interests. Injunctions, by contrast, are remedies imposed for violations (or threatened violations) of a legislative or judicial decree. See United States v. W. T. Grant Co., 345 U.S. 629, 632–633 (1953). Injunctions also carry greater risks of censorship and discriminatory application than do general ordinances. "[T]here is no more effective practical guaranty against arbitrary and unreasonable government than to require that the principles of law which officials would impose upon a minority must be imposed generally." Injunctions, of course, have some advantages over generally applicable statutes in that they can be tailored by a trial judge to afford more precise relief than a statute where a violation of the law has already occurred.

We believe that these differences require a somewhat more stringent application of general First Amendment principles in this context. In past cases evaluating injunctions restricting speech, see, e.g., NAACP v. Claiborne Hardware Co., 458 U.S. 886 (1982), Milk Wagon Drivers v. Meadowmoor Dairies, Inc., 312 U.S. 287 (1941), we have relied upon such general principles while also seeking to ensure that the injunction was no broader than necessary to achieve its desired goals. See Carroll v. President and Comm'rs of Princess Anne, 393 U.S. 175 (1968); *Claiborne Hardware*. Our close attention to the fit between the objectives of an injunction and the restrictions it imposes on speech is consistent with the general rule, quite apart from First Amendment considerations, "that injunctive relief should be no more burdensome to the defendants than necessary to provide complete relief to the plaintiffs." Accordingly, when evaluating a content-neutral injunction, we think that our standard time, place, and manner analysis is not sufficiently rigorous. We must ask instead whether the challenged provisions of the injunction burden no more speech than necessary to serve a significant government interest. See, e.g., *Claiborne Hardware* (when sanctionable "conduct occurs in the context of constitutionally protected activity ... 'precision of regulation' is demanded"); *Carroll*. * * *

The Florida Supreme Court concluded that numerous significant government interests are protected by the injunction. It noted that the State has a strong interest in protecting a woman's freedom to seek lawful medical or counseling services in connection with her pregnancy. See Roe v. Wade, 410 U.S. 113 (1973). The State also has a strong interest in ensuring the public safety and order, in promoting the free flow of traffic on public streets and sidewalks, and in protecting the property rights of all its citizens. In addition, the court believed that the State's strong interest in residential privacy, acknowledged in Frisby v. Schultz, 487 U.S. 474 (1988), applied by analogy to medical privacy. The court observed that while targeted picketing of the home threatens the psychological well-being of the "captive" resident, targeted picketing of a hospital or clinic threatens not only the psychological, but the physical well-being of the patient held "captive" by medical circumstance. We agree with the Supreme Court of Florida that the combination of these governmental interests is quite sufficient to justify an appropriately tailored injunction to protect them. We now examine each contested provision of the injunction to see if it burdens more speech than necessary to accomplish its goal.

A

1

We begin with the 36–foot buffer zone. The state court prohibited petitioners from "congregating, picketing, patrolling, demonstrating or entering" any portion of the public right-of-way or private property within 36 feet of the property line of the clinic as a way of ensuring access to the clinic. This speech-free buffer zone requires that petitioners move to the other side of Dixie Way and away from the driveway of the clinic, where the state court found that they repeatedly had interfered with the free access of patients and staff. * * *

We have noted a distinction between the type of focused picketing banned from the buffer zone and the type of generally disseminated communication that cannot be completely banned in public places, such as handbilling and solicitation. See *Frisby*, 487 U.S. at 486. * * *

The 36–foot buffer zone protecting the entrances to the clinic and the parking lot is a means of protecting unfettered ingress to and egress from the clinic, and ensuring that petitioners do not block traffic on Dixie Way. The state court seems to have had few other options to protect access given the narrow confines around the clinic. As the Florida Supreme Court noted, Dixie Way is only 21 feet wide in the area of the clinic. The state court was convinced that allowing the petitioners to remain on the clinic's sidewalk and driveway was not a viable option in view of the failure of the first injunction to protect access. And allowing the petitioners to stand in the middle of Dixie Way would obviously block vehicular traffic.

The need for a complete buffer zone near the clinic entrances and driveway may be debatable, but some deference must be given to the state court's familiarity with the facts and the background of the dispute between the parties even under our heightened review. Moreover, one of petitioners' witnesses during the evidentiary hearing before the state court conceded that the buffer zone was narrow enough to place petitioners at a distance of no greater than 10 to 12 feet from cars approaching and leaving the clinic. Protesters standing across the narrow street from the clinic can still be seen and heard from the clinic parking lots. We also bear in mind the fact that the state court originally issued a much narrower injunction, providing no buffer zone, and that this order did not succeed in protecting access to the clinic. The failure of the first order to accomplish its purpose may be taken into consideration in evaluating the constitutionality of the broader order. On balance, we hold that the 36–foot buffer zone around the clinic entrances and driveway burdens no more speech than necessary to accomplish the governmental interest at stake.

* * *

2

The inclusion of private property on the back and side of the clinic in the 36–foot buffer zone raises different concerns. * * * Patients and staff wishing to reach the clinic do not have to cross the private property abutting the clinic property * * * and nothing in the record indicates that petitioners' activities on the private property have obstructed access to the clinic. * * * We hold that on the record before us the 36–foot buffer zone as applied to the private property to the north and west of the clinic burdens more speech than necessary to protect access to the clinic.

B

In response to high noise levels outside the clinic, the state court restrained the petitioners from "singing, chanting, whistling, shouting, yelling, use of bullhorns, auto horns, sound amplification equipment or other sounds or images observable to or within earshot of the patients inside the [c]linic" during the hours of 7:30 a.m. through noon on Mondays through Saturdays. * * * Noise control is particularly important around hospitals and medical facilities during surgery and recovery periods. * * *

We hold that the limited noise restrictions imposed by the state court order burden no more speech than necessary to ensure the health and well-being of the patients at the clinic. * * *

C

The same, however, cannot be said for the "images observable" provision of the state court's order. Clearly, threats to patients or their families, however communicated, are proscribable under the First Amendment. But rather than prohibiting the display of signs that could be interpreted as threats or veiled threats, the state court issued a blanket ban on all "images observable." This broad prohibition on all "images observable" burdens more speech than necessary to achieve the purpose of limiting threats to clinic patients or their families. Similarly, if the blanket ban on "images observable" was intended to reduce the level of anxiety and hypertension suffered by the patients inside the clinic, it would still fail. * * * [I]t is much easier for the clinic to pull its curtains than for a patient to stop up her ears. * * *

D

The state court ordered that petitioners refrain from physically approaching any person seeking services of the clinic "unless such person indicates a desire to communicate" in an area within 300 feet of the clinic. The state court was attempting to prevent clinic patients and staff from being "stalked" or "shadowed" by the petitioners as they approached the clinic.

But it is difficult, indeed, to justify a prohibition on *all* uninvited approaches of persons seeking the services of the clinic, regardless of how peaceful the contact may be, without burdening more speech than necessary to prevent intimidation and to ensure access to the clinic. Absent evidence that the protesters' speech is independently proscribable (i.e., "fighting words" or threats), or is so infused with violence as to be indistinguishable from a threat of physical harm, this provision cannot stand. "As a general matter, we have indicated that in public debate our own citizens must tolerate insulting, and even outrageous, speech in order to provide adequate breathing space to the freedoms protected by the First Amendment." The "consent" requirement alone invalidates this provision; it burdens more speech than is necessary to prevent intimidation and to ensure access to the clinic.

E

The final substantive regulation challenged by petitioners relates to a prohibition against picketing, demonstrating, or using sound amplification equipment within 300 feet of the residences of clinic staff. The prohibition also covers impeding access to streets that provide the sole access to streets on which those residences are located. The same analysis applies to the use of sound amplification equipment here as that discussed above: the government may simply demand that petitioners turn down the volume if the protests overwhelm the neighborhood.

As for the picketing, our prior decision upholding a law banning targeted residential picketing remarked on the unique nature of the home, as "the last citadel of the tired, the weary, and the sick." *Frisby*.

But the 300-foot zone around the residences in this case is much larger than the zone provided for in the ordinance which we approved in *Frisby*. The ordinance at issue there made it "unlawful for any person to engage in picketing before or about the residence or dwelling of any individual." The prohibition was limited to "focused picketing taking place solely in front of a particular residence." By contrast, the 300-foot zone would ban "[g]eneral marching through residential neighborhoods, or even walking a route in front of an entire block of houses." The record before us does not contain sufficient justification for this broad a ban on picketing; it appears that a limitation on the time, duration of picketing, and number of pickets outside a smaller zone could have accomplished the desired result.

IV

Petitioners also * * * object to the portion of the injunction making it applicable to those acting "in concert" with the named parties. But petitioners themselves are named parties in the order, and they therefore lack standing to challenge a portion of the order applying to persons who are not parties. * * *

Petitioners also contend that the "in concert" provision of the injunction impermissibly limits their freedom of association guaranteed by the First Amendment.[b] But petitioners are not enjoined from associating with others or from joining with them to express a particular viewpoint. The freedom of association protected by the First Amendment does not extend to joining with others for the purpose of depriving third parties of their lawful rights. * * *

JUSTICE SOUTER, concurring.

I join the Court's opinion and write separately only to clarify two matters in the record. First, the trial judge made reasonably clear that the issue of who was acting "in concert" with the named defendants was a matter to be taken up in individual cases, and not to be decided on the basis of protesters' viewpoints. Second, petitioners themselves acknowledge that the governmental interests in protection of public safety and order, of the free flow of traffic, and of property rights are reflected in Florida law. [Citations to Florida statutes concerning public peace and obstruction of public streets.]

JUSTICE STEVENS, concurring in part and dissenting in part.* * *

I

Unlike the Court, * * * I believe that injunctive relief should be judged by a more lenient standard than legislation. As the Court notes, legislation is imposed on an entire community, regardless of individual culpability. By contrast, injunctions apply solely to an individual or a limited group of individuals who, by engaging in illegal conduct, have been judicially deprived of some liberty—the normal consequence of illegal activity.[2] Given this distinction, a statute prohibiting demonstrations within 36 feet of an abortion clinic would probably violate the First Amendment, but an injunction directed at a limited group of persons who have engaged in unlawful conduct in a similar zone might well be constitutional.

---

b. Binding nonparties acting "in concert" with defendants is considered in Chapter 3(C)(4) infra.

2. Contrary to Justice Scalia's assumption, the deprivation of liberty caused by an injunction is not a form of punishment. Moreover, there is nothing unusual about injunctive relief that includes some restriction on speech as a remedy for prior misconduct. National Society of Professional Engineers v. United States, 435 U.S. 679, 697–698 (1978).

The standard governing injunctions has two obvious dimensions. On the one hand, the injunction should be no more burdensome than necessary to provide complete relief. In a First Amendment context, as in any other, the propriety of the remedy depends almost entirely on the character of the violation and the likelihood of its recurrence. For this reason, standards fashioned to determine the constitutionality of statutes should not be used to evaluate injunctions.

On the other hand, even when an injunction impinges on constitutional rights, more than "a simple proscription against the precise conduct previously pursued" may be required; the remedy must include appropriate restraints on "future activities both to avoid a recurrence of the violation and to eliminate its consequences." Moreover, "[t]he judicial remedy for a proven violation of law will often include commands that the law does not impose on the community at large." As such, repeated violations may justify sanctions that might be invalid if applied to a first offender or if enacted by the legislature.

In this case, the trial judge heard three days of testimony and found that petitioners not only had engaged in tortious conduct, but also had repeatedly violated an earlier injunction. The injunction is thus twice removed from a legislative proscription applicable to the general public and should be judged by a standard that gives appropriate deference to the judge's unique familiarity with the facts.

II

* * *

[As to the 300-foot buffer zone around the clinic, petitioners'] argument and the Court's conclusion * * * are based on a misreading of the injunction.

[The relevant language in the injunction] does not purport to prohibit speech; it prohibits a species of conduct. * * *

The "physically approaching" prohibition entered by the trial court is no broader than the protection necessary to provide relief for the violations it found. The trial judge entered this portion of the injunction only after concluding that the injunction was necessary to protect the clinic's patients and staff from "uninvited contacts, shadowing and stalking" by petitioners. The protection is especially appropriate for the clinic patients given that the trial judge found that petitioners' prior conduct caused higher levels of "anxiety and hypertension" in the patients, increasing the risks associated with the procedures that the patients seek. Whatever the proper limits on a court's power to restrict a speaker's ability to physically approach or follow an unwilling listener, surely the First Amendment does not prevent a trial court from imposing such a restriction given the unchallenged findings in this case.

The Florida Supreme Court correctly concluded:

> "While the First Amendment confers on each citizen a powerful right to express oneself, it gives the picketer no boon to jeopardize the health, safety, and rights of others. No citizen has a right to insert a foot in the hospital or clinic door and insist on being heard-while purposefully blocking the door to those in genuine need of medical services. No picketer can force speech into the captive ear of the unwilling and disabled."

I thus conclude that, under the circumstances of this case, the prohibition against "physically approaching" in the 300–foot zone around the clinic withstands petitioners' First Amendment challenge. I therefore dissent from Part III–D.

III

Because I have joined Parts I, II, III–E, and IV of the Court's opinion and have dissented as to Part III–D after concluding that the 300–foot zone around the clinic is a reasonable time, place, and manner restriction, no further discussion is necessary. The Court, however, proceeds to address challenges to the injunction that, although arguably raised by petitioners' briefs, are not properly before the Court. [Justice Stevens dissents from the remaining portions of the opinion.]

JUSTICE SCALIA, with whom JUSTICE KENNEDY and JUSTICE THOMAS join, concurring in the judgment in part and dissenting in part.

The judgment in today's case has an appearance of moderation and Solomonic wisdom, upholding as it does some portions of the injunction while disallowing others. That appearance is deceptive. The entire injunction in this case departs so far from the established course of our jurisprudence that in any other context it would have been regarded as a candidate for summary reversal.

But the context here is abortion. * * *

Because I believe that the judicial creation of a 36–foot zone in which only a particular group, which had broken no law, cannot exercise its rights of speech, assembly, and association, and the judicial enactment of a noise prohibition, applicable to that group and that group alone, are profoundly at odds with our First Amendment precedents and traditions, I dissent.

I

The record of this case contains a videotape * * * displaying what one must presume to be the worst of the activity justifying the injunction * * *. The tape was shot by employees of, or volunteers at, the Aware Woman Clinic on three Saturdays in February and March 1993; * * * The tape was edited down (from approximately 6 to 8 hours of footage to ½ hour) * * * by the Feminist Majority Foundation.

Anyone seriously interested in what this case was about must view that tape. And anyone doing so who is familiar with run-of-the-mine labor picketing, not to mention some other social protests, will be aghast at what it shows we have today permitted an individual judge to do. I will do my best to describe it. [Justice Scalia's description is omitted.]

The videotape and the rest of the record, including the trial court's findings, show that a great many forms of expression and conduct [by demonstrators from both sides] occurred in the vicinity of the clinic. These include singing, chanting, praying, shouting, the playing of music both from the clinic and from handheld boom boxes, speeches, peaceful picketing, communication of familiar political messages, handbilling, persuasive speech directed at opposing groups on the issue of abortion, efforts to persuade individuals not to have abortions, personal testimony, interviews with the press, and media efforts to report on the protest. What the videotape, the rest of the record, and the trial court's findings do not contain is any suggestion of violence near the clinic, nor do they establish any attempt to prevent entry or exit.

II

A

Under this Court's jurisprudence, there is no question that this public sidewalk area is a "public forum," where citizens generally have a First Amendment right to speak. The parties to this case invited the Court to employ one or the other of the two well established standards applied to restrictions upon this First Amendment right. Petitioners claimed the benefit of so-called "strict scrutiny," the standard applied to content-based restrictions: the restriction must be "necessary to serve a compelling state interest and ... narrowly drawn to achieve that end." Perry Education Assn. v. Perry Local Educators' Assn., 460 U.S. 37, 45 (1983). Respondents, on the other hand, contended for what has come to be known as "intermediate scrutiny" (midway between the "strict scrutiny" demanded for content-based regulation of speech, and the "rational basis" standard that is applied-under the Equal Protection Clause-to government regulation of non-speech activities). That standard, applicable to so-called "time, place and manner regulations" of speech, provides that the regulations are permissible so long as they "are content-neutral, are narrowly tailored to serve a significant government interest, and leave open ample alternative channels of communication." Perry. The Court adopts neither of these, but creates, brand-new for this abortion-related case, an additional standard that is (supposedly) "somewhat more stringent" than intermediate scrutiny, yet not as "rigorous" as strict scrutiny. The Court does not give this new standard a name, but perhaps we could call it intermediate-intermediate scrutiny. The difference between it and intermediate scrutiny (which the Court acknowledges is inappropriate for injunctive restrictions on speech) is frankly too subtle for me to describe, so I must simply recite it: Whereas intermediate scrutiny requires that the restriction be "narrowly tailored to serve a significant government interest," the new standard requires that the restriction "burden no more speech than necessary to serve a significant government interest."

* * * [A] restriction upon speech imposed by injunction (whether nominally content based or nominally content neutral) is *at least* as deserving of strict scrutiny as a statutory, content-based restriction.

* * *

The * * * reason speech-restricting injunctions are at least as deserving of strict scrutiny is obvious enough: they are the product of individual judges rather than of legislatures—and often of judges who have been chagrined by prior disobedience of their orders. The right to free speech should not lightly be placed within the control of a single man or woman. And the third reason is that the injunction is a much more powerful weapon than a statute, and so should be subjected to greater safeguards. Normally, when injunctions are enforced through contempt proceedings, only the defense of factual innocence is available. The collateral bar rule of Walker v. Birmingham, 388 U.S. 307 (1967), eliminates the defense that the injunction itself was unconstitutional.[c] Thus, persons subject to a speech-restricting injunction who have not the money or not the time to lodge an immediate appeal face a Hobson's choice: they must remain silent, since if they speak their First Amendment rights are no defense in subsequent contempt proceedings. This is good reason to require the strictest standard for issuance of such orders.[1]

* * *

III

* * *

B

I turn now to the Court's performance in the present case. I am content to evaluate it under the lax (intermediate-intermediate scrutiny) standard that the Court has adopted, because even by that distorted light it is inadequate.

The first step under the Court's standard would be, one should think, to identify the "significant government interest" that justifies the portions of the injunction it upheld * * *.

Assuming then that the "significant interests" the Court mentioned must in fact be significant enough to be protected by state law (a concept that includes a prior court order), which law has been, or is about to be,

---

c. The collateral bar rule is discussed in Chapter 3(C)(3) of the casebook.

1. Justice Stevens believes that speech-restricting injunctions "should be judged by a more lenient standard than legislation" because "injunctions apply solely to [those] who, by engaging in illegal conduct, have been judicially deprived of some liberty." Punishing unlawful action by judicial abridgment of First Amendment rights is an interesting concept; perhaps Eighth Amendment rights could be next. I know of no authority for the proposition that restriction of speech, rather than fines or imprisonment, should be the sanction for misconduct. The supposed prior violation of a judicial order was the only thing that rendered petitioners *subject* to a personally tailored restriction on speech in the first place—not in order to punish them, but to protect the public order. To say that their prior violation not only subjects them to being singled out in this fashion, but also loosens the standards for protecting the public order through speech restrictions, is double counting.

violated, the question arises: what state law is involved here? The only one even mentioned is the original September 30, 1992, injunction,[5] which had been issued (quite rightly, in my judgment) in response to threats by the originally named parties (including petitioners here) that they would "[p]hysically close down abortion mills," "bloc[k] access to clinics," "ignore the law of the State," and "shut down a clinic." * * *

According to the Court, the state court imposed the later injunction's "restrictions on petitioner[s'] ... antiabortion message because they repeatedly violated the court's original order." Surprisingly, the Court accepts this reason as valid, without asking whether the court's findings of fact support it—whether, that is, the acts of which the petitioners stood convicted *were* violations of the original injunction.

* * *

If the original injunction is read as it must be, there is nothing in the trial court's findings to suggest that it was violated. The Court today speaks of "the failure of the first injunction to protect access." But the first injunction did not broadly "protect access." It forbade particular acts that impeded access, to-wit, intentionally "blocking, impeding or obstructing." The trial court's findings identify none of these acts, but only a mild interference with access that is the incidental by-product of leafletting and picketing. There was no sitting down, no linking of arms, no packing en masse in the driveway; the most that can be alleged (and the trial court did not even make this a finding) is that on one occasion protestors "took their time to get out of the way." If that is enough to support this one-man proscription of free speech, the First Amendment is in grave peril.

I almost forgot to address the facts showing prior violation of law (including judicial order) with respect to the other portion of the injunction the Court upholds: the no-noise-within-earshot-of-patients provision. That is perhaps because, amazingly, neither the Florida courts *nor this Court* makes the slightest attempt to link that provision to prior violations of law. The relevant portion of the Court's opinion, Part II–B, simply reasons that hospital patients should not have to be bothered with noise, from political protests or anything else (which is certainly true), and that therefore the noise restrictions could be imposed *by injunction* (which is certainly false). Since such a law is reasonable, in other words, it can be enacted by a single man to bind only a single class of social protesters. The pro-abortion demonstrators who were often making (if respondents' videotape is accurate) more noise than the petitioners, can continue to shout their chants at their opponents exiled across the street to their hearts'

---

5. Justice Souter points out that "petitioners themselves acknowledge that the governmental interests in protection of public safety and order, of the free flow of traffic, and of property rights are reflected in Florida law." This is true but quite irrelevant. As the preceding sentence of text shows, we are concerned here not with state laws in general, but with state laws that these respondents had been found to have violated. There is *no* finding of violation of any of these cited Florida statutes.

content. [When the Court has upheld an injunction restricting noise, it enforced] an *ordinance* not an *injunction*; it applied to *everyone*.

* * *

To sum up: The interests assertedly protected by the supplementary injunction did not include any interest whose impairment was a violation of Florida law or of a Florida-court injunction. Unless the Court intends today to overturn long-settled jurisprudence, that means that the interests cannot possibly qualify as "significant interests" under the Court's new standard.

* * *

What we have decided seems to be, and will be reported by the media as, an abortion case. But it will go down in the lawbooks, it will be cited, as a free-speech injunction case—and the damage its novel principles produce will be considerable. The proposition that injunctions against speech are subject to a standard indistinguishable from (unless perhaps more lenient in its application than) the "intermediate scrutiny" standard we have used for "time, place, and manner" legislative restrictions; the notion that injunctions against speech need not be closely tied to any violation of law, but may simply implement sound social policy; and the practice of accepting trial-court conclusions permitting injunctions without considering whether those conclusions are supported by any findings of fact—these latest by-products of our abortion jurisprudence ought to give all friends of liberty great concern. * * *

NOTES

1. What did the first injunction in *Madsen* prohibit? What was the rightful position it sought to protect? Did the defendants violate the first injunction? Did the defendants' conduct warrant the 36-foot buffer zone imposed by the second injunction? Is there any indication that the defendants would have violated a narrower injunction, such as proposed by Justice Scalia, one in which the defendants would have to stay out of the street and back from the driveway, but which would allow a limited number of them on the sidewalk in front of the clinic? If you were on the Court and were applying the majority's test, would you vote to sustain the 36-foot buffer zone?

2. Unlike the injunction in *Madsen*, most prophylactic injunctions do not raise first amendment issues, but they do impinge on liberty or property. What is the level of scrutiny that the majority applies in *Madsen*? Did the injunction restrict the content of speech? Where government restricts the time, place, or manner of speech, should the level of scrutiny be higher if the restriction is imposed through a statute or through an injunction? Writing before the Court decided *Madsen*, one scholar expressed concern about "the injunction's unique concentration of power [in the judge] with its dual potential for articulating public, particularly constitutional, values and for threatening individual liberty." Doug Rendleman, Irreparability Irreparably Damaged, 90 Mich.L.Rev. 1642, 1671 (1992).

3. After the U.S. Supreme Court remanded the case, the trial court issued a modified injunction in light of *Madsen*. The Florida appellate courts upheld the injunction, as modified. Johnson v. Women's Health Center, Inc., 714 So.2d 580 (Fla.App.), Fla. rev. denied, 719 So.2d 893 (1998).

4. What is the justification for the second injunction's provision on noise? Is it objectively justifiable, or is it a pretext for content discrimination? See Christina E. Wells, Bringing Structure to the Law of Injunctions Against Expression, 51 Case W.Res.L.Rev. 1 (2000).

5. The *Madsen* majority relied heavily on the finding that the defendants had violated the previous injunction in upholding the prophylactic injunction. Schenck v. Pro–Choice Network of Western NY, 519 U.S. 357, 117 S.Ct. 855, 137 L.Ed.2d 1 (1997), made clear that a prophylactic order can be issued even if there was no violation of a narrower order. The abortion clinic had a stronger case in *Schenck* than in *Madsen,* because the defendants had trespassed on clinic property, blockaded the clinic, and assaulted patients. *Schenck* also upheld fixed 15–foot buffer zones around the clinic entrances, but struck floating 15–foot buffer zones that moved with patients as they entered and left the clinic. The floating zones were not narrowly tailored because it would be too difficult for protestors to converse with patients yet avoid trespassing on the zones and the floating zones were not necessary on these facts to serve the purposes of the decree.

In contrast, Hill v. Colorado, 530 U.S. 703, 120 S.Ct. 2480, 147 L.Ed.2d 597 (2000), upheld a state statute that makes it unlawful to knowingly approach within eight feet of a person entering a health facility within 100 feet of its entrance. The Supreme Court, through Justice Stevens, distinguished *Schenck* on the basis that it dealt with a judicially created prohibition, which must be reviewed under the *Madsen* test, rather than a statutorily created prohibition, which *Madsen* held must be reviewed under the somewhat milder test of Ward v. Rock Against Racism, 491 U.S. 781, 109 S.Ct. 2746, 105 L.Ed.2d 661 (1989). The Court went on to hold that the statute was a content-neutral, valid time, place and manner regulation because it was narrowly tailored to serve the state's legitimate interest in protecting people entering a health care facility.

6. Congress subsequently enacted the Freedom of Access to Clinic Entrances Act, which makes it a federal crime to block access to a reproductive health facility or use force or threats against people using the facility. The statute has been upheld repeatedly, generally on the basis of *Madsen*. See, e.g., Norton v. Ashcroft, 298 F.3d 547 (6th Cir.2002), cert. denied, 537 U.S. 1172, 123 S.Ct. 1003, 154 L.Ed.2d 915 (2003); United States v. Gregg, 226 F.3d 253 (3d Cir.2000), cert. denied, 532 U.S. 971, 121 S.Ct. 1600, 149 L.Ed.2d 467 (2001) (statute valid as exercise of Commerce Clause power and does not violate First Amendment).

7. People ex rel. Gallo v. Acuna, 14 Cal.4th 1090, 60 Cal.Rptr.2d 277, 929 P.2d 596 (1997), cert. denied, 521 U.S. 1121, 117 S.Ct. 2513, 138 L.Ed.2d 1016 (1997), upheld injunction provisions that forbid 38 named members of a violent gang from associating with each other in a four block area that they occupied as "an urban war zone" or annoying or intimidating anyone in that area. In rejecting the argument the injunction was an overly broad constraint

on freedom of association, the California Supreme Court stated, "Like the injunction in *Madsen,* the trial court's interlocutory decree here does not embody the broad and abstract commands of a statute. Instead, it is the product of a concrete judicial proceeding prompted by particular events—inimical to the well-being of the residents of the community of Rocksprings—that led to a specific request by the City for preventive relief."

In City of Chicago v. Morales, 527 U.S. 41, 119 S.Ct. 1849, 144 L.Ed.2d 67 (1999), the Supreme Court struck down Chicago's Gang Congregation Ordinance, which prohibited "criminal street gang members" from loitering in public places. Under the ordinance, if a police officer observes a person whom he reasonably believes to be a gang member loitering in a public place with one or more persons, he shall order them to disperse. A majority of the Court concluded that the ordinance's broad sweep violated the requirement that a legislature establish minimal guidelines to govern law enforcement. In a portion of the opinion for a plurality, Justice Stevens, joined by Justices Souter and Ginsburg, also concluded that because the ordinance failed to give the ordinary citizen adequate notice of what is forbidden and what is permitted, it was impermissibly vague. The term "loiter" may have a common and accepted meaning, but the ordinance's definition of that term—"to remain in any one place with no apparent purpose"—does not. The plurality found it difficult to imagine how any Chicagoan standing in a public place with a group of people would know if he or she had an "apparent purpose." In separate opinions, other justices who joined in striking down the ordinance suggested that a more narrowly drawn statute could pass constitutional muster. In dissent, Justice Thomas, joined by Chief Justice Rehnquist and Justice Scalia, charged that by invalidating Chicago's ordinance, the Court had unnecessarily sentenced law-abiding citizens to lives of terror and misery at the hands of gangs who desired to establish dominion over the public streets. The dissent flatly denied that the ordinance was vague: "[A]ny fool would know that a particular category of conduct would be within [its] reach," quoting Kolender v. Lawson, 461 U.S. 352, 370, 103 S.Ct. 1855, 75 L.Ed.2d 903 (1983) (White, J., dissenting). Justice Thomas also rejected the claim that the ordinance violated the Due Process Clause because the asserted "freedom to loiter for innocent purposes," was in no way "deeply rooted in this Nation's history and tradition." See also Gregory S. Walston, Taking the Constitution at its Word: A Defense of the Use of Anti–Gang Injunctions, 54 U.Miami L.Rev. 47 (1999).

A recent proliferation of anti-gang injunctions seem to challenge the Supreme Court's holding in *Morales* that such injunctions are overbroad and impermissibly vague. These newer injunctions, including 40 such injunctions in San Francisco, commonly apply to the gang as an entity, rather than identified "gang members," and prohibit loitering in public places, associating with other alleged gang members, and wearing gang-related clothing. Pamela A. MacLean, Ganging Up on Gangs, National L.J. 1, June 11, 2007; Demian Bulwa, S.F. Gang Injunction Zone Controversial, S.F. Chronicle, A1, Oct. 27, 2008. A Texas appeals court upheld an anti-gang injunction, distinguishing the case from *Morales*, because the Texas ordinance provided law enforcement with guidelines to prevent arbitrary and discriminatory enforcement and limited police officers to arresting only those individuals they knew were subject to the injunction. Goyzueta v. State, 266 S.W.3d 126 (Tex.App.2008).

8. The famous attorney Johnnie L. Cochran had trouble with a former client, who began picketing him and demanding money the client thought was owed. Cochran sued for defamation and invasion of privacy. Because of the difficulty the Constitution imposes upon a public figure like Cochran to win damages (and the possibility that the client might be unable to pay), Cochran sought permanent injunctive relief. After a hearing at which it became clear that the conduct would continue absent a court order, the trial court ordered the client and others from:

"1. Standing, assembling or approaching within [300 yards] of (i) Cochran; or (ii) Cochran's place of business . . . ;

"2. In any public forum, including, but not limited to, the Los Angeles Superior Court and any other place at which Cochran appears for the purpose of practicing law: (i) picketing Cochran [or] Cochran's law firm; (ii) displaying signs, placards or other written or printed material about Cochran [or] Cochran's law firm; (iii) orally uttering statements about Cochran [or] Cochran's law firm; and

"3. Contacting, harassing, threatening, stalking, disturbing the peace of, keeping under surveillance or blocking the movements of Cochran."

After the injunction was affirmed on appeal, Cochran v. Tory, 2003 WL 22451378 (Cal.App.2003), the U.S. Supreme Court granted review, 542 U.S. 965, 125 S.Ct. 26, 159 L.Ed.2d 856 (2004). Cochran died after oral argument and Cochran's widow was substituted in his place. The Court observed that the injunction, although still in effect and not moot, "now amounts to an overly broad prior restraint upon speech, lacking plausible justification." 544 U.S. 734, 125 S.Ct. 2108, 2111, 161 L.Ed.2d 1042 (2005). The Court vacated and remanded so the lower courts could determine if any injunctive relief, narrowly tailored to the changed circumstances, was warranted. For another example of an injunction prohibiting defamatory speech, see Balboa Island Village Inn v. Lemen, 40 Cal.4th 1141, 156 P.3d 339, 57 Cal.Rptr.3d 320 (2007) (upholding permanent injunction prohibiting defamation by plaintiff against bar owners, but striking down as overbroad injunction provisions that: (1) restrict "agents and others working in concert" with plaintiff; (2) restrict plaintiff's ability to petition the government; and (3) prevent plaintiff from approaching bar employees without a time, place, or manner restriction).

(B) THE SCHOOL DESEGREGATION EXAMPLE

The Supreme Court's 1955 order in *Brown II* (at p. 107) mandated: (1) the dismantling of dual school systems; and (2) the admission of all children to unitary schools on a racially nondiscriminatory basis. After over a decade of foot dragging by school boards, the Supreme Court finally demanded prompt action: "the burden on a school board today is to come forward with a plan that promises realistically to work, and promises realistically to work *now*." Green v. School Board of New Kent County, 391 U.S. 430, 439, 88 S.Ct. 1689, 1694, 20 L.Ed.2d 716, 724 (1968). *Green* struck down a desegregation plan that complied only superficially with

Brown II's mandate. The school board in *Green* had adopted a "freedom of choice" plan, under which school children could choose which of the county's two schools (the formerly white school or the formerly African–American school) to attend. All the white children chose to attend the previously white school, and 85% of the African–American children chose the African–American school. A unanimous Court held that the freedom of choice plan perpetuated the racial identification of each school and therefore failed *Brown II*'s first criteria:

> The New Kent School Board's "freedom of choice" plan cannot be accepted as a sufficient step to "effectuate a transition" to a unitary system. * * * [T]he school system remains a dual system. Rather than further the dismantling of the dual system, the plan has operated simply to burden children and their parents with a responsibility which *Brown II* placed squarely on the School Board.

391 U.S. at 441–42, 88 S.Ct. at 1696, 20 L.Ed.2d at 725–26. Did the plan also fail to satisfy the second criteria of *Brown II*'s order—to admit children to unitary schools on a racially nondiscriminatory basis?

Neighborhood-based pupil assignments could achieve racially mixed schools relatively quickly and easily in *Green*. There, half the population was African–American, the other half white, all living in racially integrated neighborhoods. An injunction requiring the school board to assign pupils to the nearest school would integrate the schools with little or no busing.

Subsequent cases presented the courts with tougher logistic and conceptual problems. Where neighborhoods are not racially mixed, a school policy that assigns each child to the nearest school will often produce schools that are not racially mixed. In considering whether the school district has a responsibility to achieve integration, courts distinguish between segregation due to official acts or policies, which is called *de jure* segregation, and segregation due to other factors, which is called *de facto* segregation. In *Green,* the two schools in the County had been segregated due to official acts of the school board, in assigning all African–American children to one school and all white children to the other. However, residential segregation, and therefore the school segregation that results from neighborhood pupil assignment, may have many different causes: (a) past de jure discrimination by the school board; (b) past de jure discrimination by other governments, such as the state or the municipality, that are legally distinct from the school board; (c) private discrimination by real estate agents, landlords, and sellers of real estate; and (d) African–Americans' own preferences and their lower average income. These factors, in turn, have previous causes—some rooted in private actions, some rooted in public actions.

There was a dispute as to whether de facto as well as de jure segregation is unconstitutional and gives rise to liability. If so, the plaintiffs' rightful position is to attend an *integrated* school rather than a school that is *not segregated due to official action*. If not, could a court allow a school that had engaged previously in de jure segregation to adopt a desegregation plan that assigned children to schools on a nondiscriminatory basis, yet still did not produce tangible integration? Or could the court require a desegregation plan that produced integrated schools out of segregated residential patterns, even though the plaintiffs have no right, per se, to integrated schools?

SWANN v. CHARLOTTE–MECKLENBURG BOARD OF EDUCATION

Supreme Court of the United States, 1971
402 U.S. 1, 91 S.Ct. 1267, 28 L.Ed.2d 554

MR. CHIEF JUSTICE BURGER delivered the opinion of the Court.

* * * This case and those argued with it arose in States having a long history of maintaining two sets of schools in a single school system deliberately operated to carry out a governmental policy to separate pupils in schools solely on the basis of race. That was what *Brown v. Board of Education* was all about. These cases present us with the problem of defining in more precise terms than heretofore the scope of the duty of school authorities and district courts in implementing *Brown I* and the mandate to eliminate dual systems and establish unitary systems at once. * * *

I

The Charlotte–Mecklenburg school system, the 43d largest in the Nation, encompasses the city of Charlotte and surrounding Mecklenburg County, North Carolina. The area is large * * * spanning roughly 22 miles east-west and 36 miles north-south. During the 1968–1969 school year the system served more than 84,000 pupils in 107 schools. Approximately 71% of the pupils were found to be white and 29% Negro. [Most of the] Negro students attended * * * schools which were either totally Negro or more than 99% Negro.

This situation came about under a desegregation plan approved by the District Court at the commencement of the present litigation in 1965, based upon geographic zoning with a free-transfer provision. The present proceedings were initiated in September 1968 by petitioner Swann's motion for further relief based on *Green v. County School Board*. All parties now agree that in 1969 the system fell short of achieving the unitary school system that [*Green* requires].

The District Court * * * found that residential patterns in the city and county resulted in part from federal, state, and local government action other than school board decisions. School board action based on these patterns, for example, by locating schools in Negro residential areas and fixing the size of the schools to accommodate the needs of immediate neighborhoods, resulted in segregated education. These findings were subsequently accepted by the Court of Appeals.

* * * [T]he District Court was presented with two alternative pupil assignment plans—the finalized "board plan" and the "Finger plan."

The Board Plan. * * * The board plan proposed substantial assignment of Negroes to nine of the system's 10 high schools, producing 17% to 36% Negro population in each. The projected Negro attendance at the 10th school, Independence, was 2%. The proposed attendance zones for the high schools were typically shaped like wedges of a pie, extending outward from the center of the city to the suburban and rural areas of the county in order to afford residents of the center city area [which had the largest minority concentration] access to outlying schools.

As for junior high schools, the board plan rezoned the 21 school areas so that in 20 the Negro attendance would range from 0% to 38%. The other school, located in the heart of the Negro residential area, was left with an enrollment of 90% Negro.

The board plan with respect to elementary schools relied entirely upon gerrymandering of geographic zones. More than half of the Negro elementary pupils were left in nine schools that were 86% to 100% Negro; approximately half of the white elementary pupils were assigned to schools 86% to 100% white.

The Finger Plan. The plan submitted by the court-appointed expert, Dr. Finger, adopted the school board zoning plan for senior high schools with one modification: it required that an additional 300 Negro students be transported from the Negro residential area of the city to the nearly all-white Independence High School. [The Finger plan also achieved greater integration of the junior high schools and elementary schools through busing. The District Court adopted the Finger plan.] * * *

On appeal the Court of Appeals affirmed the District Court's order as to * * * the secondary school plans, but vacated the order respecting elementary schools. While agreeing that the District Court properly disapproved the board plan concerning these schools, the Court of Appeals feared that the [busing of elementary school students] would place an unreasonable burden on the board and the system's pupils. * * *

II

* * *

Over the 16 years since *Brown II,* many difficulties were encountered in implementation of the basic constitutional requirement that the State not discriminate between public school children on the basis of their race. Nothing in our national experience prior to 1955 prepared anyone for dealing with changes and adjustments of the magnitude and complexity encountered since then. Deliberate resistance of some to the Court's mandates has impeded the good-faith efforts of others to bring school systems into compliance. * * *

III

The objective today remains to eliminate from the public schools all vestiges of state-imposed segregation. * * *

If school authorities fail in their affirmative obligations under these holdings, judicial authority may be invoked. Once a right and a violation have been shown, the scope of a district court's equitable powers to remedy past wrongs is broad, for breadth and flexibility are inherent in equitable remedies. * * * Hecht Co. v. Bowles, 321 U.S. 321, 329–330, 64 S.Ct. 587, 592, 88 L.Ed. 754 (1944).

* * * [A] school desegregation case does not differ fundamentally from other cases involving the framing of equitable remedies to repair the denial of a constitutional right. The task is to correct, by a balancing of the individual and collective interests, the condition that offends the Constitution.

In seeking to define even in broad and general terms how far this remedial power extends it is important to remember that judicial powers may be exercised only on the basis of a constitutional violation. Remedial judicial authority does not put judges automatically in the shoes of school authorities whose powers are plenary. Judicial authority enters only when local authority defaults.

School authorities are traditionally charged with broad power to formulate and implement educational policy and might well conclude, for example, that in order to prepare students to live in a pluralistic society each school should have a prescribed ratio of Negro to white students reflecting the proportion for the district as a whole. To do this as an educational policy is within the broad discretionary powers of school authorities; absent a finding of a constitutional violation, however, that would not be within the authority of a federal court. As with any equity case, the nature of the violation determines the scope of the remedy. In default by the school authorities of their obligation to proffer acceptable remedies, a district court has broad power to fashion a remedy that will assure a unitary school system. * * *

IV

* * *

The construction of new schools and the closing of old ones are two of the most important functions of local school authorities and also two of the most complex. * * * The result * * *, when combined with one technique or another of student assignment, will determine the racial composition of the student body in each school in the system. Over the long run, the consequences of the choices will be far reaching. People gravitate toward school facilities, just as schools are located in response to the needs of people. The location of schools may thus influence the patterns of residential development of a metropolitan area and have important impact on composition of inner-city neighborhoods.

In the past, choices in this respect have been used as a potent weapon for creating or maintaining a state-segregated school system. In addition to the classic pattern of building schools specifically intended for Negro or white students, school authorities have sometimes, since *Brown,* closed schools which appeared likely to become racially mixed through changes in neighborhood residential patterns. This was sometimes accompanied by building new schools in the areas of white suburban expansion farthest from Negro population centers in order to maintain the separation of the races with a minimum departure from the formal principles of "neighborhood zoning." Such a policy does more than simply influence the short-run composition of the student body of a new school. It may well promote segregated residential patterns which, when combined with "neighborhood zoning," further lock the school system into the mold of separation of the races. Upon a proper showing a district court may consider this in fashioning a remedy. * * *

V

The central issue in this case is that of student assignment, and there are essentially four problem areas: * * *

(1) *Racial Balances or Racial Quotas.* * * * If we were to read the holding of the District Court to require, as a matter of substantive constitutional right, any particular degree of racial balance or mixing, that approach would be disapproved and we would be obliged to reverse. The constitutional command to desegregate schools does not mean that every school in every community must always reflect the racial composition of the school system as a whole. * * *

(2) *One-race Schools.* The record in this case reveals the familiar phenomenon that in metropolitan areas minority groups are often found concentrated in one part of the city. In some circumstances certain schools may remain all or largely of one race until new schools can be provided or neighborhood patterns change. Schools all or predominantly of one race in a district of mixed population will require close scrutiny to determine that school assignments are not part of state-enforced segregation.

In light of the above, it should be clear that the existence of some small number of one-race, or virtually one-race, schools within a district is not in and of itself the mark of a system that still practices segregation by law. The district judge or school authorities should make every effort to achieve the greatest possible degree of actual desegregation and will thus necessarily be concerned with the elimination of one-race schools. No per se rule can adequately embrace all the difficulties of reconciling the competing interests involved; but in a system with a history of segregation the need for remedial criteria of sufficient specificity to assure a school authority's compliance with its constitutional duty warrants a presumption against schools that are substantially disproportionate in their racial composition. Where the school authority's proposed plan for conversion from a dual to a unitary system contemplates the continued existence of some schools that are all or predominantly of one race, * * * [t]he court should scrutinize such schools, and the burden upon the school authorities will be to satisfy the court that their racial composition is not the result of present or past discriminatory action on their part. * * *

(3) *Remedial Altering of Attendance Zones.* The maps submitted in these cases graphically demonstrate that one of the principal tools employed by school planners and by courts to break up the dual school system has been a frank—and sometimes drastic—gerrymandering of school districts and attendance zones. An additional step was [assigning students to a school not only from its neighborhood but also from a distant neighborhood] to accomplish the transfer of Negro students out of formerly segregated Negro schools and transfer of white students to formerly all-Negro schools. * * * As an interim corrective measure, this cannot be said to be beyond the broad remedial powers of a court.

Absent a constitutional violation there would be no basis for judicially ordering assignment of students on a racial basis. All things being equal, with no history of discrimination, it might well be desirable to assign pupils to schools nearest their homes. But all things are not equal in a system that has been deliberately constructed and maintained to enforce racial segregation. * * *

In this area, we must of necessity rely to a large extent, as this Court has for more than 16 years, on the informed judgment of the district courts in the first instance and on courts of appeals. * * *

(4) *Transportation of Students.* The scope of permissible transportation of students as an implement of a remedial decree has never been defined by this Court and by the very nature of the problem it cannot be defined with precision. * * * Bus transportation has been an integral part of the public education system for years, and was perhaps the single most important factor in the transition from the one-room schoolhouse to the consolidated school. * * *

[The amount of busing under the District Court's plan] compares favorably with the transportation plan previously operated in Charlotte * * *.

An objection to transportation of students may have validity when the time or distance of travel is so great as to either risk the health of the children or significantly impinge on the educational process. District courts must weigh the soundness of any transportation plan in light of what is said in subdivisions (1), (2), and (3) above. It hardly needs stating that the limits on time of travel will vary with many factors, but probably with none more than the age of the students. The reconciliation of competing values in a desegregation case is, of course, a difficult task with many sensitive facets but fundamentally no more so than remedial measures courts of equity have traditionally employed.

VI

The Court of Appeals, searching for a term to define the equitable remedial power of the district courts, used the term "reasonableness." In

Green, this Court used the term "feasible" and by implication, "workable," "effective," and "realistic" in the mandate to develop "a plan that promises realistically to work, and ... to work *now*." On the facts of this case, we are unable to conclude that the order of the District Court is not reasonable, feasible and workable. However, in seeking to define the scope of remedial power or the limits on remedial power of courts in an area as sensitive as we deal with here, words are poor instruments to convey the sense of basic fairness inherent in equity. Substance, not semantics, must govern, and we have sought to suggest the nature of limitations without frustrating the appropriate scope of equity. * * *

The order of the District Court * * * is * * * affirmed. * * *

NOTES

1. The Court in *Swann* held that only de jure segregation gives rise to liability, but called for "the greatest possible degree of actual desegregation"—which would surely be an appropriate remedy if de facto segregation were the standard of liability. The challenge of understanding *Swann* is to explain this seeming disparity. With the standard of liability being de jure and not de facto, what is the appropriate remedy against school authorities on the facts of *Swann*?

   a. *Make the school board assign students to schools on a color-blind basis.* This remedy permits pupil assignment based upon principles such as minimizing pupils travel time. Due to housing patterns, such assignments could lead to one race schools.

   b. *Make the schools admit students on a color-blind basis, but nonetheless require color-conscious action to correct for residential segregation caused by past school segregation.* This remedy allows color-conscious action to repair racial imbalances traceable to past violations by the defendants. Such a remedy would be far more limited than that in *Swann*. According to Professor Peter Shane:

   > *Swann* clearly did more than restore the pattern of school attendance that would have prevailed but for the school authorities' racially segregative acts. * * * Although the school board's school site location decisions undoubtedly exacerbated the perpetuation of racial imbalance in the public schools after 1954, Charlotte–Mecklenburg was an urban school district with significant residential segregation that neither the district court nor the court of appeals attributed entirely to school board action. Although the precise contribution of state-required segregation to the pattern of school attendance in 1971 might have been impossible to prove, it is unlikely that the schools would all have been racially balanced, even without official segregation.

   Peter M. Shane, School Desegregation Remedies and the Fair Governance of Schools, 132 U.Pa.L.Rev. 1041, 1065–66 (1984).

   c. *Make the schools admit students on a color-blind basis, but nonetheless require color-conscious action to correct for residential segregation caused by any governmental unit, whether the school board or any other entity.* *Rizzo v. Goode* stated that a defendant that is not a proven violator cannot be held responsible for correcting the violations of others. A possible corollary is that a proven violator cannot be held responsible for correcting the separate violations of others. A series of recent school desegregation cases tend to suggest that a school board will be held responsible only for correcting its own violations and not actions of other public or private actors. E.g., Freeman v. Pitts, 503 U.S. 467, 112 S.Ct. 1430, 118 L.Ed.2d 108 (1992) (discussed at pp. 279–281); Missouri v. Jenkins (*Jenkins III*), 515 U.S. 70, 115 S.Ct. 2038, 132 L.Ed.2d 63 (1995) (see p. 165).

d. *Make defendants achieve racial balance within the school district.* Professor Shane contends that the Court has never clearly explained why its remedy seems broader than the right that it has identified. He suggests an explanation:

> Where minority students are systematically vulnerable to hostile or insensitive treatment, the racial separation of schools effectively subjugates minority students in the competition for educational resources and deprives them of any basis for reasonable confidence in the evenhanded administration of their schools.

132 U.Pa.L.Rev. at 1043. On this basis, the breadth of the remedy is prophylactic. There are hints of such prophylactic thinking in *Swann*. For example, the Court states that "in a system with a history of segregation the need for remedial criteria of sufficient specificity to assure a school authority's compliance with its constitutional duty warrants a presumption against schools that are substantially disproportionate in their racial composition." Swann v. Charlotte–Mecklenburg Board of Education, 402 U.S. 1, 26, 91 S.Ct. 1267, 1281, 28 L.Ed.2d 554 (1971). The prophylactic rationale does not necessarily mean that the broader remedy is appropriate indefinitely. See also Board of Education v. Dowell, 498 U.S. 237, 111 S.Ct. 630, 112 L.Ed.2d 715 (1991).

e. *Make defendants achieve racial balance throughout the metropolitan area.* This possibility is discussed in *Jenkins III*, at pp. 165–179.

Can you think of any other rationale for the breadth of the remedy in *Swann*?

For an excellent discussion of these possibilities, see Mark G. Yudof, School Desegregation: Legal Realism, Reasoned Elaboration, and Social Science Research in the Supreme Court, 42 L. & Contemp.Probs. 57 (Autumn 1978).

2. In comparison to these various approaches to *Swann*, consider the following approaches to a case in which an employee who is contractually obligated to keep secret an employer's client information, quits, takes a job with a rival, and divulges information about one client:

(a) Order the former employee not to divulge further client information.

(b) Order the employee not to divulge further client information and the rival not to go after that one client.

(c) Order the employee not to work for the rival.

E.g., PepsiCo v. Redmond, 54 F.3d 1262 (7th Cir.1995)(former employee ordered not to work for rival because of likelihood that trade secrets would be revealed).

3. The preceding notes dealt with ways in which the remedy might have given the plaintiffs more than their rightful position in terms of substance. The plaintiffs certainly got more than their rightful position in terms of procedure in that *Swann* does not remand the design of the desegregation plan to the school board, although the plaintiffs' rightful position is to have the school board treat them in a way that complies with the fourteenth amendment. Is supplanting the school board consistent with the rightful position concept? Professor (now U.S. Circuit Judge) William Fletcher argues that courts are supposed to supplant state and local government only to the extent that those governments have demonstrated that they cannot be trusted to remedy the wrong. William A. Fletcher, The Discretionary Constitution: Institutional Remedies and Judicial Legitimacy, 91 Yale L.J. 635, 649–650 (1982).

4. *Swann* says that how far beyond the rightful position the injunction may take the plaintiffs and push the defendants is a question without a specific answer. However, its references to balancing and citation to *Hecht* suggest that the analysis should be similar to that done when considering when relief may achieve less than the plaintiff's rightful position. The Court shows much more solicitude to the non-violator school children than to the violator school board.

5. For background on *Swann*, see Davison M. Douglas, Reading, Writing & Race: The Desegregation of the Charlotte Schools (1995). In 1999, the district court finally terminated its order in *Swann*, finding that the school system had eliminated all vestiges of de jure segregation to the extent practicable. Capacchione v. Charlotte–Mecklenburg Schools, 57 F.Supp.2d 228 (W.D.N.C.1999). The Fourth Circuit en banc affirmed. Belk v. Charlotte–Mecklenburg Board of Education, 269 F.3d 305 (4th Cir. en banc 2001), cert. denied, 535 U.S. 986, 122 S.Ct. 1537, 152 L.Ed.2d 465 (2002). The opinions also detail the subsequent history of the lengthy case.

6. The *Swann* Court stated in dicta that school authorities had "broad discretionary powers" to set educational policy, including establishing a "prescribed ratio" of students of different races in each school in the proportion found in the district as a whole. In contrast, according to Chief Justice Burger's unanimous opinion, federal courts could do no such thing "absent a finding of constitutional violation" (p. 159). This dicta is severely open to question after Parents Involved in Community Schools v. Seattle School District No. 1, 551 U.S. 701, 127 S.Ct. 2738, 168 L.Ed.2d 508 (2007). In *Parents Involved*, a plurality of the Supreme Court rejected the attempt of the Seattle and Louisville school districts to use race as an element in student assignments to schools in order to voluntarily promote racial diversity and avoid racial isolation. For Chief Justice Roberts and three other justices, these goals had not been justified as compelling governmental interests and the particular uses of race had not been shown by the respective school districts to be narrowly tailored. Without evidence of a constitutional violation, the school districts could not justify the assignment plans as remedies. Justice

Kennedy concurred in the result in *Parents Involved* because he agreed that the particular assignment systems had not been shown to be narrowly tailored. He wrote separately, however, to show that he thought that school districts could foster racial diversity without triggering strict scrutiny by not assigning students by race but instead by using techniques such as the creation of attendance zones, the placement of magnet schools, and the allocation of resources. Justice Breyer wrote an extensive and vehement dissent for himself and three other justices, which not only supported the assignment systems at issue in the case but also charged that Chief Justice Roberts' plurality opinion would effectively reverse fifty years of precedent and the remedial promise of *Brown v. Board of Education* (p. 107). In laying out his vision of what was permissible under *Brown* and its progeny, however, Justice Breyer made no attempt to justify the broad dicta from *Swann*. Whatever federal district courts may still do to remedy segregation after making a finding of a constitutional violation, the power of school districts to use race to set educational policy voluntarily today is no longer anything like what Chief Justice Burger suggested in 1971.

For some of the extensive and growing commentary on *Parents Involved*, see Jonathan Fischbach, Will Rhee & Robert Cacace, Race at the Pivot Point: The Future of Race–Based Policies to Remedy De Jure Segregation After *Parents Involved in Community Schools*, 43 Harv.Civ.Rights–Civ.Lib.L.Rev. 491 (2008); Michelle Adams, Stifling the Potential of *Grutter v. Bollinger: Parents Involved in Community Schools v. Seattle School District No. 1*, 88 Boston U.L.Rev. 937 (2008); Michael Heise, Judicial Decision-making, Social Science Evidence, and Equal Educational Opportunity: Uneasy Relations and Uncertain Futures, 31 Seattle U.L. Rev. 863 (2008); Martha Minow, After *Brown*: What Would Martin Luther King Say?, 12 Lewis & Clark L.Rev. 599 (2008).

Swann, which was decided during an era of evident resistance to the commands of *Brown*, focused on thwarting that resistance by making clear that the school boards had to take real action. *Missouri v. Jenkins,* decided during an era of concern about the scope of judicial authority, focused on defining the outer limits of the duty to desegregate.

MISSOURI v. JENKINS (*JENKINS III*)

Supreme Court of the United States, 1995
515 U.S. 70, 115 S.Ct. 2038, 132 L.Ed.2d 63

CHIEF JUSTICE REHNQUIST delivered the opinion of the Court. * * *

I

* * *

This case has been before the same United States District Judge since 1977. Missouri v. Jenkins, 491 U.S. 274, 276, 109 S.Ct. 2463, 105 L.Ed.2d 229 (1989)(*Jenkins I*). In that year, the Kansas City, Missouri, School District (KCMSD), the school board, and the children of two school board members brought suit against the State and other defendants. Plaintiffs alleged that the State, the surrounding suburban school districts (SSD's), and various federal agencies had caused and perpetuated a system of racial segregation in the schools of the Kansas City metropolitan area. The District Court realigned the KCMSD as a nominal defendant and certified as a class, present and future KCMSD students. The KCMSD brought a cross-claim against the State for its failure to eliminate the vestiges of its prior dual school system.

After a trial that lasted 7½ months, the District Court dismissed the case against the federal defendants and the SSD's, but determined that the State and the KCMSD were liable for an intradistrict violation, i.e., they had operated a segregated school system within the KCMSD. The District Court determined that prior to 1954 "Missouri mandated segregated schools for black and white children." * * *

The District Court determined that "[s]egregation ha[d] caused a system wide *reduction* in student achievement in the schools of the KCMSD." The District Court made no particularized findings regarding the extent that student achievement had been reduced or what portion of that reduction was attributable to segregation. The District Court also identified 25 schools within the KCMSD that had enrollments of 90% or more black students.

The District Court, pursuant to plans submitted by the KCMSD and the State, ordered a wide range of quality education programs for all students attending the KCMSD. * * * [Under these programs, all schools in the district would get reduced class size, full-day kindergarten, expanded summer school, before- and after-school tutoring, an early childhood development program, and substantial yearly cash grants.] The total cost for these quality education programs has exceeded $220 million.

The District Court also set out to desegregate the KCMSD but believed that "[t]o accomplish desegregation within the boundary lines of a school district whose enrollment remains 68.3% black is a difficult task." Because it had found no interdistrict violation, the District Court could not order mandatory interdistrict redistribution of students between the KCMSD and the surrounding SSD's. * * * Milliken v. Bradley, 418 U.S. 717 (1974)(*Milliken I*). The District Court refused to order additional mandatory student reassignments because they would "increase the instability of the KCMSD and reduce the potential for desegregation." * * *

In November 1986, the District Court approved a comprehensive magnet school and capital improvements plan and held the State and the KCMSD jointly and severally liable for its funding. Under the District Court's plan, every senior high school, every middle school, and one-half of the elementary schools were converted into magnet schools. The District Court adopted the magnet-school program to "provide a greater educational opportunity to *all* KCMSD students," and because it believed "that the proposed magnet plan [was] so attractive that it would draw non-minority students from the private schools who have abandoned or avoided the KCMSD, and draw in additional non-minority students from the suburbs." * * * Since its inception, the magnet school program has operated at a cost, including magnet transportation, in excess of $448 million. In April 1993, the District Court considered, but ultimately rejected, the plaintiffs' and the KCMSD's proposal seeking approval of a long-range magnet renewal program that included a 10-year budget of well over $500 million, funded by the State and the KCMSD on a joint-and-several basis.

In June 1985, the District Court ordered substantial capital improvements to combat the deterioration of the KCMSD's facilities. In formulating its capital-improvements plan, the District Court dismissed as "irrelevant" the "State's argument that the present condition of the facilities [was] not traceable to unlawful segregation." Instead, the District Court focused on its responsibility to "remed[y] the vestiges of segregation" and to "implemen[t] a desegregation plan which w[ould] maintain and attract non-minority members." [The total cost of the program was over $540 million.]

As part of its desegregation plan, the District Court has ordered salary assistance to the KCMSD. * * * [T]he District Court has ordered salary assistance to all but three of the approximately 5,000 KCMSD employees. The total cost of this component of the desegregation remedy since 1987 is over $200 million.

The District Court's desegregation plan has been described as the most ambitious and expensive remedial program in the history of school desegregation. The annual cost per pupil at the KCMSD far exceeds that of the neighboring SSD's or of any school district in Missouri. * * * These massive expenditures have financed

> "high schools in which every classroom will have air conditioning, an alarm system, and 15 microcomputers; a 2,000-square-foot planetarium; green houses and vivariums; a 25-acre farm with an air-conditioned meeting room for 104 people; a Model United Nations wired for language translation; broadcast capable radio and television studios with an editing and animation lab; a temperature controlled art gallery; movie editing and screening rooms; a 3,500-square-foot dust-free diesel mechanics room; 1,875-square-foot elementary school animal rooms for use in a zoo project; swimming pools; and numerous other facilities."

Missouri v. Jenkins (*Jenkins II*), 495 U.S. 33, 77, 110 S.Ct. 1651, 1676–77, 109 L.Ed.2d 31 (1990)(Kennedy, J., concurrence). Not surprisingly, the cost of this remedial plan has "far exceeded KCMSD's budget, or for that matter, its authority to tax." The State, through the operation of joint-and-several liability, has borne the brunt of these costs. The District Court candidly has acknowledged that it has "allowed the District planners to dream" and "provided the mechanism for th[ose] dreams to be realized." * * *

II

With this background, we turn to the present controversy. First, the State has challenged the District Court's requirement that it fund salary increases for KCMSD instructional and noninstructional staff. The State claimed that funding for salaries was beyond the scope of the District Court's remedial authority. Second, the State has challenged the District Court's order requiring it to continue to fund the remedial quality education programs for the 1992–1993 school year. The State contended that under Freeman v. Pitts, 503 U.S. 467 (1992), it had achieved partial unitary status with respect to the quality education programs already in place.[d] * * * [The District Court and Court of Appeals rejected the state's claims. The Court of Appeals] found significant the District Court's determination that although "there had been a trend of improvement in academic achievement, ... the school district was far from reaching its maximum potential because KCMSD is still at or below national norms at many grade levels." * * *

The Court of Appeals denied rehearing en banc, with five judges dissenting. * * *

Because of the importance of the issues, we granted certiorari to consider the following: (1) whether the District Court exceeded its constitutional authority when it granted salary increases to virtually all instructional and noninstructional employees of the KCMSD, and (2) whether the District Court properly relied upon the fact that student achievement test scores had failed to rise to some unspecified level when it declined to find that the State had achieved partial unitary status as to the quality education programs.

III

Respondents argue that the State may no longer challenge the District Court's remedy, and in any event, the propriety of the remedy is not before the Court. We disagree on both counts. In *Jenkins II*, we granted certiorari to review the manner in which the District Court had funded this desegregation remedy. [*Jenkins II* is reproduced in Chapter 3(C)(5).] Because we had denied certiorari on the State's challenge to review the scope of the remedial order, we resisted the State's efforts to challenge the scope of the remedy. Thus, we neither "approv[ed]" nor "disapprov[ed], the Court of Appeals' conclusion that the District Court's remedy was proper."

* * * An analysis of the permissible scope of the District Court's remedial authority is necessary for a proper determination of whether the order of salary increases is beyond the District Court's remedial authority, and thus, it is an issue subsidiary to our ultimate inquiry. * * *

Almost 25 years ago, in Swann v. Charlotte–Mecklenburg Bd. of Ed., 402 U.S. 1 (1971), * * * [a]lthough recognizing the discretion that must

---

d. *Freeman* is discussed at pp. 279–281.

necessarily adhere in a district court in fashioning a remedy [in a school desegregation case], we also recognized the limits on such remedial power. * * *

Three years later, in [Milliken v. Bradley, 418 U.S. 717 (1974) (*Milliken I*)], we held that a District Court had exceeded its authority in fashioning interdistrict relief where the surrounding school districts had not themselves been guilty of any constitutional violation. We said that a desegregation remedy "is necessarily designed, as all remedies are, to restore the victims of discriminatory conduct to the position they would have occupied in the absence of such conduct." "[W]ithout an interdistrict violation and interdistrict effect, there is no constitutional wrong calling for an interdistrict remedy." We also rejected "[t]he suggestion ... that schools which have a majority of Negro students are not 'desegregated,' whatever the makeup of the school district's population and however neutrally the district lines have been drawn and administered."

Three years later, in Milliken v. Bradley, 433 U.S. 267 (1977)(*Milliken II*), we articulated a three-part framework derived from our prior cases to guide district courts in the exercise of their remedial authority.

> In the first place, like other equitable remedies, the nature of the desegregation remedy is to be determined by the nature and scope of the constitutional violation. *Swann*. The remedy must therefore be related to 'the condition alleged to offend the Constitution....' *Milliken I*. Second, the decree must indeed be *remedial* in nature, that is, it must be designed as nearly as possible 'to restore the victims of discriminatory conduct to the position they would have occupied in the absence of such conduct.' *Milliken I*. Third, the federal courts in devising a remedy must take into account the interests of state and local authorities in managing their own affairs, consistent with the Constitution.

We added that the "principle that the nature and scope of the remedy are to be determined by the violation means simply that federal-court decrees must directly address and relate to the constitutional violation itself." * * *

Proper analysis of the District Court's orders challenged here, then, must rest upon their serving as proper means to the end of restoring the victims of discriminatory conduct to the position they would have occupied in the absence of that conduct and their eventual restoration of "state and local authorities to the control of a school system that is operating in compliance with the Constitution." We turn to that analysis.

The State argues that the order approving salary increases is beyond the District Court's authority because it was crafted to serve an "interdistrict goal," in spite of the fact that the constitutional violation in this case is "intradistrict" in nature. * * *

Here, the District Court has found, and the Court of Appeals has affirmed, that this case involved no interdistrict constitutional violation that would support interdistrict relief. Thus, the proper response by the District Court should have been to eliminate to the extent practicable the vestiges of prior de jure segregation within the KCMSD: a system-wide reduction in student achievement and the existence of 25 racially identifiable schools with a population of over 90% black students.

The District Court and Court of Appeals, however, have felt that because the KCMSD's enrollment remained 68.3% black, a purely intradistrict remedy would be insufficient. * * *

Instead of seeking to remove the racial identity of the various schools within the KCMSD, the District Court has set out on a program to create a school district that was equal to or superior to the surrounding SSD's. * * * The District Court's remedial order has all but made the KCMSD itself into a magnet district.

We previously have approved of intradistrict desegregation remedies involving magnet schools. *Milliken II.* * * *

The District Court's remedial plan in this case * * * [seeks] to attract nonminority students from outside the KCMSD schools. But this *inter*district goal is beyond the scope of the *intra*district violation identified by the District Court. In effect, the District Court has devised a remedy to accomplish indirectly what it admittedly lacks the remedial authority to mandate directly: the interdistrict transfer of students. * * *

[In *Milliken I*, Justice Stewart, who provided the Court's fifth vote,] wrote separately to underscore his understanding of that decision. In describing the requirements for imposing an "interdistrict" remedy, Justice Stewart stated: "Were it to be shown, for example, that state officials had contributed to the separation of the races by drawing or redrawing school district lines; by transfer of school units between districts; or by purposeful, racially discriminatory use of state housing or zoning laws, then a decree calling for the transfer of pupils across district lines or for restructuring of district lines might well be appropriate. In this case, however, no such interdistrict violation was shown." Justice Stewart concluded that the Court properly rejected the District Court's interdistrict remedy because "[t]here were no findings that the differing racial composition between schools in the city and in the outlying suburbs was caused by official activity of any sort."

* * * Nothing in *Milliken I* suggests that the District Court in that case could have circumvented the limits on its remedial authority by requiring the State of Michigan, a constitutional violator, to implement a magnet program designed to achieve the same interdistrict transfer of students that we held was beyond its remedial authority. Here, the District Court has done just that. * * *

Respondents argue that the District Court's reliance upon desegregative attractiveness is justified in light of the District Court's statement that segregation has "led to white flight from the KCMSD to suburban districts." The lower courts' "findings" as to "white flight" are both inconsistent internally[7], and inconsistent with the typical supposition, bolstered here by the record evidence, that "white flight" may result from desegregation, not *de jure* segregation.[8] The United States, as *amicus curiae*, argues that the District Court's finding that "de jure segregation in the KCMSD caused white students to leave the system ... is not inconsistent with the district court's earlier conclusion that the suburban districts did nothing to cause this white flight and therefore could not be included in a mandatory interdistrict remedy." But the District Court's earlier findings, affirmed by the Court of Appeals, were not so limited:

> [C]ontrary to the argument of [plaintiffs] that the [district court] looked only to the culpability of the SSDs, the scope of the order is far broader.... It noted that only the schools in one district were affected and that the remedy must be limited to that system. In examining the cause and effect issue, the court noted that "not only is plaintiff's evidence here blurred as to cause and effect, there is no 'careful delineation of the extent of the effect.' " ... The district court thus dealt not only with the issue whether the SSDs were constitutional violators but also whether there were significant interdistrict segregative effects.... When it did so, it made specific findings that negate current significant interdistrict effects, and concluded that the requirements of *Milliken* had not been met.

Jenkins v. Missouri, 807 F.2d 657, 672 (C.A.8 1986)(affirming, by an equally divided court, the District Court's findings and conclusion that there was no interdistrict violation or interdistrict effect) (en banc).[9]

In *Freeman*, we stated that "[t]he vestiges of segregation that are the concern of the law in a school case may be subtle and intangible but nonetheless they must be so real that they have a causal link to the *de jure* violation being remedied." The record here does not support the District Court's reliance on "white flight" as a justification for a permissible expansion of its intradistrict remedial authority through its pursuit of desegregative attractiveness. See *Milliken I*; see also Dayton Bd. of Ed. v. Brinkman, 433 U.S. 406, 417 (1977) (*Dayton I*).

Justice Souter claims that our holding effectively overrules Hills v. Gautreaux, 425 U.S. 284 (1976). In *Gautreaux*, the Federal Department of

---

7. Compare * * * *Jenkins*, 807 F.2d, at 662 ("[N]one of the alleged discriminatory actions committed by the State or the federal defendants ha[s] caused any significant current interdistrict segregation"), with Jenkins v. Missouri, 855 F.2d 1295, 1302 (C.A.8 1988)("These holdings are bolstered by the district court's findings that the preponderance of black students in the district was due to the State and KCMSD's constitutional violations, which caused white flight").

8. "During the hearing on the liability issue in this case there was an abundance of evidence that many residents of the KCMSD left the district and moved to the suburbs because of the district's efforts to integrate its schools."

9. Justice Souter construes the Court of Appeals' determination to mean that the violations by the State and the KCMSD did not cause segregation within the limits of each of the SSD's. But the Court of Appeals would not have decided this question at the behest of these plaintiffs-present and future KCMSD students-who have no standing to challenge segregation within the confines of the SSD's. Ergo, the Court of Appeals meant exactly what it said: the requirements of *Milliken I* had not been met because the District Court's specific findings "negate current significant interdistrict effects."

Housing and Urban Development (HUD) was found to have participated, along with a local housing agency, in establishing and maintaining a racially segregated public housing program. After the Court of Appeals ordered " 'the adoption of a comprehensive metropolitan area plan,' " we granted certiorari to consider the "permissibility in the light of [*Milliken I*] of 'inter-district relief for discrimination in public housing in the absence of a finding of an inter-district violation.' " Because the "relevant geographic area for the purposes of the [plaintiffs'] housing options [was] the Chicago housing market, not the Chicago city limits," we concluded that "a metropolitan area remedy . . . [was] not impermissible as a matter of law." 425 U.S. at 298, n.13 (distinguishing *Milliken I*, in part, because prior cases had established that racial segregation in schools is "to be dealt with in terms of 'an established geographic and administrative school system' ").

In *Gautreaux*, we did not obligate the District Court to "subjec[t] HUD to measures going beyond the geographical or political boundaries of its violation." Instead, we cautioned that our holding "should not be interpreted as requiring a metropolitan area order." We reversed appellate factfinding by the Court of Appeals that would have mandated a metropolitan-area remedy, and remanded the case back to the District Court " 'for additional evidence and for further consideration of the issue of metropolitan area relief.' "

Our decision today is fully consistent with *Gautreaux*. A district court seeking to remedy an *intra*district violation that has not "directly caused" significant interdistrict effects, *Milliken I*, exceeds its remedial authority if it orders a remedy with an interdistrict purpose. This conclusion follows directly from *Milliken II*, decided one year after *Gautreaux*, where we reaffirmed the bedrock principle that "federal-court decrees exceed appropriate limits if they are aimed at eliminating a condition that does not violate the Constitution or does not flow from such a violation." In *Milliken II*, we also emphasized that "federal courts in devising a remedy must take into account the interests of state and local authorities in managing their own affairs, consistent with the Constitution." *Gautreaux*, however, involved the imposition of a remedy upon a federal agency. Thus, it did not raise the same federalism concerns that are implicated when a federal court issues a remedial order against a State.

The District Court's pursuit of "desegregative attractiveness" cannot be reconciled with our cases placing limitations on a district court's remedial authority. It is certainly theoretically possible that the greater the expenditure per pupil within the KCMSD, the more likely it is that some unknowable number of nonminority students not presently attending schools in the KCMSD will choose to enroll in those schools. Under this reasoning, however, every increased expenditure, whether it be for teachers, noninstructional employees, books, or buildings, will make the KCMSD in some way more attractive, and thereby perhaps induce nonminority students to enroll in its schools. But this rationale is not susceptible to any objective limitation. This case provides numerous examples demonstrating the limitless authority of the District Court operating under this rationale. In short, desegregative attractiveness has been used "as the hook on which to hang numerous policy choices about improving the quality of education in general within the KCMSD."

Nor are there limits to the duration of the District Court's involvement. The expenditures per pupil in the KCMSD currently far exceed those in the neighboring SSD's. Sixteen years after this litigation began, the District Court recognized that the KCMSD has yet to offer a viable method of financing the "wonderful school system being built." Each additional program ordered by the District Court—and financed by the State—to increase the "desegregative attractiveness" of the school district makes the KCMSD more and more dependent on additional funding from the State; in turn, the greater the KCMSD's dependence on state funding, the greater its reliance on continued supervision by the District Court. But our cases recognize that local autonomy of school districts is a vital national tradition, and that a district court must strive to restore state and local authorities to the control of a school system operating in compliance with the Constitution. See *Freeman*; *Dowell*.

The District Court's pursuit of the goal of "desegregative attractiveness" results in so many imponderables and is so far removed from the task of eliminating the racial identifiability of the schools within the KCMSD that we believe it is beyond the admittedly broad discretion of the District Court. In this posture, we conclude that the District Court's order of salary increases, which was "grounded in remedying the vestiges of segregation by improving the desegregative attractiveness of the KCMSD," is simply too far removed from an acceptable implementation of a permissible means to remedy previous legally mandated segregation.

Similar considerations lead us to conclude that the District Court's order requiring the State to continue to fund the quality education programs because student achievement levels were still "at or below national norms at many grade levels" cannot be sustained. The State does not seek from this Court a declaration of partial unitary status with respect to the quality education programs. It challenges the requirement of indefinite funding of a quality education program until national norms are met, based on the assumption that while a mandate for significant educational improvement, both in teaching and in facilities, may have been justified originally, its indefinite extension is not. * * *

[Whether students in the KCMSD perform below national norms] clearly is not the appropriate test to be applied in deciding whether a previously segregated district has achieved partially unitary status. The basic task of the District Court is to decide whether the reduction in achievement by minority students attributable to prior de jure segregation has been remedied to the extent practicable. Under our precedents, the State and the KCMSD are "entitled to a rather precise statement of [their] obligations under a desegregation decree." Although the District Court has determined that "[s]egregation has caused a system wide *reduction* in achievement in the schools of the KCMSD," it never has identified the incremental effect that segregation has had on minority student achievement or the specific goals of the quality education programs. Cf. *Dayton I*.

In reconsidering this order, the District Court should * * * consider that the State's role with respect to the quality education programs has been limited to the funding, not the implementation, of those programs. As all the parties agree that improved achievement on test scores is not necessarily required for the State to achieve partial unitary status as to the quality education programs, the District Court should sharply limit, if not dispense with, its reliance on this factor. * * * Insistence upon academic goals unrelated to the effects of legal segregation unwarrantably postpones the day when the KCMSD will be able to operate on its own.

The District Court also should consider that many goals of its quality education plan already have been attained: the KCMSD now is equipped with "facilities and opportunities not available anywhere else in the country." KCMSD schools received AAA rating [the state's highest rating] eight years ago, and the present remedial programs have been in place for seven years. It may be that in education, just as it may be in economics, a "rising tide lifts all boats," but the remedial quality education program should be tailored to remedy the injuries suffered by the victims of prior *de jure* segregation. Minority students in kindergarten through grade 7 in the KCMSD always have attended AAA-rated schools; minority students in the KCMSD that previously attended schools rated below AAA have since received remedial education programs for a period of up to seven years.

On remand, the District Court must bear in mind that its end purpose is not only "to remedy the violation" to the extent practicable, but also "to restore state and local authorities to the control of a school system that is operating in compliance with the Constitution." *Freeman*.

The judgment of the Court of Appeals is reversed.

JUSTICE O'CONNOR, concurring. * * *

What the District Court did in this case, * * * and how it transgressed the constitutional bounds of its remedial powers, is to make desegregative attractiveness the underlying goal of its remedy for the specific purpose of reversing the trend of white flight. However troubling that trend may be, remedying it is within the District Court's authority only if it is "directly caused by the constitutional violation." The Court and the dissent attempt to reconcile the different statements by the lower courts as to whether white flight was caused by segregation or desegregation. One fact, however, is uncontroverted. When the District Court found that KCMSD was racially segregated, the constitutional violation from which all remedies flow in this case, it also found that there was neither an interdistrict violation nor significant interdistrict segregative effects. Whether the white exodus that has resulted in a school district that is 68% black was caused by the District Court's remedial orders or by natural, if unfortunate, demographic forces, we have it directly from the District Court that the segregative effects of KCMSD's constitutional violation did not transcend its geographical boundaries. In light of that finding, the District Court cannot order remedies seeking to rectify regional demographic trends that go beyond the nature and scope of the constitutional violation.

This case, like other school desegregation litigation, is concerned with "the elimination of the discrimination inherent in the dual school systems, not with myriad factors of human existence which can cause discrimination in a multitude of ways on racial, religious, or ethnic grounds." Swann v. Charlotte–Mecklenburg Bd. of Ed., 402 U.S. 1, 22 (1971). Those myriad factors are not readily corrected by judicial intervention, but are best addressed by the representative branches; time and again, we have recognized the ample authority legislatures possess to combat racial injustice. * * *

JUSTICE THOMAS, concurring.

It never ceases to amaze me that the courts are so willing to assume that anything that is predominantly black must be inferior. Instead of focusing on remedying the harm done to those black schoolchildren injured by segregation, the District Court here sought to convert the Kansas City, Missouri, School District (KCMSD) into a "magnet district" that would reverse the "white flight" caused by de segregation. * * *

"Racial isolation" itself is not a harm; only state-enforced segregation is. After all, if separation itself is a harm, and if integration therefore is the only way that blacks can receive a proper education, then there must be something inferior about blacks. Under this theory, segregation injures blacks because blacks, when left on their own, cannot achieve. To my way of thinking, that conclusion is the result of a jurisprudence based upon a theory of black inferiority. * * *

II

* * *

A

* * *

Our impatience with the pace of desegregation and with the lack of a good-faith effort on the part of school boards led us to approve * * * extraordinary remedial measures. But such powers should have been temporary and used only to overcome the widespread resistance to the dictates of the Constitution. The judicial overreaching we see before us today perhaps is the price we now pay for our approval of such extraordinary remedies in the past. * * *

Our willingness to unleash the federal equitable power has reached areas beyond school desegregation * * * [to include] the reconstruction of entire institutions and bureaucracies. * * *

B

* * *

Anticipating the growth of our modern doctrine, the Anti–Federalists criticized the Constitution because it might be read to grant broad equitable powers to the federal courts. In response, the defenders of the Constitution "sold" the new framework of government to the public by espousing a narrower interpretation of the equity power. * * * [T]he appropriate conclusion is that the drafters and ratifiers of the Constitution approved the more limited construction offered in response. * * *

In light of this historical evidence, it should come as no surprise that there is no early record of the exercise of broad remedial powers. * * *

D

* * *

Contrary to the dissent's conclusion, the District Court's remedial orders are in tension with two common-sense principles. First, the District Court retained jurisdiction over the implementation and modification of the remedial decree, instead of terminating its involvement after issuing its remedy. Although briefly mentioned in *Brown II* as a temporary measure to overcome local resistance to desegregation, 349 U.S., at 301 ("[d]uring this period of transition, the courts will retain jurisdiction"), this concept of continuing judicial involvement has permitted the District Courts to revise their remedies constantly in order to reach some broad, abstract, and often elusive goal. Not only does this approach deprive the parties of finality and a clear understanding of their responsibilities, but it also tends to inject the judiciary into the day-to-day management of institutions and local policies-a function that lies outside of our Article III competence. * * *

Second, the District Court failed to target its equitable remedies in this case specifically to cure the harm suffered by the victims of segregation. Of course, the initial and most important aspect of any remedy will be to eliminate any invidious racial distinctions in matters such as student assignments, transportation, staff, resource allocation, and activities. This element of most desegregation decrees is fairly straightforward and has not produced many examples of overreaching by the district courts. It is the "compensatory" ingredient in many desegregation plans that has produced many of the difficulties in the case before us.

* * * In the absence of special circumstances, the remedy for de jure segregation ordinarily should not include educational programs for students who were not in school (or were even alive) during the period of segregation. * * *

JUSTICE SOUTER, with whom JUSTICE STEVENS, JUSTICE GINSBURG, and JUSTICE BREYER join, dissenting.

* * *

II

A

* * * [N]one of the District Court's or Court of Appeals's opinions or orders requires a certain level of test scores before unitary status can be found, or indicates that test scores are the only thing standing between the State and a finding of unitary status as to the KCMSD's *Milliken II* programs. * * *

* * * The Court of Appeals refused to order the District Court to enter a finding of partial unitary status as to the KCMSD's *Milliken II* programs (and apparently, the District Court did not speak to the issue itself) simply because the State did not attempt to make the showing required for that relief. * * *

In the development of a proper unitary status record, test scores will undoubtedly play a role. It is true, as the Court recognizes, that all parties to this case agree that it would be error to require that the students in a school district attain the national average test score as a prerequisite to a finding of partial unitary status, if only because all sorts of causes independent of the vestiges of past school segregation might stand in the way of the goal. That said, test scores will clearly be relevant in determining whether the improvement programs have cured a deficiency in student achievement to the practicable extent.* * *

B

The other question properly before us has to do with the propriety of the District Court's recent salary orders. While the Court suggests otherwise, the District Court did not ground its orders of salary increases solely on the goal of attracting students back to the KCMSD. From the start, the District Court has consistently treated salary increases as an important element in remedying the systemwide reduction in student achievement resulting from segregation in the KCSMD. * * *

III

* * *

[T]he District Court did not mean by an "intradistrict violation" what the Court apparently means by it today. The District Court meant that the violation within the KCMSD had not led to segregation outside of it, and that no other school districts had played a part in the violation. * * *

[The District Court's finding that segregation caused white flight is not contradicted, as the majority asserts, by the Court of Appeals's conclusion that the District Court " 'made specific findings that negate current significant interdistrict effects....' " because the Court of Appeals meant interdistrict *segregative* effects.]

Without the contradiction, the Court has nothing to justify its rejection of the District Court's finding that segregation caused white flight but its supposition that flight results from integration, not segregation.

The supposition, and the distinction on which it rests, are untenable. At the more obvious level, there is in fact no break in the chain of causation linking the effects of desegregation with those of segregation. There would be no desegregation orders and no remedial plans without prior unconstitutional segregation as the occasion for issuing and adopting them, and an adverse reaction to a desegregation order is traceable in fact to the segregation that is subject to the remedy. When the Court quotes the District Court's reference to abundant evidence that integration caused flight to the suburbs, then, it quotes nothing inconsistent with the District Court's other findings that segregation had caused the flight. The only difference between the statements lies in the point to which the District Court happened to trace the causal sequence.

* * * [For example, property tax-paying] parents of white children, seeing the handwriting on the wall in 1985, could well have decided that the inevitable cost of clean-up would produce an intolerable tax rate and could have moved to escape it. The District Court's remedial orders had not yet been put in place. Was the white flight caused by segregation or desegregation? The distinction has no significance. * * *

B

* * *

We are not dealing here with an interdistrict remedy in the sense that *Milliken I* used the term. In the *Milliken I* litigation, the District Court had ordered 53 surrounding school districts to be consolidated with the Detroit school system, and mandatory busing to be started within the enlarged district, even though the court had not found that any of the suburban districts had acted in violation of the Constitution. * * *

[In *Gautreaux*,] HUD argued that the case should turn on the same principles governing school desegregation orders and that, under *Milliken I*, the District Court's order could not look beyond Chicago's city limits, because it was only within those limits that the constitutional violation had been committed. We agreed with HUD that the principles of *Milliken* apply outside of the school desegregation context, but squarely rejected its restricted interpretation of those principles and its view of limited equitable authority to remedy segregation. We held that a district court may indeed subject a governmental perpetrator of segregative practices to an order for relief with intended consequences beyond the perpetrator's own subdivision, even in the absence of effects outside that subdivision, so long as the decree does not bind the authorities of other governmental units that are free of violations and segregative effects:

> [*Milliken I*'s] holding that there had to be an interdistrict violation or effect before a federal court could order the crossing of district boundary lines reflected the substantive impact of a consolidation remedy on separate and independent school districts. The District Court's desegregation order in *Milliken* was held to be an impermissible remedy not because it envisioned relief against a wrongdoer

extending beyond the city in which the violation occurred but because it contemplated a judicial decree restructuring the operation of local governmental entities that were not implicated in any constitutional violation.

Id., at 296 (footnote omitted).

In the face of *Gautreaux*'s language, the Court claims that it was only because the " 'relevant geographic area for the purposes of the [plaintiffs'] housing options [was] the Chicago housing market, not the Chicago city limits,' " that we held that " 'a metropolitan area remedy [was] not impermissible as a matter of law,' " quoting *Gautreaux*. But that was only half the explanation. Requiring a remedy outside the city in the wider metropolitan area was permissible not only because that was the area of the housing market even for people who lived within the city (thus relating the scope of the remedy to the violation suffered by the victims) but also because the trial court could order a remedy in that market without binding a governmental unit innocent of the violation and free of its effects. In "reject[ing] the contention that, since HUD's constitutional and statutory violations were committed in Chicago, *Milliken* precludes an order against HUD that will affect its conduct in the greater metropolitan area," we stated plainly that "[t]he critical distinction between HUD and the suburban school districts in *Milliken* is that HUD has been found to have violated the Constitution. * * *

JUSTICE GINSBURG, dissenting. [omitted]

NOTES

1. The district court's remedy in *Jenkins* sought to integrate within the school district, as the remedy in *Swann* did, and to provide compensatory education to make up for the educational deficits caused by segregation, as the remedy in *Milliken II* did. What was new about the remedy in *Jenkins* was the scope of the compensatory education program, the effort to attract white students from private schools and the suburbs, and the attendant costs. The question was whether the ambitious scope of the remedy was appropriate.

2. One justification for the scope of the remedy in *Swann* was to integrate the schools to shield African–American students from covert discrimination by the school board. Does that rationale justify the increased scope of the remedy in *Jenkins*?

3. Another possible justification for the scope of the remedy in *Swann* was to repair the damage that segregation did to the dignity of the plaintiffs. Does that rationale justify the increased scope of the remedy?

4. Is attracting white students into the KCMSD necessary to put the plaintiffs in their rightful position?

5. In Sterling Drug, Inc. v. Bayer AG, 14 F.3d 733 (2d Cir.1994), Sterling Drug, which owned the "Bayer" name within the United States, got an injunction against Bayer AG, which owned it in most of the rest of the world, barring Bayer AG from using "Bayer" not only within the United

States but also in foreign publications and products likely to find their way into the United States. The appeals court affirmed in part, remanding with instructions that the district court narrow the decree's extraterritorial application to uses of the name likely to cause significant confusion among U.S. consumers. For a useful discussion of when a state court should enjoin out of state activity, see David S. Welkowitz, Preemption, Extraterritoriality, and the Problem of State Antidilution Laws, 67 Tulane L.Rev. 1, 70 (1992) ("An extraterritorial injunction is presumed improper absent a waiver [by the other states in which it would apply] or a showing that it regulates [matters internal to the state issuing the injunction].").

6. The reparative aspects of school desegregation remedies, such as the remedial education approved in *Milliken II*, benefit students who were not in school when the constitutional violations took place and whose parents may have come from other locales in which constitutional violations did not take place. Has *Jenkins III* implicitly overruled *Milliken II*?

7. *Jenkins III* seems to require more precision in justifying the remedy than did *Madsen* and *Swann*. Justice Thomas argues that such precision is harder to achieve with reparative than preventive remedies. It is easier to be precise in justifying a remedy to repair the damage done by an individual defendant to an individual plaintiff than a remedy to repair the damage done by society to a group. Does the difficulty of achieving much precision mean that society should let bygones be bygones, or that judgments about when and how to repair such damage are so steeped in policy that courts should leave them to legislatures? An article written years before Clarence Thomas became a Supreme Court Justice perhaps helps to understand why he favors letting bygones be:

> Thomas told me a story from his boyhood to illustrate what fairness means to him. He was on the back porch, playing blackjack for pennies with other boys. As the game went on, one boy kept winning. Thomas finally saw how: the cards were marked. The game was stopped. There were angry words. * * * From all sides fast fists snatched back lost money. There could be no equitable redistribution of the pot. The strongest, fastest hands, including those of the boy who had been cheating, got most of the pile of pennies. * * * But no one really wanted to fight—they wanted to keep playing cards. So a different deck was brought out and shuffled, and the game resumed with a simple promise of no more cheating.
>
> That story, Thomas said, is a lot like the story of race relations in America. Whites had an unfair advantage. But in 1964, with the passage of the Civil Rights Act, the government stopped the cheating. The question now is, Should the government return the ill-gotten gains to the losers? * * *
>
> Thomas believes that government simply cannot make amends, and therefore should not try. The best it can do is deal a clean deck and let the game resume, enforcing the rules as they have now come to be understood. * * * Thomas said, " * * * Use what was used to get others into the economy. Show us the precedent for all this experimentation on our race."

* * * "I would be lying to you if I said that I didn't want sometimes to be able to cheat in favor of those of us who were cheated. But you have to ask yourself, in doing that, you do violence to the safe harbor, and that is the Constitution, which says you are to protect an individual's rights no matter what."

Juan Williams, A Question of Fairness, Atlantic Monthly 70, 78–79 (Feb. 1987).

8. As *Madsen* suggests, remedies that go beyond the plaintiff's rightful position get closer scrutiny when they threaten specially protected rights. In a decision handed down the same day as *Jenkins III*, Adarand Constructors, Inc. v. Peña, 515 U.S. 200, 115 S.Ct. 2097, 132 L.Ed.2d 158 (1995), the Supreme Court held that the federal government cannot discriminate in favor of minorities except when narrowly tailored to serve a compelling governmental interest. Such an interest could include remedying past discrimination. The government program at issue in *Adarand* was voluntarily adopted rather than judicially imposed, but the Court seemed to think that similar principles would govern the remedy if it were judicially imposed. *Adarand* relied upon City of Richmond v. J.A. Croson Co., 488 U.S. 469, 491, 109 S.Ct. 706, 721, 102 L.Ed.2d 854 (1989), which stated that "[a]bsent searching judicial inquiry into the justification for such race-based measures, there is simply no way of determining what classifications are 'benign' or 'remedial' and what classifications are in fact motivated by illegitimate notions of racial inferiority or simple racial politics." Two weeks after *Adarand* and *Jenkins III* were announced, Miller v. Johnson, 515 U.S. 900, 115 S.Ct. 2475, 132 L.Ed.2d 762 (1995), applied strict scrutiny to racial gerrymandering of congressional districts to maximize African–American representation, although the gerrymandering was pursuant to a statute enacted under Congress's power to implement the fourteenth amendment. Given the degree of precision required by *Jenkins III* and given that *Madsen* threatened first amendment interests, shouldn't *Madsen* have come out the other way, except if, as Justice Scalia charges, there is a double standard for abortion cases?

Jenkins III scrutinizes the scope of the remedy far more closely than does *Swann*. The closer scrutiny in *Jenkins III* might be explained on the basis of the changing composition of the Court. But, there are other possible explanations. *Swann* was decided during an era of foot-dragging by school board defendants, while the KCMSD could not have been more enthusiastic about the remedy. The remedy in *Jenkins III* was far more aggressive than that in other school desegregation cases, both in terms of costs and its efforts to attract students from the suburbs. See Wendy Parker, The Supreme Court and Public Law Remedies: A Tale of Two Kansas Cities, 50 Hastings L.J. 482 (1999).

9. Consider the following from Judge Frank H. Easterbrook, Civil Rights and Remedies, 14 Harv.J.L. & Pub.Pol'y 103, 103–04 (1991):

When we hear an objection to the remedy, it is almost always a disguised objection to the definition of what is due, and not to the methods used to apply the balm. * * *

Because this point is *so* obvious that almost everyone will deny it, I will proceed by example through some contemporary remedial questions.

In thinking about each subject, it will help to consider three questions. First, who holds the "rights": individual persons or groups of persons? Second, what does "equality" mean: equal treatment or equal outcomes? Third, what do we expect the government to teach us: the importance of disregarding the characteristics that often are chosen as a basis of private discrimination, or the worth of a society in which persons of diverse backgrounds appear side by side? * * *

There are systematic differences in emphasis between those who think on the one hand that rights are personal, that the government should assure equal treatment, and that it should teach people the irrelevance of race (for example), and, on the other, those who believe that rights belong to groups, that equality of outcomes is most important, and that the government should assure diversity in many walks of life. * * * [T]he conclusions we reach on these questions govern the choice of remedy.

10. In Complex Justice: The Case of Missouri v. Jenkins (2008), political science professor Joshua Dunn carefully traces the underlying social history of the case. Professor Dunn sees the behind the scenes story as one of well-meaning but paternalistic white lawyers, sometimes incompetent school administrators, and increasingly hostile black community leaders. The book provides fascinating detail of how black parents, community leaders and activists resisted what they saw as misguided reforms, which were improperly aimed at attracting white families to the KCMSD rather than addressing the real educational needs of black students. Ultimately, some of the activists took over the school board and worked to end both judicial oversight and the magnet school ideals. For further information about *Jenkins*, see pp. 376–386.

11. The *Gautreaux* case originally filed in 1966 and cited in *Missouri v. Jenkins* (pp. 171–172) is still alive. Gautreaux v. Chicago Housing Authority, 491 F.3d 649 (7th Cir.2007) (affirming award of attorney fees for post-decree proceedings).

E. SPECIFIC REMEDIES OTHER THAN INJUNCTIONS

Specific performance. The contract remedy of specific performance is an order to perform under a contract. Like an injunction, specific performance is a specific, coercive, equitable remedy, enforced through the contempt power. In essence, specific performance is an injunction to perform under a contract. However, specific performance has some special requirements.

The Restatement (Second) of Contracts § 362 states that, "specific performance or an injunction will not be granted unless the terms of the contract are sufficiently certain to provide a basis for an appropriate order." Under this *certainty* requirement, a court could find that the parties had an understanding that was certain enough to be a contract and to lead to damages, but not certain enough to lead to specific performance. Although courts often recite this rule, certainty that is sufficient for liability is usually sufficient for specific performance so long as the court is certain enough of the bargain to formulate a workable decree. E.g., Naylor v. Hall, 201 Mont. 59, 67–68, 651 P.2d 1010, 1015 (1982)(absolute certainty in every detail is not a prerequisite for specific performance).

Courts will not direct specific performance of *personal service* contracts. E.g., Pierce v. Douglas School District No. 4, 297 Or. 363, 686 P.2d 332, 337 (1984)(teacher may not be compelled to perform employment contract). Specific enforcement of such contracts would impose difficult burdens of supervision on the court (see Section (B)(2) of the next chapter) and raise issues of involuntary servitude. Courts sometimes avoid these problems by forbidding the employee to work for others rather than compelling performance. E.g., Lumley v. Wagner, 42 Eng.Rep. 687 (1852) (forbidding opera singer to perform at theaters other than the one where she had contracted to perform). Professor Oman rejects the claim that specific performance of personal service contracts constitutes involuntary servitude and argues against the per se rule against enforcement, suggesting that specific performance should be available on the same basis as other contracts. Nathan Oman, Specific Performance and the Thirteenth Amendment, 93 Minn.L.Rev. __ (2008).

The doctrine of *mutuality of remedy* requires that one party be denied specific performance of a contract if the other party would be barred from that remedy. Some jurisdictions have explicitly revoked the rule. Other jurisdictions consider mutuality a relevant, but not controlling, factor in granting specific relief. Still others continue to cite the rule while recognizing broad exceptions to it. As Judge Cardozo put it:

> If there ever was a rule [of] mutuality of remedy * * *, it has been so qualified by exceptions that, viewed as a precept of general validity, it has ceased to be a rule to-day. What equity exacts today as a condition of relief is the assurance that the decree, if rendered, will operate without injustice or oppression either to plaintiff or to defendant.

Epstein v. Gluckin, 233 N.Y. 490, 493–94, 135 N.E. 861, 862 (1922). So, for instance, if there is a substantial risk that a plaintiff seeking specific performance might not perform later duties under the contract, a court might deny specific performance or condition it in such a way that the plaintiff would have to perform.

Some jurisdictions will deny specific performance because of *inadequacy of consideration*. Other jurisdictions allow this defense only upon an additional showing of fraud or unfairness.

Writs of mandamus, prohibition, and habeas corpus. A writ of mandamus is an order to a public or corporate officer to perform a ministerial duty. A writ of prohibition is an order to a judge to refrain from unwarranted conduct. A writ of habeas corpus is an order to someone who detains another person to bring that person to court and justify the detention or relinquish it. Like injunctions, these writs are specific and coercive remedies, enforced through the contempt power. Indeed, these writs can be conceived as special types of injunctions, available against certain defendants for certain purposes.

Nonetheless, the courts usually do not see these writs as the equivalent of injunctions. The most obvious but least important difference is that, unlike injunctions, they are classified as legal remedies because they were originally issued from the courts of law rather than the courts of equity. This might suggest that the writs are free from the requirement that there be no adequate remedy at law. Yet, mandamus and prohibition, but not habeas corpus, are said to be available only where there is no other adequate remedy at law. In addition, courts view mandamus and prohibition as extraordinary and accordingly set up other prerequisites to limit their availability. These prerequisites vary with both the writ and the jurisdiction, and result from both historical anachronisms and modern needs so that it is difficult to generalize about each one's availability and how it may affect the availability of other writs or an injunction to accomplish the same objective.

The writ of mandamus is available only if the plaintiff has a clear right to relief and the defendant has a clear duty to act. However, if an unclear statute, once interpreted, creates a clear duty for the officer to act, the mandamus action will lie. E.g., Swan v. Clinton, 100 F.3d 973, 978 (D.C.Cir.1996). "[C]ourts sometimes analogize between a request for mandatory injunction and a writ of mandamus, thereby triggering all of the hypertechnicalities that govern that largely outmoded remedy.... Whenever possible a petitioner should avoid requesting relief using the terms 'mandamus' or 'mandatory injunction.'" Richard J. Pierce, Jr., 3 Administrative Law Treatise 1347 (4th ed.2002). Professor Brill argues that the mandamus writ should remain as a separate remedy, but acknowledges that courts have increasingly tended to treat it as a species of injunction. Howard Brill, The Citizen's Relief Against Inactive Federal Officials: Case Studies in Mandamus, Action in the Nature of Mandamus, and Mandatory Injunctions, 16 Akron L.Rev. 339 (1983).

The writ of prohibition is available to redress judicial "usurpation of power." Will v. United States, 389 U.S. 90, 95, 88 S.Ct. 269, 273, 19 L.Ed.2d 305, 310 (1967). Because prohibition is essentially an interlocutory appeal, various limits on its availability vindicate the final judgment rule. In most jurisdictions, prohibition gets far less use than mandamus or habeas corpus.

Habeas corpus has a place in the Bill of Rights, U.S. Const. Amend. VI, because it prevents imprisonment without judicial process. Habeas corpus also provides review of criminal convictions in the judicial process supplemental to ordinary appeals and can sometimes be used in military service, immigration, and child custody cases.

Ejectment and replevin. Ejectment is an order to the sheriff to put the plaintiff in possession of real estate by, if necessary, ejecting current possessors and removing any physical obstacles. Replevin is an order to the sheriff to put the plaintiff in possession of chattels. Although the characteristics of these actions and their names sometimes vary from jurisdiction to jurisdiction, the essential point is that ejectment and replevin are specific and coercive remedies, but they are not orders to the defendant and so the defendant's failure to help put the plaintiff in possession is not contempt. Restatement (Second) of Torts § 945, Comment on Clause (a) § (a), § 946 Comment on Clause (a) § (a) (1979). However, in ejectment, resisting the sheriff, or reentry after ejectment, is contempt; in replevin, active concealment may be contempt. Moreover, injunctions may be used to supplement these remedies at law, such as by ordering the defendant to turn over a unique chattel. N.Y.Civ.Prac.L. & R. § 7109. Ejectment and replevin are remedies at law and the inadequacy rule does not apply to them.

Declaratory judgment. Declaratory judgment (covered in Chapter 4) is, as the name suggests, not a coercive remedy at all, but rather a declaration of liability or non-liability. Nonetheless, declaratory judgments often function as specific relief for reasons that you will see.

Statutory remedies for illegal administrative action. Judicial review and supervision of administrative action, an important part of modern practice, combines common law and new remedies. Milton M. Carrow, Types of Judicial Relief From Administrative Action, 58 Colum.L.Rev. 1 (1958). Where there is no exclusive statutory remedy to review administrative action, a plaintiff may ordinarily seek an injunction, a declaratory judgment, or a writ of mandamus, prohibition, or habeas corpus. Richard J. Pierce, Jr., Administrative Law Treatise ch.18 (4th ed.2002). Normally, however, the statutes that authorize administrative action provide for its judicial review. The court may "affirm"—which is in essence a declaration that it is lawful. If not, there are a number of remedial possibilities. The court may "compel agency action unlawfully withheld or unreasonably delayed." 5 U.S.C. § 706(1), which is analogous to an injunction or mandamus. Or the court may "hold unlawful and set aside" the agency action. 5 U.S.C. § 706(2). "[H]old unlawful" is in essence a declaratory judgment. "[S]et aside" goes beyond a declaration because, in their orders, courts will themselves "vacate" agency actions. Finally, if the court decides to neither affirm nor vacate the agency's action, it may "remand" the matter to the agency with directions to the agency to reconsider in light of the court's opinion.

Chapter 3

Procedures for Formulating, Administering, and Enforcing the Injunction

■ ■ ■

A. OBTAINING PRELIMINARY INJUNCTIVE RELIEF

1. TYPES OF INJUNCTIONS

The normal process for seeking a remedy from a court is to file a complaint which includes a prayer for relief specifying the remedies the plaintiff is requesting after prevailing in the action. The remedies requested may include one or more of the types of relief studied in this course, including damages or the specific relief a court may afford through an injunction. Sometimes, however, the plaintiff cannot wait for the wheels of justice to turn completely. The plaintiff may need some additional relief immediately. For example, suppose that the plaintiff and the defendant are having a dispute about who owns Blackacre and the defendant is about to tear down an old house on Blackacre that the plaintiff loves. Unless the court intervenes immediately, the plaintiff's loss due to the destruction of the beloved old house would not be rectified by either an injunction issued after a final determination on the merits or by damages. It makes sense for the court to have the power to act quickly in such a case. In this example, the court probably would order the defendant not to dismantle the house until it had decided who owned Blackacre. (If the defendant won on the merits, and was awarded title to Blackacre, she could then dismantle the house.)

Such an order is called "temporary" or "preliminary" because it lasts only long enough to give the court time to deliberate further on the merits. In contrast, an injunction issued after a final determination is called a "permanent injunction." The word "permanent" signifies not the injunction's duration but rather that it is not contingent upon some further finding on the merits. A permanent injunction continues to apply unless it expires by its own terms or is later modified or dissolved by a court of competent jurisdiction. For example, the court may find that the plaintiff did have a possessory interest in Blackacre, but that it would last for only one year; in that case, the court would issue a "permanent" injunction directing the defendant to keep off Blackacre for that year.

F.R.Civ.P. 65 (reproduced in the Appendix at p. 986), for example, distinguishes among temporary restraining orders ("TRO"), preliminary injunctions and permanent injunctions, but not because their purposes differ (all three command that a defendant do or not do some act). Instead they are distinguished by their different procedures and durations.

A TRO is an emergency order, which can be granted if, but only if, immediate and irreparable harm will result before a hearing can be held; as a result, it can be granted ex parte (i.e., without any notice to the defendant). Usually, the judge issues the TRO on the basis of affidavits or a verified complaint rather than on the basis of live testimony. Because this drastic emergency procedure is subject to abuse, especially when it is used without notice to the adverse party, there are several built-in safeguards. For example, F.R.Civ.P. 65(b) requires that a TRO may be granted without notice to the adverse party only if specific facts set forth in an affidavit or verified complaint clearly show that there will be immediate and irreparable injury to the requesting party before the adverse party can be heard. In addition, the attorney of the party seeking the TRO must certify in writing what efforts were made to give notice (formal or informal, such as by telephone or fax) to the adverse party and must provide the reasons supporting the claim that notice should not be required. (If, for example, there were a specific concern that the defendant might take some destructive action between the time notice would be given and the TRO was issued and served.). The Supreme Court has acknowledged that: "There is a place in our jurisprudence for *ex parte* issuance, without notice, of temporary restraining orders of short duration." Carroll v. President & Commissioners of Princess Anne, 393 U.S. 175, 180, 89 S.Ct. 347, 351, 21 L.Ed.2d 325, 330–331 (1968). However, the Court also observed that "there is no place within the area of basic freedoms guaranteed by the First Amendment for such orders where no showing is made that it is impossible to serve or notify the opposing parties and to give them an opportunity to participate." Id. Accordingly, it found unconstitutional a ten-day TRO that a state trial court issued prohibiting a public rally by Nazis because the order was granted ex parte and without any attempt to provide notice.

Rule 65(c) also requires the TRO applicant to post security for the costs and damages that may be incurred if it is later determined that the TRO wrongfully enjoined another party. A TRO issued without notice is valid for a very limited time—the ten-day limit (which can be extended once) established in F.R.Civ.P. 65(b)(2) is a common pattern. The enjoined party may move for the dissolution of the TRO on two days notice or even less with leave of court. Finally, the defendant is not bound by the restraining order until notified that it exists and what its terms are (see F.R.Civ.P. 65(d)(2)).

A preliminary injunction is another mechanism for granting relief before the court can conduct a full hearing on the merits; often, the preliminary injunction is granted after the TRO has expired. In contrast to the TRO, there must be both proper notice to the defendant (see, e.g., F.R.Civ.P. 65(a)(1)) and a hearing (however informal) on the motion for a preliminary injunction. See United States v. Microsoft Corp., 147 F.3d 935 (D.C.Cir.1998) (defendant did not have adequate notice that it might be the subject of a preliminary injunction). The procedural safeguards are parallel to those required for a TRO. (1) Specific facts demonstrating the need for the preliminary injunction must be established under oath; if the facts are in dispute, live testimony is often used. (2) The applicant must post security. (3) The preliminary injunction is valid for the indefinite period of time until the court conducts a full hearing on the question of whether permanent injunctive relief is warranted.

A permanent injunction cannot issue until there has been a full opportunity to hear from both sides, at a hearing or on a motion for summary judgment. Because it is issued only after the parties have had a complete opportunity to be heard, the special safeguards listed above are not applicable.

A final and important safeguard is appellate review. Despite the final judgment rule, federal and state law permit an exception for interlocutory appeal from the trial court's decision on the motion to issue a permanent or a preliminary injunction. E.g., 28 U.S.C. § 1292(a)(1); Mass.Gen.L. ch.231 § 118. Generally, courts hold that there is no interlocutory appeal from decisions regarding a TRO, because of its extremely short duration. But see Schiavo ex rel. Schindler v. Schiavo, 403 F.3d 1223, 1229 (11th Cir.) ("when a grant or denial of a TRO might have a serious, perhaps irreparable, consequence, and can be effectually challenged only by immediate appeal, we may exercise appellate jurisdiction"), stay denied, 544 U.S. 945, 125 S.Ct. 1692, 161 L.Ed.2d 518 (2005); Levine v. Comcoa, Ltd., 70 F.3d 1191 (11th Cir.1995), cert. denied, 519 U.S. 809, 117 S.Ct. 53, 136 L.Ed.2d 16 (1996) (discussing circumstances of when an extension of time can convert a TRO into a valid, and appealable, preliminary injunction). In some jurisdictions, the appeal will act as an automatic stay of the injunction until the appeal is resolved. In others, a stay must be obtained from the trial or appellate court. If there is no stay, the injunction must be obeyed pending the outcome of the appeal. See John Y. Gotanda, The Emerging Standards for Issuing Appellate Stays, 45 Baylor L.Rev. 809 (1993). The standard of review is abuse of discretion, which usually means, "[a]s long as the district court got the law right, 'it will not be reversed simply because the appellate court would have arrived at a different result if it had applied the law to the facts of the case.'" A&M Records, Inc. v. Napster, Inc., 239 F.3d 1004, 1013 (9th Cir.2001).

PROBLEM: UNAUTHORIZED MERCHANTS

Many recording artists feel plagued by entrepreneurs who show up at their live concerts and sell merchandise, especially T-shirts, to fans outside of the hall. The unauthorized merchants cut into the revenues that would be generated through the sale of souvenirs by authorized vendors inside the hall. Typically, no one connected with the recording artists knows the identities of the unauthorized merchants. Assume your clients are the members of "PILF"? Navjot Athwal, Joshua Horowitz, Thanh Ngo and Junaid Sulahryn— a capella singers who are about to go on tour to promote their new CD. They have their first big stadium concert of the tour scheduled just a few days hence. Can a TRO banning unauthorized souvenir sales be granted? Compare Billy Joel v. Various John Does, 499 F.Supp. 791 (E.D.Wis.1980) (granted) with Plant v. Doe, 19 F.Supp.2d 1316 (S.D.Fla.1998) (denied). Could the recording artists keep legal expenses down by seeking a single TRO that prohibits such unauthorized selling in all cities to be visited on a national tour? The same court that had given Billy Joel an injunction denied The Who a TRO that would apply nationally. Brockum International v. Various John Does, 551 F.Supp. 1054 (E.D.Wis.1982). Is this just a matter of the court's taste in music? SKS Merch, LLC v. Barry, 233 F.Supp.2d 841 (E.D.Ky.2002) (country music singer Toby Keith granted permanent injunction within the district and a preliminary injunction nationwide effective against any persons served); Shae Yatta Harvey, National, Multi–District Preliminary Tour Injunctions: Why The Hesitation?, 40 IDEA: J.L. & Tech. 195 (2000).

2. STANDARDS FOR GRANTING PRELIMINARY RELIEF

Appellate courts typically state that the granting of a preliminary injunction or a TRO is within the discretion of the trial court; they also note that such preliminary relief is an extraordinary and drastic remedy that should issue only if the plaintiff makes a proper showing. See 11A Charles Alan Wright, Arthur R. Miller & Mary Kay Kane, Federal Practice and Procedure § 2948 at 429 (2d ed.1995) (noting "the courts' general reluctance to impose an interim restraint on defendant before the parties' rights have been adjudicated" as well as the need to make "a sound evaluation of the factors relevant to granting relief"). For example, courts will sometimes state that a preliminary injunction may issue only if necessary to preserve the court's power to decide the merits or only to preserve the status quo. See, e.g., Morton Denlow, The Motion for a Preliminary Injunction: Time for a Uniform Federal Standard, 22 Rev.Litig. 495 (2003) (U.S. magistrate judge reviews varying standards in the circuit courts). A good summary of the historical origins and modern standards of preliminary relief is provided in Andrew Muscato, The Preliminary Injunction in Business Litigation, 3 N.Y.U.J.L. & Bus. 649 (2007). The following materials examine some of these formulations and additional factors that courts consider in making what can be a difficult decision under trying circumstances.

WINTER v. NATURAL RESOURCES DEFENSE COUNCIL

Supreme Court of the United States, 2008
555 U.S. ___, 129 S.Ct. 365, 172 L.Ed.2d 249

CHIEF JUSTICE ROBERTS delivered the opinion of the Court.

"To be prepared for war is one of the most effectual means of preserving peace." 1 Messages and Papers of the Presidents 57 (J. Richardson comp. 1897). So said George Washington in his first Annual Address to Congress, 218 years ago. One of the most important ways the Navy prepares for war is through integrated training exercises at sea. These exercises include training in the use of modern sonar to detect and track enemy submarines, something the Navy has done for the past 40 years. The plaintiffs complained that the Navy's sonar training program harmed marine mammals, and that the Navy should have prepared an environmental impact statement before commencing its latest round of training exercises. The Court of Appeals upheld a preliminary injunction imposing restrictions on the Navy's sonar training, even though that court acknowledged that "the record contains no evidence that marine mammals have been harmed" by the Navy's exercises.

The Court of Appeals was wrong, and its decision is reversed.

I

* * *

Antisubmarine warfare is currently the Pacific Fleet's top war-fighting priority. Modern diesel-electric submarines pose a significant threat to Navy vessels because they can operate almost silently, making them extremely difficult to detect and track. Potential adversaries of the United States possess at least 300 of these submarines.

The most effective technology for identifying submerged diesel-electric submarines within their torpedo range is active sonar, which involves emitting pulses of sound underwater and then receiving the acoustic waves that echo off the target. Active sonar is a particularly useful tool because it provides both the bearing and the distance of target submarines; it is also sensitive enough to allow the Navy to track enemy submarines that are quieter than the surrounding marine environment. This case concerns the Navy's use of "mid-frequency active" (MFA) sonar, which transmits sound waves at frequencies between 1 kHz and 10 kHz.

Not surprisingly, MFA sonar is a complex technology, and sonar operators must undergo extensive training to become proficient in its use. * * * The Navy conducts regular training exercises under realistic conditions to ensure that sonar operators are thoroughly skilled in its use in a variety of situations.

The waters off the coast of southern California (SOCAL) are an ideal location for conducting integrated training exercises, as this is the only area on the west coast that is relatively close to land, air, and sea bases, as well as amphibious landing areas. At issue in this case are the Composite Training Unit Exercises and the Joint Tactical Force Exercises, in which individual naval units (ships, submarines, and aircraft) train together as members of a strike group. A strike group cannot be certified for deployment until it has successfully completed the integrated training exercises, including a demonstration of its ability to operate under simulated hostile conditions. * * * The use of MFA sonar during these exercises is "mission-critical," given that MFA sonar is the only proven method of identifying submerged diesel-electric submarines operating on battery power.

Sharing the waters in the SOCAL operating area are at least 37 species of marine mammals, including dolphins, whales, and sea lions. The parties strongly dispute the extent to which the Navy's training activities will harm those animals or disrupt their behavioral patterns. The Navy emphasizes that it has used MFA sonar during training exercises in SOCAL for 40 years, without a single documented sonar-related injury to any marine mammal. The Navy asserts that, at most, MFA sonar may cause temporary hearing loss or brief disruptions of marine mammals' behavioral patterns.

The plaintiffs are the Natural Resources Defense Council, Jean-Michael Cousteau (an environmental enthusiast and filmmaker), and several other groups devoted to the protection of marine mammals and ocean habitats. They contend that MFA sonar can cause much more serious injuries to marine mammals than the Navy acknowledges, including permanent hearing loss, decompression sickness, and major behavioral disruptions. According to the plaintiffs, several mass strandings of marine mammals (outside of SOCAL) have been "associated" with the use of active sonar. They argue that certain species of marine mammals—such as beaked whales—are uniquely susceptible to injury from active sonar; these injuries would not necessarily be detected by the Navy, given that beaked whales are "very deep divers" that spend little time at the surface.

II

The procedural history of this case is rather complicated. The Marine Mammal Protection Act of 1972 (MMPA), 86 Stat. 1027, generally prohibits any individual from "taking" a marine mammal, defined as harassing, hunting, capturing, or killing it. 16 U.S.C. §§ 1362(13), 1372(a). The Secretary of Defense may "exempt any action or category of actions" from the MMPA if such actions are "necessary for national defense." § 1371(f)(1). In January 2007, the Deputy Secretary of Defense—acting for the Secretary—granted the Navy a 2-year exemption from the MMPA for the training exercises at issue in this case. The exemption was conditioned on the Navy adopting several mitigation procedures * * * [including shutting down MFA sonar in order to protect any marine mammals detected within 200 yards of a vessel during the exercises].

The National Environmental Policy Act of 1969 (NEPA) requires federal agencies "to the fullest extent possible" to prepare an environmental impact statement (EIS) for "every ... major Federal actio[n] significantly affecting the quality of the human environment." 42 U.S.C. § 4332(2)(C). An agency is not required to prepare a full EIS if it determines—based on a shorter environmental assessment (EA)—that the proposed action will not have a significant impact on the environment.

In February 2007, the Navy issued an EA concluding that the 14 SOCAL training exercises scheduled through January 2009 would not have a significant impact on the environment. The EA divided potential injury to marine mammals into two categories: Level A harassment, defined as the potential destruction or loss of biological tissue (i.e., physical injury), and Level B harassment, defined as temporary injury or disruption of behavioral patterns such as migration, feeding, surfacing, and breeding.

The Navy's computer models predicted that the SOCAL training exercises would cause only eight Level A harassments of common dolphins each year, and that even these injuries could be avoided through the Navy's voluntary mitigation measures, given that dolphins travel in large pods easily located by Navy lookouts. The EA also predicted 274 Level B harassments of beaked whales per year, none of which would result in permanent injury. * * * In light of its conclusion that the SOCAL training exercises would not have a significant impact on the environment, the Navy determined that it was unnecessary to prepare a full EIS.

Shortly after the Navy released its EA, the plaintiffs sued the Navy, seeking declaratory and injunctive relief on the grounds that the Navy's SOCAL training exercises violated NEPA, the Endangered Species Act of 1973 (ESA), and the Coastal Zone Management Act of 1972 (CZMA).[2] The District Court granted plaintiffs' motion for a preliminary injunction and prohibited the Navy from using MFA sonar during its remaining training exercises. The court held that plaintiffs had "demonstrated a probability of success" on their claims under NEPA and the CZMA. * * * Based on scientific studies, declarations from experts, and other evidence in the record, the District Court concluded that there was in fact a "near certainty" of irreparable injury to the environment, and that this injury outweighed any possible harm to the Navy.

* * * After hearing oral argument, the Court of Appeals agreed with the District Court that preliminary injunctive relief was appropriate. The appellate court concluded, however, that a blanket injunction prohibiting the Navy from using MFA sonar in SOCAL was overbroad, and remanded the case to the District Court "to narrow its injunction so as to provide mitigation conditions under which the Navy may conduct its training exercises."

---

2. The CZMA states that federal agencies taking actions "that affec[t] any land or water use or natural resources of the coastal zone" shall carry out these activities "in a manner which is consistent to the maximum extent practicable with the enforceable policies of approved State management programs." 16 U.S.C. § 1456(c)(1)(A).

On remand, the District Court entered a new preliminary injunction allowing the Navy to use MFA sonar only as long as it implemented the following mitigation measures (in addition to the measures the Navy had adopted pursuant to its MMPA exemption): (1) imposing a 12–mile "exclusion zone" from the coastline; (2) using lookouts to conduct additional monitoring for marine mammals; (3) restricting the use of "helicopter-dipping" sonar; (4) limiting the use of MFA sonar in geographic "choke points"; (5) shutting down MFA sonar when a marine mammal is spotted within 2,200 yards of a vessel; and (6) powering down MFA sonar by 6 dB during significant surface ducting conditions, in which sound travels further than it otherwise would due to temperature differences in adjacent layers of water. The Navy filed a notice of appeal, challenging only the last two restrictions.

The Navy then sought relief from the Executive Branch. The President * * * granted the Navy an exemption from the CZMA. Section 1456(c)(1)(B) permits such exemptions if the activity in question is in the paramount interest of the United States. * * *

Simultaneously, the Council on Environmental Quality (CEQ) authorized the Navy to implement "alternative arrangements" to NEPA compliance in light of "emergency circumstances." * * * Under the alternative arrangements, the Navy would be permitted to conduct its training exercises under the mitigation procedures adopted in conjunction with the exemption from the MMPA. * * *

In light of these actions, the Navy then moved to vacate the District Court's injunction with respect to the 2,200–yard shutdown zone and the restrictions on training in surface ducting conditions. The District Court refused to do so and the Court of Appeals affirmed. The Ninth Circuit held that there was a serious question regarding whether the CEQ's interpretation of the "emergency circumstances" regulation was lawful. Specifically, the court questioned whether there was a true "emergency" in this case, given that the Navy has been on notice of its obligation to comply with NEPA from the moment it first planned the SOCAL training exercises. The Court of Appeals concluded that the preliminary injunction was entirely predictable in light of the parties' litigation history. * * * The Ninth Circuit agreed with the District Court's holding that the Navy's EA—which resulted in a finding of no significant environmental impact—was "cursory, unsupported by cited evidence, or unconvincing."

The Court of Appeals further determined that plaintiffs had carried their burden of establishing a "possibility" of irreparable injury. Even under the Navy's own figures, the court concluded, the training exercises would cause 564 physical injuries to marine mammals, as well as 170,000 disturbances of marine mammals' behavior. Lastly, the Court of Appeals held that the balance of hardships and consideration of the public interest weighed in favor of the plaintiffs. The court emphasized that the negative impact on the Navy's training exercises was "speculative," since the Navy has never before operated under the procedures required by the District

Court. * * * The Ninth Circuit concluded that the District Court's preliminary injunction struck a proper balance between the competing interests at stake.

* * *

III

A

A plaintiff seeking a preliminary injunction must establish that he is likely to succeed on the merits, that he is likely to suffer irreparable harm in the absence of preliminary relief, that the balance of equities tips in his favor, and that an injunction is in the public interest. See Munaf v. Geren, 553 U.S. ___, ___, 128 S.Ct. 2207, 2218–2219, 171 L.Ed.2d 1 (2008); Amoco Production Co. v. Gambell, 480 U.S. 531, 542, 107 S.Ct. 1396, 94 L.Ed.2d 542 (1987); Weinberger v. Romero–Barcelo, 456 U.S. 305, 311–312, 102 S.Ct. 1798, 72 L.Ed.2d 91 (1982).

The District Court and the Ninth Circuit concluded that plaintiffs have shown a likelihood of success on the merits of their NEPA claim. The Navy strongly disputes this determination, arguing that plaintiffs' likelihood of success is low because the CEQ reasonably concluded that "emergency circumstances" justified alternative arrangements to NEPA compliance. * * *

The District Court and the Ninth Circuit also held that when a plaintiff demonstrates a strong likelihood of prevailing on the merits, a preliminary injunction may be entered based only on a "possibility" of irreparable harm. The lower courts held that plaintiffs had met this standard because the scientific studies, declarations, and other evidence in the record established to "a near certainty" that the Navy's training exercises would cause irreparable harm to the environment.

The Navy challenges these holdings, arguing that plaintiffs must demonstrate a likelihood of irreparable injury—not just a possibility—in order to obtain preliminary relief. On the facts of this case, the Navy contends that plaintiffs' alleged injuries are too speculative to give rise to irreparable injury, given that ever since the Navy's training program began 40 years ago, there has been no documented case of sonar-related injury to marine mammals in SOCAL. And even if MFA sonar does cause a limited number of injuries to individual *marine mammals,* the Navy asserts that plaintiffs have failed to offer evidence of species-level harm that would adversely affect *their* scientific, recreational, and ecological interests. For their part, plaintiffs assert that they would prevail under any formulation of the irreparable injury standard, because the District Court found that they had established a "near certainty" of irreparable harm.

We agree with the Navy that the Ninth Circuit's "possibility" standard is too lenient. Our frequently reiterated standard requires plaintiffs seeking preliminary relief to demonstrate that irreparable injury is *likely* in the absence of an injunction. Los Angeles v. Lyons, 461 U.S. 95, 103, 103 S.Ct. 1660, 75 L.Ed.2d 675 (1983); Granny Goose Foods, Inc. v. Teamsters, 415 U.S. 423, 441, 94 S.Ct. 1113, 39 L.Ed.2d 435 (1974); O'Shea v. Littleton, 414 U.S. 488, 502, 94 S.Ct. 669, 38 L.Ed.2d 674 (1974); see also 11A C. Wright, A. Miller, & M. Kane, Federal Practice and Procedure § 2948.1, p. 139 (2d ed.1995) (hereinafter Wright & Miller) (applicant must demonstrate that in the absence of a preliminary injunction, "the applicant is likely to suffer irreparable harm before a decision on the merits can be rendered"); id., at 155, 94 S.Ct. 669 ("a preliminary injunction will not be issued simply to prevent the possibility of some remote future injury"). Issuing a preliminary injunction based only on a possibility of irreparable harm is inconsistent with our characterization of injunctive relief as an extraordinary remedy that may only be awarded upon a clear showing that the plaintiff is entitled to such relief.

It is not clear that articulating the incorrect standard affected the Ninth Circuit's analysis of irreparable harm. Although the court referred to the "possibility" standard, and cited Circuit precedent along the same lines, it affirmed the District Court's conclusion that plaintiffs had established a "'near certainty'" of irreparable harm. At the same time, however, the nature of the District Court's conclusion is itself unclear. The District Court originally found irreparable harm from sonar-training exercises generally. But by the time of the District Court's final decision, the Navy challenged only two of six restrictions imposed by the court. The District Court did not reconsider the likelihood of irreparable harm in light of the four restrictions not challenged by the Navy. * * *

We also find it pertinent that this is not a case in which the defendant is conducting a new type of activity with completely unknown effects on the environment. * * * Part of the harm NEPA attempts to prevent in requiring an EIS is that, without one, there may be little if any information about prospective environmental harms and potential mitigating measures. Here, in contrast, the plaintiffs are seeking to enjoin—or substantially restrict—training exercises that have been taking place in SOCAL for the last 40 years. And the latest series of exercises were not approved until after the defendant took a "hard look at environmental consequences," as evidenced by the issuance of a detailed, 293–page EA.

As explained in the next section, even if plaintiffs have shown irreparable injury from the Navy's training exercises, any such injury is outweighed by the public interest and the Navy's interest in effective, realistic training of its sailors. A proper consideration of these factors alone requires denial of the requested injunctive relief. For the same reason, we do not address the lower courts' holding that plaintiffs have also established a likelihood of success on the merits.

B

A preliminary injunction is an extraordinary remedy never awarded as of right. In each case, courts "must balance the competing claims of injury and must consider the effect on each party of the granting or withholding of the requested relief." *Amoco.* "In exercising their sound discretion, courts of equity should pay particular regard for the public consequences in employing the extraordinary remedy of injunction." *Romero-Barcelo.* In this case, the District Court and the Ninth Circuit significantly understated the burden the preliminary injunction would impose on the Navy's ability to conduct realistic training exercises, and the injunction's consequent adverse impact on the public interest in national defense.

This case involves "complex, subtle, and professional decisions as to the composition, training, equipping, and control of a military force," which are "essentially professional military judgments." * * *

Here, the record contains declarations from some of the Navy's most senior officers, all of whom underscored the threat posed by enemy submarines and the need for extensive sonar training to counter this threat. Admiral Gary Roughead—the Chief of Naval Operations—stated that during training exercises:

> "It is important to stress the ship crews in all dimensions of warfare simultaneously. If one of these training elements were impacted—for example, if effective sonar training were not possible—the training value of the other elements would also be degraded...."

Captain Martin May—the Third Fleet's Assistant Chief of Staff for Training and Readiness—emphasized that the use of MFA sonar is "mission–critical." He described the ability to operate MFA sonar as a "highly perishable skill" that must be repeatedly practiced under realistic conditions. * * * Several Navy officers emphasized that realistic training cannot be accomplished under the two challenged restrictions imposed by the District Court—the 2,200–yard shutdown zone and the requirement that the Navy power down its sonar systems during significant surface ducting conditions. * * * We accept these officers' assertions that the use of MFA sonar under realistic conditions during training exercises is of the utmost importance to the Navy and the Nation.

These interests must be weighed against the possible harm to the ecological, scientific, and recreational interests that are legitimately before this Court. Plaintiffs have submitted declarations asserting that they take whale watching trips, observe marine mammals underwater, conduct scientific research on marine mammals, and photograph these animals in their natural habitats. Plaintiffs contend that the Navy's use of MFA sonar will injure marine mammals or alter their behavioral patterns, impairing plaintiffs' ability to study and observe the animals.

While we do not question the seriousness of these interests, we conclude that the balance of equities and consideration of the overall public interest in this case tip strongly in favor of the Navy. For the plaintiffs, the most serious possible injury would be harm to an unknown number of the marine mammals that they study and observe. In contrast, forcing the Navy to deploy an inadequately trained antisubmarine force jeopardizes the safety of the fleet. Active sonar is the only reliable technology for detecting and tracking enemy diesel-electric submarines, and the President—the Commander in Chief—has determined that training with active sonar is "essential to national security."

The public interest in conducting training exercises with active sonar under realistic conditions plainly outweighs the interests advanced by the plaintiffs. Of course, military interests do not always trump other considerations, and we have not held that they do. In this case, however, the proper determination of where the public interest lies does not strike us as a close question.

C

1. Despite the importance of assessing the balance of equities and the public interest in determining whether to grant a preliminary injunction, the District Court addressed these considerations in only a cursory fashion. The court's entire discussion of these factors consisted of one (albeit lengthy) sentence: "The Court is also satisfied that the balance of hardships tips in favor of granting an injunction, as the harm to the environment, Plaintiffs, and public interest outweighs the harm that Defendants would incur if prevented from using MFA sonar, absent the use of effective mitigation measures, during a subset of their regular activities in one part of one state for a limited period." * * *

The Court of Appeals held that the balance of equities and the public interest favored the plaintiffs, largely based on its view that the preliminary injunction would not in fact impose a significant burden on the Navy's ability to conduct its training exercises and certify its strike groups. The court deemed the Navy's concerns about the preliminary injunction "speculative" because the Navy had not operated under similar procedures before. But this is almost always the case when a plaintiff seeks injunctive relief to alter a defendant's conduct. The lower courts failed properly to defer to senior Navy officers' specific, predictive judgments about how the preliminary injunction would reduce the effectiveness of the Navy's SOCAL training exercises. * * *

2. The preliminary injunction requires the Navy to shut down its MFA sonar if a marine mammal is detected within 2,200 yards of a sonar-emitting vessel. The Ninth Circuit stated that the 2,200-yard shutdown zone would not be overly burdensome because sightings of marine mammals during training exercises are relatively rare. But regardless of the frequency of marine mammal sightings, the injunction will greatly increase the size of the shutdown zone. * * * Increasing the radius of the shutdown zone from 200 to 2,200 yards would * * * expand the surface area of the shutdown zone by a factor of over 100 (from 125,664 square yards to 15,205,308 square yards).

The lower courts did not give sufficient weight to the views of several top Navy officers, who emphasized that because training scenarios can take several days to develop, each additional shutdown can result in the loss of several days' worth of training. Limiting the number of sonar shutdowns is particularly important during the Joint Tactical Force Exercises, which usually last for less than two weeks. Admiral Bird explained that the 2,200–yard shutdown zone would cause operational commanders to "lose awareness of the tactical situation through the constant stopping and starting of MFA [sonar]." * * * Even if there is a low likelihood of a marine mammal sighting, the preliminary injunction would clearly increase the number of disruptive sonar shutdowns the Navy is forced to perform during its SOCAL training exercises.

* * *

3. The Court of Appeals also concluded that the Navy's training exercises would not be significantly affected by the requirement that it power down MFA sonar by 6 dB during significant surface ducting conditions. Again, we think the Ninth Circuit understated the burden this requirement would impose on the Navy's ability to conduct realistic training exercises.

Surface ducting is a phenomenon in which relatively little sound energy penetrates beyond a narrow layer near the surface of the water. When surface ducting occurs, active sonar becomes more useful near the surface but less useful at greater depths. Diesel-electric submariners are trained to take advantage of these distortions to avoid being detected by sonar.

The Ninth Circuit determined that the power-down requirement during surface ducting conditions was unlikely to affect certification of the Navy's strike groups because surface ducting occurs relatively rarely, and the Navy has previously certified strike groups that did not train under such conditions. This reasoning is backwards. Given that surface ducting is both rare and unpredictable, it is especially important for the Navy to be able to train under these conditions when they occur. Admiral Bird explained that the 6 dB power-down requirement makes the training less valuable because it "exposes [sonar operators] to unrealistically lower levels of mutual interference caused by multiple sonar systems operating together by the ships within the Strike Group." Although a 6 dB reduction may not seem terribly significant, decibels are measured on a logarithmic scale, so a 6 dB decrease in power equates to a 75% reduction.

4. The District Court acknowledged that " 'the imposition of these mitigation measures will require the Navy to alter and adapt the way it conducts antisubmarine warfare training—a substantial challenge. Nevertheless, evidence presented to the Court reflects that the Navy has employed mitigation measures in the past, without sacrificing training objectives.' " Apparently no good deed goes unpunished. The fact that the Navy has taken measures in the past to address concerns about marine mammals—or, for that matter, has elected not to challenge four additional restrictions imposed by the District Court in this case hardly means that other, more intrusive restrictions pose no threat to preparedness for war.

The Court of Appeals concluded its opinion by stating that "the Navy may return to the district court to request relief on an emergency basis" if the preliminary injunction "actually result[s] in an inability to train and certify sufficient naval forces to provide for the national defense." This is cold comfort to the Navy. The Navy contends that the injunction will hinder efforts to train sonar operators under realistic conditions, ultimately leaving strike groups more vulnerable to enemy submarines. Unlike the Ninth Circuit, we do not think the Navy is required to wait until the injunction "actually result[s] in an inability to train ... sufficient naval forces for the national defense" before seeking its dissolution. By then it may be too late.

IV

As noted above, we do not address the underlying merits of plaintiffs' claims. While we have authority to proceed to such a decision at this point, doing so is not necessary here. * * *

At the same time, what we have said makes clear that it would be an abuse of discretion to enter a permanent injunction, after final decision on the merits, along the same lines as the preliminary injunction. An injunction is a matter of equitable discretion; it does not follow from success on the merits as a matter of course. *Romero-Barcelo,* 456 U.S. at 313, 102 S.Ct. 1798 ("a federal judge sitting as chancellor is not mechanically obligated to grant an injunction for every violation of law").

The factors examined above—the balance of equities and consideration of the public interest—are pertinent in assessing the propriety of any injunctive relief, preliminary or permanent. See *Amoco Production Co.,* 480 U.S. at 546 n.12, 107 S.Ct. 1396 ("The standard for a preliminary injunction is essentially the same as for a permanent injunction with the exception that the plaintiff must show a likelihood of success on the merits rather than actual success"). Given that the ultimate legal claim is that the Navy must prepare an EIS, not that it must cease sonar training, there is no basis for enjoining such training in a manner credibly alleged to pose a serious threat to national security. This is particularly true in light of the fact that the training has been going on for 40 years with no documented episode of harm to a marine mammal. A court concluding that the Navy is required to prepare an EIS has many remedial tools at its disposal, including declaratory relief or an injunction tailored to the preparation of an EIS rather than the Navy's training in the interim. See, e.g., Steffel v. Thompson, 415 U.S. 452, 466, 94 S.Ct. 1209, 39 L.Ed.2d 505 (1974) ("Congress plainly intended declaratory relief to act as an alternative to the strong medicine of the injunction"). In the meantime, we see no basis for jeopardizing national security, as the present injunction does.

* * *

President Theodore Roosevelt explained that "the only way in which a navy can ever be made efficient is by practice at sea, under all the conditions which would have to be met if war existed." President's Annual

Message, 42 Cong.Rec. 67, 81 (1907). We do not discount the importance of plaintiffs' ecological, scientific, and recreational interests in marine mammals. Those interests, however, are plainly outweighed by the Navy's need to conduct realistic training exercises to ensure that it is able to neutralize the threat posed by enemy submarines. The District Court abused its discretion by imposing a 2,200–yard shutdown zone and by requiring the Navy to power down its MFA sonar during significant surface ducting conditions. The judgment of the Court of Appeals is reversed, and the preliminary injunction is vacated to the extent it has been challenged by the Navy.

* * *

JUSTICE BREYER, with whom JUSTICE STEVENS joins * * *, concurring in part and dissenting in part.

* * *

While a District Court is often free simply to state its conclusion in summary fashion, in this instance neither that conclusion, nor anything else I have found in the District Court's opinion, answers the Navy's documented claims that the two extra conditions the District Court imposed will, in effect, seriously interfere with its ability to carry out necessary training exercises.

* * *

JUSTICE GINSBURG, with whom JUSTICE SOUTER joins, dissenting.

The central question in this action under the National Environmental Policy Act of 1969 (NEPA) was whether the Navy must prepare an environmental impact statement (EIS). The Navy does not challenge its obligation to do so, and it represents that the EIS will be complete in January 2009—one month after the instant exercises conclude. If the Navy had completed the EIS before taking action, as NEPA instructs, the parties and the public could have benefited from the environmental analysis—and the Navy's training could have proceeded without interruption. Instead, the Navy acted first, and thus thwarted the very purpose an EIS is intended to serve.

* * *

III

A

Flexibility is a hallmark of equity jurisdiction. "The essence of equity jurisdiction has been the power of the Chancellor to do equity and to mould each decree to the necessities of the particular case. Flexibility rather than rigidity has distinguished it." Weinberger v. Romero–Barcelo, 456 U.S. 305, 312, 102 S.Ct. 1798, 72 L.Ed.2d 91 (1982) (quoting Hecht Co. v. Bowles, 321 U.S. 321, 329, 64 S.Ct. 587, 88 L.Ed. 754 (1944)). Consistent with equity's character, courts do not insist that litigants uniformly show a particular, predetermined quantum of probable success or injury before awarding equitable relief. Instead, courts have evaluated claims for equitable relief on a "sliding scale," sometimes awarding relief based on a lower likelihood of harm when the likelihood of success is very high. This Court has never rejected that formulation, and I do not believe it does so today.

Equity's flexibility is important in the NEPA context. Because an EIS is the tool for *uncovering* environmental harm, environmental plaintiffs may often rely more heavily on their probability of success than the likelihood of harm. The Court is correct that relief is not warranted "simply to prevent the possibility of some remote future injury." "However, the injury need not have been inflicted when application is made or be certain to occur; a strong threat of irreparable injury before trial is an adequate basis." I agree with the District Court that NRDC made the required showing here.

B

The Navy's own EA predicted substantial and irreparable harm to marine mammals. Sonar is linked to mass strandings of marine mammals, hemorrhaging around the brain and ears, acute spongiotic changes in the central nervous system, and lesions in vital organs. * * *

In light of the likely, substantial harm to the environment, NRDC's almost inevitable success on the merits of its claim that NEPA required the Navy to prepare an EIS, the history of this litigation, and the public interest, I cannot agree that the mitigation measures the District Court imposed signal an abuse of discretion. Cf. Amoco Production Co. v. Gambell, 480 U.S. 531, 545, 107 S.Ct. 1396, 94 L.Ed.2d 542 (1987) ("Environmental injury, by its nature, can seldom be adequately remedied by money damages and is often permanent or at least of long duration, *i.e.,* irreparable. If such injury is sufficiently likely, therefore, the balance of harms will usually favor the issuance of an injunction to protect the environment.").

* * *

NOTES

1. Courts often state that the goal of a preliminary injunction is to maintain the "status quo." But what does that mean in *Winter*? Does it mean just prior to the training exercises at issue here have commenced or the fact that the Navy has engaged in periodic training exercises in the SOCAL region for the previous 40 years? In an ordinary case, should "status quo" refer to the situation immediately prior to the filing of the suit? Before the filing of the motion for preliminary injunction? Or does the court mean by status quo the plaintiffs' rightful position? If so, how does the court know what that is in advance of deciding the case on the merits? See Thomas R. Lee, Preliminary Injunctions and the Status Quo, 58 Wash. & Lee L.Rev. 109 (2001).

2. Some courts adjust the test for granting a preliminary injunction by considering whether the request is "disfavored." This concept has been analyzed closely by the Tenth Circuit en banc. That court held that a moving party seeking a preliminary injunction falling into one of the categories of historically disfavored preliminary injunctions—which either alter the status quo, are mandatory preliminary injunctions, or afford the movant all the relief that it could recover at the conclusion of a full trial on the merits—must satisfy a heightened burden. The motion must be closely scrutinized to assure that the movants have made a strong showing both with regard to the likelihood of success on the merits and with regard to the balance of harms. O Centro Espirita Beneficiente Uniao Do Vegetal v. Ashcroft, 389 F.3d 973 (10th Cir. en banc 2004), aff'd on other grounds, 546 U.S. 418, 126 S.Ct. 1211, 163 L.Ed.2d 1017 (2006).

This treatment of certain motions for preliminary injunctive relief may help to explain the Court's posture in *Winter*. If the plaintiffs were to have obtained the preliminary injunction they desired—no Navy exercises without substantial mitigation of harm and a directive to file an EIS—they would have effectively won a complete victory. Indeed, at oral argument, the plaintiffs' lawyer confirmed that the "preliminary injunction was 'the whole ball game.'" *Winter*, 129 S.Ct. at 381.

3. As Chief Justice Roberts noted in *Winter*, the test for deciding a motion for a preliminary injunction includes consideration of whether the injunction would be adverse to the public interest. But, how do courts determine what the "public interest" is? How does the court determine what public policies and which third-party interests are relevant? In *Winter*, the Court found that the sworn statements of senior Navy personnel regarding the need for training in order to keep the Navy and the country safe from enemy submarines easily outweighed the plaintiffs' interests in whale watching trips, photography, and scientific research. But what about the public interest represented by enforcement of three federal statutes: the Marine Mammals Act, the National Environmental Policy Act and the Coastal Zone Management Act? What about harm to the marine mammals? See Laura W. Stein, The Court and Community: Why Non–Party Interests Should Count in Preliminary Injunction Actions, 16 Rev.Litig. 27 (1997); Note, "The Wild Card that is the Public Interest": Putting a New Face on the Fourth Preliminary Injunction Factor, 72 Tex.L.Rev. 849 (1994)(contending that courts should use the factor to weigh particular non–party harm which will be suffered as a direct consequence of the granting or denying of a particular preliminary injunction).

Professor John Leubsdorf addressed the question of whose interests should be weighed when applying the preliminary injunction test:

> In recent years, federal courts have given increasing attention to the effect of preliminary relief on the public interest. No doubt this reflects the flowering of broad injunctive relief which affects many persons and the judicial recognition of public interest plaintiffs. On a deeper level, it shows increasing judicial concern with the impact of legal decisions on society, as opposed to their adequacy as remedies for past misconduct.[124]

---

124. See Chayes, The Role of the Judge in Public Law Litigation, 89 Harv.L.Rev. 1281 (1976).

It does not follow, however, that the interests of everyone affected by the grant or denial of preliminary relief should figure in the interlocutory hearing. The court must determine whose interests it should consider by reference to the substantive law that will apply when the case goes to trial on the merits. An interlocutory decision about specific performance of a contract to make parts for a power plant should turn on the applicable contract law, not the plant's environmental impact. To consider interests irrelevant to the final decision at the preliminary stage will only increase the cost of the litigation and undermine the substantive law. Those whom the law excludes from protection at the final hearing have no greater claim to be taken into account earlier. This is implicit in the basic perception that preliminary relief guards against irreparable loss of rights, not against *damnum absque injuria*.

The substantive law does not always specify the objects of its protection. So long as a party with standing is present, courts granting final relief can limit their inquiry to what the law forbids. The balancing test for preliminary relief, by contrast, calls for difficult judgments about who—parties, neighbors, future generations, and so forth—have interests deserving consideration. These judgments have to be made quickly, and the law of standing provides only a partial guide. Not surprisingly, some courts avoid the problem by invoking generalizations about the public interest.

The Standard for Preliminary Injunctions, 91 Harv.L.Rev. 525, 549–50 (1978).

4. The October 2003 recall election in California, which led to the removal of Governor Gray Davis and the selection of Arnold Schwarzenegger as his successor, generated an interesting series of opinions regarding the application of preliminary injunction law where the public interest factor loomed large. A group of plaintiffs, including the Southern Christian Leadership Council and the NAACP, alleged on the basis of Bush v. Gore, 531 U.S. 98, 121 S.Ct. 525, 148 L.Ed.2d 388 (2000), that the use of obsolete punch-card voting systems in some counties in California would deny voters equal protection of the laws; up to 40,000 voters who cast ballots would not have their votes counted in what was predicted to be a close election. The plaintiffs sought a preliminary injunction which would have postponed the special recall election until the next regularly scheduled statewide election six months hence, when all counties were to be using state-approved modern voting equipment. Should the preliminary injunction have been granted? See Southwest Voter Registration Education Project v. Shelley, 278 F.Supp.2d 1131 (C.D.Cal.) (denying preliminary injunction), reversed, 344 F.3d 882 (9th Cir.) (granting preliminary injunction), panel opinion vacated, 344 F.3d 914 (9th Cir. en banc 2003) (no abuse of discretion by district court in denying request). The opinions are analyzed in James M. Fischer, "Preliminarily" Enjoining Elections: A Tale of Two Ninth Circuit Panels, 41 San Diego L.Rev. 1647 (2004).

5. How would the analysis change as the factual settings change? For example, should the district court grant a preliminary injunction to an HIV-positive elementary school teacher who does not want to be transferred from the classroom to an administrative role in the school district's offices? Chalk

v. United States District Court, 840 F.2d 701 (9th Cir.1988). To an HIV-positive prison inmate who does not wish to be segregated from the rest of the prison population for educational, religious and recreational programs? See Onishea v. Hopper, 171 F.3d 1289 (11th Cir. en banc 1999), cert. denied, 528 U.S. 1114, 120 S.Ct. 931, 145 L.Ed.2d 811 (2000). To an HIV-positive surgical technician who does not want to be transferred from the operating room to the hospital's purchasing department? Bradley v. University of Texas M.D. Anderson Cancer Center, 3 F.3d 922 (5th Cir.1993), cert. denied, 510 U.S. 1119, 114 S.Ct. 1071, 127 L.Ed.2d 389 (1994).

6. Note that the plaintiffs in *Winter* were seeking equitable relief on their federal claims in the form of an order to stop (or severely limit) the use of MFA sonar during training exercises in the future until the Navy prepared an Environmental Impact Statement. The general rule is that a court may grant interim relief only where the relief the plaintiff ultimately seeks is equitable and not legal. The modern authority for this rule is Judge Learned Hand. In Sims v. Stuart, 291 Fed. 707, 707–08 (S.D.N.Y.1922), he said: "It is, of course, true that equity will at times affirmatively restore the status quo ante pending the suit. But never, so far as I know, will it take jurisdiction over a legal claim merely to hurry it along by granting final relief at the outset of a cause." With rare exception, courts in the United States continue to follow this rule. E.g., Grupo Mexicano de Desarrollo, S.A. v. Alliance Bond Fund, Inc., 527 U.S. 308, 119 S.Ct. 1961, 144 L.Ed.2d 319 (1999)(not permissible for a federal court to use a preliminary injunction to freeze the defendant's assets for the benefit of a nonjudgment creditor asserting only a legal claim for money damages because such a remedy was beyond the relief traditionally available from a court of equity at the time the Judiciary Act of 1789 conferred equitable power on district courts). The major exception to the general rule, pre-judgment attachment of assets, is considered in Chapter 8.

7. The prerequisites for granting preliminary relief may be changed by statute. For example, under the Railway Labor Act, a carrier need not show any irreparable injury when seeking to enjoin a violation of the status quo by its employees because of the strong public interest in enforcing the Act. Delta Air Lines, Inc. v. Air Line Pilots Association, 238 F.3d 1300, 1308 (11th Cir.), cert. denied, 532 U.S. 1019, 121 S.Ct. 1958, 149 L.Ed.2d 754 (2001).

AMERICAN HOSPITAL SUPPLY CORP. v. HOSPITAL PRODUCTS LTD.

United States Court of Appeals, Seventh Circuit, 1986
780 F.2d 589

POSNER, CIRCUIT JUDGE.

* * * A district judge asked to decide whether to grant or deny a preliminary injunction must choose the course of action that will minimize the costs of being mistaken. Because he is forced to act on an incomplete record, the danger of a mistake is substantial. And a mistake can be costly. If the judge grants the preliminary injunction to a plaintiff who it later turns out is not entitled to any judicial relief—whose legal rights have not been violated—the judge commits a mistake whose gravity is measured by the irreparable harm, if any, that the injunction causes to the defendant while it is in effect. If the judge denies the preliminary injunction to a plaintiff who it later turns out is entitled to judicial relief, the judge commits a mistake whose gravity is measured by the irreparable harm, if any, that the denial of the preliminary injunction does to the plaintiff.

These mistakes can be compared, and the one likely to be less costly can be selected, with the help of a simple formula: grant the preliminary injunction if but only if $P \times H_p > (1-P) \times H_d$, or, in words, only if the harm to the plaintiff if the injunction is denied, multiplied by the probability that the denial would be an error (that the plaintiff, in other words, will win at trial), exceeds the harm to the defendant if the injunction is granted, multiplied by the probability that granting the injunction would be an error. That probability is simply one minus the probability that the plaintiff will win at trial; for if the plaintiff has, say, a 40 percent chance of winning, the defendant must have a 60 percent chance of winning ($1.00-.40 = .60$). The left-hand side of the formula is simply the probability of an erroneous denial weighted by the cost of denial to the plaintiff, and the right-hand side simply the probability of an erroneous grant weighted by the cost of grant to the defendant.

This formula, a procedural counterpart to Judge Learned Hand's famous negligence formula, see United States v. Carroll Towing Co., 159 F.2d 169, 173 (2d Cir.1947), is not offered as a new legal standard; it is intended not to force analysis into a quantitative straitjacket but to assist analysis by presenting succinctly the factors that the court must consider in making its decision and by articulating the relationship among the factors. It is actually just a distillation of the familiar four (sometimes five) factor test that courts use in deciding whether to grant a preliminary injunction. The court asks whether the plaintiff will be irreparably harmed if the preliminary injunction is denied (sometimes also whether the plaintiff has an adequate remedy at law), whether the harm to the plaintiff if the preliminary injunction is denied will exceed the harm to the defendant if it is granted, whether the plaintiff is reasonably likely to prevail at trial, and whether the public interest will be affected by granting or denying the injunction (i.e., whether third parties will be harmed—and these harms can then be added to H_p or H_d as the case may be). The court undertakes these inquiries to help it figure out whether granting the injunction would be the error-minimizing course of action, which depends on the probability that the plaintiff is in the right and on the costs to the plaintiff, the defendant, or others of granting or denying the injunction. All this is explained at length in Roland Machinery Co. v. Dresser Industries, Inc., 749 F.2d 380, 382–88 (7th Cir.1984), where a panel of this court applied the verbal counterpart to our algebraic formula, as did a different panel in Maxim's Ltd. v. Badonsky, 772 F.2d 388, 391 (7th Cir.1985). See also Leubsdorf, The Standard for Preliminary Injunctions, 91 Harv.L.Rev. 525 (1978). The formula is new; the analysis it capsulizes is standard. * * *

SWYGERT, SENIOR CIRCUIT JUDGE, dissenting.

The court today continues what it began in Roland Machinery v. Dresser Industries, 749 F.2d 380 (7th Cir.1984): a wholesale revision of the law of preliminary injunctions. * * *

I would have preferred to avoid commenting on the majority's attempt to reduce the well-developed and complex law of preliminary injunctions to a "simple" mathematical formula. But because of the potentially far-reaching and baneful consequences of today's decision, I must regretfully voice my concerns.

Henceforth, the district courts of this circuit should grant a preliminary injunction if, "but only if," $P \times H_p > (1-P) \times H_d$ * * *.

The majority describes its formula as a procedural counterpart to Judge Hand's negligence formula first appearing in United States v. Carroll Towing, 159 F.2d 169, 173 (2d Cir.1947). *Carroll Towing* was an admiralty case in which a shipowner's duty to provide against injuries resulting from the breaking of a vessel's moorings was expressed in algebraic terms. In Hand's formula the liability of the shipowner depends on whether $B < PL$, where P is the probability that the ship will break away; where L is the gravity of the resulting injury if she does; and where B is the burden of adequate precautions. Various attempts have been made to apply the Hand formula, or some derivation of it, to areas other than negligence. * * * Most courts, however, have continued to view the *Carroll Towing* opinion as a negligence formula. * * * My quarrel, however, is not with *Carroll Towing* but rather with the majority's attempt today to create its equitable analogue. A quantitative approach may be an appropriate and useful heuristic device in determining negligence in tort cases, but it has limited value in determining whether a preliminary injunction should issue. Proceedings in equity and cases sounding in tort demand entirely different responses of a district judge. The judgment of the district judge in a tort case must be definite; the judgment of the district judge in an injunction proceeding cannot, by its very nature, be as definite. The judgment of a district judge in an injunction proceeding must be flexible and discretionary—within the bounds of the now settled four-prong test.

I question the necessity and the wisdom of the court's adoption of a mathematical formula as the governing law of preliminary injunctions. The majority claims that its formula is merely a distillation of the traditional four-prong test. But if nothing is added to the substantive law, why bother? The standard four-prong test for determining whether a preliminary injunction should issue has survived for so many years because it has proven to be a workable summation of the myriad factors a district court must consider in deciding whether to grant an injunction. The test * * * may not exhibit the "precision" the majority seems to demand, but such "precision" is antithetical to the underlying principles of injunctive relief. Equity, as the majority concedes, involves the assessment of factors that cannot be quantified. A district court faced with the task of deciding whether to issue a preliminary injunction must to some extent, the majority concedes, rely on the "feel" of the case. The majority's formula will not assist the district courts in their assessment of this aspect of the decision to grant a preliminary injunction. The traditional element of discretion residing in the decision of a trial court to grant a preliminary injunction has been all but eliminated by today's decision.

Ironically, the majority never attempts to assign a numerical value to the variables of its own formula. We are never told how to measure P or Hp or Hd. I believe, and the majority appears to concede, that a numerical value could never be assigned to these variables. Who can say, for instance, what *exactly* the probability is that the granting of the injunction was an error? How then will the majority's formula ease in a meaningful way the responsibilities of the district courts? Judges asked to issue a preliminary injunction must, in large part, rely on their own judgment, not on mathematical quanta.

We must, of course, be mindful not to vest too much imprecision in the preliminary injunction standard, for law implies a system of known and generally applicable rules. The existing four-prong test, however, represents the historical balance struck by the courts between the rigidity of law and the flexibility of equity. * * *

NOTES

1. Does Judge Posner's approach change the traditional test as applied in *Winter*? If so, is the formula an improvement? If not, is it useful nevertheless? Compare, e.g., Douglas Lichtman, Uncertainty and the Standard for Preliminary Relief, 70 U.Chi.L.Rev. 197 (2003) (exploring the implications of the fact that the court will be just as uncertain about its estimates of the harms inflicted by a wrongfully-issued preliminary injunction as it is about its prediction as to the outcome of the case) and Linda J. Silberman, Injunctions by the Numbers: Less Than the Sum of Its Parts, 63 Chi–Kent L.Rev. 279, 282 (1987)(the formula "does not clarify the standard and emerges as a disguised effort to extend the heavy hand of appellate review") with Linz Audain, Of Posner, and Newton, and Twenty–First Century Law: An Economic and Statistical Analysis of the Posner Rule for Granting Preliminary Injunctions, 23 Loy.L.A.L.Rev. 1215, 1218 (1990)(comparing Judge Posner's insight favorably with Sir Isaac Newton's scientific contributions). Citations to other commentators on the *American Hospital* formula are collected in Robert J.C. Deane, Varying the Plaintiff's Burden: An Efficient Approach to Interlocutory Injunctions to Preserve Future Money Judgements, 49 U. Toronto L.J. 1, 22 (1999). Judge Posner has discussed the formula a bit more in Richard A. Posner, Economic Analysis of Law § 21.3 at 595–97 (7th ed.2007).

2. There may be less to the formula than meets the eye. In another Seventh Circuit case decided soon after *American Hospital,* Judge Eschbach (who was not a member of that panel) wrote:

> *American Hospital* does not set forth a new standard for granting preliminary injunctions. * * *

> As a distillation, the formula admirably reflects the balancing of irreparable harms inherent in the traditional test. However, a formula, of necessity cannot incorporate all of the elements of the traditional test. We note, therefore, that before the district court balances the irreparable harms suffered by the parties, the plaintiff still must establish the other prerequisites to the issuance of a preliminary injunction—namely, that the plaintiff has no adequate remedy at law; that it has a reasonable likelihood of prevailing on the merits; and that an injunction would not harm the public interest.

Brunswick Corp. v. Jones, 784 F.2d 271, 274 n. 1 (7th Cir.1986). With this "clarification," is the test in the Seventh Circuit any different from the traditional test? However, one commentator believes that *the American Hospital* test has emerged as the "triumphant, dominant theory of preliminary injunctions" because courts now overwhelmingly believe that it is proper to employ a sliding scale in which a stronger showing of irreparable harm can compensate for a smaller likelihood of success on the merits. Thomas R. Lee, Preliminary Injunctions and the Status Quo, 58 Wash. & Lee L.Rev. 110, 154 (2001). See, e.g., Scotts Co. v. United Industries Corp., 315 F.3d 264 (4th Cir.2002) (quoting and applying *American Hospital*).

Judge Posner and Judge Easterbrook have disagreed over the application of the sliding scale test in the context of a request for an injunction pending appeal. In Cavel International, Inc. v. Madigan, 500 F.3d 544 (7th Cir.2007), Judge Posner stayed enforcement of an Illinois statute making it unlawful for any person to slaughter a horse for human consumption (a delicacy in Europe). He found that the strong showing of irreparable harm (enforcement of the statute would have completely shut down Cavel International) compensated for the limited chance of success on the merits. Judge Easterbrook disagreed, believing that the sliding scale test of preliminary injunctions did not apply to a stay or injunction pending appeal, because a higher standard was required after the movant has lost at the trial level. He would have denied the injunction because of the absence of a strong showing of potential success on the merits. The same panel subsequently upheld the validity of the statute. 500 F.3d 551 (7th Cir.2007), cert. denied, 554 U.S. ___, 128 S.Ct. 2950, 171 L.Ed.2d 863 (2008).

3. In developing the formula in *American Hospital*, the court was influenced strongly by a law review article, John Leubsdorf, The Standard for Preliminary Injunctions, 91 Harv.L.Rev. 525 (1978):

> Although reducing this model to hard figures is usually impractical, an example that does so will clarify its implications. Suppose the plaintiff is an indigent who claims additional welfare payments of $20 per month. With these payments, he could buy food in bulk at reduced rates, increasing his purchasing power by $32 per month. If five months will elapse before final judgment, the defendant agency has $100 at stake and the plaintiff $160. Although calculable, these potential losses are irreparable because the plaintiff is judgment-proof and the defendant has sovereign immunity from a judgment for payments due in previous months. The judge also estimates that the plaintiff's claim has a 40% chance of success at trial. On these assumptions, the judge can calculate the

probable irreparable loss of rights resulting from the grant or denial of preliminary relief. If the defendant must pay the plaintiff's claim during the litigation, it will spend $100 with a 60% chance that the payments will be found legally unnecessary. Therefore, the defendant's probable irreparable loss of rights from the grant of relief is $60. The plaintiff's probable irreparable loss from the denial of relief, based on a similar calculation, is 40% of $160, or $64. Since the estimated $64 loss from denying relief exceeds the estimated $60 loss from granting it, the judge should grant a preliminary injunction.

This result is not trivial. A judge proceeding intuitively might well conclude that the greater potential injury to the plaintiff from the denial of interim relief does not outweigh the defendant's greater probability of success on the merits. Indeed, formulations requiring plaintiffs to show a probability of success in order to secure relief would foreclose an injunction. The intuitive approach also might encourage a judge to rely on vague generalizations about the impact of deprivations on the poor or the need to protect the public from bogus claimants.

The figures presented in the example as the probable irreparable losses of the parties are in a sense statistical myths. The defendant will not actually lose $60 no matter what happens. If the injunction issues it will pay out $100, which will turn out to be either the amount legally due the plaintiff or $100 too much. The $60 probable loss of rights can best be understood as a prediction of the average loss of rights that the defendant would sustain if similar cases were decided many times without reference to each other. Such mathematical expectations of profit or loss are familiar tools in decisionmaking theory. Judges as well as private decisionmakers often weigh alternative courses of action by considering the possible outcomes in light of their probability of occurrence.

91 Harv.L.Rev. at 542–43.

Scholars agree with the need for a court to account for the probability of error in making the preliminary injunction decision. See Joshua P. Davis, Taking Uncertainty Seriously: Revising Injunction Doctrine, 34 Rutgers L.J. 363, 369 (2003) (arguing to consider adjudicative error in both preliminary and final injunction decisions). Professor Leubsdorf defends the traditional approach of accounting for this within the evaluation of the merits and the irreparability of plaintiff's claim. Others criticize the conventional approach and suggest alternative approaches, though not that offered by Judge Posner in *American Hospital*. See Richard R.W. Brooks & Warren F. Schwartz, Legal Uncertainty, Economic Efficiency, and the Preliminary Injunction Doctrine, 58 Stan.L.Rev. 381 (2005) (proposing to grant preliminary injunctions to all plaintiffs who post a bond covering the defendant's potential damages from the injunction in order to reallocate the economic incentives by giving the plaintiff leverage to counter the defendant's likely refusal to perform where legal rights are uncertain); Douglas Lichtman, Irreparable Benefits, 116 Yale. L.J. 1284 (2007) (highlighting the inability of the conventional approach to account for irreparable benefits gained by the temporary winner from the erroneous grant or denial of a preliminary injunction).

PROBLEMS

1. How would the following case come out under *American Hospital*? What if a court was asked to prevent the Earth from being sucked into a black hole? Certain individuals brought suit under the National Environmental Policy Act to enjoin the operation of the Large Hadron Collider, a new 17-mile long subatomic particle accelerator located underground near Geneva, Switzerland, until the Collider was proven "reasonably safe." The Collider, the most expensive scientific instrument and the most powerful subatomic particle smasher ever built, was developed in hopes of resolving some fundamental questions about the universe. The plaintiffs' fear, supported by some scientists, was that the Collider might implode, creating mini-black holes, which could eventually swallow and destroy the Earth. The defendants, the consortium of international scientific organizations involved in the project, claimed that the plaintiffs had little to no chance of succeeding on their legal claims under either U.S. or European Union law. Sancho v. U.S. Department of Energy, 578 F.Supp.2d 1258 (D. Hawaii 2008).

2. Paula and Donald, who are siblings of deceased parents, each claim title to Blackacre, which is a vacation home. Should Paula get a preliminary injunction against Donald's entry onto Blackacre, under *Winter* or *American Hospital*, in the following situations?

(a) Paula, a wealthy law student who does nothing but study, has a small chance of success on the merits of who has title to Blackacre; Donald holds wild parties that would probably damage the interior, if not destroy Blackacre entirely.

(b) Take the facts as in (a) but assume that Paula is not wealthy.

(c) Assume now that Paula has a strong probability of success on the merits and neither Paula nor Donald would use Blackacre for destructive parties, but Paula, who is a practitioner of primal scream therapy when she is not in law school, intends to use Blackacre to treat patients. The neighbors write letters to the court urging that she be kept out.

3. THE SECURITY REQUIREMENT

Even if the trial court is convinced that the plaintiff is entitled to preliminary or temporary injunctive relief, it must decide to what degree the defendant deserves protection in the event that the initial decision proves to be incorrect. In particular, the court must decide the amount of security to be imposed on the plaintiff as a prerequisite to obtaining a TRO or a preliminary injunction.

(A) THE AMOUNT OF SECURITY

Rule 65(c) of the Federal Rules of Civil Procedure provides that "[t]he court may issue a preliminary injunction or a temporary restraining order only if the movant gives security * * *." Although phrased in mandatory terms, the remaining portion of the first sentence of Rule 65(c) provides that the security required shall be "in an amount that the court considers proper to pay the costs and damages sustained by any party found to have been wrongfully enjoined or restrained." This language has led some courts to conclude that the decision is discretionary, so long as the district court actually considers the question. See, e.g., SizeWise Rentals, Inc. v. Mediq/PRN Life Support Services, Inc., 216 F.3d 1088 (10th Cir.2000). The issue then becomes whether the court in exercising its discretion can waive the security requirement altogether or set the amount of the bond at a level below the estimated costs and damages that the enjoined party may actually suffer if the order is granted improperly.

While there are cases where the failure to require the posting of any bond has been considered reversible error, e.g., Maryland Department of Human Resources v. U.S. Department of Agriculture, 976 F.2d 1462 (4th Cir.1992), some courts have avoided this result by requiring a bond set at a nominal face value. This is a particularly common practice in suits to enforce important federal rights or public interests. E.g., Natural Resources Defense Council, Inc. v. Morton, 337 F.Supp. 167, 168–69 (D.D.C. 1971), aff'd on other grounds, 458 F.2d 827 (D.C.Cir.1972); 11A Charles Alan Wright, Arthur R. Miller & Mary Kay Kane, Federal Practice and Procedure: Civil § 2954 at 300 (2d ed.1995). Thus when three nonprofit environmental groups sought to prevent leasing of the Outer Continental Shelf, the district court in *NRDC* granted a preliminary injunction secured entirely by a bond of $100 instead of $750,000 for the first month and $2,500,000 for each month thereafter as requested by the government. The court noted that "the requirement of more than a nominal amount as security would * * * stifle the intent of the [1969 National Environmental Policy] Act since these three 'concerned private organizations' would be precluded from obtaining judicial review of the defendant's actions." 337 F.Supp. at 169.

Appellate courts usually state that trial courts should take the following factors into account when determining whether to waive the bond requirement or to require the posting of a bond set at a nominal sum: the possible harm to the enjoined party if the order is unlawful, the likelihood of the applicant's success on the merits, the applicant's ability to post a substantial bond or surety, and the possible adverse impact that requiring substantial security might have on the enforcement of rights created by remedial legislation. E.g., Continuum Co. v. Incepts, Inc., 873 F.2d 801 (5th Cir.1989).

Aside from the terms of F.R.Civ.P. 65(c), is it appropriate for the district court to give a plaintiff a "free ride" in seeking a preliminary injunction or a TRO? Why not estimate the cost of error realistically and force the plaintiff to decide if it is "worth it" in order to obtain preliminary relief? For discussion of the policy considerations regarding a mandatory security requirement, see James T. Carney, Rule 65 and Judicial Abuse of Power: A Modest Proposal for Reform, 19 Am.J.Tr.Advoc. 87 (1995); Note, Security for Interlocutory Injunctions Under Rule 65(c): Exceptions to the Rule Gone Awry, 46 Hastings L.J. 1863 (1995).

(B) COLLECTING ON THE SECURITY

F.R.Civ.P. 65.1 (reproduced in the Appendix at p. 988) "permits the liability of a surety to be enforced through an expeditious, summary procedure without the necessity of an independent action." 11A Charles Alan Wright, Arthur R. Miller & Mary Kay Kane, Federal Practice and Procedure: Civil § 2972 at 454 (2d ed.1995). "In the case of an injunction bond, the claim against the surety does not accrue until it is finally determined that plaintiff was not entitled to the restraining order or injunction * * *. A final determination may take the form of a decree dismissing the suit, total or partial dissolution of the injunction, or the failure to carry the burden of proof at the hearing on the preliminary injunction." Id. at 458–60.

While F.R.Civ.P. 65.1 creates a procedure for collecting damages on a bond posted in a federal court action, the rule does not address the extent of a surety's liability on the bond. See, e.g., Network Intern. L.C. v. Worldcom Technologies, Inc., 133 F.Supp.2d 713 (D.Md.2001) (discussing widely differing standards courts use to determine whether the prevailing defendant is entitled to damages on a bond). The question becomes particularly important if no bond is required or if the bond is set at a nominal sum, because a subsequent determination that the defendant was wrongfully enjoined is meaningless if the defendant's recovery of costs and damages is limited to the face value of the bond. E.g., Pharmaceutical Society of State of New York, Inc. v. New York State Department of Social Services, 50 F.3d 1168 (2d Cir.1995) (limiting recovery to amount of bond). See also Note, Recovery for Wrongful Interlocutory Injunctions Under Rule 65(c), 99 Harv.L.Rev. 828 (1986).

Finally, federal practice under F.R.Civ.P. 65.1 may conflict with the law of the forum state in two important aspects: first, the determination of what constitutes "costs and damages" payable on the bond; and second, the availability of a comparable summary procedure. 11A Charles Alan Wright, Arthur R. Miller & Mary Kay Kane, supra, § 2974 at 469. We will leave the interesting *Erie* problems that result to your civil procedure and conflicts of law classes.

B. FORMULATING AND ADMINISTERING THE INJUNCTION

PROBLEM: COUNTRY LODGE V. MILLER (REPRISED)
DRAFTING AND ADMINISTERING AN INJUNCTION

Assume that the trial court has found that Miller created a nuisance to Country Lodge by dumping too much of the unsightly apple mash waste into the Rural River. The court also finds that because Country Lodge does not have an adequate remedy at law, an injunction is the appropriate relief. According to the court, the test of a violation is whether apple mash is visible in the river as it flows past the Country Lodge property.

The following facts have been established at trial. Miller employs eighteen people. Miller and her employees usually dump apple mash into the river through a pipe leading from the apple press; occasionally they find it easier to use wheel barrows to dump excess apple mash into the river. During times of ordinary water flow, if Miller and her employees dump more than 50 pounds of apple mash per hour into the river, it is visible as the water passes by Country Lodge. However, the water flow varies greatly with the seasons and weather conditions, so there are times when just one pound of apple mash per hour is visible at Country Lodge and others when even 100 pounds per hour are not visible. There is equipment available at a cost of $28,000 that can meter the flow of apple mash through the pipe. In a prior case a few years ago, Miller was held in contempt of court for willfully violating an injunction, which was unrelated to water pollution.

(a) Who should draft the injunction? (b) What should be the precise terms of an injunction that would restore and protect Country Lodge's rightful position under these circumstances? (Try to draft the injunction). (c) How will the injunction be administered; in particular, how will the court know if Miller is violating the injunction?

1. DRAFTING THE INJUNCTION

PORTLAND FEMINIST WOMEN'S HEALTH CENTER v. ADVOCATES FOR LIFE, INC.

United States Court of Appeals, Ninth Circuit, 1988
859 F.2d 681

Hug, Circuit Judge:

* * *

Facts

* * * The clinic brought an action against [Advocates for Life, Inc and certain individuals] that was based on several spirited demonstrations in front of the clinic's building. * * * The clinic moved for a preliminary injunction, and the motion was brought before a magistrate for an evidentiary hearing.

The magistrate recommended to the district court that a preliminary injunction be issued based on his findings of fact. * * *

The district court adopted the findings in their entirety and issued the following injunction:

> IT IS HEREBY ORDERED that defendants, their agents, servants, employees, and all persons, groups, and organizations acting in concert with one or more of the defendants are enjoined from committing any of the following acts:
>
> 1. obstructing the free and direct passage of any person in or out of the Portland Feminist Women's Health Center (the Center);
>
> 2. demonstrating or distributing literature on the Foster Road sidewalk in front of the Center in a rectangular zone that extends from the Center's front door to the curb and twelve and one-half feet

on either side of a line from the middle of the Center's door to the curb;

　　3. shouting, screaming, chanting, or yelling during on-site demonstrations;

　　4. producing noise by any other means which substantially interferes with the provision of medical services within the Center, including counseling;

　　5. trespassing on Center property;

　　6. damaging the property of the Center, its employees or clients; and

　　7. interfering with the Center's receipt of public utility services.

　　This Order shall remain in effect until further order of the court.

After the injunction was issued, the demonstrations continued, and at a hearing the district court found several of the individual advocates in contempt. We are asked to determine the validity of both the injunction and the contempt citations.

Analysis

　　* * * Appellants do not seriously challenge the magistrate's findings of fact or his determination under the preliminary injunction standard. He explicitly found that the defendants engaged in the offending conduct. We proceed in our analysis on the basis that the findings of fact are not clearly erroneous, and the preliminary injunction standard was satisfied.

　　Appellants challenge the injunction's content with arguments asserting impermissible vagueness for failure to set forth an objective decibel level for prohibited shouting, yelling, chanting, and noise making. They argue that this purported vagueness has a chilling effect on protected activities and places demonstrators at the mercy of the appellees' subjective standards. Because we are dealing with an injunction, the vagueness issue is controlled by Fed.R.Civ.P. 65(d).

　　Rule 65(d) requires that injunctions "shall be specific in terms; [and] shall describe in reasonable detail ... the act or acts sought to be restrained." The Supreme Court has indicated that the policy behind the rule is "to prevent uncertainty and confusion on the part of those faced with injunctive orders, and to avoid the possible founding of a contempt citation on a decree too vague to be understood." Schmidt v. Lessard, 414 U.S. 473, 476, 94 S.Ct. 713, 715, 38 L.Ed.2d 661 (1974). We have interpreted the rule and its policy to require that "the language of injunctions ... be reasonably clear so that ordinary persons will know precisely what action is proscribed." While ambiguities in an injunction are construed in favor of the enjoined party, nonetheless "[i]njunctions are not set aside under Rule 65(d) ... unless they are so vague that they have no reasonably specific meaning."

We do not find the injunction here in dispute impermissibly vague under the applicable standards. The language that the advocates attack enjoins "shouting, screaming, chanting, or yelling during on-site demonstrations; [and] ... [p]roducing noise by any other means which substantially interferes with the provision of medical services within the Center, including counseling...." They argue that without a specific decibel level or other objective standard they cannot know whether their conduct violates the injunction. They argue further that without such a standard, the imposition of contempt sanctions under the injunction will be based on the biased and subjective interpretation of the clinic. While an enumerated decibel level certainly would provide a more specific definition of the enjoined conduct than the injunction now provides, we do not believe that such specificity is required. The terms of the injunction place the enjoined parties on fair notice of the actions that are prohibited in language that is reasonably understandable. Greater particularity, while it may be desirable, is not required under Rule 65(d). * * *

The advocates' strongest challenge to the preliminary injunction is against the third and fourth paragraphs, which prohibit shouting, screaming, chanting, yelling, and producing noise. Whether these provisions are tailored narrowly enough is a close question. The district court found that chanting, shouting, and screaming during demonstrations were audible on the second floor, where medical procedures are performed. Chanting, shouting, screaming, or yelling may be an expressive, albeit unpleasant, form of behavior. If it causes no disruption of clinic operations, such expression would not materially affect the interest at stake here. On the other hand, if the conduct rises to a volume that obstructs the provision of services in the Center, it may be enjoined. Accordingly, we modify the injunction by combining its paragraphs numbered 3 and 4 in the following fashion:

> 3. shouting, screaming, chanting, yelling, or producing noise by any other means, in a volume that substantially interferes with the provision of medical services within the Center, including counseling;....

The remainder of the preliminary injunction is not contested. We see no problem with the prohibition against trespassing, damaging property, and interfering with utility services. * * *

Appellants also challenge the injunction as constitutionally void for vagueness. However, that doctrine does not affect our decision. The vagueness doctrine is based on due process principles that require fair notice and warning. It also incorporates a requirement that specificity be sufficient to avoid arbitrary and discriminatory enforcement. The doctrine's goal is to avoid "allow[ing] policemen, prosecutors, and juries to pursue their personal predilection," by requiring legislators to promulgate specific standards in criminal statutes. These concerns arise in a different context here, where enforcement lies entirely in judicial hands. So viewed, the injunction is not unconstitutionally vague, for reasons we have already set forth. * * *

NOTES

1. *Even as modified, will the protestors know what is permissible conduct?* For example, since they are enjoined from trespassing, how will they be able to tell whether their noise "substantially interferes with the provision of medical services" on the second floor of the clinic? See, e.g., Metropolitan Opera Association v. Local 100, Hotel Employees and Restaurant Employees International Union, 239 F.3d 172 (2d Cir.2001) (vacating injunction as impermissibly vague because it failed to distinguish permissible from prohibited speech).

In this regard, consider McComb v. Jacksonville Paper Co., 336 U.S. 187, 69 S.Ct. 497, 93 L.Ed. 599 (1949). In *McComb*, the Supreme Court, contrary to the findings of the district and circuit courts below, found the defendant in contempt of an order that directed it to obey the provisions of the Fair Labor Standards Act dealing with minimum wages, overtime, and the keeping of records. The Court noted that "By its terms it enjoined any practices which were violations of those statutory provisions. Decrees of that generality are often necessary to prevent further violations where a proclivity for unlawful conduct has been shown." 336 U.S. at 192, 69 S.Ct. at 499, 93 L.Ed. at 604.

Justices Frankfurter and Jackson dissented. They noted:

> Obedience must of course be secured for the command of a court. To secure such obedience is the function of a proceeding for contempt. But courts should be explicit and precise in their commands and should only then be strict in exacting compliance. To be both strict and indefinite is a kind of judicial tyranny.
>
> * * * It is for such reasons that this Court has indicated again and again that a statute cannot properly be made the basis of contempt proceedings merely by incorporating a reference to its broad terms into a court order. These considerations become increasingly important as there is increasing use of injunctions for the enforcement of administrative orders and statutory duties.
>
> These are general principles but their application governed the decisions of the District Court and of the Circuit Court of Appeals; they should control the decision here. The two lower courts found that while the practices now complained of by the Administrator of the Wage and Hour Division of the Department of Labor constituted violations of the Fair Labor Standards Act, they were not on any fair consideration covered by the injunction, contempt of which is now charged. The injunction underlying this proceeding takes eight pages of a printed record and particularizes in great detail the violations which were enjoined. It also contains omnibus clauses prohibiting violations of the Fair Labor Standards Act. * * * In short, both courts found no contempt. They did so because there was lacking that clearness of command in the court's order which warranted a finding of its disobedience, if due regard were paid to the

proper construction of the injunction as the starting point of the contempt proceedings. * * *

One of the grievances which led to the Norris–LaGuardia Act, 29 U.S.C.A. § 101 et seq., was the generality of the terms of labor injunctions. Ambiguity lurks in generality and may thus become an instrument of severity. Behind the vague inclusiveness of an injunction like the one before us is the hazard of retrospective interpretation as the basis of punishment through contempt proceedings. The two lower courts, in finding that generally to enjoin obedience to a law is too vague a foundation for proceedings in contempt, were avoiding the very evil with which labor injunctions were justly charged. And of course it is not to be assumed that the allowable vagueness of an injunction varies with the use to which the injunction is put. This Court ought not to encourage injunctions couched in such indefinite terms by setting aside the findings of the courts below that the injunction did not forbid with explicitness sufficient to justify a finding of contempt.

336 U.S. at 195–97, 69 S.Ct. at 501–02, 93 L.Ed. at 606–07. See also S.E.C. v. Smyth, 420 F.3d 1225, 1233 n. 14 (11th Cir.2005) ("This Circuit has held repeatedly that 'obey the law' injunctions are unenforceable.").

2. One of the other important ways in which Rule 65 protects enjoined parties is the requirement that the order "describe in reasonable detail—and not by referring to the complaint or other document—the act or acts restrained or required." F.R.Civ.P. 65(d)(1)(C). Usually the court can accommodate this requirement without difficulty. However, the requirement can pose some problems and is sometimes overlooked. For example, Dupuy v. Samuels, 465 F.3d 757 (7th Cir.2006), chastised the parties and lower court for failing to enforce the commands of Rule 65(d). The plaintiff parents sought review of a preliminary injunction requiring the state department of children's services to provide informal administrative review of "safety plans" when children were taken into temporary custody; the parents contended that the injunction provided too little relief. Writing for the court, Judge Posner objected to enforcing an injunction that improperly referenced other documents:

> The injunction of which the plaintiffs complain violates Rule 65(d) of the civil rules (though that is not the plaintiffs' complaint about it), which requires that an injunction be a self-contained document rather than incorporate by reference materials in other documents. The purpose is to minimize disputes over what has been enjoined. * * *. The Ninth Circuit allows incorporation by reference if the material thus incorporated is physically attached, as by stapling, to the injunction order. There is no reason to complicate the administration of the rule by such an interpretation. There are times when literal interpretation is best; this is one of them. The Ninth Circuit's approach would encourage just the kind of mistake that the rule aims to prevent—the thoughtless attachment of separately composed documents when if the judge had integrated their contents into the injunction order he might have realized that they would not cohere with the rest of the order without changes.
>
> Rule 65(d) is simple, clear, sensible, easily complied with, and not even new; we are distressed by the failure of the parties and the district

judge to have complied with it in this case—a case that underscores the good sense of the rule.

Nevertheless, the court went on to affirm the injunction because the defendants had failed to challenge it on cross-appeal. Id. at 763.

3. In the run-of-the-mill case, where the requested relief is fairly apparent, the plaintiff drafts a proposed order and the defendant gets to approve it as to form before the trial court signs it. In many courts, the plaintiff is required to submit a proposed order with the moving papers. E.g., McKinney's New York Rules of Court, Rules of the United States District Court for the Northern District of New York, General Rule 10(d). This simple procedure forces the plaintiff to draft an order that is fairly specific (and therefore enforceable) and is not overreaching in scope. See, e.g., Developments in the Law—Injunctions, 78 Harv.L.Rev. 994, 1064 (1967)("Specificity has long been the hallmark of a well-drafted injunctive decree."). If the proposed order would impose broader relief than the plaintiff is entitled to on the basis of the moving papers, the defendant can object before it is signed and entered by the court.

4. There are cases, however, where the task of drafting the injunction is not so simple and the appropriate scope of injunctive relief is not so clearcut. In those cases, who gets to decide exactly what burdens the decree will impose on the defendants? How is the simultaneously technical and policy-making job of drafting the decree to be accomplished? Thinking back to Chapter 2, may the parties agree to write a decree that provides for more than the plaintiff's rightful position? How can the drafting process take account of the fact that events occurring after entry of the injunction may prompt one or more of the parties to seek its modification? For one answer, see Special Project—The Remedial Process in Institutional Reform Litigation, 78 Colum.L.Rev. 784 (1978). That Special Project concludes:

> The court supervising an institutional reform case must organize remedy formulation to attain two primary goals. The formulation process must produce a viable plan, and the plan must be chosen and implemented as rapidly as possible. Speedy production of an adequate and viable plan is most likely when the court maximizes the parties' participation in devising the remedy. Of course, the greater the parties' participation, the larger the amount of factual and interpretive information the court obtains from them.
>
> Although increasing party participation might be thought to slow the remedy formulation process, it frequently has the opposite effect. By provoking simultaneously the efforts of several participants a court protects itself against the failure of any one participant to produce an adequate remedy, and may goad one or more of the others to an at least minimally acceptable effort. Indeed, delay may be avoided by simultaneous, rather than sequential, adoption of a variety of formulation techniques.
>
> The infinite variety of factual circumstances in which federal district courts take responsibility for fashioning institutional relief precludes the academic prescription of any one technique of remedy formulation, or even a comparative evaluation of the alternatives. Different situations

will, of course, require different approaches. Observation suggests, however, that there are two important procedural steps courts should consider when formulating remedies. One is to involve all the parties in remedy development. The other is to obtain by the appointment of a special master a neutral source of expert information and a knowledgeable delegate who will push for a prompt and adequate remedial decree.

78 Colum. L. Rev. at 812–13.

The Columbia Special Project strongly advocated the use of a special master (see F.R.Civ.P. 53, Appendix at pp. 979–981) to aid the court in the formulation of an injunction (or decree) in complex cases. Special masters have undertaken the task in many cases, and have taken on many different roles. For a review of the roles played by masters in several different school desegregation cases, see, e.g., David L. Kirp & Gary Babcock, Judge and Company: Court–Appointed Masters, School Desegregation, and Institutional Reform, 32 Ala.L.Rev. 313 (1981). Rule 53 was revised in 2003, in part to recognize expressly and regulate such appointments. See Advisory Committee Notes to F.R.Civ.P. 53, 215 F.R.D. 158, 197–200 (2003). The court has to be careful, however, not to abdicate too much authority to an appointed special master. For example, in the Microsoft antitrust case, the Court of Appeals reversed the nonconsensual appointment of a special master where "the parties' rights must be determined, not merely enforced." United States v. Microsoft Corp., 147 F.3d 935, 954 (D.C.Cir.1998).

5. Should nonparties and members of the public have an opportunity to comment on proposed decrees that may affect them? See, e.g., Tunney Act, 15 U.S.C. § 16(b)(1981); and Consent Judgments in Actions to Enjoin Discharges of Pollutants, 28 C.F.R. § 50.7(b) (requiring, respectively, time for public comment on antitrust and pollution discharge consent decrees). Cf. F.R.Civ.P. 23(e) (class action may not be dismissed or compromised without prior notification of the class members and court approval).

Should there be any limits to such participation? In Bustop v. Superior Court, 69 Cal.App.3d 66, 137 Cal.Rptr. 793 (1977), the trial court was ordered to permit a citizen's group to intervene in the remedial phase of the Los Angeles school desegregation suit, after the California Supreme Court had affirmed that the school board had engaged in unlawful segregation. Both the African–American plaintiffs and the defendant school board opposed the intervention of Bustop, whose "prime objective [was] the prevention of mandatory reassignment of students to schools other than those which they now attend or choose to attend." Id. at 69. After *Bustop* was decided, the trial judge permitted intervention by yet another citizen's group, BEST (Better Education for Students Today). BEST "frankly disavowed any knowledge of or position toward *any* integration plan, but asserted that its members were well-intentioned citizens who would certainly have developed positions on the issues by the time they got to court." Stephen C. Yeazell, Intervention and the Idea of Litigation: A Commentary on the Los Angeles School Case, 25 U.C.L.A.L.Rev. 244, 259 (1977). However, if nonparties are not formally bound by the terms of the injunction, see Martin v. Wilks, 490 U.S. 755, 109 S.Ct. 2180, 104 L.Ed.2d 835 (1989), casebook at p. 361, why should they have any role in the process?

6. How active a role may the judge play? In United States v. Microsoft Corp., 56 F.3d 1448 (D.C.Cir.1995), the court of appeals found that the district court had exceeded its authority under the Tunney Act in refusing to enter a proposed antitrust consent decree the Department of Justice had negotiated with the computer software behemoth. The district court concluded that the decree was not in the public interest because the decree did not address certain anticompetitive practices beyond those violations alleged in the original complaint. (The judge happened to have read a book putting Microsoft's practices in a very unfavorable light.) The court of appeals saw the district court as usurping the role of the Attorney General rather than reviewing the decree itself. The appellate court even took the rare step of ordering the case remanded to a different judge, who then approved the settlement. 1995–2 Trade Cases ¶ 71,096 (D.D.C.1995). See Symposium, Pyrrhic Victories? Reexamining the Effectiveness of Antitrust Remedies in Restoring Competition and Deterring Misconduct, 69 Geo.Wash.L.Rev. 693 (2001); Lloyd C. Anderson, United States v. Microsoft, Antitrust Consent Decrees, and the Need for a Proper Scope of Judicial Review, 65 Antitrust L.J. 1 (1996).

2. ADMINISTERING THE INJUNCTION

PROBLEM: COUNTRY LODGE V. MILLER (REPRISED)
DETERMINING COMPLIANCE WITH AN INJUNCTION

Suppose that the court prohibits Miller from dumping more than 500 pounds of apple mash waste into the river every week. In the alternative, suppose that the court permits Miller to dump apple mash into the river so long as it is not visible from the Country Lodge property. How can the court determine whether Miller is in compliance with either of these injunctions?

With the average "plain vanilla" injunction, it is the plaintiff's responsibility to monitor the defendant's compliance with the terms of the injunction. If the plaintiff detects a violation, she should file for an Order to Show Cause with the court—an order directing the defendant to show cause why he should not be held in contempt of court for violating the injunction. In most cases, this monitoring system works reasonably well. It does not work so well whenever it is difficult to determine whether the defendant—be it a public entity or private corporation—is in compliance with the injunction. Other than relying entirely upon the defendant's good faith, the court needs some mechanism to help it determine whether its orders are being obeyed.

It is usually impractical for the injunction to describe precisely all that must happen to cure the violation. All of the activities of a major government department or enterprise cannot be described in any one document. Moreover, the method of administering the injunction cannot simply funnel all the conceivably relevant bits of information to the court nor should it be permitted to consume overwhelming amounts of time of the parties and counsel. If it does, the substantive progress that the court intends to achieve through the injunction will be thwarted. However, the injunction must be clear enough so that it is evident when the defendants violate its terms. Thus, the court must simultaneously avoid the twin evils of issuing an injunction that is so open ended that it is nothing more than aspirational platitudes on the one hand and so detailed as to tie everyone up in nothing but counterproductive paper work on the other. See Michael G. Starr, Accommodation and Accountability: A Strategy for Judicial Enforcement of Institutional Reform Decrees, 32 Ala.L.Rev. 399 (1981). As the next reading indicates, an injunction must be specific for other reasons as well.

JAMES A. HENDERSON, JR. & RICHARD A. PEARSON, IMPLEMENTING FEDERAL ENVIRONMENTAL POLICIES: THE LIMITS OF ASPIRATIONAL COMMANDS

78 Colum.L.Rev. 1429, 1430–36 (1978)

"Aspiration," as that concept will be employed in the following analysis, refers to the state of mind with which an actor performs a task. An actor performs "aspirationally" when he aims at accomplishing as best he can the task's underlying objectives as he perceives them. Since the objectives of many tasks are generally understood to carry limitations upon the commitment of resources, the phrase "as best he can" does not require a single-minded, "drop everything else" approach to performing the task. Instead, aspiration requires that, within these limitations, an actor will perform to the best of his ability. Nor need the task be described explicitly in aspirational terms to be aspirational. "Do your best" may accompany a request that an actor perform a given task; but even without such words the actor will be aware of the general nature of the task's purpose and will understand that he is to act in a way to achieve that purpose. * * *

A. Aspirational Commands and the Legal System

From the very beginnings of our jurisprudence, common-law judges recognized that only essentially nonaspirational patterns of conduct may effectively be compelled by threats of legal sanctions. Thus, criminal law has traditionally consisted almost entirely of commands which are negative, specific, and nonaspirational. Tort law, although vaguer in some respects, is also predominantly negative and nonaspirational. Courts have generally refused to rely upon affirmative, aspirational commands even when they are confronted with specific contexts in which such commands might have appeared to be especially desirable—where, for example, a helpless person could be rescued by the active intervention of another. This same reluctance is reflected in the traditional refusal of courts to order specific performance of personal service contracts, and in the concern in administrative law with constraining, rather than compelling, the exercise of administrative discretion. It is no less clearly reflected in the restraint with which federal lawmakers in the American system have approached the delicate task of attempting to direct the conduct of the states.

This does not mean that the American legal system is indifferent to the importance to society of aspirational conduct. However, it operates to encourage such conduct indirectly, rather than to compel it directly. The major legal institutions which the American system has traditionally relied upon to maintain sufficient levels of individual incentive have been property and contract. Together, they provide the basic common-law framework for an economic marketplace in which decisions affecting resource allocations are made by means of contract bargaining. Bargaining is a voluntary process in which each participant seeks to maximize the benefits to himself which flow from exchange transactions. The benefits which a participant derives from this process are then generally protected by the law of property. As a result, individuals are encouraged to use best efforts in their own self-interest. * * *

Nevertheless, there have been times when lawmakers have overcome their traditional reluctance to rely upon aspirational commands. * * *

B. THE DIFFICULTY OF ENFORCING ASPIRATIONAL COMMANDS

It is important to distinguish the difficulties inherent in the enforcement of aspirational commands from the problems involved in the enforcement of law generally. Even nonaspirational commands will be difficult to enforce if the resources devoted to law enforcement are inadequate to the task, or if there is a general disrespect for the source of the law. Aspirational commands present problems of a different order, however. These difficulties stem from the divergence of values between addressor and addressee, a condition which is likely to occur when a lawmaker relies upon threats of sanctions. Thus, when the addressee of an aspirational command is indifferent to, or hostile toward, the values and objectives reflected in an assigned task, aspiration of the sort desired by the addressor will typically be absent. Instead of seeking to maximize the accomplishment of the addressor's values, such an addressee may be expected to respond by either secretly resolving not to aspire in the performance of the task, masking his unwillingness with feigned sincerity, or by honestly misperceiving the addressor's objectives, which typically will only be vaguely described in an aspirational command, and consequently aspiring to perform in a manner which is only marginally useful to the addressor. Indeed, these responses have been characteristic of the experience in civil rights cases.

It must be emphasized that the addressor's problems are not ameliorated by threats of sanctions. The addressor cannot determine, with sufficient accuracy to support a consistent application of sanctions, whether the addressee has secretly refused to aspire. Furthermore, he cannot reduce the risk of the addressee's misinterpretation of his intent because generally he must keep his instructions vague if he is to leave the addressee free to aspire. Of course, both risks could be reduced by telling the addressee specifically what to do. If the addressor could have been specific, however, there would have been no need to rely upon an aspirational command. Thus, there are two basic and unavoidable problems with employing sanction-backed aspirational commands. These are, first, the problem of nonverifiability, inhering in the addressor's inability to determine whether the addressee has actually aspired in performing an assigned task; and second, the problem of vagueness, inhering in the characteristic openendedness of aspirational commands.

1. *Nonverifiability.* The problem of nonverifiability in connection with legal commands to aspire is especially acute because it threatens one of the conditions necessary to the efficacy of a system of sanction-backed legal commands—the requirement that sanctions generally be imposed in response, and only in response, to nonconforming behavior. To be sure, the addressor will be able to detect egregious instances of noncooperation—open defiance by the addressee, for example, will not pass unnoticed. However, there will usually be a range of responses available to the addressee that fall short of obvious bad faith, but that also fall considerably short of aspiration. Even assuming that the sanction is sufficient to discourage obvious bad faith responses, the addressor of a command to aspire will nevertheless be unable generally to determine whether the addressee has responded aspirationally. In a substantial majority of instances, the addressee will plausibly be able to assert that he has done his best under the circumstances, and the addressor will be unable to establish the contrary. * * *

2. *Vagueness.* The nonverifiability problem is starkest in the relatively rare instance in which there is a direct command to aspire in the performance of a simple and concretely defined task. In connection with most aspirational commands, however, the addressor will be unable to describe the task specifically, and accordingly will deliberately allow the addressee substantial discretion in the choice of how to perform. Although the problem of nonverifiability will still be present in such circumstances, vagueness adds another dimension to the addressor's problems in relying upon aspirational commands. In exercising his discretion in choosing among the alternative methods of performance, the addressee will tend to select alternatives consistent with his own values. It follows that in ways important to the addressor, the objectives sought by him will not be accomplished. This will generally occur even though the addressee honestly maintains that he is aspiring in the performance of the assigned task. The addressee may make a conscious effort to substitute the addressor's values for his own, but the more complicated the task to which he is assigned, the less likely he is to succeed with such a substitution, and the less likely it is that the performance will meet the addressor's own objectives. Nevertheless, in these circumstances the addressor could not fairly impose a sanction, although the addressee's performance departs substantially from what the addressor desired. * * *

Notes

1. Imagine that a state agency was not enforcing its own regulations in a complex area such as pollution of underground water sources. How would you draft an unvague injunction to require enforcement of the state regulations? That is not overbroad? That is neither vague nor overbroad?

2. *The prevalence of the problem.* The problem of enforcing injunctions that cannot be implemented easily without the good faith efforts of the defendant is widespread. Suppose for example that a statute requires an administrative agency to promulgate pollution control regulations for a given industry, taking into account both the pollution's consequences to health and the economic cost of its abatement. Assume that in litigation it is proved that in promulgating the regulation the agency studied only the feasibility of pollution control and not the health consequences of the pollution and the court held that as a result, the agency has violated the statute and ordered it to reconsider the regulations. Suppose that on remand to the agency for reconsideration (the customary initial remedy) the agency issued exactly the same standards as before, stating that this time the standards were based on considerations of both health *and* economics. The agency may in fact have taken account of the health consequences or it may have only gone through the motions. The court will have trouble verifying the agency's claim that it has complied with its order.

This problem is by no means limited to environmental law but rather is endemic to judicial review of administrative agencies of all sorts. Statutes that empower agencies typically demand action in light of multiple and conflicting goals. Should the agency be caught failing to consider one of these goals or in considering an illegitimate goal, it is often easy for the agency on remand to repeat its violation while feigning compliance.

The requirement under the National Labor Relations Act that employers and unions bargain in good faith, 29 U.S.C. § 158(d), is another area where this problem is encountered. Should an employer illegally refuse to bargain, the usual remedy is an order requiring the employer to bargain. This does not mean that the employer must accede to the union's position, only that the two sides attempt in good faith to reach an agreement. The employer can often feign bargaining by making offers that it believes the union will reject.

3. *One way to deal with the problem: prophylactic orders.* One way of dealing with the problem of injunctions that require good faith performance is to order the defendant to do something that cannot be feigned, even if it would put the plaintiff in something more than the rightful position. For instance, when the EPA failed for four years to meet its statutory obligation to consider a state-proposed revision of a Clean Air regulation, the court barred the agency from collecting fines for noncompliance with the existing regulation until the agency responded to the proposal. American Cyanamid v. EPA, 810 F.2d 493 (5th Cir.1987). However, the Supreme Court later rejected this approach, but only because it had not been authorized in the legislation. General Motors Corp. v. United States, 496 U.S. 530, 110 S.Ct. 2528, 110 L.Ed.2d 480 (1990). In effect, the Supreme Court concluded that the prophy-

lactic approach clashed with congressional policy goals under the particular statute in question. In other contexts, it may be possible to use a prophylactic order. See generally Tracy A. Thomas, The Prophylactic Remedy: Normative Principles and Definitional Parameters of Broad Injunctive Relief, 52 Buff. L.Rev. 301 (2004).

Given the practical and legal limitations on "overbroad" injunctions discussed supra, courts often are forced to address the problem of administering injunctions using other techniques, as the following materials illustrate.

SPECIAL PROJECT—THE REMEDIAL PROCESS IN INSTITUTIONAL REFORM LITIGATION
78 Colum.L.Rev. 784, 821–836 (1978)

Implementation of the decree involves more than judicial retention of jurisdiction and the revision of the substantive aspects of the decree that retention of jurisdiction makes possible. Additionally, there remain problems of resolving disputes, monitoring compliance, and supervising the defendant's actions. The court's response to these problems requires the choice, and sometimes the modification, of a technique of administration. Retention of jurisdiction acknowledges the necessity for judicial involvement during implementation of the remedy but does not in itself constitute a choice of administrative technique.

A wide variety of techniques are available. Traditionally, administration is party oriented, depending on adversarial interplay. However, some judges supplement this by court oriented administration, in which the court acts on its own initiative. A court acting in this latter mode may delegate to court-appointed officers some or most of the necessary functions of administration. The available techniques of judicial administration fall along a continuum between party oriented and court oriented views of implementation. * * *

1. *Party–Centered Administration.* When courts rely on the parties, implementation occurs in the traditional adversarial mode. The court assumes a passive role, playing no part in implementation unless solicited by one of the parties. This judicial passivity places a considerable burden on the plaintiff, particularly when relief is gradual or implementation is drawn out. Overseeing implementation requires a cohesive plaintiff with considerable resources, and courts sometimes act to strengthen a weak plaintiff. As a variant of this practice, with a similar effect, courts sometimes request the participation of the United States as amicus curiae.

The common requirement that the defendant submit compliance reports eases the plaintiff's burden only slightly. Since defendants are unlikely to report noncompliance frankly, the plaintiff's monitoring task remains both crucial and burdensome.

* * *

2. *Administrative Techniques with Reduced Reliance on Parties.*

* * *

a. *Direct Judicial Initiative as an Administrative Technique.* When courts give themselves a supervisory role, in which they will act without further stimulus by the parties, they have taken a step beyond their traditional passivity. On their own initiative, courts frequently set hearing dates to consider compliance reports and take any necessary action. In addition, a vigorous judge may resort to various informal methods to further implementation.

Yet such court-ordered hearings, once begun, will remain adversarial in nature, with the customary reliance on the parties, and active judicial involvement in remedy administration will be constrained by the limited expertise and time of federal judges. Direct judicial initiative can only provide a limited supplement to party-centered administration. When the latter proves inadequate, the court must often not merely assume a more active role in implementation but also delegate administrative functions to an individual or group whose duties are primarily to the court, rather than to the parties.

b. *Use of Court Appointed Agents to Administer the Remedy.* These court appointed agents are identified by a confusing plethora of titles.

* * *

In this discussion, the terms used by the courts will be replaced by terms based on the officer's principal function. The terms that will be used are master, monitor, mediator, administrator, and receiver. This function-based vocabulary provides a consistent basis for discussing the various court-appointed agents.

Masters. The master's role is to gather information and make recommendations. He reports to the court and, if required, makes findings of facts and conclusions of law. In the remedial phase of litigation, the master's principal role is to assist the court in formulating the substantive remedy, rather than in implementing it. However, masters sometimes continue to participate in the litigation, assuming implementation functions without change of title. Furthermore, because the remedy formulation and implementation phases of the lawsuit are often simultaneous, an administrator with extensive supervisory power over the defendant's activities may at the same time act as a master and be charged with developing a further plan.

Monitors. The monitor's role is to report on the defendant's compliance with the decree and on the achievement of the decree's goals. * * *

Monitors are appropriate if the remedy is complex, if compliance is difficult to measure, or if observation of the defendant's conduct is restricted. If the remedy is complex or covers many institutions, measuring compliance may be a task beyond the plaintiff's resources. If standards of compliance are not evident from the decree, a monitor can help formulate them. When the defendant is a closed institution, such as a prison or mental hospital, observing compliance may be difficult, and then monitors will be appropriate. * * *

Mediators. While the monitor's task is only to measure compliance, other court appointees play a more direct role in implementation. A mediator is a delegate whose primary responsibility is handling disputes over the decree's meaning, compliance standards, and the pace of compliance. In addition, a mediator must resolve individual grievances that arise during the remedial regime. Although retention of jurisdiction facilitates bringing such problems into court, doing so is time consuming, expensive, and strains judicial resources, even if the judicial role is informal and the procedural safeguards of a full dress evidentiary hearing are not invoked. * * *

Administrators. The administrator is the most innovative and unusual of the devices utilized by the courts for remedy implementation. The administrator's role extends beyond that of the master, monitor, or mediator but, unlike a receiver, the administrator supplements, and does not replace, the normal management of the institutional defendant. The administrator acts at his own instance to implement the remedy and has an executive role.

The authority to appoint an administrator is best grounded in the inherent power of courts "to provide themselves with appropriate instruments required for the performance of their duties" and the Supreme Court's directive that the courts make full use of their equitable powers in civil rights cases.* * *

Appointment of an administrator is most appropriate if implementation is complex and difficult to supervise. In title VII pattern and practice suits, for instance, compliance requires nondiscriminatory handling of hundreds or thousands of individual cases, a task that no judge can supervise. The complex actions required to implement comprehensive prison and mental hospital decrees are also appropriate occasions for the appointment of an administrator. An administrator may also be called for as a reaction to noncompliance with the court's orders.

The reluctance of the courts to use administrators in areas where they would be effective is probably due to considerations of equity and federalism, as the appointment of an administrator is an intrusive technique of remedy implementation. * * *

An administrator's powers normally include monitoring and mediation, but are more extensive. The variety of its functions is often obscured by the variety in terminology used, the variety of tasks a single agency sometimes performs, and the casualness with which the reported opinions describe these tasks. However, the administrator normally is given powers to supervise, coordinate, approve, or even command actions of the defendant to implement the remedy. This involves a substantial delegation of power, either with consent of the parties or imposed by the court.

The scope of this delegation varies. Some administrators are given very specific tasks, while others are granted broad and undefined power to secure implementation. * * *

Receivers. While an administrator's power derogates from the authority of the defendant's officers, these officers retain their posts. Administrators, like masters, monitors, and mediators, can only be effective if some cooperation is forthcoming from the defendant. When this is not forthcoming, a receivership may be appropriate. In a receivership, a court-appointed officer replaces the defendant's officers either completely or temporarily and for limited purposes. Imposition of a receivership is consequently a more drastic means of implementation than the appointment of an administrator or any lesser administrative agent. It is the most dramatic assertion of federal equitable power possible and courts have so regarded it. Obviously, removing state political officials from authority is more drastic than merely forcing them to act constitutionally. Receivership remains a device of last resort, used only when less intrusive devices have failed to achieve compliance, although the traditional strict restrictions on its use have been shed.

* * *

Notes

1. For a time, there was some doubt whether courts had the authority to appoint agents to oversee the implementation of judicial injunctions. See David I. Levine, The Authority for the Appointment of Remedial Special Masters in Federal Institutional Reform Litigation: The History Reconsidered, 17 U.C.Davis L.Rev. 753 (1984); Vincent M. Nathan, The Use of Masters in Institutional Reform Litigation, 10 U.Tol.L.Rev. 419 (1979)(for different reasons, both articles contended that despite the doubts expressed about the then-fairly narrow language of F.R.Civ.P. 53, there was sufficient authority to make such appointments). In 2003, F.R.Civ.P. 53 was revised to expressly authorize judicial appointment of special masters to handle post-trial matters. See F.R.Civ.P. 53(a)(1)(C), Appendix at p. 979; Advisory Committee Notes to F.R.Civ.P. 53, 215 F.R.D. 158, 197–200 (2003). As an alternative approach to the use of *ad hoc* agents, Joanna Kudisch Weinberg, The Judicial Adjunct and Public Law Remedies, 1 Yale L. & Pol'y Rev. 367 (1983), suggests that courts set up permanent offices of judicial adjuncts to handle such assignments. See also T. Willging et al., Special Masters' Incidence and Activity (Federal Judicial Center 2000).

2. For a discussion of the payment of special masters and other court appointed agents, see David I. Levine, Calculating Fees of Special Masters, 37 Hastings L.J. 141 (1985). No governmental entity—even the United States—is immune from paying for the cost of a remedial special master, as it is part of the costs of the litigation. See F.R.Civ.P. 53(g); Commodity Futures Trading Commission v. Frankwell Bullion Ltd., 99 F.3d 299 (9th Cir.1996) (costs of master or receiver may be assessed against United States).

3. As the Special Project mentions, another equitable tool, receivership, is available if the conditions precedent are established. Most commonly, a court will appoint a receiver to manage the defendant's property (such as a business in economic distress) on a temporary basis only if there is a danger that the defendant is or will become insolvent or the property at issue will be removed from the jurisdiction of the court, injured or destroyed before the merits of the dispute are decided. F.R.Civ.P. 66 (Appendix at p. 988); 12 Charles Alan Wright, Arthur R. Miller & Richard L. Marcus, Federal Practice and Procedure 2d: Civil §§ 2981–86 (1997). Sometimes, courts have used receivers to enforce compliance with the law. E.g., United States v. American Tobacco Co., 221 U.S. 106, 31 S.Ct. 632, 55 L.Ed. 663 (1911)(indicating that receiver might take charge of a company to enforce compliance with antitrust laws); United States v. Sasso, 215 F.3d 283 (2d Cir.2000) (noting use of monitors and trustees to eliminate corruption in labor unions); Plata v. Schwarzenegger, 2005 WL 2932253 (N.D.Cal.2005) (appointing receiver to take control of the delivery of medical services to all prisoners confined by the state). See generally Carolyn Hoecker Luedtke, Innovation or Illegitimacy: Remedial Receivership in Tinsley v. Kemp Public Housing Litigation, 65 Mo.L.Rev. 655 (2000); Comment, The Case for Imposing Equitable Receiverships Upon Recalcitrant Polluters, 12 U.C.L.A.J. Envt'l L. & Pol'y 207 (1993) (reviewing traditional and modern uses of receivers).

4. An injunction might specify only the goals which the defendants must achieve (e.g., provide only so many square feet per prisoner) or it may go on to indicate the milestones according to which progress toward the goals shall proceed (e.g., the defendant must commence building a new prison facility by a certain date and complete the construction by another date). Although milestones do make the injunction somewhat more complicated to write, if the defendants are dilatory, they will be in violation of the court's order at a much earlier stage. This may open the way for increased judicial intervention, in particular under F.R.Civ.P. 70 (Appendix at p. 990). See Hansford v. Maplewood Station Business Park, 621 N.E.2d 347 (Ind.App.1993)(applying Indiana's version of Rule 70); David I. Levine, The Authority for the Appointment of Remedial Special Masters in Federal Institutional Reform Litigation: The History Reconsidered, 17 U.C. Davis L.Rev. 753, 796–98 (1984)(discussing application of Rule 70)(both compare appointment under Rule 70 with use of master under Rule 53).

The following is not a written opinion but a transcript of some candid remarks from the bench. The statute in question, designed to curb the dumping of toxic wastes, imposed an absolute duty upon the Environmental Protection Agency.

ILLINOIS v. COSTLE

United States District Court for the District of Columbia, 1979
12 Env't Rep.Cas. (B.N.A.) 1597

GESSELL, DISTRICT JUDGE.

As I indicated after the discussion and argument yesterday, in view of the urgency of this matter, the Court is going today to give its ruling orally. * * *

These four proceedings are proceedings to enforce the Resource Conservation and Recovery Act of 1976, 42 U.S.C. § 9601.

The Court has previously found that the Environmental Protection Agency is in default of deadlines which were set by the Congress for the promulgation of various regulations implementing the provisions of the Act relating to hazardous and solid wastes. * * *

Plaintiffs in various forms and manner ask the Court now to establish a specific schedule for the promulgation of some ten regulations which are necessary to implement the provisions of the Act the Court has just referred to.

In response to the Court's request, EPA has submitted a proposed schedule which has been the focus of these decree proceedings.

There is no question that EPA has a duty to promulgate hazardous and solid waste regulations; and I think there is agreement that duty is to promulgate those regulations as quickly as reasonably possible.

The proposed schedule which EPA has submitted is challenged; and it is for the Court to determine whether that schedule or some other schedule is more appropriate.

Of course, the Court cannot appropriate funds; it cannot let out consulting contracts to develop the necessary technical information; it cannot hire personnel; and it cannot manage the agency's effort.

The most the Court can do is to use its influence to assure that everything reasonable is being done to carry out the obvious desire of Congress that there be prompt action to abate the hazards to our environment which the Act addresses. * * *

The agency, itself, recognizes that the estimates are nothing more than estimates; that they are subject to change; and that they are optimistic. * * *

All of the past experience indicates that it is difficult and hazardous to attempt to estimate the time required in meeting these more or less arbitrary deadlines which Congress has set in various EPA matters.

The Court cannot and should not ignore the fact that not only does EPA have other responsibilities in the regulatory area, but that it is presently under very exacting demands in other proceedings to accomplish its regulatory functions.

The Court, accordingly, has determined that it must for the time being accept the position of the agency with respect to the schedule. It appears to the Court that it is a good faith schedule which on the basis of present knowledge is in the public interest.

On the other hand, the Court has taken note and accepted the view of the Environmental Defense Fund and other Plaintiffs here that if a definite schedule is ordered by the Court, it is more likely in some vague and undefinable way that schedule will be achieved. * * *

With these considerations in mind, the Court has fashioned an order directing that the regulations be promulgated on the final dates set in the schedule submitted to the Court. The order goes further and requires that EPA shall, at the end of each quarter, commencing March 31, 1979, file with the Court in affidavit form over the signature of Mr. Costle [the EPA Administrator] a statement indicating any departures from the detailed implementing schedules that the EPA proposed on December 4, with a statement of reason or reasons therefor, together with an updated current estimate of the final promulgation date of each regulation.

The Court is also directing that whenever it appears to EPA that a date set by the Court as the outside date for promulgation of these regulations cannot be met, it shall immediately—and I emphasize, immediately—file an affidavit with the Court over the signature of the Administrator, explaining the facts and circumstances why it does not appear feasible to meet the date as ordered.

The Court is also directing that all of these filings not only, of course, be served on the parties but is directing that copies of the filings be furnished to the appropriate Oversight Committees of the Senate and the House of Representatives. * * *

Now, all of you, I think, are aware of the Court's concerns in this case but I don't want to terminate these proceedings without making it perfectly clear that in acceding to this schedule temporarily, as the Court has done, the Court is not in any respect discounting the position of the Plaintiffs, particularly of the Environmental Defense Fund, that this is a matter that can properly be labeled one approaching crisis proportions.

Well-meaning statutes are not self-implementing. We need a national will to protect the environment from the threatening health and pollution hazards which this Act addresses. There is need of a massive commitment of funds, talent and purpose to these objectives.

If the Court could do anything about it, the Court would; but these are not matters within the reach of the chancellor's foot. There is little a court of equity can do.

These are matters of national policy, political priorities; and I would urge upon the parties with everything at my command that they consider the appropriateness of continuing to rely on courts to accomplish objectives which can only be effectively accomplished in a democracy by resort to the polls, resort to the political processes which the Constitution preserves.

There is little I can do. I have done the most I can. But there are other forums where these issues could be far more properly and effectively ventilated. * * *

I will await with interest the reports from the agency pursuant to the order which I am now handing to the Deputy Clerk. * * *

NOTES

1. The plaintiffs did not even challenge the EPA's good faith even though they would not have brought and continued the suit if they had confidence that the agency was doing the best that it could. Professors Henderson and Pearson, at pp. 221–223, showed the problem of proving bad faith. In a portion of their article not reproduced here, they argue that it is somewhat easier to show the absence of good faith when the defendant is a large organization since it is hard to pass the word through an organization to obstruct a court order without the word getting out. Yet, the word may be passed by innuendo and, besides, bureaucratic inertia alone is likely to sabotage a court order that requires action unless the leaders of the organization vigorously promote the action. The absence of good faith is particularly difficult to show when the defendant is a government agency or official because most standards for review of official action put a heavy burden on the plaintiff. For example, the Administrative Procedure Act states that a judge may not overturn administrative action merely because the judge sees it as wrong-headed; it must be so wrong-headed as to be "arbitrary or capricious." 5 U.S.C. § 706(2)(A).

2. Would an injunction that granted more than the rightful position or the appointment of a receiver have been viable approaches in *Illinois v. Costle*?

3. Judge Gessell says that he will deal with the problem of getting the agency to act by using the court's "influence." What are the obstacles to agency action? How does he use his influence to deal with them? What else could he have done? For a contrary example of a court going on to use perhaps too much "influence" on a governmental agency, see Heckler v. Day, 467 U.S. 104, 104 S.Ct. 2449, 81 L.Ed.2d 88 (1984) (finding district court's injunction ordering 90-day deadlines for processing Social Security disability claims an "unwarranted judicial intrusion into a pervasively regulated area" where Congress had declined to impose deadlines). Less relief than that ordered by Judge Gessell is more commonplace, where the court simply provides judicial oversight to the defendant agency's self-determined schedule. E.g., Telecommunications Research & Action Center v. Federal Communications Commission, 750 F.2d 70 (D.C.Cir.1984) (ordering FCC to inform the court of the dates it anticipates for resolution of the disputes and advise the court of its progress every 60 days). The court in *Telecommunications Research* acknowledged that mandamus would be an appropriate remedy for "egregious delay" by an agency, but refused to find the FCC's 5–year delay to

be egregious because of the agency's assurance that it was moving expeditiously on the claims.

4. Note that this suit could be brought because Congress had imposed a categorical mandate on the EPA, ostensibly depriving the agency of all discretion. Where Congress merely exhorts the agency to issue regulations "promptly," citizen's suits are not permitted. James R. May, Now More than Ever: Trends in Environmental Citizen Suits at 30, 10 Widener L. Rev. 1 (2003).

The following article discusses an example of a fairly successful judicial intervention. What factors led to this success?

MURRAY LEVINE, CHARLES P. EWING & DAVID I. LEVINE, THE USE OF LAW FOR PREVENTION IN THE PUBLIC INTEREST
5 Prevention in Human Services 241, 265–271 (1987)

* * *

WUORI V. ZITNAY: SUCCESSFUL IMPLEMENTATION OF A CONSENT DECREE

Wuori v. Zitnay (No. 75–80, D.Me.1975) is one of the most successful of the institutional reform cases. The case is unusual because the court gave up active supervision within a relatively few years. The defendants achieved substantial, if not full, compliance with an extensive consent decree which committed the state to improve an institution for the retarded and to create new community facilities as well.

The case was brought in 1975 by Neville Woodruff, an attorney who headed the Legal Services Corporation office in Portland, Maine. In the course of visiting the Pineland Center, an institution that at its peak had housed nearly 1500 mentally retarded individuals, Woodruff received information and documents from some employees who were frustrated by their inability to provide decent care. The institution was overcrowded and in poor condition. The residents had inadequate clothing. Their personal hygiene was poor. Residents were in restraints for unconscionable periods and were overmedicated. There was a lack of both programming and professional services. Dentists were pulling teeth from some residents to prevent self-abuse or harm to others. Moreover, many who had been released to the community as part of an earlier deinstitutionalization thrust were living in inadequate homes and were not receiving adequate habilitation services.

The suit, alleging violations of the Eighth Amendment right to be free of cruel and unusual punishment, or to be free from harm at the hands of the state, was brought in 1975 on behalf of a class of all residents in the institution and all residents who had been conditionally discharged but were still under the supervision of Pineland Center. Shortly after the suit was initiated, George Zitnay was hired by the state of Maine to become Director of Pineland Center. Zitnay, an experienced and gifted institutional administrator, immediately recognized the opportunity the suit presented to gain resources and leverage to improve Pineland. When he was deposed * * * he told the full truth about the institution. Zitnay's testimony, along with the plaintiffs' fully documented case, convinced the state that it could not win. Moreover, state officials would be subject to highly adverse publicity as long as the case was in court. The state agreed to settle out of court.

For the next two years, the plaintiffs' attorney negotiated with the state to develop a satisfactory plan for correcting deficiencies. Meanwhile, Zitnay was promoted from Superintendent of Pineland to State Commissioner of Mental Health and Corrections. The then Governor, the late James B. Longley, under whom Zitnay served, sincerely supported substantial improvement in the care of the mentally retarded. Zitnay was also very able in winning support from parents' groups as well as influential private citizens throughout the state of Maine. Despite such support, progress was slow in arriving at a satisfactory plan to remedy Pineland's deficiencies.

In 1978, the plaintiff's attorney called for assistance from the Mental Health Law Project, a Washington, D.C. public interest law firm with a great deal of experience in this type of litigation. The Mental Health Law Project assisted in developing an extensive, highly detailed plan for institutional reform covering both the Pineland Center and especially community residences and programs. The plan called for the appointment of a special master to oversee implementation. Zitnay and Kevin Concannon, then Director of the Bureau of Mental Retardation, recommended that the State of Maine accept the settlement, for both men understood it could be used as a blueprint and as leverage for modernizing and improving the entire system of care for the mentally retarded throughout Maine. The State's Attorney General, Joseph Brennan, who was later to succeed Longley as governor, accepted their recommendation.

Implementation Under a Special Master

In July, 1978, United States District Court Judge Edward T. Gignoux, a highly respected jurist, entered the consent decree, based on the plan developed by the parties with the assistance of the Mental Health Law Project, as the judgment of the court. After a search, the judge appointed David Gregory, a University of Maine law professor, as special master for a period of two years. The participants believed the decree would be fully implemented by that time.

The special master began with two assumptions. The first was that the state would not have agreed to anything it did not intend to do. The second was that the limit of what he had to know was what was in the court order. He believed at the time that the total job was one of looking at what the decree required, looking at what was going on in the institution, and then reporting on the differences. As he became aware of institutional dynamics and of the organizational and political complexities of introducing change in public agencies, he soon realized that both assumptions were incorrect.

After the first six months of educating himself about the problems of mental retardation, the culture of the institution, and interagency issues, Gregory took a more active role. He not only gathered information about the state of compliance with the decree, but he began educating the heads of other agencies as to how their actions were affecting implementation of the decree. In effect, he became an advocate for the decree. He worked closely with Zitnay, who was the named defendant, and with Concannon on the task of implementation. He came to understand that although Zitnay was commissioner, he had little direct control over Pineland Center itself and no power over state agencies on the same organizational level as his department (e.g., the state personnel department, the Commissioner of Finance, and the Commissioner of Human Services, basically responsible for Medicaid and other welfare programs). As a consequence of that decision, he tended to confront some department heads vigorously, strongly intimating that he expected their cooperation. For instance, he once had a difficult confrontation with Governor Brennan (Governor Longley's successor) who, as Attorney General, had consented to the decree. Governor Brennan objected strongly to the critical tone of Gregory's reports. Gregory also worked with operators of group homes around the state to encourage them to organize politically to obtain changes in state regulations that limited their ability to program effectively. That activity, too, led to friction between Gregory and some state officials.

During this period, Zitnay and Concannon worked through the state's governmental structure to gain resources to modernize services for the retarded. They kept Gregory fully informed about barriers to implementation and other institutional problems. Gregory conducted his own investigations as to the state of compliance with the decree. He continued to receive information from some employees about deficiencies in programming or about abuses. (Other employees viewed his activities less benignly.) His reports to the court depicted the shortcomings and remaining problems in the institutions. Zitnay and Concannon could make bold requests for resources to correct deficiencies and point to the special master's reports to bolster their requests. In effect, the "blame" for the necessary large budget increases and other legislative changes could be placed on the special master. * * *

As the two year period of court supervision ended, Gregory's reports were still highly critical of the limited progress. He recommended extending the period of the court's supervision until compliance had been achieved. The plaintiffs and defendants resumed negotiations arriving at a stipulation * * * as to what further needed to be done to satisfy the terms of the decree. The state defendants agreed to the continuation of the special master's office, but in view of the friction between Gregory and the defendants, they insisted that Gregory be replaced. The change may have been at the insistence of the Governor.

In retrospect, all parties agreed that Gregory had done a superb job as special master. Although some questioned whether his reports too greatly emphasized the negatives of the defendant's actions, all agreed that had he not adopted an aggressive stance, there would have been much less progress in implementing the decree. * * *

The Next Phase

The new master was Lincoln Clark, the head of the state court mediation service. An experienced executive and a highly skilled mediator, Clark was a close friend of Judge Gignoux. He knew the major figures in state government and in the legislature. All of the major actors agreed to his appointment. Judge Gignoux appointed Clark to replace Gregory.

With a new governor taking office, Zitnay resigned as commissioner, returned to Pineland Center as superintendent, and was replaced by Kevin Concannon. Clark decided to focus first on Pineland rather than the community facilities, because it had moved far along the road to compliance under Zitnay. The most difficult part of the task was to establish criteria for deciding when the defendant had finally brought Pineland into compliance with the consent decree. Issues such as the number of beds in a room were easy to decide. Issues such as "adequate programming" required a great deal of subjective judgment.

Clark held a great many negotiating sessions among Zitnay, Concannon, and the plaintiffs' attorneys to agree to standards for compliance. Once the parties agreed, Clark brought in an outside consultant to review Pineland against the standards that had been agreed to, and to offer an opinion as to whether its programs met the standards. On the basis of an extensive review, the consultant concluded that Pineland Center was in substantial compliance with the institutional provisions of the consent decree. Clark therefore recommended that Pineland be discharged from the court's active supervision. In September, 1981, Judge Gignoux formally discharged the center from the court's direct supervision through Clark's office. Although this was an important milestone, Clark still faced correcting the remaining deficiencies in the community based treatment system, such as substandard housing, poor programming, and an insufficient number of community residences. Concannon, as Director of the Bureau of Mental Retardation, and later as Commissioner, had made progress in opening new group homes. However, persons seeking to develop group homes were faced with conflicting regulations and fiscal controls that led to great delays in opening new facilities.

In a spirit of negotiation and cooperation, Clark and the plaintiff's attorneys were willing to accept as substantial compliance the establishment of organizational means of accomplishing solutions, even if the precise program for each class member had not yet been achieved. While Clark effectively employed the skills of a mediator, he was well aware that his effectiveness depended upon the coercive power of the court. Clark also used the threat of adverse publicity, as did Gregory before him, to move matters along when progress seemed to be blocked.

Clark's reports to the court assisted the defendants' attempts to augment their budgets. Clark mailed his reports to all of the state legislators, to state officials, and to advocacy organizations. He also spoke informally with the chairman of the health committee of the state legislature, a person he knew well. Commissioner Concannon worked skillfully with the legislature as well to gain new resources and other legislation to assist the development of programs in the community.

Two years after Judge Gignoux had discharged Pineland Center from the court's active supervision, Clark believed that sufficient progress had been made in implementing the community portion of the decree. In the summer of 1983, Clark contracted with outside consultants to determine whether the defendants' claims of progress were warranted. One consultant concluded that not all of the requirements of the consent decree had been met, but that enough had been put into place that the defendants would be able to come into full compliance. Another consultant studied the lives of those class members who left Pineland Center and were living in the community. On the basis of interviews with a randomly selected sample of clients and staff, she concluded that the living, working, and learning experiences of the class members substantially adhered to the standards involved in the two major themes of the consent decree—normalization and habilitation.

An obvious concern was whether the improvements and the progress would survive if the court were to give up jurisdiction and cease supervising the programs. Two methods were developed to continue to monitor the system. A Consumer Advisory Board, created earlier as part of the consent decree, was now given greater monitoring responsibilities. The Board began developing a network of "correspondents"—people to act as next friends to those who have no families or have been abandoned by their families and to help in monitoring conditions in the many group homes scattered throughout the state. The defendants also agreed to undertake an annual, independent and public review of compliance with standards for institutional and community care incorporated into the consent decree and to publish a plan to remedy any identified deficiencies.

Clark's report, finding compliance with the terms of the consent decree as interpreted through the various stipulations, was submitted to the court in October, 1983. Shortly afterwards Judge Gignoux accepted the findings, discharged the special master, and relinquished active supervision of the case. It was one of the first cases of its kind to come to this degree of successful completion. In August, 1985, M. Levine visited Pineland Center and conducted interviews with important participants. Maine has developed a very good system of care for class members and has improved the system of care for all. Undoubtedly, one could find gaps in the provision of care, and some problems are relatively intractable, but the worst abuses have certainly been curbed, and for most, humane care at the state of the art is being provided. The state continues to identify problems in the system of care, and officials are making efforts to plan for the future. The goal of prevention is being met. * * *

NOTES

1. What are the advantages and disadvantages of the roles played respectively by Professor Gregory and Mr. Clark in *Wuori*?

2. After a long period of quiescence, there was further litigation regarding the matters addressed in *Wuori*. In October 1991, the Consumer Advisory Board that had been established in the consent decree brought an action seeking enforcement of the rights established in the 1978 consent decree. The Board's primary concerns were that the defendants had stopped making appropriate annual assessments of the medical, educational and training needs of the Pineland Center residents and outpatients, that the defendants had failed to create sufficient new community placements for residents and that basic safety at Pineland had been neglected. After some skirmishing over whether Judge Gignoux (who died in the interim) had intended to terminate jurisdiction over the case by 1986, Consumer Advisory Board v. Glover, 989 F.2d 65 (1st Cir.1993)(no such intent expressed), the district court denied the defendants' motions to dissolve the injunction and terminate the decree, 151 F.R.D. 496 (D.Me.1993), and to dismiss the Board's complaint, 151 F.R.D. 490 (D.Me.1993). The case is still active. See, e.g., Consumer Advisory Board v. Harvey, 2008 WL 4594353 (D.Me.2008) (accepting report of special master detailing to what degree the defendants were or were not in compliance with consent decree regarding adult protective services).

3. For a more detailed description of the implementation of the injunction in *Wuori*, see Murray Levine, The Role of Special Master in Institutional Reform Litigation: A Case Study, 8 Law & Policy 275 (1986). For another example of successful implementation of a detailed decree, see Judy Scales–Trent, A Judge Shapes and Manages Institutional Reform: School Desegregation in Buffalo, 17 N.Y.U.Rev.L. & Soc. Change 119 (1989–90)(showing how district court skillfully used decree implementation process to turn the Buffalo, N.Y. public schools into a "national model of integration"). But for a considerably more skeptical analysis of the use of court-appointed monitors, see Cobell v. Norton, 334 F.3d 1128 (D.C.Cir.2003) (reversing appointment). On remand, a monitor was re-appointed, but in light of the guidance from the circuit court. Cobell v. Norton, 283 F.Supp.2d 66, 214–19 (D.D.C.2003).

One attorney with extensive experience litigating institutional reform cases has specified the elements he believes are needed for any effective compliance mechanism. Considering what we have examined so far in this course, what would constrain a judge from doing all that the author recommends?

MICHAEL S. LOTTMAN, ENFORCING JUDICIAL DECREES: NOW COMES THE HARD PART

Mental Disability L.Rep. 69, 74–75 (July–August 1976)

a. An effective compliance mechanism must be established, first of all, in the context of an order, based upon a factual record, which binds the necessary officials and fixes specific responsibility on one or more of such officials for implementation of particular standards or requirements.

b. The order should be as precise and quantitative as possible, and should set forth clearly measurable, objective standards (including deadlines), so that compliance can be monitored accurately and, as far as possible, by clerical or mechanical means.

c. The order should provide for financing of required staff, physical plant improvements, development of community facilities, and other such items, and fix the responsibility for obtaining the necessary funds on the proper defendants.

d. The court should retain jurisdiction over the action.

e. If reporting requirements are included, they should serve as a starting point for compliance activity, not as an exclusive fact-gathering device. The court order, or the monitoring body, should prescribe with great specificity the format, contents, and timing of any required reports, and should structure such reports to elicit factual information rather than opinions. The reporting document should be directly related to specific provisions of the order. If feasible, such reports should be required to be verified under oath or otherwise designated as admissible in evidence, without more, in any proceeding for enforcement or contempt.

f. The monitoring body, whatever its specific form, must be on the premises of the defendant institution or otherwise in contact with the defendants on a full-time, daily basis, and must have access to all relevant records or documents and to residents or patients, defendants' employees, and other persons affected by or involved in the implementation of the order. The monitoring body must be independent of the person or agency whose conduct it is monitoring, and must owe its first allegiance to the court.

g. The monitoring body must be provided with sufficient full-time staff to monitor the defendants' operations on a daily basis, develop required plans or reports, respond to inquiries and complaints, and carry out other functions as assigned by the court. The monitoring body must also have access to professional and legal experts, either on a full-time or consulting basis.

h. While enforcement of court orders should not be made to depend solely on the efforts of attorneys for the plaintiffs, no enforcement mechanism should operate so as to interfere in any way with such attorneys' continuing duty to represent their clients. Counsel for all parties should be served with copies of any communication between the monitoring body and the court.

i. To the extent possible, monitoring bodies should not also be charged with responsibility for developing the plans and designing the requirements whose implementation they must then oversee. This "legislative-executive" role mixture is likely to dilute the effectiveness of the monitoring body.

j. Monitoring bodies should be empowered to do more than merely mediate disputes or make reports to the court; they should, at least, have the authority to make recommendations in regard to implementation of the order which must be followed unless an objection thereto is upheld by the court. The order should spell out in detail the procedure to be followed when the monitoring body identifies a violation of the order or a related problem, and the procedure for making, objecting to, and enforcing the monitoring body's recommendations—in other words, an implementation structure. The monitoring body should be given the procedural and technical weapons necessary to enable it to investigate violations and formulate recommendations.

k. Finally, the court should make it clear from the start that noncompliance with its order will be dealt with by measures of whatever severity is necessary, up to and including proceedings for contempt of court. * * *

PROBLEMS

Which techniques should a court select to administer an injunction in a case where:

(a) a local government has violated emission limits for its incinerator and the plaintiff wants the government to install pollution control equipment?

(b) a large private corporation has engaged in employment discrimination?

(c) a federal agency has failed to provide a set of documents under the Freedom of Information Act?

3. ACCOMMODATING CHANGING CIRCUMSTANCES: INTERPRETATION AND MODIFICATION OF THE DECREE

As you probably learned in your first year of law school, there are sound policy reasons for valuing the finality of judgments. Thus, it is fairly difficult to modify a final judgment of a court. See F.R.Civ.P. 60(b) (relief may be granted only upon a showing of limited conditions, such as mistake or fraud, and generally only within a limited period of time, usually one year). Similarly, the doctrine of res judicata applies even where the law which a court relied upon to render the original judgment is later changed by a higher court. E.g., Federated Department Stores, Inc. v. Moitie, 452 U.S. 394, 101 S.Ct. 2424, 69 L.Ed.2d 103 (1981). The law also values finality in private negotiations. Thus, you probably read cases in contracts that required a party to continue to perform under long-term or indefinite contracts even though economic conditions had changed and the contract was no longer economically advantageous to one party. E.g., Parev Products v. I. Rokeach, 124 F.2d 147 (2d Cir.1941)(court refused to modify a 25–year contract after 15 years of performance). Tort law also has a strong element of finality. A judgment rendered in a tort case is designed to compensate for all injury—past, present and future. A later change of circumstance (for example, after judgment, the plaintiff actually lives longer than the life expectancy assumed at trial) is not permitted to be the basis for reopening the litigation or for a modification of the judgment to change the amount awarded originally at trial. See, e.g., Pretre v. United States, 531 F.Supp. 931 (E.D.Mo.1981). As the materials in this section demonstrate, however, at times the finality of an injunction (and its close cousin, the consent decree), has been treated somewhat differently.

TIMOTHY S. JOST, FROM *SWIFT* TO *STOTTS* AND BEYOND: MODIFICATION OF INJUNCTIONS IN THE FEDERAL COURTS

64 Tex.L.Rev. 1101 (1986)

* * * The injunction is peculiarly a prospective remedy; it is a prediction based on a prediction. It is based on a prediction that unless the court intervenes the obligor will continue to violate the rights of the beneficiary. It is also itself a prediction in that it projects the power of the court into the future, promising that violation of the terms of the injunction will elicit a punitive or coercive response from the court.

Several circumstances, however, impede the court's attempt at prophecy. First, a court can only predict the obligor's future conduct based on its understanding of the obligor's present and past conduct. Even this understanding is necessarily flawed. Limited access to information, which often can be improved only at a considerable cost, and the constraints of bounded rationality hamper the court. But when the court turns from its understanding of the past or present and attempts to envision the future, it encounters even more baffling perplexities. The parties act within a dynamic socioeconomic context in which their behavior and relationship are subject to constant change. The court's vision rapidly blurs as it attempts to peer into the mists of the future and discern evolving factual developments. Moreover, not even the legal context in which the court must operate is static—new statutes and regulations constantly emerge and judicial precedents are expanded, contracted, reinterpreted, and overruled. Yet, trial courts entering injunctions are, by and large, obligated to take as given the state of the law in effect at the time the decree is entered; they have little freedom to predict the future contours of the law.

Thus, the court's assumptions about the future almost inevitably fail as the law changes. Finally, in formulating its decree the court is trammeled by the mundane limitations of drafting and by its perception of the practical and political constraints that hedge its power.

Injunctions entered by consent create further complexities. The pervasive use of consent decrees to resolve contemporary equitable litigation is striking. From 1975 through 1981, over seventy percent of Justice Department Antitrust Division case terminations were by consent decree. The [Securities and Exchange Commission] resolves about ninety percent of its cases by consent. Even when the substantive issues in a case are fully litigated to judgment by the court, the remedial resolution frequently results from negotiations by the parties based on the court's substantive decision. Relatively few complex injunctions wholly lack an element of consent.

Consent decrees are not only judicial decrees, but also long-term contracts, the products of bargaining between the parties. This bargaining process could potentially improve the predictive power of the decree. The parties presumably have better access than the court to information about their futures, particularly about their future intentions, and can avail themselves of a greater array of tools for dealing with uncertainty. But insofar as the parties have unequal power in the bargaining process, unequal access to information, or incentives to place risks and burdens on persons not represented in the negotiations, a consent decree may turn out to be even less durable than a fully litigated order. Moreover, it may be in the immediate interest of parties seeking resolution of a conflict (or their attorneys) to incorporate into a consent decree intentional ambiguity and omission, hazarding future conflict to purchase present peace.

Because the injunction is necessarily a static * * * response to a dynamic evolving problem, over time it almost inevitably becomes less responsive to the problem it addresses. * * * The future tricks the court; the injunction, the court's now outdated prediction, plods off into irrelevancy, leaving the beneficiary bereft of protection or the obligor subject to oppression.

What can the court do to accommodate change? Explicit accommodation often may be unnecessary. As time goes on the parties may themselves adjust to the future without revision of the decree. * * * When, however, an injunction's prediction of the future and the unfolding future itself begin to diverge radically, the only solution is modification.

Motions for modification are nominally brought under Federal Rule of Civil Procedure 60(b)(5), which provides that "the court may relieve a party ... from a final judgment, order, or proceeding ... [if] a prior judgment upon which it is based has been reversed or otherwise vacated, or it is no longer equitable that the judgment should have prospective application." The rule, however, merely codifies preexisting law, recognizing the inherent power of a court sitting in equity to modify its decrees prospectively to achieve equality. * * *

NOTE ON INTERPRETATION AND MODIFICATION OF A DECREE

Sometimes the court can assist the parties and avoid modification by simply interpreting the injunction or consent decree. "To interpret is to explain and elucidate, not to add or subtract from the text." 2 Milton Handler, Twenty–Five Years of Antitrust 952 (1973). As the Supreme Court has explained:

> Consent decrees are entered into by parties to a case after careful negotiation has produced agreement on their precise terms. The parties waive their right to litigate the issues involved in the case and thus save themselves the time, expense, and inevitable risk of litigation. Naturally, the agreement reached normally embodies a compromise; in exchange for the saving of cost and elimination of risk, the parties each give up something they might have won had they proceeded with the litigation. Thus the decree itself cannot be said to have a purpose; rather the parties have purposes, generally opposed to each other, and the resultant decree embodies as much of those opposing purposes as the respective parties have the bargaining power and skill to achieve. For these reasons, the scope of a consent decree must be discerned within its four corners, and not by reference to what might satisfy the purposes of one of the parties to it.

United States v. Armour & Co., 402 U.S. 673, 681–82, 91 S.Ct. 1752, 1757, 29 L.Ed.2d 256 (1971). See also United States v. New Jersey, 194 F.3d 426, 430 (3d Cir.1999) ("focus remains on the contractual language itself, rather than on the parties' subjective understanding of the language").

If interpretation will not suffice and modification is necessary, how easy should it be to modify a permanent injunction or a consent decree? Should it matter if the plaintiff or the defendant seeks the modification? Should it matter if the decree was imposed by the court in the form of a permanent injunction after a full hearing on the merits or in the form of a consent decree entered after protracted settlement negotiations and agreement by all parties? See Reynolds v. Roberts, 251 F.3d 1350 (11th Cir.2001) (emphasizing need for all parties to agree before court may approve consent decree). Should the law's general interest in valuing finality overcome the desire to do equity? Does it matter if the context is the changing circumstances of public policy involved in a large-scale public law case?

The Supreme Court's apparent stated position for many years was that it should be difficult to obtain a modification. In United States v. Swift & Co., 286 U.S. 106, 52 S.Ct. 460, 76 L.Ed. 999 (1932), the Supreme Court reversed a lower court's modification of a consent decree entered over ten years earlier in an antitrust case against the five largest meat packers in the country. Although the trial court had the power to modify consent decrees because they were judicial acts, and not private contracts, Justice Cardozo's opinion seemed to demand that the power to modify was to be used rarely. "Nothing less than a clear showing of grievous wrong evoked by new and unforeseen conditions should lead us to change what was decreed after years of litigation with the consent of all concerned." 286 U.S. at 119, 52 S.Ct. at 464. In another famous phrase from the opinion, Justice Cardozo said that there should be no modification from changed conditions unless the original dangers that were the reason for the decree originally, "once substantial, have become attenuated to a shadow." Id. The meat packer decree was not finally dissolved until 1981. United States v. Swift & Co., 1982–1 Trade Cases (CCH) ¶ 64,464 (N.D.Ill.1981).

However, in 1968, the Court appeared to relax *Swift's* "grievous wrong" standard. In United States v. United Shoe Machinery Corp., 391 U.S. 244, 88 S.Ct. 1496, 20 L.Ed.2d 562 (1968), the trial court had entered a permanent injunction designed to restore competition to the market of the manufacture of shoe machinery. Several years later, the government petitioned the trial court for further relief on the grounds that the defendant continued to dominate the market. The district court refused to grant the requested relief on the strength of *Swift*. The Supreme Court reversed, holding that the "grievous wrong" standard applied only to modifications requested by defendants seeking to avoid the responsibilities imposed by an order.

The uncertainty of when to apply the rigid standard from *Swift* to modifications of injunctions and consent decrees and when a more flexible standard is appropriate has continued. See, e.g., Thomas M. Mengler, Consent Decree Paradigms: Models Without Meaning, 29 B.C.L.Rev. 291 (1988). The cases following the problems represent the Supreme Court's contemporary efforts to clarify the standards for interpretation and modification of decrees.

PROBLEMS

How should a court rule on the following petitions?

1. Employees at a state university seek to modify a consent decree provision, which placed a $6000 cap on legal expenses that the defendant university would pay for the prosecution of successful sex discrimination suits against it, after the plaintiff-employees find that they cannot retain counsel who are willing to accept cases for that fee alone. See Rajender v. University of Minnesota, 730 F.2d 1110 (8th Cir.1984). Should it matter if the $6000 figure was arrived at by hard bargaining? May the decree be modified because the average cost of legal services in the locality has gone up substantially since the decree was entered?

2. A consent decree, which reflected the then-effective labor statutes, enjoined a railroad and its unions from requiring that all employees be members of a union. One of the union defendants later seeks to modify the decree after Congress amended the law to permit all-union worksites in railroads. See System Federation No. 91 v. Wright, 364 U.S. 642, 81 S.Ct. 368, 5 L.Ed.2d 349 (1961). Should it matter that when it amended the law, Congress did not choose to ban rules prohibiting all-union worksites? Does it make a difference whether the original order was imposed by a consent decree or through an injunction after a trial on the merits?

3. A class of African–American plaintiffs seeks interpretation or modification of a consent decree creating an affirmative action plan for the hiring of firefighters in order to protect newly hired African–Americans from the

effects of layoffs caused by unexpectedly severe budgetary constraints. See the next case.

FIREFIGHTERS LOCAL UNION NO. 1784 v. STOTTS
Supreme Court of the United States, 1984
467 U.S. 561, 104 S.Ct. 2576, 81 L.Ed.2d 483

JUSTICE WHITE delivered the opinion of the Court.

Petitioners challenge the Court of Appeals' approval of an order enjoining the City of Memphis from following its seniority system in determining who must be laid off as a result of a budgetary shortfall. Respondents contend that the injunction was necessary to effectuate the terms of a Title VII consent decree in which the City agreed to undertake certain obligations in order to remedy past hiring and promotional practices. Because we conclude that the order cannot be justified, either as an effort to enforce the consent decree or as a valid modification, we reverse.

I

In 1977 respondent Carl Stotts, a black holding the position of fire-fighting captain in the Memphis, Tennessee, Fire Department, filed a class action complaint in the United States District Court for the Western District of Tennessee. The complaint charged that the Memphis Fire Department and certain city officials were engaged in a pattern or practice of making hiring and promotion decisions on the basis of race in violation of Title VII of the Civil Rights Act of 1964, 42 U.S.C. § 2000e *et seq.*, as well as 42 U.S.C. §§ 1981 and 1983. The District Court certified the case as a class action and consolidated it with an individual action subsequently filed by respondent Fred Jones, a black fire-fighting private in the Department, who claimed that he had been denied a promotion because of his race. Discovery proceeded, settlement negotiations ensued, and in due course, a consent decree was approved and entered by the District Court on April 25, 1980.

The stated purpose of the decree was to remedy the hiring and promotion practices "of the ... Department with respect to blacks." Accordingly, the City agreed to promote 13 named individuals and to provide backpay to 81 employees of the Fire Department. It also adopted the long-term goal of increasing the proportion of minority representation in each job classification in the Fire Department to approximately the proportion of blacks in the labor force in Shelby County, Tennessee. However, the City did not, by agreeing to the decree, admit "any violations of law, rule or regulation with respect to the allegations" in the complaint. The plaintiffs waived any further relief save to enforce the decree, and the District Court retained jurisdiction "for such further orders as may be necessary or appropriate to effectuate the purposes of this decree."

The long-term hiring goal outlined in the decree paralleled the provisions of a 1974 consent decree, which settled a case brought against the

City by the United States and which applied citywide. Like the 1974 decree, the 1980 decree also established an interim hiring goal of filling on an annual basis 50 percent of the job vacancies in the Department with qualified black applicants. The 1980 decree contained an additional goal with respect to promotions: the Department was to attempt to ensure that 20 percent of the promotions in each job classification be given to blacks. Neither decree contained provisions for layoffs or reductions in rank, and neither awarded any competitive seniority. The 1974 decree did require that for purposes of promotion, transfer, and assignment, seniority was to be computed "as the total seniority of that person with the City."

In early May, 1981, the City announced that projected budget deficits required a reduction of non-essential personnel throughout the City Government. Layoffs were to be based on the "last hired, first fired" rule under which city-wide seniority, determined by each employee's length of continuous service from the latest date of permanent employment, was the basis for deciding who would be laid off. If a senior employee's position were abolished or eliminated, the employee could "bump down" to a lower ranking position rather than be laid off. As the Court of Appeals later noted, this layoff policy was adopted pursuant to the seniority system "mentioned in the 1974 decree and . . . incorporated in the City's memorandum of understanding with the Union."

On May 4, at respondents' request, the District Court entered a temporary restraining order forbidding the layoff of any black employee. The Union, which previously had not been a party to either of these cases, was permitted to intervene. At the preliminary injunction hearing, it appeared that 55 then-filled positions in the Department were to be eliminated and that 39 of these positions were filled with employees having "bumping" rights. It was estimated that 40 least-senior employees in the fire-fighting bureau of the Department would be laid off and that of these 25 were white and 15 black. It also appeared that 56 percent of the employees hired in the Department since 1974 had been black and that the percentage of black employees had increased from approximately 3 or 4 percent in 1974 to 11½ percent in 1980.

On May 18, the District Court entered an order granting an injunction. The Court found that the consent decree "did not contemplate the method to be used for reduction in rank or lay-off," and that the layoff policy was in accordance with the City's seniority system and was not adopted with any intent to discriminate. Nonetheless, concluding that the proposed layoffs would have a racially discriminatory effect and that the seniority system was not a bona fide one, the District Court ordered that the City "not apply the seniority policy proposed insofar as it will decrease the percentage of black lieutenants, drivers, inspectors and privates that are presently employed. . . ." On June 23, the District Court broadened its order to include three additional classifications. A modified layoff plan, aimed at protecting black employees in the seven classifications so as to comply with the court's order, was presented and approved. Layoffs pursuant to the modified plan were then carried out. In certain instances, to comply with the injunction, non-minority employees with more seniority than minority employees were laid off or demoted in rank.² * * *

III

The issue at the heart of this case is whether the District Court exceeded its powers in entering an injunction requiring white employees to be laid off, when the otherwise applicable seniority system would have called for the layoff of black employees with less seniority. We are convinced that the Court of Appeals erred in resolving this issue and in affirming the District Court.

A

The Court of Appeals first held that the injunction did no more than enforce the terms of the consent decree. This specific-performance approach rests on the notion that because the City was under a general obligation to use its best efforts to increase the proportion of blacks on the force, it breached the decree by attempting to effectuate a layoff policy reducing the percentage of black employees in the Department even though such a policy was mandated by the seniority system adopted by the City and the Union. A variation of this argument is that since the decree permitted the District Court to enter any later orders that "may be necessary or appropriate to effectuate the purposes of this decree," the City had agreed in advance to an injunction against layoffs that would reduce the proportion of black employees. We are convinced, however, that both of these are improvident constructions of the consent decree.

It is to be recalled that the "scope of a consent decree must be discerned within its four corners, and not by reference to what might satisfy the purposes of one of the parties to it" or by what "might have been written had the plaintiff established his factual claims and legal theories in litigation." United States v. Armour & Co., 402 U.S. 673, 681–682, 91 S.Ct. 1752, 1757, 29 L.Ed.2d 256 (1971). Here, as the District Court recognized, there is no mention of layoffs or demotions within the four corners of the decree; nor is there any suggestion of an intention to depart from the existing seniority system or from the City's arrangements with the Union. We cannot believe that the parties to the decree thought that the City would simply disregard its arrangements with the Union and the seniority system it was then following. Had there been any intention to depart from the seniority plan in the event of layoffs or demotions, it is much more reasonable to believe that there would have been an express provision to that effect. This is particularly true since the decree stated that it was not "intended to conflict with any provisions" of the 1974 decree, and since the latter decree expressly anticipated that the City would recognize seniority. It is thus not surprising that when the City

---

2. The City ultimately laid off 24 privates, 3 of whom were black. Had the seniority system been followed, 6 blacks would have been among the 24 privates laid off. Thus, three white employees were laid off as a direct result of the District Court's order. The number of whites demoted as a result of the order is not clear from the record before us.

anticipated layoffs and demotions, it in the first instance faithfully followed its preexisting seniority system, plainly having no thought that it had already agreed to depart from it. It therefore cannot be said that the express terms of the decree contemplated that such an injunction would be entered.

The argument that the injunction was proper because it carried out the purposes of the decree is equally unconvincing. The decree announced that its purpose was "to remedy past hiring and promotion practices" of the Department, and to settle the dispute as to the "appropriate and valid procedures for hiring and promotion." The decree went on to provide the agreed-upon remedy, but as we have indicated, that remedy did not include the displacement of white employees with seniority over blacks. Furthermore, it is reasonable to believe that the "remedy", which it was the purpose of the decree to provide, would not exceed the bounds of the remedies that are appropriate under Title VII, at least absent some express provision to that effect. As our cases have made clear, however, and as will be reemphasized below, Title VII protects bona fide seniority systems, and it is inappropriate to deny an innocent employee the benefits of his seniority in order to provide a remedy in a pattern-or-practice suit such as this. We thus have no doubt that the City considered its system to be valid and that it had no intention of departing from it when it agreed to the 1980 decree.

Finally, it must be remembered that neither the Union nor the non minority employees were parties to the suit when the 1980 decree was entered. Hence the entry of that decree cannot be said to indicate any agreement by them to any of its terms. Absent the presence of the Union or the non-minority employees and an opportunity for them to agree or disagree with any provisions of the decree that might encroach on their rights, it seems highly unlikely that the City would purport to bargain away non-minority rights under the then-existing seniority system. We therefore conclude that the injunction does not merely enforce the agreement of the parties as reflected in the consent decree. If the injunction is to stand, it must be justified on some other basis.

B

The Court of Appeals held that even if the injunction is not viewed as compelling compliance with the terms of the decree, it was still properly entered because the District Court had inherent authority to modify the decree when an economic crisis unexpectedly required layoffs which, if carried out as the City proposed, would undermine the affirmative action outlined in the decree and impose an undue hardship on respondents. This was true, the court held, even though the modification conflicted with a bona fide seniority system adopted by the City. The Court of Appeals erred in reaching this conclusion.[9]

---

9. The dissent seems to suggest and Justice Stevens expressly states, that Title VII is irrelevant in determining whether the District Court acted properly in modifying the consent decree. However, this was Title VII litigation, and in affirming modifications of the decree, the

Section 703(h) of Title VII provides that it is not an unlawful employment practice to apply different standards of compensation, or different terms, conditions, or privileges of employment pursuant to a bona fide seniority system, provided that such differences are not the result of an intention to discriminate because of race.[10] It is clear that the City had a seniority system, that its proposed layoff plan conformed to that system, and that in making the settlement the City had not agreed to award competitive seniority to any minority employee whom the City proposed to lay off. The District Court held that the City could not follow its seniority system in making its proposed layoffs because its proposal was discriminatory in effect and hence not a bona fide plan. Section 703(h), however, permits the routine application of a seniority system absent proof of an intention to discriminate. Teamsters v. United States, 431 U.S. 324, 352, 97 S.Ct. 1843, 1863, 52 L.Ed.2d 396 (1977). Here, the District Court itself found that the layoff proposal was not adopted with the purpose or intent to discriminate on the basis of race. Nor had the City in agreeing to the decree admitted in any way that it had engaged in intentional discrimination. The Court of Appeals was therefore correct in disagreeing with the District Court's holding that the layoff plan was not a bona fide application of the seniority system, and it would appear that the City could not be faulted for following the seniority plan expressed in its agreement with the Union. The Court of Appeals nevertheless held that the injunction was proper even though it conflicted with the seniority system. This was error. * * *

A second ground advanced by the Court of Appeals in support of the conclusion that the injunction could be entered notwithstanding its conflict with the seniority system was the assertion that "[i]t would be incongruous to hold that the use of the preferred means of resolving an employment discrimination action decreases the power of a court to order

---

Court of Appeals relied extensively on what it considered to be its authority under Title VII. That is the posture in which the cases come to us. Furthermore, the District Court's authority to impose a modification of a decree is not wholly dependent on the decree. "[T]he District's Court's authority to adopt a consent decree comes only from the statute which the decree is intended to enforce," not from the parties' consent to the decree. System Federation No. 91 v. Wright, 364 U.S. 642, 651, 81 S.Ct. 368, 373, 5 L.Ed.2d 349 (1961). In recognition of this principle, this Court in *Wright* held that when a change in the law brought the terms of a decree into conflict with the statute pursuant to which the decree was entered, the decree should be modified over the objections of one of the parties bound by the decree. By the same token, and for the same reason, a district court cannot enter a disputed modification of a consent decree in Title VII litigation if the resulting order is inconsistent with that statute.

Thus, Title VII necessarily acted as a limit on the District Court's authority to modify the decree over the objections of the City; the issue cannot be resolved solely by reference to the terms of the decree and notions of equity. Since * * * Title VII precludes a district court from displacing a non-minority employee with seniority under the contractually established seniority system absent either a finding that the seniority system was adopted with discriminatory intent or a determination that such a remedy was necessary to make whole a proven victim of discrimination, the District Court was precluded from granting such relief over the City's objection in these cases.

10. Section 703(h) provides that "it shall not be an unlawful employment practice for an employer to apply different standards of compensation, or different terms, conditions, or privileges of employment pursuant to a bona fide seniority or merit system ... provided that such differences are not the result of an intention to discriminate because of race, color, religion, sex, or national origin...." 42 U.S.C. § 2000e–2(h).

relief which vindicates the policies embodied within Title VII, and 42 U.S.C. §§ 1981 and 1983." The court concluded that if the allegations in the complaint had been proved, the District Court could have entered an order overriding the seniority provisions. Therefore, the court reasoned, "[t]he trial court had the authority to override the Firefighter's Union seniority provisions to effectuate the purpose of the 1980 Decree."

The difficulty with this approach is that it overstates the authority of the trial court to disregard a seniority system in fashioning a remedy after a plaintiff has successfully proved that an employer has followed a pattern or practice having a discriminatory effect on black applicants or employees. If individual members of a plaintiff class demonstrate that they have been actual victims of the discriminatory practice, they may be awarded competitive seniority and given their rightful place on the seniority roster. This much is clear from Franks v. Bowman Transportation Co., 424 U.S. 747, 96 S.Ct. 1251, 47 L.Ed.2d 444 (1976) and Teamsters v. United States, 431 U.S. 324, 97 S.Ct. 1843, 52 L.Ed.2d 396 (1977). *Teamsters,* however, also made clear that mere membership in the disadvantaged class is insufficient to warrant a seniority award; each individual must prove that the discriminatory practice had an impact on him. Even when an individual shows that the discriminatory practice has had an impact on him, he is not automatically entitled to have a non-minority employee laid off to make room for him. He may have to wait until a vacancy occurs, and if there are non-minority employees on layoff, the Court must balance the equities in determining who is entitled to the job. Here, there was no finding that any of the blacks protected from layoff had been a victim of discrimination and no award of competitive seniority to any of them. Nor had the parties in formulating the consent decree purported to identify any specific employee entitled to particular relief other than those listed in the exhibits attached to the decree. It therefore seems to us that in light of *Teamsters,* the Court of Appeals imposed on the parties as an adjunct of settlement something that could not have been ordered had the case gone to trial and the plaintiffs proved that a pattern or practice of discrimination existed. * * *

Finally, the Court of Appeals was of the view that the District Court ordered no more than that which the City unilaterally could have done by way of adopting an affirmative action program. Whether the City, a public employer, could have taken this course without violating the law is an issue we need not decide. The fact is that in these cases the City took no such action and that the modification of the decree was imposed over its objection.[17]

We thus are unable to agree either that the order entered by the District Court was a justifiable effort to enforce the terms of the decree to

---

17. The Court of Appeals also suggested that under United States v. Swift & Co., 286 U.S. 106, 114–115, 52 S.Ct. 460, 462, 76 L.Ed. 999 (1932), the decree properly was modified pursuant to the District Court's equity jurisdiction. But *Swift* cannot be read as authorizing a court to impose a modification of a decree that runs counter to statutory policy, see n. 9, supra, here §§ 703(h) and 706(g) of Title VII.

which the City had agreed or that it was a legitimate modification of the decree that could be imposed on the City without its consent. Accordingly, the judgment of the Court of Appeals is reversed. * * *

JUSTICE O'CONNOR, concurring. [omitted]

JUSTICE STEVENS, concurring in the judgment. [omitted]

JUSTICE BLACKMUN, with whom JUSTICE BRENNAN and JUSTICE MARSHALL join, dissenting.

* * *

III

* * * In affirming the District Court, the Court of Appeals suggested at least two grounds on which respondents might have prevailed on the merits.

A

The first of these derives from the contractual characteristics of a consent decree. Because a consent decree "is to be construed for enforcement purposes essentially as a contract," United States v. ITT Continental Baking Co., 420 U.S. 223, 238, 95 S.Ct. 926, 935, 43 L.Ed.2d 148 (1975), respondents had the right to specific performance of the terms of the decree. If the proposed layoffs violated those terms, the District Court could issue an injunction requiring compliance with them. Alternatively, the Court of Appeals noted that a court of equity has inherent power to modify a consent decree in light of changed circumstances. Thus, if respondents could show that changed circumstances justified modification of the decree, the District Court would have authority to make such a change. * * *

The Court rejects the argument that the injunctive relief was a proper exercise of the power to enforce the purposes of the decree principally on the ground that the remedy agreed upon in the consent decree did not specifically mention layoffs. This treatment of the issue is inadequate. The power of the District Court to enter further orders to effectuate the purposes of the decree was a part of the agreed remedy. The parties negotiated for this, and it is the obligation of the courts to give it meaning. In an ideal world, a well-drafted consent decree requiring structural change might succeed in providing explicit directions for all future contingencies. But particularly in civil rights litigation in which implementation of a consent decree often takes years, such foresight is unattainable. Accordingly, parties to a consent decree typically agree to confer upon supervising courts the authority to ensure that the purposes of a decree are not frustrated by unforeseen circumstances. The scope of such authority in an individual case depends principally upon the intent of the parties. Viewed in this light, recourse to such broad notions as the "purposes" of a decree is not a rewriting of the parties' agreement, but rather a part of the attempt to implement the written terms. The District Judge in these cases, who presided over the negotiation of the consent decree, is in a unique position to determine the nature of the parties' original intent, and he has a distinctive familiarity with the circumstances that shaped the decree and defined its purposes. Accordingly, he should be given special deference to interpret the general and any ambiguous terms in the decree. It simply is not a sufficient response to conclude, as the Court does, that the District Court could not enjoin the proposed layoff plan merely because layoffs were not specifically mentioned in the consent decree.

In this regard, it is useful to note the limited nature of the injunctive relief ordered by the District Court. The preliminary injunction did not embody a conclusion that the city could never conduct layoffs in accordance with its seniority policy. Rather, the District Court preliminarily enjoined a particular application of the seniority system as a basis for a particular set of layoffs. Whether the District Court would enjoin a future layoff presumably would depend on the factual circumstances of that situation. * * * There is no way of knowing whether the District Court would conclude that a future layoff conducted on the basis of seniority would frustrate the purposes of the decree sufficiently to justify an injunction. * * *

B

The Court of Appeals also suggested that respondents could have prevailed on the merits because the 1981 layoffs may have justified a modification of the consent decree. This Court frequently has recognized the inherent "power of a court of equity to modify an injunction in adaptation to changed conditions though it was entered by consent." United States v. Swift & Co., 286 U.S. 106, 114, 52 S.Ct. 460, 462, 76 L.Ed. 999 (1932); accord, Pasadena City Board of Education v. Spangler, 427 U.S. 424, 437, 96 S.Ct. 2697, 2705, 49 L.Ed.2d 599 (1976); United States v. United Shoe Machinery Corp., 391 U.S. 244, 251, 88 S.Ct. 1496, 1500, 20 L.Ed.2d 562 (1968). "The source of the power to modify is of course the fact that an injunction often requires continuing supervision by the issuing court and always a continuing willingness to apply its powers and processes on behalf of the party who obtained that equitable relief." The test for ruling on a plaintiff's request for a modification of a consent decree is "whether the change serve[s] to effectuate ... the basic purpose of the original consent decree."

The Court rejects this ground for affirming the preliminary injunction, not by examining the purposes of the *consent decree* and whether the proposed layoffs justified a modification of the decree, but rather by reference to Title VII. The Court concludes that the preliminary injunction was improper because it "imposed on the parties as an adjunct of settlement something that could not have been ordered had the case gone to trial and the plaintiffs proved that a pattern or practice of discrimination existed." Thus, the Court has chosen to evaluate the propriety of the preliminary injunction by asking what type of relief the District Court could have awarded had respondents litigated their Title VII claim and prevailed on the merits. Although it is far from clear whether that is the right question,[9] it is clear that the Court has given the wrong answer. * * *

In the instant cases, respondents' request for a preliminary injunction did not include a request for individual awards of retroactive seniority—and, contrary to the implication of the Court's opinion, the District Court did not make any such awards. Rather, the District Court order required the city to conduct its layoffs in a race-conscious manner; specifically, the preliminary injunction prohibited the city from conducting layoffs that would "decrease the percentage of black[s]" in certain job categories. The city remained free to lay off any individual black so long as the percentage of black representation was maintained.

Because these cases arise out of a consent decree, and a trial on the merits has never taken place, it is of course impossible for the Court to know the extent and nature of any past discrimination by the city. For this reason, to the extent that the scope of appropriate relief would depend upon the facts found at trial, it is impossible to determine whether the relief provided by the preliminary injunction would have been appropriate following a trial on the merits. Nevertheless, the Court says that the preliminary injunction was inappropriate because, it concludes, respondents could not have obtained similar relief had their cases been litigated instead of settled by a consent decree. * * *

For reasons never explained, the Court's opinion has focused entirely on what respondents have actually shown, instead of what they might have shown had trial ensued. It is improper and unfair to fault respondents for failing to show "that any of the blacks protected from layoff had been a victim of discrimination," for the simple reason that the claims on which such a showing would have been made never went to trial. The whole point of the consent decree in these cases—and indeed the point of most Title VII consent decrees—is for both parties to avoid the time and expense of litigating the question of liability and identifying the victims of discrimination. In the instant consent decree, the city expressly denied having engaged in any discrimination at all. Nevertheless, the consent decree in this case provided several persons with both promotions and backpay. By definition, all such relief went to persons never determined to be victims of discrimination, and the Court does not indicate that it means to suggest that the original consent decree in these cases was invalid. Any suggestion that a consent decree can provide relief only if a defendant

---

9. The Court's analysis seems to be premised on the view that a consent decree cannot provide relief that could not be obtained at trial. In addressing the Court's analysis, I do not mean to imply that I accept its premise as correct. In Steelworkers v. Weber, 443 U.S. 193, 99 S.Ct. 2721, 61 L.Ed.2d 480 (1979), this Court considered whether an affirmative action plan adopted voluntarily by an employer violated Title VII because it discriminated against whites. In holding that the plan was lawful, the Court stressed that the voluntariness of the plan informed the nature of its inquiry. Because a consent decree is an agreement that is enforceable in court, it has qualities of both voluntariness and compulsion. The Court has explained that Congress intended to encourage voluntary settlement of Title VII suits, and cooperative private efforts to eliminate the lingering effects of past discrimination. It is by no means clear, therefore, that the permissible scope of relief available under a consent decree is the same as could be ordered by a court after a finding of liability at trial.

concedes liability would drastically reduce, of course, the incentives for entering into consent decrees. Such a result would be incongruous, given the Court's past statements that "Congress expressed a strong preference for encouraging voluntary settlement of employment discrimination claims." * * *

NOTES

1. Justice Blackmun's dissent points out that the Court is reviewing the district court's decision to grant a preliminary injunction. Does the majority apply the correct standard of review? I.e., how would *Stotts* have come out under the tests applied in *Winter* (p. 190) and *American Hospital* (p. 204)?

2. The Supreme Court has held that a district court may enter a consent decree that benefits individuals who are not actual victims of an employer's discriminatory practices despite an apparent limitation in Title VII prohibiting relief to such persons because a consent decree is not an "order" within the meaning of the enforcement provisions of Title VII. Writing for the Court, Justice Brennan distinguished those situations where a district court would be barred by Title VII from providing such relief "after a trial or, as in *Stotts*, in disputed proceedings to modify a decree entered upon consent." Local No. 93 v. City of Cleveland, 478 U.S. 501, 528, 106 S.Ct. 3063, 3078, 92 L.Ed.2d 405 (1986). The Court majority acted over a dissent written by Justice Rehnquist charging that it was ignoring well-considered observations in *Stotts* that were "inconsistent with the result which the Court is apparently determined to reach in this case." Id. at 540. *Stotts* and *Local 93* are reviewed in George M. Sullivan & William A. Nowlin, The Clarification of Firefighters v. Stotts, 37 Lab.L.J. 788 (1986).

3. The facts of *Local No. 93* also raises a related problem: Under the facts of that case, the defendant city was sued by an organization of African-American and Latino firefighters, alleging that promotion practices in the fire department discriminated against minorities. The city and the plaintiffs negotiated a settlement, which provided for racial quotas on promotions, without the real participation of the largely white labor union. If the white union later seeks modification, should a trial court use a rigid or flexible standard? See Douglas Laycock, Consent Decrees Without Consent: The Rights of Nonconsenting Third Parties, 1987 U.Chi.Legal F. 103. See also Martin v. Wilks, 490 U.S. 755, 109 S.Ct. 2180, 104 L.Ed.2d 835 (1989), at p. 361.

RUFO v. INMATES OF SUFFOLK COUNTY JAIL
Supreme Court of the United States, 1992
502 U.S. 367, 112 S.Ct. 748, 116 L.Ed.2d 867

JUSTICE WHITE delivered the opinion of the Court.

* * *

I

This litigation began in 1971 when inmates sued the Suffolk County Sheriff, the Commissioner of Correction for the State of Massachusetts, the Mayor of Boston, and nine city councilors, claiming that inmates not yet convicted of the crimes charged against them were being held under unconstitutional conditions at what was then the Suffolk County Jail. The facility, known as the Charles Street Jail, had been constructed in 1848 with large tiers of barred cells. * * * The court held that conditions at the jail were constitutionally deficient:

> "As a facility for the pretrial detention of presumptively innocent citizens, Charles Street Jail unnecessarily and unreasonably infringes upon their most basic liberties, among them the rights to reasonable freedom of motion, personal cleanliness, and personal privacy. The court finds and rules that the quality of incarceration at Charles Street is 'punishment' of such a nature and degree that it cannot be justified by the state's interest in holding defendants for trial; and therefore it violates the due process clause of the Fourteenth Amendment."

The Court permanently enjoined the government defendants: "(a) from housing at the Charles Street Jail after November 30, 1973 in a cell with another inmate, any inmate who is awaiting trial and (b) from housing at the Charles Street Jail after June 30, 1976 any inmate who is awaiting trial." The defendants did not appeal.

In 1977, with the problems of the Charles Street Jail still unresolved, the District Court ordered defendants, including the Boston City Council, to take such steps and expend the funds reasonably necessary to renovate another existing facility as a substitute detention center. * * * The Court of Appeals [subsequently] ordered that the Charles Street Jail be closed on October 2, 1978, unless a plan was presented to create a constitutionally adequate facility for pretrial detainees in Suffolk County.

Four days before the deadline, the plan that formed the basis for the consent decree now before this Court was submitted to the District Court. * * *

Seven months later, the Court entered a formal consent decree in which the government defendants expressed their "desire ... to provide, maintain and operate as applicable a suitable and constitutional jail for Suffolk County pretrial detainees." The decree specifically incorporated the provisions of the Suffolk County Detention Center, Charles Street Facility, Architectural Program, which—in the words of the consent decree—"sets forth a program which is both constitutionally adequate and constitutionally required."

Under the terms of the Architectural Program, the new jail was designed to include a total of 309 "[s]ingle occupancy rooms" of 70 square feet arranged in modular units that included a kitchenette and recreation area, inmate laundry room, education units, and indoor and outdoor exercise areas. The size of the jail was based on a projected decline in inmate population, from 245 male prisoners in 1979 to 226 at present.

Although the Architectural Program projected that construction of the new jail would be completed by 1983, work on the new facility had not been started by 1984. During the intervening years, the inmate population outpaced population projections. Litigation in the state courts ensued, and defendants were ordered to build a larger jail. Thereupon, plaintiff prisoners, with the support of the sheriff, moved the District Court to modify the decree to provide a facility with 435 cells. Citing "the unanticipated increase in jail population and the delay in completing the jail," the District Court modified the decree to permit the capacity of the new jail to be increased in any amount, provided that:

> "(a) single-cell occupancy is maintained under the design for the facility; * * *

The number of cells was later increased to 453. Construction started in 1987.

In July 1989, while the new jail was still under construction, the sheriff moved to modify the consent decree to allow the double bunking of male detainees in 197 cells, thereby raising the capacity of the new jail to 610 male detainees. The sheriff argued that changes in law and in fact required the modification. The asserted change in law was this Court's 1979 decision in Bell v. Wolfish, 441 U.S. 520 (1979), handed down one week after the consent decree was approved by the District Court. The asserted change in fact was the increase in the population of pretrial detainees.

The District Court refused to grant the requested modification, holding that the sheriff had failed to meet the standard of United States v. Swift & Co., 286 U.S. 106, 119 (1932):

> "Nothing less than a clear showing of grievous wrong evoked by new and unforeseen conditions should lead us to change what was decreed after years of litigation with the consent of all concerned."

The court rejected the argument that *Bell* required modification of the decree because the decision "did not directly overrule any legal interpretation on which the 1979 consent decree was based, and in these circumstances it is inappropriate to invoke Rule 60(b)(5) to modify a consent decree." The court refused to order modification because of the increased pretrial detainee population, finding that the problem was "neither new nor unforeseen."

The District Court briefly stated that, even under the flexible modification standard adopted by other Courts of Appeals, the sheriff would not be entitled to relief because "[a] separate cell for each detainee has always been an important element of the relief sought in this litigation-perhaps even the most important element." Finally, the court rejected the argument that the decree should be modified because the proposal complied with constitutional standards, reasoning that such a rule "would undermine and discourage settlement efforts in institutional cases." The District Court never decided whether the sheriff's proposal for double celling at the new jail would be constitutionally permissible.

The new Suffolk County Jail opened shortly thereafter.

The Court of Appeals affirmed * * *. We granted certiorari.

II

In moving for modification of the decree, the sheriff relied on Federal Rule of Civil Procedure 60(b)[(5) & (6)] * * *.

There is no suggestion in these cases that a consent decree is not subject to Rule 60(b). A consent decree no doubt embodies an agreement of the parties and thus in some respects is contractual in nature. But it is an agreement that the parties desire and expect will be reflected in and be enforceable as a judicial decree that is subject to the rules generally applicable to other judgments and decrees. Railway Employees v. Wright, 364 U.S. 642, 650–651 (1961). The District Court recognized as much but held that Rule 60(b)(5) codified the "grievous wrong" standard of United States v. Swift, that a case for modification under this standard had not been made, and that resort to Rule 60(b)(6) was also unavailing. This construction of Rule 60(b) was error.

Swift was the product of a prolonged antitrust battle between the Government and the meat-packing industry. In 1920, the defendants agreed to a consent decree that enjoined them from manipulating the meat-packing industry and banned them from engaging in the manufacture, sale, or transportation of other foodstuffs. In 1930, several meat-packers petitioned for modification of the decree, arguing that conditions in the meat-packing and grocery industries had changed. The Court rejected their claim, finding that the meatpackers were positioned to manipulate transportation costs and fix grocery prices in 1930, just as they had been in 1920. It was in this context that Justice Cardozo, for the Court, set forth the much-quoted *Swift* standard, requiring "[n]othing less than a clear showing of grievous wrong evoked by new and unforeseen conditions" as a predicate to modification of the meat-packers' consent decree.

Read out of context, this language suggests a "hardening" of the traditional flexible standard for modification of consent decrees. New York State Assn. for Retarded Children, Inc. v. Carey, 706 F.2d 956, 968 (CA2), cert. denied, 464 U.S. 915 (1983). But that conclusion does not follow when the standard is read in context. The *Swift* opinion pointedly distinguished the facts of that case from one in which genuine changes required modification of a consent decree, stating that:

> "The distinction is between restraints that give protection to rights fully accrued upon facts so nearly permanent as to be substantially impervious to change, and those that involve the supervision of changing conduct or conditions and are thus provisional and tentative.... The consent is to be read as directed toward events as they then were. It was not an abandonment of the right to exact revision in

the future, if revision should become necessary in adaptation to events to be."

Our decisions since *Swift* reinforce the conclusion that the "grievous wrong" language of *Swift* was not intended to take on a talismanic quality, warding off virtually all efforts to modify consent decrees. *Railway Employees* emphasized the need for flexibility in administering consent decrees, stating: "There is ... no dispute but that a sound judicial discretion may call for the modification of the terms of an injunctive decree if the circumstances, whether of law or fact, obtaining at the time of its issuance have changed, or new ones have since arisen."

The same theme was repeated in our decision last term in Board of Education of Oklahoma City Public Schools v. Dowell, 498 U.S. 237 (1991), in which we rejected the rigid use of the *Swift* "grievous wrong" language as a barrier to a motion to dissolve a desegregation decree.

There is thus little basis for concluding that Rule 60(b) misread the *Swift* opinion and intended that modifications of consent decrees in all cases were to be governed by the standard actually applied in *Swift*. That Rule, in providing that, on such terms as are just, a party may be relieved from a final judgement or decree where it is no longer equitable that the judgment have prospective application, permits a less stringent, more flexible standard.

The upsurge in institutional reform litigation since Brown v. Board of Education, 347 U.S. 483 (1954), has made the ability of a district court to modify a decree in response to changed circumstances all the more important. Because such decrees often remain in place for extended periods of time, the likelihood of significant changes occurring during the life of the decree is increased. * * *

The government petitioners * * * assert that modification would actually improve conditions for some pretrial detainees, who now cannot be housed in the Suffolk County Jail and therefore are transferred to other facilities, farther from family members and legal counsel. In these transfer facilities, the petitioners assert that detainees may be double celled under less desirable conditions than those that would exist if double celling were allowed at the new Suffolk County Jail. The government petitioners also contend that the public interest is implicated here because crowding at the new facility has necessitated the release of some pretrial detainees and the transfer of others to halfway houses, from which many escape.

For the District Court, these points were insufficient reason to modify under Rule 60(b)(5) because its "authority [was] limited by the established legal requirements for modification...." * * * None of the changed circumstances warranted modification because it would violate one of the primary purposes of the decree which was to provide for "[a] separate cell for each detainee [which] has always been an important element of the relief sought in this litigation-perhaps even the most important element." For reasons appearing later in this opinion, this was not an adequate basis for denying the requested modification. The District Court also held that Rule 60(b)(6) provided no more basis for relief. The District Court, and the Court of Appeals as well, failed to recognize that such rigidity is neither required by *Swift* nor appropriate in the context of institutional reform litigation.

It is urged that any rule other than the *Swift* "grievous wrong" standard would deter parties to litigation such as this from negotiating settlements and hence destroy the utility of consent decrees. Obviously that would not be the case insofar as the state or local government officials are concerned. As for the plaintiffs in such cases, they know that if they litigate to conclusion and win, the resulting judgment or decree will give them what is constitutionally adequate at that time but perhaps less than they hoped for. They also know that the prospective effect of such a judgment or decree will be open to modification where deemed equitable under Rule 60(b). Whether or not they bargain for more than what they might get after trial, they will be in no worse position if they settle and have the consent decree entered. At least they will avoid further litigation and perhaps will negotiate a decree providing more than what would have been ordered without the local government's consent. And, of course, if they litigate, they may lose.

III

Although we hold that a district court should exercise flexibility in considering requests for modification of an institutional reform consent decree, it does not follow that a modification will be warranted in all circumstances. Rule 60(b)(5) provides that a party may obtain relief from a court order when "it is no longer equitable that the judgment should have prospective application," not when it is no longer convenient to live with the terms of a consent decree. Accordingly, a party seeking modification of a consent decree bears the burden of establishing that a significant change in circumstances warrants revision of the decree. If the moving party meets this standard, the court should consider whether the proposed modification is suitably tailored to the changed circumstance.[7]

A

A party seeking modification of a consent decree may meet its initial burden by showing either a significant change in factual conditions or in law.

---

7. The standard we set forth applies when a party seeks modification of a term of a consent decree that arguably relates to the vindication of a constitutional right. Such a showing is not necessary to implement minor changes in extraneous details that may have been included in a decree (*e.g.*, paint color or design of a building's facade) but are unrelated to remedying the underlying constitutional violation. Ordinarily, the parties should consent to modifying a decree to allow such changes. If a party refuses to consent and the moving party has a reasonable basis for its request, the court should modify the decree. In this case the entire architectural plan became part of the decree binding on the local authorities. Hence, any change in the plan technically required a change in the decree, absent a provision in the plan exempting certain changes. Such a provision was furnished by the 1985 modification of the decree. Of course, the necessity of changing a decree to allow insignificant changes could be avoided by not entering an overly detailed decree.

1

Modification of a consent decree may be warranted when changed factual conditions make compliance with the decree substantially more onerous. Such a modification was approved by the District Court in this litigation in 1985 when it became apparent that plans for the new jail did not provide sufficient cell space. Modification is also appropriate when a decree proves to be unworkable because of unforeseen obstacles, New York State Assn. for Retarded Children, Inc. v. Carey, 706 F.2d at 969 (modification allowed where State could not find appropriate housing facilities for transfer patients); Philadelphia Welfare Rights Organization v. Shapp, 602 F.2d at 1120–1121 (modification allowed where State could not find sufficient clients to meet decree targets); or when enforcement of the decree without modification would be detrimental to the public interest, Duran v. Elrod, 760 F.2d 756, 759–761 (C.A.7 1985) (modification allowed to avoid pretrial release of accused violent felons).

Respondents urge that modification should be allowed only when a change in facts is both "unforeseen and unforeseeable." Such a standard would provide even less flexibility than the exacting *Swift* test; we decline to adopt it. Litigants are not required to anticipate every exigency that could conceivably arise during the life of a consent decree.

Ordinarily, however, modification should not be granted where a party relies upon events that actually were anticipated at the time it entered into a decree. If it is clear that a party anticipated changing conditions that would make performance of the decree more onerous but nevertheless agreed to the decree, that party would have to satisfy a heavy burden to convince a court that it agreed to the decree in good faith, made a reasonable effort to comply with the decree, and should be relieved of the undertaking under Rule 60(b).

Accordingly, on remand the District Court should consider whether the upsurge in the Suffolk County inmate population was foreseen by the petitioners. * * *

Even if the decree is construed as an undertaking by petitioners to provide single cells for pretrial detainees, to relieve petitioners from that promise based on changed conditions does not necessarily violate the basic purpose of the decree. That purpose was to provide a remedy for what had been found, based on a variety of factors, including double celling, to be unconstitutional conditions obtaining in the Charles Street Jail. If modification of one term of a consent decree defeats the purpose of the decree, obviously modification would be all but impossible. That cannot be the rule. The District Court was thus in error in holding that even under a more flexible standard than its version of *Swift* required, modification of the single cell requirement was necessarily forbidden.

2

A consent decree must of course be modified if, as it later turns out, one or more of the obligations placed upon the parties has become impermissible under federal law. But modification of a consent decree may be warranted when the statutory or decisional law has changed to make legal what the decree was designed to prevent.

This was the case in Railway Employees v. Wright, 364 U.S. 642 (1961). A railroad and its unions were sued for violating the Railway Labor Act, 45 U.S.C. § 151 et seq., which banned discrimination against nonunion employees, and the parties entered a consent decree that prohibited such discrimination. Later, the Railway Labor Act was amended to allow union shops, and the union sought a modification of the decree. Although the amendment did not require but purposely permitted union shops, this Court held that the union was entitled to the modification because the parties had recognized correctly that what the consent decree prohibited was illegal under the Railway Act as it then read and because a "court must be free to continue to further the objectives of th[e] Act when its provisions are amended."

Petitioner Rapone urges that, without more, our 1979 decision in Bell v. Wolfish, 441 U.S. 520 (1979), was a change in law requiring modification of the decree governing construction of the Suffolk County Jail. We disagree. *Bell* made clear what the Court had not before announced: that double celling is not in all cases unconstitutional. But it surely did not cast doubt on the legality of single celling, and petitioners were undoubtedly aware that *Bell* was pending when they signed the decree. Thus, the case must be judged on the basis that it was immaterial to petitioners that double celling might be ruled constitutional, i.e., they preferred even in that event to agree to a decree which called for providing only single cells in the jail to be built.

Neither *Bell* nor the Federal Constitution forbade this course of conduct. Federal courts may not order States or local governments, over their objection, to undertake a course of conduct not tailored to curing a constitutional violation that has been adjudicated. See Milliken v. Bradley (*Milliken II*), 433 U.S. 267, 281 (1977). But we have no doubt that, to "save themselves the time, expense, and inevitable risk of litigation," United States v. Armour & Co., 402 U.S. 673, 681 (1971), petitioners could settle the dispute over the proper remedy for the constitutional violations that had been found by undertaking to do more than the Constitution itself requires (almost any affirmative decree beyond a directive to obey the Constitution necessarily does that), but also more than what a court would have ordered absent the settlement. Accordingly, the District Court did not abuse its discretion in entering the agreed upon decree, which clearly was related to the conditions found to offend the Constitution.[12]

---

12. Petitioner Rapone contends that the District Court was required to modify the consent decree because "the constitutional violation underlying the decree has disappeared and will not recur" and that "no constitutional violation [is] even alleged" at the new jail, "so there is no constitutional violation to serve as a predicate for the federal court's continued exercise of its equitable power." His argument is not well taken. The District Court did not make findings on these issues, and even if it had ruled that double celling at the new jail is constitutional and that the modification should be granted, we do not have before us the question whether the entire decree should be vacated.

To hold that a clarification in the law automatically opens the door for relitigation of the merits of every affected consent decree would undermine the finality of such agreements and could serve as a disincentive to negotiation of settlements in institutional reform litigation. * * *

While a decision that clarifies the law will not, in and of itself, provide a basis for modifying a decree, it could constitute a change in circumstances that would support modification if the parties had based their agreement on a misunderstanding of the governing law. For instance, in Pasadena City Board of Education v. Spangler, 427 U.S. 424, 437–438 (1976), we held that a modification should have been ordered when the parties had interpreted an ambiguous equitable decree in a manner contrary to the District Court's ultimate interpretation and the District Court's interpretation was contrary to intervening decisional law. And in Nelson v. Collins, 659 F.2d 420, 428–429 (C.A.4 1981)(en banc), the Fourth Circuit vacated an equitable order that was based on the assumption that double bunking of prisoners was *per se* unconstitutional.

Thus, if the Sheriff and Commissioner could establish on remand that the parties to the consent decree believed that single celling of pretrial detainees was mandated by the Constitution, this misunderstanding of the law could form a basis for modification. In this connection, we note again that the decree itself recited that it "sets forth a program which is both constitutionally adequate and constitutionally *required*." (Emphasis added).

B

Once a moving party has met its burden of establishing either a change in fact or in law warranting modification of a consent decree, the District Court should determine whether the proposed modification is suitably tailored to the changed circumstance. In evaluating a proposed modification, three matters should be clear.

Of course, a modification must not create or perpetuate a constitutional violation. Petitioners contend that double celling inmates at the Suffolk County Jail would be constitutional under *Bell*. Respondents counter that *Bell* is factually distinguishable and that double celling at the new jail would violate the constitutional rights of pretrial detainees. If this is the case—the District Court did not decide this issue—modification should not be granted.

A proposed modification should not strive to rewrite a consent decree so that it conforms to the constitutional floor. Once a court has determined that changed circumstances warrant a modification in a consent decree, the focus should be on whether the proposed modification is tailored to resolve the problems created by the change in circumstances. A court should do no more, for a consent decree is a final judgment that may be reopened only to the extent that equity requires. The court should not "turn aside to inquire whether some of [the provisions of the decree] upon separate as distinguished from joint action could have been opposed with success if the defendants had offered opposition." *Swift*.

Within these constraints, the public interest and "[c]onsiderations based on the allocation of powers within our federal system," *Dowell*, require that the district court defer to local government administrators, who have the "primary responsibility for elucidating, assessing, and solving" the problems of institutional reform, to resolve the intricacies of implementing a decree modification. Brown v. Board of Education, 349 U.S. at 299. See also Missouri v. Jenkins, 495 U.S. 33 (1990); *Milliken II*.[14] Although state and local officers in charge of institutional litigation may agree to do more than that which is minimally required by the Constitution to settle a case and avoid further litigation, a court should surely keep the public interest in mind in ruling on a request to modify based on a change in conditions making it substantially more onerous to abide by the decree. To refuse modification of a decree is to bind all future officers of the State, regardless of their view of the necessity of relief from one or more provisions of a decree that might not have been entered had the matter been litigated to its conclusion. The District Court seemed to be of the view that the problems of the fiscal officers of the State were only marginally relevant to the request for modification in this case. Financial constraints may not be used to justify the creation or perpetuation of constitutional violations, but they are a legitimate concern of government defendants in institutional reform litigation and therefore are appropriately considered in tailoring a consent decree modification.

IV

To conclude, we hold that the *Swift* "grievous wrong" standard does not apply to requests to modify consent decrees stemming from institutional reform litigation. Under the flexible standard we adopt today, a party seeking modification of a consent decree must establish that a significant change in facts or law warrants revision of the decree and that the proposed modification is suitably tailored to the changed circumstance. * * *

JUSTICE THOMAS took no part in the consideration or decision of this case.

JUSTICE O'CONNOR, concurring in the judgment.

* * * I would emphasize that we find fault only with the *method* by which the District Court reached its conclusion. The District Court may well have been justified, for the reasons suggested by Justice Stevens, in refusing to modify the decree, and the court is free, when fully exercising

---

14. The concurrence mischaracterizes the nature of the deference that we would accord local government administrators. As we have stated, the moving party bears the burden of establishing that a significant change in circumstances warrants modification of a consent decree. No deference is involved in this threshold inquiry. However, once a court has determined that a modification is warranted, we think that principles of federalism and simple common sense require the court to give significant weight to the views of the local government officials who must implement any modification.

its discretion, to reach the same result on remand. This is a case with no satisfactory outcome. The new jail is simply too small. Someone has to suffer, and it is not likely to be the government officials responsible for underestimating the inmate population and delaying the construction of the jail. Instead, it is likely to be either the inmates of Suffolk County, who will be double celled in an institution designed for single celling; the inmates in counties not yet subject to court supervision, who will be double celled with the inmates transferred from Suffolk County; or members of the public, who may be the victims of crimes committed by the inmates the county is forced to release in order to comply with the consent decree. The District Court has an extraordinarily difficult decision to make. We should not be inclined to second-guess the court's sound judgment in deciding who will bear this burden. * * *

JUSTICE STEVENS, with whom JUSTICE BLACKMUN joins, dissenting.

Today the Court endorses the standard for modification of consent decrees articulated by Judge Friendly in New York State Association for Retarded Children, Inc. v. Carey, 706 F.2d 956 (CA2), cert. denied, 464 U.S. 915 (1983). I agree with that endorsement, but under that standard I believe the findings of the District Court in this action require affirmance of its order refusing to modify this consent decree.

* * *

III

It is the terms of the 1979 consent decree, as modified and reaffirmed in 1985, that petitioners now seek to modify. The 1979 decree was negotiated against a background in which certain important propositions had already been settled. First, the litigation had established the existence of a serious constitutional violation. Second, for a period of almost five years after the entry of the 1973 injunction—which was unquestionably valid and which petitioners had waived any right to challenge—the petitioners were still violating the Constitution as well as the injunction. Third, although respondents had already prevailed, they were willing to agree to another postponement of the closing of the Charles Street Jail if petitioners submitted, and the court approved, an adequate plan for a new facility.

Obviously any plan would have to satisfy constitutional standards. It was equally obvious that a number of features of the plan, such as the site of the new facility or its particular architectural design, would not be constitutionally mandated. In order to discharge their duty to provide an adequate facility, and also to avoid the risk of stern sanctions for years of noncompliance with an outstanding court order, it would be entirely appropriate for petitioners to propose a remedy that exceeded the bare minimum mandated by the Constitution. Indeed, terms such as "minimum" or "floor" are not particularly helpful in this context. The remedy is constrained by the requirement that it not perpetuate a constitutional violation, and in this sense the Constitution does provide a "floor."

Beyond that constraint, however, the remedy's attempt to give expression to the underlying constitutional value does not lend itself to quantitative evaluation. In view of the complexity of the institutions involved and the necessity of affording effective relief, the remedial decree will often contain many, highly detailed commands. It might well be that the failure to fulfill any one of these specific requirements would not have constituted an independent constitutional violation, nor would the absence of any one element render the decree necessarily ineffective. The duty of the District Court is not to formulate the decree with the fewest provisions, but to consider the various interests involved and, in the sound exercise of its discretion, to fashion the remedy that it believes to be best.[2] Similarly, a consent decree reflects the parties' understanding of the best remedy, and, subject to judicial approval, the parties to a consent decree enjoy at least as broad discretion as the District Court in formulating the remedial decree. Cf. Firefighters v. Cleveland, 478 U.S. 501, 525–526 (1986). * * *

IV

The motion to modify that ultimately led to our grant of certiorari was filed on July 17, 1989. As I view these cases, the proponents of that motion had the burden of demonstrating that changed conditions between 1985 and 1989 justified a further modification of the consent decree. The changes that occurred between 1979 and 1985 were already reflected in the 1985 modification. Since petitioners acquiesced in that modification, they cannot now be heard to argue that pre–1985 developments—either in the law or in the facts—provide a basis for modifying the 1985 order. It is that order that defined petitioners' obligation to construct and to operate an adequate facility.

Petitioners' reliance on Bell v. Wolfish, 441 U.S. 520 (1979), as constituting a relevant change in the law is plainly misplaced * * *. [I]t was well-known to all parties when the decree was modified in 1985. It does not qualify as a changed circumstance.[5]

---

2. It is the difficulty in determining prospectively which remedy is best that justifies a flexible standard of modification. This relationship between the characteristics of a remedial decree in structural reform litigation and the flexible standard of modification is explained in the passage that Judge Friendly found to be the best statement of the applicable legal standard:

" 'The judge must search for the "best" remedy, but since his judgment must incorporate such open-ended considerations as effectiveness and fairness, and since the threat and constitutional value that occasions the intervention can never be defined with great precision, the intervention can never be defended with any certitude. It must always be open to revisions, even without the strong showing traditionally required for modification of a decree, namely, that the first choice is causing grievous hardship. A revision is justified if the remedy is not working effectively or is unnecessarily burdensome.' "

New York State Association for Retarded Children, Inc. v. Carey, 706 F.2d 956, 970 (C.A.2 1983)(quoting Fiss, The Supreme Court—1978 Term—Foreword: The Forms of Justice, 93 Harv.L.Rev. 1, 49 (1979)). The justification for modifying a consent decree is not that the decree did "too much," but that in light of later circumstances, a modified remedy would better achieve the decree's original goals.

5. As the Court agrees that Bell v. Wolfish did not constitute a change in law requiring modification of the decree, the Court does not define further the kind of changes in law that may merit modification. In particular, the Court has no occasion to draw a distinction between the type of change in law recognized in System Federation v. Wright, 364 U.S. 642 (1961), and the

The increase in the average number of pretrial detainees is, of course, a change of fact. Because the size of that increase had not been anticipated in 1979, it was appropriate to modify the decree in 1985. But in 1985, the steady progression in the detainee population surely made it foreseeable that this growth would continue. The District Court's finding that "the overcrowding problem faced by the Sheriff is neither new nor unforeseen," is amply supported by the record.

Even if the continuing increase in inmate population had not actually been foreseen, it was reasonably foreseeable. Mere foreseeability in the sense that it was an event that "could conceivably arise" during the life of the consent decree should not, of course, disqualify an unanticipated development from justifying a modification. But the parties should be charged with notice of those events that reasonably prudent litigants would contemplate when negotiating a settlement. Given the realities of today's society, it is not surprising that the District Court found a continued growth in inmate population to be within petitioners' contemplation.

Other important concerns counsel against modification of this consent decree. Petitioners' history of noncompliance after the 1973 injunction provides an added reason for insisting that they honor their most recent commitments. Petitioners' current claims of fiscal limitation are hardly new. These pleas reflect a continuation of petitioners' previous reluctance to budget funds adequate to avoid the initial constitutional violation or to avoid prolonged noncompliance with the terms of the original decree. The continued claims of financial constraint should not provide support for petitioners' modification requests.

The strong public interest in protecting the finality of court decrees always counsels against modifications. In the context of a consent decree, this interest is reinforced by the policy favoring the settlement of protracted litigation. To the extent that litigants are allowed to avoid their solemn commitments, the motivation for particular settlements will be compromised, and the reliability of the entire process will suffer.

It is particularly important to apply a strict standard when considering modification requests that undermine the central purpose of a consent decree. * * * In this action, the entire history of the litigation demonstrates that the prohibition against double celling was a central purpose of the relief ordered by the District Court in 1973, of the bargain negotiated in 1979 and embodied in the original consent decree, and of the order entered in 1985 that petitioners now seek to modify. Moreover, as the District Court found, during the history of the litigation petitioners have

---

change in law that petitioners assert was effected by *Bell*. The distinction is nevertheless significant and deserves mention. In *Wright*, the plaintiffs originally brought suit alleging that a railroad and its unions discriminated against nonunion employees, a practice prohibited by the Railway Labor Act. The defendants entered into a consent decree, promising to refrain from such discrimination. When Congress subsequently amended the Act to permit union shops, the Court concluded that a modification allowing union shops should be granted so as to further the statutory purpose. In contrast to the situation presented in *Wright*, it cannot be contended that *Bell* expressed a policy preference in favor of double celling. * * *

been able to resort to various measures such as "transfers to state prisons, bail reviews by the Superior Court, and a pretrial controlled release program" to respond to the overcrowding problem. The fact that double celling affords petitioners the easiest and least expensive method of responding to a reasonably foreseeable problem is not an adequate justification for compromising a central purpose of the decree. In this regard, the Court misses the point in its observation that "[i]f modification of one term of a consent decree defeats the purpose of the decree, obviously modification would be all but impossible." It is certainly true that modification of a consent decree would be impossible if the modification of *any* one term were deemed to defeat the purpose of the decree. However, to recognize that *some* terms are so critical that their modification would thwart the central purpose of the decree does not render the decree immutable, but rather assures that a modification will frustrate neither the legitimate expectations of the parties nor the core remedial goals of the decree. * * *

Notes

1. On remand, the district court found that although some increase was reasonably foreseeable, the specific and sustained rise in the inmate population was not actually foreseen by the parties either when the decree was originally entered in 1979 or was modified in 1985. However, the court also found that single-bunking was "at the least among the most significant objectives of the consent decree" and that the plaintiffs would not have consented to the decree without the provision for single-bunking. Moreover, double-bunking would increase the risk of violence and the risk of transmission of tuberculosis among the inmates. As a result, although the increased inmate population qualified as a change of factual circumstances, the court found that the Sheriff's proposed solution—double-bunking in 197 of the 322 cells in the jail—was not narrowly tailored to those circumstances. The court invited the Sheriff to submit a new proposal that met the objectives of the decree. The district court also denied a motion brought by the Commissioner of Corrections for the Commonwealth to entirely vacate the decree. Inmates of Suffolk County Jail v. Rufo, 148 F.R.D. 14 (D.Mass.1993). The First Circuit turned away an appeal by the Commissioner. 12 F.3d 286 (1st Cir.1993). On the Sheriff's revised motion to modify, the district court granted permission to alter up to 100 cells to permit double-bunking, and stated its intent to close the case after an additional five-year monitoring period. 844 F.Supp. 31 (D.Mass.1994). The district court partially granted the Sheriff's subsequent motion to terminate jurisdiction over the jail pursuant to the Prison Litigation Reform Act (see pp. 281–299). 129 F.3d 649 (1st Cir.1997), cert. denied, 524 U.S. 951, 118 S.Ct. 2366, 141 L.Ed.2d 735 (1998).

The Charles Street Jail was finally closed and then sold to be converted into a luxury hotel in Boston called The Liberty Hotel with rates of $325 to $4,000 per night. The jail-theme hotel invites guests to "be captivated" and includes such amenities as Do–Not–Disturb signs reading "Solitary," the "Clink" restaurant, and the "Alibi" bar. See www.libertyhotel.com; Beth Greenfield, Check In/Check Out, N.Y.Travel at 4, Dec. 23, 2007.

2. In *Rufo*, Justice White's opinion for the majority relied heavily on the need for flexibility in modifying institutional reform decrees. However, in *Stotts*, it was the dissent which took that position while Justice White's opinion for the majority took a more rigid approach. What accounts for his change of heart? Is it that "the new rule is that a *plaintiff* seeking modification has to meet an onerous burden while a *defendant* enjoys the benefits of a flexible standard?" David I. Levine, The Modification of Equitable Decrees in Institutional Reform Litigation: A Commentary on the Supreme Court's Adoption of the Second Circuit's Flexible Test, 58 Brook.L.Rev. 1239, 1267 (1993). Or is the *Rufo* Court simply returning the law of modification to a flexible standard with an ancient lineage? See Sweeton v. Brown, 27 F.3d 1162 (6th Cir. en banc 1994)(tracing flexible standard back to Sir Francis Bacon's Ordinances in Equity, written in 1618), cert. denied, 513 U.S. 1158, 115 S.Ct. 1118, 130 L.Ed.2d 1082 (1995).

3. *Rufo* has encouraged defendants to seek re-examination of many consent decrees for a variety of reasons. For examples of changes in fact, see, e.g., United States v. Eastman Kodak Co., 63 F.3d 95 (2d Cir.1995)(lifting antitrust decrees entered in 1921 and 1954); Newark Coalition for Low Income Housing v. Newark Redevelopment and Housing Authority, 524 F.Supp.2d 559 (D.N.J.2007) (terminating most of settlement agreement for low-income housing due to changed factual circumstances and inappropriateness of indefinite court monitoring of competently managed governmental agency); Evans v. Williams, 206 F.3d 1292 (D.C.Cir.2000) (requiring modification of consent decree, which obligated the District of Columbia to pay vendors of goods and services within 30 days, because the court saw a distinction between the local government's "generic inability or refusal to pay the vendors," which was well-known at the time the decree was entered, and the District's later severe and unforeseen fiscal crisis and near-bankruptcy, making it impossible to pay bills). In addition, the Supreme Court, by a 5–4 vote, allowed Rule 60(b)(5) to be used as a vehicle to seek modification of an injunction on the basis that the underlying law had been "undermined" by subsequent developments, even if it had not yet been explicitly changed by the Court. Agostini v. Felton, 521 U.S. 203, 117 S.Ct. 1997, 138 L.Ed.2d 391 (1997) (rule not limited to recognizing changes in law; may be used to effect changes). See Note, Putting the Cart Before the Horse: Agostini v. Felton Blurs the Line Between Res Judicata and Equitable Relief, 49 Case W.Res. L.Rev. 407 (1999). For an example of state defendants trying unsuccessfully to use *Rufo* as the basis for modification or termination of consent decrees, see Jeff D. v. Kempthorne, 365 F.3d 844 (9th Cir.2004). (See also *Evans v. Jeff D.*, a principal case in Chapter 10 on attorney's fees.)

4. The reach of the modification standards announced in *Rufo* is unsettled. Some courts have held that *Rufo* applies to institutional reform cases only, e.g., W.L. Gore & Associates, Inc. v. C.R. Bard, Inc., 977 F.2d 558 (Fed.Cir.1992)(refusing to apply *Rufo* to patent case). Most other courts, however, have held that *Rufo* has wider application. For example, one district court applied *Rufo* to a suit to enforce a statutory mandate directed to a government agency, focusing directly on the regulatory practices of that agency (the EPA) in the context of possible reform of those practices. The court cited to "significant authority" to support the application of *Rufo* to

non-institutional cases, even in actions brought against non-governmental entities. Cronin v. Browner, 90 F.Supp.2d 364 (S.D.N.Y.2000). In a situation highly reminiscent of *Illinois v. Costle* (p. 230), the court modified the consent decree at the request of the EPA to allow a bifurcated rulemaking process only to the extent the agency showed it was suitably tailored to address the delays in issuing regulations governing water intake structures. The court set optional deadlines for the issuance of regulations and provided for the appointment of a special master if final action on the bifurcated regulations was not agreed to by a court-set date. Other courts have applied *Rufo* to injunctions arising from a private action. E.g., V&V Food Products, Inc. v. Cacique Cheese Co., 2003 WL 255235 (N.D.Ill. 2003) (court grants motion to modify permanent injunction enjoining the defendant from using trademark to sell Mexican cheese in certain states; after modification, the defendant was permitted to advertise on nationally broadcast Spanish television networks even though advertisements would reach forbidden markets for sales).

NOTE ON BINDING SUCCESSORS IN OFFICE WITH A CONSENT DECREE

Sheriff Rufo never personally agreed to the consent decree at issue in the case which bears his name; his predecessor, Sheriff Kearney, did. Can Rufo contend that he should not be bound by that earlier decision? Some courts have rejected the contention out of hand. See, e.g., Benjamin v. Malcolm, 156 F.R.D. 561 (S.D.N.Y.1994)(rejecting argument that city should be allowed to modify consent decree concerning jails in New York City approved in previous mayor's administration).

Other courts have been more open to the position of subsequent government officials. For example, the City of Chicago successfully made such an argument in a challenge to a consent decree in which the city had agreed to pay large court judgments more promptly than it had done in the past. Later developments clarified that the city actually had no legal obligation to change its method of choosing when to pay court judgments. In Evans v. City of Chicago, 10 F.3d 474, 478–79 (7th Cir.en banc 1993), cert. denied, 511 U.S. 1082, 114 S.Ct. 1831, 128 L.Ed.2d 460 (1994), the majority released the city from the obligations it had agreed to incur in the consent decree, reasoning:

> "Chicago" did not reach a settlement with the plaintiffs. The consent decree was entered in 1984. Negotiations were conducted on Chicago's behalf by its corporation counsel, who we may suppose acted with the approval of Harold Washington, then Chicago's mayor. Although the decree purports to last for all time—and the district court's decision refusing to vacate the decree * * * reflects a belief that the commitments ought to run perpetually—democracy does not permit public officials to bind the polity forever. What one City Council enacts, another may repeal; what one mayor decrees during his four-year term, another may revoke. Today's lawmakers have just as much power to set public policy as did their predecessors. "Chicago" speaks through its elected representatives, and the people are free to upset even the most enlightened policies of earlier times. The current mayor wants to be free of his predecessor's commitment, concluding that more flexibility over budgets will promote the public welfare. People of good will could be on either

side of this disagreement; each mayor may have correctly perceived the needs of the moment.

Governments are in this respect unlike corporations or other contracting parties. A corporate board of directors may enter into commitments that continue after new directors take office; a legislature may not. True, governments may form contracts (for example, to build a new road or repay a loan) and must keep these commitments by virtue of the contract clause of the Constitution, Art. I, § 10, cl. 1. But temporary officeholders may not contract away the basic powers of government to enact laws—or in this case to adopt budgets—in the same way natural persons may make enduring promises about their own future behavior. Why then should things differ if the parties choose not the device of a seal (or even of a statute) but the imprimatur of a district judge?

Consent alone is insufficient to support a commitment by a public official that ties the hands of his successor. * * * Thus the answer to the question "why should consent decrees be enforced when contracts out of court are not?" must concentrate on legal rules that shape the parties' agreement. * * *

It depends on rules of law that govern the public official's conduct. " '[T]he District Court's authority to adopt a consent decree comes only from the statute which the decree is intended to enforce,' not from the parties' consent to the decree." Firefighters v. Stotts, 467 U.S. 561, 576 n. 9, 104 S.Ct. 2576, 2586 n. 9, 81 L.Ed.2d 483 (1984). A state official's promise to follow a rule of federal law retains its force because of the continuing effect of the law, which the state cannot alter. And a settlement of a dispute about the meaning of that law may be enforced if the agreement compromises genuine uncertainties, for then the public official actually may be enhancing or preserving the powers of the democratic branch (by avoiding a worse outcome after trial) rather than ceding the powers of the government.

This method of justifying the implementation of consent decrees implies, however, that the court must ensure that there is a substantial federal claim, not only when the decree is entered but also when it is enforced, and that the obligations imposed by the decree rest on this rule of federal law rather than the bare consent of the officeholder. * * *

The U.S. Supreme Court has sided with the Seventh Circuit's position. In Frew v. Hawkins, 540 U.S. 431, 441–42, 124 S.Ct. 899, 905, 157 L.Ed.2d 855 (2004), a unanimous Court stated:

> *Rufo* rejected the idea that the institutional concerns of government officials were "only marginally relevant" when officials moved to amend a consent decree, and noted that "principles of federalism and simple common sense require the [district] court to give significant weight" to the views of government officials. [Quoting footnote 14, p. 263, supra].
> * * *
>
> The federal court must exercise its equitable powers to ensure that when the objects of the decree have been attained, responsibility for discharging the State's obligations is returned promptly to the State and

its officials. As public servants, the officials of the State must be presumed to have a high degree of competence in deciding how best to discharge their governmental responsibilities. A State, in the ordinary course, depends upon successor officials, both appointed and elected, to bring new insights and solutions to problems of allocating revenues and resources. The basic obligations of federal law may remain the same, but the precise manner of their discharge may not. If the State establishes reason to modify the decree, the court should make the necessary changes; where it has not done so, however, the decree should be enforced according to its terms.

Does this statement square with *Rufo*? If not, how does it change the standard for modification? What sort of "reason to modify the decree" should the State establish under this statement? See O'Sullivan v. City of Chicago, 396 F.3d 843 (7th Cir.2005); Ross Sandler & David Schoenbrod, The Supreme Court, Democracy and Institutional Reform Litigation, 49 N.Y.L.Sch.L.Rev. 915 (2005) (both discussing impact of *Frew* on the law of modification).

On remand, the court in *Frew* refused to terminate the consent decree requiring the provision of adequate medical and dental care to indigent children in Texas. Frazar v. Ladd, 457 F.3d 432 (5th Cir.2006) (holding that state's alleged compliance with federal law was not, by itself, adequate ground for dissolution of consent decree and upholding district court's decision that state officials had not shown significant change in facts sufficient to warrant termination), cert. denied sub nom., Hawkins v. Frew, 549 U.S. 1118, 127 S.Ct. 1039, 166 L.Ed.2d 714 (2007).

Professors Ross Sandler and David Schoenbrod argue that consent decrees should be aimed at putting plaintiffs in their rightful position when initially entered and that defendants should be able to modify and terminate them so long as that objective is achieved. Building upon work in their book, Democracy by Decree: What Happens When Courts Run Government (2003), they argue that public officials frequently agree to relief that goes beyond putting plaintiffs in their rightful position and courts then enforce the decree too rigidly, inappropriately treating the plaintiffs as owners of contractual rights rather than more limited constitutional or statutory rights. The result is that successor officials are locked into policies agreed to by their predecessors regardless of their motives and whether the policies have worked as planned. Ross Sandler & David Schoenbrod, From Status to Contract and Back Again: Consent Decrees in Institutional Reform Litigation, 27 Rev.Lit. 115 (2007).

4. RETAINING AND CLOSING A CASE

(A) JUDICIAL DIRECTION TO TERMINATE JURISDICTION

PROBLEM: *COUNTRY LODGE V. MILLER* (REPRISED)
OBTAINING RELEASE FROM AN INJUNCTION

For six months, Miller has obeyed the terms of a permanent injunction, which ordered her to conduct an expensive clean-up and banned any further dumping of apple mash waste in the river. Miller now seeks termination of the injunction. Country Lodge opposes the motion. What result? If the injunction is vacated and Country Lodge subsequently finds a small amount of apple mash in the river (but not as much as before the court issued the injunction originally), may the court sanction Miller for violating the injunction?

In typical private law cases, such as a simple trespass action, an injunction preventing further harm (i.e., an order not to trespass) would be imposed in perpetuity. Although any reparative aspect of the order would expire of its own terms (e.g., an order to clean-up whatever damage was caused by the trespass), the court usually would retain jurisdiction to enforce the injunction at any time in the future. Without more, it would be rare to have the defendant in such a case return to court to seek dismissal of the injunction and even more unusual for the court to grant such relief.

The court certainly has the power to grant such a motion for relief. For example, F.R.Civ.P. 60(b)(5) specifically grants a court power to relieve a party from a final judgment if "applying it prospectively is no longer equitable." A typical defendant will want to be released as promptly as possible from the court's jurisdiction for several reasons. Once released, the defendant will once again have the ability to take action (and in more complex private and public law cases, make policy decisions) without judicial scrutiny or fear of judicial sanctions. Moreover, the defendant will not have to comply with monitoring rules, such as the necessity to file regular reports. Unless the conduct is independently prohibited by law (such as a statute), the defendant will be under no obligation to continue to avoid the conduct which had been proscribed by the injunction. See David I. Levine, The Latter Stages of Enforcement of Equitable Decrees: The Course of Institutional Reform Cases After Dowell, Rufo and Freeman, 20 Hastings Const.L.Q. 579, 629–32 (1993). If the trial court is convinced that the defendants are substantially in compliance with its orders, should it release them from the terms of the injunction and from the court's jurisdiction? In certain cases, must the court release the defendant? In reading the next cases, you should also have in mind the cases from Chapter 2 in which the courts decided whether it was necessary to issue an injunction against a defendant who had violated the law; in effect, the decision to release a defendant from an injunction is the reverse of the decision to impose an injunction in the first place.

BOARD OF EDUCATION OF OKLAHOMA CITY PUBLIC SCHOOLS v. DOWELL

Supreme Court of the United States, 1991
498 U.S. 237, 111 S.Ct. 630, 112 L.Ed.2d 715

CHIEF JUSTICE REHNQUIST delivered the opinion of the Court.

* * *

I

This school desegregation litigation began almost 30 years ago. [The Court reviewed the prolonged history of the case from its inception in 1961.] * * * In 1972, finding that previous efforts had not been successful at eliminating state-imposed segregation, the District Court ordered the Board [of Education of Oklahoma City, Oklahoma] to adopt the "Finger Plan," under which kindergartners would be assigned to neighborhood schools unless their parents opted otherwise; children in grades 1–4 would attend formerly all white schools, and thus black children would be bused to those schools; children in grade 5 would attend formerly all black schools, and thus white children would be bused to those schools; students in the upper grades would be bused to various areas in order to maintain integrated schools; and in integrated neighborhoods there would be stand-alone schools for all grades.

In 1977, after complying with the desegregation decree for five years, the Board made a "Motion to Close Case." The District Court held in its "Order Terminating Case":

> "The Court has concluded that [the Finger Plan] worked and that substantial compliance with the constitutional requirements has been achieved. * * *
>
> " ... The School Board, as now constituted, has manifested the desire and intent to follow the law. The court believes that the present members and their successors on the Board will now and in the future continue to follow the constitutional desegregation requirements. * * *
>
> " ... Jurisdiction in this case is terminated ipso facto subject only to final disposition of any case now pending on appeal."

This unpublished order was not appealed.

In 1984, the School Board faced demographic changes that led to greater burdens on young black children. As more and more neighborhoods became integrated, more stand-alone schools were established, and young black students had to be bused farther from their inner-city homes to outlying white areas. In an effort to alleviate this burden and to increase parental involvement, the Board adopted the Student Reassignment Plan (SRP), which relied on neighborhood assignments for students in grades K–4 beginning in the 1985–1986 school year. Busing continued for students in grades 5–12. Any student could transfer from a school where he or she was in the majority to a school where he or she would be in the minority. Faculty and staff integration was retained, and an "equity officer" was appointed.

In 1985, respondents filed a "Motion to Reopen the Case," contending that the School District had not achieved "unitary" status and that the SRP was a return to segregation. Under the SRP, 11 of 64 elementary schools would be greater than 90% black, 22 would be greater than 90% white plus other minorities, and 31 would be racially mixed. The District Court refused to reopen the case, holding that its 1977 finding of unitariness was res judicata as to those who were then parties to the action, and that the district remained unitary. * * * Because unitariness had been achieved, the District Court concluded that court-ordered desegregation must end.

The Court of Appeals for the Tenth Circuit reversed. It held that, while the 1977 order finding the district unitary was binding on the parties, nothing in that order indicated that the 1972 injunction itself was terminated. The court reasoned that the finding that the system was unitary merely ended the District Court's active supervision of the case, and because the school district was still subject to the desegregation decree, respondents could challenge the SRP. The case was remanded to determine whether the decree should be lifted or modified.

On remand, the District Court found that demographic changes made the Finger Plan unworkable, that the Board had done nothing for 25 years to promote residential segregation, and that the school district had bused students for more than a decade in good-faith compliance with the court's orders. The District Court found that present residential segregation was the result of private decisionmaking and economics, and that it was too attenuated to be a vestige of former school segregation. It also found that the district had maintained its unitary status, and that the neighborhood assignment plan was not designed with discriminatory intent. The court concluded that the previous injunctive decree should be vacated and the school district returned to local control.

The Court of Appeals again reversed, holding that " 'an injunction takes on a life of its own and becomes an edict quite independent of the law it is meant to effectuate.' " That court approached the case "not so much as one dealing with desegregation, but as one dealing with the proper application of the federal law on injunctive remedies." Relying on United States v. Swift & Co., 286 U.S. 106, 52 S.Ct. 460, 76 L.Ed. 999 (1932), it held that a desegregation decree remains in effect until a school district can show "grievous wrong evoked by new and unforeseen conditions," and "dramatic changes in conditions unforeseen at the time of the decree that ... impose extreme and unexpectedly oppressive hardships on the obligor," (quoting Jost, From *Swift* to *Stotts* and Beyond: Modification of Injunctions in the Federal Courts, 64 Tex.L.Rev. 1101, 1110 (1986)). Given that a number of schools would return to being primarily one-race schools under the SRP, circumstances in Oklahoma City had not changed enough to justify modification of the decree. * * *

We now reverse the Court of Appeals. * * *

III

The Court of Appeals relied upon language from this Court's decision in *United States v. Swift and Co.* * * *. We hold that its reliance was mistaken. * * *

United States v. United Shoe Machinery Corp., 391 U.S. 244, 88 S.Ct. 1496, 20 L.Ed.2d 562 (1968), explained that the language used in *Swift* must be read in the context of the continuing danger of unlawful restraints on trade which the Court had found still existed. * * * In the present case, a finding by the District Court that the Oklahoma City School District was being operated in compliance with the commands of the Equal Protection Clause of the Fourteenth Amendment, and that it was unlikely that the school board would return to its former ways, would be a finding that the purposes of the desegregation litigation had been fully achieved. No additional showing of "grievous wrong evoked by new and unforeseen conditions" is required of the Board. * * *

Considerations based on the allocation of powers within our federal system, we think, support our view that * * * *Swift* does not provide the proper standard to apply to injunctions entered in school desegregation cases. Such decrees, unlike the one in *Swift*, are not intended to operate in perpetuity. * * * The legal justification for displacement of local authority by an injunctive decree in a school desegregation case is a violation of the Constitution by the local authorities. Dissolving a desegregation decree after the local authorities have operated in compliance with it for a reasonable period of time properly recognizes that "necessary concern for the important values of local control of public school systems dictates that a federal court's regulatory control of such systems not extend beyond the time required to remedy the effects of past intentional discrimination."

The Court of Appeals * * * relied for its statement that "compliance alone cannot become the basis for modifying or dissolving an injunction" on our decision in United States v. W.T. Grant Co., 345 U.S. [629] at 633, 73 S.Ct. [894] at 897, [97 L.Ed. 1303 (1953)]. That case, however, did not involve the dissolution of an injunction, but the question of whether an injunction should be issued in the first place. This Court observed that a promise to comply with the law on the part of a wrongdoer did not divest a district court of its power to enjoin the wrongful conduct in which the defendant had previously engaged.

A district court need not accept at face value the profession of a school board which has intentionally discriminated that it will cease to do so in the future. But in deciding whether to modify or dissolve a desegregation decree, a school board's compliance with previous court orders is obviously relevant. * * * The test espoused by the Court of Appeals would condemn a school district, once governed by a board which intentionally discriminated, to judicial tutelage for the indefinite future. Neither the principles governing the entry and dissolution of injunctive decrees, nor the commands of the Equal Protection Clause of the Fourteenth Amendment, require any such Draconian result.

Petitioner urges that we reinstate the decision of the District Court terminating the injunction, but we think that the preferable course is to remand the case to that court so that it may decide, in accordance with this opinion, whether the Board made a sufficient showing of constitutional compliance as of 1985, when the SRP was adopted, to allow the injunction to be dissolved. The District Court should address itself to whether the Board had complied in good faith with the desegregation decree since it was entered, and whether the vestiges of past discrimination had been eliminated to the extent practicable.

In considering whether the vestiges of *de jure* segregation had been eliminated to the extent practicable, the District Court should look not only at student assignments, but "to every facet of school operations—faculty, staff, transportation, extra-curricular activities and facilities." Green [v. New Kent County School Board, 391 U.S. 430, 88 S.Ct. 1689, 20 L.Ed.2d 716 (1968)]. * * *

After the District Court decides whether the Board was entitled to have the decree terminated, it should proceed to decide respondent's challenge to the SRP. A school district which has been released from an injunction imposing a desegregation plan no longer requires court authorization for the promulgation of policies and rules regulating matters such as assignment of students and the like, but it of course remains subject to the mandate of the Equal Protection Clause of the Fourteenth Amendment. If the Board was entitled to have the decree terminated as of 1985, the District Court should then evaluate the Board's decision to implement the SRP under appropriate equal protection principles. * * *

JUSTICE SOUTER took no part in the consideration or decision of this case.

JUSTICE MARSHALL, with whom JUSTICE BLACKMUN and JUSTICE STEVENS join, dissenting.

* * * [Justice Marshall began by reviewing Oklahoma's record of segregation since the state's admission to the Union in 1907. Turning to the *Dowell* litigation, Justice Marshall found that its] history reveals nearly unflagging resistance by the Board to judicial efforts to dismantle the city's dual education system. * * *

II

I agree with the majority that the proper standard for determining whether a school desegregation decree should be dissolved is whether the purposes of the desegregation litigation, as incorporated in the decree, have been fully achieved. * * * I strongly disagree with the majority, however, on what must be shown to demonstrate that a decree's purposes have been fully realized. In my view, a standard for dissolution of a desegregation decree must take into account the unique harm associated with a system of racially identifiable schools and must expressly demand the elimination of such schools.

A

Our pointed focus in *Brown I* upon the stigmatic injury caused by segregated schools explains our unflagging insistence that formerly *de jure* segregated school districts extinguish all vestiges of school segregation. The concept of stigma also gives us guidance as to what conditions must be eliminated before a decree can be deemed to have served its purpose. * * *

Just as it is central to the standard for evaluating the formation of a desegregation decree, so should the stigmatic injury associated with segregated schools be central to the standard for dissolving a decree. The Court has indicated that "the ultimate end to be brought about" by a desegregation remedy is "a unitary, nonracial system of public education." *Green*. * * * Although the Court has never explicitly defined what constitutes a "vestige" of state-enforced segregation, the function that this concept has performed in our jurisprudence suggests that it extends to any condition that is likely to convey the message of inferiority implicit in a policy of segregation. So long as such conditions persist, the purposes of the decree cannot be deemed to have been achieved.

B

The majority suggests a more vague and, I fear, milder standard. * * *

By focusing heavily on present and future compliance with the Equal Protection Clause, the majority's standard ignores how the stigmatic harm identified in *Brown I* can persist even after the State ceases actively to enforce segregation.[6] * * * [O]ur school-desegregation jurisprudence establishes that the *effects* of past discrimination remain chargeable to the school district regardless of its lack of continued enforcement of segregation, and the remedial decree is required until those effects have been finally eliminated.

III

Applying the standard I have outlined, I would affirm the Court of Appeals' decision ordering the District Court to restore the desegregation decree. For it is clear on this record that removal of the decree will result in a significant number of racially identifiable schools that could be eliminated. * * *

It is undisputed that replacing the Finger Plan with a system of neighborhood school assignments for grades K–4 resulted in a system of racially identifiable schools. * * * Because this principal vestige of *de jure*

---

6. Faithful compliance with the decree admittedly is relevant to the standard for dissolution. The standard for dissolution should require that the school district have exhibited faithful compliance with the decree for a period sufficient to assure the District Court that the school district is committed to the ideal of integrated system. * * *

segregation persists, lifting the decree would clearly be premature at this point. * * *

In its concern to spare local school boards the "Draconian" fate of "indefinite" "judicial tutelage," the majority risks subordination of the constitutional rights of Afro–American children to the interest of school board autonomy. The courts must consider the value of local control, but that factor primarily relates to the feasibility of a remedial measure, see *Milliken II*, not whether the constitutional violation has been remedied. *Swann* establishes that if further desegregation is "reasonable, feasible, and workable," then it must be undertaken. * * * The School Board does not argue that further desegregation of the one-race schools in its system is unworkable * * *.

We should keep in mind that the court's active supervision of the desegregation process ceased in 1977. Retaining the decree does not require a return to active supervision. It may be that a modification of the decree which will improve its effectiveness and give the school district more flexibility in minimizing busing is appropriate in this case. But retaining the decree seems a slight burden on the school district compared with the risk of not delivering a full remedy to the Afro–American children in the school system. * * *

NOTES

1. The majority noted that on remand the district court first needed to decide "whether the Board made a sufficient showing of constitutional compliance as of 1985, when the SRP was adopted, to allow the injunction to be dissolved." The Supreme Court then instructed the district court that if it decided that the decree should have been terminated by 1985, the lower court "should then evaluate the Board's decision to implement the SRP under appropriate equal protection principles." What is the legal standard to be used in this portion of the proceeding? Who bears the burden of proof? For example, must the school board show that its decision to implement the SRP will not have a segregative effect? Must the plaintiffs demonstrate that the Board's decision was made with intent to re-segregate the Oklahoma City schools? See Dowell v. Board of Education of Oklahoma City Public Schools, 8 F.3d 1501 (10th Cir.1993)(affirming district court's decisions in the defendants' favor on remand).

In this second portion of the proceeding on remand, may the plaintiffs rely on the history of segregation in Oklahoma that Justice Marshall reviewed and the prior "unflagging resistance by the Board to judicial efforts to dismantle the City's dual education system"? See Price v. Austin Independent School District, 945 F.2d 1307 (5th Cir.1991).

2. Would it have made any difference to the Court's analysis if the Finger Plan had been adopted as part of a consent decree rather than as a result of complying with judicially-mandated relief? Cf. Firefighters Local Union No. 1784 v. Stotts, 467 U.S. 561, 104 S.Ct. 2576, 81 L.Ed.2d 483 (1984).

3. Should *Dowell* apply to a consent decree with proscriptive (or, in Professor Fiss' terms (p. 52 n. 4), "preventive") rather than remedial (or "reparative") goals? In Alliance to End Repression v. City of Chicago, 66 F.Supp.2d 899 (N.D.Ill.1999), the district court said no. It rejected the city's argument that compliance with a 23-year-old proscriptive consent decree, designed to prohibit the police department from engaging in political spying and harassment of citizens, in and of itself required termination or modification under *Dowell*. Instead, the defendant City had to demonstrate entitlement to modification of the consent decree under *Rufo*, which it failed to do. The Seventh Circuit panel unanimously reversed the district court. "The states and their subdivisions have a right to the restoration of control over the institutions of state and local government upon proof of decades of compliance with a decree that had shifted that control to a federal judge." 237 F.3d 799, 801 (7th Cir.2001).

4. Suppose on remand in *Dowell* that the district court finds that there are no vestiges of de jure segregation with respect to student assignments to schools (because any variation is due to changes in the housing patterns), but there are some vestiges with respect to other facets of school operations, such as faculty or staff assignments, transportation, extra-curricular activities or facilities. What should the district court do? In Freeman v. Pitts, 503 U.S. 467, 490–96, 112 S.Ct. 1430, 1445–48, 118 L.Ed.2d 108 (1992), Justice Kennedy explained for the Supreme Court:

> We hold that, in the course of supervising desegregation plans, federal courts have the authority to relinquish supervision and control of school districts in incremental stages, before full compliance has been achieved in every area of school operations. While retaining jurisdiction over the case, the court may determine that it will not order further remedies in areas where the school district is in compliance with the decree. That is to say, upon a finding that a school system subject to a court-supervised desegregation plan is in compliance in some but not all areas, the court in appropriate cases may return control to the school system in those areas where compliance has been achieved, limiting further judicial supervision to operations that are not yet in full compliance with the court decree. In particular, the district court may determine that it will not order further remedies in the area of student assignments where racial imbalance is not traceable, in a proximate way, to constitutional violations.

* * *

> That there was racial imbalance in student attendance zones was not tantamount to a showing that the school district was in noncompliance with the decree or with its duties under the law. Racial balance is not to be achieved for its own sake. It is to be pursued when racial imbalance has been caused by a constitutional violation. Once the racial imbalance due to the *de jure* violation has been remedied, the school district is under no duty to remedy imbalance that is caused by demographic factors. * * * If the unlawful *de jure* policy of a school system has been the cause of the racial imbalance in student attendance, that condition must be remedied.

The school district bears the burden of showing that any current imbalance is not traceable, in a proximate way, to the prior violation. * * *

In one sense of the term, vestiges of past segregation by state decree do remain in our society and in our schools. Past wrongs to the black race, wrongs committed by the State and in its name, are a stubborn fact of history. And stubborn facts of history linger and persist. But though we cannot escape our history, neither must we overstate its consequences in fixing legal responsibilities. The vestiges of segregation that are the concern of the law in a school case may be subtle and intangible but nonetheless they must be so real that they have a causal link to the *de jure* violation being remedied. It is simply not always the case that demographic forces causing population change bear any real and substantial relation to a *de jure* violation. And the law need not proceed on that premise.

* * *

Justice Scalia, in a concurring opinion, urged the Court to:

acknowledge that it has become absurd to assume, without any further proof, that violations of the Constitution dating from the days when Lyndon Johnson was President, or earlier, continue to have an appreciable effect upon current operation of schools. * * * We must soon revert to the ordinary principles of our law, of our democratic heritage, and of our educational tradition: that plaintiffs alleging equal protection violations must prove intent and causation and not merely the existence of racial disparity; that public schooling, even in the South, should be controlled by locally elected authorities acting in conjunction with parents; and that it is "desirable" to permit pupils to attend "schools nearest their homes".

Id. at 506–07, 112 S.Ct. at 1453–54.

Justice Souter took a very different approach in his concurring opinion. He noted that judicial control over student assignments (or some other facet of school operations) might be required in a number of situations. For example, judicial control might be needed: (a) "to remedy persisting vestiges of the unconstitutional dual system, such as remaining imbalance in faculty assignments;" (b) the dual school system were a cause of the demographic shifts; or (c) a "*Green*-type factor other than student assignments [were] a possible cause of imbalanced student assignment patterns in the future." Justice Souter would allow the district courts to reassert control over student assignments in any of these circumstances. Id. at 507–08, 112 S.Ct. at 1454–55.

Justices Blackmun, Stevens and O'Connor, concurring in the judgment, stated: "It is not enough, however, for [the school district] to establish that demographics exacerbated the problem; it must prove that its own policies did not contribute. Such contribution can occur in at least two ways: DCSS may have contributed to the demographic changes themselves, or it may have contributed directly to the racial imbalance in the schools." Id. at 512–13, 112 S.Ct. at 1457.

After taking further evidence, the district court subsequently concluded that the school district's constitutional violations had been fully remedied to the extent practicable and granted final dismissal from the court's supervision. Mills v. Freeman, 942 F.Supp. 1449, 1464 (N.D.Ga.1996).

5. Suppose that the plaintiffs in *Freeman* had initiated their suit at a time when the schools were in the condition of partial desegregation described in the majority opinion. At that point, would the district court have granted an injunction to the plaintiffs? What would its scope be? Would the scope be any different than the injunction remaining in *Freeman* after partial release from judicial supervision?

Suppose that the school district in *Freeman* had been operating some magnet schools under the terms of a consent decree, which required racial balancing of the student body in those schools. Assume that the court terminated supervision over the magnet schools, but retained jurisdiction over the remainder of the consent decree. May the school district continue to use the same race-based student assignment plan? Cavalier ex rel. Cavalier v. Caddo Parish School Board, 403 F.3d 246 (5th Cir. 2005).

6. Many courts and scholars have taken *Dowell*, *Freeman* and *Missouri v. Jenkins III* as strong signals from the Supreme Court to end supervision over school desegregation decrees. E.g., People Who Care v. Rockford Board of Education, 246 F.3d 1073, 1074 (7th Cir.2001) ("heed the admonition of the Supreme Court * * * to bend every effort to winding up school litigation and returning the operation of the schools to the local school authorities"); Bradley W. Joondeph, Skepticism and School Desegregation, 76 Wash.U.L.Q. 161 (1998) ("curtain falls on court-ordered desegregation nationwide"). Empirical work demonstrates that although several cases have been terminated, "the vast majority of school desegregation litigation continues, with no hint of impending termination." Wendy Parker, The Future of School Desegregation, 94 Nw.U.L.Rev. 1157, 1160 (2000). "The clear majority of school districts appear content with their outstanding court orders. Not seeking termination imposes only known costs, while dismissal proceedings would require additional resources and, more importantly, an examination of how the district treats minority school children." Id. Accord, David I. Levine, The Chinese American Challenge to Court–Mandated Quotas in San Francisco's Public Schools: Notes from a (Partisan) Participant–Observer, 16 Harv. Blackletter L.J. 39, 124–29 (2000) (desire of school districts to return to local control is a myth).

(B) LEGISLATIVE DIRECTION TO TERMINATE JURISDICTION

In addition to guidance from the Supreme Court of the United States regarding when lower courts are obligated to withdraw supervision over an institutional defendant, the Congress of the United States has also provided specific direction through the Prison Litigation Reform Act (PLRA). Pub. L. No. 104–134, 110 Stat. 1321–66 (April 26, 1996). The two primary purposes of the PLRA were: (i) to end what congressional sponsors perceived to be judicial micromanagement of correctional facilities across the country; and (ii) to discourage prisoners from filing what sponsors of the legislation charged was a flood of frivolous lawsuits. See Note, Peanut Butter and Politics: An Evaluation of the Separation-of-

Powers Issues in Section 802 of the Prison Litigation Reform Act, 73 Ind. L.J. 329 (1997) (noting congressional indignation at prisoner's suit complaining of being served the wrong type of peanut butter).

In order to stop what Congress considered unreasonable judicial supervision of prisons and jails nationwide, the PLRA limits the prospective relief (i.e., other than compensatory damages, 18 U.S.C. § 3626(g)(7)) that a federal district court can order in a suit concerning prison conditions in federal, state or local incarceration facilities, § 3626(g)(2)(5). The PLRA does not merely apply to suits filed after its passage into law. Because facilities in over two-thirds of the states and territories were then under federal court order, National Prison Project, Status Report: State Prisons and the Courts 1 (Jan. 1, 1996), Congress also provided that the PLRA would reach prospective relief awarded in cases even where the court had entered judgment prior to its enactment. Under 18 U.S.C. § 3626(b)(2), prospective relief in pending cases is subject to "immediate termination" unless the court approving or granting the relief had found that the relief was narrowly drawn, extended no further than necessary to correct the violation of a federal right, and was the least intrusive way to remedy this violation.

Congress did recognize that consent decrees issued prior to the existence of the PLRA would be unlikely to have the requisite judicial findings. Indeed, as Professor Branham (from whose article this summary of the PLRA was adapted) has noted, correctional officials would typically demand that consent decrees provide that their existence did not constitute an admission that conditions in the correctional facility were unconstitutional; otherwise, the officials would have been "deluged by a wave of suits for damages filed by prisoners riding on the coattails of the consent decrees awarding injunctive relief to the plaintiffs." Lynn S. Branham, Keeping the "Wolf Out of the Fold": Separation of Powers and Congressional Termination of Equitable Relief, 26 J.Legis. 185, 191 (2000). Under § 3626(b)(3), a federal district court must grant a motion to terminate jurisdiction over a correctional facility unless the court makes written findings that: (1) the prospective relief is still needed to correct a "current and ongoing" violation of a federal right; (2) the relief extends no further than necessary to correct the violation; (3) the relief is "narrowly drawn"; and (4) the relief is the "least intrusive means" of rectifying the violation. Defendants or intervenors can renew the motion to terminate on an annual basis and the court must renew its findings that the prospective relief still meets all these conditions. 18 U.S.C. § 3626(b)(1)(ii). In response, plaintiffs need an opportunity to demonstrate "current and ongoing" violations of constitutional rights that would justify a court in refusing to terminate a consent decree pursuant to § 3626(b)(3). Laaman v. Warden, New Hampshire State Prison, 238 F.3d 14 (1st Cir.2001).

As the next case discusses, the PLRA also strongly encourages district courts to act very promptly on these motions.

MILLER v. FRENCH

Supreme Court of the United States, 2000
530 U.S. 327, 120 S.Ct. 2246, 147 L.Ed.2d 326

JUSTICE O'CONNOR delivered the opinion of the Court.

The Prison Litigation Reform Act of 1995 (PLRA) establishes standards for the entry and termination of prospective relief in civil actions challenging prison conditions. If prospective relief under an existing injunction does not satisfy these standards, a defendant or intervenor is entitled to "immediate termination" of that relief. 18 U.S.C. § 3626(b)(2). And under the PLRA's "automatic stay" provision, a motion to terminate prospective relief "shall operate as a stay" of that relief during the period beginning 30 days after the filing of the motion (extendable to up to 90 days for "good cause") and ending when the court rules on the motion. §§ 3626(e)(2), (3). The superintendent of the Pendleton Correctional Facility, which is currently operating under an ongoing injunction to remedy violations of the Eighth Amendment regarding conditions of confinement, filed a motion to terminate prospective relief under the PLRA. Respondent prisoners moved to enjoin the operation of the automatic stay provision of § 3626(e)(2), arguing that it is unconstitutional. The District Court enjoined the stay, and the Court of Appeals for the Seventh Circuit affirmed. We must decide whether a district court may enjoin the operation of the PLRA's automatic stay provision and, if not, whether that provision violates separation of powers principles.

I

A

This litigation began in 1975, when four inmates at what is now the Pendleton Correctional Facility brought a class action * * * on behalf of all persons who were, or would be, confined at the facility against the predecessors in office of petitioners (hereinafter State). After a trial, the District Court found that living conditions at the prison violated both state and federal law, including the Eighth Amendment's prohibition against cruel and unusual punishment, and the court issued an injunction to correct those violations. * * *

The Court of Appeals affirmed the * * * remedial order as to those aspects governing overcrowding and double celling, the use of mechanical restraints, staffing, and the quality of food and medical services, but it vacated those portions pertaining to exercise and recreation, protective custody, and fire and occupational safety standards. This ongoing injunctive relief has remained in effect ever since, with the last modification occurring in October 1988, when the parties resolved by joint stipulation the remaining issues related to fire and occupational safety standards.

B

In 1996, Congress enacted the PLRA. As relevant here, the PLRA establishes standards for the entry and termination of prospective relief in civil actions challenging conditions at prison facilities. Specifically, a court "shall not grant or approve any prospective relief unless the court finds that such relief is narrowly drawn, extends no further than necessary to correct the violation of a Federal right, and is the least intrusive means necessary to correct the violation of the Federal right." 18 U.S.C. § 3626(a)(1)(A). The same criteria apply to existing injunctions, and a defendant or intervenor may move to terminate prospective relief that does not meet this standard. See § 3626(b)(2). In particular, § 3626(b)(2) provides:

> "In any civil action with respect to prison conditions, a defendant or intervener shall be entitled to the immediate termination of any prospective relief if the relief was approved or granted in the absence of a finding by the court that the relief is narrowly drawn, extends no further than necessary to correct the violation of the Federal right, and is the least intrusive means necessary to correct the violation of the Federal right."

A court may not terminate prospective relief, however, if it "makes written findings based on the record that prospective relief remains necessary to correct a current and ongoing violation of the Federal right, extends no further than necessary to correct the violation of the Federal right, and that the prospective relief is narrowly drawn and the least intrusive means necessary to correct the violation." § 3626(b)(3). The PLRA also requires courts to rule "promptly" on motions to terminate prospective relief, with mandamus available to remedy a court's failure to do so. § 3626(e)(1).

Finally, the provision at issue here, § 3626(e)(2), dictates that, in certain circumstances, prospective relief shall be stayed pending resolution of a motion to terminate. Specifically, subsection (e)(2), entitled "Automatic Stay," states:

> "Any motion to modify or terminate prospective relief made under subsection (b) shall operate as a stay during the period—
>
> "(A)(i) beginning on the 30th day after such motion is filed, in the case of a motion made under paragraph (1) or (2) of subsection (b); ... and
>
> "(B) ending on the date the court enters a final order ruling on the motion."

As one of several 1997 amendments to the PLRA, Congress permitted courts to postpone the entry of the automatic stay for not more than 60 days for "good cause," which cannot include general congestion of the court's docket. 18 U.S.C. § 3626(e)(3).*

---

* As originally enacted, § 3626(e)(2) provided that "[a]ny prospective relief subject to a pending motion [for termination] shall be automatically stayed during the period ... beginning on the 30th day after such motion is filed ... and ending on the date the court enters a final order ruling on the motion." The 1997 amendments to the PLRA revised the automatic stay provision to its current form, and Congress specified that the 1997 amendments "shall apply to pending cases." 18 U.S.C. § 3626 note.

C

On June 5, 1997, the State filed a motion under § 3626(b) to terminate the prospective relief governing the conditions of confinement at the Pendleton Correctional Facility. In response, the prisoner class moved for a temporary restraining order or preliminary injunction to enjoin the operation of the automatic stay, arguing that § 3626(e)(2) is unconstitutional as both a violation of the Due Process Clause of the Fifth Amendment and separation of powers principles. The District Court granted the prisoners' motion, enjoining the automatic stay. The State appealed, and the United States intervened pursuant to 28 U.S.C. § 2403(a) to defend the constitutionality of § 3626(e)(2).

The Court of Appeals for the Seventh Circuit affirmed the District Court's order. * * *

We granted certiorari to resolve a conflict among the Courts of Appeals as to whether § 3626(e)(2) permits federal courts, in the exercise of their traditional equitable authority, to enjoin operation of the PLRA's automatic stay provision and, if not, to review the Court of Appeals' judgment that § 3626(e)(2), so construed, is unconstitutional.

II

We address the statutory question first. Both the State and the prisoner class agree * * * that § 3626(e)(2) precludes a district court from exercising its equitable powers to enjoin the automatic stay. The Government argues, however, that § 3626(e)(2) should be construed to leave intact the federal courts' traditional equitable discretion to "stay the stay," invoking two canons of statutory construction. First, the Government contends that we should not interpret a statute as displacing courts' traditional equitable authority to preserve the status quo pending resolution on the merits "[a]bsent the clearest command to the contrary." Califano v. Yamasaki, 442 U.S. 682, 705, 99 S.Ct. 2545, 61 L.Ed.2d 176 (1979). Second, the Government asserts that reading § 3626(e)(2) to remove that equitable power would raise serious separation of powers questions, and therefore should be avoided under the canon of constitutional doubt. Like the Court of Appeals, we do not lightly assume that Congress meant to restrict the equitable powers of the federal courts, and we agree that constitutionally doubtful constructions should be avoided where "fairly possible." But where Congress has made its intent clear, "we must give effect to that intent."

The text of § 3626(e)(2) provides that "[a]ny motion to ... terminate prospective relief under subsection (b) *shall operate as a stay*" during a fixed period of time, i.e., from 30 (or 90) days after the motion is filed until the court enters a final order ruling on the motion. 18 U.S.C. § 3626(e)(2) (emphasis added). The stay is "automatic" once a state defendant has filed a § 3626(b) motion, and the statutory command that such a motion "shall operate as a stay during the [specified time] period" indicates that the stay is *mandatory* throughout that period of time.

Nonetheless, the Government contends that reading the statute to preserve courts' traditional equitable powers to enter appropriate injunctive relief is consistent with this text because, in its view, § 3626(e)(2) is simply a burden-shifting mechanism. That is, the purpose of the automatic stay provision is merely to relieve defendants of the burden of establishing the prerequisites for a stay and to eliminate courts' discretion to deny a stay, even if those prerequisites are established, based on the public interest or hardship to the plaintiffs. Thus, under this reading, nothing in § 3626(e)(2) prevents courts from subsequently suspending the automatic stay by applying the traditional standards for injunctive relief.

Such an interpretation, however, would subvert the plain meaning of the statute, making its mandatory language merely permissive. Section 3626(e)(2) states that a motion to terminate prospective relief "*shall operate* as a stay *during*" the specified time period from 30 (or 90) days after the filing of the § 3626(b) motion *until* the court rules on that motion. (Emphasis added.) Thus, not only does the statute employ the mandatory term "shall," but it also specifies the points at which the operation of the stay is to begin and end. In other words, contrary to Justice Breyer's suggestion that the language of § 3626(e)(2) says nothing ... about the district court's power to modify or suspend the operation of the "stay," § 3626(e)(2) unequivocally mandates that the stay "shall operate *during*" this specific interval. To allow courts to exercise their equitable discretion to prevent the stay from "operating" during this statutorily prescribed period would be to contradict § 3626(e)(2)'s plain terms. It would mean that the motion to terminate merely *may* operate as a stay, despite the statute's command that it "shall" have such effect. If Congress had intended to accomplish nothing more than to relieve state defendants of the burden of establishing the prerequisites for a stay, the language of § 3626(e)(2) is, at best, an awkward and indirect means to achieve that result.

Viewing the automatic stay provision in the context of § 3626 as a whole further confirms that Congress intended to prohibit federal courts from exercising their equitable authority to suspend operation of the automatic stay. * * *

Finally, the Government finds support for its view in § 3626(e)(3). That provision authorizes an extension, for "good cause," of the starting point for the automatic stay, from 30 days after the § 3626(b) motion is filed until 90 days after that motion is filed. The Government explains that, by allowing the court to prevent the entry of the stay for up to 60 days under the relatively generous "good cause" standard, Congress by negative implication has preserved courts' discretion to suspend the stay *after* that time under the more stringent standard for injunctive relief. To be sure, allowing a delay in entry of the stay for 60 days based on a good cause standard does not by itself necessarily imply that any other reason for preventing the operation of the stay—for example, on the basis of traditional equitable principles—is precluded. But § 3626(e)(3) cannot be read in isolation. When §§ 3626(e)(2) and (3) are read together, it is clear that the district court cannot enjoin the operation of the automatic stay. The § 3626(b) motion "shall operate as a stay during" a specific time period. Section 3626(e)(3) only adjusts the starting point for the stay, and it merely permits that starting point to be delayed. Once the 90-day period has passed, the § 3626(b) motion "shall operate as a stay" until the court rules on the § 3626(b) motion. During that time, any attempt to enjoin the stay is irreconcilable with the plain language of the statute.

Thus, although we should not construe a statute to displace courts' traditional equitable authority absent the "clearest command," or an "inescapable inference" to the contrary, we are convinced that Congress' intent to remove such discretion is unmistakable in § 3626(e)(2). And while this construction raises constitutional questions, the canon of constitutional doubt permits us to avoid such questions only where the saving construction is not "plainly contrary to the intent of Congress." * * * Like the Court of Appeals, we find that § 3626(e)(2) is unambiguous, and accordingly, we cannot adopt Justice Breyer's "more flexible interpretation" of the statute. Any construction that preserved courts' equitable discretion to enjoin the automatic stay would effectively convert the PLRA's mandatory stay into a discretionary one. Because this would be plainly contrary to Congress' intent in enacting the stay provision, we must confront the constitutional issue.

III

The Constitution enumerates and separates the powers of the three branches of Government in Articles I, II, and III, and it is this "very structure" of the Constitution that exemplifies the concept of separation of powers. While the boundaries between the three branches are not " 'hermetically' sealed," the Constitution prohibits one branch from encroaching on the central prerogatives of another. The powers of the Judicial Branch are set forth in Article III, § 1, which states that the "judicial Power of the United States shall be vested in one supreme Court and in such inferior Courts as Congress may from time to time ordain and establish," and provides that these federal courts shall be staffed by judges who hold office during good behavior, and whose compensation shall not be diminished during tenure in office. As we explained in Plaut v. Spendthrift Farm, Inc., 514 U.S. 211, 115 S.Ct. 1447, 131 L.Ed.2d 328 (1995), Article III "gives the Federal Judiciary the power, not merely to rule on cases, but to decide them, subject to review only by superior courts in the Article III hierarchy."

Respondent prisoners contend that § 3626(e)(2) encroaches on the central prerogatives of the Judiciary and thereby violates the separation of powers doctrine. It does this, the prisoners assert, by legislatively suspending a final judgment of an Article III court in violation of *Plaut* and Hayburn's Case, 2 Dall. 409, 1 L.Ed. 436 (1792). According to the prisoners, the remedial order governing living conditions at the Pendleton Correctional Facility is a final judgment of an Article III court, and § 3626(e)(2) constitutes an impermissible usurpation of judicial power because it commands the district court to suspend prospective relief under that order, albeit temporarily. An analysis of the principles underlying *Hayburn's Case* and *Plaut*, as well as an examination of § 3626(e)(2)'s interaction with the other provisions of § 3626, makes clear that § 3626(e)(2) does not offend these separation of powers principles.

Hayburn's Case arose out of a 1792 statute that authorized pensions for veterans of the Revolutionary War. The statute provided that the circuit courts were to review the applications and determine the appropriate amount of the pension, but that the Secretary of War had the discretion either to adopt or reject the courts' findings. Although this Court did not reach the constitutional issue in *Hayburn's Case*, the opinions of five Justices, sitting on Circuit Courts, were reported, and we have since recognized that the case "stands for the principle that Congress cannot vest review of the decisions of Article III courts in officials of the Executive Branch." *Plaut*; see also Morrison v. Olson, 487 U.S. 654, 677, n. 15, 108 S.Ct. 2597, 101 L.Ed.2d 569 (1988). As we recognized in *Plaut*, such an effort by a coequal branch to "annul a final judgment" is " 'an assumption of Judicial power' and therefore forbidden."

Unlike the situation in *Hayburn's Case*, § 3626(e)(2) does not involve the direct review of a judicial decision by officials of the Legislative or Executive Branches. Nonetheless, the prisoners suggest that § 3626(e)(2) falls within *Hayburn's* prohibition against an indirect legislative "suspension" or reopening of a final judgment, such as that addressed in *Plaut*. See *Plaut* (quoting *Hayburn's Case*, supra, at 413 (opinion of Iredell, J., and Sitgreaves, D.J.) (" '[N]o decision of any court of the United States can, under any circumstances, . . . be liable to a revision, or even suspension, by the [l]egislature itself, in whom no judicial power of any kind appears to be vested' ")). In *Plaut*, we held that a federal statute that required federal courts to reopen final judgments that had been entered before the statute's enactment was unconstitutional on separation of powers grounds. The plaintiffs had brought a civil securities fraud action seeking money damages. While that action was pending, we ruled in Lampf, Pleva, Lipkind, Prupis & Petigrow v. Gilbertson, 501 U.S. 350, 111 S.Ct. 2773, 115 L.Ed.2d 321 (1991), that such suits must be commenced within one year after the discovery of the facts constituting the violation and within three years after such violation. In light of this intervening decision, the *Plaut* plaintiffs' suit was untimely, and the District Court accordingly dismissed the action as time barred. After the judgment dismissing the case had become final, Congress enacted a statute providing for the reinstatement of those actions, including the *Plaut* plaintiffs', that had been dismissed under *Lampf* but that would have been timely under the previously applicable statute of limitations.

We concluded that this retroactive command that federal courts reopen final judgments exceeded Congress' authority. The decision of an inferior court within the Article III hierarchy is not the final word of the department (unless the time for appeal has expired), and "[i]t is the obligation of the last court in the hierarchy that rules on the case to give effect to Congress's latest enactment, even when that has the effect of overturning the judgment of an inferior court, since each court, at every level, must 'decide according to existing laws.'" [*Plaut*.] But once a judicial decision achieves finality, it "becomes the last word of the judicial department." And because Article III "gives the Federal Judiciary the power, not merely to rule on cases, but to decide them, subject to review only by superior courts in the Article III hierarchy," the "judicial Power is one to render dispositive judgments," and Congress cannot retroactively command Article III courts to reopen final judgments, id. (quoting Easterbrook, Presidential Review, 40 Case W.Res.L.Rev. 905, 926 (1990) (internal quotation marks omitted)).

Plaut, however, was careful to distinguish the situation before the Court in that case—legislation that attempted to reopen the dismissal of a suit seeking money damages—from legislation that "altered the prospective effect of injunctions entered by Article III courts." We emphasized that "nothing in our holding today calls ... into question" Congress' authority to alter the prospective effect of previously entered injunctions. Prospective relief under a continuing, executory decree remains subject to alteration due to changes in the underlying law. Cf. Landgraf v. USI Film Products, 511 U.S. 244, 273, 114 S.Ct. 1483, 128 L.Ed.2d 229 (1994) ("When the intervening statute authorizes or affects the propriety of prospective relief, application of the new provision is not retroactive"). This conclusion follows from our decisions in Pennsylvania v. Wheeling & Belmont Bridge Co., 54 U.S. (13 How.) 518, 14 L.Ed. 249 (1851) (*Wheeling Bridge I*) and Pennsylvania v. Wheeling & Belmont Bridge Co., 59 U.S. (18 How.) 421, 15 L.Ed. 435 (1855) (*Wheeling Bridge II*).

In *Wheeling Bridge I*, we held that a bridge across the Ohio River, because it was too low, unlawfully "obstruct[ed] the navigation of the Ohio," and ordered that the bridge be raised or permanently removed. Shortly thereafter, Congress enacted legislation declaring the bridge to be "lawful structur[e]," establishing the bridge as a "'post-roa[d] for the passage of the mails of the United States,'" and declaring that the Wheeling and Belmont Bridge Company was authorized to maintain the bridge at its then-current site and elevation. *Wheeling Bridge II*. After the bridge was destroyed in a storm, Pennsylvania sued to enjoin the bridge's reconstruction, arguing that the statute legalizing the bridge was unconstitutional because it effectively annulled the Court's decision in *Wheeling Bridge I*. We rejected that argument, concluding that the decree in *Wheeling Bridge I* provided for ongoing relief by "directing the abatement of the obstruction" which enjoined the defendants' from any continuance or reconstruction of the obstruction. Because the intervening statute altered the underlying law such that the bridge was no longer an unlawful obstruction, we held that it was "quite plain the decree of the court cannot be enforced." *Wheeling Bridge II*. The Court explained that had *Wheeling Bridge I* awarded money damages in an action at law, then that judgment would be final, and Congress' later action could not have affected plaintiff's right to those damages. But because the decree entered in *Wheeling Bridge I* provided for prospective relief—a continuing injunction against the continuation or reconstruction of the bridge—the ongoing validity of the injunctive relief depended on "whether or not [the bridge] interferes with the right of navigation." When Congress altered the underlying law such that the bridge was no longer an unlawful obstruction, the injunction against the maintenance of the bridge was not enforceable.

Applied here, the principles of *Wheeling Bridge II* demonstrate that the automatic stay of § 3626(e)(2) does not unconstitutionally "suspend" or reopen a judgment of an Article III court. Section § 3626(e)(2) does not by itself "tell judges when, how, or what to do." Instead, § 3626(e)(2) merely reflects the change implemented by § 3626(b), which does the "heavy lifting" in the statutory scheme by establishing new standards for prospective relief. Section 3626 prohibits the continuation of prospective relief that was "approved or granted in the absence of a finding by the court that the relief is narrowly drawn, extends no further than necessary to correct the violation of the Federal right, and is the least intrusive means to correct the violation," § 3626(b)(2), or in the absence of "findings based on the record that prospective relief remains necessary to correct a current and ongoing violation of a Federal right, extends no further than necessary to correct the violation of the Federal right, and that the prospective relief is narrowly drawn and the least intrusive means necessary to correct the violation," § 3626(b)(3). Accordingly, if prospective relief under an existing decree had been granted or approved absent such findings, then that prospective relief must cease, see § 3626(b)(2), unless and until the court makes findings on the record that such relief remains necessary to correct an ongoing violation and is narrowly tailored, see § 3626(b)(3). The PLRA's automatic stay provision assists in the enforcement of §§ 3626(b)(2) and (3) by requiring the court to stay any prospective relief that, due to the change in the underlying standard, is no longer enforceable, i.e., prospective relief that is not supported by the findings specified in §§ 3626(b)(2) and (3).

By establishing new standards for the enforcement of prospective relief in § 3626(b), Congress has altered the relevant underlying law. The PLRA has restricted courts' authority to issue and enforce prospective relief concerning prison conditions, requiring that such relief be supported by findings and precisely tailored to what is needed to remedy the violation of a federal right. We note that the constitutionality of § 3626(b) is not challenged here; we assume, without deciding, that the new standards it pronounces are effective. As *Plaut* and *Wheeling Bridge II* instruct, when Congress changes the law underlying a judgment awarding prospective relief, that relief is no longer enforceable to the extent it is inconsistent with the new law. Although the remedial injunction here is a "final judgment" for purposes of appeal, it is not the "last word of the judicial department." *Plaut*. The provision of prospective relief is subject to the continuing supervisory jurisdiction of the court, and therefore may be altered according to subsequent changes in the law. See Rufo v.

Inmates of Suffolk County Jail, 502 U.S. 367, 388, 112 S.Ct. 748, 116 L.Ed.2d 867 (1992). Prospective relief must be "modified if, as it later turns out, one or more of the obligations placed upon the parties has become impermissible under federal law." Ibid.; see also Railway Employees v. Wright, 364 U.S. 642, 646–647, 81 S.Ct. 368, 5 L.Ed.2d 349 (1961) (a court has the authority to alter the prospective effect of an injunction to reflect a change in circumstances, whether of law or fact, that has occurred since the injunction was entered) * * *.

The entry of the automatic stay under § 3626(e)(2) helps to implement the change in the law caused by §§ 3626(b)(2) and (3). If the prospective relief under the existing decree is not supported by the findings required under § 3626(b)(2), and the court has not made the findings required by § 3626(b)(3), then prospective relief is no longer enforceable and must be stayed. The entry of the stay does not reopen or "suspend" the previous judgment, nor does it divest the court of authority to decide the merits of the termination motion. Rather, the stay merely reflects the changed legal circumstances—that prospective relief under the existing decree is no longer enforceable, and remains unenforceable unless and until the court makes the findings required by § 3626(b)(3).

For the same reasons, § 3626(e)(2) does not violate the separation of powers principle articulated in United States v. Klein, 13 Wall. 128, 20 L.Ed. 519 (1872). In that case, Klein, the executor of the estate of a Confederate sympathizer, sought to recover the value of property seized by the United States during the Civil War, which by statute was recoverable if Klein could demonstrate that the decedent had not given aid or comfort to the rebellion. In United States v. Padelford, 9 Wall. 531, 542–543, 19 L.Ed. 788 (1870), we held that a Presidential pardon satisfied the burden of proving that no such aid or comfort had been given. While Klein's case was pending, Congress enacted a statute providing that a pardon would instead be taken as proof that the pardoned individual had in fact aided the enemy, and if the claimant offered proof of a pardon the court must dismiss the case for lack of jurisdiction. We concluded that the statute was unconstitutional because it purported to "prescribe rules of decision to the Judicial Department of the government in cases pending before it."

Here, the prisoners argue that Congress has similarly prescribed a rule of decision because, for the period of time until the district court makes a final decision on the merits of the motion to terminate prospective relief, § 3626(e)(2) mandates a particular outcome: the termination of prospective relief. As we noted in *Plaut*, however, "[w]hatever the precise scope of *Klein*, ... later decisions have made clear that its prohibition does not take hold when Congress 'amend[s] applicable law.'" The prisoners concede this point but contend that, because § 3626(e)(2) does not itself amend the legal standard, *Klein* is still applicable. As we have explained, however, § 3626(e)(2) must be read not in isolation, but in the context of § 3626 as a whole. Section 3626(e)(2) operates in conjunction with the new standards for the continuation of prospective relief; if the new standards of § 3626(b)(2) are not met, then the stay "shall operate" unless and until the court makes the findings required by § 3626(b)(3). Rather than prescribing a rule of decision, § 3626(e)(2) simply imposes the consequences of the court's application of the new legal standard.

Finally, the prisoners assert that, even if § 3626(e)(2) does not fall within the recognized prohibitions of *Hayburn's Case*, *Plaut*, or *Klein*, it still offends the principles of separation of powers because it places a deadline on judicial decisionmaking, thereby interfering with core judicial functions. Congress' imposition of a time limit in § 3626(e)(2), however, does not in itself offend the structural concerns underlying the Constitution's separation of powers. For example, if the PLRA granted courts 10 years to determine whether they could make the required findings, then certainly the PLRA would raise no apprehensions that Congress had encroached on the core function of the Judiciary to decide "cases and controversies properly before them." The respondents' concern with the time limit, then, must be its relative brevity. But whether the time is so short that it deprives litigants of a meaningful opportunity to be heard is a due process question, an issue that is not before us. We leave open, therefore, the question whether this time limit, particularly in a complex case, may implicate due process concerns.

In contrast to due process, which principally serves to protect the personal rights of litigants to a full and fair hearing, separation of powers principles are primarily addressed to the structural concerns of protecting the role of the independent Judiciary within the constitutional design. In this action, we have no occasion to decide whether there could be a time constraint on judicial action that was so severe that it implicated these structural separation of powers concerns. The PLRA does not deprive courts of their adjudicatory role, but merely provides a new legal standard for relief and encourages courts to apply that standard promptly.

Through the PLRA, Congress clearly intended to make operation of the automatic stay mandatory, precluding courts from exercising their equitable powers to enjoin the stay. And we conclude that this provision does not violate separation of powers principles. Accordingly, the judgment of the Court of Appeals for the Seventh Circuit is reversed, and the action is remanded for further proceedings consistent with this opinion.

It is so ordered.

JUSTICE SOUTER, with whom JUSTICE GINSBURG joins, concurring in part and dissenting in part.

I agree that 18 U.S.C. § 3626(e)(2) is unambiguous and join Parts I and II of the majority opinion. I also agree that applying the automatic stay may raise the due process issue, of whether a plaintiff has a fair chance to preserve an existing judgment that was valid when entered. But I believe that applying the statute may also raise a serious separation-of-powers issue if the time it allows turns out to be inadequate for a court to determine whether the new prerequisite to relief is satisfied in a particular case.[1] I thus do not join Part III of the Court's opinion and on remand would require proceedings consistent with this one. I respectfully dissent from the terms of the Court's disposition.

A prospective remedial order may rest on at least three different legal premises: the underlying right meant to be secured; the rules of procedure for obtaining relief, defining requisites of pleading, notice, and so on; and, in some cases, rules lying between the other two, such as those defining a required level of certainty before some remedy may be ordered, or the permissible scope of relief. At issue here are rules of the last variety.

Congress has the authority to change rules of this sort by imposing new conditions precedent for the continuing enforcement of existing, prospective remedial orders and requiring courts to apply the new rules to those orders. Cf. *Plaut*. If its legislation gives courts adequate time to determine the applicability of a new rule to an old order and to take the action necessary to apply it or to vacate the order, there seems little basis for claiming that Congress has crossed the constitutional line to interfere with the performance of any judicial function. But if determining whether a new rule applies requires time (say, for new factfinding) and if the statute provides insufficient time for a court to make that determination before the statute invalidates an extant remedial order, the application of the statute raises a serious question whether Congress has in practical terms assumed the judicial function. In such a case, the prospective order suddenly turns unenforceable not because a court has made a judgment to terminate it due to changed law or fact, but because no one can tell in the time allowed whether the new rule requires modification of the old order. One way to view this result is to see the Congress as mandating modification of an order that may turn out to be perfectly enforceable under the new rule, depending on judicial factfinding. If the facts are taken this way, the new statute might well be treated as usurping the judicial function of determining the applicability of a general rule in particular factual circumstances.[3] Cf. *Klein*.

Whether this constitutional issue arises on the facts of this action, however, is something we cannot yet tell, for the District Court did not address the sufficiency of the time provided by the statute to make the

---

1. The Court forecloses the possibility of a separation-of-powers challenge based on insufficient time under the PLRA: "In this action, we have no occasion to decide whether there could be a time constraint on judicial action that was so severe that it implicated these structural separation of powers concerns. The PLRA does not deprive courts of their adjudicatory role, but merely provides a new legal standard for relief and encourages courts to apply that standard promptly."

3. The constitutional question inherent in these possible circumstances does not seem to be squarely addressed by any of our cases. Congress did not engage in discretionary review of a particular judicial judgment, cf. *Plaut* (characterizing *Hayburn's Case*), or try to modify a final, non-prospective judgment. [Cf. *Plaut*.] Nor would a stay result from the judicial application of a change in the underlying law, cf. *Wheeling Bridge II*; *Plaut* (characterizing *Klein*). Instead, if the time is insufficient for a court to make a judicial determination about the applicability of the new rules, the stay would result from the inability of the Judicial Branch to exercise the judicial power of determining whether the new rules applied at all. Cf. Marbury v. Madison, 1 Cranch 137, 177, 2 L.Ed. 60 (1803) ("It is emphatically the province and duty of the judicial department to say what the law is").

findings required by § 3626(b)(3) in this particular action. Absent that determination, I would not decide the separation-of-powers question, but simply remand for further proceedings. If the District Court determined both that it lacked adequate time to make the requisite findings in the period before the automatic stay would become effective, and that applying the stay would violate the separation of powers, the question would then be properly presented.

JUSTICE BREYER, with whom JUSTICE STEVENS joins, dissenting.

* * *

The Solicitor General * * * believes that the view adopted by the majority interpretation is too rigid and calls into doubt the constitutionality of the provision. He argues that the statute is silent as to whether the district court can modify or suspend the operation of the automatic stay. He would find in that silence sufficient authority for the court to create an exception to the 90–day time limit where circumstances make it necessary to do so. As so read, the statute would neither displace the courts' traditional equitable authority nor raise significant constitutional difficulties. See Califano v. Yamasaki, 442 U.S. 682, 705, 99 S.Ct. 2545, 61 L.Ed.2d 176 (1979) (only "clearest" congressional "command" displaces courts' traditional equity powers); Edward J. DeBartolo Corp. v. Florida Gulf Coast Building & Constr. Trades Council, 485 U.S. 568, 575, 108 S.Ct. 1392, 99 L.Ed.2d 645 (1988) (the Court will construe a statute to avoid constitutional problems "unless such construction is plainly contrary to the intent of Congress").

I agree with the Solicitor General and believe we should adopt that " 'reasonable construction' " of the statute. Ibid. (quoting Hooper v. California, 155 U.S. 648, 657, 15 S.Ct. 207, 39 L.Ed. 297 (1895), stating " 'every reasonable construction must be resorted to, in order to save a statute from unconstitutionality' ").

I

At the outset, one must understand why a more flexible interpretation of the statute might be needed. To do so, one must keep in mind the extreme circumstances that at least some prison litigation originally sought to correct, the complexity of the resulting judicial decrees, and the potential difficulties arising out of the subsequent need to review those decrees in order to make certain they follow Congress' PLRA directives.

* * *

Where prison litigation is * * * complex * * *, it may prove difficult for a district court to reach a fair and accurate decision about which orders remain necessary, and are the "least intrusive means" available, to prevent or correct a continuing violation of federal law. The orders, which were needed to resolve serious constitutional problems and may still be needed where compliance has not yet been assured, are complex, interrelated, and applicable to many different institutions. Ninety days might not provide sufficient time to ascertain the views of several different parties, including monitors, to allow them to present evidence, and to permit each to respond to the arguments and evidence of the others.

It is at least possible, then, that the statute, as the majority reads it, would sometimes terminate a complex system of orders entered over a period of years by a court familiar with the local problem—perhaps only to reinstate those orders later, when the termination motion can be decided. Such an automatic termination could leave constitutionally prohibited conditions unremedied, at least temporarily. Alternatively, the threat of termination could lead a district court to abbreviate proceedings that fairness would otherwise demand. At a minimum, the mandatory automatic stay would provide a recipe for uncertainty, as complex judicial orders that have long governed the administration of particular prison systems suddenly turn off, then (perhaps selectively) back on. So read, the statute directly interferes with a court's exercise of its traditional equitable authority, rendering temporarily ineffective pre-existing remedies aimed at correcting past, and perhaps ongoing, violations of the Constitution. That interpretation, as the majority itself concedes, might give rise to serious constitutional problems.

II

The Solicitor General's more flexible reading of the statute avoids all these problems. He notes that the relevant language says that the motion to modify or terminate prospective relief "shall operate as a stay" after a period of 30 days, extendable for "good cause" to 90 days. 18 U.S.C. § 3626(e)(2). The language says nothing, however, about the district court's power to modify or suspend the operation of the "stay." In the Solicitor General's view, the "stay" would determine the legal status quo; but the district court would retain its traditional equitable power to change that status quo once the party seeking the modification or suspension of the operation of the stay demonstrates that the stay "would cause irreparable injury, that the termination motion is likely to be defeated, and that the merits of the motion cannot be resolved before the automatic stay takes effect." Where this is shown, the "court has discretion to suspend the automatic stay and require prison officials to comply with outstanding court orders until the court resolves the termination motion on the merits," subject to immediate appellate review, 18 U.S.C. § 3626(e)(4).

Is this interpretation a "reasonable construction" of the statute? I note first that the statutory language is open to the Solicitor General's interpretation. A district court ordinarily can stay the operation of a judicial order (such as a stay or injunction), when a party demonstrates the need to do so in accordance with traditional equitable criteria (irreparable injury, likelihood of success on the merits, and a balancing of possible harms to the parties and the public). There is no logical inconsistency in saying both (1) a motion (to terminate) "shall operate as a stay," and (2) the court retains the power to modify or delay the operation of the stay in appropriate circumstances. The statutory language says nothing about this last-mentioned power. It is silent. It does not direct the district court to leave the stay in place come what may.

* * *

Further, the legislative history is neutral, for it is silent on this issue. Yet there is relevant judicial precedent. That precedent does not read statutory silence as denying judges authority to exercise their traditional equitable powers. Rather, it reads statutory silence as authorizing the exercise of those powers. * * * These cases recognize the importance of permitting courts in equity cases to tailor relief, and related relief procedure, to the exigencies of particular cases and individual circumstances. In doing so, they recognize the fact that in certain circumstances justice requires the flexibility necessary to treat different cases differently—the rationale that underlies equity itself. Cf. Hecht Co. v. Bowles, 321 U.S. 321, 329, 64 S.Ct. 587, 88 L.Ed. 754 (1944) ("The essence of equity jurisdiction has been the power of the Chancellor to do equity and to mould each decree to the necessities of the particular case").

Finally, the more flexible interpretation is consistent with Congress' purposes as revealed in the statute. Those purposes include the avoidance of new judicial relief that is overly broad or no longer necessary and the reassessment of pre-existing relief to bring it into conformity with these standards. But Congress has simultaneously expressed its intent to maintain relief that is narrowly drawn and necessary to end unconstitutional practices. See 18 U.S.C. §§ 3626(a)(1), (a)(2), (b)(3). The statute, as flexibly interpreted, risks interfering with the first set of objectives only to the extent that the speedy appellate review provided in the statute fails to control district court error. The same interpretation avoids the improper provisional termination of relief that is constitutionally necessary. The risk of an occasional small additional delay seems a comparatively small price to pay (in terms of the statute's entire set of purposes) to avoid the serious constitutional problems that accompany the majority's more rigid interpretation.

* * *

Notes

1. The underlying constitutional law is somewhat difficult to parse. One student commentator has tried to harmonize the precedents later applied in *Miller*:

> Although the Framers saw the judiciary as the "least dangerous" branch, this conception was based on the judiciary remaining "truly distinct" from the legislature and the executive. As Alexander Hamilton argued, "liberty can have nothing to fear from the judiciary alone, but would have everything to fear from its union with either of the other departments." So although the Framers wanted to ensure that Congress

did not overstep its boundaries into the judicial province, they were equally concerned that the judiciary not intrude on the legislature's province.

In combination with *Plaut*, the *Wheeling Bridge* exception ensures this balance. Under *Plaut*, Congress may not overrule the courts when their judgments govern solely past conduct. Similarly, *Wheeling Bridge* dictates that the courts may not overrule Congress when the courts' judgments purport to govern future conduct. The courts only have the power of "(t)he interpretation of the laws," not the power to make the laws. It remains to the legislature to "prescrib(e) the rules by which the duties and rights of every citizen are to be regulated." If it were otherwise, a court would be able to annul a congressional act as it applied to certain individuals through "prophetic discernment," leading to the same evils courts are so concerned about when Congress is perceived to be overreaching.

Comment, The Wheeling Bridge Exception: Reopening Executory Judgments of Article III Courts, 67 U.Chi.L.Rev. 547, 560 (2000).

2. Following these principles, nine circuit courts have found the termination provisions of the PLRA to be constitutional. Ruiz v. United States, 243 F.3d 941, 945 n.6 (5th Cir.2001) (citing cases). For example, the Fifth Circuit reasoned:

When a court enters prospective injunctive relief and retains jurisdiction over the case, the judgment is not final. As long as the court retains the power to terminate or modify prospective injunctive relief in a particular case, Congress has the power to change the law and require that the change be applied with respect to the relief over which the court has retained power.

Id. at 948.

The Fifth Circuit panel joined the other circuits in rejecting the contention, based on *Klein*, that the PLRA's termination provisions unconstitutionally prescribed a rule of decision in a discrete group of cases:

By enacting the termination provisions of the PLRA, Congress has properly invoked its legislative authority to establish applicable standards and procedural rules for courts to grant or continue prospective relief regarding prison conditions. Section 3626(b) is like any other statute in that it establishes a generally applicable legal rule and allows district courts to apply that rule to the facts of specific cases. Moreover, under § 3626(b), a court is not required to terminate existing prospective relief if it finds that relief to be narrowly tailored to remedy a current and ongoing constitutional violation. Thus, the PLRA's termination provisions do not dictate results in cases pending before Article III courts.

Id. at 949.

3. Despite these principles, *Miller* perhaps has broken new ground:

Miller stands for the proposition that Congress has the power to revise or suspend judicial decisions without regard to change in underlying law, so long as the revision or suspension assists in implementing new legal standards enacted by Congress. It is crucial to understand that the automatic stay provision suspends injunctions for prospective relief against official conduct that courts have found to violate the Constitution solely upon the passage of a specified time period after the filing of a motion. The Court's assertion, that the stay operates only if such injunctions are no longer enforceable because they do not meet the new standards for injunctive relief, is simply not true. The unambiguous words of the statute state that it is the motion to terminate prospective relief that operates as a stay, not any ruling by a court that the new standards are not satisfied. Suppose, for example, a court concludes, after the enactment of the PLRA, that conditions in a prison violate the constitutional prohibition against cruel and unusual punishment. It grants injunctive relief that it expressly finds to meet the new standards of the PLRA—the relief is narrowly drawn, extends no further than necessary and is the least intrusive means to correct the unconstitutional conditions. Two years and a day later, defendants move to terminate the injunction and to stay the injunction until the motion to terminate is decided. If the court does not rule on the motion to terminate within the congressional deadline, the injunction must be stayed. Thus, the automatic stay provision will have taken effect even though the required findings were previously made and it has not been shown that the prerequisites for injunctive relief no longer exist.

Lloyd C. Anderson, Congressional Control Over the Jurisdiction of the Federal Courts: A New Threat to James Madison's Compromise, 39 Brandeis L.J. 417, 442–43 (2000–01). Compare The Supreme Court—Leading Cases, 114 Harv. L.Rev. 309, 318 (2000) (automatic stay "gives effect to the presumption that injunctions in the prison context are constitutionally suspect").

4. What is the legal effect of a judicial decision that a consent decree or injunction no longer is entitled to prospective effect because of the PLRA? Some courts have assumed that the decree must be vacated when the court is no longer entitled to enforce prospective relief. E.g., Imprisoned Citizens Union v. Ridge, 169 F.3d 178 (3d Cir.1999). Other courts have seen an important, if subtle, distinction:

> "While terminating a consent decree strips it of future potency, the decree's past puissance is preserved and certain of its collateral effects may endure. Vacating a consent decree, however, wipes the slate clean, not only rendering the decree sterile for future purposes, but also eviscerating any collateral effects and, indeed, casting a shadow on past actions taken under the decree's imprimatur.... [N]othing in the PLRA even hints that consent decrees must be vacated when prospective relief is terminated."

Benjamin v. Jacobson, 172 F.3d 144, 159 (2d Cir.en banc), cert. denied, 528 U.S. 824, 120 S.Ct. 72, 145 L.Ed.2d 61 (1999) (quoting Inmates of Suffolk County Jail v. Rouse, 129 F.3d 649, 662 (1st Cir.1997), cert. denied, 524 U.S. 951, 118 S.Ct. 2366, 141 L.Ed.2d 735 (1998)). A key practical difference will concern whether the contract which underlies the consent decree is still in existence and therefore enforceable in state court, even if a federal court may no longer grant prospective relief. Compare Gilmore v. California, 220 F.3d

987, 1003 (9th Cir.2000) (possibly enforceable in state court) with Hazen ex rel. LeGear v. Reagen, 208 F.3d 697 (8th Cir.2000) (Congress had the power to provide that PLRA prohibits state-court enforcement, on a contract theory or otherwise, of federal prison conditions consent decrees that do not meet PLRA standards).

5. The PLRA also attempted to address the concern that the defendants in certain prison conditions cases, like their counterparts in some school desegregation cases (see p. 281), may not want to seek termination of the decree. The PLRA grants the right to intervene to seek termination or to oppose the imposition or continuation of prospective relief to "any state or local official including a legislator or unit of government whose jurisdiction or function includes the appropriation of funds for ... prison facilities." 18 U.S.C. § 3626(a)(3)(F). See, e.g., Ruiz v. Estelle, 161 F.3d 814 (5th Cir.1998) (ordering intervention of individual state legislators in prison litigation even though "appropriation of funds" requires action of legislature as a unit or whole). Should this concept be extended to other types of institutional reform litigation? See David I. Levine, The Chinese American Challenge to Court–Mandated Quotas in San Francisco's Public Schools: Notes from a (Partisan) Participant–Observer, 16 Harv. Blackletter L.J. 39, 127 (2000) (creation of a comparable right to intervene in school desegregation cases "would encourage another source of interested parties to call problems to the attention of a court that might otherwise be tempted to look the other way in the name of doing good").

6. Some critics feared (and some proponents may have hoped) that the PLRA would lead to the end of all existing prison decrees. See, e.g., Ira Bloom, Prisons, Prisoners, and Pine Forests: Congress Breaches the Wall Separating Legislative from Judicial Power, 40 Ariz.L.Rev. 389, 410 (1998) (contending that the PLRA violates *Klein* because it "virtually compel[s] a decision favorable to the governmental entity involved"). A decade of experience under the PLRA shows that the actual results are more mixed. Some courts have terminated supervision over prison consent decrees. E.g., Martin v. Ellandson, 122 F.Supp.2d 1017 (S.D.Iowa 2000). Other district courts have reviewed decrees and have narrowed their scope, but have not terminated jurisdiction entirely. E.g., Ruiz v. Johnson, 154 F.Supp.2d 975 (S.D.Tex.2001) (finding persisting violations in the Texas prisons in the areas of: the conditions of confinement in administrative segregation, the failure to provide reasonable safety to inmates against assault and abuse, and the excessive use of force by correctional officers). For a careful examination of the effect of the PLRA on litigation in correctional settings, see Margo Schlanger, Civil Rights Injunctions Over Time: A Case Study of Jail and Prison Court Orders, 81 N.Y.U.L.Rev. 550 (2006) (documenting the reduction in the volume of existing and new court orders regulating jails and prisons).

C. ENFORCEMENT OF THE DECREE

The contempt power is the court's ultimate weapon to deter, overcome, or punish disobedience of an injunction. Because contempt is a powerful weapon, it may harm the defendant more than it helps the plaintiff and can require a heavy expenditure of judicial time and credibility. So, when a plaintiff complains that a defendant has violated an injunction, courts will often explore less intrusive techniques to prompt compliance, such as "clarifying" the original injunction or issuing a more prophylactic one, instead of initiating contempt proceedings. Such techniques, although nonpunitive in theory, can be quite painful to the defendant.

Just as the likelihood that the defendant will violate the plaintiff's rights helps determine whether a court will issue an injunction and its scope, so the likelihood that the defendant will continue to resist compliance with an injunction helps determine how a court will respond to allegations that the defendant has violated it in the past. Professor Robert Goldstein suggests one possible "scenario of escalating intrusiveness" in an institutional reform case:

1. Declaratory judgment with or without guidelines for compliance;

2. Time for good faith compliance;

3. A hearing on the reasons for failure to comply;

4. Plaintiff request for supplemental relief;

5. An order for defendant to submit a detailed remedial plan;

6. An order to plaintiff to submit a plan or to plaintiff and defendant to negotiate a plan;

7. Hearings on a court-ordered plan and/or the appointment of a master to formulate a plan;

8. The remedial order;

9. Appointment of a master or oversight committee with power to gather data and review and guide decree implementation;

10. Time for good faith compliance;

11. Receivership, annulment of state laws slowing relief, closing of institutions, replacement of state officials, reordering of governmental budgets, and other intrusive actions;

12. Contempt.

Robert Goldstein, A *Swann* Song for Remedies: Equitable Relief in the Burger Court, 13 Harv.C.R.-C.L.L.Rev. 1, 65–68 (1978).

This section will look first at contempt's elements, sanctions, and procedures. It will then turn to the issues of when parties are bound, the limits on enforcing decrees against persons who are not parties, and the special problems in enforcing decrees against governmental defendants.

1. THE CONTEMPT POWER

PROBLEM: COUNTRY LODGE V. MILLER (REPRISED)
CIVIL OR CRIMINAL CONTEMPT

Miller is enjoined from putting anything in the river under a statute that prohibits discharges into the waters of the state without a permit. The court holds Miller in contempt for violating the order. Would it be improper for the court to sentence Miller to five days in prison after finding her guilty of contempt by clear and convincing evidence?

———

The contempt power used to deal with violations of injunctions and other court orders is the same power used to deal with disruptive conduct in the court room, the intimidation of jurors, and other obstructions of the judicial process. As explained at the beginning of Chapter 2 (p. 34), the contempt power takes three forms: criminal contempt, coercive civil contempt, and compensatory civil contempt.

Contempt proceedings are usually triggered by the plaintiff bringing the violation of the order to the court's attention. Because criminal contempt is brought in the name of the public, the judge and not the plaintiff gets to decide whether to initiate a prosecution for criminal contempt. Indeed the court may initiate such a prosecution without any prompting from the plaintiff or continue it even if the plaintiff beseeches the court to stop the prosecution. If the court does decide to commence criminal contempt proceedings, it will generally ask the prosecutor of the jurisdiction to press the charges. The Supreme Court has invoked its supervisory powers over federal courts to forbid judges from appointing a special prosecutor unless the United States Attorney has declined the case or from appointing the plaintiff's attorney as the special prosecutor because of conflicts of interest. Young v. United States ex rel. Vuitton et Fils S.A., 481 U.S. 787, 107 S.Ct. 2124, 95 L.Ed.2d 740 (1987). In contrast to criminal contempt, where the prosecutor normally presses the charges, with compensatory or coercive civil contempt, the plaintiff usually does so.

A single proceeding may result in criminal, compensatory, and coercive sanctions. As Justice Rutledge stated:

> In any other context than one of contempt, the idea that a criminal prosecution and a civil suit for damages or equitable relief could be hashed together in a single criminal-civil hodgepodge would be shocking to every American lawyer and to most citizens.

United States v. United Mine Workers, 330 U.S. 258, 364, 67 S.Ct. 677, 730, 91 L.Ed. 884, 949–50 (1947)(Rutledge, J., dissenting). Why do you suppose that courts allow civil and criminal contempt to be "hashed"? Moreover, "no judicial opinion or statute has ever required the judge at the initiation of contempt proceedings to determine the type of sanction [criminal or civil] that may be imposed." Robert J. Martineau, Contempt of Court: Eliminating the Confusion Between Civil and Criminal Contempt, 50 U.Cin.L.Rev. 677, 684 (1981) (discussing with approval Wisconsin statute requiring such a determination). Nor can the alleged contemnor necessarily tell whether the proceedings are civil or criminal by the identity of the attorney bringing the charges. When the plaintiff is a government, the government's attorney may be competent to bring either kind of charge. Even when the plaintiff is not a government, the identity of the attorney bringing the charge may not be dispositive. For example, in the following case, Hicks, the district attorney, claims to be representing a private plaintiff in a civil contempt proceeding.

HICKS ON BEHALF OF FEIOCK v. FEIOCK

Supreme Court of the United States, 1988
485 U.S. 624, 108 S.Ct. 1423, 99 L.Ed.2d 721

JUSTICE WHITE delivered the opinion of the Court.

* * *

I

On January 19, 1976, a California state court entered an order requiring respondent, Phillip Feiock, to begin making monthly payments to his ex-wife for the support of their three children. Over the next six years, respondent only sporadically complied with the order, and by December 1982 he had discontinued paying child support altogether. His ex-wife sought to enforce the support orders. On June 22, 1984, a hearing was held in California state court on her petition for ongoing support payments and for payment of the arrearage due her. The court examined respondent's financial situation and ordered him to begin paying $150 per month commencing on July 1, 1984. The court reserved jurisdiction over the matter for the purpose of determining the arrearages and reviewing respondent's financial condition.

Respondent apparently made two monthly payments but paid nothing for the next nine months. He was then served with an order to show cause why he should not be held in contempt on nine counts of failure to make the monthly payments ordered by the court. At a hearing on August 9, 1985, petitioner made out a prima facie case of contempt against respondent by establishing the existence of a valid court order, respondent's knowledge of the order, and respondent's failure to comply with the order. Respondent defended by arguing that he was unable to pay support during the months in question. This argument was partially successful, but respondent was adjudged to be in contempt on five of the nine counts. He was sentenced to five days in jail on each count, to be served consecutively, for a total of 25 days. This sentence was suspended, however, and respondent was placed on probation for three years. As one of the conditions of his probation, he was ordered once again to make support payments of $150 per month. As another condition of his probation, he was ordered, starting the following month, to begin repaying $50 per month on his accumulated arrearage, which was determined to total $1650.

At the hearing, respondent had objected to the application of Cal.Civ. Proc.Code Ann. § 1209.5 (1982) against him, claiming that it was unconstitutional under the Due Process Clause of the Federal Constitution because it shifts to the defendant the burden of proving inability to comply with the order, which is an element of the crime of contempt.[1] This objection was rejected, and he renewed it on appeal. The intermediate state appellate court agreed with respondent and annulled the contempt order, ruling that the state statute purports to impose "a mandatory presumption compelling a conclusion of guilt without independent proof of an ability to pay," and is therefore unconstitutional because "the mandatory nature of the presumption lessens the prosecution's burden of proof." In light of its holding that the statute as previously interpreted was unconstitutional, the court went on to adopt a different interpretation of that statute to govern future proceedings: "For future guidance, however, we determine the statute in question should be construed as authorizing a permissive inference, but not a mandatory presumption." The court explicitly considered this reinterpretation of the statute to be an exercise of its "obligation to interpret the statute to preserve its constitutionality whenever possible." The California Supreme Court denied review, but we granted certiorari.

II

Three issues must be decided to resolve this case. First is whether the ability to comply with a court order constitutes an element of the offense of contempt or, instead, inability to comply is an affirmative defense to that charge. Second is whether § 1209.5 requires the alleged contemnor to shoulder the burden of persuasion or merely the burden of production in attempting to establish his inability to comply with the order. Third is whether this contempt proceeding was a criminal proceeding or a civil proceeding, i.e., whether the relief imposed upon respondent was criminal or civil in nature.

Petitioner argues that the state appellate court erred in its determinations on the first two points of state law. The court ruled that whether the individual is able to comply with a court order is an element of the offense of contempt rather than an affirmative defense to the charge, and that § 1209.5 shifts to the alleged contemnor the burden of persuasion rather than simply the burden of production in showing inability to comply. We are not at liberty to depart from the state appellate court's resolution of these issues of state law. * * *

---

1. California Civ.Proc.Code Ann. § 1209.5 (1982) states that "[w]hen a court of competent jurisdiction makes an order compelling a parent to furnish support ... for his child, proof that ... the parent was present in court at the time the order was pronounced and proof of noncompliance therewith shall be prima facie evidence of a contempt of court."

The third issue, however, is a different matter: the argument is not merely that the state court misapplied state law, but that the characterization of this proceeding and the relief given as civil or criminal in nature, for purposes of determining the proper applicability of federal constitutional protections, raises a question of federal law rather than state law. This proposition is correct as stated. The fact that this proceeding and the resultant relief were judged to be criminal in nature as a matter of state law is thus not determinative of this issue, and the state appellate court erred insofar as it sustained respondent's challenge to the statute under the Due Process Clause simply because it concluded that this contempt proceeding is "quasi-criminal" as a matter of California law.

III

A

The question of how a court determines whether to classify the relief imposed in a given proceeding as civil or criminal in nature, for the purposes of applying the Due Process Clause and other provisions of the Constitution, is one of long standing, and its principles have been settled at least in their broad outlines for many decades. When a State's proceedings are involved, state law provides strong guidance about whether or not the State is exercising its authority "in a non-punitive, non-criminal manner," and one who challenges the State's classification of the relief imposed as "civil" or "criminal" may be required to show "the clearest proof" that it is not correct as a matter of federal law. Nonetheless, if such a challenge is substantiated, then the labels affixed either to the proceeding or to the relief imposed under state law are not controlling and will not be allowed to defeat the applicable protections of federal constitutional law. This is particularly so in the codified laws of contempt, where the "civil" and "criminal" labels of the law have become increasingly blurred.[4]

Instead, the critical features are the substance of the proceeding and the character of the relief that the proceeding will afford. "If it is for civil contempt the punishment is remedial, and for the benefit of the complainant. But if it is for criminal contempt the sentence is punitive, to vindicate the authority of the court." Gompers v. Buck's Stove & Range Co., 221 U.S. 418, 441, 31 S.Ct. 492, 498, 55 L.Ed. 797 (1911). The character of the relief imposed is thus ascertainable by applying a few straightforward rules. If the relief provided is a sentence of imprisonment, it is remedial if "the defendant stands committed unless and until he performs the affirmative act required by the court's order," and is punitive if "the sentence is limited to imprisonment for a definite period." If the relief provided is a fine, it is remedial when it is paid to the complainant, and punitive when

---

4. California is a good example of this modern development, for although it defines civil and criminal contempts in separate statutes, compare Cal.Civ.Proc.Code Ann. § 1209 (Supp.1988) with Cal.Penal Code Ann. § 166 (1970), it has merged the two kinds of proceedings under the same procedural rules. See Cal.Civ.Proc.Code Ann. §§ 1209–1222 (1982 and Supp.1988).

it is paid to the court, though a fine that would be payable to the court is also remedial when the defendant can avoid paying the fine simply by performing the affirmative act required by the court's order. These distinctions lead up to the fundamental proposition that criminal penalties may not be imposed on someone who has not been afforded the protections that the Constitution requires of such criminal proceedings, including the requirement that the offense be proved beyond a reasonable doubt.[5]

The Court has consistently applied these principles. In *Gompers*, decided early in this century, three men were found guilty of contempt and were sentenced to serve 6, 9, and 12 months respectively. The Court found this relief to be criminal in nature because the sentence was determinate and unconditional. "The distinction between refusing to do an act commanded,—remedied by imprisonment until the party performs the required act; and doing an act forbidden,—punished by imprisonment for a definite term; is sound in principle, and generally, if not universally, affords a test by which to determine the character of the punishment." In the former instance, the conditional nature of the punishment renders the relief civil in nature because the contemnor "can end the sentence and discharge himself at any moment by doing what he had previously refused to do." In the latter instance, the unconditional nature of the punishment renders the relief criminal in nature because the relief "cannot undo or remedy what has been done nor afford any compensation" and the contemnor "cannot shorten the term by promising not to repeat the offense." * * *

B

In repeatedly stating and following the rules set out above, the Court has eschewed any alternative formulation that would make the classification of the relief imposed in a State's proceedings turn simply on what their underlying purposes are perceived to be. Although the purposes that lie behind particular kinds of relief are germane to understanding their character, this Court has never undertaken to psychoanalyze the subjective intent of a State's laws and its courts, not only because that effort would be unseemly and improper, but also because it would be misguided. In contempt cases, both civil and criminal relief have aspects that can be seen as either remedial or punitive or both. * * * As was noted in *Gompers*:

> "It is true that either form of [punishment] has also an incidental effect. For if the case is civil and the punishment is purely remedial, there is also a vindication of the court's authority. On the other hand, if the proceeding is for criminal contempt and the [punishment] is solely punitive, to vindicate the authority of the law, the complainant

---

5. We have recognized that certain specific constitutional protections, such as the right to trial by jury, are not applicable to those criminal contempts that can be classified as petty offenses, as is true of other petty crimes as well. This is not true, however, of the proposition that guilt must be proved beyond a reasonable doubt.

may also derive some incidental benefit from the fact that such punishment tends to prevent a repetition of the disobedience. But such indirect consequences will not change [punishment] which is merely coercive and remedial, into that which is solely punitive in character, or *vice versa*." * * *

IV

The proper classification of the relief imposed in respondent's contempt proceeding is dispositive of this case. As interpreted by the state court here, § 1209.5 requires respondent to carry the burden of persuasion on an element of the offense, by showing his inability to comply with the court's order to make the required payments. If applied in a criminal proceeding, such a statute would violate the Due Process Clause because it would undercut the State's burden to prove guilt beyond a reasonable doubt. If applied in a civil proceeding, however, this particular statute would be constitutionally valid, Maggio v. Zeitz, 333 U.S. 56, 75–76, 68 S.Ct. 401, 411–412, 92 L.Ed. 476 (1948) * * *.[9]

The state court found the contempt proceeding to be "quasi-criminal" in nature without discussing the point. There were strong indications that the proceeding was intended to be criminal in nature, such as the notice sent to respondent, which clearly labeled the proceeding as "criminal in nature," and the participation of the District Attorney in the case. Though significant, these facts are not dispositive of the issue before us, for if the trial court had imposed only civil coercive remedies, as surely it was authorized to do, then it would be improper to invalidate that result merely because the Due Process Clause, as applied in criminal proceedings, was not satisfied.[10] It also bears emphasis that the purposes underlying this proceeding were wholly ambiguous. Respondent was charged with violating nine discrete prior court orders, and the proceeding may have been intended primarily to vindicate the court's authority in the face of his defiance. On the other hand, as often is true when court orders are violated, these charges were part of an ongoing battle to force respondent to conform his conduct to the terms of those orders, and of future orders as well.

Applying the traditional rules for classifying the relief imposed in a given proceeding requires the further resolution of one factual question about the nature of the relief in this case. Respondent * * * was sentenced to five days in jail on each of the five counts, for a total of 25 days,

---

9. Our precedents are clear, however, that punishment may not be imposed in a civil contempt proceeding when it is clearly established that the alleged contemnor is unable to comply with the terms of the order.

10. This can also be seen by considering the notice given to the alleged contemnor. This Court has stated that one who is charged with a crime is "entitled to be informed of the nature of the charge against him but to know that it is a charge and not a suit." Gompers v. Buck's Stove & Range Co., 221 U.S. 418, 446, 31 S.Ct. 492, 500, 55 L.Ed. 797 (1911). Yet if the relief ultimately given in such a proceeding is wholly civil in nature, then this requirement would not be applicable. It is also true, of course, that if *both* civil and criminal relief are imposed in the same proceeding, then the " 'criminal feature of the order is dominant and fixes its character for purposes of review.' "

but his jail sentence was suspended and he was placed on probation for three years. If this were all, then the relief afforded would be criminal in nature.[11] But this is not all. One of the conditions of respondent's probation was that he begin making payments on his accumulated arrearage, and that he continue making these payments at the rate of $50 per month. At that rate, all of the arrearage would be paid before respondent completed his probation period. Not only did the order therefore contemplate that respondent would be required to purge himself of his past violations, but it expressly states that "[i]f any two payments are missed, whether consecutive or not, the entire balance shall become due and payable." What is unclear is whether the ultimate satisfaction of these accumulated prior payments would have purged the determinate sentence imposed on respondent. * * * [N]either party was able to offer a satisfactory explanation of this point at argument.[12] If the relief imposed here is in fact a determinate sentence with a purge clause, then it is civil in nature.

* * * [T]he Due Process Clause does not necessarily prohibit the State from employing this presumption [of ability to pay] as it was construed by the state court, if respondent would purge his contempt judgment by paying off his arrearage. In these circumstances, the proper course for this Court is to vacate the judgment below and remand for further consideration of § 1209.5 free from the compulsion of an erroneous view of federal law. If on remand it is found that respondent would purge his sentence by paying his arrearage, then this proceeding is civil in nature and there was no need for the state court to reinterpret its statute to avoid conflict with the Due Process Clause. * * *

JUSTICE KENNEDY took no part in the consideration or decision of this case.

JUSTICE O'CONNOR, with whom CHIEF JUSTICE [REHNQUIST] and JUSTICE SCALIA join, dissenting. * * *

" * * * In 1983, only half of custodial parents received the full amount of child support ordered; approximately 26% received some lesser

---

11. That a determinate sentence is suspended and the contemnor put on probation does not make the remedy civil in nature, for a suspended sentence, without more, remains a determinate sentence, and a fixed term of probation is itself a punishment that is criminal in nature. A suspended sentence with a term of probation is not equivalent to a conditional sentence that would allow the contemnor to avoid or purge these sanctions. A determinate term of probation puts the contemnor under numerous disabilities that he cannot escape by complying with the dictates of the prior orders, such as: any conditions of probation that the court judges to be reasonable and necessary may be imposed; the term of probation may be revoked and the original sentence (including incarceration) may be reimposed at any time for a variety of reasons without all the safeguards that are ordinarily afforded in criminal proceedings; and the contemnor's probationary status could affect other proceedings against him that may arise in the future (for example, this fact might influence the sentencing determination made in a criminal prosecution for some wholly independent offense).

12. It is also perhaps of some significance, though not binding upon us, that the parties reinforce the ambiguity on this point by entitling this contempt order, in the Joint Appendix, as "Order of the Superior Court of the State of California, County of Orange, to Purge Arrearage and Judgment of Contempt."

amount, and 24% received nothing at all." Brief for Women's Legal Defense Fund et al. as Amici Curiae 26. * * *

Contempt proceedings often will be useless if the parent seeking enforcement of valid support orders must prove that the obligor can comply with the court order. The custodial parent will typically lack access to the financial and employment records needed to sustain the burden imposed by the decision below, especially where the noncustodial parent is self-employed, as is the case here. Serious consequences follow from the California Court of Appeal's decision to invalidate California's statutory presumption that a parent continues to be able to pay the child support previously determined to be within his or her means.

* * * [T]he substance of the proceeding below and the conditions on which the sentence was suspended reveal that the proceeding was civil in nature. Mrs. Feiock initiated the underlying action in order to obtain enforcement of the child support order for the benefit of the Feiock children. The California District Attorney conducted the case under a provision of the [Uniform Reciprocal Enforcement of Support Act (URESA)] that authorizes him to act on Mrs. Feiock's behalf. As the very caption of the case in this Court indicates, the District Attorney is acting on behalf of Mrs. Feiock, not as the representative of the State of California in a criminal prosecution. Both of the provisions of California's enactment of the URESA that authorize contempt proceedings appear in a chapter of the Code of Civil Procedure entitled "Civil Enforcement." It appears that most States enforce child and spousal support orders through civil proceedings like this one, in which the burden of persuasion is shifted to the defendant to show inability to comply. * * *

It is true that the order imposing the sentence does not expressly provide that, if respondent is someday incarcerated and if he subsequently complies, he will be released immediately. The parties disagree about what will happen if this contingency arises, and there is no need to address today the question of whether the failure to grant immediate release would render the sanction criminal. In the case before us respondent carries something even better than the "keys to the prison" in his own pocket: as long as he meets the conditions of his informal probation, he will never enter the jail.

It is critical that the only conditions placed on respondent's probation, apart from the requirement that he conduct himself generally in accordance with the law, are that he cure his past failures to comply with the support order and that he continue to comply in the future.* The sanction imposed on respondent is unlike ordinary criminal probation because it is collateral to a civil proceeding initiated by a private party, and respon-

---

* Unlike the Court, I find no ambiguity in the court's sentencing order that hints that respondent can purge his jail sentence by paying off the arrearage alone. The sentencing order suspends execution of the jail sentence and places respondent on probation on the conditions that he *both* make future support payments at $150 per month *and* pay $50 per month on the arrearage. If respondent pays off the arrearage before the end of his probation period, but then fails to make a current support payment, the suspension will be revoked and he will go to jail.

dent's sentence is suspended on the condition that he comply with a court order entered for the benefit of that party. This distinguishes respondent's sentence from suspended criminal sentences imposed outside the contempt context.

This Court traditionally has inquired into the substance of contempt proceedings to determine whether they are civil or criminal, paying particular attention to whether the sanction imposed will benefit another party to the proceeding. In this case, the California Superior Court suspended respondent's sentence on the condition that he bring himself into compliance with a court order providing support for his children, represented in the proceeding by petitioner. I conclude that the proceeding in this case should be characterized as one for civil contempt, and I would reverse the judgment below.

NOTES ON *IN PERSONAM* VERSUS *IN REM* ENFORCEMENT

1. Enforcing money judgments differs fundamentally from enforcing court orders. A money judgment is not an order of the court and therefore failure to satisfy it does not constitute disobedience of the court. Rather, unless satisfied, the judgment authorizes the sheriff to seize the defendant's property, sell it, and pay the plaintiff from the proceeds. (See Chapter 8.) So a money judgment is directed against the defendant's property rather than the defendant's person. It is in rem rather than in personam. In contrast, injunctions and other court orders are generally orders to the defendant personally. This is the origin of the maxim that "equity acts in personam." But equity sometimes acts in rem. Should a defendant resist an order to convey title to real estate, the court may simply decree that the plaintiff has title. The court may also appoint a receiver to do what the injunction requires of the defendant, as was seen at p. 229 of this chapter. Would an in rem order help Ms. Feiock?

2. Although most awards of money are by money judgments, courts do sometimes directly order the payment of money. E.g., Bowen v. Massachusetts, 487 U.S. 879, 108 S.Ct. 2722, 101 L.Ed.2d 749 (1988). But an order to pay money is enforced as a money judgment because society does not want to jail debtors, as Chapter 8 will show. An exception is made for failure to pay alimony or child support, as in *Hicks*. The point of the case is, however, not whether the failure to pay alimony should be treated as contempt, but how courts should deal with alleged contempts.

NOTES ON THE CLASSIFICATION OF CONTEMPT PROCEEDINGS

1. *Hicks* holds that a jail sentence for contempt, suspended upon condition of future compliance with a court order in a civil case, is criminal unless the contemnor can purge the contempt. The dissent disagrees. Which side has the better argument?

2. *Hicks* also holds that a suspended jail sentence for contempt is civil if it can be purged. The majority remands for a determination of whether paying off the $1650 of arrearages would effect a purge. One way he might pay off

the arrearages is to make the required payments of $50 a month. But that would take 33 months of the 36 months of his probation. Another way he might purge is if he fails to make 2 payments, which would result in his being jailed and the entire balance being due immediately, and then pays off the balance. But, it seems implausible that he could come up with that much money when in jail if he could not come up with the smaller sums needed to avoid jail. No wonder the trial court did not bother to explain in advance whether paying the arrearages would purge the contempt. On the other hand, can you think of another blackletter test to determine whether the suspended sentence was imposed to punish past violations or to coerce future compliance?

3. After *Hicks*, can states use civil contempt to coerce the payment of alimony and child support? On remand, the state appellate court held that the California statute at issue in *Hicks* was "unmistakably criminal in nature." However, the court also held that the statute made ability to pay an affirmative defense in contempt proceedings. In re Feiock, 215 Cal.App.3d 141, 263 Cal.Rptr. 437 (1989). The majority opinion explained that once the alleged contemnor raises the affirmative defense by making a prima facie showing of inability to pay, the party seeking criminal contempt has the burden of proving all elements beyond a reasonable doubt, including ability to pay. The dissent charged that the majority had abandoned its original position that the possibility of compliance was an element of the offense and was, by subterfuge, putting on the alleged contemnor the burden to disprove an element of the offense.

In a later case, the state's high court embraced *In re Feoick's* holding that impossibility is an affirmative defense and not an element of the offense under the child support statute, but disagreed on the burden of proof, holding that the alleged contemnor bears the burden of persuasion. Moss v. Superior Court, 17 Cal.4th 396, 71 Cal.Rptr.2d 215, 950 P.2d 59 (1998). Finding that child support orders are obeyed in only seventeen percent of cases in California, the state legislature subsequently enacted a statute that replaced district attorneys with administrative officials in the collection process. Cal.Fam.Code § 17404.

4. Coercive civil contempt usually requires three steps: (1) the issuance of an injunction; (2) a determination of contempt and the imposition of sanctions subject to the condition that the defendant can purge; and (3) a finding as to whether the defendant has purged. *Hicks* decided that the second step can be taken civilly. Can the third step also be taken civilly? For example, suppose that Mr. Feiock receives a purgeable suspended sentence, fails to pay, is jailed, and then claims he has no money with which to purge. Should that claim be decided criminally or civilly?

5. The *Gompers* case, which is discussed at length in *Hicks*, was nationally known from extensive press coverage tracking the political struggle of the labor movement. The case, and union leader Samuel Gompers' intentional defiance of the court's injunction as a test case for secondary boycotts, is traced in Ken I. Kersch, The *Gompers v. Buck's Stove Saga*: A Constitutional Case Study in Dialogue, Resistance, and the Freedom of Speech, 31 J.Sup.Ct. History 28 (2006).

UNITED MINE WORKERS v. BAGWELL
Supreme Court of the United States, 1994
512 U.S. 821, 114 S.Ct. 2552, 129 L.Ed.2d 642

JUSTICE BLACKMUN delivered the opinion of the Court.

We are called upon once again to consider the distinction between civil and criminal contempt. Specifically, we address whether contempt fines levied against a union for violations of a labor injunction are coercive civil fines, or are criminal fines that constitutionally could be imposed only through a jury trial. We conclude that the fines are criminal and, accordingly, we reverse the judgment of the Supreme Court of Virginia.

I

Petitioners, the International Union, United Mine Workers of America and United Mine Workers of America, District 28 (collectively, the union) engaged in a protracted labor dispute with the Clinchfield Coal Company and Sea "B" Mining Company (collectively, the companies) over alleged unfair labor practices. In April 1989, the companies filed suit in the Circuit Court of Russell County, Virginia, to enjoin the union from conducting unlawful strike-related activities. The trial court entered an injunction which, as later amended, prohibited the union and its members from, among other things, obstructing ingress and egress to company facilities, throwing objects at and physically threatening company employees, placing tire-damaging "jackrocks" on roads used by company vehicles, and picketing with more than a specified number of people at designated sites. The court additionally ordered the union to take all steps necessary to ensure compliance with the injunction, to place supervisors at picket sites, and to report all violations to the court.

On May 16, 1989, the trial court held a contempt hearing and found that petitioners had committed 72 violations of the injunction. After fining the union $642,000 for its disobedience,[1] the court announced that it would fine the union $100,000 for any future violent breach of the injunction and $20,000 for any future nonviolent infraction, "such as exceeding picket numbers, [or] blocking entrances or exits." The Court early stated that its purpose was to "impos[e] prospective civil fines[,] the payment of which would only be required if it were shown the defendants disobeyed the Court's orders."

In seven subsequent contempt hearings held between June and December 1989, the court found the union in contempt for more than 400 separate violations of the injunction, many of them violent. Based on the court's stated "intention that these fines are civil and coercive," each contempt hearing was conducted as a civil proceeding before the trial judge, in which the parties conducted discovery, introduced evidence, and called and cross-examined witnesses. The trial court required that contu-

---

1. A portion of these fines was suspended conditioned on the union's future compliance. The court later vacated these fines, concluding that they were "criminal in nature."

macious acts be proved beyond a reasonable doubt, but did not afford the union a right to jury trial.

As a result of these contempt proceedings, the court levied over $64,000,000 in fines against the union, approximately $12,000,000 of which was ordered payable to the companies. Because the union objected to payment of any fines to the companies and in light of the law enforcement burdens posed by the strike, the court ordered that the remaining roughly $52,000,000 in fines be paid to the Commonwealth of Virginia and Russell and Dickenson Counties, "the two counties most heavily affected by the unlawful activity."

While appeals from the contempt orders were pending, the union and the companies settled the underlying labor dispute, agreed to vacate the contempt fines, and jointly moved to dismiss the case. A special mediator representing the Secretary of Labor, and the governments of Russell and Dickenson Counties, supported the parties' motion to vacate the outstanding fines. The trial court granted the motion to dismiss, dissolved the injunction, and vacated the $12,000,000 in fines payable to the companies. After reiterating its belief that the remaining $52,000,000 owed to the counties and the Commonwealth were coercive, civil fines, the trial court refused to vacate these fines, concluding they were "payable in effect to the public."

The companies withdrew as parties in light of the settlement and declined to seek further enforcement of the outstanding contempt fines. Because the Commonwealth Attorneys of Russell and Dickenson Counties also had asked to be disqualified from the case, the court appointed respondent John L. Bagwell to act as Special Commissioner to collect the unpaid contempt fines on behalf of the counties and the Commonwealth.

The Court of Appeals of Virginia reversed and ordered that the contempt fines be vacated pursuant to the settlement agreement. Assuming for the purposes of argument that the fines were civil, the court concluded "that civil contempt fines imposed during or as a part of a civil proceeding between private parties are settled when the underlying litigation is settled by the parties and the court is without discretion to refuse to vacate such fines."

On consolidated appeals, the Supreme Court of Virginia reversed. The court held that whether coercive, civil contempt sanctions could be settled by private parties was a question of state law, and that Virginia public policy disfavored such a rule, "if the dignity of the law and public respect for the judiciary are to be maintained." The court also rejected petitioners' contention that the outstanding fines were criminal and could not be imposed absent a criminal trial. Because the trial court's prospective fine schedule was intended to coerce compliance with the injunction and the union could avoid the fines through obedience, the court reasoned, the fines were civil and coercive and properly imposed in civil proceedings.

* * *

II

A

"Criminal contempt is a crime in the ordinary sense," Bloom v. Illinois, 391 U.S. 194, 201 (1968), and "criminal penalties may not be imposed on someone who has not been afforded the protections that the Constitution requires of such criminal proceedings." Hicks v. Feiock, 485 U.S. 624, 632 (1988). See In re Bradley, 318 U.S. 50 (1943)(double jeopardy); Cooke v. United States, 267 U.S. 517, 537 (1925)(rights to notice of charges, assistance of counsel, summary process, and to present a defense); Gompers v. Bucks Stove & Range Co., 221 U.S. 418, 444 (1911) (privilege against self-incrimination, right to proof beyond a reasonable doubt). For "serious" criminal contempts involving imprisonment of more than six months, these protections include the right to jury trial. *Bloom.* In contrast, civil contempt sanctions, or those penalties designed to compel future compliance with a court order, are considered to be coercive and avoidable through obedience, and thus may be imposed in an ordinary civil proceeding upon notice and an opportunity to be heard. Neither a jury trial nor proof beyond a reasonable doubt is required.[2]

Although the procedural contours of the two forms of contempt are well established, the distinguishing characteristics of civil versus criminal contempts are somewhat less clear.[3] In the leading early case addressing this issue in the context of imprisonment, *Gompers v. Bucks Stove & Range Co.*, the Court emphasized that whether a contempt is civil or criminal turns on the "character and purpose" of the sanction involved. * * *

The paradigmatic coercive, civil contempt sanction, as set forth in *Gompers*, involves confining a contemnor indefinitely until he complies with an affirmative command such as an order "to pay alimony, or to surrender property ordered to be turned over to a receiver, or to make a conveyance." Imprisonment for a fixed term similarly is coercive when the contemnor is given the option of earlier release if he complies. In these circumstances, the contemnor is able to purge the contempt and obtain his release by committing an affirmative act, and thus "carries the keys of his prison in his own pocket." *Gompers.*

By contrast, a fixed sentence of imprisonment is punitive and criminal if it is imposed retrospectively for a "completed act of disobedience," *Gompers*, such that the contemnor cannot avoid or abbreviate the confinement through later compliance. * * * When a contempt involves the prior

---

2. We address only the procedures required for adjudication of indirect contempts, i.e., those occurring out of court. Direct contempts that occur in the court's presence may be immediately adjudged and sanctioned summarily, and, except for serious criminal contempts in which a jury trial is required, the traditional distinction between civil and criminal contempt proceedings does not pertain.

3. Numerous scholars have criticized as unworkable the traditional distinction between civil and criminal contempt. See, e.g., Dudley, Getting Beyond the Civil/Criminal Distinction: A New Approach to Regulation of Indirect Contempts, 79 Va. L. Rev. 1025, 1033 (1993) (describing the distinction between civil and criminal contempt as "conceptually unclear and exceedingly difficult to apply").

conduct of an isolated, prohibited act, the resulting sanction has no coercive effect. "[T]he defendant is furnished no key, and he cannot shorten the term by promising not to repeat the offense."

This dichotomy between coercive and punitive imprisonment has been extended to the fine context. A contempt fine accordingly is considered civil and remedial if it either "coerce[s] the defendant into compliance with the court's order, [or] ... compensate[s] the complainant for losses sustained." United States v. United Mine Workers of America, 330 U.S. 258, 303–304 (1947). Where a fine is not compensatory, it is civil only if the contemnor is afforded an opportunity to purge. See Penfield Co. v. SEC, 330 U.S. 585, 590 (1947). Thus, a "flat, unconditional fine" totalling even as little as $50 announced after a finding of contempt is criminal if the contemnor has no subsequent opportunity to reduce or avoid the fine through compliance.

A close analogy to coercive imprisonment is a per diem fine imposed for each day a contemnor fails to comply with an affirmative court order. Like civil imprisonment, such fines exert a constant coercive pressure, and once the jural command is obeyed, the future, indefinite, daily fines are purged. Less comfortable is the analogy between coercive imprisonment and suspended, determinate fines. In this Court's sole prior decision squarely addressing the judicial power to impose coercive civil contempt fines, *United Mine Workers*, it held that fixed fines also may be considered purgeable and civil when imposed and suspended pending future compliance. See also *Penfield* ("One who is fined, unless by a day certain he [complies] ..., has it in his power to avoid any penalty"); but see *Hicks* (suspended or probationary sentence is criminal). *United Mine Workers* involved a $3,500,000 fine imposed against the union for nationwide post-World War II strike activities. Finding that the determinate fine was both criminal and excessive, the Court reduced the sanction to a flat criminal fine of $700,000. The Court then imposed and suspended the remaining $2,800,000 as a coercive civil fine, conditioned on the union's ability to purge the fine through full, timely compliance with the trial court's order. * * * [4] The Court concluded, in light of this purge clause, that the civil fine operated as "a coercive imposition upon the defendant union to compel obedience with the court's outstanding order."

This Court has not revisited the issue of coercive civil contempt fines addressed in *United Mine Workers*. Since that decision, the Court has erected substantial procedural protections in other areas of contempt law, such as criminal contempts and summary contempts. Lower federal courts and state courts such as the trial court here nevertheless have relied on *United Mine Workers* to authorize a relatively unlimited judicial power to impose noncompensatory civil contempt fines.

---

4. Although the size of the fine was substantial, the conduct required of the union to purge the suspended fine was relatively discrete. According to the Court, purgation consisted of (1) withdrawal of the union's notice terminating the Krug–Lewis labor agreement; (2) notifying the union members of this withdrawal; and (3) withdrawing and notifying the union members of the withdrawal of any other notice questioning the ongoing effectiveness of the Krug–Lewis agreement.

B

Underlying the somewhat elusive distinction between civil and criminal contempt fines, and the ultimate question posed in this case, is what procedural protections are due before any particular contempt penalty may be imposed. Because civil contempt sanctions are viewed as nonpunitive and avoidable, fewer procedural protections for such sanctions have been required. To the extent that such contempts take on a punitive character, however, and are not justified by other considerations central to the contempt power, criminal procedural protections may be in order.

The traditional justification for the relative breadth of the contempt power has been necessity: Courts independently must be vested with "power to impose silence, respect, and decorum, in their presence, and submission to their lawful mandates, and ... to preserve themselves and their officers from the approach and insults of pollution." Courts thus have embraced an inherent contempt authority, as a power "necessary to the exercise of all others."

But the contempt power also uniquely is "liable to abuse." Unlike most areas of law, where a legislature defines both the sanctionable conduct and the penalty to be imposed, civil contempt proceedings leave the offended judge solely responsible for identifying, prosecuting, adjudicating, and sanctioning the contumacious conduct. Contumacy "often strikes at the most vulnerable and human qualities of a judge's temperament," and its fusion of legislative, executive, and judicial powers "summons forth ... the prospect of 'the most tyrannical licentiousness.'" Accordingly, "in [criminal] contempt cases an even more compelling argument can be made [than in ordinary criminal cases] for providing a right to jury trial as a protection against the arbitrary exercise of official power."

Our jurisprudence in the contempt area has attempted to balance the competing concerns of necessity and potential arbitrariness by allowing a relatively unencumbered contempt power when its exercise is most essential, and requiring progressively greater procedural protections when other considerations come into play. The necessity justification for the contempt authority is at its pinnacle, of course, where contumacious conduct threatens a court's immediate ability to conduct its proceedings, such as where a witness refuses to testify, or a party disrupts the court. Thus, petty, direct contempts in the presence of the court traditionally have been subject to summary adjudication, "to maintain order in the courtroom and the integrity of the trial process in the face of an 'actual obstruction of justice.'" In light of the court's substantial interest in rapidly coercing compliance and restoring order, and because the contempt's occurrence before the court reduces the need for extensive fact-finding and the likelihood of an erroneous deprivation, summary proceedings have been tolerated.

Summary adjudication becomes less justifiable once a court leaves the realm of immediately sanctioned, petty direct contempts. If a court delays punishing a direct contempt until the completion of trial, for example, due process requires that the contemnor's rights to notice and a hearing be respected. There "it is much more difficult to argue that action without notice or hearing of any kind is necessary to preserve order and enable [the court] to proceed with its business." Direct contempts also cannot be punished with serious criminal penalties absent the full protections of a criminal jury trial. * * *

Still further procedural protections are afforded for contempts occurring out of court, where the considerations justifying expedited procedures do not pertain. Summary adjudication of indirect contempts is prohibited, and criminal contempt sanctions are entitled to full criminal process. Certain indirect contempts nevertheless are appropriate for imposition through civil proceedings. Contempts such as failure to comply with document discovery, for example, while occurring outside the court's presence, impede the court's ability to adjudicate the proceedings before it and thus touch upon the core justification for the contempt power. Courts traditionally have broad authority through means other than contempt—such as by striking pleadings, assessing costs, excluding evidence, and entering default judgment-to penalize a party's failure to comply with the rules of conduct governing the litigation process. See, e.g., Fed. Rule Civ. Proc. 11, 37. Such judicial sanctions never have been considered criminal, and the imposition of civil, coercive fines to police the litigation process appears consistent with this authority. Similarly, indirect contempts involving discrete, readily ascertainable acts, such as turning over a key or payment of a judgment, properly may be adjudicated through civil proceedings since the need for extensive, impartial factfinding is less pressing.

For a discrete category of indirect contempts, however, civil procedural protections may be insufficient. Contempts involving out-of-court disobedience to complex injunctions often require elaborate and reliable factfinding. Such contempts do not obstruct the court's ability to adjudicate the proceedings before it, and the risk of erroneous deprivation from the lack of a neutral factfinder may be substantial. Under these circumstances, criminal procedural protections such as the rights to counsel and proof beyond a reasonable doubt are both necessary and appropriate to protect the due process rights of parties and prevent the arbitrary exercise of judicial power.

C

In the instant case, neither any party nor any court of the Commonwealth has suggested that the challenged fines are compensatory. * * * The issue before us accordingly is limited to whether these fines, despite their noncompensatory character, are coercive civil or criminal sanctions.

The parties propose two independent tests for determining whether the fines are civil or criminal. Petitioners argue that because the injunction primarily prohibited certain conduct rather than mandated affirmative acts, the sanctions are criminal. Respondent in turn urges that because the trial court established a prospective fine schedule that the union could avoid through compliance, the fines are civil in character.

Neither theory satisfactorily identifies those contempt fines that are criminal and thus must be imposed through the criminal process. Petitioners correctly note that *Gompers* suggests a possible dichotomy "between refusing to do an act commanded,—remedied by imprisonment until the party performs the required act; and doing an act forbidden,—punished by imprisonment for a definite term." The distinction between mandatory and prohibitory orders is easily applied in the classic contempt scenario, where contempt sanctions are used to enforce orders compelling or forbidding a single, discrete act. In such cases, orders commanding an affirmative act simply designate those actions that are capable of being coerced.

But the distinction between coercion of affirmative acts and punishment of prohibited conduct is difficult to apply when conduct that can recur is involved, or when an injunction contains both mandatory and prohibitory provisions. Moreover, in borderline cases injunctive provisions containing essentially the same command can be phrased either in mandatory or prohibitory terms. Under a literal application of petitioners' theory, an injunction ordering the union: "Do not strike," would appear to be prohibitory and criminal, while an injunction ordering the union: "Continue working," would be mandatory and civil. In enforcing the present injunction, the trial court imposed fines without regard to the mandatory or prohibitory nature of the clause violated. Accordingly, even though a parsing of the injunction's various provisions might support the classification of contempts such as rock-throwing and placing tire-damaging "jackrocks" on roads as criminal and the refusal to place supervisors at picket sites as civil, the parties have not asked us to review the order in that manner. In a case like this involving an injunction that prescribes a detailed code of conduct, it is more appropriate to identify the character of the entire decree.

Despite respondent's urging, we also are not persuaded that dispositive significance should be accorded to the fact that the trial court prospectively announced the sanctions it would impose. Had the trial court simply levied the fines after finding the union guilty of contempt, the resulting "determinate and unconditional" fines would be considered "solely and exclusively punitive." Respondent nevertheless contends that the trial court's announcement of a prospective fine schedule allowed the union to "avoid paying the fine[s] simply by performing the ... act required by the court's order," *Hicks*, and thus transformed these fines into coercive, civil ones. Respondent maintains here, as the Virginia Supreme Court held below, that the trial court could have imposed a daily civil fine to coerce the union into compliance, and that a prospective fine schedule is indistinguishable from such a sanction.

Respondent's argument highlights the difficulties encountered in parsing coercive civil and criminal contempt fines. The fines imposed here concededly are difficult to distinguish either from determinate, punitive fines or from initially suspended, civil fines. Ultimately, however, the fact that the trial court announced the fines before the contumacy, rather than after the fact, does not in itself justify respondent's conclusion that the fines are civil or meaningfully distinguish these penalties from the ordinary criminal law. Due process traditionally requires that criminal laws provide prior notice both of the conduct to be prohibited and of the sanction to be imposed. The trial court here simply announced the penalty—determinate fines of $20,000 or $100,000 per violation—that would be imposed for future contempts. The union's ability to avoid the contempt fines was indistinguishable from the ability of any ordinary citizen to avoid a criminal sanction by conforming his behavior to the law. The fines are not coercive day fines, or even suspended fines, but are more closely analogous to fixed, determinate, retrospective criminal fines which petitioners had no opportunity to purge once imposed. We therefore decline to conclude that the mere fact that the sanctions were announced in advance rendered them coercive and civil as a matter of constitutional law.

Other considerations convince us that the fines challenged here are criminal. The union's sanctionable conduct did not occur in the court's presence or otherwise implicate the court's ability to maintain order and adjudicate the proceedings before it. Nor did the union's contumacy involve simple, affirmative acts, such as the paradigmatic civil contempts examined in *Gompers*. Instead, the Virginia trial court levied contempt fines for widespread, ongoing, out-of-court violations of a complex injunction. In so doing, the court effectively policed petitioners' compliance with an entire code of conduct that the court itself had imposed. The union's contumacy lasted many months and spanned a substantial portion of the State. The fines assessed were serious, totalling over $52,000,000.[5] Under such circumstances, disinterested factfinding and even-handed adjudication were essential, and petitioners were entitled to a criminal jury trial.

In reaching this conclusion, we recognize that this Court generally has deferred to a legislature's determination whether a sanction is civil or criminal, and that "[w]hen a State's proceedings are involved, state law provides strong guidance about whether or not the State is exercising its authority 'in a nonpunitive, noncriminal manner.'" *Hicks*. We do not deviate from either tradition today. Where a single judge, rather than a legislature, declares a particular sanction to be civil or criminal, such deference is less appropriate. Cf. Madsen v. Women's Health Center, Inc., 512 U.S. 1277 (1994). Moreover, this Court has recognized that even for

---

5. "Petty contempt like other petty criminal offenses may be tried without a jury," and the imposition only of serious criminal contempt fines triggers the right to jury trial. *Bloom*. The Court to date has not specified what magnitude of contempt fine may constitute a serious criminal sanction, although it has held that a fine of $10,000 imposed on a union was insufficient to trigger the Sixth Amendment right to jury trial. See Muniz v. Hoffman, 422 U.S. 454, 477 (1975); see also 18 U.S.C. § 1(3) (defining petty offenses as crimes "the penalty for which ... does not exceed imprisonment for a period of six months or a fine of not more than $5,000 for an individual and $10,000 for a person other than an individual, or both"). We need not answer today the difficult question where the line between petty and serious contempt fines should be drawn, since a $52,000,000 fine unquestionably is a serious contempt sanction.

state proceedings, the label affixed to a contempt ultimately "will not be allowed to defeat the applicable protections of federal constitutional law." *Hicks.* We conclude that the serious contempt fines imposed here were criminal and constitutionally could not be imposed absent a jury trial.

III

Our decision concededly imposes some procedural burdens on courts' ability to sanction widespread, indirect contempts of complex injunctions through noncompensatory fines. Our holding, however, leaves unaltered the longstanding authority of judges to adjudicate direct contempts summarily, and to enter broad compensatory awards for all contempts through civil proceedings. Because the right to trial by jury applies only to serious criminal sanctions, courts still may impose noncompensatory, petty fines for contempts such as the present ones without conducting a jury trial. We also do not disturb a court's ability to levy, albeit through the criminal contempt process, serious fines like those in this case.

Ultimately, whatever slight burden our holding may impose on the judicial contempt power cannot be controlling. The Court recognized more than a quarter-century ago:

> "We cannot say that the need to further respect for judges and courts is entitled to more consideration than the interest of the individual not be subjected to serious criminal punishment without the benefit of all the procedural protections worked out carefully over the years and deemed fundamental to our system of justice. Genuine respect, which alone can lend true dignity to our judicial establishment, will be engendered, not by the fear of unlimited authority, but by the firm administration of the law through those institutionalized procedures which have been worked out over the centuries." *Bloom.* Where, as here, "a serious contempt is at issue, considerations of efficiency must give way to the more fundamental interest of ensuring the even-handed exercise of judicial power."

* * *

JUSTICE SCALIA, concurring.

I join the Court's opinion classifying the $52,000,000 in contempt fines levied against petitioners as criminal. As the Court's opinion demonstrates, our cases have employed a variety of not easily reconcilable tests for differentiating between civil and criminal contempts. Since all of those tests would yield the same result here, there is no need to decide which is the correct one—and a case so extreme on its facts is not the best case in which to make that decision. I wish to suggest, however, that when we come to making it, a careful examination of historical practice will ultimately yield the answer. * * *

[At common law,] incarceration until compliance was a distinctive sanction, and sheds light upon the nature of the decrees enforced by civil contempt. That sanction makes sense only if the order requires performance of an identifiable act (or perhaps cessation of continuing performance of an identifiable act). A general prohibition for the future does not lend itself to enforcement through conditional incarceration, since no single act (or the cessation of no single act) can demonstrate compliance and justify release. * * *

As one would expect from this, the orders that underlay civil contempt fines or incarceration were usually mandatory rather than prohibitory, directing litigants to perform acts that would further the litigation (for example, turning over a document), or give effect to the court's judgment (for example, executing a deed of conveyance). * * * The mandatory injunctions issued upon termination of litigation usually required "a single simple act." H. McClintock, Principles of Equity § 15, pp. 32–33 (2d ed.1948). * * * And where specific performance of contracts was sought, it was the categorical rule that no decree would issue that required ongoing supervision. Compliance with these "single act" mandates could, in addition to being simple, be quick; and once it was achieved the contemnor's relationship with the court came to an end, at least insofar as the subject of the order was concerned. * * *

Even equitable decrees that were prohibitory rather than mandatory were, in earlier times, much less sweeping than their modern counterparts. Prior to the labor injunctions of the late 1800's, injunctions were issued primarily in relatively narrow disputes over property.

Contemporary courts have abandoned these earlier limitations upon the scope of their mandatory and injunctive decrees. They routinely issue complex decrees which involve them in extended disputes and place them in continuing supervisory roles over parties and institutions. See, e.g., Missouri v. Jenkins, 495 U.S. 33, 56–58 (1990); Swann v. Charlotte–Mecklenburg Bd. of Ed., 402 U.S. 1, 16 (1971). Professor Chayes has described the extent of the transformation:

> [The modern decree] differs in almost every relevant characteristic from relief in the traditional model of adjudication, not the least in that it is the centerpiece.... It provides for a complex, on-going regime of performance rather than a simple, one-shot, one-way transfer. Finally, it prolongs and deepens, rather than terminates, the court's involvement with the dispute.

Chayes, The Role of the Judge in Public Law Litigation, 89 Harv. L. Rev. 1281, 1298 (1976).

The consequences of this change for the point under discussion here are obvious: When an order governs many aspects of a litigant's activities, rather than just a discrete act, determining compliance becomes much more difficult. Credibility issues arise, for which the factfinding protections of the criminal law (including jury trial) become much more important. And when continuing prohibitions or obligations are imposed, the order cannot be complied with (and the contempt "purged") in a single act; it continues to govern the party's behavior, on pain of punishment-not unlike the criminal law.

The order at issue here provides a relatively tame example of the modern, complex decree. The amended injunction prohibited, inter alia, rock-throwing, the puncturing of tires, threatening, following or interfering with respondents' employees, placing pickets in other than specified locations, and roving picketing; and it required, inter alia, that petitioners provide a list of names of designated supervisors. Although it would seem quite in accord with historical practice to enforce, by conditional incarceration or per diem fines, compliance with the last provision-a discrete command, observance of which is readily ascertained-using that same means to enforce the remainder of the order would be a novelty. * * *

As the scope of injunctions has expanded, they have lost some of the distinctive features that made enforcement through civil process acceptable. It is not that the times, or our perceptions of fairness, have changed (that is in my view no basis for either tightening or relaxing the traditional demands of due process); but rather that the modern judicial order is in its relevant essentials not the same device that in former times could always be enforced by civil contempt. So adjustments will have to be made. We will have to decide at some point which modern injunctions sufficiently resemble their historical namesakes to warrant the same extraordinary means of enforcement. We need not draw that line in the present case, and so I am content to join the opinion of the Court.

JUSTICE GINSBURG, with whom CHIEF JUSTICE [REHNQUIST] joins, concurring in part and concurring in the judgment.

* * *

Two considerations persuade me that the contempt proceedings in this case should be classified as "criminal" rather than "civil." First, were we to accept the logic of Bagwell's argument that the fines here were civil, because "conditional" and "coercive," no fine would elude that categorization. The fines in this case were "conditional," Bagwell says, because they would not have been imposed if the unions had complied with the injunction. The fines would have been "conditional" in this sense, however, even if the court had not supplemented the injunction with its fines schedule; indeed, any fine is "conditional" upon compliance or noncompliance before its imposition.†

Second, the Virginia courts' refusal to vacate the fines, despite the parties' settlement and joint motion is characteristic of criminal, not civil proceedings. In explaining why the fines outlived the underlying civil dispute, the Supreme Court of Virginia stated: "Courts of the Commonwealth must have the authority to enforce their orders by employing coercive, civil sanctions if the dignity of the law and public respect for the

---

† Bagwell further likens the prospective fines schedule to the civil contempt fine imposed in United States v. Mine Workers, 330 U.S. 258 (1947). In that case, however, the contemnor union was given an opportunity, after the fine was imposed, to avoid the fine by "effect[ing] full compliance" with the injunction. As the Court explains, for purposes of allowing the union to avoid the fine, "full compliance" with the broad no-strike injunction, was reduced to the performance of three affirmative acts. This opportunity to purge, consistent with the civil contempt scenario described in *Gompers*, was unavailable to the unions in this case.

judiciary are to be maintained." The Virginia court's references to upholding public authority and maintaining "the dignity of the law" reflect the very purposes *Gompers* ranked on the criminal contempt side. * * *

Concluding that the fines at issue "are more closely analogous to ... criminal fines" than to civil fines, I join the Court's judgment and all but Part II–B of its opinion.

MORE NOTES ON THE CLASSIFICATION OF CONTEMPT PROCEEDINGS

1. Has the holding in *Hicks* on the classification of suspended sentences been overruled? Professor Earl C. Dudley's article, cited prominently in *Bagwell*, Getting Beyond the Civil/Criminal Distinction: A New Approach to the Regulation of Indirect Contempts, 79 Va.L.Rev. 1025, 1051 (1993), argues that *Hicks'* distinction between a suspended sentence with a period of probation and a determinate sentence with a purge clause "does not hold up," chiefly because courts "never impose a jail term and suspend it unconditionally in favor of a probationary period."

2. Has the *Hicks* test for distinguishing coercive civil contempt from criminal contempt been overruled? If so, what is the new test? In New York State National Organization of Women v. Terry, 159 F.3d 86 (2d Cir.1998), cert. denied, 527 U.S. 1003, 119 S.Ct. 2336, 144 L.Ed.2d 234 (1999), the district court levied contempt fines against Terry for violating an injunction while protesting the operation of an abortion clinic. Terry argued that the fine was criminal, and therefore unconstitutional under *Bagwell*. The court of appeals upheld the fines because the district court included in the sanction a clause that allowed Terry to purge the fine by filing and publishing in a newspaper his affirmative intention to obey the permanent injunction. See also Harris v. City of Philadelphia, 47 F.3d 1311 (3d Cir.1995) (contempt fine not criminal if the contemnor can purge through an affirmative act).

If the fine cannot be purged, what is the test? In NOW v. Operation Rescue, 37 F.3d 646, 659 (D.C.Cir.1994), the court read *Bagwell* to hold that the classification of prospective fixed fines as criminal or civil turns on "what procedural protections are due before any particular contempt penalty may be imposed, in light of the 'competing concerns' of protecting the judicial process and preventing arbitrary exercises of the contempt power." In striking that balance, courts should consider such factors as (1) whether the contempts go to the core justification of protecting the court's ability to adjudicate the proceedings before it; (2) whether the contempts consist of discrete, readily ascertainable acts so that the factfinding is less troublesome; and, (3) the characterization by the district court; however, the appeals court is not bound by the district court's characterization of the prospective nature of the fine. Reich v. Sea Sprite Boat Co., 50 F.3d 413 (7th Cir.1995), cited *Bagwell* for the proposition that sanctions for completed acts are presumptively criminal sanctions. The First Circuit, in United States v. Marquardo, 149 F.3d 36 (1st Cir.1998), cited *Bagwell* for the proposition that a "frequent scenario for civil contempt situations arises as a result of the exercise of the courts' equity jurisdiction, in which the coercive tool is often periodic monetary fines, tailored to compensate the party aggrieved for the damages suffered as a result of the contumacious conduct of the noncomplying party." Id. at 40. In a later case, the D.C. Circuit carefully emphasized another point—whether the fines imposed were non-petty. Evans v. Williams, 206 F.3d 1292 (D.C.Cir. 2000). The Ninth Circuit, in a discussion of "serious" fines, noted that the "Supreme Court has not decided where the line between serious and petty fines should be drawn." F.J. Hanshaw Enterprises, Inc. v. Emerald River Development, Inc., 244 F.3d 1128, 1139 (9th Cir.2001).

3. Professor Dudley concluded that, "we should abandon the civil/criminal distinction and instead allocate procedural protections in contempt in accord with a less complicated due process model that takes account of both the contempt process' peculiar dangers and the costs of affording those protections." 79 Va.L.Rev. at 1033, supra, Note 1. He suggests that such a model might well lead to requiring courts contemplating imposing nonpetty sanctions, whether denominated civil or criminal, to accord alleged contemnors with almost all the protections given to defendants charged with crimes. For example, he would provide appointed counsel and jury trial, but not a grand jury. To what extent has Professor Dudley convinced the Court?

4. Do you agree with the Court that there would be little lost by giving most of the criminal procedure protections to alleged contemnors subject to nonpetty sanctions? How likely is it that local juries would have convicted the union in *Bagwell* or the abortion protestors if they defied the second injunction in Madsen v. Women's Health Center, Inc., 512 U.S. 753, 114 S.Ct. 2516, 129 L.Ed.2d 593 (1994)? (Reproduced in Chapter 2.) In *Bagwell*, the union argued at the contempt hearing that it had not violated the injunction because the alleged violations were not instigated by it, but rather were caused by outsiders who were sympathetic with the goals of the strike. Some of the abortion protesters who were charged with violating the injunction in *Madsen* contended that they were independent of the named defendants. Compare Margit Livingston, Disobedience and Contempt, 75 Wash.L.Rev. 345 (2000) (contending that, by implicitly expanding the definition of criminal contempt in *Bagwell* in the name of affording heightened procedural protections to alleged contemnors, the Supreme Court has neglected to consider adequately the plaintiffs' remedial entitlements and has unduly restricted litigants from obtaining equitable relief promptly and reliably through the civil contempt procedure).

NOTES ON THE ELEMENTS OF CONTEMPT

1. The majority in *Hicks* states that a prima facie case of contempt is made out by showing a court order, of which the defendant had notice, and which the defendant violated. On the grounds that contempt requires violation of a court order, the Supreme Court held that a federal district court, which had dismissed a suit pursuant to a stipulation and dismissal order, lacks jurisdiction to enforce the underlying settlement agreement. Breach of the settlement agreement did not violate the only order in the case, which was the one dismissing it. Kokkonen v. Guardian Life Insurance Co. 511 U.S. 375, 114 S.Ct. 1673, 128 L.Ed.2d 391 (1994).

2. *Willfulness.* There is an additional element for criminal contempt—willfulness. Punishment and deterrence, which are the purposes of criminal

contempt, are inappropriate when the contempt was not willful. Should, however, "willfulness" mean that the defendant intended to do the acts that violated the order or that the defendant intended to do them knowing that they were contemptuous? In United States v. United Mine Workers, 330 U.S. 258, 67 S.Ct. 677, 91 L.Ed. 884 (1947), the government had taken over the mines, which were then as vital to the economy as the petroleum industry is today, to avert a strike. The government subsequently secured a temporary restraining order against a strike. The union and its colorful leader, John L. Lewis, conducted a strike that gripped the nation's attention. They pled that striking was not contempt because counsel had advised them that the court lacked jurisdiction to issue the order so that they intended no contempt. The trial court imposed a $10,000 fine on Lewis and a $3,500,000 fine on the union without indicating whether the fines were criminal or coercive. The Supreme Court upheld the order and the finding of criminal contempt; it provided, however, that $2,800,000 of the fine against the union was to be remitted if the strike ceased, but that the remainder of the fine against the union and the entire fine against Lewis were valid criminal sanctions. Justice Black, concurring in part and dissenting in part, wrote that:

> It is plain that the defendants acted willfully for they knew that they were disobeying the court's order. But they appear to have believed in good faith, though erroneously, that they were acting within their legal rights. Many lawyers would have so advised them. This does not excuse their conduct; the whole situation emphasizes the duty of testing the restraining order by orderly appeal instead of disobedience and open defiance. However, * * * "the intention with which acts of contempt have been committed must necessarily and properly have an important bearing on the degree of guilt and the penalty which should be imposed." * * *
>
> We should modify the District Court's decrees by making the entire amount of the fines payable conditionally.

330 U.S. at 333–34.

3. *Burdens.* Due process requires that the elements of criminal contempt be shown beyond a reasonable doubt. For civil contempt, the federal courts and many states require that the elements be shown by "clear and convincing" evidence. Many other states require only the lower preponderance of evidence standard. At least one circuit court blends the two standards together. F.T.C. v. Kuykendall, 371 F.3d 745, 754 (10th Cir. en banc 2004) ("district court judges should require proof of contempt by clear and convincing evidence and proof of the amount of compensatory damages by a preponderance of the evidence"). A few states require proof beyond a reasonable doubt for both compensatory and coercive civil contempt. Which approach is most fitting? See, e.g., Doug Rendleman, Compensatory Contempt: Plaintiff's Remedy When a Defendant Violates An Injunction, 1980 U.Ill.L.F. 971, 980; Maggio v. Zeitz, 333 U.S. 56, 79, 68 S.Ct. 401, 413, 92 L.Ed. 476, 493 (1948)(Black, J., dissenting) ("All court proceedings, whether designated as civil or criminal contempt of court or given some other name, which may result in fine, prison sentences, or both, should in my judgment require the same measure of proof, and that measure should be proof beyond a reasonable doubt.").

4. *Impossibility*. In the federal system and most states, impossibility is a defense as to which the defendant has the burden of production and persuasion for both civil and criminal contempt. If the court erroneously concludes that the contemnor can purge and has not done so, then it has functionally imposed a determinate, nonpurgable sentence through a civil process. The burden as to impossibility is critical in a case like *Hicks* where the defendant has unique access to the pertinent information. Who should have the burden? In *Hicks*, the state appellate court first held that impossibility was an element of the crime rather than a defense but that, under the statute, violation of a child support order permits but does not mandate a rebuttable presumption that compliance was possible. If the court so presumes, the burden of production would be on the alleged contemnor, but the burden of persuasion would remain on the prosecutor. On remand, the state appellate court reached a somewhat different result by treating impossibility as an affirmative defense.

NOTES ON SANCTIONS

1. *Criminal Contempt*. The majority in *United Mine Workers* stated that:

> In imposing a fine for criminal contempt, the trial judge may properly take into consideration the extent of the willful and deliberate defiance of the court's order, the seriousness of the consequences of the contumacious behavior, the necessity of effectively terminating the defendant's defiance as required by the public interest, and the importance of deterring such acts in the future. Because of the nature of these standards, great reliance must be placed upon the discretion of the trial judge.

330 U.S. at 303.

The contumacious behavior in *United Mine Workers* was a violation of the War Labor Disputes Act, which provided for a maximum penalty of either a year in jail or a $5000 fine or both. Nonetheless, the fines allowed by the Supreme Court exceeded those in the Act. Was that appropriate? See also Margaret Meriwether Cordray, Contempt Sanctions and the Excessive Fines Clause, 76 N.C.L.Rev. 407 (1998).

In some jurisdictions, statutes severely limit sanctions for criminal contempt. In a 1987 case, the New York Court of Appeals determined that the maximum sanction that could be imposed on a large utility for burning coal in defiance of a court order was $250 because of a statutory limit on criminal contempt fines that was last amended in 1981. Department of Environmental Protection v. Department of Environmental Conservation, 70 N.Y.2d 233, 519 N.Y.S.2d 539, 513 N.E.2d 706 (1987). The utility's officers might have been imprisoned, but the Court of Appeals upheld the lower court's decision not to pursue charges against them. In 1993, the statutory limit was increased to $1000. New York Judiciary Law § 751(1).

2. *Compensatory Civil Contempt*. The measure of the fine in compensatory contempt is ordinarily the plaintiff's rightful position—the measure of compensatory damages. So, in the *Country Lodge* problem, the plaintiff would receive damages that would include, chiefly, proven lost profits. See, e.g., American Airlines, Inc. v. Allied Pilots Association, 228 F.3d 574 (5th Cir.

2000), cert. denied, 531 U.S. 1191, 121 S.Ct. 1190, 149 L.Ed.2d 106 (2001) (affirming award to airline of $45.5 million dollars for compensatory civil contempt after finding that union failed to carry out a temporary restraining order mandating that it call off a "sick out" by pilots).

But what if the defendant's gain is greater than the plaintiff's loss? Restitution—which will be covered in Chapter 7—sometimes makes the measure of relief the defendant's rightful position in order to deprive the defendant of its "unjust enrichment." Because the court, in granting an injunction, denies the defendant the option of violating the plaintiff's rights for the payment of compensatory damages, isn't the excess of the defendant's gain over the plaintiff's loss unjust enrichment, especially if the defendant's violation of the injunction was willful? Some courts allow a fine pegged to unjust enrichment, some do not. Compare, e.g., A.V. by Versace, Inc. v. Gianni Versace S.p.A., 87 F.Supp.2d 281 (S.D.N.Y.2000) (fine based on profits earned by the defendant) with Jarrell v. Petoseed Co., 331 S.C. 207, 500 S.E.2d 793 (App.1998) (goal is to return injured party to status quo). See Dan B. Dobbs, Law of Remedies § 2.8(2) n.23 (2d ed.1993).

3. *Coercive Civil Contempt.* The basic rule is that the court may never apply more than "the least possible power adequate to the end proposed." Anderson v. Dunn, 19 U.S. (6 Wheat.) 204, 231, 5 L.Ed. 242 (1821). In other words, the sanction must be for coercive rather than punitive purposes. Sometimes, however, what it takes to coerce determined opposition can be awesome or even infinite, as where witnesses subpoenaed to testify against organized crime fear for their lives. There are occasionally statutory limits on coercive civil contempt sanctions. For instance, in federal court, a witness who disobeys an order to testify cannot be held for longer than the life of the proceeding, up to a maximum of eighteen months. 28 U.S.C. § 1826.

In the absence of statutory limits, coercive civil contempt sanctions can substantially exceed sanctions for the same conduct punished as criminal contempt or as an ordinary crime. For an extreme example, when a husband refused to obey an Israeli rabbinical court's order to grant his wife a divorce by saying, as is necessary under Jewish law, "I am willing," the court ordered him held in jail until he obeyed. He died in jail 32 years later without saying the words. Married to Principles, San Francisco Chronicle, Dec. 6, 1994 at A7. See also Chadwick v. Hill, 2008 WL 1886128 (E.D.Pa.2008) (rejecting husband's petition for federal habeas corpus relief from incarceration since 1995 for civil contempt for refusal to comply with state court order to return funds from offshore accounts in matrimonial proceeding).

The case of Dr. Elizabeth Morgan also illustrates the potential severity of coercive civil sanctions. Dr. Morgan, then a prominent Washington, D.C. surgeon, sought to deny her former husband, Dr. Eric Foretich, an oral surgeon, unsupervised visits with their then-six-year-old daughter. Dr. Morgan believed that Dr. Foretich had sexually abused the child. After extensive hearings that produced sharply clashing testimony, the trial court ordered Dr. Morgan to produce the child for unsupervised visits with Dr. Foretich. Dr. Morgan instead hid their daughter. The trial court held Dr. Morgan in civil contempt and, in August, 1987, incarcerated her until she produced the child. In the summer of 1989, Dr. Morgan, who by then had the most seniority among the inmates of the D.C. House of Detention, testified that she would stay in jail until the child turned 18 and would be free of the court's directives. At that point, should the trial court have freed her from incarceration for civil contempt? See, e.g., Morgan v. Foretich, 564 A.2d 1 (D.C.App. en banc 1989) (appellate court directs Dr. Morgan be freed because incarceration no longer serves coercive purpose). Before the court could act, Charles Colson (the convicted Watergate-conspirator and Prison Fellowship founder), the National Organization for Women, Ross Perot, and others successfully lobbied Congress for legislation that would forbid District of Columbia courts from incarcerating anyone for civil contempt longer than one year in a custody case. The contemnor could be held longer only after being convicted of criminal contempt before a different judge, with the right to a jury and bail. District of Columbia Civil Contempt Imprisonment Limitation Act of 1989, P.L. 101–97. Is this legislation appropriate? For a detailed account of the Morgan case, see June Carbone & Leslie J. Harris, Family Law Armageddon: The Story of Morgan v. Foretich, in Family Law Stories (2007). See also Margaret M. Mahoney, The Enforcement of Child Custody Orders by Contempt Remedies, 68 U.Pitt.L.Rev. 835 (2007).

How should courts handle confrontations with such stubborn contemnors? See Doug Rendleman, Disobedience and Coercive Contempt Confinement: The Terminally Stubborn Contemnor, 48 Wash. & Lee L.Rev. 185 (1991); Linda S. Beres, Games Civil Contemnors Play, 18 Harv. J.L. & Pub. Pol'y 795 (1995).

4. *Other responses to violations of court orders.* Other responses to violations include requiring the contemnor to pay the attorney's fees and expenses caused by the violation. E.g., Jones v. Clinton, 57 F.Supp.2d 719 (E.D.Ark.1999) (ordering President Clinton to pay in excess of $90,000 in fees and expenses to compensate court and attorneys for failure to obey discovery orders in deposition). In the case of violations of discovery orders, other sanctions, such as cutting off the contemnor's right to litigate issues connected with the violation, may be imposed. Id., 36 F.Supp.2d 1118 (E.D.Ark.1999) (finding President Clinton in contempt and listing possible sanctions pursuant to Fed.R.Civ.P. 37(b)(2)).

Notes on Procedures

1. *Criminal contempt.* As pointed out in *Hicks* and *Bagwell*, criminal contempt requires many of the same procedural safeguards as an ordinary criminal prosecution. In particular, the United States Constitution requires that alleged contemnors in state or federal court are entitled to a jury trial unless the offense is petty. The offense is serious if the contumacious behavior is a crime that carries a maximum sentence of six months or more. Nor is it petty if the contumacious behavior is not otherwise a crime, but the actual sentence imposed is of six months or more. Codispoti v. Pennsylvania, 418 U.S. 506, 94 S.Ct. 2687, 41 L.Ed.2d 912 (1974). Nonetheless, in a subsequent case, the Court held that an aggregate sentence exceeding six months is still petty if each count tried individually is a petty crime. Lewis v. United States, 518 U.S. 322, 116 S.Ct. 2163, 135 L.Ed. 2d 590 (1996). Writing for five

justices, Justice O'Connor distinguished *Codispoti* by noting that, in that case, the legislature had not given any indication of its view of the seriousness of the offense by setting a maximum penalty so that the Court's only recourse was to look at the aggregate punishment imposed. In *Lewis*, however, the defendant was tried for a crime for which Congress had set a maximum sentence of less than six months, thereby providing a basis for classifying the crime as petty. Justice Kennedy, joined by Justice Breyer, joined in the judgment only because the trial judge had stated that the accused would not serve more than 6 months in prison.

A sufficiently large fine also can make a contempt serious, but how large depends on the nature and means of the defendant. In 1966, the Supreme Court said that the rule of thumb is that a $500 fine against an individual is not petty, Cheff v. Schnackenberg, 384 U.S. 373, 375, 86 S.Ct. 1523, 1523, 16 L.Ed.2d 629 (1966), but the thumb may have swollen along with inflation. See In re Dyer, 322 F.3d 1178, 1193 (9th Cir.2003) (suggesting that any fine above $5,000, "at least in 1998 dollars," would be serious). As to organizational defendants, Muniz v. Hoffman, 422 U.S. 454, 95 S.Ct. 2178, 45 L.Ed.2d 319 (1975), held that a fine of $10,000 was petty in light of a defendant union's ability to collect dues from 13,000 members. The Second Circuit has held that a $100,000 fine against a large corporation was serious, even though it represented less than one percent of its net earnings in one year. United States v. Twentieth Century Fox Film Corp., 882 F.2d 656 (2d Cir.1989), cert. denied, 493 U.S. 1021, 110 S.Ct. 722, 107 L.Ed.2d 741 (1990).

As *Bagwell* points out, a person who disrupts a trial can summarily be held in contempt, without notice or a hearing. Pounders v. Watson, 521 U.S. 982, 117 S.Ct. 2359, 138 L.Ed.2d 976 (1997), a 7–2 per curiam decision, held that summary contempt can be used not only to ward off future disruptions, but also to punish past ones. See Note, Why Contempt is Different: Agency Costs and "Petty Crime" in Summary Contempt Proceedings, 112 Yale L.J. 1223 (2003) (comprehensive analysis of the evolution of contempt, the role of the jury, and the use of summary adjudication procedures).

2. *Civil contempt.* A small number of states, including North Carolina and California, do not allow compensatory civil contempt, apparently on the theory that compensation is really "damages" so that "the defendant ought to have a trial 'at law' with a jury * * *. On the other hand, that equity took the case in the first place is an indication that the jury trial was a secondary value in the case * * *." Dan B. Dobbs, Handbook on the Law of Remedies 100 (1973). See Doug Rendleman, Compensatory Contempt: Plaintiff's Remedy When a Defendant Violates an Injunction, 1980 U.Ill.L.F. 971, 982–83. In any event, the plaintiff may well prefer to seek compensation in an action for damages rather than in contempt in order to have a jury and to avoid the clear and convincing evidence standard.

2. WHEN ARE PARTIES BOUND?

PROBLEM: COUNTRY LODGE V. MILLER (REPRISED)
VIOLATING AN ANTICIPATED ORDER

In the early fall, the trial court denies an injunction against Miller discharging waste into the river. Country Lodge appeals. While the appeal is pending, Miller discharges waste into the river during the busy apple harvesting season. In the winter, the appellate court directs the trial court to grant the injunction. Is Miller in contempt?

GRIFFIN v. COUNTY SCHOOL BOARD OF PRINCE EDWARD COUNTY

United States Court of Appeals, Fourth Circuit, en banc, 1966
363 F.2d 206, cert. denied, 385 U.S. 960, 87 S.Ct. 395, 17 L.Ed.2d 305

BRYAN, CIRCUIT JUDGE:

[The School Board of Prince Edward County, Virginia, one of the defendants in *Brown*, reacted to the command to desegregate its public schools by closing them and making tuition grants to the Prince Edward County Educational Foundation, a private corporation conducting school for white children only. In 1962, the district court ordered the public schools reopened and enjoined the payment of tuition grants until such reopening. In 1964, the Supreme Court affirmed. In the early summer of 1964, the board announced that the public schools were no longer closed, that classes would commence in the fall, and that it would resume making tuition grants. On June 29, 1964 the plaintiffs moved the district court to enjoin the processing of tuition grants on the theory that they drained money from the public schools to perpetuate segregation. The district court refused to enjoin tuition grants for the 1964–1965 school year and plaintiffs appealed on July 17, 1964. On July 28, 1964 the plaintiffs moved the court of appeals to accelerate the appeal.] * * *

As we were then not in session, Chief Judge [Soboloff] requested the Clerk to ask the Board of Supervisors to stipulate that no tuition grants would be paid pending the appeal. On August 4, 1964 the Clerk transmitted this message to the office of the Attorney General of Virginia. In reply the Clerk was told "during the late evening of August 4", that the Board would not make the stipulation. The next morning the Clerk explained that a satisfactory stipulation would be an agreement that the grants would not be paid before the normal time for processing and paying grants, that is not until after the private schools opened in September 1964.

Meanwhile, during the night of August 4 and early morning of August 5, 1964 the Board met and decided to enlarge substantially the tuition grants for the session 1964–65, and ordered that payment of one-half of the total grants be made before September 1, 1964. That night white parents were notified of the Board's action. Checks totalling about $180,000 were distributed before 9 o'clock A.M. and most of them cashed at that hour, August 5, 1964.

On August 13, 1964 in their appeal, the appellants moved to cite the Board for contempt of this court and for an order restoring the moneys distributed during the night and morning of August 4–5, 1964. After argument of the appeal in regular course, the District Court was directed to enjoin the Board from paying any tuition grants to send children to private schools so long as these schools remained segregated.

Our decision did not pass upon the contempt motion, but remanded it to the District Court for "further inquiries into the facts surrounding the payments". [The district court found that the plan to pay the tuition grants was triggered by the Chief Judge's request for a stipulation and that the effort to receive and process 1217 applications for tuition grants required the all-night efforts of some 20 volunteers and the sale of bonds overnight, but concluded that there was no contempt.] * * *

That these acts of the Board of Supervisors constituted a contempt of this court is beyond cavil. The Board undertook to put the money then available for tuition grants—and then wholly subject to its orders—beyond its control as well as that of the court. In doing so the Board took upon itself to decide its right to exercise, in favor of the private school, the Board's general power to appropriate public funds. This use of power was, as the Board was acutely aware, an arrogation of this court's responsibility. Obviously, the aim was to thwart the impact of any adverse decree which might ultimately be forthcoming on the appeal. In effect it was a "resistance to its [this court's] lawful writ, process, order, rule, decree, or command." 18 U.S.C. § 401(3). The authorities are quite clear on the point.

The Board would escape the judgment of contempt on the argument that the statute limits the power of the court to punish violations of orders or decrees then extant. But precedent does not so contract the statute or constrict its intent. Although this court had not issued an injunction against the appropriation of the moneys to tuition grants, the Board knew that if the plaintiffs succeeded this would be its ultimate decree, as in fact it became. That potential decree was thus then within the statute. Furthermore, the appeal was itself a "process" which was alive at the time of the disbursement and was resisted by the disbursement.

In Merrimack River Savings Bank v. Clay Center, 219 U.S. 527, 31 S.Ct. 295, 55 L.Ed. 320 (1911), a temporary injunction had been issued by a Federal District Court to prevent the destruction by a municipality of a public utility's poles and wires, located in the city streets under an authorized franchise. The suit was dismissed on jurisdictional grounds. However, for and during an appeal to the Supreme Court, the injunction was continued in force. On this review the dismissal was upheld. But before the mandate of dismissal had been issued or could issue, and in the period allowed for presenting an application for a rehearing, the city cut down the poles, destroyed a large section of the wires and thus put the utility out of business. This conduct was declared to be contempt of the Supreme Court, Justice Lurton saying at 535–536, 31 S.Ct. at 296:

> It does not necessarily follow that disobedience of such an injunction, intended only to preserve the status quo pending an appeal, may not be regarded as a contempt of the appellate jurisdiction of this court, which might be rendered nugatory by conduct calculated to remove

the subject-matter of the appeal beyond its control, or by its destruction. This we need not decide, since *irrespective of any such injunction actually issued the wilful removal beyond the reach of the court of the subject-matter of the litigation ... (on) appeal ... is, in and of itself, a contempt of the appellate jurisdiction of this court....* Unless this be so, a reversal of the decree would be but a barren victory, since the very result would have been brought about by the lawless act of the defendants which it was the object of the suit to prevent. (Accent added.)

The contempt power declared in the *Merrimack* case was not suggested to be rooted in the inherent power of the Supreme Court rather than in the statute now embodied in 18 U.S.C. 401(3). * * * But *Merrimack* is not now cited to power. It is cited as warranting our finding that the putting of the subject-matter of this litigation beyond our reach was a defiance of this court, an anticipatory resistance to its ultimate orders or process. * * *

The present case is quite different factually from Berry v. Midtown Service Corp., 104 F.2d 107 (2d Cir.1939), relied upon by the Board. There the subject-matter disposed of pending appeal was the leviable assets of the judgment debtor-appellant. The Court distinguished that case from ours when it said that the appeal was not "defeated or impaired" by the defendant's assignment. Further distinction is found in its observation that the suit "was not concerned with any specific property," the judgment on appeal merely establishing a general, personal, financial liability.

In our case the disbursement of the moneys seriously impaired the appeal. The suit and the appeal were directed to a specific subject, the Board's right to apply to a certain purpose money within its power. The Board assumed the right in utter and wilful disregard of this court's views. As was said in *Merrimack* * * * such conduct constituted contempt although not formally and explicitly under injunction.

We find the Board of Supervisors and its members guilty of civil contempt. Accordingly, the Board and its constituent individuals, namely, W.W. Vaughan, C.W. Gates, H.M. Jenkins, Charles B. Pickett, John C. Steck and H.E. Carwile, Jr., personally and in their own right, will be ordered jointly and severally to restore to the County Treasurer of Prince Edward County, through recapture or otherwise, an amount equal to the disbursements authorized and made by their resolutions of August 4–5, 1964. This cause will be continued for a period of 90 days from this date for report by the Board and its members of what has been done towards compliance with this order, as well as for the passage of such further orders as may appear proper. * * *

HAYNSWORTH, CHIEF JUDGE, with whom BOREMAN, CIRCUIT JUDGE, joins (dissenting):

* * * I am not in disagreement that the conduct of the Supervisors was unconscionable. However, I must disagree with the majority in their interpretation of the power of this Court to adjudge parties in contempt.

It is clear that this Court has an inherent power to punish contempts. It was originally defined by the seventeenth section of the Judiciary Act of 1789 as the power to punish by fine or imprisonment all contempts of authority in any cause or hearing before the Court. But the power has since been limited and redefined by the Act of Congress of March 2, 1831, now 18 U.S.C. § 401. The statute prescribes:

> A court of the United States shall have power to punish by fine or imprisonment, at its discretion, such contempt of its authority, and none other, as:
>
> (1) Misbehavior of any person in its presence or so near thereto as to obstruct the administration of justice;
>
> (2) Misbehavior of any of its officers in their official transactions;
>
> (3) Disobedience or resistance to its lawful writ, process, order, rule, decree, or command.

Considerable doubt was expressed in Ex parte Robinson, 19 Wall. 505, 86 U.S. 505, as to whether this statute could limit the contempt power of the Supreme Court, which derives its existence and powers from the Constitution, and it is obvious from *Merrimack* that the Court has since gone beyond the statute. But *Robinson* made it clear that there can be no question about the limiting effect the statute has upon the courts of appeals and the district courts. As courts created, not by the Constitution, but, through the power that document vested in Congress, exercise of their inherent contempt powers must be confined to the bounds that Congress has fixed.

Measuring the facts in the present case by the word of Congress, I am unable to find a basis in the statute for a contempt citation here. Phrases (1) and (2) of the statute are not applicable here. The majority finds, under phrase (3), that there was disobedience or resistance to a lawful writ, process, order, rule, decree, or command of this Court. Yet none in fact existed to be disobeyed or resisted. The plaintiff's sought no temporary restraining order or injunction, and none was issued preventing the action taken by the Supervisors. The stipulation requested of the defendants by this court cannot be expanded to fit into any of the things specified in § 401(3).

The word "process," as used in the statute in its context of writs, orders and decrees, obviously means more than the pendency of an appeal or of some other relevant judicial proceeding. It has been traditionally used to encompass such things as a summons, a subpoena, an attachment, a warrant, a mandate, a levy and, generically, other writs and orders. In the context of other orders and writs, "process" can reasonably be understood to mean no more than the sum of more explicit terms, such as "original process," "summary process," "mesne process" and "final process," all of which clearly refer to papers issuing from the court and embodying its commands or judgments, or notice of them. Construed so expansively as the majority's suggestion of equivalence with the pendency of any relevant judicial proceeding, it would entirely contravene the clearly limiting purpose of the congressional act.

Since the suggested construction of the word "process," as used in the statute, is original with the majority, it has never been treated in any reported opinion. The suggestion is inconsistent with the substantially uniform course of decision, however, while the primary theory of the majority is explicitly at odds with the precedents in this and other courts.

This court declared itself in Ex parte Buskirk, 4 Cir., 72 F. 14. There it was held not only that an anticipatory, partial avoidance of a potential decree was not a punishable contempt within the confines of the limiting statute; violation of a stipulation made in open court, without which mesne process might, and probably would, have issued, was held not to be. Implicit in the decision is a narrow, literal reading of the word "process."

Buskirk was a party in a judicial proceeding in a district court for a determination of the ownership of a tract of timber. In open court, he entered into a stipulation that none of the timber would be cut until the court had decided the question of ownership. Nevertheless, pending the court's decision, he began cutting the timber and intentionally removed it beyond the reach of the court. This court held because of the statute, "[h]owever reprehensible such conduct . . . may have been . . . it nevertheless did not constitute a contempt to the court or its orders."

My brothers now overrule *Buskirk* without deigning to mention it.

Our own decision in *Buskirk* is not an aberration. It is the exemplar of uniform decision. Four of our sister circuits have embraced the same construction of the statute, and have done so in no uncertain terms. No court of appeals, until now, has toyed with any other reading. * * *

I would not quibble with the majority's finding of fact that the conduct of the Supervisors was contemptible, but I do dissent from their conclusion that it was contemptuous and punishable as such, when the conclusion is dependent upon a reading of the statute which relegates it to meaninglessness. Such an unsympathetic construction is particularly inappropriate when the statute was clearly intended to inhibit our authority, has been declared by the Supreme Court to have that effect and has been uniformly construed by the courts of appeals in accordance with that evident intention. Such a statute limiting the jurisdiction of the federal courts is largely enforceable only by the limited courts, themselves. Above all other statutory commands, courts should be scrupulous to conform themselves to jurisdictional statutes, so that they do not appropriate to themselves powers which have been constitutionally withdrawn from them. * * *

NOTES ON GETTING TRICKY WITH A COURT

1. Paying the tuition grants was illegal as part of a scheme to perpetuate state-sponsored segregation. As such, the plaintiffs could have gotten an

injunction requiring the school board to recover the grants. The question for the court of appeals was not whether the grants were illegal but whether they were also contempt of court. A finding of contempt offered the plaintiffs several advantages over an injunction. First, the contempt sanction provided that the individual board members had to compensate the board to the extent that they could not recover grants from parents. An injunction probably could not impose such personal liability on nonparties (for reasons that will be discussed at p. 353) and so would have given the board members no incentive to recoup the grants any more aggressively than necessary to avoid being held in contempt. Second, contempt makes the contemnor potentially liable for the other party's attorneys' fees caused by the contempt and the court of appeals awarded the plaintiffs such fees in *Griffin*. Third, contempt connotes guilt—a word usually reserved for the criminal context—even when the contempt is civil. Note that the court finds the defendants "guilty of civil contempt." Such a tinge of guilt is likely to affect the adjudication of future issues in the case. As such, contempt often boosts the plaintiffs' morale and depresses the defendants'. Morale can be an important consideration in protracted litigations, which are frequently wars of attrition.

2. In considering whether the defendants were properly held in contempt, it is useful to set out some propositions with which most attorneys would agree.

(a) Contempt includes but is not limited to violation of a valid court order. Did the defendants violate any such order?

(b) Committing an illegal act—such as breaching a contract or segregating a school—is not in itself contempt although it may give rise to ordinary civil or even criminal liability. Otherwise, all illegal acts would be contempt of court.

(c) The illegal act is not made contemptuous by a court previously declaring that it would be illegal. As you will learn in Chapter 4, a declaratory judgment is not a court order, but its issuance may enhance the civil or criminal liability by making clear that the illegal act was done knowingly.

(d) The illegal act is not made contemptuous by the violator promising in a stipulation not to do it. The stipulation is not a court order but rather a contract between the parties to it and may itself give rise to liability as well as preclude the adjudication of the issues resolved in the stipulation.

(e) Even an act that violates a stipulation that the court has approved as part of the settlement of a case is not contempt unless the court has used clear language which turned a contractual duty into an obligation to obey an operative command of the court itself. H.K. Porter Co. v. National Friction Products Corp., 568 F.2d 24, 25–27 (7th Cir.1977). For this reason, settlements that the parties intend to have enforced through the contempt power are usually styled something like "STIPULATION AND ORDER" and usually conclude with language in which the court orders the parties to abide by their stipulation. Should a party to a stipulation that is not an order violate it, the other party might, amongst other remedies, seek an injunction that the stipulation be obeyed.

3. The plaintiffs could have asked the district court for a stay of the payment of the tuition grants pending appeal and, if denied, could have sought the same relief from the court of appeals. Fed.R.App.P. 8. A stay is to an appeal what a preliminary injunction is to a complaint—an injunction designed to prevent harm pending the court's determination of the merits of the appeal or of the complaint. The standards for the issuance of a stay are similar to those for the issuance of a preliminary injunction—probability of success on the merits, potential harm to the plaintiffs if a stay is not issued, potential harm to the defendants if a stay is issued, and so on. Should a stay have been issued? Absent a stay, a defendant who succeeds in the trial court is not under court order. Why did the plaintiffs' attorneys not move for a stay? Why did Chief Judge Soboloff not issue a stay sua sponte?

4. The *Griffin* majority concluded that trying to put the money beyond the court's easy reach frustrated the appeal and thereby constituted "[d]isobedience or resistance to its lawful * * * process * * *."

(a) Under this reasoning, would it have been contempt for the defendants to have paid the money before the court clerk asked them to stipulate that they would not?

(b) Under this reasoning, would it have been contempt for the defendants to have paid the money as soon as the plaintiffs moved the district court to enjoin the payments since a motion is also a process?

(c) Does *Merrimack* support the appellate court's theory?

5. The dissent thinks that the court may well have had an inherent power to punish the defendants until Congress set out to limit that inherent power in 18 U.S.C. § 401 (1982). That section was enacted a century and a half ago, after a judge used the contempt power to punish the publication of newspaper reports that criticized him. It is unclear whether the statute applies just to criminal contempts or to civil contempts as well. The Eleventh Circuit held that as to attorneys appearing before the court the "trial judge possesses the inherent power to discipline counsel for misconduct * * * without resort[ing] to the powers of civil or criminal contempt." Kleiner v. First National Bank, 751 F.2d 1193, 1209 (11th Cir.1985).

6. So was *Griffin* rightly decided? Even on its awful facts, two of the five judges would have found no contempt. Scholars have criticized its reasoning, although not its result. E.g., Doug Rendleman, Compensatory Contempt to Collect Money, 41 Ohio State L.J. 625, 633–35 (1980). Shepardizing *Griffin* reveals no cases in which a court rested a finding of contempt upon the violation of an anticipated court order. Courts do, however, claim inherent judicial authority to punish bad faith litigation tactics, and conduct like that in *Griffin* should qualify as such. E.g., Kleiner v. First National Bank, 751 F.2d 1193 (11th Cir.1985). But, allowing judges to punish bad faith tactics gives them wider latitude, and the targets of the punishment less notice, than contemplated by 18 U.S.C. § 401.

7. *Update on Griffin*. In 2004, Virginia established the Brown v. Board of Education Scholarship Program, Va.Stat. § 30–231.1 et seq., "for the purpose of assisting students who were enrolled in the public schools of Virginia between 1954 and 1964, in jurisdictions in which the public schools

were closed to avoid desegregation, in obtaining a high school diploma" or other education. Eligible citizens, now in their late 50's and 60's, may receive scholarships of up to $5,500 to further their educations now in an effort to make up for what they were denied years ago when the schools in Prince Edward County and elsewhere were closed. Michael Janofsky, A New Hope for Dreams Suspended by Segregation, N.Y.Times, July 31, 2005.

3. THE COLLATERAL BAR RULE

Problem: Country Lodge v. Miller (Reprised)
The Collateral Bar Rule

In the early fall, the trial court enjoins Miller from discharging waste into the river. Miller continues to discharge waste while she appeals. In the winter, the appellate court overturns the injunction. Is Miller guilty of criminal contempt for violating the injunction prior to the appellate court's action?

IN RE PROVIDENCE JOURNAL CO.

United States Court of Appeals, First Circuit, 1987
820 F.2d 1342, 820 F.2d 1354, cert. dismissed, 485 U.S.
693, 108 S.Ct. 1502, 99 L.Ed.2d 785 (1988)c

Wisdom, Circuit Judge.

This appeal presents an apparent conflict between two fundamental legal principles: the hallowed First Amendment principle that the press shall not be subjected to prior restraints; the other, the sine qua non of orderly government, that, until modified or vacated, a court order must be obeyed. The district court adjudged the defendants/appellants, the Providence Journal Company and its executive editor, Charles M. Hauser, (collectively referred to as the "Journal") guilty of criminal contempt. The Journal admits that it violated the order but argues that the order was a prior restraint and that the unconstitutionality of the order is a defense in the contempt proceeding. We agree. A party subject to an order that constitutes a transparently invalid prior restraint on pure speech may challenge the order by violating it.

Facts

From 1962 to 1965, the Federal Bureau of Investigation conducted electronic surveillance of Raymond L.S. Patriarca, reputedly a prominent figure in organized crime. The FBI conducted this surveillance without a warrant in violation of his Fourth Amendment rights. The FBI later destroyed all tape recordings relating to this surveillance but retained the logs and memoranda compiled from the recordings. In 1976, the Journal requested the logs and memoranda from the FBI under the Freedom of

---

c. Certiorari was dismissed because it was filed by a special prosecutor appointed by the district court while 28 U.S.C. § 518(a) provides that only the Attorney General or the Solicitor General can conduct or argue suits "in which the United States is interested" in the Supreme Court. It was such a suit because it involved a crime against the United States, criminal contempt.

Information Act ("FOIA"). The FBI refused this request on the ground that disclosure would be an unwarranted invasion of personal privacy. * * *

In the spring of 1985, after the death of Raymond L.S. Patriarca, the Journal renewed its FOIA request to the FBI for the logs and memoranda. The FBI assented to this request and furnished the materials not only to the Journal, but also to WJAR Television Ten and other news media. On November 8, 1985, Raymond J. Patriarca ("Patriarca"), Raymond L.S. Patriarca's son, filed a summons and complaint against the FBI, WJAR, and the Journal * * * [for an injunction preventing the defendants from publishing the released material.]

On November 12, 1985, the summons, complaint, and motion were served on the Journal. One day later, the district court held a conference concerning the request for a temporary restraining order. Counsel for the Journal argued that any restraining order would constitute a prior restraint forbidden by the First Amendment. Over the objections of counsel for the Journal and the government, the court entered a temporary restraining order barring publication of the logs and memoranda by the Journal and WJAR. The district court set a hearing for November 15, 1985, at which time it would decide whether to vacate the order. The district court later vacated the order and denied preliminary injunctive relief against the Journal and WJAR.

On November 14, 1985, the day after the district court issued the order, and while that order was still in effect, the Journal published an article on the deceased Patriarca that included information taken from the logs and memoranda. The son filed a motion to judge the Journal in contempt. When he declined to prosecute the criminal contempt motion, the district court invoked Fed.R.Crim.P. 42(b) and appointed a special prosecutor. Following a hearing, the district court found the Journal guilty of criminal contempt. Subsequent to a sentencing hearing, the court imposed an 18-month jail term on Hauser, which was suspended, ordered Hauser to perform 200 hours of public service, and fined the Journal $100,000. The Journal appealed.

DISCUSSION

This appeal propounds a question that admits of no easy answer. Each party stands on what each regards as an unassailable legal principle. The special prosecutor relies on the bedrock principle that court orders, even those that are later ruled unconstitutional, must be complied with until amended or vacated.[9] This principle is often referred to as the "collateral bar" rule. The Journal relies on the bedrock principle that prior restraints against speech are prohibited by the First Amendment. In this opinion we endeavor to avoid deciding which principle should take precedence by reaching a result consistent with both principles. * * *

---

9. See Walker v. City of Birmingham, 388 U.S. 307, 87 S.Ct. 1824, 18 L.Ed.2d 1210 (1967); United States v. United Mine Workers, 330 U.S. 258, 67 S.Ct. 677, 91 L.Ed. 884 (1947).

If a publisher is to print a libelous, defamatory, or injurious story, an appropriate remedy, though not always totally effective, lies not in an injunction against that publication but in a damages or criminal action after publication. Although the threat of damages or criminal action may chill speech, a prior restraint "freezes" speech before the audience has the opportunity to hear the message. Additionally, a court asked to issue a prior restraint must judge the challenged speech in the abstract. And, as was true in the instant case, a court may issue a prior restraint in the form of a temporary restraining order or preliminary injunction without a full hearing; a judgment for damages or a criminal sanction may be imposed only after a full hearing with all the attendant procedural protections.

Equally well-established is the requirement of any civilized government that a party subject to a court order must abide by its terms or face criminal contempt. Even if the order is later declared improper or unconstitutional, it must be followed until vacated or modified. As a general rule, a party may not violate an order and raise the issue of its unconstitutionality collaterally as a defense in the criminal contempt proceeding. Rather, the appropriate method to challenge a court order is to petition to have the order vacated or amended.

In *Walker v. City of Birmingham*, the Supreme Court upheld contempt citations against Dr. Martin Luther King, Jr. and other civil rights protestors enjoined from parading without a permit. The protestors argued that the order and the ordinance upon which it was based were unconstitutional because they constituted impermissible prior restraints upon the right to free speech and assembly. The Court noted that the ordinance "unquestionably raise[d] substantial constitutional issues" and that "[t]he breadth and vagueness of the injunction itself would also unquestionably be subject to substantial constitutional question". Nonetheless, the Court ruled that the protestors could not raise those constitutional issues collaterally in the contempt proceedings. As the Supreme Court noted in *United States v. United Mine Workers*, so long as the court has jurisdiction over the parties and the subject matter of the controversy, an order it issues must be obeyed.

The *Walker* Court found it significant that the contemnors had not sought to appeal the order they violated. The Court declared: "This case would arise in quite a different constitutional posture if the petitioners, before disobeying the injunction, had challenged it in the Alabama courts, and had been met with delay or frustration of their constitutional claims." The *Walker* Court concluded by noting that "no man can be judge in his own case, however exalted his station, however righteous his motives, and irrespective of his race, color, politics, or religion".

At first glance, *Walker* would appear to control the instant case. There, as here, a party chose to violate an arguably unconstitutional prior restraint rather than to comply with the orderly process of law by seeking relief from an appellate court. *Walker* declares that the contemnors are collaterally barred from challenging the constitutionality of the order forming the basis of the contempt citation. The *Walker* Court was, however, careful to point out that the order issued by the Alabama court was not "transparently invalid". The Court specifically noted that "this is not a case where the injunction was *transparently invalid* or had only a frivolous pretense to validity". The unmistakable import of this language is that a transparently invalid order cannot form the basis for a contempt citation.

Court orders are accorded a special status in American jurisprudence. While one may violate a statute and raise as a defense the statute's unconstitutionality, such is not generally the case with a court order. Nonetheless, court orders are not sacrosanct.[28] An order entered by a court clearly without jurisdiction over the contemnors or the subject matter is not protected by the collateral bar rule.[29] Were this not the case, a court could wield power over parties or matters obviously not within its authority—a concept inconsistent with the notion that the judiciary may exercise only those powers entrusted to it by law.

The same principle supports an exception to the collateral bar rule for transparently invalid court orders. Requiring a party subject to such an order to obey or face contempt would give the courts powers far in excess of any authorized by the Constitution or Congress. Recognizing an exception to the collateral bar rule for transparently invalid orders does not violate the principle that "no man can be judge in his own case" anymore than does recognizing such an exception for jurisdictional defects. The key to both exceptions is the notion that although a court order—even an arguably incorrect court order—demands respect, so does the right of the citizen to be free of clearly improper exercises of judicial authority.

Although an exception to the collateral bar rule is appropriate for transparently void orders, it is inappropriate for arguably proper orders. This distinction is necessary both to protect the authority of the courts when they address close questions and to create a strong incentive for parties to follow the orderly process of law. No such protection or incentive is needed when the order is transparently invalid because in that instance the court is acting so far in excess of its authority that it has no right to expect compliance and no interest is protected by requiring compliance.

The line between a transparently invalid order and one that is merely invalid is, of course, not always distinct. As a general rule, if the court reviewing the order finds the order to have had any pretense to validity at the time it was issued, the reviewing court should enforce the collateral bar rule. Such a heavy presumption in favor of validity is necessary to protect the rightful power of the courts. Nonetheless, there are instances

---

28. See Cobbledick v. United States, 309 U.S. 323, 60 S.Ct. 540, 84 L.Ed. 783 (1940). In *Cobbledick,* the Supreme Court ruled that when a motion to quash a subpoena is denied, the movant may either obey its commands or violate them, and, if cited for contempt, properly contest its validity in the contempt proceeding. * * *

29. *United Mine Workers*, 330 U.S. at 293, 67 S.Ct. at 695.

where an order will be so patently unconstitutional that it will be excepted from the collateral bar rule. We now turn to consider whether the order issued by the district court on November 13, 1985, was, as the Journal contends, transparently invalid.

[The court concludes that the Supreme Court has never upheld a prior restraint on publication of news, but that it has implied that such a restraint might be appropriate in certain extreme cases.]

The special prosecutor argues, however, that the order was to last only a short period and merely preserved the status quo while allowing the court a full opportunity to assess the issues. We are sympathetic with the district court on this score. This matter came before the district court on an emergency basis. The court was forced to drop its other duties and immediately address this issue. Counsel for the Journal had received the papers less than 24 hours before they presented their arguments to the district court. Based on counsel's hastily prepared authority and without the opportunity for cool reflection, the district court was forced to make a decision. The court's natural instinct was to delay the matter temporarily so that a careful, thoughtful answer could be crafted. This approach is proper in most instances, and indeed to follow any other course of action would often be irresponsible. But, absent the most compelling circumstances, when that approach results in a prior restraint on pure speech by the press it is not allowed.

It must be said, it is misleading in the context of daily newspaper publishing to argue that a temporary restraining order merely preserves the status quo. The status quo of daily newspapers is to publish news promptly that editors decide to publish. A restraining order disturbs the status quo and impinges on the exercise of editorial discretion. News is a constantly changing and dynamic quantity. Today's news will often be tomorrow's history. This is especially true in the case of news concerning an imminent event such as an election. A restraining order lasting only hours can effectively prevent publication of news that will have an impact on that event and on those that the event affects.

Although there is no question that the Patriarca story was not news concerning an imminent event, extraneous factors required its reasonably prompt publication. The Journal had promised its readers that the Patriarca story would be forthcoming. Moreover, other media not subject to the court order had the same logs and memoranda. Were they to disseminate this information while the Journal remained silent, some readers of the Journal might lose confidence in that paper's editorial competence.[65]

* * *

---

[65]. In United States v. Dickinson, 465 F.2d 496 (5th Cir.1972), the Court of Appeals for the Fifth Circuit applied the collateral bar rule in a contempt proceeding involving a gag order against a newspaper. We decline to follow *Dickinson* for two reasons. First, *Dickinson* involved an order issued to protect a defendant's Sixth Amendment right to a fair trial, while the order in the instant matter was issued merely to protect an individual's interest in privacy. Second, *Dickinson* was decided before [the Supreme Court handed down a case that announced a particularly strict test for prior restraints].

Sec. C　　　ENFORCEMENT OF THE DECREE　　　341

Although the Journal arguably had avenues of appellate relief immediately available to it,[70] we decline to invoke the collateral bar rule because of the Journal's failure to avail itself of these opportunities. When, as here, the court order is a transparently invalid prior restraint on pure speech, the delay and expense of an appeal is unnecessary. Indeed, the delay caused by an appellate review requirement could, in the case of a prior restraint involving news concerning an imminent event, cause the restrained information to lose its value. The absence of such a requirement will not, however, lead to wide-spread disregard of court orders. Rarely will a party be subject to a transparently invalid court order. Prior restraints on pure speech represent an unusual class of orders because they are presumptively unconstitutional. And even when a party believes it is subject to a transparently invalid order, seeking review in an appellate court is a far safer means of testing the order. For if the party chooses to violate the order and the order turns out not to be transparently invalid, the party must suffer the consequences of a contempt citation.

Conclusion

We conclude that the district court's order of November 13, 1985, was transparently invalid. * * *

Because the order was transparently invalid, the appellants should have been allowed to challenge its constitutionality at the contempt proceedings.[74] A fortiori, the order cannot serve as the basis for a contempt citation. The order of the district court finding the Providence Journal Company and its executive editor, Charles M. Hauser, in criminal contempt is therefore reversed.[75]

Order

We hereby grant petitioner's suggestion for rehearing en banc. We do not, however, vacate the panel's opinion and order. Rather, we issue the

---

70. Arguably, the Journal could have immediately appealed the order to this Court under 28 U.S.C. § 1292(a)(1). And, although difficult to obtain, the Journal might have sought a writ of mandamus. 28 U.S.C. § 1651(a).

74. [In Thomas v. Collins, 323 U.S. 516, 65 S.Ct. 315, 89 L.Ed. 430 (1945)], a labor organization was enjoined from soliciting union memberships. The organizer violated the order and subsequently challenged its constitutionality arguing that the temporary restraining order constituted a prior restraint on pure speech. The Supreme Court allowed this challenge and reversed the contempt citation.

The Journal argues that *Thomas* stands for the proposition that the collateral bar rule does not apply to prior restraints on pure speech. Because the order of November 13, 1985, was transparently invalid, however, we need not address this issue. We note, however, that *Thomas* does provide support for our holding. *Thomas* held that any prior restraint on pure speech was invalid absent clear and present danger of immediate and irreparable injury to the public welfare. Moreover, *Thomas* establishes that the collateral bar rule is not impregnable in cases involving prior restraints on pure speech.

75. In reversing the contempt citation against the Journal and its executive editor, we in no way condone their conduct. From all appearances, the Journal used the presence of the court order to bolster the importance of the Patriarca story. On November 14, 1985, the day before the scheduled hearing on whether to vacate the Court order of November 13, the Journal's front page headline read: "Court restricts media use of FBI tapes on Patriarca; Journal decides to print". * * * [I]t appears to this court that the Journal published the story concerning the court order more for its publicity value than for its news value. * * *

attached en banc opinion as an addendum to, and modification of, said panel opinion; and as so modified said panel opinion and order may stand as reflecting the opinion of the en banc court. * * *

OPINION ON REHEARING

PER CURIAM.

In reflecting en banc upon the conflicting principles of "collateral bar" and "no prior restraint against pure speech," the court recognizes, with the panel, the difficulties of imposing upon a publisher the requirement of pursuing the normal appeal process. Not only would such entail time and expense, but the right sought to be vindicated could be forfeited or the value of the embargoed information considerably cheapened. Nevertheless, it seems to us that some finer tuning is available to minimize the disharmony between respect for court orders and respect for free speech.

It is not asking much, beyond some additional expense and time, to require a publisher, even when it thinks it is the subject of a transparently unconstitutional order of prior restraint, to make a good faith effort to seek emergency relief from the appellate court. If timely access to the appellate court is not available or if timely decision is not forthcoming, the publisher may then proceed to publish and challenge the constitutionality of the order in the contempt proceedings. In such event whatever added expense and time are involved, such a price does not seem disproportionate to the respect owing court processes; and there is no prolongation of any prior restraint. On the other hand, should the appellate court grant the requested relief, the conflict between principles has been resolved and the expense and time involved have vastly been offset by aborting any contempt proceedings.

We realize that our ruling means that a publisher seeking to challenge an order it deems transparently unconstitutional must concern itself with establishing a record of its good faith effort. But that is a price we should pay for the preference of court over party determination of invalidity. In the instant case, assertions have been made that some eight-and-one-half hours elapsed between the issuance of the order by the district court and the deadline for publication. Not only are we left without a clear conviction that timely emergency relief was available within the restraints governing the publisher's decision making, but we would deem it unfair to subject the publisher to the very substantial sanctions imposed by the district court because of its failure to follow the procedure we have just announced. We recognize that our announcement is technically dictum, but are confident that its stature as a deliberate position taken by us in this en banc consideration will serve its purpose.

NOTES ON THE COLLATERAL BAR RULE

1. *The collateral bar rule is not mandatory.* Walker merely held that it was permissible for states to enforce the collateral bar rule. For example, Texas recognizes an exception when the trial court's injunction unconstitu-

tionally restrains speech. In re Sheshtawy, 154 S.W.3d 114, 126 (2004). Accord, People v. Gonzalez, 12 Cal.4th 804, 50 Cal.Rptr.2d 74, 910 P.2d 1366 (1996) (citing cases from other jurisdictions declining to follow the rule). See Comment, The Collateral Bar Rule and Rule 26 Protective Orders: Overprotection of Judicial Discretion, 35 Ariz.L.Rev. 1029 (2003) (overview of collateral bar rule; comment contends that collateral bar rule should not be applied to F.R.Civ.P. 26 protective orders).

2. *Does the rule make sense?* *Providence Journal* develops an exception to the collateral bar rule, but does not question the rule itself. Unless one of the exceptions to the rule applies—more about them below—someone who violates an injunction is barred from defending a prosecution for criminal contempt by asserting that the order was invalid. In other words, one may attack the order's validity by direct appeal, but not collaterally in a criminal contempt proceeding. For example, in *Walker v. City of Birmingham,* Dr. King and others were barred from collaterally attacking the validity of an injunction enforcing a constitutionally suspect anti-parade ordinance. In contrast, other participants in the march, who were charged only with violating the ordinance because they were not named in the injunction, were not collaterally barred from making an ultimately successful attack upon the ordinance's invalidity. Shuttlesworth v. City of Birmingham, 394 U.S. 147, 89 S.Ct. 935, 22 L.Ed.2d 162 (1969). So, on account of an invalid order based upon an invalid ordinance issued by a judge who was part of a segregationist system, Dr. King and his enjoined colleagues were forced to choose. If the long-planned march were delayed until after lawyers got the order overturned or stayed on appeal, the dramatic moment for the march over the Easter weekend would have passed. Dr. King and the others chose to march and go to jail. (There he wrote the famous "Letter from Birmingham Jail." See David Benjamin Oppenheimer, Martin Luther King, and the Letter from Birmingham Jail, 26 U.C.Davis L.Rev. 791 (1993); and David Benjamin Oppenheimer, Kennedy, King, Shuttlesworth and Walker: The Events Leading to the Introduction of the Civil Rights Act of 1964, 29 U.S.F.L.Rev. 645 (1995).)

Walker v. City of Birmingham shows the harm that can result from the collateral bar rule. Yet, harm could also ensue from getting rid of it. Consider the fate of Ed Johnson. Mr. Johnson, an African–American, was convicted by an all-white jury of raping a white woman and sentenced to death. The conviction was appealed to the United States Supreme Court, which took the case on March 19, 1906. This was the first time it had ever agreed to review a state court criminal trial. Pending appeal, the Court immediately stayed the execution and telegraphed an order to Sheriff Joseph Shipp to protect Johnson. On the night of March 19, with the connivance of Sheriff Shipp, and with full knowledge of the Court's orders, a mob took Johnson out of jail and lynched him. The Supreme Court ordered the Attorney General of the United States to prosecute Sheriff Shipp for criminal contempt and he was convicted. United States v. Shipp, 214 U.S. 386, 29 S.Ct. 637, 53 L.Ed. 1041 (1909). See Mark Curriden & Leroy Phillips, Jr., Contempt of Court: The Turn-of-the-Century Lynching That Launched 100 Years of Federalism (1999). Without a collateral bar rule, Sheriff Shipp would not be guilty of contempt if the order to protect Johnson had been issued in error. The abolition of the collateral bar rule would tempt some defendants to defy a court order in the belief that later it will be found invalid. If they are wrong, however, irreparable injury will have been done to the plaintiff. The collateral bar rule reflects the judgment of appellate judges that trial court judges are generally more trustworthy than defendants in deciding whether to subject plaintiffs to such irreparable harm.

3. *Exceptions to the collateral bar rule.*

(a) *No direct appeal available.* Footnote 28 in *Providence Journal* shows that the collateral bar rule does not apply to certain discovery orders for which no direct appeal is available. The court also notes a passage in *Walker* indicating that the collateral bar rule would not apply if the demonstrators had appealed but had been given the run around. As the court acknowledges, it is difficult to appeal temporary restraining orders. Should the collateral bar rule apply to such orders? Professor Rendleman argues that the collateral bar rule should not apply to ex parte orders. Doug Rendleman, More on Void Orders, 7 Ga.L.Rev. 246 (1973).

(b) *The court lacks jurisdiction.* The collateral bar rule, in effect, puts the burden on the defendant of either obeying the order or going to the trouble of getting it overturned on appeal. The justification for this burden is that the order did not come from just anyone but rather from a judge. However, if the judge is from a low level tribunal that lacks subject matter jurisdiction to issue the injunction—say traffic court or small claims court—then putting the burden on the defendant loses plausibility. This is the rationale for the lack of jurisdiction exception. However, the most powerful trial courts sometimes may lack jurisdiction for reasons that are quite complex and difficult to evaluate. For instance, the Supreme Court in *United Mine Workers* split 5–4 in holding that the federal district court had jurisdiction to enjoin a strike against the government. Moreover, there is an exception to the no-jurisdiction-exception. Five justices in *United Mine Workers* held that even if the district court ultimately lacked jurisdiction, it had jurisdiction to issue a temporary restraining order to gain the time to determine whether it had jurisdiction. What result if the court failed to consider the jurisdictional issue at all but rather issued the temporary restraining order without mentioning it? See United States Catholic Conference v. Abortion Rights Mobilization, 487 U.S. 72, 79–80, 108 S.Ct. 2268, 2272, 101 L.Ed.2d 69 (1988).

(c) *Transparent invalidity.* *Walker* suggested transparent invalidity as an exception, but not until *Providence Journal* did a federal court base a holding on this theory. Why hadn't a case gone off on transparent invalidity in the two decades since *Walker*? Should there be a transparent invalidity exception? Should it require, as the en banc decision says, an effort to appeal? The Second Circuit Court of Appeals, in United States v. Terry, 17 F.3d 575, 579 (2d Cir.), cert. denied, 513 U.S. 946, 115 S.Ct. 355, 130 L.Ed.2d 310 (1994), joined the First Circuit in finding that a party seeking to invoke the transparent invalidity exception must make a "good faith effort to seek emergency relief from the appellate court."

(d) *Prior restraints.* *Thomas*, discussed in footnote 74, involved a union official found in contempt of an order not to violate a statute that forbade soliciting union membership. The Court struck down the statute on the grounds of prior restraint and freed the official without mention of the collateral bar rule. So *Thomas* is not square support for an exception to the collateral bar rule for prior restraints. Courts in a few states have considered whether there should be such an exception, with mixed results. See Richard E. Labunski, A First Amendment Exception to the "Collateral Bar" Rule: Protecting Freedom of Expression and the Legitimacy of Courts, 22 Pepp. L.Rev. 405 (1995). Should there be such an exception? See Christina E. Wells, Bringing Structure to the Law of Injunctions Against Expression, 51 Case W.Res.L.Rev. 1 (2000). See also McGraw–Hill Cos. v. Procter & Gamble Co., 515 U.S.1309, 116 S.Ct. 6, 132 L.Ed.2d 892 (1995)(Memorandum of Justice Stevens) (refusing to lift a prior restraint because McGraw–Hill did not seek trial court review before seeking an appeal); People v. Bryant, 94 P.3d 624 (Colo.2004) (upholding an injunction constituting a prior restraint; injunction forbid publication of a transcript of an in camera rape shield hearing in the Kobe Bryant case where the transcript was inadvertently released to the media by trial court personnel).

(e) *Inability to Comply Pending Modification.* The D.C. Circuit has held that the collateral bar rule cannot justify subjecting a defendant to liability where the party is faced with an injunction with which it is unable to comply (in this case for inability to pay). Nor can the rule justify subjecting the defendant to liability for the period in which the district court was considering the defendant's motion for modification based on inability to comply. Thus, the district court, which had granted the motion to modify on a prospective basis only, abused its discretion when it did not also make the modification retroactive. Evans v. Williams, 206 F.3d 1292 (D.C.Cir.2000).

4. *A cautionary tale.* When Cable News Network got recordings made by prison officials of conversations between General Manuel Noriega and the attorneys defending him against drug charges, the criminal trial court issued a preliminary injunction barring CNN from broadcasting the tapes for ten days or such lesser time as needed for the court to review the tapes and determine whether a restraint was warranted. To that end, the court also ordered CNN to turn over copies of the tapes. United States v. Noriega, 752 F.Supp. 1032 (S.D.Fla.1990). CNN appealed, but also broadcast portions of the tapes. The order was upheld on appeal. 917 F.2d 1543 (11th Cir.), cert. denied, 498 U.S. 976, 111 S.Ct. 451, 112 L.Ed.2d 432 (1990). After CNN finally gave the trial court copies of the tapes, the judge ruled that their contents did not justify the restraint, but that it was correct to restrain CNN because of its initial refusal to supply the tapes. 752 F.Supp. 1045 (S.D.Fla. 1990). Four years later, CNN was found guilty of criminal contempt and directed to pay a fine covering the government's legal fees incurred during the contempt prosecution and to broadcast an apology or, in alternative, pay an additional punitive fine. United States v. CNN, Inc., 865 F.Supp. 1549 (S.D.Fla.1994). CNN apologized.

5. *The attorney's liability.* The ABA Model Code of Professional Responsibility EC 7–22 (1980) states that "[r]espect for judicial rulings is essential to the proper administration of justice; however, a litigant or his lawyer may, in good faith and within the framework of the law, take steps to test the correctness of a ruling of a tribunal." If one of the exceptions to the collateral bar rule is not available, "then counsel may give his opinion that an order is

no good, or he may outline to his client the boundaries of that order and what conduct is and is not included. Except for these limited situations, it is otherwise the duty of the attorney to urge his client to comply with all orders * * *." Denise A. Lier, Liability of the Attorney Who Advises Disobedience, 6 J.Legal Prof. 333, 345 (1981).

6. *Preliminary injunctions and subsequent prosecutions.* Suppose that a trial court issues a preliminary injunction against any prosecutions under a new criminal statute, but later either the trial or appellate court determines that the statute is valid. May the government prosecute persons who engaged in the conduct while the preliminary injunction was in place, or does the injunction confer a form of temporary immunity? See Vikram David Amar, How Much Protection Do Injunctions Against Enforcement of Allegedly Unconstitutional Statutes Provide?, 31 Fordham Urb.L.J. 657 (2004). This issue was raised but not resolved in Edgar v. MITE Corp., 457 U.S. 624, 102 S.Ct. 2629, 73 L.Ed.2d 269 (1982). Compare Stevens, J., concurring (no immunity) with Marshall, J., dissenting (injunction constitutes complete defense).

4. WHO IS BOUND?

PROBLEM: COUNTRY LODGE V. MILLER (REPRISED) INJUNCTIONS THAT COERCE PERSONS WHO ARE NOT PARTIES

Assume that a court has enjoined Miller to stop discharging apple mash.

(a) Would it be proper to enforce the injunction against Miller's employees, who are not parties, if they help her continue to discharge?

(b) Is Jones, who buys Miller's cider mill, bound by the injunction that the court issued against Miller?

(c) Suppose that the defendant is the Miller County Sewage District, a municipal corporation that operates a sewage treatment plant. Miller County's discharge into the river illegally contains toxic chemicals because some users of the sewage system flush them down the drain and the treatment plant presently has no way of removing them. The culprits are probably a small number of the many thousand factories and commercial buildings in the district. Their identity is, so far, unknown. The court decides not to enjoin all discharge from the treatment plant because this would make the county uninhabitable. Instead, it enjoins anyone from putting the toxic chemicals into the sewage system and warns that it will impose heavy sanctions on any person found to violate this order. Newspapers and radio and television stations prominently report the story and a copy of the injunction is mailed to every postal address in the district. Is the injunction binding against anyone other than Miller County?

STATE UNIVERSITY OF NEW YORK v. DENTON

Supreme Court, Appellate Division, Fourth Department, New York, 1970
35 A.D.2d 176, 316 N.Y.S.2d 297

Frank Del Vecchio, Justice Presiding:

Appellants, 45 members of the faculty of the State University of New York at Buffalo, appeal from a judgment adjudging them guilty of criminal contempt for violating a preliminary injunction issued by Supreme Court, Erie County. Execution of the 30-day jail sentence has been stayed pending determination of the appeal.

In the course of student disturbances and disorders on the University campus in late February 1970 the administration requested the aid of the Buffalo city police. As a consequence, a sizable number of the public police force moved onto the campus where clashes with students ensued. Members of the University administration were barred from campus offices and a basketball game was disrupted by students demanding the removal of the police officers. The State concedes that the appellants here, as distinguished from the students, "were not party to the violent and disruptive actions leading to the injunction."

In an attempt to prevent further acts of violence, the University on February 27 * * * commenced an action against 13 named students and John Doe and Jane Doe for a permanent injunction. * * * [N]o appearance was made on behalf of the students, and an order was made enjoining the students "and all other persons receiving notice of this preliminary injunction, whether acting individually or in concert" * * * from acting within * * * plaintiff's buildings in such unlawful manner as to disrupt or interfere with plaintiff's lawful and normal operations * * *.

The preliminary injunction was served by posting copies at various locations on the campus.

* * * The judgment we are reviewing found appellants faculty members guilty of willfully violating the provisions of the preliminary injunction of March 5 in that on March 15, acting individually and in concert with each other and in concert with others with notice of the preliminary injunction, they entered the office of the president of the University located on the campus and unlawfully refused to leave the office when asked to do so. Appellants were not among the named defendants in the injunction action, were not parties to the application for the temporary injunction and were never personally served with the order of March 5.

The threshold question to be considered, therefore, is whether appellants were bound by the order of March 5, which was addressed to the named student defendants and "all persons having knowledge" of the order, and whether accordingly appellants may be found guilty of criminal contempt for its violation. Well settled principles of law require a negative answer to the inquiry. * * *

[T]he frequently cited opinion of Judge Learned Hand in Alemite Mfg. Corp. v. Staff, 2 Cir., 42 F.2d 832, [states]:

> ... (N)o court can make a decree which will bind any one but a party; a court of equity is as much so limited as a court of law; it cannot lawfully enjoin the world at large, no matter how broadly it words its decree. If it assumes to do so, the decree is *pro tanto brutum fulmen* [to that extent, harmless thunder], and the persons enjoined are free to ignore it. It is not vested with sovereign powers to declare conduct unlawful; its jurisdiction is limited to those over whom it gets personal service, and who therefore can have their day in court. Thus, the only occasion when a person not a party may be punished, is when he has helped to bring about, not merely what the decree has forbidden, because it may have gone too far, but what it has power to forbid, an act of a party. This means that the respondent must either abet the defendant, or must be legally identified with him.

Measured by these criteria, the appellants were not made subject to the preliminary injunction by the language "all persons receiving notice of this preliminary injunction." There is no basis on the facts presented for the conclusion that appellants, who had no opportunity to be heard in the injunction proceedings, were subject to punishment for violation of the order of March 5. "The courts ... may not grant an enforcement order or injunction so broad as to make punishable the conduct of persons who act independently and whose rights have not been adjudged according to law." Regal Knitwear Co. v. National Labor Relations Board, 324 U.S. 9, 13, 65 S.Ct. 478, 481, 89 L.Ed. 661.

We need not reach the question whether there was an adequate showing to justify Special Term's conclusion that appellants had knowledge of the preliminary injunction because we conclude that knowledge of a non-party alone is not sufficient without proof of agency or collusion with the named defendants to impose liability for a violation. * * * We would point out, however, that in our view there is a serious question whether posting alone, without personal service or reading aloud the provisions of the temporary injunction, was sufficient to subject appellants to the prohibition of the mandate and to make them liable to criminal contempt conviction for its violation.

The record in the instant case is devoid of any proof that the students violated the injunction and the evidence is legally insufficient to establish that the faculty members either were agents of or acted in collusion with them. The injunction was specifically aimed at the conduct of the students. The faculty members were not parties to the disruptive actions which led to the injunction nor were they charged with acting in concert with or as agents of the students. Consequently, even if they had knowledge of its provisions, they could not be held in contempt for their independent action in disobeying the injunction.

Plaintiff offered proof that after the faculty members entered the president's office one of the group handed to a University staff member a paper which stated that the group would remain until the police were removed from the campus and that they were in sympathy with the general purposes of the strike. Plaintiff argues that this established that appellants acted in concert and/or collusion with the named defendants as aiders and abettors. The concession that appellants were not parties to the disruptive actions leading to the injunction is a clear indication that they were not acting in concert and/or collusion with the students and, since there was no proof that the students themselves violated the injunction, it cannot be said that appellants aided and abetted them. The mere fact that an actor may be sympathetic to the desires of one properly bound by an injunction, or that by his conduct the former accomplishes what the party enjoined wants accomplished, is not sufficient to establish beyond a reasonable doubt that the conduct was carried out in combination or collusion with the named enjoinee. We conclude therefore that appellants were not bound by the injunction and that the application to punish appellants for contempt of court arising out of a violation of the order of March 5 should have been denied. * * *

UNITED STATES v. HALL
United States Court of Appeals, Fifth Circuit, 1972
472 F.2d 261

WISDOM, CIRCUIT JUDGE:

This case presents the question whether a district court has power to punish for criminal contempt a person who, though neither a party nor bearing any legal relationship to a party, violates a court order designed to protect the court's judgment in a school desegregation case. We uphold the District Court's conclusion that in the circumstances of this case it had this power, and affirm the defendant's conviction for contempt.

On June 23, 1971, the district court entered a "Memorandum Opinion and Final Judgment" in the case of *Mims v. Duval County School Board*. The court required The Duval County [Jacksonville], Florida School Board to complete its desegregation of Duval County Schools * * *

Among the schools marked for desegregation under the plan approved by the district court was Ribault Senior High School, a predominantly white school. * * * After the desegregation order was put into effect racial unrest and violence developed at Ribault, necessitating on one occasion the temporary closing of the school. On March 5, 1972, the superintendent of schools and the sheriff of Jacksonville filed a petition for injunctive relief in the *Mims* case with the district court. This petition alleged that certain black adult "outsiders" had caused or abetted the unrest and violence by their activities both on and off the Ribault campus. The petition identified the appellant Eric Hall, allegedly a member of a militant organization known as the "Black Front", as one of several such outsiders who, in combination with black students and parents, were attempting to prevent the normal operation of Ribault through student boycotts and other activities. As relief the petitioners requested an order "restraining all Ribault Senior High School students and any person acting independently or in concert with them from interfering with the orderly operation of the school and the Duval County School System, and for such other relief as the court may deem just and proper."

At an ex parte session on March 5, 1972, the district court entered an order [providing, inter alia, that no one may go upon the school grounds except enumerated categories of persons, such as students, faculty, and administrators.]

The order went on to provide that "[a]nyone having notice of this order who violates any of the terms thereof shall be subject to arrest, prosecution and punishment by imprisonment or fine, or both, for criminal contempt under the laws of the United States of America...." The court ordered the sheriff to serve copies of the order on seven named persons, including Eric Hall. Hall was neither a party plaintiff nor a party defendant in the *Mims* litigation, and in issuing this order the court did not join Hall or any of the other persons named in the order as parties.

On March 9, 1972, four days after the court issued its order, Hall violated that portion of the order restricting access to Ribault High School by appearing on the Ribault campus. When questioned by a Deputy United States Marshal as to the reasons for his presence, Hall replied that he was on the grounds of Ribault for the purpose of violating the March 5 order. The marshal then arrested Hall and took him into custody. After a non-jury trial, the district court found Hall guilty of the charge of criminal contempt and sentenced him to sixty days' imprisonment.

On this appeal Hall raises two related contentions. Both contentions depend on the fact that Hall was not a party to the *Mims* litigation and the fact that, in violating the court's order, he was apparently acting independently of the *Mims* parties. He first points to the common law rule that a nonparty who violates an injunction solely in pursuit of his own interests cannot be held in contempt. Not having been before the court as a party or as the surrogate of a party, he argues that in accordance with this common law rule he was not bound by the court's order. Second, he contends that Rule 65(d) of the Federal Rules of Civil Procedure prevents the court's order from binding him, since Rule 65(d) limits the binding effect of injunctive orders to "parties to the action, their officers, agents, servants, employees, and attorneys, and ... those persons in active concert or participation with them who receive actual notice of the order by personal service or otherwise." We reject both contentions.

I.

For his first contention, that a court of equity has no power to punish for contempt a nonparty acting solely in pursuit of his own interests, the appellant relies heavily on the two leading cases of Alemite Manufacturing Corp. v. Staff, 2 Cir.1930, 42 F.2d 832, and Chase National Bank v. City of Norwalk, 1934, 291 U.S. 431, 54 S.Ct. 475, 78 L.Ed. 894. In *Alemite* the district court had issued an injunction restraining the defendant and his agents, employees, associates, and confederates from infringing the plaintiff's patent. Subsequently a third person, not a party to the original suit and acting entirely on his own initiative, began infringing the plaintiff's patent and was held in contempt by the district court. The Second Circuit reversed in an opinion by Judge Learned Hand, stating that "it is not the act described which the decree may forbid, but only that act when the defendant does it." 42 F.2d at 833. In *Chase National Bank* the plaintiff brought suit against the city of Norwalk to obtain an injunction forbidding the removal of poles, wires, and other electrical equipment belonging to the plaintiff. The district court issued a decree enjoining the city, its officers, agents, and employees, "and all persons whomsoever to whom notice of this order shall come" from removing the equipment or otherwise interfering with the operation of the plaintiff's power plant. The Supreme Court held that the district court had violated "established principles of equity jurisdiction and procedure" insofar as its order applied to persons who were not parties, associates, or confederates of parties, but who merely had notice of the order. See also Regal Knitwear Co. v. NLRB, 1945, 324 U.S. 9, 13, 65 S.Ct. 478, 89 L.Ed. 661.

This case is different. In *Alemite* and *Chase National Bank* the activities of third parties, however harmful they might have been to the plaintiffs' interests, would not have disturbed in any way the adjudication of rights and obligations as between the original plaintiffs and defendants. Infringement of the *Alemite* plaintiff's patent by a third party would not have upset the defendant's duty to refrain from infringing or rendered it more difficult for the defendant to perform that duty. Similarly, the defendant's duty in *Chase National Bank* to refrain from removing the plaintiff's equipment would remain undisturbed regardless of the activities of third parties, as would the plaintiff's right not to have its equipment removed by the defendant. The activities of Hall, however, threatened both the plaintiffs' right and the defendant's duty as adjudicated in the *Mims* litigation. In *Mims* the plaintiffs were found to have a constitutional right to attend an integrated school. The defendant school board had a corresponding constitutional obligation to provide them with integrated schools and a right to be free from interference with the performance of that duty. Disruption of the orderly operation of the school system, in the form of a racial dispute, would thus negate the plaintiffs' constitutional right and the defendant's constitutional duty. In short, the activities of persons contributing to racial disorder at Ribault imperiled the court's fundamental power to make a binding adjudication between the parties properly before it.

Courts of equity have inherent jurisdiction to preserve their ability to render judgment in a case such as this. This was the import of the holding in United States v. United Mine Workers of America, 1947, 330 U.S. 258, 67 S.Ct. 677, 91 L.Ed. 884. * * * As an alternative holding the court stated that the contempt conviction would have been upheld even if the district court had ultimately been found to be without jurisdiction. This holding affirmed the power of a court of equity to issue an order to preserve the status quo in order to protect its ability to render judgment in a case over which it might have jurisdiction.

The integrity of a court's power to render a binding judgment in a case over which it has jurisdiction is at stake in the present case. In *Mine Workers* disruptive conduct prior to the court's decision could have destroyed the court's power to settle a controversy at least potentially within its jurisdiction. Here the conduct of Hall and others, if unrestrained, could have upset the court's ability to bind the parties in *Mims*, a case in which it unquestionably had jurisdiction. Moreover, the court retained jurisdiction in *Mims* to enter such further orders as might be necessary to effectuate its judgment. Thus disruptive conduct would not only jeopardize the effect of the court's judgment already entered but would also undercut its power to enter binding desegregation orders in the future.

The principle that courts have jurisdiction to punish for contempt in order to protect their ability to render judgment is also found in the use of in rem injunctions. Federal courts have issued injunctions binding on all persons, regardless of notice, who come into contact with property which is the subject of a judicial decree. A court entering a decree binding on a particular piece of property is necessarily faced with the danger that its judgment may be disrupted in the future by members of an undefinable class—those who may come into contact with the property. The in rem injunction protects the court's judgment. The district court here faced an analogous problem. The judgment in a school case, as in other civil rights actions, inures to the benefit of a large class of persons, regardless of whether the original action is cast in the form of a class action. At the same time court orders in school cases, affecting as they do large numbers of people, necessarily depend on the cooperation of the entire community for their implementation. * * *

II.

The appellant also asserts that Rule 65(d) of the Federal Rules of Civil Procedure prevents the court's order from binding him. He points out that he was not a party to the original action, nor an officer, agent, servant, employee, or attorney of a party, and denies that he was acting in "active concert or participation" with any party to the original action.

In examining this contention we start with the proposition that Rule 65 was intended to embody "the common-law doctrine that a decree of injunction not only binds the parties defendant but also those identified with them in interest, in 'privity' with them, represented by them or subject to their control." Regal Knitwear Co. v. NLRB, 1945, 324 U.S. 9, 14, 65 S.Ct. 478, 481, 89 L.Ed. 661. Literally read, Rule 65(d) would forbid the issuance of in rem injunctions. But courts have continued to issue in rem injunctions notwithstanding Rule 65(d), since they possessed the power to do so at common law and since Rule 65(d) was intended to embody rather than to limit their common law powers.

Similarly, we conclude that Rule 65(d), as a codification rather than a limitation of courts' common-law powers, cannot be read to restrict the inherent power of a court to protect its ability to render a binding judgment. We hold that Hall's relationship to the *Mims* case fell within that contemplated by Rule 65(d). By deciding *Mims* and retaining jurisdiction the district court had, in effect, adjudicated the rights of the entire community with respect to the racial controversy surrounding the school system. Moreover, as we have noted, in the circumstances of this case third parties such as Hall were in a position to upset the court's adjudication. This was not a situation which could have been anticipated by the draftsmen of procedural rules. In meeting the situation as it did, the district court did not overstep its powers.

We do not hold that courts are free to issue permanent injunctions against all the world in school cases. Hall had notice of the court's order. Rather than challenge it by the orderly processes of law, he resorted to conscious, willful defiance. See Walker v. Birmingham, 1967, 388 U.S. 307, 87 S.Ct. 1824, 18 L.Ed.2d 1210.

* * * We hold, then, that the district court had the inherent power to protect its ability to render a binding judgment between the original parties to the *Mims* litigation by issuing an interim ex parte order against an undefinable class of persons. We further hold that willful violation of that order by one having notice of it constitutes criminal contempt. The judgment of the district court is affirmed.

Notes on Injunctions Against Nonparties

1. In keeping with *SUNY*, Fed.R.Civ.P. 65(d)(2) (see Appendix at p. 987), literally read, allows courts to bind only parties, "the parties' officers, agents, servants, employees, and attorneys" and "other persons who are in active concert or participation" with one of them. The rationale is due process. E.g., Doctor's Associates, Inc. v. Reinert & Duree, P.C., 191 F.3d 297, 305 (2d Cir.1999); Richard A. Bales & Ryan A. Allison, Enjoining Nonparties, 26 Am. J. Trial Advoc. 79 (2002). See also Jeff Berryman, Injunctions: The Ability to Bind Non–Parties, 81 Canadian Bar Rev. 207 (2002) (reviewing Canadian and British authority and calling for more care in bringing representatives of non-parties into a proceeding). As a corollary, those who have not had due process usually are not barred from collaterally attacking the order for improperly purporting to bind them. *Hall*, in contrast, allows the trial court order to bind a wider group without advance notice and, correspondingly, requires those bound to challenge the order in court prior to violating its terms.

2. Suppose that the thirteen named defendants in *SUNY* were the officers of the student organization that organized the protests. Are members of the organization bound if they act at the behest of the officers? And, if so, are the officers in contempt for what the members do? See Roe v. Operation Rescue, 54 F.3d 133 (3d Cir.1995) (leader of abortion protest organization held in contempt for urging others to commit acts from which he was enjoined). Are the members bound if they act on their own initiative? In In re

Lennon, 166 U.S. 548, 17 S.Ct. 658, 41 L.Ed. 1110 (1897), a court ordered Lennon's employer, a union railroad, not to boycott the cars of a nonunion railroad. Lennon was held in contempt for failing to obey the injunction against his employer, even though his employer was unlikely to share his prounion sympathies. In Alemite Manufacturing v. Staff, 42 F.2d 832 (2d Cir. 1930), the alleged contemnor was originally bound as an employee of the defendant, but went into business for himself, and was held not to be bound because he was motivated by his own interests. One of the issues in *Madsen* (reproduced in Chapter 2) was whether nonparties who sympathize with the abortion protesters would be bound.

3. The *Hall* court attempts to distinguish *Alemite* and *Chase National Bank* on the basis that in those cases the injunction against the nonparty was not needed to protect the plaintiff's rights or to allow performance of the defendants' duties. Is Hall bound but not a nonparty who tears down the utility poles in *Chase National Bank* because: (a) the plaintiffs in *Hall* had constitutional rights and the plaintiff in *Chase National Bank* had property rights? (b) the plaintiffs in *Hall* had rights against all the world to attend an integrated school while the plaintiff in *Chase National Bank* had rights to its property only against the defendants? (c) the defendants in *Hall* had an affirmative duty to repair past segregation by setting up an integrated school system while the injunction in *Chase National Bank* was solely preventive?

4. Does *Hall* adequately address the due process concerns of Rule 65(d)? *Hall's* discussion of *United Mine Workers* is misleading. There, the district court had subject matter jurisdiction to issue a temporary restraining order to keep the peace while it determined if it had subject matter jurisdiction over the case. In *Hall*, the court argues that it has personal jurisdiction over Hall so that it can make the defendants over whom it undoubtedly has personal jurisdiction perform their duties. That *Hall* involves personal rather than subject matter jurisdiction raises due process problems that were not present in *United Mine Workers*. A portion of *Hall*, which was edited out, arguably limits its "broad sweep by noting that, since the contempt occurred within 10 days of the order's issuance, the order could be regarded as an ex parte temporary restraining order, valid under Fed.R.Civ.P. 65(b) * * *." James M. Hirschhorn, Where the Money Is: Remedies to Finance Compliance with Strict Structural Injunctions, 82 Mich.L.Rev. 1815, 1832 n.101 (1984). But, the district court did not limit the order's duration to 10 days, and no effort was made to serve Hall before issuing the order. (Recall the brief discussion of *Carroll v. President of Princess Anne County* at p. 187.)

5. What makes *Hall* a hard case is that keeping outsiders off school grounds probably is necessary to fulfill the plaintiffs' rights and prevent serious injuries. Courts, however, have a variety of techniques for controlling nonparties who may interfere with successful implementation of an injunction. Some are listed below. Would any of have them been practical in *SUNY, Hall*, or part (c) of *Country Lodge v. Miller* (p. 346).

(a) 18 U.S.C. § 1509 makes it a crime to obstruct by threats or force the performance of duties under a federal court order.

(b) Fed.R.Civ.P. 19(a)(1)(A) requires the joinder of a person subject to jurisdiction of the court if "in that person's absence, the court cannot accord complete relief among existing parties."

(c) Fed.R.Civ.P. 23 allows defendant class actions. Professor Dobbyn evaluated their feasibility to stop outsiders such as Hall:

> What makes the class action inappropriate in this type of situation is that fact that under Rule 23 of the Federal Rules of Civil Procedure the court is required to find that "the representative parties share a common interest with the class and will adequately represent the individual class members * * *" before allowing a class action. That would pose an almost insurmountable problem here, since the broad spectrum of interests that might become involved * * * from teachers, parents, students, to simple racists, each with his own peculiar reason for opposing some phase of the plan, would be nearly impossible to lump into one "class" homogeneous enough to pass the rigid test of rule 23.

John F. Dobbyn, Contempt Power of the Equity Court Over Outside Agitators, 8 St. Mary's L.J. 1, 7 (1976). Other factors to be considered under Rule 23 are whether the members of the proposed class are so numerous that it would be impractical to join them individually and whether the claims and defenses of the class representative would be typical of those of the rest of the class. See, e.g., Doctor's Associates, Inc. v. Reinert & Duree, P.C., 191 F.3d 297, 305 (2d Cir.1999) (outlining requirements for obtaining injunction against a defendant class action). Would a defendant class action be more fitting in *Hall* or *SUNY*?

6. *Jurisdiction over nonparties.* Suppose the agent, employee, or other person acting in concert with a party is not a resident of the state where the court sits. Can the court enforce an injunction against such persons consistently with the limitation due process imposes upon personal jurisdiction? The Seventh Circuit answered yes in a case where two United States citizens residing in Caribbean countries acted in concert with a defendant by helping to transfer money off-shore with knowledge that the transfer was intended to circumvent a freeze order imposed by a federal district court. "Jurisdiction over persons who knowingly violate a court's injunctive order, even those without any other contact with the forum, is 'necessary to the proper enforcement and supervision of a court's injunctive authority and offends no precept of due process.'" S.E.C. v. Homa, 514 F.3d 661, 665 (7th Cir.2008) (quoting Waffenschmidt v. MacKay, 763 F.2d 711, 714 (5th Cir.1985), cert. denied, 474 U.S. 1056, 106 S.Ct. 794, 88 L.Ed.2d 771 (1986)). Although the mandate of an injunction issued by a federal district court runs nationwide against all persons within the ambit of Rule 65(d)(2), it probably does not apply of its own accord to non-U.S. citizens acting outside of the U.S. In Reebok International Ltd. v. McLaughlin, 49 F.3d 1387 (9th Cir.), cert. denied, 516 U.S. 908, 116 S.Ct. 276, 133 L.Ed.2d 197 (1995), the Ninth Circuit distinguished *Waffenschmidt* on this basis in holding that there was no personal jurisdiction over a banking corporation with its principal place of business in Luxembourg even if the corporation had transferred assets in Luxembourg in violation of a U.S. district court's order. See Richard A. Bales & Ryan A. Allison, Enjoining Nonparties, 26 Am.J. Trial Advoc. 79 (2002).

7. *Successors to public office.* Fed.R.Civ.P. 25(d) establishes a special rule for successors to public office. It provides that "when a public officer who is a party in an official capacity dies, resigns, or otherwise ceases to hold office while the action is pending," the successor is "automatically substituted as a party." Suppose that the Supervisor of the Miller County Sewage District is defeated at the polls by a candidate who runs on a platform of protecting the river. Should the successor be obliged to follow all injunctions entered against predecessors automatically? See Statement of Douglas, J., 368 U.S. at 1012–14, 81 S.Ct. at 24–25 (dissenting from promulgation of the rule). Cf. Cobell v. Norton, 334 F.3d 1128 (D.C.Cir.2003) (cannot hold Secretary of Interior in contempt for events occurring before she took office).

8. *Successors in ownership.* In part (b) of the reprise of *Country Lodge v. Miller* (at p. 346), is Jones bound as Miller's successor in ownership? Compare Golden State Bottling Co., Inc. v. NLRB, 414 U.S. 168, 177, 94 S.Ct. 414, 421, 38 L.Ed.2d 388 (1973) (NLRB order against corporation also binding on another corporation that buys the business after a due process hearing on whether the second corporation is a successor) with Travelhost, Inc. v. Blandford, 68 F.3d 958 (5th Cir.1995) (subsequent purchaser of assets of the plaintiff's competitor not automatically bound by injunction issued against former owners of competitor). Fed.R.Civ.P. 65(d) does not explicitly mention successors.

One of the factors *Golden State Bottling* relied upon in finding that the purchaser was bound is that it knew that the previous owner of the assets had not remedied the violation. *Golden State Bottling* was distinguished in Gould, Inc. v. A & M Battery and Tire Service, 950 F.Supp. 653 (M.D.Pa.1997). The district court held that since the Comprehensive Environmental Response, Compensation and Liability Act imposed strict liability on purchasers of contaminated properties, unlike the labor statute being enforced in *Golden State Bottling*, it was not necessary that the purchaser have notice of the unremedied violation.

In reprise (c) of *Country Lodge v. Miller* (at p. 346), are users of the sewage system bound because they got their right to discharge from the Miller County Sewage District and are, in that sense, successors to it? See Puget Sound Gillnetters Association v. United States District Court, 573 F.2d 1123 (9th Cir.1978), judgment vacated by Washington v. Washington State Commercial Passenger Fishing Vessel Association, 443 U.S. 658, 99 S.Ct. 3055, 61 L.Ed.2d 823 (1979). To what extent *should* successors be bound? Professor Dobbs has stated:

> It is perfectly appropriate to bind successors in interest by earlier judicial decisions affecting the state of title or incumbrances, and both the law of res judicata and the recording statutes may do this. But an injunction with respect to property does more than adjudge title; it regulates *conduct.* Furthermore, the penalties for failing to observe the state of title and the penalties for conducting oneself in violation of an injunction aimed at another are vastly different.

Dan B. Dobbs, Contempt of Court: A Survey, 56 Cornell L.Rev. 183, 256 (1971).

9. *In rem injunctions.* *Hall* relies on in rem injunctions, which are orders directed against the whole world with respect to some property within the court's power. For example, the filing of a bankruptcy petition automatically results in the stay of any efforts to collect debts from the debtor except in bankruptcy court. 11 U.S.C. § 362. Such stays do not offend the due process concerns behind Fed.R.Civ.P. 65(d) because they do not deny creditors their day in court but determine that the day shall be spent in bankruptcy court.

Another kind of in rem decree adjudicates title. This practice was extended to regulate conduct in cases dealing with property used for illicit purposes, where injunctions sometimes enjoined the present owner and any succeeding owner from continuing the illicit use. Professor Dobbs objects to these cases on the same grounds as he objects to the successor cases. Dan B. Dobbs, Contempt of Court: A Survey, 56 Cornell L.Rev. 183, 257–58 (1971). Do these in rem cases support the result in *Hall*? See James F. Dobbyn, Contempt Power of the Equity Court Over Outside Agitators, 8 St. Mary's L.J. 1, 9 (1976).

10. Suppose that a defendant is prosecuted for murder, and the jury cannot reach a verdict. May the trial court prohibit media interviews of the members of the now-discharged jury, including interviews initiated by jury members, until after the completion of the retrial of the murder? Compare In re Hearst Newspapers Partnership, L.P., 241 S.W.3d 190 (Tex.App.2007) (finding unconstitutional an order prohibiting discharged jurors from being interviewed after the case was settled) with State v. Neulander, 173 N.J. 193, 801 A.2d 255 (2002), cert. denied, 537 U.S. 1192, 123 S.Ct. 1281, 154 L.Ed.2d 1027 (2003) (upholding gag order prohibiting jurors from being interviewed after hung jury was discharged until after re-trial could be completed with a new jury). See Nicole B. Casarez, Examining the Evidence: Post–Verdict Interviews and the Jury System, 25 Hastings Comm. & Ent.L.J. 499 (2003); Nancy S. Marder, Deliberations and Disclosures: A Study of Post–Verdict Interviews of Jurors, 82 Iowa L.Rev. 465 (1997). Or, suppose that the trial judge wants to prohibit potential witnesses from commenting upon a high-profile child molestation case before testifying in court. May she impose a gag order on all potential witnesses?

Note on *Washington v. Washington State Commercial Passenger Fishing Vessel Association*

In the 19th century, Native American tribes and the United States entered into a treaty that provided that tribal members could continue to take salmon from the rivers in what is now Washington State. The modern litigation arose because the state allowed non-tribal fishers to take so many salmon that the tribe's catch was endangered. The district court found the state liable. But the problem arose not from the state catching fish, but from many private persons doing so. The court enjoined any non-tribal fisher with notice of the injunction from taking fish except in accord with the injunction. The United States Supreme Court discussed several issues in the case at some length, but devoted only the following footnote to the propriety of enjoining nonparties:

The associations [object] that the District Court had no power to enjoin individual nontreaty fishermen, who were not parties to its decisions, from violating the allocations that it has ordered. The reason this issue has arisen is that state officials were either unwilling or unable to enforce the District Court's orders against nontreaty fishermen by way of state regulations and state law enforcement efforts. Accordingly, nontreaty fishermen were openly violating Indian fishing rights, and, in order to give federal law enforcement officials the power via contempt to end those violations, the District Court was forced to enjoin them. The commercial fishing organizations, on behalf of their individual members, argue that they should not be bound by these orders because they were not parties to (although the associations all did participate as *amici curiae* in) the proceedings that led to their issuance. * * *

In our view, the commercial fishing associations and their members are probably subject to injunction under either the rule that nonparties who interfere with the implementation of court orders establishing public rights may be enjoined, e.g., United States v. Hall, 472 F.2d 261 (C.A.5 1972), cited approvingly in Golden State Bottling Co. v. NLRB, 414 U.S. 168, 180, 94 S.Ct. 414, 423, 38 L.Ed.2d 388, or the rule that a court possessed of the res in a proceeding *in rem,* such as one to apportion a fishery, may enjoin those who would interfere with that custody. But in any case, these individuals and groups are citizens of the State of Washington, which was a party to the relevant proceedings, and "they, in their common public rights as citizens of the State, were represented by the State in those proceedings, and, like it, were bound by the judgment." Tacoma v. Taxpayers, 357 U.S. 320, 340–41, 78 S.Ct. 1209, 1221, 2 L.Ed.2d 1345 (1958). Moreover, a court clearly may order them to obey that judgment.

443 U.S. 658, 693 n. 32, 99 S.Ct. 3055, 3078 n. 32, 61 L.Ed.2d 823 (1979). For a history of the fishing rights controversy, see Shannon Bentley, Indians' Right to Fish: The Background, Impact, and Legacy of *United States v. Washington,* 17 Amer.Indian L.Rev. 1 (1992).

If the non-tribal fishers in Washington fall within the rule that "nonparties who interfere with the implementation of court orders establishing public rights may be enjoined," why not the faculty in *SUNY*? Or is the difference between the cases that non-tribal fishers really got their day in court?

If the state had not been a party but the fishing associations were parties, would their members be bound too?

So, now, what is the answer to problem (c) (p. 346)?

Note on Notice

An injunction binds neither party nor nonparty unless there is notice. Notice is obviously no problem when the alleged contemnor admits to having known of the order. Where the alleged contemnor denies notice or remains mum on that point, notice must be shown. Recall that the *SUNY* court prefers, as a means of giving notice, having the injunction read rather than posting it. If the injunction is only posted, many persons may not have read it so that it is difficult to infer notice, especially in a case of criminal contempt where the elements must be shown beyond a reasonable doubt. When, however, the notice is read, all those who can hear will have notice. The alleged contemnors may, of course, contend that they did not hear clearly enough to understand.

The party bringing the contempt action bears the burden of establishing actual knowledge of the injunction, and, at least in criminal contempt proceedings, this must be shown beyond a reasonable doubt. United States v. Baker, 641 F.2d 1311, 1317 (9th Cir.1981). The more indirect the form of communication, the harder it is to show notice. Most courts are reluctant to hold that reporting of the court order in a newspaper constitutes valid notice, unless perhaps it can be shown that the defendant read or subscribed to the publication. United States v. Gedraitis, 520 F.Supp. 84, 88 (E.D.Pa.1981), aff'd, 690 F.2d 351 (3d Cir.1982), cert. denied, 460 U.S. 1071, 103 S.Ct. 1527, 75 L.Ed.2d 949 (1983); Joint School District No. 1 v. Wisconsin Rapids Education Association, 70 Wis.2d 292, 234 N.W.2d 289, 303 (1975). In United States v. Baker, 641 F.2d 1311, 1317 n. 8 (9th Cir.1981), which grew out of the same controversy as *Washington*, the court suggested that the government consider "publication of notices of the injunctions in shore locations frequented by fishers, such as hiring halls, marinas, packing plants, post offices, and meeting halls for fishers' associations; and publication in local newspapers."

PROBLEM: COUNTRY LODGE V. MILLER (REPRISED)
INJUNCTIONS THAT HARM PERSONS
WHO ARE NOT PROVEN VIOLATORS

(a) Would it be improper to issue an injunction against Miller's employees, requiring them to clean up the mess on their own time?

(b) Would it be improper to issue an injunction that, in effect, puts Miller out of business because it would harm Wholesaler, who has a long-term contract to buy cider from Miller?

NOTE ON NON-VIOLATORS

The judgment that the defendant wronged the plaintiff legitimates the harm that coercive relief does to the defendant. But, to put the plaintiff in the rightful position, it may be useful to issue an injunction that harms persons who have not violated the plaintiff's rights. Such persons may already have been made parties by, for example, joinder or intervention. Fed.R.Civ.P. 19 & 24 (see Appendix at pp. 975–976, 978).

Injunctions that coerce non-violators. Rizzo v. Goode (reproduced in Chapter 2) held that it was improper for a district court to order the mayor and the police chief to institute a complaint process that would have helped protect the plaintiffs' rights, because the mayor and police were not liable. General Building Contractors Association v. Pennsylvania, 458 U.S. 375, 102 S.Ct. 3141, 73 L.Ed.2d 835 (1982), held that it was improper for a district court to order building contractors to join with a union to establish and fund a training program and to attain minority membership goals in the union because it had not been found that the contractors were participants in the union's discriminatory practices. The Supreme Court struck down the injunction because it treated the building contractors:

> as if they had been properly found liable for the Union's discrimination. A decree containing such provisions, we hold, is beyond the traditional equitable limitations upon the authority of a federal court to formulate such decrees.
>
> Nor does the All Writs Act, 28 U.S.C. § 1651(a), support the extensive liability imposed upon petitioners by the District Court. The District Court did not rely upon this Act, and we think it completely wide of the mark in justifying the relief granted by the District Court. That Act was most recently considered by this Court in United States v. New York Telephone Co., 434 U.S. 159, 98 S.Ct. 364, 54 L.Ed.2d 376 (1977), where we said: "This Court has repeatedly recognized the power of a federal court to issue such commands under the All Writs Act as may be necessary or appropriate to effectuate and prevent the frustration of orders it has previously issued in its exercise of jurisdiction otherwise obtained * * *." In *New York Telephone,* we held that the All Writs Act was available to require a third party to assist in the carrying out of a District Court order pertaining to the installation of [surveillance devices], and in doing so we noted that "(t)he order provided that the Company be fully reimbursed at prevailing rates, and compliance with it required minimal effort on the part of the Company and no disruption to its operations."

458 U.S. at 400–01, 102 S.Ct. at 3155–56, 73 L.Ed.2d at 856. At the same time, the Court upheld provisions of the decree that required the building contractors to submit reports to the district court as a means of checking on the union's compliance. It termed such requirements "minor and ancillary." The "minor and ancillary" provisions of the decree are analogous to a subpoena, which is after all a coercive order that one obeys because of civic duty rather than proven wrongdoing. If the building contractors were not already parties, they could have been joined under Fed.R.Civ.P. 19(a)(1)(A).

Injunctions that do not coerce but do harm non-violators. Harm to non-violators, as opposed to coercion of them, is permitted, but is weighed in the balance of equities as cases such as *Staso Milling* and *Brown II* (Chapter 2) teach. How that harm is weighed will depend on a variety of factors. Franks v. Bowman Transportation Co., 424 U.S. 747, 96 S.Ct. 1251, 47 L.Ed.2d 444 (1976), held that an injunction to remedy employment discrimination could include, in addition to requiring priority hiring of minority job applicants, that those hired be granted retroactive seniority. Faced with the contention that retroactive seniority would disadvantage some current employees, who had not been shown to have violated the statute, the majority stated:

> Without an award of seniority dating from the time when he was discriminatorily refused employment, an individual who applies for and obtains employment * * * pursuant to the District Court's order will never obtain his rightful place in the hierarchy of seniority according to which those various employment benefits are distributed. He will perpet-

ually remain subordinate to persons who, but for the illegal discrimination, would have been in respect to entitlement to these benefits his inferiors.

Id. at 767–768, 96 S.Ct. at 1266, 47 L.Ed.2d at 463.

International Brotherhood of Teamsters v. United States, 431 U.S. 324, 97 S.Ct. 1843, 52 L.Ed.2d 396 (1977), held that where the employer has discriminated an award of retroactive seniority is appropriate even though the union has not illegally discriminated and the retroactive seniority would affect innocent employees under the collective bargaining agreement that the union had negotiated. The Court did not however invalidate the seniority provisions themselves, which provided that a senior employee could not bump a junior employee from an existing job assignment. The upshot was that innocent employees were safe in their existing positions but could not get better positions until members of the plaintiff class with more seniority under the decree had their pick.

What justifies keeping the innocent employees in their present positions—by no means a "minor and ancillary" harm—is that they might not have been ahead of the plaintiffs in seniority but for the defendant's violations. Contrast the outcome in *Teamsters* with that in City of Los Angeles v. Manhart, 435 U.S. 702, 98 S.Ct. 1370, 55 L.Ed.2d 657 (1978), brought under the same statute. There, employers were found to have engaged in illegal gender discrimination by requiring higher contributions from female employees for their pensions because of actuarial findings that females lived longer and therefore would receive a pension for a longer period of time. The Court held that the remedy could not be retroactive because that would harm both the defendants and male employees, both of whom had well established expectations under prior law that differential pension contributions were proper.

PROBLEM: COUNTRY LODGE V. MILLER (REPRISED)
INJUNCTIONS THAT HARM PERSONS WHO ARE NOT
PROVEN VIOLATORS AND ARE NOT PARTIES

Country Lodge and Miller propose a consent decree that specifies a program to end Miller's pollution. The proposed consent decree states that it would "constitute a full and complete adjudication and settlement * * * and binds all parties or potential parties who had notice of the instant claims and this Consent Decree." A copy is served upon the state Environmental Protection Agency. It decides not to intervene. After the court enters the consent decree, the state EPA sues Miller, alleging the same facts and legal theories upon which Country Lodge sued. Does the consent decree preclude the second suit?

NOTE ON MARTIN V. WILKS

"Bound" by a decree might have at least four different meanings: (1) coerced to obey it; (2) precluded, by res judicata or collateral estoppel from attacking it; (3) loss of rights because the decree is a defense to otherwise illegal conduct; or (4) harmed in some more indirect way. We have dealt so far with the first and fourth possibilities, and you probably studied the second category in civil procedure class. We now come to the third possibility. In Martin v. Wilks, 490 U.S. 755, 109 S.Ct. 2180, 104 L.Ed.2d 835 (1989), a group of white firefighters brought an action alleging that the City of Birmingham and related governmental employers violated their rights by giving racially based preferences in promotions to African Americans. The employers' defense was that their promotions policy was dictated by consent decrees entered in a previous case brought by African Americans who claimed that they were the victims of racial discrimination. The Supreme Court had earlier decided that voluntary affirmative action plans do not illegally discriminate *if* they are designed to remedy past discrimination. United Steelworkers of America v. Weber, 443 U.S. 193, 99 S.Ct. 2721, 61 L.Ed.2d 480 (1979); City of Richmond v. J.A. Croson Co., 488 U.S. 469, 109 S.Ct. 706, 102 L.Ed.2d 854 (1989). The plaintiffs in *Martin v. Wilks* denied that the consent decrees were so justified. The district court held that, even if the decrees were not so justified, the government employers had a defense to the charge of racial discrimination because they could show that their hiring policy was compelled by the consent decrees and so they did not have the requisite intent to discriminate. This argument is problematic in that it would shield the employers' conduct even after a showing that the racial preferences were not justified. In a five to four decision, the Supreme Court reversed: "we think this holding contravenes the general rule that a person cannot be deprived of his legal rights in a proceeding to which he is not a party." 490 U.S. 755, 759, 109 S.Ct. 2180, 2183, 104 L.Ed.2d 835 (1989).

The majority focused on whether, under the Federal Rules of Civil Procedure, the justification for the consent decrees could be examined in the new case. The majority took the position that persons affected by a decree, such as the white firefighters, are free to attack it collaterally unless they had been joined under Fed.R.Civ.P. 19. The dissent argued that such persons cannot attack the decree except by intervening in the case in which it is entered under Fed.R.Civ.P. 24. The parties to an employment discrimination case would have grave problems joining everyone whose rights might be affected because that group includes future job applicants, some of whom do not presently live in the area. But, putting the burden on members of this group to intervene also presents grave problems because some will be unaware of the case and others may not even know that they will move to the area.

One way out of this dilemma is to count upon parties to the suit to represent the interests of nonparties whose rights might be affected. The employer cannot be counted upon to represent their interests because it often tries to minimize its exposure to damages by offering greater preferences in future hiring and promotion to members of the plaintiff class. The employer in effect saves money at the expense of nonparties. The union, which represents present employees, may not adequately represent the interests of future job applicants. On the other hand, if there is no way to cut off collateral attacks on consent decrees, employers would resist settling such cases.

In *Martin v. Wilks* itself, there were indications in the record that the City agreed to more racial preferences in the future in order to radically reduce its immediate liability for money damages. On the other hand, the interests of the white firefighters who brought the *Martin* case had, in effect, been represented by the Birmingham Firefighters Association, which, as an amicus curiae in the previous case, had raised objections to the decrees. The Association also sought to intervene, but the district court denied the motion as untimely and entered the consent decrees. The court of appeals affirmed the consent decrees in part because the firefighters could "institute an independent Title VII suit, asserting the specific violations of their rights." United States v. Jefferson County, 720 F.2d 1511, 1518 (11th Cir.1983). The majority in *Martin v. Wilks* did not address whether the white firefighters had been adequately represented in the previous case, but rather decided that, under the Federal Rules of Civil Procedure, as now written, they could not be bound unless they were joined.

The Civil Rights Act of 1991 partially reversed *Martin v. Wilks* by barring collateral objections to decrees in employment discrimination suits from persons who: (1) have actual notice of the proposed judgment and a reasonable opportunity to present objections or (2) whose interests were represented by parties. Persons satisfying these conditions are barred from later objecting to the judgment, except if there is fraud, collusion, or lack of jurisdiction. Pub. L. No. 102–166, § 108, 105 Stat. 1076 (1991) (amending 42 U.S.C. § 2000e–2(n)).

The Act has not proven to be a complete bar to collateral objections to decrees even in employment discrimination suits. On appeal after remand in *Martin*, the Eleventh Circuit upheld the district court's determination that the plaintiffs could attack the decree because, even if the new statutory bar on collateral attacks were retroactive, the conditions for its application were not present. In re Birmingham Reverse Discrimination Employment Litigation, 20 F.3d 1525, 1530 n. 1 (11th Cir.1994), cert. denied, 514 U.S. 1065, 115 S.Ct. 1695, 131 L.Ed.2d 558 (1995). The Eleventh Circuit held that the plaintiffs in the *Martin* reverse discrimination suit showed that the racial quotas on promotion of firefighters illegally discriminated because they were not tailored narrowly to remedy the wrong. 20 F.3d at 1543. In a subsequent opinion regarding the modification of the decrees' the Eleventh Circuit ordered that the decrees race-based and gender-based preferences be rewritten to be, respectively, narrowly tailored and substantially related to the objective of ending discrimination. The district court was ordered to establish a schedule for attaining neutral selection procedures within "reasonably prompt deadlines" noting that the district court could maintain affirmative action measures if it believed the action was necessary to remedy the lingering effects of discrimination. The court also remanded the determination of whether race-based affirmative action was necessary in departments other than the police and fire departments. Ensley Branch, NAACP v. Seibels, 31 F.3d 1548 (11th Cir.1994).

Martin v. Wilks continues to govern decrees in fields other than employment discrimination. For example, Baker v. General Motors, 522 U.S. 222, 118 S.Ct. 657, 139 L.Ed.2d 580 (1998), relied on it in holding that an injunction that a Michigan court issued against a former employee, forbidding him from voluntarily testifying against General Motors in products liability cases, did not bar the plaintiffs in another case in Missouri from subpoenaing him to testify. The Missouri plaintiffs were not barred because they were not parties in the Michigan case. For discussion of *Baker*, see Polly J. Price, Full Faith and Credit and the Equity Conflict, 84 Va.L.Rev. 747 (1998).

5. ENFORCEMENT AGAINST THE GOVERNMENT

PROBLEM: COUNTRY LODGE V. MILLER (REPRISED)
INJUNCTIONS THAT REQUIRE THE COOPERATION OF PUBLIC OFFICIALS

Suppose the court decides that the best of way to prevent nonparties from putting toxics in the sewage system is to make the Miller County Sewage District stop them.

(a) If the district has regulations forbidding such disposal but is not enforcing them, can the court compel it to enforce its regulations?

(b) If the state's highest court rules that the district lacks the authority, under state law, to promulgate the regulations and the state legislature refuses to grant the authority, can a federal court compel the district to promulgate the regulations, compel the state legislature to grant the district authority to promulgate the regulations, or itself promulgate regulations for the district?

Section B of this chapter considered the problems in enforcement arising from difficulties in determining what the defendant can do, stating what the defendant should do in enforceable terms, and keeping track of what defendant has done in fact. These problems can occur whether the defendant is a private person or governmental entity, as *Illinois v. Costle* (p. 230) illustrates. This section considers problems that are special to enforcement against governmental defendants.

One such problem is that sanctions against governmental defendants may harm innocent citizens. If Miller, as the private operator of an apple press, willfully violates an injunction, the court would have no compunction about fining Miller for criminal contempt because she brought the harm upon herself. But if the Miller County Sewage District violated an injunction, the fine against it would come out of the pockets of taxpayers rather than the responsible public officials. The court could theoretically jail the officials for criminal contempt, but James Hirschhorn reported that he was "aware of no federal case decided within the past twenty-five years in which a public official has been imprisoned for civil or criminal contempt for violating an injunction." James M. Hirshhorn, Where the Money Is: Remedies to Finance Compliance With Strict Structural Injunctions, 82 Mich.L.Rev. 1815, 1841 (1984). *Spallone v. United States* (reproduced at p. 394) is a subsequent example that underlines judicial reluctance to jail officials. Jailing officials is rare partly because the conflict over the jailing could well divert energies and attention from complying with the injunction. In Palmigiano v. Garrahy, 448 F.Supp. 659 (D.R.I. 1978), the court responded to contempt by threatening coercive civil fines against the state rather than punishing the officials through criminal contempt. The court emphasized that the violations arose from mismanagement and that the officials could avoid wasting the taxpayers' money on fines by obeying promptly. In this way, the judge used the threat of coercive sanctions against the state to apply political pressure on the officials; punishing the officials could have created political, practical and separation of powers problems for the judge.

Another problem special to enforcement against government is judicial reluctance to exercise powers assigned to other branches or levels of government. A narrow preventive injunction, by doing no more than stopping a governmental defendant from interfering with the plaintiff's rightful position, does not exercise the power of another branch of government but rather keeps that defendant from exceeding its powers. But, reparative injunctions as well as many of the devices for dealing with the difficulties in enforcing injunctions—such as prophylactic orders, monitors, and receivers—go beyond simply preventing future violations. Such devices, by intruding on a governmental defendant's power, raise separation of powers or federalism issues. See Gerald E. Frug, The Judicial Power of the Purse, 126 U.Pa.L.Rev. 715 (1978). If the case involves a federal court and a federal agency or a state court and a state agency, the case would raise separation of powers issues. If it involves a federal court and a state agency, it would raise federalism issues. Robert F. Nagel, Separation of Powers and the Scope of Federal Equitable Remedies, 30 Stan.L.Rev. 661 (1978).

Judges worry about separation of powers and federalism for diverse reasons. Judicial intrusion on the powers of governmental defendants shifts power from politically accountable to unaccountable hands. Moreover, a judge who strays from public expectations of the judicial role endangers the presumptive legitimacy that public opinion gives to court orders. See Colin S. Diver, The Judge as Political Powerbroker: Superintending Structural Change in Public Institutions, 65 Va.L.Rev. 43 (1979). Furthermore, the judge may not feel competent to make the necessary administrative or political decisions, either because of limited expertise or because the court lacks the fact-finding or outreach capacity of a legislature or an agency. A judge who takes over a governmental agency must conjure with the probability of disaster striking, such as a guard getting killed by a prisoner while the prison is under judicial supervision. See Geoffrey P. Alpert, Ben M. Crouch & C. Ronald Huff, Prison Reform by Judicial Decree: The Unintended Consequences of Ruiz v. Estelle, 9 Justice Sys.J. 291 (1984)(detailing rise in violence in prisons under court supervision). Although such a disaster may well have occurred anyway, the public may place the blame on the court, which would further undermine its legitimacy.

Despite separation of powers and federalism, courts still issue reparative and prophylactic orders in cases involving governmental defendants. However, sensitivity to separation of powers and federalism issues—which sometimes is called "comity"—is supposed to weigh in favor of less intrusive action. Milliken v. Bradley, 433 U.S. 267, 280, 97 S.Ct. 2749, 2757, 53 L.Ed.2d 745, 755–56 (1977) (*Milliken II*). A court is supposed to intrude only after concluding that the intrusion is necessary to protect the plaintiff's rightful position and the harm to governmental structure is less important than vindicating the plaintiff's rights. When official incompetence or resistance has gone so far that judges appoint a receiver despite comity, they tend to appoint officials already connected with the governmental defendant. E.g., United States v. Bowers, 828 F.2d 1169 (6th Cir.1987)(mayor appointed as receiver to replace commissioners), cert. denied, 486 U.S. 1006, 108 S.Ct. 1731, 100 L.Ed.2d 195 (1988); Morgan v. McDonough, 540 F.2d 527 (1st Cir.1976)(school superintendent appointed as receiver to replace board of education), cert. denied, 429 U.S. 1042, 97 S.Ct. 743, 50 L.Ed.2d 755 (1977). In such cases, the judge is not so much taking over a political branch of government as cutting the most resistant defendants out of the chain of command.

Comity affects enforcement in decisions far less dramatic than whether to appoint a receiver. Courts defer to governmental defendants in drafting injunctions and judging compliance with them. For example, the court in *Illinois v. Costle* accepted EPA's largely untested claim that it could not promulgate the mandated regulations quickly. Judges do not always accept what governmental defendants say, but a substantial burden of persuasion usually rests upon those who dispute the official pronouncement. This deference accords with the general principle of the Administrative Procedure Act that a judge should not overturn agency action simply because the judge disagrees with it; it must be so wrong as to be "arbitrary [or] capricious." 5 U.S.C. § 706(2)(A)(1988).

We now turn to two thornier problems of enforcement against governmental defendants: (1) political or bureaucratic resistance to compliance and (2) the immunity to suit of officials or institutions essential to compliance.

Note on How Politics Complicates Enforcement

The injunction must overcome the political motives or bureaucratic inertia that led the governmental defendants to violate the plaintiff's rights in the first place. The injunction in *Illinois v. Costle* (reproduced supra at p. 230) is a classic example of a judge trying to motivate the defendants by changing the political and bureaucratic milieu. EPA failed to meet the statutory deadlines for promulgating the regulations because of a lack of resources and bureaucratic inertia. To grapple with these root sources of the violation, Judge Gesell took what steps he could. He required the agency to report any further slippage to the court and he required that such reports, as well as the regular reports to the court, be signed by the EPA Administrator. He also required that all such reports be sent to the congressional oversight committees. Since the EPA Administrator would be reluctant to report bad news to Congress and more reluctant still to have to testify before Congress or the court about such failures, the decree changed the course of least resistance at EPA from letting the regulations come out when they will to getting them out on the schedule in the decree. Also, by putting the congressional committees on notice, the decree might prompt them to pressure EPA to act more quickly. Finally, by blaming Congress for some of the delay, Judge Gesell was trying to prompt the plaintiffs to get Congress to give the agency resources commensurate with the deadlines that it had imposed upon it.

More troublesome are cases when enough voters positively oppose compliance that the legislators or other politically accountable officials refuse to take necessary action. For example, the state legislature might refuse to grant a local government the authority to promulgate regulations required by an injunction or refuse to grant state officials the authority needed to raise and spend money needed to comply. The legislature might be tempted to retaliate against the court system by challenging its independence. See Michele Demary, Legislative–Judicial Relations on Contested Issues: Taxes and Same–Sex Marriage, 89 Judicature 202 (2006).

Virginia v. West Virginia, 246 U.S. 565, 38 S.Ct. 400, 59 L.Ed. 1272 (1918), is an old and striking illustration of the problems that such resistance can pose for the courts. When Virginia decided in 1861 to secede from the Union, the people living in the northwestern part of the state decided to secede from the state and form a new state, West Virginia, which would join the Union. West Virginia's constitution guaranteed to reimburse Virginia for the repayment of a share of Virginia's public debt outstanding on January 1, 1861. Congress consented in 1862 to the formation of this new state. Virginia and West Virginia failed, despite prolonged efforts, to reach agreement on West Virginia's share of the Virginia public debt. In 1906, Virginia invoked the original jurisdiction of the United States Supreme Court to sue West Virginia for reimbursement. In 1915, Virginia obtained a judgment of $12,393,929.50. However, the West Virginia legislature failed to appropriate funds to satisfy the judgment.

Money judgments are not court orders and the failure to satisfy one is not contempt. Rather, in the ordinary case, the sheriff is authorized to sell the debtor's property and use the proceeds to pay the plaintiff. (See Chapter 8(B).) Virginia did not attempt to have West Virginia's property seized because, as the parties agreed, it was all devoted to governmental purposes and such property might well be held immune from sale. Instead Virginia asked the Supreme Court to order the West Virginia legislature to levy a tax to raise funds to pay the judgment.

A unanimous opinion for the Court by Chief Justice White rejected West Virginia's contention that federalism was an insurmountable barrier to the Court's power to coerce a state. It reasoned that such a barrier would undercut the purpose of its original jurisdiction over suits between states, which is to provide an effective means of resolving such disputes. The opinion went on to say that, whatever the Court might do, Congress could enact a statute requiring West Virginia to pay. Virginia had not asked for this advisory opinion.

As for judicial action against West Virginia, the Court decided not to decide, at least for a while. The opinion noted that ordering the legislature to levy a tax was not the only means to raise money to satisfy the judgment. For instance, the Court could itself levy a tax or seize the funds of the state. But the opinion stopped short of endorsing any particular action. Rather it suggested that the rejection of West Virginia's contention that the Court may not coerce a state did not dispose of all of the possible objections to the Court's taking any one of these particular actions, such as the "discretion in the legislature of West Virginia as to taxation." Ordering the legislature to levy a tax to be used to pay Virginia would do more than decide *whether* Virginia should be put in its rightful position, but also would decide *how* the political branches of West Virginia should do so. The Court decided not to decide what judicial action, if any, should be taken, but instead set this question down for argument at the next term.

> We say this because, impelled now by the consideration of the character of the parties which has controlled us during the whole course of the litigation, the right judicially to enforce by appropriate proceedings as against a State and its governmental agencies having been determined, and the constitutional power of Congress to legislate * * * having also been pointed out, we are fain to believe that, if we refrain now from passing upon the questions stated, we may be spared in the future the necessity of exerting compulsory power against one of the States of the Union to compel it to discharge a plain duty resting upon it under the Constitution. * * * [W]e should further reserve action in order that full opportunity may be afforded to Congress to exercise the power which it undoubtedly possesses. * * *

Id. at 604–05, 38 S.Ct. at 406–07.

The pretentiousness of this language may be in part to camouflage the Court's unwillingness to decide fully the issue, which had been briefed and argued, and which would have given Virginia prompt relief. (The opinion originated the phrase "deliberate speed," later made famous in *Brown II*, reproduced in Chapter 2.) As the Court was undoubtedly aware, while the case was pending, the West Virginia Senate enacted a resolution requesting the Governor to convene a special session when the opinion came down. Shortly after the opinion issued, with the opinion itself providing some political cover, the legislature of West Virginia enacted the legislation necessary for compliance.

If the defendant in *Virginia v. West Virginia* had been a private corporation whose board of directors refused to authorize the payment of a judgment, the courts would not have hesitated for so long to override the board by allowing the seizure of the corporation's property, the garnishment of its income, or putting the corporation in the hands of a receiver to operate it for the benefit of creditors. Why did the Supreme Court hesitate to override West Virginia's "board of directors"—its legislature—by: (a) ordering the seizure and sale of public land not used for governmental purposes; (b) ordering the seizure and sale of public land used for governmental purposes; (c) ordering the seizure of state bank accounts; (d) ordering the state legislature to levy a tax; or (e) itself levying a tax? Consider what would happen in each instance if state officials and/or citizens resisted the Court's direct orders.

Should the court be any more willing to act if the defendant were a city rather than a state? The opinion in *Virginia v. West Virginia* noted "the many decided cases holding that where a municipality is empowered to levy specified taxation to pay a particular debt, the judicial power may enforce the levy of the tax to meet a judgment rendered in consequence of a default in paying the indebtedness." 246 U.S. at 594, 38 S.Ct. at 403, 62 L.Ed. at 888. Note the qualification that the municipality have the power to levy the tax. In the years following the Civil War, some municipalities attempted to defeat creditors by having the state legislature limit their power to tax. The Supreme Court approved orders to municipal officials, backed by the contempt power, to levy the necessary taxes, nonetheless. However, federal cases have not gone so far in recent decades. See James M. Hirschhorn, Where the Money Is: Remedies to Finance Compliance With Strict Structural Injunctions, 82 Mich.L.Rev. 1815, 1872–74 (1984). Compare City of Vernon v. Superior Court, 38 Cal.2d 509, 241 P.2d 243 (1952)(city council members held in contempt for refusing to levy tax to pay for sewage disposal facilities). In modern times, state constitutions and city charters make it easier for municipalities to borrow by guaranteeing that they will have the power to levy taxes to the extent necessary to pay off general obligation bonds in order to make the bonds marketable. The West Virginia legislature clearly has the power under the state constitution to levy the necessary taxes. Why does the Supreme Court treat it any differently than a municipality that has an unpaid judgment against it and the power to levy the taxes to pay it?

Even though the Supreme Court was not forceful in dealing with the West Virginia legislature's failure to pay the debt, overriding the legislature there would have been easier than in the typical case against a governmental defendant in which implementation requires an appropriation of funds or other legislative authorization. First, there was no substantial question about liability. The same was usually true in the municipal bond cases. In contrast, liability in cases arising under the equal protection clause or a regulatory statute often depends upon judicial construction of terse, vague language and disputed facts. Second, in *Virginia v. West Virginia*, the plaintiff was a state, thereby counter-balancing the political might of the defendant. In contrast, in the typical case, private persons are taking on "city hall" or the state. Third, in *Virginia v. West Virginia*, nine justices could have shared responsibility for the order to levy taxes and those who would have been adversely affected by the order lived far away. In contrast, in the typical case, the district court judge acts alone and often knows and lives among the defendant officials and citizens who would be affected by the order. Finally, there was no immunity problem in *Virginia v. West Virginia*.

NOTE ON *HOW IMMUNITY COMPLICATES ENFORCEMENT*

Resistance by governmental defendants is also complicated by the immunity of some governments to suit. Sovereign immunity bars suits against a state in its own courts, or suits against the federal government in a federal or a state court. The eleventh amendment has been read to bar suits by private persons against states in federal courts. Hans v. Louisiana, 134 U.S. 1, 10 S.Ct. 504, 33 L.Ed. 842 (1890). See generally Symposium, Shifting the Balance of Power? The Supreme Court, Federalism, and State Sovereign Immunity, 53 Stan. L. Rev. 1115 (2001). Further complications on the resistance of governmental defendants are added by the government's practical immunity for failing to enforce injunctive relief for citizens. In Town of Castle Rock v. Gonzales, 545 U.S. 748, 125 S.Ct. 2796, 162 L.Ed.2d 658 (2005), the plaintiff was held not to have a cognizable property interest in a civil restraining order obtained against her husband. Although the plaintiff theoretically had a right to protection via the injunction, the Court held that no remedy for damages applied for the police's failure to enforce the order, resulting in the horrific murder of the plaintiff's three children.

Given sovereign immunity, how is it that governmental actions can get challenged in court? For starters, the eleventh amendment does not bar suits brought by the United States or other states, which explains *Virginia v. West Virginia*, for example. Second, local governments are not generally considered sovereigns under the eleventh amendment and so are amenable to suit in federal court, which explains *Brown v. Board of Education*, for example. E.g., Northern Insurance Co. v. Chatham County, 547 U.S. 189, 126 S.Ct. 1689, 164 L.Ed.2d 367 (2006) (county not immune from federal suit unless acting as "arm of the State'). However, the courts of some states treat local governments as sovereigns. Third, Congress has circumscribed power under section 5 of the fourteenth amendment to abrogate the states' eleventh amendment immunity. E.g., United States v. Georgia, 546 U.S. 151, 126 S.Ct. 877, 163 L.Ed.2d 650 (2006). Marcia L. McCormick, Federalism Re–Constructed: The Eleventh Amendment's Illogical Impact on Congress' Power, 37 Ind.L.Rev. 345 (2004). Fourth, sovereigns can waive their immunity, although statutes that allegedly waive immunity in categories of cases are strictly construed. See, e.g., United States v. Nordic Village, Inc., 503 U.S. 30, 34, 112 S.Ct. 1011, 1014, 117 L.Ed.2d 181, 187–88 (1992). Governments are more likely to consent to suit over contracts, accidents, or specified types of administrative actions than over broader policy choices.

Fifth, and finally, the plaintiff can sometimes dispense with suing an immune government by suing governmental officials instead. Officials themselves often have some sort of immunity against suits in damages on the theory that the prospect of personal financial liability for official acts would dissuade them from taking office, or, once in office, acting decisively. (Official immunity from damages is discussed in Chapter 6.) But, official immunity generally does not stop suits for injunctive relief. In the landmark case of Ex parte Young, 209 U.S. 123, 28 S.Ct. 441, 52 L.Ed. 714 (1908), the Court allowed a private plaintiff to seek an injunction against the enforcement of an allegedly unconstitutional state statute. Although the suit challenged a state statute, the Court offered as an explanation the argument that the suit was not against the state because an state official who enforces an unconstitutional statute acts ultra vires. See Joint Anti–Fascist Refugee Committee v. McGrath, 341 U.S. 123, 71 S.Ct. 624, 95 L.Ed. 817 (1951)(applying *Ex Parte Young's* reasoning in a suit against a federal official). Compare James Leonard, Ubi Remedium Ibi Jus, or, Where There's a Remedy, There's a Right: a

Skeptic's Critique of Ex Parte Young, 54 Syracuse L.Rev. 215 (2004) (criticizing the *Ex parte Young* fiction as enabling a judicially-created federal forum for private claims against nonconsenting states, a result expressly rejected in 1787) and John Harrison, Ex Parte Young, 60 Stan.L.Rev. 989 (2008) (not an exceptional case because the plaintiff requested a traditional tool of equity, an anti-suit injunction, to restrain proceedings at law and thus it does not support a broad claim that all prospective injunctive relief is consistent with sovereign immunity) with Pratik A. Shah, Saving Section 5: Lessons Learned from Consent Decrees and Ex Parte Young, 62 Washington & Lee L.Rev. 1001 (2005) (Congress should get same judicial deference when acting against states under section 5 of the fourteenth amendment as when litigants enter into consent decrees with state officials under the *Ex Parte Young* fiction).

The key question under *Ex parte Young* is whether the relief sought is against the state and so barred by the eleventh amendment even though the state is not the defendant. In Edelman v. Jordan, 415 U.S. 651, 94 S.Ct. 1347, 39 L.Ed.2d 662 (1974), and Quern v. Jordan, 440 U.S. 332, 99 S.Ct. 1139, 59 L.Ed.2d 358 (1979), the Court decided that prospective relief, such as an injunction concerning future behavior, is permitted, while retrospective relief, such as an order that effectively awards compensation for past wrongdoing, is not because the money would come from the state treasury. Nonetheless, subsequent cases have allowed prospective relief that imposes large costs on the state. See, e.g., Frew v. Hawkins, 540 U.S. 431, 124 S.Ct. 899, 157 L.Ed.2d 855 (2004) (enforcement of consent decree obligations as a federal court order did not violate *Ex parte Young* or the eleventh amendment, even though the decree obliged Texas to provide medical services not required under federal Medicaid legislation to over one million children); Milliken v. Bradley, 433 U.S. 267, 97 S.Ct. 2749, 53 L.Ed.2d 745 (1977) (*Milliken II*) (affirming injunction requiring state officers to provide remedial education as part of reparative injunctive relief in Detroit school segregation case). So, if a sewage plant is run by a state agency rather than a local government and state law commands its officials to discharge pollution into the river but a federal regulation prohibits the same conduct, a federal court could entertain a suit by Country Lodge to enjoin those officials and would hold that the state law gives them no authority to pollute. In contrast, the court would not entertain an action by Country Lodge for damages even if captioned as against the officials because, as a practical matter, the money to pay the judgment would come from the state treasury.

Although the rule is that prospective relief against state officials is permitted, that rule has its limits. In Kelley v. Metropolitan County Board of Education, 836 F.2d 986 (6th Cir.1987), cert. denied, 487 U.S. 1206, 108 S.Ct. 2848, 101 L.Ed.2d 885 (1988), the private plaintiffs got an injunction against the school board to remedy school segregation in the county including Nashville, Tennessee. Twenty-six years later, the school board filed a third-party complaint against the State of Tennessee and various state officials alleging that the state had participated in the initial wrong-doing and seeking an injunction requiring the state to bear a share of the cost of implementing the remedy. The court of appeals ordered the complaint against the state defendants dismissed on the basis, inter alia, that its purpose was to get state funds rather than put the plaintiffs in their rightful position. The court distinguished *Milliken II* on the basis that the state officials there were brought into the case at the outset and by the plaintiffs.

This thumbnail sketch of blackletter immunity law (which is a core topic in the federal courts course) makes it evident that immunity law influences remedies. Immunity often makes it harder to attack government action through damages than through injunctive relief. Moreover, immunity can complicate successful injunctive relief against state action. Suppose that compliance with the injunction would cost money, say, to repair the state-run sewage treatment plant. If the state officials have a repair fund appropriated by the state legislature, then the federal court may make the state officials use those state funds to do the necessary repairs. But, suppose the legislature has not appropriated any money that could be used for repair of the sewage treatment plant and refuses to do so. In that context, being able to seize state assets would be useful, but the state is immune. Newman v. Alabama, 559 F.2d 283 (5th Cir.1977), illustrates the quandary. In that case, as in many others, the state did not bother to get itself dismissed as a party defendant. After all, the suit was also against state officials who can be sued for injunctive relief. But, when the judge began to talk of seizing state assets, the state was allowed to get belatedly dismissed. Alabama v. Pugh, 438 U.S. 781, 782, 98 S.Ct. 3057, 3058, 57 L.Ed.2d 1114, 1115–16 (1978) (in a suit against state officials and the state, the state "has an interest in being dismissed from th[e] action in order to eliminate the danger of being held in contempt should it fail to comply with the mandatory injunction").

This then is the ultimate problem: putting the plaintiff in the rightful position requires action that state law does not empower the defendant officials to take and the legislature refuses to grant them the necessary power. A court could conceivably react in a number of quite different ways:

1. *The court could postpone responding to the violation of its injunction in the hope that the legislature will grant the authority, the parties will settle, or Congress will act.* This was the Supreme Court's tactic in *Virginia v. West Virginia*, and it worked. See also Baker v. State, 170 Vt. 194, 744 A.2d 864 (Vt.1999) (directing state legislature to develop a remedy under the state constitution's Common Benefits Clause, which would ensure that same-sex couples would receive the same benefits and protections afforded married couples). But if patience seems unlikely to pay off, a judge who delays action may well feel that the judiciary is failing the plaintiff.

2. *The court could hold the defendant officials in contempt of court.* But, if the state law that denies the officials power to act is valid and binding, they can successfully argue that obedience is impossible. In New York State Association for Retarded Children, Inc. v. Carey, 631 F.2d 162 (2d Cir.1980), implementation of an injunction by Governor Carey of New York required funds that the legislature refused to appropriate despite his requests. The district court held the governor in contempt but the court of appeals reversed on the basis that compliance was impossible without violating provisions of the state constitution that prohibit spending public funds except pursuant to a valid appropriation. In another case, state officials were held in contempt because they had helped to create the impossibility by urging the state legislature to deny them the necessary funds. Halderman v. Pennhurst State

School & Hospital, 533 F.Supp. 631 (E.D.Pa.1981), aff'd, 673 F.2d 628 (3d Cir.1982), cert. denied, 465 U.S. 1038, 104 S.Ct. 1315, 79 L.Ed.2d 712 (1984). See also Gordon G. Young, Enforcement of Federal Private Rights Against States After Alden v. Maine: The Importance of Hutto v. Finney and Compensation Via Civil Contempt Proceedings, 59 Md.L.Rev. 440 (2000).

3. *The court could strike down whatever state law denies defendant officials the necessary authority.* That is easy if the state law is invalid quite apart from the injunction whose implementation it frustrates, as when the state law is unconstitutional or conflicts with a federal statute. For example, a state law that ordered officials to put toxic chemicals in the river, although a federal statute prohibited this, would be invalid even if no federal court had enjoined their discharge. The state statute would also be invalid if its purpose was to countermand a federal court injunction. For example, North Carolina State Board of Education v. Swann, 402 U.S. 43, 45, 91 S.Ct. 1284, 1285–86, 28 L.Ed.2d 586, 589 (1971), invalidated a state statute that prohibited busing of school children in order to frustrate school desegregation injunctions. However, in the more typical case, the state statute is neither invalid apart from the injunction nor designed to frustrate it. When the state legislature has failed to appropriate funds needed to fix the sewage discharge plant, the state law that frustrates compliance with the injunction would be the provision typically found in state constitutions prohibiting spending state funds except when the legislature has appropriated them. Or in part (b) of the *Country Lodge* problem at page 364, the state law frustrating compliance would be state constitutional or statutory provisions that limit to varying degrees the authority of local governments to promulgate regulations. Missouri v. Jenkins, 495 U.S. 33, 110 S.Ct. 1651, 109 L.Ed.2d 31 (1990) (*Jenkins II*) (reproduced at p. 376), is one of the rare examples of a case that rejects a state law of general applicability because it frustrates implementation of a federal court injunction.

4. *The court could order state officials to disregard state law.* Griffin v. County School Board, 377 U.S. 218, 233, 84 S.Ct. 1226, 1234, 12 L.Ed.2d 256, 266 (1964), said that a district court could order local officials to use the "power that is theirs" under state law to raise and spend money. The hard question arises when the power is not theirs. Federal cases have sometimes ordered state officials to disregard state law where doing so would not jeopardize the purposes of the state law. For example, in McCarthy v. Briscoe, 429 U.S. 1317, 97 S.Ct. 10, 50 L.Ed.2d 49 (1976) (p. 137), after striking down as unconstitutional a state statute that would have kept an independent candidate for President of the United States off the ballot, the court required state officials to put former U.S. Senator Eugene McCarthy on the ballot, although he did not have a nominating petition as required by a still-valid state statute. Justice Powell, acting as Circuit Justice, reasoned that the purpose of the petition requirement was served where the candidate was well-known.

Federal cases have also collected attorney's fees from states even though the legislature has appropriated no funds for this purpose. Gates v. Collier, 616 F.2d 1268 (5th Cir.1980), dealt with a state's refusal to appropriate funds to pay for an award of attorney's fees under an attorney's fees statute. "[W]here a state expresses its unwillingness to comply with a valid judgment of a federal district court, the court may use any of the weapons generally at its disposal to ensure compliance. * * * If statutory authority is needed for the court's actions, it may be found in Fed.R.Civ.P. 70." 616 F.2d at 1271. Rule 70, reproduced in the Appendix at p. 989, allows the seizure of the assets of a recalcitrant judgment debtor. *Gates* is impressive because it countermands state law. But, it would be a more useful precedent for plaintiffs if it had not involved a statute that had already stripped the state of its eleventh amendment protection and dealt with something other than attorney's fees. Fees, unlike the much larger sums usually needed to comply with injunctions, do not impact the state's budget choices in a major way. Moreover, attorney's fees are often considered a part of court costs, from which the eleventh amendment does not protect states. Hutto v. Finney, 437 U.S. 678, 695–96 nn. 24–26, 98 S.Ct. 2565, 2576 nn. 24–26, 57 L.Ed.2d 522, 537–38 nn. 24–26 (1978). Accord, Brinn v. Tidewater Transportation District Commission, 242 F.3d 227 (4th Cir.2001) (state statute prohibiting awards of attorney's fees did not apply to claims asserted under federal law because of the supremacy clause).

Only a few cases have faced the question of whether a federal court may make state officials spend money despite the lack of appropriations. The most typical reaction is to avoid giving an answer. In Welsch v. Likins, 550 F.2d 1122 (8th Cir.1977), the district court had found that unconstitutional conditions existed at a state institution for the mentally retarded and entered an injunction requiring state officials to upgrade the facility. When the state legislature failed to provide necessary funds, the district court enjoined the state commissioner of finance from complying with provisions of the state constitution forbidding expenditure of state funds without an appropriation by the state legislature. The court of appeals vacated the order in the hope that the state legislature would do better next time:

> We do not know why the Legislature that met in 1975 failed to respond more positively to the 1974 requirements of the district court. It is possible that the then Governor and the Legislature did not fully appreciate the force of those requirements; or the Governor and the Legislature may have thought that there was a better way to reach the objectives that the district court thought must be achieved.
>
> In any event, we desire to make it clear to the present Governor and the current Legislature that the [orders to improve the facility] that we uphold today are positive, constitutional requirements, and cannot be ignored. We will not presume that they will be ignored. On the contrary, we think that experience has shown that when governors and state legislatures see clearly what their constitutional duty is with respect to state institutions and realize that the duty must be discharged, they are willing to take necessary steps, including the appropriation of necessary funds.

Id. at 1132. So, as in *Virginia v. West Virginia,* the court presumes that the legislature will provide the money now that a high court has made clear that lack of appropriation does not justify the continuance of the violation. See also Robinson v. Cahill, 69 N.J. 449, 355 A.2d 129 (1976), and Abbott v. Burke, 100 N.J. 269, 495 A.2d 376 (1985), both leaving the remedy of fair funding for all public schools in New Jersey up to the legislature in the first instance. Is there any tactical advantage in avoiding the question? The court explained its reluctance to tackle the question as follows: "we are dealing with the right of a sovereign state to manage and control its own financial affairs. * * * [N]eedless direct confrontations between a federal court and a state should be avoided, particularly in a field as delicate as the one here involved." Id. at 1131–32. See also Wyatt v. Aderholt, 503 F.2d 1305, 1318 (5th Cir. 1974)("serious constitutional questions presented by federal judicial action ordering the sale of state lands, or altering the state budget * * * should not be adjudicated unnecessarily and prematurely").

The next principal case, *Jenkins II*, speaks to the propriety of directly coercing state officials to spend unappropriated funds after many attempts to solve the problem through ordinary political channels.

5. *The court could use indirect means to pressure the legislature to grant the necessary authority.* The court of appeals in *Welsch v. Likins* also displayed concern for the plaintiffs' rightful position: "The obligation of the defendants to eliminate existing unconstitutionalities does not depend upon what the Legislature may do, or upon what the Governor may do. * * *. [I]f Minnesota is going to operate institutions like Cambridge, their operation is going to have to be consistent with the Constitution of the United States." 550 F.2d at 1132.

The court went on to try to reconcile its concern for both federalism and the plaintiffs' rights by suggesting that the district court could order the closing of the state facilities for the mentally retarded unless the legislature provided the necessary funds. The result in *Welsch* can be explained entirely by the rightful position concept: the plaintiffs have a constitutional right against being held in a poor facility, but no constitutional right to being kept in a good facility. Yet, in a broader sense, the court is not out to close down state facilities for the mentally retarded. Rather it is dealing with legislative resistance indirectly rather than directly. Instead of affirmatively ordering the state to spend money that the legislature will not appropriate, the court is threatening to issue an order to prevent the state from doing something that it wants to—provide facilities for the mentally retarded. This judicial tactic is sometimes called a "negative order." The negative order circumvents the federalism problem because it leaves "the question of the expenditure of state funds in the hands of citizens of the state, not in the hands of federal judges." New York State Association for Retarded Children, Inc. v. Carey, 631 F.2d 162, 165 (2d Cir.1980). The negative order cases, like the personal service contract cases, do not require performance but do enjoin the defendant from performing except to put the plaintiffs in their rightful position (see p. 135).

The negative order is like coercive civil contempt in its reliance on coercion. However, the negative order tactic differs in some crucial respects. A finding of contempt is not a prerequisite. The basis for the negative order, as with any other injunction, must be to put the plaintiff in the rightful position rather than, as with criminal or coercive civil contempt, to seek to punish noncompliance. In *Country Lodge v. Miller*, could the court coerce the legislature to authorize the regulations by enjoining it from passing any other legislation until it provides the necessary authority? By enjoining the issuance of permits to construct any new facility in Miller County that might use toxic chemicals? See Gautreaux v. Romney, 457 F.2d 124, 128 (7th Cir.1972).

To get the attention of defendant officials, negative orders must, if carried out, have severe adverse consequences on the public. For that same reason, judges are anxious to avoid having to carry them out. So they tend to threaten where the threat is enough to bring compliance—typically where the executive and a significant minority in the legislature support providing the necessary authority. See, e.g., Robinson v. Cahill, 69 N.J. 449, 355 A.2d 129 (1976)(court enjoins schools from opening in the fall until the state legislature provides funds to equalize educational opportunity where the governor and a bit less than half of the state legislators favor enacting a state income tax to finance this program; after the threat the legislation is enacted). The negative order makes it easier for the swing votes to change by refocusing attention from the unpopular affirmative action to the still more unpopular consequences of the negative order.

MISSOURI v. JENKINS (*JENKINS II*)
Supreme Court of the United States, 1990
495 U.S. 33, 110 S.Ct. 1651, 109 L.Ed.2d 31

[This opinion deals with questions concerning how to finance the implementation of the school desegregation injunction described in *Jenkins III*, reproduced in Chapter 2. The injunction made the Kansas City Missouri School District (KCMSD) and the state jointly and severally liable for the cost of the injunction's implementation. State law limits the power of the KCMSD and other school boards to tax and borrow and gives voters a role in decisions to increase property tax rates above certain levels and to borrow. Voters had rejected all of the KCMSD's many proposals to increase taxes and sell bonds since 1969. Faced with these limits on the KCMSD's ability to raise funds, the district court itself increased the property tax rate and imposed a surcharge on the state income tax to fund implementation of the decree. The court of appeals affirmed the increase in the property tax rate for the previous year, but held that in the future the district court should not itself levy the tax, but rather should have set the KCMSD free from the state law limits on its ability to raise property tax rates. The court of appeals set aside the income tax, pointing out that the KCMSD had no power to tax income.]

JUSTICE WHITE delivered the opinion of the Court. * * *

The State's petition [for certiorari] argued that the remedies imposed by the District Court were excessive in scope and that the property tax increase violated Article III, the Tenth Amendment, principles of federal/state comity. We granted the State's petition, limited to the question of the property tax increase. * * *

III

* * *

The State urges us to hold that the tax increase violated Article III, the Tenth Amendment, and principles of federal/state comity. We find it unnecessary to reach the difficult constitutional issues, for we agree with the State that the tax increase contravened the principles of comity that must govern the exercise of the District Court's equitable discretion in this area.

It is accepted by all the parties, as it was by the courts below, that the imposition of a tax increase by a federal court was an extraordinary event. In assuming for itself the fundamental and delicate power of taxation the District Court not only intruded on local authority but circumvented it altogether. Before taking such a drastic step the District Court was obliged to assure itself that no permissible alternative would have accomplished the required task. We have emphasized that although the "remedial powers of an equity court must be adequate to the task, * * * they are not unlimited," and one of the most important considerations governing the exercise of equitable power is a proper respect for the integrity and function of local government institutions. Especially is this true where, as here, those institutions are ready, willing, and—but for the operation of state law curtailing their powers—able to remedy the deprivation of constitutional rights themselves.

The District Court believed that it had no alternative to imposing a tax increase. But there was an alternative, the very one outlined by the Court of Appeals: it could have authorized or required KCMSD to levy property taxes at a rate adequate to fund the desegregation remedy and could have enjoined the operation of state laws that would have prevented KCMSD from exercising this power. The difference between the two approaches is far more than a matter of form. Authorizing and directing local government institutions to devise and implement remedies not only protects the function of those institutions but, to the extent possible, also places the responsibility for solutions to the problems of segregation upon those who have themselves created the problems.

As Brown v. Board of Education, 349 U.S. 294, 299, 75 S.Ct. 753, 755, 99 L.Ed. 1083 (1955), observed, local authorities have the "primary responsibility for elucidating, assessing, and solving" the problems of desegregation. This is true as well of the problems of financing desegregation, for no matter has been more consistently placed upon the shoulders of local government than that of financing public schools. * * *

The District Court therefore abused its discretion in imposing the tax itself. * * *

IV

We stand on different ground when we review the modifications to the District Court's order made by the Court of Appeals. * * *

The State argues that the funding ordered by the District Court violates principles of equity and comity because the remedial order itself was excessive. As the State puts it, "the only reason that the court below needed to consider an unprecedented tax increase was the equally unprecedented cost of its remedial programs." We think this argument aims at the scope of the remedy rather than the manner in which the remedy is to be funded and thus falls outside our limited grant of certiorari in this case. * * * We accept, without approving or disapproving, the Court of Appeals' conclusion that the District Court's remedy was proper.

The State has argued here that the District Court, having found the State and KCMSD jointly and severally liable, should have allowed any monetary obligations that KCMSD could not meet to fall on the State rather than interfere with state law to permit KCMSD to meet them.[19] Under the circumstances of this case, we cannot say it was an abuse of discretion for the District Court to rule that KCMSD should be responsible for funding its share of the remedy. The State strenuously opposed efforts by respondents to make it responsible for the cost of implementing the order and had secured a reversal of the District Court's earlier decision placing on it all of the cost of substantial portions of the order. The District Court declined to require the State to pay for KCMSD's obligations because it believed that the Court of Appeals had ordered it to allocate the costs between the two governmental entities. Furthermore, if the District Court had chosen the route now suggested by the State, implementation of the remedial order might have been delayed if the State resisted efforts by KCMSD to obtain contribution.

* * * We turn to the constitutional issues. The modifications ordered by the Court of Appeals cannot be assailed as invalid under the Tenth Amendment. "The Tenth Amendment's reservation of nondelegated powers to the States is not implicated by a federal-court judgment enforcing the express prohibitions of unlawful state conduct enacted by the Fourteenth Amendment." "The Fourteenth Amendment ... was avowedly directed against the power of the States," and so permits a federal court to disestablish local government institutions that interfere with its commands.

Finally, the State argues that an order to increase taxes cannot be sustained under the judicial power of Article III. Whatever the merits of this argument when applied to the District Court's own order increasing taxes, a point we have not reached, a court order directing a local government body to levy its own taxes is plainly a judicial act within the power of a federal court. We held as much in Griffin v. Prince Edward County School Bd., [377 U.S. 218, 233, 84 S.Ct. 1226, 1234, 12 L.Ed.2d 256 (1964)], where we stated that a District Court, faced with a county's attempt to avoid desegregation of the public schools by refusing to operate those schools, could "require the county Supervisors to exercise the power that is theirs to levy taxes to raise funds adequate to reopen, operate, and maintain without racial discrimination a public school system * * *." *Griffin* followed a long and venerable line of cases in which this Court held that federal courts could issue the writ of mandamus to compel local

---

19. This suggestion was also made by the judge dissenting below [Chief Judge Lay].

governmental bodies to levy taxes adequate to satisfy their debt obligations.[20]

The State maintains, however, that even under these cases, the federal judicial power can go no further than to require local governments to levy taxes as *authorized under state law*. In other words, the State argues that federal courts cannot set aside state-imposed limitations on local taxing authority because to do so is to do more than to require the local government "to exercise the power that is theirs." We disagree. This argument was rejected as early as Von Hoffman v. City of Quincy, [4 Wall. 535, 18 L.Ed. 403 (1867)]. There the holder of bonds issued by the City sought a writ of mandamus against the City requiring it to levy taxes sufficient to pay interest coupons then due. The City defended based on a state statute that limited its power of taxation, and the Circuit Court refused to mandamus the City. This Court reversed, observing that the statute relied on by the City was passed after the bonds were issued and holding that because the City had ample authority to levy taxes to pay its bonds when they were issued, the statute impaired the contractual entitlements of the bondholders, contrary to Art. I, § 10, cl. 1 of the Constitution, under which a State may not pass any law impairing the obligation of contracts. The statutory limitation, therefore, could be disregarded and the City ordered to levy the necessary taxes to pay its bonds.

It is therefore clear that a local government with taxing authority may be ordered to levy taxes in excess of the limit set by state statute where there is reason based in the Constitution for not observing the statutory limitation. In *Von Hoffman*, the limitation was disregarded because of the Contract Clause. Here the KCMSD may be ordered to levy taxes despite the statutory limitations on its authority in order to compel the discharge of an obligation imposed on KCMSD by the Fourteenth Amendment. To hold otherwise would fail to take account of the obligations of local governments, under the Supremacy Clause, to fulfill the requirements that the Constitution imposes on them. However wide the discretion of local authorities in fashioning desegregation remedies may be, "if a state-imposed limitation on a school authority's discretion operates to inhibit or obstruct the operation of a unitary school system or impede the disestablishing of a dual school system, it must fall; state

---

20. The old cases recognized two exceptions to this rule, neither of which is relevant here. First, it was held that federal courts could not by writ of mandamus compel state officers to release funds in the state treasury sufficient to satisfy state bond obligations. The Court viewed this attempt to employ the writ of mandamus as a ruse to avoid the Eleventh Amendment's bar against exercising federal jurisdiction over the State. See Louisiana v. Jumel, 107 U.S. (17 Otto) 711, 720–721, 2 S.Ct. 128, 135–136, 27 L.Ed. 448 (1883). This holding has no application to this case, for the Eleventh Amendment does not bar federal courts from imposing on the States the costs of securing prospective compliance with a desegregation order. Milliken v. Bradley, 433 U.S. 267, 290, 97 S.Ct. 2749, 2762, 53 L.Ed.2d 745 (1977), and does not afford local school boards like KCMSD immunity from suit, Mt. Healthy City School Dist. Bd. of Education v. Doyle, 429 U.S. 274, 280–281, 97 S.Ct. 568, 572–573, 50 L.Ed.2d 471 (1977). Second, it was held that the writ of mandamus would not lie to compel the collection of taxes when there was no person against whom the writ could operate. This exception also has no application to this case, where there are state and local officials invested with authority to collect and disburse the property tax and where, as matters now stand, the District Court need only prevent those officials from applying state law that would interfere with the willing levy of property taxes by KCMSD.

policy must give way when it operates to hinder vindication of federal constitutional guarantees." North Carolina State Bd. of Education v. Swann, 402 U.S. 43, 45, 91 S.Ct. 1284, 1286, 28 L.Ed.2d 586 (1971). Even though a particular remedy may not be required in every case to vindicate constitutional guarantees, where (as here) it has been found that a particular remedy is required, the State cannot hinder the process by preventing a local government from implementing that remedy.[21] * * *

JUSTICE KENNEDY, with whom CHIEF JUSTICE [REHNQUIST], JUSTICE O'CONNOR, and JUSTICE SCALIA join, concurring in part and concurring in the judgment.

* * * Today's casual embrace of taxation imposed by the unelected, life-tenured federal judiciary disregards fundamental precepts for the democratic control of public institutions. * * *

I

* * *

The case before us represents the first in which a lower federal court has in fact upheld taxation to fund a remedial decree. * * *

Any purported distinction between direct imposition of a tax by the federal court and an order commanding the school district to impose the tax is but a convenient formalism where the court's action is predicated on elimination of state law limitations on the school district's taxing authority. As the Court describes it, the local KCMSD possesses plenary taxing powers, which allow it to impose any tax it chooses if not "hindered" by the Missouri Constitution and state statutes. This puts the conclusion before the premise. Local government bodies in Missouri, as elsewhere, must derive their power from a sovereign, and that sovereign is the State of Missouri. See Mo. Const., Art. X, § 1 (political subdivisions may exercise only "that power granted to them" by Missouri General Assembly). Under Missouri law, the KCMSD has power to impose a limited property tax levy up to $1.25 per $100 of assessed value. The power to exact a higher rate of property tax remains with the people. * * *

Whatever taxing power the KCMSD may exercise outside the boundaries of state law would derive from the federal court. The Court never confronts the judicial authority to issue an order for this purpose. Absent a change in state law, the tax is imposed by federal authority under a federal decree. The question is whether a district court possesses a power to tax under federal law, either directly or through delegation to the KCMSD.

---

21. United States v. County of Macon, 99 U.S. (9 Otto) 582, 25 L.Ed. 331 (1879), held that mandamus would not lie to force a local government to levy taxes in excess of the limits contained in a statute in effect at the time the City incurred its bonded indebtedness, for the explicit limitation in the taxing power became part of the contract, the bondholders had notice of the limitation and were deemed to have consented to it, and hence no contractual remedy was unconstitutionally impaired by observing the statute. *County of Macon* has little relevance to the present case, for KCMSD's obligation to fund the desegregation remedy arises from its operation of a segregated school system in violation of the Constitution, not from a contract between KCMSD and respondents.

II

Article III of the Constitution states that "the judicial Power of the United States, shall be vested in one supreme Court, and in such inferior Courts as the Congress may from time to time ordain and establish." The description of the judicial power nowhere includes the word "tax" or anything that resembles it. This reflects the Framers' understanding that taxation was not a proper area for judicial involvement. "The judiciary * * * has no influence over either the sword or the purse, no direction either of the strength or of the wealth of the society, and can take no active resolution whatever." The Federalist No. 78, p. 523 (J. Cooke ed.1961)(A. Hamilton).

Our cases throughout the years leave no doubt that taxation is not a judicial function. Last Term we rejected the invitation to cure an unconstitutional tax scheme by broadening the class of those taxed. We said that such a remedy "could be construed as the direct imposition of a state tax, a remedy beyond the power of a federal court." * * *

The nature of the District Court's order here reveals that it is not a proper exercise of the judicial power. The exercise of judicial power involves adjudication of controversies and imposition of burdens on those who are parties before the Court. The order at issue here is not of this character. It binds the broad class of all KCMSD taxpayers. It has the purpose and direct effect of extracting money from persons who have had no presence or representation in the suit. For this reason, the District Court's direct order imposing a tax was more than an abuse of discretion, for any attempt to collect the taxes from the citizens would have been a blatant denial of due process. * * *

The taxes were imposed by a District Court that was not "representative" in any sense, and the individual citizens of the KCMSD whose property (they later learned) was at stake were neither served with process nor heard in court. The method of taxation endorsed by today's dicta suffers the same flaw, for a district court order that overrides the citizens' state law protection against taxation without referendum approval can in no sense provide representational due process. * * *

A judicial taxation order is but an attempt to exercise a power that always has been thought legislative in nature. * * * Article I, § 1 states that "*all* legislative Powers herein granted shall be vested in a Congress of the United States, which shall consist of a Senate and House of Representatives" (emphasis added). * * *

The confinement of taxation to the legislative branches, both in our Federal and State Governments, was not random. It reflected our ideal that the power of taxation must be under the control of those who are taxed. This truth animated all our colonial and revolutionary history. * * *

[I]mposition of taxes by an authority so insulated from public communication or control can lead to deep feelings of frustration, powerlessness, and anger on the part of taxpaying citizens.

The operation of tax systems is among the most difficult aspects of public administration. It is not a function the judiciary as an institution is designed to exercise. Unlike legislative bodies, which may hold hearings on how best to raise revenues, all subject to the views of constituents to whom the legislature is accountable, the judiciary must grope ahead with only the assistance of the parties, or perhaps random amici curiae. Those hearings would be without principled direction, for there exists no body of juridical axioms by which to guide or review them. On this questionable basis, the Court today would give authority for decisions that affect the life plans of local citizens, the revenue available for competing public needs, and the health of the local economy.

Day-to-day administration of the tax must be accomplished by judicial trial and error, requisitioning the staff of the existing tax authority, or the hiring of a staff under the direction of the judge. The District Court orders in this case suggest the pitfalls of the first course. Forcing citizens to make financial decisions in fear of the fledgling judicial tax collector's next misstep must detract from the dignity and independence of the federal courts.

The function of hiring and supervising a staff for what is essentially a political function has other complications. As part of its remedial order, for example, the District Court ordered the hiring of a "public information specialist," at a cost of $30,000. The purpose of the position was to "solicit community support and involvement" in the District Court's desegregation plan. This type of order raises a substantial question whether a district court may extract taxes from citizens who have no right of representation and then use the funds for expression with which the citizens may disagree.

The Court relies on dicta from Griffin v. School Bd. of Prince Edward County, 377 U.S. 218, 84 S.Ct. 1226, 12 L.Ed.2d 256 (1964) to support its statements on judicial taxation. In *Griffin,* the Court faced an unrepentant and recalcitrant school board that attempted to provide financial support for white schools while refusing to operate schools for black schoolchildren. We stated that the district court could "require the Supervisors to exercise the power *that is theirs* to levy taxes to raise funds adequate to reopen, operate, and maintain without racial discrimination to public school system," for white schools while refusing to operate schools for black schoolchildren. There is no occasion in this case to discuss the full implications of *Griffin's* observation, for it has no application here. *Griffin* endorsed the power of a federal court to order the local authority to exercise *existing* authority to tax.

This case does not involve an order to a local government with plenary taxing power to impose a tax, or an order directed at one whose taxing power has been limited by a state law enacted in order to thwart a federal court order. An order of this type would find support in the *Griffin* dicta, and present a closer question than the one before us. Yet that order might implicate as well the "perversion of the normal legislative process" that we have found troubling in other contexts. See Spallone v. United States, 493 U.S. 265, 110 S.Ct. 625, 107 L.Ed.2d 644 (1990) [reproduced at page 394]. A legislative vote taken under judicial compulsion blurs lines of accountability by making it appear that a decision was reached by elected representatives when the reality is otherwise. For this reason, it is difficult to see the difference between an order to tax and direct judicial imposition of a tax.

* * * [T]here was no state authority in this case for the KCMSD to exercise. In this situation, there could be no authority for a judicial order touching on taxation. See United States v. County of Macon, 99 U.S. 582, 591, 25 L.Ed. 331 (1879)(where the statute empowering the corporation to issue bonds contains a limit on the taxing power, federal court has no power of mandamus to compel a levy in excess of that power; "We have no power by mandamus to compel a municipal corporation to levy a tax which the law does not authorize. We cannot create new rights or confer new powers. All we can do is to bring existing powers into operation").

The Court cites a single case, Von Hoffman v. City of Quincy, 4 Wall. 535, 18 L.Ed. 403 (1867), for the proposition that a federal court may set aside state taxation limits that interfere with the remedy sought by the district court. But the Court does not heed *Von Hoffman's* holding. There a municipality had authorized a tax levy in support of a specific bond obligation, but later limited the taxation authority in a way that impaired the bond obligation. The Court held the subsequent limitation itself unconstitutional, a violation of the Contracts Clause. Once the limitation was held invalid, the original specific grant of authority remained. There is no allegation here, nor could there be, that the neutral tax limitations imposed by the people of Missouri are unconstitutional. The majority appears to concede that the Missouri tax law does not violate a specific provision of the Constitution, stating instead that state laws may be disregarded on the basis of a vague "reason based in the Constitution." But this broad suggestion does not follow from the holding in *Von Hoffman.** * *

III

* * *

I am required in light of our limited grant of certiorari to assume that the remedy chosen by the District Court was a permissible exercise of its remedial discretion. But it is misleading to suggest that a failure to fund this particular remedy would leave constitutional rights without a remedy. * * * [Ed: The opinion argues that the remedy is broader than necessary to cure the violation in terms ultimately adopted five years later in *Jenkins III.*]

The prudence we have required in other areas touching on federal court intrusion in local government, see, e.g., Spallone v. United States, 493 U.S. 265, 110 S.Ct. 625, 107 L.Ed.2d 644 (1990), is missing here. Even on the assumption that a federal court might order taxation in an extreme case, the unique nature of the taxing power would demand that this remedy be used as a last resort. In my view, a taxation order should not even be considered, and this Court need never have addressed the question, unless there has been a finding that without the particular remedy at issue the constitutional violation will go unremedied. * * * There is no showing in this record that, faced with the revenue shortfall, the District Court gave due consideration to the possibility that another remedy among the "wide range of possibilities" would have addressed the constitutional violations without giving rise to a funding crisis. * * *

IV

* * *

In pursuing the demand of justice for racial equality, I fear that the Court today loses sight of other basic political liberties guaranteed by our constitutional system, liberties that can coexist with a proper exercise of judicial remedial powers adequate to correct constitutional violations.

NOTES

1. As the majority notes, Chief Judge Lay of the Eighth Circuit suggested below that the district court should make the state responsible for any shortfall in the funds that could have been provided by the KCMSD. The state could then decide whether to provide the funds itself or to authorize KCMSD to levy higher taxes. Giving the state this option accords with states' power to allocate funds and responsibilities among and between themselves and their subdivisions. Why did the courts take that power away from Missouri? If the district court had put the final responsibility on the state, but the legislature did not provide the necessary funds, how could the district court get the money from the state? Does footnote 20 in the majority opinion mean that the district court could order the state treasurer to disregard prohibitions in the State Constitution on releasing state funds without legislative authorization?

2. Do federal judges have the power under article III of the Constitution to impose taxes to raise money needed to remedy violations of the equal protection clause? This fundamental question puts in conflict the ideal of equal protection and the ideal of "no taxation without representation." The Civil War was fought for one; the Revolutionary War for the other. Does the majority answer this question? The majority distinguishes a judicially imposed tax from instructing the school board to disregard state law limits on its taxing power. Is there substance in this distinction? Is such an instruction more closely analogous to *Von Hoffman*, upon which the majority relies, or *Macon County*, upon which the concurring opinion relies? Does the concurring opinion explain why it is any worse to let the KCMSD disregard state law tax limits than to order an otherwise unwilling school board to tax up to the state law tax limits? See generally D. Bruce LaPierre, Enforcement of Judgments Against State and Local Governments: Judicial Control Over the Power to Tax, 61 Geo.Wash.L.Rev. 299 (1993).

One way out of the possible limits on article III power is for Congress to use its article I powers. To ensure that lack of funds will not frustrate suits brought by the United States against municipalities under the Clean Water Act, which can require them to undertake very expensive projects, the Act provides that:

> Whenever a municipality is a party to a civil action brought by the United States under this section, the State in which such municipality is located shall be joined as a party. Such a State shall be liable for payment of any judgment, entered against the municipality in such action to the extent that the laws of that State prevent the municipality from raising revenues needed to comply with such judgment.

33 U.S.C. § 1319(e).

3. The concurring opinion argues that the district court should avoid the need to confront the limits on KCMSD's taxing power by opting for a less expensive remedy. It is hard to understand why the four votes needed to grant certiorari on the appropriateness of the remedy were not available before *Jenkins III*. Acknowledging that certiorari was denied on this point, the concurring opinion argues that nonetheless comity should have been used to select a less expensive remedy.

4. Would the issue come out differently if presented to today's Supreme Court? See Janice C. Griffith, Judicial Funding and Taxation Mandates: Will Missouri v. Jenkins Survive Under the New Federalism Retraints?, 61 Ohio St.L.J. 483 (2000). Would it make a difference if the defendant was recalcitrant and no less expensive remedy was available? What if a state court were asked or authorized to impose a tax? See Idaho Schools for Equal Educational Opportunity v. State, 140 Idaho 586, 97 P.3d 453 (2004) (state law allowing trial court to impose educational necessity levy violates separation of powers provision of Idaho constitution).

5. *An update on Jenkins*. After the remand in *Jenkins III* (reproduced at p. 165), the court agreed to a settlement in which the state would be dismissed from the litigation after paying an additional $320 million. Jenkins v. Missouri, 959 F.Supp. 1151 (W.D.Mo.1997). The court, however, retained jurisdiction over the KCMSD, finding its violations were responsible for 26% of the performance gap between students of different races. Whether the decree has done much good for the plaintiffs is another question. "Billions of dollars in desegregation money had built the most expensive magnet school system in history. * * * The money had resulted in better buildings and better pay for the teachers, but hadn't brought improvement in the academic performance of students." Barbara Shelly, Schools Still a Tangled Mess, Kansas City Star (Nov. 18, 1999). The Missouri State Board of Education revoked the KCMSD's accreditation because of poor teaching and inadequate educational results. See Catherine Gewertz, Hard Lesson For Kansas City's Troubled Schools, Education Week (April 26, 2000). District Judge Dean Whipple subsequently ruled that test scores showed the school district had met the constitutional threshold for closing the achievement gap, but cautioned the district still had a "long distance to travel" even as he dismissed the case and dissolved the long-standing injunction. The plaintiffs dropped their appeal from this decision, bringing the case to a close after 26 years of litigation. Deann Smith, Plaintiff Drops Appeal in Federal School Desegregation Case, Kansas City Star (September 27, 2003). See Preston C. Green, III &

Bruce D. Baker, Urban Legends, Desegregation and School Finance: Did Kansas City Really Prove that Money Doesn't Matter?, 12 Mich.J. Race & Law 57 (2006) (using empirical study to refute claims of critics that *Jenkins* proves that exorbitant school funding has no correlation to learning outcomes).

Assuming that the order against the state officials in *Jenkins* passes eleventh amendment muster, what should the district court judge do if there is no state appropriation authorizing the payment of the necessary funds to the Kansas City school system and if such appropriation is necessary under state law? One approach might be to make the members of the state legislature parties to the suit and order them to pass the necessary statute. Consider this approach in light of the following case.

UNITED STATES v. CITY OF YONKERS

United States Court of Appeals, Second Circuit, 1988
856 F.2d 444, cert. denied in part, 489 U.S. 1065, 109 S.Ct. 1339, 103 L.Ed.2d 810 (1989), and rev'd in part, sub nom. Spallone v. United States, 493 U.S. 265, 110 S.Ct. 625, 107 L.Ed.2d 644 (1990)

JON O. NEWMAN, CIRCUIT JUDGE:

This appeal presents important issues concerning the enforcement of orders of a United States District Court requiring action by a municipality to remedy violations of the Constitution and statutes of the United States. The principal issues are whether members of the Yonkers City Council may be required to vote to implement remedies contained in a consent judgment agreed to by the City and approved by the City Council, and whether the City, in addition to the council members, may be subjected to the coercive sanctions of civil contempt when the agreed upon legislative action has not been taken. The issues arise on appeals by the City of Yonkers and four members of the Yonkers City Council from orders of the District Court for the Southern District of New York (Leonard B. Sand, Judge) adjudicating the City and the council members in civil contempt and imposing coercive sanctions. We conclude that under the circumstances of this case the recalcitrant council members may be required to vote to implement the consent judgment and that the City, in addition to the council members, may be adjudicated in contempt and subjected to coercive sanctions for failure to abide by the consent judgment and subsequent implementing orders of the District Court. We also conclude that the amount of the monetary sanctions imposed on the City, though properly substantial, should be somewhat reduced. We therefore affirm the order adjudicating the council members in contempt and affirm, as modified, the order adjudicating the City in contempt.

BACKGROUND

1. The Underlying Lawsuit

The United States filed the underlying lawsuit on December 1, 1980, against the City of Yonkers * * *. The complaint [alleges] that the City

* * * had "intentionally ... perpetuated and seriously aggravated residential racial segregation" in violation of the Constitution and Title VIII of the Civil Rights Act of 1968, 42 U.S.C. §§ 3601–3619 (1982) * * *.

The District Court found the City * * * liable * * *.

The Housing Remedy Order [entered on May 28, 1986] included provisions for the construction of 200 units of public housing and for the planning of additional units of subsidized housing. The City had previously agreed to provide acceptable sites for the 200 units of public housing as a condition of receiving its 1983 Community Development Block Grant from the United States Department of Housing and Urban Development (HUD). * * * The City was required to propose sites for 140 units within thirty days and sites for the remaining 60 units within ninety days.

[The Housing Remedy Order also required the City to present a plan for the subsidized housing by November 15, 1986]. * * *

2. *Attempts to Implement the Housing Remedy Order*

* * * [The City violated the Housing Remedy Order.] The United States and the NAACP [which had intervened] then moved for an adjudication of civil contempt and the imposition of coercive sanctions. Rather than proceed immediately to consideration of contempt sanctions, the District Court patiently endeavored to secure voluntary compliance. * * *

A consent decree was agreed to by the parties [on January 25, 1988], approved by the City Council on January 27, and entered as a consent judgment of the District Court on January 28 ("the Consent Judgment").

With respect to the 200 units of public housing, the Consent Judgment renewed the City's commitment to build the units and identified seven specific sites. * * *

[The Consent Judgment also set 800 units of subsidized housing as "an appropriate target in fulfilling its obligations" under the Housing Remedy Order, required the City to make good-faith efforts to achieve 600 of the units in annual installments of 200 units within each of the next three years. After citizens protested vehemently, the City promptly violated the Consent Decree. The City moved to modify the Consent Decree, offering to return the $30 million federal housing grant. That motion was denied and, on June 13, 1988 after prolonged consultation with the City and other parties, the District Court entered a Long Term Plan Order that specified the terms of the legislation that the City must adopt pursuant to the Consent Decree.]

On June 28 the City Council voted against a resolution "indicating [the Council's] commitment to the implementation of" the Housing Remedy Order, the Consent Judgment, and the Long Term Plan Order.

The following day the District Court directed the plaintiffs to submit an order requiring the City to take "specific implementing action" under a prescribed timetable, violation of which would subject the City to contempt sanctions. In response to the plaintiffs' proposed order setting forth such a timetable, the City argued that the defeat of the resolution on June 28 indicated that the City would not voluntarily adopt legislation contemplated by the Long Term Plan Order and suggested that the Court itself should enter an order adopting the necessary legislation. At a hearing on the proposed timetable on July 12, the District Court invited the parties' comments on the possible creation by the Court of an Affordable Housing Commission to exercise the City Council's functions concerning implementation of the housing remedy orders. The City opposed creation of the Commission because it would divest the Council of its "core legislative as well as executive functions."

3. *The Prospect of Contempt* * * *

[On July 26 the District Court issued an order that gave the City until August 1 to enact the required legislation called the Affordable Housing Ordinance. If that did not occur, the July 26 Order provided that] the City and the council members were to show cause at 10:00 a.m., August 2, why they should not be adjudged in contempt. If such cause was not shown, each council member failing to vote for such legislation would be fined $500 per day, and, if the legislation was not passed by August 10, such council member would be imprisoned on August 11. The contempt sanction against the City would be daily fines starting at $100 on August 2 and doubling in amount each day of continued noncompliance. The cumulative total of the fines against the City would exceed $10,000 by day 7, exceed $1 million by day 14, exceed $200 million by day 21, and exceed $26 billion by day 28. The order provided that a council member could be purged of contempt by voting in favor of the legislation or by enactment of the legislation. The City could be purged of contempt by enactment of the legislation. The order further provided that all fines would be paid into the Treasury of the United States and would not be refundable, that the Council would meet at least once a week to vote on the legislative package, and that any incarcerated council member would be released to attend such meetings. * * *

[On August 1, the City Council voted four to three not to comply with the July 26 Order.]

4. *The Contempt Adjudications* * * *

The Court held the City in contempt, imposed the coercive sanctions set forth in the July 26 order, and entered written findings of fact. * * *

[The District Court also held in contempt the four council members who had voted against compliance: Nicholas Longo, Edward Fagan, Peter Chema, and Henry Spallone.]

The District Court denied requests for stays by the City and the four council members. On August 9, after fines for seven days had become due, this Court stayed the contempt sanctions and ordered an expedited appeal. * * *

Discussion

A. *The Council Members*

* * *

2. *Abuse of Discretion*

* * * [T]he council members contend that the District Court exceeded its discretion in adjudicating them in contempt * * * [because] a less confrontational resolution of the matter could have been achieved had the District Court selected the alternatives of either appointing a commission to exercise the Council's housing and related powers or ordering the Affordable Housing Ordinance into effect.

These arguments blend two somewhat different propositions of law, but in the end, both are unavailing. In challenging the District Court's decision to require the Council to enact the Affordable Housing Ordinance, the contemnors are alleging an abuse of discretion in the Court's choice of remedies for the constitutional violations adjudicated in 1986. As the contemnors point out, a District Court, though endowed with broad discretion in fashioning remedies for constitutional violations, see Swann v. Charlotte–Mecklenburg Board of Education, 402 U.S. 1, 91 S.Ct. 1267, 28 L.Ed.2d 554 (1971), must exercise restraint in determining what actions ought to be required of state and local governmental officials. See Rizzo v. Goode, 423 U.S. 362, 380, 96 S.Ct. 598, 608, 46 L.Ed.2d 561 (1976). In challenging the District Court's decision to impose coercive contempt sanctions, the contemnors are alleging an abuse of discretion in the Court's method of enforcing the remedy that had been selected. Though there is no question that courts have authority to enforce their lawful orders through civil contempt, the contemnors properly point out that in selecting contempt sanctions, a court is obliged to use the " 'least possible power adequate to the end proposed.' "

In this case, however, there is a fundamental reason why the choice of implementing legislation as a remedy and the choice of coercive contempt sanctions to enforce compliance with that remedy cannot possibly be an abuse of the District Court's discretion. That reason is the blunt fact that the City agreed in the Consent Judgment to comply with the Housing Remedy Order by the adoption of necessary implementing legislation, specifically including tax abatements and zoning changes. By its approval of the Consent Judgment the City Council itself selected the remedy of implementing legislation and cannot complain that the District Court approved the agreement. Moreover, once committed by its own agreement to adopting implementing legislation, the Council cannot complain that its obligation is enforced by the coercive sanctions of civil contempt. Consent judgments are important devices for resolving difficult controversies. Their effectiveness depends on the ability of all concerned to rely on the enforcement of their terms. In the context of a consent judgment, use of civil contempt sanctions is the "least possible power *adequate* to the end proposed" because faithful performance of the agreement is precisely the end proposed.

To the extent that the council members are contending that the District Court exceeded its discretion in ordering them to adopt the precise terms of the Affordable Housing Ordinance, this argument also is unavailing. * * * The Court proceeded cautiously, according the City a full opportunity to draft the plan and ultimately accepting nearly everything that the City proposed. Similarly, with the specifics of the Affordable Housing Ordinance, the District Court afforded the City the opportunity to have its consultants draft the ordinance and accepted the draft they produced. By ordering passage of the Affordable Housing Ordinance, the District Court was carrying out the terms of the Consent Judgment under which the City agreed to adopt implementing legislation on tax abatements and zoning changes and doing so with details supplied by the City itself. The order of July 26 was well within the discretion of the District Court, as was its decision to enforce that order by civil contempt sanctions. * * *

4. *Legislative Immunity*

The major defense asserted by the council members is that they are entitled to legislative immunity and that such immunity prohibits a district court from compelling them to vote in favor of a particular ordinance. There is no doubt that state legislators enjoy immunity when engaged "in the sphere of legitimate legislative activity." * * *

Even if we assume for purposes of this appeal that city council members enjoy the same immunity available to state legislators, we would seriously doubt that such immunity insulates them from district court orders requiring them to comply with remedial decrees redressing constitutional violations. The Supreme Court has instructed a district court that, if necessary to secure compliance with a prior federal court remedial decree, it could order county legislators "to exercise the power that is theirs to levy taxes" to reopen the public schools of Prince Edward County, Virginia. Griffin v. County School Board, 377 U.S. 218, 233, 84 S.Ct. 1226, 1234, 12 L.Ed.2d 256 (1964). Though appellants minimize the force of this instruction by calling it dictum, since the need to issue such an order had not then arisen, it is especially forceful dictum when the Supreme Court specifically informs a district court what action it may take in the course of significant litigation. If it had become necessary to order the county legislators to levy taxes, there can be no doubt that the Supreme Court expected the district court to make sure that its order was enforced.

The Supreme Court has also upheld a district court's remedial order that required state and local officials to provide necessary public funds to implement a school desegregation plan. Milliken v. Bradley, 433 U.S. 267, 97 S.Ct. 2749, 53 L.Ed.2d 745 (1977) [*Milliken II*]. In *Milliken* the Court expressly rejected an immunity defense based on Eleventh Amendment sovereign immunity a claim at least as substantial as the immunity defense now asserted by the four council members. The Court pointed out that though a state enjoyed immunity from damage actions, its immunity did not insulate it from a district court judgment requiring prospective action to comply with constitutional requirements, even when compliance would have "a direct and substantial impact on the state treasury." * * *

On this appeal, however, we need not definitively decide whether as a general matter a district court may order city council members to vote in favor of a particular ordinance, even to implement remedies for constitutional violations. This appeal presents the more narrow issue whether such an order may be entered and enforced by contempt sanctions after a city has agreed to entry of a consent judgment committing itself to enact implementing ordinances and a city's legislative body has voted in favor of such a consent decree. On that narrow issue, we have no doubt that federal court authority must prevail. No litigant, least of all public officials sworn to uphold the Constitution of the United States, may be permitted to avoid compliance with solemn commitments they have made in a consent judgment entered by a federal district court to remedy constitutional violations. Without intending to cast doubt on a district court's authority to order legislative action in contested litigation concerning the appropriate choice of remedies for constitutional violations, we note that the Supreme Court has recently observed that consent judgments may contain enforceable obligations that might have been beyond the authority of a district court to enter in contested litigation. See Local No. 93, Int'l Ass'n of Firefighters v. City of Cleveland, 478 U.S. 501, 106 S.Ct. 3063, 92 L.Ed.2d 405 (1986).

Nor is there any merit in appellant Spallone's suggestion that he may not be required to implement the Consent Judgment because he voted against its approval as a member of the City Council. A federal court must be able to rely upon the assurances given by municipalities and their legislative bodies, without regard to the dissenting votes of individual local officials. Once the Yonkers City Council approved the terms of the Consent Judgment, the Council became obligated to carry out its commitments. If a member of the Council is unwilling to abide by such commitments, his option is to decline to serve on the body that is bound, not to act in defiant disregard of the commitments and the federal court judgment that memorializes them.

Whatever the scope of local legislators' immunity, it does not insulate them from compliance with a consent judgment to which their city has agreed and which has been approved by their legislative body.

5. *First Amendment*

The council members' assertion of a First Amendment defense to the July 26 order and its enforcement requires no extended discussion. Even if we acknowledge that the act of voting has sufficient expressive content to be accorded some First Amendment protection as symbolic speech, the public interest in obtaining compliance with federal court judgments that remedy constitutional violations unquestionably justifies whatever burden on expression has occurred. The council members remain free to express their views on all aspects of housing in Yonkers. But just as the First Amendment would not permit them to incite violation of federal law, it does not permit them to take action in violation of such law.

B. The City

To the extent that the City advances the same objections as the council members, particularly the contention that the District Court should have chosen to adopt the Affordable Housing Ordinance itself or to appoint a commission to exercise the City's housing functions, we need not repeat our reasons for rejecting those objections. [Some] contentions, however, require further discussion.

1. Defense of Impossibility

The claim most vigorously pressed by the City is the defense of impossibility. The City contends that enactment of the Affordable Housing Ordinance requires an affirmative vote of a majority of the City Council and that the City, as a corporate entity, is powerless to compel the council members to act. We recognize that civil contempt sanctions may not be imposed upon a person or entity unable to comply with a court's orders. Nevertheless, we conclude that the City's defense of impossibility is unavailing.

Preliminarily, we have some doubt whether the City has done everything it can, apart from securing the favorable votes of a Council majority, to obtain compliance with the orders of the District Court. The City has not requested the Governor of New York to use whatever authority he may have to remove local officials for misconduct, nor has the City requested the New York Emergency Financial Control Board for the City of Yonkers to take whatever action its broad authorizing statute permits it to take under the current circumstances, 1984 N.Y. Laws ch. 103.

More fundamentally, we agree with the position urged by the United States that the City cannot view itself as an entity separate from the City Council for purposes of complying with the Consent Judgment. The City bound itself to take necessary legislative action when it agreed to the Consent Judgment, which explicitly calls for implementing legislation. Having made that commitment, the City may properly be subjected to the coercive force of civil contempt sanctions until compliance with its commitment occurs. The suggestion that the administrative officials of the City are willing to comply but cannot take legislative action conjures up a scheme of separated powers that does not obtain in Yonkers. For purposes of taking official governmental action, the City of Yonkers is the City Council and vice versa. The Council sets municipal policy, it appoints and can replace the city manager, and it is the principal agency of governance for the City. There is not even a separately elected executive authority. The mayor is a council member elected to the Council in a citywide election; the other council members are elected from districts. Under the circumstances of this case, the Council's defiance of the Consent Judgment and the implementing orders of the District Court is the defiance of the City, and the City, along with the defiant council members, may be subject to civil contempt sanctions. As the Supreme Court has observed, "If a state agency refuses to adhere to a court order, a financial penalty may be the most effective means of insuring compliance." Hutto v. Finney, 437 U.S. 678, 691, 98 S.Ct. 2565, 2573, 57 L.Ed.2d 522 (1978). The same may be said of a city.

The City further contends that even if it can legally be held in civil contempt because of the violation of the July 26 order, it was an abuse of discretion to do so under the circumstances here presented, especially since the District Court had available the alternative of ordering the Affordable Housing Ordinance into effect. We conclude, however, that the District Court neither erred as a matter of law nor exceeded its permissible discretion by using contempt sanctions to coerce the City to fulfill commitments that it had undertaken in the Consent Judgment or by determining that such sanctions were necessary to achieve enactment of the Ordinance. * * *

3. *The Amount of the Monetary Sanctions*

The City contends that the amount of the coercive fines imposed as a remedial sanction for civil contempt is excessive and a violation of the Due Process Clause of the Fifth Amendment and the Excessive Fines Clause of the Eighth Amendment. [The court concludes that neither the Excessive Fines Clause nor the Cruel and Unusual Punishment Clause of the Eighth Amendment apply to coercive contempt sanctions.]

* * * In any event, the law of contempt itself exerts some outer limits on the normally "wide discretion" of a district court to fashion appropriate remedies to secure compliance with its lawful orders.

The fact that a coercive monetary sanction requires payment of a large daily fine does not necessarily render that sanction beyond the discretion of a district court. The Supreme Court has itself selected as an appropriate sanction a coercive fine of $2,800,000 (in 1947 dollars) to be imposed upon a union if it should fail to comply with a district court order within five days. United States v. United Mine Workers, 330 U.S. 258, 305, 67 S.Ct. 677, 702, 91 L.Ed. 884 (1947). * * *

The City of Yonkers has an annual budget of $337 million. The need for a substantial daily fine to coerce compliance is demonstrated by the City's announcement to the District Court of its willingness to pay $30 million to be relieved of its commitment to build the 200 units of public housing. Obviously, the City believes that there is a price it is willing to pay to avoid compliance with the orders of the District Court. The District Court was entitled to establish a schedule of fines that would secure compliance with its orders, and under the circumstances of this case that schedule would have to reach, without undue delay, a cumulative fine significantly above the price the City was willing to pay for noncompliance. * * * At some point, however, the doubling reaches unreasonable proportions. Under the current schedule the fine for day 25 is more than $1 billion; the fine for day 30 is more than $50 billion.

We believe that the doubling exceeds the bounds of the District Court's discretion when the level of each day's fine exceeds $1 million. The present schedule calls for a fine of more than $800,000 on day 14. We will therefore modify the contempt sanction against the City to provide that the fine shall be $1 million per day on day 15 and $1 million per day for every subsequent day of noncompliance.

CONCLUSION

* * * Unless a stay is granted by the Supreme Court or a Justice thereof, our mandate shall issue seven days from the date of this decision and our prior stay of the contempt sanctions shall at that time be vacated. On the date our mandate issues, the fines against each of the four council members shall resume at the level of $500 per day and, if noncompliance continues, each shall be imprisoned, pursuant to paragraph 5 of the Order of July 26, two days after the date our mandate issues. * * *

SPALLONE v. UNITED STATES

Supreme Court of the United States, 1990
493 U.S. 265, 110 S.Ct. 625, 107 L.Ed.2d 644

CHIEF JUSTICE REHNQUIST delivered the opinion of the Court.

* * * Both the city and the councilmembers [who were held in contempt] requested this Court to stay imposition of sanctions pending filing and disposition of petitions for certiorari. We granted a stay as to [the councilmembers (petitioners)], but denied the city's request. 487 U.S. 1251, 109 S.Ct. 14, 101 L.Ed.2d 964 (1988) [Justices Brennan and Marshall dissenting from the grant of the stay]. With the city's daily contempt sanction approaching $1 million per day, the city council finally enacted the Affordable Housing Ordinance on September 9, 1988, by a vote of 5 to 2, petitioners Spallone and Fagan voting no. Because the contempt orders raise important issues about the appropriate exercise of the federal judicial power against individual legislators, we granted certiorari [to the councilmembers but not the city], and now reverse.

II
* * *

Petitioners contend that the District Court's orders violate their rights to freedom of speech under the First Amendment, and they also contend that they are entitled as legislators to absolute immunity for actions taken in discharge of their legislative responsibilities. We find it unnecessary to reach either of these questions, because we conclude that the portion of the District Court's order of July 26 imposing contempt sanctions against the petitioners if they failed to vote in favor of the court-proposed ordinance was an abuse of discretion under traditional equitable principles.

* * * [A]s the Court of Appeals recognized, "in selecting contempt sanctions, a court is obliged to use the 'least possible power adequate to the end proposed.'"

Given that the city had entered a consent judgment committing itself to enact legislation implementing the long-term plan, we certainly cannot say it was an abuse of discretion for the District Court to have chosen contempt sanctions against the city, as opposed to petitioners, as a means of ensuring compliance. The city * * * was a party to the action from the beginning, had been found liable for numerous statutory and constitutional violations, and had been subjected to various elaborate remedial decrees which had been upheld on appeal. Petitioners, the individual city councilmen, on the other hand, were not parties to the action, and they had not been found individually liable for any of the violations upon which the remedial decree was based. * * *

It was the city, in fact, which capitulated. * * * While the District Court could not have been sure in late July that this would be the result, the city's arguments against imposing sanctions on it pointed out the sort of pressure that such sanctions would place on the city. * * *

Only eight months earlier, the District Court had secured compliance with an important remedial order through the threat of bankrupting fines against the city alone. After the city had delayed for several months the adoption of a 1987–1988 Housing Assistance Plan (HAP) vital to the public housing required by * * * the remedial order, the court ordered the city to carry out its obligation within two days. The court set a schedule of contempt fines equal to that assessed for violation of the orders in this case, and recognized that the consequence would be imminent bankruptcy for the city. Later the same day, the city council agreed to support a resolution putting in place an effective HAP and reaffirming the commitment of Yonkers to accept funds to build the 200 units of public housing mandated by * * * the remedial order.[4]

The nub of the matter, then, is whether in the light of the reasonable probability that sanctions against the city would accomplish the desired result, it was within the court's discretion to impose sanctions on the petitioners as well under the circumstances of this case.

In Tenney v. Brandhove, 341 U.S. 367, 71 S.Ct. 783, 95 L.Ed. 1019 (1951), we held that state legislators were absolutely privileged in their legislative acts in an action against them for damages. We applied this same doctrine of legislative immunity to regional legislatures in Lake Country Estates, Inc. v. Tahoe Regional Planning Agency, 440 U.S. 391, 404–405, 99 S.Ct. 1171, 1178–1179, 59 L.Ed.2d 401 (1979), and to actions

---

4. The Solicitor General distinguishes the instant sanctions from those threatened in January 1988, because in this case the city and the city council had indicated by the defeat of a resolution proposed by the court that it "Would not 'voluntarily adopt the legislation contemplated by the [court's orders].'" Before the court threatened sanctions for refusal to adopt the 1987–1988 HAP, however, the city council had twice tabled an initiative to enact the HAP and the court previously had been forced to "deem" HAPs to have been submitted for two previous years. Suffice it to say that the council's conduct with regard to the HAP hardly suggested a willingness to comply "voluntarily."

for both damages and injunctive relief in Supreme Court of Virginia v. Consumers Union of United States, Inc., 446 U.S. 719, 731–734, 100 S.Ct. 1967, 1974–1976, 64 L.Ed.2d 641 (1980). The holdings in these cases do not control the question whether local legislators such as practitioners should be immune from contempt sanctions imposed for failure to vote in favor of a particular legislative bill. But some of the same considerations on which the immunity doctrine is based must inform the District Court's exercise of its discretion in a case such as this. "Freedom of speech and action in the legislature," we observed, "was taken as a matter of course by those who severed the Colonies from the Crown and founded our Nation." *Tenney.*

In perhaps the earliest American case to consider the import of the legislative privilege, the Supreme Judicial Court of Massachusetts, interpreting a provision of the Massachusetts Constitution granting the rights of freedom of speech and debate to state legislators, recognized that "the privilege secured by it is not so much the privilege of the house as an organized body, *as of each individual member composing it, who is entitled to this privilege, even against the declared will of the house.* For he does not hold this privilege at the pleasure of the house; but derives it from the will of the people. . . ." Coffin v. Coffin, 4 Mass. 1, 27 (1808). This theme underlies our cases interpreting the Speech or Debate Clause and the federal common law of legislative immunity, where we have emphasized that any restriction on a legislator's freedom undermines the "public good" by interfering with the rights of the people to representation in the democratic process. *Lake Country Estates*; * * * Sanctions directed against the city for failure to take actions such as required by the consent decree coerce the city legislators and, of course, restrict the freedom of those legislators to act in accordance with their current view of the city's best interests. But we believe there are significant differences between the two types of fines. The imposition of sanctions on individual legislators is designed to cause them to vote, not with a view to the interest of their constituents or of the city, but with a view solely to their own personal interests. Even though an individual legislator took the extreme position or felt that his constituents took the extreme position that even a huge fine against the city was preferable to enacting the Affordable Housing Ordinance, monetary sanctions against him individually would motivate him to vote to enact the ordinance simply because he did not want to be out of pocket financially. Such fines thus encourage legislators, in effect, to declare that they favor an ordinance not in order to avoid bankrupting the city for which they legislate, but in order to avoid bankrupting themselves.

This sort of individual sanction effects a much greater perversion of the normal legislative process than does the imposition of sanctions on the city for the failure of these same legislators to enact an ordinance. In that case, the legislator is only encouraged to vote in favor of an ordinance that he would not otherwise favor by reason of the adverse sanctions imposed on the city. A councilman who felt that his constituents would rather have the city enact the Affordable Housing Ordinance than pay a "bankrupting fine" would be motivated to vote in favor of such an ordinance because the sanctions were a threat to the fiscal solvency of the city for whose welfare he was in part responsible. This is the sort of calculus in which legislators engage regularly.

We hold that the District Court, in view of the "extraordinary" nature of the imposition of sanctions against the individual councilmen, should have proceeded with such contempt sanctions first against the city alone in order to secure compliance with the remedial orders. Only if that approach failed to produce compliance within a reasonable time should the question of imposing contempt sanctions against petitioners even have been considered. * * *

JUSTICE BRENNAN, with whom JUSTICE MARSHALL, JUSTICE BLACKMUN, and JUSTICE STEVENS join, dissenting.

I understand and appreciate the Court's concern about the District Court's decision to impose contempt sanctions against local officials acting in a legislative capacity. We must all hope that no court will ever again face the open and sustained official defiance of established constitutional values and valid judicial orders that prompted Judge Sand's invocation of the contempt power in this manner. But I firmly believe that its availability for such use, in extreme circumstances, is essential. As the District Court was aware: "The issues transcend Yonkers. They go to the very foundation of the system of constitutional government. If Yonkers can defy the orders of a federal court in any case, but especially a civil rights case, because compliance is unpopular, and if that situation is tolerated, then our constitutional system of government fails. The issues before the court this morning are no less significant than that." * * *[3]

II * * *

The Court's disfavor of personal sanctions rests on two premises: (1) Judge Sand should have known when he issued the Contempt Order that there was a "reasonable probability that sanctions against the city [alone] would accomplish the desired result,"; and (2) imposing personal fines "effects a much greater perversion of the normal legislative process than does the imposition of sanctions on the city." Because personal fines were both completely superfluous to and more intrusive than sanctions against

---

3. While [the vote enacting the Housing Ordinance] terminated the contempt sanctions, it by no means heralded a lasting commitment on the part of the city council actually to follow through on the remedial obligations imposed by the Housing Ordinance. Since this date, no new public housing has been built in Yonkers. During the local city council election last November, petitioner Spallone "campaigned [for Mayor] on a pledge to continue the city's resistance to a Federal desegregation order requiring it to build low-income housing in white neighborhoods," N.Y. Times, Nov. 8, 1989, p. 31, col. 5, and Spallone was elected in a "race [that] was widely seen as a referendum on the housing desegregation plan." Petitioners Chema and Fagan were reelected to the council, and the new member filling Spallone's vacated seat also opposes compliance; thus "candidates opposed to the housing plan appea[r] to hold a majority." Whether Yonkers officials will *ever* comply with Judge Sand's orders attempting to remedy Yonkers' longstanding racial segregation remains an open question.

the city alone, the Court reasons, the personal fines constituted an abuse of discretion. Each of these premises is mistaken.

A

While acknowledging that Judge Sand "could not have been sure in late July that this would be the result," the Court confidently concludes that Judge Sand should have been sure enough that fining the city would eventually coerce compliance that he should not have personally fined the councilmembers as well. In light of the information available to Judge Sand in July, the Court's confidence is chimerical. Although the escalating city fines eventually would have seriously disrupted many public services and employment, the Court's failure even to consider the possibility that the councilmembers would maintain their defiant posture despite the threat of fiscal insolvency bespeaks an ignorance of Yonkers' history of entrenched discrimination and an indifference to Yonkers' political reality.

The Court first fails to adhere today to our longstanding recognition that the "district court has firsthand experience with the parties and is best qualified to deal with the 'flinty, intractable realities of day-to-day implementation of constitutional commands.'" Deference to the court's exercise of discretion is particularly appropriate where, as here, the record clearly reveals that the court employed extreme caution before taking the final step of holding the councilmembers personally in contempt. Judge Sand patiently weathered a whirlwind of evasive maneuvers and misrepresentations; considered and rejected alternative means of securing compliance other than contempt sanctions; and carefully considered the ramifications of personal fines. * * *

[T]he Court compounds its error by committing two more. First, the Court turns a blind eye to most of the evidence available to Judge Sand suggesting that, because of the councilmembers' continuing intransigence, sanctions against the city alone might not coerce compliance and that personal sanctions would significantly increase the chance of success. Second, the Court fails to acknowledge that supplementing city sanctions with personal ones likely would secure compliance more promptly, minimizing the overall disruptive effect of the city sanctions on city services generally and long-term compliance with the Consent Decree in particular.

As the events leading up to the Contempt Order make clear, the recalcitrant councilmembers were extremely responsive to the strong segments of their constituencies that were vociferously opposed to racial residential integration. Councilmember Fagan, for example, explained that his vote against the Housing Ordinance required by the Consent Decree "was an act of defiance. The people clearly wanted me to say no to the judge." Councilmember Spallone declared openly that "I will be taking on the judge all the way down the line. I made a commitment to my people and that commitment remains." Moreover, once Yonkers had gained national attention over its refusal to integrate, many residents made it clear to their representatives on the council that they preferred bankrupt martyrdom to integration. As a contemporaneous article observed, "[t]he defiant Councilmen are riding a wave of resentment among their white constituents that is so intense that many insist they are willing to see the city bankrupted...." N.Y.Times, Aug.5, 1988, p.B2, col.4. It thus was not evident that petitioners opposed bankrupting the city; at the very least, capitulation by any individual councilmember was widely perceived as political suicide. As a result, even assuming that each recalcitrant member sought to avoid city bankruptcy, each still had a very strong incentive to play "chicken" with his colleagues by continuing to defy the Contempt Order while secretly hoping that at least one colleague would change his position and suffer the wrath of the electorate. As Judge Sand observed, "[w]hat we have here is competition to see who can attract the greatest notoriety, who will be the political martyr ... *without regard to what is in the best interests of the city of Yonkers.*" (Emphasis added).

Moreover, acutely aware of these political conditions, the city attorney repeatedly warned Judge Sand *not* to assume that the threat of bankruptcy would compel compliance. * * *

The Court's opinion ignores this political reality surrounding the events of July 1988 and instead focuses exclusively on the fact that, eight months earlier, Judge Sand had secured compliance with another remedial order through the threat of city sanctions alone. But this remedial order had required only that the city council adopt a 1987–1988 Housing Assistance Plan, a prerequisite to the city's qualification for federal housing subsidies. In essence, Judge Sand had to threaten the city with contempt fines just to convince the Council to *accept* over $10 million in federal funds. Moreover, the city council capitulated by promising merely to accept the funds any implied suggestion that it ever intended to *use* the money for housing was, of course, proven false by subsequent events. * * *

Moreover, any confidence that city sanctions alone would ever work again was eroded even further by the public outcry against the council's approval of the Consent Decree, which magnified the councilmembers' determination to defy future judicial orders. * * *

The Court, in addition to ignoring all of this evidence before concluding that city sanctions alone would eventually coerce compliance, also inexplicably ignores the fact that imposing personal fines in addition to sanctions against the city would not only help ensure but actually *hasten* compliance. * * * Judge Sand knew that each day the councilmembers remained in contempt, the city would suffer an ever-growing financial drain that threatened not only to disrupt many critical city services but also to frustrate the long-term success of the underlying remedial scheme. * * *

B

The Court purports to bolster its judgment by contending that personal sanctions against city councilmembers effect a greater interference than city sanctions with the " 'interests of . . . local authorities in managing their own affairs, consistent with the Constitution.' "

* * * [T]he Court seems to suggest that personal sanctions constitute a "greater perversion of the normal legislative process" merely because they do not replicate that process' familiar mode of decisionmaking.

But the Court has never evinced an overriding concern for replicating the "normal" decisionmaking process when designing coercive sanctions for state and local executive officials who, like legislators, presumably are guided by their sense of public duty rather than private benefit. While recognizing that injunctions against such executive officials occasionally must be enforced by criminal or civil contempt sanctions of fines or imprisonment, see, e.g., Hutto v. Finney, 437 U.S. 678, 690–691, 98 S.Ct. 2565, 2573–2574, 57 L.Ed.2d 522 (1978), we have never held that fining or even jailing these officials for contempt is categorically more intrusive than fining their governmental entity in order to coerce compliance indirectly. * * * But the Court cannot fairly derive this premise from the principle underlying the doctrine of legislative immunity.

The doctrine of legislative immunity recognizes that, when acting collectively to pursue a vision of the public good through legislation, legislators must be free to represent their constituents "without fear of outside interference" that would result from private lawsuits. Supreme Court of Virginia v. Consumers Union of United States, Inc., 446 U.S. 719, 731, 100 S.Ct. 1967, 1974, 64 L.Ed.2d 641 (1980). Of course, legislators are bound to respect the limits placed on their discretion by the Federal Constitution; they are duty-bound not to enact laws they believe to be unconstitutional, and their laws will have no effect to the extent that courts believe them to be unconstitutional. But when acting "in the sphere of legitimate legislative activity," i.e., formulating and expressing their vision of the public good within self-defined constitutional boundaries legislators are to be "immune from deterrents to the uninhibited discharge of their legislative duty." Private lawsuits threaten to chill robust representation by encouraging legislators to avoid controversial issues or stances in order to protect themselves "not only from the consequences of litigation's results but also from the burden of defending themselves." *Supreme Court of Virginia*. To encourage legislators best to represent their constituents' interests, legislators must be afforded immunity from private suit.

But once a federal court has issued a valid order to remedy the effects of a prior, specific constitutional violation, the representatives are no longer "acting in a field where legislators traditionally have power to act."[9] At this point, the Constitution itself imposes an overriding definition of the "public good," and a court's valid command to obey constitu-

---

9. I do not mean to suggest that public policy concerns may play no role in designing the scope or content of the underlying remedial order. When each of a variety of different remedial programs would fully remedy the constitutional violation, for example, a district court should take into account relevant and important policy concerns voiced by government defendants in choosing among such remedies. * * *

tional dictates is not subject to override by any countervailing preferences of the polity, no matter how widely and ardently shared. Local legislators, for example, may not frustrate valid remedial decrees merely because they or their constituents would rather allocate public funds for other uses. More to the point here, legislators certainly may not defy court-ordered remedies for racial discrimination merely because their constituents prefer to maintain segregation: * * * Defiance at this stage results, in essence, in a perpetuation of the very constitutional violation at which the remedy is aimed.[11] Hence, once Judge Sand found that the city (through acts of its council) had engaged in a pattern and practice of racial discrimination in housing and had issued a valid remedial order, the city councilmembers became obliged to respect the limits thereby placed on their legislative independence.

* * * Moreover, even if the Court's characterization of personal fines against legislators as "perverse" were persuasive, it would still represent a myopic view of the relevant remedial inquiry. To the extent that equitable limits on federal courts' remedial power are designed to protect against unnecessary judicial intrusion into state or local affairs, it was obviously appropriate for Judge Sand to have considered the fact that the city's accrual of fines would have quickly disrupted every aspect of the daily operation of local government. Particularly when these broader effects are considered, the Court's pronouncement that fining the city is categorically less intrusive than fining the legislators personally is untenable. * * *

III

The Court's decision today that Judge Sand abused his remedial discretion by imposing personal fines simultaneously with city fines creates no new principle of law; indeed, it invokes no principle of any sort. * * * I worry that the Court's message will have the unintended effect of emboldening recalcitrant officials continually to test the ultimate reach of the remedial authority of the federal courts, thereby postponing the day when all public officers finally accept that "the responsibility of those who exercise power in a democratic government is not to reflect inflamed

---

11. See Columbus Bd. of Education v. Penick, 443 U.S. 449, 459, 99 S.Ct. 2941, 2947, 61 L.Ed.2d 666 (1979)(once court orders desegregation remedy, "[e]ach instance of a failure or refusal to fulfill this affirmative duty continues the violation of the Fourteenth Amendment"). Put another way, remedial defiance by the legislature circumvents the structural protections afforded the citizenry from unconstitutional government behavior by a multi-branch review process, by allowing the legislature de facto to override the court's ruling in a particular case that its behavior violates the Fourteenth Amendment. *Cf.* Cooper v. Aaron, 358 U.S. 1, 18, 78 S.Ct. 1401, 1409, 3 L.Ed.2d 5 (1958)("If the legislatures of the several states may, at will, annul the judgments of the courts of the United States, and destroy the rights acquired under those judgments, the constitution itself becomes a solemn mockery")(quoting United States v. Peters, 5 Cranch 115, 136, 3 L.Ed. 53 (1809)).

Indeed, even were the councilmembers to maintain that the Housing Ordinance they were required to enact itself violated the Constitution, for example, by mandating unjustified racial preferences, the members would nevertheless be bound by a court order considering yet rejecting their constitutional objection. See *Cooper, supra,* at 18, 78 S.Ct. at 1409 ("[F]ederal judiciary is supreme in the exposition of the law of the Constitution" in case adjudication). But in any event, the councilmembers raised no serious substantive objections, constitutional or otherwise, to the Ordinance (which after all was based on the city council-approved Consent Decree).

public feeling but to help form its understanding." Cooper v. Aaron, 358 U.S. 1, 26, 78 S.Ct. 1401, 1413, 3 L.Ed.2d 5 (1958) (Frankfurter, J., concurring).

NOTES ON TACTICS TO OVERRIDE LEGISLATIVE DECISIONS

1. *Yonkers* and *Spallone* illustrate a number of tactics to get unwilling governments or government officials to act and their legal and practical limitations. For a survey of others, see Daryl J. Levinson, Collective Sanctions, 56 Stan.L.Rev. 345 (2003).

2. *The court could order the government to act and use the contempt power to make it do so.* The City of Yonkers was ordered to act under a consent decree and was held in contempt for failing to comply.

(a) *The impossibility defense to contempt.* Should the city have been found in contempt if it had a separate legislature and executive and the legislature had not consented to the decree?

Delaware Valley Citizens' Council for Clean Air v. Pennsylvania, 678 F.2d 470 (3d Cir.1982), cert. denied, 459 U.S. 969, 103 S.Ct. 298, 74 L.Ed.2d 280 (*Delaware Valley I*) upheld a finding of contempt against the Commonwealth of Pennsylvania over its objection that it could not comply with a consent judgment because the legislature had not appropriated the necessary funds. The court reasoned that the Pennsylvania Department of Justice,

> members of which were signatories of this decree, has the exclusive power to compromise and settle lawsuits against the Commonwealth.
>
> * * * Neither can there be any objection to holding the Commonwealth to the terms of the decree based upon the eleventh amendment * * *. That amendment does not apply to suits brought by the United States against a state. Moreover entry of a consent judgment is a waiver of any eleventh amendment immunity that the Commonwealth might have earlier wished to claim.
>
> Because the Commonwealth, including all its branches, is bound by the consent judgment, the argument of inability to comply rings hollow. * * * [T]hose Commonwealth officials sitting in the General Assembly certainly are not incapable of insuring the Commonwealth's compliance.

Subsequently, the Pennsylvania courts held that the state officials lacked authority to enter into the consent decree and enjoined compliance with the federal order. The Third Circuit declared the state court decree of no effect because the federal decision validating the consent decree was res judicata. Delaware Valley Citizens' Council for Clean Air v. Pennsylvania, 755 F.2d 38 (3d Cir.1985), cert. denied, 474 U.S. 819, 106 S.Ct. 67, 88 L.Ed.2d 54 (*Delaware Valley II*). In a concurring opinion, Judge Stern concluded that the state decree was invalid under the Supremacy Clause. See also Badgley v. Santacroce, 800 F.2d 33, 38 (2d Cir.1986), cert. denied, 479 U.S. 1067, 107 S.Ct. 955, 93 L.Ed.2d 1003 (1987)("Even if a state court would hold the defendants in contempt for refusing to house inmates [as ordered] or if compliance would otherwise violate state law, Supremacy Clause considerations require that the judgment of the federal court be respected. * * * In any attempt by a state court to hold defendants in contempt for taking actions required by the judgment of the District Court, that judgment would provide a complete defense.")

(b) *The immunity of the state.* If the defendants are from state rather than city government and the plaintiffs are private persons, then the judge has to consider the eleventh amendment immunity of the state. In this regard, the quote from *Hutto v. Finney* in the Second Circuit opinion in *Yonkers* is somewhat misleading. *Hutto* did not penalize the state for failing to obey an order directed to it but rather awarded attorney's fees that would be paid out of Department of Correction's funds on the grounds that the state officials had litigated in bad faith. The underlying order in the case was directed against state officials rather than the state or one of its agencies. "Even if it might have been better form to omit the reference to the Department of Correction [in the award of fees], the use of that language is surely not reversible error." 437 U.S. at 692–93, 98 S.Ct. at 2574, 57 L.Ed.2d at 535.

(c) *The uncertain effect on recalcitrant officials of holding the government in contempt.* Then–Mayor of Yonkers Nicholas Wasicsko said, before the Supreme Court stayed the contempt sanctions against the Councilmen, that "if anything forces compliance, it will be the Councilmen in the cooler," rather than the fines against the City. New York Times, Aug. 27, 1988 at A1, 28. The sanctions against the government itself may or may not translate into action by the recalcitrant officials.

> YONKERS, Sept. 8—As contempt fines against Yonkers passed $1 million and one-fourth of the city work force faced lay-offs in two days, even steadfast opponents of a court-ordered housing desegregation plan seemed jolted today, and pressure grew for city officials to resolve the crisis. * * *
>
> The People's Union, a citizens' group that has supported the Council's resistance, reversed itself * * *.
>
> A councilman blocking the housing plan, Nicholas V. Longo, said the escalating fines and impending layoffs were prompting more calls for compliance. "Obviously, when the effects of the situation hit people directly, moods change," he said. "I mean the city worker who was employed yesterday, but who might be unemployed Monday has concerns. And I can't say I blame him. The same is true for residents without services."
>
> But at the same time, he added, "there are residents who feel that between the judge and the financial control board, they are being bludgeoned with a baseball bat, and their resolve only gets stronger" to resist the order.

New York Times, Sept. 9, 1988 at A1.

Some citizens will blame hardships not on the recalcitrant officials but on the judge or the plaintiffs. As one Yonkers councilman who resisted compliance said, "[c]learly the blood is on the judge's hands."

Early in the morning of September 9—although the court was willing to view it as late in the day on September 8 for the purpose of computing contempt fines—Councilmen Chema and Longo changed their votes so that the required legislation was enacted by a vote of 5 to 2. N.Y. Times, Sept. 10, 1988, at A1; New York Times, Sept. 11, 1988, at A1. The vote took place after the Supreme Court had stayed the contempt sanctions against the councilmembers. In response to the Supreme Court's decision, Mr. Spallone, who had been elected mayor while the case was pending, said that he and his allies on the city council would try to use the decision as a means of opposing implementation of Judge Sand's orders. New York Times, Jan. 11, 1990, at B9. Subsequently, the Spallone-led City Council fired the City's outside law firm, which said the City had no grounds left upon which to fight compliance, and hired new lawyers, including the lawyer for the plaintiffs in *Martin v. Wilks* (discussed supra at p. 361). New York Times, March 9, 1990. Was the *Spallone* majority correct in concluding that Judge Sand should have been reasonably sure that fines against the city alone would eventually bring compliance?

(d) *Collecting sanctions from a government*. Still another Yonkers councilman who resisted compliance said, "I say to [Judge Sand] 'if you want the money, come and get it.'" N.Y. Times, Sept. 10, 1988, at A1. The Yonkers corporation counsel responded that he assumed that the judge "would direct that the check be issued without the Council's OK, or that he could suspend the law making it illegal to transfer funds without the Council's vote—or he could move against the assets of the city." Accord, Hook v. Arizona, 907 F.Supp. 1326 (D.Ariz.)(state statute blocking payment of special master's fees was unconstitutional under Supremacy Clause), aff'd, 73 F.3d 369 (9th Cir.1995).

3. *The court could take the action itself*. In *Yonkers*, this would have meant the court declaring that the legislation was enacted by its fiat, just as the district court in *Jenkins*, in essence, enacted tax and appropriations legislation. Why do the City and Councilmen prefer the court to take the action? Why does the court want them to act? Which is a better approach? Consider what Judge Sand said on this point:

> [T]here does have to come a moment of truth, a moment of reckoning, a moment when the City of Yonkers seeks not to become the national symbol of defiance to civil rights and to heap shame upon shame upon itself, but to recognize its obligation to conform to the laws of the land and not step by step, order by order, but in the way in which any responsible community concerned about the welfare of its citizens functions. That is not going to be accomplished by this court adopting the ordinance.

Yonkers, 856 F.2d at 451.

In contrast to the fierce resistance to the 200 units of housing, Yonkers complied without great fanfare with extensive orders from Judge Sand to desegregate its 20,000 student school system. One explanation for the difference is that the schools are run by officials appointed for five-year terms, while action on the housing had to be taken by council members elected for two-year terms. Some council members made careers by feeding the flames of resistance, but then found that they could not back down without destroying their political careers. Note, Implementing Structural Injunctions: Getting a

SEC. C   ENFORCEMENT OF THE DECREE   405

Remedy When Local Officials Resist, 80 Geo.L.J. 2227 (1992), concludes that judges should take direct action. It argues that the alternative of ordering the legislators to act is fraught with first amendment and immunity problems and that the other alternative of sanctioning the government often hurts those who should benefit from the injunction.

4. *Appointing a receiver to take the action.* In *Yonkers*, Judge Sand considered appointing an Affordable Housing Commission, which would, in essence, have been a receiver. Why did the city resist this option while wanting the judge to take the action himself? Why did the judge resist this option? After the City Council backed down, Judge Sand did appoint a Fair Housing Opportunity Commission to administer parts of the decree.

5. *The court could order officials to act.* In *Yonkers*, this involved, of course, ordering the council members to vote for the required legislation and holding those who failed to do so in contempt.

(a) *Intrusiveness.* Coercing the officials is more intrusive than coercing the government because the court is requiring not only a change in the city's law but also action on the part of the legislators. Given the admonition that courts should do no more than necessary to put the plaintiffs in their rightful position, what, if anything, justifies this extra degree of intrusion?

The majority in *Spallone* found that Judge Sand went further than necessary to put the plaintiffs in their rightful position by sanctioning the council members as well as the city. Is sanctioning the councilmembers more intrusive than sanctioning the city alone? If sanctioning the councilmembers was more intrusive, was that intrusiveness justified by the need to avoid a fiscal drain on the city? If Justice Brennan is correct that there is no "independent value" to using the legislative process to implement a decree, why not just have the district court adopt the ordinance for the city, as discussed in note 3? Does *Spallone* mean that, where local executive officials refuse to obey an injunction, a district court must try sanctioning the local government before sanctioning the officials?

Spallone raises a number of questions as to how courts should decide when a decree or sanctions enforcing it are too broad. What degree of deference should an appellate court give a trial court's determination that a more intrusive decree is necessary to achieve compliance? If the least intrusive decree is insufficient to bring compliance, in what increments may a trial court become more intrusive? For example, if the least intrusive sanction is to fine Yonkers $100 if the Council does not enact the ordinance, as Judge Sand did, but the City does not respond, should the trial court double the fine each day, as Judge Sand also did? It would be less intrusive, would it not, to increase the fine by smaller amounts or to increase it less frequently?

(b) *First Amendment.* The court of appeals suggests that voting lacks first amendment significance because it is action rather than speech (are you convinced?) and that, in any event, the first amendment is no excuse for breaking the law. Two cases struck down on first amendment grounds legislation that commanded the members of inferior governmental bodies to vote in a particular way. Clarke v. United States, 886 F.2d 404 (D.C.Cir.1989); Miller v. Town of Hull, 878 F.2d 523 (1st Cir.), cert. denied, 493 U.S. 976, 110 S.Ct. 501, 107 L.Ed.2d 504 (1989). Both reasoned that the legislature could have simply enacted what it wanted rather than commanding others to vote for it. In *Clarke*, Congress enacted legislation that would stop the District of Columbia from spending any money unless the members of the District of Columbia Council voted for a measure that would weaken the District's prohibitions on discrimination against homosexuals. *Clarke* attempts to distinguish *Yonkers* on the basis that, there, "the city's failure to provide the housing was itself an illegal act" while in *Clarke* the refusal of the Council to adopt the measure was not illegal. So would *Clarke* have upheld the statute if Congress had made failure to vote for the measure a felony, rather than crippling the District's government? Justice Brennan argues that there is no first amendment problem in ordering a legislator to vote because voting pursuant to a decree is purely ministerial. Do you agree?

(c) *Legislative immunity.* The court of appeals suggests that there is no legislative immunity from being ordered to take actions necessary to implement a remedial decree. It invokes *Milliken II's* holding that, under the eleventh amendment, state officials could be forced to provide funds for prospective action. But the addressees of the *Milliken II* order were not state legislators; the issue was not whether the legislators could be forced to appropriate money but whether executive officials could be forced to use state money to comply. The possibility that the Michigan legislature would not appropriate the funds did not come up. In a broader sense, *Milliken II* stands for the proposition that there are exceptions to eleventh amendment immunity, not that court orders can countermand immunities. The court of appeals held that there was no legislative immunity because the council had voted to bind the city to the consent decree. Should Spallone, who dissented in the original vote, be bound? If not, should the members who changed their votes be bound? For an argument that consent degrees cannot abrogate legislative immunity, see Comment, The Effects of Consent Decrees on Local Legislative Immunity, 56 U.Chi.L.Rev. 1121 (1989).

The *Spallone* majority seems to conclude that state legislators are immune from injunctions when acting in their legislative capacity, while the *Spallone* dissent concludes that neither state nor local legislators should be immune from injunctions on the basis that they have no discretion to violate the Constitution. Should it make any difference that the decree orders the legislators to desist from an unconstitutional act or to take action needed to repair a past violation? Was the violation of Judge Sand's decree also a violation of the Constitution?

Subsequent to *Spallone*, the Supreme Court held that local legislators acting in their legislative capacity are entitled to the same absolute immunity previously accorded federal, state, and regional legislators. Bogan v. Scott–Harris, 523 U.S. 44, 118 S.Ct. 966, 140 L.Ed.2d 79 (1998). The plaintiff in that case contended that the legislators were not really acting in their legislative capacities because what they did was enact a budget eliminating the city department of which she was the sole employee. They were, it was alleged, firing her, and for discriminatory reasons. The Supreme Court held that enacting a budget differed fundamentally from simply firing her; terminating her employment would have left the budget line to be filled by another.

6. *Oust the recalcitrant officials.* In *Yonkers*, the judge did not claim judicial power to oust elected officials from office but rather created a situation in which the Governor would have the power to oust them under the terms of special provisions of state law and the city charter.

7. *Toss the defendants a bone.* In *Yonkers*, the councilmen who resisted the decree had vowed to their constituents to never surrender. When some of them began to have second thoughts in the face of the court's contempt power, their previous vows made it embarrassing to back down. So they urged the court to modify the decree in some way favorable to the city so they could claim that they had won something. They were less interested in the substance or size of the court's concession than in its symbolic value. The court refused to toss them a bone in the form of any sort of concession, which prolonged the drama and hard feelings. What did the court gain from its unyielding position? What should the court have done?

8. *Update on the Yonkers case.* In December 1990, a state trial judge ruled that the four council members who voted to defy Judge Sand were liable to the City under a state statute that makes government officials liable for illegal acts that waste public assets. New York's Appellate Division, however, held that the actions taken by the defendant council members "lack[ed] the necessary element of collusion, fraud, or personal gain," necessary for the attachment of personal liability on the Council members. Duffy v. Longo, 207 A.D.2d 860, 616 N.Y.S.2d 760 (1994), appeal dismissed, 86 N.Y.2d 779, 655 N.E.2d 708, 631 N.Y.S.2d 611 (1995).

After the Council backed down, Judge Sand changed the composition of those who would occupy the 200 units of public housing in a direction favoring existing residents of the neighborhoods by giving some preference to current occupants of public housing who had been model tenants. Occupancy began without more high drama, but with some tension. New York Times, June 27, 1993, at A25.

Mayor Nicholas Wasicsko, elected in 1987 at the age of 28 and a former student of one of the casebook's original authors, was defeated in his bid for reelection in 1989 by Spallone because Wasicsko favored obeying the injunction. In 1991, a candidate supported by Wasicsko defeated Spallone, and Wasicsko was elected to the City Council. In 1993, he ran for City Council President and lost, which meant he would be out of office again. The following month Wasicsko committed suicide. New York Times, Oct. 31, 1993.

The parties finally settled the housing segregation dispute 27 years after the initiation of the case. The consent plan Judge Sand approved in 2007 guaranteed that 425 owner-occupied homes, 315 private rental dwellings and 200 public housing units in Yonkers will remain affordable for at least 30 years. The city had previously settled the related school segregation claims in 2002. In reflecting on the case, Judge Sand stated: "Any efforts not to comply with the law are counterproductive to the image of the community and its well-being. The millions and millions of dollars that the City of Yonkers has spent ... could have gone to better things for the community." One of the most vocal community opponents of the integration effort commented more recently: "In a sense, the desegregation plan did work. It didn't spoil our neighborhoods; we had a lot of nice people who lived there. It wasn't the horror that we all thought it was going to be." Fernanda Santos, After 27 Years, Yonkers Housing Desegregation Battle Ends Quietly in Manhattan Court, N.Y.Times B5, May 2, 2007; Fernanda Santos, Yonkers Settles 27–Year Battle Over Desegregation, N.Y.Times A22, April 20, 2007. For a journalist's account of the events surrounding the public housing case, see Lisa Belkin, Show Me a Hero (1999); and Jonathan L. Entin, Learning from Yonkers: On Race, Class, Housing, and Courts, 44 How.L.J. 375 (2001) (review of Belkin's book).

Yonkers and *Spallone* suggest the fragility of the courts' authority, which is the subject of the following reading:

ALEXANDER BICKEL, THE LEAST DANGEROUS BRANCH
254–268 (1st ed.1962, 2d ed.1986)

* * *

POLITICAL WARFARE AND THE USES OF DECISIONS OF COURTS

The initial reaction to the Court's decision [in *Brown*], both in 1954 and in 1955, when the deliberate-speed decree came down, augured very well indeed for full acceptance, following a period of adjustment that would itself do no violence to principle. As I have indicated, the border states and especially the great border cities, as well as other marginal areas, began immediate compliance, even before issuance of the decree. In the rest of the South, the situation was this. There were some uncompromising, vaguely defiant comments * * *. But they were highly exceptional. * * * Senator Russell Long, of Louisiana, while regretting the decision, added: "My oath requires me to accept it as law.... I urge all Southern officials to avoid any sort of rash or hasty action."

* * * [A] turning point came—distinctly and unmistakably, at least in retrospect—on March 11, 1956, with issuance of the Congressional Manifesto of that date by nearly the full membership of the southern delegation. This document was a calculated declaration of political war against the Court's decision. * * *

> We regard the decision of the Supreme Court in the school cases as clear abuse of judicial power. It climaxes a trend in the Federal judiciary undertaking to legislate, in derogation of the authority of Congress, and to encroach upon the reserved rights of the states and the people. * * *

[The Manifesto] concluded as follows:

> We commend the motives of those states which have declared the intention to resist forced integration by any lawful means. * * *

Even though we constitute a minority in the present Congress, we have full faith that a majority of the American people ... will in time demand that the reserved rights of the states and of the people be made secure against judicial usurpation.

We pledge ourselves to use all lawful means to bring about a reversal of this decision which is contrary to the Constitution and to prevent the use of force in its implementation.

In this trying period, as we all seek to right this wrong, we appeal to our people not to be provoked by the agitators and trouble-makers invading our states and to scrupulously refrain from disorder and lawless acts.

From the stand taken in this document, all else flowed. With few exceptions, moderate positions previously assumed were abandoned throughout the states that had been part of the Confederacy. * * * The southern leaders understood and acted upon an essential truth, which we do not often have occasion to observe and which dawned on the southerners themselves somewhat late; hence the contrast between initial reactions and what followed. The Supreme Court's law, the southern leaders realized, could not in our system prevail—not merely in the very long run, but within the decade—if it ran counter to deeply felt popular needs or convictions, or even if it was opposed by a determined and substantial minority and received with indifference by the rest of the country. This, in the end, is how and why judicial review is consistent with the theory and practice of political democracy. This is why the Supreme Court is a court of last resort presumptively only. No doubt, in the vast majority of instances the Court prevails—not as a result of any sort of tacit referendum; rather, it just prevails, its authority is accepted more or less automatically, and no matter if grudgingly. It takes concerted effort at some risk, and hence not a little daring, to fight back, and then there is no guaranty of victory, as the Progressives and Populists found out. But given passion, vigor, and hard-headedness, it can be done and has been done. * * *

The southern purpose, therefore, was to organize and maintain unbroken the ranks of a determined and politically entrenched minority, and to test the convictions of the rest of the country. In opening this post-judgment colloquy, a colloquy searching not expedients of accommodation and compromise but the validity of the judgment itself, and in attempting this different sort of reprise, the southern leaders applied a lesson that Lincoln had taught. * * *

He and the Republican party, and, as it turned out, a goodly majority of the nation were opposed to the Supreme Court's decision in 1857 in the *Dred Scott Case.* * * * In the debates with Stephen A. Douglas in 1858, Lincoln said that he was against this decision, that he thought it wrong, that he feared its consequences, that he deemed it altogether deplorable. Douglas, on the other hand, without admitting that he necessarily thought the decision right, dwelt heavily on the argument that "whoever resists the final decision of the highest judicial tribunal aims a deadly blow at our whole republican system of government." * * *

Lincoln never advocated disobedience of judicial decrees while they were in force. * * * But he did offer resistance to the principle, in the hope and with the expectation of overturning it.

* * *

One need hardly add that all this, summed up in only somewhat milder form in Lincoln's First Inaugural, was heresy against the theoretical basis of *Marbury v. Madison*. Public officers swear to support the Constitution of the United States, and, according to *Marbury v. Madison*, as Douglas was quick to point out, the Constitution is in the Supreme Court's keeping and must be supported as declared by the Court. There can be no pursuit of contrary "political rules" except in contravention of the oath to support the Constitution, meaning the oath to support the Supreme Court's invocations of it. But that is *Marbury v. Madison*; it does not describe the system, as it is or has been. * * * [O]n the supreme occasion, when the system is forced to find ultimate self-consistency, the principle of self-rule must prevail. * * *

[Professor Bickel points out that Presidents Andrew Jackson and Franklin Roosevelt took positions similar to Lincoln's.]

Following the Lincoln–Jackson–Roosevelt tradition, southern politicians were perfectly within their rights in declining to accept the Court's decision in the *School Segregation Cases* as a political rule. They were within their rights in deploring it and arguing against it. They could hope to convert public opinion. They could vote for laws that failed to advance its principle and even failed to concur with it. They could refuse to consider the issue settled and could relitigate it at every opportunity that the judicial process offered, and of course it offers a thousand and one. * * * If they succeeded in turning public opinion, they could realistically look to the day when the principle announced by the Court would be rescinded or allowed to lapse without enforcement. * * *

Success has eluded the southern leaders, but narrowly. For a moment it seemed within reach, while the main body of northern opinion, led by President Eisenhower, mounted no defense. The chief response that was made was in terms of *Marbury v. Madison*; the President sounded almost verbatim like Stephen A. Douglas. This was an argument that could not be won—at the most it could be brought to a standstill. The Court, said the southerners just about unanswerably, had botched the job that Marshall describes in *Marbury v. Madison*; pretty obviously, the Court had performed some other function, not the one there indicated. But under *Marbury v. Madison*, ran the reply on a parallel rail, the Court is empowered to lay down the law of the land, and citizens must accept it uncritically. Whatever the Court lays down is right, even if wrong, because the Court and only the Court speaks in the name of the Constitution. Its doctrines are not to be questioned; indeed, they are hardly a fit subject for comment. The Court has spoken. The Court must be obeyed. There must be good order and peaceable submission to lawful authority. * * *

The debate was at a standstill. Both sides were right, both sides were wrong, and it didn't matter. The decisive issue, to which the southerners amply devoted their attention, going beyond the fictions of *Marbury v. Madison*, was whether what the Court had done was right or wrong, good or bad. As to this, President Eisenhower had nothing to say, except for one or two very damaging, though sheepish, admissions that he entertained some doubts of his own. And so the real point of the southern attack was missed. At best, the President—and, for its own reasons, also the Congress—politely declined the Court's invitation to join with it in ensuring the success of its now hazardous undertaking. At best, the President made a faint attempt to support the Court by drawing on *its* resources, *its* prestige and mystique, not by bringing to its aid those of the political institutions. This constituted no particular support at all. No wonder the southerners thought for a season that success was within their grasp. No one had joined the decisive issue with them. There was hardly a contest.

Having scented victory, the southern leaders, or at least a sufficient number of them, sought to assure it by turning from litigation and agitation to direct action by the use of mobs. Thus they abandoned the tradition in which they had been acting. For this no support could be found in the position of Lincoln or of those who preceded and followed him. * * * The action at Little Rock * * * raised in much bolder fashion than before the issue of order, the peace of the community as against mob rule, and it caused President Eisenhower to react. Too much cannot be made of this, however. The Executive is obliged to aid in the enforcement of specific judicial decrees that have been flouted. It is a matter of maintaining the peace. But this is an indifferent omen, at best, for the endurance of the Court's principle, if the merits of the decision are not themselves defended as right and good; and Mr. Eisenhower did not so defend them. For enforcement is a crisis of the system, not its norm. When the law summons force to its aid, it demonstrates, not its strength and stability, but its weakness and impermanence. The mob, like revolution, is an ambiguous fact. The mob is bad when it is wrong; it may be heroic when it is right. It is surely a deeply ingrained American belief that mobs of our people do not generally gather to oppose good laws, and the very fact of the mob, therefore, puts the law in question. * * *

But there was another factor in play, and it roused northern opinion, whose latent temper the southern leaders had gravely misestimated. It is this factor that lent decisive consequence to the riots in Little Rock, abetted by [riots and confrontations elsewhere]. Compulsory segregation, like states' rights and like "The Southern Way of Life," is an abstraction and, to a good many people, a neutral or sympathetic one. These riots, which were brought instantly, dramatically, and literally home to the American people, showed what it means concretely. Here were grown men and women furiously confronting their enemy: two, three, a half dozen scrubbed, starched, scared, and incredibly brave colored children. The moral bankruptcy, the shame of the thing, was evident. Television, it should be emphasized, as in the Army–McCarthy hearings, played a most significant role. There was an unforgettable scene, for example, in one CBS newscast from New Orleans, of a white mother fairly foaming at the mouth with the effort to rivet her distracted little boy's attention and teach him how to hate. And repeatedly, the ugly, spitting curse, NIGGER! The effect, achieved on an unprecedented number of people with unprecedented speed, must have been something like what used to happen to individuals (the young Lincoln among them) at the sight of an actual slave auction, or like the slower influence on northern opinion of the fighting in "Bleeding Kansas" in 1854–55.

And so the southern leaders had overplayed their hand. Mob action led to the mobilization of northern opinion in support of the Court's decision—not merely because the mob is disorderly, but because it concretized the abstraction of racism, somewhat in the manner in which the cases and controversies in whose context the Court evolves its principles concretize all abstractions. * * * One of those supreme occasions had been brought about when a decisive reprise is open to the political branches; it was for them to make the Court's decision their rule of political action, or not to do so, and thus to make or break the decision itself. The political branches * * * had independently, on their own responsibility, to speak their moral approval of the Court's decision, to support it by drawing on their own resources, and to act in pursuance of it. This was one time when hiding behind the judges' skirts would not do. The political institutions had a decision of their own to make. * * *

NOTES

1. Professor Bickel points out that the courts are vulnerable when the political branches fail to support them on the merits. This can occur not just in the great cases and in the past, but in less spectacular cases and today. In Yonkers in 1988, key opinion leaders did not support the courts on the merits.

> [T]he state's most prominent leaders have been less than outspoken. "I feel all alone," said Mayor Nicholas C. Wasicsko of Yonkers, who supports the [court's] plan but says he does not have enough clout to influence its opponents. "I need someone who has stature or patronage or whatever else it is that would get recalcitrant members [of the City Council, which has blocked implementation] to reconsider."
>
> Mr. Wasicsko says that since the contempt ruling * * * he has heard little from officials, including Andrew P. O'Rourke, the Westchester County Executive; Attorney General Robert Abrams, and Senator Alfonse M. D'Amato. Senator Daniel Patrick Moynihan has said that the court must be obeyed and has offered to help Yonkers, but has not played a prominent role.
>
> Even [New York City Mayor Edward] Koch, who has made headlines with his remarks about foreign countries, has had little to say on the Yonkers case.

[Governor Mario] Cuomo has sent what has been judged—unfairly, he suggests—to have been a mixed message, and so has John Cardinal O'Connor of the Roman Catholic Archdiocese of New York. The Cardinal has both criticized the plan and assailed the situation.

The Governor said yesterday that "the law is the law."

* * * "I am eager to help," Mr. Cuomo said. "But this is before the Court of Appeals."

Then again, Mr. Cuomo did not wait for the resolution of many court actions before taking a position on Shoreham, the nuclear power plant on Long Island that he wants to close. * * *

Joyce Purnick, Little is Said and Less Is Done About Yonkers, New York Times, Aug. 25, 1988 at B1.

2. Professor Bickel's account of the struggle to implement *Brown* divides into three periods: (1) immediately after the *Brown I* and *Brown II* decisions when there was little resistance, (2) the time of growing resistance that followed the Congressional Manifesto, and (3) the backlash against segregation after Little Rock. One might generalize to say enforcement of very controversial court injunctions decisions goes through three periods: (1) presumptive validity, (2) resistance by those opposed, and (3) a remand of the merits to the court of public opinion. The first and third periods are then windows of opportunity to implement the injunction. *Jenkins* and *Yonkers* can be seen as efforts to implement injunctions during the first of these periods—in other words, to trade on the presumptive validity of judicial decisions. *Virginia v. West Virginia* and *Welsch v. Likins* can be seen as efforts to remand to public opinion. Which approach is better? Note, however, that even in *Jenkins* and *Yonkers* the district judges did not go directly from injunction to extremely intrusive action, but, as Professor Goldstein suggests (p. 300), pursued a "scenario of escalating intrusiveness."

In the deliberations leading up to the issuance of the unanimous opinion in *Brown I*, Justice Jackson, who personally opposed segregation, urged an outcome similar to that in *Virginia v. West Virginia*—that the Court state that Congress has the power under section 5 of the fourteenth amendment to outlaw school segregation and declining, in the absence of such legislative action, to hold school segregation an unconstitutional act because the courts lack the administrative machinery to administer a remedy. Richard Kluger, Simple Justice 606–11 (2004 ed.). If a judge believes that the courts cannot offer an effective remedy, is it appropriate to decline to reach the issue of liability?

3. Barry Friedman, When Rights Encounter Reality: Enforcing Federal Remedies, 65 S.Cal.L.Rev. 735 (1992), argues that courts often intentionally give the political branches a voice in not only how, but also the extent to which constitutional wrongs are remedied. He cites the role given to Congress in deciding whether there shall be private causes of action for damages and in deciding the scope of governmental and official immunity. He also cites the opportunity that *Spallone* gives legislators to resist injunctions, although at a heavy cost to their constituents. Professor Friedman conceives of constitutional remedies as a dialogue between the courts and the political branches.

Although "dialogue" is an appealing concept, this remedial dialogue might leave voters in the dark as to who is responsible for what government does. For example, some might conclude that the Supreme Court in *Jenkins II* was less than forthright concerning whether the courts get to call the shots on how much school tax is levied, as Professor Friedman points out. Similarly, the Alabama Supreme Court issued an opinion that could have confused voters about who was responsible for school budgets in that state. Opinion of the Justices, 624 So.2d 107 (1993). After a trial court ruled that the state's funding of education produced results that were below state constitutional minima, the state senate asked the state supreme court whether the state legislature was constitutionally required to increase the budget. The court answered yes, which would help to deflect political heat from legislators for the fiscal consequences of increased school spending. The court's answer was curious because the trial court had not yet formulated any remedy and the state legislature was not a defendant. The speaker of the state assembly was a defendant, but he sought to align himself with the plaintiffs.

4. While the "Battle of Little Rock" and cases like *Jenkins II* and *Spallone* are fascinating and useful for exploring the outer limits of the remedial power, they are not typical of injunction cases against governments. According to Ross Sandler and David Schoenbrod, Democracy by Decree (2003), New York City is the target of many structural injunctions and consent decrees (as are many other municipalities). Most of the injunctions enforce state or federal statutory rights rather than constitutional rights. The cost of implementing the more important injunctions is equal to a quarter of the city's tax revenues. The impact on New York's truly discretionary spending is even larger because the bulk of the city's budget is made up of such necessities as paying interest on the city's debt and the salaries of essential employees. Although New York City does not resist compliance in the sense that neighboring Yonkers did, it rarely succeeds in fully complying with the decrees. One reason is that the statutes being enforced cumulatively require the city to do more than its resources allow. A question that such injunctions raise is who gets to make city policy and to whom are they accountable. The statutes are typically unfunded mandates, in which state and federal legislators have made large promises to be fulfilled by local government. The policy choices about the extent to which these promises will be kept, and how, are typically made in consent decrees. Frequently, elected officials consent to decrees under which the big expenses come after they are out of office. As discussed earlier in this chapter at p. 269, it can be difficult for the next official to modify the decree. E.g., Benjamin v. Malcolm, 156 F.R.D. 561 (S.D.N.Y.1994) (refusing to allow the new mayor of New York City to alter his predecessor's agreement concerning where meals for pre-trial detainees would be cooked). See also Ross Sandler & David Schoenbrod, The Supreme Court, Democracy and Institutional Reform Litigation, 49 N.Y.L.Sch.L.Rev. 915, 929 (2005) (applauding a shift in the "judicial balance toward democratic values and away from contractual rigidity" in the enforcement of consent decrees).

CHAPTER 4

DECLARATORY JUDGMENT

■ ■ ■

A declaratory judgment settles disputed issues by declaring the parties' legal rights, status and relationship without imposing any other court-ordered relief. Declaratory judgment is not a coercive remedy; it does not result in a court order requiring either party to act. The court's judgment nonetheless binds the parties because traditional rules of issue preclusion apply to prevent the parties from relitigating the issues the declaratory judgment resolves.

The declaratory judgment is an important remedy in many areas of law. In civil rights litigation, declaratory relief offers an efficient way to define constitutional norms and secure governmental compliance. Many of the cases you read in Chapters 2 and 3 on injunctive relief in fact combined a claim for declaratory relief with the claim for injunctive relief. E.g., *Brown v. Board of Education* (p. 107); *City of Los Angeles v. Lyons* (p. 62). In intellectual property law, declaratory relief can be used to define the scope of intellectual property rights without waiting for costly infringement actions to be filed. Similarly, in insurance litigation and across a range of contract disputes declaratory relief allows legal obligations to be defined in the early stages of a dispute, perhaps making further litigation unnecessary.

The declaratory judgment's value is in resolving uncertainty. What makes it a powerful remedy is its timing. It offers parties the opportunity to determine how the law will operate on the facts of a specific case *before* they act in a way that might violate the law. This ability to make legal norms particular and concrete, and thus to guide people in obeying the law, provides an essential element of fairness to the legal system. See Lawrence Slocum, Procedural Justice, 78 S.Cal.L.Rev. 181, 188–189, 219–220 (2004).

Declaratory judgments also make the legal system more efficient, allowing parties to resolve their liability without incurring the cost of litigating all aspects of a dispute, or perhaps even without waiting for the other party to sue. Suppose a creditor claims a debtor has defaulted on a debt, and has informed a credit rating company. By seeking a declaratory judgment, the alleged debtor can establish whether anything is owed, and clear her credit record without waiting for the creditor to sue. For the same reason, insurers frequently rely on the declaratory judgment to resolve coverage issues, hoping to exonerate themselves or to avoid punitive damage awards, without waiting for the underlying liability issues to be resolved. See Itzhak Zamir & Jeremy Woolf, The Declaratory Judgment (3d ed.2001).

The declaratory judgment is a statutory creation.[a] The first effective state declaratory judgment act was passed by New Jersey in 1915. Beginning in 1917, Professors Edwin M. Borchard and Edson R. Sunderland, in a series of articles and books, advocated the passage of declaratory judgment statutes. Their efforts culminated in the Uniform Declaratory Judgment Act, promulgated in 1922 and since adopted in 41 states.

The Uniform Act provides:

§ 1 Courts of record * * * shall have power to declare rights, status, and other legal relations whether or not further relief is or could be claimed. No action or proceeding shall be open to objection on the ground that a declaratory judgment or decree is prayed for. The declaration may be either affirmative or negative in form and effect; and such declarations shall have the force and effect of a final judgment or decree.

The federal Declaratory Judgment Act was not enacted until 1934, apparently because of congressional concern as to its constitutionality. The Act, as amended, is codified at 28 U.S.C. §§ 2201 & 2202. Its effective language echoes the Uniform Act:

In a case of actual controversy within its jurisdiction, [subject to certain exceptions[b]] any court of the United States, upon the filing of an appropriate pleading, may declare the rights and other legal relations of any interested party seeking such declaration, whether or not further relief is or could be sought. Any such declaration shall have the force and effect of a final judgment or decree and shall be reviewable as such.

28 U.S.C. § 2201. Both the Uniform Act and the federal act allow the court to grant further relief based on a declaratory judgment after the

---

a. Before the advent of the modern declaratory judgment, similar relief was sometimes available through specific forms of action: bills to quiet or remove a cloud from title, bills for instructions to executors or trustees as to their rights and duties, bills of interpleader to resolve conflicting rights to a fund, applications for judicial declarations of marital status, and so on. In many cases, the particular form of action was the outgrowth of a frequently repeated fact pattern, and the courts were not quick to provide analogous relief when the facts failed to match the pattern. As a result, there were a variety of forms of relief, each with its own prerequisites, resulting in considerable complexity. Sharon v. Tucker, 144 U.S. 533, 12 S.Ct. 720, 36 L.Ed. 532 (1892), in which the Court had to wade through the distinctions between three archaic forms of action before clearing the plaintiffs' title to their property, provides a nice example. In many instances, particularized forms for resolving such questions remain, though they have frequently been simplified and modernized. In the main, however, the declaratory judgment has replaced the old forms of action.

b. The Act does not authorize declaratory relief with respect to federal income taxes (for which 26 U.S.C. § 7428 provides limited declaratory relief), some anti-dumping laws and duty proceedings, and several specific provisions of the tax code.

adverse party has been given notice and an opportunity to be heard. 28 U.S.C. § 2202; U.D.J.A. § 8.

Declaratory judgment is not inherently an equitable or a legal form of action. It can be used to adjudicate both legal and equitable claims. As a consequence, the right to a jury trial will depend on whether the parallel coercive claim would be legal or equitable,[c] which it may not be easy to ascertain, particularly when counterclaims are involved. The Supreme Court has put emphasis on preserving the right to jury trial, so competing characterizations of the issues in the suit are likely to be resolved in favor of affording a jury trial. Beacon Theatres, Inc. v. Westover, 359 U.S. 500, 79 S.Ct. 948, 3 L.Ed.2d 988 (1959).

Ironically, the qualities that make declaratory relief valuable—the fact that it is available in a dispute's early stages, that it can be used to anticipate litigation that has not yet been filed, that it can define legal obligations without waiting for the law to be violated—also define the critical issues concerning the remedy's availability. If the dispute is embryonic, is there truly a case or controversy? Is it ripe? Is it appropriate for the courts to become involved at such an early stage in the dispute rather than waiting for a party who could seek coercive relief to act?

Under both the federal and the uniform acts, declaratory relief is discretionary. As you read through the following cases, try to identify the factors that will determine whether a court will grant a declaratory judgment. How would those factors suggest the following problem should be resolved?

PROBLEM: COUNTRY LODGE V. MILLER (REPRISED)
DECLARATORY JUDGMENT

Miller has operated her apple press for three years, disposing of the apple mash into the Rural River. Her downstream neighbor, Country Lodge, has complained to the newspaper about Miller's dumping, but has never approached Miller about it. Miller plans to enlarge her operation and to invest several thousand dollars in a new apple press that would discharge even more mash into the river.

If Miller sues Country Lodge, seeking a declaratory judgment that disposing of apple mash into the Rural River is not a nuisance and does not invade Country Lodge's rights as a downstream riparian owner, should the court rule on the dispute? Would your answer be different if:

(a) Country Lodge had never complained to anyone, and Miller were not contemplating a new press?

(b) Country Lodge has threatened Miller with suit each year, telling her that if she put apple mash in the river again it would get an injunction to stop her, but never following through on the threat?

On the original facts, if Country Lodge seeks a judgment declaring that the larger press and increased dumping will create a nuisance, should the

---

c. This is reflected in the language of F.R.Civ.P. 57 (reproduced in the Appendix at p. 983).

court rule on that claim? Should the law be symmetrical, so that declaratory relief would be available to both or to neither?

MEDIMMUNE, INC. v. GENENTECH, INC.

Supreme Court of the United States, 2007
549 U.S. 118, 127 S.Ct. 764, 166 L.Ed.2d 604

JUSTICE SCALIA delivered the opinion of the Court.

We must decide whether Article III's limitation of federal courts' jurisdiction to "Cases" and "Controversies," reflected in the "actual controversy" requirement of the Declaratory Judgment Act, 28 U.S.C. § 2201(a), requires a patent licensee to terminate or be in breach of its license agreement before it can seek a declaratory judgment that the underlying patent is invalid, unenforceable, or not infringed.

I

Because the declaratory-judgment claims in this case were disposed of at the motion-to-dismiss stage, we take the following facts from the allegations in petitioner's amended complaint and the unopposed declarations that petitioner submitted in response to the motion to dismiss. Petitioner MedImmune, Inc., manufactures Synagis, a drug used to prevent respiratory tract disease in infants and young children. In 1997, petitioner entered into a patent license agreement with respondent Genentech, Inc. (which acted on behalf of itself as patent assignee and on behalf of the coassignee, respondent City of Hope). The license covered an existing patent relating to the production of "chimeric antibodies" and a then-pending patent application relating to "the coexpression of immunoglobulin chains in recombinant host cells." Petitioner agreed to pay royalties on sales of "Licensed Products," and respondents granted petitioner the right to make, use, and sell them. The agreement defined "Licensed Products" as a specified antibody, "the manufacture, use or sale of which ... would, if not licensed under th[e] Agreement, infringe one or more claims of either or both of [the covered patents,] which have neither expired nor been held invalid by a court or other body of competent jurisdiction from which no appeal has been or may be taken." The license agreement gave petitioner the right to terminate upon six months' written notice.

In December 2001, the "coexpression" application covered by the 1997 license agreement matured into the "Cabilly II" patent. Soon thereafter, respondent Genentech delivered petitioner a letter expressing its belief that Synagis was covered by the Cabilly II patent and its expectation that petitioner would pay royalties beginning March 1, 2002. Petitioner did not think royalties were owing, believing that the Cabilly II patent was invalid and unenforceable, and that its claims were in any event not infringed by Synagis. Nevertheless, petitioner considered the letter to be a clear threat to enforce the Cabilly II patent, terminate the 1997 license agreement, and sue for patent infringement if petitioner did not make royalty payments as demanded. If respondents were to prevail in a patent infringement action, petitioner could be ordered to pay treble damages and attorney's fees, and could be enjoined from selling Synagis, a product that has accounted for more than 80 percent of its revenue from sales since 1999. Unwilling to risk such serious consequences, petitioner paid the demanded royalties "under protest and with reservation of all of [its] rights." This declaratory judgment action followed.

Petitioner sought the declaratory relief discussed * * * below. Petitioner also requested damages and an injunction with respect to other federal and state claims not relevant here. The District Court granted respondents' motion to dismiss the declaratory-judgment claims for lack of subject-matter jurisdiction, relying on the decision of the United States Court of Appeals for the Federal Circuit in Gen–Probe Inc. v. Vysis, Inc., 359 F.3d 1376 (2004). *Gen-Probe* had held that a patent licensee in good standing cannot establish an Article III case or controversy with regard to validity, enforceability, or scope of the patent because the license agreement "obliterate[s] any reasonable apprehension" that the licensee will be sued for infringement. The Federal Circuit affirmed the District Court * * *.

* * *

III

The Declaratory Judgment Act provides that, "[i]n a case of actual controversy within its jurisdiction ... any court of the United States ... may declare the rights and other legal relations of any interested party seeking such declaration, whether or not further relief is or could be sought." 28 U.S.C. § 2201(a). There was a time when this Court harbored doubts about the compatibility of declaratory-judgment actions with Article III's case-or-controversy requirement. We dispelled those doubts, however, in Nashville, C. & St. L.R. Co. v. Wallace, 288 U.S. 249, 53 S.Ct. 345, 77 L.Ed. 730 (1933), holding (in a case involving a declaratory judgment rendered in state court) that an appropriate action for declaratory relief *can* be a case or controversy under Article III. The federal Declaratory Judgment Act was signed into law the following year, and we upheld its constitutionality in Aetna Life Ins. Co. v. Haworth, 300 U.S. 227, 57 S.Ct. 461, 81 L.Ed. 617 (1937). Our opinion explained that the phrase "case of actual controversy" in the Act refers to the type of "Cases" and "Controversies" that are justiciable under Article III.

Aetna and the cases following it do not draw the brightest of lines between those declaratory-judgment actions that satisfy the case-or-controversy requirement and those that do not. Our decisions have required that the dispute be "definite and concrete, touching the legal relations of parties having adverse legal interests"; and that it be "real and substantial" and "admi[t] of specific relief through a decree of a conclusive character, as distinguished from an opinion advising what the law would be upon a hypothetical state of facts." In Maryland Casualty Co. v. Pacific

Coal & Oil Co., 312 U.S. 270, 273, 61 S.Ct. 510, 85 L.Ed. 826 (1941), we summarized as follows: "Basically, the question in each case is whether the facts alleged, under all the circumstances, show that there is a substantial controversy, between parties having adverse legal interests, of sufficient immediacy and reality to warrant the issuance of a declaratory judgment."

There is no dispute that these standards would have been satisfied if petitioner had taken the final step of refusing to make royalty payments under the 1997 license agreement. Respondents claim a right to royalties under the licensing agreement. Petitioner asserts that no royalties are owing because the Cabilly II patent is invalid and not infringed; and alleges (without contradiction) a threat by respondents to enjoin sales if royalties are not forthcoming. The factual and legal dimensions of the dispute are well defined and, but for petitioner's continuing to make royalty payments, nothing about the dispute would render it unfit for judicial resolution. Assuming (without deciding) that respondents here could not claim an anticipatory breach and repudiate the license, the continuation of royalty payments makes what would otherwise be an imminent threat at least remote, if not nonexistent. As long as those payments are made, there is no risk that respondents will seek to enjoin petitioner's sales. Petitioner's own acts, in other words, eliminate the imminent threat of harm.[8] The question before us is whether this causes the dispute no longer to be a case or controversy within the meaning of Article III.

Our analysis must begin with the recognition that, where threatened action by *government* is concerned, we do not require a plaintiff to expose himself to liability before bringing suit to challenge the basis for the threat—for example, the constitutionality of a law threatened to be enforced. The plaintiff's own action (or inaction) in failing to violate the law eliminates the imminent threat of prosecution, but nonetheless does not eliminate Article III jurisdiction. For example, in Terrace v. Thompson, 263 U.S. 197, 44 S.Ct. 15, 68 L.Ed. 255 (1923), the State threatened the plaintiff with forfeiture of his farm, fines, and penalties if he entered into a lease with an alien in violation of the State's anti-alien land law. Given this genuine threat of enforcement, we did not require, as a prerequisite to testing the validity of the law in a suit for injunction, that the plaintiff bet the farm, so to speak, by taking the violative action. Likewise, in Steffel v. Thompson, 415 U.S. 452, 94 S.Ct. 1209, 39 L.Ed.2d 505 (1974), we did not require the plaintiff to proceed to distribute handbills and risk actual prosecution before he could seek a declaratory

---

8. The justiciability problem that arises, when the party seeking declaratory relief is himself preventing the complained-of injury from occurring, can be described in terms of standing (whether plaintiff is threatened with "imminent" injury in fact "'fairly ... trace[able] to the challenged action of the defendant,'" Lujan v. Defenders of Wildlife, 504 U.S. 555, 560, 112 S.Ct. 2130, 119 L.Ed.2d 351 (1992)), or in terms of ripeness (whether there is sufficient "hardship to the parties [in] withholding court consideration" until there is enforcement action, Abbott Laboratories v. Gardner, 387 U.S. 136, 149, 87 S.Ct. 1507, 18 L.Ed.2d 681 (1967)). As respondents acknowledge, standing and ripeness boil down to the same question in this case.

judgment regarding the constitutionality of a state statute prohibiting such distribution. As then-Justice Rehnquist put it in his concurrence, "the declaratory judgment procedure is an alternative to pursuit of the arguably illegal activity." In each of these cases, the plaintiff had eliminated the imminent threat of harm by simply not doing what he claimed the right to do (enter into a lease, or distribute handbills at the shopping center). That did not preclude subject-matter jurisdiction because the threat-eliminating behavior was effectively coerced. The dilemma posed by that coercion—putting the challenger to the choice between abandoning his rights or risking prosecution—is "a dilemma that it was the very purpose of the Declaratory Judgment Act to ameliorate." Abbott Laboratories v. Gardner, 387 U.S. 136, 152, 87 S.Ct. 1507, 18 L.Ed.2d 681 (1967).

Supreme Court jurisprudence is more rare regarding application of the Declaratory Judgment Act to situations in which the plaintiff's self-avoidance of imminent injury is coerced by threatened enforcement action of *a private party* rather than the government. Lower federal courts, however (and state courts interpreting declaratory judgment Acts requiring "actual controversy"), have long accepted jurisdiction in such cases.

The only Supreme Court decision in point is, fortuitously, close on its facts to the case before us. Altvater v. Freeman, 319 U.S. 359, 63 S.Ct. 1115, 87 L.Ed. 1450 (1943), held that a licensee's failure to cease its payment of royalties did not render nonjusticiable a dispute over the validity of the patent. In that litigation, several patentees had sued their licensees to enforce territorial restrictions in the license. The licensees filed a counterclaim for declaratory judgment that the underlying patents were invalid, in the meantime paying "under protest" royalties required by an injunction the patentees had obtained in an earlier case. The patentees argued that "so long as [licensees] continue to pay royalties, there is only an academic, not a real controversy, between the parties." We rejected that argument and held that the declaratory-judgment claim presented a justiciable case or controversy: "The fact that royalties were being paid did not make this a 'difference or dispute of a hypothetical or abstract character.'" The royalties "were being paid under protest and under the compulsion of an injunction decree," and "[u]nless the injunction decree were modified, the only other course [of action] was to defy it, and to risk not only actual but treble damages in infringement suits." We concluded that "the requirements of [a] case or controversy are met where payment of a claim is demanded as of right and where payment is made, but where the involuntary or coercive nature of the exaction preserves the right to recover the sums paid or to challenge the legality of the claim."

The Federal Circuit's *Gen-Probe* decision distinguished *Altvater* on the ground that it involved the compulsion of an injunction. But *Altvater* cannot be so readily dismissed. Never mind that the injunction had been privately obtained and was ultimately within the control of the patentees, who could permit its modification. More fundamentally, and contrary to the Federal Circuit's conclusion, *Altvater* did not say that the coercion dispositive of the case was governmental, but suggested just the opposite.

The opinion acknowledged that the licensees had the option of stopping payments in defiance of the injunction, but explained that the *consequence* of doing so would be to risk "actual [and] treble damages in infringement suits" by the patentees. It significantly did not mention the threat of prosecution for contempt, or any other sort of governmental sanction. Moreover, it cited approvingly a treatise which said that an "actual or threatened serious injury to business or employment" by a private party can be as coercive as other forms of coercion supporting restitution actions at common law; and that "[t]o imperil a man's livelihood, his business enterprises, or his solvency, [was] ordinarily quite as coercive" as, for example, "detaining his property." F. Woodward, The Law of Quasi Contracts § 218 (1913), cited in *Altvater*.

Jurisdiction over the present case is not contradicted by Willing v. Chicago Auditorium Association, 277 U.S. 274, 48 S.Ct. 507, 72 L.Ed. 880 (1928). There a ground lessee wanted to demolish an antiquated auditorium and replace it with a modern commercial building. The lessee believed it had the right to do this without the lessors' consent, but was unwilling to drop the wrecking ball first and test its belief later. Because there was no declaratory judgment act at the time under federal or applicable state law, the lessee filed an action to remove a "cloud" on its lease. This Court held that an Article III case or controversy had not arisen because "[n]o defendant ha[d] wronged the plaintiff or ha[d] threatened to do so." It was true that one of the co-lessors had disagreed with the lessee's interpretation of the lease, but that happened in an "informal, friendly, private conversation" a year before the lawsuit was filed; and the lessee never even bothered to approach the other co-lessors. The Court went on to remark that "[w]hat the plaintiff seeks is simply a declaratory judgment," and "[t]o grant that relief is beyond the power conferred upon the federal judiciary." Had *Willing* been decided after the enactment (and our upholding) of the Declaratory Judgment Act, and had the legal disagreement between the parties been as lively as this one, we are confident a different result would have obtained. The rule that a plaintiff must destroy a large building, bet the farm, or (as here) risk treble damages and the loss of 80 percent of its business, before seeking a declaration of its actively contested legal rights finds no support in Article III.

Respondents assert that the parties in effect settled this dispute when they entered into the 1997 license agreement. When a licensee enters such an agreement, they contend, it essentially purchases an insurance policy, immunizing it from suits for infringement so long as it continues to pay royalties and does not challenge the covered patents. Permitting it to challenge the validity of the patent without terminating or breaking the agreement alters the deal, allowing the licensee to continue enjoying its immunity while bringing a suit, the elimination of which was part of the patentee's *quid pro quo*. Of course even if it were valid, this argument would have no force with regard to petitioner's claim that the agreement does not call for royalties because their product does not infringe the patent. But even as to the patent invalidity claim, the point seems to us mistaken. To begin with, it is not clear where the prohibition against challenging the validity of the patents is to be found. It can hardly be implied from the mere promise to pay royalties on patents "which have neither expired nor been held invalid by a court or other body of competent jurisdiction from which no appeal has been or may be taken." Promising to pay royalties on patents that have not been held invalid does not amount to a promise *not to seek* a holding of their invalidity.

* * *

Lastly, respondents urge us to affirm the dismissal of the declaratory-judgment claims on discretionary grounds. The Declaratory Judgment Act provides that a court "*may* declare the rights and other legal relations of any interested party," 28 U.S.C. § 2201(a) (emphasis added), not that it *must* do so. This text has long been understood "to confer on federal courts unique and substantial discretion in deciding whether to declare the rights of litigants." We have found it "more consistent with the statute," however, "to vest district courts with discretion in the first instance, because facts bearing on the usefulness of the declaratory judgment remedy, and the fitness of the case for resolution, are peculiarly within their grasp." The District Court here gave no consideration to discretionary dismissal, since, despite its "serious misgivings" about the Federal Circuit's rule, it considered itself bound to dismiss by *Gen-Probe*. Discretionary dismissal was irrelevant to the Federal Circuit for the same reason. Respondents have raised the issue for the first time before this Court, exchanging competing accusations of inequitable conduct with petitioner. Under these circumstances, it would be imprudent for us to decide whether the District Court should, or must, decline to issue the requested declaratory relief. We leave the equitable, prudential, and policy arguments in favor of such a discretionary dismissal for the lower courts' consideration on remand. Similarly available for consideration on remand are any merits-based arguments for denial of declaratory relief.

* * *

We hold that petitioner was not required, insofar as Article III is concerned, to break or terminate its 1997 license agreement before seeking a declaratory judgment in federal court that the underlying patent is invalid, unenforceable, or not infringed. The Court of Appeals erred in affirming the dismissal of this action for lack of subject-matter jurisdiction.

* * *

JUSTICE THOMAS, dissenting.

* * *

III

To reach today's result, the Court misreads our precedent and expands the concept of coercion from *Steffel* to reach voluntarily accepted contractual obligations between private parties.

* * *

No court has ever taken such a broad view of *Steffel*.

In *Steffel*, the Court held that in certain limited circumstances, a party's anticipatory cause of action qualified as a case or controversy under Article III. Based expressly on the coercive nature of governmental power, the Court found that "it is not necessary that petitioner first expose himself to *actual arrest* or *prosecution* to be entitled to challenge a *statute* that he claims deters the exercise of his constitutional rights" (emphasis added). Limited, as it is, to governmental power, particularly the power of arrest and prosecution, *Steffel* says nothing about coercion in the context of private contractual obligations. It is therefore not surprising that, until today, this Court has never applied *Steffel* and its theory of coercion to private contractual obligations; indeed, no court has ever done so.

The majority not only extends *Steffel* to cases that do not involve governmental coercion, but also extends *Steffel's* rationale. If "coercion" were understood as the Court used that term in *Steffel*, it would apply only if Genentech had threatened MedImmune with a patent infringement suit *in the absence of a license agreement*. At that point, MedImmune would have had a choice, as did the declaratory plaintiff in *Steffel*, either to cease the otherwise protected activity (here, selling Synagis) or to continue in that activity and face the threat of a lawsuit. But MedImmune faced no such choice. Here, MedImmune could continue selling its product without threat of suit because it had eliminated any risk of suit by entering into a license agreement. By holding that the voluntary choice to enter an agreement to avoid some other coerced choice is itself coerced, the Court goes far beyond *Steffel*.

The majority explains that the "coercive nature of the exaction preserves the right ... to challenge the legality of the claim." The coercive nature of what "exaction"? The answer has to be the voluntarily made license payments because there was no threat of suit here. By holding that contractual obligations are sufficiently coercive to allow a party to bring a declaratory judgment action, the majority has given every patent licensee a cause of action and a free pass around Article III's requirements for challenging the validity of licensed patents. But the reasoning of today's opinion applies not just to patent validity suits. Indeed, today's opinion contains no limiting principle whatsoever, casting aside Justice Stewart's understanding that *Steffel's* use would "be exceedingly rare."

For the foregoing reasons, I respectfully dissent.

Notes

1. Until *MedImmune*, the Federal Circuit applied a "reasonable apprehension" test to determine whether declaratory relief was available to test a patent's validity. As applied, the test required that the declaratory judgment plaintiff have undertaken steps that would lead to infringement and that the patentee explicitly or implicitly threaten to sue. Gen–Probe Inc. v. Vysis, Inc.,

359 F.3d 1376, 1380 (Fed.Cir.2004). *MedImmune* abrogates this standard. Samsung Electronics Co. v. ON Semiconductor Corp., 541 F.Supp.2d 645 (D.Del.2008).

Does this mean that there are no limits on the availability of declaratory relief in patent cases? In Prasco, LLC v. Medicis Pharmaceutical Corp., 537 F.3d 1329 (Fed.Cir.2008), a manufacturer sought a declaratory judgment that its medication did not infringe several patents the defendant held. The defendant, Medicis Pharmaceutical, marketed a similar product marked with its patents, and had sued to enforce its patent against the manufacturer of a different generic product, but did not know that the plaintiff's product existed until Prasco filed suit. On these facts, the court found there was no Article III case or controversy:

> Where Prasco has suffered no actual present injury traceable to the defendants, and the defendants have not asserted any rights against Prasco related to the patents nor taken any affirmative actions concerning Prasco's current product, one prior suit concerning unrelated patents and products and the defendants' failure to sign a covenant not to sue are simply not sufficient to establish that Prasco is at risk of imminent harm from the defendants and that there is an actual controversy between the parties. * * *

537 F.3d at 1341. According to the court, a purely subjective fear, not grounded in the defendant's actions, does not establish a case or controversy. Is *City of Los Angeles v. Lyons* (p. 62) relevant to this inquiry?

Setting the threshold for declaratory relief is not a procedural formality. In the patent context, making it easier to litigate the validity of patents will spur competition, but it may undercut innovation, because fending off more frequent challenges will make patents less valuable. See Amy Kapczynski, The Access to Knowledge Mobilization and the New Politics of Intellectual Property, 117 Yale L.J. 804 (2008) (describing *MedIummune* as one example of the Supreme Court stepping "decisively" into the debate over patent reform).

The notes that follow introduce the use of declaratory judgments in other common contexts—disputes over insurance coverage, challenges to statutes, and challenges to agency action. As each is introduced, think about the values that are in play in adjusting the interests of those who would seek declaratory relief and the interests of those who would argue declaratory relief is not proper.

2. *Insurance.* As in *MedImmune*, the Court often relies on two insurance cases, Aetna Life Insurance Co. v. Haworth, 300 U.S. 227, 57 S.Ct. 461, 81 L.Ed. 617 (1937), and Maryland Casualty Co. v. Pacific Coal & Oil Co., 312 U.S. 270, 61 S.Ct. 510, 85 L.Ed. 826 (1941), to articulate the basic standard for establishing that a case or controversy exists. In *Aetna Life*, an insured stopped paying premiums on several Aetna life insurance policies and claimed the disability benefits the policies provided included a waiver of premiums. Aetna denied his claim. The insured took no further action, but Aetna sued under the Declaratory Judgment Act to have the policies declared void. The insured had given no indication that he planned to sue over the policies; nonetheless, the Court found that the dispute presented a concrete case or controversy:

> Prior to this suit, the parties had taken adverse positions with respect to their existing obligations. * * * On the one side, the insured claimed that he had become totally and permanently disabled and hence was relieved of the obligation to continue the payment of premiums * * *. On the other side, the company made an equally definite claim that the alleged basic fact did not exist * * * and that the company was thus freed of its obligation either to pay disability benefits or to continue the insurance in force. Such a dispute is manifestly susceptible of judicial determination. It calls, not for an advisory opinion upon a hypothetical basis, but for an adjudication of present right upon established facts.

300 U.S. at 242, 57 S.Ct. at 464–465. Aetna's injury in fact was established by the need to maintain a reserve adequate to cover the insured's claim until it was resolved. Id. at 239, 57 S.Ct. at 463.

Maryland Casualty Co. is important because it resolved another major issue concerning the use of declaratory judgment actions in insurance disputes. *Maryland Casualty Co.* permitted a liability insurance company to seek a declaration that its policy did not cover a claim made against its insured, although the insured had not yet been held liable to anyone. Despite the insured's (and the injured party's) claim that they had no controversy with the insurance company until the insured's liability had been adjudicated, the court allowed the declaratory judgment action to proceed.

Following the decisions in *Aetna Life* and *Maryland Casualty Co.*, the use of declaratory judgment to resolve a wide range of disputes between insurance companies and insureds has become common. One court has described litigation seeking declaratory relief over insurance coverage as "the paradigm for asserting jurisdiction despite future contingencies that will determine whether a controversy ever becomes real." E.R. Squibb & Sons, Inc. v. Lloyd's & Cos., 241 F.3d 154 (2d Cir.2001). Insurance companies have used declaratory judgments to determine whether they have a duty to defend under the policy (see, e.g., American States Insurance Co. v. Bailey, 133 F.3d 363 (5th Cir. 1998) (no duty to defend ministers charged with sexual abuse)), to settle coverage disputes, as in *Aetna Life*, and to resolve a wide range of other disputes. Prompt resolution of these issues through declaratory judgment is of great benefit because insurers avoid the risk of subsequent punitive damage awards for failing to meet their obligations to insured parties.

The declaratory judgment action is particularly important in states that bar liability insurers who undertake the defense of an insured without a non-waiver agreement from later asserting defenses under the policy such as breach of condition, scope of coverage or continuance of coverage. In such states, a declaratory judgment action that precedes the liability action allows the insurer to have fair knowledge of its responsibilities under the policy before the liability action itself is tried. In some states, declaratory judgment actions are given preference on trial calendars and the preference is usually of greatest importance in the insurance context. See, e.g., Cal.Code Civ.Pro. § 1062.3; California Insurance Guarantee Association v. Superior Court, 231 Cal.App.3d 1617, 283 Cal.Rptr. 104 (1991).

3. Note how the declaratory judgment remedy somewhat confusingly reverses the usual positions of the parties. In *Aetna Life*, the insured—who

would usually be the plaintiff in an action to collect on the policy—becomes the defendant. In the patent context, such as in *MedImmune*, the patent holder can be the defendant in the declaratory judgment action, while in an enforcement action, the patent holder would be the plaintiff.

4. *Challenges to statutes*: As the *MedImmune* Court notes, declaratory judgments are frequently used to challenge government conduct or to avoid the risk of criminal prosecution. For a time, there was some uncertainty about how the case or controversy requirement applied to lawsuits challenging the constitutionality of statutes that had yet to be enforced. In Poe v. Ullman, 367 U.S. 497, 81 S.Ct. 1752, 6 L.Ed.2d 989 (1961), a married couple sued the State of Connecticut, seeking a declaration that a statute prohibiting the use of contraceptives or giving medical advice about them was unconstitutional. The statute had been on the books since 1879 and had never been enforced. Skeptical of the plaintiffs' claim that the statute motivated their doctor's refusal to prescribe contraceptives, the Court denied declaratory relief:

> [W]e cannot accept, as the basis of constitutional adjudication, other than as chimerical the fear of enforcement of provisions that have during so many years gone uniformly and without exception unenforced.

367 U.S. at 508, 812 S.Ct. at 1758–1759. Is this the same sort of purely subjective fear the *Prasco* court found insufficient to establish a case or controversy in note 1, above?

Following the Court's decision in *Poe*, the plaintiffs' physician, Dr. Buxton, served as Medical Director at a center run by the Planned Parenthood League of Connecticut, where he provided information and medical advice to married persons about contraception. Dr. Buxton and the Executive Director of the League were found guilty as accessories of violating the Connecticut statute that was the subject of *Poe*. Each was fined $100 and appealed. In Griswold v. Connecticut, 381 U.S. 479, 85 S.Ct. 1678, 14 L.Ed.2d 510 (1965), the Supreme Court found the statute unconstitutional. For a detailed historical account of the development of *Poe* and *Griswold*, including the reactions of the individual justices to the cases, see David J. Garrow, Liberty and Sexuality (1994).

These days, *Poe* is rarely invoked to turn back constitutional challenges to statutes; indeed, actions seeking a declaratory and injunctive relief are often filed as soon as legislation is signed into law, well before anyone has been charged with a violation. With regard to one pre-enforcement action, the Supreme Court commented:

> We are not troubled by the pre-enforcement nature of this suit. The State has not suggested that the newly enacted law will not be enforced, and we see no reason to assume otherwise. We conclude that plaintiffs have alleged an actual and well-founded fear that the law will be enforced against them. Further, the alleged danger of this statute is, in large measure, one of self-censorship; a harm that can be realized even without an actual prosecution.

Virginia v. American Booksellers Association, 484 U.S. 383, 108 S.Ct. 636, 642, 98 L.Ed.2d 782 (1988). See also Epperson v. Arkansas, 393 U.S. 97, 89 S.Ct. 266, 21 L.Ed.2d 228 (1968) (striking down a statute with no record of enforcement); Doe v. Dunbar, 320 F.Supp. 1297 (D.Colo.1970) (*Poe* does not preclude relief unless there is "a clear finding of non-enforcement").

That is not to say that *Poe* is a dead letter. See Northern Utilities, Inc. v. Lewiston Radiator Works, Inc., 2005 WL 758466 (D.Me. Feb. 3, 2005) (relying on *Poe* to find no jurisdiction over constitutional challenge to Maine's punitive damages law when declaratory judgment plaintiff had not yet been held liable for punitive damages).

5. *Ripeness and administrative rule-making.* Three 1967 Supreme Court decisions known as the *Abbott Laboratories* trilogy set out the ground rules for pre-enforcement challenges to agency rules. Abbott Laboratories v. Gardner, 387 U.S. 136, 87 S.Ct. 1507, 18 L.Ed.2d 681 (1967) (cited in *MedImmune*); Toilet Goods Association, Inc. v. Gardner, 387 U.S. 167, 87 S.Ct. 1530, 18 L.Ed.2d 704 (1967); Toilet Goods Association, Inc. v. Gardner, 387 U.S. 158, 87 S.Ct. 1520, 18 L.Ed.2d 697 (1967). The test for ripeness has two prongs: (a) the issues presented must be fit for judicial resolution; and (b) withholding judicial consideration would result in hardship to the parties. The Court described the basic rationale of the test as being "to prevent the courts, through avoidance of premature adjudication, from entangling themselves in abstract disagreement over administrative policies, and also to protect the agencies from judicial interference until an administrative decision has been formalized and its effects felt in a concrete way by the challenging parties." *Abbott Laboratories*, 387 U.S. at 148–149, 87 S.Ct. at 1515.

The Third Circuit has summarized this result in A.O. Smith Corp. v. F.T.C., 530 F.2d 515, 524 (3d Cir.1976):

> [I]t appears from the *Abbott Laboratories* trilogy that one seeking discretionary relief may not obtain pre-enforcement judicial review of agency action if there is no immediate threat of sanctions for noncompliance, or if the potential sanction is de minimis. Conversely, the court should find agency action ripe for judicial review if the action is final and clear-cut, and if it puts the complaining party on the horns of a dilemma: if he complies and awaits ultimate judicial determination of the action's validity, he must change his course of day-to-day conduct, for example, by undertaking substantial preliminary paper work, scientific testing and record-keeping, or by destroying stock; alternatively, if he does not comply, he risks sanctions or injuries including, for example, civil and criminal penalties, or loss of public confidence.

6. Even if a case or controversy is established, relief under the Declaratory Judgment Act is discretionary. On remand in *MedImmune*, what factors should guide the district court's discretion? The following case may be helpful.

MORRISON v. PARKER

United States District Court, Western District of Michigan, 2000
90 F.Supp.2d 876

McKeague, District Judge.

This case presents a claim for declaratory judgment relief under 28 U.S.C. § 2201. On March 6, 2000, after having received briefing on the issue, United States Magistrate Judge Joseph G. Scoville issued a report and recommendation recommending that this Court, in the exercise of its discretion, decline to entertain the action. * * *

[T]he report and recommendation will be adopted as the opinion of the Court. The Court, in the exercise of its discretion, declines to exercise jurisdiction over this matter. An order of dismissal shall issue forthwith.

REPORT AND RECOMMENDATION

SCOVILLE, UNITED STATES MAGISTRATE JUDGE.

* * *

Factual Background

This declaratory judgment action arises from a motor vehicle accident that occurred in Muskegon County on December 5, 1998. One motor vehicle was owned by plaintiff Hertz Corporation and operated by its lessee, Thelma Morrison. The other motor vehicle was operated by Brian Edgerton, Jr., then fifteen years old. Allegedly, Brian Edgerton, Jr. did not have a driver's license or a permit, and the vehicle that he was operating was not titled or insured. Also occupying the vehicle was defendant Gerald R. Parker, Jr., the apparent owner of the car, and members of his family. Brian Edgerton, Jr. and Gerald Parker, Jr. suffered serious injuries as a result of the accident.

In April of 1999, Gerald R. Parker, Jr. filed a negligence action in the Muskegon County Circuit Court. That action * * * alleges that Thelma Morrison was negligent in that she disregarded a stop sign and struck the vehicle occupied by Edgerton and Parker. Liability is asserted against Hertz Corporation on the basis of the Michigan owner's statute.

Brian Edgerton, Jr. is not a party to the Muskegon County Circuit Court action.[1] Brian Edgerton, Jr. has, however, made a demand against Hertz in the amount of $100,000, arising from his closed-head injury, collapsed right lung, and other injuries sustained in the accident. The demand was contained in a letter dated October 7, 1999, sent by attorney Paul Ladas on behalf of the minor. Brian Edgerton, Jr. has not, however, instituted a lawsuit.

Plaintiffs initiated the present declaratory judgment action by complaint filed December 8, 2000. In this action, plaintiffs seek a declaration of non-liability, based solely upon principles of Michigan law. Count 1 seeks a declaration that plaintiffs are not liable to Gerald R. Parker, Jr., because of his failure to insure his motor vehicle at the time of the accident. Alternatively, plaintiffs assert that Parker forfeited his right to recovery by allowing an unlicensed minor, Brian Edgerton, Jr., to operate his motor vehicle in violation of Mich.Comp.Laws § 257.904(1). Plaintiffs seek a declaration that Brian Edgerton, Jr., a minor, is foreclosed from

---

1. It is undisputed that Brian Edgerton, Jr. is under the legal disability of infancy, as he was under the age of eighteen when his claim accrued. Michigan law therefore allows him to file suit up to one year after reaching the age of majority.

recovery because of his alleged operation of a motor vehicle without a license, in violation of Mich.Comp.Laws § 257.301.

The question presently before the court is whether the court should exercise its discretion in favor of entertaining this declaratory judgment action.

Discussion

The Judicial Code empowers the federal district courts to entertain civil actions for declaratory judgment in a case of actual controversy otherwise within the court's jurisdiction. 28 U.S.C. § 2201. The Supreme Court has long held that the exercise of the jurisdiction created by section 2201 is discretionary in the district court. The Court has recently reaffirmed the breadth of discretion granted the district courts by the Declaratory Judgment Act. In Wilton v. Seven Falls Co., 515 U.S. 277, 115 S.Ct. 2137, 132 L.Ed.2d 214 (1995), the Court made the following observations:

> By the Declaratory Judgment Act, Congress sought to place a remedial arrow in the district court's quiver; it created an opportunity, rather than a duty, to grant a new form of relief to qualifying litigants. Consistent with the nonobligatory nature of the remedy, a district court is authorized, in the sound exercise of its discretion, to stay or to dismiss an action seeking a declaratory judgment before trial or after all arguments have drawn to a close. In the declaratory judgment context, the normal principle that federal courts should adjudicate claims within their jurisdiction yields to considerations of practicality and wise judicial administration.

The United States Court of Appeals for the Sixth Circuit has provided substantial guidance concerning the principles that should guide the court's exercise of its broad discretion. The Sixth Circuit has stated that the district court should exercise its discretion in favor of a declaratory judgment action (1) when the judgment will serve a useful purpose in clarifying and settling the legal relations in issue, and (2) when it will terminate and afford relief from the uncertainty, insecurity, and controversy giving rise to the proceeding. Grand Trunk Western R.R. Co. v. Consolidated Rail Corp., 746 F.2d 323, 326 (6th Cir.1984). In applying these criteria, the appellate court requires consideration by the district court of the following factors: (1) whether the declaratory action would settle the controversy; (2) whether the declaratory action would serve a useful purpose in clarifying the legal relations in issue; (3) whether the declaratory remedy is being used merely for the purpose of "procedural fencing" or "to provide an arena for a race for res judicata;" (4) whether the use of a declaratory action would increase friction between our federal and state courts and improperly encroach upon state jurisdiction; and (5) whether there is an alternative remedy which is better or more effective.

In applying the same criteria and evaluating the same factors, the federal courts have isolated two circumstances, both present in the instant case, that militate strongly against entertaining a declaratory judgment action. The first circumstance arises where, as here, a putative tortfeasor sues the victims of his negligence in an effort to force an adjudication on the tortfeasor's terms. Second is the circumstance where a coercive state-court action is already pending. * * *

In the present action, the putative tortfeasors have sued the injured parties, seeking a declaration that the injured parties cannot recover by reason of certain state-law affirmative defenses. The federal courts have long resisted such declaratory judgment actions as a perversion of the Declaratory Judgment Act. The seminal case is Cunningham Bros., Inc. v. Bail, 407 F.2d 1165 (7th Cir.1969). *Cunningham* was an action by an alleged tortfeasor against injured employees of a subcontractor, in which the tortfeasor sought a declaration that it did not have charge of the work being performed by the employees at the time of their injuries. The district court dismissed the complaint, on the ground that the case was not appropriate for the exercise of federal court discretion under the Declaratory Judgment Act. On appeal, the tortfeasor made the same argument now advanced by Hertz: instead of having to wait to be sued in different state and federal forums by the various injured parties, the tortfeasors should be allowed to bring them together in one action, and thereby adjudicate the rights of all parties in one case. The Seventh Circuit disagreed. "Regarding the individual defendants, we are of the opinion that to compel potential personal injury plaintiffs to litigate their claims at a time and in a forum chosen by the alleged tortfeasor would be a perversion of the Declaratory Judgment Act." Relying upon earlier authority, the court noted that it was not one of the purposes of the Declaratory Judgment Act "to enable a prospective negligence action defendant to obtain a declaration of non-liability." Id. at 1168 (quoting Sun Oil Co. v. Transcontinental Gas Pipe Line Corp., 108 F.Supp. 280, 282 (E.D.Pa.1952)). The Seventh Circuit acknowledged that the existence of another remedy does not automatically preclude a declaratory judgment action, but determined that the traditional personal injury action was preferable, because it would afford more effective relief. The court then made an observation that applies equally to the present case.

> Since the sustaining of plaintiff's suit in the instant case would force an injured party to litigate a claim which he may not have wanted to litigate at a time which might be inconvenient to him or which might precede his determination of the full extent of his damages, and in a forum chosen by the alleged tortfeasor, we hold the action was inappropriate for declaratory relief and was therefore properly dismissed against the individual defendants.

407 F.2d at 1169.

Following *Cunningham,* the uniform approach of the federal courts is that declaratory relief is generally inappropriate when a putative tortfeasor sues the injured party for a declaration of nonliability. The recent comments of the Eighth Circuit are instructive:

It is our view that where a declaratory plaintiff raises chiefly an affirmative defense, and it appears that granting relief could effectively deny an allegedly injured party its otherwise legitimate choice of the forum and time for suit, no declaratory judgment should issue.

BASF Corp. v. Symington, 50 F.3d 555, 559 (8th Cir.1995); accord 10B Charles Alan Wright, Arthur R. Miller & Mary Kay Kane, Federal Practice & Procedure § 2765 at 638–39 (2d ed.1998) ("The courts have also held that it is not one of the purposes of the declaratory judgments act to enable a prospective negligence action defendant to obtain a declaration of nonliability. They have felt that even though a declaratory judgment action might reduce multiple litigation with a number of injured persons, this result should not outweigh the right of a personal-injury plaintiff to choose the forum and the time, if at all, to assert his claim.").

Viewed from the perspective of the five *Grand Trunk* standards, an action by a putative tortfeasor fares poorly as a declaratory judgment action. First, the action would not necessarily settle the controversy. In their complaint, plaintiffs do not assert that Thelma Morrison was not at fault in causing defendants' injuries. Rather, they seek to raise only two state-law affirmative defenses which allegedly bar recovery as a matter of law. If plaintiffs are correct in their legal assertions, the controversy may well end. If, however, plaintiffs are incorrect, then the issues of negligence, proximate cause, and damages must still be litigated in some forum. At best, maintenance of the present case raises only the possibility of settling the controversy.

Second, this action would not serve a useful purpose in clarifying the legal relations in issue. Traditionally, affirmative defenses such as those now advanced by plaintiffs are litigated in the context of a personal injury action. I fail to see what useful purpose is served by divorcing affirmative defenses from the facts of the case and seeking an adjudication of those defenses in a vacuum.

Third, the conclusion is virtually inescapable that Hertz is using this federal court action for the purpose of procedural fencing. Plaintiffs have never explained to this court why their affirmative defenses could not be raised in response to a traditional personal injury action. In the case of Mr. Parker, such an action has been pending in the Muskegon County Circuit Court for a period of months. If plaintiffs believe that their defense is meritorious, there is nothing preventing them from raising it in a dispositive motion before the state circuit court. With regard to defendant Edgerton, a minor, the aspects of procedural fencing are even more apparent. As a minor, Mr. Edgerton is privileged under state law to wait until his nineteenth birthday before initiating a lawsuit. By bringing this action, plaintiffs would effectively force an unwilling minor to litigate his personal injury claim prematurely, perhaps before all effects of the accident become manifest. Plaintiffs have not advanced any reason why this court should be a party to depriving an injured minor of a benefit bestowed upon him by state statute.

Fourth, the maintenance of a declaratory judgment action would indeed increase friction between the federal and state courts and improperly encroach upon state jurisdiction, at least with regard to defendant Parker. As noted above, Parker presently has pending a traditional personal injury action in the state courts. The Supreme Court has long held that "ordinarily it would be uneconomical as well as vexatious for a federal court to proceed in a declaratory judgment suit where another suit is pending in a state court presenting the same issues, not governed by federal law, between the same parties." In its recent decision in *Wilton*, the Supreme Court reiterated this concept and underscored the discretion of the district court to dismiss or stay proceedings where parallel state proceedings are already pending. Presumably, plaintiffs wish to receive a declaration of nonliability from this court and then to present it to the Muskegon County Circuit Court as a bar to that court's further consideration of Parker's personal injury action. I cannot imagine the circumstances in which a federal court would choose to exercise its discretion to lecture the state courts on an issue of state law central to the resolution of a claim properly pending before those courts.

Finally, there is an alternate remedy that is better and more effective, namely, a traditional personal injury action. The Supreme Court has taught that the crucial issue is not whether the state-court action was commenced first, but whether it will most fully serve the interests of the parties and provide a comprehensive resolution of their dispute. In a personal injury action, all issues between the parties may be resolved in a comprehensive proceeding. This is certainly preferable to a federal declaratory judgment action, in which certain affirmative defenses are the only matters at issue. It is difficult to see how justice would be better served by the maintenance of this federal declaratory judgment action.

* * *

Recommended Disposition

The unanimous attitude of the federal courts is to decline to exercise declaratory judgment jurisdiction where a putative tortfeasor attempts to choose the time and forum to litigate the claims of the injured party. In these circumstances, all five of the relevant Sixth Circuit factors weigh against entertaining the action. I therefore recommend that this declaratory judgment action be dismissed without prejudice. * * *

NOTES

1. The Declaratory Judgment Act does not say that the remedy is forbidden in tort actions. *Cunningham Brothers*, which the *Morrison* court calls the seminal case, cites no authority for its conclusion that declaratory judgments are generally unavailable in tort actions. Although Congress took up bills providing for declaratory judgment repeatedly in the 1920s, when the Act was passed in 1934 no debates or hearings were held in either the House or the Senate on the bill; consideration was limited to a brief summary of the

bill by its sponsors. Given this limited direct legislative history, how is the court to determine the purposes of the Act? Should it consult the voluminous writings of Professors Borchard and Sunderland? Should it consider the history of declaratory judgment in the states, bearing in mind that the notes of the Advisory Committee to F.R.Civ.P. 57, which addresses declaratory judgments, state that the Uniform Declaratory Judgment Act "affords a guide to the scope and function of the federal act"?

2. The Supreme Court has emphasized that the Declaratory Judgment Act gives the district courts discretion to declare the parties' rights; federal courts are never required to hear an action under the statute. Wilton v. Seven Falls Co., 515 U.S. 277, 115 S.Ct. 2137, 132 L.Ed.2d 214 (1995). So long as there is a case or controversy under Article III, the district court's decision to hear or not to hear an action under the Declaratory Judgment Act will be reversed only on a showing of an abuse of discretion. *Wilton*, 515 U.S. at 289–290, 115 S.Ct. at 2144, 132 L.Ed. at 225.

What factors does the *Morrison* court consider important to its decision? The Fifth Circuit has articulated a six factor test to determine whether a declaratory judgment claim should be entertained:

> The relevant factors which the district court must consider include, but are not limited to, 1) whether there is a pending state action in which all of the matters in controversy may be fully litigated, 2) whether the plaintiff filed suit in anticipation of a lawsuit filed by the defendant, 3) whether the plaintiff engaged in forum shopping in bringing the suit, 4) whether possible inequities in allowing the declaratory plaintiff to gain precedence in time or to change forums exist, 5) whether the federal court is a convenient forum for the parties and witnesses, and 6) whether retaining the lawsuit in federal court would serve the purposes of judicial economy.

American States Insurance Co. v. Bailey, 133 F.3d 363 (5th Cir. 1998).

3. Among these factors, how much weight should be attached to who commences a lawsuit? In the *Aetna Life* case (p. 425), the court of appeals had found that: (a) the only advantage to be derived from a declaratory judgment was the adjudication of Aetna's right of cancellation; and (b) the only value of such adjudication was that it settled a defense to a lawsuit that might be filed in the future, such as after the death of the insured. Aetna Life Insurance Co. v. Haworth, 84 F.2d 695 (8th Cir.1936), rev'd, 300 U.S. 227, 57 S.Ct. 461, 81 L.Ed. 617 (1937). Of course, it is usual and unremarkable that the party who would be a defendant in a suit seeking a coercive remedy will be the plaintiff in a declaratory judgment action—it is frequently the only avenue by which the traditional defendant can initiate resolution of the legal dispute. As a result, by using declaratory judgment, the traditional defendant is also able to choose the forum. Is there any reason to disparage this result? See BASF Corp. v. Symington, 50 F.3d 555 (8th Cir.1995)(courts normally dismiss declaratory judgment actions "aimed solely at wresting the choice of forum from the 'natural' plaintiff").

In this light, consider Rule 13(a)(1) of the Federal Rules of Civil Procedure. The rule reads:

A pleading must state as a counterclaim any claim that—at the time of its service—the pleader has against an opposing party if the claim: (A) arises out of the transaction or occurrence that is the subject matter of the opposing party's claim; and (B) does not require adding another party over whom the court cannot acquire jurisdiction.

Is it unfair to force a tort plaintiff to try damages whenever the tort defendant is ready to try liability? Should Rule 13 be changed?

4. Should it change the outcome if the declaratory judgment defendant has already filed an action in state court, or if he files one while the federal declaratory judgment action is pending? If a state has begun a *criminal* prosecution while a challenge to the state statute in federal court is in its embryonic stages, the federal courts will not enjoin the state court proceedings, Younger v. Harris, 401 U.S. 37, 91 S.Ct. 756, 27 L.Ed.2d 669 (1971), or grant declaratory judgment, Samuels v. Mackell, 401 U.S. 66, 91 S.Ct. 764, 27 L.Ed.2d 688 (1971), except in the most exceptional circumstances.

Civil actions are different, however. When faced with competing state litigation, a federal district court can exercise its discretion to hear the case, or it can choose to defer to the state courts. See, e.g., Colorado River Water Conservation District v. United States, 424 U.S. 800, 96 S.Ct. 1236, 47 L.Ed.2d 483 (1976) (actions for declaratory relief brought under 28 U.S.C. § 1345 should not be stayed in deference to state court actions unless exceptional circumstances are present, because the statute evinced a clear congressional intent to have the issues decided in federal court).

5. Is it relevant that other remedies might be available to the declaratory judgment plaintiff? While the availability of other remedies can be a factor that would lead a court to exercise its discretion not to hear the case, see, e.g., Tilcon Minerals, Inc. v. Orange & Rockland Utilities, Inc., 851 F.Supp. 529 (S.D.N.Y.1994) (neither injunctive nor declaratory relief would be granted in a dispute where monetary damages were an adequate remedy), the existence of alternative remedies is not dispositive:

> [E]ngrafting upon the Declaratory Judgment Act a requirement that all of the traditional equitable prerequisites to the issuance of an injunction be satisfied before the issuance of a declaratory judgment is considered would defy Congress' intent to make declaratory relief available in cases where an injunction would be inappropriate.... Thus, the Court of Appeals was in error when it ruled that a failure to demonstrate irreparable injury—a traditional prerequisite to injunctive relief, having no equivalent in the law of declaratory judgments—precluded the granting of declaratory relief. The only occasions where this Court has disregarded these "different considerations" and found that preclusion of injunctive relief inevitably led to a denial of declaratory relief have been cases in which principles of federalism militated altogether against federal intervention in a class of adjudications.

Steffel v. Thompson, 415 U.S. 452, 471–72, 94 S.Ct. 1209, 1222, 39 L.Ed.2d 505 (1974).

The reference to "principles of federalism" in *Steffel* encompasses a series of cases in which the Court has held declaratory relief is not available if its effect would be to end-run federalism-based limitations on damages or injunctive relief. Thus, a declaratory judgment is not available where the judgment's res judicata effect would make the federal court's decision tantamount to an award of damages against the state, which the eleventh amendment would otherwise prohibit. Green v. Mansour, 474 U.S. 64, 106 S.Ct. 423, 88 L.Ed.2d 371 (1985). Neither is declaratory relief available if its effect would be to end run the Anti–Tax Injunction Act's prohibition on enjoining tax collections (Great Lakes Dredge & Dock Co. v. Huffman, 319 U.S. 293, 63 S.Ct. 1070, 87 L.Ed. 1407 (1943)), or the prohibition on enjoining ongoing criminal prosecutions (Samuels v. Mackell, 401 U.S. 66, 73, 91 S.Ct. 764, 768, 27 L.Ed.2d 688 (1971)).

Note on Jurisdiction over Declaratory Judgment Actions in Federal Court

The Federal Declaratory Judgment Act does not itself create a basis for jurisdiction in the federal district courts; it simply authorizes a court that already has jurisdiction to grant declaratory relief. So in addition to showing a justiciable controversy under Article III, a declaratory judgment plaintiff must also show some independent basis for jurisdiction—a federal statute establishing jurisdiction over the particular subject matter, for example, or diversity of citizenship, see 28 U.S.C. § 1332, or perhaps federal question jurisdiction, 28 U.S.C. § 1331.

To establish federal question jurisdiction, the plaintiff must show that the action is a "civil action arising under the Constitution, laws or treaties of the United States." 28 U.S.C. § 1331. When the right that a plaintiff asserts in a declaratory judgment action itself arises under federal law, clearly there is federal question jurisdiction. Thus, when a patent holder seeks a declaration that his patent has been infringed—a right secured by federal law—federal district courts have jurisdiction. See Talbot v. Quaker–State Oil Refining Co., 104 F.2d 967 (3d Cir.1939). Similarly, when a declaratory judgment plaintiff claims that the defendant's threatened acts would violate federal law or are preempted by federal law, the case arises under federal law, even if the plaintiff's claim is essentially defensive in nature. Verizon Maryland, Inc. v. Public Service Commission, 535 U.S. 635, 122 S.Ct. 1753, 152 L.Ed.2d 871 (2002); Shaw v. Delta Air Lines, Inc., 463 U.S. 85, 103 S.Ct. 2890, 77 L.Ed.2d 490 (1983).

On the other hand, a plaintiff's declaratory judgment action does *not* "arise under" federal law if the declaratory judgment plaintiff's complaint asserts state law claims, and the only federal question arises as a response to a potential defense. In the leading case, Skelly Oil Co. v. Phillips Petroleum Co., 339 U.S. 667, 70 S.Ct. 876, 94 L.Ed. 1194 (1950), an oil company sought a declaration that its contracts with three producers were valid. The company anticipated that the producers would defend by arguing that they had the right to terminate the contract at any time until a federal agency issued a "certificate of public convenience" relating to the contract. The federal question on which the oil company relied to establish jurisdiction was whether a valid certificate had been issued before the producers cancelled.

The Supreme Court held that the plaintiff's action did not "arise under" federal law. Invoking what has come to be known as the "well-pleaded complaint" rule, the court said that in order to establish federal question jurisdiction, "the plaintiff's claim itself must present a federal question unaided by anything alleged in anticipation of avoidance of defenses which it is thought the defendant may interpose." 339 U.S. at 672, 70 S.Ct. at 879. In *Skelly Oil*, the plaintiff's claim arose from the state law of contracts, not from federal law. The allegations raising issues of federal law were included merely in anticipation of the declaratory judgment defendant's defensive pleadings. They were not part of the plaintiff's "well-pleaded complaint," and therefore the complaint was not one "arising under federal law" for purposes of section 1331.

Given the way in which declaratory judgment actions often reverse the parties' usual roles, applying the "well-pleaded complaint" rule to a suit for declaratory relief can be a bit tricky. Say that a manufacturer, instead of waiting to be sued for patent infringement, files an action in federal court seeking a declaration that an inventor's patent is *not* valid, and that therefore he is free to develop a similar product without facing an action for infringement. Without the Declaratory Judgment Act, it is not clear that the manufacturer could plead a cause of action for coercive relief at all; at best, his "well-pleaded complaint" might assert some sort of right to be free from a patent infringement action. Is that a right "arising" under the federal law of patents?

Faced with such cases, the lower federal courts have concluded that there is jurisdiction. Rather than look at the plaintiff's well-pleaded complaint, the courts have examined whether the complaint for coercive relief that the declaratory judgment *defendant* might have filed would arise under federal law. "We determine whether there is jurisdiction in a declaratory judgment action by applying the well-pleaded complaint rule. We apply that rule not to the declaratory judgment complaint but [to] the hypothetical action the declaratory defendant would have brought." Fina Oil & Chemical Co. v. Ewen, 123 F.3d 1466 (Fed.Cir.1997). Because the declaratory judgment defendant's patent infringement claim—the coercive action the inventor might hypothetically have brought—arises under federal law, so does the plaintiff's claim that there has been no infringement.

Thus, a declaratory judgment plaintiff can bring a suit in federal court on an issue of federal law if the issue is one that would be apparent from the well-pleaded complaint for coercive relief that the defendant might have filed. Household Bank v. The JFS Group, 320 F.3d 1249, 1259 (11th Cir.2003). While the Supreme Court has not ruled directly on this issue, it has approved of its use in patent cases several times in dicta. See, e.g., Textron v. United Automobile Workers, 523 U.S. 653, 659 n.19, 118 S.Ct. 1626, 1630, 140 L.Ed.2d 863, 870 (1998).

It is not clear, however, whether the same logic can be used to establish jurisdiction in federal court over a non-federal issue, if the declaratory judgment defendant's hypothetical complaint arises under federal law. See *Textron*, 523 U.S. at 659–60 ("No decision of this Court has squarely confronted and explicitly upheld federal-question jurisdiction on the basis of the anticipated claim against which the declaratory-judgment plaintiff presents a nonfederal defense."). Some courts have also questioned whether the declaratory judgment defendant's hypothetical complaint must be one over which federal courts have exclusive jurisdiction—like a patent claim—although most courts have concluded that it need not be. Household Bank v. The JFS Group, 320 F.3d 1249, 1259 (11th Cir.2003) (collecting cases).

There is one last twist. In Franchise Tax Board v. Construction Laborers Vacation Trust, 463 U.S. 1, 103 S.Ct. 2841, 77 L.Ed.2d 420 (1983), the Court held that a declaratory judgment action could not be removed to federal court, even though a hypothetical complaint for injunctive relief by the declaratory judgment defendant would have clearly pleaded a cause of action arising under federal law. While the case's outcome seems to conflict with the "hypothetical defendant's complaint" approach, several factors in the Court's analysis suggest that the holding is more limited.

In *Franchise Tax Board*, the California Franchise Tax Board filed an action in state court alleging, first, that defendant owed a tax, and second, seeking a declaratory judgment that a federal statute, ERISA, did not preempt the tax. The defendant attempted to remove the case to federal court, asserting federal question jurisdiction.

The Supreme Court held that the case was not removable, because the dispute between the parties did not "arise" under federal law within the meaning of 28 U.S.C. § 1331. The Court recognized that ERISA gives trustees the right to sue for an injunction against a state tax that conflicted with ERISA. Further, "federal courts have regularly taken original jurisdiction over declaratory judgment suits in which, if the declaratory judgment defendant brought a coercive action to enforce its rights, that suit would necessarily present a federal question." 463 U.S. at 19, 103 S.Ct. at 2851, 77 L.Ed.2d at 437.

ERISA, however, expressly limits the parties who can sue to people like beneficiaries and trustees. The Court saw no reason why a case brought against, not by, those parties should be forced into federal court, particularly when:

> [t]here are good reasons why the federal courts should not entertain suits by the States to declare the validity of their regulations despite possibly conflicting federal law. States are not significantly prejudiced by an inability to come to federal court for a declaratory judgment in advance of a possible injunctive suit by a person subject to federal regulation. They have a variety of means by which they can enforce their own laws in their own courts, and they do not suffer if the preemption questions such enforcement may raise are tested there.

463 U.S. at 21, 103 S.Ct. at 2852, 77 L.Ed.2d at 438.

To sum up, federal district courts have federal question jurisdiction over declaratory judgment actions if:

(1) the declaratory judgment plaintiff's well-pleaded complaint alleges a cause of action that arises under federal law; or

(2) the well-pleaded complaint that the declaratory judgment defendant might have filed for coercive relief would have alleged a cause of action

that arises under federal law (at least if the declaratory judgment action itself involves a question of federal law).

A federal district court does not have federal question jurisdiction if:

(1) the federal issue the declaratory judgment plaintiff wants resolved is only an issue because it must be resolved in order to evaluate a defense that the declaratory judgment defendant might raise; or

(2) the suit is one brought by a state seeking a determination that a state law is *not* preempted by federal law (at least if the federal law is ERISA!).

NOTE ON REFORMATION

Reformation is a remedy that somewhat resembles a declaratory judgment, at least in that theoretically it is not coercive. Reformation is available when a written document—typically a contract or conveyance—does not accurately reflect the parties' actual agreement. Suppose, for example, Smith agrees to sell 100 widgets to Jones for $10,000 and tells his attorney to draw papers to that effect. Smith's attorney puts in a price of $1,000 by mistake and forwards the paper to Jones, who signs it without being aware of the error.

To correct the error, Smith could seek reformation. Once the terms of the parties' actual agreement were shown, the court would order the document reformed or corrected to reflect the parties' intentions accurately. Or the court could simply state the reformed terms of the document in its opinion, making it unnecessary to change the document physically. It is important to emphasize, however, that in a reformation action the court is not creating a new agreement, but rather simply changing the form of the agreement so that the original substance is correctly stated.

If all a reformation action achieves is correcting the documents to reflect the parties' actual intent, one might wonder why the parties need to resort to the court at all and whether there is any case or controversy for the court to resolve. Reformation is an important remedy in at least three circumstances. First, there may be an honest dispute over what terms the parties agreed to at the time.

Second, if one of the parties is a corporation or a political body, the true controversy may lie not between the individuals who reached agreement but between one party and the corporate successors of the other. Suppose Smith, as President of Widgets, Inc., agrees to supply Jones with 100 widgets for $1,000, but the written document mistakenly records a $10,000 price. If Smith then sells Widgets, Inc., to a third party without discussing the Jones contract, Jones will have a live controversy with the new owners of Widgets, Inc., in which Smith would be a central witness for Jones.

Finally, fraud or misrepresentation may be involved, not in setting the contract's terms but in recording the agreement. For example, if Smith agrees to sell a blind person 100 widgets for $1,000 but then obtains his signature on a contract in which the price is stated as $10,000, there is a good claim for reformation.

Probably because the plaintiff is asking the court to set aside the agreement's plain language, the burden of proof in reformation cases is typically one of clear and convincing evidence. In Mississippi, the case for reformation must be proved beyond a reasonable doubt. Neither the statute of frauds nor the parol evidence rule, however, is a bar to the plaintiff presenting his case as to what the actual agreement between the parties was.

CHAPTER 5

DAMAGES

■ ■ ■

A. INTRODUCTION

THE NATURE OF THE SUBJECT

The law of damages consists of the rules, standards, and methods used by the courts for measuring in money the compensation given for losses and injuries. It plays an unusually large part in Anglo–American law because of two distinctive features of the English judicial machinery. First is the presence of the jury, who award the damages under the judge's supervision and control. The rules and formulas used in the exercise of that control make up a substantial part of the law of damages. Second, in dividing jurisdiction between courts of law and courts of equity, the tradition was established that resort must be had to compensation by money damages in preference to specific relief, unless such damages are affirmatively shown to be inadequate for the just protection of the plaintiff's interest. It results from this traditional rule that a judgment for money damages is the normal and preferred remedy in our courts.

Charles McCormick, Handbook on the Law of Damages 1 (1935).

The case that follows introduces and defines the three basic types of damages awards: *nominal damages*, *compensatory damages*, and *punitive damages*. Punitive damages will be discussed in Chapter 6. Nominal damages are discussed in a note following the first case in this chapter. As a whole, this chapter focuses on compensatory damages.

As you read the case, think about the justifications for compensatory damages. What purpose does it serve to give people money when their rights are violated? What if the loss they claim is not economic in character? Can all losses be measured in money, or are some things simply beyond price?

MEMPHIS COMMUNITY SCHOOL DISTRICT v. STACHURA

Supreme Court of the United States, 1986
477 U.S. 299, 106 S.Ct. 2537, 91 L.Ed.2d 249

JUSTICE POWELL delivered the opinion of the Court.

This case requires us to decide whether 42 U.S.C. § 1983 authorizes an award of compensatory damages based on the factfinder's assessment of the value or importance of a substantive constitutional right.

I

Respondent Edward Stachura is a tenured teacher in the Memphis, Michigan, public schools. When the events that led to this case occurred, respondent taught seventh-grade life science, using a textbook that had been approved by the school board. The textbook included a chapter on human reproduction. During the 1978–1979 school year, respondent spent six weeks on this chapter. As part of their instruction, students were shown pictures of respondent's wife during her pregnancy. Respondent also showed the students two films concerning human growth and sexuality. These films were provided by the County Health Department, and the Principal of respondent's school had approved their use. Both films had been shown in past school years without incident.

After the showing of the pictures and the films, a number of parents complained to school officials about respondent's teaching methods. These complaints, which appear to have been based largely on inaccurate rumors about the allegedly sexually explicit nature of the pictures and films, were discussed at an open School Board meeting held on April 23, 1979. Following the advice of the School Superintendent, respondent did not attend the meeting, during which a number of parents expressed the view that respondent should not be allowed to teach in the Memphis school system. The day after the meeting, respondent was suspended with pay. The School Board later confirmed the suspension, and notified respondent that an "administration evaluation" of his teaching methods was underway. No such evaluation was ever made. Respondent was reinstated the next fall, after filing this lawsuit.

Respondent sued the School District, the Board of Education, various Board members and school administrators, and two parents who had participated in the April 23 School Board meeting. The complaint alleged that respondent's suspension deprived him of both liberty and property without due process of law and violated his First Amendment right to academic freedom. Respondent sought compensatory and punitive damages under 42 U.S.C. § 1983 for these constitutional violations.

At the close of trial on these claims, the District Court instructed the jury as to the law governing the asserted bases for liability. Turning to damages, the court instructed the jury that on finding liability it should award a sufficient amount to compensate respondent for the injury caused by petitioners' unlawful actions:

> "You should consider in this regard any lost earnings; loss of earning capacity; out-of-pocket expenses; and any mental anguish or emotional distress that you find the Plaintiff to have suffered as a result of conduct by the Defendants depriving him of his civil rights."

In addition to this instruction on the standard elements of compensatory damages, the court explained that punitive damages could be awarded, and described the standards governing punitive awards. Finally, at respondent's request and over petitioners' objection, the court charged that damages also could be awarded based on the value or importance of the constitutional rights that were violated:

> "If you find that the Plaintiff has been deprived of a Constitutional right, you may award damages to compensate him for the deprivation. Damages for this type of injury are more difficult to measure than damages for a physical injury or injury to one's property. There are no medical bills or other expenses by which you can judge how much compensation is appropriate. In one sense, no monetary value we place upon Constitutional rights can measure their importance in our society or compensate a citizen adequately for their deprivation. However, just because these rights are not capable of precise evaluation does not mean that an appropriate monetary amount should not be awarded. The precise value you place upon any Constitutional right which you find was denied to Plaintiff is within your discretion. You may wish to consider the importance of the right in our system of government, the role which this right has played in the history of our republic, [and] the significance of the right in the context of the activities which the Plaintiff was engaged in at the time of the violation of the right."

The jury found petitioners liable, and awarded a total of $275,000 in compensatory damages and $46,000 in punitive damages. * * *

In an opinion devoted primarily to liability issues, the Court of Appeals for the Sixth Circuit affirmed. * * *

We granted certiorari limited to the question whether the Court of Appeals erred in affirming the damages award in light of the District Court's instructions that authorized not only compensatory and punitive damages, but also damages for the deprivation of "any constitutional right" * * *.

III

A

We have repeatedly noted that 42 U.S.C. § 1983[8] creates "'a species of tort liability' in favor of persons who are deprived of 'rights, privileges,

---

8. Section 1983 reads:

"Every person who, under color of any statute, ordinance, regulation, custom, or usage, of any State or Territory or the District of Columbia, subjects, or causes to be subjected, any citizen of or immunities secured' to them by the Constitution." Accordingly, when § 1983 plaintiffs seek damages for violations of constitutional rights, the level of damages is ordinarily determined according to principles derived from the common law of torts.

Punitive damages aside,[9] damages in tort cases are designed to provide "*compensation* for the injury caused to plaintiff by defendant's breach of duty." To that end, compensatory damages may include not only out-of-pocket loss and other monetary harms, but also such injuries as "impairment of reputation..., personal humiliation, and mental anguish and suffering." Deterrence is also an important purpose of this system, but it operates through the mechanism of damages that are compensatory—damages grounded in determinations of plaintiffs' actual losses. Congress adopted this common-law system of recovery when it established liability for "constitutional torts." Consequently, "the basic purpose" of § 1983 damages is "to *compensate persons for injuries* that are caused by the deprivation of constitutional rights."

Respondent does not, and could not reasonably, contend that the separate instructions authorizing damages for violation of constitutional rights were equivalent to punitive damages instructions. In these separate instructions, the jury was authorized to find damages for constitutional violations without any finding of malice or ill will. Moreover, the jury instructions separately authorized punitive damages, and the District Court expressly labeled the "constitutional rights" damages compensatory. The instructions concerning damages for constitutional violations are thus impermissible unless they reasonably could be read as authorizing *compensatory* damages.

Carey v. Piphus [435 U.S. 247, 98 S.Ct. 1042, 55 L.Ed.2d 252 (1978)] represents a straightforward application of these principles. *Carey* involved a suit by a high school student suspended for smoking marijuana; the student claimed that he was denied procedural due process because he was suspended without an opportunity to respond to the charges against him. The Court of Appeals for the Seventh Circuit held that even if the suspension was justified, the student could recover substantial compensatory damages simply because of the insufficient procedures used to suspend him from school. We reversed, and held that the student could recover compensatory damages only if he proved actual injury caused by the denial of his constitutional rights. We noted: "[r]ights, constitutional and otherwise, do not exist in a vacuum. Their purpose is to protect

---

the United States or other person within the jurisdiction thereof to the deprivation of any rights, privileges, or immunities secured by the Constitution and laws, shall be liable to the party injured in an action at law, suit in equity, or other proper proceeding for redress."

9. The purpose of punitive damages is to punish the defendant for his willful or malicious conduct and to deter others from similar behavior. In Smith v. Wade, 461 U.S. 30, [103 S.Ct. 1625, 75 L.Ed.2d 632] (1983), the Court held that punitive damages may be available in a proper § 1983 case. As the punitive damages instructions used in this case explained, however, such damages are available only on a showing of the requisite intent. App. 94–95 (authorizing punitive damages for acts "maliciously, or wantonly, or oppressively done").

persons from injuries to particular interests...." Where no injury was present, no "compensatory" damages could be awarded.

The instructions at issue here cannot be squared with *Carey,* or with the principles of tort damages on which *Carey* and § 1983 are grounded. The jurors in this case were told that, in determining how much was necessary to "compensate [respondent] for the deprivation" of his constitutional rights, they should place a money value on the "rights" themselves by considering such factors as the particular right's "importance ... in our system of government," its role in American history, and its "significance ... in the context of the activities" in which respondent was engaged. These factors focus, not on compensation for provable injury, but on the jury's subjective perception of the importance of constitutional rights as an abstract matter. *Carey* establishes that such an approach is impermissible. The constitutional right transgressed in *Carey*—the right to due process of law—is central to our system of ordered liberty. We nevertheless held that *no* compensatory damages could be awarded for violation of that right absent proof of actual injury. *Carey,* 435 U.S. at 264, 98 S.Ct. at 1052. *Carey* thus makes clear that the abstract value of a constitutional right may not form the basis for § 1983 damages.[11]

Respondent nevertheless argues that *Carey* does not control here, because in this case a *substantive* constitutional right—respondent's First Amendment right to academic freedom—was infringed. The argument misperceives our analysis in *Carey.* That case does not establish a two-tiered system of constitutional rights, with substantive rights afforded greater protection than "mere" procedural safeguards. We did acknowledge in *Carey* that "the elements and prerequisites for recovery of damages" might vary depending on the interests protected by the constitutional right at issue. But we emphasized that, whatever the constitutional basis for § 1983 liability, such damages must always be designed "to *compensate injuries* caused by the [constitutional] deprivation." (emphasis added) That conclusion simply leaves no room for non-compensatory damages measured by the jury's perception of the abstract "importance" of a constitutional right.

Nor do we find such damages necessary to vindicate the constitutional rights that § 1983 protects. See n.11, supra. Section 1983 presupposes that damages that compensate for actual harm ordinarily suffice to deter constitutional violations. Moreover, damages based on the "value" of constitutional rights are an unwieldy tool for ensuring compliance with

---

11. We did approve an award of nominal damages for the deprivation of due process in *Carey.* Our discussion of that issue makes clear that nominal damages, and not damages based on some undefinable "value" of infringed rights, are the appropriate means of "vindicating" rights whose deprivation has not caused actual, provable injury:

"Common-law courts traditionally have vindicated deprivations of certain 'absolute' rights that are not shown to have caused actual injury through the award of a nominal sum of money. By making the deprivation of such rights actionable for nominal damages without proof of actual injury, the law recognizes the importance to organized society that those rights be scrupulously observed; but at the same time, it remains true to the principle that substantial damages should be awarded only to compensate actual injury or, in the case of exemplary or punitive damages, to deter or punish malicious deprivations of rights."

the Constitution. History and tradition do not afford any sound guidance concerning the precise value that juries should place on constitutional protections. Accordingly, were such damages available, juries would be free to award arbitrary amounts without any evidentiary basis, or to use their unbounded discretion to punish unpopular defendants. Such damages would be too uncertain to be of any great value to plaintiffs, and would inject caprice into determinations of damages in § 1983 cases. We therefore hold that damages based on the abstract "value" or "importance" of constitutional rights are not a permissible element of compensatory damages in such cases.

B

Respondent further argues that the challenged instructions authorized a form of "presumed" damages—a remedy that is both compensatory in nature and traditionally part of the range of tort law remedies. * * *

Presumed damages are a *substitute* for ordinary compensatory damages, not a *supplement* for an award that fully compensates the alleged injury. When a plaintiff seeks compensation for an injury that is likely to have occurred but difficult to establish, some form of presumed damages may possibly be appropriate. In those circumstances, presumed damages may roughly approximate the harm that the plaintiff suffered and thereby compensate for harms that may be impossible to measure. As we earlier explained, the instructions at issue in this case did not serve this purpose, but instead called on the jury to measure damages based on a subjective evaluation of the importance of particular constitutional values. Since such damages are wholly divorced from any compensatory purpose, they cannot be justified as presumed damages.[14] Moreover, no rough substitute

---

14. For the same reason, Nixon v. Herndon, 273 U.S. 536, 47 S.Ct. 446, 71 L.Ed. 759 (1927), and similar cases do not support the challenged instructions. In *Nixon,* the Court held that a plaintiff who was illegally prevented from voting in a state primary election suffered compensable injury. This holding did not rest on the "value" of the right to vote as an abstract matter; rather, the Court recognized that the plaintiff had suffered a particular injury—his inability to vote in a particular election—that might be compensated through substantial money damages.

Nixon followed a long line of cases, going back to Lord Holt's decision in Ashby v. White, 2 Ld.Raym. 938, 92 Eng.Rep. 126 (1703), authorizing substantial money damages as compensation for persons deprived of their right to vote in particular elections. Although these decisions sometimes speak of damages for the value of the right to vote, their analysis shows that they involve nothing more than an award of presumed damages for a nonmonetary harm that cannot easily be quantified:

"In the eyes of the law th[e] right [to vote] is so valuable that damages are presumed from the wrongful deprivation of it without evidence of actual loss of money, property, or any other valuable thing, and the amount of the damages is a question peculiarly appropriate for the determination of the jury, because each member of the jury has personal knowledge of the value of the right." *Ibid.*

See also Ashby v. White, *supra,* at 955, 92 Eng.Rep., at 137 (Holt, C.J.) ("As in an action for slanderous words, though a man does not lose a penny by reason of the speaking [of] them, yet he shall have an action"). The "value of the right" in the context of these decisions is the money value of the particular loss that the plaintiff suffered—a loss of which "each member of the jury has personal knowledge." It is *not* the value of the right to vote as a general, abstract matter, based on its role in our history or system of government. Thus, whatever the wisdom of these decisions in the context of the changing scope of compensatory damages over the course of this century, they do not support awards of noncompensatory damages such as those authorized in this case.

for compensatory damages was required in this case, since the jury was fully authorized to compensate respondent for both monetary and non-monetary harms caused by petitioners' conduct. * * *

IV

The judgment of the Court of Appeals is reversed, and the case is remanded for further proceedings consistent with this opinion.

JUSTICE BRENNAN and JUSTICE STEVENS join the opinion of the Court and also join JUSTICE MARSHALL's opinion concurring in the judgment.

JUSTICE MARSHALL, with whom JUSTICE BRENNAN, JUSTICE BLACKMUN, and JUSTICE STEVENS join, concurring in the judgment.

I agree with the Court that this case must be remanded for a new trial on damages. Certain portions of the Court's opinion, however, can be read to suggest that damages in § 1983 cases are necessarily limited to "out-of-pocket loss," "other monetary harms," and "such injuries as 'impairment of reputation ..., personal humiliation, and mental anguish and suffering.'" I do not understand the Court so to hold, and I write separately to emphasize that the violation of a constitutional right, in proper cases, may itself constitute a compensable injury. * * *

Following *Carey,* the courts of appeals have recognized that invasions of constitutional rights sometimes cause injuries that cannot be redressed by a wooden application of common-law damages rules. In Hobson v. Wilson, 237 U.S.App.D.C. 219, 275–281, 737 F.2d 1, 57–63 (1984), cert. denied, 470 U.S. 1084, 105 S.Ct. 1843, 85 L.Ed.2d 142 (1985), which the Court cites, plaintiffs claimed that defendant Federal Bureau of Investigation agents had invaded their First Amendment rights to assemble for peaceable political protest, to associate with others to engage in political expression, and to speak on public issues free of unreasonable government interference. The District Court found that the defendants had succeeded in diverting plaintiffs from, and impeding them in, their protest activities. The Court of Appeals for the District of Columbia Circuit held that injury to a First Amendment-protected interest could itself constitute compensable injury wholly apart from any "emotional distress, humiliation and personal indignity, emotional pain, embarrassment, fear, anxiety and anguish" suffered by plaintiffs. The court warned, however, that that injury could be compensated with substantial damages only to the extent that it was "reasonably quantifiable"; damages should not be based on "the so-called inherent value of the rights violated."

I believe that the *Hobson* court correctly stated the law. When a plaintiff is deprived, for example, of the opportunity to engage in a demonstration to express his political views, "[i]t is facile to suggest that no damage is done." Loss of such an opportunity constitutes loss of First Amendment rights "'in their most pristine and classic form.'" There is no reason why such an injury should not be compensable in damages. At the same time, however, the award must be proportional to the actual loss sustained.

The instructions given the jury in this case were improper because they did not require the jury to focus on the loss actually sustained by respondent. * * *

The Court therefore properly remands for a new trial on damages. I do not understand the Court, however, to hold that deprivations of constitutional rights can never themselves constitute compensable injuries. Such a rule would be inconsistent with the logic of *Carey*, and would defeat the purpose of § 1983 by denying compensation for genuine injuries caused by the deprivation of constitutional rights.

NOTES

1. What it means to compensate someone for an injury is at the heart of a contemporary debate over the use of the legal system to award damages, particularly in tort cases. The usual explanation for compensatory damages is that compensatory damages make the plaintiff whole. By awarding a sum of money that represents the economic value of the losses the plaintiff has suffered, the court restores the plaintiff to his or her rightful position.

When the plaintiff's losses are economic or pecuniary in nature, the concept of compensation as correcting or rectifying the wrong done makes sense intuitively. But what if the plaintiff's losses are not economic? Compensatory damages are traditionally divided into two categories: compensatory damages for pecuniary, or economic, losses and compensatory damages for nonpecuniary losses, such as emotional distress, pain and suffering, loss of consortium, and so on. Justice Marshall reads the majority's opinion to allow compensatory damages for the deprivation of constitutional rights, provided the jury's award is based on the actual injury the plaintiff suffered and not on the abstract value of the constitutional right. The majority opinion seems to endorse this view by citing *Nixon* with approval, and by referring to the common law practice of presuming damages when a person has been battered, assaulted or falsely imprisoned.

But what does it mean to say that "deprivations of constitutional rights can themselves constitute compensable injuries"? Doesn't the idea of compensation connote that the thing lost can be replaced by money, that an award of money will make the plaintiff whole? Does an award of money undo the harm when, as in *Nixon*, a person has lost the right to vote in a particular election? If money won't make the plaintiff whole, what is the point of awarding compensatory damages?

2. The practice of awarding money for non-economic harm is a target for some critics who believe litigation is out of control. According to these critics, the primary effect of awarding compensatory damages for noneconomic harm is to promote frivolous litigation by creating a jackpot for prevailing plaintiffs and their attorneys. But see Tracy A. Thomas, Restriction of Tort Remedies and the Constraints of Due Process: The Right to an Adequate Remedy, 39 Akron L.Rev. 272 (2006). Thus, the Prison Litigation Reform Act (whose limitations on injunctive relief were discussed in Chapter 3) also limits the right of prisoners to bring actions for nonpecuniary damages. In 42 U.S.C. § 1997e(e), the Act provides:

No federal civil action may be brought by a prisoner confined in a jail, prison, or other correctional facility, for mental or emotional injury suffered while in custody without a prior showing of physical injury.

Can prisoners recover compensatory damages when their constitutional rights are violated if the violation does not result in physical injury? The federal courts are divided. The D.C. and Eleventh Circuits interpret section 1997e(e) to require that prisoner suits alleging constitutional violations without accompanying physical injury be dismissed. See Harris v. Garner, 216 F.3d 970, 984 (11th Cir.2000) (en banc). Other courts have concluded that suits alleging constitutional violations are outside section 1997e(e)'s purview. Shaheed–Muhammad v. Dipaolo, 393 F.Supp.2d 80 (D.Mass.2005) (the violation of a constitutional right is an independent injury that is immediately cognizable and outside the purview of section 1997e(e)); Canell v. Lightner, 143 F.3d 1210, 1213 (9th Cir.1998) (same). Most courts have chosen a middle path, holding that claims for constitutional violations absent physical injury need not be dismissed outright, but that section 1997e(e) limits recovery to nominal and punitive damages (in addition to injunctive and declaratory relief). Royal v. Kautzky, 375 F.3d 720, 722–23 (8th Cir.2004) (citing cases), cert. denied, 544 U.S. 1061, 125 S.Ct. 2528, 161 L.Ed.2d 1111 (2005).

Does *Stachura* have any bearing on this issue? If the PLRA is intended to eliminate compensatory damages for violations of constitutional rights that do not result in physical injury, is it constitutional? Thinking back to Chapter 1 does the interpretation of the Prison Litigation Reform Act adopted by the D.C. and Eleventh Circuits leave prisoners without a remedy for some violations of their constitutional rights?

3. Doubtless, if the practice of awarding damages for the violation of constitutional rights implies that rights and money are fungible—that rights are commodities that can be replaced with money—the practice is troubling. Because most people believe rights and dollars are incommensurable, the practice of offering payment in exchange for something priceless seems arbitrary or punitive at best, and demeaning to the victim at worst. See Margaret Jane Radin, Contested Commodities 184–187 (1996).

Perhaps the problem is that "making the plaintiff whole" does not capture the full purpose of compensatory damages. As an alternative, Professor Radin suggests a "noncommodified" view of the practice of compensation. In that view, an award of damages serves a different function:

> Requiring payment is a way both to bring the wrongdoer to recognize that she has done wrong and to make redress to the victim. Redress is not restitution or rectification. "Redress" instead means showing the victim that her rights are taken seriously. It is accomplished by affirming that some action is required to symbolize public respect for the existence of certain rights and public recognition of the transgressor's fault in failing to respect those rights. In this conception of compensation, neither the harm to the victim nor the victim's right not to be harmed is commensurable with money ... even if, because of money's symbolic importance for us, large cash payments would be needed to symbolize a serious offense.

Id. at 188.

Do *Stachura* and the right to vote cases suggest that the legal system recognizes redress as a legitimate function for compensatory damages to serve? As you read this chapter, look for other evidence that would support, or challenge, Professor Radin's thesis.

4. A third way to explain the purpose of awarding compensatory damages is to focus on their deterrent effect. As the Supreme Court noted in a different context, while compensatory damages are not retributive in the sense that punitive damages are, "compensatory damages are quintessentially backward-looking. Compensatory damages may be intended less to sanction wrongdoers than to make victims whole, but they do so by a mechanism that affects the liabilities of defendants." Landgraf v. USI Film Products, 511 U.S. 244, 114 S.Ct. 1483, 128 L.Ed.2d 229 (1994).

The idea that violations of rights can be deterred by requiring wrongdoers to compensate their victims is central to the law of damages. Yet, Professor Darryl Levinson has argued that where constitutional torts are concerned, the damages remedy does not deter governmental actors, who "respond to political incentives, not financial ones." Darryl Levinson, Making Government Pay: Markets, Politics, and the Allocation of Constitutional Costs, 67 U.Chi.L.Rev. 345, 420 (2000). Regarding *Bivens* (p. 12), for example, Professor Levinson argues that remedies like the exclusionary rule are more effective than compensatory damages for fourth amendment violations, because they "eliminate * * * political rewards by derailing convictions—and in a highly visible, politically salient manner." The challenge, then, is to find remedies that control government behavior by capitalizing "on the insight that government responds to political, not market, incentives." For responses to Professor Levinson, see Symposium: Re–Examining First Principles: Deterrence and Corrective Justice in Constitutional Torts, 35 Ga.L.Rev. 837 (2001).

NOTE ON NOMINAL DAMAGES

Nominal damages are a nominal or trivial sum of money (frequently one dollar) awarded to plaintiffs who have established a cause of action, but have not shown an injury for which compensatory damages can be awarded. Nominal damages are not available for every cause of action; some wrongs are not actionable unless actual injury can be proved. For example, actual injury is part of the plaintiff's prima facie case in negligence. There is, thus, no such thing as a nominal damage award in a negligence case; if the plaintiff fails to show an actual injury, she simply loses. E.g., Right v. Breen, 277 Conn. 364, 890 A.2d 1287 (2006).

History has played an important role in determining whether nominal damages are available for a particular cause of action. Originally, actions descending from the writ of trespass were actionable without any showing of harm (perhaps because of their quasi-criminal character). Those descending from the action on the case required a showing of harm as part of the plaintiff's prima facie case. Now, however, the pattern is considerably more complex. In fact, Professor McCormick has argued that except for negligence, slander, slander of title and perhaps fraud, "in practically all other actions for torts formerly remediable in 'case' the modern decisions seem to adopt the view that, in the absence of actual damage, the defendant's misconduct renders him liable to nominal damages." Certainly it is well-accepted that nominal damages are available in contract cases, and contract is clearly descended from the action on the case. Charles McCormick, Handbook on the Law of Damages 89 (1935). For a thorough discussion, and an attempt to formulate a new rule, see Nappe v. Anschelewitz, Barr, Ansell & Bonello, 97 N.J. 37, 477 A.2d 1224 (1984)(nominal damages are available for all intentional torts, at least where the victim has suffered some injury but cannot prove an entitlement to compensatory damages).

At early common law, wrongs were actionable without any showing of injury because tort law and criminal law overlapped and shared a common purpose—sanctioning the defendant's conduct. Even if the plaintiff had not been injured, the peace had been broken. Nominal damage awards also served a purpose now served by declaratory judgment awards. By suing for nominal damages, a plaintiff could obtain a definitive adjudication of his rights before any harm occurred. This was particularly useful in disputes over property lines. By seeking nominal damages for trespass, a property owner could establish the property's boundaries and prevent others from acquiring prescriptive rights.

Nominal damages also allowed courts to provide at least some remedy to plaintiffs whose cases failed for a simple lack of proof. This can be particularly important if the case involves a fee shifting statute that awards attorney fees to the prevailing party. If the plaintiff tried to show actual damages but failed to persuade the jury, an award of nominal damages may still qualify the plaintiff as a prevailing party entitled to attorney's fees. Farrar v. Hobby, 506 U.S. 103, 113 S.Ct. 566, 121 L.Ed.2d 494 (1992). See Chapter 10(B).

The plaintiff's relative lack of success, however, can be taken into account in determining whether the plaintiff truly prevailed, and in setting the amount of the award. To determine whether a plaintiff who recovers only nominal damages should be awarded attorney's fees, several circuits rely on the framework found in Justice O'Connor's concurring opinion in *Farrar*. This framework examines: (1) the difference between the judgment recovered and the judgment sought; (2) the significance of the legal issue on which the plaintiff prevailed; and (3) the public purpose served by the litigation. Sometimes this results in a substantial fee award, as in Brandau v. Kansas, 168 F.3d 1179 (10th Cir.), cert. denied, 526 U.S. 1133, 119 S.Ct. 1808, 143 L.Ed.2d 1012 (1999) (fee award of $41,000 to a plaintiff who recovered nominal damages in a sexual harassment suit). Sometimes it does not, as in Rivera v. Horton, 7 F.Supp.2d 147 (N.D.N.Y.1998) (fee award of 66 cents to a plaintiff who recovered one dollar against each of two defendants in an action against correctional officers for excessive use of force).

Can nominal damages also serve as a "hook" for punitive damages? Where common law causes of action are concerned, most courts require a showing of actual damages before punitive damages can be awarded, although there are exceptions. See Nappe v. Anschelewitz, Barr, Ansell & Bonello, 97 N.J. 37, 477 A.2d 1224 (1984) (punitive damages may be assessed in an action for an intentional tort involving egregious conduct whether or not compensatory damages are awarded). Where constitutional rights are violated, on the other hand, it seems to be settled that punitive damages can be awarded without an award of compensatory damages. Searles v. Van Bebber, 251 F.3d 869, 880 (10th Cir.2001); Alexander v. Riga, 208 F.3d 419, 430 (3d Cir.2000). Where statutory violations are concerned, the courts are divided. See, e.g., Louisiana ACORN Fair Housing, Inc. v. LeBlanc, 211 F.3d 298 (5th Cir.2000), cert. denied, 532 U.S. 904, 121 S.Ct. 1225, 149 L.Ed.2d 136 (2001) (concluding, after reviewing the split in authority, that punitive damages cannot be awarded for a violation of the Fair Housing Act unless actual damages have been awarded).

In summary, the practical significance of nominal damage awards has always been thought to be limited to two sorts of cases: cases where the plaintiff is really after a sort of declaratory judgment, and cases where the plaintiff simply could not persuade the jury to award substantial damages. As for the first category of cases, an action for declaratory judgment now achieves the same purpose. As for the second category, given the crush of litigation that courts (allegedly) now face, isn't it right that a plaintiff who can't prove damages should go away empty-handed? Why not eliminate nominal damage awards altogether?

NOTE ON MONETARY RELIEF IN LAW AND EQUITY

In the brief quotation at the beginning of this chapter, Professor McCormick describes one of the salient characteristics of the damage award: it is a legal, as opposed to an equitable remedy. As we have seen, the equity courts sought to give a claimant *specific* relief, by undoing the harm that occurred or preventing it from happening in the first place. By contrast, the law courts relied on a *substitutionary* remedy, offering to cure the injury by offering recompense in money.

Of course, the law courts sometimes granted specific relief. Someone whose personal property had been taken, for example, could post a bond and get a writ of replevin from the law courts, which would instruct the person executing the writ to seize the property and return it. The writ of ejectment could give a landowner possession of his property. The writ of habeas corpus could release a party from confinement.

Conversely, equity courts sometimes awarded compensatory monetary relief. If a claimant sought specific performance of an obligation to pay money, and the legal remedy was inadequate, an equity court would order the money paid. Or, if an injunction had issued, and an additional award of money for past harm could dispose of the case completely, an equity court could order monetary relief under its "clean up jurisdiction." Then, there were cases in which the claimant simply had no cause of action at all in the law courts, such as cases involving trusts or mortgages, leaving all remedies up to the equity courts.

In cases like these, whether the relief sought should be characterized as legal or equitable turns on how the court's order would be enforced. Equity courts ordered defendants, personally, to act, and enforced their orders by their contempt power. Law courts relied on separate administrative proceedings to enforce their judgments. Thus, if the defendant failed to pay a money judgment, the plaintiff had to initiate separate proceedings to enforce the judgment, *garnishing* the defendant's wages, or *executing* against her property, for example. Even writs were executed by a sheriff or another administrative officer, who took possession of the property or person in question from the defendant and restored it to the plaintiff. Execution, garnishment, and other post-judgment remedies are considered further in Chapter 8.

Although only a few jurisdictions still maintain separate equity or chancery courts, there are reasons why it remains important to understand the circumstances under which equity courts would order "equitable monetary relief." One, discussed in some detail below, is that the right to a jury trial may turn on the characterization of the remedy. Another is Congress's penchant for authorizing courts to grant "appropriate equitable relief" when a statute has been violated. Then, whether courts of equity could award a particular remedy becomes a critical question.

Such an issue surfaced in the Supreme Court's opinion in Mertens v. Hewitt Associates, 508 U.S. 248, 113 S.Ct. 2063, 124 L.Ed.2d 161 (1993). In *Mertens*, beneficiaries of a pension plan alleged that an actuary's wrongdoing caused their pension plan to be underfunded. They sued under a federal statute, the Employee Retirement Income Security Act (ERISA), which provides that a plan beneficiary may bring a civil action:

> (A) to enjoin any act or practice which violates any provision of [ERISA] or the terms of the plan, or (B) *to obtain other appropriate equitable relief* (i) to redress such violations or (ii) to enforce any provisions of [ERISA] or the terms of the plan * * *.

29 U.S.C. § 1132(a)(3)(emphasis added).

The beneficiaries argued that equity courts routinely awarded compensatory monetary relief against nonfiduciaries who participated in a fiduciary breach; therefore, Congress must have intended to authorize monetary relief against nonfiduciaries when it empowered the courts to award "appropriate equitable relief."

While Justice Scalia, writing for the Court on a 5–4 vote, conceded that equity courts routinely awarded monetary damages in breach of trust cases, the Court majority held that the phrase "appropriate equitable relief" should be read more narrowly. In other sections of the statute, Congress had authorized courts to award "legal *or* equitable relief"; in § 502(a)(3), Congress authorized only equitable relief. Therefore, the Court reasoned, Congress must have intended to maintain a distinction between actions in which both legal and equitable remedies were to be available, and actions in which only equitable remedies were to be available. To allow damages, the prototypical legal remedy, in an action in which the statute authorized only equitable remedies would obliterate the distinction. Therefore, Justice Scalia wrote, in using the phrase "appropriate equitable relief" Congress must have intended to refer to "those categories of relief that were *typically* available in equity (such as injunction, mandamus, and restitution, but not compensatory damages)." 508 U.S. at 256.

Justice Scalia's understanding of equity practice and his interpretation of ERISA have been harshly criticized:

The main damage to ERISA remedy law was done in the Court's decision in *Mertens*, which construed "appropriate equitable relief" in section 502(a)(3) to preclude monetary damages for consequential injury on the ground that such relief was not "typical" of pre-fusion equity. I have explained why this holding entails a triple error: (1) make-whole monetary relief always was and remains routine in trust and other fields of equity; (2) there is no support for the suggestion that Congress intended the "unlikely" step of reviving pre-fusion equity practice; and (3) the suggestion that what Congress intended by its language was a category of "typically equitable" remedies is not only without foundation in the text or legislative history, but has unraveled in the application as well.

The blunder that invited these errors was Justice Scalia's confusion in *Mertens* about the distinction between equitable jurisdiction and equitable relief. He rightly noted that equity courts had jurisdiction in some circumstances to award money damages in common law cases. His mistake was to infer that since "money damages are ... the classic form of legal relief," when equity courts awarded money damages they were always awarding legal relief. That point is flatly wrong. Equity courts also awarded damages (sometimes called surcharge) as equitable relief in cases that were exclusively equitable, above all in breach of trust cases.

John H. Langbein, What ERISA Means by "Equitable": The Supreme Court's Trail of Error in Russell, Mertens and Great–West, 103 Colum.L.Rev. 1317, 1364 (2003). See also Colleen P. Murphy, Money as a "Specific" Remedy, 58 Ala.L.Rev. 119 (2006); Tracy A. Thomas, Justice Scalia Reinvents Restitution, 36 Loy.L.A.L.Rev. 1063 (2003).

The dispute in *Mertens* was semantic: are compensatory damages to be thought of as a fundamentally legal remedy, even if, historically, equity courts sometimes awarded them? Given how often Congress has authorized "appropriate equitable relief," the issue is not an isolated one. In other contexts, the Court has taken a fairly expansive view of the equitable power of a court to award monetary relief in order to make the plaintiff whole. For example, in employment discrimination cases, the power to award "front pay"—an award of money to replace wages lost between the time when a judgment is entered and the time the plaintiff is reinstated or, if reinstatement is not possible, finds equivalent employment—is authorized as a form of "other equitable relief," and thus is not subject to the $300,000 cap that otherwise applies to compensatory damage awards in civil rights cases. Pollard v. E.I. du Pont de Nemours & Co., 532 U.S. 843, 121 S.Ct. 1946, 150 L.Ed.2d 62 (2001). For other examples, see School Committee of Burlington v. Department of Education of Massachusetts, 471 U.S. 359, 369, 105 S.Ct. 1996, 2002, 85 L.Ed.2d 385 (1985)(grant of equitable authority in Education of the Handicapped Act empowers a court to order school authorities to reimburse parents for their expenditures on private special education); Mitchell v. Robert DeMario Jewelry, Inc., 361 U.S. 288, 80 S.Ct. 332, 4 L.Ed.2d 323 (1960)(power to enjoin discrimination in employment under the Fair Labor Standards Act includes the power to order reimbursement of wages lost because of the discrimination); Porter v. Warner Holding Co., 328 U.S. 395, 66 S.Ct. 1086, 90 L.Ed.

1332 (1946) (power to order restitution of rents collected in violation of the Emergency Price Control Act is inherent in the court's equitable power).

NOTE ON THE RIGHT TO A JURY TRIAL

One of the most important consequences of characterizing a remedy as legal or equitable is that the characterization may determine whether there is a right to a jury trial. The Seventh Amendment preserves the right to a jury trial "[i]n suits at common law, where the value in controversy shall exceed twenty dollars." The right extends beyond the common law forms of action, however; the phrase "suits at common law" includes any suit in which legal, as opposed to equitable, rights are at issue. Parsons v. Bedford, 28 U.S. (3 Pet.) 433, 447, 7 L.Ed. 732 (1830). The right to a jury trial applies even to causes of action created by Congress, if the cause of action is analogous to a suit at common law. Feltner v. Columbia Pictures Television, Inc., 523 U.S. 340, 118 S.Ct. 1279, 140 L.Ed.2d 438 (1998) (recognizing right to a jury trial in an action for statutory damages under the Copyright Act); Tull v. United States, 481 U.S. 412, 417, 107 S.Ct. 1831, 1835, 95 L.Ed.2d 365 (1987) (civil penalties).

There are two questions to be considered in deciding whether there is a right to a jury trial under a particular statute: are the rights analogous to common law rights, and is the remedy sought legal or equitable in nature? Chauffeurs, Teamsters and Helpers, Local No. 391 v. Terry, 494 U.S. 558, 110 S.Ct. 1339, 108 L.Ed.2d 519 (1990). Of the two questions, the nature of the remedy is the more important. Granfinanciera S.A. v. Nordberg, 492 U.S. 33, 109 S.Ct. 2782, 106 L.Ed.2d 26 (1989).

To illustrate the Court's approach to the jury trial question, in *Terry* the question was whether employees suing their union for failing to represent them had a right to a jury trial. The right to representation was a creature of statute, specifically section 301 of the National Labor Relations Act, unknown at common law. The Court struggled in its search for an analogous action. Writing for a plurality, Justice Marshall noted that the duty of fair representation is a fiduciary duty, and that the action was somewhat analogous to an equitable action for breach of trust. Yet, to show that the union had failed in its duty to enforce the labor agreement, the employees would first need to show that the employer had breached it. Therefore, the action was a hybrid, part legal—breach of contract—and part equitable—breach of fiduciary duty—in nature. (Justice Stevens thought the action more comparable to a legal malpractice claim, the three dissenting Justices thought the similarity to the equitable trust action was dispositive, and Justice Brennan thought the analysis should focus exclusively on the nature of the remedy sought, which he thought was legal in this case.)

As for the character of the remedy, Justice Marshall—writing for a majority of the Court on this point—concluded that the remedy sought, back pay and benefits, was essentially equivalent to compensatory damages. Because compensatory damages represented the traditional form of relief offered in courts of law, either party could demand a jury trial. While monetary relief might be characterized as equitable where it is "restitutionary, such as in actions for disgorgement of improper profits," or where it is "incidental to or intertwined with injunctive relief," neither exception was applicable in *Terry*. Therefore, as the issues in the case were neither clearly equitable nor clearly legal, the legal character of the relief sought was controlling, and the plaintiffs had a right to a jury trial. See also City of Monterey v. Del Monte Dunes, Ltd., 526 U.S. 687, 710, 119 S.Ct. 1624, 1639, 143 L.Ed.2d 882, 905 (1999) (recognizing right to a jury trial in suits seeking compensation for a regulatory taking, because compensation is legal relief, which "differs from equitable restitution and other monetary remedies available in equity, for in determining just compensation, the question is what has the owner lost, not what has the taker gained").

In passing, the *Terry* Court noted that the circuit courts have agreed that plaintiffs alleging racial or sexual discrimination in employment and seeking backpay under Title VII, however, have no right to a jury trial. The Court pointed out that in Title VII, "Congress specifically characterized backpay under Title VII as a form of 'equitable relief.' ('[T]he court may ... order * * * reinstatement or hiring of employees, with or without back pay ..., or any other equitable relief as the court deems appropriate'), and that in a discrimination case, back pay is generally restitutionary in nature." 494 U.S. at 572. Therefore, the Court felt the remedy sought in *Terry* was "clearly different from backpay sought for violations of Title VII." Id. Since the decision in *Terry*, the Civil Rights Act of 1991 has made compensatory damages and punitive damages available in Title VII and ADEA actions, and provides for a jury trial when those damages are sought. 42 U.S.C. §§ 1981a(a),(c).

To test your understanding of all this, suppose an employee argues that she was fired in retaliation for attempting to enforce her right to certain pension benefits, which would violate section 510 of ERISA and entitle her to a remedy under section 502(a)(3), the provision discussed in *Mertens* above. Because ERISA has been held to preempt state tort actions for wrongful discharge, she brings her suit in federal court, seeking back pay, reinstatement and punitive damages. If she proves her case, are these remedies available? She also asks for a jury trial. Should a jury trial be granted? For a discussion of some of the issues involved, see Thomas v. Oregon Fruit Products Co., 228 F.3d 991 (9th Cir.2000) (reviewing conflicting authorities).

B. THE BASIC ISSUES

PROBLEM: COUNTRY LODGE V. MILLER (REPRISED)
THE DAMAGES OPTION

Review the facts in *Country Lodge v. Miller*, set out in Chapter 1. Suppose that when Miller began to build her facility, the owners of Country Lodge threatened to sue for an injunction prohibiting construction of the cider mill on the grounds that it might pollute the river. The owners of Country Lodge refrained from suing when Miller wrote them a letter that said:

> I do not believe that my cider press will cause any negative environmental impact. Indeed, I share your belief that the river's integrity must be protected. If you allow construction to go forward, I will take whatever

steps are reasonably necessary to protect the interest we all share in keeping our river pristine.

Using the five inquiries identified by Professor McCormick in the excerpt that follows, plan litigation strategies to maximize and minimize Country Lodge's damages. If Country Lodge is not successful in obtaining an injunction, but does prove that Miller is liable for the pollution, what damages should Country Lodge recover? If Country Lodge does obtain an injunction, should damages also be awarded?

1. A ROADMAP TO DAMAGES

CHARLES McCORMICK, HANDBOOK ON THE LAW OF DAMAGES

2–3 (1935)

What is included in the subject of Damages? In answering this inquiry, it will be helpful to single out certain typical problems arising in a claim for damages,[15] and to consider which of these are embraced in our subject. First, the lawyer to whom is presented such a claim will consider whether the claim is enforceable at all, or, in legal parlance, whether there is a "cause of action." Examples of the matters considered here are such questions as whether an alleged contract is founded on a valid consideration, whether a trespasser on another's land can recover for injuries caused by a dangerous situation there existing, or whether a statute purporting to give a right to sue for losses sustained by one who has purchased shares of stock is constitutional. Similar in effect are all the questions relating to whether a good defense is available to the whole claim, such as the questions of release, accord and satisfaction, and contributory negligence. Needless to say, all of these matters comprised in our first group, although they determine decisively whether a given claim for damages can be successfully maintained, are outside the subject of Damages itself, as the term is traditionally used to mark off a special subject in the law.

A second inquiry which the lawyer investigating his client's claim for damages would frequently make, is this: What are the *elements* or items of the client's loss, injury, or grievance which will be recognized by the court as grounds of compensation? Will allowance be made, for example, in a contract case for disappointment due to the failure of the bargain; or, in an action for personal injury, can expense of nursing be recovered? Third, and closely allied to the last, is the inquiry: What formula of *measurement* is to be used in fixing compensation for the element or elements of loss which are recognized? The choice here may be between standards of value, e.g., whether the value of some property wrongfully appropriated shall be the market value or the value in use, or the value at the time of taking or

---

15. It is well to notice at the outset that the term "damage" is usually employed by lawyers and judges to mean the loss or injury from which the claim is asserted. "Damages," on the other hand, while sometimes used in the same sense, is more usually and conveniently limited to the meaning of the money award given as compensation for the loss.

the time of trial. Again, the standard may be one of reasonable and necessary expenditure, or the measure may be fixed, as in case of liquidated damages, by agreement of the parties. A fourth avenue of inquiry is the ascertainment of the general rules, standards, and doctrines which place *limits* upon the application of the formulas of compensation to the recognized elements. Chief among these are the requirements of certainty, and of foreseeability either at the time of the making of a contract, or as of the time of the commission of a wrong. Fifth, in examining the claim, the lawyer must inquire into the procedural rules which regulate the manner in which he can best plead and prove the elements of loss or injury, the fashion in which the judge should state the problem of compensation to the jury, and the standards to be used by the trial and appellate judges in reviewing the jury's award.

Notes

1. *What is the plaintiff's cause of action?* Although Professor McCormick is correct that the existence of a cause of action is outside the subject of damages proper, the plaintiff's cause of action is nonetheless the starting point for determining what damages are available. The purpose of any remedy, after all, is to protect the rightful position, and the rightful position is defined by the substantive law.

In tort cases, the rightful position is usually defined as the *status quo ante*; the purpose of the damage award is to give the plaintiff a sum of money that will place him in the position he occupied before the tort. In contract cases, the rightful position is usually defined as "the benefit of the bargain;" the damage award aims to place the plaintiff in the position he would have occupied had the contract been performed.

These two goals can be stated in a way that makes them seem perfectly consistent—the plaintiff in either event must be placed in the position he would have occupied had there been no tort/no breach—but there is a tension between them. The tort remedy looks backwards, to the plaintiff's pre-tort position, while the contract remedy looks ahead, and "restores" to the plaintiff a benefit that he expected to get in the future, but never in fact possessed. While in many cases the damages will be the same whether the plaintiff sues in tort or contract, and while in others only one theory may in fact be available, in many cases the plaintiff may have a choice, and that choice may affect the size of the award drastically.

Further, the goal in both tort and contract cases differs from the goal in restitution cases. The goal of the substantive law of restitution is to prevent unjust enrichment by stripping the defendant of unfairly made gains, thereby "restoring" to the plaintiff that which he neither lost nor expected to gain. Again, the size of the plaintiff's recovery may turn on the choice to pursue a cause of action in restitution instead of tort or contract.

Beyond the practical concern of choosing the cause of action that best serves the client's interests, this tension between tort, contract and restitution also raises important normative issues. That is, on particular facts, *should* an injured party be allowed to pursue restitution or compensation, whether in tort or contract? Usually, this normative question is framed as a question of substantive law: Do the facts at hand state a cause of action in tort, in contract, or for restitution? Yet, the decision to allow a cause of action in contract, but not in tort, or for restitution but not for breach of contract, really only matters because it affects the remedy, i.e., the amount that can be recovered. Therefore, the remedies course offers the perfect vantage to look back at the substantive law of torts, contracts, and restitution, and ask, why one and not the other?

2. *What elements of damages are recoverable?* In speaking of the elements of damages that are recoverable, Professor McCormick had in mind the various elements that make up the compensatory damage award. As a preliminary step, however, the lawyer investigating a damage claim should examine what other kinds of damages are available. If she cannot prove her client sustained actual loss, will nominal damages be recoverable? Are punitive damages a possibility?

Turning to compensatory damages, after the cause of action has been determined, one can begin to zero in on the elements of damages that may be recoverable. For starters, the client usually will have a very clear idea of what losses he wants to recoup. These obvious losses, however, are only a beginning. Think about the client's position. If it is a contract case, how would he have been better off if the contract had been performed? What would he have had then that he does not have now? In a tort case, where would the plaintiff be if the tort had never occurred? What would he have that he does not have now? What injuries would he have avoided? Conversely, what opportunities for gain have his injuries forced him to forgo? If the legal theory is restitution, how has the defendant profited? There is much room for creativity in building the case for damages; frequently, a little thought will reveal losses that were not at first apparent.

The next step is to look to the case law to determine which of these losses are compensable, that is, which is a proper element of damages for the plaintiff's cause of action. Here, an important distinction has developed in the cases between two categories of damages—general damages and special damages. *General damages* are defined as those damages which usually or naturally flow from the defendant's wrongful act. *Special damages,* by contrast, are damages that are peculiar to the particular plaintiff's circumstances. For example, if the defendant were held liable for destroying the plaintiff's car, the general damages would be the value of the car: any time property is destroyed, its value is lost. If the plaintiff, however, lost his job because without a car he was late for work, damages to compensate him for the loss of his job would be recoverable only as special damages, if at all. That loss is peculiar to his particular circumstances; it does not "naturally" flow from the destruction of a car.

In many cases, general damages will adequately compensate the plaintiff; after all, general damages evolved because those losses were the ones most frequently experienced. General damages, however, are not always an accurate measure of actual loss. In particular cases, general damages may over- or undercompensate the plaintiff. General damages may overcompensate the plaintiff because they are available automatically, without regard for the plaintiff's actual losses. For example, if a defendant reneges on a contract to purchase the plaintiff's house, the plaintiff is entitled to damages measured by the difference between the contract price and the house's market value, even though the plaintiff has changed her mind and is glad she did not have to sell it.

More frequently, however, general damages will undercompensate the plaintiff, because the plaintiff has suffered losses peculiar to her own circumstances and which are not included in the general damages. Returning to the example, the plaintiff who has lost her job because her car was destroyed will be undercompensated if she is limited to recovering the market value of the car. Thus, for her the critical step will be to determine if the loss of her job is compensable as *special damages*. Whether special damages are recoverable turns on the application of the doctrines of foreseeability, certainty, and avoidable consequences, discussed below.

3. *How are the damages to be measured?* Nominal damages, for obvious reasons, do not present much of a measurement problem. As for punitive damages, the standards for measuring them will be discussed in Chapter 6.

In measuring compensatory damages, at least where pecuniary losses are concerned, the central concept is that of value. The problem is, value can be measured in many ways. Professor McCormick lists just a few of the possibilities: value may mean market value, or it may mean value in use; it may mean value at the time of trial, or value at the time of the defendant's wrongdoing. The rules that dictate how to measure value, and the policies that explain them, are explored in the next section.

The concept of value is of no help, however, when compensatory damages are to be awarded for nonpecuniary losses; there is no marketplace to which one can turn to determine the "value" of pain, suffering, humiliation or distress. For this, courts simply turn to the jury, allowing the jury to determine the size of the award based upon evidence of the nature and circumstances of the defendant's wrong and its effect on the plaintiff.

4. *Is the plaintiff's recovery to be limited because his losses were unforeseeable, uncertain, avoidable, offset by benefits, or limited by agreement?*

a. *Was the loss foreseeable?* As we have seen, plaintiffs may be undercompensated if they are limited to general damages and cannot recover their particular, individualized losses as special damages. The most significant barrier to recovering a particular element of loss as special damages is the requirement that damages must be foreseeable before they can be recovered. General damages are foreseeable by definition, because they are naturally expected to flow from the defendant's act. Special damages are another matter. Before any particular element of special damages can be recovered, foreseeability must be established on the facts of the particular case.

b. *Are the plaintiff's losses reasonably certain?* The plaintiff must also prove the amount of her losses with reasonable certainty. The certainty requirement has two aspects. The first overlaps with the substantive law of causation. The plaintiff must show that it is reasonably certain (or probable) that she has suffered a loss because of the defendant's conduct. The second aspect is evidentiary. Once the fact of loss is established, she then must provide the jury with evidence from which the amount of her loss can be established with "reasonable certainty." Courts are wont to say that if the existence of a loss is clearly shown, the plaintiff must merely provide the jury with the best evidence reasonably available of the amount. So long as it is certain that the plaintiff has actually suffered a loss, the certainty rule simply requires her to provide some evidence from which the jury can make a reasonable, non-speculative estimate of the amount of her damages.

c. *Could the plaintiff, by her own actions, reasonably have avoided or limited the loss she suffered?* The plaintiff may not recover damages for any losses that could reasonably have been avoided. This rule requires the plaintiff to mitigate her damages by taking steps to limit the harm she suffers. Thus, if the defendant has wrongfully caused the plaintiff to lose her job, the plaintiff must make a reasonable effort to find other, similar work if she wishes to claim lost wages. If the plaintiff is physically injured, she will not recover damages for any aggravation of the injury that medical care reasonably available to her could have avoided. Although the avoidable consequences rule may often function to limit the plaintiff's recovery, it has a positive aspect as well. Any expenses incurred by the plaintiff in a reasonable attempt to mitigate her losses are recoverable as damages.

d. *Were the plaintiff's losses offset by benefits?* If the defendant's conduct has caused harm to the plaintiff, but at the same time has conferred a benefit on the plaintiff, under appropriate circumstances the plaintiff's recovery must be reduced by the amount of the benefit she has received. Of course, difficult issues can arise as to whether the benefit was really conferred by the defendant's wrongdoing, or whether the plaintiff would have gained the benefit in any event.

e. *Did the plaintiff agree that the defendant's liability would be limited?* Agreements may limit the plaintiff's recovery in a number of ways. In tort cases, the plaintiff may have agreed in advance to waive her right to sue, or to release the defendant from liability, or the plaintiff may have signed a release after the injury occurred. The validity and effect of releases, however, traditionally has been thought of as a matter of substantive law, and left to the torts class. In contract cases, the contract between the parties may include a limitation of liability for consequential damages, or a liquidated damages clause. Ultimately, whether such clauses are enforceable is probably also better thought of as a question of substantive law. It has, however, traditionally been included in the remedies course, so it is discussed in this chapter.

5. *How is the plaintiff's claim to be presented at trial?* One might expect damages to be the one area of the law where something approaching mathematical certainty could be achieved, with each loss tallied up and measured in accordance with generally accepted accounting principles. That expectation could hardly be farther from the truth. As Professor McCormick points out, damages are peculiarly the domain of the jury. The early practice, in fact, was for the jury to hear evidence as to all the items of loss, and simply return a verdict stating the total amount of their judgment, often not even differentiating between compensatory and punitive damages. Even the idea of giving the jury instructions as to the measure of damages is a relatively recent development, dating to the 1850's.

Modern practice at least requires the jury to differentiate between punitive and compensatory damages, and the growing fondness for the special verdict has resulted in the more frequent practice of having juries itemize various elements of the plaintiff's recovery. Still, general verdicts are common, and where damages are unliquidated and disputed, the amount of the award remains the jury's province. Except in relatively rare cases, how the jury calculates any particular item of loss is beyond the ken of all but the jurors themselves.

After the award has been announced, the trial court's review is quite limited. It can act only if an error of law has been committed (as, for example, where the jury has awarded damages for a loss that, as a matter of law, is not compensable), or if the verdict is grossly excessive or inadequate. To reject a jury verdict as excessive, the court must be convinced that the verdict is so large that it must have been the result of passion or prejudice. The standard for review of a verdict for inadequacy is less well established, but an inadequate award can be rejected if the jury's verdict is completely unsupported by the evidence.

If the trial court is convinced that the jury has erred seriously enough to justify interfering with its traditional prerogative to assess damages, the judge has two options. The judge can simply order a new trial. Or, the judge can set the amount of damages, giving the parties the option of accepting the new amount or having a new trial. When the judge decides that a verdict is excessive and offers the plaintiff the choice of a lesser amount or a new trial, it is called remittitur. When the verdict is thought inadequate, and the defendant is offered the choice of accepting a larger verdict or a new trial, it is called additur.

Both remittitur and additur threaten the right of the parties to a jury trial, because the risk and expense of a new trial coerce the party into accepting the judge's opinion on damages over the jury's. Remittitur, however, was known at common law in 1791, and because the Seventh Amendment guarantees only the right to jury as it existed at common law, the United States Supreme Court has found it constitutional. Additur, however, was unknown at common law, and so in the federal system it has been held unconstitutional. Dimick v. Schiedt, 293 U.S. 474, 55 S.Ct. 296, 79 L.Ed. 603 (1935). It is still available, though, in many state court systems. E.g., Right v. Breen, 277 Conn. 364, 890 A.2d 1287 (2006).

On appeal, review of the amount of compensatory damage awards is even more constrained, if that is possible. Most appellate courts will act only where the trial court, in rejecting a verdict or in letting it stand, has abused its discretion. In federal court, appellate review is complicated by the interaction of the *Erie* doctrine (Erie Railroad Co. v. Tompkins, 304 U.S. 64, 58 S.Ct. 817, 82 L.Ed. 1188 (1938)), requiring federal courts in diversity actions to apply the state's substantive law, and the Seventh Amendment, which requires the amount of damages to be determined by a jury. Thus, in Gasperini v. Center for Humanities, Inc., 518 U.S. 415, 116 S.Ct. 2211, 135 L.Ed.2d 659 (1996), the Court held that under *Erie*, federal courts should apply state law to evaluate the adequacy or excessiveness of a verdict in a diversity case. *Gasperini* arose in New York, and under New York law, a jury award must be set aside by the appellate court if it "materially deviates from what is reasonable compensation." The Seventh Amendment, however, only permits a federal appellate court to override a jury's judgment with regard to damages if there has been an abuse of discretion. To accommodate these conflicting standards, the Court held that the federal district court should apply the New York standard to the jury's verdict, and the court of appeals should then review the district court's decision using an abuse of discretion standard.

Given the courts' limited power over damage awards once the jury has spoken, rules evolved to provide some control over the jury during the trial. Some of these rules, like the rules concerning foreseeability, certainty and avoidability, allow the court to exclude particular items of loss altogether. The rest control the jury by limiting the evidence brought before them through rules of proof and pleading, or by providing the jury with instructions that give the formulae by which losses are to be measured.

The rules of pleading and proof, like the requirements of foreseeability and certainty, favor general damages over special damages. General damages do not need to be alleged in the complaint in order to be recovered. Because general damages "naturally flow" from the defendant's acts, the defendant should be on notice that they will be at issue even if they are not alleged.

So, when a buyer pleads that a seller has breached a contract for the sale of goods, the buyer can recover as general damages the "benefit of the bargain" (the difference between the market value of the goods and the contract price), whether or not that loss is alleged in the complaint. If, however, the plaintiff also wants to recover damages for injury to his business reputation (hoping to persuade the jury that his business reputation was injured by his inability to maintain his inventory), that item of special damages would have to be specifically alleged. Or, if the plaintiff alleges that his car has been wrongfully destroyed, he can recover general damages (the value of the car) without alleging it specifically in the complaint. If the lack of a car caused him to miss work, he would have to allege lost wages specifically.

With personal injury cases, the rules of pleading are more complex. First, damages for pain and suffering are general damages, and do not need to be alleged in order to be recovered. Beyond that, whether a particular loss needs to be alleged turns on the extent to which the injury as described in the complaint gives notice of the harm the plaintiff suffered. For example, if the plaintiff alleges that she suffered a blow to the eye, she would no doubt be allowed to prove at trial that her vision was affected, and to recover damages for that injury without having specifically alleged it. If, however, she alleged a blow to the head, and then sought to prove a loss of vision, the evidence might not be admitted on the grounds that the complaint did not give notice that her vision was at issue. In either event, if she sought to recover damages for past or future earnings, because her eyesight was critical to her work, most courts would say this was an item of special damages and needed to be specifically alleged.

Turning to matters of proof, with the exception of two categories of cases, the rules for the proof of general and special damages are the same. The plaintiff bears the burden of proving the amount of her losses with reasonable certainty. The plaintiff who seeks the benefit of her bargain must show the market value of the goods, or land, or services promised to her. The plaintiff who seeks lost earnings must prove what she would have earned had she not been injured.

In two categories of cases, "general damages" has taken on a special meaning, allowing plaintiffs to recover damages without either pleading or proving them. In some cases, general damages are synonymous with presumed damages, and plaintiffs have been allowed to recover substantial sums to compensate them for batteries, assaults and the like, without any proof of loss. Somewhat similarly, in personal injury cases, juries have been allowed to assess pain and suffering damages on the basis of their knowledge of the injury suffered, without any direct evidence of pain and suffering. The plaintiff who suffers a broken arm may recover damages for pain and suffering without either alleging or proving them. The evidence of the broken arm itself gives the jury enough to go on.

The overriding impression left by the cases on pleading and proving damages is that these rules evolved to rescue lawyers who prepared well to prove liability, but gave no thought to damages until the trial was actually underway. The lesson they teach is that a damages case should be carefully planned, beginning even before the complaint is filed. The lawyer who relies on the judge to admit evidence of an injury that was insufficiently alleged, or who allows the jury to award damages without evidence of the size of the loss risks subjecting her client to a lottery (and herself to a malpractice suit). To represent a client's best interest, counsel should plan the damages side of a case from day one. If the client's losses have been itemized, the theory of liability selected with the type of loss in mind, the evidence gathered to substantiate them, and the conduct of the trial planned with an eye toward proving damages, remembering to allege the various elements of loss and to offer proof will be the least of the plaintiff's problems.

Anticipating the damages that will be claimed is also critical for defense counsel. If the plaintiff's damage claims are anticipated, a litigation strategy can be devised to minimize them. Evidence can be gathered to challenge the plaintiff's claims; arguments that the plaintiff's losses were unforeseeable or uncertain can be developed; the lack of attempts to mitigate the loss can be documented. Neither side can afford to make damages an afterthought.

Note on Election of Remedies

Many remedies may potentially be available when a person is injured, as your analysis of the variation on the Country Lodge problem at the beginning of this section probably suggests. Beyond the basic choice between the categories of legal and equitable remedies, specific tort remedies, contract remedies, restitutionary remedies and even statutory remedies may coalesce in a single set of facts.

When multiple remedies are possible, the doctrine of "election of remedies" may come into play. The traditional formulation of the doctrine had two parts: (1) a plaintiff who has two (or more) remedies concurrently available to her must choose between those remedies if they are inconsistent; and (2) once a plaintiff has clearly elected a remedy, he or she is bound by that choice.

This traditional formulation of the rule could work harsh results. For example, the doctrine of election of remedies could put a plaintiff whose property had been converted to a very difficult choice. He could try to retrieve the property by a writ of replevin, but, having elected his remedy, he might not then be allowed to sue for consequential damages for the loss of his property's use. Or, he could sue for damages, but if the defendant turned out to have no assets to satisfy the judgment, he might be unable to get his stolen property back, having elected damages as his remedy.

Such a result might have made sense in a legal system that placed a high value on precise pleadings intended to narrow the case to a single issue for trial. It seems ludicrous in the modern system of notice pleading, in which multiple causes of action and liberal amendment are commonplace. Thus, modern courts have sharply curtailed and simplified the election of remedies doctrine.

So far as the first prong of the election doctrine is concerned, modern courts have shifted the emphasis from whether the remedies are different in form to asking whether allowing both remedies will result in double recovery or overcompensation. The cases now recognize that there is no reason not to allow a plaintiff to recover the specific property taken and also to recover damages for loss of the property's use. On the other hand, if allowing two remedies would put the plaintiff in better than the rightful position, clearly a choice must be made. Country Lodge, for example, cannot get an injunction prohibiting Miller from dumping in the river in the future, and at the same time recover damages based on the harm from future dumping.

The second prong of the traditional doctrine had to do with the timing of the choice. If a plaintiff indicated, by his pleadings or even by his actions, that he intended to pursue a particular remedy, he might be bound by that choice and precluded from pursuing an alternative, inconsistent remedy. This insistence that a plaintiff had to stick with his first choice of remedy also could work harshly, by forcing plaintiffs to commit themselves to a remedy long before all the facts were in, or by interpreting acts that were not intended as a choice of remedy as manifesting an election.

Again, the modern cases have substantially reinterpreted the rule, emphasizing that the timing of the plaintiff's choice is relevant only to the extent that the choice—or the failure to choose—may harm the defendant. This aspect of the doctrine of election of remedies is effectively a variation on the doctrine of estoppel. If the plaintiff indicates that he will pursue one remedy, and it would prejudice the defendant to allow the plaintiff to change his mind, the court may find that the plaintiff has elected his remedy. If the plaintiff has not chosen, and the defendant is prejudiced by the delay, the court may put plaintiff to the choice, or choose for him in a way that will minimize the harm. If there is no harm to the defendant, however, there is no reason not to allow the plaintiff to pursue as many remedies as he wishes, even adding new theories up to the time of trial, so long as the pleading rules allow it.

Finally, the modern cases recognize that rules of res judicata and satisfaction of judgments may be involved in election of remedies cases. Where the plaintiff's case has gone to judgment, and the plaintiff has lost, res judicata usually prevents him from bringing the same suit on a different legal theory, seeking a different remedy. Similarly, if the plaintiff has had a judgment, the rule that a judgment may be satisfied only once prevents him from suing again, on a different legal theory, for a recovery that is essentially duplicative.

On the other hand, suppose the plaintiff has won on the merits, only to discover that the remedy sought is ineffective. To return to an earlier example, suppose he sued for damages for conversion, only to discover the defendant had no assets. Is there any reason he should not be allowed to return to court and seek the return of the specific property taken, if the defendant still has it? Once it is understood that the operation of the election of remedies doctrine on these facts really has to do with preserving the finality of judgments, it becomes apparent that the same rules pertaining to modification of judgments that were studied in Chapter 3 ought simply to be applied here.

Election of remedies problems arise most frequently in cases involving deals gone sour, cases in which the plaintiff may have a choice between going ahead with the deal and suing later for damages, or calling the deal off and demanding damages or restitution. Notes following the cases on breach of contract and restitution in Chapter 7 explore restitutionary remedies in greater detail. For now, the contours of the modern doctrine of election of remedies can be sketched quickly:

(1) So far as pleading goes, a plaintiff may allege as many legal theories and alternative remedies as the facts will support, whether or not they are inconsistent.

(2) Most courts now recognize that there is no reason to require a plaintiff to elect among remedies prior to trial, unless failing to elect would harm the defendant.

(3) While it is much less important now than it once was that a plaintiff not act in a way that is inconsistent with remedies she may later want to pursue, a plaintiff must still be careful not to indicate that she is pursuing a particular remedy if she might later want to change her strategy. If changing strategy prejudices the defendant, the plaintiff may be stuck with her first choice.

(4) A plaintiff may generally now combine different forms of remedy—legal and equitable, damages and restitution—so long as the combination does not result in double recovery or overcompensation.

(5) Once a judgment is entered, rules of res judicata and satisfaction of judgments may preclude seeking additional or alternative remedies, unless changed circumstances justify modifying the judgment.

2. VALUE

My final conclusion as to the value of the company is that it is worth somewhere between $90 million and $100 million as a going concern, and to satisfy the people who want precision on the value, I fix the exact value of the company at the average of those, $96,856,850, which of course is a total absurdity that anybody could fix a value with that degree of precision, but for the lawyers who want me to make that fool estimate, I have just made it.

Citibank, N.A. v. Baer, 651 F.2d 1341, 1347 (10th Cir.1980) (quoting the trial court). See Keith Sharfman, Valuation Averaging: A New Procedure for Resolving Valuation Disputes, 88 Minn.L.Rev. 357 (2003).

The concept of value is central to the award of compensatory damages. Whatever area of substantive law is involved—contract or tort, constitutional or statutory—determining the plaintiff's loss in money is the first step in making the plaintiff whole. The cases that follow illustrate some of the tools at a court's disposal in determining value. Problems associated with valuing purely nonpecuniary losses like pain and suffering, or emotional distress are postponed until the next section.

PROBLEMS: VALUING THE PLAINTIFF'S LOSS

1. *Country Lodge v. Miller (Reprised)*: Assume that the apple mash Miller dumped into Rural River was contaminated by pesticide. If someone had standing to sue for the harm done to the river as a natural resource, how would the damages be calculated?

2. Tama's home was badly damaged in a fire for which Paul is legally responsible. The fire also destroyed most of Tama's clothing and furniture, a collection of 1960's acid rock posters from her parents' hippie days, the only manuscript of the novel she has been working on since college, and the diary she used to record the details of her high school trip to Israel.

As for her house, it is an older, single family dwelling in what has become a prized commercial area. If the house were demolished, the land could be sold for more than the pre-fire market value of the house and land together. Tama, however, loves her house, and wants to repair it. How are her damages to be established?

STATE v. BISHOP

Supreme Court of Indiana, 2003
800 N.E.2d 918

SHEPARD, CHIEF JUSTICE.

* * *

This is an eminent domain proceeding in which the State condemned land adjoining an interstate highway in order to build an interchange. We consider [a question] we have never addressed before. * * * [B]y what method does one assess the fair market value of a billboard that is taken in condemnation? * * *

STATEMENT OF FACTS

On December 6, 1996, the State of Indiana filed an action to appropriate a portion of Stephen and Molly Bishop's real estate for the purpose of constructing a cloverleaf interchange * * *. The State had previously offered the Bishops about $99,400 to purchase the land, which is located along [Interstate]–70 east of State Road 267 and is divided by I–70 into northern and southern parcels. The State condemned 1.177 acres, 0.681 acres of the northern parcel and 0.496 of the southern parcel, upon which four billboards were located. The residue of the Bishops' land was some 73 acres.

The court-appointed appraisers filed their report on November 14, 1997, assessing the fair market value of the land as $23,565 and the fair market value of improvements to the land as $167,945 (for a total value of $191,510). On December 10, 1997, the State filed exceptions to the appraisers' report as to the value of the improvements. The Bishops did not file exceptions.

In early 1998, the State deposited $191,510 with the clerk of the court. The Bishops filed a request for payment of the appraisers' amount. The State had no objection so the court ordered the clerk to pay the Bishops the amount on deposit. About this time, the Bishops sold most of the billboards to an outdoor advertising company for $2000 and gave an easement to place them along the Interstate at a price of $598,000.

* * *

On April 18, 2000, the Bishops filed a motion in limine, seeking to prohibit testimony about compensation other than fair market value, by which they meant the State's desire to pay the value of the land taken, the value of the one billboard taken, and the cost to move the remaining three billboards onto the Bishops' remaining property. The State filed a brief in opposition. After a hearing, the trial court issued an order on January 31, 2001, prohibiting the State from presenting any evidence regarding the cost of relocating the billboards or mentioning that the Bishops have billboards on their remaining property. The State subsequently filed a motion in limine to prohibit evidence of lost income or profits or the use of the capitalization of income approach to determining fair market value. The motion was denied.

The trial occurred in March 2001, and the jury returned a verdict of $595,000. The court deducted the money the State had already paid, then added $102,195.78 in interest and $2,500 in litigation expenses.

* * *

II. Fair Market Value of Billboards

* * * "It is well established in Indiana that the basic measure of damages in eminent domain cases is the fair market value of the property at the time of the take." "Fair market value is the price at which property would change hands between a willing buyer and seller, neither being under any compulsion to consummate the sale." "Anything affecting the sale value [on the date of the taking] ... is a proper matter for the jury's consideration in attempting to arrive at a 'fair market value.'"

Three widely accepted approaches to estimating the fair market value of property taken by eminent domain are:

(1) the current *cost of reproducing* the property less depreciation from all sources;

(2) the *'market data' approach* or value indicated by recent sales of comparable properties in the market, and

(3) the *'income-approach,'* or the value which the property's net earning power will support based upon the capitalization of net income.

The State argues that it was error for the trial court to exclude evidence regarding the cost to move the billboards from the condemned property to an appropriate location on the residue. We agree. The cost to move the billboards was evidence of the cost to reproduce the improvements situated on the condemned property and therefore should have been presented to the jury. Likewise, while capitalization of income is sometimes admissible to establish the fair market value of condemned billboards, for reasons which will be apparent from the discussion below, income capitalization was not relevant to market value given the facts of this case.

Prevailing Rules on Valuation. Because this Court has not previously addressed the question of the appropriate way to value billboards in an eminent domain case and because we are remanding this case for a new trial on values, we address the question now.

Other jurisdictions have treated billboards the same as other improvements to realty, adhering to the guiding principle that "improvements are compensable to the extent that they enhance the value of the land as a whole." Eminent Domain: Determination of Just Compensation for Condemnation of Billboards or Other Advertising Signs, 73 A.L.R.3d 1122, 1125. In surveying the way various jurisdictions value billboards, the A.L.R.'s editors concluded that "in arriving at this 'enhancement' value, virtually every court has appeared to limit its consideration to the evidence of the replacement or reproduction cost of the appropriated sign, less depreciation." Evidence of the rental income that the appropriated sign could be expected to produce "has been deemed admissible only where it was shown that the condemnee was unable to relocate a sign within the same market area."

* * *

Capitalization of income evidence is allowed only in limited circumstances. "Income from property is an element to be considered in determining the market value of condemned property when the income is derived from the intrinsic nature of the property itself and not from the business conducted on the property." State v. Jones, 173 Ind.App.243, 252–53, 363 N.E.2d 1028, 1024 (1977) (quoting State v. Williams, 156 Ind.App. 625, 635, 297 N.E.2d 880, 886 (1973)). *Jones* involved the appropriation of land suitable for quarrying which was part of an ongoing quarrying operation. The court distinguished the facts of that case from those in *Williams*, which involved a restaurant business being conducted on the land, because the quarrying business "derive[d] its income by processing material which is an intrinsic part of the land." Billboards are more akin to a restaurant than a quarrying operation because, like a restaurant, a billboard can be relocated to another appropriate location and continue to produce the same or similar income. Unlike a quarrying operation, its value is not tied to the land itself.

The income approach is also limited to situations where the property is being operated as a going concern, is in good condition, and is capable of producing the income to be capitalized. We do not mean to say that capitalization of income is never appropriate for determining the fair market value of billboards, but the circumstances will be rare. While it might be appropriate to consider the anticipated income from an existing lease when calculating fair market value, attempting to determine the potential future profits of an unleased billboard is inherently speculative.

Finally, we note that the purpose of these proceedings is to compensate the landowner for the value of what was taken, no less and no more. * * * In this case, the Bishops retained the ability to lease billboards on land adjacent to the highway. They are not entitled to "compensation" for something that was not taken.

[The court remanded for a new trial.]

NOTES

1. The court defines market value as the amount that a willing buyer would pay and a willing seller would accept. Research into a phenomenon known as the "endowment effect" suggests that people often value an item they have just acquired much more than they would be willing to pay to acquire it. To the extent that some seek to justify legal rules by models relying on rational actors, the endowment effect suggests an irrationality at the core of our concepts of value. Professors Owen D. Jones and Sarah F. Brosnan posit a biological basis for this phenomenon in Law, Biology, and Property: A New Theory of the Endowment Effect, 49 Wm. & Mary L.Rev. 1935 (2008). Should the rightful position necessarily be defined by market value? See Katrina Wyman, The Measure of Just Compensation, 41 U.C. Davis L.Rev. 239 (2007) (challenging the idea that the goal in eminent domain cases should be to make plaintiffs subjectively indifferent to the taking).

2. The three methods for measuring market value mentioned by the *Bishop* court—the market data approach, the cost-less-depreciation approach, and the capitalization of income approach—can be used in any context in which the market value of real or personal property is at issue. *Cost-less-depreciation* is perhaps the simplest. If the asset at issue is fungible or replaceable, its value can be determined by establishing its cost, and then adjusting the value to reflect depreciation.

Of course, few people keep detailed records about what their property cost, or schedule its depreciation. While expert testimony may be necessary to establish market value in some cases, most courts allow a property owner to testify as to the value of her own property without qualifying herself as an expert. Dan B. Dobbs, Law of Remedies § 3.5 (2d ed.1993).

3. The *market data approach* is familiar to anyone who has purchased or refinanced a home. By collecting information about the price at which similar properties are selling and then adjusting upwards or downwards to account for the particular property's unique characteristics, market value can be approximated. Expert testimony can be critical in establishing this sort of hypothetical market, and cases can turn on whether the parties' experts are qualified. For an interesting discussion, see City of Lincoln v. Realty Trust Group, 270 Neb. 587, 705 N.W.2d 432 (2005) (trial court could take judicial notice that comparable sales method of establishing value was reliable; hearing on reliability under *Daubert v. Merrell Dow Pharmaceuticals* was not required); Ventura v. Titan Sports, Inc., 65 F.3d 725 (8th Cir.1995) (expert testimony on value of licensing agreement based on survey of licensing agreements in other sports was reliable under *Daubert*).

4. The *income approach*, or discounted cash flow method, comes at the problem from a different direction. Instead of looking to a real or hypothetical market in which similar property can be bought, the income approach attempts to identify how much profit the property's owner might realize from its use. The approach then reasons backward to determine how much money—capital—invested at an appropriate rate of return it would take to generate the same income stream, or, alternatively, how much investors would pay for an investment that yielded that return. That amount of capital is the economic equivalent of the property's market value.

Why does the *Bishop* court reject the income approach as an alternative way to value the loss of the billboards?

5. Often, the market value—no matter how it is measured—may not reflect the value of property to its owner. How would the court determine the value of a family pet? Of a person's clothing or household belongings? In such cases, courts have fallen back on the somewhat amorphous concept of "actual value to the owner":

> The proper basis for assessing compensatory damages in such a case is to determine the item's actual value to [the owner] * * * who is entitled to demonstrate its value to him by such proof as the circumstances admit. * * * [T]he value to the owner may "include some element of sentimental value in order to avoid limiting the 'owner' to merely nominal damages." However * * * damages in such cases, while not merely nominal, are severely circumscribed.

Anzalone v. Kragness, 356 Ill.App.3d 365, 370, 292 Ill.Dec. 331, 336, 826 N.E.2d 472, 477 (2005) (value of a pet cat killed by a dog while boarding at a hospital). See also Victor Schwartz & Emily Laird, Non–Economic Damages in Pet Litigation: The Serious Need to Preserve a Rational Rule, 33 Pepperdine L.Rev. 227, 241–242 (2006) (cost of replacement, original cost, and investments such as immunization or training can factor into valuation of pet).

The following case presents the same problem in a context with public dimensions.

OHIO v. DEPARTMENT OF THE INTERIOR
United States Court of Appeals, District of Columbia Circuit, 1989
880 F.2d 432

WALD, CHIEF JUDGE, and ROBINSON and MIKVA, CIRCUIT JUDGES.[1]

Petitioners are 10 states, three environmental organizations ("State and Environmental Petitioners"), a chemical industry trade association, a manufacturing company and a utility company ("Industry Petitioners"), who seek review of regulations promulgated by the Department of the Interior ("DOI" or "Interior") pursuant to § 301(c)(1)-(3) of the Comprehensive Environmental Response, Compensation and Liability Act of 1980 ("CERCLA" or the "Act"), as amended, 42 U.S.C. § 9651(c). The regulations govern the recovery of money damages from persons responsible for spills and leaks of oil and hazardous substances, to compensate for injuries such releases inflict on natural resources. Damages may be recovered by state and in some cases the federal governments, as trustees for those natural resources.

Petitioners challenge many aspects of those regulations. State and Environmental Petitioners raise ten issues, all of which essentially focus on the regulations' alleged undervaluation of the damages recoverable from parties responsible for hazardous materials spills that despoil natural resources. Industry Petitioners attack the regulations from a different vantage point, claiming they will permit or encourage overstated damages. * * *

We hold that the regulation limiting damages recoverable by government trustees for harmed natural resources to 'the lesser of' (a) the cost of restoring or replacing the equivalent of an injured resource, or (b) the lost use value of the resource is directly contrary to the clearly expressed intent of Congress and is therefore invalid. We also hold that the regulation prescribing a hierarchy of methodologies by which the lost-use value of natural resources may be measured, which focuses exclusively on the market values for such resources when market values are available, is not a reasonable interpretation of the statute. * * *

I. BACKGROUND

* * *

The relevant provisions of CERCLA * * * [provide] that responsible parties may be held liable for "damages for injury to, destruction of, or loss of natural resources, including the reasonable costs of assessing such injury, destruction, or loss resulting from such a release." 42 U.S.C. § 9607(a)(C). Liability is to "the United States Government and to any State for natural resources within the State or belonging to, managed by, controlled by, or appertaining to such State." * * *

---

1. Parts I, II, III, IV, VII, VIII, IX, X, XI and XII were authored by Judge Wald. Part XIII was authored by Judge Robinson. Parts V and VI were authored by Judge Mikva.

Congress conferred on the President (who in turn delegated to Interior) the responsibility for promulgating regulations governing the assessment of damages for natural resource injuries resulting from releases of hazardous substances or oil, for the purposes of CERCLA and the Clean Water Act's § 311(f)(4)-(5) oil and hazardous substance natural resource damages provisions. * * * CERCLA as amended provides that any assessment performed in accordance with the prescribed procedure is entitled to a rebuttable presumption of accuracy in a proceeding to recover damages from a responsible party. * * *

II. STANDARD OF REVIEW

In reviewing an agency's interpretation of a statute, we first determine "whether Congress has directly spoken to the precise question at issue." Chevron U.S.A., Inc. v. Natural Resources Defense Council, Inc., 467 U.S. 837, 842 (1984). If so, then both Interior and this court "must give effect to the unambiguously expressed intent of Congress."

If, on the other hand, the statute is ambiguous or is silent on a particular issue, this court must assume that Congress implicitly delegated to the agency the power to make policy choices that " 'represent [ ] a reasonable accommodation of conflicting policies that were committed to the agency's care by the statute.' " *Chevron,* 467 U.S. at 844–45. In that event, the court must defer to the agency's interpretation of the statute so long as it is reasonable and consistent with the statutory purpose. This is "Step Two" of *Chevron* analysis. * * *

III. THE "LESSER-OF" RULE

The most significant issue in this case concerns the validity of the regulation providing that damages for despoilment of natural resources shall be "the *lesser of*: restoration or replacement costs; or diminution of use values." 43 C.F.R. § 11.35(b)(2)(1987)(emphasis added).

State and Environmental Petitioners challenge Interior's "lesser of" rule, insisting that CERCLA requires damages to be at least sufficient to pay the cost in every case of restoring, replacing or acquiring the equivalent of the damaged resource (hereinafter referred to shorthandedly as "restoration"). Because in some—probably a majority of—cases lost-use-value will be lower than the cost of restoration, Interior's rule will result in damages award too small to pay for the costs of restoration. * * *

Although our resolution of the dispute submerges us in the minutiae of CERCLA text and legislative materials, we initially stress the enormous practical significance of the "lesser of" rule. A hypothetical example will illustrate the point: imagine a hazardous substance spill that kills a rookery of fur seals and destroys a habitat for seabirds at a sealife reserve. The lost use value of the seals and seabird habitat would be measured by the market value of the fur seals' pelts (which would be approximately $15 each) plus the selling price per acre of land comparable in value to that on which the spoiled bird habitat was located. Even if, as likely, that use value turns out to be far less than the cost of restoring the rookery and seabird habitat, it would nonetheless be the only measure of damages eligible for the presumption of recoverability under the Interior rule.

After examining the language and purpose of CERCLA, as well as its legislative history, we conclude that Interior's "lesser of" rule is directly contrary to the expressed intent of Congress.

A. The Contours of "The Precise Question at Issue"

Commencing our *Chevron* analysis, we must first decide exactly what "the precise question at issue" is in the present case. * * *

That question is not what measure of damages should apply in any or all cases which are brought under the Act. As to that larger question, Interior is obviously correct in asserting that Congress delegated to it a considerable measure of discretion in formulating a standard. The precise question here is a far more discrete one: whether DOI is entitled to treat use value and restoration cost as having equal presumptive legitimacy as a measure of damages.

Interior's "lesser of" rule operates on the premise that, as the cost of a restoration project goes up relative to the value of the injured resource, at some point it becomes wasteful to require responsible parties to pay the full cost of restoration. The logic behind the rule is the same logic that prevents an individual from paying $8,000 to repair a collision-damaged car that was worth only $5,000 before the collision. Just as a prudent individual would sell the damaged car for scrap and then spend $5,000 on a used car in similar condition, DOI's rule requires a polluter to pay a sum equal to the diminution in the use value of a resource whenever that sum is less than restoration cost. What is significant about Interior's rule is the point at which it deems restoration "inefficient." Interior chose to draw the line not at the point where restoration becomes practically impossible, nor at the point where the cost of restoration becomes grossly disproportionate to the use value of the resource, but rather at the point where restoration cost exceeds—by any amount, however small—the use value of the resource. Thus, while we agree with DOI that CERCLA permits it to establish a rule exempting responsible parties *in some cases* from having to pay the full cost of restoration of natural resources, we also agree with Petitioners that it does not permit Interior to draw the line on an automatic "which costs less" basis. * * *

B. Text and Structure of CERCLA * * *

1. Section 107(f)(1) and the Measure of Damages

The strongest linguistic evidence of Congress' intent to establish a distinct preference for restoration costs as the measure of damages is contained in § 107(f)(1) of CERCLA. That section states that natural resource damages recovered by a government trustee are "for use only to restore, replace, or acquire the equivalent of such natural resources." 42 U.S.C. § 9607(f)(1). It goes on to state: "The measure of damages in any action under [§ 107(a)(C)] shall not be limited by the sums which can be used to restore or replace such resources."

a. *Limitation on Uses of Recovered Damages*

By mandating the use of all damages to restore the injured resources, Congress underscored in § 107(f)(1) its paramount restorative purpose for imposing damages at all. It would be odd indeed for a Congress so insistent that all damages be spent on restoration to allow a "lesser" measure of damages than the cost of restoration in the majority of cases. Only two possible inferences about congressional intent could explain the anomaly: Either Congress intended trustees to commence restoration projects only to abandon them for lack of funds, or Congress expected taxpayers to pick up the rest of the tab. The first theory is contrary to Congress' intent to effect a "make-whole" remedy of complete restoration, and the second is contrary to a basic purpose of the CERCLA natural resource damage provisions—that polluters bear the costs of their polluting activities. It is far more logical to presume that Congress intended responsible parties to be liable for damages in an amount sufficient to accomplish its restorative aims. Interior's rule, on the other hand, assumes that Congress purposely formulated a statutory scheme that would doom to failure its goals of restoration in a majority of cases.

In this connection, it should be noted that Interior makes no claim that a "use value" measure will provide enough money to pay for ANY of the three uses to which all damages must be assigned: restoration, replacement *or acquisition of an equivalent resource.* Nor could Interior make such a claim, because its "lesser of" rule not only calculates use value quite differently from restoration or replacement cost but it also fails to link measurement of use value in any way to the cost of acquiring an equivalent resource. For example, Interior could not possibly maintain that recovering $15 per pelt for the fur seals killed by a hazardous substance release would enable the purchase of an "equivalent" number of fur seals.

b. *The "Shall Not Be Limited by" Language*

The same section of CERCLA that mandates the expenditures of all damages on restoration (again a shorthand reference to all three listed uses of damages) provides that the measure of damages "shall not be limited by" restoration costs. § 107(f)(1), 42 U.S.C. § 9607(f)(1). This provision obviously reflects Congress' apparent concern that its restorative purpose for imposing damages not be construed as making restoration cost a damages ceiling. But the explicit command that damages "shall not be limited by" restoration costs also carries in it an implicit assumption that restoration cost will serve as the basic measure of damages in many if not most CERCLA cases. It would be markedly inconsistent with the restorative thrust of the whole section to limit restoration-based damages, as Interior's rule does, to a minuscule number of cases where restoration is cheaper than paying for lost use. * * *

C. *Legislative History of CERCLA*

The text and structure of CERCLA indicate clearly to us that Congress intended restoration costs to be the basic measure of recovery for harm to natural resources. We next examine the legislative history of CERCLA to ascertain if there are any countervailing indications to our conclusion. * * *

CERCLA's legislative history * * * shows that Congress soundly rejected the two basic premises underlying Interior's "lesser of" rule—first, that the common-law measure of damages is appropriate in the natural resource context, and second, that it is economically inefficient to restore a resource whose use value is less than the cost of restoration. * * *

Accepting for the sake of argument the contention that the "lesser of" rule reflects the common law,[37] support for the proposition that Congress adopted common-law damage standards wholesale into CERCLA is slim to nonexistent. * * * The legislative history illustrates* * * that a motivating force behind the CERCLA natural resource damage provisions was Congress' dissatisfaction with the common law. Indeed, one wonders why Congress would have passed a new damage provision at all if it were content with the common law. * * *

Alternatively, Interior justifies the "lesser of" rule as being economically efficient. Under DOI's economic efficiency view, making restoration cost the measure of damages would be a waste of money whenever restoration would cost more than the use value of the resource. Its explanation of the proposed rules included the following statement:

> [I]f use value is higher than the cost of restoration or replacement, then it would be more rational for society to be compensated for the cost to restore or replace the lost resource than to be compensated for the lost use. Conversely, if restoration or replacement costs are higher than the value of uses foregone, it is rational for society to compensate individuals for their lost uses rather than the cost to restore or replace the injured natural resource.

50 Fed.Reg. at 52,141. See also 51 Fed.Reg. at 27,704 ("lesser of" rule "promotes a rational allocation of society's assets").

This is nothing more or less than cost-benefit analysis: Interior's rule attempts to optimize social welfare by restoring an injured resource only when the diminution in the resource's value to society is greater in magnitude than the cost of restoring it. And, acknowledgedly, Congress did intend CERCLA's natural resource provisions to operate efficiently.

---

37. We note in passing that the "lesser of" standard does not apply in all non-CERCLA contexts. See, e.g., Denoyer v. Lamb, 22 Ohio App.3d 136, 490 N.E.2d 615, 618–19 (1984)(restoration cost is proper measure where property is used for a residence or for recreation, so long as restoration cost is not "grossly disproportionate" to diminution in market value); Heninger v. Dunn, 101 Cal.App.3d 858, 162 Cal.Rptr. 104, 106–09 (1980)(restoration cost is proper measure where owner has a personal reason for restoring land to its original condition, so long as restoration cost is not unreasonably disproportionate to diminution in market value); Restatement (Second) of Torts section 929, comment b (1977).

For one thing, the Act requires that the assessment of damages and the restoration of injured resources take place as cost-effectively as possible. Moreover, as we have indicated, there is some suggestion in the legislative history that Congress intended recovery not to encompass restoration cost where restoration is infeasible or where its cost is grossly disproportionate to use value.

The fatal flaw of Interior's approach, however, is that it assumes that natural resources are fungible goods, just like any other, and that the value to society generated by a particular resource can be accurately measured in every case—assumptions that Congress apparently rejected. As the foregoing examination of CERCLA's text, structure and legislative history illustrates, Congress saw restoration as the presumptively correct remedy for injury to natural resources. To say that Congress placed a thumb on the scales in favor of restoration is not to say that it forswore the goal of efficiency. "Efficiency," standing alone, simply means that the chosen policy will dictate the result that achieves the greatest value to society. Whether the particular choice is efficient depends on *how the various alternatives are valued.* Our reading of CERCLA does not attribute to Congress an irrational dislike of "efficiency"; rather, it suggests that Congress was skeptical of the ability of human beings to measure the true "value" of a natural resource. Indeed, even the common law recognizes that restoration is the proper remedy for injury to property where measurement of damages by some other method will fail to compensate fully for the injury.[41] Congress' refusal to view use value and restoration cost as having equal presumptive legitimacy merely recognizes that natural resources have value that is not readily measured by traditional means. Congress delegated to Interior the job of deciding at what point the presumption of restoration falls away, but its repeated emphasis on the primacy of restoration rejected the underlying premise of Interior's rule, which is that restoration is wasteful if its cost exceeds—by even the slightest amount—the diminution in use value of the injured resource.

* * *

VI. THE HIERARCHY OF ASSESSMENT METHODS

The regulations establish a rigid hierarchy of permissible methods for determining "use values," limiting recovery to the price commanded by the resource on the open market, unless the trustee finds that "the market for the resource is not reasonably competitive." If the trustee makes such a finding, it may "appraise" the market value in accordance with the relevant sections of the "Uniform Appraisal Standards for Federal Land Acquisition." Only when neither the market value nor the

---

41. See, e.g., Trinity Church v. John Hancock Mut. Life Ins. Co., 399 Mass. 43, 502 N.E.2d 532, 536 (1987)(restoration cost is proper measure where diminution in market value is unsatisfactory or unavailable as a measure of damages, as in the case of structural damage to a church); Weld County Bd. of Com'rs v. Slovek, 723 P.2d 1309, 1316–17 (Colo.1986) (court may, in its discretion, award restoration cost where award of diminution in market value would not adequately compensate owner for some personal reason, provided that restoration cost is not "wholly unreasonable" in relation to diminution in value); see also supra note 37.

appraisal method is "appropriate" can other methods of determining use value be employed.

Environmental petitioners maintain that Interior's emphasis on market value is an unreasonable interpretation of the statute, under the so-called "second prong" of Chevron U.S.A., Inc. v. Natural Resources Defense Council, Inc., 467 U.S. 837, 845 (1984), and we agree. While it is not irrational to look to market price as *one* factor in determining the use value of a resource, it is unreasonable to view market price as the *exclusive* factor, or even the predominant one. From the bald eagle to the blue whale and snail darter, natural resources have values that are not fully captured by the market system. * * * Courts have long stressed that market prices are not to be used as surrogates for value "when the market value has been too difficult to find, or when its application would result in manifest injustice to owner or public." We find that DOI erred by establishing "a strong presumption in favor of market price and appraisal methodologies."

We are not satisfied that the problem is solved by the provision* * * permitting nonmarket methodologies to be used when the market for the resource is not "reasonably competitive." There are many resources whose components may be traded in "reasonably competitive" markets, but whose total use values are not fully reflected in the prices they command in those markets. Interior itself provides ample proof of the inadequacy of the "reasonably competitive market" caveat. For example, DOI has noted that "the hierarchy established* * *" would dictate a use value for fur seals of $15 per seal, corresponding to the market price for the seal's pelt. Another example of DOI's erroneous equation of market price with use value is its insistence that the sum of the fees charged by the government for the use of a resource, say, for admission to a national park, constitutes "the value to the public of recreational or other public uses of the resource," because "these fees are what the government has determined to represent the value of the natural resource and represent an offer by a willing seller." This is quite obviously and totally fallacious; there is no necessary connection between the total value to the public of a park and the fees charged as admission, which typically are set not to maximize profits but rather to encourage the public to visit the park. In fact, the decision to set entrance fees far below what the traffic would bear is evidence of Congress's strong conviction that parks are priceless national treasures and that access to them ought to be as wide as possible, and not, as DOI would have it, a sign that parks are really not so valuable after all. * * *

On remand, DOI should consider a rule that would permit trustees to derive use values for natural resources by summing up all reliably calculated use values, however measured, so long as the trustee does not double count. Market valuation can of course serve as one factor to be considered, but by itself it will necessarily be incomplete.

* * *

XIII. CONTINGENT VALUATION

* * * DOI's natural resource damage assessment regulations define "use value" as

> the value to the public of recreational or other public uses of the resource, as measured by changes in consumer surplus, any fees or other payments collectable by the government or Indian tribe for a private party's use of the natural resource, and any economic rent accruing to a private party because the government or Indian tribe does not charge a fee or price for the use of the resource.

The regulations provide several approaches to use valuation. When the injured resource is traded in a market, the lost use value is the diminution in market price. When that is not precisely the case, but similar resources are traded in a market, an appraisal technique may be utilized to determine damages. When, however, neither of these two situations obtains, nonmarketed resource methodologies are available. One of these is "contingent valuation" (CV), the subject of controversy here.

The CV process "includes all techniques that set up hypothetical markets to elicit an individual's economic valuation of a natural resource." CV involves a series of interviews with individuals for the purpose of ascertaining the values they respectively attach to particular changes in particular resources. Among the several formats available to an interviewer in developing the hypothetical scenario embodied in a CV survey are direct questioning, by which the interviewer learns how much the interviewee is willing to pay for the resource; bidding formats, for example, the interviewee is asked whether he or she would pay a given amount for a resource and, depending upon the response, the bid is set higher or lower until a final price is derived; and a "take or leave it" format, in which the interviewee decides whether or not he or she is willing to pay a designated amount of money for the resource. CV methodology thus enables ascertainment of individually-expressed values for different levels of quality of resources, and dollar values of individuals' changes in well-being. * * *

Industry Petitioners point out that at common law there can be no recovery for speculative injuries, and they contend that CV methodology is at odds with that principle. CV methodology, they say, is rife with speculation, amounting to no more than ordinary public opinion polling.

We have already noted our disagreement with the proposition that the strictures of the common law apply to CERCLA. That much of Industry Petitioners' argument to the contrary thus fades away. CERCLA does, however, require utilization of the "best available procedures" for determinations of damages flowing from destruction of or injury to natural resources, and Industry Petitioners insist that CV methodology is too flawed to qualify as such. In their eyes, the CV process is imprecise, is untested, and has a built-in bias and a propensity to produce overestimation. * * *

Industry Petitioners urge * * * that even assuming that questions are artfully drafted and carefully circumscribed, there is such a high degree of variation in size of the groups surveyed, and such a concomitant fluctuation in aggregations of damages, that CV methodology cannot be considered a "best available procedure."[86] We think this attack on CV methodology is insufficient in a facial challenge to invalidate CV as an available assessment technique. The extent of damage to natural resources from releases of oil and hazardous substances varies greatly, and though the impact may be widespread and severe, it is in the mission of CERCLA to assess the public loss.[87] Certainly nothing in CV methodology itself shapes the injury inflicted by an environmental disaster, or influences identification of the population affected thereby. The argument of Industry Petitioners strikes at CERCLA, not CV's implementation, and can appropriately be considered only by Congress.

Similarly, we find wanting Industry Petitioners' protest that CV does not rise to the status of a "best available procedure" because willingness-to-pay—a factor prominent in CV methodology—can lead to overestimates by survey respondents. The premise of this argument is that respondents do not actually pay money, and likely will overstate their willingness-to-pay. One study relied upon by Industry Petitioners hypothesizes that respondents may "respond in ways that are more indicative of what they would like to see done than how they would behave in an actual market," and also observes that the converse is possible. The simple and obvious safeguard against overstatement, however, is more sophisticated questioning. Even as matters now stand, the risk of overestimation has not been shown to produce such egregious results as to justify judicial overruling of DOI's careful estimate of the caliber of worth of CV methodology.

Industry Petitioners also challenge the use of CV AFTER an oil leak or a hazardous waste release has occurred. They fear that application of CV methodology in those circumstances is fraught with a significant bias leading to overvaluation of the damaged resources. As a practical matter, it would be prohibitively expensive, if not physically impossible, to solicit individual valuations of each and every natural resource, or even a sizeable number thereof, in order to avoid any upward bias in the event that the resource is later damaged. Moreover, in light of CERCLA's preference for restoration, it would be a terrible waste of time and energy to conduct broadscale valuation interviewing beforehand. While, depend-

---

86. Industry Petitioners cite a study estimating the combined option and existence values to Texas residents of whooping cranes at $109,000,000 (13.9 million Texas residents × $7.13). The estimate rested upon responses to a survey eliciting the amount an individual would pay for a permit to visit the National Wildlife Refuge where the whooping crane winters. Had the survey been nationwide in scope, the estimate would have been $1.58 billion. Brief for Industry Petitioners at 14 n. 24 (referring to J. Stoll & L. Johnson, Concepts of Value, Nonmarket Valuation, and the Case of the Whooping Crane (Natural Resources Working Paper Series, National Resource Workgroup, Dep't of Agricultural Economics, Texas A & M Univ.)(1984) at 23–24).

87. Thus, in the whooping crane scenario referred to by industry petitioners the intent of CERCLA would be realized, not contravened, by a more expansive survey and a correspondingly higher assessment of damages if people beyond the borders of Texas were affected.

ing on whether interviewing occurs before or after damage, the results may differ somewhat, that alone does not reduce CV methodology to something less than a "best available procedure." We have no cause to overturn DOI's considered judgment that CV methodology, when properly applied, can be structured so as to eliminate undue upward biases.

We sustain DOI in its conclusion that CV methodology is a "best available procedure." As such, its conclusion in the Natural Resource Damage Assessment regulations was entirely proper. * * *

NOTES

1. The Department of the Interior issued new regulations in response to *Ohio*. The new regulations eliminate the "lesser of" rule and the hierarchy of assessment methods criticized in the case, and continue the use of contingent valuation methods. The new regulations state that the damage assessment includes the cost of "restoration, rehabilitation, replacement, and/or acquisition of the equivalent of the injured natural resource," and provide the official charged with assessment with a wide choice of methods, all focused on restoration. 43 C.F.R. § 11.82 et seq.

If contingent valuation methods were introduced in court, could they pass the *Daubert* test for admissibility of scientific evidence? See Sameer H. Doshi, Making the Sale on Contingent Valuation, 21 Tul.Envtl.L.J. 295 (2008). For further discussion of contingent valuation, see Ian Bateman and K.G. Willis (eds.), Valuing Environmental Preferences: Theory and Practice of the Contingent Valuation Method in the U.S., E.U., and Developing Countries (1999).

2. Usually, cost of repair or restoration and loss of market value amount to about the same thing. A car otherwise worth $5000 that needs $500 worth of engine work ought to be worth about $4500. Thus, in an ordinary case, where property has been damaged or destroyed, courts have generally treated the cost of repair or replacement and the loss in market value as rough equivalents:

> Where chattels have been damaged, but not destroyed, the owner can recover "(a) the difference between the value of the chattel before the harm and the value after the harm or, at his election in an appropriate case, the reasonable cost of repair or restoration, with due allowance for any difference between the original value and the value after repairs, and (b) the loss of use."

Restatement (Second) of Torts § 928. To the same effect, see Restatement (Second) of Contracts § 348 (for breach of a construction contract, damages may be "based on the diminution in the market price of the property * * * or the reasonable cost of completing performance * * * if that cost is not clearly disproportionate to the probable loss in value" to the victim of the breach).

3. In some cases, as with natural resources, the cost of repair can exceed the loss in market value. (Can you see why it is not a problem if the loss in market value exceeds the cost of repair? Recall the avoidable consequences rule.) Older decisions viewed the problem as one of waste. To use the *Ohio* court's example, if one were to spend $8,000 repairing a car that was only

worth $5,000 to begin with, $3,000 would be wasted—it would be spent without any corresponding gain in value.

Waste, however, is not really the issue. Even if, in our example, the owner of the car were given $8,000 to repair her car, she would spend the money on the repairs only *if it were worth it to her*. If the car were worth so much to her that she would spend $8,000 to repair it, there is no waste: she will get $8,000 in value for her $8,000. In such a case, if she is limited to recovering $5,000, she will be undercompensated. Or, to put it another way, we will have forced her to accept the market's values instead of her own.

On the other hand, if having her car fixed is not worth $8,000 to her, and we give her the $8,000 anyway, she will not spend the money on repairs. Instead, she will simply buy an equivalent car and pocket the difference. The problem, thus, is not waste, it is the potential for windfall. If the plaintiff is given $8,000 and she does not in fact value the car as highly as she claimed, she has gotten more than she lost (she is in better than her rightful position), and at the defendant's expense.

The tort cases are in some degree of conflict on this issue. Both views were represented in Hewlett v. Barge Bertie, 418 F.2d 654 (4th Cir.1969), cert. denied, 397 U.S. 1021, 90 S.Ct. 1261, 25 L.Ed.2d 531 (1970). In *Hewlett*, two barges collided. Hewlett sued, and recovered nominal damages from the admiralty court. On appeal, the court of appeals reversed, finding that Hewlett should have received the cost of repairing his barge: "If [a ship] is not a complete loss, and repossession or repairs are both physically and economically feasible, then the reasonable cost of recovery, including repairs and an allowance for deprivation of use, is the measure. But if the reclamation expense including repairs exceeds the ship's just value at the time of the casualty, or if repairs are not both physically and economically practicable, then it is a constructive total loss, and the limit of compensation is the value plus interest." 418 F.2d at 657. Because the tortfeasor did not show that the cost of the repairs exceeded the total value of the barge, the cost of repair should have been recoverable.

Chief Judge Haynsworth dissented. Hewlett first acquired this barge by salvaging it after it had sunk and been declared a total loss. He spent about $1300 to make it water-tight, so that he could use it as a pontoon, or, potentially, for carrying cargo on deck. The dent the barge suffered in the collision did not affect its scrap value, nor did it reduce its utility:

> In this case there is no factual equivalency between diminution in value and cost of repair. The parties and the court are agreed that there was no diminution in the market value of the barge, or in any special value it may have had to the [owner]. * * * [If the owner is awarded damages, he] is unduly enriched. He must hope greatly that another errant navigator will hit his battered barge again, and still another yet again, so that each time he may happily pocket the estimated cost of theoretical repairs which neither he nor anyone else will ever dream of undertaking while retaining all along a barge as seaworthy and useful to him and of undiminished worth if he chooses to sell it.

418 F.2d at 654. Who has the better argument? How does it bear on the problem of Tama's house, above? Should the "lesser-of" rule be applied in tort cases?

4. Would the analysis be different if the issue arose in a contract case? Peevyhouse v. Garland Coal & Mining Company, 382 P.2d 109 (Okla.1962), is a classic example. Garland Coal leased the Peevyhouses' land for a strip-mining operation. When Garland Coal returned the land, they failed to perform remedial and restorative work the lease had specifically required at the demand of the Peevyhouses. The remedial work would have cost $29,000 to perform, but market value of the land was reduced only $300 by the failure to do the work. At trial, the jury awarded the Peevyhouses $5,000 in damages.

The Supreme Court of Oklahoma reversed:

> We * * * hold that where, in a coal mining lease, lessee agrees to perform certain remedial work on the premises concerned at the end of the lease period, and thereafter the contract is fully performed by both parties except that the remedial work is not done, the measure of damages in an action by lessor against lessee for damages for breach of contract is ordinarily the reasonable cost of performance of the work; however, where the contract provision breached was merely incidental to the main purpose in view, and where the economic benefit which would result to lessor by full performance of the work is grossly disproportionate to the cost of performance, the damages which lessor may recover are limited to the diminution in value resulting to the premises because of the non-performance. * * *
>
> Under the most liberal view of the evidence herein, the diminution in value resulting to the premises because of non-performance of the remedial work was $300.00. * * * We are of the opinion that the judgment of the trial court for plaintiffs should be, and it is hereby, modified and reduced to the sum of $300.00, and as so modified it is affirmed.

382 P.2d at 114. For a thorough history of the case, see Judith L. Maute, Peevyhouse v. Garland Coal & Mining Co. Revisited: The Ballad of Willie and Lucille, 89 Nw.U.L.Rev. 1341 (1995).

On the other hand, in Groves v. John Wunder Co., 205 Minn. 163, 286 N.W. 235, 236 (1939), a contractor leased the plaintiff's land for a gravel quarry, agreeing to grade the land evenly after removing the gravel. The contractor did not do the grading, and the plaintiff sued. The evidence showed that the cost of the grading would be $60,000, while the total value of the plaintiff's property would be only $12,160 even after the grading was done. Nonetheless, the court found that the proper measure of damages was the cost of performance. Any other rule "handsomely rewards bad faith and deliberate breach of contract."

Which is the better result? Would it matter whether the land were a family farm, or property held by a developer speculating on property values? Consider Judge Posner's assessment of the result in *Groves*:

> Because the value of the plaintiff's land had fallen, the breach of contract did not actually impose any loss on him, and the only proper remedy for a harmless breach is nominal damages. The effect of the award of damages

was to shift from the owner of the land to the contractor a part of the risk of the fall in land values caused by the Depression. One expects the risk of a fall of the value of land to be borne by the owner of the land rather than by a contractor.

Youngs v. Old Ben Coal Co., 243 F.3d 387, 392 (7th Cir.2001).

The argument that awarding the cost of restoration will result in economic waste is challenged in Alan Schwartz & Robert E. Scott, Market Damages, Efficient Contracting and the Economic Waste Fallacy, 108 Colum.L.Rev. 1610 (2008), and in Juanda Lowder Daniel & Kevin S. Marshall, Avoiding Economic Waste in Contract Damages: Myths, Misunderstanding, and Malcontent, 85 Neb.L.Rev. 875 (2007). After the Louisiana Supreme Court held in Corbello v. Iowa Production, 850 So.2d 686 (La.2003), that damages for breach of a contractual obligation to restore property damaged by oil and gas production were to be measured by the cost of restoring the property, with no obligation on the landowner's part actually to undertake restoration, the Louisiana legislature enacted an elaborate regime featuring a requirement that the courts and state agencies oversee the remediation. See Loulan Petre, Jr., "Legacy Litigation" and Act 312 of 2006, 20 Tul.Envtl.L.J. 347 (2007).

C. AN OVERVIEW OF TORT DAMAGES

Many of the basic rules for tort damages are probably familiar to you already, not only from your torts class but from incidental exposure to them in property, civil procedure and elsewhere. The introduction that follows will remind you of some of the basic, black letter rules. After that, the cases in this section will give you a chance to see those rules at work in some challenging contexts.

As you read, think about the purposes served by using the legal system to compensate those harmed by wrongdoing. Over the past thirty years, the idea of using courts to "make the victim whole" has been drawn into question in a very fundamental way. From 1970's reforms limiting compensation in suits against health care providers and public entities to current campaigns for pervasive tort reform, the purpose and legitimacy of awarding compensatory damages have been challenged.

Ironically, however, when Congress responded to the horrifying events of September 11, 2001, it did so by creating a compensation scheme modeled on tort damages. Rather than, for example, establishing a benefits system for victims of 9/11, or providing a fixed payment to those who were affected, Congress established a fund to be distributed to victims according to the loss each victim suffered. In the face of this unprecedented national tragedy, Congress opted for traditional compensation.

The story of the September 11th Victim Compensation Fund has been told by Kenneth R. Feinberg, the Special Master who oversaw its operation, in a remarkable book, What is Life Worth: The Unprecedented Effort to Compensate the Victims of 9/11 (2005). Although the fund operated as an alternative to compensation through the tort system, the stories the special master has to tell and the choices he (and Congress made) put an important, human face on the concept of compensation, and we will refer to it occasionally throughout these materials.

But for now, back to the basics. According to the Restatement (Second) of Torts:

> The rules for determining the measure of damages in tort are based upon the purposes for which actions of tort are maintainable. These purposes are:
>
> (a) to give compensation, indemnity, or restitution for harms;
>
> (b) to determine rights;
>
> (c) to punish wrongdoers and deter wrongful conduct;
>
> (d) to vindicate parties and deter retaliation or violent and unlawful self-help.

Restatement (Second) of Torts § 901 (1977). The first purpose is achieved by compensatory damages; the second purpose, by nominal damages; the third by punitive damages. The standards for an award of nominal damages were discussed in connection with *Memphis Community School District v. Stachura* in section A of this chapter. The standards that govern an award of punitive damages will be discussed in Chapter 6. The rest of this section focuses on compensatory damages.

Is it self-evident why compensating the victims of wrongdoing is a legitimate public policy goal? Is there an intrinsic value in restoring the victim of wrongdoing to his or her rightful position? Is the answer to be found, alternatively, in the idea of deterrence? If an activity must absorb—internalize, in the language of the economists—the costs of the harms for which it is responsible, the cost of that activity will rise, creating an incentive to find a safer way to undertake it. See Guido Calabresi, The Costs of Accidents (1970). Although there is vigorous debate over this insight's implications, it has had a profound impact on current thought about the purposes served by tort law. For a useful summary of the debate, see Gary T. Schwartz, Mixed Theories of Tort Law: Affirming Both Deterrence and Corrective Justice, 75 Tex.L.Rev. 1801 (1997). Are there other ways to justify awarding compensation to tort victims? Exploring the justification for compensatory damages is one of the section's major themes, and other important possibilities will be introduced in the notes following the cases.

Broadly speaking, tort cases can be divided into cases involving harm to the person, and cases involving harm to real or personal property. In tort cases involving personal harm, compensatory damages typically include damages for:

> (1) Past and future bodily harm and emotional distress;
>
> (2) Lost earnings and loss of earning capacity;
>
> (3) Reasonable past and future medical and other expenses; and
>
> (4) Harm to property or business.

Restatement (Second) of Torts § 924 (1977).

In cases involving harm to property, damages include compensation for

(1) the difference between the property's pre-and post-tort market value, or the cost of repairing the harm; and

(2) where real property is harmed, the occupant's discomfort and annoyance.

Restatement (Second) of Torts §§ 928, 929 (1977).

All of these elements of loss and more are combined in the case that follows, which will provide you an overview of compensatory damages in tort. The rest of this section addresses tort damages in greater detail, and is organized to track the five inquiries identified by Professor McCormick in section B.

AYERS v. JACKSON TOWNSHIP

Supreme Court of New Jersey, 1987
106 N.J. 557, 525 A.2d 287

STEIN, JUSTICE.

In this case we consider the application of the New Jersey Tort Claims Act (the Act), N.J.S.A. 59:1–1 to 12–3, to the claims asserted by 339 residents of Jackson Township against that municipality.

The litigation involves claims for damages sustained because plaintiffs' well water was contaminated by toxic pollutants leaching into the Cohansey Aquifer from a landfill established and operated by Jackson Township. After an extensive trial, the jury found that the township had created a "nuisance" and a "dangerous condition" by virtue of its operation of the landfill, that its conduct was "palpably unreasonable,"—a prerequisite to recovery under N.J.S.A. 59:4–2—and that it was the proximate cause of the contamination of plaintiffs' water supply. The jury verdict resulted in an aggregate judgment of $15,854,392.78, to be divided among the plaintiffs in varying amounts. The jury returned individual awards for each of the plaintiffs that varied in accordance with such factors as proximity to the landfill, duration and extent of the exposure to contaminants, and the age of the claimant.

The verdict provided compensation for three distinct claims of injury: $2,056,480 was awarded for emotional distress caused by the knowledge that they had ingested water contaminated by toxic chemicals for up to six years; $5,396,940 was awarded for the deterioration of their quality of life during the twenty months when they were deprived of running water; and $8,204,500 was awarded to cover the future cost of annual medical surveillance that plaintiffs' expert testified would be necessary because of plaintiffs' increased susceptibility to cancer and other diseases. * * *

I

* * * A substantial number—more than 150—of the plaintiffs gave testimony with respect to damages, describing in detail the impairment of

their quality of life during the period that they were without running water, and the emotional distress they suffered. With regard to the emotional distress claims, the plaintiffs' testimony detailed their emotional reactions to the chemical contamination of their wells and the deprivation of their water supply, as well as their fears for the health of their family members. Expert psychological testimony was offered to document plaintiffs' claims that they had sustained compensable psychological damage as a result of the contamination of their wells.

We now consider each of the plaintiffs' damage claims in the context of the evidence adduced at trial and the legal principles that should inform our application of the Tort Claims Act.

QUALITY OF LIFE

[The court described how, for nearly two years, the plaintiffs' water was provided in 40 gallon, 100 pound barrels, the inconvenience that entailed, and the inevitable discomfort and tension the lack of running water produced among household members.]

The trial court charged the jury that plaintiffs' claim for "quality of life" encompassed "inconveniences, aggravation, and unnecessary expenditure of time and effort related to the use of the water hauled to their homes, as well as to other disruption in their lives, including disharmony in the family unit." The aggregate jury verdict on this claim was $5,396,940. This represented an average award of slightly over $16,000 for each plaintiff; thus, a family unit consisting of four plaintiffs received an average award of approximately $64,000.

* * *

[D]efendant argues that this segment of the verdict is barred by the New Jersey Tort Claims Act, which provides:

> No damages shall be awarded against a public entity or public employee for pain and suffering resulting from any injury; provided, however, that this limitation on the recovery of damages for pain and suffering shall not apply in cases of permanent loss of a bodily function, permanent disfigurement or dismemberment where the medical treatment expenses are in excess of $1,000.00.

Defendant contends that the legislative intent in restricting damages for "pain and suffering" was to encompass claims for all "non-objective" injuries, unless the statutory threshold of severity of injury or expense of treatment is met. The township asserts that the inconvenience, aggravation, effort and disruption of the family unit that resulted from the loss of plaintiff's water supply was but a form of "pain and suffering" and therefore uncompensable under the Act.

The Appellate Division rejected the township's contention, concluding that there was a clear distinction between

> the subjectively measured damages for pain and suffering, which are not compensable by the Tort Claims Act, and those which objectively

affect quality of life by causing an interference with the use of one's land through inconvenience and the disruption of daily activities.

We agree with the Appellate Division's conclusion. The Tort Claims Act's ban against recovery of damages for "pain and suffering resulting from any injury" is intended to apply to the intangible, subjective feelings of discomfort that are associated with personal injuries. It was not intended to bar claims for inconvenience associated with the invasion of a property interest. * * * [T]he interest invaded here, the right to obtain potable running water from plaintiffs' own wells, is qualitatively different from "pain and suffering" related to a personal injury.

As the Appellate Division acknowledged, plaintiffs' claim for quality of life damages is derived from the law of nuisance. It has long been recognized that damages for inconvenience, annoyance, and discomfort are recoverable in a nuisance action. The Restatement (Second) of Torts section 929 (1977) sets out three distinct categories of compensation with respect to invasions of an interest in land:

> (a) the difference between the value of the land before the harm and the value after the harm, or at [plaintiff's] election in an appropriate case, the cost of restoration that has been or may be reasonably incurred;
>
> (b) the loss of use of the land, and
>
> (c) discomfort and annoyance to him as occupant.

While the first two of these components constitute damages for the interference with plaintiff's use and enjoyment of his land, the third category compensates the plaintiff for his personal losses flowing directly from such an invasion. As such, damages for inconvenience, discomfort, and annoyance constitute "distinct grounds of compensation for which in ordinary cases the person in possession is entitled to recover in addition to the harm to his proprietary interests." Restatement Second of Torts section 929 comment e (1977).

Accordingly, we conclude that the quality of life damages represent compensation for losses associated with damage to property, and agree with the Appellate Division that they do not constitute pain and suffering under the Tort Claims Act. We therefore sustain the judgment for quality of life damages.

Emotional Distress

The jury verdict awarded plaintiffs damages for emotional distress in the aggregate amount of $2,056,480. The individual verdicts ranged from $40 to $14,000.

Many of the plaintiffs testified about their emotional reactions to the knowledge that their well-water was contaminated. * * * [T]he consistent thrust of the testimony offered by numerous witnesses was that they suffered anxiety, stress, fear, and depression, and that these feelings were directly and causally related to the knowledge that they and members of their family had ingested and been exposed to contaminated water for a substantial time period. * * *

[T]he township contended that the jury verdict for emotional distress constituted damages for "pain and suffering resulting from any injury," recovery for which is expressly barred by the Tort Claims Act. The Appellate Division, without deciding the issue of the sufficiency of plaintiffs' proofs, agreed that the verdict for emotional distress was barred by the Act:

> We cannot conceive how plaintiffs' concern that their exposure to toxic wastes might have precipitated a serious illness can be characterized as anything other than pain and suffering. It is a measure of their entirely subjective responses to a situation which, though threatening, never materialized into objective manifestations of injury. Under the circumstances, we conclude that although damages for these intangible harms might be recoverable from a non-governmental entity, as consequential to a nuisance, the language of N.J.S.A. 59:9B2(d), barring damages from a public entity "for pain and suffering resulting from any injury," clearly precludes recovery herein.

* * *

[W]e reject plaintiffs' assertion that the Tort Claims Act's limitation against recovery for "pain and suffering resulting from any injury" does not apply to claims based on emotional distress. * * *

Addressing first plaintiffs' contention that emotional distress is not an "injury" as that term is used in the Tort Claims Act, we observe that the Act broadly defines injury to include

> death, injury to a person, damage to or loss of property or any other injury that a person may suffer that would be actionable if inflicted by a private person.

The statutory definition is expansive and unqualified and clearly accommodates "emotional distress" as an injury "that a person may suffer that would be actionable if inflicted by a private person." The term "injury" is also used in N.J.S.A. 59:4–2, which defines the scope of public entity liability. Plainly, if emotional distress did not constitute an injury under this section, plaintiffs could not have asserted a cause of action for emotional distress under the Act. We discern no basis in the legislative history or in the statutory scheme of the Act for assigning a more restrictive meaning to the term "injury" as used in N.J.S.A. 59:9–2(d), the section that limits liability for pain and suffering, than that accorded to the same word in the section of the Act that imposes liability on a public entity. Accordingly, we hold that claims for emotional distress are encompassed by the term "injury" in N.J.S.A. 59:9–2(d).

The term "pain and suffering" is not defined in the Act. The Comment to N.J.S.A. 59:9–2 describes the limitation on damages for pain and suffering as reflecting "the policy judgment that in view of the economic burdens presently facing public entities a claimant should not be reimbursed for non-objective types of damages, such as pain and suffering, except in aggravated circumstances * * *." We are in full accord with the conclusion of the Appellate Division that the subjective symptoms of depression, stress, health concerns, and anxiety described by the plaintiffs and their expert witness constitute "pain and suffering resulting from any injury" as that phrase is used in N.J.S.A. 59:9–2(d). * * *

CLAIMS FOR ENHANCED RISK AND MEDICAL SURVEILLANCE

No claims were asserted by plaintiffs seeking recovery for specific illnesses caused by their exposure to chemicals. Rather, they claim damages for the enhanced risk of future illness attributable to such exposure. They also seek to recover the expenses of annual medical examinations to monitor their physical health and detect symptoms of disease at the earliest possible opportunity.

Before trial, the trial court granted defendant's motion for summary judgment dismissing the enhanced risk claim. * * *

With regard to the claims for medical surveillance expenses, the trial court denied defendant's summary judgment motion, and the jury verdict included damages of $8,204,500 for medical surveillance. * * *

1.

Our evaluation of the enhanced risk and medical surveillance claims requires that we focus on a critical issue in the management of toxic tort litigation: at what stage in the evolution of a toxic injury should tort law intercede by requiring the responsible party to pay damages?

[The court first concludes that any plaintiffs who do incur cancer at a later date will be able to sue the Township. The statute of limitations will not have run, because under New Jersey's discovery rule, the cause of action does not accrue until the victim is aware of the injury. Neither will the state's single controversy rule bar plaintiffs from suing. Usually, the single controversy rule would require the plaintiffs to raise all their claims—property claims and personal injury claims—in the same proceeding. According to the Court, however, the single controversy rule, "cannot sensibly be applied to a toxic-tort claim filed when disease is manifested years after the exposure, merely because the same plaintiff sued previously to recover for property damage or other injuries. In such a case, the rule is literally inapplicable since, as noted, the second cause of action does not accrue until the disease is manifested; hence, it could not have been joined with the earlier claims."] * * *

2.

Much of the same evidence was material to both the enhanced risk and medical surveillance claims. Dr. Joseph Highland, a toxicologist * * * testified concerning the health hazards posed by the chemicals and the exposure levels at which adverse health effects had been experimentally observed. * * *

Dr. Highland testified that the Legler area residents, because of their exposure to toxic chemicals, had an increased risk of cancer; that unborn children and infants were more susceptible to the disease because of their immature biological defense systems; and that the extent of the risk was variable with the degree of exposure to the chemicals. Dr. Highland testified that he could not quantify the extent of the enhanced risk of cancer because of the lack of scientific information concerning the effect of the interaction of the various chemicals to which plaintiffs were exposed. However, the jury could reasonably have inferred from his testimony that the risk, although unquantified, was medically significant. * * *

Dr. Highland also testified that the exposure to chemicals had already caused actual physical injury to plaintiffs through its adverse effects on the genetic material within their cells.

Dr. Susan Daum, a physician * * * specializing in the diagnosis and treatment of diseases induced by toxic substances, testified that plaintiffs required a program of regular medical surveillance. Acknowledging her reliance on the report of Dr. Highland, Dr. Daum stated that plaintiffs' exposure to chemicals had produced "a reasonable likelihood that they have now or will develop health consequences from this exposure." * * *

Although both the enhanced risk and medical surveillance claims are based on Dr. Highland's testimony, supplemented by Dr. Daum's testimony in the case of the surveillance claim, these claims seek redress for the invasion of distinct and different interests. The enhanced risk claim seeks a damage award, not because of any expenditure of funds, but because plaintiffs contend that the unquantified injury to their health and life expectancy should be presently compensable, even though no evidence of disease is manifest. Defendant does not dispute the causal relationship between the plaintiffs' exposure to toxic chemicals and the plaintiffs' increased risk of diseases, but contends that the probability that plaintiffs will actually become ill from their exposure to chemicals is too remote to warrant compensation under principles of tort law.

By contrast, the claim for medical surveillance does not seek compensation for an unquantifiable injury, but rather seeks specific monetary damages measured by the cost of periodic medical examinations. The invasion for which redress is sought is the fact that plaintiffs have been advised to spend money for medical tests, a cost they would not have incurred absent their exposure to toxic chemicals. Defendant contends that the claim for medical surveillance damages cannot be sustained, as a matter of law, if the plaintiffs' enhanced risk of injury is not sufficiently probable to be compensable. In our view, however, recognition of the medical surveillance claim is not necessarily dependent on recognition of the enhanced risk claim.

3.

The trial court declined to submit to the jury the issue of defendant's liability for the plaintiffs' increased risk of contracting cancer, kidney or liver damage, or other diseases associated with the chemicals that had migrated from the landfill to their wells. If the issue had not been withheld, the jury could have concluded from the evidence that most or all of the plaintiffs had a significantly but unquantifiably enhanced risk of the identified diseases, and that such enhanced risk was attributable to defendant's conduct. * * *

[N]either the trial court nor the Appellate Division challenged the contention that the enhanced risk of disease was a tortiously-inflicted injury, but both concluded that the proof quantifying the likelihood of disease was insufficient to submit the issue to the jury. As the Appellate Division observed:

> While it is true that damages are recoverable for the prospective consequences of a tortious injury, it must be demonstrated that the apprehended consequences are reasonably probable. * * *

Our disposition of this difficult and important issue requires that we choose between two alternatives, each having a potential for imposing unfair and undesirable consequences on the affected interests. A holding that recognizes a cause of action for unquantified enhanced risk claims exposes the tort system, and the public it serves, to the task of litigating vast numbers of claims for compensation based on threats of injuries that may never occur. It imposes on judges and juries the burden of assessing damages for the risk of potential disease, without clear guidelines to determine what level of compensation may be appropriate. It would undoubtedly increase already escalating insurance rates. It is clear that the recognition of an "enhanced risk" cause of action, particularly when the risk is unquantified, would generate substantial litigation that would be difficult to manage and resolve.

Our dissenting colleague, arguing in favor of recognizing a cause of action based on an unquantified claim of enhanced risk, points out that "courts have not allowed the difficulty of quantifying injury to prevent them from offering compensation for assault, trespass, emotional distress, invasion of privacy or damage to reputation." Although lawsuits grounded in one or more of these causes of action may involve claims for damages that are difficult to quantify, such damages are awarded on the basis of events that have occurred and can be proved at the time of trial. In contrast, the compensability of the enhanced risk claim depends upon the likelihood of an event that has not yet occurred and may never occur—the contracting of one or more diseases the risk of which has been enhanced by defendant's conduct. It is the highly contingent and speculative quality of an unquantified claim based on enhanced risk that renders it novel and difficult to manage and resolve. If such claims were to be litigated, juries would be asked to award damages for the enhanced risk of a disease that may never be contracted, without the benefit of expert testimony sufficient to establish the likelihood that the contingent event will ever occur.

On the other hand, denial of the enhanced-risk cause of action may mean that some of these plaintiffs will be unable to obtain compensation for their injury. Despite the collateral estoppel effect of the jury's finding that defendant's wrongful conduct caused the contamination of plaintiffs' wells, those who contract diseases in the future because of their exposure to chemicals in their well water may be unable to prove a causal relationship between such exposure and their disease. * * * Dismissal of the enhanced risk claims may effectively preclude any recovery for injuries caused by exposure to chemicals in plaintiffs' wells because of the difficulty of proving that injuries manifested in the future were not the product of intervening events or causes. * * *

In deciding between recognition or nonrecognition of plaintiffs' enhanced-risk claim, we feel constrained to choose the alternative that most closely reflects the legislative purpose in enacting the Tort Claims Act. We are conscious of the admonition that in construing the Act courts should "exercise restraint in the acceptance of novel causes of action against public entities." In our view, the speculative nature of an unquantified enhanced risk claim, the difficulties inherent in adjudicating such claims, and the policies underlying the Tort Claims Act argue persuasively against the recognition of this cause of action. Accordingly, we decline to recognize plaintiffs' cause of action for the unquantified enhanced risk of disease, and affirm the judgment of the Appellate Division dismissing such claims. We need not and do not decide whether a claim based on enhanced risk of disease that is supported by testimony demonstrating that the onset of the disease is reasonably probable could be maintained under the Tort Claims Act.

4.

The claim for medical surveillance expenses stands on a different footing from the claim based on enhanced risk. It seeks to recover the cost of periodic medical examinations intended to monitor plaintiffs' health and facilitate early diagnosis and treatment of disease caused by plaintiffs' exposure to toxic chemicals. At trial, competent medical testimony was offered to prove that a program of regular medical testing and evaluation was reasonably necessary and consistent with contemporary scientific principles applied by physicians experienced in the diagnosis and treatment of chemically-induced injuries.

The Appellate Division's rejection of the medical surveillance claim is rooted in the premise that even if medical experts testify convincingly that medical surveillance is necessary, the claim for compensation for these costs must fall, as a matter of law, if the risk of injury is not quantified, or, if quantified, is not reasonably probable. This analysis assumes that the reasonableness of medical intervention, and, therefore, its compensability, depends solely on the sufficiency of proof that the occurrence of the disease is probable. We think this formulation unduly impedes the ability of courts to recognize that medical science may necessarily and properly intervene where there is a significant but unquantified risk of serious disease.

This point is well-illustrated by the hypothetical case discussed in the opinion of the Court of Appeals in Friends for All Children v. Lockheed Aircraft Corp., 746 F.2d 816 (D.C.Cir.1984):

> Jones is knocked down by a motorbike when Smith is riding through a red light. Jones lands on his head with some force. Understandably shaken, Jones enters a hospital where doctors recommend that he undergo a battery of tests to determine whether he has suffered any internal head injuries. The tests prove negative, but Jones sues Smith solely for what turns out to be the substantial cost of the diagnostic examinations.
>
> From our example, it is clear that even in the absence of physical injury Jones ought to be able to recover the cost for the various diagnostic examinations proximately caused by Smith's negligent action. A cause of action allowing recovery for the expense of diagnostic examinations recommended by competent physicians will, in theory, deter misconduct, whether it be negligent motorbike riding or negligent aircraft manufacture. The cause of action also accords with commonly shared intuitions of normative justice which underlie the common law of tort. The motorbike rider, through his negligence, caused the plaintiff, in the opinion of medical experts, to need specific medical services–a cost that is neither inconsequential nor of a kind the community generally accepts as part of the wear and tear of daily life. Under these principles of tort law, the motorbike should pay.

* * *

Compensation for reasonable and necessary medical expenses is consistent with well-accepted legal principles. It is also consistent with the important public health interest in fostering access to medical testing for individuals whose exposure to toxic chemicals creates an enhanced risk of disease. The value of early diagnosis and treatment for cancer patients is well-documented.* * *

Accordingly, we hold that the cost of medical surveillance is a compensable item of damages where the proofs demonstrate, through reliable expert testimony predicated upon the significance and extent of exposure to chemicals, the toxicity of the chemicals, the seriousness of the diseases for which individuals are at risk, the relative increase in the chance of onset of disease in those exposed, and the value of early diagnosis, that such surveillance to monitor the effect of exposure to toxic chemicals is reasonable and necessary. In our view, this holding is thoroughly consistent with our rejection of plaintiffs' claim for damages based on their enhanced risk of injury. That claim seeks damages for the impairment of plaintiffs' health, without proof of its likelihood, extent, or monetary value. In contrast, the medical surveillance claim seeks reimbursement for the specific dollar costs of periodic examinations that are medically necessary notwithstanding the fact that the extent of plaintiffs' impaired health is unquantified.

We find that the proofs in this case were sufficient to support the trial court's decision to submit the medical surveillance issue to the jury, and were sufficient to support the jury's verdict.

5.

The medical surveillance issue was tried as if it were a conventional claim for compensatory damages susceptible to a jury verdict in a lump sum. The jury was so instructed by the trial court, and neither plaintiffs' nor defendant's request to charge on this issue sought a different instruction.

In the Appellate Division, defendant argued for the first time that a lump-sum damage award for medical surveillance was inappropriate. Defendant contended that if the court were to uphold all or any part of the medical surveillance award, it should "create an actuarially-sound fund, to which the plaintiffs may apply in the future for the cost of medical surveillance upon proof that those costs are not otherwise compensable * * * or after deduction of the amounts so reimbursed," and should leave to the trial court, on remand, the task of establishing "details of the creation and supervision of such a fund." * * *

In our view, the use of a court-supervised fund to administer medical-surveillance payments in mass exposure cases, particularly for claims under the Tort Claims Act, is a highly appropriate exercise of the Court's equitable powers. Such a mechanism offers significant advantages over a lump-sum verdict. For Tort Claims Act cases, it provides a method for offsetting a defendant's liability by payments from collateral sources. Although the parties in this case sharply dispute the availability of insurance coverage for surveillance-type costs, a fund could provide a convenient method for establishing credits in the event insurance benefits were available for some, if not all, of the plaintiffs.

In addition, a fund would serve to limit the liability of defendants to the amount of expenses actually incurred. A lump-sum verdict attempts to estimate future expenses, but cannot predict the amounts that actually will be expended for medical purposes. Although conventional damage awards do not restrict plaintiffs in the use of money paid as compensatory damages, mass-exposure toxic-tort cases involve public interests not present in conventional tort litigation. The public health interest is served by a fund mechanism that encourages regular medical monitoring for victims of toxic exposure. Where public entities are defendants, a limitation of liability to amounts actually expended for medical surveillance tends to reduce insurance costs and taxes, objectives consistent with the legislature's admonition to avoid recognition of novel causes of action. * * *

In litigation involving public-entity defendants, we conclude that the use of a fund to administer medical-surveillance damages should be the general rule, in the absence of factors that render it impractical or inappropriate.

However, we decline to upset the jury verdict awarding medical-surveillance damages in this case. Such a result would be unfair to these plaintiffs, since the medical-surveillance issue was tried conventionally, and neither party requested the trial court to withhold from the jury the power to return a lump-sum verdict for each plaintiff in order that relief by way of a fund could be provided. * * *

HANDLER, J., concurring in part and dissenting in part.

* * * The essence of the claim for damages here is the reality of the physical injury caused by the wrongful exposure to toxic chemicals and the increased peril of cancer and other serious diseases that the residents have incurred. * * *

The Court cannot, and does not, dispute or denigrate the expert testimony presented at trial "that the exposure to chemicals had already caused actual physical injury to plaintiffs through its adverse effects on the genetic material within their cells" and that plaintiffs' exposure to chemicals had produced "a reasonable likelihood that they have now and will develop health consequences from this exposure." Dr. Joseph Highland gave uncontested testimony that plaintiffs had already suffered physical injury from the damage to their cellular and genetic material caused by the chemicals to which they were exposed. These chemicals are mutagenic agents: they destroy parts of the genetic material of cells they contact. This destruction may affect only the function of a few cells or it may lead to the failure of major organs. It may make the cells likely starting points for cancer, and it may lead to mutations in the victims' children.

The majority recognizes that plaintiffs have suffered injury. It is self-evident that exposure to highly toxic chemicals is the "infliction of ... harm," "an invasion of a legally protected interest." Nevertheless, the majority concludes that plaintiffs' injury cannot be redressed. Its reasons for treating their claims different from other injury claims are an unsupported fear of "vast numbers of claims" and a belief that no "clear guidelines [exist] to determine what level of compensation may be appropriate."

These reasons are an evasion of the challenge posed by tortious injury that carries with it an enhanced risk of even greater injury, and the need to provide fair compensation for innocent victims suffering this form of injury. The Court postponed a similar determination in Evers v. Dollinger, 95 N.J. 399, 471 A.2d 405 (1984). There a woman brought suit claiming that her doctor's negligent diagnosis and treatment enhanced the risk that her cancer would recur. While her appeal of the trial court's judgment was pending, she suffered a recurrence of the cancer. The majority decided that it need not decide whether enhanced risk, standing alone, is an actionable element. Nevertheless, the Court held that because the disease had recurred, plaintiff would be allowed to recover damages for enhanced risk.

Allowing recovery for enhanced risk in *Evers* where the plaintiff suffered subsequent harm cannot be reconciled with the denial of recovery for enhanced risk in the present case. The majority professes to deny compensation because it cannot "measure" or "quantify" the enhanced risk of future injury. The fact that the plaintiffs in the present case have not–yet–suffered extreme symptoms is no justification for denying recovery. As in *Evers v. Dollinger*, "[t]he Court is . . . troubled by a seeming inability to quantify the risk of future cancer. But, adding the incurrence of future harm as a requirement for the recovery for such increased risk does not resolve the dilemma since the risk still remains unquantified." Id. at 421, 471 A.2d 405 (Handler, J., concurring). When the Court allowed recovery for enhanced risk in *Evers*, it did not in the slightest way insist that the risk be quantified.

The majority reasons that plaintiffs' claim is not cognizable in part because the risk of future disease does not rise to the level of "reasonable probability." Yet the court concedes that the plaintiffs have proven that they have a "significantly . . . enhanced risk" of contracting serious diseases. It nowhere explains why a risk that generates the "reasonable probability" of future injury can be compensated while one that "significantly enhances" the likelihood of future injury cannot. * * *

The courts have not allowed the difficulty of quantifying injury to prevent them from offering compensation for assault, trespass, emotional distress, invasion of privacy, or damage to reputation. * * * Where new forms of injury have been put before the courts, the courts have developed procedures, standards, and formulas for determining appropriate compensation. This perception was expressed in Capron, Tort Liability in Genetic Counseling, 79 Colum.L.Rev. 618, 649 (1979):

> [T]he collective wisdom of the community on the proper redress for a particular harm, informed by experience, common sense, and a desire to be fair to the parties, seems an acceptable way of arriving at a damage verdict and probably one that is preferable to a more scientific (and sterile) process that excludes nonquantifiable elements to achieve an aura of objectivity and precision.

The plaintiffs' claim of an unquantified enhanced risk should not be characterized as "depend[ing] upon the likelihood of an event that has not yet occurred and may never occur." The injury involved is an actual event: exposure to toxic chemicals. The tortious contamination, moreover, is an event that has surely occurred; it is not a speculative or remote possible happening. Among the consequences of this unconsented-to invasion are genetic damage and a tangible risk of a major disease, a peril that is real even though it cannot be precisely measured or weighed. The peril, moreover, is unquestionably greater than that experienced by persons not similarly exposed to toxic chemicals. The toxic injury and claim for damages are not attributable only to some possible future event. Like claims based on the doctrines of trespass, assault, invasion of privacy, or defamation, the damages suffered are not solely actual consequential damages, but also the disvalue of being subjected to an intrinsically harmful event. The risk of dreadful disease resulting from toxic exposure and contamination is more frightening and palpable than any deficits we may feel or imagine from many other wrongful transgressions. * * *

In deciding whether to recognize plaintiffs' claims, the majority focuses on the problem of sovereign defendants in tort suits involving the unquantified nature of certain injuries. The majority, however, fails to note the long-term benefits lost when compensation is not allowed for injuries caused. Compensation serves to deter negligent behavior. We disserve this policy in this case, where the defendant municipality has engaged not simply in negligent conduct, but in "palpably unreasonable" conduct causing real and serious injury to its residents. * * *

"A tortfeasor should not be allowed to escape responsibility for causing an increased risk that would not have existed but for his negligence simply because of the statistical uncertainty of the risk." * * *

The majority speaks of the speculative nature of compensating claims of enhanced risk as if such would be an anomaly in the logical and orderly work of tort law compensation. The truth is to the contrary. There are relatively few injuries that can be easily or logically quantified. It is not merely the relatively new tort claims like "pain and suffering" and "emotional distress" that are difficult to quantify. What is the logical method of evaluation for compensating a claim of trespass on land, the battery of unconsented-to surgery, a violation of personal privacy, or an insult to character? When a jury awards $50,000 for an accident that led to the loss of a limb, how is that $50,000 a logical quantification of that injury?

The severe limitation of damages imposed by the Court in this case is inadequate and unfair. No person in her right mind would trade places with any one of these plaintiffs. Does this not suggest that a person would have to be paid a considerable sum of money, more than that permitted here by the Court, before tolerating the injuries suffered by these plaintiffs? Why should not a jury be permitted to make this determination? * * *

Notes

1. *The Plaintiff's Cause of Action.* Studying remedies as a separate course presumes that it is possible to draw a bright line between right and remedy, that issues bearing on the proper remedy and issues of substantive law are separate and distinct. In fact, the line between remedial principles and substantive law can be smudged and gray.

For example, is the recovery of damages for medical surveillance and enhanced risk in *Ayers* a remedies question, or a question of substantive tort law? The defendant characterized the issue as a question of substantive tort law. Because the plaintiffs had not shown an enhanced risk of cancer with sufficient certainty, the defendant argued, they had not shown a personal injury. The plaintiffs therefore could not recover the costs of medical surveillance because they had no cause of action against the defendants in the first place. The court, on the other hand, characterized the issue as a remedies question. The plaintiffs were harmed by the exposure to toxic chemicals, which established their cause of action. Whether particular items of loss were recoverable was a question of the appropriate remedy.

Not all courts agree, however, at least where the plaintiff has not yet suffered a physical injury from the exposure. Thus, in Henry v. Dow Chemical Co., 473 Mich. 63, 78, 701 N.W.2d 684, 691 (2005), the Michigan Supreme Court rejected a claim for medical monitoring expenses by plaintiffs who had been exposed to a carcinogen—dioxin—but who had not demonstrated any physical injury:

> It is no answer to argue, as plaintiffs have, that the need to pay for medical monitoring is itself a present injury sufficient to sustain a cause of action for negligence. In so doing, plaintiffs attempt to blur the distinction between "injury" and "damages." While plaintiffs arguably demonstrate economic losses that would otherwise satisfy the "damages" element of a traditional tort claim, the fact remains that these economic losses are wholly derivative of a possible, future injury rather than an actual, present injury. A financial "injury" is simply not a present physical injury, and thus not cognizable under our tort system. Because plaintiffs have not alleged a present physical injury, but rather, "bare" damages, the medical expenses plaintiffs claim to have suffered (and will suffer in the future) are not compensable.

For a summary of recent cases, see Chris P. Guzelian, Bruce E. Hillner & Philip Guzelian, A Quantitative Methodology for Determining the Need for Exposure–Prompted Medical Monitoring, 79 Ind.L.J. 57, 59–60 nn. 3,4 (2004); Richard Bourne, Medical Monitoring Without Physical Injury: The Least Justice can do for Those Industry has Terrorized with Poisonous Products, 58 S.M.U. L.Rev. 251, 252 n.10 (2005).

Courts have drawn the same line for plaintiffs seeking emotional distress damages for exposure to toxic or carcinogenic substances. If the plaintiff has no immediate physical injuries, the question is one of substantive tort law, and courts have typically denied recovery. If the plaintiff has suffered a physical injury, and therefore has a cause of action, remedies principles govern; recovery can be allowed if the loss was foreseeable and reasonably certain. See Norfolk and Western Railway v. Ayers, 538 U.S. 135, 123 S.Ct. 1210, 155 L.Ed.2d 261 (2003) (railroad workers whose exposure to asbestos in the workplace caused asbestosis could recover damages for their resulting fear of cancer and mental anguish).

Does it make sense for physical injury to serve as the condition precedent for recovering damages for economic and emotional loss? Thinking back to the purposes of tort law as outlined in the introduction to this section, how might the *Henry* court respond to concerns that denying compensation to those who have been exposed to carcinogens but are not yet ill will lead to underdeterrence?

2. *Elements of the Damage Award.* The plaintiff's rightful position provides the starting point in determining what elements of damages are

recoverable. To get started simply ask: What items of loss must be replaced to restore the plaintiff to her rightful position? In cases involving economic harm, a sort of balance sheet can be employed:

> In determining the measure of recovery, aside from harm to body, emotions or reputation, a balance sheet is in effect set up by the court in which are stated the items of assets and liabilities that have been affected by the tort, (a) before the tort and (b) as they appear at the time of trial. In this are put on one side such assets of the injured person as have been affected by the tort, including his capacity to make profitable use of his time, and on the other side, the same assets at the time of the trial and any existing or prospective liabilities imposed upon him as a result of the tort. The difference, to the extent that it results from the tort, constitutes the theoretical measure of recovery.

Restatement (Second) of Torts § 906 comment a. While nonpecuniary harms are not susceptible of such precise measurement, the theory remains the same: restore the plaintiff to the pre-tort position.

What elements of loss should be compensated to restore the plaintiffs in *Ayers v. Jackson Township* to their rightful positions? The plaintiffs identified three sorts of losses for which they sought compensation: harm to the quality of their lives, exposure to suspected and known carcinogens, and the costs of medical surveillance that this exposure necessitated. Could they have been more ambitious? What other sorts of losses might they have claimed?

Would the *Ayers* plaintiffs be recovering double damages if they were compensated once for injury to quality of life and again for emotional distress?

3. *Measuring the Damages.* How might the *Ayers* jury have arrived at its figures for injury to quality of life? How much would you have awarded the plaintiffs if they had been allowed to recover damages for their emotional distress? Strategies for measuring nonpecuniary loss are discussed in part 2 of this section.

4. *Limits on the Award: Are the damages foreseeable, certain, unavoidable and not offset by benefits?*

a. *Foreseeability.* According to Professor McCormick, whose framework for thinking about damage issues introduces section B, damages must be foreseeable to be recoverable. Foreseeability is one of several doctrines on which courts rely to exclude damages that are too remote. See Dan B. Dobbs, The Law of Remedies § 3.3 (2d ed.1993). For various reasons, however, foreseeability has come to be viewed as more the province of the substantive law of contracts and torts than of the law of remedies. Thus, Hadley v. Baxendale, 156 Eng. Rep. 145 (Ex.1854), which gives meaning to foreseeability as a limit on contract damages, is a staple of the first year contracts course.

Similarly, the concept of foreseeability permeates tort law. The plaintiff must be foreseeable before the defendant owes her a duty. Some harm must be foreseeable before the defendant's behavior will be labeled negligent. If the injury that results was unforeseeable, the court may declare it too remote to be considered proximately caused by the defendant's conduct.

Unsurprisingly, there isn't much left to foreseeability at the remedies stage in tort cases. If foreseeability is a real issue, typically it will bear on whether the plaintiff has a cause of action, not on the damages that might be available. Thus, as discussed in Note 1, above, whether a plaintiff who has been exposed to a potentially harmful substance as a result of defendant's wrongdoing can recover has largely been treated as raising a question of substantive tort law. If the plaintiff has suffered a physical injury as a result of the exposure, pain and suffering damages, including fear of future consequences, are routinely available as parasitic damages.

Once a cause of action in tort has been established, the general rule has been that if the type of harm the plaintiff suffered was foreseeable, the extent of the harm need not have been. The classic case is McCahill v. New York Transportation Co., 201 N.Y. 221, 94 N.E. 616 (1911), in which the plaintiff was so weakened by his preexisting alcoholism that he unexpectedly died from the relatively minor injuries the defendant caused. Because of the rule that "you take your plaintiff as you find him" (also known as the "eggshell" or "thin skull" plaintiff rule), the defendant was liable for the plaintiff's death, although the death was unforeseeable.

Foreseeability can be an issue, however, when a plaintiff attempts to recover damages for an injury that is different in kind, not merely in extent, from the injury that gave rise to his cause of action. In *Ayers*, for example, the court assumed that emotional distress damages "might be recoverable from a non-governmental entity as consequential to a nuisance." Not everyone would agree: The Restatement (Second) of Torts takes a narrower view, allowing only the person in possession of property, not members of the household, to recover damages for bodily harm in a nuisance action.

Plaintiffs who have attempted to include emotional distress damages as consequential damages in a suit for injury to property have gotten mixed results. Most courts simply deny recovery. See Dan B. Dobbs, Law of Remedies § 5.15(3) (2d ed.1993). Others allow recovery if special circumstances, like a preexisting relationship between the parties or the personal character of the property, make the harm particularly foreseeable. E.g., Windeler v. Scheers Jewelers, 8 Cal.App.3d 844, 88 Cal.Rptr. 39 (1970). Of course, keep in mind that a court that denies recovery for mental distress as a separate item of damages may turn around and measure the value of the property by its "intrinsic" or "actual" value to the owner. See p. 471.

b. *Certainty.* Damages cannot be recovered unless the amount of the loss has been established with reasonable certainty. Restatement (Second) of Torts § 912. The traditional rule requires the plaintiff to show that the future loss is probable, i.e., more likely than not, the loss will come to pass. For the *Ayers* court, the prospect of future losses attributable to an unquantified risk of future disease was too uncertain to permit recovery. For a different view, see Dillon v. Evanston Hospital, 199 Ill.2d 483, 771 N.E.2d 357, 264 Ill.Dec. 653 (2002) (reproduced at p. 538).

Yet, how certain were the losses for which the *Ayers* court did allow recovery? How certain is it that the amount awarded as quality of life damages was accurate? How about the damages for medical monitoring? Those were based on the plaintiffs' life expectancy. Is it certain that any of the plaintiffs will live exactly that long? See David Faigman et al., 1 Modern Scientific Evidence § 9.59 (2008–2009 ed.) (methods of estimating life expectancy).

The court's solution to the indeterminacy problem in *Ayers* is to require the defendant to pay for the cost of medical surveillance, and preserve the plaintiffs' cause of action should cancer eventually occur. This sort of claim-splitting has garnered significant support. At least in cases involving exposure to asbestos, the majority of jurisdictions now allow plaintiffs to bring a second suit if they later develop a second disease. Comment, Medical Monitoring Plaintiffs and Subsequent Claims for Disease, 66 U.Chi.L.Rev. 969 (1999).

c. *Avoidable Consequences*. According to the unavoidable consequences rule, a plaintiff cannot recover damages for any harm that could have been avoided by taking reasonable steps to mitigate the harm. Restatement (Second) of Torts § 918. In personal injury cases, the rule's main effect is to give the plaintiff an incentive to seek reasonable medical care to limit the consequences of the injury. In cases involving damage to property, the rule requires reasonable steps to repair or replace the damaged property if that will limit the plaintiff's losses.

As *Ayers* neatly demonstrates, the rule has a positive corollary: If reasonable steps are taken to limit losses (here, medical surveillance to detect cancer while it is still treatable), the costs of those steps are recoverable as damages.

d. *Offsetting Benefits and Collateral Sources*. "When the defendant's tortious conduct * * * has conferred a special benefit to the interest of the plaintiff that was harmed, the value of the benefit conferred is considered in mitigation of damages, to the extent that this is equitable." Restatement (Second) of Torts § 920. For example, if a doctor performs an unauthorized operation that actually improves the plaintiff's health, the amount of damages the plaintiff recovers from the doctor will be reduced by the amount of benefit conferred. Id. comment a, illustration 1. The same principle applies in contract cases, if the breach in fact confers a benefit on the nonbreaching party. See Restatement (Second) of Contracts § 347, comment c.

So, if the plaintiffs in *Ayers* have health insurance that will pay for the costs of medical monitoring, should the award of damages for medical monitoring be reduced? No, according to the collateral source rule. The collateral source rule provides that "[p]ayments made to or benefits conferred on the injured party from other sources are not credited against the tortfeasor's liability, although they cover all or part of the harm for which the tortfeasor is liable." Note, California's Collateral Source Rule and Plaintiff's Receipt of Uninsured Motorist Benefits, 37 Hastings L.J. 667, 670 (1986). In other words, the amount of the plaintiffs' recovery is not reduced even though the plaintiffs may be compensated for the same loss again through their insurance, or by some other collateral source.

When an injured plaintiff is compensated by a collateral source for injuries the defendant caused, the stage is set for a conflict between two of the purposes of compensatory damages. If the plaintiff is allowed to keep the benefit from the collateral source and to recover again from the defendant, the plaintiff has a windfall. To the extent that compensatory damages are supposed to "make the plaintiff whole," the rule that collateral sources are ignored puts the plaintiff in better than his rightful position.

On the other hand, consider the effect on deterrence if benefits from a collateral source reduce the defendant's obligation to pay. If compensatory damages are intended to deter defendants by making them bear the full cost of the harm they cause, letting them off the hook in cases where the plaintiff was wise enough to insure, or fortunate enough to have friends to help out financially, would result in under-deterrence. Further, given the expense of litigation, compensatory damages don't really make the plaintiff whole anyway, and why should the defendant benefit from the insurance premiums the plaintiff wisely invested? After all, people should have an incentive to buy insurance, and a rule that deprived them of its benefits would discourage its purchase. See Helfend v. Southern California Rapid Transit District, 2 Cal.3d 1, 15, 84 Cal.Rptr. 173, 465 P.2d 61 (1970). Finally, many plaintiffs will not be overcompensated, because their insurance policies will have subrogation clauses that allow the insurer to recapture any benefits for which the plaintiff later receives compensation. So, double recovery is less common than the statement of the rule would suggest.

Remember, however, that an insurance company is likely to be on both sides of a personal injury lawsuit. As the rule operates, the plaintiff is likely to be compensated by two insurance companies: his own and the defendants'. Thus, the collateral source rule, which after all evolved before insurance was widely available, is often criticized as contributing to unnecessary increases in the cost of insurance. See, e.g., Nora J. Pasman–Green & Ronald D. Richards Jr., Who is Winning the Collateral Source Rule War? The Battleground in the Sixth Circuit States, 31 U.Tol.L.Rev. 425 (2000).

Eliminating the collateral source rule is high on the agenda of the current movement for tort reform. Legislation limiting the application of the rule has been enacted in at least thirty states. Some sixteen have enacted legislation eliminating or modifying the collateral source rule in all civil actions. Other states have been more selective, eliminating it in actions against public entities (Pennsylvania), construction defect cases (Alaska) or in medical malpractice actions (fifteen states). Interestingly, most of these statutes acknowledge the policy of encouraging potential plaintiffs to insure either by excluding collateral sources for which the plaintiff has paid premiums, or by offsetting the cost of some or all of the premiums paid to the collateral source. Like most tort reform statutes, these provisions have been challenged, sometimes successfully, on constitutional grounds. See Sorrell v. Thevenir, 69 Ohio St.3d 415, 633 N.E.2d 504 (1994) (early version of Ohio statute unconstitutional under open courts and right to remedy provisions of state constitution); Thompson v. KFB Insurance Co., 252 Kan. 1010, 850 P.2d 773 (1993) (statute eliminating rule only where damages exceed $150,000 violates equal protection and due process); but see Marsh v. Green, 782 So.2d 223 (Ala.2000) (statute making evidence of collateral benefits admissible is constitutional); Germantown Savings Bank v. City of Philadelphia, 98 Pa.Cmwlth. 508, 512 A.2d 756 (1986), aff'd 517 Pa. 313, 535 A.2d 1052 (1988) (statute abrogating collateral source rule in actions against political subdivisions is constitutional).

The Air Transportation Safety and System Stabilization Act, Pub.L. 107–42, Sept. 22, 2001, 115 Stat. 237, which established the September 11th Victim Compensation Fund, mandated that the Fund "reduce the amount of compensation * * * by the amount of the collateral source compensation the claimant has received or is entitled to receive" as a result of the terrorist attacks. According to the Fund's Final Report, "the deduction of collateral source payments from awards proved to be one of the Fund's most contentious issues." Final Report of the Special Master for the September 11th Compensation Fund (Vol. I) at 43. Can you see why this would be the case? The Special Master developed detailed regulations intended to ensure that savings—as distinguished from forms of insurance—were not deducted, that benefits were valued conservatively so that awards would be maximized, and that victim contributions, like premiums, were fully taken into account. Is it possible that the Fund's experience will give momentum or direction for future reform? See Kenneth S. Abraham & Kyle D. Logue, The Genie and the Bottle: Collateral Sources Under the September 11th Victim Compensation Fund, 53 DePaul L.Rev. 591 (2003); Stephan Landsman, A Chance to be Heard: Thoughts About Schedules, Caps, and Collateral Source Deductions in the September 11th Victim Compensation Fund, 53 DePaul L.Rev. 393 (2003).

Thinking about the effect of the collateral source rule on insurance brings up, however, another of compensation's purposes. Often it is said that tort law itself functions as a kind of insurance. When the cost of injuries is included in the price of an activity or a product, the price rises, spreading the cost among participants or consumers. With the collateral source rule in place, are consumers paying for the same insurance twice, once in their insurance premiums, and once in the product's price? Which is the more efficient way to insure? The implications of the idea that compensatory damages are a form of insurance are explored further in part 3 of this section.

5. *Caps on Damage Awards: Balancing the Hardships?* In Chapter 2, at p. 90, the idea of balancing the hardships—leaving the plaintiff short of the rightful position because of the hardship that full relief would cause to the defendant—was characterized as a peculiarly equitable notion. Surely, the note asked, no one would advocate paying the plaintiff less than the damages she was owed because of concerns about the effect on the defendant's wealth. Is the New Jersey Tort Claims Act's prohibition on pain and suffering damages in actions against public entities and public employees a form of balancing the hardships, insofar as it leaves the plaintiffs short of their rightful position in order to conserve the public's wealth? Do you see a similarity to the trade-off Congress made in the statutory scheme in *Schweiker v. Chilicky*, p. 20? The Ohio Supreme Court upheld Ohio's tort reform statute—which includes a cap on noneconomic damages, changes to the collateral source rule, and a limit on punitive damages—in Arbino v. Johnson & Johnson, 116 Ohio St.3d 468, 880 N.E.2d 420 (2007) (principal case in Chapter 6, p. 691). For discussions of how caps may disproportionately affect disadvantaged groups, see Stephen Daniels & Joanne Martin, The Texas Two-Step: Evidence on the Link Between Damage Caps and Access to the Civil Justice System, 55 DePaul L. Rev. 635 (2006); Michael L. Rustad, Neglecting the Neglected: The Impact of Noneconomic Damage Caps on Meritorious Nursing Home Lawsuits, 14 Elder L.J. 331 (2006).

Pain and suffering damages are a popular target for those who believe the tort system is in need of reform. Caps on pain and suffering damages in medical malpractice cases are discussed at p. 524.

6. *Managing the Damage Award.* Tort damages have traditionally been awarded in a lump sum for past, present and future losses. The *Ayers* court suggests that were it not for the unfairness of changing the rules at such a late date in the litigation, it would abandon this practice. Instead of awarding a lump sum for medical surveillance, the court would create a fund against which the plaintiffs could make claims as they incur costs.

The idea of a judicially administered fund for medical monitoring costs has turned out to be an attractive solution to the problem of uncertainty. For example, in Metro–North Commuter Railroad Co. v. Buckley, 521 U.S. 424, 117 S.Ct. 2113, 138 L.Ed.2d 560 (1997), the Court rejected awarding lump sum damages for medical monitoring, but specifically reserved the question of whether a trust fund for medical monitoring expenses would have been an appropriate remedy.

Tort reformers have found the notion of replacing lump sum awards with judgments that are paid out periodically, over time, to be attractive. That way, the defendant maintains control over the award, and gains the benefit of any expenses that, for one reason or another, do not eventuate. In return, the plaintiff gains a measure of security. If expenses exceed what might have been predicted, there is some protection, and the plaintiff is saved the burden of investing the award against future need. On the other hand, such paternalism may be unjustified, and it is not clear how periodically paid judgments are to accommodate the plaintiff's lawyer's fee, given that contingency fees predominate in personal injury litigation. Nonetheless, some tort reform statutes specifically provide for periodic payment of judgments. For an attempt to work out the problems periodic payment of judgments raises, see the Model Periodic Payment of Judgments Act.

Ayers does not present very complicated problems in managing a damage award, compared to cases that may involve thousands or tens of thousands of claims, like asbestos, DES, or Agent Orange litigation. The problems in *Ayers* are sensitive primarily because a public entity is the defendant, and the public fisc can be jealously guarded. Should the rules of damages be responsive to the type of litigation involved? Should there be one set of damage rules when the defendant is a public entity, another for private defendants? Should there be a separate set of rules for mass disasters, toxic torts, and the like? How about for cases in which children too young to manage a lump sum award are involved? See Kush v. Lloyd, 616 So.2d 415 (Fla.1992) (parents who recover future extraordinary expenses for an impaired child must hold the award in segregated trust account).

Could the plaintiffs in cases like *Henry v. Dow Chemical*, p. 499, in which the Michigan Supreme Court rejected a medical monitoring claim, prevail by characterizing their claim as a claim for equitable relief? In their article, Unrealized Torts, 88 Va. L.Rev. 1625 (2002), Professors John C.P. Goldberg and Benjamin C. Zipursky suggest that plaintiffs seeking creation of a medical monitoring fund are in effect seeking a form of injunctive relief, requiring a defendant who has created an ongoing danger to take steps to prevent future harm to those affected. When the argument was made in *Henry*, however, the court was unconvinced: "Regardless of whether the relief plaintiffs seek is equitable or legal in nature, defendant was entitled to summary disposition regarding plaintiffs' medical monitoring cause of action because plaintiffs have not stated a valid cause of action." 701 N.W.2d at 702.

For the *Henry* court, allowing recovery of medical monitoring expenses raised a series of issues best resolved by the legislature. First, the availability of such relief "would create a potentially limitless pool of plaintiffs," given the wide range of exposure to toxins, diverting resources from those who may actually be injured. Id at 694. The court was especially concerned with the effect on the state's economy: "[H]owever much equity might favor lightening the economic burden now borne by [the plaintiffs], we have no assurance that a decision in plaintiffs' favor * * * will not wreak enormous harm on Michigan's citizens and its economy." Finally, the court was concerned that practical details of administering a medical monitoring system would overwhelm the courts. Id. at 699. For similar concerns, see James A. Henderson, Jr. & Aaron D. Twerski, Asbestos Litigation Gone Mad: Exposure–Based Recovery for Increased Risk, Mental Distress, and Medical Monitoring, 53 S.C.L.Rev. 815 (2002).

Do these concerns suggest that the form of public law litigation Chayes described in Chapter 1 now reaches into private tort litigation? Having seen courts struggle with complex injunctive remedies in areas from school desegregation to prison reform and beyond, how would you evaluate the court's concerns? The overlap between public law and private law is a focus of the last section of this chapter.

1. ELEMENTS OF THE AWARD

The next case introduces two statutory forms of action—wrongful death and survival actions—created to fill an important gap in tort recovery. It also provides an opportunity to think further about the purposes compensation serves. One of the characteristics that sets tort damages apart is the availability of monetary recovery for nonmonetary harms. What purpose is served by awarding money damages for a loss that money cannot make good?

BELL v. CITY OF MILWAUKEE
United States Court of Appeals, Seventh Circuit, 1984
746 F.2d 1205

CUMMINGS, CHIEF JUDGE.

* * *

[Daniel Bell was shot in the back as he fled from police officer Grady. His family brought a civil rights action to recover damages for the shooting and the subsequent racially motivated cover-up. Daniel Bell's estate was awarded $100,000 for compensatory damages for "loss of life," and $25,000 in punitive damages. Bell's father's estate recovered $475,000 for the loss of the son's society and companionship. (Bell's father happened to die subsequent to Bell.) Bell's siblings were awarded $100,000 for loss of society and companionship. On appeal, the awards were affirmed, except for the award for loss of society and companionship to Bell's siblings. With regard to that award, the court of appeals held that while the fourteenth amendment protected Bell's father's liberty interest in his son's society and companionship, the siblings' interests were not constitutionally protected.[a]

V. SECTION 1983 CLAIM OF DANIEL BELL'S ESTATE

The district court allowed the plaintiffs to include a special verdict question regarding the violation of Daniel Bell's constitutional rights. The jury found a violation, and awarded $100,000 in damages to the estate of Daniel Bell for the loss of his life and enjoyment thereof. Defendants contend that Wisconsin law does not permit recovery by the estate for the death of Daniel Bell. The district court in ruling upon defendants' post-verdict motions disagreed, holding without explaining that Wis.Stat. § 895.04 allows the personal representative of Daniel Bell's estate to recover for loss of life for the benefit of the estate. The district court also noted that if the Wisconsin wrongful death statute could not be read as allowing the estate to recover, state law would be inconsistent with the deterrent policies of Section 1983 and therefore could not be applied. While the district court's interpretation of Section 895.04 may be in error, its evaluation of the policies behind Section 1983 in regard to Daniel Bell's estate's claim is correct.

Wisconsin survival statute Section 895.01 provides that wrongful death actions survive the death of the victim (as well as the death of the wrongdoer), and wrongful death statute Section 895.04(1) states that "[a]n action for wrongful death may be brought by the personal representative of the deceased person or by the person to whom the amount recovered belongs." What the district court seemingly overlooked, however, is that Wisconsin law does not allow separate recovery for both the estate and the beneficiaries—the very result obtained below. It is well settled under Sections 895.01 and 895.04, and those Sections' predecessors that recovery in a Wisconsin wrongful death action, even if brought in name by the personal representative, cannot include damages for the loss of life itself. The allowed recovery in Wisconsin compensates for the injury to the beneficiaries, within certain statutory recovery limitations, and not for the loss of life of the victim. * * *

The policy behind this rule is that "the cause of action belongs to the beneficiary * * *." As stated in Prunty v. Schwantes, 40 Wis.2d 418, 424–425, 162 N.W.2d 34, 38–39, "After a person dies, he can no longer be compensated * * *. [O]ur legislature has decided that the survivors of the deceased are the ones that have actually been damaged, and they are the

---

[a]. In Russ v. Watts, 414 F.3d 783 (7th Cir.2005), the Seventh Circuit held that parents have no constitutional right to recover damages for loss of a child's society and companionship, overruling *Bell* on that point.

ones that should be compensated * * *." The rationale implicit in the Wisconsin rule is that the victim once deceased cannot practicably be compensated for the loss of life to be made whole. Thus if the particular compensation policy embodied in Wisconsin wrongful death law were to be applied, Daniel Bell's estate could not raise a claim for loss of life.

Though damages for loss of life are not recoverable by Daniel Bell's estate under Wisconsin law, Wis.Stat. § 895.01 allows the estate to recover for injuries suffered by Daniel Bell prior to death by virtue of, for example, excessive use of force in the course of arrest. Section 895.01 allows survival of actions for "damage to the person". The jury considered the question, however, and found no deprivation of Daniel Bell's rights occurring prior to death. * * *

In short, the Wisconsin statutory scheme creates a survival action in favor of the estate for pre-death injuries and a wrongful death action in favor of the victim's survivors, and neither type of action traditionally allows recovery of damages for loss of life itself. The district court's apparent misconstruction of Wisconsin law, however, has no practical impact on plaintiffs' claims since the application and policy of this point of Wisconsin law are inconsistent with those of Section 1983 and the Fourteenth Amendment protection of life. Therefore, Wisconsin law cannot be applied to preclude the estate's recovery for loss of life, for the reasons set out below. Where the constitutional deprivation sought to be remedied in a Section 1983 action causes death and the applicable state law would deem the action to survive or would allow recovery for the damage claim at issue, courts generally apply the state law. But the more difficult question, the question presented here and addressed by Section 1988[b] is whether a state law is "inconsistent" with federal civil rights law and therefore does not apply where state law would not allow the estate to recover for the loss of life. * * *

The Supreme Court has yet to decide squarely this issue. * * *

In a case where plaintiff died but not as a result of the putatively unconstitutional act, the Supreme Court has confirmed that restrictive state statutes apply to Section 1983 actions. In Robertson v. Wegmann, 436 U.S. 584, 98 S.Ct. 1991, 56 L.Ed.2d 554, the plaintiff who brought a Section 1983 action for malicious prosecution died while his suit was pending. The Court held that pursuant to Section 1988 the applicable Louisiana law governed the survivability issue. Under the state law, the decedent's action abated because no person with the requisite relationship

---

b. 42 U.S.C.A. § 1988 provides: The jurisdiction in civil and criminal matters conferred on the district courts by the provisions of this Title * * * for the protection of all persons in the United States in their civil rights * * * shall be exercised and enforced in conformity with the laws of the United States, so far as such laws are suitable to carry the same into effect; but in all cases where they are not adapted to the object, or are deficient in the provisions necessary to furnish suitable remedies and punish offenses against law, the common law, as modified and changed by the constitution and statutes of the State wherein the court having jurisdiction of such civil or criminal cause is held, so far as the same is not inconsistent with the Constitution and laws of the United States, shall be extended to and govern the said courts in the trial and disposition of the cause. * * *

to him was alive at the time of his death. Concluding that this outcome was not inconsistent with the policies of Section 1983, the Court ruled that the action did not survive but explicitly declined to express any view on the particular issue before us, i.e., whether a cause of action exists in favor of the estate despite state law which precludes such, where the alleged deprivation of constitutional rights caused death. * * *

In a *Bivens* action, i.e., an action brought not against state or local officials under Section 1983 but against federal officials directly under the Constitution, the Supreme Court has allowed recovery by the estate notwithstanding restrictive state law. Carlson v. Green, 446 U.S. 14, 100 S.Ct. 1468, 64 L.Ed.2d 15. *Carlson* involved a *Bivens*-type suit brought by a mother on behalf of the estate of her deceased son, alleging that federal prison officials grossly neglected his asthmatic condition and administered drugs which worsened his condition, with defendants' indifference in part attributable to racial prejudice. Plaintiff argued that defendants' acts and omissions violated the deceased's Eighth and Fourteenth Amendment rights. Under Indiana law no recovery was available where the acts complained of caused the victim's death. * * * Although not explicitly discussing the component of damages for loss of life, the Supreme Court found that a uniform federal rule was necessary to achieve the *Bivens* policies of deterring federal officials from violating federal constitutional rights, and held that whenever a state survival statute would extinguish the action brought against defendants whose conduct results in death, federal law permits survival of the action. The Court distinguished *Robertson* on the rationales that in *Carlson* the plaintiff's death was caused by the defendant's acts upon which the suit was based, and no state interests are implicated by applying purely federal law to federal officials who violate the "federal Constitution". * * *

Supreme Court precedent expressing the policies underlying Section 1983 and the guarantees of the Fourteenth Amendment indicate that allowing the estate of Daniel Bell to recover is the proper result under federal policy, and that restrictive state law at issue in this case is inconsistent with the federal policy.

It is axiomatic that the Fourteenth Amendment protects individuals from deprivation by the state of life without due process. Regarding the egregiousness of Grady's conduct, on the basis of his conviction for reckless homicide and the record in general, Grady was at least grossly reckless in the commission of the killing. Under Parratt v. Taylor, 451 U.S. 527, 531–535, 101 S.Ct. 1908, 1910–1913, 68 L.Ed.2d 420, in which the Supreme Court held that even a negligent deprivation of a constitutional right is sufficient for plaintiff to invoke that right, Grady's recklessness clearly suffices, and Daniel Bell most assuredly was denied due process in the deprivation of his life.

Further, the fundamental policies behind Section 1983 are twofold: compensation for and deterrence of unconstitutional acts committed under state law. One of the primary reasons Section 1983 was enacted was to remedy and deter racial killing and other acts violative of the Fourteenth Amendment. The legislative history behind Section 1983 expresses an unequivocal concern for protecting life. * * * The deterrence objective of Section 1983 was not paramount in *Robertson v. Wegmann* as it is here. In *Robertson* death was an intervening circumstance, and thus the Court did not perceive any significant loss of deterrence if the restrictive Louisiana statute were applied, commenting that:

> In order to find even a marginal influence on behavior as a result of Louisiana's survivorship provisions, one would have to make the rather farfetched assumptions that a state official had both the desire and the ability deliberately to select as victims only those persons who would die before conclusion of the § 1983 suit for reasons entirely unconnected with the official illegality and who would not be survived by any close relatives.

Robertson, 436 U.S. at 592 n.10, 98 S.Ct. at 1996 n.10. But since in the instant case the killing is the unconstitutional act, there would result more than a marginal loss of influence on potentially unconstitutional actors and therefore on the ability of Section 1983 to deter official lawlessness if the victim's estate could not bring suit to recover for loss of life. Moreover, if Section 1983 did not allow recovery for loss of life notwithstanding inhospitable state law, deterrence would be further subverted since it would be more advantageous to the unlawful actor to kill rather than injure. As the Supreme Court observed in Carey v. Piphus, 435 U.S. 247, 258, 98 S.Ct. 1042, 1049, 55 L.Ed.2d 252, "[I]t is not clear * * * that common-law tort rules of damages will provide a complete solution to the damages issue in every § 1983 case." Therefore it is appropriate, as the Supreme Court has noted in regard to Section 1983 damage issues, to fashion "a federal rule responsive to the need whenever a federal right is impaired."

In sum, we hold that Wis.Stat. §§ 895.01 and 895.04, along with Wisconsin decisions construing those provisions, which would preclude recovery to Daniel Bell's estate for loss of life, are inconsistent with the deterrent policy of Section 1983[41] and the Fourteenth Amendment's protection of life.[42] The Wisconsin law therefore cannot be applied to preclude the $100,000 damages recovered by Daniel Bell's estate for loss of life. * * *

---

41. Deterrence of wrongful or negligent conduct is also a policy objective of tort law, but as in Wisconsin, survival and wrongful death statutes generally do not seek to deter wrongful deaths through the imposition of damages for loss of life itself. The rationale is typically the extraordinary difficulty in measuring the value of the loss; and in the context of a survival action, there is the additional inability to restore a deceased to the state he would have enjoyed but for his death. See R. Posner, Tort Law: Cases and Economic Analysis 121–122 (1982). Yet given the stated tort policy of deterrence and the conceivable reduction of the incidence of tortious conduct created by the threat of substantial damages, these dilemmas amount to less than a compelling argument against awarding any damages at all for loss of life.

42. Our holding that Daniel Bell's estate may properly raise a Section 1983 claim is based upon the Fourteenth Amendment's protection of life and the deterrence objective underlying Section 1983; it is unnecessary to address whether Section 1983 compensation policy is necessarily inconsistent with the Wisconsin policy of noncompensation where the victim by virtue of death cannot be made whole.

The above-cited decisions also support plaintiffs' contention that the $25,000 punitive damages awarded against Grady in favor of Daniel Bell's estate should be upheld, even though Wis.Stat. § 895.04 does not allow the victim's estate to recover punitive damages. To disallow punitive damages in Section 1983 actions solely on the basis of restrictive state tort law would seriously hamper the deterrence effect of Section 1983. * * *

NOTES

1. *The Purpose of the Damage Award: Compensation and Deterrence.* Only five or six states allow recovery of damages for "loss of life"—sometimes known as hedonic damages—in a wrongful death action. See Eric A. Posner & Cass R. Sunstein, Dollars and Death, 72 U.Chi.L.Rev. 537, 545 (2005) (listing Arkansas, Connecticut, Hawai'i, New Hampshire and New Mexico); see also Choctaw Maid Farms, Inc. v. Hailey, 822 So.2d 911 (Miss.2002) (hedonic damages are recoverable in wrongful death action even where death is instantaneous). After all, if the plaintiff is dead—or comatose (compare McDougald v. Garber, 73 N.Y.2d 246, 538 N.Y.S.2d 937, 536 N.E.2d 372 (1989) (no recovery) with Holston v. Sisters of the Third Order of St. Francis, 247 Ill.App.3d 985, 187 Ill.Dec. 743, 618 N.E.2d 334, 347 (1993), aff'd, 165 Ill.2d 150, 209 Ill.Dec. 12, 650 N.E.2d 985 (Ill.1995) (damages recoverable))—can an award of damages for the lost value of his life be justified as compensation?

Of course, without an award of damages for the lost value of life, damages in cases where the decedent has no dependents or has limited earning capacity—elders, homemakers or children for example—will be minimal. See, e.g., McGowan v. Estate of Wright, 524 So.2d 308 (Miss.1988) (upholding a jury verdict that awarded only funeral expenses to the estranged spouse of a man who was instantly killed in a car accident). Consider:

> [The loss to the victim in a wrongful death case] consists of the utility or satisfaction that the victim would have derived, net of any disutility, over the remaining course of his life. * * * [This] type of loss cannot, strictly speaking, be compensated. No award of damages will restore a dead person to the state of happiness he would have enjoyed but for his death. This is not a compelling argument against awarding damages, provided the purpose of tort damages is deterrent rather than compensatory. The threat of having to pay heavy damages will reduce the incidence of tortious conduct, and so increase social welfare, even though the payment of damages in a case where the victim dies will not compensate him.

Richard A. Posner, Tort Law: Cases and Economic Analysis 121–22 (1982).

On the other hand, does awarding damages for the value of a life commodify life in a way that is fundamentally offensive?

> Many people believe that a human life is uniquely precious and therefore cannot be given a monetary valuation. See, for example, Frank Ackerman and Lisa Heinzerling, Priceless: On Knowing the Price of Everything and the Value of Nothing 61 (New Press 2004) ("Putting a price on human life ... is clearly unacceptable to virtually all religions and moral philoso-

phies.")". Calculating the value of a human life demeans the victim of the wrong rather than vindicating his memory.

Eric A. Posner & Cass R. Sunstein, Dollars and Death, 72 U.Chi.L.Rev. 537, 553 (2005). The Special Master encountered this feeling in administering the September 11th Victim Compensation Fund:

> Claimant after claimant referred to the disconnect between a life lost and the inadequacy of mere compensation: "Whatever award we receive will obviously never come close to the worth of our son. To be perfectly honest, this whole matter of victims' compensation is ghoulish and repulsive. We are in a no-win situation. Whatever we receive is not enough. The only way we win is if you had some magical power to bring [him] back."

Kenneth R. Feinberg, What is Life Worth? 141 (2005).

Yet in ways the idea of individualized compensation for harm done is equally fundamental—think back to Hammurabi's Code ("if he dies ... and he is a free born man, he shall pay one half mina of silver.") Is the alternative acceptable? "Awarding zero damages for wrongful death is hardly less demeaning, and an award of an 'arbitrary' amount of money—in which either the jury or the legislature picks a number out of thin air—is no better. Similarly, it is hard to believe that regulatory policy should assume that human life is worth nothing or, alternatively, that it has some arbitrary value." Eric A. Posner & Cass R. Sunstein, Dollars and Death, 72 U.Chi. L.Rev. 537, 553 (2005). Can you see a way out of this dilemma?

2. *The Purpose of the Damage Award (continued): The Insurance Perspective.* As an earlier note suggested, compensatory damages can function as a form of insurance. Richard A. Epstein, The Legal and Insurance Dynamics of Mass Tort Litigation, 13 J.Legal Stud. 475 (1984); W. Kip Viscusi, The Value of Life: Has Voodoo Economics Come to the Courts, 1990 J. Forensic Economics 1, 3. Having to pay damage awards increases the price of goods and services, shifting the losses associated with those goods and services and spreading the cost among all those who consume them. The price the consumer pays, thus, is the price of the product plus the price of the insurance.

But while people often insure against possible economic losses, especially against the losses their death would cause to their dependents, no one would buy insurance against the kind of loss that was the focus of *Bell*. That is to say, it would not make sense to buy an insurance policy that, in addition to taking care of the decedent's dependents, paid damages to the deceased. Surely, people would rather save the premiums, and have the money while they are alive, rather than shifting the income to a time when they cannot enjoy it.

Following out the implications of this argument, some economists argue that many forms of compensation for nonpecuniary loss effectively require consumers to purchase an irrational form of insurance. John E. Calfee & Paul H. Rubin, Some Implications of Damage Payments for Nonpecuniary Losses, 21 J.Legal Stud. 371 (1992). Of course, others argue that rational people would sometimes insure against nonpecuniary loss, and that there is in fact evidence that forms of insurance against these kinds of losses exist. Ronen Avraham, Should Pain-and-Suffering Damages be Abolished from Tort Law? More Experimental Evidence, 55 U. Toronto L.J. 941 (2005).

Whichever economists have the best of this empirical argument, does it make sense to evaluate the practice of awarding damages as a form of insurance? Or, is making the plaintiff whole a goal tort law should pursue regardless of whether people insure against a particular form of injury? See Heidi Li Feldman, Harm and Money: Against the Insurance Theory of Tort Compensation, 75 Tex.L.Rev. 1567 (1997).

3. *The Purpose of the Damage Award (continued): Redress.* Perhaps the availability of "loss of life" damages in a case like *Bell*, or of pain and suffering damages more generally, suggests that compensatory damages in tort cases serve purposes beyond compensation and deterrence. Recall Professor Radin's argument—raised in connection with the *Stachura* case in the first section of this chapter—that "requiring payment is a way both to bring the wrongdoer to recognize that she has done wrong and to make redress to the victim." Margaret Jane Radin, Contested Commodities (1996). According to Professor John C.P. Goldberg, the right to have access to a legal forum for the redress of private wrongs is an aspect of liberty so fundamental as to be protected by the Fourteenth Amendment's due process clause. John C.P. Goldberg, The Constitutional Status of Tort Law, 115 Yale L.J. 524 (2005). Cf. Emily Sherwin, Compensation and Revenge, 43 S.D.L.Rev. 1387 (2003) (nonpecuniary damage awards are among the features of compensatory damage awards that suggest "an affinity to revenge").

Interestingly, the Special Master of the September 11th Victim Compensation Fund established noneconomic awards of $250,000 as presumed compensation for the pain and suffering each victim experienced before their deaths. 28 CFR § 104.44. What purpose does an award of noneconomic damages to the deceased serve in that context? See Martha Chamallas, The September 11th Victim Compensation Fund: Rethinking the Damages Element in Injury Law, 71 Tenn.L.Rev. 51, 76–77 (2003) (lump sum award "treats victims more like heroes than like tort victims * * * [and is] akin to a memorial").

4. *The Plaintiff's Cause of Action: Survival and Wrongful Death Actions.* At English common law, actions for personal injury and other injuries to other personal interests terminated if either of the parties to the action died. (Causes of action based on property rights—like breach of contract—survived.) Further, there was no independent cause of action for causing a person's death. So at least until the middle of the nineteenth century, neither Daniel Bell's estate nor his family would have had a cause of action in tort. Daniel Bell's action would have terminated with his death, and any injuries his family claimed to have suffered because of his death would not have been actionable. Although there were early decisions in America departing from these rules, generally they were adopted as part of the common law. Dan B. Dobbs, The Law of Torts § 294 at 803 (2000).

Then, in 1846 Parliament enacted Lord Campbell's Act, 9 & 10 Vic., c. 93, which established a cause of action against one who wrongfully caused another's death for the benefit of those dependent on the decedent for support. Following this lead, every state now has a statutory remedy for wrongful death. See Stuart M. Speiser et al., Recovery for Wrongful Death and Injury (3d ed.1992).

Wrongful death statutes in this country fall roughly into two categories. The majority follow the pattern set by Lord Campbell's Act. They designate certain beneficiaries, and compensate them for the loss of the decedent's support. In other states, however, the wrongful death action is for the benefit of the decedent's estate, and damages aim at compensating the estate for the amounts the decedent would have saved from his earnings and bequeathed to his heirs had he lived his expected life span. See Theodore A. Smedley, Some Order Out of Chaos in Wrongful Death Law, 37 Vand.L.Rev. 273 (1984).

In addition, every state has also changed the common law rule that most tort causes of action do not survive the death of either party by enacting survival statutes. Although what specific causes of action survive varies from state to state, personal injury actions survive in most. Under a survival statute, a suit for personal injuries can be maintained by the plaintiff's estate if the plaintiff dies, and against the defendant's estate if he dies.

Where the defendant's wrong caused the plaintiff's death, the survival statute and the wrongful death statute may overlap. Then, generally, as in *Bell,* the decedent's cause of action for damages sustained before his death is prosecuted under the survival statute for the benefit of his estate, and a wrongful death action is maintained for the benefit of his dependents. (Procedurally, many states allow both actions to be prosecuted at the same time by the decedent's personal representative.)

5. *The Elements of Damages in Wrongful Death and Survival Actions.* The elements of damages in a survival action or a wrongful death action are fixed by statute. Many survival statutes expressly limit the damages that can be recovered. Prohibitions on punitive damages, like that in *Bell,* and on pain and suffering damages, for example, are common. See, e.g., Rufo v. Simpson, 86 Cal.App.4th 573, 617, 103 Cal.Rptr.2d 492 (2001) (applying Cal.Code Civ.Pro. § 377.34, which provides that damages for pain, suffering or disfigurement of decedent prior to death may not be awarded in an action brought by a decedent's personal representative).

As for wrongful death statutes, the damages available depend on the theory of the action. Where the wrongful death action is for the estate's benefit (effectively extending the survival action to include all the damage done to the decedent, not simply the damage up to the time of death), the damages are determined by subtracting the decedent's projected lifetime expenses from his projected lifetime earnings. Dan B. Dobbs, Law of Remedies § 8.3(4)(2d ed.1993).

Wrongful death statutes premised on compensating the decedent's dependents are more complicated. The elements vary widely from jurisdiction to jurisdiction. All, of course, recognize that the financial support the decedent would have provided to his dependents must be replaced. Many jurisdictions have gone beyond this, however, to recognize that the decedent's non-monetary contributions to his family—his society, comfort and support—should also be compensated, although the language of the statutes has sometimes forced courts to rationalize recovery by positing that the deceased's society, comfort and services have a financial value that can be determined. See, e.g., Krouse v. Graham, 19 Cal.3d 59, 137 Cal.Rptr. 863, 562 P.2d 1022 (1977). Very few jurisdictions have taken the next step to award damages for the mental anguish of the survivors, although the number may be increasing. Dan B. Dobbs, The Law of Torts § 297 at 812 (2000). Finally, a few jurisdictions have recognized that complete compensation requires that both the estate and the dependents be made whole, allowing the heirs to recover lost inheritance and the dependents to recover lost support. Yowell v. Piper Aircraft, 703 S.W.2d 630 (Tex.1986); Martin v. Atlantic Coast Line R.R., 268 F.2d 397 (5th Cir.1959)(Federal Employees Liability Act).

6. *The Elements of Damages in a Personal Injury Case.* Damages for harm to the plaintiff's quality of life or lost enjoyment of life are less controversial in personal injury cases. It seems to be generally settled that general damages can include compensation for loss of the ability to participate in or to enjoy the ordinary activities of life. See, e.g., Ogden v. J.M. Steel Erecting, Inc., 201 Ariz. 32, 31 P.3d 806, 813 (Ct.App.2001) (damages for loss of enjoyment of life "compensate the individual not only for the subjective knowledge that one can not [any] longer enjoy all of life's pursuits, but also for the objective loss of the ability to engage in these activities"). Two issues on which courts are divided, however, are: (1) whether damages for lost enjoyment or quality of life are a separate element of damages requiring a separate jury instruction, or whether they are subsumed within pain and suffering damages; and (2) whether a separate award of damages should be made for "lost years" in cases in which the plaintiff's life expectancy has been shortened by the defendant's negligence. On the first issue, see Golden Eagle Archery v. Jackson, 116 S.W.3d 757, 769 (Tex.2003) (reviewing cases taking each position, and concluding hedonic damages are recoverable as part of the award for permanent injury). On the second, compare Downie v. U.S. Lines Co., 359 F.2d 344 (3d Cir.1966) (not recoverable) with Alexander v. Scheid, 726 N.E.2d 272 (Ind.2000) (shortened life expectancy is a compensable element of damages, citing cases).

2. MEASURING THE DAMAGES

Elements of tort damages that are economic in character—medical expenses, lost earnings, harm to property, and so on—usually do not present measurement problems beyond those identified in section B of this chapter. The same cannot be said for two elements of loss: nonpecuniary damages and economic losses that lie in the future, like harm to earning capacity. If you are persuaded there are good reasons to compensate plaintiffs for nonpecuniary loss, how do you calculate the worth of pain, suffering or quality of life? So long as plaintiffs are required to recover damages in a single trial, how do you determine what the future would have held had the plaintiff not been injured?

TULLIS v. TOWNLEY ENGINEERING & MANUFACTURING CO.

United States Court of Appeals, Seventh Circuit, 2001
243 F.3d 1058

FLAUM, CHIEF JUDGE.

[William Tullis sued his employer for retaliatory discharge, alleging that he was fired for pursuing a workers compensation claim after injuring his back. At trial, he prevailed, recovering $80,185.58 in nonpecuniary damages. The Court of Appeals found that there was sufficient evidence to support the jury verdict in his favor on liability.]

* * *

B. COMPENSATORY DAMAGES

Townley contends that the $80,185.68 nonpecuniary damages jury award for "mental anguish and inconvenience" was the product of passion and prejudice and so it requests a new trial or reduction of the damages through remittitur. Townley is concerned about the massive and excessive size of the jury award. The district court reviewed Townley's request for a new trial based upon the nonpecuniary damage award and determined that the award should be upheld. We review the district court's refusal to grant a new trial on the basis that the damages the jury awarded were excessive for an abuse of discretion.

When we review a compensatory damages award, we employ the following three-part test: (1) whether the award is monstrously excessive; (2) whether there is no rational connection between the award and the evidence; and (3) whether the award is roughly comparable to awards made in similar cases. Townley argues that the jury award for $80,185.68 fails all three prongs of this test.

Specifically, Townley claims that the award is monstrously excessive because it is based exclusively upon Tullis' own testimony. No physician or other professional testified that Tullis suffered psychologically from Townley's conduct nor did Tullis or a family member, friend, or other lay witness testify to his emotional injury. * * * Townley asserts that Tullis' testimony was not very detailed and thus does not support the award. Further, Townley notes that Tullis did not claim that he suffered from periodic depression, fits of anger, or other physical symptoms. According to Townley, all of this combined displays that Tullis' award for mental anguish and inconvenience was monstrously excessive.

Townley also maintains that the award is not rationally related to the evidence and that Tullis did not make a specific request with regard to compensatory damages; rather he asked the jury to "do what's fair." Townley argues that the problem is that the evidence does not support the amount awarded. For instance, in Avitia v. Metropolitan Club of Chicago, Inc., 49 F.3d 1219, 1229–30 (7th Cir.1995), the court found damages for

$21,000 because of emotional distress were excessive, even though the plaintiff in that case cried as a result of being discharged from a job that he had been at for 13 years and experienced such distress several years after he had been fired. Tullis, according to Townley, has provided far less compelling evidence regarding the intensity and duration of his emotional distress. Similarly, in Fleming v. County of Kane, 898 F.2d 553, 561–62 (7th Cir.1990), the Court found a $40,000 award, which had been reduced to this figure from the jury's amount of $80,000 by the trial court, was proper. The plaintiff in Fleming had been discharged for his whistle-blowing activities. Fleming testified to feelings of embarrassment, humiliation, certain depression, serious headaches, and sleeplessness. His wife and fellow department employees supported his testimony concerning his physical and emotional condition. Once again, Townley asserts that Tullis did not provide nearly the same type of evidence as was presented in Fleming, yet he received a substantially greater award, and these cases suggest that Tullis' nonpecuniary damage award is not rationally related to the evidence that he presented.

Finally, Townley advances that the jury award is not comparable to awards in similar cases. As previously discussed, the award in this case is larger than in *Avitia*, 49 F.3d at 1230 ($10,500 award after remittitur), and *Fleming*, 898 F.2d at 561–62 ($40,000 award). While it may be true that in Kasper v. Saint Mary of Nazareth Hosp., 135 F.3d 1170, 1174 (7th Cir.1998), a compensatory damage award for a retaliatory discharge claim in the amount of $150,000 was upheld, this was because the award was not challenged. Similarly, in *Jackson*, 40 F.3d at 245 n. 5, a case involving a retaliatory discharge claim under the Illinois Workers' Compensation Act, the parties agreed to compensatory damages in the amount of $75,000. Finally, in Peeler v. Village of Kingston Mines, 862 F.2d 135 (7th Cir.1988), the court addressed a $50,000 award for emotional distress based upon a retaliatory discharge claim. In that case, the evidence presented relayed "[p]oignant scenes of distress and abysmal poverty," while the plaintiff was unemployed. There, the plaintiff was evicted from his house, forced to live in a truck for three days, depended in part on charity to feed his family, used rags to diaper his child, friends donated clothes for his five children, could not afford a doctor when his children were sick, and suffered health problems. Townley argues that Tullis' experience does not rise nearly to this level and thus $80,185.68 is simply not warranted.

* * *

Although Townley characterizes Tullis' testimony regarding his emotional distress and inconvenience as relatively meager and scant, the jury obviously did not perceive it this way considering the award they granted Tullis. An award for nonpecuniary loss can be supported, in certain circumstances, solely by a plaintiff's testimony about his or her emotional distress. The jury was able to observe Tullis when he was testifying and they apparently found his testimony to be sincere and sufficient to convince them that he merited the award they gave him.

The jury, as seen by the amount they awarded Tullis, which some may even characterize as exceedingly generous, must have not believed that Tullis needed to show that he sought the help of psychologists or friends for his emotional distress or that he was required to provide more detail about either his emotional distress or the inconvenience that he experienced. Tullis' testimony did reveal he felt "low" and "degraded" when he was laid off and "back-stabbed" when the company opposed his unemployment claim. He also said that he was without work for nine to ten months, and this affected his personal life, including that he had to borrow money from family and friends and he had his lights and phone shut off. The jury could have determined that these were not minor events. The jury also may have taken into account that his family life was disrupted in that he was not able to buy his children new schools clothes, pay his child support, or take his children out dining and shopping. Tullis also did find a new job, but it was as a trucker, which required him to be away from home, and he even said that Townley "was a very convenient place for [him] to work at because it was close to the house. It was five minutes from the house." The jury may very well have found that these types of changes were significant to Tullis' family situation. Because it is within the jury's domain to assess the credibility of witnesses, specifically in this case the testimony of Tullis, we cannot find that the award was monstrously excessive or not rationally connected to the evidence. Further, since we have determined that the verdict was supported by the evidence, then necessarily it was not a result of passion and prejudice.

Thus, our remaining task is to examine "whether the award is out of line with other awards in similar cases." Townley cites *Avitia* and *Fleming* as cases that are roughly comparable and resulted in damage awards that were not nearly as substantial as the award in this case. *Avitia*, however, involved emotional distress only and not inconvenience. Similarly, in *Fleming* the damages concerned emotional distress, and unlike in this case, we affirmed the trial court's determination that a remittitur, reducing the damages to $40,000, was appropriate. More recently, we affirmed without much commentary, a $50,000 compensatory award (presumably for emotional distress) for retaliatory discharge brought under the Illinois Workers' Compensation Act. The most troubling case presented by Townley with regard to the issue is *Peeler*, 862 F.2d at 139, in which rather egregious facts led to the affirmation of a $50,000 compensatory award for the plaintiff. One must remember that this jury award is from 1988 and the current dollar value of this award is greater than $50,000; it is worth approximately $70,000 in 1999. The *Peeler* award is roughly comparable to Tullis' compensatory damage award, if one takes into account the jury's right to make awards based upon its view of a witness's demeanor and credibility. We cannot conclude that $80,185.68 is not roughly comparable to the small number of similar cases (albeit in most instances distinguishable) that we have discussed. Therefore, we affirm the district court's decision not to grant a new trial or remittitur on the issue of the $80,185.68 compensatory damage award.

NOTES

1. In tort cases, special damages consist of the plaintiff's economic losses: past and future medical expense, loss of earnings and earning capacity, and damage to property. Everything else falls into the catchall of general damages. The entire range of human responses to injury can be found there, from the pain and suffering associated with physical injury, to the emotional and psychological consequences of disability, to harm to the quality of life and the value of life itself, as in *Ayers* and *Bell*.

Very little law exists on the proper measurement of nonpecuniary losses, except to say that the amount of the award is in the fact-finder's discretion. What discussion there is in the cases focuses on the admissibility of evidence and the propriety of various jury arguments. Because the loss is intangible and subjective, the plaintiff's testimony as to the discomfort, annoyance, and so on that the injury has caused is central. Family and friends may also testify as to the injury's effects. Simply seeing the plaintiff, who may be disfigured or disabled, provides the jury something to go on.

Appellate courts have allowed lawyers a free hand in presenting demonstrative evidence to influence the jury's award. Some plaintiffs' lawyers place great stock in "day-in-the-life" films that show how the plaintiff's daily activities have been affected by the injury. The use of these films can raise a number of discovery and evidentiary issues. For example, must the opposing party be allowed to attend the filming or have access to all unused footage? See, e.g., Cisarik v. Palos Community Hospital, 144 Ill.2d 339, 162 Ill.Dec. 59, 579 N.E.2d 873 (1991) (no). What evidentiary standards must be met for a film to be admissible? See Jones v. City of Los Angeles, 20 Cal.App.4th 436, 24 Cal.Rptr.2d 528 (1993) (standard is the same as that for authentication of a writing; the proponent must show that the videotape accurately portrays what it purports to portray, for example by offering testimony by a person who was present at the filming).

As for jury arguments, appeals to the jury's sympathy and attempts to arouse the jury's passion and prejudice are impermissible. Beyond this vague restriction, the controversy has focused on two very specific types of jury argument. One of these is known as the Golden Rule argument. In a Golden Rule argument, counsel asks the jury to place itself in the shoes of the plaintiff, or defendant, and to ask, were I him, how much would I demand as compensation, or were I sued, how much would I think it fair for me to pay? Golden Rule arguments are generally not permitted.

Opinion is divided as to the other traditional argument, the per diem argument. In a per diem argument, counsel suggests a specific amount of compensation for each day, or hour, or minute that the plaintiff will suffer, and then demonstrates to the jury what the award should be by multiplying that amount by the plaintiff's life expectancy in days, hours, or minutes. With this calculation, a small amount can rapidly inflate into an astronomical award. Some jurisdictions permit the per diem argument, provided that the jury is instructed that the figures used are not evidence, but are simply offered by way of argument and illustration. Other jurisdictions do not allow it, because the technique gives a misleading impression of precision.

For examination of the way in which juries evaluate non-pecuniary loss, see Ronen Avraham, Putting a Price on Pain-and-Suffering Damages: A Critique of the Current Approaches and a Preliminary Proposal for Change, 100 Nw.U.L.Rev. 87 (2006); Nicole L. Mott, Valerie P. Hans & Lindsay Solomon, What's Half a Lung Worth? Civil Jurors' Accounts of Their Award Decision Making, 24 L. & Hum.Behav. 401 (2000); Roselle L. Wissler, Patricia F. Kuehn & Michael J. Saks, Instructing Jurors on General Damages in Personal Injury Cases: Problems and Possibilities, 6 Psych.Pub.Pol'y & L. 712 (2000).

2. Does the indeterminacy associated with measuring nonpecuniary loss undermine the goals of tort law?

> The paramount contemporary efficiency based goals of tort law contemplate that the costs of accidents be allocated to the most suitable actors and enterprises whose activities and products generate them, thereby spreading the costs of accidents to the consumers of the products and services. * * * The attainment of [these] economic goals hinges on the integrity and soundness of the process of valuing victims' losses. Loss allocation and spreading are undermined by the incommensurability of pain and money. The deterrence-incentive-based goals depend on a rational foundation that individuals and enterprises can summon in making their cost-benefit analyses so as to optimize the expenditure of resources on loss avoidance. Deterrence and incentive goals of tort law are corrupted when the assessment of damages is arbitrary and lacks any objective referent.

Joseph H. King, Pain and Suffering, Noneconomic Damages, and the Goals of Tort Law, 57 S.M.U.L.Rev. 163, 209 (2004). Does the problem have a constitutional dimension? Paul DeCamp, Beyond State Farm: Due Process Constraints on Noneconomic Compensation Damages, 27 Harv. J.L. & Pub. Pol'y 231 (2003) (arguing due process may limit nonpecuniary damage awards, as it does punitive damage awards).

Professor King suggests that instead of awarding general damages, economic damages be expanded to ensure that medical and rehabilitative strategies for coping with pain and loss are available, and attorneys fees be awarded to prevailing plaintiffs. See also John L. Diamond, Dillon v. Legg, Revisited: Toward a Unified Theory of Compensating Bystanders and Relatives for Intangible Injuries, 35 Hastings L.J. 477 (1984). Keep Professor King's point in mind when studying the next case:

ARPIN v. UNITED STATES
United States Court of Appeals, Seventh Circuit, 2008
521 F.3d 769

POSNER, CIRCUIT JUDGE.

The plaintiff's husband was a patient at the Belleville Family Practice Clinic, in southern Illinois. The clinic is jointly operated by the U.S. Air

Force and St. Louis University, the defendants in this suit for wrongful death arising from alleged medical malpractice. * * * After a three-day bench trial, the district judge found the defendants jointly and severally liable and awarded the plaintiff damages in excess of $8 million, consisting of some $500,000 for medical care and lost wages, $750,000 for pain and suffering, and $7 million for loss of consortium by her and the couple's four children. The appeals challenge both the finding of liability and the amount of damages awarded for loss of consortium.

[The plaintiff's husband fell at work, injuring his hip. Because the pain worsened overnight, he went to a hospital, where the injury treated with painkillers. The pain continued to worsen, so the plaintiff took her husband to the defendants' family practice clinic. According to the appellate court, the evidence supported the trial court's determination that the defendants' doctors negligently diagnosed his hip pain as a muscle strain, rather than recognizing that it was a symptom of a serious infection. Had the infection been properly diagnosed, it would have been easily treated with antibiotics. Two days later, plaintiff's husband was admitted to a hospital with symptoms of septic shock and multiple organ failure. He died two weeks later.]

* * *

So both defendants were liable for Arpin's death, and the liability was joint and several; we now consider whether the judge's award of $7 million in damages for loss of consortium was so excessive as to "shock the judicial conscience," which is the test under Illinois law. The awarding of damages, such as for pain and suffering and loss of consortium, that do not merely replace a financial loss has been criticized, especially in medical malpractice cases because of concern with the high and rising costs of health care. Damages awards in malpractice cases drive up liability insurance premiums and, what may be the greater cost, promote "defensive medicine" that costs a lot but may do patients little good. Daniel P. Kessler & Mark B. McClellan, "Do Doctors Practice Defensive Medicine?," 111 Q.J. Econ. 353 (1998). A reaction has set in that includes the recent passage of an Illinois law capping noneconomic damages in malpractice cases at $1 million for hospitals and hospital affiliates and $500,000 for physicians and other health-care professionals, 735 ILCS 5/2–1706.5(a)(1), (2), though the law was passed too recently to be applicable to this case and a judge has ruled that it violates the Illinois constitution. LeBron v. Gottlieb Memorial Hospital, 2007 WL 3390918 (Ill.Cir.Ct. Nov. 13, 2007).

It used to be thought that noneconomic losses were arbitrary because incommensurable with any dollar valuation. That is not true. People are constantly trading off hazards to life and limb against money; consider combat pay and re-enlistment bonuses in the army. Even when the tradeoff is between two nonmonetary values, such as danger and convenience (as when one crosses a street against the lights because one is in a hurry, or drives in excess of the speed limit), it may be possible to express the tradeoff in monetary terms, for example by estimating, on the basis of hourly wage rates, the value of the time saving. And if we know both the probability of a fatal accident and the benefit that a person would demand to bear it we can estimate a value of life and use that value to calculate damages in wrongful death cases. See W. Kip Viscusi and Joseph E. Aldy, "The Value of a Statistical Life: A Critical Review of Market Estimates Throughout the World," 27 J. Risk & Uncertainty 5 (2003). Suppose a person would demand $7 to assume a one in one million chance of being killed. Then we would estimate the value of his life at $7 million. Not that he would sell his life for that (or for any) amount of money, but that if the risk could be eliminated at any cost under $7 he would be better off. Suppose it could be eliminated by the potential injurer at a cost of only $5. Then we would want him to do so and the prospect of a $7 million judgment if he failed to would give him the proper incentive.

Loss of life is a real loss even when it has no financial dimension (the decedent might have had no income). So is the loss of the companionship ("consortium") of a loved one. The problem is the lack of a formula for calculating appropriate damages for loss of consortium. The plaintiff's lawyer presented a good deal of evidence of the close and loving relationship between Mr. Arpin and his wife and children, but did not attempt—how could he?—to connect the evidence to the specific figures that he requested in his closing argument. He requested $5 million for Arpin's widow and $1 million for each of the children; the judge awarded $4 million to her and $750,000 to each child. All the judge said in explanation of his award of these amounts was that "it is difficult to put a value on something that is priceless. Mrs. Arpin is far more dependent on her husband than are her children. Her children have suffered the loss of a father that is great and the devastation to this family is immeasurable."

When a federal judge is the trier of fact, he, unlike a jury, is required to explain the grounds of his decision. Fed.R.Civ.P. 52(a). "This means, when the issue is the amount of damages, that the judge must indicate the reasoning process that connects the evidence to the conclusion." Jutzi–Johnson v. United States, 263 F.3d 753, 758 (7th Cir.2001). One cannot but sympathize with the inability of the district judge in this case to say more than he did in justification of the damages that he assessed for loss of consortium. But the figures were plucked out of the air, and that procedure cannot be squared with the duty of reasoned, articulate adjudication imposed by Rule 52(a).

The judge should have considered awards in similar cases, both in Illinois and elsewhere. * * *

Courts may be able to derive guidance for calculating damages for loss of consortium from the approach that the Supreme Court has taken in recent years to the related question of assessing the constitutionality of punitive damages. The Court has ruled that such damages are presumptively limited to a single-digits multiple of the compensatory damages, and perhaps to no more than four times those damages. State Farm Mutual

Automobile Ins. Co. v. Campbell, 538 U.S. 408, 424–25, 123 S.Ct. 1513, 155 L.Ed.2d 585 (2003). The first step in taking a ratio approach to calculating damages for loss of consortium would be to examine the average ratio in wrongful-death cases in which the award of such damages was upheld on appeal. The next step would be to consider any special factors that might warrant a departure from the average in the case at hand. Suppose the average ratio is 1:5—that in the average case, the damages awarded for loss of consortium are 20 percent of the damages awarded to compensate for the other losses resulting from the victim's death. The amount might then be adjusted upward or downward on the basis of the number of the decedent's children, whether they were minors or adults, and the closeness of the relationship between the decedent and his spouse and children. In the present case the first and third factors would favor an upward adjustment, and the second a downward adjustment because all of Arpin's children were adults when he died.

We suspect that such an analysis would lead to the conclusion that the award in this case was excessive, but it is not our place to undertake the analysis. It is a task for the trial judge in the first instance, though we cannot sustain the award of damages for loss of consortium on the meager analysis in the judge's opinion; it does not satisfy the requirements of Rule 52(a). We have suggested (without meaning to prescribe) an approach that would enable him to satisfy them.

We affirm the joint and several liability of the defendants. and the award of damages other than for loss of consortium. With regard to those damages we vacate the judgment and remand the case for further proceedings consistent with this opinion.

NOTES

1. Loss of consortium is a separate cause of action brought by a person whose spouse has suffered debilitating injuries. The action protects the interest in intimate relationships. Elements of damages typically include loss of the spouse's society and comfort, physical and emotional support, physical intimacy and diminished social activity. Loss of consortium is a derivative action. Defenses that are good against the physically injured person's case will also defeat the spouse's action for loss of consortium.

A controversial issue is whether relationships other than marriage deserve protection. Generally, courts have denied loss of consortium recovery to unmarried cohabitants whose partners suffer injuries that affect the relationship. Dan B. Dobbs, Law of Remedies § 8.1(5)(2d ed.1993); but see Cal. Code Civ.Pro. § 377.60 (permitting claims related to wrongful death by persons who have filed declaration of domestic partnership). The most common controversy is over whether harm to the parent-child relationship should give rise to a cause of action for loss of consortium. Compare Rolf v. Tri State Motor Transit Co., 91 Ohio St.3d 380, 745 N.E.2d 424 (Ohio 2001) (emancipated adult children have action for loss of consortium based on parent's death, as do minor children) and Rufo v. Simpson, 86 Cal.App.4th 573, 614,

103 Cal.Rptr.2d 492, 520 (2001) (parents of adult child have action for loss of society based on child's death) with In re Air Crash at Little Rock, Arkansas, June 1, 1999, 170 F.Supp.2d 861, 862 (E.D.Ark.2001) (Arkansas included among twenty-two states denying right of child to claim loss of consortium of parent).

2. As Judge Posner mentions, nonpecuniary damages are a popular target for tort reform. Thirty-two states limit the recovery of pain and suffering damages by statute. While some states cap recovery in all cases, in most states the limit applies to a particular defendant—the government, for example, as in *Ayers*—or to a particular kind of case, typically medical malpractice actions. Pain and suffering awards in medical malpractice cases are capped in 22 states, with the caps ranging from $250,000 in California to $1 million for especially severe injuries in Florida.

Federal statutes can involve caps as well. The Civil Rights Act of 1991, for example, gives victims of intentional discrimination a right to compensatory damages, including nonpecuniary damages, but limits the amount of the award according to the size of the employer's enterprise, in order to protect defendants with fewer assets from huge liability. 42 U.S.C. § 1981a.

Is it appropriate to undercompensate plaintiffs in order to avoid tapping the defendant's wallet too deeply? Balancing the hardships—leaving the plaintiff short of the rightful position because of the hardship that full relief would cause—is usually justified by concerns of avoiding economic waste. The plaintiff may be denied specific relief—an injunction—but recovers compensatory damages aimed at making the plaintiff as whole as possible. In Ferdon ex rel. Petrucelli v. Wisconsin Patients Compensation Fund, 284 Wis.2d 573, 701 N.W.2d 440 (2005), the Wisconsin Supreme Court partially invalidated the state's cap on pain and suffering damages in medical malpractice cases. While leaving intact an earlier decision holding the cap constitutional in wrongful death cases, the court found the cap unconstitutional as applied to claims for personal injury. Noting that the cap's effect was felt most harshly by young, severely injured plaintiffs, whose awards were potentially large because their life expectancy was so long, and that the cap applied to each occurrence of medical malpractice, limiting the entire family's recovery, the court observed:

> The legislature enjoys wide latitude in economic regulation. But when the legislature shifts the economic burden of medical malpractice from insurance companies and negligent health care providers to a small group of vulnerable, injured patients, the legislative action does not appear rational. Limiting a patient's recovery on the basis of youth or how many family members he or she has does not appear to be germane to any objective of the law.

701 N.W.2d at 446. The Wisconsin court went on to find that the cap was not rationally related to any of the legislature's stated objectives—fair compensation, lowering malpractice premiums, keeping the state insurance fund solvent, reducing health care costs or ensuring quality health care. See also Catherine M. Sharkey, Unintended Consequences of Medical Malpractice Damages Caps, 80 N.Y.U.L.Rev. 391 (2005); Elizabeth Stewart Poisson, Comments Addressing the Impropriety of Statutory Caps on Pain and Suffering Awards in the Medical Liability System, 82 N.C.L.Rev. 759 (2004).

> Other courts have disagreed:
>
>> Despite this court's concerns about the wisdom of depriving a few badly injured plaintiffs of full recovery, the cap is also constitutionally reasonable. Rather than cap all damages, like the cap struck down in Condemarin v. University Hospital, 775 P.2d 348 (Utah 1989), the limitation on recoverable damages in this case is narrowly tailored, by limiting quality of life damages alone. While Judd notes that Utah has not seen large damage awards in significant numbers, this position ignores at least one important factor. Although quality of life damages are very real, they are also less susceptible to quantification than purely economic damages. * * * The difficulty of predicting quality of life damages must be considered by insurers when setting rates and planning reserves. At least in some measure, then, predicting and controlling future costs can result in lower insurance rates. Taken as one of a number of measures enacted to help control health care costs, the cap on quality of life damages is thus a reasonable approach.

Judd v. Drezga, 103 P.3d 135, 141 (Utah 2004) (upholding cap's reduction of jury award from $1.25 million to $250,000).

Caps have been attacked on other constitutional grounds as well. State constitutional guarantees of the right to a jury trial, of open access to courts, and of a right to a remedy have all been invoked in challenges to caps, sometimes successfully, more often not. See Ferndon ex rel. Petrucelli v. Wisconsin Patients Compensation Fund, 284 Wis.2d 573, 701 N.W.2d 440, 459 n.12 (2005)(collecting cases). Courts, however, have not always had the last word. Often, legislatures have responded by modifying the cap, see, e.g., Fl.Stat. § 766.118; in Texas and Louisiana, the state constitutions were amended to authorize caps after the courts had struck them down. See Texas Const. Art. 3 § 66; Louisiana Const. Art. XII § 10(C).

3. Does Judge Posner's approach satisfy Professor King's concerns about indeterminacy described in the notes following *Tullis* at p. 520? How persuasive is the court's explanation of the monetary value of life and love? Elsewhere, Judge Posner has advocated the same approach to understanding the monetary value of avoiding pain and suffering:

> Awarding any amount of damages for pain and suffering has long been criticized as requiring the trier of fact to monetize a loss that is incommensurable with any monetary measure. We do not agree with the criticism. Pain and suffering are perceived as costs, in the sense of adversities that one would pay to be spared, by the people who experience them. Unless tortfeasors are made to bear these costs, the cost of being adjudged careless will fall and so there will be more accidents and therefore more pain and suffering. The problem of figuring out how to value pain and suffering is acute, however. Various solutions, none wholly satisfactory, have been suggested, such as asking the trier of fact, whether jurors or judge, to imagine how much they would pay to avoid the kind of pain and suffering that the victim of the defendant's negligence experienced or how much they would demand to experience it willingly; or to estimate how much it would cost the victim (if he survived) to obtain counseling or therapy to minimize the pain and suffering, or how

much they would demand to assume the risk of the pain and suffering that the victim experienced. If they said they would demand $1,000 to assume a .01 risk of such a misfortune, this would imply that the victim should receive an award of $100,000, as that is the judgment that, if anticipated, would have induced the defendant to spend up to $1,000 to prevent. Talk is cheap, though; and maybe a better approach would be to present the jury with evidence of how potential victims themselves evaluate such risks, an approach that has been used to infer the value of life from people's behavior in using safety devices such as automobile seatbelts or in demanding risk premiums to work at hazardous jobs.

Jutzi–Johnson v. United States, 263 F.3d 753, 758–759 (7th Cir.2001).

Administrative agencies often rely on the idea that the "value of a statistical life" can be derived from people's behavior when they must place a value on avoiding injury in order to justify regulations. By reasoning backward from the willingness of people to invest in safety devices that might save a life, a figure for the value of life can be calculated. Similarly, a figure can be calculated by examining the premium people are paid for engaging in risky occupations.

Experts routinely offer to testify about the value of a statistical life in personal injury cases. Should the testimony be admissible? In Mercado v. Ahmed, 974 F.2d 863 (7th Cir.1992), a trial court had refused to allow an expert to testify that based on a survey of 75 studies, a boy's diminished enjoyment of life could be valued at between $2.2 million and $2.7 million. The Seventh Circuit affirmed:

> A survey of attitudes and views of others as a basis for concluding something is true is not necessarily wrong. * * * [W]hat is wrong here is not that the evidence is founded on consensus or agreement, it is that the consensus is that of persons who are no more expert than are jurors on the value of life.

Id. at 869. No scientific consensus exists as to the appropriate methodology to value a life. Therefore, the trial judge was correct to exclude the testimony of the expert proffered by the plaintiff, who was "no more expert in valuing life than the average person." Other courts have agreed, finding government and private industry studies unhelpful in establishing the hedonic value of an individual's life. First, the range of values the studies report—from a low of $450,000 to a high of $9 million—is so wide as to give the jury no helpful guidance. Ayers v. Robinson, 887 F.Supp. 1049 (N.D.Ill.1995). Second, the purpose of the studies—to evaluate regulations or safety devices—is so different from the purpose of individualized damage calculations as to make the studies' relevance suspect. Government agencies frequently do not reveal their methodologies, and the numbers they settle on may be as much the result of political compromise as of science. Id. at 1061 n.4.

While a few jurisdictions do admit expert testimony on the value of life, see, e.g., Kansas City Southern Railway Co. v. Johnson, 798 So.2d 374 (Miss.), cert. denied, 534 U.S. 816, 122 S.Ct. 43, 151 L.Ed.2d 15 (2001), many have agreed with *Mercado* that expert testimony is unnecessary, and may mislead the jury. See, e.g., Dorn v. Burlington Northern Santa Fe Railroad Co., 397

F.3d 1183, 1194 n.5 (9th Cir.2005) (citing cases holding expert testimony on the value of life not admissible).

4. Could contingent valuation techniques like those used in *Ohio v. Department of the Interior*, at p. 479, be the answer? Is it possible that empirical research could generate answers? Both possibilities are discussed in Eric A. Posner & Cass R. Sunstein, Dollars & Death, 72 U.Chi.L.Rev. 537 (2005) (describing various approaches to the problem, including psychological and economic research using simple, subjectively reported scales to quantify happiness).

5. There are two components to the problem of measuring damages for nonpecuniary loss. One component is accuracy. How can we be sure that the amount of damages awarded bears any real relationship to the loss? Contingent valuation techniques and statistical calculations of the value of a life attempt to address that problem.

The second component is consistency. Even if there is a general agreement that plaintiffs deserve compensation for nonpecuniary harms, is there any way to be sure that similarly injured plaintiffs receive similar awards? Would Professor King be satisfied if it was assured that similarly injured plaintiffs would receive similar awards?

The Seventh Circuit's solution is to compare awards in similar cases. Not all courts agree. For example, the California Court of Appeal rejected O.J. Simpson's argument that an $8.5 million award to Ron Goldman's parents for Ron's wrongful death was excessive:

> Simpson's argument on appeal essentially comes down to this: the largest award his counsel could find in California reported cases for the loss of comfort and society in the wrongful death of an adult child was $2 million. This method of attacking a verdict was disapproved by our Supreme Court in Bertero v. National General Corp., 13 Cal.3d 43, 65, footnote 12, where it said,
>
> "* * * The vast variety of and disparity between awards in other cases demonstrate that injuries can seldom be measured on the same scale. The measure of damages suffered is a factual question and as such is a subject particularly within the province of the trier of fact. For a reviewing court to upset a jury's factual determination on the basis of what other juries awarded to other plaintiffs for other injuries in other cases based upon different evidence would constitute a serious invasion into the realm of factfinding. Thus, we adhere to the previously announced and historically honored standard of reversing as excessive only those judgments which the entire record, when viewed most favorably to the judgment, indicates were rendered as the result of passion and prejudice on the part of the jurors."

Rufo v. Simpson, 86 Cal.App.4th 573, 103 Cal.Rptr.2d 492, 522 (2001). See also Epping v. Commonwealth Edison Co., 315 Ill.App.3d 1069, 248 Ill.Dec. 625, 734 N.E.2d 916 (2000) (clear weight of authority in Illinois rejects comparing awards to determine excessiveness); JoEllen Lind, The End of Trial on Damages? Intangible Losses and Comparability Review, 51 Buffalo

L.Rev. 251 (2003). For an example of the problem, see the disagreement between the majority and the dissent in Jutzi–Johnson v. United States, 263 F.3d 753 (7th Cir.2001), over whether suffocation by hanging is comparable to drowning for purposes of comparing awards.

6. Judge Posner suggests not simply comparing the size of the awards, but comparing the ratio between the wrongful death award and the award for loss of consortium. Is there a logical relationship between the two? Judge Posner's approach is modeled on the Supreme Court's approach to punitive damages, which we will examine in Chapter 6.

7. The legislation creating the September 11th Victim Compensation Fund defined noneconomic loss broadly, including pain and suffering, disfigurement, loss of enjoyment of life, loss of consortium and more. Air Transportation Safety and System Stabilization Act, Pub. L. No. 107–42, § 402(7), 115 Stat. 230, 237 (2001). The fund's final regulations, however, provided for a presumptive award of $250,000 in survival damages for the pre-death pain and suffering of victims, and $100,000 for the spouse and for each dependent. 28 CFR § 104.44. Would a fixed award make sense in tort cases?

WALKER v. RITCHIE

Ontario Court of Appeal, 2005
[2005] W.D.F.L. 2682, 197 O.A.C. 81

[Stephanie Walker was 17 years old and in Grade 12. Her car struck the rear end of a trailer as the defendant, Ritchie, tried to maneuver his tractor-trailer into a narrow driveway off a two-lane country road at night. As a result of the crash, Stephanie sustained catastrophic, permanent injuries, leaving her with residual paralysis and irreversible cognitive deficits. The trial court found that as a result of her injuries, Stephanie would be unable ever to work in a competitive job. The court found Ritchie and his employer liable, and awarded Stephanie $4,959,901 (Canadian) in damages.]

* * *

E. DAMAGES ISSUES

Of the total damages award of approximately $4.9 million, the appellants challenge $1,140,679.00. That challenge relates only to certain components of the award for pecuniary damages. In particular, the appellants argue that the trial judge erred in:

1) assuming that Stephanie would have attended university;

2) applying earning statistics for all university graduates;

* * *

1) The University Assumption

The trial judge was alert to the principles of law applicable to the assessment of non-pecuniary losses, including loss of future income. He recognized that the assessment of future income loss is, by its nature, somewhat speculative, particularly in predicting a future career for an adolescent who has not yet set her long-term education goals or embarked on a specific career path. In acknowledging these difficulties, the trial judge cited Graham v. Rourke (1990), 75 O.R. (2d) 622 (Ont. C.A.), at 634, which establishes that a plaintiff is not required to prove her future income loss on a balance of probabilities but rather to prove "a real and substantial risk of future pecuniary loss". Stephanie was accordingly not required to show that, but for the accident, she would have achieved a university education and therefore lost the earning capacity of a university graduate. Rather, the onus was on her to establish a real and substantial risk that she lost the earning capacity available to a person with that education.

As found by the trial judge, Stephanie was injured at a time when her post-secondary course was undecided. In those circumstances, the trial judge was required to ask himself if Stephanie had established a real and substantial risk that she lost the benefits of a university education.

To set a basis for Stephanie's loss of income, the trial judge considered Stephanie in the context of her familial and educational background. He dismissed the possibility that Stephanie would have stopped her education after grade twelve. Such a discontinuance of her education would have been inconsistent with her accomplishments to the date of the accident, inconsistent with her motivation to achieve, and inconsistent with the expectations of her parents and the accomplishments of her siblings.

If Stephanie had continued her education, the evidence established that she could have chosen from among a number of options: returning to high school to obtain [sufficient credits for admission to a Canadian university;] entering community college to pursue a career such as that of her younger sister; entering community college and then transferring to university; pursuing a soccer scholarship at a U.S. university; or entering university, when she was able to do so, as a mature student. All these options were open to Stephanie.

In choosing among these options, there were many unknowns, but the known factors were Stephanie's tenacity, significant academic potential, established athletic accomplishments, and a supportive family who expected her to continue her education. In deciding among the possible options, the trial judge had the benefit of evidence from Stephanie's family and her experienced high school guidance counselor. He decided that Stephanie's most reasonable and substantial possible option was the attainment of a university education.

* * *

Had Stephanie pursued a university education, as an average university graduate she would have expected, as a starting point, a salary of $57,190.00 annually, with an average annual salary over her lifetime of $65,769.00.

After setting a base annual earnings loss, a trial judge must refine the award by properly considering the potential negative and positive contingencies. Examples of negative contingencies that impede the production of income are job loss, forced retirement, disability prior to normal retirement age, and the possibility that a plaintiff may, after all, have pursued a different path. At least to some extent, however, these negative contingencies are offset by employer- or government-provided benefits programs. Factors that might improve the plaintiff's potential income (i.e. positive contingencies), include promotion, labour productivity increases, and continuing employment after normal retirement age. To some greater or lesser extent, negative contingencies and positive contingencies may be found to offset each other.

* * *

Looking at those contingencies, the trial judge recognized that Stephanie might not have gone to university, but instead pursued a community college education, an education that statistically would have resulted in lower average earnings. To reflect that contingency, he deducted 10% from Stephanie's award for loss of future income. As well, the trial judge made a further deduction from the award to reflect that, with her post-accident limitations, Stephanie might earn income in the future. He found such employment would likely be part-time clerical work in a supportive environment at or near the minimum wage. He quantified the appropriate deduction at $100,000 on evidence that Stephanie's future employment would be limited to about one-third of normal working hours and would not likely extend beyond age 60.

There was ample evidence to support the trial judge's conclusion that Stephanie might well, after some delay, have proceeded through university. There was also evidence to support the adjustments made by the trial judge by way of deductions for contingencies. Accordingly, this ground of appeal cannot succeed.

2) Earnings Statistics

The appellants argue that the trial judge erred in assessing Stephanie's income loss on the basis of gender-neutral earnings statistics. * * * They submit that the trial judge erred in basing his award on statistics for all university graduates, as opposed to statistics for all female university graduates. * * *

On the first ground, the trial judge discussed the legal principles. He considered Tucker (Public Trustee of) v. Asleson, [1991] B.C.J. No. 954 (B.C. S.C.), where Finch J. applied the average university earnings of male graduates to an eight year-old girl who suffered serious brain injury. In doing so, he found that "no educational or vocational opportunities were excluded to her", although he subsequently applied a significant deduction for negative contingencies. In Terracciano (Guardian ad litem of) v. Etheridge, [1997] B.C.J. No. 1051 (B.C. S.C.) at para. 80, Saunders J. queried the applicability of average female earnings statistics, which he noted, "have hidden in them serious discounts for lower and sporadic participation in the labour market which are duplicated by many of the negative contingencies used by economists to massage the numbers downward". Finally, the trial judge considered Gray v. Macklin, [2000] O.J. No. 4603 (Ont. S.C.J.), where evidence was called about the diminishing differential in men's and women's earnings. In *Gray*, the trial judge commented at para. 197 on historical wage inequities and the need for the court to "ensure as much as possible that the appropriate weight is given to societal trends in the labour market in order that the future loss of income properly reflects future circumstances." In that case, the trial judge also discounted the award by a total of 30% for negative contingencies.

* * *

As in the other authorities that have considered this issue, the trial judge decided damages on the evidence before him. On the first objection, while damages awards are compensatory in nature and cannot be calculated in a manner that overcompensates a particular individual, a court must be equally cognizant of the fact that gender-based earnings statistics are grounded in retrospective historical data that may no longer accurately project the income a person would achieve in the future.

In this case, the trial judge cannot be said to have erred in applying gender-neutral earnings tables to Stephanie's income loss. He did so on the basis of the evidence before him, which he accepted. In doing so, he noted that at least two of Stephanie's potential options—teaching and kinetics—were areas where pay equity had been achieved. Further, he noted at para. 135 that female earnings tables were based on historical data and might be inappropriate "where the court is attempting to make a forecast stretching many years into the future".

* * *

In this case, as in most, an individual approach is required to the assessment of future loss of income. The trial judge applied an individual approach to his assessment of Stephanie's loss of income. He chose to apply gender-neutral statistics. We see no error in his decision to do so or in his application of those statistics.

* * *

NOTES

1. While *Walker* is a Canadian case, its approach to the problem of earning capacity is typical of U.S. courts. If the plaintiff has a history of earnings on which to rely, that earning history provides a benchmark for evaluating future earning capacity. See, e.g., Pretre v. United States, 531 F.Supp. 931 (E.D.Mo.1981) (auto plant worker).

On the other hand, where the plaintiff is young or unemployed, the court may have to rely on guesswork about the plaintiff's future plans and ambitions. As *Walker* points out, the determination is highly individualized. For example, in Snow v. Villacci, 2000 Me. 127, 754 A.2d 360 (2000), the plaintiff was injured in a car accident. His injuries limited his ability to participate in a two-year training program at a stock brokerage, which he alleged would have led to a position as a financial consultant. Because he did not do well in the rest of the training program, he was offered a less lucrative position in the brokerage. Although he had not earned any income at either job at the time of the accident, the plaintiff claimed damages for "loss of an earning opportunity."

Snow could not make out a traditional claim for loss of earning capacity, because he had no ongoing impairment that limited his ability to earn income. Nonetheless, the Supreme Court of Maine permitted the claim to proceed:

> Although we recognize that proof of this type of loss may be more complex than proof of other traditional losses, we are confident that trial judges will exercise appropriate discretion in excluding evidence that is nothing more than mere hope or speculation. Accordingly, recovery may be had for the loss of an earning opportunity if the claimant proves, by a preponderance of the evidence, that: (1) the opportunity was real and not merely a hoped-for prospect; (2) the opportunity was available not just to the public in general but to the plaintiff specifically; (3) the plaintiff was positioned to take advantage of the opportunity; (4) the income from the opportunity was measurable and demonstrable; and (5) the wrongdoer's negligence was a proximate cause of the plaintiff's inability to pursue the opportunity.

754 A.2d at 365. What was it that persuaded the *Walker* court that Stephanie would have successfully completed her university education?

2. *Walker* is one of a series of Canadian cases attempting to come to grips with the fact that according to employment statistics, a woman is likely to earn much less money than a man. Presented with the same argument, albeit thirty years ago, an American court had a different response:

> I am constrained to agree with the defense that the present value of prospective earnings, female wages, before taxes must be used. However sympathetic this Court may be to equality in employment, it must look to the reality of the situation and not be controlled by its own convictions. One does not need expert testimony to conclude that there is inequality in the average earnings of the sexes. There is no criterion to help us predict when this unwarranted condition will be remedied and as a consequence I feel compelled to adopt the defendant's position.

Caron v. United States, 410 F.Supp. 378 (D.R.I.1975). Which court is more persuasive?

On the related issue of using race-based earning tables, at least two federal decisions line up with *Walker*. United States v. Serawop, 505 F.3d 1112 (10th Cir.2007) (affirming trial court's order for a race-and gender-neutral recalculation of lost income after expert provided a report that reduced estimated damages on the basis that the victim was Native American); Wheeler Tarpeh–Doe v. United States, 771 F.Supp. 427 (D.D.C.1991) (refusing to use race-based wage-earnings predictions), rev'd on other grounds, 28 F.3d 120 (D.C.Cir.1994). Are the issues different for race and gender? For a thorough discussion, see Martha Chamallas, Civil Rights in Ordinary Tort Cases: Race, Gender, and the Calculation of Economic Loss, 38 Loy.L.A.L.Rev. 1435 (2005); Jennifer B. Wriggins, Damages In Tort Litigation: Thoughts on Race and Remedies 1865–2007, 27 Rev.Litig. 37 (2007) (analysis of how black and white plaintiffs historically were treated unequally by the tort compensation system).

3. In Greyhound Lines, Inc. v. Sutton, 765 So.2d 1269, 1277 (2000), the Mississippi Supreme Court reviewed an award for lost earning capacity for a child. The court of appeals had reversed a wrongful death award, instructing the trial court that damages for a child's lost earning capacity should have been based upon "some type of average income for persons in the community." The Mississippi Supreme Court reversed:

> The conclusion by the Court of Appeals that the income for the children should be based on some sort of average income for persons of the community in which they lived, as far as we can find, has no basis in our law. Additionally, such a method is just as speculative as basing the recovery on the earning history of the parents. It is both unfair and prejudicial to ground the projected future income of a deceased child on either basis. Both methods result in potentially disparate recoveries for children from affluent communities or with affluent parents, as opposed to children from less affluent areas or with less affluent parents.

> Who is to say that a child from the most impoverished part of the state or with extremely poor parents has less of a future earnings potential than a child from the wealthiest part of the state or with wealthy parents? Today's society is much more mobile than in the past. Additionally, there are many more educational and job-training opportunities available for children as a whole today. We must not assume that individuals forever remain shackled by the bounds of community or class. The law loves certainty and economy of effort, but the law also respects individual aptitudes and differences.

> Therefore, we hold that in cases brought for the wrongful death of a child where there is no past income upon which to base a calculation of projected future income, there is a rebuttable presumption that the deceased child's income would have been the equivalent of the national average as set forth by the United States Department of Labor. This presumption will give both parties in civil actions a reasonable benchmark to follow in assessing damages. Either party may rebut the presumption by presenting relevant credible evidence to the finder of fact. Such evidence might include, but is certainly not limited to, testimony regarding the child's age, life expectancy, precocity, mental and physical health, intellectual development, and relevant family circumstances. This evidence will allow the litigants to tailor their proof to the aptitudes and talents of the individual's life being measured.

Is the court's decision consistent with the *Walker* court's treatment of Stephanie Walker's family background and resources? See August McCarthy, The Lost Futures of Lead–Poisoned Children: Race–Based Damage Awards and the Limits of Constitutionality, 14 Geo. Mason U.Civ.Rts.L.J. 75 (2004).

4. The September 11th Victim Compensation Fund used male work-life expectancy and income growth rate tables to calculate the presumed awards for economic loss for both male and female victims. See Final Report of the Special Master for the September 11th Victim Compensation Fund 33 (Volume I). Would this be a promising approach for tort cases? See Martha Chamallas, The September 11th Victim Compensation Fund: Rethinking the Damages Element in Injury Law, 71 Tenn.L.Rev. 51 (2003); Martha F. Davis, Valuing Women: A Case Study, 23 Women's Rts.L.Rep. 219 (2002).

5. Tort victims who do not work outside the home have presented particular problems in calculating earning capacity. Two points are clear. The award for earning capacity is an award for just that—capacity—and does not require an established employment record if the plaintiff can meet the burden of showing that a return to work was likely, but for the injury. Second, compensation for the value of replacement services for the victim's household work is commonplace. Martha Chamallas, The September 11th Victim Compensation Fund: Rethinking the Damages Element in Injury Law, 71 Tenn. L.Rev. 51, 73 (2003).

6. Determining a plaintiff's life expectancy in a personal injury case makes similar demands on the court's clairvoyance. For example, in McMillan v. City of New York, 253 F.R.D. 247 (E.D.N.Y.2008), an African American was paralyzed in a ferry crash and required life-long care. The defendants introduced actuarial evidence to show that African Americans with spinal cord injuries have a shorter life expectancy than similarly injured persons of other races.

Judge Jack Weinstein rejected the use of race-based data to determine life expectancy. Race, Judge Weinstein observed, is a social construct, not a biological category. Moreover, in a society with hundreds of years of racial mixing, assigning individuals to single racial categories to predict their lifespan is arbitrary:

> In the United States, there has been "racial mixing" among "Whites," "Africans," "Native Americans," and individuals of other "racial" and "ethnic" backgrounds for more than three and a half centuries. * * * Statistical reliance on "race" leads to such questions as whether [the plaintiff in *Plessy v. Ferguson*, who was apparently ⅞ "white" and ⅛ "black"] would have been categorized today as "African–American" for life expectancy purposes. In a more recent example, "racially" characterizing for statistical purposes in a negligence lawsuit the current [President], born of a "White" American mother and an "African" citizen of Kenya, would be considered absurd by most Americans. See Colm Tóibín, James Baldwin & Barack Obama, N.Y. Rev. of Books, Oct. 23, 2008, at 18 ("When Obama was a child, he wrote, 'my father . . . was black as pitch, my mother white as milk.' "). Reliance on "race"-based statistics in estimating life expectancy of individuals for purposes of calculating dam-

ages is not scientifically acceptable in our current heterogeneous population.

Citing studies showing that socio-economic status—not race—accounts for most variation in life expectancy among groups, Judge Weinstein concluded that to use race-based statistics to determine plaintiff's life expectancy would deny the plaintiff both equal protection and substantive due process:

A. *Equal Protection*

As Professor Martha Chamallas notes, "when experts rely on race or gender-based statistics to calculate tort damages, we tend not to notice the discrimination and to accept it as natural and unproblematic." Civil Rights in Ordinary Tort Cases: Race, Gender, and the Calculation of Economic Loss, 38 Loy. L.A. L.Rev. 1435, 1442 (2005). "Racial" classifications of individuals are "suspect categories," meaning that state action in reliance on "race"-based statistics triggers strict scrutiny. Judicial reliance on "racial" classifications constitutes state action. See also Chamallas, Questioning the Use of Race–Specific and Gender–Specific Economic Data in Tort Litigation: A Constitutional Argument, [63 Fordham L.Rev. 73, 106 (1994)] ("By conceding the relevance of race-based or gender-based data through its admission into evidence ... the judge necessarily leads the jury to believe that gender and race are legally permissible factors and thus cannot be said to be neutral on the issue."). Equal protection in this context demands that the claimant not be subjected to a disadvantageous life expectancy estimate solely on the basis of a "racial" classification.

B. *Due Process*

There is a right—in effect a property right—to compensation in cases of negligently caused damage to the person under state and federal law. See Martinez v. State of California, 444 U.S. 277, 282, 100 S.Ct. 553, 62 L.Ed.2d 481 (1980) ("[a]rguably" a tort cause of action created by a State constitutes "a species of 'property' protected by the Due Process Clause" and there is a federal "interest in protecting the individual citizen from state action that is wholly arbitrary or irrational").

By allowing use of "race"-based statistics at trial, a court would be creating arbitrary and irrational state action. * * * Were the court to apply an ill-founded assumption, automatically burdening on "racial" grounds a class of litigants who seek compensation, there would be a denial of due process.

253 F.R.D. at 255–256. See Debra Sydnor & Shirlethia Franklin, Calculating the Damages: Race and Socio–Economic Status, 26 Med. Malpractice L. & Strategy 3 (2009).

According to actuarial tables, women have a longer life-expectancy than men. If a man were to argue that the use of life-expectancy tables that distinguish between men and women violates his rights, would he have a good claim?

3. LIMITS ON RECOVERY: FORESEEABLE, CERTAIN AND UNAVOIDABLE

STEINHAUSER v. HERTZ CORP.
United States Court of Appeals, Second Circuit, 1970
421 F.2d 1169

FRIENDLY, CIRCUIT JUDGE:

On September 4, 1964, plaintiff Cynthia Steinhauser, a New Jersey citizen then 14 years old, her mother and father were driving south through Essex County, N.Y. A northbound car, owned by defendant Hertz Corporation, a Delaware corporation authorized to do business in New York, and operated by defendant Ponzini, a citizen of New York, crossed over a double yellow line in the highway into the southbound lane and struck the Steinhauser car heavily on the left side. The occupants did not suffer any bodily injuries.

The plaintiffs' evidence was that within a few minutes after the accident Cynthia began to behave in an unusual way. Her parents observed her to be 'glassy-eyed,' 'upset,' 'highly agitated,' 'nervous' and 'disturbed.' When Ponzini came toward the Steinhauser car, she jumped up and down and made menacing gestures until restrained by her father. On the way home she complained of a headache and became uncommunicative. In the following days things went steadily worse. Cynthia thought that she was being attacked and that knives, guns and bullets were coming through the windows. She was hostile toward her parents and assaulted them; becoming depressed, she attempted suicide.

The family physician recommended hospitalization. After observation and treatment in three hospitals, with a final diagnosis of 'schizophrenic reaction—acute—undifferentiated,' she was released in December 1964 under the care of a psychiatrist, Dr. Royce, which continued until September 1966. His diagnosis, both at the beginning and at the end, was of a chronic schizophrenic reaction; he explained that by 'chronic' he meant that Cynthia was not brought to him because of a sudden onset of symptoms. She then entered the Hospital of the University of Pennsylvania and, one month later, transferred to the Institute of Pennsylvania Hospital for long-term therapy. Discharged in January 1968, she has required the care of a psychiatrist. The evidence was that the need for this will continue, that reinstitutionalization is likely, and that her prognosis is bad.

As the recital makes evident, the important issue was the existence of a causal relationship between the rather slight accident and Cynthia's undoubtedly serious ailment. The testimony was uncontradicted that prior to the accident she had never displayed such exaggerated symptoms as thereafter. * * *

Dr. Royce testified that a person may have a predisposition to schizophrenia which, however, requires a 'precipitating factor' to produce an outbreak. As a result of long observation he believed this to have been Cynthia's case—that 'she was a rather sensitive child and frequently exaggerated things and distorted things that happened within in the family' but that the accident was 'the precipitating cause' of her serious mental illness. Under cross-examination he stated that prior to the accident Cynthia had a 'prepsychotic' personality but might have been able to lead a normal life. Dr. Stevens, attending psychiatrist at the Institute of Pennsylvania Hospital, who had treated Cynthia, in answer to a hypothetical question which included the incidents relied on by the defendants to show prior abnormality, was of the opinion that the accident 'was the precipitating cause of the overt psychotic reaction,' 'the last straw that breaks the camel's back.' In contrast defendants' expert, Dr. Brock, while agreeing that 'with a background of fertile soil' schizophrenia can be induced by emotional strain, was of the opinion * * * that Cynthia was already schizophrenic at the time of the accident.

* * *

After several hours of deliberation the jury propounded the following question:

If we find the auto accident was the precipitating factor, but not the cause of the illness (schizophrenia) must we find for the plaintiff?

The judge responded by rereading what he had already said on proximate cause. Ten minutes later the jury brought in a defendants' verdict.

It is plain enough that plaintiffs were deprived of a fair opportunity to have the jury consider the case on the basis of the medical evidence they had adduced. The testimony was that before the accident Cynthia was neither a 'perfectly normal child' nor a schizophrenic, but a child with some degree of pathology which was activated into schizophrenia by an emotional trauma although it otherwise might not have blossomed. Whatever the medical soundness of this theory may or may not be, and there does not seem in fact to have been any dispute about it, see Guttmacher and Weihofen, Psychiatry and the Law 43–55 (1952), plaintiffs were entitled to have it fairly weighed by the jury. They could not properly be pinioned on the dilemma of having either to admit that Cynthia was already suffering from active schizophrenia or to assert that she was wholly without psychotic tendencies. The jury's question showed how well they had perceived the true issue. When they were told in effect that plaintiffs could recover only if, contrary to ordinary experience, the accident alone produced the schizophrenia, the result was predestined.

It is unnecessary to engage in exhaustive citation of authority sustaining the legal validity of plaintiffs' theory of the case. Since New York law governs, the oft-cited decision in McCahill v. New York Transportation Co., 201 N.Y. 221, 94 N.E. 616 (1911), which plaintiffs' appellate counsel has discovered, would alone suffice. There the defendant's taxicab negligently hit McCahill, broke his thigh and injured his knee. After being hospitalized, he died two days later of delirium tremens. A physician testified that 'the injury precipitated his attack of delirium tremens, and understand I mean precipitated not induced'; he explained that by 'precipitated,' he meant 'hurried up,'—just what plaintiffs' experts testified to be the role of the accident here. The Court of Appeals allowed recovery for wrongful death.

* * *

We add a further word that may be of importance on a new trial. Although the fact that Cynthia had latent psychotic tendencies would not defeat recovery if the accident was a precipitating cause of schizophrenia, this may have a significant bearing on the amount of damages. The defendants are entitled to explore the probability that the child might have developed schizophrenia in any event. While the evidence does not demonstrate that Cynthia already had the disease, it does suggest that she was a good prospect. Judge Hiscock said in *McCahill*, 'it is easily seen that the probability of later death from existing causes for which a defendant was not responsible would probably be an important element in fixing damages, but it is not a defense.' In *Evans v. S. J. Groves & Sons Company*, supra, we noted that if a defendant 'succeeds in establishing that the plaintiff's pre-existing condition was bound to worsen * * * an appropriate discount should be made for the damages that would have been suffered even in the absence of the defendant's negligence.' 315 F.2d at 347–348. * * * It is no answer that exact prediction of Cynthia's future apart from the accident is difficult or even impossible. However taxing such a problem may be for men who have devoted their lives to psychiatry, it is one for which a jury is ideally suited.

Reversed for a new trial.

DILLON v. EVANSTON HOSPITAL

Supreme Court of Illinois, 2002
199 Ill.2d 483, 771 N.E.2d 357, 264 Ill.Dec. 653

JUSTICE FREEMAN delivered the opinion of the court:

[The plaintiff brought a medical malpractice action against Dr. Sener, Evanston Hospital, and others. The trial court found that Dr. Sener negligently failed to completely remove a catheter that he had inserted in patient's vein as means to administer chemotherapy. The catheter migrated to plaintiff's heart.]

* * *

V. DAMAGES: INCREASED RISK OF FUTURE INJURY

Dr. Sener and the hospital next contend that the trial court erred in instructing the jury that it could award plaintiff damages for "[t]he increased risk of future injuries." * * *

There was evidence presented at trial establishing the proximate causal connection between the actions of Dr. Sener and the hospital and the catheter fragment becoming embedded in plaintiff's heart. On medical advice, plaintiff chose not to attempt removal of the fragment. All the expert witnesses but one believed that the risks of injury from an attempted removal of the fragment outweighed the risks that would exist if the catheter remained in the heart. The attendant risks of the catheter remaining were infection, perforation of the heart, arrhythmia, embolization, and further migration of the fragment. At the time of trial, plaintiff had not suffered from any of these conditions, although she did suffer from anxiety over the fragment's presence.

The evidence was that it was not reasonably certain that plaintiff would in the future suffer the injuries for which she was at risk due to the fragment's presence in her heart. Several physicians testified about the risk of infection, with the lowest estimated risk being close to zero and the highest being 20%. The risk of arrhythmia was less than 5%. The risks of perforation and migration were also small. The risk of embolization was low to nonexistent.

The jury instruction that addressed compensation for plaintiff's increased risks stated in relevant part:

> If you decide for the plaintiff on the question of liability, you must then fix the amount of money which will reasonably and fairly compensate her for any of the following elements of damages proved by the evidence to have resulted from the negligence of one or more of the defendants, taking into consideration the nature, extent, and duration of the injury:
>
> *The increased risk of future injuries.*
>
> The pain and suffering experienced and reasonably certain to be experienced in the future as a result of the injuries.

(Emphasis added.)

* * *

The jury awarded plaintiff $500,000 for her increased risk of future injuries. * * *

This court has historically rejected assessing damages for future injuries. This court has explained: "It would be plainly unjust to require a defendant to pay damages for results that may or may not ensue and that are merely problematical. To justify a recovery for future damages the law requires proof of a reasonable certainty that they will be endured in the future." [This position] represents the majority rule.

* * *

Not all jurisdictions follow the majority rule. For example, in Petriello v. Kalman, 215 Conn. 377, 576 A.2d 474 (1990), the Supreme Court of Connecticut provided an analysis that revealed the problems inherent with the majority approach. That court criticized the "all-or-nothing" approach as follows:

"In essence, if a plaintiff can prove that there exists a 51 percent chance that his injury is permanent or that future injury will result, he may receive full compensation for that injury as if it were a certainty. If, however, the plaintiff establishes only a 49 percent chance of such a consequence, he may recover nothing for the risk to which he is presently exposed. Although this all or nothing view has been adopted by a majority of courts faced with the issue, the concept has been severely criticized by numerous commentators. By denying any compensation unless a plaintiff proves that a future consequence is more likely to occur than not, courts have created a system in which a significant number of persons receive compensation for future consequences that never occur and, conversely, a significant number of persons receive no compensation at all for consequences that later ensue from risks not rising to the level of probability. This system is inconsistent with the goal of compensating tort victims fairly for all the consequences of the injuries they have sustained, while avoiding, so far as possible, windfall awards for consequences that never happen."

Petriello, 215 Conn. at 393–94, 576 A.2d at 482–83.

* * * Our review of cases from other jurisdictions indicates a trend toward allowing compensation for increased risk of future injury as long as it can be shown to a reasonable degree of certainty that the defendant's wrongdoing created the increased risk.

* * *

[We] believe that the Connecticut court's approach to this issue better comports with this state's principle of single recovery. An entire claim arising from a single tort cannot be divided and be the subject of several actions, regardless of whether or not the plaintiff has recovered all that he or she might have recovered. This is true even as to prospective damages. There cannot be successive actions brought for a single tort as damages in the future are suffered, but the one action must embrace prospective as well as accrued damages. * * *

Also, this court has previously held in a different context:

"There is nothing novel about requiring health care professionals to compensate patients who are negligently injured while in their care. To the extent a plaintiff's chance of recovery or survival is lessened by the malpractice, he or she should be able to present evidence to a jury that the defendant's malpractice, to a reasonable degree of medical certainty, proximately caused the increased risk of harm or lost chance of recovery. We therefore reject the reasoning of cases which hold, as a matter of law, that plaintiffs may not recover for medical malpractice injuries if they are unable to prove that they would have enjoyed a greater than 50% chance of survival or recovery absent the alleged malpractice of the defendant. To hold otherwise would free health care providers from legal responsibility for even the grossest acts of negligence, as long as the patient upon whom the malpractice was performed already suffered an illness or injury that could be quantified by experts as affording that patient less than a 50% chance of recovering his or her health."

Holton v. Memorial Hospital, 176 Ill.2d 95, 119, 223 Ill.Dec. 429, 679 N.E.2d 1202 (1997).

The theories of lost chance of recovery and increased risk of future injury have similar theoretical underpinnings. * * *

Accordingly, we hold simply that a plaintiff must be permitted to recover for all demonstrated injuries. The burden is on the plaintiff to prove that the defendant's negligence increased the plaintiff's risk of future injuries. A plaintiff can obtain compensation for a future injury that is not reasonably certain to occur, but the compensation would reflect the low probability of occurrence. * * * "The defendant's proper remedy lies in objecting to the excessiveness of the verdict in an appropriate case."

Having determined that this element of damages is compensable, we now consider whether the jury was properly instructed thereon. * * * [We] conclude that the instruction which the jury received on this element of damages did not adequately state the law. * * *

[The] instruction fails to instruct the jury on several important legal requirements, e.g., the increased risk must be based on evidence and not speculation, and, more importantly, the size of the award must reflect the probability of occurrence. * * * Accordingly, we reverse plaintiff's damages award for the increased risk of future injury, and remand the cause to the trial court for a new trial solely on that element of damages.

* * *

NOTES

1. Do *Dillon* and *Steinhauser* have anything in common?

2. Think back to *Ayers v. Jackson Township* at p. 486, in which the court denied recovery for enhanced risk of cancer stemming from exposure to carcinogens in a town's drinking water. Would *Dillon* support recovery in such a case?

As *Dillon* notes, courts have shown increasing acceptance of probabilistic recovery, particularly in medical malpractice cases. When doctors misdiagnose an illness and deny the plaintiff the opportunity to undergo treatment, many courts allow the plaintiff to recover damages even if the treatment she was denied is successful much less than half the time. See Alexander v. Scheid, 726 N.E.2d 272, 277 (Ind.2000) (physician who negligently failed to diagnose lung cancer liable for increased risk of harm); Roberts v. Ohio Permanente Medical Group, 76 Ohio St.3d 483, 668 N.E.2d 480 (1996)(delay in diagnosis of lung cancer deprived plaintiff of a less than 50% chance of survival, proportional recovery allowed); Delaney v. Cade, 255 Kan. 199, 873 P.2d 175, 177–78, 182 (Kan.1994) (allowing paraplegic plaintiff to recover where risk of spinal cord injury was increased five to ten percent by prolonged period of shock following car accident and prior to surgery). In Scafidi v. Seiler, 119 N.J. 93, 574 A.2d 398 (1990), the court characterized the view that damages may be recovered for the loss of a chance at a better outcome as "the clear majority." See, e.g., David A. Fischer, Tort Recovery for Loss of a Chance, 36 Wake Forest L.Rev. 605 (2001); Joseph King, Jr., "Reduction of Likelihood" Reformulation and Other Retrofitting of the Loss-of-a-Chance Doctrine, 28 U.Mem.L.Rev. 491 (1998).

In toxic exposure cases, even when the risk can be quantified, most courts refuse to allow recovery for future consequences of exposure unless the loss is reasonably certain to occur. Sterling v. Velsicol Chemical Corp., 855 F.2d 1188, 1205 (6th Cir.1988)(under Tennessee law, a 25% or 30% increase in the risk of cancer "does not constitute a reasonable medical certainty, but rather a mere possibility or speculation," and therefore damages for future cancer are not recoverable).

Yet, consider:

[I]t seems * * * likely from his remarks that the district judge thought that all probabilities are too uncertain to provide a basis for awarding damages. Yet most knowledge, and almost all legal evidence, is probabilistic. Even the proposition that [the plaintiff] will die some day is merely empirical. It is of course highly probable that he will die but it is not certain in the way it is certain that 10^3 is 1000 * * *.

All this has long been recognized in personal-injury cases, as it is throughout the law. If a tort victim is seriously injured and will require medical attention for the rest of his life, the court in deciding how much to award him for future medical expenses will have to estimate how long he can be expected to live, and it will make this estimate by consulting a mortality table, which is to say by looking at a statistical summation of the experience of thousands or millions of people. * * *

DePass v. United States, 721 F.2d 203, 207 (7th Cir.1983)(Posner, J. dissenting). If most damages for future loss are probabilistic in character, what's wrong with awarding damages for the future of cancer? Lars Noah, An Inventory of Mathematical Blunders in Applying the Loss-of-a-Chance Doctrine, 24 Rev.Litig. 369 (2005).

Of course, some jurisdictions continue to reject the loss of a chance approach altogether. See Dumas v. Cooney, 235 Cal.App.3d 1593, 1 Cal. Rptr.2d 584 (1991)(plaintiff alleging negligent diagnosis must show that with a correct diagnosis he would have had a better than 50% chance of survival); Fennell v. Southern Maryland Hosp. Center, Inc., 320 Md. 776, 580 A.2d 206 (1990)(same). An extreme example is Duarte v. Zachariah, 22 Cal.App.4th 1652, 28 Cal.Rptr.2d 88 (1994). Duarte was referred to Dr. Zachariah for chemotherapy after she had a mastectomy to remove a breast cancer. Dr. Zachariah negligently prescribed an overdose of a drug which damaged Duarte's bone marrow, making further chemotherapy dangerous to her health. As the court of appeal interpreted the evidence, without chemotherapy, 10% of patients in Duarte's condition suffer a recurrence of cancer. With chemotherapy, only 5% suffer a recurrence. Duarte's cancer recurred, but on this evidence, she could only show that there was a 50% chance that the doctor's negligence caused the recurrence. In other words, it was just as likely that she was in the group that would have had a recurrence despite chemotherapy as it was that she was in the group that would have been benefitted from chemotherapy. Because she could not show that more likely than not chemotherapy would have made a difference, her case failed.

MUNN v. SOUTHERN HEALTH PLAN, INC.

United States District Court, Northern District of Mississippi, 1989
719 F.Supp. 525, aff'd, 924 F.2d 568 (5th Cir.), cert. denied,
502 U.S. 900, 112 S.Ct. 277, 116 L.Ed.2d 229 (1991).

L.T. SENTER, JR., CHIEF UNITED STATES DISTRICT JUDGE.

This wrongful death case presents some of the most difficult questions which this court has ever been asked to resolve. The case arose from an automobile accident which the defendant admits resulted from her negligence in attempting to pass another vehicle in dense fog. The plaintiff's wife was severely injured as a result of the collision and died approximately two hours after the accident. The problem arises because the plaintiff and his wife, both adherents to the Jehovah's Witness faith, refused on religious grounds to allow the doctors who were treating Mrs. Munn to administer a blood transfusion which the defendant contends would have saved her life.

The defendant seeks summary judgment to the effect that if the jury should find, for whatever reason, that she is not liable for damages for Mrs. Munn's death, then the plaintiff is not entitled to recover for any prospective harm beyond the point of Mrs. Munn's death. Because the answer to this question depends, at least in part, upon the legal doctrine which is to be applied to the facts of this case, the court will begin by attempting to resolve that issue.

The defendant has raised three theories which she insists apply under the facts of this case to bar, at least in part, the plaintiff's recovery. These are contributory negligence, assumption of the risk, and the doctrine of avoidable consequences. Only the latter of these clearly applies to the facts of this case.

The doctrine of avoidable consequences, sometimes referred to as the duty of the plaintiff to mitigate damages, "functions as a negative rule, denying an injured person recovery of damages for any reasonably avoidable consequences of the injury." The basic rule is that the plaintiff may not recover from the defendant for injuries which flow from the defendant's wrongful conduct but which could have been avoided by the plaintiff's availing herself of reasonable measures to limit the harm. Simply stated, once the injury has occurred, the plaintiff may not stand idly by and allow her damages to accumulate when she could take reasonable steps to minimize them. The doctrine of avoidable consequences comes into play only after the defendant has committed the wrongful act, but at a time when the plaintiff still has an opportunity to avoid the consequences in whole or in part. * * *

The doctrine is often referred to as the plaintiff's duty to mitigate damages, but such reference lacks legal precision and can lead to confusion with other concepts in the law of damages. The doctrine of avoidable consequences should not be confused with the doctrine of contributory negligence. The latter focuses on issues of proximate causation of, and ultimate liability for, an accident, whereas the former focuses only on measurement of damages resulting from the injury-producing event.

The distinction noted above makes it clear that the present case is not one where the doctrine of contributory negligence should be applied. There has been no allegation that any action or inaction of Mrs. Munn was causally related to the accident which resulted in her injuries. * * *

The other theory raised by the defendant is that by refusing the transfusion, Mrs. Munn assumed the risk of her own death. The doctrine of assumption of the risk provides that a plaintiff who voluntarily assumes a risk of harm arising from the negligent or reckless conduct of the defendant cannot recover for such harm. * * * [T]he risk that is being assumed is the known risk that the defendant does not intend to act, or has already failed to act, in accordance with a duty imposed on him by law. "The result is that the defendant is relieved of all legal duty to the plaintiff; and being under no duty, he cannot be charged with negligence." Prosser [Handbook of the Law of Torts § 68 (4th ed. 1971)] at 440. In the instant case, by assuming the risk that she would die if she did not agree to a blood transfusion, Mrs. Munn did not relieve the defendant of any duty because the defendant had no duty in relation to the transfusion. * * *

In an earlier motion for summary judgment, the plaintiff raised two issues in relation to the defense based on the doctrine of avoidable consequences which were not addressed by the court in its order denying the motion. Those issues need to be addressed prior to trial and both are relevant to the issue currently before the court. First, the plaintiff contends that the egg-shell or thin skull rule should be applied in this case. The "rule" is actually an exception to the more general rule that a defendant is liable only for those consequences which were the reasonably foreseeable results of an anticipated action. As stated by Prosser, a "defendant is held liable when his negligence operates upon a concealed *physical* condition, such as pregnancy, or a latent disease, or susceptibility to disease, to produce consequences which he could not reasonably anticipate." Prosser, Handbook of the Law of Torts § 43, p. 261 (4th ed.1971) (emphasis added). The statement of the rule in the Restatement is much the same:

> The negligent actor is subject to liability for harm to another although a *physical condition* of the other which is neither known nor should be known to the actor makes the injury greater than that which the actor as a reasonable man should have foreseen as a probable result of his conduct.

Restatement (2d) Torts § 461. (Emphasis added.)

Every authority which this court can find which states the "eggshell skull rule" speaks only of physical conditions which pre-exist the injury for which compensation is sought and lead to unforeseeably severe results. The religious beliefs of the plaintiff simply are not covered by this rule.

The plaintiff also presses a first amendment argument. This argument is not fleshed out and relies entirely on cases where a state attempted to force a Jehovah's Witness to accept a blood transfusion. There is a clear distinction, however, between the overt attempt by a state actor to force an individual to take some action which her religion forbids her to take and the application of a universally applied tort doctrine which leaves the person "free to make [her] choice between the practice of [her] religion and the acceptance of treatment that may be contrary thereto." Martin v. Industrial Accident Commission, 304 P.2d 828, 831 (Cal.1956) (upholding denial of worker's comp. death benefits where death was found to be result of refusal of transfusion on religious grounds). An individual has a right under the first amendment to hold religious beliefs and live by them, but that does not mean that anyone who commits a tort against that individual must suffer the consequences of decisions made by the victim based upon those religious beliefs.

It has been argued that persons who refuse medical treatment on religious grounds should be exempted on first amendment grounds from the operation of the doctrine of avoidable consequences. Comment, Medical Care, Freedom of Religion, and Mitigation of Damages, 87 Yale L.J. 1466 (1978). The author contends that the application of this facially neutral doctrine to a tort victim who refuses medical treatment for religious reasons is a denial of a state benefit on religious grounds. The argument is basically that putting the tort victim to the choice of acting in violation of his religious beliefs or losing the right conferred by state law to obtain complete recovery for all harm which results from the wrongful conduct of another places an undue burden on the victim's free exercise rights. Cited in support of this argument are Sherbert v. Verner, 374 U.S. 398 (1963), and Wisconsin v. Yoder, 406 U.S. 205 (1972). *Sherbert* involved the denial of state unemployment benefits to a woman who refused on religious grounds to accept a job which required her to work on Saturday. The Court held that this was an impermissible burden on her free exercise rights. In *Yoder,* the Court held that a state mandatory school attendance law violated the free exercise rights of people of the Amish faith. Each of these cases involves direct state action. If an exception to the doctrine of avoidable consequences is made for those who refuse medical treatment on religious grounds, payment for the harm which could have been avoided will come from the pockets of the tortfeasor, not from the coffers of the state. To adopt an absolute rule which required one citizen to pay damages for the consequences of another's exercising her religious freedom would favor an establishment of religion in a way which seems constitutionally unsupportable. Additionally, the doctrine of avoidable consequences does not automatically bar the plaintiff from recovering the losses sustained after the refusal of medical treatment; it bars recovery of those losses only when the refusal is found to be unreasonable under all of the circumstances known to the tort victim at the time of the refusal. In what has come to be considered as the leading case on this point, the Connecticut Supreme Court upheld the lower court's decision to submit the question of the objective reasonableness of the plaintiff's refusal of medical treatment to the jury with the instruction that the jurors were to consider the fact that the refusal was based on religious belief as one of the circumstances. Lange v. Hoyt, 114 Conn. 590, 159 A. 575 (1932). The author of the comment also takes exception to this procedure, arguing that the jury is, in effect, being asked to pass upon the reasonableness of the plaintiff's religious belief. This indeed presents a problem. However, neither of the parties have adequately addressed this issue, so the court will delay any attempt to resolve it until the parties may be heard at the jury instruction conference after the evidence is in.

The court holds that the doctrine of avoidable consequences is the appropriate standard to be applied in this case and that its application does not violate the first amendment.

APPLICATION OF THE DOCTRINE OF AVOIDABLE CONSEQUENCES IN A WRONGFUL DEATH CASE

As stated earlier, the doctrine of avoidable consequences prevents the plaintiff from recovering for that part of her injury which could have been avoided by taking reasonable steps after the injury occurred.[2] How does this rule operate when the harm which the defendant contends was avoidable is death?

Neither party has presented the court with a single authority on this point, nor has exhaustive research turned up a single case where any court has addressed the issues presented by this case. Simply stated, the question is: if the jury should find that the refusal of the blood transfusion was unreasonable and that Mrs. Munn would have lived had she taken the transfusion, then what damages may the plaintiff recover.

The defendant's argument is that if the jury makes this dual finding, then there is no wrongful death and the plaintiff's cause of action is under the survival statute. From a purely technical standpoint, this is a compelling argument. At common law, "if a tortfeasor killed a man, neither the victim's losses before his death nor the losses to his survivors caused by his death were compensable." Because the statutes which have been passed to abrogate this rule are in derogation of the common law, they must be strictly construed. If recovery is not expressly provided for in either the wrongful death or survival statute, then there can be no recovery for the losses suffered by either the survivors or the estate. Given this backdrop, if Mrs. Munn's refusal to accept the transfusion is seen as cutting off the defendant's liability for her death, then the plaintiff must

---

2. Several courts have expanded the doctrine to include measures which if taken prior to the injury would have lessened the severity of the injury. The most common example is the application of the doctrine in cases where the injury resulting from an auto accident was aggravated by the plaintiff's failure to use a seat belt.

fall back on the Mississippi Survival Statute, Miss.Code Ann. § 91–7–233 (1972).

Section 91–7–233 provides: Executors, administrators, and temporary administrators may commence and prosecute any personal action whatever, at law or in equity, which the testator or intestate might have commenced and prosecuted. Mrs. Munn could clearly have commenced an action against Ms. Algee to recover for the injuries she sustained as a result of Ms. Algee's wrongful conduct. Included in her recovery, if any, would have been prospective relief for the future effects of the injuries which were received in the accident, such as lost income, future pain and suffering, and future medical expenses. However, in the usual survival action, the calculation of these damages is based, not upon a mortality table, but upon the actual date of the tort victim's death. In survival actions, "damages must of course be based upon the known period of life, and no recovery may be had for any prospective loss of earnings, expenses, or suffering based upon any probable life expectancy of the deceased, such as would be appropriate if the deceased were prosecuting the case in his lifetime." McCormick, Damages, 337–38 (1935). This rule clearly applies where the death results from an intervening cause which is deemed sufficient to break the causal connection between the tort and the death; but it is not so clear that it applies in this case.

In the usual personal injury case, in addition to the action under the survival statute, the plaintiff, as the husband of the decedent, would have a claim for his own losses which were caused by the injury to his wife—i.e., loss of services, loss of consortium, etc. This claim could be brought "at common law without the aid of statute." However, once again, recovery could be had only for the losses incurred by the plaintiff during the time period between the commission of the tort and the death of Mrs. Munn, if the damages resulting from the death are not attributable to the defendant.

The plaintiff counters with the argument that a straightforward application of the doctrine of avoidable consequences would allow him, both on his own behalf and on behalf of the decedent's estate, to recover damages for any harm which could not have been avoided by allowing the transfusion. A perfunctory reading of the rule, as generally stated, supports this argument. Generally, it is said that the plaintiff may recover for the harm which resulted from the defendant's wrongful act and which could not have been avoided by the plaintiff's acting reasonably after the injury has occurred. The plaintiff alleges that his wife suffered severe physical injury, including a broken pelvis, broken ribs, a punctured and collapsed lung, and a severed artery, which would have resulted in long term disability, pain and suffering, and future medical expenses if she had survived. These consequences could not have been avoided by allowing the transfusion and, therefore, should be recoverable. On a purely emotional level, this argument is appealing; however, any attempt to ground such a holding on legal principles is thwarted by the stark reality that these consequences were never actually suffered by the plaintiff's decedent. This court can find no authority for allowing recovery of purely hypothetical losses.

The argument for recovery of damages for injuries to Mr. Munn which were actually suffered as a result of the death, at least to the extent that they would have occurred even if the plaintiff had taken the transfusion and survived, does not share this infirmity. Clearly, given the extent of the decedent's injuries, if she had lived, there would have been some loss of consortium and services to her husband and quite possibly lost earnings which under this argument ought now to be recoverable by her estate. There are serious problems with allowing recovery of damages for these elements of the loss. Whether the problem is addressed in terms of proximate cause or simply in terms of a public policy against allowing recovery from this defendant for consequences which the plaintiff could have avoided matters little. The doctrine of avoidable consequences operates to relieve the defendant of any legal obligation to pay damages for harm which the victim of her wrongful act could have avoided. The damages which the plaintiff seeks to recover did not occur as a result of the personal injuries suffered by the decedent but as a result of Mrs. Munn's death—a death for which the defendant has no legal obligation to pay damages if the jury should find that the death was avoidable and that the refusal of the transfusion was unreasonable.

Conclusion

The court holds that the doctrine of avoidable consequences is the appropriate standard to be applied in this case and that its application does not violate the plaintiff's first amendment rights. The court further holds that this question should be submitted to the jury through an appropriate instruction telling the jurors that they may consider the fact that it was based on religious belief. The court also holds that the plaintiff may not recover for purely hypothetical injuries which never occurred because of her death if the jury should find that the refusal of the transfusion was unreasonable and that the decedent would have survived had she taken the transfusion; nor may he recover for the harm actually suffered which resulted from his wife's death even though it would have been suffered to some extent even if she had taken the transfusion and lived.

Notes

1. How is the jury to decide whether decedent's refusal was reasonable? In Small v. Combustion Engineering, 209 Mont. 387, 681 P.2d 1081 (1984), the plaintiff had refused low-risk knee surgery that was nearly certain to restore his ability to walk. The plaintiff, who was manic-depressive, considered only the operation's risks and ignored its benefits. The court found his choice objectively unreasonable, but reasonable for the plaintiff personally. The court felt obliged to take the plaintiff's point of view, and allowed him to recover. Is that the right result? The Restatement (Second) of Torts says

reasonableness is to be judged by the same reasonable person standard that defines negligence. "Thus [the plaintiff's] physical and mental condition after an injury are considered in determining whether he was unreasonable in failing to take steps to reduce the harm or in refusing aid." § 918 comment c. Yet, when determining whether someone has been negligent, insanity and other mental deficiencies do "not relieve the actor from liability for conduct which does not conform to the standard of a reasonable" person. Restatement (Second) of Torts § 283B. For a thorough discussion of these issues, see Guido Calabresi, Ideals, Beliefs, Attitudes and the Law (1985).

2. Requiring an injured party to take reasonable steps to limit his losses avoids waste. Look again at the notes following *Ohio v. Department of Interior*, p. 481, especially those discussing the *Hewlett v. Barge Bertie* case (p. 482). If Mrs. Munn valued her religious principles more than her life, wouldn't sacrificing those principles be the greater harm? If she had undergone the transfusion, could she recover for the damage to her principles?

3. If the jury decides Mrs. Munn behaved unreasonably, what damages are recoverable? Normally, one who fails to take reasonable steps to mitigate his losses can nonetheless recover damages for those losses that were unavoidable. Here, however, there is a paradox. Because of the way in which wrongful death damages are calculated, Mrs. Munn's recovery would probably have been greater had she lived. The focus on pecuniary loss and the exclusion of damages for loss of life mean that wrongful death recoveries for injured children or for non-working spouses can be shockingly small.

4. Mr. Munn's claim is also barred by his wife's unreasonable behavior. Loss of consortium is a derivative claim. Defenses that prevail against the injured party also bar an action by the spouse. Similarly, wrongful death claims are derivative.

5. Only a minority of jurisdictions follow the seat belt rule adverted to in the main case. In most jurisdictions, the plaintiff's failure to wear a seat belt does not reduce her damages. Dan B. Dobbs, The Law of Torts § 205 (2000).

6. At trial, the jury in *Munn* was instructed,

> In determining whether or not Elaine Munn's decision to refuse the blood transfusion was unreasonable, you may consider that the blood transfusions were medically recommended. But, you may also consider her religious beliefs and related teachings, together with the known risks of blood transfusions, if you find that to be a factor in her decision.

The jury awarded damages of $241.44 for Mr. Munn's medical expenses, $10,411 for Mrs. Munn's medical expenses, and $10,000 for Mrs. Munn's pain and suffering.

On appeal, the Fifth Circuit (2–1) affirmed. The trial court had erred by allowing the defendant to question Mr. Munn about religious beliefs and practices completely unrelated to medical treatment (such as the refusal of Jehovah's Witnesses to salute the flag or "do service to their country"). Nonetheless, the error was harmless, because the jury was clearly persuaded that Mrs. Munn's objectively unreasonable refusal of treatment caused her death, and because the amount of the jury's award was not, in the court's opinion, influenced by the improperly admitted evidence. Munn v. Algee, 924 F.2d 568 (5th Cir.), cert. denied, 502 U.S. 900, 112 S.Ct. 277, 116 L.Ed.2d 229 (1991).

The court did question the trial court's jury instruction on avoidable consequences, however: "[A] case-by-case approach to religiously motivated refusals to mitigate damages can involve weighing the reasonableness of religious beliefs and thus arguably violate the establishment clause." 924 F.2d at 574–75. Therefore, a purely objective approach—one that avoids any mention of religious beliefs—is preferable. As for the Munns' argument that ignoring religious beliefs entirely impermissibly burdens free exercise rights, "generally applicable rules imposing incidental burdens on particular religions do not violate the free exercise clause." 924 F.2d at 574.

7. Does the purely objective test proposed by the Fifth Circuit adequately protect the plaintiff's right to free exercise of religion? What of the trial court's concern with *Sherbert v. Verner* and *Wisconsin v. Yoder* at p. 545? On this point, the Court of Appeals' silence speaks loudly. The opinion merely cites two 1961, pre-*Sherbert* cases, and Employment Division, Department of Human Resources v. Smith, 494 U.S. 872, 110 S.Ct. 1595, 108 L.Ed.2d 876 (1990)(free exercise clause does not prohibit application of Oregon Drug laws to ceremonial ingestion of peyote). See Note, Refusal of Medical Treatment on the Basis of Religion and an Analysis of the Duty to Mitigate Damages Under Free Exercise Jurisprudence, 25 Ohio N.U.L.Rev. 381 (1999).

By contrast with *Munn*, in Williams v. Bright, 167 Misc.2d 312, 632 N.Y.S.2d 760 (Sup.Ct.1995), a New York trial court held that subjecting the refusal of a Jehovah's Witness to have a transfusion to a "reasonableness" test would burden the exercise of her religion and served no compelling governmental interest.[c] Noting that all damage awards are tailored to the injured individual's circumstances, the court concluded:

> [T]he plaintiff's devout belief * * * was as much a part of her as her age, her gender, her physical condition * * *. She may not be penalized for her beliefs, and the defendants are no more unfairly burdened than if the fortuitously injured party had been a brain surgeon, [or] a ballet dancer. * * *

Therefore, the trial court instructed the jury:

---

c. In part, the trial court's decision in *Williams* rested on its interpretation of the Religious Freedom Restoration Act of 1993 (RFRA), which required any substantial burden on the exercise of religion to be justified by a compelling governmental interest. In City of Boerne v. Flores, 521 U.S. 507, 117 S.Ct. 2157, 138 L.Ed.2d 624 (1997), the Court declared RFRA unconstitutional as applied to the States, finding it was not a legitimate exercise of Congress's Fourteenth Amendment enforcement powers. In Cutter v. Wilkinson, 544 U.S. 709, 125 S.Ct. 2113, 161 L.Ed.2d 1020 (2005), however, the Court upheld a portion of the Religious Land Use and Institutionalized Persons Act (RLUIPA), which required prisons to show a compelling interest to apply otherwise neutral regulations to prisoners, if the application would substantially burden the right to free exercise. According to the Court, RLUIPA was a permissible accommodation of religious exercise, and not an impermissible establishment of religion, even though it favored religion-based claims to exemption for regulation over claims that were not religious in character.

You have to accept as a given that the dictates of her religion forbid blood transfusions. And so you have to determine ... whether she ... acted reasonably as a Jehovah's Witness in refusing surgery which would involve blood transfusions. Was it reasonable for her, not what you would do or your friends or family, was it reasonable for her given her beliefs, without questioning the validity or the propriety of her beliefs?

The appellate division disagreed, finding serious Establishment Clause problems with the way in which the trial court's decision would effectively burden the defendant with the cost of the plaintiff's religious beliefs:

The trial court's instruction to the jurors on mitigation directed them to pass upon the reasonableness of plaintiff Robbins' objection, on religious grounds, to a blood transfusion. The fallacy in this instruction was that the jury never received any evidence pertaining to the rationale of her religious convictions, nor how universally accepted they may have been by members of her faith. * * * The charge thus created a sham inquiry; instead of framing an issue on how plaintiff Robbins' religious beliefs impacted on mitigation, the court foreclosed the issue in her favor without any supporting evidence. Let us recall, the jurors were told that they must ask themselves whether this plaintiff's refusal to accept a blood transfusion was reasonable, "given her beliefs, without questioning the validity" of those beliefs. Having thus removed from the jury's consideration any question as to the validity (that is to say, the reasonableness) of plaintiff Robbins' religious convictions, the court effectively directed a verdict on the issue.

Of course, the alternative—the receipt of "expert" testimony on this subject—presents an even worse prospect. Such evidence, if any conflict developed, would present a triable issue as to whether the conviction against transfusions was heretical—or orthodox—within the Jehovah's Witness faith.

On the other hand, the appellate division noted, applying the reasonable person test without any reference to the plaintiff's religious beliefs, leaving the jury without any explanation of the plaintiff's reasons, would be unfair. Therefore, the court held that the New York pattern jury instruction should be modified:

In considering whether the plaintiff acted as a reasonably prudent person, you may consider the plaintiff's testimony that she is a believer in the Jehovah's Witness faith, and that as an adherent of that faith, she cannot accept any medical treatment which requires a blood transfusion. I charge you that such belief is a factor for you to consider, together with all the other evidence you have heard, in determining whether the plaintiff acted reasonably in caring for her injuries, keeping in mind, however, that the overriding test is whether the plaintiff acted as a reasonably prudent person, under all the circumstances confronting her.

Williams v. Bright, 230 A.D.2d 548, 658 N.Y.S.2d 910 (App.Div.), app. dism'd, 90 N.Y.2d 935, 686 N.E.2d 1368, 664 N.Y.S.2d 273 (1997). For a general discussion, see Jared Goldstein, Is There a "Religious Question" Doctrine? Judicial Authority to Examine Religious Practices and Beliefs, 54 Cath. U.L.Rev. 497 (2005).

8. Is it relevant that while the Munns and many Jehovah's Witnesses are African–Americans, their case was tried before a predominantly white jury? Dissenting from the Fifth Circuit's opinion in *Munn*, Judge Alvin B. Rubin found it hard to believe that irrelevant evidence about the Jehovah's Witnesses' controversial ideology did not affect the verdict. "I see no way that a reviewing court could be sure—other than by substituting its own views for those of the jury or by inventing some post-hoc rationalization for the verdict—that Algee's appeal to the jury's religious prejudice and nationalism had but slight effect on the verdict." 924 F.2d at 583 (Rubin, J., dissenting).

4. MANAGING DAMAGES ACTIONS: THE NEW PUBLIC LAW LITIGATION?

Throughout this section, we have alluded to legislative and judicial reforms that respond to perceived problems with tort damages—damages caps, changes to the collateral source rule, restrictions on damages for pain and suffering and so on. What these reforms have in common is a sense that fully compensating injured victims is not important enough to justify what the reformers see as a potential harm to the public in terms of higher insurance rates, fewer doctors entering risky specialties, curtailed public services, and so on. If one were to seek an analogy to equitable remedies, the logical candidate would be balancing the hardships, which fine-tunes the remedy to limit its impact, not just on the defendant, but on the public generally.

As the Court noted in *Brown II*, p. 107, it is equity—not law—that traditionally "has been characterized by a * * * facility for adjusting and reconciling public and private needs," and it was this equitable facility to which Professor Chayes drew attention with his argument that a new creation, public law litigation, had arrived on the scene. As legislatures and courts become aware that tort law is indeed public law, are suits for damages taking on some of the characteristics of public law litigation?

Mass tort litigation—litigation over harms caused by asbestos, Agent Orange, Bendectin and so on—is the most obvious candidate for a comparison between institutional reform litigation and tort litigation. As you read about the Agent Orange cases in the excerpts that follow, look back to Chayes' account of the central features of public law litigation in Chapter 1. Can you identify similar features in mass tort litigation?

Occasionally, the September 11th Victim Compensation Fund has served as a foil in this chapter for considering the nature of compensation and the effect of particular tort damage doctrines. The Special Master for the Fund, Kenneth Feinberg, was a Special Master for Judge Weinstein in the Agent Orange case described in the next excerpt. How might Mr. Feinberg's experience with the Agent Orange claims have shaped his approach to the Fund?

PETER H. SCHUCK, THE ROLE OF JUDGES IN SETTLING COMPLEX CASES: THE AGENT ORANGE EXAMPLE
53 U.Chi.L.Rev. 337, 341–48 (1986)

I.

On May 7, 1984, Chief Judge Jack B. Weinstein of the Eastern District of New York, flanked by his special masters, announced that the Agent Orange class action had been settled only a few hours earlier, just before jury selection was to begin. The settlement of that action, which was then probably the largest single personal injury litigation in history, created a fund that now totals about $200 million and increases by over $40,000 each day. Approximately 250,000 individual and group claims have been lodged against this fund, and in May of 1985 the court established the framework for the complicated administrative apparatus that is to resolve and administer those claims. * * *

The class was defined to include some 2.4 million American veterans exposed to Agent Orange during the war in Vietnam, the wives and children (born and unborn) of those veterans, and exposed Vietnam veterans from Australia and New Zealand. The seven defendants (pared down from an original twenty-four) were the chemical companies that manufactured Agent Orange. The United States, not named by plaintiffs as a defendant, was joined by the defendants on an indemnity-contribution theory. Judge Pratt, who originally presided over the case, dismissed the government as a party in 1980. Although Judge Weinstein brought the government back into the case just before the settlement, he subsequently dismissed the claims against it.

* * * From the moment that Judge Weinstein replaced Judge Pratt on October 21, 1983, the goal of settlement was uppermost in his mind. He believed that toxic tort cases like Agent Orange, involving mass exposures and causal relationships that are extremely difficult and costly to prove, could not be litigated properly or at an acceptable social cost under traditional rules. Absent settlement, he predicted a one-year trial with results that would remain inconclusive for years to come. Although he harbored genuine doubts about the veterans' evidence on causation, he deeply sympathized with their plight. In open court and in his written opinions, he denounced the "injustices" they suffered, believed that "[t]hey and their families should receive recognition, medical treatment and financial support," and shared the now-conventional view that the American people had failed to discharge "the nation's obligations to Vietnam veterans and their families." The prospect of having either to direct a verdict for the chemical companies or to reverse a jury verdict in favor of the veterans could not have been an appealing one. Unquestionably, he was prepared to do his duty if necessary, but a negotiated settlement offered the far more attractive possibility: everyone would gain something, soon, and at an acceptable social cost.

Earlier settlement discussions between the parties had failed. The court, however, had not been involved in those negotiations. And since then, circumstances had changed—most particularly, the identity and judicial style of the presiding judge. Weinstein immediately established a May 7, 1984 trial date—a little more than six months away—and left no doubt of his implacable determination to hold to it. He did this despite—or perhaps because of—the fact that the parties had to that point conducted little discovery except on a single issue, the government contract defense. He dragged the United States back into the case, believing that the government's presence would greatly facilitate settlement. He also indicated that he would submit the issue of government liability to the jury on an "advisory" basis (the Federal Tort Claims Act precluded a binding jury decision). Finally, he revealed to the parties, albeit only as a "tentative," "preliminary," and, as it turned out, non-appealable matter, how he intended to rule on a number of important and complex legal issues, such as choice-of-law and governmental immunity.

In February 1984, Weinstein requested and obtained permission to retain, at the defendants' expense, an unnamed consultant to develop a settlement strategy and plan. That consultant was later revealed to be Ken Feinberg, a lawyer whom Weinstein knew and trusted. Feinberg was not only knowledgeable about toxic tort litigation, but also had a reputation as an effective mover, shaker, and conciliator. By mid-March, he had prepared a settlement plan. It stated no dollar amount but contained three sections: an analysis of the elements for determining the aggregate settlement amount, especially the various sources of uncertainty and the likely number and nature of claims; a discussion of alternative criteria for allocating any liability among the chemical companies; and a discussion of alternative criteria for distributing any settlement fund to claimants. This document, which the judge made available to the lawyers, occasioned considerable disagreement but succeeded in setting the terms for the negotiations that followed.

On April 10, less than three weeks before trial, Weinstein appointed three special masters for settlement. Feinberg and David I. Shapiro, a prominent class action expert and skillful negotiator, would work with the lawyers. Leonard Garment, a Washington political insider, would explore what resources the government might contribute to a settlement. Feinberg and Shapiro immediately identified three major obstacles to settlement: the parties were more than a quarter of a billion dollars apart; each side was deeply divided internally over whether and on what terms to settle (and in defendants' case, how to allocate liability); and the government was manifestly unwilling to contribute toward a settlement fund or even to participate in settlement negotiations.

The judge and special masters decided to convene an around-the-clock negotiating marathon at the courthouse during the weekend before the trial. The lawyers were ordered to appear on Saturday morning, May 5, with their "toothbrushes and full negotiating authority." On that morning, while preliminary jury selection work was proceeding in another room, Weinstein met with the lawyers and gave them a "pep talk" about settlement. Then the special masters undertook a grueling two-day course of shuttle diplomacy, holding separate meetings with each side interspersed with private conferences with Judge Weinstein. On several occasions, the judge met privately with each side.

Several features of the discussion were particularly salient in generating the settlement agreement. First, the court did not permit the two sides to meet face-to-face until the very end, after the terms of the deal had been defined. This strategy preserved the court's control over the negotiations and prevented them from fragmenting. In particular, it stymied the plaintiffs' lawyers in their last-ditch effort to improve on the deal by settling with five of the defendants and isolating Monsanto and Diamond Shamrock, the two companies they thought most vulnerable to liability and punitive damages.

Second, the masters attempted to break log-jams in the negotiations by helping the lawyers to predict the consequences of the various approaches under consideration, and by proposing alternative solutions. * * *

Third, when especially difficult issues arose that threatened to derail the settlement, the parties agreed to be bound by the judge's decision. The most important example of the judge acting as arbitrator involved perhaps the most difficult question facing the defendants—how to allocate liability among themselves. * * *

Fourth, the judge and his special masters, while being careful not to be duplicitous, did emphasize different things to each side. In their discussions with plaintiffs' lawyers, they stressed the weakness of the evidence on causation, the novelty of many questions of law in the case, the consequent risk of reversal on appeal of a favorable verdict, the prospect that they might lose everything if they rejected settlement, and the enormous costs of continued litigation. To the defendants' lawyers, they stressed the presumed pro-plaintiff sympathies of Brooklyn juries, the reputational damage that protracted litigation and unfavorable publicity would cause their clients, and the high costs of the trial and of the inevitable appeals.

Fifth, a common theme in all discussions was the pervasive uncertainty that surrounded the law, the facts, the duration and ultimate outcome of the litigation, and the damages likely to be awarded. By almost all accounts, it was this uncertainty that proved to be the decisive inducement to settlement. On one count, however, Judge Weinstein left little doubt in the lawyers' minds: the court, having crafted and taken responsibility for the settlement, was in a position to make it stick.

Sixth, the imminence and ineluctability of trial "concentrated the minds" of the lawyers as nothing else could have done. This deadline imparted to their deliberations an urgency and a seriousness that swept aside objections that might have undermined negotiations in less compelling circumstances. The lawyers' growing physical and mental exhaustion during that weekend of feverish intensity abetted the conciliatory effect. As one plaintiff's lawyer later complained in his challenge to the validity of the settlement, "the Judge wore us all down with that tactic."

Seventh, the judge and special masters displayed a degree of skill, sophistication, imagination, and artistry in fashioning the settlement that almost all the participants viewed as highly unusual. But even this would not have availed had Judge Weinstein not inspired an extraordinary measure of respect, even awe, in the lawyers, and had the special masters not been viewed as enjoying the authority to speak and make commitments for him.

Eighth, the settlement was negotiated without any agreement (or even any serious discussion) of how the settlement fund would be distributed among the claimants, and without reliable information as to the number of claims that would be filed. The first, of course, was of great interest to the plaintiffs and a matter of indifference to the defendants. The second, however, was significant to both sides. It is not at all certain that settlement could have been reached had the parties been required to resolve these issues in advance. The problem was not simply that preparation of a distribution plan required an immense amount of analysis. A protracted process of political compromise and education was also needed to gain support for the plan, a process whose results even now remain doubtful and perhaps legally vulnerable.

Ninth, the lawyers on the PMC [plaintiffs' management committee] at the time of the settlement possessed very different personalities, ideologies, and incentives than those of the group of lawyers that had launched the case and carried it through its first five years. These differences likely affected the lawyers' disposition to settle. The veterans' passionate desire for vindication at trial, quite apart from their wish for compensation, had strongly driven their chosen lawyer, Victor Yannacone, during the earlier stages of the litigation. Yet the PMC's deliberations concerning the settlement were strongly influenced by lawyers who had only the most attenuated relationship to the veterans. And under the terms of an internal fee-sharing agreement, these lawyers would be secured financially by even a "low" settlement.

Finally, the court was prepared to allocate substantial resources to the quest for a settlement. Judge Weinstein devoted a great deal of his own time to thinking through and implementing a settlement strategy. His three special masters for settlement commanded high compensation and worked long hours. Their billings to the court totaled hundreds of thousands of dollars, even excluding the massive amount of work they later invested in connection with the distribution plan.

[The settlement reached was for $180 million, although, as the article indicates, the fund increased as interest accrued. The distribution plan called for nearly $150 million to be distributed through a payment program that distributed death and disability benefits to individual veterans and family members like an insurance policy but without requiring proof of causation or otherwise adhering to traditional tort principles. Another portion, roughly $45 million, was to be turned over to a class assistance foundation benefitting both veterans and family members.

On appeal, the Second Circuit upheld the plan to distribute funds to individual disabled veterans and families of deceased veterans without requiring a particularized showing of individual causation. In re Agent Orange Litigation, 818 F.2d 179 (2d Cir.1987), cert. denied, 487 U.S. 1234, 108 S.Ct. 2899, 101 L.Ed.2d 932 (1988). The court did find it was improper, however, to devote $45 million to the class assistance foundation. Because there would be no assurance that the foundation's self-governing and self-perpetuating board of directors would possess the independent, disinterested judgment required to allocate the funds fairly, the appellate court held that the district court must either directly supervise the class assistance programs, or add the money to the fund for distribution.]

Notes

1. How does the settlement reached in the *Agent Orange* case compare to the traditional tort remedy? Should settlements be thought of as remedies at all? Does it make a difference that the case is a class action, in which any settlement must be approved by the judge?

2. For a more detailed description and analysis of the Agent Orange litigation, see Peter H. Schuck, Agent Orange on Trial: Mass Toxic Disasters in the Courts (1986); Philip Jones Griffiths, Agent Orange: "Collateral Damage" in Viet Nam (2003).

ABRAM CHAYES, THE ROLE OF THE JUDGE IN PUBLIC LAW LITIGATION

89 Harv.L.Rev. 1281 (1976)

Reproduced at pages 5–8.

RICHARD L. MARCUS, *PUBLIC LAW LITIGATION AND LEGAL SCHOLARSHIP*

21 U.Mich.J.L.Reform 647, 671–81 (1988)

* * *

B. Treating Public Law Litigation Differently: The Link Between Chayes and Current Issues

* * *

1. The tort "crisis"—Personal injury litigation seems to display few of the features that Chayes found peculiar to public law litigation. The legal rules have evolved over time, but they certainly look different from the high-toned constitutional principles that typify the school desegregation or prison conditions suit. The relief seems to be prototypically private—a single transfer of money from defendant to plaintiff if plaintiff wins.

But tort law has changed. The nineteenth-century individualism that supported doctrines like the fellow-servant rule and made contributory negligence a complete defense has yielded to a different attitude that views tort remedies as ways to shift the costs of accidents. More significantly, products liability, scarcely an important part of the docket fifty years ago, has emerged as the major focus of innovation in tort law. Pathbreaking scholars and courts have propelled plaintiffs into new theories not solely to improve the plaintiffs' chances of compensation, but also and explicitly to alter the behavior of providers of goods and services. Thus courts are increasingly willing to entertain the idea of punitive damages in products liability cases, explicitly endorsing relief designed to alter conduct.

These developments have, not surprisingly, provoked spirited opposition. The insurance industry, in particular, has regularly complained that shifts in the law have undermined its ability to make the calculations necessary to set premium levels. A few notable bankruptcies resulting from massive tort litigation (e.g., Manville Corp. and A.H. Robins) seem to lend substance to arguments that tort liability has gotten out of hand. Even the instrumental argument has been turned on its head by those who assert that regulation through jury verdicts is stifling innovation in technology. It is harder to say now than it was in 1976 that "conventional" tort litigation has only private significance; in terms of social importance, it may rival the sort of cases Chayes had in mind. * * * That, in turn, leads judges presiding over all types of litigation to engage in what Chayes observed in public law litigation—managerial judging.

2. *Managerial judging*—There can be little doubt that Chayes was correct in perceiving a great shift in judicial behavior from the classical model in which the judge was a passive arbiter. He saw this change as resulting from the judge's need to fashion a remedy for unconstitutional conditions, a development that made the judge step in and take over matters that formerly would have been left to the parties. Active judicial involvement, then, was a response to necessity.

In retrospect, it seems that Chayes perceived the necessity and the response too narrowly. The features of public law litigation that prompted judicial efforts to control litigation cannot meaningfully be limited to that kind of litigation. As might have been expected, judges promptly applied the lessons they had learned from their public law litigation experiences outside that realm. Having found a significant public interest in most civil litigation, judges reacted by taking charge of ordinary cases in a way somewhat similar to that in which they had taken control of the cases Chayes described. * * *

The obvious result of this protean role for the judge is to expand the judge's control over the development of the case, sometimes including responsibility for the proper preparation of the case. On a much broader scale than Chayes realized, then, modern judging raises problems of legitimacy of the investigating magistrate when measured against the classical model. Ad hoc judicial activity is hard to square with the notion that the Federal Rules of Civil Procedure should be applied in the same manner in all cases; the triumph of equity now seems to mean that the rules are merely guideposts. As a result, there is a troubling possibility that judges may indulge their own preferences about kinds of litigation in expanding or contracting litigation opportunities. The 1983 amendments even provide some support for that by inviting judges to restrict discovery if the expense seems unwarranted by "the importance of the issues at stake in the litigation."

Without seeming to realize it, Chayes hit upon a fundamental shift in judicial behavior. The theoretical ramifications of that shift are increasingly important in the academy, and resolution of these issues turns largely on reassessing the Fulleresque view of litigation, as Chayes suggested.

3. *Adjudication v. mediation*—Another feature of public law litigation that Chayes focused on may be even more fundamental than managerial judging. Chayes noted the tendency of judges to sidestep their responsibility to devise remedies by pressuring the parties to negotiate a consent decree. He properly perceived that this sort of prodding could not easily be fit into the classical image of the judge as a decision maker, not a facilitator.

As with the judicial management phenomenon, the idea of the judge as mediator was gaining popularity at the time Chayes was writing, and it also applied to a much greater range of cases than Chayes appreciated. In part, this was a reaction to the increasing pressures of growing caseloads, but it also represented the feeling of some judges that all or nothing outcomes in court often were inferior as a matter of justice to the negotiated outcomes that could result from mediation. The relation between the flexibility of negotiated outcomes and the incentives to settle litigation was hardly a new insight, but judges did not begin acting on that insight in large numbers until the late 1970's. By 1983 the practice had achieved such acceptance that it was enshrined in the amendments to the federal rules.

Managerial judging was originally designed to speed adjudication, but it lends itself to mediation as well because it provides the judge with much information about the case and many occasions for inviting or persuading the litigants to consider alternatives. But mediation is even more difficult to fit into the classical model of litigation. Thus, for decades after the federal rules were adopted in 1938, many judges felt that judicial involvement in the settlement process was inappropriate. The insight that the all or nothing results dictated by the law often will be less attractive to the parties than a compromise in no way undermines this traditional reluctance. To the contrary, the law's preference for all or nothing results suggests that compromises are to be shunned.

It is not surprising that public law litigation would strain the traditional view, however, because the remedy so often seems detached from the finding of a violation. As a consequence, one could say the all or nothing motif does not apply in such cases because it is so hard to know what the "all" might be, and always possible that the court will fashion something less than "all."

But the ambivalence in public law cases ran deeper; very often the consent decree was a negotiated resolution of *both* violation and remedy. This reality flowed easily from the nature of the problem courts confronted in framing decrees. The remedy problem in a prison conditions case, for example, arises because no single aspect of the prison's operations is necessarily unconstitutional if considered apart from all the others. In *Hutto v. Finney,* for example, the district court found the Arkansas prison system to violate the eighth amendment because it was "a dark and evil world completely alien to the free world." It then tried to prod the defendants to improve conditions. When that failed, the court imposed a specific injunction which, in part, set thirty days as the maximum sentence for confinement in isolation. The problem was that confining inmates in isolation for more than thirty days was not, standing alone, a constitutional violation. The Supreme Court nevertheless upheld the thirty day limitation because "[t]he length of time each inmate spent in isolation was simply one consideration among many" and, "taking the long and unhappy history of the litigation into account, the court was justified in entering a comprehensive order to insure against the risk of inadequate compliance."

If the problem with fashioning a decree is caused by the difficulty of identifying exactly which features of the defendant's conduct constitute a violation, it is a short step to prodding the parties to make a deal on both violation and remedy. In taking that step, the court can build on the long history of consent decrees in antitrust and employment discrimination cases. But once that step is taken, the distinguishing features of public law litigation seem to recede; if hard liability decisions can be avoided in those cases, they can be escaped in others as well. Moreover, to the extent the public law litigation cases take up a lot of judicial time and energy, it is attractive to use mediation to dispose of the other less weighty portion of the docket.

The current tort crisis atmosphere reinforces this trend. Should tort plaintiffs be left to pursue the all or nothing result at trial or encouraged to accept a "fair" settlement? Where the main uncertainty is the proper amount of compensation, the judge can feel relatively comfortable urging acceptance of a fair amount, based on the verdicts obtained in similar cases, whether or not that suggestion can be backed up with punishment for the party who resists the judge's suggestions. But liability is often unclear; in such cases, judges may have more effective tools to capitalize on uncertainty, because liability often depends more on the judge's decisions than does the measure of damages, which is usually left to the jury. By suggesting proplaintiff or prodefendant inclinations on the legal issues, the judge can powerfully affect the settlement atmosphere. Where the judge's influence is greatest, however, there are no referents like jury verdicts in other cases to guide the judge in selecting a settlement figure. What is the right amount to settle a weak case? How does a judge develop rules for that? What will rules regarding "fair" settlements of weak cases do to the substantive law, with its increasingly regulatory impetus, if they dilute the distinction between cases in which there should and should not be liability? * * *

NOTES

1. Looking at the traditional model of adjudication and the characteristics of public law litigation identified by Professor Chayes, where does the *Agent Orange* litigation fit? How does it depart from the traditional model? Would you call *Agent Orange* public law litigation?

What other damages actions have you seen in this course that might be characterized as "public law litigation"?

2. Is it a good idea to import the active judicial role and emphasis on settlement that characterize public law litigation into cases like *Agent Orange,* or into ordinary tort or contract cases, for that matter? Professor David Rosenberg has argued that mass exposure cases in fact demand "public law mechanisms":

> Public law mechanisms would accomplish the same general purposes in mass exposure litigation that they achieve in civil rights or consumer fraud cases—regulating institutional policies or systematic practices that violate external substantive norms, and assuring access for the critical mass of claims necessary to generate appropriate levels of deterrence for enhancing the tort system's utilitarian and rights-based objectives. The keystone of the public law process is the class action and the managerial role for the judiciary that class action procedure authorizes. Public law adjudication of mass exposure claims would also entail remedial innovations, such as the use of scheduled or nonindividualized damages and insurance fund judgments. * * * [A]pplying public law process to mass exposure cases would likely enhance the system's functional productivity considerably. By enabling courts to exploit the aggregative nature of mass exposure claims, public law procedures would fulfill not only the utilitarian goals of the tort system, but the system's rights-based objectives as well—for such procedures would afford courts the greatest possible opportunity to remedy and prevent tortiously imposed risks of disease and would thus make the system more, not less, responsive to individual rights.

David Rosenberg, The Causal Connection in Mass Exposure Cases: A "Public Law" Vision of the Tort System, 97 Harv.L.Rev. 851 (1984). Similarly, Judge Weinstein himself has called for reforms to enable courts to cope with this sort of litigation, emphasizing, inter alia, the need for class actions; active, managerial judges; mechanisms to limit the total damages awarded; and distribution systems that provide scheduled recoveries without further adjudication, along the lines of worker's compensation systems. Jack B. Weinstein,

Individual Justice in Mass Tort Litigation: The Effect of Class Actions, Consolidations, and Other Multiparty Devices (1995).

3. If tort law is taking on the characteristics of public law litigation, is that a positive or a negative development? On the substantive side, so far as promoting public values goes, critics of the tort system have argued that tort law is ineffective, if not counterproductive, at creating incentives to safety. See Peter W. Huber, Liability: The Legal Revolution and its Consequences (1988); Stephen Sugarman, Doing Away with Personal Injury Litigation (1989). On the procedural side, the managerial role the public law model forces on judges also has its critics. See Judith A. Resnik, Managerial Judges, 96 Harv.L.Rev. 374 (1982); Stephen H. Subrin, How Equity Conquered Common Law: The Federal Rules of Civil Procedure in Historical Perspective, 135 U.Pa.L.Rev. 909 (1987).

As for the remedy, the strongest similarity between institutional reform cases and cases like *Agent Orange* is the pressure for settlement generated by the complexity, expense, and controversial character of the lawsuit. See Peter H. Schuck, Agent Orange on Trial 340 (1986). As the *Agent Orange* litigation demonstrates, that pressure operates on the judge as well as on the parties. In this, however, public law litigation is not really unique. As the costs of litigation have spiraled upwards, and as dockets have become increasingly crowded, the pressure to settle has come to bear on all kinds of litigation, and the responsibility for promoting settlement has increasingly landed on the judge. See Wayne D. Brazil, Effective Approaches to Settlement: A Handbook for Lawyers and Judges (1988).

Is an active role for judges in settling cases necessarily a good thing, however? In a part of the article that has been omitted, Professor Schuck argues that the judge's active participation in settling cases raises problems, if the judge overreaches his power to coerce settlement, becomes unable to assess the settlement fairly because he is overinvolved, or fails to protect against the risk of procedural unfairness inherent in informal settlement proceedings. Did Judge Weinstein successfully avoid these problems? For example, how did the judge reach the conclusion that $180 million was an appropriate amount for the settlement? At one point in the settlement discussion, one of the masters pressed the judge to urge a $200 million settlement, but the judge refused because the plaintiffs' case was so "shaky." Richard L. Marcus, Apocalypse Now? (Book Review: Agent Orange on Trial), 85 Mich.L.Rev. 1267 (1987). Is this troubling?

Professor Marcus also notes that the pressure to settle can "blur the distinction between cases in which there should and should not be liability." There are also federalism issues. "Rule 23 is not a warrant for tort reform in federal court in order to cure 'defects' in state tort law." Richard L. Marcus, They Can't Do That, Can They? Tort Reform Via Rule 23, 80 Cornell L.Rev. 858 (1995). Professor Owen Fiss has also argued that there may be reasons why final adjudication is preferable to settlement. Owen Fiss, Against Settlement, 93 Yale L.J. 1073 (1984). Do you agree?

4. The Supreme Court has clarified the ground rules for settling mass tort cases somewhat. In Amchem Products v. Windsor, 521 U.S. 591, 117 S.Ct. 2231, 138 L.Ed.2d 689 (1997), the parties sought certification as a class in

order to obtain judicial approval of an already-negotiated settlement. The settlement would have disposed of the claims of a class that included all persons who had been exposed to the defendants' asbestos products, but who had not yet filed suit, and their families. According to the Court, the class did not meet Federal Rule of Civil Procedure 23(b)(3)'s requirement that common questions of law or fact predominate over questions affecting only individual members. The millions of claims involved were disparate in important respects. Each claim involved different types of exposure and different types of injuries, and these sorts of issues predominated over the common interest in speedy resolution of claims. Further, Rule 23(a)(4)'s requirement that the named parties will fairly and adequately protect the interests of the class was not met. The small number of parties named in the action each served generally as a representative of the whole, and without distinct representatives for each sub group, the structural assurance of fair and adequate representation for the diverse groups that Rule 23 requires was not present.

Then, in Ortiz v. Fibreboard, 527 U.S. 815, 119 S.Ct. 2295, 144 L.Ed.2d 715 (1999), the Supreme Court invalidated an asbestos class action settlement that had been approved by the lower courts under Rule 23(b)(1)(B), which does not require that common claims predominate. Rule 23(b)(1)(B) class actions are authorized when multiple claims are made against a limited fund that is inadequate to pay them all. In *Ortiz*, however, the fund was limited only by the parties' agreement to establish a settlement fund. Further, Rule 23(b)(1)(B) contemplates that fund will be equitably divided among all claimants. The settlement in *Ortiz* excluded certain classes of claimants, and lacked safeguards for the rights of those excluded. In reaching its decision, the Court recognized that mass tort litigation demands creative solutions, and expressed the hope that Congress would act to resolve the asbestos case crisis legislatively. Recent scholarship on mass torts includes Richard A. Nagareda, Mass Torts in a World of Settlement (2007) (arguing that exchanging a class's right to sue for a compensation scheme is effectively an act of governance); David Marcus, Some Realism About Mass Torts, 75 U.Chi.L.Rev. 1949 (2008); Douglas G. Smith, An Administrative Approach to the Resolution of Mass Tort Claims, 2009 U.Ill.L.Rev. __; Samuel Issacharoff & Richard A. Nagareda, Class Settlements Under Attack, 156 U.Pa.L.Rev. 1649 (2008).

5. After thoughtful consideration, the Special Master for the September 11th Victim Compensation Fund has argued that it would be unwise to attempt to replicate the fund's success in other areas; it "should remain limited to the unique circumstances that gave it birth." Kenneth R. Feinberg, What is Life Worth 181 (2005). At the same time, by all accounts the fund was extraordinarily successful:

> Nearly every family of an individual killed in the September 11th attacks chose to participate in the Fund. To the extent that participation is a measure of success, the Fund was extraordinarily successful. What factors contributed to this success? In our view, there are five major factors that resulted in this overwhelming acceptance of the Fund as a means of compensation. First, the alternative of litigation presented both uncertainty and delay. Second, the Fund took extraordinary steps to assure that families could obtain detailed information about their likely recovery from the Fund. Third, the Fund took a proactive approach—personally

contacting each claimant, ensuring that claimants were able to obtain and present the best information in support of the claim; assisting claimants to obtain helpful information; explaining to claimants information that would assist the Fund in maximizing the computation of economic loss and resolving uncertainties in favor of the claimant. Fourth, the Fund offered in-person informal meetings along with hearings so that claimants could "have their day in court" and explain the magnitude of their loss and their views about the way in which the Fund should treat their particular situation. Fifth, the Fund offered certainty without significant delay, allowing families the option of a type of "closure." * * * Claimants had a personal stake and involvement in the process. Had the Fund opted to curtail access or failed to offer explanations of the manner in which the Fund would treat each individual's situation, some portion of claimants would likely have been sufficiently uncomfortable or uncertain to commit to the Fund.

Kenneth R. Feinberg, 1 Final Report of the Special Master for the September 11th Victim Compensation Fund of 2001 pp. 1–2 (http://www.usdoj.gov/final_report.pdf). Are there lessons that mass tort litigation generally could learn from the fund's success?

D. AN OVERVIEW OF CONTRACT DAMAGES

The next case gives an overview of the issues that arise when damages are sought as the remedy for a breach of contract. Once again, the notes that follow the case are organized along the lines suggested by the excerpt from McCormick on Damages at pp. 457–458. Contract damages are covered extensively in the first year contracts course; after this overview, our focus is on the gray areas in which tort, contract and, in Chapter 7, restitution overlap.

1. THE BASIC RULES

GREAT AMERICAN MUSIC MACHINE, INC. v. MID–SOUTH RECORD PRESSING CO.

United States District Court, Middle District of Tennessee, 1975
393 F.Supp. 877

MORTON, DISTRICT JUDGE.

This suit is brought by plaintiffs Great American Music Machine, Inc. (GrAMM), a Colorado corporation, and Ralph Harrison, a citizen and resident of Colorado, against Mid–South Record Pressing Company, a division of GRT Corporation, with its principal place of business in Davidson County, Tennessee. The complaint seeks monetary damages, based upon breach of contract and implied warranty in connection with some record albums which plaintiffs allege were defectively pressed by Mid–South. The defendant counterclaims on its open account with the plaintiff corporation in the stipulated amount of thirteen thousand and twenty-five dollars and thirty-nine cents ($13,025.39). Jurisdiction of this court is properly invoked under 28 U.S.C. § 1332.

Findings of Fact

In August of 1971, plaintiff Harrison and several of his close friends and business associates formed "Crossroads Limited Partnership," the predecessor to plaintiff corporation. The partnership was formed for the purpose of promoting and exploiting the musical talents of Harrison as a songwriter and singer, although he was then unknown in the entertainment field and had never performed professionally. The business plan of the partnership was to finance the production of a master tape for an album by Ralph Harrison, convert the partnership into a corporation, produce and promote the album and Harrison as an artist, and raise additional capital through a public offering of the stock of the corporation. GrAMM was incorporated by the Crossroads venture in March of 1972, and all the rights of Crossroads were merged into the new corporation.

In the fall of 1971, Harrison went to New York City to produce the master tape for an album featuring himself as the singing artist. The production cost of the master tape was thirty-one thousand and eighty-eight dollars ($31,088.00). The title of the album was to be "Free Spirit Movin'."

In early February of 1972, Harrison and an investor in the venture came to Nashville, Tennessee, to contract for the pressing and packaging of the record album. On behalf of GrAMM, they contracted orally with the defendant, Mid–South Record Pressing Company, for the pressing of forty thousand (40,000) record albums, at a cost of thirteen thousand and twenty-five dollars and thirty-nine cents ($13,025.39). GrAMM received assurances that the records would be of high quality. Although there was some dispute in the testimony at trial, it appears to the satisfaction of this court that there was some discussion with Janet Tabor, manager of defendant company, concerning the overall business plan of GrAMM. It is the finding of this court that GrAMM's plan to offer stock to the public in June of 1972 was mentioned in this discussion.

Under the terms of the oral agreement between the parties, Mid–South was to mail directly to members of ESA, a national sorority, some thirty-two thousand (32,000) copies of the album. (One of Harrison's songs on the record had been adopted by ESA as its theme song.) GrAMM supplied the postage in advance for this mailing. To be enclosed with the albums sent to ESA members was a letter requesting that five dollars ($5.00) be remitted to GrAMM, of which one dollar ($1.00) would be donated to a certain service project of the sorority. The bulk of the remaining 8,000 albums was to be sent to Gambit Records, a Nashville company with whom GrAMM had contracted for nationwide distribution. By mid-February of 1972, a test pressing of good quality had been approved by GrAMM, and Mid–South commenced production of the album. Though there was some dispute in the testimony at trial, the court finds that the contemplated delivery date was the first week of April, 1972.

On April 3, 1972, GrAMM received a shipment of the records at its office in Denver, Colorado. At that time it was discovered by Harrison and others that the records were defective in that they were warped, pitted and blistered, producing excessive surface noises when played. GrAMM immediately sent two representatives to Nashville on April 4, 1972, to investigate the situation. Upon arrival, the GrAMM representatives learned that some eight thousand (8,000) of the records had already been shipped to ESA members; roughly four thousand (4,000) records had been delivered to Gambit, from which an undetermined number had been sent to distributors and disc jockeys around the country.

The court finds as a matter of fact that the first pressing of the record by Mid–South was for the most part commercially unacceptable. Witnesses for both the plaintiff and the defendant testified as to this fact. Gordon Close, one of the GrAMM representatives sent to Nashville in early April, and Janet Tabor of Mid–South both agreed that the larger part of the records still on hand at Mid–South were unusable and that the entire lot should be scrapped and new records pressed. To be included in the new pressing were replacements for the defective albums which had already been shipped out. * * *

Although GrAMM did not complain of the quality of the second pressing nor reject the second batch of albums, it has refused to pay its open account with Mid–South. The amount due on the account is $13,025.39.

In relation to the contemplated stock offering by GrAMM, plaintiff introduced evidence at trial attempting to show that Mr. Mike McBride of Equidyne, Inc., a brokerage firm in Salt Lake City, Utah, had agreed to a firm underwriting of five hundred thousand dollars ($500,000.00) worth of GrAMM securities. * * *

From the evidence developed at trial with regard to the underwriting offer, it is difficult for this court to ascertain exactly why the underwriting did not go through. * * *

CONCLUSIONS OF LAW

The court finds that the defendant company breached implied warranties of merchantability and fitness for a particular purpose, T.C.A. § 47–2–314 and § 47–2–315, in the first pressing of the record albums. Defendant also breached its express contractual agreement to produce records of high quality. * * *

The court finds as a matter of law that plaintiff justifiably rejected the entire first pressing of the record albums as nonconforming goods. T.C.A. § 47–2–602. This rejection included the 12,000 records which had already been shipped out to ESA members and Gambit. Plaintiff notified the defendant of the defects as soon as it became aware of them, on the day it received initial shipment. The defective records had only negligible value as scrap, and defendant made no request that they be returned to it. The cost of retrieving the records already distributed would have greatly exceeded their value as scrap. Any revenue from the records that were shipped to ESA members appears to have been from the second "replacement" batch of records.

With regard to the second pressing of the record albums, the court finds that plaintiff GrAMM is liable on its open account with defendant in the amount of $13,025.39. Plaintiff's liability is predicated upon the fact that it accepted the repressed records and under T.C.A. § 47–2–607 must pay at the contract rate for goods accepted by it. The fact that plaintiff accepted the second batch of records does not, however, in any way preclude its suit for damages occasioned by the defective pressing of the first batch of records. The delivery of the second batch of records did not constitute a cure within the meaning of T.C.A. § 47–2–508, as the damage had already occurred and the time set for performance had expired.

Having previously determined that defendant Mid–South breached express and implied warranties, we now turn to the question of damages. Plaintiff GrAMM has elected to sue for breach of contract, rather than suing in tort for negligence. The damages recoverable for a breach of contract " ... are limited to those reasonably within the contemplation of the defendant when the contract was made, while in a tort action a much broader measure of damages is applied." Prosser, Handbook on the Law of Torts, p. 613.

The standard measure of damages under the Uniform Commercial Code, as adopted in Tennessee, is not particularly helpful under the facts of this case. Under T.C.A. § 47–2–714(2):

> The measure of damages for breach of warranty is the difference at the time and place of acceptance between the value of the goods accepted and the value they would have had if they had been as warranted....

In the instant case, no credible evidence was proffered to the court to reflect the difference between the value that the records would have had if they had been perfectly pressed the first time and delivered on time, as warranted, and the value of the repressed records which were delivered late, after some of the defective records had already been distributed.

Fortunately, the drafters of the Code anticipated such unique factual circumstances and added the following provision to § 47–2–714(2):

> ... unless special circumstances show proximate damages of a different amount.

Additionally, T.C.A. § 47–2–714(3) provides:

> In a proper case any incidental and consequential damages under the next section may also be recovered.

T.C.A. § 47–2–715 explains what may be included as incidental and consequential damages:

(1) Incidental damages resulting from the seller's breach include expenses reasonably incurred in inspection, receipt, transportation and care and custody of goods rightfully rejected, any commercially reasonable charge, expenses or commissions in connection with effecting cover and *any other reasonable expense incident to the delay or other breach.*

(2) Consequential damages resulting from the seller's breach include

(a) any loss resulting from general or particular requirements and needs of which the seller at the time of contracting had reason to know and which could not reasonably be prevented by cover or otherwise; and

(b) injury to person or property proximately resulting from any breach of warranty. (emphasis added)

According to Comment 4 to the above-quoted section:

The burden of proving the extent of loss incurred by way of consequential damage is on the buyer, but the section on liberal administration of remedies rejects any doctrine of certainty which requires almost mathematical precision in the proof of loss. *Loss may be determined in any manner which is reasonable under the circumstances.* (emphasis added)

With regard to certainty of proof required on damage questions generally, Tennessee law provides:

... there is a clear distinction between the measure of proof necessary to establish the fact that plaintiff had sustained some damage, and the measure of proof necessary to enable the jury to fix the amount. The rule which precludes the recovery of uncertain damages applies to such damages as are not the certain result of the wrong, not to those damages which are definitely attributable to the wrong and only uncertain in respect of their amount.

Acuff v. Vinsant, 59 Tenn.App. 727, 443 S.W.2d 669 (Tenn.App.1969), at 674.

The question of allowable damages in this case is made more difficult by the speculative nature of the business venture undertaken by GrAMM. It is undisputed that Harrison had not demonstrated that his talents as a songwriter and artist had any appreciable market value prior to the production of the record, "Free Spirit Movin'." The proof clearly indicates the extremely hazardous nature of an undertaking to produce a "hit" record and create a "star" in the entertainment world.

Plaintiff GrAMM contends that the defective first pressing and resultant delay and confusion virtually destroyed the market for the "Free Spirit Movin'" album, and that Mid–South's breach also caused the failure of the firm underwriting of $500,000 by Equidyne. Plaintiff concedes that it is impossible to project with reasonable certainty what the future profits of the new corporation might have been. Instead, plaintiff asks for (1) the cost of laying the ground work for the manufacture and distribution of the album, including production costs of the record, plus advertising and promotional costs; (2) the cost of keeping the corporation going as a business entity from the date of the breach until the date that plaintiff finally had a successful public offering and began producing music for commercial use; (3) the capital lost from the projected underwriting which failed to materialize, less that realized from a subsequent stock offering; and (4) expenses allegedly incurred following the breach in an attempt by GrAMM to rehabilitate the record, including: advertising expenses, promotional salaries, telephone costs, office supplies, payroll taxes, and salaries of management personnel and secretaries.

As previously noted, while the amount of damages may be approximated, the fact of damage attributable to the wrong must be proven with reasonable certainty. The court rejects the first two elements of damages propounded by the plaintiff, for the reason that the plaintiff did not prove to the court's satisfaction that there was ever any appreciable market for the record, nor that any such market was destroyed.

With regard to the existence of any market for the record, it is noteworthy that 32,000 of the 40,000 records pressed were to be shipped to ESA members as a promotional gimmick, with the request that $5.00 be remitted. The ESA members were, of course, under no legal obligation to pay the requested price for this unordered merchandise. 39 U.S.C. § 3010. There was no proof as to what percentage of the ESA members was likely to send in the requested price.

It was shown at trial that the usual practice among unknown artists in the record industry is to first put out a "single" record, as this is less expensive than an album. In this manner, the marketability of the artist can be tested prior to the production of an album. Ralph Harrison had never produced a single record, nor even performed professionally, prior to the production of the "Free Spirit Movin'" album. Therefore, the court must necessarily rely on the proof at trial with regard to the marketability potential of "Free Spirit Movin'."

James Fogelsong, President of Dot Records and an expert in the music field, testified that the lyrics and artist's performance in "Free Spirit Movin'" were not exceptional in any way; that its production was ordinary or worse; and that the musical instruments in the album "were not in time." Paul Perry, a disc jockey for a popular Nashville radio station, testified that he was impressed with the jacket of the album, but not with the ingredients of the record. He testified that he found no fault with the pressing of the album, and that the ingredients on the record couldn't measure up to the programming standards of his station in any event. He further testified that, in his opinion, the album "would not have had any major marketization," even with an initial pressing of highest quality.

Plaintiff offered no credible expert witnesses to refute the testimony of Fogelsong and Perry. No market survey or other reliable evidence with regard to market potential was introduced by plaintiff. Based upon the proof, the court concludes that no appreciable market existed for the "Free Spirit Movin'" album.

Although GrAMM proved the amount of its investment and the cost of operating its business during the period in question, it offered no convincing proof that, with an initial pressing of high quality, it would in all probability have sold a sufficient number of records to recoup its investment. "Ordinarily, damages are said to be speculative when the probability that a circumstance will exist as an element for compensation becomes conjectural." 25 C.J.S. § 2. In the absence of credible proof that the album had a probability of success, the court cannot speculate that this would have been the case. In fact, the proof at trial convinced the court that the album had a far greater chance of failure than of success.

* * *

The law is well settled that the injured party is not to be put in a better position by a recovery of damages for breach of contract than he would have been in if there had been full performance. 25 C.J.S. Damages § 3. In this case, to grant plaintiff its entire investment in the album as damages for the breach by defendant would in all probability be to put GrAMM in a far better financial position than it would have been in had there been no breach. This the court will not do. It does not appear that plaintiff would have recouped the investment even if there had been no breach.

The court also rejects plaintiff's damages claim with regard to the failure of the $500,000.00 firm stock underwriting to materialize. First, the proof was not sufficiently clear as to why the underwriting did not go through. In absence of such satisfactory proof, the court cannot hold defendant liable for the failure.

Secondly, the court finds that such damages are too remote to have reasonably been within the contemplation of the parties at the time the contract was made. Although it appears from the proof that some mention was made of the stock offering in the conversation between GrAMM and Mid-South representatives, it does not appear that it was discussed in such detail that defendant would have had any idea that it might be held liable for the failure of the underwriting. As noted by the court in Baker v. Riverside Church of God, 61 Tenn.App. 270, 453 S.W.2d 801 (1970), in quoting from Squire et al. v. Western Union Telegraph Co., 98 Mass. 232 (1867):

> A rule of damages which should embrace within its scope all the consequences which might be shown to have resulted from a failure or omission to perform a stipulated duty or service would be a serious hindrance to the operations of commerce and to the transaction of the common business life. The effect would often be to impose a liability wholly disproportionate to the nature of the act or service which a

party had bound himself to perform and to the compensation paid and received therefore.

453 S.W.2d 801, 810.

In the case currently before the court, plaintiff asks damages in excess of $200,000 for breach of a $13,000 contract. The breach of the contract has not been satisfactorily proven to be the cause of the alleged loss. Certainly, these damages may not be allowed.

Under the circumstances peculiar to this case, the court finds the best measure of allowable damages to be the expenses reasonably incurred by GrAMM in its efforts to rehabilitate the record following the breach.

The court concludes that the following elements may be included in the expenses of rehabilitating the record:

(1) salaries and travel expenses of GrAMM representatives sent to Nashville to negotiate the re-pressing of the record album and act as GrAMM's quality control agents;

(2) salaries of other GrAMM employees for the period in which they were actively engaged in the rehabilitation of the record;

(3) extra mailing and handling costs attributable to the defective first pressing;

(4) reasonable telephone costs;

(5) advertising and promotional expenses reasonably incurred by GrAMM in rehabilitating the record; and

(6) a reasonable amount for office supplies and various other miscellaneous expenses.

* * *

NOTES

1. *The Plaintiff's Cause of Action.* Tort law is to some extent an aggregation of many distinct causes of action, each defining distinct legally protected interests and potentially calling for distinct remedies. By contrast, at least since the late nineteenth century contract law has been seen as a unified field. Whatever the subject matter of the particular contract, the law of contracts governs. The same principles, substantive and remedial, are determinative in all cases, although the application of those principles turns on the specific contract at hand.

There have always been those who have argued that the unity of the field of contracts is illusory, largely the product of overactive academic imaginations. See, e.g., Grant Gilmore, Death of Contract (1974). Indeed, recent developments provide some support for the argument that there is less a single Law of Contracts than a law of insurance contracts, of employment contracts, of commercial contracts, and so on, with separate remedies for each.

The codification of the law of sales in Article Two of the Uniform Commercial Code, the Tennessee version of which governs in *GrAMM,* suggests this diversity by providing a framework of substantive and remedial principles peculiar to contracts for the sale of goods. Paradoxically, however, Article Two also confirms the universality of contract remedies; its provisions generally mirror the common law of contracts closely enough that a case like *GrAMM* may be used to study those general principles. Still, Article Two does frequently depart from the general principles of substantive and remedial contract law in order to reflect the demands of the commercial field to which it applies. Where relevant, those departures have been noted, although any detailed treatment of the law of sales perforce is left to the commercial law courses. For detailed discussion of Article Two, see James J. White & Robert S. Summers, Uniform Commercial Code (5th ed.2002).

2. *The Purpose of the Damage Award: Protecting the Expectation, Reliance, and Restitution Interests.* According to the Restatement (Second) of Contracts § 344:

> Judicial remedies under the rules stated in this Restatement serve to protect one or more of the following interests of a promisee:
>
> (a) his "expectation interest," which is his interest in having the benefit of his bargain by being put in as good a position as he would have been in had the contract been performed,
>
> (b) his "reliance interest," which is his interest in being reimbursed for loss caused by reliance on the contract by being put in as good a position as he would have been in had the contract not been made, or
>
> (c) his "restitution interest," which is his interest in having restored to him any benefit that he has conferred on the other party.

The vehicle that promotes these purposes is the compensatory damage award, and that is the primary focus of this section. Nominal damages are available in contract cases, however, when no actual injury to one of these three interests can be shown. Punitive damages are another matter. Any interest in punishing or deterring the breaching party is noticeably absent from the Restatement's summary of the purposes of contract remedies, and traditional wisdom would have it that punitive damages are not available unless the plaintiff can recast his cause of action to sound in tort:

> Punitive damages are not recoverable for a breach of contract unless the conduct constituting the breach is also a tort for which punitive damages are recoverable.

Restatement (Second) of Contracts § 355. Considerable inroads have been made on the traditional rule, as the materials starting at page 585 discuss.

Focusing for a moment on the purposes compensatory damage awards are intended to serve, think about this hypothetical: Suppose you are offered a job in another city, and you must sell your car to cover the moving expenses. You have advertised it in the paper for several days at a price of $2800, with no success. Time is short, and realizing your predicament, your roommate offers to buy it from you for $2600, which is all she can afford. You agree to sell it to her. Ten minutes later, someone calls, offers to buy it for $2800, and when told it has been sold, ups the offer to $2900. You agree to sell it to the caller, and immediately inform your roommate. Being a law student, she immediately sues you. Assuming an enforceable contract was formed, what damages should she recover?

As we have seen, contract damages ostensibly protect the promisee's reliance, expectation, and restitution interests, interests that are usually consistent. In fact, the article that first identified how contract damages protect these three interests did so precisely to show that they frequently overlap. Lon Fuller & William Perdue, The Reliance Interest in Contract Damages, 46 Yale L.J. 52 (1936). For example:

> [W]here the reliance interest is conceived to embrace the loss of the opportunity to enter similar contracts with other persons, the reliance and expectation interests will have a tendency to approach one another, the precise degree of their correspondence depending upon the extent to which other opportunities of similar nature were open to the plaintiff when he entered the contract on which suit is brought. The physician who by making one appointment deprives himself of the opportunity of making a precisely similar appointment with another patient presents a case of a complete correspondence between the reliance and expectation interests. The tendency of the expectation and reliance interests to coalesce in cases of this sort has the consequence that the same item of damages may often be classified under either heading. Thus, where the defendant's breach of contract results in the plaintiff's property remaining idle for a period, the courts in awarding the plaintiff the rental value of the premises have sometimes considered that they were granting reimbursement for the loss of the opportunity to employ the property for other purposes (the reliance interest), and sometimes that they were granting compensation for the loss of profits which would have been made had the defendant performed his promise (expectation interest).

Id. at 74–75. Observing this overlap, Professors Fuller and Perdue argued that the express measure of contract damages and the unstated motives of the courts had diverged. Often, though courts measured damages by expectation, what they were actually compensating was the plaintiff's reliance. The expectation measure simply relieved plaintiffs of the burden of *proving* reliance, lost opportunities being inherently difficult to establish.

Thus, Professors Fuller and Perdue argued that the expectation measure of damages was justified because by protecting reliance even where it could not be shown, the expectation measure both served the ends of corrective justice by undoing the harm caused by the breach, and promoted contracting by encouraging reliance. At the same time, however, Professors Fuller and Perdue's thesis posed a substantial challenge to traditional contract doctrine: "It may be said parenthetically that [our] discussion * * *, though directed primarily to the normal measure of recovery where damages are sought, also has relevance to the more general question, why should a promise which has not been relied on ever be enforced at all * * *?" Id. at 57. See also Patrick S. Atiyah, The Rise and Fall of Freedom of Contract (1979)(arguing that expectancies based merely on a promise have little claim to the law's protection, and in fact are rarely enforced).

So, in a case such as that posed at the beginning of this Note, where there has been no reliance, should the promisee recover damages? Without reliance, why should we say there is a contract at all? Do promises have some independent moral and legal force that makes them enforceable even without reliance, a force that the expectation measure acknowledges? See Ernest J. Weinrib, Punishment and Disgorgement as Contract Remedies, 78 Chi.-Kent L.Rev. 55 (2003) (arguing that the expectation measure of damages is justified on corrective justice grounds); Charles Fried, Contract as Promise (1981). Can economics provide an answer? See David W. Barnes, The Anatomy of Contract Damages and Efficient Breach Theory, 6 S.Cal.Interdisc.L.J. 397 (1997–98) (expectation measure of damages is justified because it allows economically efficient breaches to occur); Avery Katz, Reflections on Fuller and Perdue's The Reliance Interest in Contract Damages: A Positive Economic Framework, 21 U.Mich.J.L.Ref. 541, 542 (1988).

The scholarship discussing the relationship between expectation and reliance, and the merits and demerits of each as a basis for contract damages, has been described as "vast and daunting, and * * * of a remarkably high quality." Christopher T. Wonnell, Symposium: "W(h)ither The Reliance Interest?": Expectation, Reliance, and the Two Contractual Wrongs, 38 San Diego L.Rev. 53, 55 (2001). Currently, theories focusing on expectation interests, and downplaying the role of reliance, seem to be in the ascendancy. See, e.g., W. David Slawson, Why Expectation Damages for Breach of Contract Must Be the Norm: A Refutation of the Fuller and Perdue "Three Interests" Thesis, 81 Neb.L.Rev. 839 (2003); Melvin A. Eisenberg & Brett H. McDonnell, Expectation Damages and the Theory of Overreliance, 54 Hastings L.J. 1335 (2003).

If the answer to Professors Fuller and Perdue is that for moral or economic reasons, contracts must be enforced even where there is no reliance, why stop with expectation damages? If breaching a contract is wrong, and the defendant did it deliberately, shouldn't punitive damages be available? If a promisor earns a profit by breaching a contract, and breaching a contract is wrong, shouldn't the defendant have to give up any profit earned by his wrongdoing? Are there interests that Fuller and Purdue (and the Restatement) overlooked? See Eyal Zamir, The Missing Interest: Restoration of the Contractual Equivalence, 93 Va.L Rev. 59 (2007) (when courts, for example, prorate the contract price when a parcel of land contains fewer acres than were promised, their aim is to restore the parties to a position equivalent to the bargain they might have made, which is neither expectation nor reliance.)

Instead of looking to the plaintiff's rightful position, should the court aim for the defendant's rightful position, perhaps requiring the defendant to disgorge the benefits of a breach? See the discussion in Chapter 7 and Melvin A. Eisenberg, The Disgorgement Interest in Contract Law, 105 Mich.L.Rev. 559 (2006). These questions are explored in sections that follow.

3. *Elements of the Damage Award.* Turning to the elements of compensatory damages that may be available when contract damages are sought, the idea of a balance sheet may again be helpful. On one side of the ledger would be the plaintiff's losses: the value of the lost performance, plus any incidental or consequential damages. On the other side of the ledger are the plaintiff's savings. First, the plaintiff may have saved the cost of his own performance when the defendant's breach made it unnecessary for him to perform. Second,

the plaintiff may be able to act to avoid some losses; the wrongly fired worker may be able to find another job or the manufacturer whose customer has breached may be able to find a new buyer for his goods. These "losses avoided" must be added to the plaintiff's savings. Then, after the various elements have been identified, the expectation damages may be calculated by subtracting the plaintiff's savings from the plaintiff's losses, or as the Restatement puts it:

> [T]he injured party has a right to damages based on his expectation interest as measured by
>
> > (a) the loss in the value to him of the other party's performance caused by its failure or deficiency, plus
> >
> > (b) any other loss, including incidental or consequential loss, caused by the breach, less
> >
> > (c) any cost or other loss that he has avoided by not having to perform.

Restatement (Second) of Contracts § 347.

The Restatement's formula for calculating expectation is universal; it can be applied to any type of contract. In practice, however, more specific formulae have evolved as the measure of damages for specific types of contracts. To borrow an example from Professor E. Allan Farnsworth, when a property owner breaches a construction contract before the work is completed, the Restatement would measure the builder's expectation as the unpaid contract price minus the cost of completing the house (assuming for the sake of simplicity that the builder suffered neither incidental nor consequential damages, and was unable to avoid any losses). Practically speaking, however, it can be very difficult to show the cost of completing a half-built house. It is much easier for the contractor to show how much profit he expected to make when he entered the contract, and how much he has spent on performance so far (his reliance). Therefore, he would prefer to measure his damages by his expected profit plus his costs so far, and indeed, the cases support such a measure. E. Allan Farnsworth, Contracts § 12.10 (4th ed.2004). Because the builder's expected profit is equal to the contract price minus his costs so far minus the cost of completion, the "profits plus reliance" measure is the algebraic equivalent of the Restatement's "loss of value minus costs saved" measure.

The materials in this chapter include the damage measures for most of the basic types of contracts. As you encounter them, it may be helpful to relate each to the Restatement's basic measure of expectation. It is also important to understand that in most cases damages that protect the plaintiff's expectation interest—the benefit of the bargain—simultaneously protect his reliance and restitution interests. For example, if a defendant promises to sell the plaintiff a car worth $6,000 for only $5,000, and then breaches after accepting the plaintiff's deposit of $500, one way to measure the damages would be the value of the car ($6,000) less the cost the plaintiff avoided by not having to pay the balance of the purchase price ($4500), or $1,500. An award of $1,500 protects the plaintiff's expectation by giving him the $1,000 profit he expected; it protects his reliance interest by returning his $500 deposit;

and it protects his restitution interest by taking the $500 away from the defendant. In other cases, however, reliance or restitution damages may be alternative remedies for a contract breach; the plaintiff may choose to sue for damages measured by his reliance, or for restitution, instead of seeking expectation damages.

Does the Restatement's generic formulation adequately capture the losses that are to be expected when a contract is breached, or are there obvious omissions? What about the inconvenience and annoyance that are inevitable when a deal goes sour? See Leonard E. Gross, Time and Tide Wait for No Man: Should Lost Personal Time be Compensable? 33 Rutgers L.J. 683 (2002). In contract cases, the loss of the value of the defendant's performance is the measure of general damages; other items of loss are considered special damages.

Ignoring limitations like foreseeability, certainty, etc., what would the damages have been in *Great American Music Machine (GrAMM)*? What award would be necessary to protect Harrison's expectation interest? His reliance interest? His restitution interest? If Harrison is given the "benefit of the bargain," are his reliance and restitutionary interests adequately protected? See Robert M. Lloyd, Contract Damages in Tennessee, 69 Tenn.L.Rev. 837 (2002).

4. *Measuring the Damages.* Because non-pecuniary losses are rarely recoverable in contract cases, the primary problem in measuring the damages lies in supplying the values necessary to fill in the relevant general damages formula, and in establishing the amount of whatever special damages have been incurred with reasonable certainty. See, e.g., John Y. Gotanda, Recovering Lost Profits in International Disputes, 36 Geo.J. Int'l L. (2004) (describing use of the discounted cash flow method for determining the value of lost profits). For a discussion of the concept of value generally, and of how courts have handled cases in which market value and cost of completion diverge, review the materials in section B(2) of this chapter.

5. *Limits on the Award.*

a. *Foreseeability.* Consideration of the role of foreseeability in contract damages begins with Hadley v. Baxendale, 156 Eng.Rep. 145 (1854), a fixture of the basic course in contracts. In *Hadley,* the defendant breached a contract to deliver a mill shaft to be repaired. The delay that resulted caused the mill owner to lose profits, because his mill was unable to operate without the shaft. Yet the court denied the mill owner recovery, because the loss of profits was unforeseeable:

> When two parties have made a contract which one of them has broken, the damages which the other party ought to receive in respect of such breach of contract should be such as may fairly and reasonably be considered either arising naturally, i.e., according to usual course of things, from such breach of contract itself, or such as may reasonably be supposed to have been in the contemplation of both parties, at the time they made the contract as the probable result of the breach of it. Now, if the special circumstances under which the contract was actually made were communicated by the plaintiffs to the defendants, and thus known to both parties, the damages resulting from the breach of such a contract,

which they would reasonably contemplate, would be the amount of the injury which would ordinarily follow from a breach of contract under these special circumstances so known and communicated.

156 Eng.Rep. at 151.

Because of *Hadley*, the distinction between general and special (or consequential) damages in contract cases takes on added importance. General damages are those that, under the first prong of *Hadley*'s test, arise "naturally" from that breach, and are foreseeable by definition. Special, or consequential, damages fall under *Hadley*'s second prong, and must be proven to have been foreseeable based on special circumstances known to the breaching party at the time the contract was formed.

For a time, the requirement that special damages be shown to be foreseeable was interpreted to require the plaintiff to show that the loss was more than objectively foreseeable. The plaintiff had to show that, by entering into the contract knowing the circumstances, the breaching party at least tacitly consented to be liable for that loss in the event of a breach. The tacit agreement variation of the *Hadley* rule, however, has been rejected by virtually every state that has considered it, and by the Restatement of Contracts and the UCC as well. Note, The Tacit Agreement Test—Arkansas Clings to a Dinosaur, 40 Ark.L.Rev. 403, 406 (1986). The Restatement (Second) of Contracts § 351, states the settled rule:

(2) Loss may be foreseeable as a probable result of a breach because it follows from the breach

(a) in the ordinary course of events

(b) as a result of special circumstances, beyond the ordinary course of events, that the party in breach had reason to know.

(3) A court may limit damages for foreseeable loss by excluding recovery for loss of profits, by allowing recovery only for loss incurred in reliance, or otherwise, if it concludes that in the circumstances justice so requires in order to avoid disproportionate compensation.

The UCC's version of *Hadley* is in § 2–715(2)(a), which is quoted in *GrAMM*. Does it differ from the Restatement's formulation? See Paul S. Turner, Consequential Damages: Hadley v. Baxendale Under the Uniform Commercial Code, 54 S.M.U.L.Rev. 655 (2001). Was the court in *GrAMM* correct in holding that the damages with regard to the failure of the stock underwriting were too remote, given its finding that the plan to make a public offering of the stock was mentioned in discussions with Mid–South?

One of the challenges of studying remedies is to account for the ways in which the same concept—here, foreseeability—is treated differently in tort and contract suits. For example, Harrison also attempted to cast his suit in negligence, but failed because of the statute of limitations. Had he been successful, would it have made any difference? How do the rules governing foreseeability in tort compare to the rule derived from *Hadley?* If Harrison had been allowed to pursue his negligence claim, would damages attributable to the underwriting failure have been recoverable? See *Evra Corp. v. Swiss Bank Corp.* at p. 600.

The comparison of tort and contract remedies is the subject of the next section of this chapter. To give a quick answer, because Harrison's losses were purely economic, most courts would have held that no cause of action in negligence could be stated. That is simply to say, a court would probably decide that contract rules ought to govern this loss. But why?

b. *Certainty.* Damages can be recovered for a particular element of loss "only to the extent that the evidence affords a sufficient basis for estimating their amount in money with reasonable certainty." Restatement (Second) of Contracts § 352. Although both tort and contract damages must be certain, courts may apply the requirement somewhat differently in different contexts. For example, in Evergreen Amusement Corp. v. Milstead, 206 Md. 610, 112 A.2d 901 (1955), a contractor breached an agreement to clear and grade a site for a drive-in movie theater. The property owner sued, seeking damages measured by the profits he lost because the theater's opening was delayed. The court denied recovery of this element of damages. The plaintiff pointed to a number of antitrust cases that seemed to support recovery, and the court responded:

> "While the opinions do not articulate that the damages were allowed to make effective the civil sanctions of the anti-trust statutes and, indeed, in one case, perhaps self-consciously, suggest that there is no distinction in the rules as to damages between anti-trust cases and others, nevertheless, it seems clear that the courts, in order to lay a basis for punitive triple damages, have relaxed the standards of proof in anti-trust suits to permit the establishment of lost profits as basic damages."

Does it make sense to allow an item of loss in an antitrust or tort case, and deny the same element in a contract case as too uncertain, on basically the same proof? Keep in mind that contract liability is strict, although it can be argued that courts could—and do—use doctrines like foreseeability, certainty and avoidability to respond to different degrees of fault. George M. Cohen, The Fault Lines in Contract Damages, 80 Va.L.Rev. 1225 (1994).

The requirement that the amount of the plaintiff's losses be shown with sufficient certainty has always posed particular problems for plaintiffs involved in new or entrepreneurial ventures, as in *Evergreen* or *GrAMM*. In fact, lost profits from a new business have sometimes been considered *per se* uncertain and unrecoverable. This *per se* rule is supported by the notion that while an established business can use its past earning records to show lost profits with reasonable certainty, a new business has no track record and thus cannot provide any non-speculative basis for calculating damages. See John Y. Gotanda, Recovering Lost Profits in International Disputes, 36 Geo.J. Int'l L. (2004) (describing application of the certainty requirement to lost profit claims in international tribunals).

Two developments have led to a relaxation of the certainty requirement. First, according to Professor McCormick, the certainty requirement evolved to control speculation by the jury. Yet,

> "with increasing confidence in other developing doctrines which are used to control verdicts, such as the doctrines of 'contemplation of the parties' in contract cases and of 'proximate cause' in tort cases, and with increasing flexibility in controlling the size of the verdict on the motion

for new trial or on appeal, the judges have come to relax their strict insistence that the jury shall not 'speculate' as to the amount. 'Certainty' becomes 'reasonable certainty' and then 'reasonable probability.'"

Charles McCormick, Handbook on the Law of Damages 118 (1935). See also Note, Averting the New Business' Battle to Prove Lost Profits: A Reintroduction of the Traditional Reasonable Certainty Rule as a Penalty Default, 67 S.Cal.L.Rev. 1573 (1994). Professor McCormick was writing in 1935, however; the advent of cases involving radiation, toxins, and carcinogens has brought certainty back into the spotlight. See *Ayers v. Jackson Township* at p. 486; *In re: Agent Orange Litigation* at p. 553.

Second, as economic forecasting has become more sophisticated—and as courts have become more comfortable with economic experts—the *per se* rule regarding new businesses has declined, and what was a *per se* rule has become a rule of evidence, in most jurisdictions. With regard to losses suffered by a new business, as with any other loss, the plaintiff must simply provide evidence from which the jury may estimate the amount with reasonable certainty, and without speculation. What sort of evidence might the plaintiff in *GrAMM* have produced to persuade the court that recovery was appropriate? How about in *Evergreen?*

When expectation damages are unavailable because they are too uncertain, courts often fall back upon the concept of general damages. Thus, in *Evergreen*, instead of recovering damages based on his lost profits, the plaintiff recovered general damages for the loss of the use of his land, that is, the land's rental value for the period of the delay. Is it clear that the rental value of an unused parcel can be established with any greater certainty than the profits it might generate? After all, what is the rental value if not a projection of the profits that might be available from the various uses to which the land might be put? Professor Dobbs has argued that the certainty rule simply confirms that the law is biased to favor capital investments over entrepreneurial ventures. Dan B. Dobbs, Law of Remedies § 3.4 (2d ed.1993).

If even general damages are unavailable or unsatisfactory, as in *GrAMM*, an alternative measure of damages may be available. In contract cases, for example, if expectation damages are too uncertain, the plaintiff may recover damages measured by the plaintiff's reliance, in order at least to protect the plaintiff from losses suffered because he relied on the defendant's promise. In *GrAMM*, the plaintiff relied on the defendant's promise by paying the production, advertising, and promotional costs of the record; by paying the operating costs of the corporation; and by investing capital in the underwriting venture. Yet, the court denies recovery for these losses. Why?

Even the reliance measure is limited by the overall remedial goal of placing the plaintiff in the position he would have occupied if the contract had been performed. Where the plaintiff is involved in a losing deal, reliance damages may overcompensate him; they may leave him in a better position than if the contract had been performed. So, reliance damages are limited in losing contracts:

> Under the rule stated [in section 349], the injured party may, if he chooses, ignore the element of profit and recover as damages his expenditures in reliance. He may choose to do this if he cannot prove his profit

with reasonable certainty. He may also choose to do this in the case of a losing contract, one under which he would have had a loss rather than a profit. In that case, however, it is open to the party in breach to prove the amount of the loss, to the extent that he can do so with reasonable certainty, * * * and have it subtracted from the injured party's damages.

Restatement (Second) of Contracts § 349, comment a. Note, however, on whom the Restatement places the burden of showing that a loss was expected and its amount. In light of this, was *GrAMM* rightly decided?

Another alternative to compensating the plaintiff for his lost expectations is restitution. That alternative is discussed, along with restitution generally, in Chapter 7 (although in fact it has never been quite clear whether restitution should be considered an alternative remedy for breach of contract, or a distinct substantive right).

c. *Avoidable Consequences.* The rule regarding avoidable consequences is the same in contract as in tort: if, through reasonable efforts, a loss could have been avoided, damages for that amount cannot be recovered. Restatement (Second) of Contracts § 350; UCC § 2–715(1)(consequential damages which "could not reasonably be avoided by cover or otherwise" may be recovered). The usual effect of the avoidable consequences rule is to promote cover, to give plaintiffs the incentive to continue to pursue their presumably profitable enterprises by obtaining an equivalent performance from someone else.

There are, however, exceptions to the rule. For one, a majority of states continue to adhere to a common law rule that allows landlords to recover damages from a lessee who has abandoned the property even though others stand ready to rent it. See 21 A.L.R.3d 534 for a summary of the jurisdictions that continue to follow this rule.

Again, the rule also has a positive side: reasonable sums expended in attempting to avoid the loss can be recovered. Are there any items of recovery in *GrAMM* that fall into this category?

d. *Offset by benefits.* The offset rule, too, applies in contract cases. Restatement (Second) of Contracts § 347, comment e. As the following excerpt demonstrates, the difficulty in applying the offset rule lies in determining whether the benefit was actually the product of the defendant's actions.

CHARLES J. GOETZ & ROBERT E. SCOTT, MEASURING SELLERS' DAMAGES: THE LOST PROFITS PUZZLE

31 Stanford L.Rev. 323, 323–27 (1979)

A buyer repudiates a fixed-price contract to purchase goods, and the seller sues for damages. How should a court measure the seller's loss? The answer seems simple: The seller should be awarded damages sufficient to place it in the same economic position it would have enjoyed had the buyer performed the contract. But the seductive conceptual simplicity of the compensation principle disguises substantial practical problems in measuring seller's damages.

Contract law has traditionally minimized measurement difficulties by basing damages in most cases on the difference between the contract price and market value of the repudiated goods. The common law courts generally limited the seller to such market damages whenever the seller had a resale market for the contract goods. These courts assumed that combining this damage award with proceeds from a resale would give the seller the profits that performance would have earned it. * * *

But as the Uniform Commercial Code damages scheme supplanted the common law, the notion was advanced that the common law rule erroneously used the contract-market formula to measure loss in several circumstances in which the compensation principle demanded that the seller recover by direct proof the profit lost because of the breach. * * *

The "lost-volume seller" is the second category where market damages are frequently believed to measure true losses inadequately. Market resales do not replace or substitute for the breached contract when such resales would have been made even if the buyer had not breached. The seller may contend that, while it did in fact resell the contract goods, the other buyer would have purchased anyway. Therefore, if the breaching buyer had fully performed the contract, the seller would have realized two profits from two sales. Since selling the goods to the second buyer produced only one profit for the seller, the breaching party ought to pay over the other profit in order to put the seller in the position it would have achieved had the buyer performed. Conventional analysis has assumed that whenever the seller is able to supply all available buyers at the prevailing price, its damages are presumptively equal to the entire expected profit lost on the breached contract.

* * *

e. *Limiting damages by agreement.* Parties to a contract have the power to limit liability expressly in the agreement, or to alter the measure of damages the common law would impose. See UCC § 2–719(2). The power, however, is not unlimited. Most jurisdictions have limited the power of the parties to exclude consequential damages, as in the UCC:

> Consequential damages may be limited or excluded unless the limitation or exclusion is unconscionable. Limitation of consequential damages for injury to the person in the case of consumer goods is prima facie unconscionable but limitation of damages where the loss is commercial is not.

UCC § 2–719(3).

Another technique for limiting exposure to damages in the event of breach is the liquidated damages clause. A liquidated damages clause sets a specific amount of damages that will be recoverable in the event of a breach. Not all liquidated damages clauses are enforceable, however:

> Damages for breach by either party may be liquidated in the agreement but only at an amount that is reasonable in the light of the anticipated or actual loss caused by the breach and the difficulties of

proof of loss. A term fixing unreasonably large liquidated damages is unenforceable on grounds of public policy as a penalty.

Restatement (Second) of Contracts § 356.

JUSTIN SWEET, LIQUIDATED DAMAGES IN CALIFORNIA
60 Calif.L.Rev. 84, 85–90 (1972)

* * *

Policy Considerations and Trends in Party Autonomy

The question of how much autonomy the law should give parties to employ clauses that control the amount of damages recoverable for contract breach is part of the general issue of party autonomy. Even in periods of maximum party autonomy, there have been some controls on contract-making, such as the Statute of Frauds, capacity requirements, legality requirements, and usury laws. Also, the consideration doctrine limited pure contractual freedom by not enforcing gift promises and by balancing extremely unequal bargaining power through the mutuality concept. Until the 20th century, however, the general norm was party autonomy.

The most important reason for the modern trend away from autonomy is that much of 19th century contract law was predicated upon the model of a contract between two parties of relatively equal bargaining power who negotiate and conclude a mutually acceptable agreement. Instead, the bulk of contracts today are various forms of adhesion contracts, the mass-produced, nonnegotiated contracts pioneered by the insurance, utilities, and transportation industries. The consent in these adhesion contracts is a fiction. The party handed a form usually has no time to read it, would not understand it if he took the time, would not be able to find anyone with authority to change it if he wished to, and very likely would not be able to make the transaction if he insisted upon a change from the standard form.

Largely because of adhesion contracts, the past 20 years have seen a proliferation of legal controls on contracts. There is more judicial intervention through the back door of interpretation and, increasingly now, direct intervention through refusal to enforce contracts that courts think are unjust.

A. Reasons for Liquidated Damages Provisions

As the norm has changed from negotiated contract to adhesion contract, the reasons for employing liquidated damages clauses have changed, and accompanying this has been a change in judicial attitude toward enforcement. First, consider the use of liquidation clauses in the model of a negotiated contract. Both contracting parties often wish to control their risk exposure, and permitting them to do so encourages risk-taking. The performing party may also wish to avoid the feared irrationality of the judicial process in determining actual damages. He may also be fearful that the court will give insufficient consideration to legitimate excuses for nonperformance, that the court may be unduly sympathetic to plaintiff's claim that any loss he incurred should be paid for by the party whose nonperformance caused the loss or that the court may consider contract breach an immoral act.

There are also reasons why the nonperforming party as well may wish to use a liquidated damages clause. Sometimes a breach will cause damage, but the amount of damages cannot be proven under damage rules. For example, in wartime procurement contracts it may be impossible to establish the damages caused by delayed or defective performance by the contractor. Without an enforceable clause purporting to liquidate damages, the nonperforming party may fear that the performing party will have insufficient incentive to perform if the latter realizes that damages he has caused are not sufficiently provable to be collected. Such a clause is a penalty in that its principal function is to coerce performance. Yet if it is reasonable—not disproportionate to actual, although unprovable, damages or to the contract price—it will be enforced. Without a liquidated damages clause there is also a danger that contractor may recover the full contract price despite a breach that caused some unprovable losses. Thus while the nonperforming party may be motivated principally by the penalty aspects of the clause, he may to a lesser degree be motivated by the desire to prevent what appears to him to be unjust enrichment.

Liquidated damages clauses may also be inserted to improve upon what the parties believe to be a deficiency in the litigation process: the cost and difficulty of judicially proving damages. Through a liquidation clause the parties attempt to use contract to settle the amount of damages involved and thus improve the normal rules of damages. Also, when the clause is phrased in such a way as to indicate that the breaching party will pay a specified amount if a particular breach occurs, troublesome problems involved in proving causation and foreseeability may be avoided.

In the adhesion contract situation there are some similarities in objectives; the desire to control the irrationality and expense of the litigation process and the need to know the extent of risk exposure are still involved. There are, however, obvious additional objectives of the stronger party. He can dictate the terms of the contract; if he is the performing party, he is likely to use the contract clause to limit his exposure almost to the vanishing point, and if he is the nonperforming party, he may try to use a penalty clause to coerce performance, or he may try to use a genuine liquidation clause to make vindication of his legal rights as convenient and inexpensive as possible. In the adhesion context, then, the stronger party may try to limit his own liability and to set an agreed amount that is sufficiently high to coerce performance. In the event performance is not rendered, the clause may obtain a settlement or win the case.

B. *Judicial Responses to Liquidated Damages Provisions*

Moving from the reasons why liquidated damages clauses are used by the parties, let us consider what motivates courts to uphold or reject these clauses. Some courts undoubtedly are persuaded by the argument that the parties have paid their money and taken their chances. Since the parties have assumed certain risks, courts often see no particular reason to relieve them from the risks they have taken. Treating the liquidated damages clauses as any other, such courts uphold the clauses to reward the party who has guessed best on the question of damages. Other courts enforce these clauses because they believe that protecting the reasonable expectations of the contracting parties encourages risk-taking and assists in planning. Still other courts look at the contract as a package and enforce the liquidation clause because they feel that the party attacking the clause has received benefits under the contract. This is especially likely when such a clause is directly related to the contract price. For example, in one important case, a gun manufacturer offered to supply guns at different prices depending upon when delivery had to be made. The government chose the quickest delivery at the highest price. Nonenforcement of the delay-damage liquidation clause in this case would have disturbed the package arrangement and created unjust enrichment.

Courts also enforce these clauses because they believe liquidated damages clauses help the courts achieve just results. Sometimes the computation of damages in litigation is no better than a guess; as long as the amount selected by the parties is within a reasonable range, the courts feel that enforcing the amount selected is likely to be as fair as any amount determined by the court. Furthermore, courts believe that if such agreements are enforced, at least in theory the use of such clauses should expand, resulting in fewer breaches, fewer law suits, fewer or easier trials, and in many cases, at least as just a result.

Finally, courts recognize that enforcement of these clauses can cure defects in the litigation process. For example, the requirements as to certainty may seem too restrictive. A court may enforce a liquidation clause to ensure that a party will get a just recovery that might otherwise be denied him because he cannot establish the loss with sufficient certainty.

Many purported liquidated damages clauses, however, are not enforced. The traditional rationale for nonenforcement is that courts will not aid in coercion, oppression, or unjust enrichment; courts seek only to compensate, and enforcement of penalty clauses is contrary to that purpose. Thus, enforcement of a clause not based upon an estimate of proper compensation would cause an unconscionable result.

Refusal to enforce these clauses may recognize the protection contracting parties need from their own unfortunate optimism and their failure to consider in advance the possibility that subsequent events may affect their performance. Like the doctrines of consideration, frustration, impossibility, and mistake, not enforcing a liquidation clause reflects the idea that the performing party should not be held strictly to his promise. The refusal to enforce a liquidation clause does not preclude the plaintiff from recovering actual damages. This method of relieving a party from his contractual promise gives the judge the comfortable feeling that he is not upsetting traditional law but merely putting the plaintiff to his proof of damages.

Moreover, modern courts are beginning to look at the realities of the contract–making process. They realize that if the clause is part of an adhesion contract, some of the reasons for permitting and encouraging party autonomy do not apply. When one party is under great compulsion and has no choice, it is not likely that the amount is fair risk assumption. Party autonomy is less attractive in such a context, especially when enforcing the clause would do violence to a damages rule that the court believes to be salutary.

NOTES

1. In determining whether a liquidated damages clause is enforceable, should the court consider actual damages that would be too uncertain or remote to be recoverable as compensatory damages? See Gregory Scott Crespi, Measuring "Actual Harm" for the Purpose of Determining the Enforceability of Liquidated Damages Clauses, 41 Hous.L.Rev. 1579 (2005).

2. When courts are convinced that ordinary contract damage measures fall far short of compensation, they sometimes require the parties to perform on pain of contempt by awarding specific performance, or create economic incentives to perform by awarding supercompensatory remedies like punitive damages or disgorgement of profits (see the next section). Why should parties be free to decide whether to settle for the legal measure of damages or not? See Aaron S. Edlin & Alan Schwartz, Optimal Penalties in Contracts, 78 Chi.-Kent L.Rev. 33 (2003) (to promote economic efficiency, liquidated damages clauses should be enforced unless they violate some independent norm, like the prohibition on unconscionable agreements or antitrust laws).

2. CONTRACT OR TORT? THE UNCERTAIN BOUNDARY

FREEMAN & MILLS, INC. v. BELCHER OIL CO.
Supreme Court of California, 1995
11 Cal.4th 85, 900 P.2d 669, 44 Cal.Rptr.2d 420

LUCAS, CHIEF JUSTICE.

* * *

I. FACTS
* * *

In June 1987, defendant Belcher Oil Company retained the law firm of Morgan, Lewis & Bockius (Morgan) to defend it in a Florida lawsuit.

Pursuant to a letter of understanding * * * Belcher Oil was to pay for costs incurred on its behalf, including fees for accountants. [Morgan] hired plaintiff, the accounting firm of Freeman & Mills, Incorporated, to provide a financial analysis and litigation support for Belcher Oil in the Florida lawsuit.

* * * In April 1988, [Neil] Bowman [Belcher Oil's general counsel] became dissatisfied with Morgan's efforts and the lawyers were discharged. Bowman asked Morgan for a summary of the work performed by Freeman & Mills and, at the same time, directed [Morgan] to have Freeman & Mills stop their work for Belcher Oil. * * * Freeman & Mills's final statement was for $70,042.50 in fees, plus $7,495.63 for costs, a total of $77,538.13.

Freeman & Mills billed Morgan, but no payment was forthcoming. Freeman & Mills then billed Belcher Oil directly and, for about a year, sent monthly statements and regularly called Bowman about the bill, but no payment was forthcoming. In August 1989, [Morgan] finally told Freeman & Mills that Belcher Oil refused to pay their bill. Freeman & Mills then wrote to Bowman asking that the matter be resolved. In September 1989, Bowman responded, complaining that Belcher Oil had not been consulted about the extent of Freeman & Mills's services and suggesting Freeman & Mills should look to Morgan for payment of whatever amounts were claimed due.

Ultimately, Freeman & Mills filed this action against Belcher Oil, alleging * * * causes of action for breach of contract, "bad faith denial of contract," and quantum meruit. Belcher Oil answered and the case was presented to a jury in a bifurcated trial, with punitive damages reserved for the second phase. * * *

The jury returned its first phase verdict. On Freeman & Mills's breach of contract claim, the jury found [that Belcher Oil had breached the contract], and that the amount of damages suffered by Freeman & Mills was $25,000. The jury also [found that] Belcher Oil had denied the existence of the contract and had acted with oppression, fraud, or malice. Thereafter, the jury returned its verdict awarding $477,538.13 in punitive damages and judgment was entered consistent with the jury's verdicts.

[The trial court granted a motion to correct the jury's verdict to award] Freeman & Mills $131,614.93 in compensatory damages (the $25,000 actually awarded by the jury, plus the $77,538.13 included in the punitive damage award, plus $29,076.80 for prejudgment interest), and $400,000 * * * in punitive damages.

Belcher Oil appealed from the "corrected" judgment. * * *

II. THE *SEAMAN'S* DECISION

The tort of bad faith "denial of contract" was established in a per curiam opinion in Seaman's [Direct Buying Service v. Standard Oil Co., 36 Cal.3d 752 (1984)]. These were the facts before the court in that case: In 1971, Seaman's Direct Buying Service, a small marine fueling station in

Eureka, wanted to expand its operation by developing a marine fuel dealership in conjunction with a new marina under development by the City of Eureka. When Seaman's approached the city about a long term lease of a large parcel of land in the marina, the city required Seaman's to obtain a binding commitment from an oil supplier. To that end, Seaman's negotiated with several companies and, by 1972, reached a tentative agreement with Standard Oil.

Both Seaman's and Standard Oil signed a letter of intent setting forth the basic terms of their arrangement but that letter was subject to government approval of the contract, continued approval of Seaman's credit status, and future agreement on specific arrangements. Seaman's showed the letter to the city and, shortly thereafter, signed a 40–year lease with the city.

Shortly thereafter, an oil shortage dramatically reduced the available supplies of oil and, in November 1973, Standard Oil told Seaman's that new federal regulations requiring allocation of petroleum products to those that had been customers since 1972 precluded its execution of a new dealership agreement. In response, Seaman's obtained an exemption from the appropriate federal agency. Standard Oil appealed and persuaded the agency to reverse the order, but Seaman's eventually had the exemption reinstated contingent on a court determination that a valid contract existed between the parties.

Seaman's then asked Standard Oil to stipulate to the existence of a contract, stating that a refusal would force it to discontinue operations. Standard Oil's representative refused the request, telling Seaman's, "See you in court." Seaman's business collapsed and it sued Standard Oil for damages on four theories—breach of contract, fraud, breach of the implied covenant of good faith and fair dealing, and interference with Seaman's contractual relationship with the City.

The case was tried to a jury, which returned its verdicts in favor of Seaman's on all theories except fraud, awarding compensatory and punitive damages. Standard Oil appealed. We considered "whether, and under what circumstances, a breach of the implied covenant of good faith and fair dealing in a commercial contract may give rise to an action in tort." For purposes of completeness, we quote from *Seaman's* at some length:

"It is well settled that, in California, the law implies in every contract a covenant of good faith and fair dealing. Broadly stated, that covenant requires that neither party do anything which will deprive the other of the benefits of the agreement. California courts have recognized the existence of this covenant, and enforced it, in cases involving a wide variety of contracts...." In the seminal cases of Comunale v. Traders & General Ins. Co. [(1958)] 50 Cal.2d 654, and Crisci v. Security Ins. Co. [(1967)] 66 Cal.2d 425, this court held that a breach of the covenant of good faith and fair dealing by an insurance carrier may give rise to a cause of action in tort as well as in contract.

"While the proposition that the law implies a covenant of good faith and fair dealing in all contracts is well established, the proposition advanced by Seaman's—that breach of the covenant always gives rise to an action in tort—is not so clear. In holding that a tort action is available for breach of the covenant in an insurance contract, we have emphasized the 'special relationship' between insurer and insured, characterized by elements of public interest, adhesion, and fiduciary responsibility. No doubt there are other relationships with similar characteristics and deserving of similar legal treatment.

"When we move from such special relationships to consideration of the tort remedy in the context of the ordinary commercial contract, we move into largely uncharted and potentially dangerous waters. Here, parties of roughly equal bargaining power are free to shape the contours of their agreement and to include provisions for attorney fees and liquidated damages in the event of breach. They may not be permitted to disclaim the covenant of good faith but they are free, within reasonable limits at least, to agree upon the standards by which application of the covenant is to be measured. In such contracts, it may be difficult to distinguish between breach of the covenant and breach of contract, and there is the risk that interjecting tort remedies will intrude upon the expectations of the parties. This is not to say that tort remedies have no place in such a commercial context, but that it is wise to proceed with caution in determining their scope and application.

"For the purposes of this case it is unnecessary to decide the broad question which Seaman's poses. Indeed, it is not even necessary to predicate liability on a breach of the implied covenant. It is sufficient to recognize that a party to a contract may incur tort remedies when, in addition to breaching the contract, it seeks to shield itself from liability by denying, in bad faith and without probable cause, that the contract exists.

"It has been held that a party to a contract may be subject to tort liability, including punitive damages, if he coerces the other party to pay more than is due under the contract terms through the threat of a lawsuit, made 'without probable cause and with no belief in the existence of the cause of action.' There is little difference, in principle, between a contracting party obtaining excess payment in such manner, and a contracting party seeking to avoid all liability on a meritorious contract claim by adopting a 'stonewall' position ('see you in court') without probable cause and with no belief in the existence of a defense. Such conduct goes beyond the mere breach of contract. It offends accepted notions of business ethics. Acceptance of tort remedies in such a situation is not likely to intrude upon the bargaining relationship or upset reasonable expectations of the contracting parties."

Seaman's concluded that, because a good faith denial of the existence of a binding contract is not a tort, the trial court's failure to instruct the jury on the requirement of bad faith was error, and that error was prejudicial.

III. STARE DECISIS

* * * As we explain below, developments occurring subsequent to the *Seaman's* decision convince us that it was incorrectly decided, that it has generated unnecessary confusion, costly litigation, and inequitable results, and that it will continue to produce such effects unless and until we overrule it.

IV. SUBSEQUENT DEVELOPMENTS

A. California Supreme Court Decisions—Subsequent opinions of this court indicate a continuing reluctance, originally reflected in *Seaman's* itself, to authorize tort recovery for noninsurance contract breaches.

In Foley v. Interactive Data Corp. (1988) 47 Cal.3d 654, we * * * refused to afford such remedies for the essentially contractual claim of breach of the implied covenant arising in [the employment] context.

In reaching our conclusion in *Foley,* we relied in part on certain basic principles relevant to contract law, including the need for "predictability about the cost of contractual relationships," and the purpose of contract damages to compensate the injured party rather than punish the breaching party. Focusing on the implied covenant, we observed that, with the exception of insurance contracts, "[b]ecause the covenant is a contract term, ... compensation for its breach has almost always been limited to contract rather than tort remedies." * * *

Most recently, in Applied Equipment Corp. v. Litton Saudi Arabia Ltd. (1994) 7 Cal.4th 503, we held that a contracting party may not be held liable in tort for conspiring with another to interfere with his own contract. * * * We noted that limiting contract breach damages to those within the reasonably foreseeable contemplation of the parties when the contract was formed "serves to encourage contractual relations and commercial activity by enabling parties to estimate in advance the financial risks of their enterprise."

Our decisions in *Foley* * * * and *Applied Equipment* each contain language that strongly suggests courts should limit tort recovery in contract breach situations to the insurance area, at least in the absence of violation of an independent duty arising from principles of tort law other than denial of the existence of, or liability under, the breached contract. * * *

B. Court of Appeal Decisions

* * * Many of the pertinent Court of Appeal decisions recognize compelling policy reasons supporting the preclusion of tort remedies for contractual breaches outside the insurance context. * * * For example, * * * [in] Harris [v. Atlantic Richfield Co. (1993) 14 Cal.App.4th 70], the Court of Appeal denied a tort recovery for bad faith contract breach in violation of public policy. The court elaborated on the applicable policy considerations as follows: "The traditional goal of contract remedies is compensation of the promisee for the loss resulting from the breach, not compulsion of the promisor to perform his promises. Therefore, 'willful' breaches have not been distinguished from other breaches. The restrictions on contract remedies serve purposes not found in tort law. They protect the parties' freedom to bargain over special risks and they promote contract formation by limiting liability to the value of the promise. This encourages efficient breaches, resulting in increased production of goods and services at lower cost to society. * * *

C. *Criticism by Courts of Other Jurisdictions*

We decided *Seaman's* in 1984. Since then, courts of other jurisdictions have either criticized or declined to follow our *Seaman's* analysis. Of all the states, only Montana has recognized the tort of bad faith in typical arm's length commercial contracts, and recently even that state has qualified the tort by requiring a showing of a special relationship between the contracting parties. (See Story v. Bozeman (Mont.1990) 791 P.2d 767, 776.).

Ninth Circuit Judge Kozinski expressed his candid criticism of *Seaman's* in a concurring opinion in Oki America, Inc. v. Microtech Intern., Inc. (9th Cir.1989) 872 F.2d 312, 314–317. Among other criticism, Judge Kozinski found the *Seaman's* holding unduly imprecise and confusing. As he stated, "It is impossible to draw a principled distinction between a tortious denial of a contract's existence and a permissible denial of liability under the terms of the contract. The test ... seems to be whether the conduct 'offends accepted notions of business ethics.' This gives judges license to rely on their gut feelings in distinguishing between a squabble and a tort. As a result, both the commercial world and the courts are needlessly burdened...."

Judge Kozinski also mentioned the substantial costs associated with *Seaman's* litigation, and the resulting interference with contractual relationships. "Perhaps most troubling, the willingness of courts to subordinate voluntary contractual arrangements to their own sense of public policy and proper business decorum deprives individuals of an important measure of freedom. The right to enter into contracts—to adjust one's legal relationships by mutual agreement is too easily smothered by government officers eager to tell us what's best for us." * * *

V. *Seaman's* Should be Overruled

As previously indicated, the *Seaman's* decision has generated uniform confusion and uncertainty regarding its scope and application, and widespread doubt about the necessity or desirability of its holding. * * *

For all the foregoing reasons, we conclude that *Seaman's* should be overruled. We emphasize that nothing in this opinion should be read as affecting the existing precedent governing enforcement of the implied covenant in insurance cases. Further, nothing we say here would prevent the Legislature from creating additional civil remedies for noninsurance contract breach, including such measures as providing litigation costs and attorney fees in certain aggravated cases, or assessing increased compensatory damages covering lost profits and other losses attributable to the breach, as well as restoration of the *Seaman's* holding if the Legislature deems that course appropriate

Concurring and Dissenting Opinion by MOSK, J.:

I concur in the judgment. I disagree, however, with the majority's conclusion that *Seaman's Direct Buying Service, Inc. v. Standard Oil Co.* (1984) 36 Cal.3d 752, was wrongly decided. * * *

I will discuss below the various circumstances under which courts have found or may find a breach of contract to be tortious—circumstances broader than may be suggested by the majority's holding. As I will explain, a tortious breach of contract outside the insurance context may be found when (1) the breach is accompanied by a traditional common law tort, such as fraud or conversion; (2) the means used to breach the contract are tortious, involving deceit or undue coercion; or (3) one party intentionally breaches the contract intending or knowing that such a breach will cause severe, unmitigatable harm in the form of mental anguish, personal hardship, or substantial consequential damages. I will then explain why in my view *Seaman's* was correctly decided. Finally, I will explain why *Seaman's* is distinguishable from the present case.

I.

The notion that a breach of contract might be tortious causes conceptual difficulty because of the fundamental difference between the objectives of contract and tort law. "[Whereas] [c]ontract actions are created to protect the interest in having promises performed," "[t]ort actions are created to protect the interest in freedom from various kinds of harm. The duties of conduct which give rise to them are imposed by law, and are based primarily on social policy, not necessarily based upon the will or intention of the parties...."

This difference in purpose has its greatest practical significance in the differing types of damages available under the two bodies of law. "Contract damages are generally limited to those within the contemplation of the parties when the contract was entered into or at least reasonably foreseeable by them at that time; consequential damages beyond the expectations of the parties are not recoverable." Damages for emotional distress and mental suffering, as well as punitive damages, are also generally not recoverable. "This limitation on available damages serves to encourage contractual relations and commercial activity by enabling parties to estimate in advance the financial risks of their enterprise." "In contrast, tort damages are awarded to compensate the victim for injury suffered. For the breach of an obligation not arising from contract, the measure of damages ... is the amount which will compensate for all the detriment proximately caused thereby, whether it could have been anticipated or not. (Civ.Code § 3333.)" Both emotional distress damages and punitive damages are, under the proper circumstances, available to the tort victim.

Tort and contract law also differ in the moral significance that each places on intentional injury. Whereas an intentional tort is seen as reprehensible—the deliberate or reckless harming of another—the intentional breach of contract has come to be viewed as a morally neutral act, as exemplified in Justice Holmes's remark that "[t]he duty to keep a contract at common law means a prediction that you must pay damages if you do not keep it—and nothing else." (Holmes, The Path of the Law (1897) 10 Harv.L.Rev. 457, 462.) This amoral view is supported by the economic insight that in intentional breach of contract may create a net benefit to society. The efficient breach of contract occurs when gain to the breach party exceeds the loss to the party suffering the breach, allowing the movement of resources to their more optimal use. (See Posner, Economic Analysis of Law (1986) 107–108.) * * *

But while the purposes behind contract and tort law are distinct, the boundary line between the two areas of the law is neither clear not fixed. * * *. The courts "have extended the tort liability for misfeasance to virtually every type of contract where defective performance may injure the promisee. An attorney or abstractor examining a title, a physician treating a patient, a surveyor, an agent collecting a note or lending money or settling a claim, or a liability insurer defending a suit, all have been held liable in tort for their negligence." * * *

Nor are the rules that determine whether the action will sound in tort or contract, or both, clear cut. When the breach of contract also involves physical injury to the promisee, or the destruction of tangible property, as opposed to damage to purely economic interests, then the action will generally sound in tort. Thus, a manufacturer that sells defective automobiles may be liable to an automobile dealer in contract for delivery of nonconforming goods, but will be liable in tort if one of the nonconforming automobiles leads to an accident resulting in physical injury. * * *

It is also true that public policy does not always favor a limitation on damages for intentional breaches of contract. The notion that society gains from an efficient breach must be qualified by the recognition that many intentional breaches are not efficient. As Judge Posner explained in Patton [v. Mid–Continent Systems, Inc. (7th Cir.1988) 841 F.2d 742, 751]: "Not all breaches of contract are involuntary or otherwise efficient. Some are opportunistic; the promisor wants the benefit of the bargain without bearing the agreed-upon costs, and exploits the inadequacies of purely compensatory remedies (the major inadequacies being that pre-and post-judgment interest rates are frequently below market levels when the risk of nonpayment is taken into account and that the winning party cannot recover ... attorney's fees)." Commentators have also pointed to other "inadequacies of purely compensatory remedies" that encourage inefficient breaches (i.e. breaches that result in greater losses to the promisee than gains for the promisor): the lack of emotional distress damages, even when such damages are the probable result of the breach, and the restriction of consequential damages to those in the contemplation of the parties at the time the contract was formed.

In addition to fully compensating contract plaintiffs and discouraging inefficient breaches, the imposition of tort remedies for certain intentional breaches of contract serves to punish and deter business practices that constitute distinct social wrongs independent of the breach. For example, we permit the plaintiff to recover exemplary damages in cases in which the breached contract was induced through promissory fraud, even though the plaintiff has incurred the same loss whether the contract was fraudulently induced or not. Our determination to allow the plaintiff to sue for fraud and to potentially recover exemplary damages is not justified by the plaintiffs [sic] greater loss, but by the fact that the breach of a fraudulently induced contract is a significantly greater wrong, from society's standpoint, than an ordinary breach. * * *

As the above illustrate, the rationale for limiting actions for intentional breaches of contract to contract remedies—that such limitation promotes commercial stability and predictability and hence advances commerce—is not invariably a compelling one. Breaches accompanied by deception or infliction of intentional harm may be so disruptive of commerce and so reprehensible in themselves that the value of deterring such actions through the tort system outweighs the marginal loss in the predictability of damages that may result. But in imposing tort duties to deter intentionally harmful acts among contracting parties, courts must be cautious not to fashion remedies which overdeter the illegitimate and as a result chill legitimate activities. Thus, courts should be careful to apply tort remedies only when the conduct in question is so clear in its deviation from socially useful business practices that the effect of enforcing such tort duties will be, as in the case of fraud, to aid rather than discourage commerce.

[N]ot all tortious breaches of contract arise from conventional torts. Numerous courts have recognized types of intentionally tortious activity that occur exclusively or distinctively within the context of a contractual relationship. The most familiar type of tortious breach of contract in this state is that of the insurer, whose unreasonable failure to settle or resolve a claim has been held to violate the covenant of good faith and fair dealing. Tort liability is imposed primarily because of the distinctive characteristics of the insurance contract: the fiduciary nature of the relationship, the fact that the insurer offers a type of quasi-public service that provides financial security and peace of mind, and the fact that the insurance contract is generally one of adhesion. In these cases, the special relationship between insurer and insured supports the elevation of the covenant of good faith and fair dealing, a covenant implied by law in every contract and generally used as an aid to contract interpretation, into a tort duty.

Because the good faith covenant is so broad and all-pervasive, this court and others have been reluctant to expand recognition of the action for tortious breach of the covenant beyond the insurance context. Unfortunately, the preoccupation of California courts with limiting the potentially enormous scope of this tort has diverted attention away from the useful task of identifying specific practices employed by contracting parties that merit the imposition of tort remedies. Other jurisdictions not so preoccupied have made greater progress in developing a common law of tortious breach of contract. While the cases are not easily amenable to classification, they appear to fit into two broad categories.

The first category focuses on tortious means used by one contracting party to coerce or deceive another party into foregoing its contractual rights. For example, in Advanced Medical v. Arden Medical Systems (3d Cir.1992) 955 F.2d 188, Advanced Medical, Inc. (Advanced), a distributor of medical products, entered into an agreement with a manufacturer of a high-technology blood analysis device, whereby the former was designated as the latter's exclusive distributor for the mid-Atlantic region. The manufacturing company was eventually acquired by Johnson & Johnson, which disapproved of the exclusive distributorship. Instead of merely breaching the agreement, Johnson & Johnson used a variety of questionable tactics to "drive Advanced out of the contract," including marketing competing products not made available to Advanced, and withholding its support services. The court, applying Pennsylvania law, held that in addition to a breach of contract, there was sufficient evidence to submit the question of punitive damages to a jury on a theory of Johnson & Johnson's "tortious interference" with its own contract. * * *

A second type of tortious intentional breach has been found when the consequences of the breach are especially injurious to the party suffering the breach, and the breaching party intentionally or knowingly inflicts such injury. Cases of this type have generally occurred outside the commercial context, involving manifestly unequal contracting parties and contracts concerning matters of vital personal significance, in which great mental anguish or personal hardship are the probable result of the breach. In these cases, courts have permitted substantial awards of emotional distress damages and/or punitive damages, both as a means of providing extra sanctions for a defendant engaging in intentionally injurious activities against vulnerable parties, and as a way of fully compensating plaintiffs for types of injury that are neither readily amendable to mitigation nor generally recoverable as contract damages. For example, in K Mart Corp. v. Ponsock (Nev.1987) 732 P.2d 1364, 1370, disapproved on other grounds by Ingersoll–Rand Co. v. McClendon (1990) 498 U.S. 133, 137, the Nevada Supreme Court allowed a $50,000 award of punitive damages to stand when an employer discharged a long-term employee on a fabricated charge for the purpose of defeating the latter's contractual entitlement to retirement benefits. * * *

The principle that certain contractual interests of vulnerable parties deserve greater protection than ordinary contract damages would otherwise provide has led our Legislature to authorize special sanctions for various types of intentional breaches. For example, one who is the victim of an intentional breach of warranty of consumer goods may recover twice the amount of actual damages (Civ.Code, § 1794, subd. (c)) and treble damages may be awarded to a retail seller who is injured by "willful or repeated" warranty violations (id., § 1794.1, subd. (a)). Labor Code section 206 provides for treble damages for the willful failure to pay wages after the Labor Commissioner determines the wages are owing. * * *

II.

* * * [Turning to the *Seaman's* case,] there are some commercial cases in which the harm intentionally inflicted on an enterprise cannot be mitigated, and in which ordinary contract damages are insufficient compensation. *Seaman's* is such a case. In *Seaman's*, because of the unusual combination of market forces and government regulation set in motion by the 1973 oil embargo, Standard's conduct had a significance beyond the ordinary breach: its practical effect was to shut Seaman's out of the oil market entirely, forcing it out of business. In other words, Standard intentionally breached its contract with Seaman's with the knowledge that the breach would result in Seaman's demise. Having thus breached its contract with blithe disregard for the severe and, under these rare circumstances, unmitigatable injury it caused Seaman's, Standard was justly subject to tort damages.

* * * A breach should not be considered tortious if the court determines that it was justified by avoidance of some substantial, unforeseen cost on the part of the breaching party, even if such cost does not excuse that party's nonperformance. Nor should a tortious breach under these circumstances be recognized if it is clear that the party suffering the harm voluntarily accepted that risk under the contract. But the intentional or knowing infliction of severe consequential damages on a business enterprise through the unjustified, bad faith breach of a contract is reprehensible and costly both for the party suffering the breach and for society as a whole, and is therefore appropriately sanctioned through the tort system.

III.

The present case, on the other hand, is essentially a billing dispute between two commercial entities. Belcher Oil claimed, apparently in bad faith and without probable cause, that it had no contractual agreement with Freeman & Mills. That is, Belcher Oil not only intentionally breached its contract, but then asserted a bad faith defense to its liability. As explained above, the solution which the Legislature has devised for this kind of transgression is the awarding of the other party's attorney fees, and this is precisely what occurred—Freeman & Mills was awarded $212,891 in attorney fees pursuant to Code of Civil Procedure sections 128.5 and 2033, subdivision (c). To permit the award of punitive damages in addition to this sum would upset the legislative balance established in the litigation sanctions statutes and make tortious actions—intentional breach of contract and the assertion of a bad faith defense—which we have consistently held not to be tortious.

On this basis, I concur in the majority's disposition in favor of Belcher Oil on the bad faith denial of contract cause of action.* * *

NOTES

1. The exchange between the majority and Justice Mosk thoroughly reviews the differences between tort and contract damages, and suggests some explanations for them. Which of the justifications do you find most persuasive? For an alternative justification, see Steven Thel & Peter Siegelman, Wilfulness vs. Expectation: A Promisor–Based Defense of Wilful Breach Doctrine, 107 U.Mich.L.Rev. ___ (2009).

2. As Justice Mosk points out, a basic difference between tort and contract remedies is that the fact that contract damages are to the benefit of the bargain may in fact encourage breach under some circumstances. Does it make sense to have a remedy that effectively encourages breach of contract?

Consider Judge Posner's view:

[I]n some cases a party is tempted to break his contract simply because his profit from breach would exceed his profit from completing performance. He will do so if the profit would also exceed the expected profit to the other party from completion of the contract, and hence the damages from breach. So in this case awarding damages will not deter a breach of contract. It should not. It is an efficient breach. Suppose I sign a contract to deliver 100,000 custom-ground widgets at 10¢ apiece to A for use in his boiler factory. After I have delivered 10,000, B comes to me, explains that he desperately needs 25,000 custom-ground widgets at once since otherwise he will be forced to close his pianola factory at great cost, and offers me 15¢ apiece for them. I sell him the widgets and as a result do not complete timely delivery to A, causing him to lose $1,000 in profits. Having obtained an additional profit of $1,250 on the sale to B, I am better off even after reimbursing A for his loss, and B is also better off. The breach is therefore Pareto superior. True, had I refused to sell to B he could have gone to A and negotiated an assignment to him of part of A's contract with me. But this would have introduced an additional step, with additional transaction costs—and high ones, because it would be a bilateral-monopoly negotiation.

Could not the danger of deterring efficient breaches of contract be eliminated simply by redefining the legal concept of breach of contract so that only inefficient terminations counted as breaches? No. Remember that an important function of contracts is to assign risks to superior risk bearers. If the risk materializes, the party to whom it was assigned must pay. It is no more relevant that he could not have prevented the risk from occurring at a reasonable, perhaps at any, cost than that an insurance company could not have prevented the fire that destroyed the building it insured. The breach of contract corresponds to the occurrence of the event that is insured against.

Let us consider the case in which the expectation loss—that is, the loss of the expected profit of the contract—exceeds the reliance loss, that is, the expense that the victim of the breach incurred in performing his side of the contract. Seller agrees to sell a machine for $100,000, delivery to be made in six months. The day after the contract is signed he defaults, realizing that he would lose $5,000 at the contract price. The buyer's reliance loss—the costs he has irretrievably incurred as a result of the contract—is zero, but it would cost him, let's assume, $112,000 to obtain a substitute machine. So $12,000 is his expectation loss. Why should he be allowed to insist on a measure of damages that gives him more (by $12,000) than he has actually lost? Because awarding the reliance loss would encourage inefficient breaches. The net gain to the buyer from contractual performance, $12,000, would have exceeded by $7,000 the net loss to the seller, so if we make the buyer's net expected gain the cost of breach to the seller we discourage an inefficient breach.

Richard A. Posner, Economic Analysis of Law (7th ed.2007) § 4.10 at pp. 120–121. For a basic treatment of economic analysis, see A. Mitchell Polinsky, An Introduction to Law and Economics (4th ed.2009).

Of course, not all breaches are efficient. Some breaches are opportunistic; that is to say, some parties breach because they can get away with it. The potential for opportunistic breach arises because contract damage rules sometimes undercompensate the victim of a breach. Then, a rational party might conclude that the damages it will actually have to pay are less than the cost of performance. For an argument that punitive damages should be available in contract actions to forestall opportunistic breach, see William S. Dodge, The Case for Punitive Damages in Contracts, 48 Duke L.J. 629 (1999); but see Nicholas J. Johnson, The Boundaries of Extracompensatory Relief for Abusive Breach of Contract, 33 Conn.L.Rev. 181 (2000) (allowing punitive damages would make the cost of contract-making too high, creating disincentives to trade). Are either *Seaman's* or *Belcher Oil* examples of efficient breaches? Opportunistic breaches?

Although economic explanations of the contract remedy have gained wide acceptance, see Restatement (Second) of Contracts § 344, they are not without their detractors. See, e.g., Marco J. Jimenez, The Value of a Promise: A Utilitarian Approach to Contract Law Remedies, 56 U.C.L.A.L.Rev. 59 (2008); Ian R. Macneil, Efficient Breach of Contract: Circles in the Sky, 68 Va.L.Rev. 947 (1982).

3. For some years, tort law and tort remedies had been expanding into areas formerly dominated by contract. The majority's opinion in *Freeman & Mills* was no doubt intended to signal the end of that expansion. Interestingly, Canadian courts may be headed in the opposite direction. In Whiten v. Pilot Insurance Co., [2002] 209 D.L.R. (4th) 257 (S.C.C.), the Supreme Court of Canada upheld a punitive damage award against an insurer who attempted to gain a favorable settlement by refusing to pay off on a fire insurance policy. In a companion case, the court indicated that punitive damages would not be recoverable if compensatory damages were adequate, even if the breach was deliberate and fraudulent. Sylvan Lake Golf & Tennis Club, Ltd. v. Performance Industries, Ltd., [2002] 209 D.L.R. (4th) 318 (S.C.C.) ("Punitive damages are rational only if compensatory damages do not adequately achieve the

objectives of retribution, deterrence, and denunciation, which was not the case here. This case involved a commercial relationship between businessmen who were equals. Although the individual defendant's misconduct was planned and deliberate and lasted for four and one-half years, the plaintiff obtained full compensation plus costs on a solicitor and client basis, which had a punitive effect on the individual defendant."). See John D. McCamus, Prometheus Bound or Loose Cannon? Punitive Damages for Pure Breach of Contract in Canada, 41 San Diego L.Rev. 1491 (2004).

4. The two Canadian cases fall into a common pattern, refusing to allow punitive damages in commercial contracts but providing for them in the insurance context. Note that the *Freeman & Mills* majority does not question the soundness of the cases holding that a breach of the covenant of good faith and fair dealing by an insurer gives rise to tort liability and tort damages. Many jurisdictions recognize that bad faith breach can give rise to tort liability in insurance cases. John Sebert, Punitive and Nonpecuniary Damages in Actions Based upon Contract: Toward Achieving the Objective of Full Compensation, 33 U.C.L.A.L.Rev. 1565, 1614 n.178 (1986) (15 jurisdictions).

If compelling performance, other than by compensating the promisee for her lost expectation, is a bad idea, why should insurance contracts be treated any differently? Consider:

> What are the features of the insurance contract which distinguish it from the ordinary commercial contract? * * * An obvious difference * * * is a party's motivation for entering the contract. In insurance contracts, a party does not seek "to obtain a commercial advantage but to protect [him or herself] against the risk of accidental losses * * *. Among considerations in purchasing liability insurance, as insurers are well aware, is the peace of mind and security it will provide in the event of an accidental loss * * *".
>
> Another oft repeated difference is that there exists a "great disparity in the economic situations and bargaining abilities of the insurer and the insured." Thus, the normal protections provided a party by the open marketplace are absent in these contracts.
>
> A further very important characteristic of the insurance contract is that ordinary contract damages are inadequate to protect the insured's rights. In the first place, they offer no motivation whatsoever for the insurer *not* to breach. If the only damages an insurer will have to pay upon a judgment of breach are the amounts that it would have owed under the policy plus interest, it has every interest in retaining the money, earning the higher rates of interest on the outside market, and hoping eventually to force the insured into a settlement for less than the policy amount. * * *
>
> Secondly, contract damages do not adequately protect the insured's interest. Unlike a party to an ordinary commercial contract who can turn to the marketplace to replace necessary "widgets" not delivered by a breaching seller, an insured has nowhere to turn to replace monthly disability payments. Money damages paid pursuant to a judgment years after the insurer has initially reneged on payment do not remedy the

harm suffered by the insured, namely the immediate inability to support oneself and its attendant horrors.

Wallis v. Superior Court, 160 Cal.App.3d 1109, 1117–18, 207 Cal.Rptr. 123, 128–29 (1984). Would Judge Posner agree that insurance contracts should be treated differently? See Note 2 at p. 596.

5. The Canadian cases focus on whether compensatory damages adequately protect the nonbreaching party's interests. If the problem is that contract damages undercompensate, are punitive damages the right solution? As an alternative, why not recognize that the insurer who breaches in bad faith violates two contractual obligations—the obligation to perform the contract, and the obligation to act in good faith—and award separate compensatory damages for the second breach? Ernest J. Weinrib, Punishment and Disgorgement as Contract Remedies, 78 Chi.-Kent L.Rev. 55, 97–98 (2003).

What sorts of damages would be appropriate? In Giampapa v. American Family Insurance Co., 64 P.3d 230 (Colo.2003), the Colorado Supreme Court held that damages for nonpecuniary loss, including damages for emotional distress and impaired quality of life, are recoverable elements of contract damages when an insurance company willfully and wantonly breaches. Because the insured's peace of mind is the focus of the contract, such damages are foreseeable. See also Michael Traynor, Bad Faith Breach of a Commercial Contract: A Comment on the Seaman's Case, 8 Bus.L.News (1984) (arguing for an expanded definition of foreseeability to forestall bad faith); C. Delos Putz & Nona Klippen, Commercial Bad Faith: Attorney Fees—Not Tort Liability—Is the Remedy for Stonewalling, 21 U.S.F.L.Rev. 419 (1987). These issues are thoroughly reviewed in Symposium, The Law of Bad Faith in Contract and Insurance, 72 Tex.L.Rev. 1203 (1994).

6. Justice Mosk notes in *Freeman & Mills* that punitive damages can be recovered when "the breach is accompanied by a traditional common law tort, such as fraud or conversion." Almost all jurisdictions recognize that if the plaintiff can plead an independent tort for which punitive damages are recoverable in addition to the breach of contract, punitive damages may be recovered. See Restatement (Second) of Contracts § 355; Ernest J. Weinrib, Punishment and Disgorgement as Contract Remedies, 78 Chi.-Kent L.Rev. 55 (2003). The tort of promissory fraud is particularly powerful, at least if the court is willing to infer from the defendant's nonperformance that he entered the contract without the intent ever to perform. See Rosener v. Sears, Roebuck & Co., 110 Cal.App.3d 740, 168 Cal.Rptr. 237 (1980). One or two courts have gone farther, finding tort liability "where elements of tort mingle with the breach," so long as an award of punitive damages would serve the public interest. Hibschman Pontiac, Inc. v. Batchelor, 266 Ind. 310, 362 N.E.2d 845 (1977).

7. As Justice Mosk notes, another way in which tort law has expanded into contractual relationships is by imposing tort liability when a party to a contract behaves negligently. The next case suggests that there, too, contract law may now be regaining lost ground.

EVRA CORP. v. SWISS BANK CORP.
United States Court of Appeals, Seventh Circuit, 1982
673 F.2d 951, cert. denied, 459 U.S. 1017, 103 S.Ct. 377, 74 L.Ed.2d 511

POSNER, CIRCUIT JUDGE.

The question—one of first impression—in this diversity case is the extent of a bank's liability for failure to make a transfer of funds when requested by wire to do so. The essential facts are undisputed. In 1972 Hyman–Michaels Company, a large Chicago dealer in scrap metal, entered into a two-year contract to supply steel scrap to a Brazilian corporation. Hyman–Michaels chartered a ship, the Pandora, to carry the scrap to Brazil. The charter was for one year, with an option to extend the charter for a second year; specified a fixed daily rate of pay for the hire of the ship during both the initial and the option period, payable semi-monthly "in advance"; and provided that if payment was not made on time the Pandora's owner could cancel the charter. Payment was to be made by deposit to the owner's account in the Banque de Paris et des Pays–Bas (Suisse) in Geneva, Switzerland.

The usual method by which Hyman–Michaels, in Chicago, got the payments to the Banque de Paris in Geneva was to request the Continental Illinois National Bank and Trust Company of Chicago, where it had an account, to make a wire transfer of funds. Continental would debit Hyman–Michaels' account by the amount of the payment and then send a telex to its London office for retransmission to its correspondent bank in Geneva—Swiss Bank Corporation—asking Swiss Bank to deposit this amount in the Banque de Paris account of the Pandora's owner. The transaction was completed by the crediting of Swiss Bank's account at Continental by the same amount.

When Hyman–Michaels chartered the Pandora in June 1972, market charter rates were very low, and it was these rates that were fixed in the charter for its entire term-two years if Hyman–Michaels exercised its option. Shortly after the agreement was signed, however, charter rates began to climb and by October 1972 they were much higher than they had been in June. The Pandora's owners were eager to get out of the charter if they could. At the end of October they thought they had found a way, for the payment that was due in the Banque de Paris on October 26 had not arrived by October 30, and on that day the Pandora's owner notified Hyman–Michaels that it was canceling the charter because of the breach of the payment term. Hyman–Michaels had mailed a check for the October 26 installment to the Banque de Paris rather than use the wire-transfer method of payment. It had done this in order to have the use of its money for the period that it would take the check to clear, about two weeks. But the check had not been mailed in Chicago until October 25 and of course did not reach Geneva on the twenty-sixth.

When Hyman–Michaels received notification that the charter was being canceled it immediately wired payment to the Banque de Paris, but the Pandora's owner refused to accept it and insisted that the charter was indeed canceled. The matter was referred to arbitration in accordance with the charter. On December 5, 1972, the arbitration panel ruled in favor of Hyman–Michaels. The panel noted that previous arbitration panels had "shown varying degrees of latitude to Charterers":

> "In all cases, a pattern of obligation on Owners' part to protest, complain, or warn of intended withdrawal was expressed as an essential prerequisite to withdrawal, in spite of the clear wording of the operative clause. No such advance notice was given by Owners of M/V Pandora."

One of the three members of the panel dissented; he thought the Pandora's owner was entitled to cancel.

Hyman–Michaels went back to making the charter payments by wire transfer. On the morning of April 25, 1973, it telephoned Continental Bank and requested it to transfer $27,000 to the Banque de Paris account of the Pandora's owner in payment for the charter hire period from April 27 to May 11, 1973. Since the charter provided for payment "in advance," this payment arguably was due by the close of business on April 26. The requested telex went out to Continental's London office on the afternoon of April 25, which was nighttime in England. Early the next morning a telex operator in Continental's London office dialed, as Continental's Chicago office had instructed him to do, Swiss Bank's general telex number, which rings in the bank's cable department. But that number was busy, and after trying unsuccessfully for an hour to engage it the Continental telex operator dialed another number, that of a machine in Swiss Bank's foreign exchange department which he had used in the past when the general number was engaged. We know this machine received the telexed message because it signaled the sending machine at both the beginning and end of the transmission that the telex was being received. Yet Swiss Bank failed to comply with the payment order, and no transfer of funds was made to the account of the Pandora's owner in the Banque de Paris.

No one knows exactly what went wrong. One possibility is that the receiving telex machine had simply run out of paper, in which event it would not print the message although it had received it. Another is that whoever took the message out of the machine after it was printed failed to deliver it to the banking department. Unlike the machine in the cable department that the Continental telex operator had originally tried to reach, the machines in the foreign exchange department were operated by junior foreign exchange dealers rather than by professional telex operators, although Swiss Bank knew that messages intended for other departments were sometimes diverted to the telex machines in the foreign exchange department.

At 8:30 a.m. the next day, April 27, Hyman–Michaels in Chicago received a telex from the Pandora's owner stating that the charter was canceled because payment for the April 27–May 11 charter period had not been made. Hyman–Michaels called over to Continental and told them to keep trying to effect payment through Swiss Bank even if the Pandora's owner rejected it. This instruction was confirmed in a letter to Continental dated April 28, in which Hyman–Michaels stated: "please instruct your London branch to advise their correspondents to persist in attempting to make this payment. This should be done even in the face of a rejection on the part of Banque de Paris to receive this payment. It is paramount that in order to strengthen our position in an arbitration that these funds continue to be readily available." Hyman–Michaels did not attempt to wire the money directly to the Banque de Paris as it had done on the occasion of its previous default. Days passed while the missing telex message was hunted unsuccessfully. Finally Swiss Bank suggested to Continental that it retransmit the telex message to the machine in the cable department and this was done on May 1. The next day Swiss Bank attempted to deposit the $27,000 in the account of the Pandora's owner at the Banque de Paris but the payment was refused.

Again the arbitrators were convened and rendered a decision. In it they ruled that Hyman–Michaels had been "blameless" up until the morning of April 27, when it first learned that the Banque de Paris had not received payment on April 26, but that "being faced with this situation," Hyman–Michaels had "failed to do everything in [its] power to remedy it. The action taken was immediate but did not prove to be adequate, in that [Continental] Bank and its correspondent required some 5–6 days to trace and effect the lost instruction to remit. [Hyman–Michaels] could have ordered an immediate duplicate payment—or even sent a Banker's check by hand or special messengers, so that the funds could have reached owner's Bank, not later than April 28th." By failing to do any of these things Hyman–Michaels had "created the opening" that the Pandora's owner was seeking in order to be able to cancel the charter. It had "acted imprudently." The arbitration panel concluded, reluctantly but unanimously, that this time the Pandora's owner was entitled to cancel the agreement. * * *

Hyman–Michaels then brought this diversity action against Swiss Bank, seeking to recover its expenses in the second arbitration proceeding plus the profits that it lost because of the cancellation of the charter. The contract by which Hyman–Michaels had agreed to ship scrap steel to Brazil had been terminated by the buyer in March 1973 and Hyman–Michaels had promptly subchartered the Pandora at market rates, which by April 1973 were double the rates fixed in the charter. Its lost profits are based on the difference between the charter and subcharter rates. * * *

The case was tried to a district judge without a jury. [The judge ruled that] under Illinois law [Swiss Bank] was liable to Hyman–Michaels for $2.1 million in damages. This figure was made up of about $16,000 in arbitration expenses and the rest in lost profits on the subcharter of the Pandora. * * *

[Under Swiss law, Hyman–Michaels could not have prevailed because it was not in privity with Swiss Bank. Illinois law does not require privity. The court avoided the choice of law problem, however, by concluding that the trial court had erred in allowing Hyman–Michaels to recover even under Illinois law.]

When a bank fails to make a requested transfer of funds, this can cause two kinds of loss. First, the funds themselves or interest on them may be lost, and of course the fee paid for the transfer, having bought nothing, becomes a loss item. These are "direct" (sometimes called "general") damages. Hyman–Michaels is not seeking any direct damages in this case and apparently sustained none. It did not lose any part of the $27,000; although its account with Continental Bank was debited by this amount prematurely, it was not an interest-bearing account so Hyman–Michaels lost no interest; and Hyman–Michaels paid no fee either to Continental or to Swiss Bank for the aborted transfer. A second type of loss, which either the payor or the payee may suffer, is a dislocation in one's business triggered by the failure to pay. Swiss Bank's failure to transfer funds to the Banque de Paris when requested to do so by Continental Bank set off a chain reaction which resulted in an arbitration proceeding that was costly to Hyman–Michaels and in the cancellation of a highly profitable contract. It is those costs and lost profits—"consequential" or, as they are sometimes called, "special" damages—that Hyman–Michaels seeks in this lawsuit, and recovered below. It is conceded that if Hyman–Michaels was entitled to consequential damages, the district court measured them correctly. The only issue is whether it was entitled to consequential damages. * * *

The rule of *Hadley v. Baxendale*—that consequential damages will not be awarded unless the defendant was put on notice of the special circumstances giving rise to them—has been applied in many Illinois cases, and *Hadley* cited approvingly. In Siegel v. Western Union Tel. Co., 312 Ill.App. 86, 92B93, 37 N.E.2d 868, 871 (1941), the plaintiff had delivered $200 to Western Union with instructions to transmit it to a friend of the plaintiff's. The money was to be bet (legally) on a horse, but this was not disclosed in the instructions. Western Union misdirected the money order and it did not reach the friend until several hours after the race had taken place. The horse that the plaintiff had intended to bet on won and would have paid $1650 on the plaintiff's $200 bet if the bet had been placed. He sued Western Union for his $1450 lost profit, but the court held that under the rule of *Hadley v. Baxendale*, Western Union was not liable, because it "had no notice or knowledge of the purpose for which the money was being transmitted."

The present case is similar, though Swiss Bank knew more than Western Union knew in *Siegel;* it knew or should have known, from Continental Bank's previous telexes, that Hyman–Michaels was paying the Pandora Shipping Company for the hire of a motor vessel named Pandora. But it did not know when payment was due, what the terms of the charter were, or that they had turned out to be extremely favorable to Hyman–

Michaels. And it did not know that Hyman–Michaels knew the Pandora's owner would try to cancel the charter, and probably would succeed, if Hyman–Michaels was ever again late in making payment, or that despite this peril Hyman–Michaels would not try to pay until the last possible moment and in the event of a delay in transmission would not do everything in its power to minimize the consequences of the delay. Electronic funds transfers are not so unusual as to automatically place a bank on notice of extraordinary consequences if such a transfer goes awry. Swiss Bank did not have enough information to infer that if it lost a $27,000 payment order it would face a liability in excess of $2 million.

It is true that in both *Hadley* and *Siegel* there was a contract between the parties and here there was none. We cannot be certain that the Illinois courts would apply the principles of those cases outside of the contract area. As so often in diversity cases, there is an irreducible amount of speculation involved in attempting to predict the reaction of a state's courts to a new issue. The best we can do is to assume that the Illinois courts would look to the policies underlying cases such as *Hadley* and *Siegel* and, to the extent they found them pertinent, would apply those cases here. We must therefore ask what difference it should make whether the parties are or are not bound to each other by a contract. On the one hand, it seems odd that the absence of a contract would enlarge rather than limit the extent of liability. After all, under Swiss law the absence of a contract would be devastating to Hyman–Michaels' claim. Privity is not a wholly artificial concept. It is one thing to imply a duty to one with whom one has a contract and another to imply it to the entire world.

On the other hand, contract liability is strict. A breach of contract does not connote wrongdoing; it may have been caused by circumstances beyond the promisor's control—a strike, a fire, the failure of a supplier to deliver an essential input. And while such contract doctrines as impossibility, impracticability, and frustration relieve promisors from liability for some failures to perform that are beyond their control, many other such failures are actionable although they could not have been prevented by the exercise of due care. The district judge found that Swiss Bank had been negligent in losing Continental Bank's telex message and it can be argued that Swiss Bank should therefore be liable for a broader set of consequences than if it had only broken a contract. But *Siegel* implicitly rejects this distinction. Western Union had not merely broken its contract to deliver the plaintiff's money order; it had "negligently misdirected" the money order. "The company's negligence is conceded." 312 Ill.App. at 88, 91, 37 N.E.2d at 869, 871. Yet it was not liable for the consequences.

Siegel, we conclude, is authority for holding that Swiss Bank is not liable for the consequences of negligently failing to transfer Hyman–Michaels' funds to Banque de Paris; reason for such a holding is found in the animating principle of *Hadley v. Baxendale*, which is that the costs of the untoward consequence of a course of dealings should be borne by that party who was able to avert the consequence at least cost and failed to do so. In *Hadley* the untoward consequence was the shutting down of the mill. The carrier could have avoided it by delivering the engine shaft on time. But the mill owners, as the court noted, could have avoided it simply by having a spare shaft. 9 Ex. at 355–56, 156 Eng.Rep. at 151. Prudence required that they have a spare shaft anyway, since a replacement could not be obtained at once even if there was no undue delay in carting the broken shaft to and the replacement shaft from the manufacturer. The court refused to imply a duty on the part of the carrier to guarantee the mill owners against the consequences of their own lack of prudence, though of course if the parties had stipulated for such a guarantee the court would have enforced it. The notice requirement of *Hadley v. Baxendale* is designed to assure that such an improbable guarantee really is intended.

This case is much the same, though it arises in a tort rather than a contract setting. Hyman–Michaels showed a lack of prudence throughout. It was imprudent for it to mail in Chicago a letter that unless received the next day in Geneva would put Hyman–Michaels in breach of a contract that was very profitable to it and that the other party to the contract had every interest in canceling. It was imprudent thereafter for Hyman–Michaels, having narrowly avoided cancellation and having (in the words of its appeal brief in this court) been "put . . . on notice that the payment provision of the Charter would be strictly enforced thereafter," to wait till [sic] arguably the last day before payment was due to instruct its bank to transfer the necessary funds overseas. And it was imprudent in the last degree for Hyman–Michaels, when it received notice of cancellation on the last possible day payment was due, to fail to pull out all the stops to get payment to the Banque de Paris on that day, and instead to dither while Continental and Swiss Bank wasted five days looking for the lost telex message. Judging from the obvious reluctance with which the arbitration panel finally decided to allow the Pandora's owner to cancel the charter, it might have made all the difference if Hyman–Michaels had gotten payment to the Banque de Paris by April 27 or even by Monday, April 30, rather than allowed things to slide until May 2.

This is not to condone the sloppy handling of incoming telex messages in Swiss Bank's foreign department. But Hyman–Michaels is a sophisticated business enterprise. It knew or should have known that even the Swiss are not infallible; that messages sometimes get lost or delayed in transit among three banks, two of them located 5000 miles apart, even when all the banks are using reasonable care; and that therefore it should take its own precautions against the consequences—best known to itself—of a mishap that might not be due to anyone's negligence.

We are not the first to remark the affinity between the rule of *Hadley v. Baxendale* and the doctrine, which is one of tort as well as contract law and is a settled part of the common law of Illinois, of avoidable consequences. If you are hurt in an automobile accident and unreasonably fail to seek medical treatment, the injurer, even if negligent, will not be held liable for the aggravation of the injury due to your own unreasonable behavior after the accident. If in addition you failed to fasten your seat belt, you may be barred from collecting the tort damages that would have been prevented if you had done so. Hyman–Michaels' behavior in steering close to the wind prior to April 27 was like not fastening one's seat belt; its failure on April 27 to wire a duplicate payment immediately after disaster struck was like refusing to seek medical attention after a serious accident. The seat-belt cases show that the doctrine of avoidable consequences applies whether the tort victim acts imprudently before or after the tort is committed.

The rule of *Hadley v. Baxendale* links up with tort concepts in another way. The rule is sometimes stated in the form that only foreseeable damages are recoverable in a breach of contract action. So expressed, it corresponds to the tort principle that limits liability to the foreseeable consequence of the defendant's carelessness. The amount of care that a person ought to take is a function of the probability and magnitude of the harm that may occur if he does not take care. If he does not know what that probability and magnitude are, he cannot determine how much care to take. That would be Swiss Bank's dilemma if it were liable for consequential damages from failing to carry out payment orders in timely fashion. To estimate the extent of its probable liability in order to know how many and how elaborate fail-safe features to install in its telex rooms or how much insurance to buy against the inevitable failures, Swiss Bank would have to collect reams of information about firms that are not even its regular customers. It had no banking relationship with Hyman–Michaels. It did not know or have reason to know how at once precious and fragile Hyman–Michaels' contract with the Pandora's owner was. These were circumstances too remote from Swiss Bank's practical range of knowledge to have affected its decisions as to who should man the telex machines in the foreign department or whether it should have more intelligent machines or should install more machines in the cable department, any more than the falling of a platform scale because a conductor jostled a passenger who was carrying fireworks was a prospect that could have influenced the amount of care taken by the Long Island Railroad. See Palsgraf v. Long Island R.R., 248 N.Y. 339, 162 N.E. 99 (1928).

In short, Swiss Bank was not required in the absence of a contractual undertaking to take precautions or insure against a harm that it could not measure but that was known with precision to Hyman–Michaels, which could by the exercise of common prudence have averted it completely. As Chief Judge Cardozo (the author of *Palsgraf*) remarked in discussing the application of *Hadley v. Baxendale* to the liability of telegraph companies for errors in transmission, "The sender can protect himself by insurance in one form or another if the risk of nondelivery or error appears to be too great.... The company, if it takes out insurance for itself, can do no more than guess at the loss to be avoided." Kerr S.S. Co. v. Radio Corp. of America, 245 N.Y. 284, 291–92, 157 N.E. 140, 142 (1927). * * *

The legal principles that we have said are applicable to this case were not applied below. Although the district judge's opinion is not entirely clear, he apparently thought the rule of *Hadley v. Baxendale* inapplicable and the imprudence of Hyman–Michaels irrelevant. He did state that the damages to Hyman–Michaels were foreseeable because "a major international bank" should know that a failure to act promptly on a telexed request to transfer funds could cause substantial damage; but *Siegel* * * * make[s] clear that that kind of general foreseeability, which is present in virtually every case, does not justify an award of consequential damages.

We could remand for new findings based on the proper legal standard, but it is unnecessary to do so. The undisputed facts, recited in this opinion, show as a matter of law that Hyman–Michaels is not entitled to recover consequential damages from Swiss Bank. * * *

Notes

1. Both tort and contract rely on foreseeability to limit liability for remote losses. In contract, foreseeability is defined by *Hadley v. Baxendale*: the party charged with liability must be on notice of the special circumstances giving rise to the loss. See also UCC § 2–715(2) ("Consequential damages resulting from the seller's breach include, (a) any loss resulting from general or particular requirements and needs of which the seller at the time of contracting had reason to know * * * "). In tort, foreseeability casts its net farther: so long as the type of harm that occurs is foreseeable, the extent of harm or the manner in which it occurs is irrelevant. A defendant whose negligence causes harm will be liable for all the consequences that follow, so long as the damage that occurs is of the same general sort, from the same physical forces as the harm that was foreseeable. See, e.g., Petition of Kinsman Transit Co., 338 F.2d 708 (2d Cir.1964).

If *Evra* were analyzed as a tort case, what would be the outcome? Keep in mind that remoteness of the loss is not the only question foreseeability bears upon. For example, did Swiss Bank owe Hyman–Michaels, who after all was not its customer, a duty? Foreseeability is one among a number of factors courts examine to determine whether one person owes another a duty to use reasonable care; others important factors are whether the plaintiff's loss was certainly caused by the wrong, whether the causal connection was close, whether the defendant's behavior was morally wrong, the social policy of deterring negligent behavior and the availability of insurance. J'Aire Corp. v. Gregory, 24 Cal.3d 799, 157 Cal.Rptr. 407, 598 P.2d 60 (1979)(one who contracts with the owner of a building to make repairs has a duty to the owner's lessees to use reasonable care to avoid economic loss to their businesses).

There has been a general trend to limit the availability of purely economic damages in both negligence and strict liability actions. The logic has been, basically, that actions for purely economic loss should be brought as contract actions, even if the loss is the result of negligence. At least at the time of *Evra*, however, Illinois had apparently not joined that trend, if the trial court was correct in its conclusion that Hyman–Michaels could sue without establishing privity. On the recovery of pure economic loss in tort and contract, see David Gruning, Pure Economic Loss in American Tort Law: An Unstable Consensus, 54 Am.J.Comp.L. 187 (2006). Symposia on the topic appear at 27

Int'l Rev. L. & Econ. 1 (2007); and Dan B. Dobbs, Conference on Economic Tort Law, 48 Ariz.L.Rev. 689 (2006).

Assuming that the Illinois decisions abolishing the privity requirement establish a duty, was Swiss Bank negligent? Did they fail to act reasonably in light of their customers' foreseeable losses? Was Hyman–Michaels contributorily negligent? Did Hyman–Michaels act reasonably to mitigate its losses?

Uniform Commercial Code § 4A–305 (c)–(d) provides that consequential damages are available in connection with a late or improper execution of payment orders only if provided for in an express, written contract between the sender and the receiving bank. Is that a better solution to the problem in *Evra*?

2. At points, Judge Posner hints at each of the above—duty, due care, contributory negligence, and avoidable consequences—as explaining why Hyman–Michaels cannot recover its special damages. It is not surprising that he believes they overlap; as an advocate of an economic approach to law, Judge Posner believes that all of these doctrines share the same goal—economic efficiency. Formal distinctions between tort and contract notwithstanding, the goal of each is to insure that the costs of accidents fall on those who most cheaply could have avoided them. See also Richard A. Posner, Economic Analysis of Law (7th ed.2007). Thus, the rule in *Hadley v. Baxendale* is "animated" by the principle "that the costs of the untoward consequences of a course of dealings should be borne by that party who was able to avert the consequence at least cost and failed to do so."

But, how does Judge Posner know that the miller was the cheapest cost avoider? How expensive are mill shafts, and how often do they break? How long does it usually take to repair one? Do the repairs always mean lost profits, or are millers sometimes able to defer work until the shaft is repaired, without a loss? Doesn't Judge Posner need more facts before he can conclude that the rule in *Hadley* placed the loss on the cheapest cost avoider? See Richard A. Epstein, Beyond Foreseeability: Consequential Damages in the Law of Contract, 18 J.Legal Stud. 105 (1989).

More importantly, how does Judge Posner know that Hyman–Michaels was the cheapest cost avoider? Is that the kind of decision that can or should be made in the first instance on appeal?

3. Economic explanations of *Hadley v. Baxendale* usually focus on how the rule promotes efficiency by giving the party who has better information about what is at stake an incentive to share that information. Then, the parties can bargain over who will take precautions against that loss, and at what cost. Knowing what steps to take to avoid a loss, however, requires two sorts of information: information about the size of the loss, and information about how likely the loss is to occur. In most contract contexts, it makes sense to encourage the party in possession of information about the size of the loss to disclose, because few promisors are likely to disclose candidly the probability that they will fail to perform. See Benjamin E. Hermalin et al., Contract Law in A. Mitchell Polinsky & Steven Shavell, 1 Handbook of Law and Economics (2007).

In *Evra,* only Hyman–Michaels knew what was at stake, but only Swiss Bank knew how likely it was that the telex would go astray. Is efficiency better served by a rule that requires all of a bank's customers (or, as here, a bank's customer's customers) to inform the bank of the nature of their transactions, or by a rule that would encourage banks to warn of or take steps to prevent unreasonable delays? Is it realistic to expect Hyman–Michaels to notify Swiss Bank of what was at stake? See Note, Evra Corp. v. Swiss Bank Corp.: Consequential Damages for Bank Negligence in Wire Transfers, 9 Rutgers Comp. & Tech.L.J. 369 (1983) (arguing that notice is impractical). If Hyman–Michaels cannot reasonably notify Swiss Bank, how is Hyman–Michaels to know what steps to take to insure against the loss, without knowing how likely the loss is to occur? See Note, An Economic Approach to Hadley v. Baxendale, 62 Neb.L.Rev. 157 (1983) (without information as to the risks, customers are likely to over- or under-insure).

Hadley continues to inspire commentary. See, e.g., Symposium, The Common Law of Contracts as a World Force in Two Ages: A Conference Celebrating the 150th Anniversary of Hadley v. Baxendale, 11 Tex. Wesleyan L.Rev. 421 (2005); Barry E. Adler, The Questionable Ascent of Hadley v. Baxendale, 51 Stan.L.Rev. 1547 (1999); Melvin Aron Eisenberg, Probability and Chance in Contract Law, 45 U.C.L.A.L.Rev. 1005 (1998).

4. Does *Evra* suggest that contract law is reclaiming some lost ground from tort law? Arguably, the courts' increasing reluctance to allow plaintiffs to bring tort actions when a defendant's defective product or even negligent behavior causes purely economic harm represents a similar development. Even the area of professional negligence, identified by Justice Mosk in his concurrence in *Freeman & Mills* as occupying the gray area between tort and contract, is perhaps shifting back toward a contract approach. For example, recent decisions have taken the position that emotional distress damages are not available in legal malpractice actions, unless special circumstances make them particularly foreseeable. E.g., Wehringer v. Powers & Hall, 874 F.Supp. 425 (D.Mass.) (discussing the cases), aff'd, 65 F.3d 160 (1st Cir.1995). Compare B & M Homes v. Hogan, 376 So.2d 667 (Ala.1979) (mental distress is foreseeable, recoverable element of contract damages when builder's faulty construction of home results in severe defects) with Erlich v. Menezes, 21 Cal.4th 543, 87 Cal.Rptr.2d 886, 981 P.2d 978 (1999) (emotional distress is unforeseeable when a builder's negligence severely damages a home; emotional concerns were not "the essence of the contract").

E. ADJUSTMENTS TO THE DAMAGE AWARD

1. TIME AND VALUE: PREJUDGMENT INTEREST

PROBLEM: COUNTRY LODGE V. MILLER (REPRISED)
PREJUDGMENT INTEREST

The court has declared Miller's operation a nuisance and enjoined it. In addition, the court has awarded Country Lodge damages for: (1) the cost of restoring the riverfront to its original condition; (2) the profits Country Lodge lost; and (3) the Lodge owner's annoyance and discomfort. Should prejudgment interest be awarded on all or any part of the award?

KANSAS v. COLORADO

Supreme Court of the United States, 2001
533 U.S. 1, 121 S.Ct. 2023, 150 L.Ed.2d 72

JUSTICE STEVENS delivered the opinion of the Court.

The Arkansas River rises in the mountains of Colorado just east of the Continental Divide, descends for about 280 miles to the Kansas border, then flows through that State, Oklahoma, and Arkansas and empties into the Mississippi River. On May 20, 1901, Kansas first invoked this Court's original jurisdiction to seek a remedy for Colorado's diversion of water from the Arkansas River. In opinions written during the past century, we have described the history and the importance of the river. For present purposes it suffices to note that two of those cases led to the negotiation of the Arkansas River Compact (Compact), an agreement between Kansas and Colorado that in turn was approved by Congress in 1949. The case before us today involves a claim by Kansas for damages based on Colorado's violations of that Compact.

* * *

[The Court-appointed Special Master determined that groundwater well pumping in Colorado had materially depleted the river's waters, violating the Compact.]

[T]he Special Master recommends that damages be measured by Kansas' losses, rather than Colorado's profits, attributable to Compact violations after 1950; that the damages be paid in money rather than water; and that the damages should include prejudgment interest from 1969 to the date of judgment. Colorado has filed four objections to the report. It contends (1) that the recommended award of damages would violate the Eleventh Amendment to the United States Constitution; (2) that the damages award should not include prejudgment interest; (3) that the amount of interest awarded is excessive; and (4) that the Special Master improperly credited flawed expert testimony, with the result that Kansas' crop production losses were improperly calculated. On the other hand, Kansas has filed an objection submitting that prejudgment interest should be paid from 1950, rather than 1969. The United States, which intervened because of its interest in the operation of flood control projects in Colorado, submits that both States' objections should be overruled.

I

[The Court rejected Colorado's argument that because damages were measured by the losses Kansas farmers incurred, the suit was barred by the Eleventh Amendment. The Eleventh Amendment does not bar suits by one state seeking damages from another state, so long as the state suing is more than a nominal party merely forwarding its citizens' claims to avoid the Eleventh Amendment. Enforcing a water compact is in the public interest whatever damage measure might ultimately apply, and Kansas was in full control of the litigation throughout.]

* * *

II

Colorado next excepts to the Special Master's conclusion that the damages award should include prejudgment interest despite the fact that Kansas' claim is unliquidated.[2] At one point in time, the fact that the claim was unliquidated would have been of substantial importance. As a general matter, early common-law cases drew a distinction between liquidated and unliquidated claims and refused to allow interest on the latter. This rule seems to have rested upon a belief that there was something inherently unfair about requiring debtors to pay interest when they were unable to halt its accrual by handing over to their creditors a fixed and unassailable amount.

This common-law distinction has long since lost its hold on the legal imagination. Beginning in the early part of the last century, numerous courts and commentators have rejected the distinction for failing to acknowledge the compensatory nature of interest awards. This Court allied itself with the evolving consensus in 1933, when we expressed the opinion that the distinction between cases of liquidated and unliquidated damages "is not a sound one." The analysis supporting that conclusion gave no doubt as to our reasoning: "Whether the case is of the one class or the other, the injured party has suffered a loss which may be regarded as not fully compensated if he is confined to the amount found to be recoverable as of the time of breach and nothing is added for the delay in obtaining the award of damages." Our cases since 1933 have consistently acknowledged that a monetary award does not fully compensate for an injury unless it includes an interest component.

Relying on our cases, the Special Master "concluded that the unliquidated nature of Kansas' money damages does not, in and of itself, bar an award of prejudgment interest." In reaching that conclusion, the Special Master was fully cognizant of both the displaced common-law rule and the subsequent doctrinal evolution. In addition, he gave careful consideration to equitable considerations that might mitigate against an award of interest, concluding that "considerations of fairness," supported the award of at least some prejudgment interest in this case.

---

2. Though final damages have not yet been calculated, the importance of this issue is illustrated by breaking down the damages claimed by Kansas. Of $62,369,173 in damages so claimed, $9,218,305 represents direct and indirect losses in actual dollars when the damage occurred. Of the remaining $53,150,868, about $12 million constitutes an adjustment for inflation (a type of interest that Colorado concedes is appropriate) while the remaining amount (approximately $41 million) represents additional interest intended to compensate for lost investment opportunities. Third Report of Special Master 87–88 (hereinafter Third Report). The magnitude of prejudgment interest ultimately awarded in this case will, of course, turn on the date from which interest accrues. See Part III–B, infra.

We find no fault in the Special Master's analysis of either our prior cases or the equities of this matter. While we will deal with the amount of prejudgment interest below, to answer Colorado's second objection it is sufficient to conclude that the Special Master was correct in determining that the unliquidated nature of the damages does not preclude an award of prejudgment interest.

Colorado's second exception is overruled.

III

Colorado's third exception takes issue with both the rate of interest adopted by the Special Master and the date from which he recommended that interest begin to accrue. As to the second of these two concerns, Colorado submits that, if any prejudgment interest is to be awarded, it should begin to accrue in 1985 (when Kansas filed its complaint in this action), rather than in 1969 (when, the Special Master concluded, Colorado knew or should have known that it was violating the Compact).

On the other hand, Kansas has entered an exception, arguing that the accrual of interest should begin in 1950. We first address the rate question, then the timing issue.

A

The Special Master credited the testimony of Kansas' three experts who calculated the interest rates that they thought necessary to provide full compensation for the damages caused by Colorado's violations of the Compact in the years since 1950. As a result of inflation and changing market conditions those rates varied from year to year. In their calculation of the damages suffered by Kansas farmers, the experts used the interest rates that were applicable to individuals in the relevant years rather than the (lower) rates available to States.

Colorado argues that the lower rates should have been used because it is the State, rather than the individual farmers, that is maintaining the action and will receive any award of damages. But if, as we have already decided, see Part I, supra, it is permissible for the State to measure a portion of its damages by losses suffered by individual farmers, it necessarily follows that the courts are free to utilize whatever interest rate will most accurately measure those losses. The money in question in this portion of the damages award is revenue that would—but for Colorado's actions—have been earned by individual farmers. Thus, the Special Master correctly concluded that the economic consequences of Colorado's breach could best be remedied by an interest award that mirrors the cost of any additional borrowing the farmers may have been forced to undertake in order to compensate for lost revenue.

B

Although the Special Master rejected Colorado's submission that there is a categorical bar to the award of prejudgment interest on unliquidated claims, he concluded that such interest should not "be awarded according to [any] rigid theory of compensation for money withheld," but rather should respond to "'considerations of fairness.'" Kansas argues that our decisions * * * have effectively foreclosed the equities–balancing approach that the Special Master adopted. There is some merit to Kansas' position. See [City of Milwaukee v. National Gypsum Co., 515 U.S. 189, 193, 115 S.Ct. 2091 (1995)] (affirming a decision of the Court of Appeals that had read our cases as "disapproving of a 'balancing of the equities' as a method of deciding whether to allow prejudgment interest").

However, despite the clear direction indicated by some of our earlier opinions, we cannot say that by 1949 our case law had developed sufficiently to put Colorado on notice that, upon a violation of the Compact, we would automatically award prejudgment interest from the time of injury. Given the state of the law at that time, Colorado may well have believed that we would balance the equities in order to achieve a just and equitable remedy, rather than automatically imposing prejudgment interest in order to achieve full compensation. While we are confident that, when it signed the Compact, Colorado was on notice that it might be subject to prejudgment interest if such interest was necessary to fashion an equitable remedy, we are unable to conclude with sufficient certainty that Colorado was on notice that such interest would be imposed as a matter of course. We, therefore, believe that the Special Master acted properly in carefully analyzing the facts of the case and in only awarding as much prejudgment interest as was required by a balancing of the equities.

We also agree with the Special Master that the equities in this case do not support an award of prejudgment interest from the date of the first violation of the Compact, but rather favor an award beginning on a later date. In reaching this conclusion, the Special Master appropriately considered several factors. In particular, he relied on the fact that in the early years after the Compact was signed, no one had any thought that the pact was being violated. In addition, he considered the long interval that passed between the original injuries and these proceedings, as well as the dramatic impact of compounding interest over many years.

In its exception, Kansas argues that the Special Master's reasoning would be appropriate if damages were being awarded as a form of punishment, but does not justify a refusal to provide full compensation to an injured party. Moreover, Kansas argues, a rule that rewards ignorance might discourage diligence in making sure that there is full compliance with the terms of the Compact. Kansas' argument is consistent with a "rigid theory of compensation for money withheld," but, for the reasons discussed above, we are persuaded that the Special Master correctly declined to adopt such a theory. The equitable considerations identified by the Special Master fully justify his view that in this case it would be inappropriate to award prejudgment interest for any years before either party was aware of the excessive pumping in Colorado.

In its third exception, Colorado argues that, if prejudgment interest is to be awarded at all, the equities are best balanced by limiting such interest to the time after the complaint was filed, rather than the time after which Colorado knew or should have known that it was violating the Compact. Specifically, Colorado suggests that prejudgment interest should begin to accrue in 1985 rather than 1969. The choice between the two dates is surely debatable; it is a matter over which reasonable people can—and do—disagree. After examining the equities for ourselves, however, a majority of the Court has decided that the later date is the more appropriate.[5]

When we overruled Colorado's objections to the Special Master's first report, we held that Kansas was not guilty of inexcusable delay in failing to complain more promptly about post-Compact well pumping. In saying that the delay was not inexcusable, we recognized that the nature and extent of Colorado's violations continued to be unclear even in the years after which it became obvious that the Compact was being violated. That conclusion is something of a two-edged sword, however. While Kansas' delay was understandable given the amorphous nature of its claims, there is no doubt that the interests of both States would have been served if the claim had been advanced promptly after its basis became known. Once it became obvious that a violation of the Compact had occurred, it was equally clear that the proceedings necessary to evaluate the significance of the violations would be complex and protracted. Despite the diligence of the parties and the Special Master, over 15 years have elapsed since the complaint was filed. Given the uncertainty over the scope of damages that prevailed during the period between 1968 and 1985 and the fact that it was uniquely in Kansas' power to begin the process by which those damages would be quantified, Colorado's request that we deny prejudgment interest for that period is reasonable.

For these reasons, we overrule Kansas' exception. We also overrule Colorado's third exception insofar as it challenges the interest rates recommended by the Special Master, but we sustain that objection insofar as it challenges the award of interest for the years prior to 1985.

[The Court's discussion of Colorado's objection to the method by which crop losses were determined is omitted.]

JUSTICE O'CONNOR, with whom JUSTICE SCALIA and JUSTICE THOMAS join, concurring in part and dissenting in part.

* * * We are dealing with an interstate compact apportioning the flow of a river between two States. A compact is a contract. It represents a bargained-for exchange between its signatories and "remains a legal

---

5. Justice O'Connor, Justice Scalia, and Justice Thomas would not allow any prejudgment interest. Justice Kennedy and Chief Justice [Rehnquist] are of the opinion that prejudgment interest should run from the date of the filing of the complaint. Justice Souter, Justice Ginsburg, Justice Breyer, and the author of this opinion agree with the Special Master's view that interest should run from the time when Colorado knew or should have known that it was violating the Compact. In order to produce a majority for a judgment, the four Justices who agree with the Special Master have voted to endorse the position expressed in the text.

document that must be construed and applied in accordance with its terms." It is a fundamental tenet of contract law that parties to a contract are deemed to have contracted with reference to principles of law existing at the time the contract was made. The basic question before the Court is thus one of "the fair intendment of the contract itself." Specifically, the question is whether, at the time the Compact was negotiated and approved, Colorado and Kansas could fairly be said to have intended, or at least to have expected or assumed, that Colorado might be exposing itself to liability for prejudgment interest in the event of the Compact's breach.

I fail to see how Colorado and Kansas could have contemplated that prejudgment interest would be awarded. * * * To be sure, we had by then, along with other courts, criticized the common law rule that prejudgment interest was recoverable on claims for liquidated, but not for unliquidated, damages. But in the absence of a statute providing for such interest, many courts, including our own, still denied and would continue to deny prejudgment interest on claims for unliquidated and unascertainable damages in a great many, and probably most, circumstances.

* * * [U]ntil 1987, we had never even suggested that monetary damages could be recovered from a State as a remedy for its violation of an interstate compact apportioning the flow of an interstate stream. * * * How, then, can one say that, at the time the Compact was negotiated and approved, its signatories could fairly be said to have intended, or at least could reasonably be said to have expected or assumed, that Kansas might recover prejudgment interest on damages caused by Colorado's breach? * * * As both the Compact itself and the parties' post-Compact course of dealing make clear, the "fair intendment" of the Compact very probably was simply for the in-kind recovery of water as a remedy for its breach. * * *

The Court ignores all of this in awarding prejudgment interest to Kansas, seizing instead upon the compensatory rationale behind the criticism of the common law rule and awards of prejudgment interest on unliquidated claims for damages in general. I do not dispute that awards of interest are compensatory in nature or that, as a general matter, "a monetary award does not fully compensate for an injury unless it includes an interest component." But, as the Court itself recognizes, our precedents make clear that, at least today and in the absence of a governing statute, awards of prejudgment interest on unliquidated claims for damages are governed not by any "rigid theory of compensation for money withheld," but rather by "considerations of fairness." This is especially so where, as here, we are dealing with suits by one governmental body against another.

There is nothing fair about awarding prejudgment interest as a remedy for the Compact's breach when all available evidence suggests that the signatories to the Compact neither intended nor contemplated such an unconventional remedy. * * *

NOTES

1. In a subsequent appeal, Kansas argued that prejudgment interest should have been awarded from 1985 until the date of the judgment on the entire award. The Special Master disagreed, and calculated interest only on damages that accrued after 1985. The Court upheld the Special Master:

> After all, says Kansas, "[p]rejudgment interest serves to compensate for the loss of use of money due as damages ... thereby achieving full compensation for the injury those damages are intended to redress." Why then, asks Kansas, calculate post 1985 interest on only some of the damages then due? * * * Kansas' argument would make good sense in an ordinary case. But the question here is not about the ordinary case * * *. [L]ike the Special Master, we did not seek to provide compensation for all lost investment opportunities; rather, we sought to weigh the equities.

Kansas v. Colorado, 543 U.S. 86, 96, 125 S.Ct. 526, 160 L.Ed.2d 418 (2004).

2. As the *Kansas* Court recognizes, an award of prejudgment interest is necessary to ensure that the plaintiff is fully compensated, given the inevitable delay between injury and recovery:

> If justice were immediate, there would never be an award of prejudgment interest. The injured party would receive an enforceable judgment immediately, with no loss in value from the time value of money. Because justice often takes many years to achieve, interest is added to the original judgment to ensure that compensation is complete.

Michael S. Knoll, Primer on Prejudgment Interest, 75 Tex.L.Rev. 293, 294 (1996). Depending on the length of the delay, the amount at stake can be considerable. In Cayuga Indian Nation of New York v. Pataki, 165 F.Supp.2d 266 (N.D.N.Y.2001), for example, the court awarded a tribe that had been deprived of its land for 204 years $211,000,326.80 in prejudgment interest. And that was after balancing the hardships and reducing the award by 60%! On appeal, however, the claim was found to be barred by laches, an equitable defense that is discussed in Chapter 9. Cayuga Indian Nation of New York v. Pataki, 413 F.3d 266 (2d Cir.2005), cert. denied, 547 U.S. 1128, 126 S.Ct. 2021, 164 L.Ed.2d 780 (2006).

If an award of prejudgment interest is required in order to compensate the plaintiff fully for its losses, why doesn't interest begin to accrue when the harm was suffered? What factors were most important in persuading the majority to balance the equities in Colorado's favor? What factors were most important to the dissent? The dissent's focus on the "fair intendment of the parties" is consistent with the history of prejudgment interest:

> Because interest was generally presumed not to be within the contemplation of the parties, common-law courts in England allowed interest by way of damages only when founded upon agreement of the parties.

Library of Congress v. Shaw, 478 U.S. 310, 314–315, 106 S.Ct. 2957, 92 L.Ed.2d 250 (1986). Would the Court be willing to balance the equities if liability were based on tort instead of contract? Will the Court balance the equities again if the same breach recurs?

3. Prejudgment interest was originally limited to cases in which the damages were liquidated, or at least ascertainable before judgment by reference to market values. Why would courts have distinguished between liquidated and unliquidated damages for purposes of awarding prejudgment interest? Consider:

> Most courts have refused to allow interest in the case of damages which are not liquidated or cannot be determined by computation or reference to market values, because the defendant should not be considered at fault for not paying a sum which he could not have ascertained with any degree of certainty. If this statement of the reason underlying the rule requiring certainty is correct it suggests that the primary concern of the courts has not been compensation for the plaintiff, but rather one or both of two other objectives: punishment of the defendant for his fault in failing to pay a sum which was ascertainable, or protection of the defendant from liability for withholding payment of an uncertain amount.

Note, Interest as Damages in California, 5 U.C.L.A. L.Rev. 262, 262–64 (1958).

Once the compensatory nature of prejudgment interest is recognized, the distinction between liquidated and unliquidated claims becomes difficult to defend. Nonetheless, some courts adhere to it. See, e.g., Ventura v. Titan Sports, Inc., 65 F.3d 725 (8th Cir.1995) (under Minnesota law, prejudgment interest is available only for claims that are liquidated or readily ascertainable by reference to objective market values); Coho Resources v. McCarthy, 829 So.2d 1 (Miss.2002) (no prejudgment interest where principal amount has not been fixed prior to judgment).

4. Generally speaking, prejudgment interest is not available for noneconomic losses. As one student commentator explained:

> Under the modern theory, moreover, interest would not be given upon those elements of damages representing an injury to personality or feelings. Even though the jury attempts to measure such injuries in monetary terms, the measurement is only an arbitrary one and the addition of interest would serve little purpose.

Note, Interest as Damages in California, 5 U.C.L.A.L.Rev. 262, 264 (1958). Some jurisdictions give the judge or the jury broad discretion to award prejudgment interest in cases in which prejudgment interest would not have been available at common law. See, e.g., Cal.Civ.Code § 3288 (jury has discretion to award prejudgment interest in cases "not arising from contract and in every case of oppression, fraud or malice").

5. Can prejudgment interest be awarded for a statutory violation, if the statute itself is silent? See Wickham Contracting v. Local Union No. 3, IBEW, 955 F.2d 831, 834 (2d Cir.1992) (interest can be recovered for violation of the federal Labor Management Relations Act):

> The award should be a function of (i) the need to fully compensate the wronged party for actual damages suffered, (ii) considerations of fairness and the relative equities of the award, (iii) the remedial purpose of the statute involved and/or (iv) such other general principles as are deemed relevant by the court.

"Other general principles" can include evidence of legislative intent, whether the statute already provides for full compensation or punitive damages, and the certainty of the plaintiff's damages. Id.

6. At common law, prejudgment interest has always been simple interest at the legal rate. The legal rate of interest is typically set by statute. Courts of equity would sometimes award compound interest where there was a breach of a fiduciary duty involving misuse of trust funds, or a failure to invest trust funds. See Restatement (Second) of Trusts § 207(2). In some circumstances, compound interest at the market rate can be constitutionally required. See Redevelopment Agency of Burbank v. Gilmore, 38 Cal.3d 790, 214 Cal.Rptr. 904, 700 P.2d 794 (1985) (compound interest at the market rate must be awarded as damages for delay in eminent domain action). How did the Special Master determine the interest rate in *Kansas v. Colorado*?

7. Delay affects a damage award in two ways. First, if the amount of the loss is measured as of the date of the injury, and there has been inflation since then, inflation will have eroded the purchasing power of the award. Second, even if there has been no inflation, without an award of prejudgment interest the plaintiff will be under-compensated because he will have lost the ability to use the money he deserved. "Wholly independent of inflation, any rational person values a promise to pay a dollar next year less than a promise to pay a dollar right away. Wimpy's offer to Popeye—'I would gladly pay you Tuesday for a hamburger today'—is always a bad deal." Jim Chen, The Price of Macroeconomic Imprecision: How Should the Law Measure Inflation?, 54 Hastings L.J. 1375, 1380 (2003). Thus, as the *Kansas* Court explains in footnote 2, to compensate the plaintiff fully, both inflation and the time value of money need to be taken into account.

Market-based interest rates theoretically reflect both inflation and the time value of money. "[M]arket interest rates include two components—an estimate of anticipated inflation, and a desired 'real' rate of return on investment." Jones & Laughlin Steel Corp. v. Pfeifer, 462 U.S. 523, 542, 103 S.Ct. 2541, 76 L.Ed.2d 768 (1983). If the court adjusts the award for inflation, what rate of return should it use in awarding prejudgment interest?

In that light, consider Anchorage Asphalt Paving Co. v. Lewis, 629 P.2d 65 (Alaska 1981). There, the defendant breached a contract to pave a road in 1970. For various reasons, the case did not go to trial until 1979. While contract damages are ordinarily measured at the time of the breach, the trial court awarded damages based on the cost of paving the road at the time of the trial. The trial court also awarded prejudgment interest, but the Alaska Supreme Court reversed:

> The award of damages at 1979 values suffices, in our view, to give Lewis what he initially bargained for, an acceptable paved road system. Ordinarily his award would be his cost of repair at or near the time of the breach, plus prejudgment interest up to the time of trial. Here, for the reasons previously explained, the court was justified in deviating from this standard method. However, to calculate the cost of repair at 1979 values and award prejudgment interest on that from 1970 strikes us as an unwarranted and unjustifiable compounding of damages.

Id. at 70. Is that the right result?

8. The policy of promoting settlements also comes into play in thinking about prejudgment interest. Without an award of prejudgment interest, the defendant has an incentive to drag out the proceedings while having use of the amount in dispute. So, some jurisdictions have expanded the availability of prejudgment interest in order to promote settlement.

An extreme example is in Ruff v. Weintraub, 105 N.J. 233, 519 A.2d 1384 (1987). There, the court affirmed an award of prejudgment interest in a personal injury case, even though much of the award was for future losses, such as injury to earning capacity. The court recognized that interest could hardly be justified as damages for delay when the loss had not yet occurred, but the New Jersey Rules of Court provided for prejudgment interest on the entire judgment in all but "exceptional" tort cases. The court rationalized the award as encouraging settlement (and requested the New Jersey Civil Practice Commission to reconsider the rule). To the same effect, see LaPlante v. American Honda Motor Co., 27 F.3d 731 (1st Cir.1994) (Rhode Island law).

For a more moderate attempt to use prejudgment interest to promote settlement, see Cal.Civ.Code § 3291 (if plaintiff makes a statutory offer of settlement that the defendant refuses, and plaintiff's recovery at trial exceeds his demand, plaintiff may claim interest on the judgment at 10% from the time of the offer).

9. Prejudgment interest cannot be awarded against the United States without its consent. Further, a general waiver of sovereign immunity will not be interpreted as consent to an award of interest. The "no interest" rule requires a separate, express waiver:

> "[T]here can be no consent by implication or by use of ambiguous language. Nor can an intent on the part of the framers of a statute or contract to permit the recovery of interest suffice where the intent is not translated into affirmative statutory or contractual terms. The consent necessary to waive the traditional immunity must be express, and it must be strictly construed."

United States v. New York Rayon Importing Co., 329 U.S., 654, 659, 67 S.Ct., 601, 604, 91 L.Ed. 577 (1947).

10. Almost all jurisdictions have statutes calling for the award of postjudgment interest when there is a delay between the entry of a judgment and its satisfaction. See, e.g., Cal.Code Civ.Pro. § 685.010 (interest accrues at a rate of 10% per year on the amount of an unsatisfied money judgment).

2. TIME AND MONEY: DISCOUNTING TO PRESENT VALUE

JONES & LAUGHLIN STEEL CORPORATION v. PFEIFER

Supreme Court of the United States, 1983
462 U.S. 523, 103 S.Ct. 2541, 76 L.Ed.2d 768

JUSTICE STEVENS delivered the opinion of the Court.

Respondent was injured in the course of his employment as a loading helper on a coal barge. As his employer, petitioner was required to compensate him for his injury under § 4 of the Longshoremen's and Harbor Workers' Compensation Act (the Act). We granted certiorari * * * to consider whether the Court of Appeals correctly upheld the trial court's computation of respondent's damages.

* * *

I

* * *

The District Court's calculation of damages was predicated on a few undisputed facts. At the time of his injury respondent was earning an annual wage of $26,065. He had a remaining work expectancy of 12 ½ years. On the date of trial (October 1, 1980), respondent had received compensation payments of $33,079,14. If he had obtained light work and earned the legal minimum hourly wage from July 1, 1979 until his 65th birthday, he would have earned $66,350.

The District Court arrived at its final award by taking 12½ years of earnings at respondent's wage at the time of injury ($325,312.50), subtracting his projected hypothetical earnings at the minimum wage ($66,-352) and the compensation payments he had received under § 4 ($33,-079.14), and adding $50,000 for pain and suffering. The court did not increase the award to take inflation into account, and it did not discount the award to reflect the present value of the future stream of income. The Court instead decided to follow a decision of the Supreme Court of Pennsylvania, which had held "as a matter of law that future inflation shall be presumed equal to future interest rates with these factors offsetting." Kaczkowski v. Bolubasz, 491 Pa. 561, 583, 421 A.2d 1027, 1038–1039 (1980). Thus, although the District Court did not dispute that respondent could be expected to receive regular cost-of-living wage increases from the date of his injury until his presumed date of retirement, the Court refused to include such increases in its calculation, explaining that they would provide respondent "a double consideration for inflation." For comparable reasons, the Court disregarded changes in the legal minimum wage in computing the amount of mitigation attributable to respondent's ability to perform light work.

* * *

The Damages Issue

The District Court found that respondent was permanently disabled as a result of petitioner's negligence. He therefore was entitled to an award of damages to compensate him for his probable pecuniary loss over the duration of his career, reduced to its present value. It is useful at the outset to review the way in which damages should be measured in a hypothetical inflation-free economy. We shall then consider how price inflation alters the analysis. Finally, we shall decide whether the District Court committed reversible error in this case.

In calculating damages, it is assumed that if the injured party had not been disabled, he would have continued to work, and to receive wages at periodic intervals until retirement, disability, or death. An award for impaired earning capacity is intended to compensate the worker for the diminution in that stream of income. The award could in theory take the form of periodic payments, but in this country it has traditionally taken the form of a lump sum, paid at the conclusion of the litigation. The appropriate lump sum cannot be computed without first examining the stream of income it purports to replace.

* * *

Each annual installment in the lost stream comprises several elements. The most significant is, of course, the actual wage. In addition, the worker may have enjoyed certain fringe benefits, which should be included in an ideal evaluation of the worker's loss but are frequently excluded for simplicity's sake. On the other hand, the injured worker's lost wages would have been diminished by state and federal income taxes. Since the damages award is tax-free, the relevant stream is ideally of after-tax wages and benefits. See Norfolk & Western R. Co. v. Liepelt, 444 U.S. 490, 100 S.Ct. 755, 62 L.Ed.2d 689 (1980). Moreover, workers often incur unreimbursed costs, such as transportation to work and uniforms, that the injured worker will not incur. These costs should also be deducted in estimating the lost stream.

In this case the parties appear to have agreed to simplify the litigation, and to presume that in each installment all the elements in the stream would offset each other, except for gross wages. However, in attempting to estimate even such a stylized stream of annual installments of gross wages, a trier of fact faces a complex task. The most obvious and most appropriate place to begin is with the worker's annual wage at the time of injury. Yet the "estimate of loss from lessened earnings capacity in the future need not be based solely upon the wages which the plaintiff was earning at the time of his injury." C. McCormick, Damages § 86 (1935). Even in an inflation-free economy—that is to say one in which the prices of consumer goods remain stable—a worker's wages tend to "inflate." This "real" wage inflation reflects a number of factors, some linked to the specific individual and some linked to broader societal forces.

With the passage of time, an individual worker often becomes more valuable to his employer. His personal work experiences increase his hourly contributions to firm profits. To reflect that heightened value, he will often receive "seniority" or "experience" raises, "merit" raises, or even promotions. Although it may be difficult to prove when, and whether, a particular injured worker might have received such wage increases, they may be reliably demonstrated for some workers.

Furthermore, the wages of workers as a class may increase over time. Through more efficient interaction among labor, capital, and technology, industrial productivity may increase, and workers' wages may enjoy a share of that growth. Such productivity increases—reflected in real increase in the gross national product per worker-hour—have been a permanent feature of the national economy since the conclusion of World War II. Moreover, through collective bargaining, workers may be able to negotiate increases in their "share" of revenues, at the cost of reducing shareholders' rate of return on their investments. Either of these forces could affect the lost stream of income in an inflation-free economy. In this case, the plaintiff's proffered evidence on predictable wage growth may have reflected the influence of either or both of these two factors.

To summarize, the first stage in calculating an appropriate award for lost earnings involves an estimate of what the lost stream of income would have been. The stream may be approximated as a series of after-tax payments, one in each year of the worker's expected remaining career. In estimating what those payments would have been in an inflation-free economy, the trier of fact may begin with the worker's annual wage at the time of injury. If sufficient proof is offered, the trier of fact may increase that figure to reflect the appropriate influence of individualized factors (such as foreseeable promotions) and societal factors (such as foreseeable productivity growth within the worker's industry).

Of course, even in an inflation-free economy the award of damages to replace the lost stream of income cannot be computed simply by totaling up the sum of the periodic payments. For the damages award is paid in a lump sum at the conclusion of the litigation, and when it—or even a part of it—is invested, it will earn additional money. It has been settled since our decision in Chesapeake & Ohio R. Co. v. Kelly, 241 U.S. 485, 36 S.Ct. 630, 60 L.Ed. 1117 (1916) that "in all cases where it is reasonable to suppose that interest may safely be earned upon the amount that is awarded, the ascertained future benefits ought to be discounted in the making up of the award."

The discount rate should be based on the rate of interest that would be earned on "the best and safest investments." Once it is assumed that the injured worker would definitely have worked for a specific term of years, he is entitled to a risk-free stream of future income to replace his lost wages; therefore, the discount rate should not reflect the market's premium for investors who are willing to accept some risk of default. Moreover, since under *Liepelt*, supra, the lost stream of income should be estimated in after-tax terms, the discount rate should also represent the after-tax rate of return to the injured worker.

Thus, although the notion of a damage award representing the present value of a lost stream of earnings in an inflation-free economy rests on some fairly sophisticated economic concepts, the two elements that determine its calculation can be stated fairly easily. They are: (1) the amount that the employee would have earned during each year that he could have been expected to work after the injury; and (2) the appropriate discount rate, reflecting the safest available investment. The trier of fact should apply the discount rate to each of the estimated installments in the lost stream of income, and then add up the discounted installments to determine the total award.

II

Unfortunately for triers of fact, ours is not an inflation-free economy. Inflation has been a permanent fixture in our economy for many decades, and there can be no doubt that it ideally should affect both stages of the calculation described in the previous section. The difficult problem is how it can do so in the practical context of civil litigation under [the Longshoreman's Act].

The first stage of the calculation requires an estimate of the shape of the lost stream of future income. For many workers, including respondent, a contractual "cost-of-living adjustment" automatically increases wages each year by the percentage change during the previous year in the consumer price index calculated by the Bureau of Labor Statistics. Such a contract provides a basis for taking into account an additional societal factor—price inflation—in estimating the worker's lost future earnings.

The second stage of the calculation requires the selection of an appropriate discount rate. Price inflation—or more precisely, anticipated price inflation—certainly affects market rates of return. If a lender knows that his loan is to be repaid a year later with dollars that are less valuable than those he has advanced, he will charge an interest rate that is high enough both to compensate him for the temporary use of the loan proceeds and also to make up for their shrinkage in value.

At one time many courts incorporated inflation into only one stage of the calculation of the award for lost earnings. In estimating the lost stream of future earnings, they accepted evidence of both individual and societal factors that would tend to lead to wage increases even in an inflation-free economy, but required the plaintiff to prove that those factors were not influenced by predictions of future price inflation. No increase was allowed for price inflation, on the theory that such predictions were unreliably speculative. In discounting the estimated lost stream of future income to present value, however, they applied the market interest rate.

The effect of these holdings was to deny the plaintiff the benefit of the impact of inflation on his future earnings, while giving the defendant the benefit of inflation's impact on the interest rate that is used to discount those earnings to present value. Although the plaintiff in such a situation could invest the proceeds of the litigation at an "inflated" rate of interest, the stream of income that he received provided him with only enough dollars to maintain his existing nominal income; it did not provide him with a stream comparable to what his lost wages would have been in an inflationary economy. This inequity was assumed to have been minimal because of the relatively low rates of inflation.

In recent years, of course, inflation rates have not remained low. There is now a consensus among courts that the prior inequity can no longer be tolerated. There is no consensus at all, however, regarding what form an appropriate response should take.

Our sister common law nations generally continue to adhere to the position that inflation is too speculative to be considered in estimating the lost stream of future earnings; they have sought to counteract the danger of systematically undercompensating plaintiffs by applying a discount rate that is below the current market rate. Nevertheless, they have each chosen different rates, applying slightly different economic theories. In England, Lord Diplock has suggested that it would be appropriate to allow for future inflation "in a rough and ready way" by discounting at a rate of 4¾%. He accepted that rate as roughly equivalent to the rates available "[i]n times of stable currency." The Supreme Court of Canada has recommended discounting at a rate of seven percent, a rate equal to market rates on long-term investments minus a government expert's prediction of the long-term rate of price inflation. And in Australia, the High Court has adopted a 2% rate, on the theory that it represents a good approximation of the long-term "real interest rate."

In this country, some courts have taken the same "real interest rate" approach as Australia. They have endorsed the economic theory suggesting that market interest rates include two components—an estimate of anticipated inflation, and a desired "real" rate of return on investment—and that the latter component is essentially constant over time. They have concluded that the inflationary increase in the estimated lost stream of future earnings will therefore be perfectly "offset" by all but the "real" component of the market interest rate.

Still other courts have preferred to continue relying on market interest rates. To avoid undercompensation, they have shown at least tentative willingness to permit evidence of what future price inflation will be in estimating the lost stream of future income.

Finally, some courts have applied a number of techniques that have loosely been termed "total offset" methods. What these methods have in common is that they presume that the ideal discount rate—the after-tax market interest rate on a safe investment—is (to a legally tolerable degree of precision) completely offset by certain elements in the ideal computation of the estimated lost stream of future income. They all assume that the effects of future price inflation on wages are part of what offsets the market interest rate. The methods differ, however, in their assumptions regarding which if any other elements in the first stage of the damages calculation contribute to the offset.

The litigants and the amici in this case urge us to select one of the many rules that have been proposed and establish it for all time as the exclusive method in all federal trials for calculating an award for lost earnings in an inflationary economy. We are not persuaded, however, that such an approach is warranted. For our review of the foregoing cases leads us to draw three conclusions. First, by its very nature the calculation of an award for lost earnings must be a rough approximation. Because the lost stream can never be predicted with complete confidence, any lump sum represents only a "rough and ready" effort to put the plaintiff in the position he would have been in had he not been injured. Second, sustained price inflation can make the award substantially less precise. Inflation's current magnitude and unpredictability create a substantial risk that the damage award will prove to have little relation to the lost wages it purports to replace. Third, the question of lost earnings can arise in many different contexts. In some sectors of the economy, it is far easier to assemble evidence of an individual's most likely career path than in others.

These conclusions all counsel hesitation. Having surveyed the multitude of options available, we will do no more than is necessary to resolve the case before us. We limit our attention to suits under * * * the Act, noting that Congress has provided generally for an award of damages but has not given specific guidance regarding how they are to be calculated. Within that narrow context, we shall define the general boundaries within which a particular award will be considered legally acceptable.

III

* * * In calculating an award for a longshoreman's lost earnings caused by the negligence of a vessel, the discount rate should be chosen on the basis of the factors that are used to estimate the lost stream of future earnings. If the trier of fact relies on a specific forecast of the future rate of price inflation, and if the estimated lost stream of future earnings is calculated to include price inflation along with individual factors and other societal factors, then the proper discount rate would be the after-tax market interest rate. But since specific forecasts of future price inflation remain too unreliable to be useful in many cases, it will normally be a costly and ultimately unproductive waste of longshoremen's resources to make such forecasts the centerpiece of litigation under [the Act]. As Judge Newman has warned, "The average accident trial should not be converted into a graduate seminar on economic forecasting." For that reason, both plaintiffs and trial courts should be discouraged from pursuing that approach.

On the other hand, if forecasts of future price inflation are not used, it is necessary to choose an appropriate below-market discount rate. As long as inflation continues, one must ask how much should be "offset" against the market rate. Once again, that amount should be chosen on the basis of the same factors that are used to estimate the lost stream of future earnings. If full account is taken of the individual and societal factors (excepting price inflation) that can be expected to have resulted in wage increases, then all that should be set off against the market interest rate is an estimate of future price inflation. This would result in one of the "real interest rate" approaches described above. Although we find the economic evidence distinctly inconclusive regarding an essential premise of those approaches, we do not believe a trial court adopting such an approach in a suit under § 5(b) should be reversed if it adopts a rate between one and three percent and explains its choice.[30]

* * *

As a result, the judgment below must be set aside. In performing its damages calculation, the trial court applied the theory of *Kaczkowski*, supra, as a mandatory federal rule of decision, even though the petitioner had insisted that if compensation was to be awarded, it "must be reduced to its present worth." Moreover, this approach seems to have colored the trial court's evaluation of the relevant evidence. At one point, the court noted that respondent had offered a computation of his estimated wages from the date of the accident until his presumed date of retirement, including projected cost-of-living adjustments. It stated, "We do not disagree with these projections, but feel they are inappropriate in view of the holding in *Kaczkowski*." Later in its opinion, however, the court declared, "We do not believe that there was sufficient evidence to establish a basis for estimating increased future productivity for the plaintiff, and therefore we will not inject such a factor in this award."

On remand, the decision on whether to reopen the record should be left to the sound discretion of the trial court. It bears mention that the present record already gives reason to believe a fair award may be more confidently expected in this case than in many. The employment practices in the longshoring industry appear relatively stable and predictable. The parties seem to have had no difficulty in arriving at the period of respondent's future work expectancy, or in predicting the character of the work that he would have been performing during that entire period if he had not been injured. Moreover, the record discloses that respondent's wages were determined by a collective bargaining agreement that explicitly provided for "cost of living" increases, and that recent company history also included a "general" increase and a "job class increment increase." Although the trial court deemed the latter increases irrelevant during its first review because it felt legally compelled to assume they would offset any real interest rate, further study of them on remand will allow the court to determine whether that assumption should be made in this case.

IV

We do not suggest that the trial judge should embark on a search for "delusive exactness." It is perfectly obvious that the most detailed inquiry can at best produce an approximate result. And one cannot ignore the fact that in many instances the award for impaired earning capacity may be overshadowed by a highly impressionistic award for pain and suffering. But we are satisfied that whatever rate the District Court may choose to discount the estimated stream of future earnings, it must make a deliberate choice, rather than assuming that it is bound by a rule of state law.

---

30. The key premise is that the real interest rate is stable over time. It is obviously not perfectly stable, but whether it is even relatively stable is hotly disputed among economists. * * *

The judgment of the Court of Appeals is vacated and the case is remanded for further proceedings consistent with this opinion.

It is so ordered.

NOTES

1. The Court points out in a footnote that the arithmetic of discounting is simple if present value tables are used. Present value tables state the present value of $1 for any period at any discount rate. The present value of any sum is simply that sum multiplied by the present value of $1. See Stuart M. Speiser et al., Recovery for Wrongful Death and Injury (3d ed.1992). For the more mathematically inclined, the present value of $1 due in n periods, where the rate of interest is i, is $1/(1 + i)^n$. As the table below shows, the choice of a discount rate can affect the plaintiff's award dramatically:

PRESENT VALUE OF FUTURE RECEIPTS OF $25,000 A YEAR, FOR VARIOUS PERIODS AND DISCOUNT RATES

Period	Discount Rate			
	2%	5%	10%	12%
10 years	$224,565	$193,043	$153,615	$141,255
20 years	408,785	311,555	212,840	186,735
30 years	501,603	384,313	235,673	201,138

Richard A. Posner, Economic Analysis of Law § 6.11 at 194 (7th ed.2007).

2. The court notes three approaches to accounting for inflation: increasing the award to account for inflation and then discounting by the market rate of interest, partially offsetting inflation against interest and discounting by the real rate of interest, and totally offsetting inflation and interest. Each approach has its adherents. See, e.g., Calva–Cerqueira v. United States, 281 F.Supp.2d 279 (D.D.C.2003) (because some expenses increase faster than inflation, proper approach is to calculate the likely escalation of expenses and then discount to present value using an after tax market rate); Nesmith v. Texaco, 727 F.2d 497 (5th Cir.1984) (proper approach is to exclude evidence of price inflation and discount by a below-market rate); Kaczkowski v. Bolubasz, 491 Pa. 561, 421 A.2d 1027 (1980) (total offset). See David Faigman et al., 1 Modern Scientific Evidence §§ 9.70–9.78 (2008–2009 ed.).

3. Discounting to determine the value of future events plays an important and controversial role in policy analysis, as well as in the calculation of damages. See Symposium, Intergenerational Equity and Discounting, 74 U.Chi.L.Rev. 1 (2007).

4. Why does the Court choose a discount rate based on the interest rate that could be earned by the "best and safest available investments"? Consider the following case.

ENERGY CAPITAL CORP. v. UNITED STATES

United States Court of Appeals, Federal Circuit, 2002
302 F.3d 1314

SCHALL, CIRCUIT JUDGE.

[The Department of Housing and Urban Development agreed to eliminate certain regulatory barriers so Energy Capital could originate loans to allow owners of HUD properties to install energy efficient heating. Energy Capital agreed to structure the loans so that the savings from reduced utility bills would more than cover the annual loan payment. HUD terminated the agreement after a newspaper suggested that the contract had been entered in exchange for Energy Capital's principals' fund-raising efforts on President Clinton's behalf. The newspaper corrected the story the next day to clarify that there were no allegations that HUD officials knew that the principals were Democratic fund-raisers. Four days later, HUD cancelled the agreement. Energy Capital sued for breach of contract, and prevailed. The Court of Claims found that the breach deprived Energy Capital of the profits it would have made on the loans, which were capped by the agreement at $200 million.]

* * *

C. *The Computation of Damages*

Finally, the government contends that the Court of Federal Claims made the following two errors when it discounted the damages award: (i) discounting damages to the date of judgment instead of the date of breach of contract; and (ii) using a risk-free discount rate rather than a risk-adjusted discount rate.

(i) Date of Discounting

The government argues that by discounting to the date of judgment, the trial court effectively awarded prejudgment interest against the United States—a practice which is prohibited by Library of Congress v. Shaw, 478 U.S. 310, 314, 106 S.Ct. 2957, 92 L.Ed.2d 250 (1986), unless there has been an explicit waiver of sovereign immunity. We disagree.

"The time when performance should have taken place is the time as of which damages are measured." In many cases, the appropriate date for calculation of damages is the date of breach. That rule does not apply, however, to anticipated profits or to other expectancy damages that, absent the breach, would have accrued on an ongoing basis over the course of the contract. In those circumstances, damages are measured throughout the course of the contract. To prevent unjust enrichment of the plaintiff, the damages that would have arisen after the date of judgment ("future lost profits") must be discounted to the date of judgment. Discounting future lost profits to the date of judgment merely converts future dollars to an equivalent amount in present dollars at the date of judgment; it is not an award of prejudgment interest and does not violate sovereign immunity.

Almost all of Energy Capital's lost profits would have been earned after the date of judgment. Accordingly, we hold that the trial court did not err in discounting Energy Capital's lost profits to the date of judgment instead of the date of breach.

(ii) Discounting for Risk

The government also argues that the trial court incorrectly applied a risk-free discount rate of 5.9 percent, the rate of return on 10–year Treasury notes with constant maturity. The government contends that the discount rate represents the return an investor would require in order to risk investing capital in a particular venture and that such a rate must incorporate any risk that cash flows would not be realized.

[The court reviewed the parties' experts' testimony. Energy Capital's expert] used what is referred to as the "discounted cash flow" ("DCF") method. "The DCF method is currently in wide use in the analysis of capital stock, acquisition candidates, capital projects, financial instruments, and contract rights. The DCF method measures the value of a business by forecasting its anticipated net cash flows. Such cash flows are then discounted to present value to account for both: (i) the time value of money; and (ii) business and financial risks."

In applying the DCF method, [the expert] began by calculating that the AHELP venture would have produced $24.6 million in profits absent the breach. Mr. Arcy then discounted the $24.6 million amount to present value using a risk-adjusted discount rate. He determined that the most appropriate risk-adjusted discount rate was based on the average rate of return on mortgage real estate investment trusts ("REITs"). An REIT is a legal entity recognized by the Internal Revenue Code. A mortgage REIT is a REIT that chooses to own mortgage interests in real estate, as opposed to owning the encumbered real estate itself.

[The expert] relied on mortgage REITs because a mortgage REIT would be interested in acquiring AHELP loans. During the appropriate time, the average dividend yield (i.e. the rate of return) for mortgage REITs was approximately 8.5 percent. Mr. Arcy then added 2 percent to that rate in order to account for the debt component and profit component, thereby arriving at a risk-adjusted discount rate of 10.5 percent.

[The government's expert, Mr. Hisey,] agreed * * * that a risk-adjusted discount rate was appropriate, but opined that a higher risk-adjusted discount rate of 25% should be used. Mr. Hisey considered the AHELP Program to be a form of specialized lending. Mr. Hisey, accordingly, averaged the returns of five specialized lending companies.

In post-trial briefing, Energy Capital backed away from a portion of the valuation method used by its own expert, Mr. Arcy. Specifically, Energy Capital objected to the use of a risk-adjusted discount rate; Energy Capital argued instead that LaSalle Talman Bank v. United States, 45

Fed. Cl. 64, 109 n. 69 (1999), mandates the use of a risk-free rate of return, which LaSalle suggests is the current rate of interest on Treasury securities.

The Court of Federal Claims * * * agreed with Energy Capital that the appropriate discount rate was the rate of return on "conservative investment instruments." * * * The court thereby took judicial notice of the rate of return on 10-year Treasury notes with constant maturity on the date of judgment (5.9%) and discounted the damages award to present value using this conservative discount rate. * * *

* * *

The purpose of the lost profits damages calculation is to put Energy Capital "in as good a position as [it] would have been in had the contract been performed." Restatement (Second) of Contracts § 344(a). * * *

Energy Capital argues that once the Court of Federal Claims determined that its profits were reasonably certain, no further consideration of risk was appropriate, because risk already had been considered in determining whether there would have been profits. We disagree. A venture that is anticipated to produce $1 million in profits and that has a 95% chance of success is obviously more valuable than a venture that is anticipated to produce $1 million in profits with only a 90% chance of success—and yet, both ventures would most likely be determined to have a reasonable certainty of producing profits. Therefore, the fact that the trial court has determined that profits were reasonably certain does not mean that risk should play no role in valuing the stream of anticipated profits. In other words, by finding that Energy Capital's lost profits were reasonably certain, the trial court determined that the probability that the AHELP venture would be successful was high enough that a determination of profits would not be unduly speculative. The determination of the amount of those profits, however, could still be affected by the level of riskiness inherent in the venture.

Energy Capital argues that the sole purpose in discounting is to account for the time value of money. Again, we disagree. When calculating the value of an anticipated cash flow stream pursuant to the DCF method, the discount rate performs two functions: (i) it accounts for the time value of money; and (ii) it adjusts the value of the cash flow stream to account for risk.

We do not hold that in every case a risk-adjusted discount rate is required. Rather, we merely hold that the appropriate discount rate is a question of fact. In a case where lost profits have been awarded, each party may present evidence regarding the value of those profits, including an appropriate discount rate.

* * *

In the case before us, both parties presented CPA experts who agreed that a risk-adjusted discount rate was appropriate. Neither expert suggested that using a risk-free discount rate would accurately represent the value of the AHELP venture. Because the trial court found that [the plaintiff's expert's] discount rate was more credible, we hold that 10.5% is the appropriate discount rate in this case.

* * *

Notes

1. The discounted cash flow method was introduced in connection with the discussion of value in section B of this chapter. Why does the court decide that a risk-adjusted discount rate is more appropriate than the risk-free rate used in *Jones & Laughlin Steel Corporation v. Pfeifer*?

2. Do you see a connection between the issue in this case and the issues raised in *Steinhauser* (p. 536) and *Dillon* (p. 538)?

3. TAXATION OF DAMAGE AWARDS

COMMISSIONER OF INTERNAL REVENUE v. BANKS

Supreme Court of the United States, 2005
543 U.S. 426, 125 S.Ct. 826, 160 L.Ed.2d 859

JUSTICE KENNEDY delivered the opinion of the Court.

The question in these consolidated cases is whether the portion of a money judgment or settlement paid to a plaintiff's attorney under a contingent-fee agreement is income to the plaintiff under the Internal Revenue Code, 26 U.S.C. § 1 et seq.

* * *

We hold that, as a general rule, when a litigant's recovery constitutes income, the litigant's income includes the portion of the recovery paid to the attorney as a contingent fee. * * *

I

A. *Commissioner v. Banks*

In 1986, respondent John W. Banks, II, was fired from his job as an educational consultant with the California Department of Education. He retained an attorney on a contingent-fee basis and filed a civil suit against the employer in a United States District Court. The complaint alleged employment discrimination * * *. After trial commenced in 1990, the parties settled for $464,000. Banks paid $150,000 of this amount to his attorney pursuant to the fee agreement.

Banks did not include any of the $464,000 in settlement proceeds as gross income in his 1990 federal income tax return. In 1997 the Commissioner of Internal Revenue issued Banks a notice of deficiency for the 1990 tax year. The Tax Court upheld the Commissioner's determination, finding that all the settlement proceeds, including the $150,000 Banks had paid to his attorney, must be included in Banks' gross income.

The Court of Appeals for the Sixth Circuit reversed in part. It agreed the net amount received by Banks was included in gross income but not the amount paid to the attorney. * * * [T]he court held the contingent-fee agreement was not an anticipatory assignment of Banks' income because the litigation recovery was not already earned, vested, or even relatively certain to be paid when the contingent-fee contract was made. A contingent-fee arrangement, the court reasoned, is more like a partial assignment of income-producing property than an assignment of income. The attorney is not the mere beneficiary of the client's largess, but rather earns his fee through skill and diligence. This reasoning, the court held, applies whether or not state law grants the attorney any special property interest (e.g., a superior lien) in part of the judgment or settlement proceeds.

B. *Commissioner v. Banaitis*

After leaving his job as a vice president and loan officer at the Bank of California in 1987, Sigitas J. Banaitis retained an attorney on a contingent-fee basis and brought suit in Oregon state court against the Bank of California and its successor in ownership, the Mitsubishi Bank. The complaint alleged that Mitsubishi Bank willfully interfered with Banaitis' employment contract, and that the Bank of California attempted to induce Banaitis to breach his fiduciary duties to customers and discharged him when he refused. The jury awarded Banaitis compensatory and punitive damages. After resolution of all appeals and post-trial motions, the parties settled. The defendants paid $4,864,547 to Banaitis; and, following the formula set forth in the contingent-fee contract, the defendants paid an additional $3,864,012 directly to Banaitis' attorney.

Banaitis did not include the amount paid to his attorney in gross income on his federal income tax return, and the Commissioner issued a notice of deficiency. The Tax Court upheld the Commissioner's determination, but the Court of Appeals for the Ninth Circuit reversed. In contrast to the Court of Appeals for the Sixth Circuit, the Banaitis court viewed state law as pivotal. Where state law confers on the attorney no special property rights in his fee, the court said, the whole amount of the judgment or settlement ordinarily is included in the plaintiff's gross income. Oregon state law, however, like the law of some other States, grants attorneys a superior lien in the contingent-fee portion of any recovery. As a result, the court held, contingent-fee agreements under Oregon law operate not as an anticipatory assignment of the client's income but as a partial transfer to the attorney of some of the client's property in the lawsuit.

II

To clarify why the issue here is of any consequence for tax purposes, two preliminary observations are useful. The first concerns the general issue of deductibility. For the tax years in question the legal expenses in these cases could have been taken as miscellaneous itemized deductions subject to the ordinary requirements, but doing so would have been of no help to respondents because of the operation of the Alternative Minimum Tax (AMT). For noncorporate individual taxpayers, the AMT establishes a tax liability floor equal to 26 percent of the taxpayer's "alternative minimum taxable income" (minus specified exemptions) up to $175,000, plus 28 percent of alternative minimum taxable income over $175,000. Alternative minimum taxable income, unlike ordinary gross income, does not allow any miscellaneous itemized deductions.

Second, after these cases arose Congress enacted the American Jobs Creation Act of 2004. Section 703 of the Act amended the Code * * *. The amendment allows a taxpayer, in computing adjusted gross income, to deduct "attorney fees and court costs paid by, or on behalf of, the taxpayer in connection with any action involving a claim of unlawful discrimination." The Act defines "unlawful discrimination" to include a number of specific federal statutes, any federal whistle-blower statute, and any federal, state, or local law "providing for the enforcement of civil rights" or "regulating any aspect of the employment relationship ... or prohibiting the discharge of an employee, the discrimination against an employee, or any other form of retaliation or reprisal against an employee for asserting rights or taking other actions permitted by law." These deductions are permissible even when the AMT applies. Had the Act been in force for the transactions now under review, these cases likely would not have arisen. The Act is not retroactive, however, so while it may cover future taxpayers in respondents' position, it does not pertain here.

III

The Internal Revenue Code defines "gross income" for federal tax purposes as "all income from whatever source derived." The definition extends broadly to all economic gains not otherwise exempted. A taxpayer cannot exclude an economic gain from gross income by assigning the gain in advance to another party. The rationale for the so-called anticipatory assignment of income doctrine is the principle that gains should be taxed "to those who earn them," a maxim we have called "the first principle of income taxation." The anticipatory assignment doctrine is meant to prevent taxpayers from avoiding taxation through "arrangements and contracts however skillfully devised to prevent [income] when paid from vesting even for a second in the man who earned it." The rule is preventative and motivated by administrative as well as substantive concerns, so we do not inquire whether any particular assignment has a discernible tax avoidance purpose. * * *

In an ordinary case attribution of income is resolved by asking whether a taxpayer exercises complete dominion over the income in question. In the context of anticipatory assignments, however, the assignor often does not have dominion over the income at the moment of receipt. In that instance the question becomes whether the assignor retains dominion over the income-generating asset, because the taxpayer "who owns or controls the source of the income, also controls the disposition of that which he could have received himself and diverts the payment from himself to others as the means of procuring the satisfaction of his wants." Looking to control over the income-generating asset, then, preserves the principle that income should be taxed to the party who earns the income and enjoys the consequent benefits.

In the case of a litigation recovery the income-generating asset is the cause of action that derives from the plaintiff's legal injury. The plaintiff retains dominion over this asset throughout the litigation. We do not understand respondents to argue otherwise. Rather, respondents advance two counterarguments. First, they say that * * * the value of a legal claim is speculative at the moment of assignment, and may be worth nothing at all. Second, respondents insist that the claimant's legal injury is not the only source of the ultimate recovery. The attorney, according to respondents, also contributes income-generating assets—effort and expertise—without which the claimant likely could not prevail. On these premises respondents urge us to treat a contingent-fee agreement as establishing, for tax purposes, something like a joint venture or partnership in which the client and attorney combine their respective assets—the client's claim and the attorney's skill—and apportion any resulting profits.

We reject respondents' arguments. Though the value of the plaintiff's claim may be speculative at the moment the fee agreement is signed, the anticipatory assignment doctrine is not limited to instances when the precise dollar value of the assigned income is known in advance. * * * In the cases before us * * * the taxpayer retained control over the income-generating asset, diverted some of the income produced to another party, and realized a benefit by doing so. * * * That the amount of income the asset would produce was uncertain at the moment of assignment is of no consequence.

We further reject the suggestion to treat the attorney-client relationship as a sort of business partnership or joint venture for tax purposes. The relationship between client and attorney, regardless of the variations in particular compensation agreements or the amount of skill and effort the attorney contributes, is a quintessential principal-agent relationship. The client may rely on the attorney's expertise and special skills to achieve a result the client could not achieve alone. That, however, is true of most principal-agent relationships, and it does not alter the fact that the client retains ultimate dominion and control over the underlying claim. The control is evident when it is noted that, although the attorney can make tactical decisions without consulting the client, the plaintiff still must determine whether to settle or proceed to judgment and make, as well, other critical decisions. Even where the attorney exercises independent judgment without supervision by, or consultation with, the client, the attorney, as an agent, is obligated to act solely on behalf of, and for the exclusive benefit of, the client-principal, rather than for the benefit of the attorney or any other party.

The attorney is an agent who is duty bound to act only in the interests of the principal, and so it is appropriate to treat the full amount of the recovery as income to the principal. * * * The portion paid to the agent may be deductible, but absent some other provision of law it is not excludable from the principal's gross income.

This rule applies whether or not the attorney-client contract or state law confers any special rights or protections on the attorney, so long as these protections do not alter the fundamental principal-agent character of the relationship. State laws vary with respect to the strength of an attorney's security interest in a contingent fee and the remedies available to an attorney should the client discharge or attempt to defraud the attorney. No state laws of which we are aware, however, even those that purport to give attorneys an "ownership" interest in their fees, convert the attorney from an agent to a partner.

* * *

IV

The foregoing suffices to dispose of Banaitis' case. Banks' case, however, involves a further consideration. Banks brought his claims under federal statutes that authorize fee awards to prevailing plaintiffs' attorneys. He contends that application of the anticipatory assignment principle would be inconsistent with the purpose of statutory fee shifting provisions. In the federal system statutory fees are typically awarded by the court under the lodestar approach, and the plaintiff usually has little control over the amount awarded. Sometimes, as when the plaintiff seeks only injunctive relief, or when the statute caps plaintiffs' recoveries, or when for other reasons damages are substantially less than attorney's fees, court-awarded attorney's fees can exceed a plaintiff's monetary recovery. See, e.g., Riverside v. Rivera, 477 U.S. 561, 564–565, 91 L.Ed.2d 466, 106 S.Ct. 2686 (1986) (compensatory and punitive damages of $33,350; attorney's fee award of $245,456.25). Treating the fee award as income to the plaintiff in such cases, it is argued, can lead to the perverse result that the plaintiff loses money by winning the suit. Furthermore, it is urged that treating statutory fee awards as income to plaintiffs would undermine the effectiveness of fee-shifting statutes in deputizing plaintiffs and their lawyers to act as private attorneys general.

We need not address these claims. After Banks settled his case, the fee paid to his attorney was calculated solely on the basis of the private contingent-fee contract. There was no court-ordered fee award, nor was there any indication in Banks' contract with his attorney, or in the settlement agreement with the defendant, that the contingent fee paid to Banks' attorney was in lieu of statutory fees Banks might otherwise have been entitled to recover. Also, the amendment added by the American Jobs Creation Act redresses the concern for many, perhaps most, claims governed by fee-shifting statutes.

* * *

For the reasons stated, the judgments of the Courts of Appeals for the Sixth and Ninth Circuits are reversed, and the cases are remanded for further proceedings consistent with this opinion.

It is so ordered.

Notes

1. Generally speaking, how a damage award is characterized for tax purposes depends on what the award replaces. Thus, Banks' and Banaitas' awards, which replaced taxable wages, had to be included in their gross taxable income. See, e.g., Gail v. United States, 58 F.3d 580 (10th Cir. 1995)(portion of a judgment representing unpaid gas royalties characterized as income, portion representing diminution in real property value characterized as capital gain); Commissioner v. Gillette Motor Transport, Inc., 364 U.S. 130, 80 S.Ct. 1497, 4 L.Ed.2d 1617 (1960).

Damages in some personal injury cases, however, can be excluded from gross income even when they replace otherwise taxable income. Section 104(a)(2) of the Internal Revenue Code, as amended in 1996, provides:

§ 104. Compensation for injuries or sickness.

(a) In general. Except in the case of amounts attributable to (and not in excess of) deductions allowed under section 213 (relating to medical, expenses, etc.) for any prior taxable year, gross income does not include:

* * *

(2) the amount of any damages (other than punitive damages) received or agreement and whether as lump sums or as periodic payments on account of personal physical injuries or physical sickness; * * *

For purposes of paragraph (2), emotional distress shall not be treated as a physical injury or physical sickness. The preceding sentence shall not apply to an amount of damages not in excess of the amount paid for medical care (described in subparagraph (A) or (B) of section 213(d)(1)) attributable to emotional distress. * * *

To attempt a rough translation: punitive damages are to be included as gross income.[a] Otherwise, damages received "on account of personal physical injuries or physical sickness" are excluded from gross income (unless they represent compensation for medical expenses that have already been deducted).

Emotional distress damages, however, are included in gross income, although damages awarded for medical care attributable to emotional distress are excluded. (As above, if those medical expenses were deducted from gross income when they were incurred, they are not excluded.)

---

a. There is one exception. In wrongful death actions in some states, the plaintiff cannot recover compensatory damages; only punitive damages are permitted. Section 104(c) provides that punitive damages are to be excluded from gross income if they are awarded in a wrongful death action in a state that allows only punitive damages in wrongful death actions.

The Conference Committee report on the 1996 amendment, which was part of the Small Business Act of 1996, is very helpful in sorting this all out. The report can be found in CCH Standard Federal Tax Reporter, Vol. 2, § 1.104–1, 6660.137 (1996).

2. For a brief time, section 104(a)(2)'s constitutionality was in doubt. In *Murphy v. IRS,* the plaintiff recovered damages for emotional distress in a whistle-blower action. She challenged the authority of the Internal Revenue Service to tax her award, first arguing that the recovery was compensation "on account of personal physical injury or sickness," and second that taxing her award was unconstitutional because her damages were not income within the meaning of the Sixteenth Amendment. Initially, the D.C. Circuit agreed with her constitutional argument. Murphy v. IRS, 460 F.3d 79 (D.C.Cir.2006). After much outcry, the court reversed course, granting a rehearing sua sponte and vacating its earlier opinion. 493 F.3d 170 (D.C.Cir.2007), cert. denied, 554 U.S. ___, 128 S.Ct. 2050, 170 L.Ed.2d 793 (2008). The critical question, according to the court, was not whether nonpecuniary damages are income in the sense of accession to wealth, but rather whether Congress intended to, and had the power to, include them in the definition of gross income. The court found that as a matter of statutory interpretation, Congress intended nonpecuniary damages to be included in the definition of gross income, and that Congress had the power to do so under art. I, § 9 of the Constitution.

3. *Income taxes, lost wages and jury instructions.* Under section 104, if the plaintiff recovers damages for lost wages or lost earning capacity "on account of personal physical injury or sickness," the amount of the award is excluded from gross income, even though the wages would have been taxed had they been earned. Thus, as the Court in Jones & Laughlin Steel Corp. v. Pfeifer, 462 U.S. 523, 534, 103 S.Ct. 2541, 2549, 76 L.Ed.2d 768 (1983), noted (at p. 621), "Since the damages award is tax-free, the relevant stream is ideally of after-tax wages and benefits."

Despite this, most courts do not consider taxes when calculating lost earning capacity. The traditional rule has been that lost earning capacity is based on gross earnings, because evidence as to future tax rates and the plaintiff's future tax status is too speculative. In Norfolk & Western Railway v. Liepelt, 444 U.S. 490, 100 S.Ct. 755, 62 L.Ed.2d 689 (1980), the Supreme Court challenged the traditional rule, and held that in a wrongful death case arising under the Federal Employers' Liability Act (where federal and not state law controls), damages for lost support should be based on net earnings after taxes, to avoid overcompensation. Since *Norfolk,* a few states have followed the Supreme Court's lead. See, e.g., Slater v. Skyhawk Transportation, Inc., 77 F.Supp.2d 580 (D.N.J.1999) (New Jersey bases damages on net earnings). Most, however, continue to exclude evidence that the plaintiff's wages would have been taxed. E.g., Estevez v. United States, 72 F.Supp.2d 205 (S.D.N.Y.1999) (applying New York law).

If the jury is not going to hear evidence about the taxes the plaintiff is avoiding, should the jury at least be instructed that the award itself is not taxable, so they won't assume the award will be taxed and inflate it? Again, although *Norfolk* held it was error to refuse to instruct the jury that their award would not be taxed, most courts refuse to do so. See Stover v. Lakeland

Square Owners Association, 434 N.W.2d 866 (Iowa 1989) (citing cases). Although *Norfolk* has had some impact, see, e.g., Bussell v. DeWalt Products Corp., 105 N.J. 223, 519 A.2d 1379 (1987), most courts continue to believe that an instruction that awards are not taxable is unnecessary and unwise. It presumes that the jury will not heed its mandate to decide the case only on the evidence before it, opens a "Pandora's box" of possible cautionary instructions, and introduces confusion and speculation.

4. *Damages "on account of personal physical injury or physical sickness."* Before the 1996 amendments, section 104(a)(2) excluded from gross income "damages received on account of personal injury." Internal Revenue Service regulations interpreting section 104(a)(2) provide that "the term 'damages received' * * * means an amount received through prosecution of a legal suit or action based upon tort or tort-type rights, or through a settlement agreement entered into in lieu of such prosecution." 26 C.F.R. § 1.104–1(c)(1994).

Applying this earlier version of section 104(a)(2), the Supreme Court had held that back pay awards in age discrimination cases were not "damages received on account of personal injury" because the wage loss was caused by discrimination, not by a personal injury. Commissioner of Internal Revenue v. Schleier, 515 U.S. 323, 115 S.Ct. 2159, 132 L.Ed.2d 294 (1995); see also United States v. Burke, 504 U.S. 229, 112 S.Ct. 1867, 119 L.Ed.2d 34 (1992) (back pay in Title VII case is not excludable from gross income because Title VII's remedial scheme does not address a tort-like personal injury). Under the amended version of section 104(a)(2), which requires that the award be "on account of a personal physical injury," damage awards in discrimination cases would be even more clearly includable in gross income. See Laura Sager & Stephen Cohen, How the Income Tax Undermines Civil Rights Law, 73 S.Cal.L.Rev. 1075 (2000).

Before the 1996 amendments, damages awards in slander, libel, constitutional tort cases and so on were arguably awards "on account of personal injury" and thus excludable from gross income. See, e.g., Fabry v. Commissioner, 223 F.3d 1261 (11th Cir.2000)(damages for injury to reputation are "on account of personal injury" and excludable from gross income in 1992 tax year); Greer v. United States, 207 F.3d 322 (6th Cir.2000) (damages for wrongful termination, injury to reputation, and mental anguish could be excluded from gross income in 1995 tax year); Bent v. Commissioner of Internal Revenue, 835 F.2d 67 (3d Cir.1987) (damages for violation of first amendment rights are "on account of personal injury"). The 1996 amendment's requirement that the award be "on account of personal *physical* injury" would seem to foreclose any argument in the future that such awards are excludable from gross income.

5. *Taxes and Interest.* Is prejudgment or postjudgment interest excludable from gross income if it is awarded in a personal injury case? The consensus seems to be that it is not. In three circuits, courts of appeals have concluded that prejudgment interest on a personal injury award is not received "on account of" personal injury, and therefore is not excludable from gross income. See Rozpad v. Commissioner, 154 F.3d 1 (1st Cir. 1998)(prejudgment interest award under Rhode Island law); Brabson v. Unit-

ed States, 73 F.3d 1040 (10th Cir.) (prejudgment interest award under Colorado law), cert. denied, 519 U.S. 1039, 117 S.Ct. 607, 136 L.Ed.2d 533 (1996); Kovacs v. Commissioner, 25 F.3d 1048 (6th Cir.1993) (prejudgment interest award under Michigan law), cert. denied, 513 U.S. 963, 115 S.Ct. 424, 130 L.Ed.2d 338 (1994). See also Francisco v. United States, 267 F.3d 303 (3d Cir.2001) (under Pennsylvania law, prejudgment interest could not be recovered for loss of consortium, therefore, prejudgment interest authorized by statute in cases where defendant delayed trial or did not make an adequate settlement offer was not an award of damages "on account of personal injury").

In each of these cases, the determination that prejudgment interest was not "damages on account of personal injury" turned on the fact that at common law, prejudgment interest was not recoverable in personal injury cases where the amount of damages was unliquidated. Therefore, the award of prejudgment interest in a personal injury case was seen as attributable to the defendant's delay, rather than "on account of" the personal injuries. Is this understanding of prejudgment interest consistent with the understanding of prejudgment interest in *Kansas v. Colorado?*

Chapter 6

Punishment and Punitive Damages

■ ■ ■

Both civil and criminal law provide certain remedies not measured by the rightful position of either the plaintiff or the defendant. Among these remedies are imprisonment, fines, civil penalties, punitive damages, and forfeitures. The imposition of these sanctions does not depend solely on a showing of injury or damage but rather are focused on penalizing the wrongful conduct of the defendant. Punishment is a familiar concept under criminal law, where defendants are imprisoned or fined for illegal conduct deemed unacceptable by society. Punishment is also available under the civil law primarily through the remedy of punitive damages, which are monetary penalties designed to punish the defendant and deter the defendant and others from similar conduct in the future. This chapter explores the contours of punitive damages: why they are awarded, when they are awarded, and how the proper amount of punishment is determined.

A. DISTINGUISHING CIVIL AND CRIMINAL PUNISHMENT

Where the law gives the court discretion in imposing sanctions, particularly criminal sanctions, judges typically consider the gravity of the offense and the harm or injury it has caused. Driving the calculus is the underlying theory of the purpose of the sanction: punishment, protection, or rehabilitation. Judges consider the impact of the sanction on the defendant and the community in terms of the ultimate purposes of the penalty: (a) seeking retribution against the defendant by providing "just desserts" for committing morally reprehensible acts; (b) deterring the defendant from committing other crimes; (c) deterring others who know of the sanction from committing such violations; (d) preventing the defendant through incarceration or supervision on parole or probation from committing such violations; and (e) rehabilitating or reforming the personality and character of the defendant so that he will not commit further violations and will lead a socially beneficial life.

These theories of criminal punishment are evident in the rationales underlying civil penalties. As the Supreme Court explains in the case of

Exxon Shipping Co. v. Baker (p. 673), American law has historically identified three justifications for punitive damages: retribution, deterrence, and compensation for intangible injuries. Modern scholars are in disagreement as to which of these theories should drive the award of punitive damages. See Mark Geistfeld, Punitive Damages, Retribution, and Due Process, 81 S.Cal.L.Rev. 263 (2008) (justifying punitive damages as retribution or "vindictive" damages); Dan Markel, Retributive Damages: A Theory of Punitive Damages as Intermediate Sanction, 94 Cornell L.Rev. 2 (2009) (providing a normative account of the theory of punitive damages as retribution); Anthony Sebok, Punitive Damages: From Myth to Theory, 92 Iowa L.Rev. 957 (2007) (urging a return to the theoretical emphasis on the retributive element of punitive damages in rectifying a private wrong); Benjamin C. Zipursky, A Theory of Punitive Damages, 84 Tex.L.Rev. 105 (2005) (grounding punitive damages in a theory of civil recourse and right of plaintiff to be punitive in response to a wrong); Dan B. Dobbs, Ending Punishment in "Punitive" Damages: Deterrence–Measured Remedies, 40 Ala.L.Rev. 831 (1989) (arguing for specific deterrence theory that would measure punitive damages by defendant's gain or plaintiff's litigation costs). New theories have also been advanced, such as using punitive damages as societal damages or to advance the greater public good. See Christopher J. Robinette, Peace: A Public Purpose for Punitive Damages?, 2 Charleston L.Rev. 327 (2008); Catherine M. Sharkey, Punitive Damages as Societal Damages, 113 Yale L.J. 347 (2003). The underlying theory for punitive damages is critical to many ongoing debates about these damages: whether they should be awarded at all or whether the criminal law will suffice; what the proper measure of relief is given the underlying goal; and, whether there are or should be limitations upon awards.

In many cases, it may be difficult to distinguish between sanctions that are punitive to the defendant and those that are remedial in the sense that they return a plaintiff to his rightful position or further a public policy such as safety or preventing fraud. Frequently, a sanction serves both purposes. David Yellen & Carl V. Mayer, Coordinating Sanctions for Corporate Misconduct: Civil or Criminal Punishment?, 29 Am. Crim.L.Rev. 961 (1992) (discussing examples from government contracting). Treble damages are a good example. Treble damages are monetary remedies awarded in the amount of three times the proven damage to the plaintiff. Often these are automatically provided by statute; for example, the antitrust statute, 15 U.S.C. § 15, provides that successful plaintiffs can recover their damages plus treble damages. Treble damages serve multiple purposes, as they work to punish the defendant and also further remedial goals of facilitating the plaintiff's litigation where the damage award is small and the governmental burden would be larger in pursuing the case. The U.S. Supreme Court recognized in PacifiCare Health Systems, Inc. v. Book, 538 U.S. 401, 123 S.Ct. 1531, 155 L.Ed.2d 578 (2003), that treble damages can be construed as either punitive or compensatory, depending upon the context:

Our cases have placed different statutory treble-damages provisions on different points along the spectrum between purely compensatory and strictly punitive awards. Thus, in Vermont Agency of Natural Resources v. United States ex rel. Stevens, 529 U.S. 765, 784, 120 S.Ct. 1858, 146 L.Ed.2d 836 (2000), we characterized the treble-damages provision of the False Claims Act, 31 U.S.C. §§ 3729–3733, as "essentially punitive in nature." In Brunswick Corp. v. Pueblo Bowl–O–Mat, Inc., 429 U.S. 477, 485, 97 S.Ct. 690, 50 L.Ed.2d 701 (1977), on the other hand, we explained that the treble-damages provision of § 4 of the Clayton Act, 15 U.S.C. § 15, "is in essence a remedial provision." Likewise in American Soc. of Mechanical Engineers, Inc. v. Hydrolevel Corp., 456 U.S. 556, 575, 102 S.Ct. 1935, 72 L.Ed.2d 330 (1982), we noted that "the antitrust private action [which allows for treble damages] was created primarily as *a remedy* for the victims of antitrust violations." (Emphasis added.) And earlier this Term, in Cook County v. United States ex rel. Chandler, 538 U.S. 119, 130, 123 S.Ct. 1239, we stated that "it is important to realize that treble damages have a compensatory side, serving remedial purposes in addition to punitive objectives." Indeed, we have repeatedly acknowledged that the treble-damages provision contained in RICO itself is remedial in nature. In Agency Holding Corp. v. Malley–Duff & Associates, Inc., 483 U.S. 143, 151, 107 S.Ct. 2759, 97 L.Ed.2d 121 (1987), we stated that "[b]oth RICO and the Clayton Act are designed *to remedy* economic injury by providing for the recovery of treble damages, costs, and attorney's fees." (Emphasis added.) And in Shearson/American Express Inc. v. McMahon, 482 U.S. 220, 241, 107 S.Ct. 2332, 96 L.Ed.2d 185 (1987) we took note of the "remedial function" of RICO's treble-damages provision.

Given this ambiguity as to the nature of treble damages, the Court rejected the assertion that arbitration was not compelled in the case because treble damages under RICO were punitive and prohibited by the parties' arbitration agreements which precluded the arbitrator from awarding "punitive or exemplary damages." *PacifiCare*, 538 U.S. at 406. Thus, the distinction between criminal and civil sanctions can be important to a critical issue in the case, as illustrated further in *Hudson v. United States*.

HUDSON v. UNITED STATES

Supreme Court of the United States, 1997
522 U.S. 93, 118 S.Ct. 488, 139 L.Ed.2d 450

CHIEF JUSTICE REHNQUIST delivered the opinion of the Court.

The Government administratively imposed monetary penalties and occupational debarment on petitioners for violation of federal banking statutes, and later criminally indicted them for essentially the same conduct. We hold that the Double Jeopardy Clause of the Fifth Amendment is not a bar to the later criminal prosecution because the administrative proceedings were civil, not criminal. Our reasons for so holding in large part disavow the method of analysis used in United States v. Halper, 490 U.S. 435, 448, 109 S.Ct. 1892, 1901–1902, 104 L.Ed.2d 487 (1989), and reaffirm the previously established rule exemplified in United States v. Ward, 448 U.S. 242, 248–249, 100 S.Ct. 2636, 2641–2642, 65 L.Ed.2d 742 (1980). * * *

[Hudson and two others were officers and/or shareholders of the First National Bank of Tipton and the First National Bank of Hammon. In 1989 the Office of the Comptroller of the Currency (OCC) brought administrative civil claims against the three alleging that loans nominally made to third parties were in reality made to Hudson in violation of various federal banking statutes and regulations. The OCC also sought to bar the three from any further management of federally insured banks. The matter was settled for individual civil penalties between $12,500 and $16,500 and an agreement not to participate in any manner in a banking institution. In August 1992, the three were indicted on 22 counts of conspiracy, misapplication of bank funds, and making false bank entries. The violations charged rested on the same transactions that formed the basis of the administrative actions brought by the OCC.]

The Double Jeopardy Clause provides that no "person [shall] be subject for the same offence to be twice put in jeopardy of life or limb." We have long recognized that the Double Jeopardy Clause does not prohibit the imposition of any additional sanction that could, " 'in common parlance,' " be described as punishment. The Clause protects only against the imposition of multiple criminal punishments for the same offense, * * * and then only when such occurs in successive proceedings. Whether a particular punishment is criminal or civil is, at least initially, a matter of statutory construction. A court must first ask whether the legislature, "in establishing the penalizing mechanism, indicated either expressly or impliedly a preference for one label or the other." Even in those cases where the legislature "has indicated an intention to establish a civil penalty, we have inquired further whether the statutory scheme was so punitive either in purpose or effect," as to "transfor[m] what was clearly intended as a civil remedy into a criminal penalty," Rex Trailer Co. v. United States, 350 U.S. 148, 154, 76 S.Ct. 219, 222, 100 L.Ed. 149 (1956).

In making this latter determination, the factors listed in Kennedy v. Mendoza–Martinez, 372 U.S. 144, 168–169, 83 S.Ct. 554, 567–568, 9 L.Ed.2d 644 (1963), provide useful guideposts * * * It is important to note, however, that "these factors must be considered in relation to the statute on its face," and "only the clearest proof" will suffice to override legislative intent and transform what has been denominated a civil remedy into a criminal penalty. *Ward*.

Our opinion in *United States v. Halper* marked the first time we applied the Double Jeopardy Clause to a sanction without first determining that it was criminal in nature. * * * [In United States v. Halper, 490

U.S. 435, 109 S.Ct. 1892, 104 L.Ed.2d 487 (1989), a laboratory manager was convicted of 65 counts of making false claims under the Medicare program resulting in a total over-payment to the laboratory of $585. He was sentenced to two years imprisonment and a $5000 fine. The government then brought a civil action against him under the False Claims Act, 31 U.S.C. §§ 3729–3731. The District Court found that the statutory civil penalty of more than $130,000 would violate the Double Jeopardy Clause. The Supreme Court unanimously reached the same conclusion: "We * * * hold that under the Double Jeopardy Clause a defendant who already has been punished in a criminal prosecution may not be subjected to an additional civil sanction to the extent that the second sanction may not fairly be characterized as remedial, but only as a deterrent or retribution."]

As the *Halper* Court saw it, the imposition of "punishment" of any kind was subject to double jeopardy constraints, and whether a sanction constituted "punishment" depended primarily on whether it served the traditional "goals of punishment," namely "retribution and deterrence." Any sanction that was so "overwhelmingly disproportionate" to the injury caused that it could not "fairly be said solely to serve [the] remedial purpose" of compensating the government for its loss, was thought to be explainable only as "serving either retributive or deterrent purposes."

The analysis applied by the *Halper* Court deviated from our traditional double jeopardy doctrine in two key respects. First, the *Halper* Court bypassed the threshold question: whether the successive punishment at issue is a "criminal" punishment. Instead, it focused on whether the sanction, regardless of whether it was civil or criminal, was so grossly disproportionate to the harm caused as to constitute "punishment." In so doing, the Court elevated a single *Kennedy* factor—whether the sanction appeared excessive in relation to its nonpunitive purposes—to dispositive status. But as we emphasized in *Kennedy* itself, no one factor should be considered controlling as they "may often point in differing directions." The second significant departure in *Halper* was the Court's decision to "asses[s] the character of the actual sanctions imposed," rather than, as *Kennedy* demanded, evaluating the "statute on its face" to determine whether it provided for what amounted to a criminal sanction.

We believe that *Halper's* deviation from longstanding double jeopardy principles was ill considered. As subsequent cases have demonstrated, *Halper's* test for determining whether a particular sanction is "punitive," and thus subject to the strictures of the Double Jeopardy Clause, has proved unworkable. We have since recognized that all civil penalties have some deterrent effect. See Department of Revenue of Mont. v. Kurth Ranch, 511 U.S. 767, 777, n. 14, 114 S.Ct. 1937, 1945, n. 14, 128 L.Ed.2d 767 (1994); United States v. Ursery, 518 U.S. 267, 284, n. 2, 116 S.Ct. 2135, 2145, n. 2, 135 L.Ed.2d 549 (1996). If a sanction must be "solely" remedial (i.e., entirely nondeterrent) to avoid implicating the Double Jeopardy Clause, then no civil penalties are beyond the scope of the Clause. Under *Halper's* method of analysis, a court must also look at the "sanction actually imposed" to determine whether the Double Jeopardy Clause is implicated. Thus, it will not be possible to determine whether the Double Jeopardy Clause is violated until a defendant has proceeded through a trial to judgment. But in those cases where the civil proceeding follows the criminal proceeding, this approach flies in the face of the notion that the Double Jeopardy Clause forbids the government from even "attempting a second time to punish criminally."

Finally, it should be noted that some of the ills at which *Halper* was directed are addressed by other constitutional provisions. The Due Process and Equal Protection Clauses already protect individuals from sanctions which are downright irrational. The Eighth Amendment protects against excessive civil fines, including forfeitures. The additional protection afforded by extending double jeopardy protections to proceedings heretofore thought to be civil is more than offset by the confusion created by attempting to distinguish between "punitive" and "nonpunitive" penalties.

Applying traditional double jeopardy principles to the facts of this case, it is clear that the criminal prosecution of these petitioners would not violate the Double Jeopardy Clause. It is evident that Congress intended the OCC money penalties and debarment sanctions imposed for violations of 12 U.S.C. §§ 84 and 375b to be civil in nature. As for the money penalties, both 12 U.S.C. §§ 93(b)(1) and 504(a), which authorize the imposition of monetary penalties for violations of §§ 84 and 375b respectively, expressly provide that such penalties are "civil." While the provision authorizing debarment contains no language explicitly denominating the sanction as civil, we think it significant that the authority to issue debarment orders is conferred upon the "appropriate Federal banking agenc[ies]." §§ 1818(e)(1)–(3). That such authority was conferred upon administrative agencies is prima facie evidence that Congress intended to provide for a civil sanction. * * *

Turning to the second stage of the *Ward* test, we find that there is little evidence, much less the clearest proof that we require, suggesting that either OCC money penalties or debarment sanctions are "so punitive in form and effect as to render them criminal despite Congress' intent to the contrary." First, neither money penalties nor debarment have historically been viewed as punishment. We have long recognized that "revocation of a privilege voluntarily granted," such as a debarment, "is characteristically free of the punitive criminal element." Similarly, "the payment of fixed or variable sums of money [is a] sanction which ha[s] been recognized as enforceable by civil proceedings since the original revenue law of 1789." Second, the sanctions imposed do not involve an "affirmative disability or restraint," as that term is normally understood. While petitioners have been prohibited from further participating in the banking industry, this is "certainly nothing approaching the 'infamous punishment' of imprisonment." Third, neither sanction comes into play "only" on a finding of scienter. The provisions under which the money penalties were imposed, 12 U.S.C. §§ 93(b) and 504, allow for the assessment of a penalty against any person "who violates" any of the underlying banking statutes, without regard to the violator's state of mind. "Good faith" is considered by OCC in determining the amount of the penalty to be imposed, § 93(b)(2), but a penalty can be imposed even in the absence of bad faith. The fact that petitioners' "good faith" was considered in determining the amount of the penalty to be imposed in this case is irrelevant, as we look only to "the statute on its face" to determine whether a penalty is criminal in nature. *Kennedy*. Similarly, while debarment may be imposed for a "willful" disregard "for the safety or soundness of [an] insured depository institution," willfulness is not a prerequisite to debarment; it is sufficient that the disregard for the safety and soundness of the institution was "continuing."

Fourth, the conduct for which OCC sanctions are imposed may also be criminal (and in this case formed the basis for petitioners' indictments). This fact is insufficient to render the money penalties and debarment sanctions criminally punitive particularly in the double jeopardy context, see *United States v. Dixon*, 509 U.S. 688, 704, 113 S.Ct. 2849, 2860, 125 L.Ed.2d 556 (1993) (rejecting "same-conduct" test for double jeopardy purposes).

Finally, we recognize that the imposition of both money penalties and debarment sanctions will deter others from emulating petitioners' conduct, a traditional goal of criminal punishment. But the mere presence of this purpose is insufficient to render a sanction criminal, as deterrence "may serve civil as well as criminal goals." *Ursery*, 116 S.Ct., at 2149; see also *Bennis v. Michigan*, 516 U.S. 442, 452, 116 S.Ct. 994, 1000, 134 L.Ed.2d 68 (1996) ("[F]orfeiture ... serves a deterrent purpose distinct from any punitive purpose"). For example, the sanctions at issue here, while intended to deter future wrongdoing, also serve to promote the stability of the banking industry. To hold that the mere presence of a deterrent purpose renders such sanctions "criminal" for double jeopardy purposes would severely undermine the Government's ability to engage in effective regulation of institutions such as banks.

In sum, there simply is very little showing, to say nothing of the "clearest proof" required by *Ward*, that OCC money penalties and debarment sanctions are criminal. The Double Jeopardy Clause is therefore no obstacle to their trial on the pending indictments, and it may proceed.
* * *

JUSTICE SCALIA, with whom JUSTICE THOMAS joins, concurring. [Omitted.]

JUSTICE STEVENS, concurring in the judgment. [Omitted.]

JUSTICE SOUTER, concurring in the judgment. [Omitted.]

JUSTICE BREYER, with whom JUSTICE GINSBURG joins, concurring in the judgment.

* * * I disagree with the Court's reasoning in two respects. First, unlike the Court I would not say that "only the clearest proof" will

"transform" into a criminal punishment what a legislature calls a "civil remedy." I understand that the Court has taken this language from earlier cases. But the limitation that the language suggests is not consistent with what the Court has actually done. Rather, in fact if not in theory, the Court has simply applied factors of the *Kennedy* variety to the matter at hand. * * *

Second, I would not decide now that a court should evaluate a statute only "on its face," rather than "assessing the character of the actual sanctions imposed." *Halper* involved an ordinary civil-fine statute that as normally applied would not have created any "double jeopardy" problem. It was not the statute itself, but rather the disproportionate relation between fine and conduct as the statute was applied in the individual case that led this Court, unanimously, to find that the "civil penalty" was, in those circumstances, a second "punishment" that constituted double jeopardy. See 490 U.S., at 439, 452, 109 S.Ct., at 1896–1897, 1903–1904 (finding that $130,000 penalty was "sufficiently disproportionate" to $585 loss plus approximately $16,000 in government expenses caused by Halper's fraud to constitute a second punishment in violation of double jeopardy). Of course, the Court in *Halper* might have reached the same result through application of the constitutional prohibition of "excessive fines." * * * But that is not what the Court there said. And nothing in the majority's opinion today explains why we should abandon this aspect of *Halper*'s holding. Indeed, in context, the language of *Kennedy* that suggests that the Court should consider the statute on its face does not suggest that there may not be further analysis of a penalty as it is applied in a particular case. Most of the lower court confusion and criticism of *Halper* appears to have focused on the problem of characterizing—by examining the face of the statute—the purposes of a civil penalty as punishment, not on the application of double jeopardy analysis to the penalties that are imposed in particular cases. It seems to me quite possible that a statute that provides for a punishment that normally is civil in nature could nonetheless amount to a criminal punishment as applied in special circumstances. And I would not now hold to the contrary. * * *

NOTES

1. In United States v. Mackby, 261 F.3d 821 (9th Cir.2001), the Ninth Circuit addressed a case reminiscent of *Halper*. The defendant had obtained an overpayment of $58,152 from Medicare through submitting false claims. Under the False Claims Act which provides for civil penalties of $5,000 for each Medicare claim that exceeds the annual monetary limit and also for triple damages for overpayments, the court awarded a total of $729,455 to the government. Congress has not characterized the False Claims Act sanctions as either remedial or punitive. The Ninth Circuit found the fines per claim to have a punitive purpose because no damages to the government needed to be shown; it also found the treble damages to be at least partially punitive.

Consequently, relying on *Hudson* and United States v. Bajakajian, 524 U.S. 321, 118 S.Ct. 2028, 141 L.Ed.2d 314 (1998) (reproduced at p. 651), the circuit court found the civil fines were subject to analysis under the Eighth Amendment's excessive fines clause. The reasoning in *Halper* has been overruled; it is not so clear that the result has also been overruled.

2. In 1987, Montana passed a Dangerous Drug Act, Mont.Code Ann. §§ 15–21–101 et seq., which imposed a large tax on the possession of certain drugs. Taxpayers were not required to file a return or pay any tax until 72 hours after they had been arrested for possession of any of the proscribed drugs. Six members of the Kurth family were arrested for growing and selling marijuana. After pleading guilty, two went to prison and the others received suspended or deferred sentences. In addition, $18,000 was forfeited in an associated civil action. When Montana sought to collect the tax, the Kurths successfully claimed protection under the Double Jeopardy Clause. Department of Revenue v. Kurth Ranch, 511 U.S. 767, 114 S.Ct. 1937, 128 L.Ed.2d 767 (1994). Although the Supreme Court noted that the high rate of taxation and its deterrent purpose did not alone make the tax a punishment, the additional features of imposing the tax only after commission of the crime and basing the tax on the possession of goods which the Kurths could not lawfully possess were sufficient to make the tax punitive. *Kurth Ranch* expressly extended *Halper* from civil penalties to taxes. Given the different purposes of penalties and taxes, will this extension of *Halper* survive *Hudson*? Is Montana now free to relabel the tax a mandatory criminal fine and collect it in the initial criminal proceeding?

3. States have also required released sexual offenders to register with the police and provide detailed personal information. Much of this information, including name, address and photograph, are published on the Internet. The Supreme Court has followed *Hudson* in finding these measures civil in nature. Smith v. Doe, 538 U.S. 84, 123 S.Ct. 1140, 155 L.Ed.2d 164 (2003) (because Alaska's act was nonpunitive, it did not violate the Ex Post Facto Clause). See also Connecticut Department of Public Safety v. Doe, 538 U.S. 1, 123 S.Ct. 1160, 155 L.Ed.2d 98 (2003) (no procedural due process right to a hearing on current dangerousness because registration is premised on offender's prior conviction alone). Critics charge that these results are wrong. For example, one student writer argues that when considering actions such as sex offender registration and criminal alien detention, "regardless of the civil or criminal label, the government cannot have its cake and eat it too: either a collateral consequence is punitive and thus subject to a host of constitutional provisions reserved for criminal sanctions, or it is regulatory and thus requires an individualized assessment of whether the deprivation of liberty will actually serve its purported regulatory purpose." Note, Making Outcasts Out of Outlaws: The Unconstitutionality of Sex Offender Registration and Criminal Alien Detention, 117 Harv.L.Rev. 2731, 2732 (2004).

NOTES ON DIFFERENCES BETWEEN CIVIL AND CRIMINAL PROCEEDINGS

The cases suggest that whether a remedy in the nature of a sanction is civil or criminal may be determined at least in part by whether the defendant's liability for the sanction is established by a civil or criminal proceeding.

There is a basic notion that the more severe the sanction or remedy that can be imposed on a defendant, the more formal, thorough and unassailable in its fact-finding nature the procedure for establishing liability should be. In some regards this is borne out in the way American law operates. Obviously, the proof beyond a reasonable doubt required in a criminal trial puts a greater weight on being sure of the facts before a criminal penalty is imposed than does the proof by preponderance of the evidence, which is typical in civil trials. Alternatively, the differences between civil and criminal proceedings may be explained by the greater value our legal system puts on liberty, though this does little to explain the protections afforded a corporation in a criminal trial. Of course, the differences between civil and criminal procedures may be little more than the result of historical practice, particularly insofar as criminal procedure is constrained by the Constitution.

It may be equally accurate to consider criminal and civil procedure as simply different systems for establishing or defeating a claim of liability with a different array of tools provided to the two sides to the dispute. Without attempting to provide a detailed review of civil or criminal procedure, the following differences between the two systems should be borne in mind, particularly with regard to whether they justify or explain differences in the type of remedy that a judge may impose.

1. *Commencement of the action.* No formal procedure prior to the filing of the complaint is required of the government or a private party in a civil action. F.R.Civ.P. 3. A federal misdemeanor charge, carrying a possible term of imprisonment not in excess of one year, may be brought by the government through an information which requires no pre-charging procedure by the prosecutor. A federal felony charge, carrying a possible term of imprisonment in excess of one year, requires presentation of evidence by the prosecutor to a grand jury consisting of 16 to 23 citizens and the affirmative vote of 12 or more grand jurors as well as the assent of the prosecutor. U.S. Const., amend. V; F.R.Crim.P. 6 & 7.

2. *Discovery.* Modern civil discovery is, of course, wide-ranging and is equally available to both the plaintiff and the defendant. Federal criminal discovery is entirely different. Through the powers of the grand jury, the government has the ability to conduct extensive discovery before returning an indictment. The grand jury has the power to issue subpoenas both for the production of documents and things and for the taking of testimony. There is no territorial limit within the United States on such subpoenas. Under the Fifth Amendment, anyone claiming in good faith that his testimony may incriminate him may not be compelled to testify, but the government may obtain from such a party virtually anything relevant to its inquiry other than testimony, including documents, blood samples and voice or handwriting exemplars. Pennsylvania v. Muniz, 496 U.S. 582, 110 S.Ct. 2638, 110 L.Ed.2d 528 (1990); Schmerber v. California, 384 U.S. 757, 86 S.Ct. 1826, 16 L.Ed.2d 908 (1966). Prior to indictment, a person who believes or has been informed that he or she is the target of a grand jury investigation has no power to conduct discovery against the government or third parties.

Following the return of the indictment, the government can no longer make use of the investigatory power of the grand jury. Discovery by deposition is open to the parties only upon motion to the court and in "exceptional circumstances," such as the reasonable likelihood that a witness will not be able to appear at trial because of illness or death. F.R.Crim.P. 15. Generally, discovery provided for in the rules is limited and, in part, is reciprocal but may be commenced only by the defendant. The defendant may obtain any record of his own statements in the possession of the government and his prior criminal record. F.R.Crim.P. 16. He may also obtain documents and tangible objects in the government's possession which the government intends to offer at trial and reports of examinations or tests, but if he requests such disclosure, he will be subject to reciprocal discovery. The defendant is not entitled to obtain copies of grand jury testimony or exhibits if they do not fall into one of the categories for which discovery is provided. The prior statements and reports of the government's witnesses are not discoverable by the defendant until after the witness has testified. 18 U.S.C. § 3500. But the government must make evidence in its possession which is materially favorable to the accused available to the defendant. Brady v. Maryland, 373 U.S. 83, 83 S.Ct. 1194, 10 L.Ed.2d 215 (1963).

In the real world of criminal trials, less restrictive practice may be followed. In the typical white collar criminal case there is in fact considerable exchange of documents prior to or during trial, but this arises from agreement between the parties or the instructions of judges facing the exigencies of modern trial calendars.

3. *Bail.* Unlike the civil system, a criminal defendant may be required to post bail in an amount or form that will assure his appearance at trial. Failure to post such bail will result in the defendant's pre-trial incarceration. 18 U.S.C. § 3141 et seq.; F.R.Crim.P. 46. In some circumstances, a defendant may be detained prior to trial for reasons unrelated to the likelihood of his failure to appear for trial.

4. *Trial.* The government's burden of proof at trial in a criminal case is to prove the defendant committed the crime beyond a reasonable doubt. United States v. Regan, 232 U.S. 37, 34 S.Ct. 213, 58 L.Ed. 494 (1914). But one should note that there is a distinction between the liability phase and the remedy phase of a criminal trial. The government need not prove facts at a sentencing hearing beyond a reasonable doubt and hearsay evidence may be used at a sentencing hearing. McMillan v. Pennsylvania, 477 U.S. 79, 106 S.Ct. 2411, 91 L.Ed.2d 67 (1986); Williams v. New York, 337 U.S. 241, 69 S.Ct. 1079, 93 L.Ed. 1337 (1949). Grand jury proceedings are also not controlled by the rules of evidence; hearsay is routinely used in presentations to the grand jury. A trial before a jury drawn from the district in which the alleged crime was committed is assured by the Sixth Amendment and the defendant may not be compelled to testify nor may the prosecutor draw to the attention of the jury or comment on the defendant's failure to testify. 18 U.S.C. § 3481; Griffin v. California, 380 U.S. 609, 85 S.Ct. 1229, 14 L.Ed.2d 106 (1965). Corporations and other organizations are not protected by the Fifth Amendment privilege. Bellis v. United States, 417 U.S. 85, 94 S.Ct. 2179, 40 L.Ed.2d 678 (1974).

5. *Effect of conviction.* Remedies following conviction are not limited to fines or imprisonment. Conviction of a felony may carry collateral conse-

quences such as loss of the right to serve on a grand jury, forfeiture of the instruments or proceeds of a crime, e.g., 18 U.S.C. §§ 3665–67, 3681, and other disabilities. For example, in 1988, Congress markedly increased the collateral consequences of convictions for distribution or possession of narcotics. 21 U.S.C. § 853(a). The statute has a graduated scheme of increasing disabilities. After a first conviction for drug possession, the court has discretion to make the defendant ineligible for any or all federal benefits for a year; require that the defendant successfully complete a drug treatment program with periodic testing; and/or require that the defendant perform appropriate community service. A third conviction for drug distribution results in ineligibility for all federal benefits. Federal benefits are defined to include issuance of a grant, contract, loan, professional license or commercial license by the federal government or by use of federal funds; but federal benefits do not include any retirement, welfare, social security, health, disability or veterans benefit, public housing or any other benefit for which payments or services are required for eligibility.

6. *Administrative proceedings.* Numerous statutes give the government the authority to seek civil penalties not only through proceedings in the district court, but also through administrative proceedings. Often the choice of forum is placed in the hands of the agency. E.g., Resource Conservation and Recovery Act, 42 U.S.C. § 6928 (1983). This choice may carry important procedural consequences: in the administrative forum discovery may be much more limited than in a district court proceeding; cross-examination of witnesses may be limited or prohibited; the opportunity for jury trial is obviously not present; direct evidence may be presented in writing rather than through live witnesses; ultimately, the hearing provided may be of a legislative rather than an adjudicatory type. Appellate courts have also held that sanctions imposed by administrative agencies are reviewable in court only on the ground that the agency acted outside its legal authority or abused its discretion. Butz v. Glover Livestock Commission Co., 411 U.S. 182, 93 S.Ct. 1455, 36 L.Ed.2d 142 (1973); Moffer v. Watt, 690 F.2d 1037 (D.C.Cir.1982).

UNITED STATES v. BAJAKAJIAN

Supreme Court of the United States, 1998
524 U.S. 321, 118 S.Ct. 2028, 141 L.Ed.2d 314

JUSTICE THOMAS delivered the opinion of the Court.

Respondent Hosep Bajakajian attempted to leave the United States without reporting, as required by federal law, that he was transporting more than $10,000 in currency. Federal law also provides that a person convicted of willfully violating this reporting requirement shall forfeit to the government "any property ... involved in such offense." 18 U.S.C. § 982(a)(1). The question in this case is whether forfeiture of the entire $357,144 that respondent failed to declare would violate the Excessive Fines Clause of the Eighth Amendment. We hold that it would, because full forfeiture of respondent's currency would be grossly disproportional to the gravity of his offense.

I

On June 9, 1994, respondent, his wife, and his two daughters were waiting at Los Angeles International Airport to board a flight to Italy; their final destination was Cyprus. Using dogs trained to detect currency by its smell, customs inspectors discovered some $230,000 in cash in the Bajakajians' checked baggage. A customs inspector approached respondent and his wife and told them that they were required to report all money in excess of $10,000 in their possession or in their baggage. Respondent said that he had $8,000 and that his wife had another $7,000, but that the family had no additional currency to declare. A search of their carry-on bags, purse, and wallet revealed more cash; in all, customs inspectors found $357,144. The currency was seized and respondent was taken into custody.

A federal grand jury indicted respondent on three counts. Count One charged him with failing to report, as required by 31 U.S.C. § 5316(a)(1)(A), that he was transporting more than $10,000 outside the United States, and with doing so "willfully," in violation of § 5322(a). * * * Count Three sought forfeiture of the $357,144 pursuant to 18 U.S.C. § 982(a)(1), which provides:

> "The court, in imposing sentence on a person convicted of an offense in violation of section . . . 5316, . . . shall order that the person forfeit to the United States any property, real or personal, involved in such offense, or any property traceable to such property." 18 U.S.C. § 982(a)(1). * * *

Although § 982(a)(1) directs sentencing courts to impose full forfeiture, the District Court concluded that such forfeiture would be "extraordinarily harsh" and "grossly disproportionate to the offense in question," and that it would therefore violate the Excessive Fines Clause. The court instead ordered forfeiture of $15,000, in addition to a sentence of three years of probation and a fine of $5,000—the maximum fine under the Sentencing Guidelines—because the court believed that the maximum Guidelines fine was "too little" and that a $15,000 forfeiture would "make up for what I think a reasonable fine should be." * * *

II

The Eighth Amendment provides: "Excessive bail shall not be required, nor excessive fines imposed, nor cruel and unusual punishments inflicted." This Court has had little occasion to interpret, and has never actually applied, the Excessive Fines Clause. We have, however, explained that at the time the Constitution was adopted, "the word 'fine' was understood to mean a payment to a sovereign as punishment for some offense." The Excessive Fines Clause thus "limits the government's power to extract payments, whether in cash or in kind, 'as punishment for some offense.'" Austin v. United States, 509 U.S. 602, 609–610, 113 S.Ct. 2801, 2805, 125 L.Ed.2d 488 (1993). Forfeitures—payments in kind—are thus "fines" if they constitute punishment for an offense.

We have little trouble concluding that the forfeiture of currency ordered by § 982(a)(1) constitutes punishment. * * *

The United States argues, however, that the forfeiture of currency under § 982(a)(1) "also serves important remedial purposes." The Government asserts that it has "an overriding sovereign interest in controlling what property leaves and enters the country." It claims that full forfeiture of unreported currency supports that interest by serving to "dete[r] illicit movements of cash" and aiding in providing the Government with "valuable information to investigate and detect criminal activities associated with that cash." Deterrence, however, has traditionally been viewed as a goal of punishment, and forfeiture of the currency here does not serve the remedial purpose of compensating the Government for a loss. * * * Although the Government has asserted a loss of information regarding the amount of currency leaving the country, that loss would not be remedied by the Government's confiscation of respondent's $357,144.[4]

The United States also argues that the forfeiture mandated by § 982(a)(1) is constitutional because it falls within a class of historic forfeitures of property tainted by crime. * * * In so doing, the Government relies upon a series of cases involving traditional civil in rem forfeitures that are inapposite because such forfeitures were historically considered nonpunitive.

The theory behind such forfeitures was the fiction that the action was directed against "guilty property," rather than against the offender himself.[5] Historically, the conduct of the property owner was irrelevant; indeed, the owner of forfeited property could be entirely innocent of any crime. As Justice Story explained:

"The thing is here primarily considered as the offender, or rather the offence is attached primarily to the thing; and this, whether the offence be malum prohibitum, or malum in se.... [T]he practice has been, and so this Court understands the law to be, that the proceeding in rem stands independent of, and wholly unaffected by any criminal proceeding in personam." The Palmyra, 12 Wheat., at 14–15, 6 L.Ed. 531.

Traditional in rem forfeitures were thus not considered punishment against the individual for an offense. Because they were viewed as nonpunitive, such forfeitures traditionally were considered to occupy a place outside the domain of the Excessive Fines Clause. Recognizing the non-

---

4. We do not suggest that merely because the forfeiture of respondent's currency in this case would not serve a remedial purpose, other forfeitures may be classified as nonpunitive (and thus not "fines") if they serve some remedial purpose as well as being punishment for an offense. Even if the Government were correct in claiming that the forfeiture of respondent's currency is remedial in some way, the forfeiture would still be punitive in part. (The Government concedes as much.) This is sufficient to bring the forfeiture within the purview of the Excessive Fines Clause.

5. The "guilty property" theory behind in rem forfeiture can be traced to the Bible, which describes property being sacrificed to God as a means of atoning for an offense. See Exodus 21:28. In medieval Europe and at common law, this concept evolved into the law of deodand, in which offending property was condemned and confiscated by the church or the Crown in remediation for the harm it had caused.

punitive character of such proceedings, we have held that the Double Jeopardy Clause does not bar the institution of a civil, in rem forfeiture action after the criminal conviction of the defendant. *Ursery.*[6]

The forfeiture in this case does not bear any of the hallmarks of traditional civil in rem forfeitures. The Government has not proceeded against the currency itself, but has instead sought and obtained a criminal conviction of respondent personally. The forfeiture serves no remedial purpose, is designed to punish the offender, and cannot be imposed upon innocent owners.

Section 982(a)(1) thus descends not from historic in rem forfeitures of guilty property, but from a different historical tradition: that of in personam, criminal forfeitures. Such forfeitures have historically been treated as punitive, being part of the punishment imposed for felonies and treason in the Middle Ages and at common law. Although in personam criminal forfeitures were well established in England at the time of the Founding, they were rejected altogether in the laws of this country until very recently.

The Government specifically contends that the forfeiture of respondent's currency is constitutional because it involves an "instrumentality" of respondent's crime. According to the Government, the unreported cash is an instrumentality because it "does not merely facilitate a violation of law," but is " 'the very sine qua non of the crime.' " The Government reasons that "there would be no violation at all without the exportation (or attempted exportation) of the cash."

Acceptance of the Government's argument would require us to expand the traditional understanding of instrumentality forfeitures. This we decline to do. Instrumentalities historically have been treated as a form of "guilty property" that can be forfeited in civil in rem proceedings. In this case, however, the Government has sought to punish respondent by proceeding against him criminally, in personam, rather than proceeding in rem against the currency. It is therefore irrelevant whether respondent's currency is an instrumentality; the forfeiture is punitive, and the test for the excessiveness of a punitive forfeiture involves solely a proportionality determination.

III

Because the forfeiture of respondent's currency constitutes punishment and is thus a "fine" within the meaning of the Excessive Fines Clause, we now turn to the question of whether it is "excessive."

---

6. It does not follow, of course, that all modern civil in rem forfeitures are nonpunitive and thus beyond the coverage of the Excessive Fines Clause. Because some recent federal forfeiture laws have blurred the traditional distinction between civil in rem and criminal in personam forfeiture, we have held that a modern statutory forfeiture is a "fine" for Eighth Amendment purposes if it constitutes punishment even in part, regardless of whether the proceeding is styled in rem or in personam. See *Austin v. United States,* supra, at 621–622, 113 S.Ct. at 2811–2812 (although labeled in rem, civil forfeiture of real property used "to facilitate" the commission of drug crimes was punitive in part and thus subject to review under the Excessive Fines Clause).

A

The touchstone of the constitutional inquiry under the Excessive Fines Clause is the principle of proportionality: The amount of the forfeiture must bear some relationship to the gravity of the offense that it is designed to punish. * * * Until today, however, we have not articulated a standard for determining whether a punitive forfeiture is constitutionally excessive. We now hold that a punitive forfeiture violates the Excessive Fines Clause if it is grossly disproportional to the gravity of a defendant's offense.

The text and history of the Excessive Fines Clause demonstrate the centrality of proportionality to the excessiveness inquiry; nonetheless, they provide little guidance as to how disproportional a punitive forfeiture must be to the gravity of an offense in order to be "excessive." Excessive means surpassing the usual, the proper, or a normal measure of proportion. The constitutional question that we address, however, is just how proportional to a criminal offense a fine must be, and the text of the Excessive Fines Clause does not answer it.

Nor does its history. The Clause was little discussed in the First Congress and the debates over the ratification of the Bill of Rights.

* * *

We must therefore rely on other considerations in deriving a constitutional excessiveness standard, and there are two that we find particularly relevant. The first, which we have emphasized in our cases interpreting the Cruel and Unusual Punishments Clause, is that judgments about the appropriate punishment for an offense belong in the first instance to the legislature. See, e.g., Solem v. Helm ("Reviewing courts ... these are peculiarly questions of legislative policy"). The second is that any judicial determination regarding the gravity of a particular criminal offense will be inherently imprecise. Both of these principles counsel against requiring strict proportionality between the amount of a punitive forfeiture and the gravity of a criminal offense, and we therefore adopt the standard of gross disproportionality articulated in our Cruel and Unusual Punishments Clause precedents.

In applying this standard, the district courts in the first instance, and the courts of appeals, reviewing the proportionality determination de novo, must compare the amount of the forfeiture to the gravity of the defendant's offense. If the amount of the forfeiture is grossly disproportional to the gravity of the defendant's offense, it is unconstitutional.

B

Under this standard, the forfeiture of respondent's entire $357,144 would violate the Excessive Fines Clause. Respondent's crime was solely a reporting offense. It was permissible to transport the currency out of the country so long as he reported it. Section 982(a)(1) orders currency to be forfeited for a "willful" violation of the reporting requirement. Thus, the essence of respondent's crime is a willful failure to report the removal of currency from the United States. Furthermore, as the District Court found, respondent's violation was unrelated to any other illegal activities. The money was the proceeds of legal activity and was to be used to repay a lawful debt. Whatever his other vices, respondent does not fit into the class of persons for whom the statute was principally designed: He is not a money launderer, a drug trafficker, or a tax evader. And under the Sentencing Guidelines, the maximum sentence that could have been imposed on respondent was six months, while the maximum fine was $5,000. Such penalties confirm a minimal level of culpability.

The harm that respondent caused was also minimal. Failure to report his currency affected only one party, the Government, and in a relatively minor way. There was no fraud on the United States, and respondent caused no loss to the public fisc. Had his crime gone undetected, the Government would have been deprived only of the information that $357,144 had left the country. The Government and the dissent contend that there is a correlation between the amount forfeited and the harm that the Government would have suffered had the crime gone undetected. We disagree. There is no inherent proportionality in such a forfeiture. It is impossible to conclude, for example, that the harm respondent caused is anywhere near 30 times greater than that caused by a hypothetical drug dealer who willfully fails to report taking $12,000 out of the country in order to purchase drugs.

Comparing the gravity of respondent's crime with the $357,144 forfeiture the Government seeks, we conclude that such a forfeiture would be grossly disproportional to the gravity of his offense. It is larger than the $5,000 fine imposed by the District Court by many orders of magnitude, and it bears no articulable correlation to any injury suffered by the Government.

C

Finally, we must reject the contention that the proportionality of full forfeiture is demonstrated by the fact that the First Congress enacted statutes requiring full forfeiture of goods involved in customs offenses or the payment of monetary penalties proportioned to the goods' value. It is argued that the enactment of these statutes at roughly the same time that the Eighth Amendment was ratified suggests that full forfeiture, in the customs context at least, is a proportional punishment. The early customs statutes, however, do not support such a conclusion because, unlike § 982(a)(1), the type of forfeiture that they imposed was not considered punishment for a criminal offense.

Certain of the early customs statutes required the forfeiture of goods imported in violation of the customs laws, and, in some instances, the vessels carrying them as well. These forfeitures, however, were civil in rem forfeitures, in which the Government proceeded against the property itself on the theory that it was guilty, not against a criminal defendant. Such forfeitures sought to vindicate the Government's underlying property right in customs duties, and like other traditional in rem forfeitures, they were not considered at the Founding to be punishment for an offense. They therefore indicate nothing about the proportionality of the punitive forfeiture at issue here.

Other statutes, however, imposed monetary "forfeitures" proportioned to the value of the goods involved. * * *

These "forfeitures" were similarly not considered punishments for criminal offenses. This Court so recognized in Stockwell v. United States, 13 Wall. 531, 20 L.Ed. 491 (1871), a case interpreting a statute that * * * provided that a person who had concealed goods liable to seizure for customs violations should "forfeit and pay a sum double the amount or value of the goods." The *Stockwell* Court rejected the defendant's contention that this provision was "penal," stating instead that it was "fully as remedial in its character, designed as plainly to secure [the] rights [of the Government], as are the statutes rendering importers liable to duties." * * *

The early monetary forfeitures, therefore, were considered not as punishment for an offense, but rather as serving the remedial purpose of reimbursing the Government for the losses accruing from the evasion of customs duties. They were thus no different in purpose and effect than the in rem forfeitures of the goods to whose value they were proportioned. Cf. One Lot Emerald Cut Stones v. United States, 409 U.S. 232, 237, 93 S.Ct. 489, 493, 34 L.Ed.2d 438 (1972) (per curiam) (customs statute requiring the forfeiture of undeclared goods concealed in baggage and imposing a monetary penalty equal to the value of the goods imposed a "remedial, rather than [a] punitive sanctio[n]").[19] By contrast, the full forfeiture mandated by § 982(a)(1) in this case serves no remedial purpose; it is clearly punishment. The customs statutes enacted by the First Congress, therefore, in no way suggest that § 982(a)(1)'s currency forfeiture is constitutionally proportional.

* * *

For the foregoing reasons, the full forfeiture of respondent's currency would violate the Excessive Fines Clause.

JUSTICE KENNEDY, with whom CHIEF JUSTICE [REHNQUIST], JUSTICE O'CONNOR, and JUSTICE SCALIA join, dissenting.

For the first time in its history, the Court strikes down a fine as excessive under the Eighth Amendment. The decision is disturbing both for its specific holding and for the broader upheaval it foreshadows. At issue is a fine Congress fixed in the amount of the currency respondent

---

19. *One Lot Emerald Cut Stones* differs from this case in the most fundamental respect. We concluded that the forfeiture provision in *Emerald Cut Stones* was entirely remedial and thus nonpunitive, primarily because it "provide[d] a reasonable form of liquidated damages" to the Government. 409 U.S. at 237, 93 S.Ct. at 493. The additional fact that such a remedial forfeiture also serves to "reimburse the Government for investigation and enforcement expenses," is essentially meaningless, because even a clearly punitive criminal fine or forfeiture could be said in some measure to reimburse for criminal enforcement and investigation. * * *

sought to smuggle or to transport without reporting. If a fine calibrated with this accuracy fails the Court's test, its decision portends serious disruption of a vast range of statutory fines. The Court all but says the offense is not serious anyway. This disdain for the statute is wrong as an empirical matter and disrespectful of the separation of powers. The irony of the case is that, in the end, it may stand for narrowing constitutional protection rather than enhancing it. To make its rationale work, the Court appears to remove important classes of fines from any excessiveness inquiry at all. This, too, is unsound; and with all respect, I dissent.

I

A

In striking down this forfeiture, the majority treats many fines as "remedial" penalties even though they far exceed the harm suffered. Remedial penalties, the Court holds, are not subject to the Excessive Fines Clause at all. Proceeding from this premise, the majority holds customs fines are remedial and not at all punitive, even if they amount to many times the duties due on the goods. In the majority's universe, a fine is not a punishment even if it is much larger than the money owed. This confuses whether a fine is excessive with whether it is a punishment.

This novel, mistaken approach requires reordering a tradition existing long before the Republic and confirmed in its early years. The Court creates its category to reconcile its unprecedented holding with a six-century-long tradition of in personam customs fines equal to one, two, three, or even four times the value of the goods at issue.

In order to sweep all these precedents aside, the majority's remedial analysis assumes the settled tradition was limited to "reimbursing the Government for" unpaid duties. The assumption is wrong. Many offenses did not require a failure to pay a duty at all. None of these in personam penalties depended on a compensable monetary loss to the government. True, these offenses risked causing harm, ante, but so does smuggling or not reporting cash. A sanction proportioned to potential rather than actual harm is punitive, though the potential harm may make the punishment a reasonable one. The majority nonetheless treats the historic penalties as nonpunitive and thus not subject to the Excessive Fines Clause, though they are indistinguishable from the fine in this case. (It is a mark of the Court's doctrinal difficulty that we must speak of nonpunitive penalties, which is a contradiction in terms.)

* * *

B

The majority's novel holding creates another anomaly as well. The majority suggests in rem forfeitures of the instrumentalities of crimes are not fines at all. The point of the instrumentality theory is to distinguish goods having a "close enough relationship to the offense" from those incidentally related to it. Austin v. United States, 509 U.S. 602, 628, 113

S.Ct. 2801, 2815, 125 L.Ed.2d 488 (Scalia, J., concurring in part and concurring in judgment). From this, the Court concludes the money in a cash smuggling or non-reporting offense cannot be an instrumentality, unlike, say, a car used to transport goods concealed from taxes. There is little logic in this rationale. The car plays an important role in the offense but is not essential; one could also transport goods by jet or by foot. The link between the cash and the cash-smuggling offense is closer, as the offender must fail to report while smuggling more than $10,000. The cash is not just incidentally related to the offense of cash smuggling. It is essential, whereas the car is not. Yet the car plays an important enough role to justify forfeiture, as the majority concedes. A fortiori, the cash does as well. Even if there were a clear distinction between instrumentalities and incidental objects, when the Court invokes the distinction it gets the results backwards.

II

Turning to the question of excessiveness, the majority states the test: A defendant must prove a gross disproportion before a court will strike down a fine as excessive. This test would be a proper way to apply the Clause, if only the majority were faithful in applying it. The Court does not, however, explain why in this case forfeiture of all of the cash would have suffered from a gross disproportion. The offense is a serious one, and respondent's smuggling and failing to report were willful. The cash was lawful to own, but this fact shows only that the forfeiture was a fine; it cannot also prove that the fine was excessive.

* * *

NOTES

1. The Court did not address the question of whether the $15,000 forfeiture actually ordered by the district court would have been grossly disproportionate. If the question had been raised, how do you think the Court would have decided?

2. For a time, scholars argued that punitive damages were "fines" that, if excessive, run afoul of the Eighth Amendment's prohibition on excessive fines. Calvin Massey, The Excessive Fines Clause and Punitive Damages: Some Lessons from History, 40 Vanderbilt L.Rev. 1233 (1987); Note, The Constitutionality of Punitive Damages Under the Excessive Fines Clause of the Eighth Amendment, 85 Mich.L.Rev. 1699 (1987). The Court rejected that argument, finding that the amendment does not apply to litigation between private parties. Browning–Ferris Industries of Vermont, Inc. v. Kelco Disposal, Inc., 492 U.S. 257, 109 S.Ct. 2909, 106 L.Ed.2d 219 (1989). If the Court had not rejected this argument, its parallel rules regarding proportionality review for both criminal fines and punitive damages might be more defensible. See Colleen P. Murphy, Comparison to Criminal Sanctions in the Constitutional Review of Punitive Damages, 41 San Diego L.Rev. 1443 (2004). Dean Chemerinsky argues there are unjustifiable inconsistencies in the Supreme

Court's decisions regarding the "four major types of punishment that courts can impose: death sentences, imprisonment, fines, and punitive damages." Erwin Chemerinsky, The Constitution and Punishment, 56 Stan. L.Rev. 1049 (2004).

3. The Supreme Court has adopted a similar proportionality analysis for criminal sentences. Ewing v. California, 538 U.S. 11, 123 S.Ct. 1179, 155 L.Ed.2d 108 (2003). (Note, however, that Justice Thomas, the author of *Bajakajian*, voted against the use of proportionality as a constitutional limitation on criminal punishment in *Ewing*.) The Eighth Amendment's prohibition of "cruel and unusual punishment" prohibits sentences that are disproportionate to the severity of the crime committed. In *Ewing*, a split majority of the Court upheld a sentence of 25 years to life under California's "Three Strikes You're Out" law, finding it was not unconstitutionally disproportionate to the offense of shoplifting three golf clubs valued at $1,200. In Harmelin v. Michigan, 501 U.S. 957, 111 S.Ct. 2680, 115 L.Ed.2d 836 (1991), the Supreme Court rejected a proportionality challenge brought by a first-time offender convicted under Michigan law for possession of more than 650 grams of a mixture containing cocaine who received a mandatory term of life in prison without the possibility of parole.

4. Justice Scalia has been vocal in his opposition to proportionality analysis for any punishment, civil or criminal, outside of the death penalty context. In his concurring opinion in *Ewing*, he explained:

> In my opinion in Harmelin v. Michigan, 501 U.S. 957, 984, 985, 111 S.Ct. 2680, 115 L.Ed.2d 836 (1991), I concluded that the Eighth Amendment's prohibition of "cruel and unusual punishments" was aimed at excluding only certain *modes* of punishment, and was not a "guarantee against disproportionate sentences." Out of respect for the principle of stare decisis, I might nonetheless accept the contrary holding of Solem v. Helm, 463 U.S. 277, 103 S.Ct. 3001, 77 L.Ed.2d 637 (1983)—that the Eighth Amendment contains a narrow proportionality principle—if I felt I could intelligently apply it. This case demonstrates why I cannot.
>
> Proportionality—the notion that the punishment should fit the crime—is inherently a concept tied to the penological goal of retribution. "[I]t becomes difficult even to speak intelligently of 'proportionality,' once deterrence and rehabilitation are given significant weight,"—not to mention giving weight to the purpose of California's three strikes law: incapacitation. In the present case, the game is up once the plurality has acknowledged that "the Constitution does not mandate adoption of any one penological theory," and that a "sentence can have a variety of justifications, such as incapacitation, deterrence, retribution, or rehabilitation." That acknowledgment having been made, it no longer suffices merely to assess "the gravity of the offense compared to the harshness of the penalty;" that classic description of the proportionality principle (alone and in itself quite resistant to policy-free, legal analysis) now becomes merely the "first" step of the inquiry. Having completed that step (by a discussion which, in all fairness, does not convincingly establish that 25–years-to-life is a "proportionate" punishment for stealing three golf clubs), the plurality must then *add* an analysis to show that "Ew-

ing's sentence is justified by the State's public-safety interest in incapacitating and deterring recidivist felons."

> Which indeed it is—though why that has anything to do with the principle of proportionality is a mystery. Perhaps the plurality should revise its terminology, so that what it reads into the Eighth Amendment is not the unstated proposition that all punishment should be reasonably proportionate to the gravity of the offense, but rather the unstated proposition that all punishment should reasonably pursue the multiple purposes of the criminal law. That formulation would make it clearer than ever, of course, that the plurality is not applying law but evaluating policy.

Ewing, 538 U.S. at 31–32 (Scalia, J., dissenting). Professor Tracy Thomas agrees, and argues that proportionality analysis, while seeming to be an objective calculus, is instead a subjective inquiry with potential for judicial abuse. Proportionality and the Supreme Court's Jurisprudence of Remedies, 59 Hastings L.J. 73 (2007). A similar rule of proportionality, which emerges in the Supreme Court's opinions on punitive damages, is explored in Section C.

B. PUNITIVE DAMAGES AT COMMON LAW

Claims for and awards of punitive damages exhibit aspects of both tort and criminal law. Punitive or exemplary damages "are not compensation for injury. Instead, they are private fines levied by civil juries to punish reprehensible conduct and to deter its future occurrence." Gertz v. Robert Welch, Inc., 418 U.S. 323, 350, 94 S.Ct. 2997, 3012, 41 L.Ed.2d 789 (1974). The Restatement (Second) of Torts § 908 provides a similar definition:

> (1) Punitive damages are damages, other than compensatory or nominal damages, awarded against a person to punish him for his outrageous conduct and to deter him and others like him from similar conduct in the future.
>
> (2) Punitive damages may be awarded for conduct that is outrageous, because of the defendant's evil motive or his reckless indifference to the rights of others. In assessing punitive damages, the trier of fact can properly consider the character of the defendant's act, the nature and extent of the harm to the plaintiff that the defendant caused or intended to cause and the wealth of the defendant.

Many of the recurring issues raised by punitive damages reflect the unsure marriage of tort and criminal law that generated this remedy. If the remedy is a punishment of the defendant, should the trial procedures and the plaintiff's burden of proof differ from the civil law? Since the punitive award is generally thought to be over and above what the plaintiff receives to be made whole, what facts or conduct concerning the defendant are relevant to determining the amount of damages to be awarded? Is it appropriate for the successful plaintiff to retain all of a punitive award or should some or all of it pass to the government or to some organization devoted to countering the sort of injurious conduct in which the defendant engaged? In a mass tort, are multiple punitive awards against the same defendant for the same course of conduct fair to either the defendant or to a late-arriving plaintiff who finds the defendant insolvent? Is there any practical and realistic mechanism to address this problem?

Punitive damages have been the focus of public debate and extensive legal commentary in recent years. Until the middle of the last century, punitive damages were generally restricted to intentional and dignitary torts. Michael L. Rustad, Happy No More: Federalism Derailed by the Court that Would be King of Punitive Damages, 64 Md.L.Rev. 461 (2005). Since then, there has been a growth of punitive damage awards in other areas:

Contracts. The black letter rule for 200 years has been that punitive damages are not available for breach of contract. Restatement (First) of Contracts § 342 (1932). The reasoning developed in modern times is based on the theory of efficient breach and the conclusion that in many cases, it is "uneconomical to induce completion of performance of a contract" by the threat of punitive damages. Richard A. Posner, Economic Analysis of Law 119 (7th ed.2007). Beginning in the 1960s, courts permitted the award of punitive damages for bad faith breach of insurance contract, and such awards are now allowed in a majority of jurisdictions. E.g., Giampappa v. American Family Mutual Insurance Co., 64 P.3d 230 (Colo.2003). It is now the general rule that punitive damages are available when the conduct constituting the breach of contract is also an independent tort. Restatement (Second) of Contracts § 355 (1979); William S. Dodge, The Case for Punitive Damages in Contracts, 48 Duke L.J. 629 (1999). Indeed, it appears that punitive damages are now awarded more frequently, and in higher amounts, in cases involving contract-related torts (e.g., tortious interference with contract, fraud, employment discrimination) than in tort cases not involving contractual relationships. See U.S. Department of Justice, Bureau of Justice Statistics, "Civil Bench and Jury Trials in State Courts," 6–7 (2005).

Products Liability. Prior to 1976, there were very few punitive damage awards in product liability cases. There was limited comment on this, but since punishment was traditionally associated with wilful or intentional acts, it may have appeared anomalous to the courts to punish a defendant for negligence or for tortious conduct for which he was strictly liable. In addition, in Roginsky v. Richardson–Merrell, Inc., 378 F.2d 832 (2d Cir.1967), Judge Friendly raised three other problems as he struck down a punitive damage award: (1) the inequity of punishing shareholders for the misdeeds of low-level employees; (2) the possibility that the defendant would be insured against punitive damage liability; and (3) the risk of excessive punishment through repeated punitive awards involving a single defective product. In 1976, Professor David G. Owen published his massive and seminal article, Punitive Damages in Products Liability Litigation, 74 Mich.L.Rev. 1257 (1976), arguing in favor of punitive damages in appropriate products liability cases. Such cases are no longer unusual. E.g., Grimshaw v. Ford Motor Co., 119 Cal.App.3d 757, 174 Cal.Rptr. 348 (1981) (reproduced infra).

Mass Torts. The first mass tort action in which punitive damages issues arose was brought in 1961 to challenge the sale of an allegedly defective anti-cholesterol drug. Such cases are now common and raise the issue of multiple punitive damage claims. E.g., Dunn v. HOVIC, 1 F.3d 1371 (3d Cir. en banc), cert. denied, 510 U.S. 1031, 114 S.Ct. 650, 126 L.Ed.2d 608 (1993) (asbestos manufacturer).

GRIMSHAW v. FORD MOTOR CO.
California Court of Appeal, Fourth District, 1981
119 Cal.App.3d 757, 174 Cal.Rptr. 348

TAMURA, ACTING PRESIDING JUSTICE.

A 1972 Ford Pinto hatchback automobile unexpectedly stalled on a freeway, erupting into flames when it was rear ended by a car proceeding in the same direction. Mrs. Lilly Gray, the driver of the Pinto, suffered fatal burns and 13–year-old Richard Grimshaw, a passenger in the Pinto, suffered severe and permanently disfiguring burns on his face and entire body. Grimshaw and the heirs of Mrs. Gray (Grays) sued Ford Motor Company and others. Following a six-month jury trial, verdicts were returned in favor of plaintiffs against Ford Motor Company. Grimshaw was awarded $2,516,000 compensatory damages and $125 million punitive damages; * * * On Ford's motion for a new trial, Grimshaw was required to remit all but $3½ million of the punitive award as a condition of denial of the motion.

Ford appeals from the judgment and from an order denying its motion for a judgment notwithstanding the verdict as to punitive damages. Grimshaw appeals from the order granting the conditional new trial and from the amended judgment entered pursuant to the order. * * *

FACTS
* * *

The Accident

At the moment of impact, the Pinto caught fire and its interior was engulfed in flames. According to plaintiffs' expert, the impact of the Galaxie had driven the Pinto's gas tank forward and caused it to be punctured by the flange or one of the bolts on the differential housing so that fuel sprayed from the punctured tank and entered the passenger compartment through gaps resulting from the separation of the rear wheel well sections from the floor pan. By the time the Pinto came to rest after the collision, both occupants had sustained serious burns. When they emerged from the vehicle, their clothing was almost completely burned off. Mrs. Gray died a few days later of congestive heart failure as a result of the burns. Grimshaw managed to survive but only through heroic medical

measures. He has undergone numerous and extensive surgeries and skin grafts and must undergo additional surgeries over the next 10 years. He lost portions of several fingers on his left hand and portions of his left ear, while his face required many skin grafts from various portions of his body.
* * *

Design of the Pinto Fuel System

In 1968, Ford began designing a new subcompact automobile which ultimately became the Pinto. Mr. Iacocca, then a Ford Vice President, conceived the project and was its moving force. Ford's objective was to build a car at or below 2,000 pounds to sell for no more than $2,000. * * *

It was then the preferred practice in Europe and Japan to locate the gas tank over the rear axle in subcompacts because a small vehicle has less "crush space" between the rear axle and the bumper than larger cars. The Pinto's styling, however, required the tank to be placed behind the rear axle leaving only 9 or 10 inches of "crush space"—far less than in any other American automobile or Ford overseas subcompact. In addition, the Pinto was designed so that its bumper was little more than a chrome strip, less substantial than the bumper of any other American car produced then or later. The Pinto's rear structure also lacked reinforcing members known as "hat sections" (2 longitudinal side members) and horizontal cross-members running between them such as were found in cars of larger unitized construction and in all automobiles produced by Ford's overseas operations. The absence of the reinforcing members rendered the Pinto less crush resistant than other vehicles. Finally, the differential housing selected for the Pinto had an exposed flange and a line of exposed bolt heads. These protrusions were sufficient to puncture a gas tank driven forward against the differential upon rear impact. * * *

Crash Tests

During the development of the Pinto, prototypes were built and tested. Some were "mechanical prototypes" which duplicated mechanical features of the design but not its appearance while others, referred to as "engineering prototypes," were true duplicates of the design car. These prototypes as well as two production Pintos were crash tested by Ford to determine, among other things, the integrity of the fuel system in rear-end accidents. Ford also conducted the tests to see if the Pinto as designed would meet a proposed federal regulation requiring all automobiles manufactured in 1972 to be able to withstand a 20–mile-per-hour fixed barrier impact without significant fuel spillage and all automobiles manufactured after January 1, 1973, to withstand a 30–mile-per-hour fixed barrier impact without significant fuel spillage.

The crash tests revealed that the Pinto's fuel system as designed could not meet the 20–mile-per-hour proposed standard. * * *

The Cost to Remedy Design Deficiencies

When a prototype failed the fuel system integrity test, the standard of care for engineers in the industry was to redesign and retest it. The vulnerability of the production Pinto's fuel tank at speeds of 20 and 30–miles-per-hour fixed barrier tests could have been remedied by inexpensive "fixes," but Ford produced and sold the Pinto to the public without doing anything to remedy the defects. Design changes that would have enhanced the integrity of the fuel tank system at relatively little cost per car included the following: Longitudinal side members and cross members at $2.40 and $1.80, respectively; a single shock absorbent "flak suit" to protect the tank at $4; a tank within a tank and placement of the tank over the axle at $5.08 to.$5.79; a nylon bladder within the tank at $5.25 to $8; placement of the tank over the axle surrounded with a protective barrier at a cost of $9.95 per car; substitution of a rear axle with a smooth differential housing at a cost of $2.10; imposition of a protective shield between the differential housing and the tank at $2.35; improvement and reenforcement of the bumper at $2.60; addition of eight inches of crush space a cost of $6.40. Equipping the car with a reinforced rear structure, smooth axle, improved bumper and additional crush space at a total cost of $15.30 would have made the fuel tank safe in a 34 to 38–mile-per-hour rear end collision by a vehicle the size of the Ford Galaxie. If, in addition to the foregoing, a bladder or tank within a tank were used or if the tank were protected with a shield, it would have been safe in a 40 to 45–mile-per-hour rear impact. If the tank had been located over the rear axle, it would have been safe in a rear impact at 50 miles per hour or more.

FORD'S APPEAL

* * *

II

Other Evidentiary Rulings

Ford contends that the court erroneously admitted irrelevant documentary evidence highly prejudicial to Ford. We find the contention to be without merit. * * *

Exhibit No. 125:

Exhibit No. 125 was a report presented at a Ford production review meeting in April 1971, recommending action to be taken in anticipation of the promulgation of federal standards on fuel system integrity. The report recommended, inter alia, deferral from 1974 to 1976 of the adoption of "flak suits" or "bladders" in all Ford cars, including the Pinto, in order to realize a savings of $20.9 million. The report stated that the cost of the flak suit or bladder would be $4 to $8 per car. The meeting at which the report was presented was chaired by Vice President Harold MacDonald and attended by Vice President Robert Alexander and occurred sometime before the 1972 Pinto was placed on the market. A reasonable inference may be drawn from the evidence that despite management's knowledge that the Pinto's fuel system could be made safe at a cost of but $4 to $8 per car, it decided to defer corrective measures to save money and enhance profits. The evidence was thus highly relevant and properly received.

* * *

VI

Punitive Damages

Ford contends that it was entitled to a judgment notwithstanding the verdict on the issue of punitive damages on two grounds: First, punitive damages are statutorily and constitutionally impermissible in a design defect case; second, there was no evidentiary support for a finding of malice or of corporate responsibility for malice. In any event, Ford maintains that the punitive damage award must be reversed because of erroneous instructions and excessiveness of the award.

(1) "Malice" Under Civil Code Section 3294:

The concept of punitive damages is rooted in the English common law and is a settled principle of the common law of this country. (Owen, Punitive Damages in Products Liability Litigation, 74 Mich.L.Rev. 1258 (hereafter Owen); Mallor & Roberts, Punitive Damages, Towards A Principled Approach, 31 Hastings L.J. 639 (hereafter Mallor & Roberts); Note, Exemplary Damages in the Law of Torts, 70 Harv.L.Rev. 517.) The doctrine was a part of the common law of this state long before the Civil Code was adopted. When our laws were codified in 1872, the doctrine was incorporated in Civil Code section 3294, which at the time of trial read: "In an action for the breach of an obligation not arising from contract, where the defendant has been guilty of oppression, fraud, or malice, express or implied, the plaintiff, in addition to the actual damages, may recover damages for the sake of example and by way of punishing the defendant."

Ford argues that "malice" as used in section 3294 and as interpreted by our Supreme Court in Davis v. Hearst, 160 Cal. 143, 116 P. 530, requires *animus malus* or evil motive—an intention to injure the person harmed—and that the term is therefore conceptually incompatible with an unintentional tort such as the manufacture and marketing of a defectively designed product. This contention runs counter to our decisional law. As this court recently noted, numerous California cases after *Davis v. Hearst*, have interpreted the term "malice" as used in section 3294 to include, not only a malicious intention to injure the specific person harmed, but conduct evincing "a conscious disregard of the probability that the actor's conduct will result in injury to others."

In Taylor v. Superior Court, 24 Cal.3d 890, 157 Cal.Rptr. 693, 598 P.2d 854, our high court's most recent pronouncement on the subject of punitive damages, the court observed that the availability of punitive damages has not been limited to cases in which there is an actual intent to harm plaintiff or others. The court concurred with the *Searle* (G.D. Searle & Co. v. Superior Court, 49 Cal.App.3d 22, 122 Cal.Rptr. 218) court's suggestion that conscious disregard of the safety of others is an appropriate description of the *animus malus* required by Civil Code section 3294, adding: "In order to justify an award of punitive damages on this basis, the plaintiff must establish that the defendant was aware of the probable dangerous consequences of his conduct, and that he wilfully and deliberately failed to avoid those consequences." * * *

The interpretation of the word "malice" as used in section 3294 to encompass conduct evincing callous and conscious disregard of public safety by those who manufacture and market mass produced articles is consonant with and furthers the objectives of punitive damages. The primary purposes of punitive damages are punishment and deterrence of like conduct by the wrongdoer and others. In the traditional noncommercial intentional tort, compensatory damages alone may serve as an effective deterrent against future wrongful conduct but in commerce-related torts, the manufacturer may find it more profitable to treat compensatory damages as a part of the cost of doing business rather than to remedy the defect. (Owen, supra p. 1291; Note, Mass Liability and Punitive Damages Overkill, 30 Hastings L.J. 1797, 1802.) Deterrence of such "objectionable corporate policies" serves one of the principal purposes of Civil Code section 3294. Governmental safety standards and the criminal law have failed to provide adequate consumer protection against the manufacture and distribution of defective products. Punitive damages thus remain as the most effective remedy for consumer protection against defectively designed mass produced articles. They provide a motive for private individuals to enforce rules of law and enable them to recoup the expenses of doing so which can be considerable and not otherwise recoverable.

We find no statutory impediments to the application of Civil Code section 3294 to a strict products liability case based on design defect. * * *

(2) Constitutional Attacks on Civil Code Section 3294

[Ford's] contention that the potential liability for punitive damages in other cases for the same design defect renders the imposition of such damages violative of Ford's due process rights also lacks merit. Followed to its logical conclusion, it would mean that punitive damages could never be assessed against a manufacturer of a mass produced article. No authorities are cited for such a proposition; indeed, as we have seen, the cases are to the contrary. We recognize the fact that multiplicity of awards may present a problem, but the mere possibility of a future award in a different case is not a ground for setting aside the award in this case, particularly as reduced by the trial judge. If Ford should be confronted with the possibility of an award in another case for the same conduct, it may raise the issue in that case. We add, moreover, that there is no necessary unfairness should the plaintiff in this case be rewarded to a greater extent than later plaintiffs. As Professor Owen has said in response to such a charge of unfairness: "This conception ignores the enormous diligence, imagination, and financial outlay required of initial plaintiffs to uncover and to prove the flagrant misconduct of a product manufacturer. In fact, subsequent plaintiffs will often ride to favorable verdicts and settlements on the coattails of the firstcomers." That observation fits the instant case. * * *

(3) Sufficiency of the Evidence to Support the Finding of Malice and Corporate Responsibility

Ford contends that its motion for judgment notwithstanding the verdict should have been granted because the evidence was insufficient to support a finding of malice or corporate responsibility for such malice. The record fails to support the contention.* * * There was ample evidence to support a finding of malice and Ford's responsibility for malice.

Through the results of the crash tests Ford knew that the Pinto's fuel tank and rear structure would expose consumers to serious injury or death in a 20 to 30 mile-per-hour collision. There was evidence that Ford could have corrected the hazardous design defects at minimal cost but decided to defer correction of the shortcomings by engaging in a cost-benefit analysis balancing human lives and limbs against corporate profits. Ford's institutional mentality was shown to be one of callous indifference to public safety. There was substantial evidence that Ford's conduct constituted "conscious disregard" of the probability of injury to members of the consuming public.

Ford's argument that there can be no liability for punitive damages because there was no evidence of corporate ratification of malicious misconduct is equally without merit. California follows the Restatement rule that punitive damages can be awarded against a principal because of an action of an agent if, but only if, " '(a) the principal authorized the doing and the manner of the act, or (b) the agent was unfit and the principal was reckless in employing him, or (c) the agent was employed in a managerial capacity and was acting in the scope of employment, or (d) the principal or a managerial agent of the principal ratified or approved the act.' " The present case comes within one or both of the categories described in subdivisions (c) and (d).

There is substantial evidence that management was aware of the crash tests showing the vulnerability of the Pinto's fuel tank to rupture at low speed rear impacts with consequent significant risk of injury or death of the occupants by fire. There was testimony from several sources that the test results were forwarded up the chain of command * * *. It may be inferred from the testimony * * * that * * * two engineers had approached management about redesigning the Pinto or that, being aware of management's attitude, they decided to do nothing. In either case the decision not to take corrective action was made by persons exercising managerial authority. Whether an employee acts in a "managerial capacity" does not necessarily depend on his "level" in the corporate hierarchy. As the *Egan* court said: " 'Defendant should not be allowed to insulate itself from liability by giving an employee a nonmanagerial title and relegating to him crucial policy decisions.' "

* * *

(6) Amount of Punitive Damage Award

Ford's final contention is that the amount of punitive damages awarded, even as reduced by the trial court, was so excessive that a new trial on that issue must be granted. Ford argues that its conduct was less reprehensible than those for which punitive damages have been awarded in California in the past; that the $3½ million award is many times over the highest award for such damages ever upheld in California; and that the award exceeds maximum civil penalties that may be enforced under federal or state statutes against a manufacturer for marketing a defective automobile. We are unpersuaded.

In determining whether an award of punitive damages is excessive, comparison of the amount awarded with other awards in other cases is not a valid consideration. * * * In deciding whether an award is excessive as a matter of law or was so grossly disproportionate as to raise the presumption that it was the product of passion or prejudice, the following factors should be weighed: The degree of reprehensibility of defendant's conduct, the wealth of the defendant, the amount of compensatory damages, and an amount which would serve as a deterrent effect on like conduct by defendant and others who may be so inclined. Applying the foregoing criteria to the instant case, the punitive damage award as reduced by the trial court was well within reason.[20]

In assessing the propriety of a punitive damage award, as in assessing the propriety of any other judicial ruling based upon factual determinations, the evidence must be viewed in the light most favorable to the judgment. Viewing the record thusly in the instant case, the conduct of Ford's management was reprehensible in the extreme. It exhibited a conscious and callous disregard of public safety in order to maximize corporate profits. Ford's self-evaluation of its conduct is based on a review of the evidence most favorable to it instead of on the basis of the evidence most favorable to the judgment. Unlike malicious conduct directed toward a single specific individual, Ford's tortious conduct endangered the lives of thousands of Pinto purchasers. Weighed against the factor of reprehensibility, the punitive damage award as reduced by the trial judge was not excessive.

Nor was the reduced award excessive taking into account defendant's wealth and the size of the compensatory award. Ford's net worth was 7.7 billion dollars and its income after taxes for 1976 was over 983 million dollars. The punitive award was approximately .005% of Ford's net worth

---

20. A quantitative formula whereby the amount of punitive damages can be determined in a given case with mathematical certainty is manifestly impossible as well as undesirable. (Mallor & Roberts, supra, 31 Hastings L.J. 639, 666–667, 670.) The authors advocate abandonment of the rule that a reasonable relationship must exist between punitive damages and actual damages. They suggest that courts balance society's interest against defendant's interest by focusing on the following factors: Severity of threatened harm; degree of reprehensibility of defendant's conduct, profitability of the conduct, wealth of defendant, amount of compensatory damages (whether it was high in relation to injury), cost of litigation, potential criminal sanctions and other civil actions against defendant based on same conduct. In the present case, the amount of the award as reduced by the judge was reasonable under the suggested factors, including the factor of any other potential liability, civil or criminal.

and approximately .03% of its 1976 net income. The ratio of the punitive damages to compensatory damages was approximately 1.4 to one. Significantly, Ford does not quarrel with the amount of the compensatory award to Grimshaw.

Nor was the size of the award excessive in light of its deterrent purpose. An award which is so small that it can be simply written off as a part of the cost of doing business would have no deterrent effect. An award which affects the company's pricing of its product and thereby affects its competitive advantage would serve as a deterrent. The award in question was far from excessive as a deterrent against future wrongful conduct by Ford and others.

Ford complains that the punitive award is far greater than the maximum penalty that may be imposed under California or federal law prohibiting the sale of defective automobiles or other products. For example, Ford notes that California statutes provide a maximum fine of only $50 for the first offense and $100 for a second offense for a dealer who sells an automobile that fails to conform to federal safety laws or is not equipped with required lights or brakes; that a manufacturer who sells brake fluid in this state failing to meet statutory standards is subject to a maximum of only $50; and that the maximum penalty that may be imposed under federal law for violation of automobile safety standards is $1,000 per vehicle up to a maximum of $800,000 for any related series of offenses. It is precisely because monetary penalties under government regulations prescribing business standards or the criminal law are so inadequate and ineffective as deterrents against a manufacturer and distributor of mass produced defective products that punitive damages must be of sufficient amount to discourage such practices. Instead of showing that the punitive damage award was excessive, the comparison between the award and the maximum penalties under state and federal statutes and regulations governing automotive safety demonstrates the propriety of the amount of punitive damages awarded.

Grimshaw's Appeal

Grimshaw has appealed from the order conditionally granting Ford a new trial on the issue of punitive damages and from the amended judgment entered pursuant to that order.

Grimshaw contends that the new trial order is erroneous because (1) the punitive damages awarded by the jury were not excessive as a matter of law, (2) the specification of reasons was inadequate; and (3) the court abused its discretion in cutting the award so drastically. For reasons to be stated, we have concluded that the contentions lack merit.

The court prefaced its specification of reasons with a recitation of the judicially established guidelines[16] for determining whether a punitive

---

16. The court stated that "the principles by which the propriety of the amount of punitive damages awarded will be judged are threefold: (1) Is the sum so large as to raise a presumption that the award was the result of passion and prejudice and therefore excessive as a matter of law;

award is excessive. The court then observed that there was evidence in the record (referring to Exhibit 125) which might provide a possible rational basis for the 125 million dollar jury verdict which would dispel any presumption of passion or prejudice, adding, however, that the court was not suggesting that the amount was warranted "or that the jury did utilize Exhibit 125, or any other exhibits, and if they did, that they were justified in so doing." The court then noted, based on the fact that Ford's net worth was 7.7 billion and its profits during the last quarter of the year referred to in the financial statement introduced into evidence were more than twice the punitive award, that the award was not disproportionate to Ford's net assets or to its profit generating capacity. The court noted, however, that the amount of the punitive award was 44 times the compensatory award, the court stated that while it did not consider that ratio alone to be controlling because aggravating circumstances may justify a ratio as high as the one represented by the jury verdict, it reasoned that the ratio coupled with the amount by which the punitive exceeded the compensatory damages (over 122 million dollars) rendered the jury's punitive award excessive as a matter of law.

Grimshaw contends that the court erred in determining that the ratio of punitive to compensatory damages rendered the punitive excessive as a matter of law. The trial court, however, did not base its decision solely on the ratio of punitive to compensatory. It took into account the ratio, the "aggravating circumstances" (the degree of reprehensibility), the wealth of the defendant and its profit generating capacity, the magnitude of the punitive award, including the amount by which it exceeded the compensatory. Those were proper considerations for determining whether the award was excessive as a matter of law. When a trial court grants a new trial for excessive damages, either conditionally or outright, a presumption of correctness attaches to the order and it will not be reversed unless it plainly appears that the judge abused his discretion. In the case at bench, we find no abuse of discretion. * * *

Finally, Grimshaw contends the court abused its discretion in reducing the award to $3½ million as a condition of its new trial order and urges this court to restore the jury award or at least require a remittitur of substantially less than that required by the trial court. * * *

Here, the judge, exercising his independent judgment on the evidence, determined that a punitive award of $3½ million was "fair and reasonable." Evidence pertaining to Ford's conduct, its wealth and the savings it realized in deferring design modifications in the Pinto's fuel system might have persuaded a different fact finder that a larger award should have been allowed to stand. Our role, however, is limited to determining whether the trial judge's action constituted a manifest and unmistakable abuse of discretion. Here, the judge referred to the evidence bearing on those factors in his new trial order and obviously weighed it in deciding

---

(2) Does the award bear a reasonable relationship to the net assets of the defendant; and (3) Does the award bear a reasonable relationship to the compensatory damages awarded."

what was a "fair and reasonable" award. We cannot say that the judge abused the discretion vested in him by Code of Civil Procedure section 662.5 or that there is "no substantial basis in the record" for the reasons given for the order. Finally, while the trial judge may not have taken into account Ford's potential liability for punitive damages in other cases involving the same tortious conduct in reducing the award, it is a factor we may consider in passing on the request to increase the award. Considering such potential liability, we find the amount as reduced by the trial judge to be reasonable and just.

* * *

NOTES

1. Exhibit 125, the report by Ford engineers showing savings which would be realized by deferring design and safety changes, has been called "possibly the most remarkable document ever produced in an American lawsuit." Stuart Speiser, Lawsuit 357 (1980). The *Grimshaw* case has taken on mythical proportions showing how disturbed jurors are by common business practices that balance life and safety against monetary cost. Gray T. Schwartz, The Myth of the Ford Pinto Case, 43 Rutgers L.Rev. 1013 (1991).

2. As a general rule, where a statutory scheme does not limit the remedies that a court may impose, punitive or exemplary damages have been found to be available to a plaintiff. E.g., Smith v. Wade, 461 U.S. 30, 103 S.Ct. 1625, 75 L.Ed.2d 632 (1983) (inmate in reformatory for youthful first offenders beaten and sexually assaulted by cellmates; punitive damages available against prison guard in action brought under 42 U.S.C. § 1983); Reich v. Cambridgeport Air Systems, Inc., 26 F.3d 1187 (1st Cir.1994) (Secretary of Labor bringing action under whistleblower provision of Occupational Safety and Health Act on behalf of employee may be awarded exemplary damages).

There are exceptions where the award of such damages would be at odds with effectuating the purposes of the statute. For example, the Supreme Court has held that punitive damages are not an available remedy in private suits under either Title VI of the Civil Rights Act of 1964, section 202 of the Americans with Disabilities Act or section 504 of the Rehabilitation Act. It reasoned that a remedy is "appropriate relief" in private suits under Spending Clause legislation, such as these acts, only if the funding recipient is on notice that, by accepting federal funding, it exposes itself to liability of that nature. A funding recipient is generally on notice that it is subject not only to those remedies explicitly provided in the relevant legislation, but also to those remedies traditionally available in suits for breach of contract, of which punitive damages is not one. Barnes v. Gorman, 536 U.S. 181, 122 S.Ct. 2097, 153 L.Ed.2d 230 (2002).

3. States and cities may recover punitive damages under the common law. United States v. Hooker Chemicals & Plastics Corp., 748 F.Supp. 67 (W.D.N.Y.1990) (punitive damages available on claim defendant had committed a public nuisance in disposing of toxic waste); City of New York ex rel. People v. Taliaferrow, 144 Misc.2d 649, 544 N.Y.S.2d 273 (Sup.Ct.1989), aff'd,

158 A.D.2d 445, 551 N.Y.S.2d 253 (2d Dept.1990) (in public nuisance action to stop use of premises for prostitution, $100,000 in punitive damages awarded). On the other hand, punitive damages are generally not available *against* the government unless authorized by statute. Newport v. Fact Concerts, Inc., 453 U.S. 247, 101 S.Ct. 2748, 69 L.Ed.2d 616 (1981); Cook County, Illinois v. United States ex rel. Chandler, 538 U.S. 119, 123 S.Ct. 1239, 155 L.Ed.2d 247 (2003) (municipalities, but not States, are subject to treble damages and civil penalties of up to $10,000 per claim under the False Claims Act, 31 U.S.C. § 3729).

4. Whether insurance is available to cover punitive damage awards turns on a number of issues: the explicit language of the insurance contract; the implicit exceptions to the contract (e.g., one is not insured against intentional acts); the legal standard of liability in a case; and the common and statutory law of insurance in the relevant jurisdiction. The law in different states varies greatly on these issues. See Tom Baker, Reconsidering Insurance for Punitive Damages, 1998 Wis.L.Rev. 101 (1998); Christopher Wilson, Lazenby After Hodges—Insurability of Punitive Damages Awards in Tennessee: A Continuing Question of Public Policy, 36 U.Mem.L.Rev. 463 (2006).

EXXON SHIPPING CO. v. BAKER

Supreme Court of the United States, 2008
554 U.S. ___, 128 S.Ct. 2605, 171 L.Ed.2d 570

JUSTICE SOUTER delivered the opinion of the Court.

* * *

I

On March 24, 1989, the supertanker *Exxon Valdez* grounded on Bligh Reef off the Alaskan coast, fracturing its hull and spilling millions of gallons of crude oil into Prince William Sound. The owner, petitioner Exxon Shipping Co. (now SeaRiver Maritime, Inc.), and its owner, petitioner Exxon Mobil Corp. (collectively, Exxon), have settled state and federal claims for environmental damage, with payments exceeding $1 billion, and this action by respondent Baker and others, including commercial fishermen and native Alaskans, was brought for economic losses to individuals dependent on Prince William Sound for their livelihoods.

A

The tanker was over 900 feet long and was used by Exxon to carry crude oil from the end of the Trans–Alaska Pipeline in Valdez, Alaska, to the lower 48 States. On the night of the spill it was carrying 53 million gallons of crude oil, or over a million barrels. Its captain was one Joseph Hazelwood, who had completed a 28–day alcohol treatment program while employed by Exxon, as his superiors knew, but dropped out of a prescribed follow-up program and stopped going to Alcoholics Anonymous meetings. According to the District Court, "[t]here was evidence presented to the jury that after Hazelwood was released from [residential treatment], he drank in bars, parking lots, apartments, airports, airplanes, restaurants, hotels, at various ports, and aboard Exxon tankers." The jury also heard contested testimony that Hazelwood drank with Exxon officials and that members of the Exxon management knew of his relapse. Although Exxon had a clear policy prohibiting employees from serving onboard within four hours of consuming alcohol, Exxon presented no evidence that it monitored Hazelwood after his return to duty or considered giving him a shoreside assignment. Witnesses testified that before the *Valdez* left port on the night of the disaster, Hazelwood downed at least five double vodkas in the waterfront bars of Valdez, an intake of about 15 ounces of 80–proof alcohol, enough "that a non-alcoholic would have passed out."

The ship sailed at 9:12 p.m. on March 23, 1989, guided by a state-licensed pilot for the first leg out, through the Valdez Narrows. At 11:20 p.m., Hazelwood took active control and, owing to poor conditions in the outbound shipping lane, radioed the Coast Guard for permission to move east across the inbound lane to a less icy path. Under the conditions, this was a standard move, which the last outbound tanker had also taken, and the Coast Guard cleared the *Valdez* to cross the inbound lane. The tanker accordingly steered east toward clearer waters, but the move put it in the path of an underwater reef off Bligh Island, thus requiring a turn back west into the shipping lane around Busby Light, north of the reef.

Two minutes before the required turn, however, Hazelwood left the bridge and went down to his cabin in order, he said, to do paperwork. This decision was inexplicable. There was expert testimony that, even if their presence is not strictly necessary, captains simply do not quit the bridge during maneuvers like this, and no paperwork could have justified it. And in fact the evidence was that Hazelwood's presence was required, both because there should have been two officers on the bridge at all times and his departure left only one, and because he was the only person on the entire ship licensed to navigate this part of Prince William Sound. To make matters worse, before going below Hazelwood put the tanker on autopilot, speeding it up, making the turn trickier, and any mistake harder to correct.

As Hazelwood left, he instructed the remaining officer, third mate Joseph Cousins, to move the tanker back into the shipping lane once it came abeam of Busby Light. Cousins, unlicensed to navigate in those waters, was left alone with helmsman Robert Kagan, a nonofficer. For reasons that remain a mystery, they failed to make the turn at Busby Light, and a later emergency maneuver attempted by Cousins came too late. The tanker ran aground on Bligh Reef, tearing the hull open and spilling 11 million gallons of crude oil into Prince William Sound.

After Hazelwood returned to the bridge and reported the grounding to the Coast Guard, he tried but failed to rock the *Valdez* off the reef, a maneuver which could have spilled more oil and caused the ship to founder. The Coast Guard's nearly immediate response included a blood test of Hazelwood (the validity of which Exxon disputes) showing a blood-alcohol level of .061 eleven hours after the spill. Experts testified that to have this much alcohol in his bloodstream so long after the accident, Hazelwood at the time of the spill must have had a blood-alcohol level of around three times the legal limit for driving in most States.

In the aftermath of the disaster, Exxon spent around $2.1 billion in cleanup efforts. * * * Exxon pleaded guilty to violations of the Clean Water Act, the Refuse Act, and the Migratory Bird Treaty Act and agreed to pay a $150 million fine, later reduced to $25 million plus restitution of $100 million. A civil action by the United States and the State of Alaska for environmental harms ended with a consent decree for Exxon to pay at least $900 million toward restoring natural resources, and it paid another $303 million in voluntary settlements with fishermen, property owners, and other private parties.

B

* * *

[T]he jury awarded $287 million in compensatory damages to the commercial fishermen. * * * The jury awarded $5,000 in punitive damages against Hazelwood and $5 billion against Exxon. * * * [T]he [Ninth] Circuit remanded twice for adjustments in light of this Court's due process cases before ultimately itself remitting the award to $2.5 billion.

* * *

IV

Exxon challenges the size of the remaining $2.5 billion punitive damages award. * * * [I]t does not offer a legal ground for concluding that maritime law should never award punitive damages, or that none should be awarded in this case, but it does argue that this award exceeds the bounds justified by the punitive damages goal of deterring reckless (or worse) behavior and the consequently heightened threat of harm. The claim goes to our understanding of the place of punishment in modern civil law and reasonable standards of process in administering punitive law * * *.

A

The modern Anglo–American doctrine of punitive damages dates back at least to 1763, when a pair of decisions by the Court of Common Pleas recognized the availability of damages "for more than the injury received." Wilkes v. Wood, Lofft 1, 18, 98 Eng.Rep. 489, 498 (1763). In *Wilkes*, one of the foundations of the Fourth Amendment, exemplary damages awarded against the Secretary of State, responsible for an unlawful search of John Wilkes's papers, were a spectacular £4,000. And in Huckle v. Money, 95 Eng.Rep. 768, 768–769 (K.B. 1763), the same judge who is recorded in *Wilkes* gave an opinion upholding a jury's award of 300 (against a government officer again) although "if the jury had been confined by their oath to consider the mere personal injury only, perhaps [£20] damages would have been thought damages sufficient."

Awarding damages beyond the compensatory was not, however, a wholly novel idea even then, legal codes from ancient times through the Middle Ages having called for multiple damages for certain especially harmful acts. See, e.g., Code of Hammurabi § 8 (R. Harper ed. 1904) (tenfold penalty for stealing the goat of a freed man); Statute of Gloucester, 1278, 6 Edw. I, ch. 5, 1 Stat. at Large 66 (treble damages for waste). But punitive damages were a common law innovation untethered to strict numerical multipliers, and the doctrine promptly crossed the Atlantic, to become widely accepted in American courts by the middle of the 19th century.

B

Early common law cases offered various rationales for punitive-damages awards, which were then generally dubbed "exemplary," implying that these verdicts were justified as punishment for extraordinary wrongdoing, as in Wilkes's case. Sometimes, though, the extraordinary element emphasized was the damages award itself, the punishment being "for example's sake," Tullidge v. Wade, 3 Wils. 18, 19, 95 Eng.Rep. 909 (K.B. 1769) "to deter from any such proceeding for the future." See also Coryell at 77 (instructing the jury "to give damages for *example's* sake, to prevent such offences in [the] future").

A third historical justification * * * was the need "to compensate for intangible injuries, compensation which was not otherwise available under the narrow conception of compensatory damages prevalent at the time." Cooper Industries, Inc. v. Leatherman Tool Group, Inc., 532 U.S. 424, 437–438, n. 11 (2001). But see Sebok, What Did Punitive Damages Do? 78 Chi.-Kent L.Rev. 163, 204 (2003) (arguing that "punitive damages have never served the compensatory function attributed to them by the Court in *Cooper*"). As the century progressed, and "the types of compensatory damages available to plaintiffs ... broadened," the consequence was that American courts tended to speak of punitive damages as separate and distinct from compensatory damages.

Regardless of the alternative rationales over the years, the consensus today is that punitives are aimed not at compensation but principally at retribution and deterring harmful conduct. This consensus informs the doctrine in most modern American jurisdictions, where juries are customarily instructed on twin goals of punitive awards. See, e.g., * * * N. Y. Pattern Jury Instr., Civil, No. 2:278 (2007) ("The purpose of punitive damages is not to compensate the plaintiff but to punish the defendant ... and thereby to discourage the defendant ... from acting in a similar way in the future"). The prevailing rule in American courts also limits punitive damages to cases of what the Court in *Day* spoke of as "enormity," where a defendant's conduct is "outrageous," 4 Restatement § 908(2), owing to "gross negligence," "willful, wanton, and reckless indifference for the rights of others," or behavior even more deplorable, 1 Schlueter § 9.3(A).

Under the umbrellas of punishment and its aim of deterrence, degrees of relative blameworthiness are apparent. Reckless conduct is not intentional or malicious, nor is it necessarily callous toward the risk of harming others, as opposed to unheedful of it. See, e.g., 2 Restatement § 500, Comment *a*, pp. 587–588 (1964) ("Recklessness may consist of either of two different types of conduct. In one the actor knows, or has reason to know ... of facts which create a high degree of risk of ... harm to another, and deliberately proceeds to act, or to fail to act, in conscious disregard of, or indifference to, that risk. In the other the actor has such knowledge, or reason to know, of the facts, but does not realize or appreciate the high degree of risk involved, although a reasonable man in his position would do so"). Action taken or omitted in order to augment profit represents an enhanced degree of punishable culpability, as of course does willful or malicious action, taken with a purpose to injure.* * *

Regardless of culpability, however, heavier punitive awards have been thought to be justifiable when wrongdoing is hard to detect (increasing chances of getting away with it), or when the value of injury and the corresponding compensatory award are small (providing low incentives to sue), 4 Restatement § 908, Comment *c*, p. 465 ("Thus an award of nominal damages ... is enough to support a further award of punitive damages, when a tort, ... is committed for an outrageous purpose, but no significant harm has resulted"). And, with a broadly analogous object, some regulatory schemes provide by statute for multiple recovery in order to induce private litigation to supplement official enforcement that might fall short if unaided.

C

State regulation of punitive damages varies. A few States award them rarely, or not at all. Nebraska bars punitive damages entirely, on state constitutional grounds. Four others permit punitive damages only when authorized by statute: Louisiana, Massachusetts, and Washington as a matter of common law, and New Hampshire by statute codifying common law tradition. Michigan courts recognize only exemplary damages supportable as compensatory, rather than truly punitive, while Connecticut courts have limited what they call punitive recovery to the "expenses of bringing the legal action, including attorney's fees, less taxable costs."

As for procedure, in most American jurisdictions the amount of the punitive award is generally determined by a jury in the first instance, and that "determination is then reviewed by trial and appellate courts to ensure that it is reasonable." Pacific Mut. Life Ins. Co. v. Haslip, 499 U.S. 1, 15 (1991); see also Honda Motor Co. v. Oberg, 512 U.S. 415, 421–426 (1994). Many States have gone further by imposing statutory limits on punitive awards, in the form of absolute monetary caps, see, e.g., Va. Code Ann. § 8.01–38.1 ($350,000 cap), a maximum ratio of punitive to compensatory damages, see, e.g., Ohio Rev. Code Ann. § 2315.21(D)(2)(a) (2:1 ratio in most tort cases), or, frequently, some combination of the two, see, e.g., Alaska Stat. § 09.17.020(f) (2006) (greater of 3:1 ratio or $500,000 in most actions). The States that rely on a multiplier have adopted a variety of ratios, ranging from 5:1 to 1:1.

Despite these limitations, punitive damages overall are higher and more frequent in the United States than they are anywhere else. * * * And some legal systems not only decline to recognize punitive damages themselves but refuse to enforce foreign punitive judgments as contrary to public policy. See, e.g., Gotanda, Charting Developments Concerning Punitive Damages: Is the Tide Changing? 45 Colum. J. Transnat'l L. 507 (2007) (noting refusals to enforce judgments by Japanese, Italian, and German courts, positing that such refusals may be on the decline, but concluding, "American parties should not anticipate smooth sailing when seeking to have a domestic punitive damages award recognized and enforced in other countries").

D

American punitive damages have been the target of audible criticism in recent decades, see, e.g., Note, Developments, The Paths of Civil Litigation, 113 Harv.L.Rev. 1783, 1784–1788 (2000) (surveying criticism), but the most recent studies tend to undercut much of it. A survey of the literature reveals that discretion to award punitive damages has not mass-produced runaway awards, and although some studies show the dollar amounts of punitive-damages awards growing over time, even in real terms, by most accounts the median ratio of punitive to compensatory awards has remained less than 1:1. Nor do the data substantiate a marked increase in the percentage of cases with punitive awards over the past several decades. The figures thus show an overall restraint and suggest that in many instances a high ratio of punitive to compensatory damages is substantially greater than necessary to punish or deter.

The real problem, it seems, is the stark unpredictability of punitive awards. Courts of law are concerned with fairness as consistency, and evidence that the median ratio of punitive to compensatory awards falls within a reasonable zone, or that punitive awards are infrequent, fails to tell us whether the spread between high and low individual awards is acceptable. The available data suggest it is not. A recent comprehensive study of punitive damages awarded by juries in state civil trials found a median ratio of punitive to compensatory awards of just 0.62:1, but a mean ratio of 2.90:1 and a standard deviation of 13.81. Even to those of us unsophisticated in statistics, the thrust of these figures is clear: the spread is great, and the outlier cases subject defendants to punitive damages that dwarf the corresponding compensatories. The distribution of awards is narrower, but still remarkable, among punitive damages assessed by judges: the median ratio is 0.66:1, the mean ratio is 1.60:1, and the standard deviation is 4.54. Other studies of some of the same data show that fully 14% of punitive awards in 2001 were greater than four times the compensatory damages, with 18% of punitives in the 1990s more than trebling the compensatory damages, see Ostrom, Rottman, & Goerdt, A Step Above Anecdote: A Profile of the Civil Jury in the 1990s, 79

Judicature 233, 240 (1996). And a study of "financial injury" cases using a different data set found that 34% of the punitive awards were greater than three times the corresponding compensatory damages.

Starting with the premise of a punitive-damages regime, these ranges of variation might be acceptable or even desirable if they resulted from judges' and juries' refining their judgments to reach a generally accepted optimal level of penalty and deterrence in cases involving a wide range of circumstances, while producing fairly consistent results in cases with similar facts. Cf. TXO Production Corp. v. Alliance Resources Corp., 509 U.S. 443, 457–458 (1993) (plurality opinion). But anecdotal evidence suggests that nothing of that sort is going on. One of our own leading cases on punitive damages, with a $4 million verdict by an Alabama jury, noted that a second Alabama case with strikingly similar facts produced "a comparable amount of compensatory damages" but "no punitive damages at all." See *Gore*, 517 U.S. at 565, n. 8. As the Supreme Court of Alabama candidly explained, "the disparity between the two jury verdicts ... [w]as a reflection of the inherent uncertainty of the trial process." BMW of North America, Inc. v. Gore, 646 So.2d 619, 626 (1994). We are aware of no scholarly work pointing to consistency across punitive awards in cases involving similar claims and circumstances.

E

The Court's response to outlier punitive damages awards has thus far been confined by claims at the constitutional level * * *.

Today's enquiry differs from due process review because the case arises under federal maritime jurisdiction, and we are reviewing a jury award for conformity with maritime law, rather than the outer limit allowed by due process; we are examining the verdict in the exercise of federal maritime common law authority, which precedes and should obviate any application of the constitutional standard. Our due process cases, on the contrary, have all involved awards subject in the first instance to state law. See, e.g., *State Farm* (fraud and intentional infliction of emotional distress under Utah law); *Gore* (fraud under Alabama law); *TXO* (plurality opinion) (slander of title under West Virginia law); *Haslip* (fraud under Alabama law). These, as state-law cases, could provide no occasion to consider a "common-law standard of excessiveness," *Browning-Ferris Industries*, and the only matter of federal law within our appellate authority was the constitutional due process issue.

Our review of punitive damages today, then, considers not their intersection with the Constitution, but the desirability of regulating them as a common law remedy for which responsibility lies with this Court as a source of judge-made law in the absence of statute. Whatever may be the constitutional significance of the unpredictability of high punitive awards, this feature of happenstance is in tension with the function of the awards as punitive, just because of the implication of unfairness that an eccentrically high punitive verdict carries in a system whose commonly held notion of law rests on a sense of fairness in dealing with one another.

Thus, a penalty should be reasonably predictable in its severity, so that even Justice Holmes's "bad man" can look ahead with some ability to know what the stakes are in choosing one course of action or another. See The Path of the Law, 10 Harv.L.Rev. 457, 459 (1897). And when the bad mans counterparts turn up from time to time, the penalty scheme they face ought to threaten them with a fair probability of suffering in like degree when they wreak like damage. Cf. Koon v. United States, 518 U.S. 81, 113 (1996) (noting the need "to reduce unjustified disparities" in criminal sentencing "and so reach toward the evenhandedness and neutrality that are the distinguishing marks of any principled system of justice"). The common sense of justice would surely bar penalties that reasonable people would think excessive for the harm caused in the circumstances.

F

1

With that aim ourselves, we have three basic approaches to consider, one verbal and two quantitative. As mentioned before, a number of state courts have settled on criteria for judicial review of punitive-damages awards that go well beyond traditional "shock the conscience" or "passion and prejudice" tests. Maryland, for example, has set forth a nonexclusive list of nine review factors under state common law that include "degree of heinousness," "the deterrence value of [the award]," and "[w]hether [the punitive award] bears a reasonable relationship to the compensatory damages awarded." Alabama has seven general criteria, such as "actual or likely harm [from the defendants conduct]," "degree of reprehensibility," and "[i]f the wrongful conduct was profitable to the defendant." * * *

These judicial review criteria are brought to bear after juries render verdicts under instructions offering, at best, guidance no more specific for reaching an appropriate penalty. In Maryland, for example, which allows punitive damages for intentional torts and conduct characterized by "actual malice," juries may be instructed that

"An award for punitive damages should be:

"(1) In an amount that will deter the defendant and others from similar conduct.

"(2) Proportionate to the wrongfulness of the defendant's conduct and the defendant's ability to pay.

"(3) But not designed to bankrupt or financially destroy a defendant."

Md. Pattern Jury Instr., Civil, No. 10:13 (4th ed. 2007).

In Alabama, juries are instructed to fix an amount after considering "the character and degree of the wrong as shown by the evidence in the case, and the necessity of preventing similar wrongs." 1 Ala. Pattern Jury Instr., Civil, No. § 23.21 (Supp. 2007).

These examples leave us skeptical that verbal formulations, superimposed on general jury instructions, are the best insurance against unpredictable outliers. Instructions can go just so far in promoting systemic consistency when awards are not tied to specifically proven items of damage (the cost of medical treatment, say), and although judges in the States that take this approach may well produce just results by dint of valiant effort, our experience with attempts to produce consistency in the analogous business of criminal sentencing leaves us doubtful that anything but a quantified approach will work. A glance at the experience there will explain our skepticism.

The points of similarity are obvious. "[P]unitive damages advance the interests of punishment and deterrence, which are also among the interests advanced by the criminal law." *Browning-Ferris Industries*, 492 U.S., at 275. See also 1977 Restatement § 908, Comment *a*, at 464 (purposes of punitive damages are "the same" as "that of a fine imposed after a conviction of a crime"); 18 U.S.C. § 3553(a)(2) (requiring sentencing courts to consider, inter alia, "the need for the sentence imposed ... to provide just punishment for the offense" and "to afford adequate deterrence to criminal conduct"); United States Sentencing Commission, Guidelines Manual § 1A1.1, comment. (Nov. 2007).

It is instructive, then, that in the last quarter century federal sentencing rejected an "indeterminate" system, with relatively unguided discretion to sentence within a wide range, under which "similarly situated offenders were sentenced [to], and did actually serve, widely disparate sentences." Instead it became a system of detailed guidelines tied to exactly quantified sentencing results, under the authority of the Sentencing Reform Act of 1984, 18 U.S.C. § 3551 et seq.

The importance of this for us is that in the old federal sentencing system of general standards the cohort of even the most seasoned judicial penalty-givers defied consistency. Judges and defendants alike were "[l]eft at large, wandering in deserts of uncharted discretion," M. Frankel, Criminal Sentences: Law Without Order 7–8 (1973), which is very much the position of those imposing punitive damages today, be they judges or juries, except that they lack even a statutory maximum; their only restraint beyond a core sense of fairness is the due process limit. This federal criminal law development, with its many state parallels, strongly suggests that as long "as there are no punitive-damages guidelines, corresponding to the federal and state sentencing guidelines, it is inevitable that the specific amount of punitive damages awarded whether by a judge or by a jury will be arbitrary."

2

This is why our better judgment is that eliminating unpredictable outlying punitive awards by more rigorous standards than the constitutional limit will probably have to take the form adopted in those States that have looked to the criminal-law pattern of quantified limits. One option would be to follow the States that set a hard dollar cap on punitive damages, a course that arguably would come closest to the criminal law, rather like setting a maximum term of years. The trouble is, though, that there is no "standard" tort or contract injury, making it difficult to settle upon a particular dollar figure as appropriate across the board. And of course a judicial selection of a dollar cap would carry a serious drawback; a legislature can pick a figure, index it for inflation, and revisit its provision whenever there seems to be a need for further tinkering, but a court cannot say when an issue will show up on the docket again. See, e.g., Jones & Laughlin Steel Corp. v. Pfeifer, 462 U.S. 523, 546–547 (1983) (declining to adopt a fixed formula to account for inflation in discounting future wages to present value, in light of the unpredictability of inflation rates and variation among lost-earnings cases).

The more promising alternative is to leave the effects of inflation to the jury or judge who assesses the value of actual loss, by pegging punitive to compensatory damages using a ratio or maximum multiple. See, e.g., 2 ALI Enterprise Responsibility for Personal Injury: Reporters' Study 258 (1991) (hereinafter ALI Reporters' Study) ("[T]he compensatory award in a successful case should be the starting point in calculating the punitive award"); ABA, Report of Special Comm. on Punitive Damages, Section of Litigation, Punitive Damages: A Constructive Examination 64–66 (1986) (recommending a presumptive punitive-to-compensatory damages ratio). As the earlier canvass of state experience showed, this is the model many States have adopted, and Congress has passed analogous legislation from time to time, as for example in providing treble damages in antitrust, racketeering, patent, and trademark actions, see 15 U.S.C. §§ 15, 1117; 18 U.S.C. § 1964(c); 35 U.S.C. § 284. And of course the potential relevance of the ratio between compensatory and punitive damages is indisputable, being a central feature in our due process analysis. See, e.g., *State Farm*; *Gore*.

Still, some will murmur that this smacks too much of policy and too little of principle. But the answer rests on the fact that we are acting here in the position of a common law court of last review, faced with a perceived defect in a common law remedy. Traditionally, courts have accepted primary responsibility for reviewing punitive damages and thus for their evolution, and if, in the absence of legislation, judicially derived standards leave the door open to outlier punitive-damages awards, it is hard to see how the judiciary can wash its hands of a problem it created, simply by calling quantified standards legislative. See *State Farm* (Ginsburg, J., dissenting) ("In a legislative scheme or a state high court's design to cap punitive damages, the handiwork in setting single-digit and 1-to-1 benchmarks could hardly be questioned"); 2 ALI Reporters' Study 257 (recommending adoption of ratio, "probably legislatively, although possibly judicially").

History certainly is no support for the notion that judges cannot use numbers. The 21-year period in the rule against perpetuities was a judicial innovation, see, e.g., Cadell v. Palmer, 1 Clark & Finnelly 372, 6 Eng.Rep. 956, 963 (H.L.1833), and so were exact limitations periods for civil actions, sometimes borrowing from statutes, but often without any statutory account to draw on. For more examples, see 1 W. Blackstone, Commentaries on the Laws of England 451 (1765) (listing other common law age cut-offs with no apparent statutory basis). And of course, adopting an admiralty-law ratio is no less judicial than picking one as an outer limit of constitutionality for punitive awards. See *State Farm*.

Although the legal landscape is well populated with examples of ratios and multipliers expressing policies of retribution and deterrence, most of them suffer from features that stand in the way of borrowing them as paradigms of reasonable limitations suited for application to this case. While a slim majority of the States with a ratio have adopted 3:1, others see fit to apply a lower one, see, e.g., Colo. Rev. Stat. Ann. § 13–21–102(1)(a) (2007) (1:1); Ohio Rev. Code Ann. § 2315.21(D)(2)(a) (2:1), and a few have gone higher, see, e.g., Mo. Ann. Stat. § 510.265(1) (5:1). Judgments may differ about the weight to be given to the slight majority of 3:1 States, but one feature of the 3:1 schemes dissuades us from selecting it here. With a few statutory exceptions, generally for intentional infliction of physical injury or other harm, see, e.g, Ala. Code § 6–11–21(j); Ark. Code Ann. § 16–55–208(b), the States with 3:1 ratios apply them across the board (as do other States using different fixed multipliers). That is, the upper limit is not directed to cases like this one, where the tortious action was worse than negligent but less than malicious, exposing the tortfeasor to certain regulatory sanctions and inevitable damage actions; the 3:1 ratio in these States also applies to awards in quite different cases involving some of the most egregious conduct, including malicious behavior and dangerous activity carried on for the purpose of increasing a tortfeasors financial gain. We confront, instead, a case of reckless action, profitless to the tortfeasor, resulting in substantial recovery for substantial injury. Thus, a legislative judgment that 3:1 is a reasonable limit overall is not a judgment that 3:1 is a reasonable limit in this particular type of case.

For somewhat different reasons, the pertinence of the 2:1 ratio adopted by treble-damages statutes (offering compensatory damages plus a bounty of double that amount) is open to question. Federal treble-damages statutes govern areas far afield from maritime concerns (not to mention each other); the relevance of the governing rules in patent or trademark cases, say, is doubtful at best. And in some instances, we know that the considerations that went into making a rule have no application here. We know, for example, that Congress devised the treble damages remedy for private antitrust actions with an eye to supplementing official enforcement by inducing private litigation, which might otherwise have been too rare if nothing but compensatory damages were available at the end of the day. That concern has no traction here, in this case of staggering damage inevitably provoking governmental enforcers to indict and any number of private parties to sue. To take another example, although 18 U.S.C. § 3571(d) provides for a criminal penalty of up to twice a crime victim's loss, this penalty is an alternative to other specific fine amounts which courts may impose at their option, see §§ 3571(a)–(c), a fact that makes us wary of reading too much into Congress's choice of ratio in one provision. State environmental treble-damages schemes offer little more support: for one thing, insofar as some appear to punish even negligence, while others target only willful conduct, some undershoot and others may overshoot the target here. For another, while some States have chosen treble damages, others punish environmental harms at other multiples. See, e.g., N.H. Rev. Stat. Ann. § 146–A:10 (damages of one-and-a-half times the harm caused to private property by oil discharge); Minn. Stat. Ann. § 115A.99 (2005) (civil penalty of 2 to 5 times the costs of removing unlawful solid waste). All in all, the legislative signposts do not point the way clearly to 2:1 as a sound indication of a reasonable limit.

3

There is better evidence of an accepted limit of reasonable civil penalty, however, in several studies mentioned before, showing the median ratio of punitive to compensatory verdicts, reflecting what juries and judges have considered reasonable across many hundreds of punitive awards. We think it is fair to assume that the greater share of the verdicts studied in these comprehensive collections reflect reasonable judgments about the economic penalties appropriate in their particular cases.

These studies cover cases of the most as well as the least blameworthy conduct triggering punitive liability, from malice and avarice, down to recklessness, and even gross negligence in some jurisdictions. The data put the median ratio for the entire gamut of circumstances at less than 1:1, meaning that the compensatory award exceeds the punitive award in most cases. In a well-functioning system, we would expect that awards at the median or lower would roughly express jurors' sense of reasonable penalties in cases with no earmarks of exceptional blameworthiness within the punishable spectrum (cases like this one, without intentional or malicious conduct, and without behavior driven primarily by desire for gain, for example) and cases (again like this one) without the modest economic harm or odds of detection that have opened the door to higher awards. It also seems fair to suppose that most of the unpredictable outlier cases that call the fairness of the system into question are above the median; in theory a factfinder's deliberation could go awry to produce a very low ratio, but we have no basis to assume that such a case would be more than a sport, and the cases with serious constitutional issues coming to us have naturally been on the high side, see, e.g., *State Farm* (ratio of 145:1); *Gore* (ratio of 500:1). On these assumptions, a median ratio of punitive to compensatory damages of about 0.65:1 probably marks the line near which cases like this one largely should be grouped. Accordingly, given the need to protect against the possibility (and the disruptive cost to the legal system) of awards that are unpredictable and unnecessary, either for deterrence or for measured retribution, we consider that a 1:1 ratio, which is above the median award, is a fair upper limit in such maritime cases.

The provision of the CWA respecting daily fines confirms our judgment that anything greater would be excessive here and in cases of this type. Congress set criminal penalties of up to $25,000 per day for negligent violations of pollution restrictions, and up to $50,000 per day for knowing ones. 33 U.S.C. §§ 1319(c)(1), (2). Discretion to double the penalty for knowing action compares to discretion to double the civil liability on conduct going beyond negligence and meriting punitive treatment. And our explanation of the constitutional upper limit confirms that the 1:1 ratio is not too low. In *State Farm*, we said that a single-digit maximum is appropriate in all but the most exceptional of cases, and "[w]hen compensatory damages are substantial, then a lesser ratio, perhaps only equal to compensatory damages, can reach the outermost limit of the due process guarantee."

V

Applying this standard to the present case, we take for granted the District Court's calculation of the total relevant compensatory damages at $507.5 million. A punitive-to-compensatory ratio of 1:1 thus yields maximum punitive damages in that amount.

JUSTICE ALITO took no part in the consideration or decision of this case.

JUSTICE SCALIA, with whom JUSTICE THOMAS joins, concurring.

I join the opinion of the Court, including the portions that refer to constitutional limits that prior opinions have imposed upon punitive damages. While I agree with the argumentation based upon those prior holdings, I continue to believe the holdings were in error. See State Farm Mut. Automobile Ins. Co. v. Campbell, 538 U.S. 408, 429, 123 S.Ct. 1513, 155 L.Ed.2d 585 (2003) (Scalia, J., dissenting).

JUSTICE STEVENS, concurring in part and dissenting in part.

While I join Parts I, II, and III of the Court's opinion, I believe that Congress, rather than this Court, should make the empirical judgments expressed in Part IV. While maritime law " 'is judge-made law to a great extent,' " it is also statutory law to a great extent; indeed, "[m]aritime tort law is now dominated by federal statute." Miles v. Apex Marine Corp., 498 U.S. 19, 36 (1990). For that reason, when we are faced with a choice between performing the traditional task of appellate judges reviewing the acceptability of an award of punitive damages, on the one hand, and embarking on a new lawmaking venture, on the other, we "should carefully consider whether [we], or a legislative body, are better equipped to perform the task at hand."

Evidence that Congress has affirmatively chosen *not* to restrict the availability of a particular remedy favors adherence to a policy of judicial restraint in the absence of some special justification. The Court not only fails to offer any such justification, but also ignores the particular features of maritime law that may counsel against imposing the sort of limitation the Court announces today. Applying the traditional abuse-of-discretion standard that is well grounded in the common law, I would affirm the judgment of the Court of Appeals * * *

II

* * * [B]oth caps and ratios of the sort the Court relies upon in its discussion are typically imposed by legislatures, not courts. Although the Court offers a great deal of evidence that States have acted in various ways to limit punitive damages, it is telling that the Court fails to identify a single state *court* that has imposed a precise ratio, as the Court does today, under its common-law authority. State legislatures have done so, of course; and indeed Congress would encounter no obstacle to doing the same as a matter of federal law. But Congress is far better situated than is this Court to assess the empirical data, and to balance competing policy interests, before making such a choice.

The Court concedes that although "American punitive damages have been the target of audible criticism in recent decades," "most recent studies tend to undercut much of [that criticism]." It further acknowledges that "[a] survey of the literature reveals that discretion to award punitive damages has not mass-produced runaway awards." The Court concludes that the real problem is large *outlier* awards, and the data seem to bear this out. But the Court never explains why abuse-of-discretion review is not the precise antidote to the unfairness inherent in such excessive awards. * * *

On an abuse-of-discretion standard, I am persuaded that a reviewing court should not invalidate this award. In light of Exxon's decision to permit a lapsed alcoholic to command a supertanker carrying tens of millions of gallons of crude oil through the treacherous waters of Prince William Sound, thereby endangering all of the individuals who depended upon the sound for their livelihoods, the jury could reasonably have given expression to its "moral condemnation" of Exxon's conduct in the form of this award.

JUSTICE GINSBURG, concurring in part and dissenting in part.

* * *

While recognizing that the question is close, I share Justice Stevens' view that Congress is the better equipped decisionmaker.

First, I question whether there is an urgent need in maritime law to break away from the "traditional common-law approach" under which punitive damages are determined by a properly instructed jury, followed by trial-court, and then appellate-court review, "to ensure that [the award] is reasonable." Pacific Mut. Life Ins. Co. v. Haslip, 499 U.S. 1, 15 (1991). The Court acknowledges that the traditional approach "has not mass-produced runaway awards," or endangered settlement negotiations. Nor has the Court asserted that outlier awards, insufficiently checked by abuse-of-discretion review, occur more often or are more problematic in maritime cases than in other areas governed by federal law.

Second, assuming a problem in need of solution, the Court's lawmaking prompts many questions. The 1:1 ratio is good for this case, the Court believes, because Exxon's conduct ranked on the low end of the blameworthiness scale: Exxon was not seeking "to augment profit," nor did it act "with a purpose to injure." What ratio will the Court set for defendants who acted maliciously or in pursuit of financial gain? Should the magnitude of the risk increase the ratio and, if so, by how much? Horrendous as the spill from the *Valdez* was, millions of gallons more might have spilled as a result of Captain Hazelwood's attempt to rock the boat off the reef; cf. TXO Production Corp. v. Alliance Resources Corp., 509 U.S. 443, 460–462 (1993) (plurality opinion) (using potential loss to plaintiff as a guide in determining whether jury verdict was excessive). In the end, is the Court holding only that 1:1 is the maritime-law ceiling, or is it also signaling that any ratio higher than 1:1 will be held to exceed "the constitutional outer limit"? On next opportunity, will the Court rule, definitively, that 1:1 is the ceiling due process requires in all of the States, and for all federal claims?

* * *

JUSTICE BREYER, concurring in part and dissenting in part.

* * *

Like the Court, I believe there is a need, grounded in the rule of law itself, to assure that punitive damages are awarded according to meaningful standards that will provide notice of how harshly certain acts will be punished and that will help to assure the uniform treatment of similarly situated persons. Legal standards, however, can secure these objectives without the rigidity that an absolute fixed numerical ratio demands. In setting forth constitutional due process limits on the size of punitive damages awards, for example, we said that *"few* awards exceeding a single-digit ratio between punitive and compensatory damages, to a significant degree, will satisfy due process." State Farm Mut. Automobile Ins. Co. v. Campbell, 538 U.S. 408, 425 (2003) (emphasis added). We thus foresaw exceptions to the numerical constraint.

In my view, a limited exception to the Court's 1:1 ratio is warranted here. As the facts set forth in Part I of the Court's opinion make clear, this was no mine-run case of reckless behavior. The jury could reasonably have believed that Exxon knowingly allowed a relapsed alcoholic repeatedly to pilot a vessel filled with millions of gallons of oil through waters that provided the livelihood for the many plaintiffs in this case. Given that conduct, it was only a matter of time before a crash and spill like this occurred. And as Justice Ginsburg points out, the damage easily could have been much worse.

* * *

NOTES

1. The punitive award—even as reduced by the Supreme Court to $507.7 million—is still about the third largest award ever upheld. See Hilao v. Estate of Marcos, 103 F.3d 767 (9th Cir.1996) ($1.2 billion against estate of Ferdinand Marcos for human rights violations in the Philippines); Motorola Credit Corp. v. Uzan, 509 F.3d 74 (2d Cir.2007) ($1 billion against Turkish corporations and one of the world's richest families for fraudulent financial scheme); Time Warner Entertainment v. Six Flags Over Georgia, 254 Ga.App. 598, 563 S.E.2d 178 (2002), cert. denied, 538 U.S. 977, 123 S.Ct. 1783, 155 L.Ed.2d 665 (2003) ($257 million for dishonest business conduct for parent company's preference of own financial interest as against limited partnership). The Alaska jury originally awarded $5 billion in punitive damages against Exxon, which was halved to $2.5 billion by the Ninth Circuit.

2. The Supreme Court holds that the 3:1 is generally an appropriate ratio for punitive damages, but that the 1:1 ratio between compensatory and punitive damages is appropriate for "this particular type of case." What type of case is that? Does Justice Ginsburg agree?

3. The Supreme Court was evenly divided on whether the Exxon Corporation could be held vicariously liable for the actions of its managerial employee, the alcoholic captain. (Only 8 Justices considered the case as Justice Alito recused himself because of his ownership of Exxon stock.) This left standing a lower court decision affirming the jury instruction that permitted the jury to assign vicarious liability based on the involvement of an employee acting in a managerial capacity. In re Exxon Valdez, 270 F.3d 1215, 1233–36 (9th Cir. 2001) (*Valdez I*). Given what we know about vicarious liability from *Grimshaw* and the *Restatement*, should Exxon be liable here? In Kolstad v. American Dental Association, 527 U.S. 526, 545–46, 119 S.Ct. 2118, 144 L.Ed.2d 494 (1999), the Supreme Court rejected the managerial scope of employment rule for imposing liability for punitive damages upon an employer for a discriminatory employment decision by a manager that was contrary to the employer's policies and good faith efforts to comply with Title VII's prohibition of workplace sex discrimination.

4. In assigning derivative liability, the Ninth Circuit in *Exxon Shipping* distinguished cases denying punitive damages in maritime cases involving "maintenance and cure," worker's compensation type payments for food and living expenses for injured sailors. The U.S. Supreme Court has taken up the question of whether punitive damages are permitted under maritime common law where the relevant federal maritime statutes limit recovery to the sailor's direct loss. The Eleventh Circuit allowed recovery for punitives when a shipowner willfully failed to pay maintenance and cure to an injured sailor. Atlantic Sounding Co. v. Townsend, 496 F.3d 1282 (11th Cir.2007), cert. granted, 555 U.S. ___, 129 S.Ct. 490, 172 L.Ed.2d 355 (2008). Justice Stevens, in an omitted part of his dissent in *Exxon Shipping*, suggested that there might be something special about maritime law that made punitive damages particularly appropriate in these kinds of cases. He noted the lack of available recovery under maritime law for many non-pecuniary injuries that are stan-

dard recoveries in other tort law that could be awarded as punitive damages to compensate the plaintiff's intangible injuries.

5. After the Supreme Court's decision, the parties finally settled the 19-year old case for $383.4 million. Exxon Mobil Agrees to Partial Settlement: $383 Million in Punitives for Valdez Spill, Legal News, BNA (Sept. 16, 2008). This reduced amount subtracted payments previously made to corporate plaintiffs who settled early in the case in exchange for not executing on compensatory damages and ceding back to Exxon any punitive damages they might later be awarded. Each remaining plaintiff will receive approximately $11,000 in punitive damages, adding to the $15,000 awarded for compensatory damages. At the same time, Exxon reported its greatest corporate profits ever. Jad Mouawad, Exxon's Profit Jumped to a Record in a Quarter, N.Y. Times B3, Oct. 31, 2008 (setting record for most profitable American corporation).

Notes on Tort Reform

As the Court notes in *Exxon Shipping*, many states have legislatively limited punitive damages. There has been an active public debate over the last decade as to whether there has been a substantial growth of punitive damage awards and whether the large size and uneven imposition of punitive awards support the "reform" of punitive damages. A large amount of empirical material, including studies of the size and frequency of punitive awards, an examination of the effect of punitive awards on settlement behavior, and an examination of the relation of punitive awards to business decisions and economic outcomes is found in Special Issue: The Future of Punitive Damages, 1998 Wis.L.Rev. 1. For some of the recent empirical work, see Theodore Eisenberg, et al., Juries, Judges and Punitive Damages: Empirical Analysis Using the Civil Justice Survey of State Courts, 1992, 1996, and 2001, 3 J.Emp.Leg.Stud. 263 (2006) (concluding that the level of punitive damages has not increased over time, the awards of punitives are infrequent and awarded in only 2.4% of cases tried, and that 24% of awards were under $10,000 and 60% under $100,000); Martin T. Wells & Theodore Eisenberg, The Significant Association Between Punitive and Compensatory Damages in Blockbuster Cases: A Methodological Primer, 3 J.Emp.Leg.Stud. 169 (2006) (showing a strong, statistically significant relation between punitive and compensatory awards contrary to conventional assertions).

With some statutory exceptions, no punitive damages are allowed in Nebraska, New Hampshire, and Washington. Kansas limits punitive damage awards in professional liability actions to 25% of the annual gross income of the defendant or $3 million; any award is divided equally between the plaintiff and a state fund. Missouri, Mo.Rev.Stat. § 537.675(2), Oregon, Or.Rev.Stat. § 18.540(1), and Utah, Utah Code Ann. § 78–18–1(3), also have statutes requiring payment of a portion of a punitive damage award to the state. Some of these legislative efforts to address windfalls to successful plaintiffs have had a mixed reception in the courts. In Kirk v. Denver Publishing Co., 818 P.2d 262 (Colo.1991), the Colorado Supreme Court held that a state statute that directed one-third of the exemplary damages collected by a plaintiff be paid to the state general fund was an unconstitutional taking of the plaintiff's property, i.e., his judgment against the defendant. But in Hoskins v. Business

Men's Assurance, 79 S.W.3d 901 (Mo.2002), the Missouri Supreme Court upheld a statute allowing the state to assert a 50% lien on any final judgment for punitive damages. It rejected claims that this was an excessive fine prohibited under the Excessive Fines Clause of the Eighth Amendment, or the Takings Clause or the Due Process Clause because the state's award was entirely derivative of a final judgment.

There are other ways to avoid windfall to one plaintiff. Illinois gives the trial court discretion to apportion a punitive damage award between the plaintiff, her attorney, and the Illinois Department of Rehabilitation Services. Ill.Rev.Stat. Ch. 100 par. 2–1207 (1986). The Ohio Supreme Court ordered sua sponte the diversion of the bulk of a $30 million punitive damage award (less $10 million awarded to the plaintiff and the contractual attorney's fees) to a cancer research fund, to be named after the decedent and to be established at a cancer hospital at the Ohio State University. Dardinger v. Anthem Blue Cross & Blue Shield, 98 Ohio St.3d 77, 781 N.E.2d 121 (2002). Lawyers and courts are thus recasting punitive damages as "curative damages" used to cure a problem by directing funds to charitable organizations. Molly McDonough, Handing Down Help: In Ohio, "Curative Damages" Are Embraced by Tort Plaintiffs and the Supreme Court, 91 ABA J.24 (Oct. 2005). Another way for the legislature to address this issue would be to tax the awards at a high rate. See James Serven, The Taxation of Punitive Damages: Horton Lays an Egg?, 72 Den.U.L.Rev. 215 (1995) (discussing federal taxation of punitive damage awards).

A number of states have adopted procedural mechanisms in an effort to attain more clearly defensible results in punitive damage cases. In an asbestos case with the possibility of multiple punitive damage awards against the defendant, the Florida Supreme Court bifurcated the issue of the amount of punitive damages from the trial of other issues. Thus, the defendant can put previous punitive damage awards before the jury and build a record for a due process argument on the cumulative effect of the awards with a reduced risk. W.R. Grace & Co. v. Waters, 638 So.2d 502 (Fla.1994). Several states have adopted statutes requiring a stricter standard of proof for punitive damages and at least eight states have adopted a requirement that trial courts explain their refusal to disturb a jury award of punitive damages. See Transportation Insurance Co. v. Moriel, 879 S.W.2d 10 (Tex.1994). See also Developments—The Paths of Civil Litigation: Problems and Proposals in Punitive Damages Reform, 113 Harv.L.Rev. 1783 (2000). And other states place a cap on the defendant's bond posted during the appeal of a punitive damages award. Doug Rendleman, A Cap on the Defendant's Appeal Bond? Punitive Damages Tort Reform, 39 Akron L.Rev. 1089 (2006).

The most common legislative reform of punitive damages has been to limit the total measure of recovery, often at three times the compensatory damages awarded. These damages caps, seen also in statutory limitations on non-economic compensatory damages, have been challenged under numerous grounds arguing that they essentially deny plaintiffs their right to fair procedural and substantive result for their injuries.

ARBINO v. JOHNSON & JOHNSON
Supreme Court of Ohio, 2007
116 Ohio St.3d 468, 880 N.E.2d 420

MOYER, CHIEF JUSTICE.

I

INTRODUCTION

Petitioner Melisa Arbino initiated a products-liability action against respondents Johnson & Johnson, Ortho–McNeil Pharmaceutical, Inc., and Johnson & Johnson Pharmaceutical Research & Development, L.L.C. in 2006. She alleges that she suffered blood clots and other serious medical side effects from using the Ortho Evra Birth Control Patch, a hormonal birth-control medication that Johnson & Johnson created. * * *

II

TORT REFORM IN OHIO AND STARE DECISIS

Before engaging in a specific analysis of these issues, it is necessary to briefly review the major tort-reform laws enacted by the General Assembly in recent history. Doing so provides the proper context for our decision and frames the necessary discussion of stare decisis.

Since 1975, the General Assembly has adopted several so-called tort-reform acts, which were inevitably reviewed by this court. In the course of this review, we have examined several specific provisions that are similar in language and purpose to those at issue here; all of these similar statutes have been declared unconstitutional. The first reform provision we reviewed was former R.C. 2307.43, which was passed in the Ohio Medical Malpractice Act of 1975. This statute placed a $200,000 cap on general medical-malpractice damages not involving death, with no exceptions for those suffering severe injuries. See Morris v. Savoy (1991), 576 N.E.2d 765. The General Assembly passed this legislation to combat a perceived malpractice-insurance crisis. Although it took several years for a challenge to be raised, we ultimately held that R.C. 2307.43 violated the due-process protections of the Ohio Constitution. We specifically noted that " '[i]t is irrational and arbitrary to impose the cost of the intended benefit to the general public solely upon a class consisting of those most severely injured by medical malpractice.' "

The General Assembly's next major enactment was the Tort Reform Act of 1987, which sought to change civil-justice and insurance law to alleviate another "insurance crisis." See Sorrell v. Thevenir (1994), 633 N.E.2d 504. In *Sorrell*, we examined one facet of this law, R.C. 2317.45, which placed a significant limitation on the collateral-source rule adopted in Pryor v. Webber (1970), 263 N.E.2d 235. The H.B. 1 version of R.C. 2317.45 required the trial court to subtract certain collateral benefits from a plaintiff's final award of compensatory damages. We held that this mandatory deduction of collateral benefits violated the right to a jury trial, due process, equal protection, and the right to a remedy. * * *

We returned to our review of H.B. 1 in Zoppo v. Homestead Ins. Co. (1994), 644 N.E.2d 397, in which we examined former R.C. 2315.21(C)(2). That statute required a trial judge to determine the amount of punitive damages to be awarded in a tort action, even when the trier of fact was a jury. We struck this section as a violation of the right to a jury trial in the Ohio Constitution.

Finally, the General Assembly passed substantial reforms in 1997 with Am.Sub.H.B. No. 350. * * * Among other things, it modified the collateral-source rule in tort actions to require the trier of fact to consider but not automatically set off collateral benefits, capped punitive damages and allowed the trier of fact to determine damages up to the cap in tort and products-liability claims, and capped noneconomic damages at different levels, with higher limits for permanent injuries. Although we examined and discussed several subsections of the law in our review, we ultimately found H.B. 350 to be unconstitutional in toto as a violation of the separation of powers and the single-subject clause of the Ohio Constitution. State ex rel. Ohio Academy of Trial Lawyers v. Sheward (1999), 715 N.E.2d 1062.

Arbino argues that the portions of S.B. 80 at issue here are functionally identical to the statutes this court held to be unconstitutional in those cases. She alleges that the principle of stare decisis therefore requires us to declare the statutes here unconstitutional as well. We disagree.

The protracted interbranch tension on this subject establishes at least two key points. First, tort reform has been a major issue of concern in this state over the past several decades and remains one today. Ohio is hardly unique in this regard, as such reforms have been raised in nearly every state in the nation. State legislatures and judiciaries have differed widely in their responses to this issue, and a definite split in authority is clear. The federal judiciary has been drawn to the issue as well, with the United States Supreme Court offering guidance on several key issues over the past few years, most notably regarding punitive-damages awards.

A fundamental principle of the constitutional separation of powers among the three branches of government is that the legislative branch is "the ultimate arbiter of public policy." It necessarily follows that the legislature has the power to continually create and refine the laws to meet the needs of the citizens of Ohio. The fact that the General Assembly has repeatedly sought to reform some aspects of the civil tort system for over 30 years demonstrates the continuing prominence of this issue.

Second, even considering the numerous opinions by this court on this issue, the basic constitutionality of tort-reform statutes is hardly settled law. Our prior review has focused on certain unconstitutional facets of the prior tort-reform laws that can be addressed to create constitutionally valid legislation. We have not dismissed all tort reform as an unconstitutional concept. * * *

A careful review of the statutes at issue here reveals that they are more than a rehashing of unconstitutional statutes. In its continued pursuit of reform, the General Assembly has made progress in tailoring its legislation to address the constitutional defects identified by the various majorities of this court.

* * *

C
Punitive–Damages Limits in R.C. 2315.21
* * *

The statute limits punitive damages in tort actions to a maximum of two times the total amount of compensatory damages awarded to a plaintiff per defendant. However, these limitations do not apply if the defendant committed a felony in causing the injury, one of the elements of the felony is that it was committed purposely or knowingly, and the defendant was convicted of or pleaded guilty to the felony. If the limitations do apply, punitive damages may be limited further if the defendant is a "small employer"[6] or an individual. In that case, the punitive damages may not exceed "the lesser of two times the amount of the compensatory damages awarded to the plaintiff from the defendant or ten percent of the employer's or individual's net worth when the tort was committed, up to a maximum of three hundred fifty thousand dollars."

Additionally, punitive damages may not be awarded more than once against the same defendant for the same act or course of conduct once the maximum amount of damages has been reached. However, this restriction can be overcome if the plaintiff offers new and substantial evidence of previously undiscovered behaviors for which punitive damages are appropriate or the prior awards against the defendant were "totally insufficient" to punish the defendant.

Arbino presents the same constitutional challenges to this statute that she raised against R.C. 2315.18. [limits on non-pecuniary damages].

* * *

2. Right to a Remedy and Right to an Open Court

Arbino also argues that R.C. 2315.21 violates the right to a remedy in an open court. This right protects against laws that completely foreclose a cause of action for injured plaintiffs or otherwise eliminate the ability to receive a meaningful remedy. Like the noneconomic-damages limits in R.C. 2315.18, the punitive-damages limits in R.C. 2315.21 do not deny plaintiffs the right to seek a remedy for their tort claims. Further, they do not eliminate the ability to seek a "meaningful" remedy for their injuries, primarily because punitive damages "are not compensation for injury. Instead, they are private fines levied by civil juries to punish reprehensible conduct and to deter its future occurrence." Gertz v. Robert Welch, Inc.

---

6. "Small employer" is defined as an entity with not more than 100 full-time permanent employees or, if the company qualifies as a manufacturer, with not more than 500 full-time permanent employees. R.C. 2315.21(A)(5).

(1974), 418 U.S. 323, 350, 94 S.Ct. 2997, 41 L.Ed.2d 789. "The purpose of punitive damages is not to compensate a plaintiff, but to punish and deter certain conduct." Because punitive damages are separate and apart from any remedy for a plaintiff's injuries, and because R.C. 2315.21 does not prevent potential plaintiffs from bringing a successful cause of action for their injuries, it does not violate Section 16, Article I of the Ohio Constitution.

3. *Due Course of Law/Due Process*

Arbino also alleges that R.C. 2315.21 violates the "due course of law" provision in Section 16, Article I of the Ohio Constitution.* * *

a. *Real and substantial relation to the general welfare of the public*

R.C. 2315.21 does not offend due process under this test. The General Assembly cited several studies and other forms of evidence upon which it relied in concluding that the civil justice system as it then existed was harming the state's economy. It then reviewed punitive damages in view of this evidence and concluded that such awards were part of the problem. Section 3(A)(4)(a) and (b). The General Assembly noted that while punitive damages serve the purpose of punishing tortfeasors for certain wrongful actions and omissions, the "absence of a statutory ceiling upon recoverable punitive or exemplary damages in tort actions has resulted in occasional multiple awards * * * that have no rational connection to the wrongful actions or omissions of the tortfeasor." The uncodified section further explained the basis for limitations on awards against small employers and stated that the ratio used for the limitation derived from recent United States Supreme Court precedent.

[W]e accept that the evidence cited sufficiently demonstrated the need to reform the civil litigation system in the state. Using this evidence, the General Assembly found that the uncertainty and subjectivity associated with the civil justice system were harming the state' economy. The reforms codified in R.C. 2315.21 were an attempt to limit the subjective process of punitive-damages calculation, something the General Assembly believed was contributing to the uncertainty. Arbino assails these findings, arguing that the General Assembly relied on "generalizations about the dilemma of punitive damages, without citation to any specific testimony or evidence supporting its claims." While we agree with Arbino that the legislative record is thin in this regard, it nonetheless offers justifications sufficient to meet the requirement of a "real and substantial relation" to the general welfare of the public. The general goal of making the civil justice system more predictable is logically served by placing limits that ensure that punitive damages generally cannot exceed a certain dollar figure. Based on its review of the economic evidence, the General Assembly believes that such predictability will aid the state economy. That reasoning is sufficient under the first prong of the analysis.

b. *Neither arbitrary nor unreasonable*

Under the second prong, we find that the statute is neither arbitrary nor unreasonable. Setting the limitation at double the amount of compensatory damages received by the plaintiff ensures that the defendant may still be punished. Further, the exceptions for small employers and individuals strike a balance between imposing punishment and ensuring that lives and businesses are not destroyed in the process. This careful compromise represents a level of thought and attention to detail not seen in arbitrary or unreasonable statutes. For the foregoing reasons, R.C. 2315.21 does not offend the due-process protections in Section 16, Article I of the Ohio Constitution.

* * *

IV

Conclusion

The decision in this case affirms the General Assembly's efforts over the last several decades to enact meaningful tort reforms. It also places Ohio firmly with the growing number of states that have found such reforms to be constitutional.[8] However, the issue remains a contentious one across the nation, with several states finding such statutes unconstitutional.[9]

We appreciate the policy concerns Arbino and her amici have raised. However, the General Assembly is responsible for weighing those concerns and making policy decisions; we are charged with evaluating the constitutionality of their choices. Issues such as the wisdom of damages limitations and whether the specific dollar amounts available under them best serve the public interest are not for us to decide. Using a highly deferential standard of review appropriate to a facial challenge to these statutes, we conclude that the General Assembly has responded to our previous decisions and has created constitutionally permissible limitations.

C. CONSTITUTIONAL LIMITATIONS ON PUNITIVE DAMAGES

The U.S. Supreme Court has joined in the refrain about the excessiveness of some punitive damage awards. In a series of relatively recent cases, the Court has crafted a judicial inquiry to assess when punitive

---

8. As of the date of this opinion, courts have upheld limits on noneconomic damages in at least 19 other jurisdictions [citations omitted]. At least ten states have upheld limitations on punitive damages, including provisions requiring that a certain percentage of awards be allotted to a designated public fund.

9. Among those finding such attempts at reform unconstitutional are Illinois (Best v. Taylor Machine Works (1997), 689 N.E.2d 1057 (striking down caps on noneconomic damages)); New Hampshire (Brannigan v. Usitalo (1991), 587 A.2d 1232 (same)); North Dakota (Arneson v. Olson (N.D.1978), 270 N.W.2d 125 (striking down cap on all damages)); South Dakota (Knowles v. United States, 1996 SD 10, 544 N.W.2d 183 (same)); and Wisconsin (Ferdon v. Wisconsin Patients Comp. Fund, 2005 WI 125, 284 Wis.2d 573, 701 N.W.2d 440 (striking down cap on noneconomic damages)).

damages are so grossly excessive as to violate the Constitution's due process guarantee against arbitrary state action. Many have criticized the Court's venture into punitive damages review, arguing that constitutional analysis does not extend to this type of judicial tort reform. A. Benjamin Spencer, Due Process and Punitive Damages: The Error of Federal Excessiveness Jurisprudence, 79 S.Cal.L.Rev. 1085 (2006) (arguing that the excessiveness review is defective because it conflicts with important rules of constitutional construction and goes beyond the procedural protections demanded by due process); Benjamin C. Zipursky, A Theory of Punitive Damages, 84 Tex.L.Rev. 105 (2005) (contending that the Court's heightened constitutional scrutiny of punitive damages is inappropriate where a private plaintiff is exercising her right to be punitive rather than where the state is imposing punishment); Kevin S. Marshall & Patrick Fitzgerald, Punitive Damages and the Supreme Court's Reasonable Relationship Test: Ignoring the Economics of Deterrence, 19 St. John's J. Legal Comment. 237 (2005) (arguing that Supreme Court rulings that limit punitive damages to an award "reasonably related" to actual damages eliminates the economic foundations of deterrence); but see Mark Geistfeld, Constitutional Tort Reform, 38 Loy.L.A.L.Rev. 1093 (2005) (endorsing the Court's expanded substantive due process review to limit tort damages).

STATE FARM MUTUAL AUTOMOBILE INSURANCE CO. v. CAMPBELL

Supreme Court of the United States, 2003
538 U.S. 408, 123 S.Ct. 1513, 155 L.Ed.2d 585

JUSTICE KENNEDY delivered the opinion of the Court.

We address once again the measure of punishment, by means of punitive damages, a State may impose upon a defendant in a civil case. The question is whether, in the circumstances we shall recount, an award of $145 million in punitive damages, where full compensatory damages are $1 million, is excessive and in violation of the Due Process Clause of the Fourteenth Amendment to the Constitution of the United States.

I

In 1981, Curtis Campbell (Campbell) was driving with his wife, Inez Preece Campbell, in Cache County, Utah. He decided to pass six vans traveling ahead of them on a two-lane highway. Todd Ospital was driving a small car approaching from the opposite direction. To avoid a head-on collision with Campbell, who by then was driving on the wrong side of the highway and toward oncoming traffic, Ospital swerved onto the shoulder, lost control of his automobile, and collided with a vehicle driven by Robert G. Slusher. Ospital was killed, and Slusher was rendered permanently disabled. The Campbells escaped unscathed.

In the ensuing wrongful death and tort action, Campbell insisted he was not at fault. Early investigations did support differing conclusions as to who caused the accident, but "a consensus was reached early on by the investigators and witnesses that Mr. Campbell's unsafe pass had indeed caused the crash." Campbell's insurance company, petitioner State Farm Mutual Automobile Insurance Company, nonetheless decided to contest liability and declined offers by Slusher and Ospital's estate to settle the claims for the policy limit of $50,000 ($25,000 per claimant). State Farm also ignored the advice of one of its own investigators and took the case to trial, assuring the Campbells that "their assets were safe, that they had no liability for the accident, that State Farm would represent their interests, and that they did not need to procure separate counsel." To the contrary, a jury determined that Campbell was 100 percent at fault, and a judgment was returned for $185,849, far more than the amount offered in settlement.

At first State Farm refused to cover the $135,849 in excess liability. Its counsel made this clear to the Campbells: " 'You may want to put for sale signs on your property to get things moving.' " Nor was State Farm willing to post a supersedeas bond to allow Campbell to appeal the judgment against him. Campbell obtained his own counsel to appeal the verdict. During the pendency of the appeal, in late 1984, Slusher, Ospital, and the Campbells reached an agreement whereby Slusher and Ospital agreed not to seek satisfaction of their claims against the Campbells. In exchange the Campbells agreed to pursue a bad faith action against State Farm and to be represented by Slusher's and Ospital's attorneys. The Campbells also agreed that Slusher and Ospital would have a right to play a part in all major decisions concerning the bad faith action. No settlement could be concluded without Slusher's and Ospital's approval, and Slusher and Ospital would receive 90 percent of any verdict against State Farm.

In 1989, the Utah Supreme Court denied Campbell's appeal in the wrongful death and tort actions. State Farm then paid the entire judgment, including the amounts in excess of the policy limits. The Campbells nonetheless filed a complaint against State Farm alleging bad faith, fraud, and intentional infliction of emotional distress. * * * At State Farm's request the trial court bifurcated the trial into two phases conducted before different juries. In the first phase the jury determined that State Farm's decision not to settle was unreasonable because there was a substantial likelihood of an excess verdict.

Before the second phase of the action against State Farm we decided BMW of North America, Inc. v. Gore, 517 U.S. 559, 116 S.Ct. 1589, 134 L.Ed.2d 809 (1996), and refused to sustain a $2 million punitive damages award which accompanied a verdict of only $4,000 in compensatory damages. Based on that decision, State Farm * * * moved for the exclusion of evidence of dissimilar out-of-state conduct. The trial court denied State Farm's motion.

The second phase addressed State Farm's liability for fraud and intentional infliction of emotional distress, as well as compensatory and punitive damages. The Utah Supreme Court aptly characterized this phase of the trial:

> "State Farm argued during phase II that its decision to take the case to trial was an 'honest mistake' that did not warrant punitive damages. In contrast, the Campbells introduced evidence that State Farm's decision to take the case to trial was a result of a national scheme to meet corporate fiscal goals by capping payouts on claims company wide. This scheme was referred to as State Farm's 'Performance, Planning and Review,' or PP & R, policy. To prove the existence of this scheme, the trial court allowed the Campbells to introduce extensive expert testimony regarding fraudulent practices by State Farm in its nation-wide operations. Although State Farm moved prior to phase II of the trial for the exclusion of such evidence and continued to object to it at trial, the trial court ruled that such evidence was admissible to determine whether State Farm's conduct in the Campbell case was indeed intentional and sufficiently egregious to warrant punitive damages."

Evidence pertaining to the PP & R policy concerned State Farm's business practices for over 20 years in numerous States. Most of these practices bore no relation to third-party automobile insurance claims, the type of claim underlying the Campbells' complaint against the company. The jury awarded the Campbells $2.6 million in compensatory damages and $145 million in punitive damages, which the trial court reduced to $1 million and $25 million respectively. Both parties appealed.

The Utah Supreme Court sought to apply the three guideposts we identified in *Gore* and it reinstated the $145 million punitive damages award. Relying in large part on the extensive evidence concerning the PP & R policy, the court concluded State Farm's conduct was reprehensible. The court also relied upon State Farm's "massive wealth" and on testimony indicating that "State Farm's actions, because of their clandestine nature, will be punished at most in one out of every 50,000 cases as a matter of statistical probability," and concluded that the ratio between punitive and compensatory damages was not unwarranted. Finally, the court noted that the punitive damages award was not excessive when compared to various civil and criminal penalties State Farm could have faced, including $10,000 for each act of fraud, the suspension of its license to conduct business in Utah, the disgorgement of profits, and imprisonment. We granted certiorari.

II

We recognized in Cooper Industries, Inc. v. Leatherman Tool Group, Inc., 532 U.S. 424, 121 S.Ct. 1678, 149 L.Ed.2d 674 (2001), that in our judicial system compensatory and punitive damages, although usually awarded at the same time by the same decisionmaker, serve different purposes. Compensatory damages "are intended to redress the concrete loss that the plaintiff has suffered by reason of the defendant's wrongful conduct." By contrast, punitive damages serve a broader function; they are aimed at deterrence and retribution.* * *

While States possess discretion over the imposition of punitive damages, it is well established that there are procedural and substantive constitutional limitations on these awards. The Due Process Clause of the Fourteenth Amendment prohibits the imposition of grossly excessive or arbitrary punishments on a tortfeasor. * * * To the extent an award is grossly excessive, it furthers no legitimate purpose and constitutes an arbitrary deprivation of property. * * *

Although these awards serve the same purposes as criminal penalties, defendants subjected to punitive damages in civil cases have not been accorded the protections applicable in a criminal proceeding. This increases our concerns over the imprecise manner in which punitive damages systems are administered. We have admonished that "[p]unitive damages pose an acute danger of arbitrary deprivation of property. Jury instructions typically leave the jury with wide discretion in choosing amounts, and the presentation of evidence of a defendant's net worth creates the potential that juries will use their verdicts to express biases against big businesses, particularly those without strong local presences." * * * Our concerns are heightened when the decisionmaker is presented, as we shall discuss, with evidence that has little bearing as to the amount of punitive damages that should be awarded. Vague instructions, or those that merely inform the jury to avoid "passion or prejudice," do little to aid the decisionmaker in its task of assigning appropriate weight to evidence that is relevant and evidence that is tangential or only inflammatory.

In light of these concerns, in *Gore* we instructed courts reviewing punitive damages to consider three guideposts: (1) the degree of reprehensibility of the defendant's misconduct; (2) the disparity between the actual or potential harm suffered by the plaintiff and the punitive damages award; and (3) the difference between the punitive damages awarded by the jury and the civil penalties authorized or imposed in comparable cases. We reiterated the importance of these three guideposts in *Cooper Industries* and mandated appellate courts to conduct *de novo* review of a trial court's application of them to the jury's award. Exacting appellate review ensures that an award of punitive damages is based upon an " 'application of law, rather than a decisionmaker's caprice.' "

III

Under the principles outlined in *BMW of North America, Inc. v. Gore*, this case is neither close nor difficult. It was error to reinstate the jury's $145 million punitive damages award. We address each guidepost of *Gore* in some detail.

A

"[T]he most important indicium of the reasonableness of a punitive damages award is the degree of reprehensibility of the defendant's conduct." *Gore*. We have instructed courts to determine the reprehensibility of a defendant by considering whether: the harm caused was physical as opposed to economic; the tortious conduct evinced an indifference to or a reckless disregard of the health or safety of others; the target of the conduct had financial vulnerability; the conduct involved repeated actions or was an isolated incident; and the harm was the result of intentional malice, trickery, or deceit, or mere accident. The existence of any one of these factors weighing in favor of a plaintiff may not be sufficient to sustain a punitive damages award; and the absence of all of them renders any award suspect. It should be presumed a plaintiff has been made whole for his injuries by compensatory damages, so punitive damages should only be awarded if the defendant's culpability, after having paid compensatory damages, is so reprehensible as to warrant the imposition of further sanctions to achieve punishment or deterrence.

Applying these factors in the instant case, we must acknowledge that State Farm's handling of the claims against the Campbells merits no praise. The trial court found that State Farm's employees altered the company's records to make Campbell appear less culpable. State Farm disregarded the overwhelming likelihood of liability and the near-certain probability that, by taking the case to trial, a judgment in excess of the policy limits would be awarded. State Farm amplified the harm by at first assuring the Campbells their assets would be safe from any verdict and by later telling them, postjudgment, to put a for-sale sign on their house. While we do not suggest there was error in awarding punitive damages based upon State Farm's conduct toward the Campbells, a more modest punishment for this reprehensible conduct could have satisfied the State's legitimate objectives, and the Utah courts should have gone no further.

This case, instead, was used as a platform to expose, and punish, the perceived deficiencies of State Farm's operations throughout the country. The Utah Supreme Court's opinion makes explicit that State Farm was being condemned for its nationwide policies rather than for the conduct direct toward the Campbells. ("[T]he Campbells introduced evidence that State Farm's decision to take the case to trial was a result of a national scheme to meet corporate fiscal goals by capping payouts on claims company wide"). This was, as well, an explicit rationale of the trial court's decision in approving the award, though reduced from $145 million to $25 million. * * *

A State cannot punish a defendant for conduct that may have been lawful where it occurred. *Gore* * * *. Nor, as a general rule, does a State have a legitimate concern in imposing punitive damages to punish a defendant for unlawful acts committed outside of the State's jurisdiction. Any proper adjudication of conduct that occurred outside Utah to other persons would require their inclusion, and, to those parties, the Utah courts, in the usual case, would need to apply the laws of their relevant jurisdiction. Phillips Petroleum Co. v. Shutts, 472 U.S. 797, 821–822, 105 S.Ct. 2965, 86 L.Ed.2d 628 (1985).

Here, the Campbells do not dispute that much of the out-of-state conduct was lawful where it occurred. They argue, however, that such evidence was not the primary basis for the punitive damages award and was relevant to the extent it demonstrated, in a general sense, State Farm's motive against its insured. * * * This argument misses the mark. Lawful out-of-state conduct may be probative when it demonstrates the deliberateness and culpability of the defendant's action in the State where it is tortious, but that conduct must have a nexus to the specific harm suffered by the plaintiff. A jury must be instructed, furthermore, that it may not use evidence of out-of-state conduct to punish a defendant for action that was lawful in the jurisdiction where it occurred. * * * A basic principle of federalism is that each State may make its own reasoned judgment about what conduct is permitted or proscribed within its borders, and each State alone can determine what measure of punishment, if any, to impose on a defendant who acts within its jurisdiction. * * *

For a more fundamental reason, however, the Utah courts erred in relying upon this and other evidence: The courts awarded punitive damages to punish and deter conduct that bore no relation to the Campbells' harm. A defendant's dissimilar acts, independent from the acts upon which liability was premised, may not serve as the basis for punitive damages. A defendant should be punished for the conduct that harmed the plaintiff, not for being an unsavory individual or business. Due process does not permit courts, in the calculation of punitive damages, to adjudicate the merits of other parties' hypothetical claims against a defendant under the guise of the reprehensibility analysis, but we have no doubt the Utah Supreme Court did that here. ("Even if the harm to the Campbells can be appropriately characterized as minimal, the trial court's assessment of the situation is on target: 'The harm is minor to the individual but massive in the aggregate' "). Punishment on these bases creates the possibility of multiple punitive damages awards for the same conduct; for in the usual case nonparties are not bound by the judgment some other plaintiff obtains. *Gore* (Breyer, J., concurring) ("Larger damages might also 'double count' by including in the punitive damages award some of the compensatory, or punitive, damages that subsequent plaintiffs would also recover").

The same reasons lead us to conclude the Utah Supreme Court's decision cannot be justified on the grounds that State Farm was a recidivist. Although "[o]ur holdings that a recidivist may be punished more severely than a first offender recognize that repeated misconduct is more reprehensible than an individual instance of malfeasance," in the context of civil actions courts must ensure the conduct in question replicates the prior transgressions.

The Campbells have identified scant evidence of repeated misconduct of the sort that injured them. Nor does our review of the Utah courts' decisions convince us that State Farm was only punished for its actions toward the Campbells. Although evidence of other acts need not be identical to have relevance in the calculation of punitive damages, the

Utah court erred here because evidence pertaining to claims that had nothing to do with a third-party lawsuit was introduced at length. Other evidence concerning reprehensibility was even more tangential. For example, the Utah Supreme Court criticized State Farm's investigation into the personal life of one of its employees and, in a broader approach, the manner in which State Farm's policies corrupted its employees. The Campbells attempt to justify the courts' reliance upon this unrelated testimony on the theory that each dollar of profit made by underpaying a third-party claimant is the same as a dollar made by underpaying a first-party one. * * * [T]his argument is unconvincing. The reprehensibility guidepost does not permit courts to expand the scope of the case so that a defendant may be punished for any malfeasance, which in this case extended for a 20–year period. In this case, because the Campbells have shown no conduct by State Farm similar to that which harmed them, the conduct that harmed them is the only conduct relevant to the reprehensibility analysis.

B

Turning to the second *Gore* guidepost, we have been reluctant to identify concrete constitutional limits on the ratio between harm, or potential harm, to the plaintiff and the punitive damages award. ("[W]e have consistently rejected the notion that the constitutional line is marked by a simple mathematical formula, even one that compares actual *and potential* damages to the punitive award"). We decline again to impose a bright-line ratio which a punitive damages award cannot exceed. Our jurisprudence and the principles it has now established demonstrate, however, that, in practice, few awards exceeding a single-digit ratio between punitive and compensatory damages, to a significant degree, will satisfy due process. In [Pacific Mutual Life Insurance Co. v. Haslip, 499 U.S. 1, 111 S.Ct. 1032, 113 L.Ed.2d 1 (1991)] in upholding a punitive damages award, we concluded that an award of more than four times the amount of compensatory damages might be close to the line of constitutional impropriety. We cited that 4–to–1 ratio again in *Gore*. The Court further referenced a long legislative history, dating back over 700 years and going forward to today, providing for sanctions of double, treble, or quadruple damages to deter and punish. While these ratios are not binding, they are instructive. They demonstrate what should be obvious: Single-digit multipliers are more likely to comport with due process, while still achieving the State's goals of deterrence and retribution, than awards with ratios in range of 500 to 1, or, in this case, of 145 to 1.

Nonetheless, because there are no rigid benchmarks that a punitive damages award may not surpass, ratios greater than those we have previously upheld may comport with due process where "a particularly egregious act has resulted in only a small amount of economic damages." See also [*Gore*] (positing that a higher ratio *might* be necessary where "the injury is hard to detect or the monetary value of noneconomic harm might have been difficult to determine"). The converse is also true, however. When compensatory damages are substantial, then a lesser ratio, perhaps only equal to compensatory damages, can reach the outermost limit of the due process guarantee. The precise award in any case, of course, must be based upon the facts and circumstances of the defendant's conduct and the harm to the plaintiff.

In sum, courts must ensure that the measure of punishment is both reasonable and proportionate to the amount of harm to the plaintiff and to the general damages recovered. In the context of this case, we have no doubt that there is a presumption against an award that has a 145–to–1 ratio. The compensatory award in this case was substantial; the Campbells were awarded $1 million for a year and a half of emotional distress. This was complete compensation. The harm arose from a transaction in the economic realm, not from some physical assault or trauma; there were no physical injuries; and State Farm paid the excess verdict before the complaint was filed, so the Campbells suffered only minor economic injuries for the 18–month period in which State Farm refused to resolve the claim against them. The compensatory damages for the injury suffered here, moreover, likely were based on a component which was duplicated in the punitive award. Much of the distress was caused by the outrage and humiliation the Campbells suffered at the actions of their insurer; and it is a major role of punitive damages to condemn such conduct. Compensatory damages, however, already contain this punitive element. See Restatement (Second) of Torts § 908, Comment *c,* p. 466 (1977) ("In many cases in which compensatory damages include an amount for emotional distress, such as humiliation or indignation aroused by the defendant's act, there is no clear line of demarcation between punishment and compensation and a verdict for a specified amount frequently includes elements of both").

* * *

The remaining premises for the Utah Supreme Court's decision bear no relation to the award's reasonableness or proportionality to the harm. They are, rather, arguments that seek to defend a departure from well-established constraints on punitive damages. While States enjoy considerable discretion in deducing when punitive damages are warranted, each award must comport with the principles set forth in *Gore*. Here the argument that State Farm will be punished in only the rare case, coupled with reference to its assets (which, of course, are what other insured parties in Utah and other States must rely upon for payment of claims) had little to do with the actual harm sustained by the Campbells. The wealth of a defendant cannot justify an otherwise unconstitutional punitive damages award. *Gore* ("The fact that BMW is a large corporation rather than an impecunious individual does not diminish its entitlement to fair notice of the demands that the several States impose on the conduct of its business"); see also id., at 591 (Breyer, J., concurring) ("[Wealth] provides an open-ended basis for inflating awards when the defendant is wealthy.... That does not make its use unlawful or inappropriate; it simply means that this factor cannot make up for the failure of other factors, such as 'reprehensibility,' to constrain significantly an award that purports to punish a defendant's conduct"). The principles set forth in *Gore* must be implemented with care, to ensure both reasonableness and proportionality.

C

The third guidepost in *Gore* is the disparity between the punitive damages award and the "civil penalties authorized or imposed in comparable cases." We note that, in the past, we have also looked to criminal penalties that could be imposed. The existence of a criminal penalty does have bearing on the seriousness with which a State views the wrongful action. When used to determine the dollar amount of the award, however, the criminal penalty has less utility. Great care must be taken to avoid use of the civil process to assess criminal penalties that can be imposed only after the heightened protections of a criminal trial have been observed, including, of course, its higher standards of proof. Punitive damages are not a substitute for the criminal process, and the remote possibility of a criminal sanction does not automatically sustain a punitive damages award.

Here, we need not dwell long on this guidepost. The most relevant civil sanction under Utah state law for the wrong done to the Campbells appears to be a $10,000 fine for an act of fraud, an amount dwarfed by the $145 million punitive damages award. The Supreme Court of Utah speculated about the loss of State Farm's business license, the disgorgement of profits, and possible imprisonment, but here again its references were to the broad fraudulent scheme drawn from evidence of out-of-state and dissimilar conduct. This analysis was insufficient to justify the award.

IV

An application of the *Gore* guideposts to the facts of this case, especially in light of the substantial compensatory damages awarded (a portion of which contained a punitive element), likely would justify a punitive damages award at or near the amount of compensatory damages. The punitive award of $145 million, therefore, was neither reasonable nor proportionate to the wrong committed, and it was an irrational and arbitrary deprivation of the property of the defendant. The proper calculation of punitive damages under the principles we have discussed should be resolved, in the first instance, by the Utah courts.

* * *

JUSTICE SCALIA, dissenting.

I adhere to the view expressed in my dissenting opinion in BMW of North America, Inc. v. Gore, 517 U.S. 559, 598–99, 116 S.Ct. 1589, 134 L.Ed.2d 809 (1996), that the Due Process Clause provides no substantive protections against "excessive" or "unreasonable" awards of punitive damages. I am also of the view that the punitive damages jurisprudence which has sprung forth from *BMW v. Gore* is insusceptible of principled application; accordingly, I do not feel justified in giving the case stare decisis effect. I would affirm the judgment of the Utah Supreme Court.

JUSTICE THOMAS, dissenting.

I would affirm the judgment below because "I continue to believe that the Constitution does not constrain the size of punitive damages awards." Accordingly, I respectfully dissent.

JUSTICE GINSBURG, dissenting.

Not long ago, this Court was hesitant to impose a federal check on state-court judgments awarding punitive damages. In Browning–Ferris Industries of Vermont, Inc. v. Kelco Disposal, Inc., 492 U.S. 257, 109 S.Ct. 2909, 106 L.Ed.2d 219 (1989), the Court held that neither the Excessive Fines Clause of the Eighth Amendment nor federal common law circumscribed awards of punitive damages in civil cases between private parties. Two years later, in Pacific Mut. Life Ins. Co. v. Haslip, 499 U.S. 1, 111 S.Ct. 1032, 113 L.Ed.2d 1 (1991), the Court observed that "unlimited jury [or judicial] discretion ... in the fixing of punitive damages may invite extreme results that jar one's constitutional sensibilities;" the Due Process Clause, the Court suggested, would attend to those sensibilities and guard against unreasonable awards. Nevertheless, the Court upheld a punitive damages award in *Haslip* "more than 4 times the amount of compensatory damages, ... more than 200 times [the plaintiff's] out-of-pocket expenses," and "much in excess of the fine that could be imposed." And in TXO Production Corp. v. Alliance Resources Corp., 509 U.S. 443, 113 S.Ct. 2711, 125 L.Ed.2d 366 (1993), the Court affirmed a state-court award "526 times greater than the actual damages awarded by the jury." * * *

It was not until 1996, in BMW of North America, Inc. v. Gore, 517 U.S. 559, 116 S.Ct. 1589, 134 L.Ed.2d 809 (1996), that the Court, for the first time, invalidated a state-court punitive damages assessment as unreasonably large. If our activity in this domain is now "well-established," it takes place on ground not long held.

In *Gore*, I stated why I resisted the Court's foray into punitive damages "territory traditionally within the States' domain." I adhere to those views, and note again that, unlike federal habeas corpus review of state-court convictions under 28 U.S.C. § 2254, the Court "work[s] at this business of checking state courts alone," unaided by the participation of federal district courts and courts of appeals. It was once recognized that "the laws of the particular State must suffice [to superintend punitive damages awards] until judges or legislators authorized to do so initiate system-wide change." *Haslip* (Kennedy, J., concurring in judgment). I would adhere to that traditional view.

I

The large size of the award upheld by the Utah Supreme Court in this case indicates why damage-capping legislation may be altogether fitting and proper. Neither the amount of the award nor the trial record, however, justifies this Court's substitution of its judgment for that of Utah's competent decisionmakers. In this regard, I count it significant that, on the key criterion "reprehensibility," there is a good deal more to the story than the Court's abbreviated account tells.

Ample evidence allowed the jury to find that State Farm's treatment of the Campbells typified its "Performance, Planning and Review" (PP & R) program; implemented by top management in 1979, the program had "the explicit objective of using the claims-adjustment process as a profit center." "[T]he Campbells presented considerable evidence," the trial court noted, documenting "that the PP & R program . . . has functioned, and continues to function, as an unlawful scheme . . . to deny benefits owed consumers by paying out less than fair value in order to meet preset, arbitrary payout targets designed to enhance corporate profits." That policy, the trial court observed, was encompassing in scope; it "applied equally to the handling of both third-party and first-party claims."

* * *

Regarding liability for verdicts in excess of policy limits, the trial court referred to a State Farm document titled the "Excess Liability Handbook"; written before the Campbell accident, the handbook instructed adjusters to pad files with "self-serving" documents, and to leave critical items out of files, for example, evaluations of the insured's exposure. Divisional superintendent Bill Brown used the handbook to train Utah employees. While overseeing the Campbell case, Brown ordered adjuster Summers to change the portions of his report indicating that Mr. Campbell was likely at fault and that the settlement cost was correspondingly high. The Campbells' case, according to expert testimony the trial court recited, "was a classic example of State Farm's application of the improper practices taught in the Excess Liability Handbook."

The trial court further determined that the jury could find State Farm's policy "deliberately crafted" to prey on consumers who would be unlikely to defend themselves. In this regard, the trial court noted the testimony of several former State Farm employees affirming that they were trained to target "the weakest of the herd"—"the elderly, the poor, and other consumers who are least knowledgeable about their rights and thus most vulnerable to trickery or deceit, or who have little money and hence have no real alternative but to accept an inadequate offer to settle a claim at much less than fair value."

The Campbells themselves could be placed within the "weakest of the herd" category. The couple appeared economically vulnerable and emotionally fragile. At the time of State Farm's wrongful conduct, "Mr. Campbell had residuary effects from a stroke and Parkinson's disease."

* * *

State Farm's "wrongful profit and evasion schemes," the trial court underscored, were directly relevant to the Campbells' case:

"The record fully supports the conclusion that the bad-faith claim handling that exposed the Campbells to an excess verdict in 1983, and resulted in severe damages to them, was a product of the unlawful profit scheme that had been put in place by top management at State Farm years earlier. The Campbells presented substantial evidence showing how State Farm's improper insistence on claims-handling employees' reducing their claim payouts ... regardless of the merits of each claim, manifested itself ... in the Utah claims operations during the period when the decisions were made not to offer to settle the Campbell case for the $50,000 policy limits—indeed, not to make any offer to settle at a lower amount. This evidence established that high-level manager Bill Brown was under heavy pressure from the PP & R scheme to control indemnity payouts during the time period in question. * * * There was ample basis for the jury to find that everything that had happened to the Campbells—when State Farm repeatedly refused in bad-faith to settle for the $50,000 policy limits and went to trial, and then failed to pay the 'excess' verdict, or at least post a bond, after trial—was a direct application of State Farm's overall profit scheme, operating through Brown and others."

State Farm's "policies and practices," the trial evidence thus bore out, were "responsible for the injuries suffered by the Campbells," and the means used to implement those policies could be found "callous, clandestine, fraudulent, and dishonest." * * * The Utah Supreme Court, relying on the trial court's record-based recitations, understandably characterized State Farm's behavior as "egregious and malicious."

* * *

NOTES

1. On remand, the Utah Supreme Court did not completely take the hint at the end of Justice Kennedy's opinion (p. 704) that applying the *Gore* factors to the *State Farm* facts, "likely would justify a punitive damages award at or near the amount of compensatory damages," that is, about $1 million. Reviewing the evidence in light of the guidance the U.S. Supreme Court gave in its opinion, the Utah Supreme Court concluded that a punitive award of just over $9 million was appropriate. The Utah court focused on the reprehensibility of the insurer's conduct as well as the need to observe the single digit ratio Justice Kennedy prescribed. Campbell v. State Farm Mutual Automobile Insurance Co., 98 P.3d 409 (Utah), cert. denied, 543 U.S. 874, 125 S.Ct. 114, 160 L.Ed.2d 123 (2004). But see Walker v. Farmers Insurance Exchange, 153 Cal.App.4th 965, 63 Cal.Rptr.3d 507 (2007) (*State Farm's* 9:1 ratio not binding and a 1:1 ratio of punitive to compensatory damages was more appropriate in the case because fewer reprehensible factors were present).

2. The three guideposts to constitutional punitive damages were first articulated by the Court in BMW of North America, Inc. v. Gore, 517 U.S. 559, 116 S.Ct. 1589, 134 L.Ed.2d 809 (1996). In *Gore*, a wealthy doctor who purchased a BMW discovered that the company had fraudulently failed to

disclose that the new car had been repainted. Dr. Gore discovered the fraud when he took the car to Mr. Slick at Slick Finish for detailing and finishing. Under state consumer law, such disclosure was not required. The diminution in market value to the car was $4,000, and the Alabama jury originally awarded him $4 million in punitive damages. That amount was reduced to $2 million on appeal as the court found that it was inappropriate to compute punitive damages by multiplying the number of repainted cars sold nationally (approximately 1000) by $4,000 or the amount of economic harm per consumer. (It did not explain where $2 million came from). After reversal by the Supreme Court, the state court remitted the amount of punitives to $50,000. After *State Farm*, is this punitive award to Dr. Gore justified? Before *Gore*, the Supreme Court had decided TXO Production Corp. v. Alliance Resources Corp., 509 U.S. 443, 113 S.Ct. 2711, 125 L.Ed.2d 366 (1993), which upheld a ten million dollar punitive damages award, 526 times the amount of compensatory damages, finding that the jury could have rationally considered the potential harm that might have occurred from the defendant's conduct.

3. In *State Farm*, the Court did not address the role of the more extensive list of factors it had approved a few years before in Pacific Mutual Life Insurance Co. v. Haslip, 499 U.S. 1, 111 S.Ct. 1032, 113 L.Ed.2d 1 (1991). In particular, the Court said little in *State Farm* of the importance of the financial position of the defendant or the profitability to the defendant of the wrongful conduct. Justice Kennedy briefly observed, "The wealth of a defendant cannot justify an otherwise unconstitutional punitive damages award" (p. 703). Should these wealth factors play a role in deciding how much punishment is constitutional? See Jane Mallor & Barry S. Roberts, Punitive Damages: On the Path to a Principled Approach?, 50 Hastings L.J. 1001 (1999).

The California Supreme Court concluded that some consideration of the defendant's financial condition would still be relevant to satisfying the state's legitimate objectives, even as it recognized that wealth cannot substitute for *State Farm's* guideposts in limiting awards. Simon v. San Paolo U.S. Holding Co., 35 Cal.4th 1159, 113 P.3d 63, 29 Cal.Rptr.3d 379 (2005) (reducing $1.7 million punitive damage award to $50,000). In a companion case, the California Supreme Court affirmed the right of the state to protect the public from harmful corporate policies and practices; nevertheless, the court refused to measure punitive damages by the disgorgement of all profits due to the wrongful conduct. Johnson v. Ford Motor Co., 35 Cal.4th 1191, 113 P.3d 82, 29 Cal.Rptr.3d 401 (2005) (remanding for reconsideration the appellate court's reduction of punitive damages from $10 million to $53,000 based upon a compensatory award of $17,000). See Keith N. Hylton, A Theory of Wealth and Punitive Damages, 17 Widener L.J. 927 (2008) (arguing that wealth will tend to be a relevant factor when optimal deterrence requires elimination of the defendant's gain); Kathleen S. Kizer, California's Punitive Damages Law: Continuing to Punish and Deter Despite *State Farm v. Campbell*, 57 Hastings L.J. 827 (2006).

Should the defendant's *lack* of wealth impact the judgment? In Engle v. Liggett Group, Inc., 945 So.2d 1246 (Fla. 2006), cert. denied, 552 U.S. ___, 128 S.Ct. 96, 169 L.Ed.2d 244 (2007), the Florida Supreme Court invalidated a $145 billion punitive damages award to the class of smokers concluding, without analysis, that it would "result in an unlawful crippling" of the defendant tobacco companies. The court's main basis for overturning the award was the inability to assess the reasonableness of the ratio because compensatory damages had only been determined for 3 of the class plaintiffs in the amount of $12.7 million.

4. The requirement that state trial and appellate courts review the amount of punitive damage awards was established in Honda Motor Co., Ltd. v. Oberg, 512 U.S. 415, 114 S.Ct. 2331, 129 L.Ed.2d 336 (1994). In that case, the Supreme Court found that the practice under the Oregon Constitution of allowing the courts to vacate a judgment only when there was no evidence to support the jury decision, but not permitting review for excessive awards, was not consistent with due process standards.

5. The Supreme Court has ruled that appellate courts are to review de novo the trial court's application of the *Gore* factors in determining the constitutionality of an award of punitive damages. The re-examination clause of the Seventh Amendment is not implicated because an assessment of punitive damages is not a finding of historical or predictive fact. Cooper Industries, Inc. v. Leatherman Tool Group, Inc., 532 U.S. 424, 121 S.Ct. 1678, 149 L.Ed.2d 674 (2001). Colleen P. Murphy, Judicial Assessment of Legal Remedies, 94 Nw.U.L.Rev. 153 (1999), provides a discussion of the decline in the deference which judges have shown to jury damage awards over the last several decades. The question of the division of authority between juries and judges in determining remedies is also present in judicial review of jury verdicts. The Court had much earlier held that the Seventh Amendment allowed remittitur but not additur. Dimick v. Schiedt, 293 U.S. 474, 55 S.Ct. 296, 79 L.Ed. 603 (1935). Remittitur, the procedure by which the trial judge reviews jury awards for excessiveness, ordering a new trial unless the plaintiff accepts a reduction in the award, dates back to the early nineteenth century. Blunt v. Little, 3 F.Cas. 760 (C.C.Mass.1822).

6. There is a division among federal appellate courts on the procedure for reducing a jury's excessive punitive damage award. The Supreme Court has held that the Seventh Amendment requires that the plaintiff be given the option of a new trial in lieu of remitting a portion of the jury's compensatory award. Hetzel v. Prince William County, 523 U.S. 208, 118 S.Ct. 1210, 140 L.Ed.2d 336 (1998). With respect to an excessive award of punitive damages, some circuits follow the same rule and give the plaintiff the choice between a new trial or accepting the amount the court deems proper (commonly called remittitur). E.g., Riley v. Kurtz, 194 F.3d 1313 (6th Cir.1999); Ace v. Aetna Life Insurance Co., 139 F.3d 1241 (9th Cir.), cert. denied, 525 U.S. 930, 119 S.Ct. 338, 142 L.Ed.2d 279 (1998). Other circuits have held that, despite *Hetzel*, the district court should direct entry of judgment for a set amount as part of its independent responsibility to review an award of punitive damages for excessiveness. Ross v. Kansas City Power & Light Co., 293 F.3d 1041 (8th Cir.2002); Johansen v. Combustion Engineering, Inc., 170 F.3d 1320 (11th Cir.), cert. denied, 528 U.S. 931, 120 S.Ct. 329, 145 L.Ed.2d 256 (1999). The question of the appropriate procedure in light of the re-examination clause of the Seventh Amendment ("no fact tried by a jury, shall be otherwise re-examined in any Court of the United States, than according to the rules of the

common law") is addressed in Colleen P. Murphy, Judgment as a Matter of Law on Punitive Damages, 75 Tulane L.Rev. 459 (2000).

The Supreme Court has not directly ruled on the deference the trial court owes the jury verdict when applying the *Gore* factors. In Atlas Food Systems and Services, Inc. v. Crane National Vendors, Inc., 99 F.3d 587, 595 (4th Cir.1996), the Fourth Circuit has ruled that the trial court's review under F.R.Civ.P. 59 is not terribly deferential. "The court's review of the amount of a punitive damages award should involve comparison of the court's independent judgment on the appropriate amount with the jury's award to determine whether the jury's award is so excessive as to work an injustice." The appellate court emphasized the trial judge's greater knowledge of other punitive damage awards and her extensive experience in imposing penalties in criminal and civil contexts. Of course, information on other punitive damage awards is usually withheld from juries. Presumably judges may rely on facts which the jury may not see because they are less prone to emotion and better able to compare one case to another.

7. The Supreme Court quickly elaborated upon the question presented in *State Farm* as to when conduct outside of the case might appropriately be the basis for a punitive damages award. In Philip Morris USA v. Williams, 549 U.S. 346, 127 S.Ct. 1057, 166 L.Ed.2d 940 (2007), the Court reversed an award of $79.5 million in punitives, roughly a ratio of 100–to–1 with the $821,000 in compensatory damages, for the company's conduct in leading the plaintiff's deceased husband to believe it was safe to smoke. The Court held that it was an unconstitutional taking of the defendant's property without due process for a jury to base a punitive award upon its desire to punish the defendant for harming non-parties. In *Williams*, the jury calculated punitive damages, in part, upon the number of other people similar to the plaintiff in the state who had suffered physical harm or death of family members because of the tobacco company's fraud. The evidence did not suffer from the *State Farm* problem because it was the exact same conduct at issue in the case. The Court held that the jury instruction should have excluded these other possible harms to nonparties from factoring into the punishment. See Thomas B. Colby, Clearing the Smoke from *Philip Morris v. Williams*: The Past, Present, and Future of Punitive Damages, 118 Yale L.J. 392 (2008) (supporting the Court's return to a theory of punitive damages for only private, and not public, wrongs). However, the Court noted that evidence of harm to others is permitted to assess the reprehensibility of the defendant's conduct. As Justice Stevens observed in his dissent, "This nuance eludes me." See also Symposium on *Philip Morris v. Williams*, 2 Charleston L.Rev. 287–519 (2008).

On remand, the Oregon Supreme Court found that Philip Morris's requested jury instruction excluding consideration of harm to other persons was appropriately rejected by the court because of state procedural default rules that preclude adoption of instructions that are commingled with erroneous propositions of law. The court affirmed its prior decision leaving the $79.5 million punitive damages award in place. Williams v. Philip Morris, Inc., 344 Or. 45, 176 P.3d 1255 (2008). The U.S. Supreme Court then granted Philip Morris' subsequent petition for certiorari in this case on the question of whether Oregon may apply an alternative state law basis to deny a party's claim after the Court has adjudicated the merits of the party's federal claim and remanded to the state court with instructions to apply the correct constitutional standard. Philip Morris USA, Inc. v. Williams, 554 U.S. ___, 128 S.Ct. 2904, 171 L.Ed.2d 840 (2008).

8. Does Justice Kennedy's opinion in *State Farm* suggest that a similar 3:1 ratio should be imposed on non-pecuniary damages? See Michael Rustad, The Uncert–Worthiness of the Court's Unmaking of Punitive Damages, 2 Charleston L.Rev. 459 (2008) (predicting that the Court will extend its punitive damages jurisprudence to curtail the award of non-economic damages); Paul DeCamp, Beyond *State Farm*: Due Process Constraints on Noneconomic Compensatory Damages, 27 Harv. J.L. & Pub. Policy 231 (2003) (arguing for similar due process review of non-economic damages, but rejecting the *State Farm* criteria in favor of a standard of review comparing the award with the range of prior decisions in similar cases).

MATHIAS v. ACCOR ECONOMY LODGING, INC.

United States Court of Appeals, Seventh Circuit, 2003
347 F.3d 672

POSNER, CIRCUIT JUDGE.

The plaintiffs brought this diversity suit governed by Illinois law against affiliated entities that own and operate the "Motel 6" chain of hotels and motels. One of these hotels (now a "Red Roof Inn," though still owned by the defendant) is in downtown Chicago. The plaintiffs, a brother and sister, were guests there and were bitten by bedbugs, which are making a comeback in the U.S. as a consequence of more conservative use of pesticides. The plaintiffs claim that in allowing guests to be attacked by bedbugs in a motel that charges upwards of $100 a day for a room and would not like to be mistaken for a flophouse, the defendant was guilty of "willful and wanton conduct" and thus under Illinois law is liable for punitive as well as compensatory damages. The jury agreed and awarded each plaintiff $186,000 in punitive damages though only $5,000 in compensatory damages. The defendant appeals, complaining primarily about the punitive-damages award. * * *

The defendant argues that at worst it is guilty of simple negligence, and if this is right the plaintiffs were not entitled by Illinois law to any award of punitive damages. It also complains that the award was excessive-indeed that any award in excess of $20,000 to each plaintiff would deprive the defendant of its property without due process of law. The first complaint has no possible merit, as the evidence of gross negligence, indeed of recklessness in the strong sense of an unjustifiable failure to avoid a *known* risk was amply shown. In 1998, EcoLab, the extermination service that the motel used, discovered bedbugs in several rooms in the motel and recommended that it be hired to spray every room, for which it would charge the motel only $500; the motel refused. The next year, bedbugs were again discovered in a room but EcoLab was asked to spray just that room. The motel tried to negotiate "a building sweep [by EcoLab] free of charge," but, not surprisingly, the negotiation failed. By the spring of 2000, the motel's manager "started noticing that there were refunds being given by my desk clerks and reports coming back from the guests that there were ticks in the rooms and bugs in the rooms that were biting." She looked in some of the rooms and discovered bedbugs. The defendant asks us to disregard her testimony as that of a disgruntled ex-employee, but of course her credibility was for the jury, not the defendant, to determine.

Further incidents of guests being bitten by insects and demanding and receiving refunds led the manager to recommend to her superior in the company that the motel be closed while every room was sprayed, but this was refused. This superior, a district manager, was a management-level employee of the defendant, and his knowledge of the risk and failure to take effective steps either to eliminate it or to warn the motel's guests are imputed to his employer for purposes of determining whether the employer should be liable for punitive damages. The employer's liability for compensatory damages is of course automatic on the basis of the principle of respondeat superior, since the district manager was acting within the scope of his employment.

The infestation continued and began to reach farcical proportions, as when a guest, after complaining of having been bitten repeatedly by insects while asleep in his room in the hotel, was moved to another room only to discover insects there; and within 18 minutes of being moved to a third room he discovered insects in that room as well and had to be moved still again. (Odd that at that point he didn't flee the motel.) By July, the motel's management was acknowledging to EcoLab that there was a "major problem with bed bugs" and that all that was being done about it was "chasing them from room to room." Desk clerks were instructed to call the "bedbugs" "ticks," apparently on the theory that customers would be less alarmed, though in fact ticks are more dangerous than bedbugs because they spread Lyme Disease and Rocky Mountain Spotted Fever. Rooms that the motel had placed on "Do not rent, bugs in room" status nevertheless were rented.

It was in November that the plaintiffs checked into the motel. They were given Room 504, even though the motel had classified the room as "DO NOT RENT UNTIL TREATED," and it had not been treated. Indeed, that night 190 of the hotel's 191 rooms were occupied, even though a number of them had been placed on the same don't-rent status as Room 504. One of the defendant's motions in limine that the judge denied was to exclude evidence concerning all other rooms—a good example of the frivolous character of the motions and of the defendant's pertinacious defense of them on appeal.

Although bedbug bites are not as serious as the bites of some other insects, they are painful and unsightly. Motel 6 could not have rented any rooms at the prices it charged had it informed guests that the risk of being bitten by bedbugs was appreciable. Its failure either to warn guests or to take effective measures to eliminate the bedbugs amounted to fraud and probably to battery as well, as in the famous case of Garratt v. Dailey, 279 P.2d 1091, 1093–94 (Wash. 1955), appeal after remand, 304 P.2d 681 (Wash. 1956), which held that the defendant would be guilty of battery if he knew with substantial certainty that when he moved a chair the plaintiff would try to sit down where the chair had been and would land on the floor instead. There was, in short, sufficient evidence of "willful and wanton conduct" within the meaning that the Illinois courts assign to the term to permit an award of punitive damages in this case.

But in what amount? In arguing that $20,000 was the maximum amount of punitive damages that a jury could constitutionally have awarded each plaintiff, the defendant points to the U.S. Supreme Court's recent statement that "few awards [of punitive damages] exceeding a single-digit ratio between punitive and compensatory damages, to a significant degree, will satisfy due process." State Farm Mutual Automobile Ins. Co. v. Campbell, 538 U.S. 408, 123 S.Ct. 1513, 1524, 155 L.Ed.2d 585 (2003). The Court went on to suggest that "four times the amount of compensatory damages might be close to the line of constitutional impropriety." Hence the defendant's proposed ceiling in this case of $20,000, four times the compensatory damages awarded to each plaintiff. The ratio of punitive to compensatory damages determined by the jury was, in contrast, 37.2 to 1.

The Supreme Court did not, however, lay down a 4–to–1 or single-digit-ratio rule—it said merely that "there is a presumption against an award that has a 145–to–1 ratio," *State Farm*, 123 S.Ct. at 1524—and it would be unreasonable to do so. We must consider why punitive damages are awarded and why the Court has decided that due process requires that such awards be limited. The second question is easier to answer than the first. The term "punitive damages" implies punishment, and a standard principle of penal theory is that "the punishment should fit the crime" in the sense of being proportional to the wrongfulness of the defendant's action, though the principle is modified when the probability of detection is very low (a familiar example is the heavy fines for littering) or the crime is potentially lucrative (as in the case of trafficking in illegal drugs). Hence, with these qualifications, which in fact will figure in our analysis of this case, punitive damages should be proportional to the wrongfulness of the defendant's actions.

Another penal precept is that a defendant should have reasonable notice of the sanction for unlawful acts, so that he can make a rational determination of how to act; and so there have to be reasonably clear standards for determining the amount of punitive damages for particular wrongs. And a third precept, the core of the Aristotelian notion of corrective justice, and more broadly of the principle of the rule of law, is that sanctions should be based on the wrong done rather than on the status of the defendant; a person is punished for what he does, not for who he is, even if the who is a huge corporation.

What follows from these principles, however, is that punitive damages should be admeasured by standards or rules rather than in a completely ad hoc manner, and this does not tell us what the maximum ratio of punitive to compensatory damages should be in a particular case. To determine that, we have to consider why punitive damages are awarded in the first place.

England's common law courts first confirmed their authority to award punitive damages in the eighteenth century, see Dorsey D. Ellis, Jr., "Fairness and Efficiency in the Law of Punitive Damages," 56 S.Cal. L.Rev. 1, 12–20 (1982), at a time when the institutional structure of criminal law enforcement was primitive and it made sense to leave certain minor crimes to be dealt with by the civil law. And still today one function of punitive-damages awards is to relieve the pressures on an overloaded system of criminal justice by providing a civil alternative to criminal prosecution of minor crimes. An example is deliberately spitting in a person's face, a criminal assault but because minor readily deterrable by the levying of what amounts to a civil fine through a suit for damages for the tort of battery. Compensatory damages would not do the trick in such a case, and this for three reasons: because they are difficult to determine in the case of acts that inflict largely dignitary harms; because in the spitting case they would be too slight to give the victim an incentive to sue, and he might decide instead to respond with violence—and an age-old purpose of the law of torts is to provide a substitute for violent retaliation against wrongful injury—and because to limit the plaintiff to compensatory damages would enable the defendant to commit the offensive act with impunity provided that he was willing to pay, and again there would be a danger that his act would incite a breach of the peace by his victim.

When punitive damages are sought for billion-dollar oil spills and other huge economic injuries, the considerations that we have just canvassed fade. As the Court emphasized in *Campbell*, the fact that the plaintiffs in that case had been awarded very substantial compensatory damages—$1 million for a dispute over insurance coverage—greatly reduced the need for giving them a huge award of punitive damages ($145 million) as well in order to provide an effective remedy. Our case is closer to the spitting case. The defendant's behavior was outrageous but the compensable harm done was slight and at the same time difficult to quantify because a large element of it was emotional. And the defendant may well have profited from its misconduct because by concealing the infestation it was able to keep renting rooms. Refunds were frequent but may have cost less than the cost of closing the hotel for a thorough fumigation. The hotel's attempt to pass off the bedbugs as ticks, which some guests might ignorantly have thought less unhealthful, may have postponed the instituting of litigation to rectify the hotel's misconduct. The award of punitive damages in this case thus serves the additional purpose of limiting the defendant's ability to profit from its fraud by escaping detection and (private) prosecution. If a tortfeasor is "caught" only half the time he commits torts, then when he is caught he should be punished twice as heavily in order to make up for the times he gets away.

Finally, if the total stakes in the case were capped at $50,000 (2 x [$5,000 + $20,000]), the plaintiffs might well have had difficulty financing this lawsuit. It is here that the defendant's aggregate net worth of $1.6 billion becomes relevant. A defendant's wealth is not a sufficient basis for awarding punitive damages. *State Farm*; *Gore* (concurring opinion); Zazu Designs v. L'Oreal, S.A., 979 F.2d 499, 508–09 (7th Cir.1992). That would be discriminatory and would violate the rule of law, as we explained earlier, by making punishment depend on status rather than conduct. Where wealth in the sense of resources enters is in enabling the defendant to mount an extremely aggressive defense against suits such as this and by doing so to make litigating against it very costly, which in turn may make it difficult for the plaintiffs to find a lawyer willing to handle their case, involving as it does only modest stakes, for the usual 33–40 percent contingent fee.

In other words, the defendant is investing in developing a reputation intended to deter plaintiffs. It is difficult otherwise to explain the great stubborness with which it has defended this case, making a host of frivolous evidentiary arguments despite the very modest stakes even when the punitive damages awarded by the jury are included.

As a detail (the parties having made nothing of the point), we note that "net worth" is not the correct measure of a corporation's resources. It is an accounting artifact that reflects the allocation of ownership between equity and debt claimants. A firm financed largely by equity investors has a large "net worth" (= the value of the equity claims), while the identical firm financed largely by debt may have only a small net worth because accountants treat debt as a liability.

All things considered, we cannot say that the award of punitive damages was excessive, albeit the precise number chosen by the jury was arbitrary. It is probably not a coincidence that $5,000 + $186,000 = $191,000/191 = $1,000: i.e., $1,000 per room in the hotel. But as there are no punitive-damages guidelines, corresponding to the federal and state sentencing guidelines, it is inevitable that the specific amount of punitive damages awarded whether by a judge or by a jury will be arbitrary. (Which is perhaps why the plaintiffs' lawyer did not suggest a number to the jury.) The judicial function is to police a range, not a point. See *Gore*; TXO Production Corp. v. Alliance Resources Corp., 509 U.S. 443, 458, 113 S.Ct. 2711, 125 L.Ed.2d 366 (1993) (plurality opinion).

But it would have been helpful had the parties presented evidence concerning the regulatory or criminal penalties to which the defendant exposed itself by deliberately exposing its customers to a substantial risk of being bitten by bedbugs. That is an inquiry recommended by the Supreme Court. But we do not think its omission invalidates the award. We can take judicial notice that deliberate exposure of hotel guests to the health risks created by insect infestations exposes the hotel's owner to sanctions under Illinois and Chicago law that in the aggregate are comparable in severity to the punitive damage award in this case.

"A person who causes bodily harm to or endangers the bodily safety of an individual by any means, commits reckless conduct if he performs recklessly the acts which cause the harm or endanger safety, whether they otherwise are lawful or unlawful." 720 ILCS 5/12–5(a). This is a misdemeanor, punishable by up to a year's imprisonment or a fine of $2,500, or both. (For the application of the reckless-conduct criminal statute to corporate officials, see Illinois v. Chicago Magnet Wire Corp., 534 N.E.2d 962, 963 (Ill. 1989).) Of course a corporation cannot be sent to prison, and $2,500 is obviously much less than the $186,000 awarded to each plaintiff in this case as punitive damages. But this is just the beginning. Other guests of the hotel were endangered besides these two plaintiffs. And, what is much more important, a Chicago hotel that permits unsanitary conditions to exist is subject to revocation of its license, without which it cannot operate. Chi. Munic. Code §§ 4–4–280, 4–208–020, 050, 060, 110. We are sure that the defendant would prefer to pay the punitive damages assessed in this case than to lose its license.

NOTES

1. For further insight into *Mathias*, see Colleen P. Murphy, The "Bedbug" Case and *State Farm v. Campbell*, 9 Roger Williams U.L.Rev. 579 (2004) (comparing the approaches of Justice Kennedy and Judge Posner).

2. Some courts have adhered to the single digit ratio. E.g., Eden Electrical, Ltd. v. Amana Co., 370 F.3d 824 (8th Cir.2004) (affirming district court's reduction of punitive damages from $17 million to $10 million), cert. denied, 543 U.S. 1150, 125 S.Ct. 1322, 161 L.Ed.2d 112 (2005); see Lauren R. Goldman & Nickholai G. Levin, *State Farm* at Three: Lower Courts' Application of the Ratio Guidepost, 2 N.Y.U.J.L & Bus. 509 (2006) (concluding that *State Farm* has altered the landscape of punitive damages litigation in a wide variety of cases). Others have found exceptions to the rule. E.g., Saunders v. Branch Banking & Trust Co., 526 F.3d 142 (4th Cir.2008) (upholding punitive damages with 80:1 ratio, $80,000 punitives/$1,000 statutory damages under Fair Credit Reporting Act because of need for meaningful deterrent in case of trivial compensatory damages and reprehensibility of bank preying on financially vulnerable car loan customer); Kemp v. American Telephone & Telegraph Co., 393 F.3d 1354 (11th Cir.2004) (upholding punitive award of $250,000 for mere $115 in compensatory damages to plaintiff's grandson who rang up telephone charges for playing a 900 number "Let's Make a Deal" game that violated state gambling laws); Timm v. Progressive Steel Treating, Inc., 137 F.3d 1008 (7th Cir.1998) (upholding punitive damages in a sex discrimination suit with no compensatory damages where jury may have thought employee quit to take a higher paying job); Alexandra B. Klass, Punitive Damages and Valuing Harm, 92 Minn.L.Rev. 83 (2007) (arguing that courts should depart from a single-digit ratio where harm is "undervalued" as when compensatory damages are small or difficult to determine).

CHAPTER 7

RESTITUTION AND RESTITUTIONARY REMEDIES

■ ■ ■

A. INTRODUCTION

RESTATEMENT OF RESTITUTION
(1937)

Section One. Unjust Enrichment.

A person who has been unjustly enriched at the expense of another is required to make restitution to the other.

DOUGLAS LAYCOCK, THE SCOPE AND SIGNIFICANCE OF RESTITUTION
67 Tex.L.Rev. 1277, 1277–84 (1989)

The law of restitution offers substantive and remedial principles of broad scope and practical significance. In an outline of the sources of civil liability, the principal headings would be tort, contract, and restitution. * * * [Yet] [d]espite its importance, restitution is a relatively neglected and underdeveloped part of the law. In the mental map of most lawyers, restitution consists largely of blank spaces with undefined borders and only scattered patches of familiar ground. * * *

I. THE DEFINING CONCEPTS OF RESTITUTION

A. *An Historical Definition*

The rules of restitution developed much like the rules of equity. Restitution arose to avoid unjust results in specific cases—as a series of innovations to fill gaps in the rest of the law. Consequently, any definition of restitution risks the self-conscious circularity of Maitland's definition of equity[6]: restitution consists of those rules that originated in writs and equitable remedies that lawyers think of as restitutionary.

The Restatement [of Restitution, published in 1937] attempted to induce a unifying principle and thus to provide a more satisfactory

---

6. "Equity is that body of rules which is administered only by those courts which are known as Courts of Equity." F. Maitland, Equity 1 (2d ed.1936).

definition. The Restatement legitimated three insights: that a seemingly great variety of specific rules serve a common purpose, that these rules can be thought of as a single body of law under the name 'restitution,' and that these rules support a general principle that unjust enrichment must be disgorged. This was a major accomplishment; it created the field.

But the effort succeeded only in part. Drafting decisions that were probably inevitable in 1937 have become increasingly problematic over the years, in part because of the other great legal publication of 1937, the Federal Rules of Civil Procedure. The subtitle of the Restatement, and of its two great subdivisions, is "Quasi Contracts and Constructive Trusts." These categories depend in part on the separation of law and equity, and even more on a categorization of claims rooted in the forms of action and dependent on fictional pleadings. Yet the Federal Rules merged law and equity, put the last nail in the coffin of the forms of action, and embodied both the realist emphasis on substantial justice and a modern distaste for legal fiction.

The reporters of the Restatement were sympathetic to these trends, but they could not yet escape the past. Their work is laden with references to the pre–1937 roots of restitution, and they did not fully avoid the view that restitution is the body of law historically available under the label of quasi-contract or constructive trust. But a definition in terms of common-law writs is little help to modern lawyers. It is also misleading: restitution is both broader and narrower than the historic scope of quasi-contract and constructive trust. The search for definition must be conceptual rather than historical.

B. A Conceptual Definition

Lawyers use the word "restitution" in at least two senses. "Restitution" means recovery based on and measured by unjust enrichment. * * * It follows from the focus on enrichment that restitution measures recovery by defendant's gain rather than plaintiff's loss. * * *

"Restitution" also retains its original literal meaning, which is simply restoration of something lost or taken away. Thus, restitution continues to include remedies that restore to plaintiff the specific thing he lost or that undo disrupted transactions and restore both parties to their original positions in kind. The Restatement refers to in-kind restoration of specific property as "specific restitution." * * *

"Restitution" is sometimes used in a third sense—to restore the value of what plaintiff lost. The Restatement employs the term this way at least occasionally, and the usage is common in the statutes requiring criminals to make restitution to their victims. But restitution of the value of what plaintiff lost is simply compensatory damages. Used in this sense, "restitution" loses all utility as a means of distinguishing one body of law from another. Restitution must be distinguished from compensation, either by its focus on restoration of the loss in kind or by its focus on defendant's gain as the measure of recovery. * * *

Restitution is also commonly distinguished from injunctions and specific performance, even though these remedies also grant specific relief and are premised on the inadequacy of substitutionary remedies such as damages. An injunction can order defendant to return specific property to plaintiff, and in this simple case, the injunction is a means of achieving specific restitution.

But most injunctive remedies are not restitutionary in this sense. Injunctions prevent future wrongdoing or ameliorate the future consequences of a past wrong by some means more complex than restoring possession of misappropriated property or reversing a transaction. Specific performance decrees award plaintiff something he has never had, because it was promised to him and cannot be obtained elsewhere. Thus, injunctions and specific performance are more often preventive than restorative. They are historically subject to different rules, and they raise different policy considerations. The occasional restitutionary use of injunctions is part of restitution and should be recognized as such, but most of the law of injunctions and specific performance is outside the field.

II. THE PRACTICAL SIGNIFICANCE OF RESTITUTION

Many cases of unjust enrichment are also covered by other principles, including the basic rules of tort and contract. If defendant steals a hundred-dollar bill, he is unjustly enriched in the amount of one hundred dollars. But he has also committed a tort; indeed, it is the tort that makes his enrichment unjust. The tort damages are also one hundred dollars. If defendant is solvent, it will rarely matter whether plaintiff recovers one hundred dollars in damages for the tort or one hundred dollars in restitution of the unjust enrichment.

Because of such overlaps, one gets little sense of the practical significance of restitution by systematically developing all applications of the unjust enrichment and specific restitution principles. It is more enlightening to ask what restitution adds to the other sources of civil liability. The restitutionary claim matters in three sets of cases: (1) when unjust enrichment is the only source of liability; (2) when plaintiff prefers to measure recovery by defendant's gain, either because it exceeds plaintiff's loss or because it is easier to measure; and (3) when plaintiff prefers specific restitution, either because defendant is insolvent, because the thing plaintiff lost has changed in value, or because plaintiff values the thing he lost for nonmarket reasons. * * *

NOTE ON APPROACHING RESTITUTION CASES

After many relatively dormant years, academic attention to restitution and unjust enrichment has increased sharply. Domestically, at least part of the impetus for the renewed interest in the field is the anticipated appearance of the American Law Institute's Restatement (Third) of Restitution and Unjust Enrichment. As of this writing, tentative drafts covering the first seven chapters of the new Restatement have been approved.[a] On the Restatement, see Doug Rendleman, Restating Restitution: The Restatement Process and Its Critics, 65 Wash. & Lee L.Rev. 933 (2008); Andrew Kull, Restitution and Reform, 32 So.Ill.U.L.J. 83–92 (2007); and Chaim Saiman, Restating Restitution: A Case of Contemporary Common Law Conceptualism, 52 Vill.L Rev. 487 (2007) (arguing that the Restatement has more in common with the high formalism of the nineteenth century than with contemporary modes of private law discourse). The interest in restitution is international in scope. See, e.g., Peter Birks, Unjust Enrichment (2d rev.ed.2005) (Great Britain); Chaim Saiman, Restitution in America: Why the U.S. Refuses to Join the Global Restitution Party, 28 Oxford J.Leg.Stud. 99 (2008); I.M. Jackman, The Varieties of Restitution (1998) (Australia); Ross B. Grantham & Charles E.F. Rickett, Enrichment and Restitution in New Zealand (2000).

Another reason for the apparent revival of the law of unjust enrichment and restitution is a sense that unjust enrichment may be today's "new frontier" in the development of the common law. As Professor Rendleman has explained, where the limits of tort and contract have been reached, characterizing a case as involving unjust enrichment and requiring a restitutionary remedy can open the court's eyes to new possibilities. Doug Rendleman, Common Law Restitution in the Mississippi Tobacco Settlement: Did the Smoke Get in Their Eyes?, 33 Ga.L.Rev. 847, 848–49 (1999). In this way, restitution has been explored as a solution to problems ranging from reparations for slavery to crime to employment discrimination to destructive products to human rights. See, e.g., Gareth Jones, Restitution and Unjust Enrichment: Stripping a Criminal of the Profits of Crime, 1 Theoretical Inq.L. 59 (2000); Candace S. Kovacic–Fleisher, Restitution in Public Concern Cases, 36 Loy.L.A.L.Rev. 901 (2003); Anthony J. Sebok, Two Concepts of Injustice in Restitution for Slavery, 84 B.U.L.Rev. 1405 (2004).

But to begin at the beginning, as you read the cases that follow you may find it helpful to focus on three issues. The first is procedural: Did the plaintiff bring his or her case in law or in equity, and how did he or she plead it? The second is substantive: What was the plaintiff required to show in order to establish a right to restitution? The third is remedial: What remedy did the plaintiff get?

Procedure. Professor Laycock notes that the Restatement of Restitution is divided into two parts, quasi-contract and constructive trust, corresponding to the two kinds of actions that lawyers then used most frequently to bring claims based on a theory of unjust enrichment. Quasi-contract claims were closely associated with the common law form of action known as assumpsit. In assumpsit, the plaintiff alleged that the defendant had received some benefit—money, goods, services—from the plaintiff, and that defendant had implicitly promised to pay for it. Using assumpsit, the plaintiff could avoid procedural entanglements that made the common law action on the debt cumbersome by asking the court to enforce the new, implied promise to pay.

---

a. Each of the tentative drafts has been approved "subject to the discussion at the [American Law Institute's Annual] Meeting and to appropriate editorial revision" as is the ALI's practice. A summary of the discussion and comments on specific sections can be found in the annual ALI Proceedings, or on the ALI's website at www.ali.org, by accessing the Fall issue of the ALI Reporter in the year of the annual meeting at which the draft was presented.

In some cases, this promise was implied (more accurately, inferred) from the parties' own dealings and behavior; it was a contract "implied in fact," no different in legal effect from an express contract. In other cases, the contract was said to be "implied in law." Then, the law court imposed an obligation to pay based, essentially, on the notion that unjust enrichment ought to be avoided:

> In quasi contracts the obligation arises, not from consent of the parties, as in the case of contracts, express or implied in fact, but from the law of natural immutable justice and equity. * * * Where a case shows that it is the duty of the defendant to pay, the law imputes to him a promise to fulfill that obligation. The duty, which thus forms the foundation of a quasi-contractual obligation, is frequently based on the doctrine of unjust enrichment.

66 Am.Jur.2d: Restitution and Implied Contracts §§ 5–6. See Candace Saari Kovacic–Fleischer, Quantum Meruit and the Restatement (Third) of Restitution and Unjust Enrichment, 27 Rev.Litig. 127 (2007). Although some early common law forms of action were also restitutionary in character (the legal action of replevin, for example, by which a plaintiff could recover specific property taken from him), it was with quasi-contract that the concept of unjust enrichment as an independent source of obligation entered the common law.

In the equity courts, the constructive trust was the primary vehicle for enforcing the obligation to return benefits unjustly acquired. If an equity court concluded that the defendant was in possession of property that it was unjust for him to retain, it would declare that the property was held in constructive trust for the person to whom it equitably belonged, and order the property returned. The name constructive "trust" is thus somewhat misleading. Just as "implied in law" quasi-contracts did not rest on an actual promise, the obligation to return the property did not arise from a true trust. Rather, it arose from the courts' desire to avoid unjust enrichment. See Colleen P. Murphy, Misclassifying Monetary Restitution, 55 S.M.U.L.Rev. 1577 (2002) (helpful discussion of the taxonomy of restitution).

Substance. By now, the Restatement's characterization of restitution as constituting—along with torts and contracts—the third main branch of civil liability has gained wide acceptance. Yet, while torts and contracts are mainstays of the first year curriculum, it usually falls to the remedies course to cover the substantive law of restitution.

The substantive law of restitution operates at two extremes. At one extreme are narrow rules, adequate to the case before the court, but too narrow to function as rules of decision as new cases arise. At the other extreme are broad principles that invoke the majesty of the law, but function more to justify results than to decide cases. Thus, in Moses v. Macferlan, 2 Burr. 1005, 1012, 97 Eng.Rep. 676, 681 (K.B.1760), the case generally credited as the seminal restitution case, Lord Mansfield explained that the obligation to make restitution comes into being when "the defendant, upon the circumstances of the case, is obliged by the ties of natural justice and equity to refund the money." The Restatement of Restitution relies on equally broad principles, such as the principle that restitution will be awarded whenever a defendant is unjustly enriched, and the principle that volunteers and officious intermeddlers may not recover in restitution. Restatement of Restitution §§ 1, 2.

The tentative draft of the Restatement (Third) of Restitution and Unjust Enrichment attempts to avoid this problem by defining unjust enrichment in terms of legal, rather than moral obligations:

> The concern of restitution is not, in fact, with unjust enrichment in this broad sense, but with a narrower set of circumstances giving rise to what is more appropriately called unjustified enrichment * * *. Unjustified enrichment is enrichment that lacks an adequate legal basis: it results from a transfer that the law treats as ineffective to work a conclusive alteration in ownership rights. Because the legal basis that makes a transfer effective is ordinarily a consensual exchange, a valid gift, or a legal duty (such as a liability in tort or an obligation to pay taxes), the concern of restitution is predictably with those anomalous transfers that cannot be justified by the terms of a valid and enforceable exchange transaction; by the intention of the transferor to make a gift; or by the existence of a legal duty to the transferee.

Restatement (Third) of Restitution, § 1 comment *b* (Tentative Draft No. 1, 2001). See Doug Rendleman, When Is Enrichment Unjust? Restitution Visits An Onyx Bathroom, 36 Loy.L.A.L.Rev. 991 (2003) (discussing broad and narrow concepts of unjust enrichment). On the normative underpinnings of the law of restitution generally, see Hanoch Dagan, The Law and Ethics of Restitution (2005).

Part of the problem in defining unjust enrichment is that the conditions under which restitution has been sought are infinitely variable. Three patterns, however, tend to be repeated. In the first, the plaintiff has conferred a benefit on the defendant that the defendant did not request. In the second pattern, the plaintiff has conferred a benefit on the defendant at the defendant's request—perhaps pursuant to a contract—and, rather than attempting to enforce the contract, the plaintiff prefers to seek the return of his performance or its value. In the third pattern, the defendant has acquired a benefit tortiously or by other wrongdoing. The cases that follow illustrate each of these patterns.

Remedy. As with tort and contract remedies, the concept of rightful position is critical to understanding restitutionary remedies. Instead of aiming at the plaintiff's rightful position, however, restitution aims at the defendant's. Disgorgement is the key concept. By making the defendant disgorge the benefits she cannot justly retain, the law of restitution returns the defendant to the position she should, "in equity and good conscience," have occupied.

This chapter ends with a discussion of the restitutionary remedies derived from equity—in particular, the constructive trust. It is important to recognize that the constructive trust cases provide more than just a discussion of an alternative remedy for unjust enrichment. Because the law of restitution evolved concurrently in the law courts and the equity courts, much of the substantive law of restitution developed in the equity courts. Thus, it is important to recognize as you read the constructive trust cases that the cases are defining the terms of the obligation itself.

B. RESTITUTION AND UNSOLICITED BENEFITS

PROBLEM: COUNTRY LODGE V. MILLER (REPRISED)
RESTITUTION FOR BENEFITS CONFERRED

Suppose that after Country Lodge threatened to sue Miller for polluting the river, Miller built settling ponds down river from her plant to clear the water. Because the ponds also remove silt from the river, the water flowing past Country Lodge now is even clearer and purer than it was before the apple mill began operation. For the first time in years, Country Lodge's guests are able to enjoy wading and swimming in the water. Can Miller recover in restitution for the benefit she has bestowed on Country Lodge? Can Miller recover in restitution from her property insurer, if the insurer would have been liable for any damages recovered by Country Lodge had the pollution been allowed to continue?

KOSSIAN v. AMERICAN NATIONAL INSURANCE CO.

Court of Appeal of California, Fifth District, 1967
254 Cal.App.2d 647, 62 Cal.Rptr. 225

STONE, ASSOCIATE JUSTICE.

On February 19, 1964, fire destroyed a portion of the Bakersfield Inn, owned by one Reichert. At the time, the property was subject to a first deed of trust in which defendant was the beneficiary. Pursuant to the requirements of the deed of trust, defendant's interest in the property was protected by policies of fire insurance. On March 16, 1964, Reichert, as owner in possession, entered into a written contract with plaintiff whereby plaintiff agreed to clean up and remove the debris from the fire damaged portion of the Inn for the sum of $18,900. Defendant had no knowledge of the execution of the agreement between plaintiff and Reichert.

Plaintiff commenced work in the middle of March 1964, and completed it in early April. During the entire time work was in progress Reichert was in possession of the premises as owner, although defendant caused a notice of Reichert's default under the deed of trust to be filed four days after the contract for demolition was entered into between plaintiff and Reichert. The record does not reflect that plaintiff had actual knowledge of the notice of default until after the work was completed.

Some time after plaintiff had fully performed the contract, Reichert filed a petition in bankruptcy. The trustee in bankruptcy abandoned the premises comprising the Bakersfield Inn, together with any interest in the four fire insurance policies up to the amount of $424,000. Each policy contained a provision insuring against the cost of cleaning up and removing debris caused by fire damage.

Following abandonment of the policies by the trustee in bankruptcy, Reichert and his wife assigned their interest in them to defendant in accordance with the terms of the deed of trust. Defendant submitted proofs of loss, claiming a total of $160,000, including the sum of $18,000 as the estimated cost for removing and cleaning up debris. These claims were rejected by the carriers; negotiations followed; the compromise figure of $135,620 was agreed upon and this amount paid to defendant. We do not have an itemization of the adjusted claims of loss upon which the compromised loss settlement was made, so that the record is not clear as to what part of the $18,900 cost of debris removal defendant received. It is clear, however, that the insurance payment included at least a part of the cost of debris removal and demolition.

Defendant demonstrates, by a careful analysis of the facts, that there was no direct relationship between plaintiff and defendant in regard to either the work performed on the property after the fire or in relation to the fire insurance policies. The contract for debris removal was between plaintiff and Reichert, and defendant did not induce plaintiff, directly or indirectly, to enter into that contract. Plaintiff had no lien against the property resulting from his work, and if he had such a lien it would have been wiped out by defendant's foreclosure of its first deed of trust.

Had the circumstances been simply that defendant, by foreclosure, took the property improved by plaintiff's debris removal, there would be a benefit conferred upon defendant by plaintiff, but no unjust enrichment. It is the additional fact that defendant made a claim to the insurance carriers for the value of work done by plaintiff that is the nub of the case.

Defendant argues that plaintiff was not a party to the insurance contracts, while defendant had a contract right to collect indemnity for losses resulting from the fire, including the debris removal cost. This contract right was embodied in the insurance policies. Defendant relies upon Russell v. Williams, 58 Cal.2d 487 at page 490, 24 Cal.Rptr. 859, at page 861, 374 P.2d 827, at page 829 where it is said:

> "It is a principle of long standing that a policy of fire insurance does not insure the property covered thereby, but is a personal contract indemnifying the insured against loss resulting from the destruction of or damage to his interest in that property. This principle gives rise to the supplemental rule that, in the absence of a special contract, the proceeds of a fire insurance policy are not a substitute for the property the loss of which is the subject of indemnity."

Defendant says it made no agreement, express or implied, with plaintiff that it would pay for the debris removal or that any part of the insurance proceeds would be applied for that purpose. Therefore, concludes defendant, there being no privity of relationship between it and plaintiff, and no fraud or deceit alleged or proved, defendant has the right to the property benefitted by plaintiff's work and labor expended in removing the debris and to the insurance payments as well.

Plaintiff makes no claim to the insurance "fund" upon the ground he relied thereon similar to the reliance of a mechanic or materialman that forms the basis of an equitable claim to a building fund. He relies upon the basic premise that defendant should not be allowed to have the fruits of plaintiff's labor and also the money value of that labor. This, of course, is a simplified pronouncement of the doctrine of unjust enrichment, a theory which can, in some instances, have validity without privity of relationship.

The most prevalent implied-in-fact contract recognized under the doctrine of unjust enrichment is predicated upon a relationship between the parties from which the court infers an intent. However, the doctrine also recognizes an obligation *imposed* by law regardless of the intent of the parties. In these instances there need be no relationship that gives substance to an implied intent basic to the "contract" concept, rather the obligation is imposed because good conscience dictates that under the circumstances the person benefitted should make reimbursement.

Plaintiff's claim does not rest upon a quasi contract implied in fact but upon an equitable obligation *imposed* by law. It is true that defendant's right to the insurance payment was a contract right embodied in the policies of insurance, as explicated in *Russell v. Williams*, supra, nevertheless the indemnity payment was based in part upon a claim of loss that did not exist because plaintiff had already remedied the loss by his work for which he was not paid.

We are cited no California cases that are close aboard, and independent research reveals none. Lack of precedent applicable to the facts peculiar to this case is not surprising, however, as the authors of the Restatement recognize that the essential nature of equity cases concerned with problems of restitution makes definitive precedent unlikely. We are guided by the "Underlying Principles" delineated in the Restatement on Restitution: "The rules stated in the Restatement of this subject depend for their validity upon certain basic assumptions in regard to what is required by justice in the various situations. In this Topic, these are stated in the form of principles. They cannot be stated as rules since either they are too indefinite to be of value in a specific case or, for historical or other reasons, they are not universally applied. They are distinguished from rules in that they are intended only as general guides for the conduct of the courts * * *."

The governing principle is expressed in the opening sentence of the Restatement on Restitution, as follows: "The Restatement of this subject deals with situations in which one person is accountable to another on the ground that otherwise he would unjustly benefit or the other would unjustly suffer loss."

The question, simply stated, is whether in a jurisdiction that recognizes the equitable doctrine of unjust enrichment one party should be indemnified twice for the same loss, once in labor and materials and again in money, to the detriment (forfeiture) of the party who furnished the labor and materials. We conclude that the doctrine of unjust enrichment is applicable to the facts of this case, and that plaintiff is entitled to reimbursement out of the insurance proceeds paid defendant for work done by plaintiff.

The facts concerning the amount of insurance recovered by defendant and the percentage of the total proof of loss attributable to plaintiff's work are not altogether clear, probably because this is a proceeding for summary judgment before trial of the action. In any event, it is clear that defendant, in addition to taking over the property which plaintiff cleared of debris, also received indemnity insurance payments covering at least part of the cost for clearing that property of debris. The amount can be made certain by a trial on the merits, and if it develops that defendant recovered only a part of the cost for debris removal, this fact does not preclude a partial recovery by plaintiff. We learn from the Restatement, page 611: "Where a person is entitled to restitution from another because the other, without tortious conduct, has received a benefit, the measure of recovery for the benefit thus received is the value of what was received * * *."

Thus, to the extent defendant received insurance for debris removal performed by plaintiff, plaintiff should recover. If defendant received less than the value of plaintiff's work, as defendant seems to contend, then plaintiff should recover pro tanto.

The judgment is reversed.

Notes

1. In the excerpt that begins this chapter, Professor Laycock identifies three practical advantages to seeking restitution. Which of those three applies here?

2. *On procedure:* The *Kossian* court's references to "the most prevalent implied-in-fact contract recognized under the law of unjust enrichment" and to "a quasi-contract implied in fact" display a confusion about the difference between contracts implied-in-fact and contracts implied-in-law that unfortunately is not uncommon. As the Note on Approaching Restitution Cases, at p. 719 explained, implied-in-fact and implied-in-law contracts rest on different foundations. A contract is implied-in-fact when the parties' past dealings and relationship suggest that the recipient of a benefit implicitly promised to pay for it. By contrast, an implied-in-law contract, or quasi-contract, is created by a court to avoid unjust enrichment. Because both types of action were brought using the common law form of action known as assumpsit, the early cases easily confused them. Nonetheless, the distinction is important because quasi-contracts are "implied in law;" "implied-in-fact" contracts have to do with carrying out the parties' intent, not with avoiding unjust enrichment.

The *Kossian* court is also cavalier in its treatment of the distinction between law and equity. Although the courts of law and equity have been merged into a single judicial system in most jurisdictions, the historical distinction between law and equity can still have significant effects, as section A of Chapter 5 pointed out. The *Kossian* court mixes the language of law and equity fairly indiscriminately. So, is restitution legal or equitable?

The answer is both. An action seeking restitution could be brought in the law courts or in the equity courts, depending on the nature of the case and the remedy sought. *Kossian*, for example, is a legal action, with a legal remedy: a money judgment for the amount of the benefit the defendant unjustly received.

Yet, *Kossian* is not unusual in the way the opinion mixes the language of law and equity. This mixture can seem confusing, until one realizes that the word "equity" can be used in two senses. In one sense, it refers to the historical courts of equity, as distinguished from the courts of law. In that sense, restitution is not solely equitable in character.

Equity, however, has a broader sense, a sense in which it simply refers to fairness or justice. Restitution, with its focus on *unjust* enrichment, is equitable in character in the sense that both the law courts and the courts of equity focused on considerations of fairness and justice—equity—in order to "do the right thing."

3. *On the substantive law:* The plaintiff in *Kossian* had no claim against the insurance policies themselves, had no express or implied contract with the defendant, and was not defrauded or deceived by the defendant. Under those circumstances, why do the "ties of natural justice and equity" oblige the defendant to share the insurance proceeds?

According to the court, the reason is that the defendant will be "unjustly enriched" unless part of the insurance proceeds are paid over to the plaintiff. Because the insurance claim was compromised, however, it is almost certain that at trial the plaintiff will receive less than the contract price he agreed upon with Reichert, and perhaps even less than it cost him in labor and materials to do the job. Yet, the court indicates that Kossian will recover only the insurance proceeds for debris removal, and intimates that the defendant would not have an obligation to pay the plaintiff for his labor at all if no insurance proceeds were earmarked for the removal.

Is that the right result? The defendant has received more than just the insurance proceeds; the defendant has the benefit of the plaintiff's labor as well. There is nothing to suggest that the original contract price Kossian negotiated was out of line, and the defendant's property is certainly worth more as a result of the work that was done. Therefore, shouldn't there be an obligation to pay for the work, regardless of whether the defendant collected on the policy? Would it have mattered if the defendant knew of the plaintiff's contract with Reichert at some point after Reichert's default?

4. The Restatement provides that "officious intermeddlers" and "volunteers" are not entitled to restitution for the benefits they confer on another. Restatement of Restitution § 2. How would you determine whether the benefit in *Kossian* was conferred officiously or voluntarily? The case law is not much help: it seems to be generally accepted that "intermeddler" and "volunteer" are little more than labels used to justify, rather than to explain,

the result in a particular case. Saul Levmore, Explaining Restitution, 71 Va.L.Rev. 65 (1985).

Professor Levmore offers several insights as to why courts may require restitution in some cases of unsolicited benefits and not in others. His premise is that requiring restitution effectively creates a bargain between the parties, by requiring the defendant to pay the plaintiff for the value of the benefit received. Courts may be reluctant to create such a bargain for a number of reasons. It may be difficult for the court to decide on the actual value of the benefit that has been conferred. Further, even if the value of the benefit can be determined, it may not be clear that the recipient desired it or could afford it. Finally, by requiring the provider of services to bargain rather than allowing him to act first and get paid later, the courts support the development of active markets that promote efficient resource allocation.

Would Professor Levmore agree with the result in *Kossian?*

5. Professor Dan Dobbs has suggested a slightly different set of principles to decide these sorts of restitution cases:

> The first principle is that one who has conferred a benefit upon another with an intention to make a gift, has no equitable claim for relief against the recipient of the benefit in the absence of fraud, mistake, duress or undue influence. * * * The second principle is that one who confers a benefit upon another without affording that other the opportunity to reject the benefit, has no equitable claim for relief against the recipient of the benefit in the absence of some special policy that would outweigh the right of free choice in the benefited party.

Dan B. Dobbs, Handbook on the Law of Remedies 229 (1973). See also Dan B. Dobbs, 1 Law of Remedies § 4.9 (2d ed.1993). Would Professor Dobbs agree with the result in *Kossian?*

6. The tentative draft of the Restatement (Third) of Restitution and Unjust Enrichment provides that where real property is improved by mistake, the resulting enrichment lacks an adequate legal basis and is therefore unjust. If the remedy, however, would result in a forced exchange, the remedy will be limited to prevent undue prejudice to the property owner. Restatement (Third) of Restitution and Unjust Enrichment § 10 (Tentative Draft No. 1, 2001). Evaluating the prejudice or hardship to the property owner requires a case-by-case analysis in which the problems stressed by Professors Dobbs and Levmore—that if the owner cannot remove the improvements, he will have to raise the cash to pay for something he did not choose to have—play a central role. How would *Kossian* be decided under this provision?

7. In *Kossian*, the plaintiff performed his services under a mistaken belief that "one Reichert," with whom he contracted, still owned the property. Would it have made a difference if the plaintiff had known, before he started work, that Reichert had defaulted and the defendant had taken possession? Should a plaintiff ever get restitution if he knowingly performs services for someone who has not solicited them? According to the Restatement, a person who confers a benefit on another without mistake, coercion or request generally cannot claim restitution, "except where the benefit was necessary for the protection of the interests of the other or third persons." Restatement

of Restitution § 112. On acting to protect self-interest, see Daniel Friedmann, Unjust Enrichment, Pursuance of Self-Interest and the Limits of Free Riding, 36 Loy.L.A.L.Rev. 831 (2003).

In Berry v. Barbour, 279 P.2d 335 (Okla.1954), the defendant hired plaintiff to do some repairs on a building defendant owned. While plaintiff was working on the property, a fire broke out. (The plaintiff was not at fault in any way for the fire.) In extinguishing the blaze, firefighters cut several holes in the building's roof. Plaintiff repaired the holes without contacting defendant, who was in Germany at the time. Should the plaintiff have a valid claim for restitution?

According to the Restatement, a person who preserves the property of another can claim restitution if he was: (1) in possession of the property at the time; (2) it was not reasonably possible to communicate with the owner; (3) he had no reason to think that the services were unwanted; (4) he intended to charge for his services or to retain the property if it was not claimed; and (5) the owner accepted possession of the repaired or improved property. Restatement of Restitution § 117. The Restatement applies a similar rule when unsolicited services are provided to another in order to preserve life or health; the services must be necessary to prevent serious harm, and the person providing the services must expect compensation, and have no reason to believe the services are unwanted. Restatement of Restitution § 115.

How would the Restatement's principles apply in *Berry*? Would Professors Dobbs and Levmore agree that these factors should determine the result?

The tentative draft of the Restatement (Third) of Restitution and Unjust Enrichment takes a flexible approach to these questions, in each case authorizing restitution if the claimant intervenes effectively, "the circumstances justify the claimant's decision to intervene without prior agreement for payment" and it is reasonable to assume that the defendant would want the services performed. See Restatement (Third) of Restitution and Unjust Enrichment § 20 (Tentative Draft No. 2, 2002) (protection of other), § 21 (protection of property). To determine whether circumstances justify the decision, four factors are important: (1) the propriety of the claimant's intervention in the absence of contract; (2) the hardship to the defendant in being required to meet a noncontractual liability; (3) the potential for unjust enrichment if restitution is withheld; and (4) the social interest in encouraging the transaction in question. Restatement (Third) of Restitution and Unjust Enrichment, Part II, Introductory Note (Tentative Draft No. 2, 2002).

8. *Other cases of mistake.* So far, all of the cases discussed have involved improvements to real property. Similar principles apply to other services conferred on a defendant by mistake. For example, the Tentative Draft for the Restatement (Third) of Restitution and Unjust Enrichment § 9 provides that unjust enrichment occurs to the extent that:

(a) specific restitution is feasible;

(b) the benefit is subsequently realized in money or its equivalent;

(c) the recipient has revealed a willingness to pay for the benefit; or

(d) the recipient has been spared an otherwise necessary expense.

Generally speaking, the case for unjust enrichment is stronger when money, rather than services, is involved. Where a person pays money to another in the mistaken belief that he has a duty to do so, he can usually get restitution. Restatement of Restitution § 15. Why should it be easier to get restitution for money paid by mistake than for services rendered by mistake? Do the principles Professors Levmore and Dobbs advocate suggest an explanation?

9. In DCB Construction Co., Inc. v. Central City Development Co. ("CCDC"), 965 P.2d 115 (Colo.1998), CCDC leased an historic building to Tenant, to be used only for limited stakes gambling. The lease provided that Tenant would pay all costs of remodeling the building, that CCDC had the right to approve all plans, and that the historic character of the site would be preserved. Tenant contracted with DCB Construction ("DCB") to do the work, and CCDC approved the plans. As the lease required, Tenant posted a notice informing everyone involved in the improvements that CCDC was not liable for the improvements, and that CCDC's interest in the property could not be subjected to a lien for the improvements.

In November, 1992, DCB stopped work on the project because of Tenant's failure to pay. At that point, Tenant owed nearly $300,000 on the contract. In December, Tenant stopped paying rent. In February, CCDC evicted Tenant, but CCDC was unable to find another Tenant. DCB obtained a judgment against Tenant for just over $300,000, but Tenant was insolvent.

DCB sued CCDC for unjust enrichment. The trial court found in favor of DCB, and entered judgment against CCDC for $333,191, the amount Tenant owed for the work, plus interest and costs. On appeal, the Colorado Supreme Court applied the test found in Restatement of Restitution § 1: Did the defendant (1) receive a benefit, (2) at plaintiff's expense, which (3) it would be unjust for him to retain? The trial court had found that the improvements increased the value of CCDC's property, even though CCDC had been unable to re-lease it. Turning to whether the enrichment was unjust, however, the Court paused:

> The notion of what is or is not "unjust" is an inherently malleable and unpredictable standard. Because tenants frequently contract for improvements to leased property, the law must be sufficiently predictable so that the appropriate parties can adequately calculate and make adjustments for the risks they face. Landlords need to know, with some degree of certainty, what behavior and circumstances will subject them to these claims; and contractors likewise should be able to make risk-adjusted pricing decisions and implement appropriate payment-protection provisions. Thus, we think it is important to articulate a general rule, applicable in this context, that provides more stability and predictability than an ad hoc review.

965 P.2d at 120. Taking note of policies of protecting autonomy and rights of choice, the court concluded that "injustice in this context requires some type of improper, deceitful, or misleading conduct by the landlord." Id. at 122.

Chief Justice Mullarkey dissented. "There are many situations which fall short of wrongful conduct but are so unjust that the claim should lie," he argued. Id. at 123. Here, for example, there was evidence that CCDC had requested the improvements, that the lease provided for CCDC to retain the improvements, and that CCDC knew of and assisted in DCB's work. Therefore, it would be inequitable to allow CCDC to keep the improvements without paying for them.

Who has the better of the argument? How would the majority decide *Kossian*? The dissent? A similar problem can arise when a subcontractor performs services and is not paid by the contractor. If the property owner has not yet paid the contractor, can the subcontractor seek restitution? See Reisenfeld & Co. v. The Network Group, Inc., 277 F.3d 856 (6th Cir.2002) (under Ohio law, the type of wrongdoing required by *DCB Construction* would not be required in order to show that it would be unjust for a sub-broker to go unpaid when payment to the broker was excused by the broker's fraud); see also Doug Rendleman, Quantum Meruit for the Subcontractor: Has Restitution Jumped Off Dawson's Dock?, 79 Tex.L.Rev. 2055 (2001).

10. *On the remedy.* The remedy for unjust enrichment in *Kossian* would be a money judgment. As in the case of compensatory damages, the remedy would be substitutionary in character, giving the plaintiff an award of money as a substitute for the value of the benefit conferred on the defendant.

With restitution, as with compensatory damages, questions of how the benefit to the defendant is to be measured inevitably arise. Here, the court measures the defendant's unjust enrichment by the amount of the insurance proceeds attributable to the cost of cleaning up the property. Is that the proper measure? Why not the price the plaintiff and Reichert had negotiated? Why not the reasonable value of the plaintiff's services?

Think about what the appropriate measure of damages might be in some of the other situations suggested in the notes. If a doctor saves an unconscious person's life, is the measure of restitutionary recovery the value of the doctor's services, or the value of the person's life? Principles that determine the measure of damages are discussed in the next case.

C. RESTITUTION AND WRONGFULLY ACQUIRED BENEFITS

PROBLEM: COUNTRY LODGE V. MILLER (REPRISED) A RESTITUTION OPTION?

During the first year of the cider mill's operation, Miller saved $20,000 by dumping her apple mash into the river instead of installing an alternative means of disposal. Country Lodge lost $10,000 as a result of the pollution. Assuming that Country Lodge can establish that dumping the apple mash was a nuisance, could Country Lodge seek restitution rather than tort damages? In the language of the case that follows, could Miller waive the tort of nuisance and sue Miller in assumpsit? If so, how would the award be measured?

OLWELL v. NYE & NISSEN

Supreme Court of Washington, 1946
26 Wash.2d 282, 173 P.2d 652

MALLERY, JUSTICE.

On May 6, 1940, plaintiff, E.L. Olwell, sold and transferred to the defendant corporation his one-half interest in Puget Sound Egg Packers, a Washington corporation having its principal place of business in Tacoma. By the terms of the agreement, the plaintiff was to retain full ownership in an "Eggsact" egg-washing machine, formerly used by Puget Sound Egg Packers. The defendant promised to make it available for delivery to the plaintiff on or before June 15, 1940. It appears that the plaintiff arranged for and had the machine stored in a space adjacent to the premises occupied by the defendant but not covered by its lease. Due to the scarcity of labor immediately after the outbreak of the war, defendant's treasurer, without the knowledge or consent of the plaintiff, ordered the egg washer taken out of storage. The machine was put into operation by defendant on May 31, 1941, and thereafter for a period of three years was used approximately one day a week in the regular course of the defendant's business. Plaintiff first discovered this use in January or February of 1945 when he happened to be at the plant on business and heard the machine operating. Thereupon plaintiff offered to sell the machine to defendant for $600 or half of its original cost in 1929. A counter offer of $50 was refused and approximately one month later this action was commenced to recover the reasonable value of defendant's use of the machine, and praying for $25 per month from the commencement of the unauthorized use until the time of trial. * * * The court entered judgment for plaintiff in the amount of $10 per week for the period of 156 weeks covered by the statute of limitations, or $1,560, and gave the plaintiff his costs.

The theory of the respondent was that the tort of conversion could be "waived" and suit brought in quasi-contract, upon a contract implied in law, to recover, as restitution, the profits which inured to appellant as a result of its wrongful use of the machine. With this the trial court agreed and in its findings of facts found that the use of the machine "resulted in a benefit to the users, in that said use saves the users approximately $1.43 per hour of use as against the expense which would be incurred were eggs to be washed by hand; that said machine was used by Puget Sound Egg Packers and defendant, on an average of one day per week from May of 1941, until February of 1945 at an average saving of $10.00 per each day of use."

In substance, the argument presented by the assignments of error is that the principle of unjust enrichment, or quasi-contract, is not of universal application, but is imposed only in exceptional cases because of special facts and circumstances and in favor of particular persons; that respondent had an adequate remedy in an action at law for replevin or claim and delivery; that any damages awarded to the plaintiff should be based upon the use or rental value of the machine and should bear some reasonable relation to its market value. * * *

It is uniformly held that in cases where the defendant *tortfeasor* has benefitted by his wrong, the plaintiff may elect to "waive the tort" and bring an action in assumpsit for restitution. Such an action arises out of a duty imposed by law devolving upon the defendant to repay an unjust and unmerited enrichment.

It is clear that the saving in labor cost which appellant derived from its use of respondent's machine constituted a benefit.

According to the Restatement of Restitution, § 1(b), p. 12,

"A person confers a benefit upon another if he gives to the other possession of or some other interest in money, land, chattels, or choses in action, performs services beneficial to or at the request of the other, satisfies a debt or a duty of the other, or in any way adds to the other's security or advantage. *He confers a benefit not only where he adds to the property of another, but also where he* saves the other from expense or loss. The word 'benefit', therefore denotes any form of advantage." (Italics ours)

It is also necessary to show that while appellant benefitted from its use of the egg-washing machine, respondent thereby incurred a loss. It is argued by appellant that since the machine was put into storage by respondent, who had no present use for it, and for a period of almost three years did not know that appellant was operating it and since it was not injured by its operation and the appellant never adversely claimed any title to it, nor contested respondent's right of repossession upon the latter's discovery of the wrongful operation, that the respondent was not damaged because he is as well off as if the machine had not been used by appellant.

The very essence of the nature of property is the right to its exclusive use. Without it, no beneficial right remains. However plausible, the appellant cannot be heard to say that his wrongful invasion of the respondent's property right to exclusive use is not a loss compensable in law. To hold otherwise would be subversive of all property rights since his use was admittedly wrongful and without claim of right. The theory of unjust enrichment is applicable in such a case.

We agree with appellant that respondent could have elected a "common garden variety of action," as he calls it, for the recovery of damages. It is also true that except where provided for by statute, punitive damages are not allowed, the basic measure for the recovery of damages in this state being compensation. If, then, respondent had been *limited* to redress *in tort* for damages, as appellant contends, the court below would be in error in refusing to make a finding as to the value of the machine. In such case the award of damages must bear a reasonable relation to the value of the property.

But respondent here had an election. He chose rather to waive his right of action *in tort* and to sue *in assumpsit* on the implied contract. Having so elected, he is entitled to the measure of restoration which accompanies the remedy.

"Actions for restitution have for their primary purpose taking from the defendant and restoring to the plaintiff something to which the plaintiff is entitled, or if this is not done, causing the defendant to pay the plaintiff an amount which will restore the plaintiff to the position in which he was before the defendant received the benefit. If the value of what was received and what was lost were always equal, there would be no substantial problem as to the amount of recovery, since actions of restitution are not punitive. In fact, however, the plaintiff frequently has lost more than the defendant has gained, and sometimes the defendant has gained more than the plaintiff has lost.

"In such cases the measure of restitution is determined with reference to the tortiousness of the defendant's conduct or the negligence or other fault of one or both of the parties in creating the situation giving rise to the right to restitution. If the defendant was tortious in his acquisition of the benefit he is required to pay for what the other has lost although that is more than the recipient benefitted. *If he was consciously tortious in acquiring the benefit, he is also deprived of any profit derived from his subsequent dealing with it.* If he was no more at fault than the claimant, he is not required to pay for losses in excess of benefit received by him and he is permitted to retain gains which result from his dealing with the property." (Italics ours)

Restatement of Restitution, pp. 595, 596.

Respondent may recover the profit derived by the appellant from the use of the machine.

[The court then held that the plaintiff could not recover more than he had prayed for in the complaint, and directed the trial court to reduce the judgment to $25.00 per month, or $900.]

Notes

1. In the excerpt that begins this chapter, Professor Laycock identifies three practical advantages to seeking restitution. Which of those three applies here?

2. *On procedure.* "Assumpsit" was the common law form of action used to bring a quasi-contract claim. As you might remember from your civil procedure class, the forms of action were pleading devices. To bring a case in the law courts, the plaintiff had to fit it to one of the recognized forms, which were often highly technical.

Most jurisdictions have abandoned the forms of action in favor of modern rules of code or notice pleading. Under modern pleading, to bring a restitution case, or any other case, it is simply necessary to set forth the facts that entitle the plaintiff to relief. Nonetheless, some understanding of the forms of action is helpful, particularly in reading the older cases.

The form of action of assumpsit required the plaintiff to allege that the defendant had received some benefit from the plaintiff, and (implicitly) promised to pay for it. Assumpsit could be further broken down into what were known as the "common counts" based on the nature of the benefit received: money had and received, goods sold and delivered, quantum meruit (the value of labor done), and so on. Thus, by "waiving" the tort form of action and suing in assumpsit, the plaintiff could base his claim on the benefit the defendant had received rather than on the harm the plaintiff had suffered.

Yet, the phrase "waiving the tort and suing in assumpsit" is potentially misleading, if "waiving" is taken to mean relinquishing a right or claim against the defendant. By choosing to sue in assumpsit for unjust enrichment rather than in tort for the harm caused, the plaintiff is in no sense relinquishing any right to recover from the defendant. Indeed, frequently it is the tortious character of the defendant's actions that makes the enrichment clearly unjust.

The phrase is also troublesome in connection with the notion of election of remedies, which was introduced earlier at p. 464. Apparently unaware that the "promise to pay" is a fiction forced on plaintiffs by the need to plead in assumpsit, some courts have held that a plaintiff who seeks relief on a quasi-contract theory has "elected" to affirm the transaction, and cannot later change to a tort theory of recovery. The better view would recognize that it is unjust enrichment, not a promise, that justifies restitution; so long as there is no double recovery, there is no inconsistency between tort and restitution in this context.

3. *On the substantive law.* Not all torts can be "waived." For example, it is generally agreed that the plaintiff in a defamation suit does not have the option of foregoing damages in order to recover the profits the defendant's publication earned. Hart v. E.P. Dutton & Co., 197 Misc. 274, 93 N.Y.S.2d 871 (Sup.Ct.1949), aff'd, 277 A.D. 935, 98 N.Y.S.2d 773 (1950); Dan B. Dobbs, Law of Remedies § 7.2 (2d ed.1993). How should a court go about deciding what torts can be waived? That is, when can a plaintiff sue in restitution to recover the benefits of defendant's tortious conduct?

According to Professor Palmer, courts are slowly moving away from the notion that assumpsit is only available as an alternative cause of action for a select number of torts, and toward recognizing that an action in restitution should always be available when the defendant has acquired a benefit through tortious wrongdoing. George E. Palmer, Law of Restitution § 2.1 (1978). As this idea becomes more generally accepted, however, courts will need to develop some principle to determine whether the defendant's benefit actually was derived from the invasion of the plaintiff's right.

Professor Friedmann has attempted to articulate such a principle:

[R]estitution may be justified on the general principle that a person who obtains—though not necessarily tortiously—a benefit at the expense of another through appropriation of a property or quasi-property interest held by the other person is unjustly enriched and should be liable to the other for any benefit attributable to the appropriation. This principle draws its strength from fundamental concepts of property that prohibit exploitation of another's right—even if the other is unable or unwilling to exploit the right himself—without his consent. But unlike an approach based on traditional property concepts, it permits restitution in cases involving "nonexclusive" interests—quasi-property—and may even be extended * * * to certain kinds of contract rights that may, for purposes of this analysis, be considered to be proprietary. In addition, the principle abandons the waiver-of-tort concept altogether, permitting restitution even if the defendant's act is not a tort or, if prima facie a tort, excused or justified.

Daniel Friedmann, Restitution of Benefits Obtained Through the Appropriation of Property or the Commission of a Wrong, 80 Colum.L.Rev. 504, 509 (1980). See also James S. Rogers, Restitution for Wrongs and the Restatement (Third) of the Law of Restitution and Unjust Enrichment, 42 Wake Forest L.Rev. 55 (2007).

Would Professor Friedmann allow restitution in the *Country Lodge* problem? Does the interest in being free from pollution qualify as a "quasi-property" interest?

4. According to the doctrine of balancing the hardships, a court might not order Miller to install pollution control devices that cost $20,000 in order to avoid a $10,000 harm, although it would order her to pay damages to Country Lodge. This result is frequently justified as economically efficient: it would be wasteful to expend $20,000 to avoid the loss of $10,000. If Country Lodge is granted restitution, won't that undercut the economically efficient result? Does this explain why the tort of nuisance is not "waivable"?

Wouldn't the same argument apply to *Olwell,* however? Isn't using an egg-washing machine—especially in war-time—more socially valuable than letting it sit in a shed? Shouldn't Puget Sound Egg Packers be encouraged to put this machine to use, contingent on their willingness to pay the plaintiff's damages?

5. Professor Friedmann's principle would allow restitution even where the defendant's act is not wrongful. Does this seem correct? Suppose that during a storm, a ship owner orders the plaintiff's goods jettisoned in order to save the lives of the crew and passengers. Should the owner pay restitution to the plaintiff? If the owner jettisons the plaintiff's goods to save his own? If the owner jettisons goods that he promised to sell to the plaintiff at the voyage's end? What if the plaintiff was planning to resell those goods in his store?

6. *On the remedy: Measuring the restitutionary recovery.* If the ship owner in Note 5 above, or Miller in the *Country Lodge* problem, owes restitution to the plaintiff, how is the recovery to be measured? As *Olwell* notes, there are three possibilities, depending on the facts of the particular case:

The plaintiff's loss and the defendant's gain may be equal. In such a case, "There [is] no substantial problem as to the amount of recovery, since actions of restitution are not punitive." Of course, if the plaintiff's loss and the defendant's gain are equal, there is also no immediately apparent reason to sue in restitution. The plaintiff can sue in tort and recover the same amount. In such cases, there may be a conceptual difference between tort and restitution, but there is no practical difference in the amount recovered.

There may, however, be other practical consequences to the choice. Because of quasi-contract's distinct historical roots, some technical distinctions between tort and quasi-contract still exist. Thus, in some states, different rules with regard to the statute of limitations, survivorship, and sovereign immunity may apply depending on the plaintiff's choice of tort or quasi-contract.

The plaintiff's loss may be greater than the defendant's gain. Then, "If the defendant was tortious in his acquisition of the benefit he is required to pay for what the other has lost although that is more than the recipient benefitted."

If the theory of the plaintiff's case is unjust enrichment, why should his recovery ever exceed the benefit the defendant received? Measuring recovery by the plaintiff's loss is inconsistent with the conceptual goal of preventing unjust enrichment, to the extent the plaintiff's loss exceeds the defendant's gain. Suppose the defendant has converted the plaintiff's property and sold it, foolishly, for far less than it was worth. If the plaintiff sues in assumpsit, should he recover the value of the item, or the amount the defendant actually received? According to *Olwell*, the answer has been the former, but is that really consistent with a theory of preventing unjust enrichment?

Formal pleadings aside, another way to look at the issue would be, where restitution and tort point to inconsistent results, which should predominate? Should the goal of tort law—restoring the plaintiff to her rightful position—be undercut because the plaintiff selected the wrong legal theory? Allowing the plaintiff to recover her losses even when they exceed the defendant's gain effectively means that in cases where both tort and restitution actions are available, at a minimum the tort goal of restoring the plaintiff to her rightful position will be served.

The defendant's gain may be greater than the plaintiff's loss. "If [the defendant] was consciously tortious in acquiring the benefit, he is also deprived of any profit derived from his subsequent dealing with it."

Depriving the defendant of profits is usually justified by invoking the principle that "No one should profit from his own wrongdoing." Restatement of Restitution § 3. But while this principle may justify requiring the defendant to disgorge profits, does it necessarily justify handing them over to the plaintiff?

Often, awarding the plaintiff the defendant's profits is justified because the defendant has deprived the plaintiff of an opportunity to make a profit himself. Thus, in cases of unfair competition, or interference with contract, where the plaintiff and the defendant are in the same business, awarding the plaintiff the defendant's profits in a way simply acknowledges that if the defendant had not interfered, the plaintiff might have made those profits himself. Similarly, in trademark cases, an award of profits is often justified as compensating the plaintiff for the loss of profits he might have made himself, had the defendant not violated his trademark.

Where an award of profits can be thought of as compensating the plaintiff for the loss of the opportunity to make the same profit himself, justifying restitution is straightforward. As in the first of *Olwell*'s categories, the defendant's gain is equal to the plaintiff's loss. In other cases, however, this justification may not be available. In *Olwell* itself, for example, the plaintiff lacked the capacity to make use of the machine the defendant converted, and so his loss—even in terms of opportunity—was clearly less than the defendant's gain. The only loss Olwell suffered was the loss of the opportunity to rent or sell the machine. Why should he recover more? The defendant may have profited, but not at the plaintiff's expense!

Thus, if the plaintiff has done nothing to earn a profit, didn't expect to earn one, and couldn't have earned it himself had he tried, why should he get a windfall? Consider the following remarks, made in a copyright infringement case:

> It is true that if the infringer makes greater profits than the copyright owner lost, because the infringer is a more efficient producer than the owner or sells in a different market, the owner is allowed to capture the additional profit even though it does not represent a loss to him. It may seem wrong to penalize the infringer for his superior efficiency and give the owner a windfall. But it discourages infringement. By preventing infringers from obtaining any net profit it makes any would-be infringer negotiate directly with the owner of a copyright that he wants to use, rather than bypass the market by stealing the copyright and forcing the owner to seek compensation from the courts for his loss. Since the infringer's gain might exceed the owner's loss, especially as loss is measured by a court, limiting damages to that loss would not effectively deter this kind of forced exchange.

Taylor v. Meirick, 712 F.2d 1112 (7th Cir.1983). Does this justification sound familiar? What is the relationship between disgorgement and punitive damages? See Gail Heriot, Civilizing Punitive Damages: Lessons from Restitution, 36 Loy.L.A.L.Rev. 869 (2003); Andrew Kull, Restitution's Outlaws, 78 Chicago–Kent L.Rev. 17 (2003).

Some statutory schemes rely on disgorgement to punish and deter violations. E.g., Balance Dynamics Corp. v. Schmitt Industries, Inc., 204 F.3d 683 (6th Cir.) (disgorgement available under Lanham Act where bad faith is shown); cert. denied, 531 U.S. 927, 121 S.Ct. 306, 148 L.Ed.2d 245 (2000). A consensus seems to be forming that agencies that are authorized to seek equitable relief are also authorized to seek disgorgement, even if the statute does not expressly convey that authority. See FTC v. Verity International, Ltd., 443 F.3d 48 (2d Cir.2006), cert. denied, 549 U.S. 1278, 127 S.Ct. 1868, 167 L.Ed.2d 317 (2007) (collecting cases). See also George P. Roach, A Default Rule of Omnipotence: Implied Jurisdiction and Exaggerated Remedies in Equity for Federal Agencies, 12 Fordham J.Corp. & Fin.L. 1 (2007). On SEC efforts to seek disgorgement under Sarbanes–Oxley, including a good discussion of accounting and offset problems, see Elaine Buckberg & Frederick C. Dunbar, Disgorgement: Punitive Demands and Remedial Offers, 63 Bus.Law. 347–381 (2008). On antitrust, see Einer Elhauge, Disgorgement as an Antitrust Remedy, 76 Antitrust L.J. ___ (2009).

Not all conscious tortfeasors, however, are required to give up their profits. The classic hypothetical exploring the limits of disgorgement runs along these lines: If an artist steals paint, brushes and canvas and creates a masterpiece, can the victim of the theft recover the entire market value of the painting by way of restitution? The answer is no. The painting's value is largely the product of the artist's skill, not of the theft. Thus, at some point, it is inappropriate to measure restitution by profits, if the profits are primarily attributable to the defendant's skill and efforts, not to the wrongdoing. The plaintiff's recovery would be limited to the value of the stolen property.

By this logic, in *Olwell,* the plaintiff would recover the rental value of the egg-washing machine. (Of course, even this award can be conceptualized as restitutionary. The defendant benefitted, at a minimum, by not having to rent or buy a machine to wash his eggs. Although the rental value is general damages for a temporary taking of property, on the facts of *Olwell,* rental value exceeded the plaintiff's actual losses, because the plaintiff had no plans to rent the machine. Thus, on the facts of a case like *Olwell,* general damages in tort are actually restitutionary in character.) Similarly, in patent cases, recovery is limited by statute to a reasonable royalty or licensing fee, and in trademark cases, the court may, in its discretion, so limit the recovery.

Even if a court decides that disgorgement is appropriate, it may still take the defendant's efforts into account in two ways. First, it may consider the defendant's efforts in choosing how to measure his profits. For example, in *Olwell,* why didn't the court measure the recovery by the percentage of the plant's profits proportionate to the increased production the machine made possible? Wouldn't that be a more accurate measure of the defendant's profits than the labor costs saved? Although the court did not explicitly consider the possibility, profits above the labor expenses saved are more directly attributable to the defendant's skill in marketing than to the egg-washing machine. After all, the defendant could have made those profits without infringing the plaintiff's rights simply by hiring more workers.

A second way to take the defendant's efforts into account is to apportion the profits between the defendant's efforts and the product of the plaintiff's property. The leading case is Sheldon v. Metro–Goldwyn Pictures Corp., 309 U.S. 390, 60 S.Ct. 681, 84 L.Ed. 825 (1940). Metro–Goldwyn produced a movie that plagiarized the plaintiff's play. While Metro–Goldwyn was clearly liable to the plaintiff for the profits attributable to the infringement of plaintiff's copyright, the Court found it necessary to apportion the profits, because, "The testimony showed quite clearly that in the creation of profits from the exhibition of a motion picture, the talent and popularity of the 'motion picture stars' generally constitutes the main drawing power of the picture, and that this is especially true where the title of the picture is not identified with any well-known play or novel." 309 U.S. at 407, 60 S.Ct. at 687. Therefore, the Court affirmed an award of twenty per cent of the net profits to the plaintiffs. See also Boardman v. Phipps, [1967] 2 A.C. 46 (House of Lords 1966) (requiring disgorgement of profits, but allowing "liberal recovery" in quantum meruit for the defendants' work and skill); Victor P. Goldberg, The Net Profits Puzzle, 97 Colum.L.Rev. 524 (1997) (discussing Buchwald v. Paramount Pictures Corp., 13 U.S.P.Q.2d 1497 (Cal.Super.Ct.1990) (stolen idea for a movie)).

Thus, *Olwell*'s assertion that a conscious wrongdoer will always be stripped of his profits is probably over broad. As Professor Palmer has noted, there are "no easy formulas" to determine "whether, or the extent to which, the defendant's gain is the product not solely of the plaintiff's interest but also of contributions made by the defendant. * * * Instead, the court must resort to general considerations of fairness, taking into account the nature of the defendant's wrong, the relative extent of his contribution, and the feasibility of separating this from the contribution traceable to the plaintiff's interest." George E. Palmer, Law of Restitution § 2.12 at 161 (1978).

Despite *Olwell*'s assertions, restitution in quasi-contract for conversion has usually been measured by the value of the chattel. Restatement of Restitution § 151. If the property itself has increased in value, or generated direct profits, those profits may be recovered, but where the defendant has used the property, the recovery has generally been measured by the reasonable value of the property's use. Restatement of Restitution § 157 comment d. Similarly, in patent cases, and at the court's discretion in trademark cases, an infringer's "profits" are measured by a reasonable royalty (the equivalent of rental value) rather than by the infringer's actual profits.

Another alternative to a profit-based measure is to measure recovery by the expenses the defendant saved. An interesting example is City of Chicago v. Roppolo, 113 Ill.App.3d 602, 69 Ill.Dec. 435, 447 N.E.2d 870 (1983). In *Roppolo,* the defendant, a developer, had promised to move and rehabilitate a landmark building in order to get a zoning amendment critical to his project approved. Instead, he just tore down the building. The court imposed a "constructive trust" on the developer, in the amount of the expenses he saved by not having to move and rehabilitate the building. See also Daniel Farber, Reassessing *Boomer*: Justice, Efficiency, and Nuisance Law, in Property Law and Legal Education: Essays in Honor of John Cribbet (P. Hay & M. Hoeflich, eds. 1988)(damages in nuisance cases should be measured by the amount the defendant would have had to pay to acquire the right to pollute).

Sometimes, however, recovery is measured by the defendant's actual profits. In quasi-contract, the leading example is Edwards v. Lee's Administrator, 265 Ky. 418, 96 S.W.2d 1028 (1936). There, a property owner recovered a part of the profits his neighbor had earned by offering tours of a cave that extended under both parcels. By analogy, there are a number of tort causes of action in which the tort measure of damages arguably allows profits to be recovered, interference with contract and appropriation of the right of publicity being the most common examples. See George E. Palmer, Law of Restitution § 2.9. (1978). And in trademark, copyright, and insider trading cases, profits are frequently recovered. See Douglas Laycock, Modern American Remedies 583–85 (3d ed.2002).

For a review of these issues, see Daniel Friedmann, Restitution for Wrongs: The Measure of Recovery, 79 Tex.L.Rev. 1879 (2001). For a discussion of how a society's underlying values might be reflected in the way it determines the measure of restitution, see Hanoch Dagan, Unjust Enrichment: A Study of Private Law and Public Values (1998). For a British perspective, see James Edelman, Gain–Based Damages: Contract, Tort, Equity and Intellectual Property (2002).

D. RESTITUTION AND SOLICITED BENEFITS

HUTCHISON v. PYBURN
Court of Appeals of Tennessee, 1977
567 S.W.2d 762

DROWOTA, JUDGE.

This is a case involving fraud in the sale of realty in which plaintiffs-vendees were awarded both rescission of the deed and punitive damages by the Chancery Court of Davidson County. Since the case is before us without a bill of exceptions, our recitation of the facts follows the allegations of plaintiffs-appellees and the findings of the Chancellor.

In January of 1973, plaintiffs William and Jo Lynn Hutchison purchased a house and lot from defendants Robert and Carol Pyburn for $24,000.00. Of this amount, $23,500.00 represented a loan from Home Federal Savings & Loan Association which was secured by a deed of trust. Defendant Jack Williams built the house and sold the property to the Pyburns, and his brother, defendant John Williams, was real estate agent for the Pyburns in the sale of the property to plaintiffs. In July of 1973, plaintiffs noticed seepage from their sewage disposal system, investigated, and discovered that their property had not been approved as a home site by the Metropolitan Board of Health because it lacked the requisite topsoil to sustain the septic tank and overflow field needed for sewage disposal. Further, the Metropolitan Department of Code Administration had been informed of the problem, and had issued a building permit to defendant Jack Williams only by mistake. Evidently defendant Pyburn had become aware of the sewage problem after purchasing the property from Williams and had prevailed on Williams to release him from his obligation to purchase it, whereupon Pyburn and Williams negotiated the sale to plaintiffs.

Plaintiffs brought suit, alleging that the defendants Pyburn and Williams knew of the property's condition and that there was no practical means of correcting it at the time of the sale. They charged that defendants' failure to inform them of the sewage problem amounted to fraud and deceit, and that the condition of the property represented a breach of the warranties contained in the deed. The Chancellor dismissed the case against defendant John Williams, but entered a decree in favor of plaintiffs against the Pyburns and Jack Williams. The decree allowed plaintiffs rescission of the contract, incidental damages in the form of expenses incurred in connection with the property, moving costs, and attorney's fees, from all of which was deducted the reasonable rental value of the property for the period of plaintiffs' occupancy. In addition to the sum due plaintiffs in incidental damages, which was set at $3,168.94, the Chancellor assessed $5,000.00 in punitive damages against the defendants and made a specific finding that defendants' misrepresentation was fraudulent. * * *

Defendants * * * assert that the trial court erred in awarding punitive damages for misrepresentations incident to a contract when rescission of the contract and deed was also decreed. * * *

In Tennessee it is established that courts of equity are empowered to award punitive damages. * * *

One objection raised to the award of punitive damages in this case is that it is inconsistent with rescission of the deed under the doctrine of election of remedies. That doctrine estops a plaintiff who has clearly chosen to pursue one of two inconsistent and irreconcilable remedies from later resorting to the other. The "essential element" here is "that the remedies be inconsistent." * * * There is no such inconsistency, however, between the remedy of rescission and an award of punitive damages. The latter * * * is designed to penalize and deter, and results from the nature of defendant's conduct rather than from the harm it causes. The character of punitive damages, then, is in no wise inconsistent with rescission and its concomitant remedies of restitution and incidental damages. The latter are all aimed at *redressing* the harm done the plaintiff and, while this means they may be considered inconsistent with a remedy such as compensatory damages, which also aims at redress but by a different method, they may not be so considered with respect to the *deterrent* sanction of punitive damages. Thus, plaintiffs' choice of rescission as a means of redress is not inconsistent with their request for punitive damages and does not estop them from making that request.

Similarly, punitive damages do not conflict with the theoretical aim of equitable rescission, which is to return the parties to the status in which they were prior to the transaction. That aim is simply one approach to redressing the wrong done to plaintiff, an approach that differs from that of compensatory damages, which are intended to redress the wrong by directly compensating the plaintiff for what he has lost. But again, punitive damages are not intended to redress the plaintiff's wrong, but to make an example of the defendant's conduct. Since they thus relate to considerations totally different from those of rescission, punitive damages neither frustrate rescission's redressing of plaintiff's wrong by return of the parties to the *status quo,* nor are they inconsistent with it.

Cases often announce the rule that there must be proof of "actual damages" before punitive damages may be awarded. The cases are unclear, however, as to the meaning of "actual damages" in this context. It has been logically suggested that the phrase should mean no more than that the plaintiff cannot get punitive damages without proving a valid cause of action, that is, without showing that he has been legally injured in some way, which is really a roundabout way of saying that there can be no cause of action for punitive damages alone. * * * That approach, applied broadly, would allow recovery of punitive damages if plaintiff, in addition to showing the requisite degree of bad conduct and intent by defendant, could merely prove his entitlement to injunctive relief or nominal damages. But we need not go so far here in construing "actual damages" not to mean strictly an award of compensatory damages. Returning to the case before us, we hold simply that plaintiffs' proof of their entitlement to rescission of the deed, refund of the purchase price, and incidental damages such as moving expenses, shows sufficient harm and loss to them to satisfy the "actual damages" prerequisite to recovery of punitive damages in Tennessee.

Finally, defendants point to a proposition which we agree is the general rule in Tennessee and elsewhere: punitive damages may not be recovered in an action for breach of contract. This case, however, is not one for breach of contract, for plaintiffs asked that the contract be made a nullity by rescission. Further, the pleadings and memorandum of the trial court indicate that the main thrust of the action is a claim of fraud and misrepresentation against all the defendants, although an additional claim of breach of warranty was asserted against the Pyburns, with whom plaintiffs were in privity. Thus, regardless of any overtones of contract that may appear in this suit, there also clearly exists here a cause of action against all defendants for the sort of tortious misconduct required as a basis for recovery of punitive damages * * *. For this reason, such a recovery cannot be defeated by the rule that punitive damages are unavailable in contract actions. * * *

NOTES

1. In the excerpt that begins this chapter, Professor Laycock identifies three practical advantages to seeking restitution. Which of those three applies here?

To understand why a plaintiff might seek restitution instead of damages, some background on the tort of fraud is necessary. In most jurisdictions, the measure of damages for fraud is the difference between the value the plaintiff expected to receive if the defendant's representations had been true, and the value the plaintiff did receive. This "benefit of the bargain" measure would seem to belong more to the law of contracts than to the law of torts. Its adoption by a majority of jurisdictions represents the recognition that fraud in the inducement to a contract lies on the border between tort and contract.

A few jurisdictions, however, keep to a more "tort-like" measure, measuring damages by how much the plaintiff is "out-of-pocket"; that is, by the difference between the value of what the plaintiff had before the tort and the value of what he has after.

Both of these measures, however, require that the misrepresentation affect the value of what the plaintiff bargained for. If that is not the case, perhaps because some other factor intervened to affect the values involved, rescission may offer a better chance at recovery. For example, in Goodwin v. Dick, 220 Mass. 556, 107 N.E. 925 (1915), the plaintiff bought stock on the intentionally false representation that it was treasury stock. The stock was worthless, but it would also have been worthless if it had actually been treasury stock. Under the benefit of the bargain measure, the value of what plaintiff was promised and the value of what he got were the same, so the plaintiff would recover nothing. Under an "out-of-pocket" approach, the result would be the same, because the misrepresentation did not cause the stock to be worthless. Yet, if the plaintiff had sued for rescission, he would have recovered the purchase price. In such a case, so far as the plaintiff is concerned, it is rescission or nothing at all.

In *Hutchison*, of course, causation is not a problem. The misrepresentations clearly affected the value of the property. So, why did the plaintiffs rescind instead of seeking damages?

2. *On procedure.* The remedy of rescission avoids, or cancels, a transaction. Where the transaction is executory, rescission amounts to no more than an announcement that the deal is off. More commonly, rescission is sought when a plaintiff has transferred something of value to a defendant and then wants it, or its equivalent in money, returned. Thus, restitution usually goes hand in hand with rescission, as each party is required to give up the benefits it acquired under the voided transaction in order to return the other to the status quo ante.

Although *Hutchison* speaks of rescission as an equitable remedy, rescission was not restricted to the equity courts. At law, rescission was available by an action in quasi-contract. Thus, in *Hutchison,* the plaintiff could have rescinded the contract by offering to return the property, and then sued in quasi-contract for the return of the purchase price. (One of the distinctions between legal and equitable rescission is that, at law, the plaintiff rescinded the contract by tendering restitution to the defendant and then suing. In the equity courts, tender was not required; the plaintiff sued, and the court rescinded the contract if the plaintiff prevailed.)

Depending on the case, there can be advantages to seeking equitable rescission. In a case like *Hutchison*, rescission, or cancellation, of the deed is the type of remedy that would not have been available at law. While the law courts effected restitution by entering a money judgment in the plaintiff's favor, the equity courts could order the defendant to return the specific property he had received. As a result, equitable rescission gave the plaintiff an advantage over the defendant's creditors, if the defendant was insolvent. Indeed, a court of equity could create a lien on the property in order to secure the plaintiff's entitlement to return of the purchase price and incidental damages.

The choice between an equitable and legal remedy raises an issue discussed in Chapter 2. In order to have the benefits of equitable rescission, must the plaintiff show that the legal remedy is inadequate? The answer to that question is complex. Certainly, there are cases in which the availability of rescission in equity has turned on the adequacy of the legal remedy. Thus, plaintiffs have been allowed an equitable remedy where they could show that they sought the return of specific, unique property, or that complete relief required cancellation of a document (which could not be accomplished by a law court), or that the defendant was insolvent and only an equitable remedy could guarantee recovery. Conversely they have been denied equitable relief when they simply sought return of the purchase price.

At the same time, however, equitable rescission has been allowed in many cases without any discussion of the inadequacy requirement. In part, this may be because for a time there was no way to rescind a contract for fraud at common law. Thus, equity courts originally took cognizance of claims for rescission based on fraud because there was no equivalent action at law and never let go, even after the law courts developed one.

If this explanation were completely accurate, however, equitable rescission would always be available for contracts induced by fraud. Oddly, it is not. While almost all courts allow the defrauded purchaser of land to seek rescission in equity, without concern for the adequacy of the legal remedy, many jurisdictions limit the defrauded purchaser of goods to his legal, quasi-contract remedy unless the legal remedy is inadequate. At bottom, the best one can say is that sometimes an adequate legal remedy bars equitable rescission, sometimes it does not, largely without rhyme or reason.

3. *On the substantive law.* Rescission and restitution are potentially available as remedies in a variety of contract cases. As *Hutchison* indicates, a contract can be rescinded for fraud, or, for that matter, for duress or coercion. When a contract is induced by merely innocent or negligent misrepresentation, rescission and restitution may be the only remedy available, if the jurisdiction does not recognize a tort action for negligent or innocent misrepresentation. See Emily Sherwin, Nonmaterial Misrepresentation: Damages, Rescission, and the Possibility of Efficient Fraud, 36 Loy.L.A.L.Rev. 1017 (2003). Rescission and restitution are also available as remedies for a substantial breach of contract, as discussed in the notes following the next case.

Restitution is also an important remedy in cases of failed contracts. For example, where a plaintiff has conferred a benefit on a defendant pursuant to a contract that turns out to be invalid or unenforceable, restitution may be the only appropriate remedy. Thus, in Pyeatte v. Pyeatte, 135 Ariz. 346, 661 P.2d 196 (App.1982), Mr. and Ms. Pyeatte agreed that she would support him through law school, and that after he graduated, he would support her further education. One year after Mr. Pyeatte's graduation, however, he and Ms. Pyeatte dissolved their marriage. In the dissolution proceeding, the trial court awarded Ms. Pyeatte $23,000 in damages for the husband's breach of their oral contract.

On appeal, the court found that the terms of the oral agreement were not sufficiently certain to create a binding contract. Nonetheless, the court remanded the matter to the trial court, holding that Ms. Pyeatte stated a cause of action for restitution:

> Appellee * * * argues that appellant's education, which she subsidized and which he obtained through the exhaustion of community assets constitutes a benefit for which he must, in equity, make restitution. * * *
>
> Restitution is available to a party to an agreement where he performs services for the other believing that there is a binding contract. * * *
>
> In Wisner [v. Wisner, 129 Ariz. 333, 631 P.2d 115 (App.1981)] we observed that "[i]n our opinion, unjust enrichment, as a legal concept, is not properly applied in the setting of a marital relationship." Our observation was directed to the wife's claim in that case for restitution for

the value of her *homemaking services* during the couple's 15-year marriage and for the couple's reduced income during the husband's lengthy training period. Where both spouses perform the usual and incidental activities of the marital relationship, upon dissolution there can be no restitution for performance of these activities. Where, however, the facts demonstrate an agreement between the spouses and an extraordinary or unilateral effort by one spouse which inures solely to the benefit of the other by the time of the dissolution, the remedy of restitution is appropriate.

When a party seeks restitution of benefits conferred under an agreement, the interaction between the law of restitution and the law of contracts can be problematic. In *Pyeatte*, for example, given that the Pyeattes' contract was unenforceably vague, it may seem that requiring Mr. Pyeatte to pay Ms. Pyeatte for her services is tantamount to enforcing the contract, therefore violating the rule against enforcing vague agreements.

Where the agreement is unenforceable because it is indefinite, that should not be a concern, however. The policy of the law of contracts is simply not to allow a party to recover the benefit of an indefinite bargain. So long as Ms. Pyeatte's recovery is limited to restitution, that policy is not contravened.

In other cases, though, restitution may be inconsistent with the policies that make the underlying contract unenforceable. For example, if the contract is unenforceable because its end is illegal, it may be appropriate also to deny restitution in order to discourage such contracts. For discussion of whether restitution is available for benefits conferred under unenforceable contracts, see Dan B. Dobbs, Law of Remedies §§ 13.1 to 13.5 (2d ed.1993); Peter Birks, Recovering Value Transferred Under an Illegal Contract, 1 Theoretical Inq.L. 155 (2000).

4. *On the remedy: The elements of restitutionary recovery.* The plaintiff's award in *Hutchison* can be divided into several components: (1) rescission of the deed, (2) refund of the purchase price, (3) incidental damages, (4) punitive damages and (5) attorney's fees. That the defendant should refund the purchase price seems obvious: that is the restitutionary element of the action for rescission and restitution.

But is it so clear that the plaintiff should recover incidental damages, if this is an action for restitution? The court draws a distinction between compensatory damages, which it says would be inconsistent with the restitutionary nature of plaintiff's claim, and incidental damages, which it says are not. What is the difference between compensatory damages and incidental damages? Aren't incidental damages a form of compensatory damages? If this is an action for restitution, in which the theory is to avoid unjust enrichment, how was the defendant enriched by the plaintiff's moving expenses? If damages are premised on letting the deal stand while compensating the injured party, while restitution is premised on undoing the deal, is it fair to let the plaintiff seek both in the same action? See generally Peter Linzer, Rough Justice: A Theory of Restitution and Reliance, Contracts and Torts, 2001 Wis.L.Rev. 695, 697 ("the specific legal form used to find liability is not really as important jurisprudentially as the court's willingness or unwillingness to hold someone responsible").

Consider the court's response in Utemark v. Samuel, 118 Cal.App.2d 313, 317, 257 P.2d 656, 659 (1953):

> It appears to have been the purpose of the court to place the *defendants* in *status quo* regardless of any loss *plaintiffs* might suffer, but it was the plaintiffs, not the defendants, who were entitled to be restored to their former position. This is the purpose of rescission. Equity is solicitous that the innocent party who rescinds be not made to suffer. It exercises no such solicitude for the wrongdoer who has brought about a situation in which one or the other must lose.

Recall *Olwell*'s account of the appropriate measure of damages: where the plaintiff's loss is greater than the defendant's gain, and the defendant's conduct was tortious, the measure is the plaintiff's loss.

What this means is that the restitutionary goal and the tort goal end up the same: to restore the status quo ante. There is, however, an important difference for the Hutchisons. If they sued for tort damages, their award (in a jurisdiction that followed the "out of pocket" rule) would be a money judgment for the difference between what they paid for the land and its value. They would be stuck with the land. A restitutionary remedy returns them the full purchase price, and leaves the defendants holding the bag.

This raises an interesting conceptual problem. Should we conceive of cases where the restitutionary remedy simply gives the plaintiff back what she parted with as restitution cases, or should we reserve the label "restitution" for cases that truly aim at disgorging profits?

5. Suppose, in *Hutchison*, the plaintiffs had planned on operating a business on the property purchased from the defendant and, as a result of the defendant's fraud, they were unable to operate for several months? Following the logic of *Utemark,* should they be able to recover the profits they lost as consequential damages?

While many courts allow plaintiffs to recover incidental damages such as moving expenses, costs incurred in attempting to put the property to use, or consequential damages for harm caused by the misrepresented condition, lost profits have been routinely denied. With regard to contracts for the sale of goods, however, the Uniform Commercial Code § 2–711 now expressly allows recovery of lost profits in addition to incidental and consequential damages when a buyer rescinds a contract for breach of warranty. When a buyer rescinds because of fraud, lost profits are recoverable under the Code in jurisdictions following the benefit of the bargain rule, but not in jurisdictions where fraud damages are limited to out of pocket losses. See George E. Palmer, Law of Restitution § 3.9 at 280 (1978).

6. The award of attorney's fees to the plaintiffs in *Hutchison* is enigmatic. As Chapter 10 discusses, under the American rule, each party is liable for its own attorney's fees unless one of a limited number of exceptions applies. There is no general exception for restitution cases. Possibly, the Hutchisons' contract contained a clause providing for the payment of attorneys' fees to the prevailing party in the event of a dispute. Although courts occasionally deny enforcement of such clauses on the grounds that the contract has been rescinded, most courts recognize that restitution is simply an alternative

remedy for the underlying fraud or breach, and that the fiction of rescission does not change the character of the action. Compare Bodenhamer v. Patterson, 278 Or. 367, 563 P.2d 1212 (1977)(denying attorney's fees) with Katz v. Van Der Noord, 546 So.2d 1047 (Fla.1989)(fees awarded).

7. Should punitive damages be recoverable in a restitution case? Courts are divided. See, e.g., Madrid v. Marquez, 131 N.M. 132, 33 P.3d 683, 685 (App.2001) (while majority rule is that punitive damages are not permitted in equity, court follows the "modern trend" of allowing punitive damages in equity, without prerequisite of an award of compensatory damages); Dan B. Dobbs, Law of Remedies § 4.5(5) (2d ed.1993). Some see the doctrine of election of remedies as a bar, although the discussion at p. 464, should make it clear that it need not be. Others deny recovery because punitive damages cannot be awarded without actual, compensatory damages (see p. 451), or because punitive damages were not awarded in equity courts. See Alcorn County, Mississippi v. U.S. Interstate Supplies, Inc., 731 F.2d 1160 (5th Cir.1984). None of these reasons can really withstand critical scrutiny, and the trend is probably to allow punitive damages where fraud, oppression or malice is shown.

EARTHINFO, INC. v. HYDROSPHERE RESOURCE CONSULTANTS, INC.

Supreme Court of Colorado, 1995
900 P.2d 113

JUSTICE SCOTT delivered the Opinion of the Court.

In January 1990, Hydrosphere Resource Consultants, Inc. (Hydrosphere), filed this action against petitioner, EarthInfo, Inc. (EarthInfo), seeking to rescind the parties' software development contracts due to EarthInfo's failure to make royalty payments. The trial court determined that EarthInfo had breached its contracts with Hydrosphere, ordered the contracts rescinded, and ordered that EarthInfo repay to Hydrosphere all the net profits it realized as a result of its breach. The court of appeals affirmed the trial court. * * *

I

Between 1986 and 1988, Hydrosphere entered into several contracts with US West, Inc. (US West) * * * to develop a number of products that employ CD–ROM technology. The products were designed to exploit hydrological and meteorological information collected by government agencies and to make that information available to the general public through Hydrosphere. Under the Contracts, Hydrosphere was to develop the CD–ROM units and create the software that enables end-users to access the otherwise public information on line from the CD–ROM units.

The Contracts vested all rights of ownership, copyrights, and patents in the products to US West. Under the terms of the Contracts, Hydrosphere had an ongoing obligation to provide technical support to end-users of the products, and US West was to create user manuals, and package and market the products. US West was also to pay Hydrosphere a fixed hourly development fee as well as royalties, calculated as a percentage of net sales, for "inventive product ideas." Payments under the Contracts were made on a quarterly basis.

On February 10, 1989, US West assigned its interest in the Contracts to EarthInfo. * * * EarthInfo agreed to pay US West $60,432. EarthInfo also entered into a separate agreement with Hydrosphere in which it agreed to honor US West's obligations under the Contracts, including the continued payment of royalties on the products already developed by Hydrosphere. EarthInfo fulfilled its contractual obligations through June 30, 1990. Hydrosphere then claimed that sales of a new derivative product were subject to royalty payments; EarthInfo claimed that the Contracts did not address derivative products, and therefore objected to increasing its royalty obligation. On October 30, 1990, when the third-quarter royalty payments were due, EarthInfo informed Hydrosphere that it was withholding these payments and any further royalty payments pending clarification of the basis for the royalty payments. EarthInfo continued to make payments of the fixed hourly development fees. A total of $19,000 in fixed fees was paid to Hydrosphere after June 30, 1990. After strained negotiations, Hydrosphere notified EarthInfo by letter on December 12, 1990, that it was rescinding the Contracts.

On January 11, 1991, Hydrosphere filed a breach of contract action against EarthInfo * * *. [After trial], the trial court ruled that EarthInfo did not owe royalties on sales of the derivative product, but the court determined that EarthInfo had breached its Contracts with Hydrosphere when it unilaterally suspended royalty payments on the other products. In a subsequent hearing, both parties sought rescission of the Contracts and restitution as a remedy. The trial court found "the breach was substantial" and that "due to the nature of the contracts between the parties and the depth of their disputes, damages would be inadequate." The trial court determined that the appropriate remedy would be rescission. * * * [The court] set June 30, 1990, the date through which EarthInfo had paid royalties, as the date of rescission.

As restitution between the parties, the court ordered EarthInfo to return to Hydrosphere all tangible property developed under the Contracts. In addition, the court found that "since rescission is an equitable remedy the court has discretion in determining the appropriate relief for the parties," and ordered EarthInfo to return to Hydrosphere all property, promotional materials and proprietary information related to the Hydrodata products. In addition, the court held EarthInfo responsible in equity "for the repayment to Hydrosphere of the net profits realized by EarthInfo" from June 30, 1990, until the date of the order, totaling $265,204.91. The court found Hydrosphere "in equity responsible for the repayment to EarthInfo of amounts paid by EarthInfo" in acquiring the Hydrodata product line from US West, totaling $60,432, and in fixed hourly development fees paid by EarthInfo after June 30, 1990, in the amount of $19,000. The costs incurred by EarthInfo were deducted from the net profits, resulting in a judgment in favor of Hydrosphere in the amount of $185,772.91.

EarthInfo appealed * * *.

II

This case presents a question of first impression for this court: whether a party that breaches a contract can be required to disgorge to the non-breaching party any benefits received as a result of the breach. Because this issue has remained largely unexplored, the rules of application are neither settled nor uniform. The difficulty in resolving this issue stems from a subtle conflict between the law of restitution and the law of contracts. This conflict is well articulated in what has become a leading article on the disgorgement principle:

> It is a principle of the law of restitution that one should not gain by one's own wrong; it is a principle of the law of contracts that damages for breach should be based on the injured party's lost expectation. In many cases, the principles are mutually consistent. If, on breach, the injured party's lost expectation equals or exceeds the gain by the party in breach, then damages based on expectation strip the party in breach of all gain, and make the injured party whole. But if the injured party's lost expectation is less than the gain realized by the party in breach, then damages based on expectation do not strip the party in breach of all gain. This situation brings the two principles into conflict.

E. Allan Farnsworth, Your Loss or My Gain? The Dilemma of the Disgorgement Principle in Breach of Contract, 94 Yale L.J. 1339, 1341 (1985). According to Farnsworth, courts have been reluctant to award profits to a nonbreaching party in a breach of contract action, thus allowing the party in breach to keep part of the gain, since in effect "a 'mere' breach of contract is not a 'wrong.'" Many others, however, have suggested that if the gain realized by the party in breach exceeds the injured party's loss, the measure of damages should strip the party in breach of all gain. We adopt neither approach as a general rule, and hold instead that whether profits are awarded to a nonbreaching party shall be determined within the discretion of the trial court on a case by case basis.

A

Rescission of a contract may be granted if the facts show a substantial breach, that the injury caused by the breach is irreparable, and that damages are inadequate, difficult or impossible to assess. A contract can also be rescinded by the "mutual consent" or "actions" of the parties.

Here, the trial court found not only that EarthInfo's breach was substantial, but that "due to the nature of the contracts between the parties and the depth of their disputes, damages would be inadequate." The trial court also found that although the Contracts "contemplate an ongoing relationship" between the parties, "[i]t is unrealistic to assume that damages could be computed and awarded and that the parties could then resume that relationship in a productive manner." The trial court found further that both parties sought rescission of the Contracts. Thus, the trial court concluded that rescission was necessary.[7] Since evidence in the record supports the trial court's findings, we conclude that rescission of the Contracts was warranted.

Rescission of a contract normally is accompanied by restitution on both sides. The contract is "being unmade, so restoration of benefits received under the contract seems to follow." Restitution measures the remedy by the defendant's gain and seeks to force disgorgement of that gain in order "to prevent the defendant's unjust enrichment." Restitution, which seeks to prevent unjust enrichment of the defendant, differs in principle from damages, which measure the remedy by the plaintiff's loss and seek to provide compensation for that loss. As a consequence, "in some cases the defendant gains more than the plaintiff loses, so that the two remedies may differ in practice as well as in principle."[9]

A party seeking to rescind a contract must return the opposite party to the status quo ante, or the position in which he or she was prior to entering into the contract. The rule of returning the parties to the status quo ante is equitable and it requires the use of practicality in the readjustment of the parties' rights. Since rescission is an equitable remedy, it is within the trial court's sound discretion to determine the method for accomplishing a return to the status quo ante based upon the facts as determined by the trier of fact. All uncertainties as to the amount of benefit are to be resolved against the party committing the material breach.

The main options for measurement of the benefit conferred on the breaching party are these:

> (1) the increased assets in the hands of the defendant from the receipt of property;
>
> (2) the market value of services or intangibles provided to the defendant, without regard to whether the defendant's assets were actually increased; that is, the amount which it would cost to obtain similar services, whether those services prove to be useful or not;

---

7. The trial court held: The court finds not only that the breach was substantial, but that due to the nature of the contracts between the parties and the depth of their disputes, damages would be inadequate. The contracts contemplate an ongoing relationship. It is unrealistic to assume that damages could be computed and awarded and that the parties could then resume that relationship in a productive manner.... Rescission is, therefore, an appropriate remedy. The court explained further that "[a] principal reason why a remedy limited to damages is inappropriate is that it would leave the products developed by Hydrosphere in the hands of a hostile and uncooperative EarthInfo, with the latter under a continuing duty to pay royalties, and also with an interest in promoting its own product line."

9. In the event a defendant's gains in a transaction exceed the plaintiff's losses and the plaintiff recovers the defendant's gains as restitution, the plaintiff will receive a greater reward and will be better off than if he or she were awarded damages for the defendant's breach. Thus, the plaintiff's expectations are exceeded because recovery is not based on the loss in value to the plaintiff, but rather on the benefit to the breaching defendant.

(3) the use value of any benefits received, as measured by (i) market indicators such as rental value or interest or (ii) actual gains to the defendant from using the benefits, such as the gains identified in item (5) below;

(4) the gains realized by the defendant upon sale or transfer of an asset received from the plaintiff;

(5) collateral or secondary profits earned by the defendant by use of an asset received from the plaintiff, or, what is much the same thing, the savings effected by the use of the asset.

Dan B. Dobbs, Law of Remedies § 4.1(4) at 566–67 (footnote omitted). It is the fifth option, disgorgement of profits, which is principally at issue in this case.

No easy formulas exist for determining when restitution of profits realized by a party is permissible. Instead, the court must resort to general considerations of fairness, taking into account the nature of the defendant's wrong, the relative extent of his or her contribution, and the feasibility of separating this from the contribution traceable to the plaintiff's interest. 1 George E. Palmer, The Law of Restitution § 2.12 at 161 (1978) [hereinafter "Palmer"]. Thus, the more culpable the defendant's behavior, and the more direct the connection between the profits and the wrongdoing, the more likely that the plaintiff can recover all defendant's profits. See, e.g., Douglas Laycock, The Scope and Significance of Restitution, 67 Tex.L.Rev. 1277, 1289 (1989). The trial court must ultimately decide whether the whole circumstances of a case point to the conclusion that the defendant's retention of any profit is unjust.

Generally, the mere breach of a contract will not make the defendant accountable for benefits thereby obtained, whether through dealings with a third person or otherwise. As noted by Dobbs § 4.1(4) at 566–67:

> [t]o require a defendant to give up profits may operate with particular severity because at least some of the profits would almost always be attributable to the defendant's efforts or investment. So the profit recovery as a measure of restitution is extraordinary. In general, the defendant who is not a serious wrongdoer is held only to make restitution measured by actual gains in assets or in gains of services or intangibles which he [or she] in fact sought in the relevant transaction.

If, however, the defendant's wrongdoing is intentional or substantial, or there are no other means of measuring the wrongdoer's enrichment, recovery of profits may be granted. See generally George E. Palmer, Law of Restitution § 2.12 at 164–65.

B

The trial court determined that EarthInfo's breach of the Contracts was substantial, damages were difficult to assess, and the parties mutually consented to rescission. Thus, the trial court required EarthInfo to disgorge all the profits it realized as a result of the breach. The court returned to EarthInfo the consideration it agreed to pay for the Hydrodata product line and also allowed it to retain the profits it earned when it was making the royalty payments. The court held EarthInfo responsible, however, for the repayment to Hydrosphere of the net profits it realized from June 30, 1990 until the date of the order, determining that to be the most equitable treatment of the parties given the nature of the dispute. We agree that EarthInfo must be required to disgorge the profits it accrued as a result of its breach since its breach was conscious and substantial.

The trial court found that the Contracts between EarthInfo and Hydrosphere did not require EarthInfo to pay royalties on sales of the derivative product. EarthInfo was still required, however, to pay royalties on all other products under the written Contracts. The trial court determined that EarthInfo's repudiation of its long-standing royalty obligations to Hydrosphere was a substantial breach of the Hydrodata Contracts. The trial court's factual determinations are supported by the evidence and should not be disturbed on appeal absent a clear showing of abuse of discretion. The trial court's order represents a permissible exercise of its discretion.

Since the record supports the trial court's findings that EarthInfo consciously and substantially breached its Contracts with Hydrosphere, damages were difficult to assess, and the parties mutually agreed to rescission, retention of profits by EarthInfo would be an unjust enrichment. Accordingly, we find that the extraordinary remedy of restitution and disgorgement of profits is justified.

III

The remaining issue then is the determination of the profits to be returned to Hydrosphere. The petitioner contends that the trial court erred in failing to apportion the net profits in a way that reflected the relative contributions to those profits by the parties. We agree.

"Courts have recognized that some apportionment must be made between those profits attributable to the plaintiff's property and those earned by the defendant's efforts and investment, limiting the plaintiff to the profits fairly attributable to his share." "Even the wilful wrongdoer should not be made to give up that which is his [or her] own; the principle is disgorgement, not plunder." The defendant's personal efforts in contributing to profits must be taken into account, but are often difficult to measure. For example, if the defendant uses the plaintiff's machine in producing goods, which it packages, distributes and sells to retail customers, it may increase its profits, but we are not so sure that the increase has much if any connection with the plaintiff's machine. We can be sure, however, that the defendant's profits relate in part to the defendant's own investments, efforts, or enterprising attitude. [Dobbs § 4.5(3)] at 647.

Dobbs' example of profit-making complexity is similar to the profit-making in the case at hand. EarthInfo used Hydrosphere's software programming in five items produced, packaged, distributed, and sold by EarthInfo. EarthInfo's marketing, packaging and enhancement of the products presumably contributed to the earning of the net profits; that contribution should be accounted for and withheld from the disgorgement of those profits by Hydrosphere.

No single rule governing the burden of proving apportionment is adequate for all cases or all facets of a single case. Profit claims can be calculated first by identifying and deducting legitimate business expenses from gross income. The defendant usually has the best access to this information and may properly be required to prove such expenses. Second, gross income of the defendant is produced at least in part "by investment, enterprise, and management skill of the defendant," and the defendant should receive credit for its own efforts and investments. * * * The court must determine which part of the profit results from the defendant's own independent efforts and which part results from the benefits provided by the plaintiff. The court must seek to determine a fair apportionment that will result in a reasonable approximation or informed estimate of the relative contributions of the two parties. The allocation of the burden of establishing such approximation, and degree of specificity of proof required, may be affected by such factors as the seriousness of the defendant's wrongdoing and the extent to which the plaintiff's contribution was at risk in the profit making enterprise. Where the relative contributions of the two parties are inseparable or untraceable, there should be no recovery of profits by the plaintiff unless the defendant is a very serious wrongdoer. In the present case, considering the nature and extent of the breach as well as the other relevant factors, we hold that it is the burden of the plaintiff to establish facts sufficient to permit the trial court to determine the relative contributions of the parties so that profits can be fairly apportioned. * * *

The trial court made no findings with respect to the relative contributions of each party and whether they are inseparable. Thus, this case should be remanded to the trial court for further proceedings so that the court's order that EarthInfo disgorge its profits is limited to those profits attributable to Hydrosphere. Accordingly, we affirm in part, reverse in part, and return this case to the court of appeals with directions that it remand the case to the trial court for recalculation of wrongful profits attributable to Hydrosphere and entry of a new order of restitution.

NOTES

1. According to the Restatement (Second) of Contracts, the victim of a serious breach or repudiation of contract is entitled "to restitution for any benefit that he has conferred on the other party by way of part performance or reliance." Restatement (Second) of Contracts § 373(a). The only exception is that there is no right to restitution if the victim has completely performed

and the only obligation owing is the payment of a definite sum of money for the performance. Id. § 373(b). *EarthInfo* simply takes this principle to its logical extreme, by measuring the restitutionary recovery according to principles developed in restitution cases like *Olwell* (p. 732).

2. Restitutionary recovery is particularly valuable—and controversial—when a party finds itself in a losing contract. When enmeshed in a losing deal, there is a strong incentive for a party to find a way out, if that can be done without risking liability for damages. Think back, for example, to *Evra Corp. v. Swiss Bank* at p. 600. Once the market rate for charters rose higher than the rate in the long-term charter the parties had agreed to, the ship owner had a strong incentive to insist on strict performance of the charter agreement. If the charterer could be induced to breach, then the ship owner would be free to call off the deal and charter the ship at market rates.

This incentive to induce the other party to breach when you find yourself in a losing contract is exacerbated if the nonbreaching party can also sue for restitution. Consider Mobil Oil Exploration and Producing Southeast, Inc. v. United States, 530 U.S. 604, 120 S.Ct. 2423, 147 L.Ed.2d 528 (2000). In *Mobil Oil*, the oil company plaintiffs paid the United States $156 million for leases giving them exploration rights off the North Carolina coast, provided the companies received permission from the relevant federal agencies. It was understood that even with these permissions, exploration would not be possible if the State of North Carolina did not consent.

While the oil companies' permit applications were pending, Congress passed legislation that changed the requirements for permits, imposing additional delays. For two months, North Carolina refused to give its consent. The oil companies sued, alleging that Congress's action amounted to a repudiation of the contract, and requesting restitution. The Court agreed, and ordered the Government to pay back the $156 million. Justice Stevens disagreed:

> The risk that North Carolina would frustrate performance of the leases executed in 1981 was foreseeable from the date the leases were signed. It seems clear to me that the State's objections, rather than the enactment of [the legislation that effectively repudiated the contract], is the primary explanation for petitioners' decision to take steps to avoid suffering the consequences of the bargain they made. As a result of the Court's action today, petitioners will enjoy a windfall reprieve that Congress foolishly provided them in its decision to pass legislation that, while validly responding to a political constituency that opposed the development of the Outer Banks, caused the Government to breach its own contract. Viewed in the context of the entire transaction, petitioners may well be entitled to a modest damages recovery for the two months of delay attributable to the Government's breach. But restitution is not a default remedy; it is available only when a court deems it, in all of the circumstances, just. A breach that itself caused at most a delay of two months in a protracted enterprise of this magnitude does not justify the $156 million draconian remedy that the Court delivers.

Id. at 639, 120 S.Ct. at 2445, 147 L.Ed.2d at 553 (Stevens, J., dissenting).

To give another example, suppose a builder agrees to build a house for a contract price of $200,000. When the house is about half finished, the builder realizes the construction has cost her $120,000 so far, and it will take another $100,000 in labor and materials to finish the house. She has made a bad deal. If she walks away and is sued for breach, she will have to pay the cost of completing the house, less the unpaid contract price, and she will lose $20,000.

Consider, however, what happens if she can induce the owner to breach. If the owner has made partial payments, and the jurisdiction prohibits restitution in favor of a breaching party, she may come out ahead. Or, she can sue for breach and seek reliance damages, but as we have already seen, her reliance damages will be limited in order to prevent giving her more than the benefit of her bargain.

So, suppose instead of suing for breach of contract damages, she asks for rescission of the contract, and restitution. She escapes from her obligation to complete the performance, and recovers damages based upon the value of the performance she has conferred on the owner. Assuming the value of her labor and materials is closer to the $120,000 it cost her to perform than to the contract price, she walks away without any loss.

Does that seem like the right result? The question is controversial. On the one hand, if recovery is based on unjust enrichment, it seems only logical that the plaintiff should recover the full value of the benefits the defendant received. On the other hand, full restitutionary recovery effectively rewrites the parties' bargain, obliging the defendant to pay full value when he promised—with the plaintiff's consent—to pay less. It invites opportunism, giving the party who made a bad deal a tremendous incentive to induce a breach by the other party. It complicates reaching fair settlements, and is not a remedy either party to a contract would agree to in advance of a breach. Andrew Kull, Restitution as a Remedy for Breach of Contract, 67 S.C.L.Rev. 1465 (1994).

Professor Kull argues that the Restatement's position rests on a misunderstanding of rescission as a remedy for breach. Rescission, properly understood, is a remedy that simply unwinds an agreement that can no longer go forward, and it traditionally was available as a remedy only where the transaction was still capable of being unwound. The early cases thus limited rescission to cases in which: (1) the breach was substantial, tantamount to a repudiation of the contract, (2) the transaction could be fully unwound by returning the benefits received, *in specie*, and (3) the performance had not gone so far as to make unwinding the deal impracticable. Id. at 1515–16. While these restrictions may be too strict, Professor Kull urges that limitations along these lines are necessary to avoid inefficiency and inequity. Does he have a point?

3. When a defendant breaches in order to make a profit from the breach, it raises a different question. Then, allowing restitution measured by the defendant's profits—disgorgement—would seem to be at odds with another basic premise of contract damages, the notion of efficient breach. See pp. 596–597. Can the result in *EarthInfo* be reconciled with the notion that it is sound policy to encourage economically efficient breaches?

The commentators are divided about whether disgorgement is either widely available or appropriate as a remedy for breach of contract. Professor

Palmer acknowledged that courts required disgorgement in a few cases—for example, when a seller in a land sale agreement breaches to sell to a third party at a higher price, or where an employee breaches by revealing trade secrets—but concluded that "the evidence points to the rejection of any general principle" that disgorgement is available as a remedy for breach of contract. George E. Palmer, Law of Restitution § 4.9(e) at 449 (1978).

Professor Melvin Eisenberg, however, believes that the Restatement (Second) of Contracts' failure to recognize disgorgement as an interest protected by contract law was misguided. "[M]ore than a dozen appellate cases decided by various state appellate courts, the United States Supreme Court, the House of Lords, and the highest courts of other common law jurisdictions have awarded disgorgement in a contract setting." Melvin Eisenberg, The Disgorgement Interest in Contract Law, 105 Mich.L.Rev. 559, 565–566 (2006). While disgorgement should not be routinely available, under some circumstances disgorgement can promote both economic efficiency and fairness. The critical question? "When performance is promised under a contract, is the promisee "entitled" to it in such a way that if this performance is withheld, appropriated, or otherwise "taken," the promisee can be regarded as having been deprived of an interest that "belonged" to him?" If so, according to Eisenberg, disgorgement is an appropriate remedy. Is *Earthinfo* such a case?

4. What should be made of the fact that Earthinfo's breach was deliberate and unexcused? After all, Earthinfo had no apparent reason not to pay the royalties it acknowledged were due, except perhaps to exert settlement leverage over Hydrosphere in its dispute over the new products. Without a restitutionary remedy, does the threat of contract damages provide any disincentive to this type of behavior?

Other commentators also believe disgorgement is an appropriate remedy for breach of contract in some cases. Professor Farnsworth, for example, has argued that in cases of "abuse of contract," where the defendant's breach has left the plaintiff with no way to obtain a reasonable substitute for the defendant's performance, restitution measured by the defendant's savings from breach should be available, because expectation damages present a significant risk of undercompensation. E. Allan Farnsworth, Your Loss or My Gain? The Dilemma of the Disgorgement Principle in Breach of Contract, 94 Yale L.J. 1339 (1985). Would this be such a case?

Professor Farnsworth's justification for disgorgement is very similar to an explanation sometimes offered for allowing punitive damages for bad faith breach of an insurance contract. See pp. 598–599; Richard E. Speidel, The Borderland of Contract, 10 N.Ky.L.Rev. 163, 192–93 (1983)(punitive damages are appropriate "where the breaching party captures an immediate gain under circumstances where the prospect of full compensation to the aggrieved party is low.") Does disgorgement offer an appealing alternative to punitive damages in some of the situations discussed at pp. 596–599?

The Restatement (Third) of Restitution and Unjust Enrichment opts for disgorgement when a contract is willfully breached, at least under some circumstances:

> (1) If a breach of contract is both material and opportunistic, the injured promisee has a claim in restitution to the profit realized by the defaulting

promisor as a result of the breach. Liability in restitution with disgorgement of profit is an alternative to liability for contract damages measured by injury to the promisee.

(2) A breach is "opportunistic" if

(a) the breach is deliberate;

(b) the breach is profitable by the test of subsection (3); and

(c) the promisee's right to recover damages for the breach affords inadequate protection to the promisee's contractual entitlement. In determining the adequacy of damages for this purpose,

(i) damages are ordinarily an adequate remedy if they can be used to acquire a full equivalent to the promised performance in a substitute transaction; and

(ii) damages are ordinarily an inadequate remedy if they cannot be used to acquire a full equivalent to the promised performance in a substitute transaction.

(3) A breach is "profitable" when it results in gains to the defaulting promisor (net of potential liability in damages) greater than the promisor would have realized from performance of the contract. Profits from breach include saved expenditure and consequential gains that the defaulting promisor would not have realized but for the breach. The amount of such profits must be proved with reasonable certainty.

(4) Disgorgement by the rule of this Section will be denied

(a) if the parties' agreement authorizes the promisor to choose between performance of the contract and a remedial alternative such as payment of liquidated damages; or

(b) to the extent that disgorgement would result in an inappropriate windfall to the promisee, or would otherwise be inequitable in a particular case.

Restatement (Third) of Restitution and Unjust Enrichment § 39 (Tentative Draft No. 4, 2005).

5. Alternatively, isn't EarthInfo's behavior—using the property without paying for it—almost like a conversion, for which disgorgement is an appropriate remedy? What result would the rule Professor Daniel Friedmann advocates, at pp. 735–736, reach?

6. Could restitution offer a way out of the *Peevyhouse/Groves* dilemma, discussed at pp. 483–484 in the text? Recovery could be measured by the defendant's savings; that is, "the saving of the costs of modification." E. Allan Farnsworth, Your Loss or My Gain? The Dilemma of the Disgorgement Principle in Breach of Contract, 94 Yale L.J. 1339, 1393 (1985). In other words, the plaintiff should be able to recover whatever amount she would have charged had the defendant requested a modification of the contract to conform with her performance. Id. at 1389.

7. Can the party who has breached a contract ever seek restitution? For example, a builder may have performed a substantial amount of work on a landowner's property before breaching; or the buyer of goods may have paid

part of the purchase price, and then reneged. If the breaching party is sued, the value of his part performance is generally offset from the nonbreaching party's damages. But if the nonbreaching party does not sue, and the breaching party seeks restitution, the traditional rule denies recovery. The fairness of this result is questionable, and inroads have been made on the traditional rule (always with the caveat that restitution must be limited to benefits that the nonbreaching party actually received). Thus, the Uniform Commercial Code allows the breaching buyer to recover payments in excess of damages owed to the seller, UCC § 2–718(2), and a number of cases support restitution in favor of the breaching builder, if the landowner is actually enriched. See Dan B. Dobbs, Law of Remedies § 12.24 (2d ed.1993).

E. EQUITABLE RESTITUTIONARY REMEDIES

PROBLEM: MOORE v. REGENTS OF THE UNIVERSITY OF CALIFORNIA

John Moore suffered from hairy cell leukemia. As part of his treatment, a doctor at one of the University of California's hospitals removed Moore's spleen, which had swollen from its normal weight of a few ounces to more than fifteen pounds. Using various bioengineering techniques, the doctor and his research colleagues developed a cell line using Moore's spleen that has extraordinary research and therapeutic potential. It has already been patented and sold to biotech firms, and the cell line's worth is probably measured in the tens, if not hundreds of millions of dollars. Assuming that the doctor violated his fiduciary duty to disclose his research and economic interests before obtaining Moore's consent to the operation (see Moore v. Regents of University of California, 51 Cal.3d 120, 271 Cal.Rptr. 146, 793 P.2d 479 (1990), cert. denied, 499 U.S. 936, 111 S.Ct. 1388, 113 L.Ed.2d 444 (1991)), what remedies may be available to Moore?

LATHAM v. FATHER DIVINE

Court of Appeals of New York, 1949
299 N.Y. 22, 85 N.E.2d 168

DESMOND, J.

* * * For present purposes, then, we have a case where one possessed of a large property and having already made a will leaving it to certain persons, expressed an intent to make a new testament to contain legacies to other persons, attempted to carry out that intention by having a new will drawn which contained a large legacy to those others, but was, by means of misrepresentations, undue influence, force, and indeed, murder, prevented, by the beneficiaries named in the existing will, from signing the new one. Plaintiffs say that those facts, if proven, would entitle them to a judicial declaration, which their prayer for judgment demands, that defendants, taking under the already probated will, hold what they have so taken as constructive trustees for plaintiffs, whom decedent wished to, tried to, and was kept from, benefitting.* * *

A constructive trust will be erected whenever necessary to satisfy the demands of justice. Since a constructive trust is merely "the formula through which the conscience of equity finds expression" its applicability is limited only by the inventiveness of men who find new ways to enrich themselves unjustly by grasping what should not belong to them. Nothing short of true and complete justice satisfies equity, and, always assuming these allegations to be true, there seems no way of achieving total justice except [by the imposition of a constructive trust].

SNEPP v. UNITED STATES
Supreme Court of the United States, 1980
444 U.S. 507, 100 S.Ct. 763, 62 L.Ed.2d 704

Per Curiam.

* * *

I

Based on his experiences as a CIA agent, Snepp published a book about certain CIA activities in South Vietnam. Snepp published the account without submitting it to the Agency for prepublication review. As an express condition of his employment with the CIA in 1968, however, Snepp had executed an agreement promising that he would "not ... publish ... any information or material relating to the Agency, its activities or intelligence activities generally, either during or after the term of [his] employment ... without specific prior approval by the Agency." The promise was an integral part of Snepp's concurrent undertaking "not to disclose any classified information relating to the Agency without proper authorization." Thus, Snepp had pledged not to divulge *classified* information and not to publish *any* information without prepublication clearance. The Government brought this suit to enforce Snepp's agreement. It sought a declaration that Snepp had breached the contract, an injunction requiring Snepp to submit future writings for prepublication review, and an order imposing a constructive trust for the Government's benefit on all profits that Snepp might earn from publishing the book in violation of his fiduciary obligations to the Agency.

The District Court found that Snepp had "willfully, deliberately and surreptitiously breached his position of trust with the CIA and the [1968] secrecy agreement" by publishing his book without submitting it for prepublication review. The court also found that Snepp deliberately misled CIA officials into believing that he would submit the book for prepublication clearance. Finally, the court determined as a fact that publication of the book had "caused the United States irreparable harm and loss." The District Court therefore enjoined future breaches of Snepp's agreement and imposed a constructive trust on Snepp's profits.

The Court of Appeals accepted the findings of the District Court and agreed that Snepp had breached a valid contract. It specifically affirmed the finding that Snepp's failure to submit his manuscript for prepublication review had inflicted "irreparable harm" on intelligence activities vital to our national security. Thus, the court upheld the injunction against future violations of Snepp's prepublication obligation. The court, however, concluded that the record did not support imposition of a constructive trust. The conclusion rested on the court's perception that Snepp had a First Amendment right to publish unclassified information and the Government's concession—for the purposes of this litigation—that Snepp's book divulged no classified intelligence. In other words, the court thought that Snepp's fiduciary obligation extended only to preserving the confidentiality of classified material. It therefore limited recovery to nominal damages and to the possibility of punitive damages if the Government—in a jury trial—could prove tortious conduct. * * *

II

Snepp's employment with the CIA involved an extremely high degree of trust. In the opening sentence of the agreement that he signed, Snepp explicitly recognized that he was entering a trust relationship. The trust agreement specifically imposed the obligation not to publish *any* information relating to the Agency without submitting the information for clearance. Snepp stipulated at trial that—after undertaking this obligation—he had been "assigned to various positions of trust" and that he had been granted "frequent access to classified information, including information regarding intelligence sources and methods." Snepp published his book about CIA activities on the basis of this background and exposure. He deliberately and surreptitiously violated his obligation to submit all material for prepublication review. Thus, he exposed the classified information with which he had been entrusted to the risk of disclosure.

Whether Snepp violated his trust does not depend upon whether his book actually contained classified information. The Government does not deny—as a general principle—Snepp's right to publish unclassified information. Nor does it contend—at this stage of the litigation—that Snepp's book contains classified material. The Government simply claims that, in light of the special trust reposed in him and the agreement that he signed, Snepp should have given the CIA an opportunity to determine whether the material he proposed to publish would compromise classified information or sources. Neither of the Government's concessions undercuts its claim that Snepp's failure to submit to prepublication review was a breach of his trust.

Both the District Court and the Court of Appeals found that a former intelligence agent's publication of unreviewed material relating to intelligence activities can be detrimental to vital national interests even if the published information is unclassified. When a former agent relies on his own judgment about what information is detrimental, he may reveal information that the CIA—with its broader understanding of what may expose classified information and confidential sources—could have identified as harmful. In addition to receiving intelligence from domestically based or controlled sources, the CIA obtains information from the intelligence services of friendly nations and from agents operating in foreign countries. The continued availability of these foreign sources depends upon the CIA's ability to guarantee the security of information that might compromise them and even endanger the personal safety of foreign agents.

Undisputed evidence in this case shows that a CIA agent's violation of his obligation to submit writings about the Agency for prepublication review impairs the CIA's ability to perform its statutory duties. Admiral Turner, Director of the CIA, testified without contradiction that Snepp's book and others like it have seriously impaired the effectiveness of American intelligence operations. He said:

> "Over the last six to nine months, we have had a number of sources discontinue work with us. We have had more sources tell us that they are very nervous about continuing work with us. We have had very strong complaints from a number of foreign intelligence services with whom we conduct liaison, who have questioned whether they should continue exchanging information with us, for fear it will not remain secret. I cannot estimate to you how many potential sources or liaison arrangements have never germinated because people were unwilling to enter into business with us."

In view of this and other evidence in the record, both the District Court and the Court of Appeals recognized that Snepp's breach of his explicit obligation to submit his material—classified or not—for prepublication clearance has irreparably harmed the United States Government.

III

The decision of the Court of Appeals denies the Government the most appropriate remedy for Snepp's acknowledged wrong. Indeed, as a practical matter, the decision may well leave the Government with no reliable deterrent against similar breaches of security. No one disputes that the actual damages attributable to a publication such as Snepp's generally are unquantifiable. Nominal damages are a hollow alternative, certain to deter no one. The punitive damages recoverable after a jury trial are speculative and unusual. Even if recovered, they may bear no relation to either the Government's irreparable loss or Snepp's unjust gain.

The Government could not pursue the only remedy that the Court of Appeals left it without losing the benefit of the bargain it seeks to enforce. Proof of the tortious conduct necessary to sustain an award of punitive damages might force the Government to disclose some of the very confidences that Snepp promised to protect. The trial of such a suit, before a jury if the defendant so elects, would subject the CIA and its officials to probing discovery into the Agency's highly confidential affairs. Rarely would the Government run this risk. In a letter introduced at Snepp's trial, former CIA Director Colby noted the analogous problem in criminal cases. Existing law, he stated, "requires the revelation in open court of confirming or additional information of such a nature that the potential damage to the national security precludes prosecution." When the Government cannot secure its remedy without unacceptable risks, it has no remedy at all.

A constructive trust, on the other hand, protects both the Government and the former agent from unwarranted risks. This remedy is the natural and customary consequence of a breach of trust. It deals fairly with both parties by conforming relief to the dimensions of the wrong. If the agent secures prepublication clearance, he can publish with no fear of liability. If the agent publishes unreviewed material in violation of his fiduciary and contractual obligation, the trust remedy simply requires him to disgorge the benefits of his faithlessness. Since the remedy is swift and sure, it is tailored to deter those who would place sensitive information at risk. And since the remedy reaches only funds attributable to the breach, it cannot saddle the former agent with exemplary damages out of all proportion to his gain. The decision of the Court of Appeals would deprive the Government of this equitable and effective means of protecting intelligence that may contribute to national security. We therefore reverse the judgment of the Court of Appeals insofar as it refused to impose a constructive trust on Snepp's profits, and we remand the cases to the Court of Appeals for reinstatement of the full judgment of the District Court.

MR. JUSTICE STEVENS, with whom MR. JUSTICE BRENNAN and MR. JUSTICE MARSHALL join, dissenting.

In 1968, Frank W. Snepp signed an employment agreement with the CIA in which he agreed to submit to the Agency any information he intended to publish about it for prepublication review. The purpose of such an agreement, as the Fourth Circuit held, is not to give the CIA the power to censor its employees' critical speech, but rather to ensure that classified, nonpublic information is not disclosed without the Agency's permission.

In this case Snepp admittedly breached his duty to submit the manuscript of his book, *Decent Interval*, to the CIA for prepublication review. However, the Government has conceded that the book contains no classified, nonpublic material. Thus, by definition, the interest in confidentiality that Snepp's contract was designed to protect has not been compromised. Nevertheless, the Court today grants the Government unprecedented and drastic relief in the form of a constructive trust over the profits derived by Snepp from the sale of the book. Because that remedy is not authorized by any applicable law and because it is most inappropriate for the Court to dispose of this novel issue summarily on the Government's conditional cross-petition for certiorari, I respectfully dissent.

I

The rule of law the Court announces today is not supported by statute, by the contract, or by the common law. Although Congress has enacted a number of criminal statutes punishing the unauthorized dissemination of certain types of classified information, it has not seen fit to authorize the constructive trust remedy the Court creates today. Nor does either of the contracts Snepp signed with the Agency provide for any such remedy in the event of a breach. The Court's per curiam opinion seems to suggest that its result is supported by a blend of the law of trusts and the law of contracts. But neither of these branches of the common law supports the imposition of a constructive trust under the circumstances of this case.

Plainly this is not a typical trust situation in which a settlor has conveyed legal title to certain assets to a trustee for the use and benefit of designated beneficiaries. Rather, it is an employment relationship in which the employee possesses fiduciary obligations arising out of his duty of loyalty to his employer. One of those obligations, long recognized by the common law even in the absence of a written employment agreement, is the duty to protect confidential or "classified" information. If Snepp had breached that obligation, the common law would support the implication of a constructive trust upon the benefits derived from his misuse of confidential information.

But Snepp did not breach his duty to protect confidential information. Rather, he breached a contractual duty, imposed in aid of the basic duty to maintain confidentiality, to obtain prepublication clearance. In order to justify the imposition of a constructive trust, the majority attempts to equate this contractual duty with Snepp's duty not to disclose, labeling them both as "fiduciary." I find nothing in the common law to support such an approach. * * *

[E]ven assuming that Snepp's covenant to submit to prepublication review should be enforced, the constructive trust imposed by the Court is not an appropriate remedy. If an employee has used his employer's confidential information for his own personal profit, a constructive trust over those profits is obviously an appropriate remedy because the profits are the direct result of the breach. But Snepp admittedly did not use confidential information in his book; nor were the profits from his book in any sense a product of his failure to submit the book for prepublication review. For, even if Snepp had submitted the book to the Agency for prepublication review, the Government's censorship authority would surely have been limited to the excision of classified material. In this case, then, it would have been obliged to clear the book for publication in precisely the same form as it now stands. Thus, Snepp has not gained any profits as a result of his breach; the Government, rather than Snepp, will be unjustly enriched if he is required to disgorge profits attributable entirely to his own legitimate activity.

Despite the fact that Snepp has not caused the Government the type of harm that would ordinarily be remedied by the imposition of a constructive trust, the Court attempts to justify a constructive trust remedy on the ground that the Government has suffered *some* harm. The Court states that publication of "unreviewed material" by a former CIA agent "can be detrimental to vital national interests even if the published information is unclassified." * * * I do not believe, however, that the Agency has any authority to censor its employees' publication of unclassified information on the basis of its opinion that publication may be "detrimental to vital national interests" or otherwise "identified as harmful." * * *

The Court also relies to some extent on the Government's theory at trial that Snepp caused it harm by flouting his prepublication review obligation and thus making it appear that the CIA was powerless to prevent its agents from publishing any information they chose to publish, whether classified or not. * * *

In any event, to the extent that the Government seeks to punish Snepp for the generalized harm he has caused by failing to submit to prepublication review and to deter others from following in his footsteps, punitive damages is, as the Court of Appeals held, clearly the preferable remedy "since a constructive trust depends on the concept of unjust enrichment rather than deterrence and punishment." * * *

Notes

1. In the excerpt that begins this chapter, Professor Laycock identifies three practical advantages to seeking restitution. Which of those three applies here?

2. *On procedure.* The constructive trust is an equitable remedy. Must there be an independent basis for equitable jurisdiction—an inadequate legal remedy, for example—before a constructive trust can be imposed? Nominally, the answer may be yes, but at least according to Professor Palmer, courts frequently ignore the requirement. See George E. Palmer, Law of Restitution § 1.6 at 36 (1978).

Further, where a case involves wrongdoing by a trustee or other fiduciary, there was no adequate remedy at law. At common law, no form of action existed to enforce a trust. If a grantor conveyed legal title to a grantee, intending the property to be held in trust for some beneficiary, so far as the law courts were concerned the property belonged to the trustee. If the beneficiary wished to compel the trustee to honor the terms of the trust, he had to seek relief in equity, where the beneficiary's "equitable ownership" would be acknowledged. The equity courts, thus, got into the business of supervising trustees to ensure that they observed their fiduciary duties in the handling of funds and property entrusted to them.

Yet, it is important to recognize that the constructive trust and the express trust have little but the name in common. An express trust is a substantive (and potentially complex) legal arrangement. Establishing a trust creates property rights in the beneficiary, and imposes substantive duties on the trustee. Does the recognition of a constructive trust similarly impose duties and create rights? Although occasionally courts will talk about the duties of a constructive trustee, it has generally been recognized that with regard to duties, the constructive trust is a remedy, not a substantive legal arrangement. A constructive trustee's only "duty" is to comply with the court's order to transfer the property to the plaintiff.

3. *On the substantive law.* According to the Restatement of Restitution § 190, "Where a person in a fiduciary relationship to another acquires property, and the acquisition or retention of the property is in violation of his duty as fiduciary, he holds it upon a constructive trust for the other." On the other hand, a mere breach of contract does not give rise to a constructive trust. Bear Kaufman Realty, Inc. v. Spec Development, Inc., 268 Ill.App.3d 898, 206 Ill.Dec. 239, 645 N.E.2d 244 (Ill.App.1994). According to Professor Palmer, the employer-employee relationship is not enough, standing alone, to impose an obligation to disgorge profits made from a breach. George E. Palmer, Law of Restitution § 1.5 at 26 (1978), citing Williams v. Herring, 183 Iowa 127, 165 N.W. 342 (1917). On what basis, then, did the Court find that Snepp was a fiduciary? For a discussion of some of the problems in defining fiduciary relationships, see Deborah DeMott, Beyond Metaphor: An Analysis of Fiduciary Obligation, 1988 Duke L.J. 879.

Employees do stand in a fiduciary relationship to their employers for some purposes. Employers have recovered awards based on the profits former employees garnered by revealing trade secrets or confidential information, or by violating covenants not to compete. (The cases are collected in George E. Palmer, Law of Restitution § 2.8(b)(1978)). The information Snepp revealed, however, was not classified. How did Snepp do anything more than merely breach his contract? Suppose an employee breached his contract by quitting when he had promised to work for a specific period of time. Should his employer be able to assert a constructive trust over the wages he earns at his new job? Is the Court persuasive in its argument that Snepp violated his duty as fiduciary, as opposed to simply breaching his employment contract?

Trustees have a duty not to use a fiduciary position for personal profit. Thus, where trustees abscond with trust property, or use it for their own purposes, the constructive trust recaptures the misappropriated property, along with any profits or income derived from it by the trustee. The information Snepp used in his book, however, was conceded not to be classified or proprietary, so it is not clear that he used his fiduciary position for profit in this sense.

The duties of a fiduciary, however, go farther: a fiduciary may not use her position for personal profit even where the profit is not obtained at the principal's expense. Mosser v. Darrow, 341 U.S. 267, 71 S.Ct. 680, 95 L.Ed. 927 (1951). Thus, trustees have been held accountable when they acquire an asset so related to the principal's business as to create a conflict of interest, even though the principal was offered and refused the asset. Pratt v. Shell Petroleum Corp., 100 F.2d 833 (10th Cir.1938). Similarly, fiduciaries who accept secret rewards or commissions have been held to hold them in constructive trust, though clearly the principal could never have received the benefit himself. Even profits obtained by a violation of law have been subject to a constructive trust, as in Diamond v. Oreamuno, 24 N.Y.2d 494, 301 N.Y.S.2d 78, 248 N.E.2d 910 (1969), where a constructive trust was imposed for a corporation's benefit on profits corporate officers realized through insider trading.

Plainly, the rationale of these cases is deterrence. So, essentially, is the rationale of *Snepp*. Fiduciaries must not be allowed to profit from their wrongs, and, if they are to be stripped of their profits, the only logical party to receive the profits is the principal, windfall or no.

Stripping defendants of their profits is a powerful deterrent, attractive to the proponents of many policy goals. Thus, restitutionary remedies have been pressed into the service of crime prevention (see United States v. Banco Cafetero Panama, 797 F.2d 1154 (2d Cir.1986)(forfeiture of proceeds of drug transactions)); environmental protection (William Drayton, Economic Law Enforcement, 4 Harv.Envr.L.Rev. 1 (1980) (advocating a recapture standard that would measure the penalty for noncompliance with pollution regulations by the profits made by noncompliance)), and even architectural preservation (see Jane P. Kourtis, The Constructive Trust: Equity's Answer to the Need for a Strong Deterrent to the Destruction of Historic Landmarks, 16 B.C.Envtl.Aff.L.Rev. 793 (1989)). How does restitution stack up against punitive damages as a deterrent? What are the advantages and disadvantages of each?

One objection to using the constructive trust to cause the defendant to disgorge profits is that profit-based restitution strikes too broadly, depriving the wrongdoer not only of the profits generated by his wrong, but also of the profits his efforts, skill and talent generated. See Daniel Friedmann, Restitution for Wrongs: The Measure of Recovery, 79 Tex.L.Rev. 1879 (2001). Indeed, the remedy has sometimes been denied precisely because sorting out the defendant's own contributions to the profit is impossibly complex. Dan B. Dobbs, Law of Remedies § 4.5(3) (2d ed.1993). Should some effort be made, therefore, to determine what profits Snepp would have made had he submitted the book for review and then published it? As the government conceded that the book contained no classified information, shouldn't it be presumed that the very same book would eventually have been published, only a little later? In some cases, it is possible to argue that it is appropriate to use the constructive trust to strip fiduciaries of their profits, because the principal in fact has a right to the fiduciary's efforts, skill and talent. Does that logic hold for *Snepp*? If so, shouldn't some effort be made to compensate Snepp for the time he spent writing the book? See, e.g., Boardman v. Phipps, [1967] 2 A.C. 46 (H.L.1966) (requiring disgorgement of profits, but allowing "liberal recovery" in quantum meruit for defendants' work and skill). For British and Canadian cases allowing disgorgement for breach (in one case, on facts nearly identical to *Snepp*), see John McCamus, Disgorgement for Breach of Contract: A Comparative Perspective, 36 Loy.L.A.L.Rev. 943 (2003).

4. *On the remedy*. The constructive trust imposed on Snepp's royalties strikingly resembles another equitable remedy available to redress unjust enrichment, the equitable accounting. One of the duties equity imposed upon trustees was the duty to account to the beneficiary for the disposition of the trust's property. Equitable accounting enforced that duty, allowing the beneficiary of a trust to hold the trustee to answer for the property entrusted to him; if the property was income-generating, the trustee could be held answerable for the profits through an accounting for profits. Dan B. Dobbs, Law of Remedies § 4.3(5) (2d ed.1993). The difference between a constructive trust (which, through tracing can also reach profits generated by the property held

in trust) and an accounting is that an accounting typically resulted in a money judgment against the trustee personally. Dale Oesterle, Deficiencies of the Restitutionary Right to Trace Misappropriated Property in Equity and in UCC § 9–306, 68 Cornell L.Rev. 172, 173 n.4 (1983).

From its origins in the law of trusts, the accounting for profits later became available as a remedy whenever a fiduciary profited wrongfully from his position, or whenever profit-generating property was acquired wrongfully and the legal remedy was inadequate, either because tracing was involved or because the accounts involved were so complex that the simple forms of accounting available at law were inadequate. Dale Oesterle, Restitution and Reform, 79 Mich.L.Rev. 336, 351 (1979). For example, accounting for profits became available as a remedy in cases of unfair competition, trademark infringement and copyright infringement, among others. Dan B. Dobbs, Law of Remedies § 4.3 (2d ed.1993).

5. In a footnote in *Snepp*, the Court upheld the prepublication agreement at issue against constitutional attack. Snepp's voluntary agreement to submit to prepublication screening obviated any first amendment problems. Could the government require all its employees to sign prepublication agreements? In 1983, the Reagan Administration issued National Security Decision Directive 84, which suggested that anyone with access to sensitive information would have to sign a lifetime prepublication screening agreement. The directive was never implemented because of the controversy it engendered. Would the directive have withstood a first amendment challenge? See Lee C. Bollinger, "Government Secrets: The First Amendment Implications of Prepublication Review Agreement," Statement for the Committee on Government Operations, U.S. House of Representatives, Oct. 19, 1983. In Agee v. Central Intelligence Agency, 500 F.Supp. 506 (D.D.C.1980), a constructive trust over the royalties from a book published without prepublication review was denied because the government was enforcing prepublication agreements selectively, demonstrating that the enforcement decision was "clouded by content considerations rather than wholly legitimate concerns for security."

Over half of the states have enacted statutes impressing an "involuntary trust" on any profits generated by novels, movies, plays, etc. written by criminals about their crimes. See, e.g., Cal. Civ. Code § 2225; N.Y. Executive Law § 632–A. These statutes require that the profits be held in trust for a specified number of years for the benefit of victims who may establish damage claims against the criminal. Thus, they are not truly restitutionary; rather, they operate as a form of garnishment. (Garnishment is discussed in Chapter 8.)

The New York statute was found unconstitutional by a unanimous Court, however, in Simon and Schuster, Inc. v. Members of the New York State Crime Victims Board, 502 U.S. 105, 112 S.Ct. 501, 116 L.Ed.2d 476 (1991). The first two steps in Justice O'Connor's opinion are straightforward. First, the statute imposed a content-based restriction on speech, which could only be justified by a compelling state interest. Second, while the state has a compelling interest in compensating the victims from the fruit of the crime, it has "little if any interest" in singling out speech as the sole source of compensation.

Therefore, the question becomes, is the statute narrowly tailored to reach the goal of ensuring that victims are compensated from the proceeds of the crime? Justice O'Connor concluded that New York's statute was not. The opinion reviews a list of works from Thoreau's Civil Disobedience to The Confessions of St. Augustine that might have been subject to a trust under the statute's definitions, and concludes that the statute was over inclusive: "The Son of Sam law clearly reaches a wide range of literature that does not enable a criminal to profit from his crime while a victim remains uncompensated." 505 U.S. at 122, 112 S.Ct. at 511. Justice Blackmun concurred, but urged that the Court, in light of the fact that many jurisdictions have similar statutes, should have given the lower courts additional guidance by finding the statute unconstitutionally under-inclusive as well. Justice Kennedy concurred, arguing that even a compelling interest cannot justify a direct, content-based burden on speech protected by the first amendment.

TORRES v. EASTLICK (IN RE NORTH AMERICAN COIN & CURRENCY, LTD.)

United States Court of Appeals, Ninth Circuit, 1985
767 F.2d 1573, cert. denied, 475 U.S. 1083, 106 S.Ct. 1462, 89 L.Ed.2d 719 (1986)

CANBY, CIRCUIT JUDGE:

North American Coin and Currency, Ltd. (hereinafter NAC or debtor) was an Arizona corporation in the business of buying and selling precious metals. The appellants are former customers of NAC who placed orders with the company and paid for them during the week of September 13, 1982, immediately before NAC filed for voluntary reorganization under Chapter 11 of the Bankruptcy Code. They brought this class action against the Bankruptcy Trustee, seeking to recover their funds from the bankruptcy estate. They claim that the trustee holds the funds in constructive trust for them because the debtor obtained the money by fraud or misrepresentation. On cross-motions for summary judgment, the bankruptcy court found for the trustee. The district court affirmed. We have jurisdiction over the appeal pursuant to 28 U.S.C. § 1291, and we affirm.
* * *

[After discovering that NAC was threatened with insolvency, several people affiliated with NAC ("the principals") decided that they should try to operate the company for one more week until a scheduled board of director's and shareholder's meeting. To keep the company operating, while protecting new customers in case the company did not survive, the principals placed all receipts from new transactions during the week before the shareholder's meeting in a new bank account, labeled "Special Trust Account." If the board of directors voted to keep the company going and the shareholders infused the necessary new capital, the trust account funds were to be used to fill the customers' precious metals orders. If the company failed, the principals anticipated that the customers would get their money back.]

* * * NAC filed a Chapter 11 petition for reorganization on September 23, 1982. The funds in the "Special Trust Account" remain intact.

The plaintiffs now assert that the trustee for NAC holds those funds in constructive trust for them.

Property that is truly in trust is not "property of the [trustee's] estate" within the meaning of section 541 of the Bankruptcy Code, 11 U.S.C. § 541. Plaintiffs argue that the same result must follow for property that is subject to a constructive trust. They further contend that, because the existence and nature of the debtor's interests in property are determined by reference to state law, they are entitled to all of the funds in the Special Account if Arizona law would view those funds as subject to a constructive trust.

While we agree that any constructive trust that is given effect must be a creature of Arizona law, we cannot accept the proposition that the bankruptcy estate is automatically deprived of any funds that state law might find subject to a constructive trust. * * * A constructive trust is not the same kind of interest in property as a joint tenancy or a remainder. It is a remedy, flexibly fashioned in equity to provide relief where a balancing of interests in the context of a particular case seems to call for it. Moreover, in the case presented here it is an inchoate remedy; we are not dealing with property that a state court decree has in the past placed under a constructive trust. We necessarily act very cautiously in exercising such a relatively undefined equitable power in favor of one group of potential creditors at the expense of other creditors, for ratable distribution among all creditors is one of the strongest policies behind the bankruptcy laws.

While state law must be applied in a manner consistent with federal bankruptcy law, we do not suggest that it is irrelevant. Arizona law permits the imposition of a constructive trust "whenever title to property has been obtained through actual fraud, misrepresentation, concealment, undue influence, duress, or through any other means which render it unconscionable for the holder of legal title to retain and enjoy its beneficial interest."

In permitting the imposition of a constructive trust for actions amounting to actual fraud, Arizona law is not inconsistent with federal bankruptcy law. Bankruptcy trustees have been held to have no interest in property acquired by fraud of bankrupts, as against the rightful owners of the property. The principle underlying this rule is that the creditors should not benefit from fraud at the expense of those who have been defrauded. * * *

In Arizona, as elsewhere, "actual fraud" is characterized by a willful intent to deceive. The debtor commits fraud, even though he has made no affirmative false representations, if he commits himself to a transaction with no intention of carrying it out. An intention not to carry out the transaction—in other words, a fraudulent intent—may be inferred where the debtor conceals his insolvency knowing that his financial situation is so hopeless that he can never meet the obligation he has acquired. However, the debtor's mere failure to disclose his insolvency, without more, does not constitute a fraud entitling the creditor to rescind the transaction. If the debtor believes in good faith that he will be able to carry out the transaction, he lacks the deceptive intent necessary for a finding of fraud.

We conclude that the evidence on which the plaintiffs rely does not support an inference that NAC intended to defraud them. * * *

Plaintiffs' final contention is that, even if the circumstances do not amount to actual fraud, we should impose a constructive trust on the ground that plaintiffs' funds were obtained by "means which render it unconscionable for the holder of legal title to retain and enjoy its beneficial interest." For reasons of federal bankruptcy policy to which we have already referred, we are reluctant so to exercise a general equitable power in the circumstances here presented. We fully recognize that plaintiffs have sustained substantial losses as a result of the NAC bankruptcy. Plaintiffs, however, comprise only one of several comparable groups of creditors who sustained substantial losses. Plaintiffs happened to place their orders during the week of September 13, with the result that their funds were placed in a "trust" account (even though it was contemplated that the funds might later be removed to complete the transactions). Another group of customers placed their orders shortly before September 13, but sent in their purchase money during the week of September 13. Their funds were not placed in a special account, and they must look to the bankruptcy proceeding for their relief. Other customers both placed their orders and sent in their funds prior to September 13, but their orders had not been executed at the time of the bankruptcy. They, too, are treated as general creditors in the bankruptcy. We fail to discern the equitable principle that requires us to protect the plaintiffs' investments fully, at the expense of these other creditors. Indeed, the equities, as well as the principles underlying the bankruptcy laws, point in the other direction. * * *

Notes

1. In the excerpt that begins this chapter, Professor Laycock identifies three practical advantages to seeking restitution. Which of those three applies here?

2. *On procedure.* Frequently, constructive trusts are asserted against defendants whose obligations exceed their assets, as here. A legal remedy would be inadequate, because a money judgment would be unenforceable, so there is no problem with establishing that an equity court could have taken cognizance of the case.

If the defendant was not insolvent, the Restatement at least made a distinction between a constructive trust arising and a constructive trust being specifically enforceable. While a constructive trust might arise whenever an actor was subject to an equitable duty to convey property to another (see the discussion of the substantive law, below), that trust would only be specifically enforced if the legal remedy was inadequate. See Restatement of Restitution § 160 comment *e*.

The Restatement took this view because it viewed the constructive trust as a substantive legal arrangement that comes into being when property is wrongfully acquired and that "exists" even if a court of equity would not have taken cognizance of the case. For example, suppose a defendant obtains the plaintiff's car by fraud, and still has it in his possession. If the plaintiff sought specific relief in equity, it is generally accepted that it would not be forthcoming; his legal remedy, replevin, would be adequate. George E. Palmer, Law of Restitution § 1.4 at 18 (1978). According to the Restatement of Restitution, however, the defendant would nonetheless have been a "constructive trustee." Restatement of Restitution § 160 comment *e*. Thus, the Restatement of Restitution treats the constructive trust as "arising" when the property subject to the trust is acquired by the defendant, even though no court of equity would enforce it specifically. In the Restatement's terms, whether a constructive trust exists and how it will be enforced are two separate questions, and only the latter turns on the existence of a ground for equity jurisdiction.

The difference between calling the constructive trust a remedy and calling it a substantive legal arrangement seems largely semantic, if not metaphysical. See Stephen Smith, The Structure of Unjust Enrichment Law: Is Restitution a Right or a Remedy?, 36 Loy.L.A.L.Rev. 1037 (2003). An occasional case, however, may turn on the difference. Compare United States v. Fontana, 528 F.Supp. 137 (S.D.N.Y.1981)(if the property in question was acquired by a breach of fiduciary duty, then a constructive trust arose at that time, and the property therefore was not subject to the government's tax lien, even if the beneficiary of the constructive trust did not file suit until after the tax lien was filed) with Taylor Associates v. Diamant, 178 B.R. 480 (9th Cir.BAP 1995)(because constructive trust is inchoate remedy until it is imposed by court, property is subject to trustee's strong arm powers and can be recovered for the debtor's estate).

9. *On the substantive law.* Although the constructive trust is often used as a remedy for wrongdoing—fraud, breach of fiduciary duty, and the like—it is not limited to those situations. Unjust enrichment is all that is required. "Where a person holding title to property is subject to an equitable duty to convey it to another on the ground that he would be unjustly enriched if he were permitted to retain it, a constructive trust arises." Restatement of Restitution § 160. A constructive trust can be used to recover benefits conferred by mistake, Citizens Federal Bank v. Cardian Mortgage Corp., 122 B.R. 255 (Bankr.E.D.Va.1990)(Virginia law)(money credited to account by bookkeeping error), or simply to avoid unfairness, Carr v. Carr, 120 N.J. 336, 576 A.2d 872 (1990)(constructive trust imposed over a portion of the decedent's estate in favor of the spouse who, because decedent died while their divorce was pending, had no claim under New Jersey statutes).

On the other hand, the fact that the defendant owes the plaintiff a debt is not, standing alone, sufficient to give rise to a constructive trust. If money were paid or property delivered to another under circumstances that merely gave rise to a debt, the fact that the defendant was insolvent would not make that debt specifically enforceable. Restatement of Restitution § 160, comment f. Thus, the plaintiffs in *North American Coin and Currency* failed because they could not show that the money had been obtained by fraud, and under Arizona law, without fraud, a constructive trust could not arise. They were left with a mere debt.

In refusing to impose a constructive trust, however, is the court applying Arizona law or federal bankruptcy law? See Thomas H. Jackson, Statutory Liens & Constructive Trust in Bankruptcy: Undoing the Confusion, 61 Am. Bankruptcy L.J. 287 (1987). For a time, the Ninth Circuit's opinion in *North American Coin and Currency* generated some confusion on that point. The Ninth Circuit attempted to clarify the situation in Mitsui Manufacturers Bank v. Unicom Computer Corp., 13 F.3d 321 (9th Cir.1994). Holding that under California law a constructive trust could arise when a debtor negligently detained another's property, the court commented: "[W]e reject the [view] that our opinion in *In re North Am. Coin & Currency, Ltd.* created an elaborate, multi-part test to determine whether and under what circumstances a constructive trust may be imposed on property of a debtor * * *. Our decision should not be read as saying more than what it actually says; viz., that while state law must be the starting point in determining whether a constructive trust may arise in a federal bankruptcy case, that law must be applied in a manner not inconsistent with federal bankruptcy law." Is that clear? See Andrew Kull, Restitution in Bankruptcy: Reclamation and Constructive Trust, 72 Am.Bankr.L.J. 265 (1998).

4. *On the remedy.* As discussed above, a constructive trust can be specifically enforced, at least when the property in question is unique or the defendant insolvent. Then, it results in an order, directed to the defendant, to turn the wrongfully acquired property over to the plaintiff. Because the constructive trust gives the plaintiff the subject property *in specie,* the plaintiff acquires an advantage over an insolvent defendant's other creditors. Thus, had a constructive trust been imposed in *North American Coin & Currency,* the account in question would simply have been turned over to the plaintiffs. Similarly, the constructive trust can allow a plaintiff to reach property that would otherwise be exempt from a money judgment under a homestead or other exemption.

Without the constructive trust, the account remains in the debtor's estate. The plaintiffs are free to pursue their claim by seeking a money judgment for the amounts they are owed, but that judgment will simply establish them as general creditors, entitled to a share of the debtor's assets.

In order to establish a constructive trust, according to the court, they must show that the money was acquired by fraud. Why should that be the case? If NAC still has the plaintiffs' money, shouldn't NAC return it?

On the other hand, why should the plaintiffs have an advantage over NAC's other creditors, even if they can show fraud? According to the court, property acquired by fraud never becomes part of the bankrupt's estate because, in a sense, it is never his property. Why, though, does the manner in which the property was acquired make a difference? The court says that creditors should not benefit from the debtor's fraud at the expense of the one

THE CORPORATION OF THE PRESIDENT OF THE CHURCH OF JESUS CHRIST OF LATTER-DAY SAINTS v. JOLLEY

Supreme Court of Utah, 1970
24 Utah 2d 187, 467 P.2d 984

CROCKETT, CHIEF JUSTICE.

This appeal challenges a judgment and decree of the district court which impressed against the defendant Vickie C. Jolley a constructive trust upon two new automobiles, a 1968 Pontiac Firebird and a 1968 Chevrolet Corvette which had been given her by one LaMar Kay, who had purchased the cars with money embezzled from the plaintiff church. On appeal defendant makes two contentions: 1) that a constructive trust can be imposed only on a fiduciary or confidant and not upon a third person with respect to whom no such relationship exists; and 2) that even if such a constructive trust could be imposed it should extend only to the amount of funds which were identified as being embezzled from the plaintiff and traced into that property.

Where the evidence is in dispute it is surveyed in the light favorable to the trial court findings. The said LaMar Kay was an accountant employed by the plaintiff church. During 1967 and 1968, by the use of fictitious firm names and pretended payment of claims he was engaged in a scheme of embezzling funds. In April of 1968 he drew from a fictitious account in the name of "Barker and Clayton" in the Murray State Bank a check in the amount of $4,305.57 made payable to Peck and Shaw, automobile dealers, with which he paid $4,224.62 for the Pontiac Firebird in question.

In August, 1968, he drew another check on the same account in the amount of $3,000 with which he purchased a cashier's check payable to Capital Chevrolet; this check was then presented to the latter company as part payment for the 1968 Chevrolet Corvette which had a total purchase price of $5,008.87. The balance on this car was paid by $50 cash on August 26, 1968, and $1,958.87 on August 30, 1968. The latter two cash payments admittedly were not traced directly through the "Barker and Clayton" account of embezzled funds into the Corvette automobile. But the evidence does show that a few days before he made those cash payments on that automobile, LaMar Kay had drawn $2,700 in cash from that account.

Upon completion of the purchases as above stated, the titles to both of these automobiles were transferred to the defendant Vickie C. Jolley; and there is no evidence nor contention made that she gave any legal consideration for them. Inasmuch as she is not a bona fide purchaser for value, her defenses in raising the question as to her lack of knowledge of the source of the funds which purchased the automobiles, and her averment that a constructive trust can only be impressed upon the wrongdoing fiduciary or confidant are of no avail to her. Where one has stolen or embezzled the money or property of another, he obtains no title whatsoever. A constructive trust may be impressed upon it in his hands; and equity may continue the trust effective against any subsequent transferee, unless transferred to a bona fide purchaser and under circumstances where equity would require a different result. The evidence in this case justified the court in its conclusion that the defendant had no better title to these automobiles than LaMar Kay had, and that they were held in constructive trust for the benefit of the plaintiff.

As to the defendant's second contention: that the plaintiff is not entitled to recover an equitable portion of the Corvette represented by the $1,958.87 and $50 cash payments which were not traced directly to the embezzled funds, this is to be said: Such direct tracing of funds is not an indispensable requisite to the conclusion arrived at. In the nature of the function of determining facts it is essential that the court or jury have the prerogative of finding not only facts based upon direct evidence, but also those which may be established from the reasonable inferences that may be deduced therefrom. The circumstances here shown concerning the associations of the defendant with LaMar Kay, including the facts that she went with him on the occasion of the purchase of the automobile; and that a few days previous to making the payments in question he had withdrawn $2,700 from the embezzled funds account, provide a reasonable basis for the trial court to believe that it was paid for entirely by money embezzled from plaintiff.

Affirmed.

HENRIOD, JUSTICE (dissenting).

Without expressing any opinion as to the rest of the main opinion and its conclusion, I dissent from that portion which includes $50 and $1,958.87 cash, in any amount upon which a purported trust could be impressed. The main opinion's own language reflects the weakness of the decision with respect to those amounts, which is compounded by the obvious conjecture indulged by 'guessing' that such amounts must have been a part of a much greater withdrawal. * * *

NOTES

1. *Jolley* demonstrates another advantage of the equitable remedies for unjust enrichment. To prevent unjust enrichment, the equity courts would follow, or "trace," the wrongfully held property through changes both in form (from money to car) and in possession (from Kay to Jolley), so long as a bona fide purchase for value did not intervene. The benefits of tracing are obvious. If the property has changed forms, only by tracing can the plaintiff obtain a specific restitutionary remedy and the advantage over general creditors that goes with it. The same is true if the property has changed hands. Tracing allows a specific remedy against the new holder, as to whom there might otherwise be no remedy at all.

Moreover, in the right circumstances, following property into its product can turn a neat profit for the plaintiff. Suppose Kay had bought stock with the church's money, instead of buying the cars. The stock would then be the product of the embezzled funds, and the church would be able to assert a constructive trust over it, profiting from any appreciation in its value. The church would get a windfall, which would be justified by adverting to the maxim that a wrongdoer should not profit from his wrongdoing.

Thus, while a profit-based measure of recovery has been the exception rather than the rule where legal restitution is concerned, equity has always admitted the possibility through the constructive trust. Both the profit-based measure of damages, however, and the capture of profits through the constructive trust have been restricted to cases of conscious wrongdoing. If the defendant acquired the plaintiff's property innocently and exchanged it for more valuable property, a constructive trust would not be enforced over the acquired property. That is, if Jolley, not knowing the cars were bought with embezzled money, had exchanged the cars for stock, and the stock appreciated in value, the church could not enforce a constructive trust over the stock. The church, instead, would be limited to another equitable remedy, the *equitable lien*.

An *equitable lien*, like any lien, is a security interest in another's property; it gives the lien holder the right to sell the property and have the proceeds applied to his claim. If the proceeds of the sale exceed the claim, the excess belongs to the property owner (and his creditors). If the proceeds of the sale are insufficient to satisfy the claim, the lienholder may, at least in the case of an equitable lien, have a money judgment for the deficiency.

In some circumstances, as where the innocent recipient of property subject to a constructive trust has exchanged it for more valuable property, an equitable lien may be the only equitable remedy available to a plaintiff. In other cases, however, the plaintiff may actually prefer an equitable lien even though a constructive trust would also be available. For example, if Kay had used the embezzled funds to purchase stock and the stock's value had depreciated, should the church seek a constructive trust over the stock, an equitable lien against it, or a money judgment for the amount embezzled?

A third equitable remedy, *subrogation,* may also come into play in cases where property subject to a constructive trust is exchanged. Where property subject to a constructive trust has been used to satisfy a debt, neither the constructive trust nor the equitable lien is available as a remedy because the property is no longer in the defendant's possession. (Nor would any remedy lie against the creditor whose debt was satisfied, because unless he had notice of the defendant's wrongdoing, he would have given value in exchange for the property and thus would be a bona fide purchaser for value.) In such a case, the only equitable remedy open to the plaintiff is subrogation. Subrogation places the plaintiff in the same position occupied by the creditor whose debt was satisfied, giving the plaintiff the advantage of whatever security or priorities that creditor might have had. For example, if Kay used the embezzled funds to pay off the mortgage on his home, subrogation would place the church in the mortgagee's position, with its claim secured by Kay's home. See

Restatement (Third) of Restitution and Unjust Enrichment § 41 (Misappropriation of Financial Assets) (Tentative Draft No. 4, 2005).

2. The right to a constructive trust, an equitable lien, or subrogation turns on the plaintiff's ability to trace the wrongfully acquired property into some property currently in the defendant's possession (or in the case of subrogation, into a discharged debt). For example, the inability to trace unjust enrichment to a wrongful act inflicted on any plaintiff prevented recovery in a case in which the plaintiffs sought restitution for the unjust enrichment gained by companies from slavery. In re African–American Slave Descendants Litigation, 471 F.3d 754, 760 (7th Cir.2006), cert. denied, 552 U.S. ___, 128 S.Ct. 92, 169 L.Ed.2d 243 (2007).

As the dissent in *Jolley* points out, if the plaintiff cannot show that the second car was bought with the embezzled funds, it cannot impose a constructive trust on the car. But why should that be the case? Why should it make a difference whether Kay bought the car with his own money, and spent the church's money on fast living, or if he bought the car with the church's money and wasted his own? Consider the following:

* * * [I]n this case we are asked * * * to hold that, where one's property has been wrongfully applied and dissipated by another, a charge remains upon the estate of the latter for the amount thus wrongfully taken, upon the ground that his estate is thereby so much larger, and that the trust property is really and clearly there, in a substituted form, although it cannot be directly traced. * * * While one who has been wronged may follow and take his own property, or its visible product, it is quite a different thing to say that he may take the property of somebody else. The general property of an insolvent debtor belongs to his creditors, as much as particular trust property belongs to a cestui que trust. * * *

"Suppose that an insolvent debtor, D., has only $1,000 of property, but is indebted to the amount of $2,000, one-half of which is due to A., and the other half to B. In this condition of things D.'s property can only pay fifty per cent of his debts. By such distribution A. and B. would each be equitably entitled to $500. Now, suppose D., while in that condition, collects $1,000 for F., but instead of remitting the money, as he should, he uses it in paying his debt in full to A. By doing so, D. has not increased his assets a penny, nor diminished his aggregate indebtedness a penny. The only difference is that he now owes $1,000 each to B. and F., whereas he previously owed $1,000 each to A. and B. Now if F. is to have preference over B., then his claim will absorb the entire amount of D.'s property, leaving nothing whatever for B. In other words, the $500 to which B. was equitably entitled from his insolvent debtor, upon a fair distribution of the estate, has, without any fault of his, been paid to another, merely in consequence of the wrongful act of the debtor." [Francis v. Evans, 69 Wis. 115, 33 N.W. 93 (1887) (Taylor J. dissenting).]
* * * The illustration demonstrates that the mere fact that a trustee has used the money does not show that it has gone into his estate. If used to pay debts, he has simply turned it over to a creditor, thereby giving him a preference, while his own estate and indebtedness remains exactly as before. Suppose he had stolen the money, and turned it over to somebody

from whom it could not be reclaimed. Can anyone say the owner should have an equitable lien upon the thief's insolvent estate in preference to his creditors? They and the owner are equally innocent, and each must bear his own misfortune.

Slater v. Oriental Mills, 18 R.I. 352, 27 A. 443, 444 (1893). The theory that the plaintiff's assets are "still in" the defendant's estate even if they cannot be traced specifically (the "swollen assets" theory) has generally been rejected. The plaintiff must be able to trace in order to assert a constructive trust or other equitable restitutionary remedy. Only if F. can show that D. used his own money to pay A., and kept F.'s, can F. assert a constructive trust over the remaining $1000.

But should the result really turn on which specific dollar bills D. used to pay A.? Professor Oesterle thinks not:

> Assume that Wrongdoer, with ten dollars in his pocket, steals ten dollars from Owner. Wrongdoer then deposits his ten dollars in an interest-bearing bank account and exchanges Owner's ten dollars for a hat. At the time Owner gets a judgment against Wrongdoer, the bank account has produced one dollar of interest and the hat is worth fifteen dollars. Owner traces into the hat and realizes a profit of five dollars from his stolen money. Tracing conclusively presumes that Wrongdoer's benefit from the conversion is the traceable product—the hat. Wrongdoer argues that his real benefit from the conversion is not fifteen dollars but eleven dollars, for had he not stolen Owner's money, Wrongdoer would have purchased the hat with his ten dollars and foregone the one dollar of interest. His profit from the conversion, Wrongdoer contends, was the money stolen, plus the one dollar of interest that he was able to earn as a result of depositing his own ten dollars with a bank at market rates of interest. * * *

> Objectively, the wealth that Wrongdoer gained as the result of the conversion depends on whether he still would have bought the hat had he not taken Owner's money. If so, then the actual benefits arising from the misappropriation are measured more accurately by the difference between Wrongdoer's wealth after the misappropriation and Wrongdoer's wealth had he purchased the misappropriated property with available funds or lines of credit. Wrongdoer's actual benefit arising from the conversion is his ability to forego use of the other available sources of capital to purchase the hat. The four dollar gain, representing what Wrongdoer would have realized if he had acted lawfully in purchasing the hat with his own ten dollars (or with a borrowed ten dollars) is not a benefit derived from the conversion; rather, the benefit is attributable to extraneous factors, such as smart trading, or favorable market conditions. On the other hand, if Wrongdoer would not have bought the hat without Owner's money, then he can be said to have the hat solely as the result of the conversion. * * *

Dale Oesterle, Deficiencies of the Restitutionary Right to Trace Misappropriated Property in Equity and in UCC § 9–306, 68 Corn.L.Rev. 172, 198 (1983). According to Professor Oesterle, if the goal is to prevent unjust enrichment, tracing based on physical exchanges (which dollars were spent for what) is unprincipled. Because tracing ignores causation, it may deprive the defendant of gains that are not "unjust," because they are not the result of the defendant's misappropriation, but rather the result of his efforts, skill or luck. To do so cannot be justified as necessary to prevent unjust enrichment; it is simply punitive.

3. Tracing can also be used to capture profits generated by the misappropriated property itself. Where the misappropriated property has generated dividends, interest, rents, or any other form of income, those profits may be recovered. Restatement of Restitution §§ 158, 205. If the profits are to some extent attributable to the defendant's efforts, should that be taken into account? See supra at pp. 739, 767; Dale Oesterle, Deficiencies of the Restitutionary Right to Trace Misappropriated Property in Equity and in UCC § 9–306, 68 Corn.L.Rev. 172 (1983).

4. In tracing cases, the burden of showing that the defendant exchanged property subject to a constructive trust for other property is on the plaintiff. Was the church's evidence sufficient to establish the right to a constructive trust over Jolley's Corvette? To aid plaintiffs who must trace wrongfully acquired property through various incarnations in order to get some equitable remedy, a number of tracing fictions have evolved, as the next case illustrates.

IN RE MUSHROOM TRANSPORTATION CO.

United States Bankruptcy Court, Eastern District of Pennsylvania, 1998
227 B.R. 244

By BRUCE FOX, BANKRUPTCY JUDGE:

The chapter 7 trustee of the consolidated entities known as Mushroom Transportation, Jeoffrey L. Burtch, has brought suit against a number of defendants, [asserting] that [the] defendants received the proceeds of property stolen from the estate of Mushroom Transportation by former counsel to the debtor, Jonathan Ganz. Further, the trustee averred that these * * * defendants "knew or reasonably should have known that the monies received" by them from Mr. Ganz did not belong to him. His complaint sought * * * monetary relief in four separate counts: two in common law—conversion and constructive trust; and two statutory claims—turnover (under 11 U.S.C. § 542 or 543) and "unauthorized transfer" pursuant to 11 U.S.C. §§ 549, 550.

In their opposition to the trustee's claims, the four defendants asserted that they had lent money to Mr. Ganz, they had been properly repaid by him, and there was no evidence that he had repaid them with money stolen from Mushroom Transportation. Further, Fidelity argued at trial that if it had been repaid with stolen money, it neither knew nor should have known of this fact and so were entitled to be treated as a good faith transferee who received the property for fair value.

* * *

I.

* * *

A.

The four causes of action stated against the defendants have a common evidentiary element: each of them requires a showing that the proceeds of funds stolen from the now consolidated estate of Mushroom Transportation were paid to the defendants. That is, the plaintiff here cannot prevail unless he can establish that the proceeds of estate funds from the debtor were transferred by Mr. Ganz to the defendants. * * *

Here, of course, Mr. Ganz deposited the funds he stole from the Mushroom estate into his personal bank account with Fidelity Bank. These funds were then commingled with other deposits (both before and after the thefts) and used to pay a large number of individuals and entities. Many of the other deposits were derived from legitimate sources; some were derived from thefts from other bankruptcy estates.

Obviously, Mr. Ganz, by his embezzlement of Mushroom funds, converted property of the bankruptcy estates to his own use as a matter of Pennsylvania law. Pennsylvania law would apply in this adversary proceeding because the theft of funds arose from Pennsylvania corporations, occurred in Pennsylvania, and the misappropriated funds were deposited in Pennsylvania. Since the proceeding here does not involve competing creditor claims to bankruptcy estate property, there are no federal bankruptcy policies which suggest that state law should be preempted. Thus, the bankruptcy trustee, acting on behalf of the Mushroom estate, has a claim against Mr. Ganz due to his theft of property.

* * *

Under state law, the bankruptcy estates, acting through the bankruptcy trustee, had the right to claim that the funds stolen by Mr. Ganz were held in trust by the thief on their behalf. Such a claim would prefer them to other creditors of Mr. Ganz. That is, even if Mr. Ganz were insolvent, the bankruptcy trustee could validly assert under Pennsylvania law that he should be repaid first from all funds stolen by Mr. Ganz and still in his possession, because those funds as a matter of state law were held by Mr. Ganz in trust for the Mushroom estate. However, in order to prevail on any trust claim against Ganz, the bankruptcy trustee must "trace the proceeds received from the conversion and identify them as contained in some specific fund or property in possession [of the wrongdoer.]" If the stolen funds were no longer in the possession of Mr. Ganz when the bankruptcy trustee made demand for their return, no such recovery would be ordered and the bankruptcy trustee would hold but a general unsecured claim against Ganz for conversion.

Were a third party to receive the converted funds from Ganz with knowledge that they were converted (either actual or presumed knowledge) then the bankruptcy trustee could recover the converted property from the third party recipient on the common law claims of conversion or constructive trust.

The fact that Ganz deposited the stolen funds into a bank account does not preclude the imposition of a constructive trust being established. However, it is necessary that the stolen funds be traced into that particular account. Where improperly converted assets of a trust estate are traced into the fund for distribution, a preference has always been allowed on the theory that such assets have never become a part of those of the trustee but at all times have remained, whether in their original or substituted form, the property of the cestui que trust, and therefore the trustee's general creditors are not entitled to any share in their distribution.

The fact that Ganz commingled the stolen Mushroom funds by depositing other funds, derived from both legitimate and illegitimate sources, into this bank account does not by itself preclude the imposition of a trust. However, tracing the amount of stolen funds remaining in the account at any given time involves the application of a number of common law presumptions.

As a general rule, in tracing the origins of funds withdrawn from a bank account, Pennsylvania applies the rule established in Clayton's Case, 1 Merrival 572 (Ch. 1816), that the funds first deposited are the funds first withdrawn.

This principle has been modified by application of the presumptions articulated in English common law in In re Hallett's Estate [Knatchbull v. Hallett], 13 Ch.D. 696 (1879) when tracing funds which have been commingled by a tortfeasor into a bank account. There are two related presumptions derived from *Hallett's Estate* and accepted in Pennsylvania (and federal) common law. First, if the fiduciary (i.e., tortfeasor/depositor) has a choice of withdrawing either the proceeds of trust funds or legitimate funds, then the fiduciary will withdraw the legitimate funds. Second, once the proceeds of the trust (i.e., stolen funds) are spent by the fiduciary, new deposits made are not treated as replenishing the trust proceeds. Together, these two tracing presumptions are sometimes referred to as the "lowest intermediate balance" rule.

As summarized by the Third Circuit Court of Appeals:

> The lowest intermediate balance rule, a legal construct, allows trust beneficiaries to assume that trust funds are withdrawn last from a commingled account. Once trust money is removed, however, it is not replenished by subsequent deposits. Therefore, the lowest intermediate balance in a commingled account represents trust funds that have never been dissipated and which are reasonably identifiable.

* * *

Counsel for the trustee in this adversary proceeding assumed at the end of the trial that certain commingled bank account presumptions, which as a matter of equity were established to resolve disputes regarding claims to property held by a tortfeasor, were applicable to the instant litigation. That is, the tracing decisions cited above generally involved disputes over claims to funds remaining on deposit in bank accounts still in the possession of the tortfeasor, rather than to claims against innocent third parties who dealt with the tortfeasor. Here, the application of the intermediate balance rule in any claim by the trustee for a constructive trust against Mr. Ganz would result in a conclusion that he no longer held any funds in trust, since his account balance reached zero on October 10, 1989—years before this litigation commenced.

Nonetheless, if I accept plaintiff's position, arguendo, and apply commingled bank account tracing presumptions to this dispute, there remain two defects to his claims against these four defendants on the evidence presented.

First, the evidence does not support the bankruptcy trustee's argument that the defendants here received the proceeds of funds stolen from the Mushroom estate. Not only does the plaintiff overlook the intermediate balance rule, but he also ignores the principle accepted in Pennsylvania that when trust funds from various estates are commingled, there is a presumption that they are treated on a "first in, first out" basis. See Fischbach & Moore v. Philadelphia Nat. Bank, 134 Pa. Super. at 91; see also Empire State Surety Co. v. Carroll County:

> Where a trustee has mingled in a common fund the moneys of many separate cestuis que trustent and then made payments out of this common fund, the legal presumption is that the moneys were paid out in the order in which they were paid in, and the cestuis que trustent are equitably entitled to any allowable preference in the inverse order of the times of their respective payments into the fund.

194 F. at 605.

Recently, the Pennsylvania Superior Court was faced with competing claims of two fraud victims to the remaining funds in a bank account of a tortfeasor who had deposited funds wrongfully obtained from both victims. Certain withdrawals had been made leaving a balance insufficient to repay both claimants. The appellate court concluded that, under Pennsylvania law, the funds withdrawn were derived from the first victim only based upon the "first in, first out" presumption:

> In attempting to trace funds, the rule in Pennsylvania is "first in, first out." Pursuant to this rule, "the legal presumption is that the moneys were paid out in the order which they were paid in, and [the parties claiming ownership] are equitably entitled to any allowable preference in the inverse order of the times of their respective payments into the fund." * * *

Here, the government audit of Mr. Ganz's Fidelity account makes clear that, upon application of the intermediate balance rule along with the first in, first out principle for the proceeds of stolen funds, there were no Mushroom funds remaining in that account at the time of Mr. Ganz's challenged payments to these defendants. If any stolen funds were presumptively in the Fidelity account at the time the two challenged transfers were made, using the intermediate balance rule that legitimate funds were dispersed first, and then using the first in, first out principle regarding stolen funds, the proceeds of stolen funds on hand at the time of the two transfers could only have been derived from bankruptcy estates other than Mushroom; Mr. Ganz deposited the proceeds of those other thefts after he deposited the Mushroom proceeds, and the Mushroom proceeds would have been spent.

Accordingly, the defendants did not receive any of the proceeds of funds stolen from the Mushroom estate. Since these four defendants never received any estate property, the trustee has no right to recover any funds paid to them based upon the four theories he has asserted. Therefore, the defendants are entitled to judgment.

B.

Second, even if the trustee had proven that the defendants had received the proceeds of Mr. Ganz's theft from the Mushroom estates, plaintiff's claims founder on a second requirement: that any recovery be against third parties who were not bona fide transferees for value.

* * *

As explained recently by the Pennsylvania Superior Court:

A cause of action for money had and received entitles a party to relief where money is wrongfully diverted from its proper use and that money subsequently falls into the hands of a third person who has not given valuable consideration for it.... The cause of action fails, however, where the recipient of the money has given consideration in exchange for the funds and is unaware that the money was procured by fraudulent means.

Under the Restatement of Restitution, the cause of action is defined as follows:

A person who, non-tortiously and without notice that another has the beneficial ownership of it, acquires property which it would not have been wrongful for him to acquire with notice of the facts and of which he is not a purchaser for value is, upon discovery of the facts, under a duty to account to the other for the direct product of the subject matter and the value of the use to him, if any, and in addition, to

    a) return the subject matter in specie, if he has it;

    b) pay its value to him, if he has non-tortiously consumed it in beneficial use;

    c) pay its value or what he received therefor at his election, if he has disposed of it.

Restatement of Restitution § 123

Therefore, had Fidelity Bank and the A–1 defendants received funds from Mr. Ganz which could be traced to the proceeds of funds stolen from the Mushroom estates, there is no evidence that these defendants were not bona fide purchasers for value under state law.

Further, under Pennsylvania law it is well established that a tortfeasor's payments to third parties in satisfaction of antecedent debts represent fair value for the payments received.

* * *

In this proceeding there was no evidence presented to demonstrate that the four defendants involved in the instant trial received any payments from Mr. Ganz for which fair consideration was not given, or that they knew or should have known that the funds used to pay them did not belong to Mr. Ganz. On the contrary, the evidence is unrebutted that the defendants had lent money either to Mr. Ganz or an entity for which he provided a guarantee, and that the challenged transfers were simply repayments of those earlier obligations. * * *

Based upon this evidence, I conclude that the defendants were good faith transferees for value. As such, the plaintiff is not entitled to any relief.

* * *

Notes

1. Another advantage of tracing is that it can allow a plaintiff to recover misappropriated money that has been commingled with other money. Tracing, however, may be difficult when the commingled account has been subject to multiple deposits and withdrawals. Courts have developed a number of tracing fictions to be used in such cases. The first of these, the rule in *Clayton's Case*, or first-in, first-out (FIFO), is basically an accounting principle. FIFO posits that withdrawals are made in the same order as deposits, so that the money first deposited is first withdrawn. Suppose Thief steals $100 from Owner, and deposits it in an account, to which he adds $100 of his own. He then withdraws $100, and spends it, leaving $100 in the account. Under FIFO, the $100 remaining in the account belongs to Thief. The first money deposited (Owner's) is presumed to have been the first money withdrawn.

2. Whatever its merits as an accounting principle, FIFO has little to recommend it in restitution cases, if equity and the prevention of unjust enrichment are the goals. In cases involving the commingling of a claimant's and a wrongdoer's funds, it has largely been replaced by the rule in *Hallett's Estate* (Knatchbull v. Hallett, 13 Ch.Div. 356 (1879)). According to *Hallett's Estate*, the wrongdoer is presumed to spend his own money first, whatever the order of deposits. Thus, in the above example, Thief would be presumed to have spent his own money first, and the $100 remaining in the account would be presumed to be Owner's.

The rule in *Hallett's Estate* is qualified, however, by the *lowest intermediate balance* rule. Once all the wrongdoer's money has been withdrawn, subsequent withdrawals can only have been from the misappropriated funds. Even if the balance in the account later increases, the claimant's stake cannot exceed the lowest balance in the account between the time of the original deposit and the present. Subsequent deposits to the account are not treated as restoring the claimant's funds, unless there is specific evidence that they were so intended. Thus, to continue with the example, if Thief withdraws an additional $25 from the account, reducing the balance to $75, the $25 withdrawal must have been Owner's money, as Thief's money has all already been withdrawn. Even if the balance in the account later increases to $100 or more because of subsequent deposits, Owner's claim against the account is limited to $75, the lowest intermediate balance. (It is important to keep in mind, however, that tracing is only required when an equitable remedy is sought. Owner can only impose a constructive trust on $75 in the account. He can, of course, seek a money judgment to compensate him for the additional $25.)

Applying the lowest intermediate balance rule, however, can be complicated. See, e.g., Republic Supply Co. v. Richfield Oil Co., 79 F.2d 375 (9th Cir.1935)(rule is to be applied not by looking at the precise order of deposits and withdrawals, but by the account's daily closing balance). Also, some courts have made it relatively easy to establish that subsequent deposits to an account were intended to restore the trust fund, in which case the lowest intermediate balance rule does not preclude recovery. See, e.g., Mitchell v. Dunn, 211 Cal. 129, 294 P. 386 (1930).

3. Thieves are not necessarily wastrels. Suppose Thief's first withdrawal from the account is invested lucratively, rather than wasted. Should it then be presumed that he spent his own money first? In *In re: Oatway* (Hertslet v. Oatway [1903] 2 Ch.Div. 356), an English case that has been followed in many American jurisdictions, the court developed the "option rule." The option rule allows the claimant against a fund that has commingled trust funds and the wrongdoer's funds to choose whether to treat any particular withdrawal as his, so long as his money could be traced to the account at the time of the withdrawal, consistent with the lowest intermediate balance rule.

4. When funds belonging to more than one claimant are commingled in an account, the *averaging approach* can provide an attractive, though sometimes complicated, alternative to FIFO. Suppose Thief embezzles $100 from Owner One and $100 from Owner Two and deposits it all in one account. Then, Thief spends $100 from the account on stock, which has appreciated by the time of trial to a value of $150. Finally, Thief withdraws the remaining $100, and spends it. Under the FIFO approach, the stock (the first withdrawal) would be presumed to have been purchased with Owner One's money (the first deposit). Owner One would have a claim to the stock, and Owner Two (whose money remained in the account, according to the fiction) would have a money judgment against the presumably insolvent Thief. (The *Hallett's Estate* approach is irrelevant because there is no reason to presume that Thief would spend one claimant's money before another's.)

The *averaging,* or *pro rata,* approach attempts to treat all claimants equitably by giving each a proportionate claim against any withdrawal in an amount determined by the claimant's share in the account at the time the withdrawal was made. Thus, since Owner One and Owner Two each had a claim to half of the account at the time of the withdrawal, each would have a claim to half of the stock.

5. Keep in mind that the tracing fictions are equitable devices, and their use may be limited to avoid harm to creditors. See Bank of Alex Brown v. Goldberg, 158 B.R. 188 (Bankr.E.D.Cal.1993)(creditor must show his property was specifically and directly exchanged for the property subject to the trust if defendant is insolvent, unless tracing will not harm other creditors), aff'd, 168 B.R. 382 (9th Cir.BAP 1994); Emily Sherwin, Unjust Enrichment and Creditors, 27 Rev.Litig. 141 (2007).

6. The Restatement of Restitution attempted to develop an approach to tracing that would simplify and rationalize the law by eliminating tracing fictions, but its approach proved to be difficult to apply in complex cases and was not well-received by the courts. See George E. Palmer, Law of Restitution § 2.17 at 208 (1978). The Restatement (Third) of Restitution and Unjust Enrichment § 59 (Tentative Draft No. 7, 2008) returns to more familiar ground, largely following traditional tracing rules. Within the limits of the lowest intermediate balance rule, it endorses the "marshalling" or "option" approach of *In re Oatway,* allowing a claimant whose funds are commingled with a wrongdoer's to follow his funds into any traceable product of the commingled account. As between claimants whose funds are commingled, the rule in *Clayton's Case* (*FIFO*) is rejected in favor of the averaging approach, giving each claimant a share of the account or its traceable products in proportion to the claimant's stake.

7. Courts have adapted many of the tracing fictions in implementing statutory forfeiture schemes. See, e.g., United States v. Banco Cafetero Panama, 797 F.2d 1154 (2d Cir.1986)(using tracing fictions to determine if funds in an account are "proceeds" of a drug transaction.); United States v. All Funds, 832 F.Supp. 542 (E.D.N.Y.1993). See also 18 U.S.C. § 984 (abrogating the lowest intermediate balance rule in forfeiture cases).

A Tracing Problem

Arielle is an accountant who keeps the books for several small businesses. On August 17, she embezzled $10,000 from Grady, one of her clients. She used $4,000 to make the last payment on her car loan, and deposited the remaining $6,000 in her personal checking account. On August 30, she wrote a check to her landlord, George Mazel, for $1,000. On September 1, she deposited $2,000 of her own money in the account. On September 15, she bought 30 shares of common stock in Notachance, Inc., for $100 a share, paying for it with money from the account. On September 19, she embezzled $8,000 from a second client, Brennan, and deposited it in the account. On October 1, she deposited $2,000 of her own money in the account. On October 3, she purchased 600 shares of common stock in Quikbux, Inc., for $10 a share.

Grady and Brennan have discovered Arielle's embezzling. Identify the remedies available to them. (Notachance, Inc. is currently selling for $50 a share; Quikbux is going for $20.)

CHAPTER 8

COLLECTION OF MONETARY JUDGMENTS

■ ■ ■

A. PROVISIONAL RELIEF

In many instances, a plaintiff cannot wait for the wheels of justice to turn completely. Time may be of the essence. As we have seen in Chapter 3, the court has power, in equity, to issue TROs and preliminary injunctions. Where money rather than equitable relief is at issue, courts have other specialized procedures to make certain that assets do not disappear pending a full consideration on the merits. Because the purpose is to make sure that the defendants will be able to satisfy any money judgment which the court may render, the assets do not even have to be related to the underlying controversy. E.g., Maine R.Civ.Proc. 4A(c). See also F.R.Civ.P. 64 ("all remedies providing for seizure of person or property for the purpose of securing satisfaction of judgment ultimately to be entered * * * are available * * * in the manner provided by the law of the state in which the district court is held"). If necessary, the court can even appoint a receiver to operate the asset (such as a business) until the right to ownership is decided on the merits. See F.R.Civ.P. 66.

The Supreme Court has held, however, that the district courts may not use Rule 65 to issue a preliminary injunction preventing defendants from disposing of assets pending the adjudication of a contract claim for money damages. Justice Scalia, for a majority of five justices, held that this use of a preliminary injunction was not permissible because such a remedy was historically unavailable from a court of equity. The dissent of four justices, while recognizing that enjoining the disposal of assets was an uncommon use of equity power, would have permitted it as being within the basic principles of the use of equity power. Grupo Mexicano de Desarrollo S.A. v. Alliance Bond Fund, Inc., 527 U.S. 308, 119 S.Ct. 1961, 144 L.Ed.2d 319 (1999). Other common law countries permit its courts to issue preliminary injunctions under these circumstances. Mark S.W. Hoyle, Freezing and Search Orders (4th ed.2006); Stephen B. Burbank, The Bitter with the Sweet: Tradition, History, and Limitations on Federal Judicial Power—A Case Study, 75 Notre Dame L. Rev. 1291 (2000). Where state law allows the use of injunctive relief for freezing assets in aid of satisfying the ultimate judgment, however, the federal court may invoke that power pursuant to F.R.Civ.P. 64. United States ex rel. Rahman v. Oncology Associates P.C., 198 F.3d 489 (4th Cir.1999).

An important concern about any provisional legal relief that may be available has been that it be fair to both sides in the legal dispute. As the next cases indicate, the Supreme Court of the United States has assessed the constitutionality of many of the most commonly used procedures.

CONNECTICUT v. DOEHR

Supreme Court of the United States, 1991
501 U.S. 1, 111 S.Ct. 2105, 115 L.Ed.2d 1

JUSTICE WHITE delivered an opinion, Parts I, II, and III of which are the opinion of the Court.*

This case requires us to determine whether a state statute that authorizes prejudgment attachment of real estate without prior notice or hearing, without a showing of extraordinary circumstances, and without a requirement that the person seeking the attachment post a bond, satisfies the Due Process Clause of the Fourteenth Amendment. We hold that, as applied to this case, it does not.

I

On March 15, 1988, Petitioner John F. DiGiovanni submitted an application to the Connecticut Superior Court for an attachment in the amount of $75,000 on respondent Brian K. Doehr's home in Meridan, Connecticut. DiGiovanni took this step in conjunction with a civil action for assault and battery that he was seeking to institute against Doehr in the same court. The suit did not involve Doehr's real estate nor did DiGiovanni have any pre-existing interest either in Doehr's home or any of his other property.

Connecticut law authorizes prejudgment attachment of real estate without affording prior notice or the opportunity for a prior hearing to the individual whose property is subject to the attachment. The State's prejudgment remedy statute provides, in relevant part:

> "The court or a judge of the court may allow the prejudgment remedy to be issued by an attorney without hearing * * * upon verification by oath of the plaintiff or of some competent affiant, that there is probable cause to sustain the validity of the plaintiff's claims and (1) that the prejudgment remedy requested is for an attachment of real property...." Conn.Gen.Stat. § 52–278e (1991).

The statute does not require the plaintiff to post a bond to insure the payment of damages that the defendant may suffer should the attachment prove wrongfully issued or the claim prove unsuccessful.

As required, DiGiovanni submitted an affidavit in support of his application. In five one-sentence paragraphs, DiGiovanni stated that the

---

* CHIEF JUSTICE [REHNQUIST], JUSTICE BLACKMUN, JUSTICE KENNEDY, and JUSTICE SOUTER join Parts I, II, and III of this opinion, and JUSTICE SCALIA joins Parts I and III.

facts set forth in his previously submitted complaint were true; that "I was willfully, wantonly and maliciously assaulted by the defendant, Brian K. Doehr"; that "[s]aid assault and battery broke my left wrist and further caused an ecchymosis to my right eye, as well as other injuries"; and that "I have further expended sums of money for medical care and treatment." The affidavit concluded with the statement, "In my opinion, the foregoing facts are sufficient to show that there is probable cause that judgment will be rendered for the plaintiff."

On the strength of these submissions the Superior Court judge, by an order dated March 17, found "probable cause to sustain the validity of the plaintiff's claim" and ordered the attachment on Doehr's home "to the value of $75,000." The sheriff attached the property four days later, on March 21. Only after this did Doehr receive notice of the attachment. He also had yet to be served with the complaint, which is ordinarily necessary for an action to commence in Connecticut. As the statute further required, the attachment notice informed Doehr that he had the right to a hearing: (1) to claim that no probable cause existed to sustain the claim; (2) to request that the attachment be vacated, modified, or that a bond be substituted; or (3) to claim that some portion of the property was exempt from execution.

Rather than pursue these options, Doehr filed suit against DiGiovanni in Federal District Court, claiming that § 52–278e(a)(1) was unconstitutional under the Due Process Clause of the Fourteenth Amendment. The District Court upheld the statute and granted summary judgment in favor of DiGiovanni. On appeal, a divided panel of the United States Court of Appeals for the Second Circuit reversed. * * * We granted certiorari * * *.

II

With this case we return to the question of what process must be afforded by a state statute enabling an individual to enlist the aid of the State to deprive another of his or her property by means of the prejudgment attachment or similar procedure. Our cases reflect the numerous variations this type of remedy can entail. In Sniadach v. Family Finance Corp. of Bay View, 395 U.S. 337, 89 S.Ct. 1820, 23 L.Ed.2d 349 (1969), the Court struck down a Wisconsin statute that permitted a creditor to effect prejudgment garnishment of wages without notice and prior hearing to the wage earner. In Fuentes v. Shevin, 407 U.S. 67, 92 S.Ct. 1983, 32 L.Ed.2d 556 (1972), the Court likewise found a Due Process violation in state replevin provisions that permitted vendors to have goods seized through an *ex parte* application to a court clerk and the posting of a bond. Conversely, the Court upheld a Louisiana *ex parte* procedure allowing a lienholder to have disputed goods sequestered in Mitchell v. W.T. Grant Co., 416 U.S. 600, 94 S.Ct. 1895, 40 L.Ed.2d 406 (1974). *Mitchell*, however, carefully noted that *Fuentes* was decided against "a factual and legal background sufficiently different ... that it does not require the invalidation of the Louisiana sequestration statute." Those differences included

Louisiana's provision of an immediate postdeprivation hearing along with the option of damages; the requirement that a judge rather than a clerk determine that there is a clear showing of entitlement to the writ; the necessity for a detailed affidavit; and an emphasis on the lien-holder's interest in preventing waste or alienation of the encumbered property. In North Georgia Finishing, Inc. v. Di–Chem, Inc., 419 U.S. 601, 95 S.Ct. 719, 42 L.Ed.2d 751 (1975), the Court again invalidated an *ex parte* garnishment statute that not only failed to provide for notice and prior hearing but that also failed to require a bond, a detailed affidavit setting out the claim, the determination of a neutral magistrate, or a prompt postdeprivation hearing.

These cases "underscore the truism that '[d]ue process unlike some legal rules, is not a technical conception with a fixed content unrelated to time, place and circumstances.'" Mathews v. Eldridge, 424 U.S. [319] at 334, 96 S.Ct., at 902 [(1976)] (quoting Cafeteria Workers v. McElroy, 367 U.S. 886, 895, 81 S.Ct. 1743, 1748, 6 L.Ed.2d 1230 (1961)). In *Mathews*, we drew upon our prejudgment remedy decisions to determine what process is due when the government itself seeks to effect a deprivation on its own initiative. That analysis resulted in the now familiar threefold inquiry requiring consideration of "the private interest that will be affected by the official action"; "the risk of an erroneous deprivation of such interest through the procedures used, and the probable value, if any, of additional or substitute safeguards"; and lastly "the Government's interest, including the function involved and the fiscal and administrative burdens that the additional or substitute procedural requirement would entail."

Here the inquiry is similar but the focus is different. Prejudgment remedy statutes ordinarily apply to disputes between private parties rather than between an individual and the government. Such enactments are designed to enable one of the parties to "make use of state procedures with the overt, significant assistance of state officials," and they undoubtedly involve state action "substantial enough to implicate the Due Process Clause." Tulsa Professional Collection Services, Inc. v. Pope, 485 U.S. 478, 486, 108 S.Ct. 1340, 1345, 99 L.Ed.2d 565 (1988). Nonetheless, any burden that increasing procedural safeguards entails primarily affects not the government, but the party seeking control of the other's property. For this type of case, therefore, the relevant inquiry requires, as in *Mathews*, first, consideration of the private interest that will be affected by the prejudgment measure; second, an examination of the risk of erroneous deprivation through the procedures under attack and the probable value of additional or alternative safeguards; and third, in contrast to *Mathews*, principal attention to the interest of the party seeking the prejudgment remedy, with, nonetheless, due regard for any ancillary interest the government may have in providing the procedure or forgoing the added burden of providing greater protections.

We now consider the *Mathews* factors in determining the adequacy of the procedures before us, first with regard to the safeguards of notice and a prior hearing, and then in relation to the protection of a bond.

III

We agree with the Court of Appeals that the property interests that attachment affects are significant. For a property owner like Doehr, attachment ordinarily clouds title; impairs the ability to sell or otherwise alienate the property; taints any credit rating; reduces the chance of obtaining a home equity loan or additional mortgage; and can even place an existing mortgage in technical default where there is an insecurity clause. Nor does Connecticut deny that any of these consequences occurs.

Instead, the State correctly points out that these effects do not amount to a complete, physical, or permanent deprivation of real property; their impact is less than the perhaps temporary total deprivation of household goods or wages. But the Court has never held that only such extreme deprivations trigger due process concern. To the contrary, our cases show that even the temporary or partial impairments to property rights that attachments, liens, and similar encumbrances entail are sufficient to merit due process protection. Without doubt, state procedures for creating and enforcing attachments, as with liens, "are subject to the strictures of due process."[4]

We also agree with the Court of Appeals that the risk of erroneous deprivation that the State permits here is substantial. By definition, attachment statutes premise a deprivation of property on one ultimate factual contingency—the award of damages to the plaintiff which the defendant may not be able to satisfy. For attachments before judgment, Connecticut mandates that this determination be made by means of a procedural inquiry that asks whether "there is probable cause to sustain the validity of the plaintiff's claim." Conn.Gen.Stat. § 52–278e(a). The statute elsewhere defines the validity of the claim in terms of the likelihood "that judgment will be rendered in the matter in favor of the plaintiff." Conn.Gen.Stat. § 52–278c(a)(2)(1991). What probable cause means in this context, however, remains obscure. * * *

We need not resolve this confusion since the statute presents too great a risk of erroneous deprivation * * *. If the statute demands inquiry into the sufficiency of the complaint, or, still less, the plaintiff's good-faith belief that the complaint is sufficient, requirement of a complaint and a factual affidavit would permit a court to make these minimal determina-

---

4. Our summary affirmance in Spielman–Fond, Inc. v. Hanson's Inc., 417 U.S. 901, 94 S.Ct. 2596, 41 L.Ed.2d 208 (1974), does not control. In *Spielman–Fond*, the District Court held that the filing of a mechanic's lien did not amount to the taking of a significant property interest. A summary disposition does not enjoy the full precedential value of a case argued on the merits and disposed of by a written opinion. The facts of *Spielman–Fond* presented an alternative basis for affirmance in any event. Unlike the case before us, the mechanic's lien statute in *Spielman–Fond* required the creditor to have a pre-existing interest in the property at issue. As we explain below, a heightened plaintiff interest in certain circumstances can provide a ground for upholding procedures that are otherwise suspect.

tions. But neither inquiry adequately reduces the risk of erroneous deprivation. Permitting a court to authorize attachment merely because the plaintiff believes the defendant is liable, or because the plaintiff can make out a facially valid complaint, would permit the deprivation of the defendant's property when the claim would fail to convince a jury, when it rested on factual allegations that were sufficient to state a cause of action but which the defendant would dispute, or in the case of a mere good-faith standard, even when the complaint failed to state a claim upon which relief could be granted. The potential for unwarranted attachment in these situations is self-evident and too great to satisfy the requirements of due process absent any countervailing consideration.

Even if the provision requires the plaintiff to demonstrate, and the judge to find, probable cause to believe that judgment will be rendered in favor of the plaintiff, the risk of error was substantial in this case. As the record shows, and as the State concedes, only a skeletal affidavit need be and was filed. The State urges that the reviewing judge normally reviews the complaint as well, but concedes that the complaint may also be conclusory. It is self-evident that the judge could make no realistic assessment concerning the likelihood of an action's success based upon these one-sided, self-serving, and conclusory submissions. And as the Court of Appeals said, in a case like this involving an alleged assault, even a detailed affidavit would give only the plaintiff's version of the confrontation. Unlike determining the existence of a debt or delinquent payments, the issue does not concern "ordinarily uncomplicated matters that lend themselves to documentary proof." The likelihood of error that results illustrates that "fairness can rarely be obtained by secret, one-sided determination of facts decisive of rights.... [And n]o better instrument has been devised for arriving at truth than to give a person in jeopardy of serious loss notice of the case against him and an opportunity to meet it."

What safeguards the State does afford do not adequately reduce this risk. Connecticut points out that the statute also provides an "expeditiou[s]" postattachment adversary hearing; notice for such a hearing; judicial review of an adverse decision; and a double damages action if the original suit is commenced without probable cause. Similar considerations were present in *Mitchell* where we upheld Louisiana's sequestration statute despite the lack of predeprivation notice and hearing. But in *Mitchell*, the plaintiff had a vendor's lien to protect, the risk of error was minimal because the likelihood of recovery involved uncomplicated matters that lent themselves to documentary proof, and plaintiff was required to put up a bond. None of these factors diminishing the need for a predeprivation hearing is present in this case. It is true that a later hearing might negate the presence of probable cause, but this would not cure the temporary deprivation that an earlier hearing might have prevented. "The Fourteenth Amendment draws no bright lines around three-day, 10–day or 50–day deprivations of property. Any significant taking of property by the State is within the purview of the Due Process Clause." *Fuentes.*

Finally, we conclude that the interests in favor of an *ex parte* attachment, particularly the interests of the plaintiff, are too minimal to supply such a consideration here. Plaintiff had no existing interest in Doehr's real estate when he sought the attachment. His only interest in attaching the property was to ensure the availability of assets to satisfy his judgment if he prevailed on the merits of his action. Yet there was no allegation that Doehr was about to transfer or encumber his real estate or take any other action during the pendency of the action that would render his real estate unavailable to satisfy a judgment. Our cases have recognized such a properly supported claim would be an exigent circumstance permitting postponing any notice or hearing until after the attachment is effected. Absent such allegations, however, the plaintiff's interest in attaching the property does not justify the burdening of Doehr's ownership rights without a hearing to determine the likelihood of recovery.

No interest the government may have affects the analysis. The State's substantive interest in protecting any rights of the plaintiff cannot be any more weighty than those rights themselves. Here the plaintiff's interest is *de minimis*. Moreover, the State cannot seriously plead additional financial or administrative burdens involving predeprivation hearings when it already claims to provide an immediate post-deprivation hearing.

Historical and contemporary practice support our analysis. Prejudgment attachment is a remedy unknown at common law. Instead, "it traces its origin to the Custom of London, under which a creditor might attach money or goods of the defendant either in the plaintiff's own hands or in the custody of a third person, by proceedings in the mayor's court or in the sheriff's court." Generally speaking, attachment measures in both England and this country had several limitations that reduced the risk of erroneous deprivation which Connecticut permits. Although attachments ordinarily did not require prior notice or a hearing, they were usually authorized only where the defendant had taken or threatened to take some action that would place the satisfaction of the plaintiff's potential award in jeopardy. Attachments, moreover, were generally confined to claims by creditors. As we and the Court of Appeals have noted, disputes between debtors and creditors more readily lend themselves to accurate *ex parte* assessments of the merits. Tort actions, like the assault and battery claim at issue here, do not. Finally, as we will discuss below, attachment statutes historically required that the plaintiff post a bond.

Connecticut's statute appears even more suspect in light of current practice. A survey of state attachment provisions reveals that nearly every State requires either a preattachment hearing, a showing of some exigent circumstance, or both, before permitting an attachment to take place.
* * *

We do not mean to imply that any given exigency requirement protects an attachment from constitutional attack. Nor do we suggest that the statutory measures we have surveyed are necessarily free of due process problems or other constitutional infirmities in general. We do believe, however, that the procedures of almost all the States confirm our view that the Connecticut provision before us, by failing to provide a preattachment hearing without at least requiring a showing of some exigent circumstance, clearly falls short of the demands of due process.

IV

A

Although a majority of the Court does not reach the issue, Justices Marshall, Stevens, O'Connor, and I deem it appropriate to consider whether due process also requires the plaintiff to post a bond or other security in addition to requiring a hearing or showing of some exigency.[7]

As noted, the impairments to property rights that attachments affect merit due process protection. Several consequences can be severe, such as the default of a homeowner's mortgage. In the present context, it need only be added that we have repeatedly recognized the utility of a bond in protecting property rights affected by the mistaken award of prejudgment remedies.

Without a bond, at the time of attachment, the danger that these property rights may be wrongfully deprived remains unacceptably high even with such safeguards as a hearing or exigency requirement. The need for a bond is especially apparent where extraordinary circumstances justify an attachment with no more than the plaintiff's *ex parte* assertion of a claim. We have already discussed how due process tolerates, and the States generally permit, the otherwise impermissible chance of erroneously depriving the defendant in such situations in light of the heightened interest of the plaintiff. Until a postattachment hearing, however, a defendant has no protection against damages sustained where no extraordinary circumstance in fact existed or the plaintiff's likelihood of recovery was nil. Such protection is what a bond can supply. Both the Court and its individual members have repeatedly found the requirement of a bond to play an essential role in reducing what would have been too great a degree of risk in precisely this type of circumstance.

But the need for a bond does not end here. A defendant's property rights remain at undue risk even when there has been an adversarial hearing to determine the plaintiff's likelihood of recovery. At best, a court's initial assessment of each party's case cannot produce more than an educated prediction as to who will win. This is especially true when, as

---

7. Ordinarily we will not address a contention advanced by a respondent that would enlarge his or her rights under a judgment, without the respondent filing a cross-petition for certiorari. Here the Court of Appeals rejected Doehr's argument that § 52–278e(a)(1) violates due process in failing to mandate a preattachment bond. Nonetheless, this case involves considerations that in the past have prompted us "to consider the question highlighted by respondent." First, as our cases have shown, the notice and hearing question and the bond question are intertwined and can fairly be considered facets of same general issue. Thus, "[w]ithout undue strain, the position taken by respondent before this Court ... might be characterized as an argument in support of the judgment below" insofar as a discussion of notice and a hearing cannot be divorced from consideration of a bond. Second, this aspect of prejudgment attachment "plainly warrants our attention, and with regard to which the lower courts are in need of guidance." Third, "and perhaps most importantly, both parties have briefed and argued the question."

here, the nature of the claim makes any accurate prediction elusive. In consequence, even a full hearing under a proper probable-cause standard would not prevent many defendants from having title to their homes impaired during the pendency of suits that never result in the contingency that ultimately justifies such impairment, namely, an award to the plaintiff. Attachment measures currently on the books reflect this concern. All but a handful of States require a plaintiff's bond despite also affording a hearing either before, or (for the vast majority, only under extraordinary circumstances) soon after, an attachment takes place. Bonds have been a similarly common feature of other prejudgment remedy procedures that we have considered, whether or not these procedures also included a hearing.

The State stresses its double damages remedy for suits that are commenced without probable cause. This remedy, however, fails to make up for the lack of a bond. As an initial matter, the meaning of "probable cause" in this provision is no more clear here than it was in the attachment provision itself. Should the term mean the plaintiff's good faith or the facial adequacy of the complaint, the remedy is clearly insufficient. A defendant who was deprived where there was little or no likelihood that the plaintiff would obtain a judgment could nonetheless recover only by proving some type of fraud or malice or by showing that the plaintiff had failed to state a claim. Problems persist even if the plaintiff's ultimate failure permits recovery. At best a defendant must await a decision on the merits of the plaintiff's complaint, even assuming that a [statutory] action may be brought as a counterclaim. Settlement, under Connecticut law, precludes seeking the damages remedy, a fact that encourages the use of attachments as a tactical device to pressure an opponent to capitulate. An attorney's advice that there is probable cause to commence an action constitutes a complete defense, even if the advice was unsound or erroneous. Finally, there is no guarantee that the original plaintiff will have adequate assets to satisfy an award that the defendant may win.

Nor is there any appreciable interest against a bond requirement. Section 52–278e(a)(1) does not require a plaintiff to show exigent circumstances nor any pre-existing interest in the property facing attachment. A party must show more than the mere existence of a claim before subjecting an opponent to prejudgment proceedings that carry a significant risk of erroneous deprivation.

B

Our foregoing discussion compels the four of us to consider whether a bond excuses the need for a hearing or other safeguards altogether. If a bond is needed to augment the protections afforded by preattachment and postattachment hearings, it arguably follows that a bond renders these safeguards unnecessary. That conclusion is unconvincing, however, for it ignores certain harms that bonds could not undo but that hearings would prevent. The law concerning attachments has rarely, if ever, required defendants to suffer an encumbered title until the case is concluded without any prior opportunity to show that the attachment was unwarranted. Our cases have repeatedly emphasized the importance of providing a prompt postdeprivation hearing at the very least. Every State but one, moreover, expressly requires a preattachment or postattachment hearing to determine the propriety of an attachment.

The necessity for at least a prompt postattachment hearing is self-evident because the right to be compensated at the end of the case, if the plaintiff loses, for all provable injuries caused by the attachment is inadequate to redress the harm inflicted, harm that could have been avoided had an early hearing been held. An individual with an immediate need or opportunity to sell a property can neither do so, nor otherwise satisfy that need or recreate the opportunity. The same applies to a parent in need of a home equity loan for a child's education, an entrepreneur seeking to start a business on the strength of an otherwise strong credit rating, or simply a homeowner who might face the disruption of having a mortgage placed in technical default. The extent of these harms, moreover, grows with the length of the suit. Here, oral argument indicated that civil suits in Connecticut commonly take up to four to seven years for completion. Many state attachment statutes require that the amount of a bond be anywhere from the equivalent to twice the amount the plaintiff seeks. These amounts bear no relation to the harm the defendant might suffer even assuming that money damages can make up for the foregoing disruptions. It should be clear, however, that such an assumption is fundamentally flawed. Reliance on a bond does not sufficiently account for the harms that flow from an erroneous attachment to excuse a State from reducing that risk by means of a timely hearing.

If a bond cannot serve to dispense with a hearing immediately after attachment, neither is it sufficient basis for not providing a preattachment hearing in the absence of exigent circumstances even if in any event a hearing would be provided a few days later. The reasons are the same: a wrongful attachment can inflict injury that will not fully be redressed by recovery on the bond after a prompt postattachment hearing determines that the attachment was invalid.

Once more, history and contemporary practice support our conclusion. Historically, attachments would not issue without a showing of extraordinary circumstances even though a plaintiff bond was almost invariably required in addition. Likewise, all but eight States currently require the posting of a bond. Out of this 42 State majority, all but one requires a preattachment hearing, a showing of some exigency, or both, and all but one expressly require a postattachment hearing when an attachment has been issue *ex parte*. This testimony underscores the point that neither a hearing nor an extraordinary circumstance limitation eliminates the need for a bond, no more than a bond allows waiver of these other protections. To reconcile the interests of the defendant and the plaintiff accurately, due process generally requires all of the above. * * *

CHIEF JUSTICE REHNQUIST with whom JUSTICE BLACKMUN joins, concurring in part and concurring in the judgment.

I agree with the Court that the Connecticut attachment statute, "as applied in this case," fails to satisfy the Due Process Clause of the Fourteenth Amendment. I therefore join Parts I, II and III of its opinion. Unfortunately, the remainder of the Court's opinion does not confine itself to the facts of this case, but enters upon a lengthy disquisition as to what combination of safeguards are required to satisfy Due Process in hypothetical cases not before the Court. I therefore do not join Part IV.

As the Court's opinion points out, the Connecticut statute allows attachment not merely for a creditor's claim, but for a tort claim of assault and battery; it affords no opportunity for a pre-deprivation hearing; it contains no requirement that there be "exigent circumstances," such as an effort on the part of the defendant to conceal assets; no bond is required from the plaintiff; and the property attached is one in which the plaintiff has no pre-existing interest. The Court's opinion is, in my view, ultimately correct when it bases its holding of unconstitutionality of the Connecticut statute as applied here on our cases of *Sniadach*; *Fuentes*; *Mitchell*; and *North Georgia Finishing*. But I do not believe that the result follows so inexorably as the Court's opinion suggests. All of the cited cases dealt with personalty—bank deposits or chattels—and each involved the physical seizure of the property itself, so that the defendant was deprived of its use. These cases, which represented something of a revolution in the jurisprudence of procedural due process, placed substantial limits on the methods by which creditors could obtain a lien on the assets of a debtor prior to judgment. But in all of them the debtor was deprived of the use and possession of the property. In the present case, on the other hand, Connecticut's pre-judgment attachment on real property statute, which secures an incipient lien for the plaintiff, does not deprive the defendant of the use or possession of the property.

The Court's opinion therefore breaks new ground, and I would point out, more emphatically than the Court does, the limits of today's holding. In Spielman–Fond, Inc. v. Hanson's, Inc., 379 F.Supp. 997, 999 (D.Ariz.1973), the District Court held that the filing of a mechanics' lien did not cause the deprivation of a significant property interest of the owner. We summarily affirmed that decision. Other courts have read this summary affirmance to mean that the mere imposition of a lien on real property, which does not disturb the owner's use or enjoyment of the property, is not a deprivation of property calling for procedural due process safeguards. I agree with the Court, however, that upon analysis the deprivation here is a significant one, even though the owner remains in undisturbed possession. "For a property owner like Doehr, attachment ordinarily clouds title; impairs the ability to sell or otherwise alienate the property; taints any credit rating; reduces the chance of obtaining a home equity loan or additional mortgage; and can even place an existing mortgage in technical default when there is an insecurity clause." Given the elaborate system of title records relating to real property which prevails in all of our states, a lienor need not obtain possession or use of real property belonging to a debtor in order to significantly impair its value to him.

But in *Spielman–Fond, Inc.*, there was, as the Court points out in fn. 4, an alternate basis available to this Court for affirmance of that decision. Arizona recognized a pre-existing lien in favor of unpaid mechanics and materialmen who had contributed labor or supplies which were incorporated in improvements to real property. The existence of such a lien upon the very property ultimately posted or noticed distinguishes those cases from the present one, where the plaintiff had no pre-existing interest in the real property which he sought to attach. Materialman's and mechanic's lien statutes award an interest in real property to workers who have contributed their labor, and to suppliers who have furnished material, for the improvement of the real property. Since neither the labor nor the material can be reclaimed once it has become a part of the realty, this is the only method by which workmen or small businessmen who have contributed to the improvement of the property may be given a remedy against a property owner who has defaulted on his promise to pay for the labor and the materials. To require any sort of a contested court hearing or bond before the notice of lien takes effect would largely defeat the purpose of these statutes.

Petitioner in its brief relies in part on our summary affirmance in Bartlett v. Williams, 464 U.S. 801, 104 S.Ct. 46, 78 L.Ed.2d 67 (1983). That case involved a *lis pendens*, in which the question presented to this Court was whether such a procedure could be valid when the only protection afforded to the owner of land affected by the *lis pendens* was a post-sequestration hearing. A notice of *lis pendens* is a well established traditional remedy whereby a plaintiff (usually a judgment creditor) who brings an action to enforce an interest in property to which the defendant has title gives notice of the pendency of such action to third parties; the notice causes the interest which he establishes, if successful, to relate back to the date of the filing of the *lis pendens*. The filing of such notice will have an effect upon the defendant's ability to alienate the property, or to obtain additional security on the basis of title to the property, but the effect of the lis pendens is simply to give notice to the world of the remedy being sought in the lawsuit itself. The *lis pendens* itself creates no additional right in the property on the part of the plaintiff, but simply allows third parties to know that a lawsuit is pending in which the plaintiff is seeking to establish such a right. Here, too, the fact that the plaintiff already claims an interest in the property which he seeks to enforce by a lawsuit distinguishes this class of cases from the Connecticut attachment employed in the present case. * * *

It is both unwise and unnecessary, I believe, for the Court to proceed, as it does in Part IV, from its decision of the case before it to discuss abstract and hypothetical situations not before it. This is especially so where we are dealing with the Due Process Clause which, as the Court recognizes, "unlike some legal rules, is not a technical conception with a fixed content unrelated to time, place and circumstances. And it is even more true in a case involving constitutional limits on the methods by which the states may transfer or create interests in real property; in other areas of the law, dicta may do little damage, but those who insure titles or write title opinions often do not enjoy the luxury of distinguishing between dicta and holding."

The two elements of due process with which the Court concerns itself in Part IV—the requirement of a bond, and of "exigent circumstances"—prove to be upon analysis so vague that the discussion is not only unnecessary, but not particularly useful. Unless one knows what the terms and conditions of a bond are to be, the requirement of a "bond" in the abstract means little. The amount to be secured by the bond and the conditions of the bond are left unaddressed—is there to be liability on the part of a plaintiff if he is ultimately unsuccessful in the underlying lawsuit, or is it instead to be conditioned on some sort of good faith test? The "exigent circumstances" referred to by the Court are admittedly equally vague; nonresidency appears to be enough in some states, an attempt to conceal assets is required in others, an effort to flee the jurisdiction in still others. We should await concrete cases which present questions involving bonds and exigent circumstances before we attempt to decide when and if the Due Process Clause of the Fourteenth Amendment requires them as prerequisites for a lawful attachment.

JUSTICE SCALIA, concurring in part and concurring in the judgment.

Since the manner of attachment here was not a recognized procedure at common law, I agree that its validity under the Due Process Clause should be determined by applying the test we set forth in Mathews v. Eldridge, 424 U.S. 319, 96 S.Ct. 893, 47 L.Ed.2d 18 (1976); and I agree that it fails that test. I join Parts I and III of the Court's opinion, and concur in the judgment of the Court.

NOTES

1. *Afterword:* DiGiovanni ultimately recovered $3,422.34 plus costs in his state court suit. Pinsky v. Duncan, 79 F.3d 306, 308 (2d Cir.1996). In the federal suit, the Second Circuit held that Doehr could not recover damages unless he could demonstrate that DiGiovanni was liable for malicious prosecution in instituting the attachment proceeding and continuing the attachment (for fifteen days) after the Supreme Court's ruling. Id. at 313. DiGiovanni prevailed on summary judgment, Doehr v. DiGiovanni, 1997 WL 835067 (D.Conn.1997), but did not recover any attorney's fees, 8 F.Supp.2d 172 (D.Conn.1998).

2. What is the holding in *Doehr*? See Note, Connecticut v. Doehr and Procedural Due Process Values: The Sniadach Tetrad Revisited, 79 Cornell L.Rev. 1603 (1994). Given that the Court says that the statute violates due process, "as applied to this case" (p. 788), may Connecticut's *lis pendens* practice still be applied in other circumstances? For example, suppose a Connecticut home owner contracts for her house to be painted for a set price,

but then refuses to pay because she is dissatisfied with the quality of the work. The painter files suit for breach of contract and obtains an attachment on the house without hearing or bond. Does the homeowner have a claim under the due process clause? See, e.g., Shaumyan v. O'Neill, 987 F.2d 122 (2d Cir.1993); New Destiny Development Corp. v. Piccione, 802 F.Supp. 692 (D.Conn.1992)(both holding Connecticut's *lis pendens* statute constitutional as applied to different factual circumstances than were present in *Doehr*).

To put an end to such case-by-case litigation, Connecticut amended the statute at issue in *Doehr*. A plaintiff seeking to attach property must now file an affidavit showing facts sufficient to demonstrate probable cause that the plaintiff will obtain a favorable judgment. The affidavit must also show exigent circumstances, such as the defendant's likely removal of the property from the state or hiding or disposal of the property. The defendant may request that a bond be posted. Conn.Gen.Stat. § 52–278e (1994).

3. The "Denver Boot" is used to immobilize automobiles that the police have determined are owned by people who owe numerous parking tickets. The boot, which is much cheaper to use than a towing service, cannot be removed without special equipment. Naturally, it is not removed until the parking tickets are cleared. Is this a violation of due process? See Patterson v. Cronin, 650 P.2d 531 (Colo.1982) (although a hearing is not constitutionally mandated prior to the immobilization of a motor vehicle, a prompt and adequate proceeding must be available upon demand after the immobilization has occurred, and before the tickets and fees must be paid). How prompt must the hearing be held after towing? City of Los Angeles v. David, 538 U.S. 715, 123 S.Ct. 1895, 155 L.Ed.2d 946 (2003) (no due process violation for a thirty-day delay in holding a hearing). Cf. Florida v. White, 526 U.S. 559, 119 S.Ct. 1555, 143 L.Ed.2d 748 (1999) (police not required under fourth amendment to obtain a warrant before seizing an automobile from a public place when there was probable cause to believe that it was forfeitable contraband).

Consider Judge Posner's views:

> Suppose, for example, that the issue is whether the owner of an apparently abandoned car should be notified, and given an opportunity for a hearing, *before* the car is towed away and sold for scrap. The chance that the car wasn't really abandoned, but broke down or was stolen, is not trivial, and the cost of a hearing is modest relative to the value of the car * * *. But suppose we are speaking of * * * illegally parked cars. Since the cars are not about to be destroyed, the deprivation is much less than in the case of the abandoned car. The probability of error is also much lower, because ordinarily the determination of whether a car is illegally parked is cut and dried. And the cost of a predeprivation hearing is very high; if the owner has to be notified before the car is towed, he'll remove it and the deterrent effect will be eliminated.

Richard Posner, Economic Analysis of Law § 21.1 at 594 (7th ed.2007). How might the person who wrote *American Hospital* (p. 204) reduce the question of whether to grant a pre-seizure hearing to another "simple formula"?

4. What is the status of self-help remedies under the line of cases discussed in *Doehr*? For example, section 9–609 of the Uniform Commercial Code for Secured Transactions provides:

> (a) After default, a secured party:
>
> > (1) may take possession of the collateral; and
> >
> > (2) without removal, may render equipment unusable and dispose of collateral on a debtor's premises * * *.
>
> (b) A secured party may proceed under subsection (a):
>
> > (1) pursuant to judicial process; or
> >
> > (2) without judicial process, if it proceeds without breach of the peace.
>
> (c) If so agreed, and in any event after default, a secured party may require the debtor to assemble the collateral and make it available to the secured party at a place to be designated by the secured party which is reasonably convenient to both parties.

Does this provision pass muster? Compare Flagg Brothers, Inc. v. Brooks, 436 U.S. 149, 98 S.Ct. 1729, 56 L.Ed.2d 185 (1978)(self-help does not invoke any state action) with Lugar v. Edmondson Oil Co., 457 U.S. 922, 102 S.Ct. 2744, 73 L.Ed.2d 482 (1982)(state officers helping private creditor invokes state action). See Comment, The Electronic Self-help Provisions of UCITA: A Virtual Repo Man?, 33 J. Marshall L. Rev. 663 (2000).

5. Many of the cases the Court relied upon in *Doehr* concerned consumer credit transactions. What does the imposition of these requirements do to the cost of credit or goods sold on credit? Is this desirable from the point of view of sellers, such as department stores? From the point of view of those buyers who have every intention of making their installment payments? See Peter V. Letsou, The Political Economy of Consumer Credit Regulation, 44 Emory L.J. 587 (1995)(contending that coercive remedies enhance lender-borrower relationships). Does it matter that few debtors actually have a defense on the merits? See James J. White, The Abolition of Self–Help Repossession: The Poor Pay More, 1973 Wis.L.Rev. 503 (estimating that only 6 of every 1000 people whose cars are repossessed have a meritorious defense to non-payment). Or, even if the risk of error is low, is there value in the hearing itself, at least in terms of the dignity of the individual whose property is at risk? Compare Jerry L. Mashaw, The Supreme Court's Due Process Calculus for Administrative Adjudication in Mathews v. Eldridge: Three Factors in Search of a Theory of Value, 44 U.Chi.L.Rev. 28 (1976) (yes) with Louis Kaplow & Steven Shavell, Fairness Versus Welfare, 114 Harv.L.Rev. 961, 1211–25 (2001) (questioning "dignity" arguments).

6. Prejudgment seizure is a powerful tool because it shifts the strategic balance of subsequent litigation: time now becomes the creditor's friend. A debtor who needs the seized property quickly may settle on terms worse than could be achieved through litigation or negotiation with the creditor. A dramatic example of the power of frozen assets to induce a prompt settlement is a case involving an eminent New York law firm. Kaye, Scholer, Fierman, Hays & Handler paid $41 million to settle with the government only six days

after the federal Office of Thrift Supervision filed a lawsuit alleging that the firm had withheld information concerning its client, a failed savings and loan association. The key to the huge and quick settlement was the seizure order, which prevented the partners from disposing of law firm or individual assets pending the outcome of the suit. The use of the seizure order was surprising, given the fact that the firm was hardly likely to disappear or to be judgment proof. See Marshall L. Small, Limitations Imposed by the Federal Debt Collection Procedures Act on Use of Pre-Judgment Remedies to Enforce Federal Administrative Agency Claims for Monetary Payments, 49 Bus.Law. 1541 (1994); In The Matter of Kaye, Scholer, Fierman, Hays & Handler: A Symposium on Government Regulation, Lawyers' Ethics, and the Rule of Law, 66 So.Cal.L.Rev. 977 (1993).

How might a state limit the grounds for effecting prejudgment seizure of property to protect abuse? Should the law distinguish between residents and non-residents? See British International Insurance Co. Ltd. v. Seguros La Republica, S.A, 212 F.3d 138 (2d Cir.), cert. denied, 531 U.S. 1010, 121 S.Ct. 564, 148 L.Ed.2d 484 (2000) (to be permitted to defend a case on the merits in New York state courts, unauthorized foreign or alien insurers must post bond or other security). Individuals and corporations? Perpetrators of fraud and upstanding citizens? See, e.g., Robert J. Kheel, New York's Amended Attachment Statute: A Prejudgment Remedy in Need of Further Revision, 44 Brook.L.Rev. 199 (1978). What about alleged terrorists? R. Colgate Seleden, The Executive Protection: Freezing the Financial Assets of Alleged Terrorists, the Constitution, and Foreign Participation in U.S. Financial Markets, 8 Fordham J.Corp. & Fin.L. 491 (2003) (analyzing the federal authority to seize property of non-citizens suspected of terrorist activity).

7. As states have changed their prejudgment statutes to conform with the Supreme Court's line of decisions in this area, prejudgment attachment procedure has come to resemble the temporary restraining order (TRO) even more than before. However, the two remedies still retain some differences, which yield advantages to those plaintiffs who are able to choose between legal and equitable relief and therefore are not constricted by *Grupo Mexicano* (p. 787). For example, one difference between prejudgment replevin and a TRO is that a writ of replevin serves as a lien on the defendant's property from the time the writ is issued, thus putting the plaintiff creditor ahead of other unsecured creditors with respect to the replevied property in the event the creditor files for bankruptcy. Furthermore, often a writ of replevin must be served on the holder of the defendant's property by a sheriff, or a United States Marshal for federal court cases, while a TRO may be served by any non-party. Because of crowded court calendars, it may take a day or longer to find a sheriff or marshal to serve the writ of replevin. Finally, a writ of replevin attaches only to so much property as is actually seized, while, if it is available, preliminary relief may bar the disposition of property simply by serving the person in possession or control.

Are there situations in which a creditor with legal and equitable claims might wish to use both remedies? Should there be any differences or should attachment look exactly like a TRO? Recall Rule 65(b)'s requirement that a TRO without notice may not issue unless it clearly appears from specific sworn facts that immediate, irreparable injury, loss or damage will result to the applicant before the adverse party can be heard in opposition. Also recall that in deciding whether to grant an injunction, a court must balance the hardships to the opposing parties.

8. Abusive use of attachment statutes may subject the abuser to liability. Thus, the Supreme Court unanimously permitted a suit under 42 U.S.C. § 1983 that alleged that the owner and manager of a trailer park conspired with local deputy sheriffs to illegally evict—and thus unreasonably seize—the plaintiffs' trailer home in violation of their constitutional rights under the fourth and fourteenth amendments. The trailer home was badly damaged during the eviction, which the deputy sheriffs knew was illegal because no eviction order had been issued. Soldal v. Cook County, 506 U.S. 56, 113 S.Ct. 538, 121 L.Ed.2d 450 (1992).

In a similar vein, the Court has held that private defendants charged with liability under 42 U.S.C. § 1983 for invoking state replevin, garnishment and attachment statutes later declared unconstitutional are not entitled to the qualified immunity that governmental officials enjoy. Wyatt v. Cole, 504 U.S. 158, 112 S.Ct. 1827, 118 L.Ed.2d 504 (1992). However, one court has held that plaintiffs seeking to hold private actors liable for invoking an unconstitutional state procedure must demonstrate that the defendants failed to act in good faith. Thus, the Fifth Circuit dismissed *Wyatt* on remand because the plaintiffs failed to show that the defendants knew or should have known that the state's replevin statute was unconstitutional prior to its invalidation by a court. Wyatt v. Cole, 994 F.2d 1113 (5th Cir.), cert. denied, 510 U.S. 977, 114 S.Ct. 470, 126 L.Ed.2d 421 (1993).

9. One of the tools that the government has used in the "war on drugs" has been to seize the assets of those suspected to be drug dealers. If the alleged dealers are found to be not guilty, the assets are returned. The seizures even include the money that alleged dealers would use to pay their attorneys to represent them in their criminal trials. What form of due process must be included in these seizure statutes to withstand scrutiny? See the next case.

UNITED STATES v. JAMES DANIEL GOOD REAL PROPERTY

Supreme Court of the United States, 1993
510 U.S. 43, 114 S.Ct. 492, 126 L.Ed.2d 490

JUSTICE KENNEDY delivered the opinion of the Court.

The principal question presented is whether, in the absence of exigent circumstances, the Due Process Clause of the Fifth Amendment prohibits the Government in a civil forfeiture case from seizing real property without first affording the owner notice and an opportunity to be heard. We hold that it does. * * *

I

On January 31, 1985, Hawaii police officers executed a search warrant at the home of claimant James Daniel Good. The search uncovered about

89 pounds of marijuana, marijuana seeds, vials containing hashish oil, and drug paraphernalia. About six months later, Good pleaded guilty to promoting a harmful drug in the second degree, in violation of Hawaii law. He was sentenced to one year in jail and five years' probation, and fined $1,000. Good was also required to forfeit to the State $3,187 in cash found on the premises.

On August 8, 1989, four and one-half years after the drugs were found, the United States filed an *in rem* action in the United States District Court for the District of Hawaii, seeking to forfeit Good's house and the four-acre parcel on which it was situated. The United States sought forfeiture under 21 U.S.C. § 881(a)(7), on the ground that the property had been used to commit or facilitate the commission of a federal drug offense.[1]

On August 18, 1989, in an *ex parte* proceeding, a United States Magistrate Judge found that the Government had established probable cause to believe Good's property was subject to forfeiture under § 881(a)(7). A warrant of arrest *in rem* was issued, authorizing seizure of the property. The warrant was based on an affidavit recounting the fact of Good's conviction and the evidence discovered during the January 1985 search of his home by Hawaii police.

The Government seized the property on August 21, 1989, without prior notice to Good or an adversary hearing. At the time of the seizure, Good was renting his home to tenants for $900 per month. The Government permitted the tenants to remain on the premises subject to an occupancy agreement, but directed the payment of future rents to the United States Marshal.

Good filed a claim for the property and an answer to the Government's complaint. He asserted that the seizure deprived him of his property without due process of law and that the forfeiture action was invalid because it had not been timely commenced under the statute. The District Court granted the Government's motion for summary judgment and entered an order forfeiting the property.

The Court of Appeals for the Ninth Circuit affirmed in part, reversed in part, and remanded for further proceedings. The court was unanimous in holding that the seizure of Good's property, without prior notice and a hearing, violated the Due Process Clause. * * *

We now affirm the due process ruling * * *.

---

1. Title 21 U.S.C. § 881(a)(7) provides: "(a) The following shall be subject to forfeiture to the United States and no property right shall exist in them:

* * *

"(7) All real property, including any right, title, and interest (including any leasehold interest) in the whole of any lot or tract of land and any appurtenances or improvements, which is used, or intended to be used, in any manner or part, to commit, or to facilitate the commission of, a violation of this subchapter punishable by more than one year's imprisonment, except that no property shall be forfeited under this paragraph, to the extent of an interest of an owner, by reason of any act or omission established by that owner to have been committed or omitted without the knowledge or consent of that owner."

II

The Due Process Clause of the Fifth Amendment guarantees that "[n]o person shall ... be deprived of life, liberty, or property, without due process of law." Our precedents establish the general rule that individuals must receive notice and an opportunity to be heard before the Government deprives them of property.

The Government does not, and could not, dispute that the seizure of Good's home and four-acre parcel deprived him of property interests protected by the Due Process Clause. By the Government's own submission, the seizure gave it the right to charge rent, to condition occupancy, and even to evict the occupants. Instead, the Government argues that it afforded Good all the process the Constitution requires. The Government makes two separate points in this regard. First, it contends that compliance with the Fourth Amendment suffices when the Government seizes property for purposes of forfeiture. In the alternative, it argues that the seizure of real property under the drug forfeiture laws justifies an exception to the usual due process requirement of preseizure notice and hearing. We turn to these issues.

A

The Government argues that because civil forfeiture serves a "law enforcement purpos[e]," the Government need comply only with the Fourth Amendment when seizing forfeitable property. We disagree. The Fourth Amendment does place restrictions on seizures conducted for purposes of civil forfeiture, One 1958 Plymouth Sedan v. Pennsylvania, 380 U.S. 693, 696, 85 S.Ct. 1246, 1248, 14 L.Ed.2d 170 (1965)(holding that the exclusionary rule applies to civil forfeiture), but it does not follow that the Fourth Amendment is the sole constitutional provision in question when the Government seizes property subject to forfeiture.

We have rejected the view that the applicability of one constitutional amendment pre-empts the guarantees of another. As explained in Soldal v. Cook County, 506 U.S. 56, 70, 113 S.Ct. 538, 548, 121 L.Ed.2d 450 (1992):

> "Certain wrongs affect more than a single right and, accordingly, can implicate more than one of the Constitution's commands. Where such multiple violations are alleged, we are not in the habit of identifying as a preliminary matter the claim's 'dominant' character. Rather, we examine each constitutional provision in turn."

Here, as in *Soldal*, the seizure of property implicates two " 'explicit textual source[s] of constitutional protection,' " the Fourth Amendment and the Fifth. The proper question is not which Amendment controls but whether either Amendment is violated.

Nevertheless, the Government asserts that when property is seized for forfeiture, the Fourth Amendment provides the full measure of process due under the Fifth. The Government relies on Gerstein v. Pugh, 420 U.S. 103, 95 S.Ct. 854, 43 L.Ed.2d 54 (1975), and Graham v. Connor, 490 U.S. 386, 109 S.Ct. 1865, 104 L.Ed.2d 443 (1989), in support of this proposition.

That reliance is misplaced. *Gerstein* and *Graham* concerned not the seizure of property but the arrest or detention of criminal suspects, subjects we have considered to be governed by the provisions of the Fourth Amendment without reference to other constitutional guarantees. In addition, also unlike the seizure presented by this case, the arrest or detention of a suspect occurs as part of the regular criminal process, where other safeguards ordinarily ensure compliance with due process.

Gerstein held that the Fourth Amendment, rather than the Due Process Clause, determines the requisite post-arrest proceedings when individuals are detained on criminal charges. Exclusive reliance on the Fourth Amendment is appropriate in the arrest context, we explained, because the Amendment was "tailored explicitly for the criminal justice system," and its "balance between individual and public interests always has been thought to define the 'process that is due' for seizures of person or property in criminal cases." Furthermore, we noted that the protections afforded during an arrest and initial detention are "only the *first* stage of an elaborate system, unique in jurisprudence, designed to safeguard the rights of those accused of criminal conduct." (Emphasis in original.)

So too, in *Graham* we held that claims of excessive force in the course of an arrest or investigatory stop should be evaluated under the Fourth Amendment reasonableness standard, not under the "more generalized notion of 'substantive due process.'" Because the degree of force used to effect a seizure is one determinant of its reasonableness, and because the Fourth Amendment guarantees citizens the right "to be secure in their persons ... against unreasonable ... seizures," we held that a claim of excessive force in the course of such a seizure is "most properly characterized as one invoking the protections of the Fourth Amendment."

Neither *Gerstein* nor *Graham*, however, provides support for the proposition that the Fourth Amendment is the beginning and end of the constitutional inquiry whenever a seizure occurs. That proposition is inconsistent with the approach we took in Calero–Toledo v. Pearson Yacht Leasing Co., 416 U.S. 663, 94 S.Ct. 2080, 40 L.Ed.2d 452 (1974), which examined the constitutionality of *ex parte* seizures of forfeitable property under general principles of due process, rather than the Fourth Amendment. And it is at odds with our reliance on the Due Process Clause to analyze prejudgment seizure and sequestration of personal property. See, e.g., Fuentes v. Shevin, 407 U.S. 67, 92 S.Ct. 1983, 32 L.Ed.2d 556 (1972); Mitchell v. W.T. Grant Co., 416 U.S. 600, 94 S.Ct. 1895, 40 L.Ed.2d 406 (1974).

It is true, of course, that the Fourth Amendment applies to searches and seizures in the civil context and may serve to resolve the legality of these governmental actions without reference to other constitutional provisions. * * * But the purpose and effect of the Government's action in the present case go beyond the traditional meaning of search or seizure. Here the Government seized property not to preserve evidence of wrongdoing, but to assert ownership and control over the property itself. Our cases establish that government action of this consequence must comply with the Due Process Clauses of the Fifth and Fourteenth Amendments.

* * *

B

Whether *ex parte* seizures of forfeitable property satisfy the Due Process Clause is a question we last confronted in *Calero–Toledo*, which held that the Government could seize a yacht subject to civil forfeiture without affording prior notice or hearing. Central to our analysis in *Calero–Toledo* was the fact that a yacht was the "sort [of property] that could be removed to another jurisdiction, destroyed, or concealed, if advance warning of confiscation were given." The ease with which an owner could frustrate the Government's interests in the forfeitable property created a " 'special need for very prompt action' " that justified the postponement of notice and hearing until after the seizure.

We had no occasion in *Calero–Toledo* to decide whether the same considerations apply to the forfeiture of real property, which, by its very nature, can be neither moved nor concealed. * * *

The right to prior notice and a hearing is central to the Constitution's command of due process. "The purpose of this requirement is not only to ensure abstract fair play to the individual. Its purpose, more particularly, is to protect his use and possession of property from arbitrary encroachment—to minimize substantively unfair or mistaken deprivations of property...." *Fuentes*.

We tolerate some exceptions to the general rule requiring predeprivation notice and hearing, but only in " 'extraordinary situations where some valid governmental interest is at stake that justifies postponing the hearing until after the event.' " Whether the seizure of real property for purposes of civil forfeiture justifies such an exception requires an examination of the competing interests at stake, along with the promptness and adequacy of later proceedings. The three-part inquiry set forth in Mathews v. Eldridge, 424 U.S. 319, 96 S.Ct. 893, 47 L.Ed.2d 18 (1976), provides guidance in this regard. The *Mathews* analysis requires us to consider the private interest affected by the official action; the risk of an erroneous deprivation of that interest through the procedures used, as well as the probable value of additional safeguards; and the Government's interest, including the administrative burden that additional procedural requirements would impose.

Good's right to maintain control over his home, and to be free from governmental interference, is a private interest of historic and continuing importance. The seizure deprived Good of valuable rights of ownership, including the right of sale, the right of occupancy, the right to unrestricted use and enjoyment, and the right to receive rents. All that the seizure left him, by the Government's own submission, was the right to bring a claim for the return of title at some unscheduled future hearing.

In *Fuentes*, we held that the loss of kitchen appliances and household furniture was significant enough to warrant a predeprivation hearing. And in Connecticut v. Doehr, 501 U.S. 1, 111 S.Ct. 2105, 115 L.Ed.2d 1 (1991), we held that a state statute authorizing prejudgment attachment of real estate without prior notice or hearing was unconstitutional, in the absence of extraordinary circumstances, even though the attachment did not interfere with the owner's use or possession and did not affect, as a general matter, rentals from existing leaseholds.

The seizure of a home produces a far greater deprivation than the loss of furniture, or even attachment. It gives the Government not only the right to prohibit sale, but also the right to evict occupants, to modify the property, to condition occupancy, to receive rents, and to supersede the owner in all rights pertaining to the use, possession, and enjoyment of the property.

The Government makes much of the fact that Good was renting his home to tenants, and contends that the tangible effect of the seizure was limited to taking the $900 a month he was due in rent. But even if this were the only deprivation at issue, it would not render the loss insignificant or unworthy of due process protection. The rent represents a significant portion of the exploitable economic value of Good's home. It cannot be classified as *de minimis* for purposes of procedural due process. In sum, the private interests at stake in the seizure of real property weigh heavily in the *Mathews* balance.

The practice of *ex parte* seizure, moreover, creates an unacceptable risk of error. Although Congress designed the drug forfeiture statute to be a powerful instrument in enforcement of the drug laws, it did not intend to deprive innocent owners of their property. The affirmative defense of innocent ownership is allowed by statute. * * *

The *ex parte* preseizure proceeding affords little or no protection to the innocent owner. In issuing a warrant of seizure, the magistrate judge need determine only that there is probable cause to believe that the real property was "used, or intended to be used, in any manner or part, to commit, or to facilitate the commission of" a felony narcotics offense. The Government is not required to offer any evidence on the question of innocent ownership or other potential defenses a claimant might have. * * *

The purpose of an adversary hearing is to ensure the requisite neutrality that must inform all governmental decisionmaking. That protection is of particular importance here, where the Government has a direct pecuniary interest in the outcome of the proceeding.[2] Moreover, the

---

2. The extent of the Government's financial stake in drug forfeiture is apparent from a 1990 memo, in which the Attorney General urged United States Attorneys to increase the volume of forfeitures in order to meet the Department of Justice's annual budget target: "We must significantly increase production to reach our budget target. '... Failure to achieve the $470 million projection would expose the Department's forfeiture program to criticism and undermine confidence in our budget projections. Every effort must be made to increase forfeiture income during the remaining three months of [fiscal year] 1990.'"

availability of a postseizure hearing may be no recompense for losses caused by erroneous seizure. Given the congested civil dockets in federal courts, a claimant may not receive an adversary hearing until many months after the seizure. And even if the ultimate judicial decision is that the claimant was an innocent owner, or that the Government lacked probable cause, this determination, coming months after the seizure, "would not cure the temporary deprivation that an earlier hearing might have prevented." *Doehr*.

This brings us to the third consideration under *Mathews*, "the Government's interest, including the function involved and the fiscal and administrative burdens that the additional or substitute procedural requirement would entail." The governmental interest we consider here is not some general interest in forfeiting property but the specific interest in seizing real property before the forfeiture hearing. The question in the civil forfeiture context is whether *ex parte* seizure is justified by a pressing need for prompt action. We find no pressing need here.

This is apparent by comparison to *Calero–Toledo*, where the Government's interest in immediate seizure of a yacht subject to civil forfeiture justified dispensing with the usual requirement of prior notice and hearing. Two essential considerations informed our ruling in that case: first, immediate seizure was necessary to establish the court's jurisdiction over the property, and second, the yacht might have disappeared had the Government given advance warning of the forfeiture action. * * * Neither of these factors is present when the target of forfeiture is real property.

Because real property cannot abscond, the court's jurisdiction can be preserved without prior seizure. * * *

In the case of real property, the res may be brought within the reach of the court simply by posting notice on the property and leaving a copy of the process with the occupant. In fact, the rules which govern forfeiture proceedings under § 881 already permit process to be executed on real property without physical seizure * * *.

Nor is the *ex parte* seizure of real property necessary to accomplish the statutory purpose of § 881(a)(7). The Government's legitimate interests at the inception of forfeiture proceedings are to ensure that the property not be sold, destroyed, or used for further illegal activity prior to the forfeiture judgment. These legitimate interests can be secured without seizing the subject property.

Sale of the property can be prevented by filing a notice of *lis pendens* as authorized by state law when the forfeiture proceedings commence. If there is evidence, in a particular case, that an owner is likely to destroy his property when advised of the pending action, the Government may obtain an *ex parte* restraining order, or other appropriate relief, upon a proper showing in district court. See Fed.Rule Civ.Proc. 65. The Government's policy of leaving occupants in possession of real property under an occupancy agreement pending the final forfeiture ruling demonstrates that there is no serious concern about destruction in the ordinary case.

Finally, the Government can forestall further illegal activity with search and arrest warrants obtained in the ordinary course.

In the usual case, the Government thus has various means, short of seizure, to protect its legitimate interests in forfeitable real property. There is no reason to take the additional step of asserting control over the property without first affording notice and an adversary hearing.

Requiring the Government to postpone seizure until after an adversary hearing creates no significant administrative burden. A claimant is already entitled to an adversary hearing before a final judgment of forfeiture. No extra hearing would be required in the typical case, since the Government can wait until after the forfeiture judgment to seize the property. From an administrative standpoint it makes little difference whether that hearing is held before or after the seizure. And any harm that results from delay is minimal in comparison to the injury occasioned by erroneous seizure.

C

It is true that, in cases decided over a century ago, we permitted the *ex parte* seizure of real property when the Government was collecting debts or revenue. See, e.g., Springer v. United States, 102 U.S. 586, 593–594, 26 L.Ed. 253 (1881); Murray's Lessee v. Hoboken Land & Improvement Co., 18 How. 272, 15 L.Ed. 372 (1856). Without revisiting these cases, it suffices to say that their apparent rationale—like that for allowing summary seizures during wartime, and seizures of contaminated food,—was one of executive urgency. "The prompt payment of taxes," we noted, "may be vital to the existence of a government." *Springer*. See also G.M. Leasing Corp. v. United States, 429 U.S. 338, 352, n. 18, 97 S.Ct. 619, 628, n. 18, 50 L.Ed.2d 530 (1977)("The rationale underlying [the revenue] decisions, of course, is that the very existence of government depends upon the prompt collection of the revenues").

A like rationale justified the *ex parte* seizure of tax-delinquent distilleries in the late nineteenth century, since before passage of the Sixteenth Amendment, the Federal Government relied heavily on liquor, customs, and tobacco taxes to generate operating revenues. In 1902, for example, nearly 75 percent of total federal revenues—$479 million out of a total of $653 million—was raised from taxes on liquor, customs, and tobacco.

The federal income tax code adopted in the first quarter of this century, however, afforded the taxpayer notice and an opportunity to be heard by the Board of Tax Appeals before the Government could seize property for nonpayment of taxes. In Phillips v. Commissioner, 283 U.S. 589, 51 S.Ct. 608, 75 L.Ed. 1289 (1931), the Court relied upon the availability, and adequacy, of these preseizure administrative procedures in holding that no judicial hearing was required prior to the seizure of property. These constraints on the Commissioner could be overridden, but only when the Commissioner made a determination that a jeopardy assessment was necessary. Writing for a unanimous Court, Justice Brandeis explained that under the tax laws "[f]ormal notice of the tax liability is thus given; the Commissioner is required to answer; and there is a complete hearing *de novo*.... These provisions amply protect the [taxpayer] against improper administrative action." * * *

Similar provisions remain in force today. The current Internal Revenue Code prohibits the Government from levying upon a deficient taxpayer's property without first affording the taxpayer notice and an opportunity for a hearing, unless exigent circumstances indicate that delay will jeopardize the collection of taxes due.

Just as the urgencies that justified summary seizure of property in the 19th century had dissipated by the time of *Phillips*, neither is there a plausible claim of urgency today to justify the summary seizure of real property under § 881(a)(7). Although the Government relies to some extent on forfeitures as a means of defraying law enforcement expenses, it does not, and we think could not, justify the prehearing seizure of forfeitable real property as necessary for the protection of its revenues.

D

The constitutional limitations we enforce in this case apply to real property in general, not simply to residences. That said, the case before us well illustrates an essential principle: Individual freedom finds tangible expression in property rights. At stake in this and many other forfeiture cases are the security and privacy of the home and those who take shelter within it.

Finally, the suggestion that this one petitioner must lose because his conviction was known at the time of seizure, and because he raises an as applied challenge to the statute, founders on a bedrock proposition: fair procedures are not confined to the innocent. The question before us is the legality of the seizure, not the strength of the Government's case.

In sum, based upon the importance of the private interests at risk and the absence of countervailing Government needs, we hold that the seizure of real property under § 881(a)(7) is not one of those extraordinary instances that justify the postponement of notice and hearing. Unless exigent circumstances are present, the Due Process Clause requires the Government to afford notice and a meaningful opportunity to be heard before seizing real property subject to civil forfeiture.[3]

To establish exigent circumstances, the Government must show that less restrictive measures—i.e., a *lis pendens*, restraining order, or bond— would not suffice to protect the Government's interests in preventing the sale, destruction, or continued unlawful use of the real property. We agree with the Court of Appeals that no showing of exigent circumstances has

---

3. We do not address what sort of procedures are required for preforfeiture seizures of real property in the context of criminal forfeiture. We note, however, that the federal drug laws now permit seizure before entry of a criminal forfeiture judgment only where the Government persuades a district court that there is probable cause to believe that a protective order "may not be sufficient to assure the availability of the property for forfeiture." 21 U.S.C. § 853(f).

been made in this case, and we affirm its ruling that the *ex parte* seizure of Good's real property violated due process.

III

We turn now to the question whether a court must dismiss a forfeiture action that the Government filed within the statute of limitations, but without complying with certain other statutory timing directives. * * *

We hold that courts may not dismiss a forfeiture action filed within the five-year statute of limitations for noncompliance with the internal timing requirements of [the relevant statute]. The Government filed the action in this case within the five-year statute of limitations, and that sufficed to make it timely. We reverse the contrary holding of the Court of Appeals. * * *

CHIEF JUSTICE REHNQUIST, with whom JUSTICE SCALIA joins, and JUSTICE O'CONNOR joins in Parts II and III, concurring in part and dissenting in part.

I concur in Parts I and III of the Court's opinion and dissent with respect to Part II. The Court today departs from longstanding historical precedent and concludes that the *ex parte* warrant requirement under the Fourth Amendment fails to afford adequate due process protection to property owners who have been convicted of a crime that renders their real property susceptible to civil forfeiture under 21 U.S.C. § 881(a)(7). It reaches this conclusion although no such adversary hearing is required to deprive a criminal defendant of his liberty before trial. And its reasoning casts doubt upon long settled law relating to seizure of property to enforce income tax liability. I dissent from this ill-considered and disruptive decision.

I

The Court applies the three-factor balancing test for evaluating procedural due process claims set out in Mathews v. Eldridge, 424 U.S. 319, 96 S.Ct. 893, 47 L.Ed.2d 18 (1976), to reach its unprecedented holding. I reject the majority's expansive application of *Mathews*. *Mathews* involved a due process challenge to the adequacy of administrative procedures established for the purpose of terminating Social Security disability benefits, and the *Mathews* balancing test was first conceived to address due process claims arising in the context of modern administrative law. No historical practices existed in this context for the Court to consider. The Court has expressly rejected the notion that the *Mathews* balancing test constitutes a "one-size-fits-all" formula for deciding every due process claim that comes before the Court. More importantly, the Court does not work on a clean slate in the civil forfeiture context involved here. It has long sanctioned summary proceedings in civil forfeitures. See, e.g., Dobbins' Distillery v. United States, 96 U.S. 395, 24 L.Ed. 637 (1878)(upholding seizure of a distillery by executive officers based on *ex parte* warrant); and G.M. Leasing Corp. v. United States, 429 U.S. 338, 97 S.Ct. 619, 50 L.Ed.2d 530 (1977)(upholding warrantless automobile seizures).

A

The Court's fixation on *Mathews* sharply conflicts with both historical practice and the specific textual source of the Fourth Amendment's "reasonableness" inquiry. The Fourth Amendment strikes a balance between the people's security in their persons, houses, papers, and effects and the public interest in effecting searches and seizures for law enforcement purposes. Compliance with the standards and procedures prescribed by the Fourth Amendment constitutes all the "process" that is "due" to respondent Good under the Fifth Amendment in the forfeiture context. We made this very point in *Gerstein* with respect to procedures for detaining a criminal defendant pending trial:

> "The historical basis of the probable cause requirement is quite different from the relatively recent application of variable procedural due process in debtor-creditor disputes and termination of government-created benefits. The Fourth Amendment was tailored explicitly for the criminal justice system, and its balance between individual and public interests always has been thought to define the 'process that is due' for seizures of person *or property* in criminal cases, including the detention of suspects pending trial."

The *Gerstein* Court went on to decide that while there must be a determination of probable cause by a neutral magistrate in order to detain an arrested suspect prior to trial, such a determination could be made in a nonadversarial proceeding, based on hearsay and written testimony. It is paradoxical indeed to hold that a criminal defendant can be temporarily deprived of liberty on the basis of an *ex parte* probable cause determination, yet respondent Good cannot be temporarily deprived of property on the same basis. As we said in United States v. Monsanto, 491 U.S. 600, 615–616, 109 S.Ct. 2657, 2666–2667, 105 L.Ed.2d 512 (1989):

> "[I]t would be odd to conclude that the Government may not restrain property, such as the home and apartment in respondent's possession, based on a finding of probable cause, when we have held that (under appropriate circumstances), the Government may restrain persons where there is a finding of probable cause to believe that the accused has committed a serious offense."

Similarly, in *Graham* the Court faced the question of what constitutional standard governs a free citizen's claim that law enforcement officials used excessive force in the course of making an arrest, investigatory stop, or other "seizure" of his person. We held that the Fourth Amendment, rather than the Due Process Clause, provides the source of any specific limitations on the use of force in seizing a person: "Because the Fourth Amendment provides an explicit textual source of constitutional protection against this sort of physically intrusive governmental conduct, that Amendment, not the more generalized notion of 'substantive due process' must be the guide for analyzing these claims." The "explicit textual source of constitutional protection" found in the Fourth Amendment should also guide the analysis of respondent Good's claim of a right to additional procedural measures in civil forfeitures.

B

The Court dismisses the holdings of *Gerstein* and *Graham* as inapposite because they concern "the arrest or detention of criminal suspects." But we have never held that the Fourth Amendment is limited only to criminal proceedings. In *Soldal*, we expressly stated that the Fourth Amendment "applies in the civil context as well." Our historical treatment of civil forfeiture procedures underscores the notion that the Fourth Amendment specifically governs the process afforded in the civil forfeiture context, and it is too late in the day to question its exclusive application. As we decided in *Calero–Toledo*, there is no need to look beyond the Fourth Amendment in civil forfeitures proceedings involving the Government because *ex parte* seizures are "too firmly fixed in the punitive and remedial jurisprudence of the country to be now displaced."

The Court acknowledges the long history of *ex parte* seizures of real property through civil forfeiture, and says "[w]ithout revisiting these cases,"—whatever that means—that they appear to depend on the need for prompt payment of taxes. The Court goes on to note that the passage of the Sixteenth Amendment alleviated the Government's reliance on liquor, customs, and tobacco taxes as sources of operating revenue. Whatever the merits of this novel distinction, it fails entirely to distinguish the leading case in the field, *Phillips*, a unanimous opinion authored by Justice Brandeis. That case dealt with the enforcement of income tax liability, which the Court says has replaced earlier forms of taxation as the principle source of governmental revenue. There the Court said:

> "The right of the United States to collect its internal revenue by summary administrative proceedings has long been settled ... [w]here, as here, adequate opportunity is afforded for a later judicial determination of the legal rights, summary proceedings to secure prompt performance of pecuniary obligations to the government have been consistently sustained."

> "Where only property rights are involved, mere postponement of the judicial enquiry is not a denial of due process, if the opportunity given for the ultimate judicial determination of the liability is adequate."

Thus today's decision does not merely discard established precedence regarding excise taxes, but deals at least a glancing blow to the authority of the Government to collect income tax delinquencies by summary proceedings.

II

The Court attempts to justify the result it reaches by expansive readings of *Fuentes* and *Doehr*. In *Fuentes*, the Court struck down state replevin procedures, finding that they served no important state interest that might justify the summary proceedings. Specifically, the Court noted that the tension between the private buyer's use of the property pending final judgment and the private seller's interest in preventing further use and deterioration of his security tipped the balance in favor of a prior hearing in certain replevin situations. "[The provisions] allow summary seizure of a person's possessions when no more than private gain is directly at stake." Cf. Mitchell v. W.T. Grant Co., 416 U.S. 600, 94 S.Ct. 1895, 40 L.Ed.2d 406 (1974)(upholding Louisiana sequestration statute that provided immediate postdeprivation hearing along with the option of damages).

The Court in *Fuentes* also was careful to point out the limited situations in which seizure before hearing was constitutionally permissible, and included among them "summary seizure of property to collect the internal revenue of the United States." Certainly the present seizure is analogous, and it is therefore quite inaccurate to suggest that *Fuentes* is authority for the Court's holding in the present case.

Likewise in *Doehr*, the Court struck down a state statute authorizing prejudgment attachment of real estate without prior notice or hearing due to potential bias of the self-interested private party seeking attachment. The Court noted that the statute enables one of the private parties to "make use of state procedures with the overt, significant assistance of state officials," that involve state action "substantial enough to implicate the Due Process Clause." *Doehr*. The Court concluded that, absent exigent circumstances, the private party's interest in attaching the property did not justify the burdening of the private property owner's rights without a hearing to determine the likelihood of recovery. In the present case, however, it is not a private party but the Government itself which is seizing the property.

The Court's effort to distinguish *Calero–Toledo* is similarly unpersuasive. The Court says that "[c]entral to our analysis in *Calero–Toledo* was the fact that a yacht was the 'sort [of property] that could be removed to another jurisdiction, destroyed, or concealed, if advanced warning of confiscation were given.' " But this is one of the *three* reasons given by the Court for upholding the summary forfeiture in that case: the other two— "fostering the public interest and preventing continued illicit use of the property," and the fact that the "seizure is not initiated by self-interested private parties; rather, Commonwealth officials determine whether seizure is appropriate ...," are both met in the present case. And while not capable of being moved or concealed, the real property at issue here surely could be destroyed or damaged. Several dwellings are located on the property that was seized from respondent Good, and these buildings could easily be destroyed or damaged to prevent them from falling into the hands of the Government if prior notice were required.

The government interests found decisive in *Calero–Toledo* are equally present here: the seizure of respondent Good's real property serves important governmental purposes in combatting illegal drugs; a preseizure notice might frustrate this statutory purpose by permitting respondent Good to destroy or otherwise damage the buildings on the property; and Government officials made the seizure rather than self-interested private parties seeking to gain from the seizure. * * *

III

This is not to say that the Government's use of civil forfeiture statutes to seize real property in drug cases may not cause hardship to innocent individuals. But I have grave doubts whether the Court's decision in this case will do much to alleviate those hardships, and I am confident that whatever social benefits might flow from the decision are more than offset by the damage to settled principles of constitutional law which are inflicted to secure these perceived social benefits. I would reverse the decision of the Court of Appeals *in toto*.

JUSTICE O'CONNOR, concurring in part and dissenting in part.

JUSTICE THOMAS, concurring in part and dissenting in part.

[opinions omitted]

NOTES

1. Does Judge Posner's analysis (p. 800) help to decide whether people like Mr. Good should have the preseizure hearing the Court mandates here?

2. *James Daniel Good* concerned real estate. Should the holding be extended to personal property? See, e.g., United States v. Daccarett, 6 F.3d 37 (2d Cir.1993), cert. denied, 510 U.S. 1191, 114 S.Ct. 1294, 127 L.Ed.2d 648 (1994)(allowing seizure of electronic funds transfers to bank account due to exigent circumstances); Waiste v. State, 10 P.3d 1141 (Alaska 2000) (*James Daniel Good* does not require hearing before seizing fishing boat). But if a hearing is generally required when personal property is seized, is the dissent in *James Daniel Good* correct to charge that the decision deals "at least a glancing blow to the authority of the Government to collect income tax delinquencies by summary proceedings"?

3. The Supreme Court has rejected an extension of *James Daniel Good*'s hearing requirement to statutes authorizing the government, without notice or a special hearing, to withhold money and impose penalties on a public works subcontractor. In Lujan v. G & G Fire Sprinklers, Inc., 532 U.S. 189, 121 S.Ct. 1446, 149 L.Ed.2d 391 (2001), the Court held unanimously that if a party's only relevant property interest is a claim of entitlement to bring a legal action for breach of contract, the provision of a forum for hearing that action is all that is required to vindicate that property interest.

4. *Another parking problem.* Consider the plight of Ilana Love. She found a parking ticket on her car for parking illegally in a handicapped space. The fine is $275. She cannot obtain an administrative hearing without prepaying the fine. Is this procedure a deprivation of property without due

process under *James Daniel Good*? Love v. City of Monterey, 37 Cal.App.4th 562, 43 Cal.Rptr.2d 911 (1995).

5. What should be the remedy for improperly failing to provide a preseizure hearing? Dismissal of the forfeiture action with prejudice? Dismissal, but without prejudice to refile, if the statute of limitations, or some exception to the statute, permits? E.g., Kadonsky v. United States, 216 F.3d 499 (5th Cir.2000), cert. denied, 531 U.S. 1176, 121 S.Ct. 1151, 148 L.Ed.2d 1013 (2001). The exclusion from the forfeiture proceeding of any evidence obtained as a result of the pre-hearing seizure? See, e.g., United States v. Parcel of Property, 337 F.3d 225 (2d Cir.2003). Damages under *Bivens* or § 1983? E.g., Conkey v. Reno, 885 F.Supp. 1389 (D.Nev.1995). The use value of the property seized until a hearing is held? E.g., United States v. 47 West 644 Route 38, Maple Park, Ill., 190 F.3d 781 (7th Cir.1999), cert. denied, 529 U.S. 1005, 120 S.Ct. 1270, 146 L.Ed.2d 220 (2000). The court may require the United States to pay interest on improperly seized funds and other property because Congress waived the federal government's sovereign immunity against paying interest in the Civil Asset Forfeiture Reform Act of 2000, 28 U.S.C. § 2465(b)(1)(C).

6. How much information must be furnished to someone whose property is seized by the police? The Supreme Court has held that law enforcement officers who seize property for criminal investigations are not required by the fourteenth amendment to provide the property owner with individualized notice of available state law remedies for reacquiring the seized property, so long as the information is available from public sources, such as statutes. West Covina v. Perkins, 525 U.S. 234, 119 S.Ct. 678, 142 L.Ed.2d 636 (1999). The Supreme Court (by a 5–to–4 vote) has also held that due process does not require actual notice to an incarcerated prisoner of intended forfeiture of property; notice reasonably calculated to inform the prisoner of the pendency of the seizure is constitutionally adequate. Dusenbery v. United States, 534 U.S. 161, 122 S.Ct. 694, 151 L.Ed.2d 597 (2002). However, the Court later qualified *Dusenbery* when addressing the government's due process obligation if, prior to taking and selling property, it becomes aware that its otherwise reasonable method of attempting to notify the property owner had actually failed (here, certified letters were returned unclaimed). Chief Justice Roberts held for the majority that the government must take additional reasonable steps to attempt to provide notice. Jones v. Flowers, 547 U.S. 220, 126 S.Ct. 1708, 164 L.Ed.2d 415 (2006).

B. POST–JUDGMENT RELIEF

1. BASIC COLLECTION STRATEGY

JAMES J. BROWN, COLLECTING A JUDGMENT
13 Litigation 31 (Fall 1986)

You win the big one: a $5 million judgment. With it comes rave reviews from clients, colleagues, friends, and relatives. You have the judgment framed and hang it on your wall.

But wait a second. "Where's the money?" the managing partner asks. The real world rears its ugly head. It dawns on you that the defendant isn't going to stroll into your office with a certified check for five million bucks.

You close your door, take the judgment off your wall, and replace it with the certificate you got for coaching your daughter's little league team. You stop taking phone calls and start looking for the rules on collecting judgments.

Begin with Federal Rule of Civil Procedure 69 [reproduced in the Appendix at p. 989]. It says that procedures for enforcing judgments follow state law, except when a federal statute specifically governs.

Under state law, the first step is to record the judgment in the county where the debtor resides or owns property. A federal judgment may be recorded in the same manner as a state judgment in any locality within the federal district where the judgment was entered. File a certified copy of the judgment in the county land records, usually at the registry of deeds or county recorder's office, and pay the filing fee. The judgment becomes a lien on the debtor's property in the county where you record it. * * *

Say you have a federal judgment from the United States District Court for the District of Maryland at Baltimore. If the debtor owns property in Howard County, Maryland (which does not encompass Baltimore, but is in the same federal district), you would record the judgment by filing a certified copy with the appropriate office of Howard County. The judgment will then be a lien against the debtor's Howard County property.

* * * If you know the debtor has property in other counties in the same state but outside the federal district where the judgment was entered, follow the state procedures for registering the judgment there. Registering the judgment means enrolling it on the court docket. Then record the judgment in the new county so it becomes a lien on any real property the debtor owns there.

Judgments obtained in a federal district court may also be registered in other federal districts once they become final by appeal or otherwise. * * *

So once you register the judgment in another district, you can record it and get the resulting lien against the debtor's property in any county within the registering district. * * *

Now you have liens on the debtor's property in various places. That is a good start, because it will establish your priority interest in that property if you get into a scuffle with creditors who come along later. But how do you get your money?

If the debtor has property in the jurisdiction where the judgment was entered or registered, have the court clerk issue a writ of execution against the property (sometimes called an attachment writ or a garnishment writ). Then present the writ to the U.S. marshal, who will attach the property to satisfy your judgment. * * *

You should describe the property to the marshal as specifically as possible. If there are different kinds of property, request different writs from the clerk. For example, in the federal district courts, there are usually separate forms of writs for: Attachment on Judgment (personal property, goods, chattels); Attachment on Judgment (credits); and Attachment on Judgment (garnishment of wages, earnings, salary, commissions and pensions). Consult the clerk on what writs should be issued.

If the debtor's property is in the hands of a third party such as a bank, proceed in accordance with state law (unless a particular federal statute applies) to attach (or garnish) those credits and have them applied against your judgment. (You should check applicable state and federal law on exemptions, especially when garnishing wages.) Writs of attachment on a judgment may be obtained from each court where your judgment is registered, and the process can be repeated until your judgment is satisfied. * * *

If the debtor owns personal property, recording the judgment in the county courthouse or registry of deeds may not be enough. For example, if the property is an aircraft, the U.S. marshal should attach it in accordance with state law.

* * * Once the marshal has attached and levied on the property, he will auction the property, sell it, and apply the sale proceeds, after expenses, to the judgment. Any excess proceeds are distributed to other lienholders in the order of their priorities, and, if there is anything left, to the debtor. * * *

To find the debtor's assets, you may use the same discovery devices available in prejudgment litigation, and more. * * * Rule 69 entitles a judgment creditor to use the discovery procedures found in Rules 26 through 37. In addition, you may use applicable state discovery procedures and state supplementary proceedings. As usual, the timing and sequence of discovery is your choice. An examination of the judgment debtor in supplementary proceedings is an excellent way to begin post-judgment discovery.

To start the process, file a petition for supplementary proceedings. In that petition, recite the facts concerning your judgment, and include a request to examine the judgment debtor and have him bring documents. * * *

If the debtor is a publicly held company, your request should call for quarterly and annual reports filed with the Securities and Exchange Commission. If the debtor is required to file other disclosure documents with local, state or federal agencies, get those too.

In post-judgment discovery, more than one examination of the debtor is often necessary, and you may have to move for sanctions under Rule 37 to get all the necessary documents from a recalcitrant debtor. You should also go after other sources of information about the debtor and his finances.

If the debtor has an accountant, subpoena the accountant and his records concerning the debtor. * * *

Even if the debtor has "lost" his financial statements or tax returns, you will find them in the accountant's files. If the debtor does not have an accountant, and still has not produced tax returns, move the court for an order requiring the debtor to give you written authorization to obtain copies of his returns from the Internal Revenue Service.

In some cases, you may suspect that the debtor has not produced all his bank records. When that happens, go right to the source. If you know where the debtor banks, subpoena the records from the bank.

* * * Credit card account statements are clues to the debtor's spending patterns, and they can help you trace exactly where he was on a given day. The records might show that the debtor stopped at a marina for food and gas, using a boat you did not realize that he or his alter ego corporation owned. * * *

During post-judgment litigation, you can often get injunctions or writs to freeze or attach assets that the debtor has transferred to others. This will prevent the assets from being further dissipated while your post-judgment litigation proceeds.

You should consider restraining asset transfers during a post-judgment appeal by invoking Federal Civil Procedure Rule 62 [reproduced in the Appendix at pp. 984–985]. If the debtor is unable to post a supersedeas bond, you can move the court to set other conditions for securing the judgment pending appeal. This will make it easier to collect the judgment if the debtor's appeal is unsuccessful. If the debtor does post a bond, the judgment can be satisfied against the bond. * * *

Under certain state and federal laws, receiverships may be established to administer the affairs and conserve the assets of financially troubled companies. More often than not, bankruptcy is the preferred method of administering and reorganizing insolvent companies. In [one] case, we proceeded under federal receivership statutes to give us quick access to the debtor's business and to prevent further dissipation of assets. * * *

The postjudgment litigation may be lengthy and expensive. There is no easy way at the beginning to assure your client that the money he spends in post-judgment discovery and litigation will produce an even bigger recovery. Usually, the preliminary post-judgment discovery, if done properly, will tell you how much of the judgment you can collect. * * *

Notes

1. Collection problems can be quite involved. For example, does the legal definition of "property" include intangible property such as the ownership of securities? If so, how can a creditor find and collect upon such intangible property? If the registered holder of stock has sold the certificate representing his shares subsequent to a judgment against him but before collection has been accomplished, can a creditor reach the certificate? Robert D. Hillman,

Other People's Money: Problems in Attaching Securities Under Three Versions of U.C.C. Article 8, 16 J.L. & Com. 89 (1996).

The UCC permits attachment or levy upon a security only if the certificate which represents the debtors' shares is itself seized. This hinders creditors in their efforts at collection, but protects bona fide purchasers of securities and promotes free transferability. However, certain securities fall outside the ambit of the UCC, for example, if they represent shares which are not commonly traded on securities exchanges. In such cases, for example in Arkansas, the law provides that creditors may "seize" the corporate securities merely by having a sheriff leave a writ of execution with the corporation; there is no need to seize the certificates themselves. Thus, in Arkansas at least, a creditor would wish to maintain that securities owned by a debtor are not securities under the terms of the UCC so that even transfers to bona fide purchasers can be thwarted. See Robert Laurence, Enforcing a Money Judgment Against the Defendant's Stocks and Bonds: A Brief Foray into the Forbidding Realms of Article Eight and the Fourth Amendment, 38 Ark. L.Rev. 561 (1985).

2. In some states, creditors can reach intangible property that otherwise cannot be readily seized through a device known as a turnover statute. Thus, in Renger Memorial Hospital v. State, 674 S.W.2d 828 (Tex.App.1984), the trial court granted the plaintiffs partial satisfaction of a judgment in the form of an order requiring the defendant hospital to turn over a cause of action the hospital owned against its former directors. See generally Bradley J.B. Toben & Elizabeth A. Toben, Using Turnover Relief To Reach The Nonexempt Paycheck, 40 Baylor L.Rev. 195 (1988); Philip K. Maxwell & Tim Labadie, Insurance Law, 48 S.M.U.L.Rev. 1351, 1387–91 (1995)(reviewing requirements for turnover of causes of action).

Not all causes of action may be transferred, however. For example, the Utah Supreme Court has held that, although a malpractice claim against a law firm may be acquired by a creditor through attachment and execution, it was against public policy of the state to allow the very law firm against whom the claim had been brought to purchase the cause of action at a sheriff's sale. As the firm obviously would not be going on to sue itself, the court believed that "public confidence in both the legal profession and the legal process as a whole would be damaged if lawyers were allowed to execute on legal malpractice claims brought against them." Snow, Nuffer, Engstrom & Drake v. Tanasse, 980 P.2d 208, 212 (Utah 1999).

The types of intangible property that may be reached with forms of the turnover device are otherwise fairly open-ended. For example, intellectual property is an important source of potentially valuable intangible assets, which may be reached with turnover. Thus, the family of Ron Goldman obtained the intangible rights of O.J. Simpson in a book, "If I Did It," in which the former pro football star explained how he hypothetically might have committed the slayings of Goldman and Nicole Brown, Simpson's ex-wife. While Simpson was acquitted of the murders, he was found liable in the subsequent civil trial for the wrongful death of Goldman, a waiter who had come to Brown's house to return a pair of glasses. The Goldman family was awarded a judgment of $33.5 million in 1997, but has been unable to collect much of the award from Simpson because his major assets, his Florida home and pensions from his football and movie careers, are not subject to levy for the satisfaction of civil court judgments. Jennifer Kay, Goldmans Get Rights to Simpson Book, AP, June 15, 2007. See also Juliet M. Moringiello, Seizing Domain Names to Enforce Judgments: Looking Back to Look to the Future, 72 U.Cin.L.Rev. 95 (2003) (reviewing how the law of enforcement of judgments has been applied to intangible property and concluding that an Internet domain name should be treated as an intangible asset subject to a collection action).

3. Another consideration is the fact that in most states, a judgment is valid for only a set length of time. For example, Minnesota provides for judgments that are valid for 10 years. Minn.Stat.Ann. § 550.01. Maine, however, provides instead a presumption of payment of a judgment once 20 years have elapsed since it was issued. Me.Rev.Stat.Ann. tit. 14, § 864. Thus, even if a debtor is paying off a judgment, she may escape paying off some of it if the validity of the judgment ends. On the other hand, even if a debtor is without seizable assets at the time the judgment is rendered, and is apparently "judgment-proof," the debtor may bear watching over the time that the judgment is valid in the event she does acquire some assets that can be seized. See Goldman v. Simpson, 160 Cal.App.4th 255, 72 Cal.Rptr.3d 729 (2008) (renewing judgment against O.J. Simpson for an additional ten years).

4. New York has created a device to ease the burden on creditors who want to locate the assets of judgment debtors while the judgments remain valid. Rather than searching for the actual bank branch where a debtor has an account, collection lawyers can send an information subpoena consisting of electronic lists of unpaid court judgments to willing banks located in the state. N.Y.C.P.L.R. § 5224 (a)(4). The bank makes an electronic comparison with the accounts in all of its branches and informs the creditor of any matches. The creditors' attorney, "as an officer of the court," § 5222 (a), responds by electronically serving, § 5222 (g), a restraining order on the bank for up to twice the amount owed, which then freezes the account for up to a year. § 5222 (b). The creditor must also notify the debtor of the freeze and certain rights under the statute, § 5222 (d) & (e), before proceeding to satisfy the judgment, including interest and the costs of collection. This system is very cheap, making it highly efficient for creditors (usually collection agencies with large lists of unpaid judgments) to search frequently for bank accounts of debtors. Lucette Lagnado, Cold-Case Files: Dunned for Old Bills, Poor Find Some Hospitals Never Forget, Wall Street J. June 8, 2004 at A1. See also David Gray Carlson, Critique of Money Judgment Part One: Liens on New York Real Property, 82 St. John's L.Rev. 1291 (2008) (analyzing the fine points of New York state execution procedures and criticizing several aspects as unconstitutional). Other states are trying other methods to make the collection of judgments more efficient in the computer era. See Joseph D. Bolton & Maxine M. Long, What Do I Do with My Judgment Now? A Primer on the New Centralized Judgment Lien Law, 75 Fla.B.J. 73 (Nov.2001) ("In addition to simplifying the judgment collection process, the public nature of the new centralized lien filing system may facilitate satisfaction of judgments

by putting additional pressure on debtors to pay" because of the effect on their credit rating.).

5. Additional practical advice on collection strategy is available in Robert L. Haig & Patricia O. Kahn, Representing the Judgment Creditor, 16 Am.J.Tr.Advoc. 1 (1992). More theoretical material is available in Stephen B. Burbank, Federal Judgments Law: Sources of Authority and Sources of Rules, 70 Tex.L.Rev. 1551 (1992). For advice on collecting judgments in foreign contexts, see, e.g., Dennis Campbell & Suzanne Rodriguez (eds.), International Execution Against Judgment Debtors (1998).

KAHN v. BERMAN

California Court of Appeal, First District, 1988
198 Cal.App.3d 1499, 244 Cal.Rptr. 575

SABRAW, ASSOCIATE JUSTICE.

* * *

I. THE FACTUAL AND PROCEDURAL HISTORY

William and John Kahn contracted with William Berman, Carl Pecson and Ace Truck & Equipment Rental, Inc., for the purchase of the Ace rental business in Las Vegas, Nevada. After disputes arose between the parties, litigation ensued in the Nevada state courts. * * *

A money judgment was entered on July 19, 1984, against William and Nana Berman in an amount greater than $1.2 million and against Carl and Shirley Pecson in an amount greater than $900,000. The judgment included significant punitive damages based on the jury's verdict that fraud had been committed. It was appealed on December 17, 1984.

The Kahns recorded the entire Nevada money judgment in the San Mateo County Recorder's Office on July 20, 1984. Five days later, on July 25, 1984, a purported $500,000 first deed of trust was recorded against the Berman's [sic] Hillsborough, California, residence by an entity named "The Berman Corporation." The deed of trust bore a date of December 15, 1983, but the notary's acknowledgment of William and Nana Berman's signatures was dated July 20, 1984, just one day after the Nevada judgment was entered. The address listed for the Berman Corporation on the deed of trust was 585 Remillard Drive, Hillsborough, California, the same property purportedly being encumbered.

On March 6, 1985, the Kahns filed an application in the San Mateo County Superior Court requesting entry of a judgment based on the Nevada judgment. A new California judgment was entered on the sister-state judgment by the clerk of the court on March 13, 1985. Notice of entry of the judgment was served on the Bermans on March 14, 1985. However, the notice contained a typographical error—rather than correctly reflecting that judgment had been entered in the amount of $1,237,433.38, it stated that the judgment was for $123,744.38. On September 5, 1985, the Berman's counsel accepted service of a corrected notice of entry of judgment on the sister-state judgment.

The Kahns had a writ of execution against a dwelling house (the Berman's Hillsborough residence) issued by the San Mateo County Superior Court on February 27, 1986. The writ of execution was levied by the sheriff and recorded on March 7, 1986. Notice of the levy was mailed the same day.

On March 31, 1986, the Kahns applied for an order authorizing the sale of the Berman residence. William Berman recorded a declaration of homestead on his Hillsborough residence on April 18, 1986. An abstract of judgment reflecting the Kahns' new California judgment was recorded in the San Mateo County Recorder's Office on May 1, 1986.

The Bermans opposed the Kahns' application for an order of sale on several grounds. Among other things, they argued that they were entitled to a $55,000 homestead exemption based on the April 18, 1986, declaration of homestead. They took the position that the declaration of homestead was senior to any judgment lien based on the Nevada judgment because no *abstract* of the Nevada judgment had been filed in San Mateo by April 18, 1986. In the event the court rejected their declared homestead argument, the Bermans alternatively asserted that they were entitled to claim the statutory homestead exemption authorized by section 704.720. Finally, they argued that, if an order of sale was granted, the minimum bid was required to be at least $555,644.23 (homestead exemption of $55,000, property taxes of $644.23, and the $500,000 Berman Corporation deed of trust).

On July 24, 1986, following a contested hearing, the Kahns obtained an order for the sale of the Bermans' Hillsborough residence pursuant to Code of Civil Procedure section 704.780. Among other things, the order stated that: (1) the sheriff had completed levy on the Bermans' residence in the form and manner required by law; (2) although the property was a valid homestead, the Kahn's judgment lien had priority because the declaration of homestead was not recorded until April 19, 1986 [sic; April 18, 1986]; (3) the fair market value of the dwelling was $450,000; and (4) the Bermans were not entitled to claim the statutory homestead exemption. * * *

II. ANALYSIS

A. *Recordation in California of a Sister State Judgment Does Not Create a Judgment Lien on Real Property in California*

* * * There is presently no single statute which clearly and explicitly lists those money judgments (i.e., California, sister-state, federal or foreign) that may serve as the basis for creation of a judgment lien by recordation. * * *

Reading all of these statutes together with the statutory history, it is apparent that recordation of a sister state judgment cannot directly give rise to a judgment lien on real property located in California—a sister state money judgment must first be reduced to a California judgment.

In the present case, rather than immediately filing an application for entry of a new California judgment based on the Nevada judgment entered on July 19, 1984, plaintiffs recorded a certified copy of the entire Nevada judgment in San Mateo County. Because plaintiffs did not initially comply with the Sister State Money Judgments Act by obtaining a California judgment, the recordation had no effect.

B. The Full Faith and Credit Clause of the United States Constitution Does Not Require California to Follow Nevada Procedures for Creation of a Judgment Lien

Anticipating the difficulty presented by their initial failure to have a California judgment entered on the Nevada judgment and to then record an abstract of such a California judgment, the Kahns argue in their cross appeal that requiring them to follow California rather than Nevada procedures for enforcement of the Nevada judgment violates the full faith and credit clause of the United States Constitution. (U.S. Const., art. IV, § 1.) They further assert that recording of a certified copy of the Nevada judgment was sufficient under the law of Nevada to create a judgment lien in California.

Although the Kahns correctly recite Nevada law regarding creation of a judgment lien on real property located in Nevada, we disagree with their constitutional assertion that Nevada procedural law must be followed when enforcing a Nevada judgment in California. The Kahns cite only the bare language of Article IV of the Constitution for the proposition that California is required to follow Nevada procedures for creation of a judgment lien in such a case. They fail to provide any other authority on this point. However, our own research reveals that a contrary interpretation was rendered by the United States Supreme Court in the early days of the Constitution.

In McElmoyle v. Cohen (1839) 38 U.S. (13 Pet.) 312, [10 L.Ed. 177], the Supreme Court held that a South Carolina judgment could not be directly enforced by execution in Georgia. The court explained that "To give it the force of a judgment in another State, it must be made a judgment there, and can only be executed in the latter as its laws may permit. It must be conceded that the judgment of a State court cannot be enforced out of the State by an execution issued within it." (Id. 13 Pet. at p. 325; see also * * * Huntington v. Attrill (1892) 146 U.S. 657, 685, 13 S.Ct. 224, 234, 36 L.Ed. 1123, 1134 [Article IV, section 1, of the Constitution does not "put the judgments of other States upon the footing of domestic judgments, to be enforced by execution; but [it leaves] the manner in which they may be enforced to the law of the State in which they are sued on, pleaded, or offered in evidence"], citing *McElmoyle v. Cohen*, supra, 38 U.S. (13 Pet.) 312, 325 * * *.)

It follows from these authorities that the Kahns' argument must be rejected. The full faith and credit clause is not violated by requiring that a sister-state judgment first be reduced to a California judgment before it may serve as the basis for a judgment lien on real property located in California.

C. The Order Authorizing the Sale of the Bermans' Residence Was Erroneous

The traditional method for enforcing a money judgment obtained in a sister state was to institute an independent action on the sister-state judgment in a California court. In 1974 the Sister State Money Judgments Act created a simpler alternative method for registration of such judgments.

Section 1710.15, subdivision (a), provides "A judgment creditor may apply for entry of a judgment based on a sister state judgment by filing an application pursuant to Section 1710.20." Once an application is properly filed in an appropriate venue, the clerk of the court is required to enter California judgment. With certain statutory exceptions, the new judgment has the same effect as an original California money judgment and "may be enforced or satisfied in like manner."

The next step in the process is for notice of entry of the California judgment to be served "promptly" by the judgment creditor upon the judgment debtor in the same manner as provided for service of summons. Within 30 days after service of the notice of entry, the judgment debtor is entitled to make a motion to have the new judgment vacated. The judgment can be vacated "on any ground which would be a defense to an action in this state on the sister state judgment...." In most cases, a judgment creditor cannot have a writ of execution issued until at least 30 days after the judgment creditor has been served with notice of entry of the new judgment.

The Kahns completed the statutory prerequisites for enforcement of the Nevada judgment on September 5, 1985, when notice of entry of their new California judgment was accepted by the Bermans' counsel. Rather than creating a judgment lien by recording an abstract of the new judgment, the Kahns next proceeded with execution against the Bermans' residence.[7]

The first step for execution on a dwelling house is for the judgment creditor to have the superior court issue a writ of execution. The judgment creditor then delivers the writ to the levying officer with instructions for service. Next, the officer levies on the real property. After the levy, the officer is required to promptly serve notice on the judgment creditor that the levy has been made. Within 20 days after the notice is served, the judgment creditor must apply for an order of sale or the property will be released. The application must state whether the dwelling is a homestead and must also state the amount of any liens or encumbrances on the dwelling. If the court thereafter determines that the dwelling is exempt, it must also determine the fair market value and make an order for its sale

---

7. Nothing in the statutory scheme requires a judgment creditor to create a judgment lien. The creditor can simply choose to levy execution, thereby creating an execution lien.

subject to the homestead exemption.[8] If no bid is received at the sale which exceeds the amount of the homestead exemption plus the amount needed to satisfy all liens and encumbrances, the homestead cannot be sold.[9] Finally if no bid in excess of 90 percent of the fair market value of the dwelling is received, the creditor must return to court and seek an order permitting the sale for the highest bid that exceeds the total amount of the homestead exemption and all liens and encumbrances.

Although portions of the foregoing statutory scheme were followed in this case, the correct result was not reached. The March 7, 1986, levy on the Bermans' residence gave rise to an execution lien (even though no judgment lien had previously been created). The Kahns thereafter applied for an order of sale * * *. The trial court correctly determined that the Kahns' March 7, 1986, execution lien had priority over the Bermans' April 18, 1986, declaration of homestead. However, in their response to the application for an order of sale, the Bermans had filed a declaration which established that the property in question was a homestead as defined in section 704.710, subdivision (c),[10] because: (1) it was the principal dwelling where they resided on March 7, 1986 (the date the Kahns' execution lien arose); and (2) they had continuously resided there since that time. The declaration also established that the Bermans were over the age of 65. As a result, the trial court erred when it concluded that the Bermans were not entitled to the $55,000 statutory exemption provided by sections 704.720 and 704.730, subdivision (a)(3).

When the court issued its order of sale * * *, it should have first determined that the property was exempt (i.e., subject to a statutory homestead exemption), next determined the fair market value of the property (found to be $450,000) and the amount of the homestead exemption ($55,000), and finally specified the amounts of the proceeds of the sale to be distributed to the lien and encumbrance holders. Thus, the order of sale should have properly listed, inter alia, the $55,000 homestead exemption, the property tax lien of $644.23, and the $500,000 Berman Corporation deed of trust.[11]

---

8. Section 704.780, subdivision (b) provides: "The court shall determine whether the dwelling is exempt. If the court determines that the dwelling is exempt, the court shall determine the amount of the homestead exemption and the fair market value of the dwelling and shall make an order for sale of the dwelling subject to the homestead exemption. The order for sale of the dwelling subject to the homestead exemption shall specify the amount of the proceeds of the sale that is to be distributed to each person having a lien or encumbrance on the dwelling and shall include the name and address of each such person." * * *

9. Section 704.800, subdivision (a) provides: "(a) If no bid is received at a sale of a homestead pursuant to a court order for sale that exceeds the amount of the homestead exemption plus any additional amount necessary to satisfy all liens and encumbrances on the property, including but not limited to any attachment or judgment lien, the homestead shall not be sold and shall be released and is not hereafter subject to a court order for sale upon subsequent application by the same judgment creditor for a period of one year."

10. Section 704.710, subdivision (c) provides in relevant part: "(c) 'Homestead' means the principal dwelling (1) in which the judgment debtor or the judgment debtor's spouse resided on the date the judgment creditor's lien attached to the dwelling, and (2) in which the judgment debtor or the judgment debtor's spouse resided continuously thereafter until the date of the court determination that the dwelling is a homestead."

11. Needless to say, such an order might have prevented the sale of the property. As we have already noted, section 704.800, subdivision (a), prohibits the sale of a homestead unless a

It follows that the order of sale must be and is reversed.

NOTES

1. *Kahn* is representative of the kind of steps that a creditor must follow in any state in order to execute upon a judgment. *Kahn* also demonstrates that there is usually a priority list of who would receive the proceeds from any sheriff's sale. First, the costs of the sale itself are deducted. There may be other liens, such as for the payment of back taxes, mechanics' liens, mortgages, or other judgment creditors. As *Kahn* indicates, the court must rank these liens according to their statutory priority and see that they are paid off in full from the proceeds of the sale in order from first to last until the money runs out. If there is any money left after all the expenses and liens are paid, it goes to the debtor. Thus, in a situation where there are many creditors and limited assets, creditors want to get in the queue as close to the front as possible. See David Gray Carlson & Paul M. Shupack, Judicial Lien Priorities under Article 9 of the Uniform Commercial Code: Part I, 5 Cardozo L.Rev. 287 (1984). However, a creditor who is relegated to the end of the queue may end up with more money by driving the debtor into bankruptcy court where most new liens (typically less than 90 days old) and certain state-law exemptions are not honored and unsecured creditors share on a pro rata basis any funds remaining after the fully secured creditors are reimbursed.

2. Did the Kahns' attorney commit malpractice? Consider how the minutiae of collection law trip up practitioners with alarming frequency. For example, in Republic National Bank v. United States, 506 U.S. 80, 113 S.Ct. 554, 121 L.Ed.2d 474 (1992), the bank failed to perfect its claim on the proceeds of the sale of property that the federal government had seized from its owner, who was alleged to have purchased the property with the proceeds of narcotics sales. The proceeds were deposited in the U.S. Treasury and the U.S. moved to dismiss for lack of subject matter jurisdiction. In a deeply divided decision (there were two majority opinions because of the vote splitting on different aspects of the case), the Supreme Court allowed the lower court to continue to exercise jurisdiction in the *in rem* civil forfeiture after the *res* was removed from the custody of the U.S. Marshal and placed in the U.S. Treasury.

In United States v. McDermott, 507 U.S. 447, 113 S.Ct. 1526, 123 L.Ed.2d 128 (1993), a judgment creditor had filed a state-law judgment lien on the McDermotts' existing and any subsequently acquired property. The Internal Revenue Service then filed a tax lien against all real and personal property owned or subsequently acquired by the McDermotts, and later still the McDermotts acquired a piece of property. The Court held, 6–3, that the tax lien was "first in time" and therefore first in right as to the subsequently acquired property because a judgment lien is perfected only when property is

---

minimum bid sufficient to cover all of the liens and encumbrances is received. At the same time, however, we do not intend to pass on the validity or legitimacy of the $500,000 deed of trust recorded by the "Berman Corporation." It is sufficient to say that the circumstances of the recording were suspicious. Finally, the Kahns have access to other statutory remedies for challenging that deed of trust. (Civ.Code, § 3439 *et seq.* [the Uniform Fraudulent Transfer Act].)

seized, while, in contrast, a tax lien created under the Tax Lien Act, 26 U.S.C. § 6323, is perfected when filed.

3. In addition to execution, the remedy at issue in *Kahn,* probably the other most commonly used collection device is garnishment. In garnishment, the creditor obtains money that a third party (the garnishee), usually a bank or an employer, owes to the debtor. The garnishee's obligation to the debtor (and the debtor's obligation to the creditor) are satisfied to the extent the garnishee pays the creditor. Usually only a percentage of the garnishee's debt to the debtor may be used at any one time to satisfy the creditor. E.g., Consumer Credit Protection Act, 15 U.S.C. §§ 1673 (limiting garnishment to 25% of take home pay, unless garnishment is for support of a spouse or child where 60% limitation applies).

2. EXEMPT PROPERTY

As the *Kahn* opinion indicates, state law exempts (or partially exempts) certain properties from legal attachment and sale, which as a result cannot be used to satisfy judgments. Besides the homestead exemption discussed in *Kahn,* the most common exemption protects some or all of an individual debtor's wages. The concept of exemption is simple enough to understand: although the state wants creditors to be able to collect judgments against debtors, it does not want to permit the debtor to become totally impoverished in the process. However, as the next cases and materials indicate, deciding whether property is exempt is not always as simple as consulting a statute. In addition, states vary in how generous they are with exemptions. In this section, we first read an example of a court interpreting an exemption statute. Then we will consider how exemptions are affected by the interaction of the laws of our two complementary legal regimes—the federal and state governments.

GUTTERMAN v. FIRST NATIONAL BANK OF ANCHORAGE

Supreme Court of Alaska, 1979
597 P.2d 969

RABINOWITZ, CHIEF JUSTICE.

The First National Bank of Anchorage obtained a default judgment against Michael Gutterman. That judgment provided that three paintings owned by Gutterman, then in the possession of an art dealer, were to be delivered to the custody of the clerk of the superior court and sold at an execution sale, with the proceeds to be applied toward satisfaction of the judgment.

Prior to the execution sale, Gutterman notified the court of his claim * * * of an exemption from execution in the paintings in the amount of $300. The sale of the paintings was postponed at the Bank's request, and the Bank subsequently filed a motion to disallow the claim of exemption in the superior court.

The relevant statutory section, AS 09.35.080(a)(2), provides:

Exemptions (a) The following property is exempt from execution, except as otherwise specifically provided when selected and reserved by the judgment debtor or his agent at the time of the levy, or as soon after levy and before sale as the existence of the levy becomes known to him:

* * * (2) books, pictures, and musical instruments belonging to the judgment debtor not to exceed $300 in value....

The parties stipulated that each of the paintings in question was worth more than the $300 exemption provided in the statute. The question thus presented to the superior court was whether Gutterman was entitled to the benefit of the exemption provision and to receive $300 from the proceeds of the sale of the paintings. The superior court held that "pictures" exceeding $300 in value are not property exempt from execution by the terms of the statute and that Gutterman therefore had no exemption right in the proceeds of the execution sale.[1] It is from this decision of the superior court that Gutterman brings this appeal.

In order to properly discuss the question raised by Gutterman as to the nature of the exemption granted by AS 09.35.080(a)(2), it is necessary to briefly place exemption laws in their social and historical context. Exemption laws emerged from bankruptcy law policies concerned with both maintaining a certain basic level of economic vitality in individual debtors and reasonably protecting creditors' rights to satisfaction of legally incurred debt.

In order to protect debtors and their families from pauperism and to facilitate rehabilitation, state laws universally provide for the exemption of certain property, or a certain value of property, from seizure for general debts. The laws range in liberality from the most spartan subsistence standard to the extremes reflected in unlimited exemptions for homesteads and life insurance.

A debtor's property which is not exempted from execution in satisfaction of debt by applicable state or federal laws is subject to the rights of creditors.[5]

---

1. The superior court noted that, unlike the provisions of AS 09.35.090 concerning the residence exemption, AS 09.35.080 contained no express exemption for the proceeds of a sale of "pictures" or other exempt items enumerated therein. The court reasoned that, accordingly, the legislature "apparently intended ... (a) different treatment with respect to categorical exemptions." It concluded that a picture that exceeds $300.00 in value is not exempt. It is the picture, and not the value, to which the exemption is directed.

5. AS 09.35.070 expresses this principle in the following terms:

Property Liable. All goods, chattels, money, or other property, both real and personal, or an interest in the property of the judgment debtor not exempt by law, and all property and rights of property seized and held under attachment in the action are liable to execution.

The federal law of exemptions has no applicability to this case. The recently revised federal Bankruptcy Act, which takes effect October 1, 1979, contains specific provisions relating to exemptions under bankruptcy law. * * * The historical and revision notes to that section list some of the items that may be exempted under other federal laws. The revised Act specifically provides that a bankrupt debtor retains exemptions allowed under applicable state law. Prior to

While the scope of state exemption laws varies considerably among the states, certain categories of debtors' property are provided some degree of exemption in most states. Prominent among state exemptions is the homestead or residence exemption, which exempts the debtor's homestead from execution sale either entirely or to the extent of a certain specified value.[6] Among the other forms of debtors' property provided varying degrees of protection from creditors are life insurance policies and proceeds; earnings and subsistence allowances; and various types of non-wage income, including welfare payments, retirement income, alimony and child support, or other compensation payments. In addition, some states, though not Alaska, provide general dollar amount exemptions, with the particular assets to be included in the dollar amount left to the debtor's choice.[8]

The exemption which is the subject of this appeal is one of the specific personal property exemptions provided for in AS 09.35.080(a).[9] * * *

---

enactment of the revised Act, the federal Bankruptcy Act contained no uniform scheme of exemptions, but, instead, deferred to other federal and state law as to exemptions.

6. Alaska's residence exemption is defined in AS 09.35.090. A homestead exemption is provided by Section 4 of the Uniform Exemptions Act, approved by the National Conference of Commissioners on Uniform State Laws in 1976. Vukovich reports that all but six jurisdictions provide a homestead exemption. [See Vukovich, Debtors' Exemption Rights, 62 Geo.L.J. 779, 797 (1974).]

8. Alaska's exemptions provisions contain no such general dollar amount exemptions, but provide value limitations for specific categories of exempt property. Several commentators have recommended that exemption statutes should prescribe a value limitation for personal property to be chosen by the debtor without restriction as to form or kind. However, this approach has been rejected by both the Uniform Exemptions Act and the revised federal Bankruptcy Act.

9. AS 09.35.080(a) provides:

(a) The following property is exempt from execution, except as otherwise specifically provided when selected and reserved by the judgment debtor or his agent at the time of the levy, or as soon after levy and before sale as the existence of the levy becomes known to him:

* * *

(2) books, pictures, and musical instruments belonging to the judgment debtor not to exceed $300 in value;

(3) necessary wearing apparel belonging to the judgment debtor for the use of himself or his family; watches or jewelry not to exceed $200 in value;

(4) the tools, implements, apparatus, motor vehicles, books, office furniture, business files, animals, laboratory and any other article necessary to enable any person to carry on the trade, occupation, or profession by which that person habitually earns his living to the value of $2,500, including sufficient quantity of foods to support the animals, if any, for six months;

(5) the following property belonging to the judgment debtor and in actual use or kept for use by and for his family: animals, household goods, furniture, and utensils to the value of $1,200, including food sufficient to support the animals, if any, for six months, and provisions actually provided for family use and necessary for the support of that person and family for six months;

(6) all property of a public or municipal corporation;

(7) no article of property mentioned in this section is exempt from execution issued on a judgment recovered for its price, and, in the event the article of property [h]as been sold or exchanged for other property, the proceeds of the sale or the article for which it was exchanged is not exempt from execution.

Personal and household property exemptions such as those provided in AS 09.35.080(a)(2) are designed to ensure that debtors will have necessary items for living in reasonable comfort and for earning a living. The statutes vary as to the types of items that are exempt and as to the amount of their exempt value. * * *

Alaska's limited value exemption for "pictures" thus represents a legislative judgment that such items are among the amenities of life in which a debtor may preserve at least a limited investment.[11]

Gutterman does not assert a right to preserve the paintings themselves, which have in fact been sold, but argues that he nonetheless should retain the benefit of the $300 exemption granted to debtors owning "pictures." Resolution of this issue rests on an interpretation of the statutory phrase in AS 09.35.080(a)(2) granting an exemption for "pictures ... belonging to the judgment debtor not to exceed $300 in value." As the superior court's order denying an exemption recognized, the meaning of this statutory phrase is neither clear nor unambiguous.[12]

It is an accepted general rule that "exemption laws are remedial in character and should be liberally construed in favor of the debtor." We therefore conclude that the statute should not be interpreted in a way which completely eliminates a debtor's exemption rights in an item of property within an exempt category because that item's value exceeds the statutory allowance. Instead, we agree with the reasoning and conclusion advanced by one commentator on exemption laws:

> The few statutes which regulate the forced sale of exempt personalty worth more than the statutory maximum provide that the exempt amount is to be paid to the debtor from the proceeds of sale prior to any payment to the execution creditor. The exemption clearly should extend to the proceeds of an involuntary sale of personalty. Otherwise, the exemption is meaningless whenever the value of the personalty exceeds the statutory allowance, since the levying creditor immediately could order the sheriff to pay the total amount to him. Moreover, if the sheriff is forced to sell exempt property, it is likely that the debtor has no nonexempt property. This is a situation where the protection of the exemption laws is needed and appropriate. Accordingly, the courts should afford the debtor a reasonable time to purchase other property with the proceeds.

In addition to useful household items, the exemption statutes also commonly apply to more personalized, arguably less necessary, items such as family pictures, Bibles, wedding rings and other jewelry, books, historical and scientific collections, guns, church pews, and cemetery lots. The states also allow debtors and members of their families to keep all of their clothing or such as is necessary.

11. Compare AS 09.35.080(a)(2) with Cal.Civ.Proc.Code § 690.1 (West 1955 & Supp. 1979)("Works of art shall not be exempt unless of or by the debtor and his resident family") and Or.Rev.Stat. § 23.160(1)(a)(1977) ("pictures ... to the value of $150"). See also Uniform Exemptions Act § 8(a)(3)("family portraits and heirlooms of particular sentimental value to the individual").

12. The superior court's order noted that "[a]t first blush, the Court frankly was inclined to [Gutterman's] position."

Faced with a similar question as to the interpretation of a Massachusetts statute granting an exemption for an "automobile ... not exceeding seven hundred dollars in value," a federal district court observed that:

> If nothing else is clear, it is beyond serious dispute that the statutory phrase 'not exceeding seven hundred dollars in value' is ambiguous on its face, at least with respect to the controlling issue in this case.

Levin v. Mauro, 425 F.Supp. 205, 206 (D.Mass.1977).

This is the approach adopted by the Uniform Exemptions Act. The comment to that Act's provision defining a debtor's personal property exemptions, Section 8, makes it

> clear that if an item within any of the categories listed has a value exceeding $500, the individual is nonetheless entitled to an exemption in the items to the extent of $500, and the creditor is entitled to levy only on the excess value. * * *

More helpful to the precise question of statutory interpretation presented here is *Levin v. Mauro,* interpreting a Massachusetts exemption statute worded much like AS 09.35.080(a)(2). The Massachusetts statute provided an exemption in an automobile "not exceeding seven hundred dollars in value;" the Alaska statute provides an exemption in pictures "not to exceed $300 in value." The *Levin* court, after noting the ambiguity of this language and the remedial purpose of exemption statutes, concluded that the Massachusetts statute should be construed to allow "a debtor owning a car in excess of the limit ... to turn it over to the trustee for liquidation ... (and) to purchase another vehicle with $700 derived from liquidation proceeds." In reaching this conclusion, the court rejected as "legitimate, but by no means conclusive," the argument that the Massachusetts legislature had expressly provided setoff schemes with regard to other exemptions and that "if the legislature wanted a setoff it knew how to write one." * * *

We find this analysis and authority persuasive and hold that Gutterman should receive the $300 amount of the exemption from the proceeds of the sale of the paintings. A contrary result would be unreasonable because it would provide no exemption for a debtor whose picture has a value of $300.01 and a full exemption for a debtor owning the same type of property worth just one penny less. We think our resolution of this question fairly balances the rights of debtors and creditors, since their respective interests in such exempt categories of property will be uniform and not dependent on very small differences in the value of such items of property.

The $300 exemption benefit provided by AS 09.35.080(a)(2) does not, however, confer an unrestricted right to that portion of the proceeds from the execution sale. The terms of AS 09.35.080(a)(7) provide that "in the event the article of property has been sold or exchanged the proceeds of the sale or the article for which it was exchanged is not exempt from execution." Thus, the $300 in proceeds to which Gutterman is entitled is not in itself exempt and does not assume the generic exemption afforded the "pictures" from which it is derived.

Notwithstanding this principle, as a matter of exemption law a debtor is allowed and encouraged to convert nonexempt property into exempt property and to change the types of exempt property he or she owns without losing the benefit of the relevant exemptions. * * *

Only in cases of actual fraud as to creditors, such as attempting to convert secured collateral to exempt property, is the practice not recognized by law.

Gutterman's interest in these proceeds is identical to that recognized in several jurisdictions for the proceeds from a voluntary sale of exempt property. More than fifty years ago, the Kansas Supreme Court, in the context of such voluntary sales, stated that:

> It is well settled that the proceeds of exempt property are exempt to the debtor for a reasonable time, to enable him ... to invest the money in other exempt property.

Gutterman shall therefore receive the $300 exemption from the sale proceeds and be allowed a reasonable time in which to reinvest those proceeds in other exempt property. * * *

NOTES

1. As *Gutterman* indicates, states can and do exempt certain tangible property from seizure by creditors. For example, one of the most "debtor-friendly" states is Texas. Section 41.001 of the Texas Property Code exempts a homestead and burial lots and exempts the proceeds of sale of a homestead for six months. Section 41.002 defines an urban homestead as not more than ten acres of land, together with any improvements, which is used for a dwelling or for a business. A rural family is entitled to 200 acres, while a single person is entitled to 100. If the property is larger, the owner may designate which portion shall be considered the homestead. Section 42.001(a) also exempts from attachment by creditors up to $60,000 of personal property owned by a family (or $30,000 by an individual). The list of eligible personal property includes the following items, among others: home furnishings including family heirlooms, provisions for consumption, farming or ranching implements, tools and equipment, including a boat, used in a trade or profession, clothing, jewelry (not to exceed 25 percent of the aggregate limitation), two firearms, athletic and sporting equipment, one motor vehicle for each member of the family, two horses, mules or donkeys, household pets and twelve head of cattle, sixty head of other livestock and 120 fowl. Importantly, Texas also exempts current wages for personal services. Id. § 42.001(b).

Under such a generous statutory scheme, what is the actual dollar value of a judgment issued against an ordinary individual living in that state likely to be? For discussion of the effect of variations in state exemptions on the conduct of debtors, compare Teresa A. Sullivan, Elizabeth Warren and Jay L. Westbrook, As We Forgive Our Debtors 241 (1989)(empirical studies suggest that there is little effect) with Stephen G. Gilles, The Judgment–Proof Society, 63 Wash. & Lee L.Rev. 603 (2006) (proposing reforms because the widespread state and federal exemptions "seriously undermine the deterrence and corrective justice goals of tort law"). See also Symposium, Judgment Proofing, 52 Stan.L.Rev. 1 (1999).

The Bankruptcy Abuse Prevention and Consumer Protection Act of 2005, Pub.L. 109–8, 119 Stat. 62, 216, addressed congressional concern that debtors have sometimes moved to states with generous exemptions in an effort to protect their assets from creditors. For example, a debtor now must have lived in a state for at least two years before filing for bankruptcy in order to claim the exemptions available in that state. 11 U.S.C. § 522(b)(3)(A). A debtor who has lived fewer than 39 months in a state before filing for bankruptcy cannot claim more than $125,000 (inflation-adjusted) as a homestead or residential exemption. 11 U.S.C. § 522(p).

2. Henry W. Farnam, Chapters in the History of Social Legislation in the United States to 1860, 148–52 (1938), provides some background on the development of exemptions and an explanation for why Texas law is particularly generous to debtors. Farnam traces the U.S. exemption system from its origins in Texas, which in turn took the concept from Spanish law. Soon after gaining independence in 1829, Texas used the homestead exemption as a device to attract immigrants, who would be debtors as they got their farms and ranches started. Starting in 1841, other states followed suit. Farnam notes that although a form of exemption appears in Leviticus, he believes that the system developed in Texas out of reaction to the harsh English law, rather than a conscious attempt to follow the Biblical institution.

3. As the provisions from Texas indicate, exemption statutes tend to reflect a very particular image of the locality. This tends to hold true for even newly revised statutes. For example, when the Vermont Legislature revised its statute in 1988, it retained exemptions that reflect that state's self-image as a land of subsistence farmers. See, e.g., Parrotte v. Sensenich, 22 F.3d 472 (2d Cir.1994)(dairy farmer's bulls used as breeding stock are exempt under Vermont law as "tools of the trade," even though the cows which produce the milk are not exempt under this category); Note, Vermont's New Debtor's Exemption Statute, 13 Vt.L.Rev. 609 (1989)(new statute protects, inter alia, $5000 in growing crops, ten cords of firewood, various animals and feed for the animals to survive through one winter, three swarms of bees, and one yoke of animals used for team work). What property exemptions might be suited to a more urbanized setting? Note, Making a Bad Situation Worse: Going Against the Current, Have Tennessee and Mississippi Floundered in Their Approach to the "Tools of the Trade" Exemption?, 31 U.Mem.L.Rev. 401 (2001) (reviewing various interpretations of the exemption). What other policy considerations might prompt a state to retain these perhaps outdated exemptions? See Richard M. Hynes et al., The Political Economy of Property Exemption Laws, 47 J.L. & Econ. 19 (2004).

4. Can exemption statutes be written to avoid becoming quaint anachronisms as society changes? Is the only solution to have the legislature revise the list periodically? One potential solution is called the "wild card." It allows a debtor to transfer some or all of the value of certain unclaimed exemptions to other property that otherwise would be unprotected from creditors. Thus, a Vermont debtor who does not happen to own $5000 in growing crops can transfer that value to some other property. Vt.Stat.Ann. tit. 12, § 2740(7). The federal exemption plan, which is often used in bankruptcy, allows the transfer of a modest portion of any unused homestead exemption. 11 U.S.C. § 522(d)(5). Besides maintaining flexibility, "wild cards" also equalize the treatment of debtors who do and do not happen to own the specific categories of exempted properties.

5. How is a judgment debtor, who may be unsophisticated, to know of the existence of the exemptions available? The Tenth Circuit has held that New Mexico's postjudgment execution statutes violated due process because they did not require the sheriff to inform the debtor, upon seizure of property, that various exemptions exist and that a procedure is available to protect exempt property. Aacen v. San Juan County Sheriff's Department, 944 F.2d 691 (10th Cir.1991). See also Diana Gribbon Motz & Andrew H. Baida, The Due Process Rights of Postjudgment Debtors and Child Support Obligors, 45 Md.L.Rev. 61 (1986).

LAWS v. LAWS

Superior Court of Pennsylvania, 2000
758 A.2d 1226, 2000 PA Super. 248

POPOVICH, JUSTICE.

This is an appeal from the order of the Court of Common Pleas, Cambria County, entered on December 2, 1999, which ordered Appellant Laura D. Laws to pay $425.00 per month in child support. Appellant contends that the trial court abused its discretion by ordering her to pay a confiscatory amount of support and by attaching her wages in an amount that exceeded the Consumer Credit Protection Act's limit on garnishment. For the following reasons, we affirm.

On May 12, 1999, Appellee Michael E. Laws filed for modification of the child support order for the parties' three minor children. At that time, Appellee had primary custody of the children. On June 16, 1999, a conference was held with the Domestic Relations section of the Cambria County Court of Common Pleas. By interim support order dated June 23, 1999, Appellant was directed to pay $400.00 in child support and $10.00 for arrears per month to Appellee.

Appellant appealed from the child support order, and a hearing was held before a master on August 13, 1999. At the time of the hearing, Appellee was employed as a welder for Johnstown America Corporation. On average, his net monthly income was $2,075.00. Appellant worked part-time at McDonald's Restaurant and earned $476.00 net income per month. However, the master found that Appellant had a monthly earning capacity of $800.00. This was based upon Appellant's prior earnings at Reese Brothers of $900.00 per month for telemarketing and her employment skills and experience as a secretary and a letter carrier. The master found that Appellant lost employment because of alcohol addiction and substance abuse. The master found that Appellant did not demonstrate that she was unable to work full-time and therefore assessed her an $800.00 per month earning capacity. In addition, the master determined that Appellee had reasonable day care expenses of $432.00 per month.

Based upon these findings, the master determined that Appellant was required to pay $311.00 per month in child support, as well as $151.00 per month towards day care. Since this amount of $462.00 per month exceeded 50% of her earning capacity, the master determined that Appellant was entitled to a deviation from the guidelines to a support amount of $400.00 per month. The final recommendation of the master was that Appellant was required to pay an aggregate total of $425.00 in child support, allocated as $300.00 for child support, $100.00 for day care expenses and $25.00 for arrears. Appellant's wages were to be attached in the amount of $212.49 semi-monthly.

The lower court adopted the master's recommendation. * * * This appeal followed.

Appellant raises the following issues for our review:

1. Whether the trial court abused its discretion ordering the Defendant–Appellant to pay child support in the amount of $425.00 per month, which is confiscatory under the circumstances in this case.

2. Whether the trial court abused its discretion in ordering that the Defendant–Appellant's wages be attached in the amount of $212.49 semi-monthly, which exceeds 65% of the Defendant–Appellant's disposable earnings.

* * *

We will not interfere with the broad discretion afforded the trial court absent an abuse of that discretion or insufficient evidence to sustain the support order. * * *

First, Appellant contends that the lower court erred in ordering support payments that were confiscatory because the payments do not provide Appellant with reasonable living expenses. * * *

At the time of the support hearing, Appellant was working part-time. Previously, she had been working full-time and earned approximately $900.00 per month. The master found that Appellant did not demonstrate that she was unable to work full-time. Therefore, Appellant voluntarily reduced her income. "Ordinarily, a party who willfully fails to obtain appropriate employment will be considered to have an income equal to the parties earning capacity." Pa.R.Civ.P. 1910.16–2(d)(4). The determination of a parent's ability to provide child support is based upon the parent's earning capacity rather than the parent's actual earnings. * * * Appellant does not contest the lower court's determination that she had an earning capacity of $800.00 per month.

* * * [W]e find that the lower court did not err in failing to consider Appellant's actual living expenses because Appellant's earning capacity exceeds $550 and does not trigger [the Pennsylvania threshold].

Second, Appellant contends that the lower court abused its discretion by attaching Appellant's wages in an amount that exceeded the garnishment limit as permitted under federal law.

The Federal Consumer Credit Protection Law states that the maximum part of the aggregate disposable earnings of an individual for any workweek shall not exceed 65%. See 15 U.S.C.A. § 1673(b)(2)(B). "Disposable earnings" is defined as "that part of the earnings of any individual remaining after the deduction from those earnings of any amounts required by law to be withheld." Earnings are defined as "compensation paid or payable for personal services, whether denominated as wages, salary, commission, bonus, or otherwise." Appellant argues that since her net monthly income was $476.00, the lower court violated this restriction on garnishment when it ordered her to pay $425.00 in child support that exceeded 65% of her disposable income.

After extensive review of Pennsylvania law, we have determined that the issue of whether the Federal Consumer Credit Protection Act's disposable earnings equates to Pennsylvania's earning capacity for the purpose of limitation on garnishment has not been addressed by the Pennsylvania Courts. After examining the purpose of the Consumer Credit Protection Act and the manner in which other jurisdictions handled this issue, we find that when an obligor's disposable earnings are less than his or her earning capacity because the obligor voluntarily reduced his or her income, the earning capacity should be used when determining the limit on garnishment of wages under the Consumer Credit Protection Act. In reaching this conclusion, we are guided by our concern that obligors could reduce or avoid their child support obligation by voluntarily reducing their earnings so insufficient funds remained available for garnishment.

The legislative history of the Consumer Credit Protection Act indicates Congress intended a dual purpose regarding support payments: (1) to protect debtors from unscrupulous creditors and (2) to assure that dependent children receive support payments. Congress had certain types of creditors in mind in enacting this legislation. It did not seek to shackle such legitimate debt collection as child support. "Its purpose is to protect consumers from a host of unfair, harassing and deceptive debt collection practices without imposing unnecessary restraints on ethical debt collectors." Senate Report No. 95–382, 95th Cong. 1st session, 1977 U.S.Code Cong. & Ad.News 1695, 1696. Protection of debtors was balanced by allowing for a higher percentage of payroll deduction for child support. Congress wanted "to assure an effective program of child support."

When determining the intent of the Consumer Credit Protection Act regarding child support, we are persuaded by a similar case of New York State. In Carol J. v. William J., 119 Misc.2d 739, 464 N.Y.S.2d 635 (Fam.Ct.1983), an obligor had his wages garnished to pay child support. The garnishment exceeded 50% of his disposable income. He argued that this violated the Consumer Credit Protection Act. However, the court noted that the obligor voluntarily minimized his earnings. The court held that an obligor could not rely on the Consumer Credit Protection Act provision prohibiting garnishment of wages exceeding 50% of his disposable income since such reliance would allow him to circumvent his legal obligation due to his own act. The court concluded, "Respondent will not be allowed to thwart both Federal and New York State policy to assure support of dependents by perverting the Consumer Credit Protection Act."

The court in New York interpreted the Consumer Credit Protection Act as to not permit an obligor who has voluntarily reduced his or her income from reducing his or her child support payments by using the obligor's potential earnings not actual earnings. "One who purposefully minimizes his income, may have his duty to support based upon potential not just actual earnings. To afford respondent the relief of the Consumer Credit Protection Act would be to allow him to circumvent this legal obligation through his own acts."

Likewise, we are convinced that an obligor should not be permitted to circumvent child support payments by voluntarily taking an income reduction. * * * The Federal garnishment law does not expressly include such an adjustment. However, we are convinced that an obligor who voluntarily took an income reduction should not be able to circumvent a valid court order to pay child support by perverting the Consumer Credit Protection Act. Allowing such a result would undermine the power of Pennsylvania's child support orders and the dual purpose of the Consumer Credit Protection Act. We are guided in our determination by recognizing that the ultimate purpose of the child support order is to provide for the best interests and welfare of children from broken homes, and not to punish the obligor parent. In order to advance this purpose, we find that the Consumer Credit Protection Act's garnishment limitation should equate disposable earnings with earning capacity as determined by Pa.R.Civ.P. 1910.16–2(d)(4) when an obligor voluntarily reduces his or her earnings.

The record demonstrates that the lower court determined Appellant's earning capacity to be $800.00 per month. The maximum amount attachable under the Consumer Credit Protection Act ($800 x 65%) is $520 per month. Appellant was ordered to pay $425.00 per month. Therefore, we find that the trial court did not abuse its discretion in that the child support order does not exceed 65% of Appellant's monthly income. Cf. *Carol J.*, 464 N.Y.S.2d at 637 (court used obligor's previous annual income in determining child support award when obligor purposefully reduced his annual income from $45,000 to $15,000).

Order affirmed.[1]

NOTES

1. As *Laws* indicates, federal statutes may affect to what extent assets of debtors are available to creditors for attachment or garnishment. For example, except for child support, the Consumer Credit Protection Act generally limits any garnishment to 25% of disposable income. Another important source of wealth for many people is their retirement income, such as their pension benefits. However, these assets are generally not accessible to credi-

---

1. We note that Appellee argued that Appellant's appeal should be quashed for failing to file a reproduced record. However, Appellant was granted leave to proceed In Forma Pauperis. The Rules of Appellate Procedure state that if a party is granted leave to proceed IFP, such party shall not be required to reproduce the record. Therefore, we deny Appellee's request for this appeal to be dismissed.

tors. As another example, the Employee Retirement Income Security Act of 1974 (ERISA), 29 U.S.C. § 1056(d)(1), forbids the assignment or alienation of pension fund benefits. A similar source of retirement income, an Individual Retirement Account, is also off-limits. Rousey v. Jacoway, 544 U.S. 320, 125 S.Ct. 1561, 161 L.Ed.2d 563 (2005) (rejecting contention that creditors should be able to reach IRA accounts because they are accessible to owners at all times, subject only to ten percent tax penalty). See Patricia E. Dilley, Hidden in Plain View: The Pension Shield Against Creditors, 74 Ind.L.J. 355 (1999).

2. If a debtor were to retire, start to receive some of those accumulated pension benefits or withdraw some IRA funds, and put them into a separate bank account, should those withdrawn funds still be exempt from garnishment? Compare Robbins ex rel. Robbins v. DeBuono, 218 F.3d 197 (2d Cir.2000), cert. denied, 531 U.S. 1071, 121 S.Ct. 760, 148 L.Ed.2d 662 (2001) (no longer protected) with United States v. Smith, 47 F.3d 681 (4th Cir. 1995)(still protected) and Guidry v. Sheet Metal Workers National Pension Fund, 39 F.3d 1078 (10th Cir.en banc 1994), cert. denied, 514 U.S. 1063, 115 S.Ct. 1691, 131 L.Ed.2d 556 (1995)(no longer protected under federal law, but 75% protected under state law as "disposable earnings"). Cf. Gutterman v. First National Bank of Anchorage, 597 P.2d 969 (Alaska 1979)(court grants debtor time to put proceeds from sale of exempt property into other exempt property).

3. Should creditors be permitted to garnish students' bank accounts? Accounts whose funds are traceable to federally guaranteed student loans? See Schaerrer v. Westman Commission Company, 769 P.2d 1058 (Colo.1989). What about collecting on unpaid student loans by later withholding social security benefits? Lockhart v. United States, 545 U.S. 142, 126 S.Ct. 699, 163 L.Ed.2d 557 (2005) (Debt Collection Improvement Act clearly makes Social Security benefits subject to offset to secure repayment of government educational loans; other legislation had already overridden the 10–year statute of limitations generally applicable to the collection of debt in the case of student loans).

4. In *Carol J.*, the case the *Laws* court relied upon, the New York court based the support payment on what the husband should have been earning in his profession as a stock broker, rather than what he reported, largely because of the suspicion that Mr. J. was fraudulently concealing income. But what if he needed to leave the stress of the brokerage business in New York City for health reasons, as well as to fulfill his dream of becoming the captain of a sport fishing boat in Florida? Could the court order Mr. J. to get back to selling pork-belly futures at the brokerage? To pay Ms. J. as if he were still at the brokerage? In *Laws*, the court treated Ms. Laws' alcohol and substance abuse problems as if they were entirely of her own making. Is that fair?

Ms. Laws was ordered to pay as if she were working full time as a telemarketer, secretary and/or letter carrier. What about overtime work? At least one court has held that a spouse cannot be forced to work overtime and on weekends to maintain a certain level of spousal and child support. The father had been working sixteen-hour days as a theatrical stage-hand while the couple was still married, but he changed to the shorter hours and lower pay of television work shortly after they were separated and a trial court issued a temporary support order. A unanimous California Supreme Court held that, although it would be appropriate under these suspicious facts to base support on the father's ability to earn rather than his actual income, the support payments had to be based on objectively reasonable hours and not on an extraordinary work regimen. In re Marriage of Simpson, 4 Cal.4th 225, 14 Cal.Rptr.2d 411, 841 P.2d 931 (1992).

Suppose Mr. Laws believes that Ms. Laws could earn more money, and pay more support, if she moved from rural Cambria County, where unemployment is high and wages are low, to Pittsburgh (50+ miles away) or Philadelphia (200+ miles), where prevailing wages are much higher. Can the court base an order on what theoretically she could earn in a big city? Compare Johansen v. State, 491 P.2d 759 (Alaska 1971) (could not order move from fishing village where the ex-husband was born and raised) with Moss v. Superior Court, 17 Cal.4th 396, 71 Cal.Rptr.2d 215, 950 P.2d 59 (1998) (may impose contempt sanction on parent who willfully fails to seek employment to be able to pay child support).

3. FORECLOSURE SALES

GRIGGS v. MILLER

Supreme Court of Missouri, Division No. 2, 1963
374 S.W.2d 119

WALTER H. BOHLING, SPECIAL COMMISSIONER.

[The original defendant in this case, W.A. Brookshire, was sued separately by Ray Crouch and by Dorothy Contestible for debts allegedly owed. Plaintiff Crouch won a judgment of nearly $2,000. Contestible's $17,000 judgment was under appeal.

Missouri law provides that winning plaintiffs may immediately "execute" on defendant's property to pay the judgment, unless defendant posts a bond. Missouri law also permits the defendant to choose which property is to be sold at execution sale and to decide the order of sale, with the sale proceeding until the debt is satisfied.

Defendant Brookshire owned a 322 acre farm, more than 200 head of cattle, and corporate stock. Additionally, Brookshire had deposited collateral with an insurance company sufficient to satisfy Crouch's judgment. Sheriff Powell and Crouch knew of defendant's assets and collateral. Furthermore, Crouch had in his possession more than $10,000 worth of defendant's cattle.

Defendant Brookshire requested the sheriff to sell only one 40 acre section of the farm, which Brookshire contended would satisfy his debts because the entire farm was worth between $50,000 and $90,000. The sheriff, however, held an execution sale for the entire farm. Brookshire warned the participants not to purchase the farm because the judgment was on appeal. He advised them that he had other assets "probably" sufficient to cover the debt, including the collateral and the cattle that Crouch was holding.

Nonetheless, the entire farm was sold to Bill Griggs for $20,600. Defendant withheld possession, and Griggs sued him. The court appointed Miller as trustee to represent Brookshire's interests when Brookshire was confined to state prison and could not defend himself.] * * *

A sheriff conducting an execution sale is the agent of the property owner and the judgment creditor, and his duty is to protect the interests of both and to see that the property is not sacrificed. We said in Gordon v. Hickman, 96 Mo. 350, 356, 9 S.W. 920, 921, 922: "If the property can be divided without prejudice, and a part will sell for the debt and costs, a part only shall be sold." Forced sales of property usually do not bring full value.

Sheriff Powell's advertisement of the sale of defendant's 322 acre farm was to "sell all of said real estate or as much thereof as *it* be necessary to pay the judgment of $1,966.69," in the Henry County Circuit Court, which, with interest and costs, amounted to $2,308.16 on the day of sale.

Defendant's farm was never advertised for sale under the Audrain County (Contestible) execution. * * *

Sheriff Powell testified he paid out the $20,600.00 purchase money about two hours after the sale. * * *

It is not questioned but that this 322 acre farm, consisting of approximately eight forties, could have been offered for sale in parcels. Rule 76.24 contemplates that the officer "divide such property, if susceptible of division, and sell so much thereof as will be sufficient to satisfy such execution." This was not done, and we hold that it should have been so divided. In Brookshire v. Powell, Mo., 335 S.W.2d 176, 181, the disparity between the market value of this farm and a bid of $2,300 was considered so great as to require setting aside that execution sale and sheriff's deed. In the case at bar the Henry County judgment, interest and costs amounted to $2,308.16; and for that amount under said execution and the constructive levy of the Audrain County execution, but without an advertisement for sale under Rule 76.36, under said Audrain County execution, it is sought to justify this forced sale for $20,600 of property valued at about $46,000. * * *

Defendant is entitled to relief upon doing equity. Accordingly, if defendant will, within thirty days, deposit in this court, for the use and benefit of those entitled thereto, the sum of $20,600 with interest at the rate of 6% per annum from the date of sale until the same is paid, the decree appealed from will be reversed and the cause remanded with directions to cancel the sheriff's sale and the sheriff's deed to plaintiff made pursuant thereto; otherwise the decree will stand affirmed. In either event the costs are assessed against the estate of defendant Brookshire. * * *

NOTES

1. Note that the defendant protested that he "probably" had sufficient cattle to satisfy the Crouch judgment. Should the creditors (and their agent, the sheriff) have to satisfy the judgment against property in a particular order, such as personal property before real estate? See, e.g., Evcco Leasing Corp. v. Ace Trucking Co., 828 F.2d 188 (3d Cir.1987). For centuries, this has been true. "Bailiffs shall [not] seize any land or rent for any debt, so long as the chattels of the debtor are sufficient to repay the debt * * *." Magna Carta, chapter 9, signed by King John at Runnymede, 1215 A.D.

Feudal England was based on tenure in land. It was viewed as disruptive of society to permit the Crown to repossess land which had been granted to a tenant who later went into debt, if the tenant had chattel sufficient to satisfy the debt. Thus, the Magna Carta sought to limit the power of creditors to seize land in payment of debt. Other provisions of the Magna Carta sought to prevent abuse by sheriffs, who rented their jurisdictions—bailiwicks—from the Crown and derived income from debt collection. Thus, not unlike the Missouri statute discussed in *Griggs,* the Magna Carta prohibited a sheriff from attaching any more of a deceased debtor's chattels than were necessary to satisfy the claims against him, and required the attachment to be done in front of witnesses after showing proper authorization from the Crown. See William F. Swindler, Magna Carta: Legend and Legacy (1965).

Given the structural changes that have occurred in Anglo–American society from the time of King John to the present, what are some arguments for and against retention of the rule that the debtor is permitted to choose which property will be levied upon?

2. Why did it matter to the *Griggs* court whether all of the judgments were advertised before the sale? See, e.g., Ford & Vlahos v. ITT Commercial Finance Corp., 8 Cal.4th 1220, 1233, 885 P.2d 877, 885, 36 Cal.Rptr.2d 464, 472 (1994):

> In contrast to notice, one purpose of which is to alert the debtor and other secured creditors to take steps to protect their interests, possibly including locating bidders for their collateral, the purpose of requiring adequate advertising of a foreclosure sale is to force the secured party to ensure the auction is well attended by legitimate bidders, so the highest commercially reasonable price for the collateral will be obtained.

Compare Deibler v. Atlantic Properties Group, Inc., 652 A.2d 553 (Del.), cert. denied, 516 U.S. 809, 116 S.Ct. 55, 133 L.Ed.2d 20 (1995)(no due process violation where skeletal requirements of Delaware notice statute were met because debtors themselves could publicize sheriff's sale of stock and provide additional information to entice potential bidders).

3. In Guardian Loan Co. v. Early, 47 N.Y.2d 515, 419 N.Y.S.2d 56, 392 N.E.2d 1240 (1979), the New York Court of Appeals refused to set aside a transfer of the debtors' house, which was sold for about seven percent of its estimated value. The debtors, the Earlys, had obtained postponements of two previous sheriff's sales, but never satisfied the judgment against them. In petitioning the court to revoke the transfer, it was alleged that a flat tire

caused the Earlys to be late to the sale, and that the couple had nearly enough cash to satisfy the judgment. The court held that it had broad authority to prevent misuse of sheriff's sales, but it lacked any statutory grounds for setting aside a sale that complied "with the notice, time or manner of such sale."

What factors must a court consider in deciding whether to cancel a deed created by a sheriff's sale of the debtor's property? Apart from statutory considerations, what public policy concerns might a court look to in deciding whether to overturn the results of such sales? Whose interests does the court protect in declining to cancel deed transfers effected by sheriff's sales? For one answer, see Robert R. Wisdom Oil Co. v. Gatewood, 682 S.W.2d 882, 885 (Mo.App.1984):

> Execution sales may be set aside upon motion of parties, not only in cases of fraud or where inadequacy in the sales price is so great as to shock the judicial conscience, but also in cases of irregularity in the conduct of the sale to the prejudice of any party having an interest in the action, or cases of accident or surprise where because of some misunderstanding, mistake, misapprehension or other fortuity, the parties are prevented from being present at the sale to protect their interests. Or stated another way, mere inadequacy of consideration will not justify the setting aside of a judicial sale unless accompanied by some irregularity. Irregularities that have been recognized to fall within this rule include, a mortgagor's mistake as to the date of the sale; a misleading description of the property to be sold; the sale of an excessive portion of real property; a sale made after the sheriff announced sales were concluded; and a sale at an unusual hour.

4. Previously, we noted that a creditor who was last in the queue might find that bankrupting the debtor might net the creditor more money. For a few years in the 1980s and 1990s, another reason to consider bankruptcy was that in some federal circuits, the bankruptcy court could set aside certain sheriff's sales of property if there was reason to believe that the sales price did not reach a set amount (usually 70%) of the fair market value of the property. When the asset was resold by the bankruptcy court, pro rata distribution rules applied. The Supreme Court ultimately decided (by a 5–4 vote) that a bankruptcy court has no power to set aside a forced sale conducted in accordance with state foreclosure law. According to Justice Scalia's opinion for the majority, the consideration received in a noncollusive and regularly conducted nonjudicial foreclosure sale establishes the "reasonably equivalent value" of property as a matter of law. Justice Souter's dissent would have read a 1984 amendment to the Bankruptcy Code, 11 U.S.C. § 542(a)(2)(A), as specifically authorizing a trustee in bankruptcy to avoid certain pre-bankruptcy transfers, including those on foreclosure sales, that a bankruptcy court determined were not made in exchange for a reasonably equivalent value. BFP v. Resolution Trust Corp., 511 U.S. 531, 114 S.Ct. 1757, 128 L.Ed.2d 556 (1994). For analysis of *BFP*, compare Michael H. Rubin & Stephen P. Stronchein, Security Devices, 55 La.L.Rev. 611 (1995) (generally supportive of decision, but noting questions left unanswered) with William N. Eskridge, Jr. & Philip P. Frickey, The Supreme Court, 1993 Term—Foreword: The Law as Equilibrium, 108 Harv.L.Rev. 26, 83 (1994) (calling *BFP* "an astonishing decision for a textualist").

4. BODY EXECUTION

LANDRIGAN v. McELROY
Supreme Court of Rhode Island, 1983
457 A.2d 1056

WEISBERGER, JUSTICE.

The defendant appeals from a Superior Court order granting the plaintiff's motion for a body execution pursuant to G.L.1956 (1969 Reenactment) § 9-25-15. The defendant contends that the body execution statute contravenes the Fourteenth Amendment to the Constitution of the United States. We agree that a portion of the statute is unconstitutional. Accordingly, we sustain the defendant's appeal, vacate the order that granted the plaintiff's motion for a body execution, and remand the case to the Superior Court.

The facts that led to the issuance of the body execution in this case are undisputed. A civil action for assault and battery in the Superior Court resulted in a jury verdict for plaintiff. Judgment was entered in the amount of $42,029.28 plus interest on December 3, 1976. The trial justice denied defendant's motion for a new trial, and defendant appealed to this court. On February 22, 1979, we summarily denied and dismissed defendant's appeal. The plaintiff then requested that the clerk of the Superior Court prepare an execution on the judgment. During March and April of 1979 two executions were issued, but both were returned unsatisfied.

Thereupon, plaintiff moved pursuant to § 9-25-15 for an execution against the body of defendant.[1] Arguing that the body execution statute was unconstitutional, defendant objected. After a hearing, a Superior Court justice granted plaintiff's motion and on April 29, 1980, ordered that an execution issue against the body of defendant. On the same day, a stay pending appeal to this court was granted.

The arguments of defendant on appeal can be summarized as follows: (1) section 9-25-15 denies defendant the equal protection of the laws by depriving him of his fundamental right to physical liberty without a compelling state interest, [and] (2) the issuance of a body execution without a prior hearing concerning defendant's ability to pay the tort judgment does not comport with the requirements of procedural due process * * *. Before we address the merits of these claims, however, we must discuss the background of the body execution statute.

HISTORY OF THE BODY EXECUTION STATUTE

Imprisonment for debt is an ancient remedy. Note, Body Attachment and Body Execution: Forgotten But Not Gone, 17 Wm. & Mary L.Rev. 543

---

1. General Laws 1956 (1969 Reenactment) § 9-25-15 provides in part: "An execution, original, alias, or pluries, may issue against the body of a defendant not exempt from arrest in an action * * * sounding in tort in which the title to real estate was not in dispute * * * provided, however, that no execution, original, alias or pluries, shall issue against the body of a defendant unless so ordered by a justice of the superior court or a justice of a district court upon the written ex parte motion of a party named in the action."

(1976); see Howe, Studies in the Civil Law 205–06 (2d ed. 1905). Indeed, under Roman law creditors could seize and imprison even insolvent debtors and sell them into slavery; if more than one creditor had a claim against a debtor, they could partition the debtor's body into proportionate shares. At common law, the writs of *capias ad respondendum* and *capias ad satisfaciendum* authorized the arrest of the debtor at the initiation of the lawsuit or after judgment had been rendered respectively. Vestiges of these procedures existed in colonial America and in the United States during the post-Revolutionary War period. In response to abusive utilization of body execution statutes by creditors during the late-eighteenth and nineteenth centuries, state legislatures enacted statutory and constitutional provisions that limited or entirely prohibited imprisonment for debt. See generally, Note, Imprisonment for Debt: In the Military Tradition, 80 Yale L.J. 1679, 1679 n. 1 (1971) (listing statutory and constitutional provisions concerning body execution). The Constitution of the State prohibits, absent a strong presumption of fraud, continued imprisonment of a judgment debtor "after he shall have delivered up his property for the benefit of his creditors * * *." R.I. Const., art. I, sec. 11. Moreover, once a contract judgment debtor is imprisoned pursuant to a body execution, he or she may obtain release almost immediately by taking the "poor debtor's oath."[3] In addition, the creditor for whose benefit the debtor is imprisoned must pay in advance for the prisoner's board.[4]

Section 9–25–15 must be examined in light of these limitations and its own legislative history. The body execution statute originated in the Court and Practice Act of 1905. * * * In 1961 the Legislature amended the statute to enable judgment creditors to obtain through ex parte motion execution against the bodies of judgment debtors. Clearly, this amendment was intended "to deprive judgment creditors of arbitrary power to issue, through their counsel, body executions against judgment debtors and to require submission of the petitions to judicial scrutiny." Martin v. Estrella, 110 R.I. 368, 370, 292 A.2d 884, 886 (1972). We have held, however, that once a judgment creditor sets forth one of the statutory grounds for issuance of a body execution, the trial justice has no choice but to grant the creditor's motion. As will become evident, our decision today overrules *Martin v. Estrella* to the extent that the court's opinion in that case deprives a trial justice of any discretion to deny a motion for a body execution.

The Constitutional Validity of § 9–25–15

The defendant bases his equal-protection challenge to § 9–25–15 on the doctrine enunciated by the United States Supreme Court in Williams

---

3. The defendant in this case, however, is a debtor on a tort judgment. He therefore would not be subject to discharge pursuant to the "poor debtor's oath" until six months after imprisonment.

4. In 1975 the Legislature increased the amount that a creditor must pay in advance for the board of a debtor imprisoned pursuant to a body execution from $4.00 per week to $210.00 per week. In our opinion, this evinces a legislative intent to discourage the use of body execution as a means for satisfying judgments. We note further that supplementary proceedings in aid of execution are more readily available to assist judgment creditors in obtaining satisfaction. * * *

v. Illinois, 399 U.S. 235, 90 S.Ct. 2018, 26 L.Ed.2d 586 (1970), and Tate v. Short, 401 U.S. 395, 91 S.Ct. 668, 28 L.Ed.2d 130 (1971). In both cases the Court addressed the constitutionality of imprisoning a defendant beyond the statutorily authorized term solely because the defendant was unable to pay a fine that accompanied his sentence. The Court determined that such imprisonment constituted invidious discrimination in violation of the equal-protection clause. These cases make clear that the state cannot imprison an individual solely because of a lack of money.

The defendant points out that a federal district court relied on *Williams* and *Tate* to strike down, as facially repugnant to the equal-protection clause, the body execution statute of another state. In Abbit v. Bernier, 387 F.Supp. 57 (D.Conn.1974), the court found that even though the Connecticut statute did not expressly exclude a preincarceration hearing to determine ability to pay, the state courts implemented the statute without providing for such hearings. Consequently, the court struck down the statute as unconstitutional. Subsequently, a Connecticut state court found that the *Abbit* court erroneously concluded that court practices in the state did not include a hearing to determine the judgment debtor's ability to pay. Palumbo v. Manson, 35 Conn.Supp. 130, 133, 400 A.2d 288, 289–90 (Super.Ct.1979). Accordingly, the state court upheld the body execution statute by interpreting it as requiring such a hearing.[6]

The body execution statute at issue in *Abbit* and *Palumbo* was silent concerning a preincarceration hearing to determine the judgment debtor's ability to pay. The "ex parte" amendment to our statute, on the other hand, implicitly excludes such a hearing. Moreover, this court's interpretation of that amendment in *Martin v. Estrella, supra,* deprives a trial justice of any discretion to deny issuance of a body execution once a creditor sets forth the existence of a statutory ground. We are of the opinion, therefore, that § 9–25–15 is incapable of an interpretation upholding its validity as long as the "ex parte" language is an effective part of the statute.

* * * By failing to provide for a preincarceration hearing to determine ability to pay, the statute in effect enables only tort judgment debtors who are able to pay to obtain immediate release from imprisonment. These individuals need only comply with the judgments and executions against them. On the other hand, tort judgment debtors who are unable to pay must remain in prison for at least six months.[7] They are, therefore, incarcerated solely because of their lack of money. This disparate treatment is precisely the type of invidious discrimination prohibited by the Court in *Williams* and *Tate*.

---

6. Subsequently, the Connecticut Legislature repealed the body execution statute.

7. Certain poor debtors may obtain post-body execution release almost immediately by taking the "poor debtor's oath." We do not limit our opinion, however, to the application of the body execution statute only to tort judgment debtors. The requirements of equal protection and due process apply equally to the application of the body execution statute to debtors who are unable to pay nontort judgments.

Moreover, imprisoning a tortfeasor who is unable to pay a judgment does not implement the governmental interest in enforcing judgments and executions. Supplemental proceedings in aid of execution more effectively further this interest because such proceedings enable a creditor to obtain satisfaction of a judgment on an installment payment basis. In short, imprisoning debtors who are unable to pay judgments against them does not have a rational connection with enforcement of the obligation to pay. This court will not attribute to the Legislature an intent that would result in absurdities or would defeat the underlying purpose of legislation.

We hold that the ex parte hearing provision of the 1961 amendment to § 9–25–15 is unconstitutional as violative of the equal-protection clause. We assume, however, that the Legislature would prefer that this court strike down only the unconstitutional portion if such a construction is reasonably possible. Accordingly, we shall sever the ex parte hearing portion of the 1961 amendment to § 9–25–15 from the rest of the statute, strike down this element as unconstitutional, and interpret the remaining portion of the statute as requiring a hearing to determine the judgment debtor's ability to pay. [The Court then explained the basis for its power to sever the unconstitutional portion of the statute.] * * *

NOTES

1. Similarly, the Supreme Court of the United States has addressed what a court may do to a felon who was fined and placed on probation on the condition that he make restitution to his victim but who does not pay. The trial court may not order the felon back to prison for that reason alone without first determining why the felon did not pay the victim and whether alternative orders, such as extending the time to pay, might be appropriate. Bearden v. Georgia, 461 U.S. 660, 103 S.Ct. 2064, 76 L.Ed.2d 221 (1983). Compare Hicks on Behalf of Feiock v. Feiock, 485 U.S. 624, 108 S.Ct. 1423, 99 L.Ed.2d 721 (1988)(allowing the use of jail as a coercive remedy where a defendant failed to obey a court order requiring the payment of child support).

2. Is a broader attack on body execution statutes appropriate? In Kinsey v. Preeson, 746 P.2d 542 (Colo.1987), the Supreme Court of Colorado struck down that state's body execution statute on the grounds that it failed the rational basis test. The court noted:

> [A]n indigent judgment debtor will suffer imprisonment based solely on an involuntary inability to pay the judgment and still owe the entire amount of the judgment after serving time in jail. Imprisoning an indigent debtor will not serve the coercive purpose of the body execution statute. In fact, jailing the indigent debtor defeats the purpose of obtaining payment for the judgment creditor by precluding gainful employment during the period of incarceration.

746 P.2d at 549. What if the real effect of imprisonment under such statutes is to create a family-wide scramble to find money to pay the debt? Even if effective, is it fair? See, e.g., Coetzee v. South Africa, CCT 19–94 (1995) (Constitutional Court of South Africa bans use of debtors' prison).

3. If body execution is unavailable, what is the court to do to a debtor who is not indigent, but is able to protect assets so that they are not subject to levy or garnishment? If the debtor is determined enough, perhaps not much. E.g., Lepak v. McClain, 844 P.2d 852 (Okla.1992) (Oklahoma Constitution prohibits statute allowing incarceration to be used to enforce money judgments in civil contempt proceedings). However, despite its constitutional prohibition against "imprisonment for debt," the Oklahoma Supreme Court has held that unpaid child support payments, even those that have been reduced to judgment, may be enforced by a jail sentence imposed for indirect contempt of court. Sommer v. Sommer, 947 P.2d 512 (Okla.1997). Accord, United States v. Ballek, 170 F.3d 871 (9th Cir.1999), cert. denied, 528 U.S. 853, 120 S.Ct. 318, 145 L.Ed.2d 114 (1999) (Child Support Recovery Act does not violate the constitutional prohibition against slavery or imprisonment for debt). See also Robert C. Davis & Tanya M. Bannister, Improving Collection of Court–Ordered Restitution, 79 Judicature 30 (1995)(simple reminder letters sent to convicted offenders will improve the rate of restitution obtained by crime victims). Some have called for more stringent measures. Note, Putting Fear Back Into the Law and Debtors Back Into Prison: Reforming the Debtors' Prison System, 42 Washburn L.J. 143 (2002) (calling for harsh penalties when a debtor intentionally withholds money after a court has determined that the payment of the debt is just).

Chapter 9

Conduct of the Plaintiff: Bars to Obtaining Relief

■ ■ ■

In both equity and law there are traditional rules, principles, and maxims that focus on the behavior of the plaintiff and, when applicable, bar the plaintiff from obtaining relief. Ultimately all of the principles and rules that we examine in this chapter involve misconduct by the plaintiff, but the degree and type of misconduct varies and traditionally a number of different maxims or principles have been invoked by the courts to bar a plaintiff from obtaining relief. Stated in their boldest traditional form, these rules and principles bar the plaintiff from all relief; in some circumstances they are used to modify or adjust a remedy. Frequently law and equity expressed the same root idea in different terms and applied different tests to the plaintiff's behavior. The categories established by the various principles are frequently not well defined at the margin, so that one category shades imperceptibly into another. For instance, the proposition that in order to obtain relief one must come into a court with "clean hands" is a very broad proposition. It can include the stricture against misleading another party to his detriment, which is found in equitable estoppel, or the prohibition against delaying the commencement of an action while the defendant proceeds with the activity that the plaintiff complains of, which is part of laches. The principles which have been inherited from equity are typically more flexible and less distinct than those which are derived from law.

The group of principles and maxims that we examine in this chapter are typically included in remedies courses, but they are often combined with other principles such as that of undue hardship or *de minimis non curat lex*. They are frequently dealt with in conjunction with undue hardship and similar concepts because a legal procedure that balances the equities between the plaintiff and the defendant requires the examination of the plaintiff's conduct and where that examination results in the plaintiff receiving no relief, the cases become very like those in this chapter. When you have finished this chapter, re-examine Smith v. Staso Milling Co., 18 F.2d 736 (2d Cir.1927), which is set out beginning at p. 101, and ask yourself how many of the issues in that case could be categorized or argued under the headings of unclean hands, equitable estoppel, or laches. To a large extent, the framing of the issues in dispute determines whether the court "balances the equities" or decides the case under one of the principles examined in this chapter.

The connection to *de minimis* cases lies in the fact that the principles and maxims discussed in this chapter are conceived of as defenses. If a remedies course is organized to focus in one place on defenses, the cases here become naturally grouped with the *de minimis* cases.

We have addressed the cases in this chapter with the emphasis on the plaintiff's conduct for two reasons. First, these cases develop the theme of determining remedies by focusing on what will return the plaintiff to her rightful position by taking up the issue of what sort of conduct by the plaintiff will lead a court to conclude that the plaintiff should obtain nothing from the defendant. Second, some of these cases deal with the conduct of the plaintiff toward the court or third parties so that they do not always fit neatly with cases which focus on the relations between the plaintiff and the defendant. There are some forms of conduct that may defeat the plaintiff's claim for relief regardless of the defendant's behavior.

PROBLEM: COUNTRY LODGE V. MILLER (REPRISED)
PLAINTIFF'S CONDUCT

Country Lodge has sued, seeking to enjoin Miller from polluting the Rural River which flows from Miller's property past that of Country Lodge. Country Lodge also claims damages for loss of business, alleging that numerous customers have complained of the unsightly river in the fall when Miller discharges her apple mash. Miller first defends by claiming that Country Lodge has unclean hands since it, too, is discharging garbage into the river. Should Country Lodge be denied relief in the following circumstances:

a) Country Lodge's discharges are only one-tenth the volume of Miller's?

b) Miller, being upstream, is not directly affected by Country Lodge's discharges?

Would your answers be different if Country Lodge's discharges were a breeding ground for insects which harmed Miller's apples?

What if Miller had gone to Country Lodge before beginning the discharges, told Country Lodge what she planned to do, and Country Lodge said it had no objection to Miller discharging apple mash?

Assume Country Lodge's owner had read in the newspaper that Miller was about to install a big apple press and discharge mash into the river and that experience in a neighboring county showed that the discharge would be unsightly. If Country Lodge waited to sue until Miller starting discharging the apple mash, should that delay bar Country Lodge from obtaining relief? Should it matter whether the relief sought was damages or an injunction?

On the same set of facts, suppose the Environmental Protection Agency sued Miller for discharging apple mash without a permit; should EPA be barred from obtaining relief? Would it make a difference to your answer if

Miller had applied to EPA for a discharge permit a year before but, despite a statutory requirement that EPA act on all permit applications within six months, EPA had failed to act because it considered other permit applications more important? What if EPA's Director of Water Pollution had erroneously, but in good faith, told Miller that she came within an exception to the statute and did not need a permit for her apple mash discharge?

A. UNCLEAN HANDS AND IN PARI DELICTO

"He who comes into equity must come with clean hands" is a central maxim of equity with a direct effect on the plaintiff's ability to obtain relief: the court will not provide relief to one who does not come with clean hands. While the metaphor of the maxim is a powerful image, it is, of course, remarkably uninformative as to the legal principle involved. As the Seventh Circuit has noted, "Today, 'unclean hands' really just means that in equity as in law the plaintiff's fault, like the defendant's, is relevant to the question of what if any remedy the plaintiff is entitled to." Scheiber v. Dolby Laboratories, Inc., 293 F.3d 1014, 1021 (7th Cir.2002), cert. denied, 537 U.S. 1109, 123 S.Ct. 853, 154 L.Ed.2d 781 (2003). The "unclean hands" maxim could be reformulated to state that the courts will not grant relief to plaintiffs who have committed improper conduct with regard to the matter in litigation. But this reformulation of the maxim still leaves a central issue vague: what conduct might be considered "improper"? Moreover, it may too narrowly restrict the sweep of the maxim, which has been interpreted elastically when considering how closely the plaintiff's behavior must be connected to the matter in litigation.

"*In pari delicto potior est conditio defendentis*"—in a case of equal or mutual fault, the position of the defending party is the better one—is the common law parallel to the clean hands doctrine. A plaintiff who is *in pari delicto* with the defendant will receive no relief from the court. *In pari delicto* carries a greater emphasis on equality of fault than does the unclean hands defense and involves a mutuality of wrongdoing.

These defenses have important common threads. First, their successful invocation leads to the denial of relief to the plaintiff. Second, this result is not justified by the defendant's conduct, which may be reprehensible, but by the plaintiff's misconduct. Third, the basis on which the maxims are applied is often not the rights of the litigant to the case but the interests of the public and the protection of the integrity of the court. But it is an open question in many cases whether the decision of the court to accept one of these defenses and leave things as it found them clearly serves the interests of the public. Frequently the court has to rely on long-term arguments to the effect that its refusal to grant relief to plaintiffs who behave in an unacceptable manner will discourage others from such behavior in the future. Not only do these arguments look to the long-term impacts, they ignore the windfall that the defendant obtains. Ideally, the doctrine will be simultaneously just to the plaintiff, defendant and the public. In reading these cases, consider whether there are other mechanisms that would more fairly balance those interests.

KEYSTONE DRILLER CO. v. GENERAL EXCAVATOR CO.

Supreme Court of the United States, 1933
290 U.S. 240, 54 S.Ct. 146, 78 L.Ed. 293

MR. JUSTICE BUTLER delivered the opinion of the Court.

The question presented is whether the Circuit Court of Appeals rightly applied the maxim, He who comes into equity must come with clean hands.

Petitioner owns five patents which may be conveniently identified as the Clutter patent and the four Downie patents. They all cover devices constituting parts of a ditching machine operated on the principle of a mechanical hoe or mattock. The Clutter patent is basic and the Downie patents are for claimed improvements.

Prior to the commencement of these suits, the petitioner brought a suit in the Eastern Division of the Northern Ohio District against the Byers Machine Company for infringement of the first three patents. January 31, 1929, the court held them valid and infringed, and granted injunction. Defendant appealed.

[In February 1929 Keystone brought suit against, inter alia, General Excavator alleging infringement of the same three patents.] Plaintiff immediately applied for temporary injunctions to restrain further infringement. The applications were based upon the complaints, supporting affidavits and the pleadings, opinion and decree in the *Byers* Case. The court filed a memorandum in which it is stated that, while plaintiff had sustained its patents as against the defenses of an alleged impecunious infringer, defendants were in good faith pressing new defenses that seemed to have merit enough to prevent the application of the rule permitting a temporary injunction merely because of the prior adjudication. The court denied the injunctions, but upon condition that defendants give bonds to pay the profits or damages that might be decreed against them. * * * November 5, 1930, the Circuit Court of Appeals affirmed the decree in the *Byers* Case. * * * The district court held the Clutter patent and the first and fourth Downie patents valid and infringed, the second Downie not infringed, and the third Downie patent invalid.

At the trial of these cases, defendants introduced evidence that plaintiff did not come into court with clean hands. It was sufficient to sustain findings of fact made by both courts, in substance as follows: June 27, 1921, Downie filed the application on which was issued his first patent. In the preceding winter he had learned of a possible prior use at Joplin, Mo., by Bernard R. Clutter. The latter is a brother of the patentee of the Clutter patent and had then recently been in the service of plaintiff as demonstrator in the use of ditching machinery. Downie made the application and assigned his rights to plaintiff, of which he was secretary and general manager. The patent issued, and plaintiff, contemplating the bringing of an infringement suit thereon against the Byers Machine Company, was advised that the prior use at Joplin was sufficient to cast doubt upon the validity of the patent. Downie then went to Bernard R. Clutter and for valuable considerations * * * obtained from Clutter an affidavit prepared by Downie to the effect that Clutter's use of the device was an abandoned experiment, and also obtained Clutter's agreement to assign plaintiff any rights he might have as inventor, to keep secret the details of the prior use, and, so far as he was able, to suppress the evidence. No proof of such use was produced at the trial of that case. The defendants in these suits took Clutter's deposition early in 1930. He did not then disclose his arrangement with plaintiff for concealment of evidence in the *Byers* Case. Their suspicions being aroused by his testimony, defendants in the latter part of that year again examined him and secured facts upon which they were able to compel the plaintiff to furnish the details of the corrupt transaction.

The district court characterized Downie's conduct as highly reprehensible, and found that his purpose was to keep Clutter silent. But it also found that the plaintiff did nothing to suppress evidence in these cases. It expressed the opinion that matters pertaining to the motion for preliminary injunction had no bearing upon the merits, and that plaintiff's use of the *Byers* decree was not a fraud upon the court. And it ruled the maxim did not apply. The Circuit Court of Appeals held the contrary, reversed the decrees of the District Court, and remanded the cases, with instructions to dismiss the complaints without prejudice.

Plaintiff contends that the maxim does not apply unless the wrongful conduct is directly connected with and material to the matter in litigation, and that, where more than one cause is joined in a bill and plaintiff is shown to have come with unclean hands in respect of only one of them, the others will not be dismissed.

The meaning and proper application of the maxim are to be considered. As authoritatively expounded, the words and the reasons upon which it rests extend to the party seeking relief in equity. "It is one of the fundamental principles upon which equity jurisprudence is founded, that before a complainant can have a standing in court he must first show that not only has he a good and meritorious cause of action, but he must come into court with clean hands. He must be frank and fair with the court, nothing about the case under consideration should be guarded, but everything that tends to a full and fair determination of the matters in controversy should be placed before the court." Story's Equity Jurisprudence (14th Ed.) § 98. * * * This court has declared: "It is a principle in chancery, that he who asks relief must have acted in good faith. The equitable powers of this court can never be exerted in behalf of one who has acted fraudulently, or who by deceit or any unfair means has gained an advantage. To aid a party in such a case would make this court the abetter of iniquity." Bein v. Heath, 6 How. 228, 247, 12 L.Ed. 416. * * *

But courts of equity do not make the quality of suitors the test. They apply the maxim requiring clean hands only where some unconscionable act of one coming for relief has immediate and necessary relation to the equity that he seeks in respect of the matter in litigation. They do not close their doors because of plaintiff's misconduct, whatever its character, that has no relation to anything involved in the suit, but only for such violations of conscience as in some measure affect the equitable relations between the parties in respect of something brought before the court for adjudication. They apply the maxim, not by way of punishment for extraneous transgressions, but upon considerations that make for the advancement of right and justice. They are not bound by formula or restrained by any limitation that tends to trammel the free and just exercise of discretion.

Neither the plaintiff's corruption of Clutter in respect of the first Downie patent nor its use in these cases of the *Byers* decree can fairly be deemed to be unconnected with causes of action based on the other patents.

Its bills show the devices covered by the five patents to be important, if not essential, parts of the same machine. And its claims warrant the inference that each supplements the others. This is made plain by mere reference to the things patented. The Clutter device is for the hoe or mattock arrangement. The first Downie is for an improvement designed, by a drop bottom scoop and other means, to permit more accurate dumping. The second Downie had for its main purpose the elimination of a "blind spot" in the unloading operation. The third Downie makes possible and convenient the use of scoops of different widths upon the same machine. The fourth Downie device consists of detachable rake teeth for a scoop.

Had the corruption of Clutter been disclosed at the trial of the *Byers* Case, the court undoubtedly would have been warranted in holding it sufficient to require dismissal of the cause of action there alleged for the infringement of the Downie patent. Promptly after the decision in that case plaintiff brought these suits and immediately applied for injunctions *pendente lite*. It used the decree of validity there obtained in support, if not indeed as the basis, of its applications. And plaintiff's misconduct in the *Byers* suit remaining undisclosed, that decree was given weight on the motions for preliminary injunctions. As the litigation was to continue for years and the use of the devices in question was essential to the ditching machinery, it is clear that the injunctions would have been a burdensome detriment to defendants. The amounts of the bonds required in lieu of injunctions attest the importance of the advantage obtained by use of the decree. While it is not found, as reasonably it may be inferred from the circumstances, that from the beginning it was plaintiff's intention through suppression of Clutter's evidence to obtain decree in the *Byers* Case for use in subsequent infringement suits against these defendants and others, it does clearly appear that the plaintiff made the *Byers* Case a part of his preparation in these suits. The use actually made of that decree is sufficient to show that plaintiff did not come with clean hands in respect of any cause of action in these cases.

The relation between the device covered by the first Downie patent and those covered by the other patents, taken in connection with the use to which plaintiff put the *Byers* decree, is amply sufficient to bring these cases within the maxim.

Decrees affirmed.

NOTES

1. It appears the plaintiff owned four good patents and one perhaps obtained by misrepresentation. The Court found that the patented devices were each an important, if not essential, part of the same machine. This suggests that if infringement of the four good patents were enjoined, the defendant would not be able to manufacture a machine that would be competitive with the plaintiff's. Why should the plaintiff's unclean hands with regard to one patent deprive him of the benefit of the other four? Would the result have been different if the suppression of evidence had been brought to light earlier? Namely, if the first Downie patent had been held invalid in the *Byers* case, would an injunction against the infringement of the other four patents have been upheld?

2. The U.S. Supreme Court recognized the defense of inequitable conduct by the patent applicant as a bar to enforcement of a patent in Precision Instrument Manufacturing Co. v. Automotive Maintenance Machinery Co., 324 U.S. 806, 65 S.Ct. 993, 89 L.Ed. 1381 (1945). The formulation of the defense developed by the courts focuses on the intent of the patentee to mislead or deceive the Patent and Trademark Office and on the materiality of the deceptive act to issuance of the patent. As the Federal Circuit has explained:

> A party asserting that a patent is unenforceable due to inequitable conduct must prove materiality and intent by clear and convincing evidence. Once threshold findings of materiality and intent are established, the trial court must weigh them to determine whether the equities warrant a conclusion that inequitable conduct occurred. This requires a careful balancing: when the misrepresentation or withheld information is highly material, a lesser quantum of proof is needed to establish the requisite intent. In contrast, the less material the information, the greater the proof must be.

Purdue Pharma L.P. v. Endo Pharmaceuticals, Inc., 438 F.3d 1123, 1128 (Fed.Cir.2006) (directing trial court on how to assess whether patents for OxyContin® are enforceable).

An administrative rule defines materiality and indicates how much adverse information a patent applicant must disclose. 37 C.F.R. §§ 1.56(a)-(b)(2004). The rule is stated in general terms, meaning that the interpretation of "materiality" by the courts will continue. The extensive case law on this issue is surveyed and analyzed in, e.g., Comment, Inequitable Conduct: Persistent Problems and Recommended Resolutions, 82 Marq.L.Rev. 845 (1999).

What should the result be when a patent applicant fails to disclose material facts, which the patent examiner discovers prior to determining that the patent should issue? In A.B. Dick Company v. Burroughs Corp., 798 F.2d 1392 (Fed.Cir.1986), a patent issued under such circumstances was held unenforceable. What should the result be for the applicant who makes appropriate disclosure after filing? Should it matter whether the examiner has detected the failure to disclose before it is cured? See Rohm & Haas v. Crystal Chemical Co., 722 F.2d 1556 (Fed.Cir.1983), cert. denied, 469 U.S. 851, 105 S.Ct. 172, 83 L.Ed.2d 107 (1984).

Is fraudulently obtaining a patent a greater wrong than obstructing the processes of the court? See Aptix Corp. v. Quickturn Design Systems, Inc., 269 F.3d 1369 (Fed.Cir.2001) (using *Keystone Driller* to distinguish between the dismissal of a patent infringement action on the basis of unclean hands because of misconduct during litigation from extinguishing the patent entirely due to misconduct in obtaining the patent). What about patent misuse, which is defined as "an impermissible attempt to extend the time or scope of the patent grant"? Robin C. Feldman, The Insufficiency of Antitrust Analysis for Patent Misuse, 55 Hastings L.J. 399, 402 (2003). The affirmative defense of patent misuse leads to the remedy of a refusal by courts to enforce the patent "until the abusive practice has been abandoned and the effects of the practice have dissipated." Id. See MedPointe Healthcare Inc. v. Hi–Tech Pharmacal Co., 380 F.Supp.2d 457 (D.N.J.2005) ("patent misuse" is an extension of the equitable doctrine of unclean hands).

3. It may well be that unsuccessful fraud will not have the serious consequences that the plaintiff faced in *Keystone*. In Niner v. Hanson, 217 Md. 298, 142 A.2d 798 (1958), the plaintiff had perjured himself in earlier litigation between the same parties but had recanted before the termination of the first proceeding. In rejecting an unclean hands defense, the majority noted: "It has been held in a number of well-considered cases that dismissal is not required even where the complainant was guilty of fraud, perjury or suppression of evidence, where the wrongdoing does not result in benefit to the wrongdoer, or operate as a fraud or imposition upon the court in which relief is sought." The dissent believed the court had misstated the issue: "the question to be resolved in this action is whether the [plaintiff's] wrongful conduct is connected with, or related to, the dispute and not whether the [defendant] has been injured." What interests are served by these differing formulations of the rule?

4. The unclean hands doctrine derives from the maxims of the equity court. If the plaintiff in *Keystone* sued for damages rather than for an injunction to prevent further infringement of its patents, would the result in the case be the same? Would it make sense for the court to grant damages but not an injunction?

CLINTON E. WORDEN & CO. v. CALIFORNIA FIG SYRUP CO.

Supreme Court of the United States, 1903
187 U.S. 516, 23 S.Ct. 161, 47 L.Ed. 282

Mr. Justice Shiras delivered the opinion of the Court.

The courts below concluded, upon the evidence, that the defendants sold a medical preparation named, marked, and packed, in imitation of the complainant's medicine, for the purpose and with the design and intent of deceiving purchasers and inducing them to buy defendant's preparation instead of the complainant's. We see no reason to dissent from that conclusion, and if there were no other questions in the case, we should be ready to affirm the decree, awarding a perpetual injunction and an account of the profits and gains derived from such unfair and dishonest practices.

Another ground, however, is urged against the complainant's right to invoke the aid of a court of equity, in that the California Fig Syrup Company, the complainant, has so fraudulently represented to the public the nature of its medical preparation that it is not entitled to equitable relief.

Some courts have gone so far as to hold that courts of equity will not interfere by injunction in controversies between rival manufacturers and dealers in so-called quack medicines.

It may be said, in support of such a view, that most, if not all, the States of this Union have enactments forbidding and making penal the practice of medicine by persons who have not gone through a course of appropriate study, and obtained a license from a board of examiners; and there is similar legislation in respect to pharmacists. And it would seem to be inconsistent, and to tend to defeat such salutary laws, if medical preparations, often and usually containing powerful and poisonous drugs, are permitted to be widely advertised and sold to all who are willing to purchase. Laws might properly be passed limiting and controlling such traffic by restraining retail dealers from selling such medical preparations, except when prescribed by regular medical practitioners.

But we think that, in the absence of such legislation, courts cannot declare dealing in such preparations to be illegal, nor the articles themselves to be not entitled, as property, to the protection of the law.

We find, however, more solidity in the contention, on behalf of the appellants, that when the owner of a trade-mark applies for an injunction to restrain the defendant from injuring his property by making false representations to the public, it is essential that the plaintiff should not in his trade-mark, or in his advertisements and business, be himself guilty of any false or misleading representation; that if the plaintiff makes any material false statement in connection with the property which he seeks to protect, he loses his right to claim the assistance of a court of equity; that where any symbol or label claimed as a trade-mark is so constructed or worded as to make or contain a distinct assertion which is false, no property can be claimed on it, or, in other words, the right to the exclusive use of it cannot be maintained. * * *

In the Circuit Court of the United States for the Eastern District of Michigan, April 1, 1895, the California Fig Syrup Company filed a bill, seeking to restrain Frederick Stearns & Company from infringing complainant's trade-mark. The court declined to grant an injunction, and dismissed the bill with costs, holding that the words "Syrup of Figs" or "Fig Syrup," if descriptive of a syrup, one of the characteristic ingredients of which is the juice of the fig, cannot be sustained as a valid trade-mark or trade name, and that, under the facts of the case, the use of the name "Syrup of Figs," in connection with a description of the preparation as a fruit remedy, "nature's pleasant laxative," applied to a compound, whose active ingredient is senna, and containing but a small proportion of fig juice, which has no considerable laxative properties, is deceptive, and deprives one so using it of any claim to equitable relief.

On appeal to the Circuit Court of Appeals of the Sixth Circuit the decree * * * was affirmed. In his opinion Circuit Judge Taft, after stating that the term "Syrup of Figs," if intended to describe the character of the article considered, could not be used as a trade-mark, proceeded to say:

> But the second ground presented, and that upon which the court below rested its decision, prevents the complainant from having any relief at all. That ground is that the complainant has built up its business and made it valuable by an intentional deceit of the public. It has intended the public to understand that the preparation which it sells has, as an important medicinal agent in its composition, the juice of California figs. This has undoubtedly led the public into the purchase of the preparation. The statement is wholly untrue. Just a suspicion of fig juice has been put into the preparation, not for the purpose of changing its medicinal character, or even its flavor, but merely to give a weak support to the statement that the article sold is syrup of figs. This is a fraud upon the public. It is true it may be a harmless humbug to palm off upon the public as syrup of figs what is syrup of senna, but it is nevertheless of such a character that a court of equity will not encourage it by extending any relief to the person who seeks to protect a business which has grown out of and is dependent upon such deceit. It is well settled that if a person wishes his trade-mark property to be protected by a court of equity, he must come into court with clean hands, and if it appears that the trade-mark for which he seeks protection is itself a misrepresentation to the public, and has acquired a value with the public by fraudulent misrepresentations in advertisements, all relief will be denied to him. This is the doctrine of the highest court of England, and no court has laid it down with any greater stringency than the Supreme Court of the United States. * * *

The argument for complainant is, that because fig juice or syrup has no laxative property everybody ought to understand that when the term is used to designate a laxative medicine it must have only a fanciful meaning. But the fact is admitted that the public believe that fig juice or syrup has laxative medicinal properties. It is to them that the complainant seeks to sell its preparation, and it is with respect to their knowledge and impressions that the character, whether descriptive or fanciful, of the term used, is to be determined.

* * * That the complainant company, years after it had established a popular demand for its product, issued statements in medical journals and newspapers and circulars, that the medical properties of their compound were derived from senna, does not relieve it from the charge of deceit and misrepresentation to the public. Such publications went only to giving information to wholesale dealers. The company by the use of the terms of its so-called trade-mark on its bottles, wrappers, and cartons continued to appeal to the consumers, out of whose credulity came the profits of their business. And, indeed, it was the imitation by the defendants of such false and misleading representations that led to the present suit.

* * * [U]pon the entire evidence in the case, and in the light of the authorities cited by the counsel of the respective parties, our conclusions are that the name "Syrup of Figs" does not, in fact, properly designate or describe the preparation made and sold by the California Fig Syrup Company, so as to be susceptible of appropriation as a trade-mark, and that the marks and names, used upon the bottles containing complainant's preparation, and upon the cartons and wrappers containing the bottles, are so plainly deceptive as to deprive the complainant company of a right to a remedy by way of an injunction by a court of equity. * * *

Mr. Justice McKenna dissented.

Notes

1. There appears to be no claim in this case that the California Fig Syrup Co. acted in any improper manner with regard to the defendant. Is it appropriate for the defendant, in effect, to claim that since both it and the plaintiff are defrauding the public, the Court should not restrain its injury to the plaintiff?

2. Since the rationale of the Court's decision rests on the misrepresentation to the public by the plaintiff, would it be improper for the Court to fashion a decree that prohibited both the plaintiff and the defendant from engaging in misrepresentation? Could a court invite a public authority or a member of the consuming public to intervene in the action and request such relief? If the Court is unable or unwilling to take such action when it has identified misrepresentation to the public as the wrong that controls the case, how has the Court's decision served the interest of equity or justice? If the public authorities or misled consumers do not choose to bring an action against the California Fig Syrup Co., why should the Court use this case as a vehicle to protect them? Is the issue of the plaintiff's behavior likely to be

fully and effectively developed by the litigants in this case? Should standards of standing or justiciability be applied to unclean hands controversies?

3. Assume the *Worden* court had before it a plaintiff who was seeking to recover a debt and the defendant offered persuasive evidence that the money he had borrowed from the plaintiff was the proceeds of an illegal drug transaction. Are the plaintiff's hands sufficiently clean to allow recovery?

4. The Supreme Court addressed an unclean hands defense in the context of a claim based on a statute in McKennon v. Nashville Banner Publishing Co., 513 U.S. 352, 115 S.Ct. 879, 130 L.Ed.2d 852 (1995). McKennon alleged that she was fired because of her age in violation of the Age Discrimination in Employment Act of 1967. In her deposition in the case, McKennon revealed that she had removed confidential financial documents from her employer's premises to use in her lawsuit. The employer sought summary judgment because removing the papers was a basis for discharging McKennon from employment. The Court found the purpose of the statute to be both to provide compensation to employees who suffered age discrimination and to deter employers from discriminating; in that context the Court rejected the unclean hands defense but held that the plaintiff's misconduct was still relevant to the remedy. The Court found that reinstatement or front pay would not be an appropriate remedy in this case, but that backpay was compensation to restore McKennon to her rightful position absent discrimination and that in fashioning its remedy the district court should start with backpay from the date of firing to discovery of the removal of the documents and then consider extraordinary equitable circumstances in the case.

5. The criminal law has some doctrines that sound analogous to unclean hands. The exclusionary rule that holds evidence obtained in violation of the defendant's Fourth Amendment rights inadmissible is an obvious example. United States v. Tucker, 28 F.3d 1420 (6th Cir.1994), cert. denied, 514 U.S. 1049, 115 S.Ct. 1426, 131 L.Ed.2d 308 (1995), explains the basis and limits of the defense of entrapment, which focuses on the predisposition of the defendant to commit the crime, not on the overzealous or outrageous nature of the government's conduct. The possibility that the Supreme Court would dismiss an indictment on the basis of outrageous government conduct in inducing a crime remains a possibility only in the sense that the Court is reluctant to announce that a remedy will never be available under any circumstances. United States v. Russell, 411 U.S. 423, 93 S.Ct. 1637, 36 L.Ed.2d 366 (1973); Hampton v. United States, 425 U.S. 484, 96 S.Ct. 1646, 48 L.Ed.2d 113 (1976).

BATEMAN EICHLER, HILL RICHARDS, INC. v. BERNER

Supreme Court of the United States, 1985
472 U.S. 299, 105 S.Ct. 2622, 86 L.Ed.2d 215

JUSTICE BRENNAN delivered the opinion of the Court.

The question presented by this case is whether the common-law in pari delicto defense bars a private damages action under the federal securities laws against corporate insiders and broker-dealers who fraudulently induce investors to purchase securities by misrepresenting that they are conveying material nonpublic information about the issuer.

I

The respondent investors filed this action in the United States District Court for the Northern District of California, alleging that they incurred substantial trading losses as a result of a conspiracy between Charles Lazzaro, a registered securities broker employed by the petitioner Bateman Eichler, Hill Richards, Inc. (Bateman Eichler), and Leslie Neadeau, President of T.O.N.M. Oil & Gas Exploration Corporation (TONM), to induce them to purchase large quantities of TONM over-the-counter stock by divulging false and materially incomplete information about the company on the pretext that it was accurate inside information. Specifically, Lazzaro is alleged to have told the respondents that he personally knew TONM insiders and had learned, inter alia, that (a) "[v]ast amounts of gold had been discovered in Surinam, and TONM had options on thousands of acres in gold-producing regions of Surinam"; (b) the discovery was "not publically known, but would subsequently be announced"; (c) TONM was currently engaged in negotiations with other companies to form a joint venture for mining the Surinamese gold; and (d) when this information was made public, "TONM stock, which was then selling from $1.50 to $3.00/share, would increase in value from $10 to $15/share within a short period of time, and ... might increase to $100/share" within a year. Some of the respondents aver that they contacted Neadeau and inquired whether Lazzaro's tips were accurate; Neadeau stated that the information was "not public knowledge" and "would neither confirm nor deny those claims," but allegedly advised that "Lazzaro was a very trustworthy and a good man."

The respondents admitted in their complaint that they purchased TONM stock, much of it through Lazzaro, "on the premise that Lazzaro was privy to certain information not otherwise available to the general public." Their shares initially increased dramatically in price, but ultimately declined to substantially below the purchase price when the joint mining venture fell through.

Lazzaro and Neadeau are alleged to have made the representations set forth above knowing that the representations "were untrue and/or contained only half-truths, material omissions of fact and falsehoods," intending that the respondents would rely thereon, and for the purpose of "influenc[ing] and manipulat[ing] the price of TONM stock" so as "to profit themselves through the taking of commissions and secret profits." The respondents contended that this scheme violated, inter alia, § 10(b) of the Securities Exchange Act of 1934, 48 Stat. 891, 15 U.S.C. § 78j(b),[7] and

---

7. That section provides:

"It shall be unlawful for any person, directly or indirectly, by the use of any means or instrumentality of interstate commerce or of the mails, or of any facility of any national securities exchange—

* * *

SEC Rule 10b–5 promulgated thereunder, 17 CFR § 240.10b–5 (1984).[8] They sought capital losses and lost profits, punitive damages, and costs and attorney's fees. * * *

II

The common-law defense at issue in this case derives from the Latin, in pari delicto potior est conditio defendentis: "In a case of equal or mutual fault ... the position of the [defending] party ... is the better one." The defense is grounded on two premises: first, that courts should not lend their good offices to mediating disputes among wrongdoers; and second, that denying judicial relief to an admitted wrongdoer is an effective means of deterring illegality. In its classic formulation, the in pari delicto defense was narrowly limited to situations where the plaintiff truly bore at least substantially equal responsibility for his injury, because "in cases where both parties are in delicto, concurring in an illegal act, it does not always follow that they stand in pari delicto; for there may be, and often are, very different degrees in their guilt." 1 J. Story, Equity Jurisprudence 304–305 (13th ed.1886)(Story). Thus there might be an "inequality of condition" between the parties, id., at 305, or "a confidential relationship between th[em]" that determined their "relative standing" before a court, 3 J. Pomeroy, Equity Jurisprudence § 942a, p. 741 (5th ed.1941). In addition, the public policy considerations that undergirded the in pari delicto defense were frequently construed as precluding the defense even where the plaintiff bore substantial fault for his injury: "there may be on the part of the court itself a necessity of supporting the public interests or public policy in many cases, however reprehensible the acts of the parties may be." 1 Story 305. Notwithstanding these traditional limitations, many courts have given the in pari delicto defense a broad application to bar actions where plaintiffs simply have been involved generally in "the same sort of wrongdoing" as defendants.

In [Perma Life Mufflers, Inc. v. International Parts Corp., 392 U.S. 134, 88 S.Ct. 1981, 20 L.Ed.2d 982 (1968)], we emphasized "the inappropriateness of invoking broad common-law barriers to relief where a private suit serves important public purposes." That case involved a treble-damages action against a Midas Muffler franchisor by several of its

---

"(b) To use or employ, in connection with the purchase or sale of any security registered on a national securities exchange or any security not so registered, any manipulative or deceptive device or contrivance in contravention of such rules and regulations as the Commission may prescribe as necessary or appropriate in the public interest or for the protection of investors."

8. That Rule provides:

"It shall be unlawful for any person, directly or indirectly, by the use of any means or instrumentality of interstate commerce, or of the mails or of any facility of any national securities exchange,

"(a) To employ any device, scheme, or artifice to defraud,

"(b) To make any untrue statement of a material fact or to omit to state a material fact necessary in order to make the statements made, in the light of the circumstances under which they were made, not misleading, or

"(c) To engage in any act, practice, or course of business which operates or would operate as a fraud or deceit upon any person, in connection with the purchase or sale of any security."

dealers, who alleged that the franchise agreement created a conspiracy to restrain trade in violation of the Sherman and Clayton Acts. The lower courts barred the action on the grounds that the dealers, as parties to the agreement, were in pari delicto with the franchisor. In reversing that determination, the opinion for this Court emphasized that there was no indication that Congress had intended to incorporate the defense into the antitrust laws, which "are best served by insuring that the private action will be an ever-present threat to deter anyone contemplating [illegal] business behavior." Accordingly, the opinion concluded that "the doctrine of in pari delicto, with its complex scope, contents, and effects, is not to be recognized as a defense to an antitrust action." The opinion reserved the question whether a plaintiff who engaged in "truly complete involvement and participation in a monopolistic scheme"—one who "aggressively support[ed] and further[ed] the monopolistic scheme as a necessary part and parcel of it"—could be barred from pursuing a damages action, finding that the muffler dealers had relatively little bargaining power and that they had been coerced by the franchisor into agreeing to many of the contract's provisions.

In separate opinions, five Justices agreed that the concept of "equal fault" should be narrowly defined in litigation arising under federal regulatory statutes. "[B]ecause of the strong public interest in eliminating restraints on competition, ... many of the refinements of moral worth demanded of plaintiffs by ... many of the variations of in pari delicto should not be applicable in the antitrust field." Id., at 151, 88 S.Ct., at 1991 (Marshall, J., concurring in result). The five Justices concluded, however, that where a plaintiff truly bore at least substantially equal responsibility for the violation, a defense based on such fault—whether or not denominated in pari delicto—should be recognized in antitrust litigation.[17]

Bateman Eichler argues that *Perma Life*—with its emphasis on the importance of analyzing the effects that fault-based defenses would have on the enforcement of congressional goals—is of only marginal relevance to a private damages action under the federal securities laws. Specifically, Bateman Eichler observes that Congress expressly provided for private antitrust actions—thereby manifesting a "desire to go beyond the common law in the antitrust statute in order to provide substantial encouragement to private enforcement and to help deter anticompetitive conduct"— whereas private rights of action under § 10(b) of the Securities Exchange Act of 1934 are merely implied from that provision—thereby, apparently, supporting a broader application of the in pari delicto defense. * * *

---

17. Justice White concluded that "the in pari delicto defense in its historic formulation is not a useful concept" in antitrust law, but emphasized that he "would deny recovery where plaintiff and defendant bear substantially equal responsibility for injury resulting to one of them." The other four Justices would have allowed explicit, though limited, use of the in pari delicto defense itself. Id., at 147, 88 S.Ct., at 1988 (Fortas, J., concurring in result); id., at 148–149, 88 S.Ct., at 1989 (Marshall, J., concurring in result); id., at 153, 88 S.Ct., at 1991 (Harlan, J., joined by Stewart, J., concurring in part and dissenting in part).

We disagree. Nothing in *Perma Life* suggested that public policy implications should govern only where Congress expressly provides for private remedies; the classic formulation of the in pari delicto doctrine itself required a careful consideration of such implications before allowing the defense. Moreover, we repeatedly have emphasized that implied private actions provide "a most effective weapon in the enforcement" of the securities laws and are "a necessary supplement to Commission action." J.I. Case Co. v. Borak, 377 U.S. 426, 432, 84 S.Ct. 1555, 1560, 12 L.Ed.2d 423 (1964). * * * We therefore conclude that the views expressed in *Perma Life* apply with full force to implied causes of action under the federal securities laws. Accordingly, a private action for damages in these circumstances may be barred on the grounds of the plaintiff's own culpability only where (1) as a direct result of his own actions, the plaintiff bears at least substantially equal responsibility for the violations he seeks to redress, and (2) preclusion of suit would not significantly interfere with the effective enforcement of the securities laws and protection of the investing public.

A

The District Court and Court of Appeals proceeded on the assumption that the respondents had violated § 10(b) and Rule 10b–5, an assumption we accept for purposes of resolving the issue before us. Bateman Eichler contends that the respondents' delictum was substantially par to that of Lazzaro and Neadeau for two reasons. First, whereas many antitrust plaintiffs participate in illegal restraints of trade only "passively" or as the result of economic coercion, as was the case in *Perma Life,* the ordinary tippee acts voluntarily in choosing to trade on inside information. Second, § 10(b) and Rule 10b–5 apply literally to "any person" who violates their terms, and do not recognize gradations of culpability.

We agree that the typically voluntary nature of an investor's decision impermissibly to trade on an inside tip renders the investor more blameworthy than someone who is party to a contract solely by virtue of another's overweening bargaining power. We disagree, however, that an investor who engages in such trading is necessarily as blameworthy as a corporate insider or broker-dealer who discloses the information for personal gain. Notwithstanding the broad reach of § 10(b) and Rule 10b–5, there are important distinctions between the relative culpabilities of tippers, securities professionals, and tippees in these circumstances. The Court has made clear in recent Terms that a tippee's use of material nonpublic information does not violate § 10(b) and Rule 10b–5 unless the tippee owes a corresponding duty to disclose the information. * * * In the context of insider trading, we do not believe that a person whose liability is solely derivative can be said to be as culpable as one whose breach of duty gave rise to that liability in the first place.

Moreover, insiders and broker-dealers who selectively disclose material nonpublic information commit a potentially broader range of violations than do tippees who trade on the basis of that information. A tippee trading on inside information will in many circumstances be guilty of fraud against individual shareholders, a violation for which the tipper shares responsibility. But the insider, in disclosing such information, also frequently breaches fiduciary duties toward the issuer itself. And in cases where the tipper intentionally conveys false or materially incomplete information to the tippee, the tipper commits an additional violation: fraud against the tippee. Such conduct is particularly egregious when committed by a securities professional, who owes a duty of honesty and fair dealing toward his clients. * * * Absent other culpable actions by a tippee that can fairly be said to outweigh these violations by insiders and broker-dealers, we do not believe that the tippee properly can be characterized as being of substantially equal culpability as his tippers.

There is certainly no basis for concluding at this stage of this litigation that the respondents were in pari delicto with Lazzaro and Neadeau. The allegations are that Lazzaro and Neadeau masterminded this scheme to manipulate the market in TONM securities for their own personal benefit, and that they used the purchasing respondents as unwitting dupes to inflate the price of TONM stock. The respondents may well have violated the securities laws, and in any event we place no "stamp of approval" on their conduct. But accepting the facts set forth in the complaint as true—as we must in reviewing the District Court's dismissal on the pleadings—Lazzaro and Neadeau "awakened in [the respondents] a desire for wrongful gain that might otherwise have remained dormant, inspired in [their] mind[s] an unfounded idea that [they were] going to secure it, and then by fraud and false pretenses deprived [them] of [their] money," * * * actions that, if they occurred, were far more culpable under any reasonable view than the respondents' alleged conduct.

B

We also believe that denying the in pari delicto defense in such circumstances will best promote the primary objective of the federal securities laws—protection of the investing public and the national economy through the promotion of "a high standard of business ethics ... in every facet of the securities industry." SEC v. Capital Gains Research Bureau, Inc., 375 U.S. 180, 186–187, 84 S.Ct. 275, 280, 11 L.Ed.2d 237 (1963). Although a number of lower courts have reasoned that a broad rule of caveat tippee would better serve this goal, we believe the contrary position adopted by other courts represents the better view.

To begin with, barring private actions in cases such as this would inexorably result in a number of alleged fraudulent practices going undetected by the authorities and unremedied. The Securities and Exchange Commission has advised us that it "does not have the resources to police the industry sufficiently to ensure that false tipping does not occur or is consistently discovered," and that "[w]ithout the tippees' assistance, the Commission could not effectively prosecute false tipping—a difficult practice to detect." * * * Thus it is particularly important to permit "litigation among guilty parties [that will serve] to expose their unlawful conduct and render them more easily subject to appropriate civil, administrative, and criminal penalties." Kuehnert v. Texstar Corp., 412 F.2d 700, 706, n. 3 (C.A.5 1969)(Godbold, J., dissenting). The in pari delicto defense, by denying any incentive to a defrauded tippee to bring suit against his defrauding tipper, would significantly undermine this important goal.[28]

Moreover, we believe that deterrence of insider trading most frequently will be maximized by bringing enforcement pressures to bear on the sources of such information—corporate insiders and broker-dealers.

> "The true insider or the broker-dealer is at the fountainhead of the confidential information.... If the prophylactic purpose of the law is to restrict the use of all material inside information until it is made available to the investing public, then the most effective means of carrying out this policy is to nip in the bud the source of the information, the tipper, by discouraging him from 'making the initial disclosure which is the first step in the chain of dissemination.' This can most readily be achieved by making unavailable to him the defense of in pari delicto when sued by his tippee upon charges based upon alleged misinformation." Nathanson v. Weis, Voisin, Cannon, Inc., 325 F.Supp. 50, 57–58 (S.D.N.Y.1971).

In addition, corporate insiders and broker-dealers will in many circumstances be more responsive to the deterrent pressure of potential sanctions; they are more likely than ordinary investors to be advised by counsel and thereby to be informed fully of the "allowable limits on their conduct." *Kuehnert* (Godbold, J., dissenting). Although situations might well arise in which the relative culpabilities of the tippee and his insider source merit a different mix of deterrent incentives, we therefore conclude that in tipper-tippee situations such as the one before us the factors discussed above preclude recognition of the in pari delicto defense.

Lower courts reaching a contrary conclusion have typically asserted that, absent a vigorous allowance of the in pari delicto defense, tippees would have, "in effect, an enforceable warranty that secret information is true," and thus no incentive not to trade on that information. These courts have reasoned, in other words, that tippees in such circumstances would be in "the enviable position of 'heads-I-win tails-you-lose,' "—if the tip is correct, the tippee will reap illicit profits, while if the tip fails to yield the expected return, he can sue to recover damages.

---

28. Our analysis is buttressed by reference to § 9(e) of the Securities Exchange Act of 1934, 48 Stat. 890, 15 U.S.C. § 78i(e), which allows co-conspirators a right of contribution against "any person who, if joined in the original suit, would have been liable to make the same payment." This provision overrides the common-law rule against contribution from co-conspirators, which was grounded on the premise that "parties generally in pari delicto should be left where they are found." Texas Industries, Inc. v. Radcliff Materials, Inc., 451 U.S. 630, 635, 101 S.Ct. 2061, 2064, 68 L.Ed.2d 500 (1981). As the Commission observes, "[s]urely, the Congress that provided that a brokerage professional such as Lazzaro could recover from his fellow manipulators should be understood to have also permitted the victims of Lazzaro's manipulative scheme to sue him." Brief for SEC as Amicus Curiae at 26.

We believe the "enforceable warranty" theory is overstated and overlooks significant factors that serve to deter tippee trading irrespective of whether the in pari delicto defense is allowed. First, tippees who bring suit in an attempt to cash in on their "enforceable warranties" expose themselves to the threat of substantial civil and criminal penalties for their own potentially illegal conduct.[32] Second, plaintiffs in litigation under § 10(b) and Rule 10b–5 may only recover against defendants who have acted with scienter. * * * Thus "if the tip merely fails to 'pan out' or if the information itself proves accurate but the stock fails to move in the anticipated direction, the investor stands to lose all of his investment. Only in the situation where the investor has been deliberately defrauded will he be able to maintain a private suit in an attempt to recoup his money."

We therefore conclude that the public interest will most frequently be advanced if defrauded tippees are permitted to bring suit and to expose illegal practices by corporate insiders and broker-dealers to full public view for appropriate sanctions. As the Ninth Circuit emphasized in this case, there is no warrant to giving corporate insiders and broker-dealers "a license to defraud the investing public with little fear of prosecution."

CHIEF JUSTICE [REHNQUIST] concurs in the judgment.

JUSTICE MARSHALL took no part in the decision of this case.

NOTES

1. The Supreme Court addressed the availability of the *in pari delicto* defense under the securities laws a second time in Pinter v. Dahl, 486 U.S. 622, 108 S.Ct. 2063, 100 L.Ed.2d 658 (1988). Dahl had purchased a $310,000 interest in oil and gas leases from Pinter and told various friends and relatives of the venture; they in turn, without meeting or speaking to Pinter, invested $7,500 each in the leases. When the venture failed, Dahl and the other investors sued Pinter for rescission under Section 12(1) of the Securities Act of 1933, 45 U.S.C. § 771(1), for the unlawful sale of unregistered securities. Pinter contended that Dahl's active solicitation of the other investors and his knowledge that the securities were unregistered put him *in pari delicto* and barred recovery. The Court continued its retreat from the expansive language of Justice Black's opinion for the Court in *Perma Life* stating that five Justices in that case recognized that a narrow, traditional formulation of the *in pari delicto* defense was available in private antitrust actions. The Court found the defense available in *Pinter* as well, after applying the *Bateman Eichler* test. The facts before the Court in *Pinter* were insufficient to determine whether Dahl was at equal fault with Pinter and the case was remanded for further factual development. Thus the Court is clearly holding open the prospect that, in an appropriate case, the *in pari delicto* defense will

---

32. In addition to potential liability under § 10(b) and Rule 10b–5, investors also are subject to liability under §§ 2 and 3 of the Insider Trading Sanctions Act of 1984, 98 Stat. 1264–1265, 15 U.S.C.A. §§ 78u(d)(2), 78ff(a)(Supp.1985), which imposes severe civil sanctions on persons who have illegally used inside information, as well as criminal fines of up to $100,000.

be available in a private action brought under regulatory statutes such as the securities and antitrust laws.

2. Equality of fault is often not easy to measure. For instance, in a state in which gambling is illegal and the winner of a wager does not obtain legal title to his winnings, should it be a defense to a charge of robbery that the defendant was recouping his own property? The courts have divided on the answer. See People v. Rosen, 11 Cal.2d 147, 78 P.2d 727 (1938). Sometimes, courts solve the measuring problem by dispensing with a strict weighing of fault. See, e.g., Quick v. Samp, 697 N.W.2d 741 (S.D.2005) (even if an attorney were slightly more culpable than his client in using a forged document in court, where the wrongful conduct was obvious to all, *in pari delicto* was not a public policy justification requiring indemnity).

3. If the plaintiffs in *Bateman Eichler* had been more fortunate and the price of their stock had risen, they might have been sued by the people from whom they bought the stock. If the *Bateman Eichler* plaintiffs then brought an action in contribution against Lazzaro and Neadeau, should that suit be barred by an *in pari delicto* defense? Would it serve the purposes of the securities acts to allow the original tipper to suffer no monetary consequences for providing good tips?

Should it make any difference whether Congress has provided for an action in contribution under the securities laws? In Northwest Airlines, Inc. v. Transport Workers Union of America, AFL–CIO, 451 U.S. 77, 101 S.Ct. 1571, 67 L.Ed.2d 750 (1981), and Texas Industries, Inc. v. Radcliff Materials, Inc., 451 U.S. 630, 101 S.Ct. 2061, 68 L.Ed.2d 500 (1981), the Supreme Court held that where a common law claim to contribution is raised under a federal statute and Congress has neither indicated that such a remedy was to be available nor that courts were to develop substantive law, then the old American common law rule of no right to contribution among joint tortfeasors was to apply.

4. Some courts have suggested that even where a narrow *in pari delicto* defense is made out by a defendant in an insider trading case, the defense should be rejected if it appears that the defendant's unlawful activities were of a sort likely to have a substantial impact on the investing public and the primary legal responsibility for and ability to control that impact is with the defendant. Do you agree?

5. In Mascenic v. Anderson, 53 Ill.App.3d 971, 11 Ill.Dec. 718, 369 N.E.2d 172 (1977), the plaintiff placed real property in a land trust of which his lover, the defendant, was the sole beneficiary. This was done solely to prevent the plaintiff's wife from obtaining any interest in the property in the event of a divorce. The defendant then conspired with an attorney to defraud the plaintiff of his beneficial interest in the property. An unclean hands defense succeeded in the trial court but failed on appeal where the court held that under the defense the conduct of the plaintiff must be connected to the transaction complained of and must be directed to the defendant making the contention. Would the court have reached the same result if the defendant had raised an *in pari delicto* defense?

6. If the Court in *Worden* had employed the analysis adopted in *Perma Life* and *Bateman Eichler,* which emphasizes promoting the objective of the

relevant statute, how would that case have been decided? Are the relevant statutes the trademark laws or the laws regulating the practice of medicine? Would it make any difference if the plaintiff's actions were alleged to be in violation of state law rather than federal law? What if the plaintiff's actions violate common law but not statutory law?

7. In *Perma Life,* Justice Black emphasized that Congress had not adopted the *in pari delicto* defense in passing the antitrust laws. Would it be a sound approach to recognize none of the defenses which turn on the plaintiff's misconduct in cases under regulatory statutes where Congress has not explicitly adopted the defense?

B. ESTOPPEL

The definition of equitable estoppel or estoppel in pais varies among the courts. In the case that follows, the Ninth Circuit sets out a four-part test. Other courts have expressed closely similar standards in different language. The Fifth Circuit stated the principle in narrative form in Central Bank and Trust Company v. General Finance Corporation, 297 F.2d 126, 129 (5th Cir.1961): "The doctrine of estoppel applies where, by words or conduct, one person wilfully, culpably or negligently causes another to believe in the existence of a state of things by which the other may be induced to act so as to change his previous position to his injury." Another form of the doctrine is judicial estoppel, an equitable doctrine that a court may use to preclude a party from taking a position in a judicial proceeding that is inconsistent with a claim taken by that party in a previous proceeding. New Hampshire v. Maine, 532 U.S. 742, 121 S.Ct. 1808, 149 L.Ed.2d 968 (2001).

Equitable estoppel is distinct from the defense of waiver. Waiver is the voluntary and intentional abandonment of a known right by the plaintiff. There are three elements that differ between estoppel and waiver: first, waiver does not require any alteration of position by the defendant to be effective; second, estoppel may typically arise even if the plaintiff acted negligently and did not intend to give up his rights; and finally, consideration is generally necessary for a waiver to be effective.

As the following case shows, one should not be misled by the rubric "equitable estoppel" to believe that this defense is limited to cases that arise in equity.

JOHNSON v. WILLIFORD
United States Court of Appeals, Ninth Circuit, 1982
682 F.2d 868

BETTY FLETCHER, CIRCUIT JUDGE.

The government appeals from the district court's order granting Johnson's writ of habeas corpus. Johnson was convicted and sentenced under a federal statute requiring a minimum term of ten years, without possibility of parole. Neither the sentencing order nor the initial sentence computation report noted Johnson's ineligibility for parole. After numerous reviews by the Parole Commission and various other federal officers, none of whom uncovered the error, Johnson was released on parole.

Some 15 months later when the error was discovered, he was arrested and his parole revoked. In response, Johnson petitioned for a writ of habeas corpus. The district court ordered his immediate release pending action on the petition. * * *

FACTS

Johnson was convicted in the Northern District of Florida of conspiring to import marijuana, importing marijuana, and engaging in a continuing criminal enterprise in violation of 21 U.S.C. § 848 (1976). On May 25, 1977, he was sentenced to consecutive terms of five, five, and ten years, respectively, for these three convictions. * * *

From August 30, 1977 to September 18, 1978, Johnson was imprisoned at the Federal Correctional Institution (F.C.I.) at McNeil Island, Washington. While there, his sentence computation record was prepared, indicating parole eligibility on September 18, 1980. Johnson was moved to Lompoc F.C.I., and authorities there reviewed his sentence computation on October 11, 1978. On May 17, 1979, the sentence computation was reviewed by the administrative systems manager of the western regional office of the Bureau of Prisons. On July 23, 1979, Johnson's case manager recommended a presumptive parole date of September 18, 1980. This recommendation was reviewed by the unit manager at Terminal Island F.C.I. Copies of the recommendation were supplied to the United States Parole Offices in the Northern District of Florida and the Southern District of California. On September 14, 1979, after a Parole Commission hearing, Johnson's release was continued to the presumptive parole date of September 18, 1980. On February 25, 1980, a case manager at Terminal Island F.C.I. recommended a parole date of September 18, 1980, with prior release to a half-way house. * * * Johnson was released on parole on September 18, 1980, and remained on parole for fifteen months. At the time of his release, Johnson was 39 years old. Aside from the marijuana related offenses for which he was convicted, the record reveals only one prior incident of criminal conduct—a 10 year old drunk driving conviction. The district court found that he had made an "excellent" adjustment to parole, living with his wife and his two teenage children, operating an agricultural business, reporting regularly to his parole officer and keeping his court appearances. In the words of the district court, "[H]is reintegration into society has been good."

ANALYSIS

I. Violation of 21 U.S.C. § 848 is a Non–Parolable Offense.

At the time of Johnson's conviction, 21 U.S.C. § 848(c) provided, in pertinent part, that:

In the case of any sentence imposed under this section, imposition or execution of such sentence shall not be suspended, probation shall not be granted and section 4202 of Title 18 [making parole available] * * * shall not apply. * * *

II. The Government is Estopped From Enforcing the Non–Parolability Provision of § 848 in This Case.

A. The Government is Not Immune from Estoppel in This Case

In general, equitable estoppel is not available as a defense against the government, especially when the government is acting in its sovereign, as opposed to its proprietary, capacity. Nevertheless, this court has held that "where justice and fair play require it," estoppel will be applied against the government, even when the government acts in its sovereign capacity if the effects of estoppel do not unduly damage the public interest. * * * The Supreme Court has never explicitly endorsed this theory, although "no fewer than eight circuits ... have stated that there are some circumstances in which the Government will be estopped," Hansen v. Harris, 619 F.2d 942, 959 (2d Cir.1980)(Newman, J., concurring) (collecting cases), rev'd per curiam, 450 U.S. 785, 101 S.Ct. 1468, 67 L.Ed.2d 685 (1981), and [Moser v. United States, 341 U.S. 41, 71 S.Ct. 553, 95 L.Ed. 729 (1951)] has been cited as a case wherein the Supreme Court by its holding, in fact, estopped the Government. [United States v.] Lazy FC Ranch, 481 F.2d [985 (9th Cir.1973)] at 989.

In a recent decision, Miranda v. INS, 673 F.2d 1105 (9th Cir.1982), our court reaffirmed the application of equitable estoppel against the government acting in its sovereign capacity. The court, relying on an estoppel theory, had originally reversed a decision of the Board of Immigration Appeals. Miranda v. INS, 638 F.2d 83 (9th Cir.1980). The Supreme Court vacated the panel's original decision and remanded for further consideration in light of *Hansen*. INS v. Miranda, 454 U.S. 808, 102 S.Ct. 81, 70 L.Ed.2d 77 (1981). Upon reconsideration, the *Miranda* panel adhered to its original judgment. It described *Hansen* as a case in which application of estoppel would circumvent "the conditions defined by Congress for charging the public treasury," Miranda, 673 F.2d at 1105–06 (quoting Federal Crop Insurance Corp. v. Merrill, 332 U.S. 380, 385, 68 S.Ct. 1, 3, 92 L.Ed. 10 (1947)), while application of estoppel in *Miranda* would not create a drain on the public fisc. In this respect, the instant case is indistinguishable from *Miranda*.

We turn now to an examination of whether the threshold requirements for estoppel against the government described in *Lazy FC Ranch* are present here. Under *Lazy FC Ranch,* the government's wrongful conduct must threaten "to work a serious injustice" and the public's interest must not "be unduly damaged by the imposition of estoppel." 481 F.2d at 989. The Parole Commission's deliberate decision to release Johnson on parole, and his subsequent successful reintegration into the community, suggest that his continuation on parole status does not seriously threaten the public interest. The injustice to Johnson if he is reincarcerated is apparent. The government says in its brief, "petitioner's case is in some respects a sympathetic one." We think this is an understatement. The record discloses at least eight separate administrative reviews of Johnson's projected parole date. Each review confirmed that Johnson could be paroled. His expectation of release on parole on September 18, 1980, was raised almost as soon as he began to serve his sentence, and was encouraged and heightened by the successive administrative reviews. The government argues that Johnson has received a windfall, and that while a return to custody would disappoint his expectations, "those expectations were not justified in any event," in light of his conviction and sentencing under § 848. This assertion is plainly incorrect. The progress of Johnson's case through eight administrative reviews culminating in 15 months of parole release surely justified him in expecting to continue, during good behavior, in that status. The frustration of those expectations would be a serious injustice. Even convicted criminals are entitled to be treated by their government in a fair and straightforward manner. We find that under these facts appellee may raise the defense of estoppel against the Government.

B. *The Elements of Equitable Estoppel Are Present in This Case*

Our inquiry so far has focused on whether this is the kind of case in which estoppel may be asserted against the government. Having concluded that it is, we now turn to an examination of whether the traditional elements giving rise to equitable estoppel are present. The four required elements were described by this court in United States v. Georgia–Pacific Company, 421 F.2d 92, 96 (9th Cir.1970):

> (1) The party to be estopped must know the facts;
>
> (2) he must intend that his conduct shall be acted on or must so act that the party asserting the estoppel has a right to believe it is so intended;
>
> (3) the latter must be ignorant of the facts; and
>
> (4) he must rely on the former's conduct to his injury.

The first element is present. Johnson's initial sentence computation report indicates plainly that he was convicted under § 848. The progress reports prepared from time to time all include recitations of his offenses. Prior to Johnson's release, the government had been treating all other prisoners in the same position as Johnson as ineligible for parole. Although there was no case holding that § 848 convictions were nonparolable in the wake of the 1976 Parole Commission and Reorganization Act until United States v. Valenzuela, 646 F.2d 352 (9th Cir.1980), the government can hardly deny knowledge of what it has always treated as settled law.

The second element is also present. Johnson surely had a right to believe, after his parole computation had passed successfully through as many as eight administrative reviews, culminating in his ultimate release on parole for a period of 15 months, that he would remain on parole during good behavior.

The difficult question concerns the third element. The government argues that the crucial "fact" is simply the proper meaning of § 848, and that Johnson should be charged with constructive knowledge despite the fact that the government, the expert here, has misinterpreted or misapplied the statute in eight separate reviews in this case. In Brandt v. Hickel, 427 F.2d 53, 56 (9th Cir.1970), this court observed that "some forms of erroneous advice are so closely connected to the basic fairness of the administrative decision making process that the government may be estopped from disavowing the misstatement." In the instant case, the Government's active misadvice to Johnson regarding his eligibility for parole prevents us from charging appellee with even constructive knowledge of the proper meaning of section 848. Accordingly, we find the third element of estoppel present.

Finally, there is obvious detrimental reliance in this case. Johnson has been reunited with his family and has left the safe haven of steady employment as a fruit packer in order to start and operate his own fruit packing business. By the time of his rearrest, he had hired five employees, was solely responsible for the business banking accounts, and had been extended credit by local businesses.

In summary, we find that the requisite elements of equitable estoppel are all present and that the government should be estopped. * * *

Notes

1. The circuit court accurately states that the Supreme Court has not held that the government may be estopped by the actions of its agents. It is an open question whether the Supreme Court is ever likely to find a case in which it would hold the government estopped. This issue was considered in Heckler v. Community Health Services of Crawford County, Inc., 467 U.S. 51, 60–61, 104 S.Ct. 2218, 2224, 81 L.Ed.2d 42 (1984), in which Justice Stevens wrote for the majority:

> When the Government is unable to enforce the law because the conduct of its agents has given rise to an estoppel, the interest of the citizenry as a whole in obedience to the rule of law is undermined. It is for this reason that it is well settled that the Government may not be estopped on the same terms as any other litigant. Petitioner urges us to expand this principle into a flat rule that estoppel may not in any circumstances run against the Government. We have left the issue open in the past,[12] and do

---

12. See INS v. Miranda, 459 U.S. 14, 19, 103 S.Ct. 281, 284, 74 L.Ed.2d 12 (1982)(per curiam); Schweiker v. Hansen, 450 U.S. 785, 788, 101 S.Ct. 1468, 1470, 67 L.Ed.2d 685 (1981)(per curiam); Montana v. Kennedy, 366 U.S. 308, 315, 81 S.Ct. 1336, 1341, 6 L.Ed.2d 313 (1961). In fact, at least two of our cases seem to rest on the premise that when the Government acts in misleading ways, it may not enforce the law if to do so would harm a private party as a result of governmental deception. See United States v. Pennsylvania Industrial Chemical Corp., 411 U.S. 655, 670–675, 93 S.Ct. 1804, 1814–1817, 36 L.Ed.2d 567 (1973)(criminal defendant may assert as a defense that the Government led him to believe that its conduct was legal); Moser v. United

so again today. Though the arguments the Government advances for the rule are substantial, we are hesitant, when it is unnecessary to decide this case, to say that there are *no cases* in which the public interest in ensuring that the Government can enforce the law free from estoppel might be outweighed by the countervailing interest of citizens in some minimum standard of decency, honor, and reliability in their dealing with their Government.[13]

Justice Rehnquist replied in a concurring opinion:

> Sixty-seven years ago, in Utah Power & Light Co. v. United States, 243 U.S. 389, 37 S.Ct. 387, 61 L.Ed. 791 (1917), private parties argued that they had acquired rights in federal lands, contrary to the law, because Government employees had acquiesced in their exercise of those rights. In that case the Court laid down the general principle governing claims of estoppel on behalf of private individuals against the Government:
>
>> As a general rule, laches or neglect of duty on the part of officers of the Government is no defense to a suit by it to enforce a public right or protect a public interest. And, if it be assumed that the rule is subject to exceptions, we find nothing in the cases in hand which fairly can be said to take them out of it as heretofore understood and applied in this court. A suit by the United States to enforce and maintain its policy respecting lands which it holds in trust for all the people stands upon a different plane in this and some other respects from the ordinary private suit to regain the title to real property or to remove a cloud from it.
>
> Since then we have applied that principle in a case where a private party relied on the misrepresentation of a Government agency as to the coverage of a crop insurance policy, a misrepresentation which the Court agreed would have estopped a private insurance carrier. We have applied it in a case where a private party relied on a misrepresentation by a Government employee as to Social Security eligibility, a misrepresentation which resulted in the applicant's losing 12 months of Social Security benefits. And we have applied it on at least three occasions to claims of estoppel in connection with the enforcement of the immigration laws and

---

States, 341 U.S. 41, 71 S.Ct. 553, 95 L.Ed. 729 (1951)(applicant cannot be deemed to waive right to citizenship on the basis of a form he signed when he was misled as to the effect signing would have on his rights). This principle also underlies the doctrine that an administrative agency may not apply a new rule retroactively when to do so would unduly intrude upon reasonable reliance interests.

13. See generally St. Regis Paper Co. v. United States, 368 U.S. 208, 229, 82 S.Ct. 289, 301, 7 L.Ed.2d 240 (1961)(Black, J., dissenting)("Our Government should not by picayunish haggling over the scope of its promise, permit one of its arms to do that which, by any fair construction, the Government has given its word that no arm will do. It is no less good morals and good law that the Government should turn square corners in dealing with the people than that the people should turn square corners in dealing with their government"); Federal Crop Insurance Corporation v. Merrill, 332 U.S. 380, at 387–388, 68 S.Ct. 1, at 4–5, 92 L.Ed. 10 (1947)(Jackson, J., dissenting)("It is very well to say that those who deal with the Government should turn square corners. But there is no reason why the square corners should constitute a one-way street"); Brandt v. Hickel, 427 F.2d 53, 57 ([9th Cir].1970)("To say to these appellants, 'The joke is on you. You shouldn't have trusted us', is hardly worthy of our great government"); Menges v. Dentler, 33 Pa. 495, 500 (1859)("Men naturally trust in their government, and ought to do so, and they ought not to suffer for it").

the denial of citizenship because of the conduct of immigration officials. In none of these cases have we ever held the Government to be estopped by the representations or conduct of its agents. In INS v. Hibi, [414 U.S. 5, 94 S.Ct. 19, 38 L.Ed.2d 7 (1973)(per curiam)], we noted that it is still an open question whether, in some future case, "affirmative misconduct" on the part of the Government might be grounds for an estoppel.

I agree with the Court that there is no need to decide in this case whether there are circumstances under which the Government may be estopped, but I think that the Court's treatment of that question gives an impression of hospitality towards claims of estoppel against the Government which our decided cases simply do not warrant. In footnote 12, the Court intimates that two of our decisions have allowed the Government to be estopped: United States v. Pennsylvania Industrial Chemical Corp., 411 U.S. 655, 93 S.Ct. 1804, 36 L.Ed.2d 567 (1973), and Moser v. United States, 341 U.S. 41, 71 S.Ct. 553, 95 L.Ed. 729 (1951). But these cases are not traditional equitable estoppel cases. *Pennsylvania Industrial Chemical Corp.* was a criminal prosecution, and we held that "to the extent that [Government regulations] deprived [the defendant] of fair warning as to what conduct the Government intended to make criminal, we think there can be no doubt that traditional notions of fairness inherent in our system of criminal justice prevent the Government from proceeding with the prosecution." And the Court's rather cryptic opinion in *Moser,* holding that an alien who declined to serve in the Armed Forces was not barred from United States citizenship pursuant to a federal statute, expressly rejected any doctrine of estoppel, and rested on the absence of a knowing and intentional waiver of the right to citizenship.

We do not write on a clean slate in this field, and our cases have left open the possibility of estoppel against the Government only in a rather narrow possible range of circumstances. Because I think the Court's opinion, in its efforts to phrase new statements of the circumstances under which the Government may be estopped, casts doubt on these decided cases, I concur only in the judgment.

467 U.S. at 66–68, 104 S.Ct. at 2227–2228. See also Office of Personnel Management v. Richmond, 496 U.S. 414, 110 S.Ct. 2465, 110 L.Ed.2d 387 (1990)(holding there can be no estoppel against the government by a claimant seeking public funds not otherwise authorized by law).

2. As is apparent from the cases discussed in the preceding note, the courts have found the law governing an agent and principal to be different when the principal is the government rather than a private party. What makes the government different? If it is to protect the government or the public fisc from the negligence or malfeasance of government agents, why shouldn't a corporate treasury have equal protection? Wouldn't the government have an action against its agent in damages if the public was injured monetarily? Why is such a remedy not adequate?

If the central interest is protection of the public from non-monetary injury or ensuring that the will of Congress is carried out, isn't *Johnson v. Williford* wrongly decided?

What interest is served by the result in a case like *Schweiker v. Hansen*, where a private party loses 12 months of Social Security benefits? What principle justifies the government in benefiting from the negligence or misconduct of its officers and employees?

3. Green v. Christiansen, 732 F.2d 1397 (9th Cir.1984), is another case involving release of a federal prisoner before his sentence was complete. The Ninth Circuit did not find the government estopped from reincarcerating Green because he had no expectation that he should be released and he was not so misled that it would be improper to charge him with constructive knowledge that he had time to serve. How does one establish a reliance interest in his freedom? Given the clarity of the statute in the *Johnson* case, why did Johnson not have constructive knowledge of being liable to reincarceration?

4. The Ninth Circuit returned to the issue of equitable estoppel against the government in Watkins v. United States Army, 875 F.2d 699 (9th Cir. en banc 1989), cert. denied, 498 U.S. 957, 111 S.Ct. 384, 112 L.Ed.2d 395 (1990). Watkins was drafted into the Army in 1967. He re-enlisted in 1970, 1974 and 1979. He was denied re-enlistment in 1982. Watkins was an exemplary soldier. From the time of his pre-induction medical exam, he had routinely informed the Army that he was a homosexual. Throughout the period of his Army service the Army's regulations prohibited the re-enlistment of homosexuals. The 1982 denial of re-enlistment was based solely on Watkins' homosexuality.

In determining whether there was a basis for invoking equitable estoppel against the government, the court posed a two prong test before addressing the traditional elements of estoppel laid out in *Johnson v. Williford*: first, a party seeking to estop the government must establish affirmative misconduct going beyond mere negligence; and second, estoppel is only available where the government's act will cause serious injustice and the public's interest will not suffer undue damage by the imposition of liability. The majority found that Watkins prevailed on both of these tests as well as on the traditional elements of estoppel and enjoined the Army from relying on its regulation barring homosexuals from re-enlistment as a basis for refusing re-enlistment to Watkins.

In what sense was the Army's prior re-enlistment of Watkins affirmative misconduct? While it may plainly have been misconduct with regard to the regulations, was it misconduct that was harmful to Watkins? In Sulit v. Schiltgen, 213 F.3d 449 (9th Cir.2000), the Ninth Circuit held that neither the failure to inform an individual of his or her legal rights nor the negligent provision of misinformation constituted affirmative misconduct. Why should a party seeking to bar the government from changing its course of conduct have to show that the government had engaged in affirmative misconduct rather than acted negligently?

In addressing the fourth element of its traditional estoppel test, Watkins' reliance on the Army's course of action, the court found that Watkins was injured because he developed military rather than civilian skills and had invested fourteen years toward a pension. These injuries could be compensated by providing funds for retraining and quantifying the value of the forfeited pension interest. If the Army's regulation against re-enlisting homosexuals is constitutionally sound, would it be better to give Watkins money damages and not carve out an exception to the regulation? Other homosexuals will not be able to obtain a position in the Army. Why should Watkins get a job in the future rather than damages for the Army's past conduct?

Watkins ultimately settled his case, accepting voluntary retirement with an honorable discharge. He received approximately $135,000 in back pay and full retirement benefits as well as a retroactive promotion to sergeant first class.

NOTE ON THE GOVERNMENT AS PLAINTIFF

The Clean Air Act, 42 U.S.C §§ 7401 et seq. controls air pollution through a division of responsibility between the federal government and the states. The federal EPA sets national standards for permissible concentrations of pollutants in the ambient air and the states develop implementation plans establishing emission limits for particular plants or types of facilities; these state implementation plans ("SIPs") are to ensure that the national ambient air quality standards are met. EPA approves SIPs, which are then enforceable both under state law and by EPA under the Clean Air Act. The states may choose to revise their SIPs to reflect changed circumstances and those revisions are submitted to EPA for approval. A SIP revision becomes effective as a matter of state law when it is adopted by the state regardless of EPA's approval or failure to act on the proposed revision; but the revision only becomes effective as a matter of federal law when EPA approves the revision. Courts have held that, under the statute, EPA has four months in which to approve or reject a SIP revision.

EPA has been notoriously slow in acting on proposed SIP revisions, frequently taking much longer than four months. This puts an industrial operator in a difficult position: if it complies with the revised SIP which is state law, it may be subject to an action for penalties or injunctive relief by EPA for violation of federal law during the period in which EPA failed to act on the proposed SIP revision. In these circumstances, if EPA brings an action to enforce the unrevised federal SIP, having failed to carry out its statutory duty to approve or reject the SIP revision, EPA comes into the court with the sort of cloud upon its claim that in a private suit would lead the court to consider whether the agency should obtain the full relief to which it would be entitled in a case where there was simply a violation of a SIP.

The courts of appeals have dealt with these circumstances in different ways. The District of Columbia Circuit decided that penalties accrued in the period after the statutory deadline for EPA action had passed but before EPA acted on a SIP revision, should be held in abeyance pending EPA's final action on the proposed SIP revision. If the revision were approved, no penalty would be collected; if it were rejected, penalties for the entire period would be collected. The court reasoned that if the revision were approved, then the post-deadline penalties were the result of EPA's failure to act on time; if the revision were rejected, the defendant would not benefit undeservedly. Duquesne Light Co. v. Environmental Protection Agency, 698 F.2d 456, 470–72 (D.C.Cir.1983).

The Fifth Circuit, putting particular emphasis on the important role played by the states under the Clean Air Act, ruled that EPA was barred from collecting any penalties for violation of the federal SIP for the period from the four month statutory deadline for acting on SIP revisions to the date on which EPA acted on the proposed revision. The court believed the possibility of collecting penalties might improperly influence EPA to disapprove SIP revisions and found it unacceptable to leave a company, which was complying with state law, open to a penalty because of delays within EPA. American Cyanamid Co. v. U.S. Environmental Protection Agency, 810 F.2d 493 (5th Cir.1987); see General Motors Corp. v. Environmental Protection Agency, 871 F.2d 495 (5th Cir.1989)(applying the *American Cyanamid* reasoning to other provisions of the Clean Air Act).

The First Circuit chose a third path, setting out two remedies. First, the affected manufacturer could bring an action under the Clean Air Act to compel EPA to act on the proposed SIP revision. Second, the court considering EPA's enforcement action should take the agency's delay in acting on the proposed SIP revision into account in setting penalties. The court believed this gave EPA the necessary incentive to act without unreasonable delay but protected the interest of the public in enforcing clean air regulations where SIP revisions were rejected after delay by EPA. United States v. General Motors Corp., 876 F.2d 1060 (1st Cir.1989).

None of these cases speaks in terms of traditional principles or maxims in other areas of public or private law such as unclean hands. Indeed an unclean hands defense is unlikely to succeed: "The general principles of equity are applicable in a suit by the United States to secure the cancellation of a conveyance or the rescission of a contract. But they will not be applied to frustrate the purpose of its laws or to thwart public policy." Pan American Petroleum & Transport Co. v. United States, 273 U.S. 456, 506, 47 S.Ct. 416, 424, 71 L.Ed. 734 (1927). Nevertheless, the underlying fact situation is clearly akin to the cases in this chapter: the plaintiff has engaged in misconduct and the question for the court is whether the misconduct is sufficiently extreme or relevant to the dispute before the court so that the plaintiff should be barred from receiving relief.

The First Circuit case went to the Supreme Court, which held that EPA is not required to act on a proposed SIP revision within four months as that requirement refers only to actions required on the original SIP and not on a revision. Moreover, the Court held that even though the Administrative Procedure Act required EPA to conclude matters "within a reasonable time," EPA is not barred from bringing suit to enforce an existing SIP on the ground that it has unreasonably delayed action on a proposed revision. The Court did not reach the issue of remedies. General Motors Corp. v. United States, 496 U.S. 530, 110 S.Ct. 2528, 110 L.Ed.2d 480 (1990). The problem of how to address the errant government plaintiff remains.

C. LACHES AND STATUTES OF LIMITATIONS

By statutes of limitations, the legislature bars the commencement of lawsuits after a set period of time from the events which give rise to the controversy or from the discovery of facts that provide the plaintiff with the factual basis to pursue her claim. For example, the general rule under federal criminal law is that suit is barred if an indictment is not returned within five years after the offense is committed. 18 U.S.C. § 3282. But there are exceptions; for instance, there is no limitation on the bringing of indictments for offenses punishable by death. 18 U.S.C. § 3281. The states typically have limitation periods applicable to different categories of lawsuits: torts, money damages, criminal offenses and so on. The basic rationale of statutes of limitation is two-fold: with the passage of time evidence becomes less reliable—memories fade, witnesses die, documents can no longer be found—and there is an interest in ensuring repose and finality even in potential disputes. In selecting a limitation period, the legislature balances the substantive policies behind the cause of action with the interest in repose. There is, of course, a great deal of dispute over how the limitation periods are to be measured. See The Law Commission, Limitation of Actions (Consultation Paper No. 151) (1998) (reviewing the law in many common law countries and suggesting reforms for England and Wales); Adam Bain & Ugo Colella, Interpreting Federal Statutes of Limitations, 37 Creighton L.Rev. 493 (2004).

The legislative bars to commencing a lawsuit are paralleled by the equitable defense of laches. As with the other equitable principles explored in this chapter, there are numerous formulations of the principle of laches. Laches is fairly defined as delay by a plaintiff in asserting his rights that is not excusable or reasonable and that works to the prejudice or injury of the defendant. Prejudice comes in a variety of forms; changing one's economic position based on the belief that there is no live controversy with the plaintiff and the routine destruction of documents through a corporate document retention policy are two common examples. Laches bars pursuit of her claim by the plaintiff. Laches obviously differs from a statute of limitation by considering the conduct of the plaintiff and its effect on the defendant rather than simply measuring a period of time. Laches is a defense to equitable actions; some courts following the merger of law and equity will allow the laches defense in legal actions, Borland By and Through Utah State Dept. of Social Services v. Chandler, 733 P.2d 144 (Utah 1987), but generally the defense is limited to equitable actions, e.g., Turner v. Guy, 2 Mass.App.Ct. 343, 311 N.E.2d 921 (1974).

TRW INC. v. ANDREWS

Supreme Court of the United States, 2001
534 U.S. 19, 122 S.Ct. 441, 151 L.Ed.2d 339

JUSTICE GINSBURG delivered the opinion of the Court.

This case concerns the running of the two-year statute of limitations governing suits based on the Fair Credit Reporting Act (FCRA or Act), as added, 84 Stat. 1127, and amended, 15 U.S.C. § 1681 et seq.[1] The time prescription appears in § 1681p, which sets out a general rule and an exception. Generally, an action to enforce any liability created by the Act may be brought "within two years from the date on which the liability arises." The exception covers willful misrepresentation of "any information required under [the Act] to be disclosed to [the plaintiff]": when such a representation is material to a claim under the Act, suit may be brought "within two years after [the plaintiff's] discovery . . . of the misrepresentation."

Section 1681p's exception is not involved in this case; the complaint does not allege misrepresentation of information that the FCRA "require[s] . . . to be disclosed to [the plaintiff]." Plaintiff-respondent Adelaide Andrews nevertheless contends, and the Ninth Circuit held, that § 1681p's generally applicable two-year limitation commenced to run on Andrews' claims only upon her discovery of defendant-petitioner TRW Inc.'s alleged violations of the Act.

We hold that a discovery rule does not govern § 1681p. That section explicitly delineates the exceptional case in which discovery triggers the two-year limitation. We are not at liberty to make Congress' explicit exception the general rule as well.

I

A

Congress enacted the FCRA in 1970 to promote efficiency in the Nation's banking system and to protect consumer privacy. As relevant here, the Act seeks to accomplish those goals by requiring credit reporting agencies to maintain "reasonable procedures" designed "to assure maximum possible accuracy of the information" contained in credit reports, § 1681e(b), and to "limit the furnishing of [such reports] to" certain statutorily enumerated purposes, § 1681e(a); 15 U.S.C. § 1681b. The Act creates a private right of action allowing injured consumers to recover "any actual damages" caused by negligent violations and both actual and punitive damages for willful noncompliance.

B

The facts of this case are for the most part undisputed. On June 17, 1993, Adelaide Andrews visited a radiologist's office in Santa Monica,

---

1. Congress has revised the FCRA extensively since the events at issue, but has not altered the provisions material to this case.

California. She filled out a new patient form listing certain basic information, including her name, birth date, and Social Security number. Andrews handed the form to the office receptionist, one Andrea Andrews (the Impostor), who copied the information and thereafter moved to Las Vegas, Nevada. Once there, the Impostor attempted on numerous occasions to open credit accounts using Andrews' Social Security number and her own last name and address.

On four of those occasions, the company from which the Impostor sought credit requested a report from TRW. Each time, TRW's computers registered a match between Andrews' Social Security number, last name, and first initial and therefore responded by furnishing her file. TRW thus disclosed Andrews' credit history at the Impostor's request to a bank on July 25, 1994; to a cable television company on September 27, 1994; to a department store on October 28, 1994; and to another credit provider on January 3, 1995. All recipients but the cable company rejected the Impostor's applications for credit.

Andrews did not learn of these disclosures until May 31, 1995, when she sought to refinance her home mortgage and in the process received a copy of her credit report reflecting the Impostor's activity. Andrews concedes that TRW promptly corrected her file upon learning of its mistake. She alleges, however, that the blemishes on her report not only caused her inconvenience and emotional distress, they also forced her to abandon her refinancing efforts and settle for an alternative line of credit on less favorable terms.

On October 21, 1996, almost 17 months after she discovered the Impostor's fraudulent conduct and more than two years after TRW's first two disclosures, Andrews filed suit in the United States District Court for the Central District of California. Her complaint stated two categories of FCRA claims against TRW, only the first of which is relevant here. Those claims alleged that TRW's four disclosures of her information in response to the Impostor's credit applications were improper because TRW failed to verify, predisclosure, that Adelaide Andrews of Santa Monica initiated the requests or was otherwise involved in the underlying transactions. Andrews asserted that by processing requests that matched her profile on Social Security number, last name, and first initial but did not correspond on other key identifiers, notably birth date, address, and first name, TRW had facilitated the Impostor's identity theft. According to Andrews, TRW's verification failure constituted a willful violation of § 1681e(a), which requires credit reporting agencies to maintain "reasonable procedures" to avoid improper disclosures. She sought injunctive relief, punitive damages, and compensation for the "expenditure of time and money, commercial impairment, inconvenience, embarrassment, humiliation and emotional distress" that TRW had allegedly inflicted upon her.

TRW moved for partial summary judgment, arguing, inter alia, that the FCRA's statute of limitations had expired on Andrews' claims based on the July 25 and September 27, 1994, disclosures because both occurred more than two years before she brought suit. Andrews countered that her claims as to all four disclosures were timely because the limitations period did not commence until May 31, 1995, the date she learned of TRW's alleged wrongdoing. The District Court, agreeing with TRW that § 1681p does not incorporate a general discovery rule, held that relief stemming from the July and September 1994 disclosures was time barred.

The Court of Appeals for the Ninth Circuit reversed this ruling, applying what it considered to be the "general federal rule ... that a federal statute of limitations begins to run when a party knows or has reason to know that she was injured." The court rejected the District Court's conclusion that the text of § 1681p, and in particular the limited exception set forth in that section, precluded judicial attribution of such a rule to the FCRA. "[U]nless Congress has expressly legislated otherwise," the Ninth Circuit declared, "the equitable doctrine of discovery is read into every federal statute of limitations." Finding no such express directive, the Court of Appeals held that "none of [Andrews'] injuries were stale when suit was brought." * * *

II

* * *

The Appeals Court principally relied on our decision in Holmberg v. Armbrecht, 327 U.S. 392, 66 S.Ct. 582, 90 L.Ed. 743 (1946). In that case, we instructed with particularity that "where a plaintiff has been injured by fraud and remains in ignorance of it without any fault or want of diligence or care on his part, the bar of the statute does not begin to run until the fraud is discovered." *Holmberg* thus stands for the proposition that equity tolls the statute of limitations in cases of fraud or concealment; it does not establish a general presumption applicable across all contexts. The only other cases in which we have recognized a prevailing discovery rule, moreover, were decided in two contexts, latent disease and medical malpractice, "where the cry for [such a] rule is loudest," Rotella v. Wood, 528 U.S. 549, 555, 120 S.Ct. 1075, 145 L.Ed.2d 1047 (2000). See United States v. Kubrick, 444 U.S. 111, 100 S.Ct. 352, 62 L.Ed.2d 259 (1979); Urie v. Thompson, 337 U.S. 163, 69 S.Ct. 1018, 93 L.Ed. 1282 (1949).

We have also observed that lower federal courts "generally apply a discovery accrual rule when a statute is silent on the issue." [S]ee also Klehr v. A.O. Smith Corp., 521 U.S. 179, 191, 117 S.Ct. 1984, 138 L.Ed.2d 373 (1997) (citing Connors v. Hallmark & Son Coal Co., 935 F.2d 336, 342 (C.A.D.C.1991), for the proposition that "federal courts generally apply [a] discovery accrual rule when [the] statute does not call for a different rule"). But we have not adopted that position as our own. And, beyond doubt, we have never endorsed the Ninth Circuit's view that Congress can convey its refusal to adopt a discovery rule only by explicit command, rather than by implication from the structure or text of the particular statute.

The Ninth Circuit thus erred in holding that a generally applied discovery rule controls this case. The FCRA does not govern an area of the law that cries out for application of a discovery rule, nor is the statute "silent on the issue" of when the statute of limitations begins to run. Section 1681p addresses that precise question; the provision reads:

> "An action to enforce any liability created under [the Act] may be brought ... within two years from the date on which the liability arises, except that where a defendant has materially and willfully misrepresented any information required under [the Act] to be disclosed to an individual and the information so misrepresented is material to the establishment of the defendant's liability to that individual under [the Act], the action may be brought at any time within two years after discovery by the individual of the misrepresentation."

We conclude that the text and structure of § 1681p evince Congress' intent to preclude judicial implication of a discovery rule.

"Where Congress explicitly enumerates certain exceptions to a general prohibition, additional exceptions are not to be implied, in the absence of evidence of a contrary legislative intent." Andrus v. Glover Constr. Co., 446 U.S. 608, 616–617, 100 S.Ct. 1905, 64 L.Ed.2d 548 (1980). Congress provided in the FCRA that the two-year statute of limitations runs from "the date on which the liability arises," subject to a single exception for cases involving a defendant's willful misrepresentation of material information. The most natural reading of § 1681p is that Congress implicitly excluded a general discovery rule by explicitly including a more limited one. See Leatherman v. Tarrant County Narcotics Intelligence and Coordination Unit, 507 U.S. 163, 168, 113 S.Ct. 1160, 122 L.Ed.2d 517 (1993) ("Expressio unius est exclusio alterius."). We would distort § 1681p's text by converting the exception into the rule. Cf. United States v. Brockamp, 519 U.S. 347, 352, 117 S.Ct. 849, 136 L.Ed.2d 818 (1997) ("explicit listing of exceptions" to running of limitations period considered indicative of Congress' intent to preclude "courts [from] read[ing] other unmentioned, open-ended, 'equitable' exceptions into the statute").

At least equally telling, incorporating a general discovery rule into § 1681p would not merely supplement the explicit exception contrary to Congress' apparent intent; it would in practical effect render that exception entirely superfluous in all but the most unusual circumstances. A consumer will generally not discover the tortious conduct alleged here—the improper disclosure of her credit history to a potential user—until she requests her file from a credit reporting agency. If the agency responds by concealing the offending disclosure, both a generally applicable discovery rule and the misrepresentation exception would operate to toll the statute of limitations until the concealment is revealed. Once triggered, the statute of limitations would run under either for two years from the discovery date. In this paradigmatic setting, then, the misrepresentation exception would have no work to do.

Both Andrews and the Government, appearing as amicus in her support, attempt to generate some role for the express exception independent of that filled by a general discovery rule. They conceive of the exception as a codification of the judge-made doctrine of equitable estoppel, which, they argue, operates only after the discovery rule has triggered the limitations period, preventing a defendant from benefiting from its misrepresentation by tolling that period until the concealment is uncovered.

To illustrate this supposed separate application, Andrews and the Government frame the following scenario: A credit reporting agency injures a consumer by disclosing her file for an improper purpose. The consumer has no reason to suspect the violation until a year later, when she applies for and is denied credit as a result of the agency's wrongdoing. At that point, the Government asserts, "the consumer would presumably be put on inquiry notice of the violation, and the discovery rule would start the running of the normal limitation period." Some days or months later, the consumer follows up on her suspicions by requesting a copy of her credit report, to which the agency responds by concealing the initial improper disclosure. According to Andrews and the Government, the misrepresentation exception would then operate to toll the already-commenced limitations period until the agency reveals its wrongdoing.

We reject this argument for several reasons. As an initial matter, we are not persuaded by this effort to distinguish the practical function of a discovery rule and the express exception, because we doubt that the supporting scenario is likely to occur outside the realm of theory. The fatal weakness in the narrative is its assumption that a consumer would be charged with constructive notice of an improper disclosure upon denial of a credit application. If the consumer habitually paid her bills on time, the denial might well lead her to suspect a prior credit agency error. But the credit denial would place her on "inquiry notice," and the discovery rule would trigger the limitations period at that point, only if a reasonable person in her position would have learned of the injury in the exercise of due diligence. See Stone v. Williams, 970 F.2d 1043, 1049 (C.A.2 1992) ("The duty of inquiry having arisen, plaintiff is charged with whatever knowledge an inquiry would have revealed."); 2 C. Corman, Limitation of Actions § 11.1.6, p. 164 (1991) ("It is obviously unreasonable to charge the plaintiff with failure to search for the missing element of the cause of action if such element would not have been revealed by such search.").

In the usual circumstance, the plaintiff will gain knowledge of her injury from the credit reporting agency. The scenario put forth by Andrews and the Government, however, requires the assumption that, even if the consumer exercised reasonable diligence by requesting her credit report without delay, she would not in fact learn of the disclosure because the credit reporting agency would conceal it. The uncovering of that concealment would remain the triggering event for both the discovery rule and the express exception. In this scenario, as in the paradigmatic one, the misrepresentation exception would be superfluous.

In any event, both Andrews and the Government concede that the independent function one could attribute to the express exception would arise only in "rare and egregious case[s]." The result is that a rule nowhere contained in the text of § 1681p would do the bulk of that provision's work, while a proviso accounting for more than half of that text would lie dormant in all but the most unlikely situations.

It is "a cardinal principle of statutory construction" that "a statute ought, upon the whole, to be so construed that, if it can be prevented, no clause, sentence, or word shall be superfluous, void, or insignificant." Duncan v. Walker, 533 U.S. 167, 174, 121 S.Ct. 2120, 2125 150 L.Ed.2d 251 (2001). "[W]ere we to adopt [Andrews'] construction of the statute," the express exception would be rendered "insignificant, if not wholly superfluous." Id., 121 S.Ct., at 2125. We are "reluctant to treat statutory terms as surplusage in any setting," id., and we decline to do so here.[5]

Andrews advances two additional arguments in defense of the decision below, neither of which we find convincing. She contends, first, that the words "date on which the liability arises"—the phrase Congress used to frame the general rule in § 1681p—"literally expres[s]" a discovery rule because liability does not "arise" until it "present[s] itself" or comes to the attention of the potential plaintiff. The dictionary definition of the word "arise" does not compel such a reading; to the contrary, it can be used to support either party's position. See Webster's Third New International Dictionary 117 (1966) (arise defined as "to come into being"; "to come about"; or "to become apparent in such a way as to demand attention"); Black's Law Dictionary 138 (rev. 4th ed.1968) ("to come into being or notice"). And TRW offers a strong argument that we have in fact construed that word to imply the result Andrews seeks to avoid. See Brief for Petitioner 16–20 (citing, inter alia, McMahon v. United States, 342 U.S. 25, 72 S.Ct. 17, 96 L.Ed. 26 (1951) (statute of limitations triggered on date "cause of action arises" incorporates injury-occurrence rule)). On balance, we conclude, the phrase "liability arises" is not particularly instructive, much less dispositive of this case.

Similarly unhelpful, in our view, is Andrews' reliance on the legislative history of § 1681p. She observes that early versions of that provision, introduced in both the House and Senate, keyed the start of the limitations period to "the date of the occurrence of the violation." From the disappearance of that language in the final version of § 1681p, Andrews infers a congressional intent to reject the rule that the deleted words would have plainly established.

As TRW notes, however, Congress also heard testimony urging it to enact a statute of limitations that runs from "the date on which the violation is discovered" but declined to do so. Hearings before the Subcom-

---

5. Similarly, even if we agreed that the discovery and equitable estoppel doctrines could comfortably coexist in this setting, we would reject the contention that we are therefore free to incorporate both into the FCRA. As we have explained, we read Congress' codification of one judge-made doctrine not as a license to imply others, but rather as an intentional rejection of those it did not codify.

mittee on Consumer Affairs of the House Committee on Banking and Currency, 91st Cong., 2d Sess., 188 (1970). In addition, the very change to § 1681p's language on which Andrews relies could be read to refute her position. The misrepresentation exception was added at the same time Congress changed the language "date of the occurrence of the violation" to "liability arises." We doubt that Congress, when it inserted a carefully worded exception to the main rule, intended simultaneously to create a general discovery rule that would render that exception superfluous. In sum, the evidence of the early incarnations of § 1681p, like the "liability arises" language on which Congress ultimately settled, fails to convince us that Congress intended sub silentio to adopt a general discovery rule in addition to the limited one it expressly provided.

III

* * *

For the reasons stated, the judgment of the Court of Appeals for the Ninth Circuit is reversed, and the case is remanded for further proceedings consistent with this opinion.

JUSTICE SCALIA, with whom JUSTICE THOMAS joins, concurring in the judgment.

As the Court notes, the Court of Appeals based its decision on what it called the "general federal rule ... that a federal statute of limitations begins to run when a party knows or has reason to know that she was injured." The Court declines to say whether that expression of the governing general rule is correct. There is in my view little doubt that it is not, and our reluctance to say so today is inexplicable, given that we held, a mere four years ago, that a statute of limitations which says the period runs from "the date on which the cause of action arose," 29 U.S.C. § 1451(f)(1), "incorporates the standard rule that the limitations period commences when the plaintiff has a complete and present cause of action," Bay Area Laundry and Dry Cleaning Pension Trust Fund v. Ferbar Corp., 522 U.S. 192, 201, 118 S.Ct. 542, 139 L.Ed.2d 553 (1997).

Bay Area Laundry quoted approvingly our statement in Clark v. Iowa City, 20 Wall. 583, 589, 22 L.Ed. 427 (1875), that "[a]ll statutes of limitation begin to run when the right of action is complete...." This is unquestionably the traditional rule: absent other indication, a statute of limitations begins to run at the time the plaintiff "has the right to apply to the court for relief...." 1 H. Wood, Limitation of Actions § 122a, p. 684 (4th ed.1916). "That a person entitled to an action has no knowledge of his right to sue, or of the facts out of which his right arises, does not postpone the period of limitation." 2 Wood, supra, § 276c(1), at 1411.

The injury-discovery rule applied by the Court of Appeals is bad wine of recent vintage. Other than our recognition of the historical exception for suits based on fraud, e.g., Bailey v. Glover, 21 Wall. 342, 347–350, 22 L.Ed. 636 (1875), we have deviated from the traditional rule and imputed an injury-discovery rule to Congress on only one occasion. Urie v. Thompson, 337 U.S. 163, 169–171, 69 S.Ct. 1018, 93 L.Ed. 1282 (1949).[2] We did so there because we could not imagine that legislation as "humane" as the Federal Employers' Liability Act would bar recovery for latent medical injuries. We repeated this sentiment in Rotella v. Wood, 528 U.S. 549, 555, 120 S.Ct. 1075, 145 L.Ed.2d 1047 (2000), saying that the "cry for a discovery rule is loudest" in the context of medical-malpractice suits; and we repeat it again today with the assertion that the present case does not involve "an area of the law that cries out for application of a discovery rule." These cries, however, are properly directed not to us, but to Congress, whose job it is to decide how "humane" legislation should be— or (to put the point less tendentiously) to strike the balance between remediation of all injuries and a policy of repose. See Amy v. Watertown (No. 2), 130 U.S. 320, 323–324, 9 S.Ct. 537, 32 L.Ed. 953 (1889) ("[T]he cases in which [the statute of limitations may be suspended by causes not mentioned in the statute itself] are very limited in character, and are to be admitted with great caution; otherwise the court would make the law instead of administering it").

Congress has been operating against the background rule recognized in *Bay Area Laundry* for a very long time. When it has wanted us to apply a different rule, such as the injury-discovery rule, it has said so. To apply a new background rule to previously enacted legislation would reverse prior congressional judgments; and to display uncertainty regarding the current background rule makes all unspecifying new legislation a roll of the dice. Today's opinion, in clarifying the meaning of 15 U.S.C. § 1681p, casts the meaning of innumerable other limitation periods in doubt.

Because there is nothing in this statute to contradict the rule that a statute of limitations begins to run when the cause of action is complete, I concur in the judgment of the Court.

NOTES

1. What is a person such as Andrews supposed to do to protect her rights under the Court's interpretation of the FCRA? Why would Congress require such action on the part of so many citizens?

2. In the footnotes to *TRW*, the majority sparred with Justices Scalia and Thomas concerning the meaning of the Court's 1997 decision in *Bay Area Laundry*. Justice Ginsburg responded to their concurring opinion:

> The opinion concurring in the judgment rips *Bay Area Laundry* from its berth; we here set the record straight. The question presented in *Bay Area Laundry* was whether a statute of limitations could commence to run on one day while the right to sue ripened on a later day. We answered

---

2. As the Court accurately notes, in one other case we simply observed (without endorsement) that several Courts of Appeals had substituted injury-discovery for the traditional rule in medical-malpractice actions under the Federal Tort Claims Act, see United States v. Kubrick, 444 U.S. 111, 120, and n. 7, 100 S.Ct. 352, 62 L.Ed.2d 259 (1979), and in two other cases observed (without endorsement) that lower federal courts "generally apply" an injury-discovery rule, see Rotella v. Wood, 528 U.S. 549, 555, 120 S.Ct. 1075, 145 L.Ed.2d 1047 (2000); Klehr v. A.O. Smith Corp., 521 U.S. 179, 191, 117 S.Ct. 1984, 138 L.Ed.2d 373 (1997).

that question, and only that question, "no," unless the statute indicates otherwise. Continuing on beyond the place where the concurrence in the judgment leaves off, we clarified:

> "Unless Congress has told us otherwise in the legislation at issue, a cause of action does not become 'complete and present' for limitations purposes until the plaintiff can file suit and obtain relief. See Reiter v. Cooper, 507 U.S. 258, 267, 113 S.Ct. 1213, 122 L.Ed.2d 604 (1993) ('While it is theoretically possible for a statute to create a cause of action that accrues at one time for the purpose of calculating when the statute of limitations begins to run, but at another time for the purpose of bringing suit, we will not infer such an odd result in the absence of any such indication in the statute.')."

534 U.S. at 34 n. 6, 122 S.Ct. at 450 n. 6.

The concurring justices replied:

> The question presented on which certiorari was granted in [*Bay Area Laundry*] was not, as the Court now recharacterizes it, the generalized inquiry "whether a statute of limitations could commence to run on one day while the right to sue ripened on a later day," but rather (as set forth in somewhat abbreviated form in petitioner Bay Area Laundry's merits brief) the much more precise question, "When does the statute of limitations begin to run on an action under the Multiemployer Pension Plan Amendments Act, 29 U.S.C. § 1381 et seq., to collect overdue employer withdrawal liability payments?" * * * The Court's *Bay Area Laundry* opinion introduced its discussion of the merits as follows:
>
> > "[T]he Ninth Circuit's decision conflicts with an earlier decision of the District of Columbia Circuit [which] held that the statute of limitations ... runs from the date the employer misses a scheduled payment, not from the date of complete withdrawal.... The Third and Seventh Circuits have also held that the statute of limitations runs from the failure to make a payment.... We granted certiorari ... to resolve these conflicts."
>
> The Court's assertion that we did not answer the question presented, and did not resolve the conflicts—held only that the Ninth Circuit was wrong to say that the limitations period commenced before there was a right of action, and not that the other circuits were right to say that the period commenced upon the failure to make a payment—is as erroneous as it is implausible. *Bay Area Laundry* held that the cause of action arose when "the employer violated an obligation owed the plan," because "the standard rule" is that the period begins to run when the plaintiff has a "complete and present cause of action."

534 U.S. at 36 n. 1, 122 S.Ct. at 451 n. 1.

3. Another example of the Supreme Court concluding that Congress has demanded extreme vigilance on the part of potential plaintiffs is Ledbetter v. Goodyear Tire & Rubber Co., 550 U.S. 618, 127 S.Ct. 2162, 167 L.Ed.2d 982 (2007). The Court held that the continuing effects of a discriminatory act did not extend the time period for filing an employment discrimination claim under Title VII of the Civil Rights Act of 1964. Instead, the Court interpreted

the Act to mean that the time period was triggered by the initial discrete act, in this instance the defendant's original decision to deny a female manager a raise granted to male managers. The time period was not extended by the continued receipt of paychecks issued under that discriminatory pay-setting decision. This interpretation effectively gave employees only 180 or 300 days (depending on the jurisdiction) to learn of a discriminatory pay decision and to timely file a complaint. Legislation to reverse this decision, the Lilly Ledbetter Fair Pay Restoration Act, passed in January 2009. Obama Signs First Piece of Legislation Into Law, Washington Post at A1 (Jan. 29, 2009).

4. For many years, Congress did not provide a general statute of limitations. In 1990, Congress provided a general statute of limitation for civil cases under future federal statutes, 28 U.S.C. § 1658:

> Except as otherwise provided by law, a civil action arising under an Act of Congress enacted after [December 1, 1990] may not be commenced later than 4 years after the cause of action accrues.

This statute applies if a plaintiff's claim against a defendant was made possible by any post–1990 congressional enactment, whether in the form of an amendment to an existing statute or passage of a wholly new statute. Jones v. R.R. Donnelley & Sons Co., 541 U.S. 369, 124 S.Ct. 1836, 158 L.Ed.2d 645 (2004). Does this fallback statute provide any assistance in determining what Congress may have thought was "the background rule" with respect to statutes of limitation? See, e.g., Skwira v. United States, 344 F.3d 64 (1st Cir.2003) (applying discovery rule after rejecting proposition that *TRW* requires a strict time-of-injury rule in wrongful death cases).

The most specific statute of limitations will govern a cause of action. Thus, the Supreme Court refused to allow taxpayer plaintiffs to proceed under the longer statute of limitations for general tax refund actions where their claims were more precisely wrongful levy claims for which a shorter, 9–month limitations period applied. EC Term of Years Trust v. United States, 550 U.S. 429, 127 S.Ct. 1763, 167 L.Ed.2d 729 (2007).

5. In litigation under older federal statutes where no limitation period has been provided, it is settled practice to borrow the local time limitation for the parallel state cause of action if no federal statute expressly applies. Graham County Soil & Water Conservation District v. United States ex rel. Wilson, 545 U.S. 409, 125 S.Ct. 2444, 162 L.Ed.2d 390 (2005). The question of the characterization of a federal cause of action for limitation borrowing purposes is ultimately a question of federal law, so it is important to remain consistent with federal policy. DelCostello v. International Brotherhood of Teamsters, 462 U.S. 151, 103 S.Ct. 2281, 76 L.Ed.2d 476 (1983) (court borrowed a federal statute of limitation where it appeared to more closely reflect congressional balance between repose and substantive policies behind claim). In Wilson v. Garcia, 471 U.S. 261, 105 S.Ct. 1938, 85 L.Ed.2d 254 (1985), addressing the federal remedial statute for violations of civil rights under 42 U.S.C. § 1983, the Supreme Court decided that practical considerations favored characterizing all claims under section 1983 as falling in one category with one statute of limitation applicable in a given state rather than attempting to parse each particular claim and determine the appropriate state limitation period for that claim. In contrast, in *Graham County Soil & Water*

Conservation District, the Supreme Court held that the six-year statute of limitations in the False Claims Act, 31 U.S.C. § 3731(b)(1), does not govern False Claims Act civil actions for retaliation; these instead must be brought in the time provided by the most closely analogous state limitations period to avoid creating the possible result that the cause of action would expire before it accrued.

Limitations taken from state law do not bar suits by the United States when it sues to vindicate a public right or interest, absent a clear showing of congressional intent to the contrary. United States v. Summerlin, 310 U.S. 414, 416–17, 60 S.Ct. 1019, 1020–21, 84 L.Ed. 1283 (1940). This doctrine has its origins in the common law principle that time does not run against the king. Today it is justified on the ground that public rights and revenues should not be lost due to the negligence of public officials. Guaranty Trust Co. v. United States, 304 U.S. 126, 132, 58 S.Ct. 785, 788–789, 82 L.Ed. 1224 (1938); SEC v. Rind, 991 F.2d 1486, 1491 (9th Cir.), cert. denied, 510 U.S. 963, 114 S.Ct. 439, 126 L.Ed.2d 372 (1993). But the government is subject to applicable federal statutes of limitation and the courts have not generally been willing to carve out exceptions to the limitation periods on the grounds that it is difficult for the government to discover statutory or regulatory violations and bring its claims within the applicable limitation period. E.g., 3M Co. v. Browner, 17 F.3d 1453 (D.C.Cir.1994). Some courts, however, have accepted the argument that the statute of limitations should run from the time the defendant reports the violation to the government, because it would have been "practically impossible" to discover the violation and the remedial benefits of the statute would be lost. E.g., Atlantic States Legal Foundation v. A1 Tech Specialty Steel Corp., 635 F.Supp. 284 (N.D.N.Y.1986). Further discussion can be found in Abner J. Mikva and James E. Pfander, On the Meaning of Congressional Silence: Using Federal Common Law to Fill the Gap in Congress's Residual Statute of Limitations, 107 Yale L.J. 393 (1997).

6. The Louisiana Supreme Court has held that the bar imposed by a statute of limitation may be overcome by showing that the defendant has acted so as to prevent the plaintiff from bringing his cause of action. This is part of the equitable doctrine of *"contra non valentem agere nulla currit praescriptio"*: a prescription or limitation does not run against a party who is unable to act. Wimberly v. Gatch, 635 So.2d 206 (La.1994). A suit against a child molester by the parents of the child was not barred by a limitation period where research showed that the normal reaction of a sexually abused child was secrecy and delayed disclosure. The court viewed the equitable doctrine as an application of the principle that one should not be able to take advantage of one's own wrongful act.

7. The Supreme Court has held that a law enacted after expiration of a previously applicable limitations period violated the Ex Post Facto Clause when applied to revive a previously time-barred prosecution. Under this holding, California could not pass legislation extending the time in which prosecution for sex-related child abuse was authorized where the law was enacted after the prior limitations periods for the defendant's alleged offenses had expired. Stogner v. California, 539 U.S. 607, 123 S.Ct. 2446, 156 L.Ed.2d 544 (2003). Courts have distinguished *Stogner* in finding no Ex Post Facto Clause violation when the legislature has either extended an unexpired

statute of limitations, e.g., State v. Martin, 151 N.H. 107, 849 A.2d 138 (2004), or revived civil actions, e.g., DeLonga v. Diocese of Sioux Falls, 329 F.Supp.2d 1092 (D.S.D.2004).

8. Congress did not exceed its enumerated powers when it passed 28 U.S.C. § 1367(d), which requires the tolling and extending of the state statute of limitations on a state law claim during the period in which the cause of action was pending under the federal court's supplemental jurisdiction. The statute was necessary and proper to execute Congress's power to constitute tribunals inferior to the Supreme Court, and to ensure that those tribunals may fairly and efficiently exercise the judicial power of the United States. Jinks v. Richland County, 538 U.S. 456, 123 S.Ct. 1667, 155 L.Ed.2d 631 (2003). The Court also held that the statute applied to political subdivisions of the State, such as a county, even though the Court had held in Raygor v. Regents of the University of Minnesota, 534 U.S. 533, 122 S.Ct. 999, 152 L.Ed.2d 27 (2002), that the same statute did not apply to claims filed in federal court against the States themselves.

9. Legislatures sometimes provide an alternate means of measuring whether an action is timely. A statute of repose "provides that a cause of action must be commenced within a specified amount of time after the defendant's action which allegedly led to injury, regardless of whether the plaintiff has discovered the injury or wrongdoing." In contrast, a statute of limitations, "bars an action not commenced within a specified amount of time after the cause of action 'accrues.'" Castellani v. Bailey, 218 Wis.2d 245, 252, 578 N.W.2d 166, 170 (1998); Dennis J. LaFave, Remedying the Confusion Between Statutes of Limitations and Statutes of Repose in Wisconsin—A Conceptual Guide, 88 Marq.L.Rev. 927 (2005). For example, the General Aviation Revitalization Act of 1994, 49 U.S.C. § 40101, bars state and federal tort claims brought against the manufacturer of certain light aircraft (or components thereof) more than eighteen years after the product is first sold. This can mean that the plaintiff has no cause of action. "The harm that has been done is damnum absque injuria—a wrong for which the law affords no redress." McIntosh v. Melroe Co., 729 N.E.2d 972, 978 (Ind.2000) (upholding the ten-year statute of repose for products liability actions under Indiana law).

PRO–FOOTBALL, INC. v. HARJO

United States Court of Appeals, District of Columbia Circuit, 2005
415 F.3d 44

PER CURIAM.

In 1992, seven Native Americans petitioned the Trademark Trial and Appeal Board ("TTAB") to cancel the registrations of six trademarks used by the Washington Redskins football team. After the TTAB granted their petition, the team's owner, Pro–Football, Inc., brought suit seeking reversal of the TTAB's decision. The district court granted summary judgment to Pro–Football on two alternate grounds, holding that the TTAB should have found the Native Americans' petition barred by laches and that in any event the TTAB's cancellation decision was unsupported by substantial evidence. The Native Americans now appeal. Because we find that the district court applied the wrong standard in evaluating laches as to at least one of the Native Americans, we remand the record for the district court to revisit this issue.

I.

The Lanham Trademark Act provides protection to trademark owners. See generally 15 U.S.C. §§ 1051–1127, 1141–1141n. To take advantage of many of its provisions, trademark owners must register their marks with the Patent and Trademark Office. Not all marks, however, can be registered. Under 15 U.S.C. § 1052, the PTO must deny registration to certain types of marks, including those which, in subsection (a)'s language, "may disparage or falsely suggest a connection with persons, living or dead, institutions, beliefs, or national symbols, or bring them into contempt, or disrepute."

Another section, 15 U.S.C. § 1064(3), provides that if a mark is registered in violation of section 1052(a), "any person who believes that he is or will be damaged by the registration" may file a petition "[a]t any time" with the PTO to cancel the registration. This triggers a proceeding before the TTAB, which takes evidence and determines whether to cancel the mark. Yet another provision, 15 U.S.C. § 1069, states that "[i]n all ... proceedings equitable principles of laches, estoppel, and acquiescence, where applicable may be considered and applied."

This case concerns the registrations of six trademarks owned by Pro–Football, the corporate owner of the Washington Redskins football team, that include the word "Redskin." The first—"The Redskins" written in a stylized script—was registered in 1967, three more in 1974, another in 1978, and the sixth—the word "Redskinettes"—in 1990. Pro–Football uses all these marks in connection with goods and services related to its football team, including merchandise and entertainment services.

In 1992, seven Native Americans petitioned for cancellation of the registrations, claiming that the marks had disparaged Native Americans at the times of registration and had thus been registered in violation of section 1052(a). Pro–Football defended its marks, arguing among other things that laches barred the Native Americans' claim. Rejecting this argument, the TTAB found laches inapplicable due to the "broader interest—an interest beyond the personal interest being asserted by the present petitioners—in preventing a party from receiving the benefits of registration where a trial might show that respondent's marks hold a substantial segment of the population up to public ridicule."

On the merits, the parties presented the TTAB with a variety of evidence, including (1) dictionary entries for "redskin," some of which contained usage labels identifying the term as offensive and others of which did not; (2) book and media excerpts from the late nineteenth century through the 1940s that used the term "redskin" and portrayed Native Americans in a pejorative manner; (3) a study that found derogatory use of the term in Western-genre films from before 1980; (4) petitioners' testimony about their views of the term; (5) results from a 1996 survey of the general population and Native Americans that asked whether various terms, including "redskin," were offensive; (6) newspaper articles and game program guides from the 1940s onward using Native American imagery in connection with Washington's football team; and (7) testimony and documents relating to Native American protests, including one in 1972, aimed specifically at the team. In a lengthy opinion, the TTAB concluded that a preponderance of the evidence showed the term "redskin" as used by Washington's football team had disparaged Native Americans from at least 1967 onward. The TTAB cancelled the registrations. Cancellation did not require Pro–Football to stop using the marks, but it did limit the team's ability to go after infringers under the Lanham Act.

Pursuant to 15 U.S.C. § 1071(b), Pro–Football filed suit in the U.S. District Court for the District of Columbia, seeking reinstatement of its registrations on the grounds that: (1) laches barred the Native Americans' petition; (2) the TTAB's finding of disparagement was unsupported by substantial evidence; and (3) section 1052(a) violates the First and Fifth Amendments to the U.S. Constitution both facially and as applied by the TTAB. Although in suits challenging TTAB decisions parties may introduce new evidence in the district court, in this case the only such evidence of note related to laches. After discovery, the parties cross-moved for summary judgment. Without reaching the constitutional issues, the district court granted summary judgment to Pro–Football on the alternate grounds that laches barred the Native Americans' petition and that the TTAB's conclusion of disparagement was unsupported by substantial evidence. This appeal followed.

II.

An equitable doctrine, "[l]aches is founded on the notion that equity aids the vigilant and not those who slumber on their rights." NAACP v. NAACP Legal Def. & Educ. Fund, Inc., 753 F.2d 131, 137 (D.C.Cir.1985). This defense, which Pro–Football has the burden of proving, "requires proof of (1) lack of diligence by the party against whom the defense is asserted, and (2) prejudice to the party asserting the defense." Nat'l R.R. Passenger Corp. v. Morgan, 536 U.S. 101, 121–22, 122 S.Ct. 2061, 153 L.Ed.2d 106 (2002). In this case, the Native Americans contend both that the statute bars the defense of laches and that even were laches an available defense, Pro–Football has failed to prove it.

The Native Americans' statutory argument runs as follows: because section 1064(3) permits petitions alleging wrongful registration under section 1052(a) to be filed "[a]t any time," laches is not a valid defense in cancellation proceedings. We disagree. The words "[a]t any time" demonstrate only that the act imposes no statute of limitations for bringing petitions. Those words have nothing to do with what equitable defenses may be available during cancellation proceedings. Indeed, under the

Native Americans' logic, equitable defenses would never be available as long as cancellation petitions are brought within the specified statute of limitations—"[a]t any time" for petitions alleging wrongful registration under section 1052(a) or certain other grounds, and "[w]ithin five years" of registration for petitions brought for all other reasons, see id. § 1064(1). This would make section 1069, which explicitly permits consideration of laches and other equitable doctrines, meaningless as to cancellation petitions. For this reason, we disagree with the Third Circuit's suggestion that laches is not an available defense to cancellation petitions brought pursuant to section 1064(3). Instead, we join the Federal Circuit and our own district court, see Pro–Football, Inc. v. Harjo, 57 U.S.P.Q.2d 1140, 1145 (D.D.C.2000), in concluding that the statute does not bar the equitable defense of laches in response to section 1064(3) cancellation petitions.

The Native Americans also offer several reasons why, in their view, the district court erred in its assessment of laches in this case. At this point, we need only consider one: their claim that the district court mistakenly started the clock for assessing laches in 1967—the time of the first mark's registration—for *all* seven Native Americans, even though one, Mateo Romero, was at that time only one year old.

We agree with the Native Americans that this approach runs counter to the well-established principle of equity that laches runs only from the time a party has reached his majority. The Supreme Court first embraced this principle in 1792, holding in a case dealing with conflicting 1761 land grants that "*laches* cannot ... be imputed" as the "rights do not seem to have been abandoned; for in 1761, the children were infants, and were hardly of age, when this action was brought." Gander's Lessee v. Burns, 4 U.S.(4 Dall.) 122, 1 L.Ed. 768 (1792). The Court has since held to this principle. See Hoyt v. Sprague, 103 U.S. 613, 636–37, 26 L.Ed. 585 (1880) (evaluating laches "after [complainants] came of age"); * * * cf. Wagner v. Baird, 48 U.S. (7 How.) 234, 242, 12 L.Ed. 681 (1849) (noting that equity makes allowances for "circumstances to account for a party's neglect, such as imprisonment, infancy, coverture, or by having been beyond seas") * * *.

Pro–Football asserts that were we to apply this principle here, it "would logically mean that trademark owners could never have certainty, since a disparagement claim could be brought by an as yet unborn claimant for an unlimited time after a mark is registered." At the least, this assertion is overstated—only owners of those trademarks that may disparage a population that gains new members (as opposed to one that disparages, say, a single corporate entity), would face such a prospect. But even if registrations of some marks would remain perpetually at risk, it is unclear why this fact authorizes—let alone requires—abandonment of equity's fundamental principle that laches attaches only to parties who have unjustifiably delayed in bringing suit. Pro–Football forgets that "laches is not, like limitation, a mere matter of time," but rather turns on whether the party seeking relief "delayed inexcusably or unreasonably in filing suit" in a way that was "prejudicial" to the other party. Why should equity give more favorable treatment to parties that harm expanding numbers of people (in which case, under Pro–Football's theory, laches runs from the date of harm) than it gives to parties that harm only a few people (in which case laches runs from whenever those people are free of legal disabilities)? Why should equity elevate Pro–Football's perpetual security in the unlawful registration of a trademark over the interest of a Native American who challenged this registration without lack of diligence? Why should laches bar *all* Native Americans from challenging Pro–Football's "Redskins" trademark registrations because *some* Native Americans may have slept on their rights?

The fact that Pro–Football may never have security in its trademark registrations stems from Congress's decision not to set a statute of limitations and instead to authorize petitions for cancellation based on disparagement "[a]t any time." See 15 U.S.C. § 1064(3). Congress knew perfectly well how to set statutes of limitations—as noted earlier, it required that petitions for cancellations on many other grounds be brought "[w]ithin five years" of registration—but consciously declined to do so with respect to cancellation petitions based on disparagement. Indeed, Congress may well have denied companies the benefit of a statute of limitations for potentially disparaging trademarks for the very purpose of discouraging the use of such marks. * * * Cf. In re Riverbank Canning Co., 25 C.C.P.A. 1028, 95 F.2d 327, 329 (1938) (noting that the "field is almost limitless from which to select words for use as trade-marks, and one who uses debatable marks does so at the peril that his mark may not be entitled to registration").

Here, Romero has brought his own claim, and there is no reason why the laches of others should be imputed to him. In accordance with the context-specific approach required by equity, the district court should have measured both his delay and the resulting prejudice to Pro–Football based on the period between his attainment of majority and the filing of the 1992 cancellation petition.

In assessing prejudice, the district court should address both trial and economic prejudice. As to trial prejudice, the court should consider the extent to which Romero's post-majority delay resulted in a "loss of evidence or witnesses supporting [Pro–Football's] position." As to economic prejudice, we express no view as to how such prejudice should be measured where, as here, what is at stake is not the trademark owner's right to use the marks but rather the owner's right to Lanham Act protections that turn on registration. We encourage the district court to take briefing on whether economic prejudice should be measured based on the owner's investment in the marks during the relevant years, on whether the owner would have taken a different course of action—e.g., abandoned the marks—had the petitioner acted more diligently in seeking cancellation, or on some other measure.

III.

While retaining jurisdiction over the case, we remand the record to the district court for the purpose of evaluating whether laches bars Mateo Romero's claim.

NOTES

1. The district court found that the seven Native American petitioners all admitted to being long aware of the Washington Redskins team name and the name of the cheerleaders, the Redskinettes. Suzan Shown Harjo, born in 1945, was aware of the team name since she was a child. Others knew of the team as far back as World War II. Pro–Football, Inc. v. Harjo, 284 F.Supp.2d 96, 112 (D.D.C.2003), remanded, 415 F.3d 44 (D.C.Cir.2005). On remand, the district court found that Mateo Romero did not conduct due diligence in the nearly eight years after he reached the age of majority and that the NFL demonstrated prejudice due to the delay. Therefore, Romero's complaint, filed in 1992, was dismissed because it was barred by laches. Pro–Football, Inc. v. Harjo, 567 F.Supp.2d 46 (D.D.C.2008). Even if all of the plaintiffs involved in *Harjo* were barred by laches, what is to stop someone else from bringing the same claim again? Is it fair for the marks to remain perpetually at risk, as the circuit court acknowledges? See Lynda J. Oswald, Challenging the Registration of Scandalous and Disparaging Marks Under the Lanham Act: Who Has Standing to Sue?, 41 Am.Bus.L.J. 251 (2004).

2. For another example of laches as a bar to recovery, see Tillamook Country Smoker, Inc. v. Tillamook County Creamery Association, 465 F.3d 1102 (9th Cir.2006):

> The Tillamook County Creamery Association, the maker of the Tillamook brand of cheese for nearly a hundred years, has a beef with a company called Tillamook Country Smoker ["Smoker"], a purveyor of smoked meats and jerky. In 1976, Smoker began selling its meat products under its name. The cheese people had actual knowledge of Smoker's activities, but never said a word. Not only that, the cheese folks even sold Smoker's products in its own gift shop and its mail-order catalog.
>
> Twenty-five years later, when Smoker began selling its meat snacks in supermarkets, the cheese people for the first time claimed trademark infringement and sought to enjoin the meat people from making any further use of the Smoker name. The cheese people explain their quarter-century delay in taking action against Smoker by contending that they are victims of "progressive encroachment." The district court ruled that the cheese people are barred by laches. We agree.

3. In Environmental Defense Fund, Inc. v. Alexander, 614 F.2d 474 (5th Cir.), cert. denied, 449 U.S. 919, 101 S.Ct. 316, 66 L.Ed.2d 146 (1980), laches was found to be a good defense to a suit by an environmental group seeking to enjoin the Corps of Engineers from proceeding with construction of the Tennessee–Tombigbee Waterway with a 300 foot channel rather than the 170 foot channel authorized by Congress. The plaintiffs' response to the laches claim reduced to the assertion that they did not realize for a long period that it was illegal for the Corps to do what it had done. The court held that laches

did not depend on subjective awareness of the legal basis on which a claim could be made.

In examining the prejudicial aspect of laches in the case, the court balanced the equities, weighing the expenditure by the defendants against the benefits claimed by the plaintiffs. Is such balancing appropriate in all cases where laches is raised as a defense or only in public law cases?

Is there any conflict between this approach to laches in a public law environmental case and the emphasis in *Bateman Eichler* on furthering the intent of Congress? Wouldn't the intent of Congress in the *Environmental Defense Fund* case be furthered by rejecting the laches defense and requiring the Corps to build the channel authorized by Congress?

4. The prejudicial aspect of laches may affect certain claims, but not others. In Sanders v. Dooly County, 245 F.3d 1289 (11th Cir.2001), the Eleventh Circuit held that laches barred voters from seeking injunctive relief from racially gerrymandered voting districts when they waited to bring suit over six years after the first use of the districts. The officials were prejudiced by the fact that redistricting late in the decade would lead to back-to-back redistrictings and the available census data was old. However, the voters' claims for declaratory relief were not barred because there was no similar prejudice to officials. Edward Yorio, A Defense of Equitable Defenses, 51 Ohio St.L.J. 1201 (1990), provides an extensive analysis of the flexibility provided to courts in calculating damages or determining relief when equitable defenses come into play.

5. In Fitzgerald v. O'Connell, 120 R.I. 240, 386 A.2d 1384 (1978), a case in which specific performance for the purchase of real estate was prayed for, the court summarized the grounds on which laches is usually found:

> In the past, typical examples of prejudice that have supported the defense of laches have been the loss of evidence, a change of title, or the death of a key witness. Evidence that a defendant expended sums of money in constructing improvements has also been held to be sufficient prejudice to support a finding of laches. Where the subject matter is speculative and subject to rapid fluctuation in value, such as oil and mining properties, the doctrine of "speculative delay" may bar a claim to ownership if the claimant asserts his interest only after the risk has passed and the value of the property has become apparent.

6. It is a long-standing principle that the defense of laches is not available against the government when it acts in its sovereign capacity or where it has a direct pecuniary interest in a matter. Costello v. United States, 365 U.S. 265, 81 S.Ct. 534, 5 L.Ed.2d 551 (1961); United States v. Summerlin, 310 U.S. 414, 60 S.Ct. 1019, 84 L.Ed. 1283 (1940). But the immunity to the defense does not extend to those cases in which a government sues for the use and benefit of an individual or in which a government acts like a business in a commercial transaction or in its proprietary capacity. E.g., Clearfield Trust Co. v. United States, 318 U.S. 363, 63 S.Ct. 573, 87 L.Ed. 838 (1943). See also City of Sherrill v. Oneida Indian Nation of New York, 544 U.S.197, 125 S.Ct. 1478, 1492, 161 L.Ed.2d 386 (2005) (applying laches to two hundred year old claims of Indian tribe to revive its ancient sovereignty over certain lands because, "When a party belatedly asserts a right to present and future

sovereign control over territory, longstanding observances and settled expectations are prime considerations.").

The Second Circuit recently joined the Seventh Circuit in categorizing the:

> three main possibilities for when laches might apply against the United States: first, "that only the most egregious instances of laches can be used to abate a government suit"; second, "to confine the doctrine to suits against the government in which ... there is no statute of limitations"; and third, "to draw a line between government suits in which the government is seeking to enforce either on its own behalf or that of private parties what are in the nature of private rights, and government suits to enforce sovereign rights, and to allow laches as a defense in the former class of cases but not the latter."

Cayuga Indian Nation of New York v. Pataki, 413 F.3d 266, 278 (2d Cir.2005) (quoting United States v. Administrative Enterprises, 46 F.3d 670, 673 (7th Cir.1995)), cert. denied, 547 U.S. 1128, 126 S.Ct. 2022, 164 L.Ed.2d 780 (2006). Do these cases amount to saying that in theory governmental entities are not usually barred by laches but in fact the court is free to weigh the elements of a laches defense in order to reach a "just" result?

7. In contrast, the equitable estoppel cases involving the government do not appear to make these distinctions between the various capacities in which the government acts. Is there a sound reason for recognizing these differences in laches but not in estoppel?

It is probable that in *Environmental Defense Fund v. Alexander*, the Fund would claim that it was acting as a private attorney general representing the interests of all citizens in protecting public property and public rights. If the government is not subject to a laches defense when it acts in that capacity, why should the laches defense be applicable to plaintiffs like the Fund?

8. In an appropriate case, the unequivocal deadline of a statute of limitations may be lengthened against any defendant by the doctrine of "equitable tolling." Bowen v. City of New York, 476 U.S. 467, 106 S.Ct. 2022, 90 L.Ed.2d 462 (1986) (equitable tolling of statute of limitations appropriate where consistent with congressional intent and called for by the facts of the case); United States v. Clymore, 245 F.3d 1195 (10th Cir.2001) (equitable tolling allowed where claimant actively pursued his remedies by filing a defective pleading during the statutory period or where he was induced or tricked by his adversary's misconduct into allowing the filing deadline to pass). See Adam Bain & Ugo Colella, Interpreting Federal Statutes of Limitations, 37 Creighton L.Rev. 493 (2004) (considering how to determine when Congress intends to include or exclude equitable considerations in applying a statute of limitations).

Chapter 10

Attorney's Fees

■ ■ ■

Court-awarded attorney's fees are an important aspect of many types of litigation. Where fees are available, compiling, negotiating and litigating a fee request can take perhaps as much as a tenth of the time spent on the case, or more if fee issues are hotly disputed. Most awards are measured in the tens of thousands of dollars, but seven- and even eight-figure awards are not unknown in certain areas of the law, such as antitrust cases.

Attorney's fees are important for reasons beyond the time and money involved. Just as the availability of damages tends to encourage or discourage particular conduct by would-be plaintiffs and defendants, the possible award of fees affects, and is intended to affect, the behavior of the litigants and their attorneys. Fees can prompt litigation which could not be paid for otherwise or fund the expansion of a private firm or public interest group after a successful suit. The availability of fees for supervising compliance with a decree can radically enlarge the plaintiff's role in decree administration and enforcement. At the same time, the availability of fees to a prevailing defendant, or even the threat of such fees, can discourage suits altogether or prompt plaintiffs to delete from complaints less promising causes of action.

Working on a fee application is a time for retrospection. It forces the attorneys and the judge to think back on a train of events that often goes back years. Since the application should document how each block of hours was used, the process makes one recall events that were so intense when they happened that one would have never believed that they could be forgotten. Moreover, it is now the prevailing attorney who is on trial: did she use her time prudently or could she have conducted the case in a more cost-effective manner? Perhaps it is these elements, as much as the amounts of money involved, that makes the fee application so hotly contested in some cases; the case in chief is over, but the attorneys fight on, reviewing their own behavior in the suit.

Just as the fees stage of the case provides a thoughtful lawyer with a chance to come to terms with the end of a significant involvement, it also should provide students of remedies with a chance to reflect on what they have been studying. Fees litigation, after all, involves the courts self-consciously writing about the entire litigation process and its place in public policy. Moreover, it involves two themes of recurring importance in this book. One theme is equity. Once courts determine that they have the power to award fees, their thinking as to who gets them and in what amount represents the height of equitable decision-making. A second theme is the source and limits of remedial powers. What are the appropriate roles of the legislature and the courts in making fees decisions?

For citations to some of the voluminous attorney's fee literature, see Symposium, Contingency Fee Financing of Litigation in America, 47 DePaul L. Rev. 227 (1998); Judith Resnik, Dennis E. Curtis & Deborah R. Hensler, Individuals Within the Aggregate: Relationships, Representation, and Fees, 71 N.Y.U.L.Rev. 296 (1996). Comprehensive and updated treatment of the topic is available in: Mary F. Derfner & Arthur D. Wolf, Court Awarded Attorneys Fees (2003)(three volumes); Alba Conte, Attorney Fee Awards (3d ed.2004).

A. THE POWER OF THE COURT TO AWARD ATTORNEY'S FEES

PROBLEM: COUNTRY LODGE V. MILLER (REPRISED)
PAYING THE ATTORNEYS

Assume that Country Lodge prevails in its suit against Miller and wins a judgment for $8500 for lost profits. Country Lodge's attorney submits a bill for 28 hours of work at $100 per hour ($2800). If that bill is paid out of the judgment, has the law restored Country Lodge to its rightful position?

Now assume that Miller prevails because the court determines that she had a legal right to put biodegradable apple mash into the river. Miller's attorneys billed her $2000 to defend her in the suit Country Lodge brought. Should Country Lodge have to reimburse Miller for the cost of the defense?

The basic "American Rule" regarding attorney's fees has long been that each side pays its own unless the parties have agreed otherwise in advance, or unless a court is authorized by a statute or by a recognized equitable exception to shift payment of the fees to the opposing party. Arcambel v. Wiseman, 3 U.S. (3 Dall.) 306, 1 L.Ed. 613 (1796), is recognized as the judicial source of the American Rule. In contrast, under the "English Rule," prevailing parties recover fees as a matter of course from the losing party. The English Rule is followed in most common law countries and in Europe. See Robert G. Bone, The Economics of Civil Procedure 158–86 (2003) (considering whether the U.S. should adopt the English rule); Charles E. Hyde & Philip L. Williams, Necessary Costs and Expenditure Incentives Under the English Rule, 22 Int'l L. & Econ. 133 (2002) (under English rule, the sum awarded to winning party is actually based upon the amount the court finds was "necessary" for the attainment of justice); Virginia G. Maurer, Robert E. Thomas & Pamela A.

DeBooth, Attorney Fee Arrangements: The U.S. and Western European Perspectives, 19 Nw. J. Int'l L. & Bus. 272 (1999). Japan is one of the very few other major industrial countries in the world to have adopted the American Rule. See Kojima & Taniguchi, Access to Justice in Japan: Japanese National Report on Access to Justice, 1 Access to Justice 689, 705 (1978)(significant exception of fee shifting in favor of prevailing tort plaintiffs). Alaska is an example of the rare state where the English Rule has been adopted in a modified form—prevailing parties are partially compensated for productive work performed by their attorneys. Susanne Di Pietro & Teresa W. Carns, Alaska's English Rule: Attorney's Fee Shifting in Civil Cases, 13 Alaska L. Rev. 33 (1996).

The Supreme Court of the United States has offered several reasons for its adherence to the American Rule. These include: 1) to avoid discouraging the poor from bringing a meritorious lawsuit because of the possibility of having to pay the other side's fees; 2) not penalizing any party merely for bringing a suit; and 3) not imposing a great burden on judicial administration due to the inherent difficulty in computing fees. See, e.g., Fleischmann Distilling Corp. v. Maier Brewing Co., 386 U.S. 714, 87 S.Ct. 1404, 18 L.Ed.2d 475 (1967); Oelrichs v. Spain, 82 U.S. (15 Wall.) 211, 21 L.Ed. 43 (1872). Thus, "[i]n combination with the contingent fee, the American Rule has opened the courthouse door to individuals who would have lacked either adequate resources or ability to tolerate (let alone diversify) risk to bring a lawsuit." Stephen B. Burbank & Linda J. Silberman, Civil Procedure Reform in Comparative Context: The United States of America, 45 Am. J. Comp. L. 675, 691–92 (1997). On the other hand, because application of the American Rule means that a vindicated party usually pays its own fees, critics note that it fails to restore the parties to their rightful positions by making prevailing parties whole. E.g., Walter Olson & David Bernstein, Loser–Pays: Where Next?, 55 Md.L.Rev. 1161 (1996) (contending that more legislatures should experiment with the English Rule). Combined with that other unique American device, the contingency fee, the American Rule almost certainly contributes to the increased quantity and cost of litigation in the United States as compared to other industrialized countries. Robert A. Kagan, Adversarial Legalism: The American Way of Law (2001). See also Herbert M. Kritzer, Risks, Reputations and Rewards: Contingency Fee Legal Practice in the United States (2004) (using empirical data to assess to what degree the contingency fee contributes to litigiousness in the United States).

Perhaps because there are situations where the American Rule appears to be unfair, the courts have created and applied certain exceptions to the rule, and thereby have allowed some parties to obtain fees. These equitable exceptions include: (1) *Bad Faith*—where fees are awarded because the losing party has brought the suit in bad faith, vexatiously or for oppressive reasons, see, e.g., Kansas City Southern Ry. Co. v. Guardian Trust Co., 281 U.S. 1, 50 S.Ct. 194, 74 L.Ed. 659 (1930); (2) *Contempt*—where fees are awarded against a party who willfully disobeys a court order which leads to additional legal expenses for the prevailing party, see, e.g., Trustees v. Greenough, 105 U.S. (15 Otto) 527, 26 L.Ed. 1157 (1881); (3) *Common Fund*—where fees are awarded to a party who preserves or generates a common fund for a class of plaintiffs, see, e.g., Alyeska Pipeline Service Co. v. Wilderness Society, 421 U.S. 240, 95 S.Ct. 1612, 44 L.Ed.2d 141 (1975); and (4) *Substantial Benefit*—where fees are awarded to a prevailing party when the suit has benefited the defendant, such as in a shareholders' derivative suit, see, e.g., Mills v. Electric Auto–Lite Co., 396 U.S. 375, 90 S.Ct. 616, 24 L.Ed.2d 593 (1970). For discussion of exceptions to the American Rule, see Charles Silver, A Restitutionary Theory of Attorneys' Fees in Class Actions, 76 Cornell L.Rev. 656 (1991).

In *Alyeska*, the Supreme Court held that it must wait for Congress to create additional federal exceptions to the American Rule. Therefore, the Court rejected an opportunity to establish a new exception for federal courts, the "private attorney general" theory, which would shift fees in cases where private citizens brought suits benefiting society as a whole. The Court held that Congress had made specific and explicit provisions for the allowance of attorney's fees under selected statutes granting or protecting various federal rights. For the Court to make an exception where Congress had not would be an unwarranted intrusion of the judicial branch into the legislature's domain. Justice Marshall's dissent took the position that the private attorney general theory was simply a version of the substantial benefit theory, which the Court had previously recognized.

Congress responded to *Alyeska* by creating a plethora of targeted fee shifting statutes, including: Civil Rights Attorney's Fees Awards Act of 1976, 42 U.S.C. § 1988, Toxic Substance Control Act, 15 U.S.C. § 2619, Truth in Lending Act, 15 U.S.C. § 1640, and many more. Nearly two hundred federal statutes now authorize courts to award attorney's fees in particular circumstances. See Mary F. Derfner & Arthur D. Wolf, Court Awarded Attorney Fees at chs. 29–43 (2003). The bulk of attorney's fees litigation at the Supreme Court level now consists of interpreting congressional intent in these statutes.

While *Alyeska* means that most fee awards now are by statute, the judge-made exceptions are, of course, of continuing importance. For example, even after *Alyeska*, the Supreme Court has held consistently that the courts have the inherent power to make a lawyer who has litigated in bad faith pay fees. E.g., Chambers v. NASCO, Inc., 501 U.S. 32, 111 S.Ct. 2123, 115 L.Ed.2d 27 (1991)(can use inherent power in diversity case, even where the law of the state forbids fee shifting, to sanction bad faith litigation); Willy v. Coastal Corp., 503 U.S. 131, 112 S.Ct. 1076, 117 L.Ed.2d 280 (1992)(allowing fees under F.R.Civ.P. 11, even if it is later determined that the court did not have subject matter jurisdiction over the action). In addition, parties remain free to enter into enforceable contracts which would alter the American Rule in the event of a dispute. E.g., Travelers Casualty & Surety Co. v. Pacific Gas & Electric Co., 549 U.S. 443, 127 S.Ct. 1199, 167 L.Ed.2d 178 (2007) (upholding award of attorney's fees pursuant to contract in bankruptcy litigation, finding nothing in the Bankruptcy Code disallowing such relief).

The Supreme Court's interpretation of the American Rule in *Alyeska* is a limit on federal courts only; state courts have more freedom to create new equitable exceptions. Thus in Serrano v. Priest, 20 Cal.3d 25, 141 Cal.Rptr. 315, 569 P.2d 1303 (1977), the California Supreme Court adopted the private attorney general theory soon after *Alyeska* rejected it. But see Lloyd C. Anderson, Equitable Power to Award Attorney's Fees: The Seductive Appeal of "Benefit," 48 S.D.L.Rev. 217 (2003) (contending that both the private attorney general theory and the common benefit theory exceed the equitable power of state courts). When should state appellate judges create other exceptions?

BERNHARD v. FARMERS INSURANCE EXCHANGE

Supreme Court of Colorado, 1996
915 P.2d 1285

JUSTICE KOURLIS delivered the Opinion of the Court.

* * *

I.

This is an action by the insured, Sandra Bernhard, against her automobile liability insurer, Farmers Insurance Exchange ("Farmers"), for bad faith breach of insurance contract. * * *

On two separate occasions the [plaintiffs] made time-limited offers to settle their claims against Bernhard: first for the applicable policy limits of $200,000 and later, for $230,000. Farmers did not accept either of these settlement offers. At trial, the jury found against Bernhard * * * and awarded the [plaintiffs] damages substantially in excess of the policy limits. * * *

Bernhard brought this suit for bad faith breach of contract against Farmers for its failure to settle with the [plaintiffs]. She sought a damage award for the excess judgment of $82,000 and additional damages for emotional distress. The case initially resulted in a hung jury but was retried in July of 1992. The jury did not award Bernhard any damages for emotional distress, but did award her $108,911.30 for the excess judgment and for the attorney fees she had incurred in bringing the bad faith breach of contract case against Farmers.

Farmers moved for a new trial or to amend the judgment, arguing that the jury could not award attorney fees. Bernhard agreed that the jury's verdict should not have included attorney fees, but filed a separate motion seeking an award of attorney fees from the court. At the hearing, the trial court judge awarded Bernhard $32,000 for attorney fees incurred in the pursuit of her bad faith claim against Farmers. Farmers appealed and the court of appeals reversed the trial court's award of attorney fees.

* * * We hold that, unless specifically provided for in the insurance contract, attorney fees are not recoverable upon successful litigation of a bad faith breach of insurance contract claim. We therefore affirm the court of appeals' reversal of the trial court's award of attorney fees to Bernhard and remand the case for proceedings consistent with this opinion.

II.

As a general rule, in the absence of a statute, court rule, or private contract to the contrary, attorney fees are not recoverable by the prevailing party in either a contract or tort action. This reasoning is based on the American rule, which requires each party in a lawsuit to bear its own legal expenses.

* * *

Colorado does recognize several exceptions to the general rule,[1] however, Bernhard's claim for attorney fees does not fit within any established exception. Permitting Bernhard to recover attorney fees would represent the creation of a new exception to the American rule: a function better addressed by the legislative than the judicial branch of government.

Bernhard argues that her situation is analogous to that discussed in Farmers Group, Inc. v. Trimble, 658 P.2d 1370 (Colo.App.1982) (*Trimble I*), Farmers Group, Inc. v. Trimble, 691 P.2d 1138 (Colo.1984) (*Trimble II*), and Farmers Group, Inc. v. Trimble, 768 P.2d 1243 (Colo.App.1988) (*Trimble III*), and that since attorney fees were awarded in that line of cases, they should be awarded in her case as well. Bernhard, however, misapplies the *Trimble* cases.

The *Trimble* cases were related to a third party personal injury lawsuit brought against the insured, Trimble, based on several claims including one of negligent entrustment. Trimble's insurer, Farmers Group, Inc., was contractually required to provide for Trimble's legal defense. Farmers Group, Inc., did hire an attorney to defend Trimble. However, while this third party case was ongoing, Farmers Group, Inc., filed a declaratory judgment action against Trimble seeking a determination that Trimble's policy did not provide coverage for the negligent entrustment claim. As a result, Trimble was unable to discuss the third party proceedings with the attorney retained by Farmers Group, Inc., and because he was facing an imminent deposition in the third party suit, he was forced to retain a private attorney to defend himself. * * *

---

[1]. Exceptions to the American rule recognized in Colorado include those based on: the "common fund" doctrine; a party's bad faith and lack of candor in dealing with the court; breach of fiduciary duty or breach of trust; and a party's wrongful act proximately causing the wronged party to become engaged in litigation with others.

In this last exception, the fees incurred by the wronged party in the third party suit may be recovered in a later action against the wrongdoer, whereas the fees incurred in bringing the actual action against the wrongdoer are not recoverable. This exception encompasses attorney fees arising out of a variety of actions including: a quiet title action; an action in fraud; and a malicious prosecution; see also Technical Computer Servs., Inc. v. Buckley, 844 P.2d 1249 (Colo.App.1992) (attorney fees incurred in defending false criminal charges are recoverable in later malicious prosecution action against party that caused false charges to be brought, but fees incurred in bringing the malicious prosecution action itself are not recoverable).

* * *

The court of appeals in *Trimble I* held that Trimble could recover his costs in hiring an attorney to defend him against the claims brought by the third party. * * * [I]n *Trimble I,* Trimble sought reimbursement for the fees that he was forced to incur due to the insurer's failure to provide counsel. These fees were a specific and direct benefit of the contract breached by the insurer. Thus, they were not incidental to the bringing of the lawsuit but rather were the subject of the action itself.

* * *

A.

In *Trimble II,* this court concluded that a quasi-fiduciary relationship exists between an insurer and insured within the context of defense of a third party claim.

Attorney fees may be recoverable in an action for breach of fiduciary duty as a recognized exception to the American rule. * * * This court reasoned that, as in a breach of trust action, the goal in a breach of fiduciary duty action is to make the injured party whole. Hence, the injured party is entitled to recover attorney fees if necessary to restore that party to his or her pre-injury status.

The question raised here is whether an action based on a breach of a *quasi*-fiduciary duty should be analogized to an action based on breach of a fiduciary duty and thus be treated as an exception to the American rule. We find significant and dispositive distinctions between the quasi-fiduciary duty of an insurer and the duty of a true fiduciary, and conclude that the exception does not apply.

In *Trimble II* we held that the quasi-fiduciary duty of an insurer toward an insured stems specifically from the insurer's control over the defense of actions brought against the insured by third parties. The determination of whether a true fiduciary relationship exists depends upon the degree of control exercised by the fiduciary over the affairs of the other person. The quasi-fiduciary relationship between an insurer and an insured is limited to areas in which the insurer exercises a strong degree of control over the insured's interests. Even though the insurer may have control over the defense of a third party lawsuit, the insurer lacks any such control over many other aspects of its relationship with the insured. Thus, we refrain from characterizing the insurer/insured relationship as quasi-fiduciary for all purposes, for doing so would impose duties on the insurer that this court has not endorsed.

Furthermore, even in the context of defending a third party lawsuit, the relationship between an insurer and an insured falls short of a true fiduciary relationship. An insured can regain some control over her defense by retaining independent counsel, either at her own cost and expense or by later suing the insurer for collection of those fees. Also, the extent of the duty required of an insurer in the quasi-fiduciary relationship differs from what would be required in a true fiduciary relationship. One who is acting as a fiduciary for another has the duty to act with the utmost good faith and loyalty on behalf of, and for the benefit of, the other person. The duty required of an insurer towards the insured is much more constrained. In *Trimble II,* this court held that an insurer's actions are governed by general principles of negligence and that the quasi-fiduciary relationship between an insurer and its insured requires only reasonable conduct on the part of the insurer, nothing more.

The insurer-insured relationship is a contractual one, created for the mutual benefit of the parties. The insured retains some responsibilities for, and control over, decision-making that distinguish the relationship from one of a true fiduciary nature. To hold otherwise would be to deprive both the insured and the insurer of the mutuality of the contract. Thus, we conclude that the duty of an insurer and that of a true fiduciary are not similar enough to warrant including the quasi-fiduciary duty of the insurer within the breach of fiduciary duty exception to the American rule.

B.

In addition to finding a quasi-fiduciary relationship between the insurer and the insured, *Trimble II* found an implied covenant of good faith and fair dealing in every insurance contract. It is from this implied covenant of good faith and fair dealing that bad faith breach of insurance contract as a tort cause of action may arise.

Bernhard argues that, based on *Trimble II,* good faith and fair dealing is a benefit of her insurance contract, and that the language in *Trimble III* allows recovery of attorney fees whenever an insured reasonably hires an attorney to obtain benefits of the contract. We disagree with both steps of Bernhard's argument.

First, we disagree with her assertion that good faith and fair dealing is a benefit of the insurance contract. *Trimble II* imposes a legal duty on an insurer to deal with its insured in good faith. It does not find good faith or fair dealing to be a benefit of the contract itself. Instead, *Trimble II* creates a tort cause of action based on a bad faith breach of an insurance contract, but it does not give rise to a claim that failure to deal in good faith is a denial of a contract benefit.

We also disagree with Bernhard's contention that *Trimble III* allows recovery of attorney fees when any benefit of a contract has been denied. *Trimble III* holds, in pertinent part, that expenditure of attorney's fees in defending a third party tort action could serve as the economic loss from which emotional distress damages resulted. In so holding, the court of appeals states "When an insured is reasonably compelled to hire an attorney to obtain benefits tortiously denied by his insurer, the attorney fees so incurred constitute economic loss caused by the tort and are recoverable as damages." *Trimble III,* 768 P.2d at 1246 (citing Brandt v. Superior Court, 37 Cal.3d 813, 210 Cal.Rptr. 211, 693 P.2d 796 (1985)).

We disapprove this particular language in *Trimble III* and its reliance on *Brandt.* The *Brandt* case stands for a much broader exception than we choose to adopt in this case. *Brandt* concerned an insured who was injured in an accident. The insured made a demand upon the disability insurer for payment of benefits, but the insurer unreasonably refused to pay. The insured then filed an action against the insurer for: 1) breach of contract, 2) breach of the covenant of good faith and fair dealing, and 3) violation of California statutory prohibitions against unfair claims practices. Under his cause of action for breach of good faith and fair dealing, the insured included as damages the attorney fees he incurred in connection with his breach of contract claim. The insurer successfully moved to strike the portion of the complaint requesting attorney fees. The California Supreme Court then exercised jurisdiction over the case and issued a writ of mandate directing the trial court to reinstate the demand for attorney fees as damages.

The reasoning employed by the *Brandt* majority in allowing the claim for attorney fees to stand was as follows: if the insurer's tortious conduct compelled the insured to retain an attorney to obtain benefits due under the contract, then the attorney fees would be recoverable damages proximately caused by the tort. This diverges from the exception recognized in Colorado and applied in the *Trimble* line of cases. In the *Trimble* cases, the insured was forced to provide his own legal defense even though his insurance policy explicitly stated that the insurer would provide it. Thus, the attorney fees he sought to recover represented the actual legal defense the insurer should have provided for him. Under the *Brandt* facts, however, the insured did not hire legal representation in order to defend against a third party claim, but instead hired legal representation to force the insurer to provide him with disability payments. Thus, while the disability payments were an actual benefit of the contract denied to him, the attorney fees were only incidental to his efforts to gain this benefit.

We find the dissent in *Brandt* persuasive in reasoning that if recovery were allowed for attorney fees stemming from a suit to enforce any wrongful withholding of benefits under an insurance contract, this would effectively swallow the entire American rule on attorney fees. Unless we are prepared to abandon the American rule for the English rule of automatically awarding attorney fees to the prevailing party, it would be difficult to carve out an exception that allows an award of attorney fees that are incidental to the bringing of a bad faith breach of contract action. Attorney fees are incurred by most parties to most lawsuits. If the goal were always to make the prevailing party genuinely whole, these fees would be an element of damage. But such is not the law. Thus, we confine the applicable exception in Colorado to where the attorney fees directly represent a benefit of the contract wrongfully denied by the opposing party.

* * *

SCOTT, J., does not participate.

JUSTICE LOHR dissenting:

* * *

II.

* * *

A.

* * *

In arriving at our decision in *Trimble II,* we held that "[t]he standard of conduct on the part of the insurer when dealing with claims arising under an insurance policy is shaped by, and must reflect, the quasi-fiduciary relationship that exists between the insurer and the insured by virtue of the insurance contract." We stated: "Particularly when handling claims of third persons that are brought against the insured, an insurance company stands in a position similar to that of a fiduciary." We reasoned that this is so because under the insurance contract, "the insurer retains the absolute right to control the defense of actions brought against the insured, and the insured is therefore precluded from interfering with the investigation and negotiation for settlement."

The issue now before us is whether an insured can recover attorney fees incurred in successfully pursuing a bad faith breach of insurance contract claim against an insurer. * * *

The majority asserts that the insurer lacks any control over many aspects of its relationship with the insured and therefore the majority "refrain[s] from characterizing the insurer/insured relationship as quasi-fiduciary for all purposes." This statement creates confusion regarding the nature of the quasi-fiduciary relationship and I believe misconstrues the term as intended by this Court in *Trimble II*. The relevant context for consideration of the relationship of insurer and insured for purposes of the present case is the defense of third party claims against the insured. In this context, the analogy of the relationship of insurer and insured to a fiduciary relationship is at its strongest. This is because of the degree of control ceded to the insurer by the insured pursuant to the insurance contract in conducting such defense. The fact that in other aspects of their relationship the insurer may have no such duty to its insured is not relevant for the purpose of the present case.

In refusing to recognize an analogy to a fiduciary relationship, the majority determines that the relationship between the insurer and the insured is simply a contractual relationship. However, I believe two important distinctions exist in this type of contractual relationship. First, we have recognized the disparity of control between the contracting parties in the insurance contract as contrasted with that existing in other contractual relationships. Second, a consumer's expectation in entering into an insurance contract is to be freed from liability and to obtain security from economic catastrophe. Therefore, although the relationship is founded in contract, a quasi-fiduciary relationship arises because of the unique characteristics of the mutual obligations and expectations of the parties.

* * *

In the context in which the quasi-fiduciary duty applies, the insurer must act in good faith and take the interests of the insured into account in its conduct of the defense and of settlement negotiations. This is only a natural and fair consequence of the terms of the insurance contract, where the insured relinquishes control of the defense of third party claims and the insurer assumes responsibility for the defense.

Because a breach of a fiduciary duty is a recognized exception to the American rule, I likewise would include breach of the heightened duty associated with the quasi-fiduciary relationship of an insurance contract as an exception to the American rule that generally bars the recovery of attorney fees in a contract or tort action.

B.

The majority opinion disagrees with Bernhard's assertion that good faith and fair dealing is a benefit of her insurance contract and that the language in *Trimble III* allows recovery of attorney fees whenever an insured reasonably hires an attorney to obtain the benefits of such contract.

Trimble III was an appeal by the insurer following a verdict for Trimble on his claim for bad faith breach of insurance contract following our remand in *Trimble II*. The court of appeals recognized that the damages for emotional distress at issue on appeal could be awarded only if sufficient economic loss was also established. The court held that the attorney fees incurred by the insured "to obtain the benefits tortiously denied by his insurer ... constitute economic loss caused by the tort and are recoverable as damages." *Trimble III,* 768 P.2d at 1246. In so holding, the court of appeals relied upon Brandt v. Superior Court, 37 Cal.3d 813, 210 Cal.Rptr. 211, 693 P.2d 796 (1985).

Brandt involved an action by an employee who was a beneficiary of a group disability policy provided by his employer. The employee became totally disabled, but the insurance carrier refused to pay any benefits. The employee filed a complaint, alleging both a contract claim, seeking to be paid the benefits due under the policy, and a tort claim, seeking additional damages based upon the insurer's breach of the covenant of good faith and fair dealing. The court in *Brandt* held that an insured is entitled to recover attorney fees in an action to obtain benefits under the policy, including attorney fees when the insurer's tortious conduct reasonably compels the insured to retain an attorney to obtain the benefits due under a policy. The court reasoned that "[w]hen an insurer's tortious conduct reasonably compels the insured to retain an attorney to obtain the benefits due under a policy, it follows that the insurer should be liable in a tort action for that expense." The court in *Brandt* allowed recovery of attorney fees as damages proximately caused by the tort.

Similarly, in *Trimble III,* the court of appeals determined that attorney fees are proper damages where the insured "is reasonably compelled to hire an attorney to obtain benefits tortiously denied by his insurer" because these fees "constitute economic loss caused by the tort and are recoverable as damages." *Trimble III* stated this principle of law relying on *Brandt* without any limitations as the majority here now wishes to establish. Nowhere did either *Trimble III* or *Brandt* limit the recovery of attorney fees to securing benefits explicitly listed in the contract. Farmer's tortious conduct compelled Bernhard to hire an attorney to obtain the benefit of the implied covenant of good faith and fair dealing. According to the explicit language in *Brandt,* relied upon and restated in *Trimble III,* Bernhard is entitled to recover her attorney fees.

* * *

NOTES

1. Should the *Bernhard* decision have any effect on the availability of punitive damages? Of emotional distress damages? In terms of restoring someone to the rightful position, is it better to compensate for these two items of non-pecuniary damage, for the out-of-pocket attorney's fees, or for all three?

2. The majority in Brandt v. Superior Court, 37 Cal.3d 813, 817, 210 Cal.Rptr. 211, 213, 693 P.2d 796, 798 (1985), reasoned, "What we consider here is attorney's fees that are recoverable as damages resulting from a tort in the same way that medical fees would be part of the damages in a personal injury action." In contrast, the dissent in *Brandt,* which the *Bernhard* majority found persuasive, rejected the contention that an insured has separate causes of action against the insurance company for breach of contract and for violation of the duty of good faith and fair dealing:

> The contract suit is regarded as if it were a prior suit and the tort suit as if it were a later suit; since the insurer's tort is what caused it to deny benefits, the suit to recover benefits was occasioned by the tort and therefore in the tort suit the insured should be allowed to recover the attorney fees he expended in the contract suit.

> But this analysis appears to mistake the nature of the bad faith tort. When an insurance company withholds payments in bad faith its actions amount to both a breach of contract and a tort, but two separate breaches of duty are not involved. The single duty breached—the covenant of good faith and fair dealing—"springs from the contractual relationship between the parties." The plaintiff may bring suit on both contract and tort theories, but ultimately he must elect which remedy to pursue. There simply is no collateral suit from which attorney fees may be recovered.

Id. at 823, 210 Cal.Rptr. at 217, 693 P.2d at 802. Is this class of tort cases truly distinguishable from all others? Or, would the exception the *Brandt* court and the *Bernhard* dissent saw ultimately swallow the American rule? See Dan B. Dobbs, 1 Law of Remedies § 3.10(3) (2d ed.1993).

3. The law of other states is mixed on whether an insured may recover attorney's fees incurred to obtain benefits due under a policy and those incurred in prosecuting a bad faith claim against the insurer to obtain damages that are not included in the policy benefits. See, e.g., Polselli v. Nationwide Mutual Fire Insurance Co., 126 F.3d 524 (3d Cir.1997) (predicting that Pennsylvania would permit recovery of fees); Biegler v. American Family Mutual Insurance Co., 621 N.W.2d 592 (2001) (South Dakota permits recovery of fees from insurance company pursuant to statute); Campbell v. State Farm Mutual Automobile Insurance Co., 2001 Ut. 89, 65 P.3d 1134, 1169 (2001) (permitting recovery of fees from insurers in these circumstances), rev'd on other grounds, 538 U.S. 408, 123 S.Ct. 1513, 155 L.Ed.2d 585 (2003); Fleming v. Quigley, 2003 Guam 4, 2003 WL 554665 (Guam Terr. 2003) (same). Compare Tynes v. Bankers Life Co., 224 Mont. 350, 730 P.2d 1115 (1986) (rejecting recovery of fees).

4. The New Jersey Supreme Court has created a similar exception to the American Rule outside of the insurance context. That court allows the recovery of fees expended when an executor or trustee of an estate reaps substantial financial benefit from the exercise of undue influence and the estate then has to incur attorney's fees in litigation against the fiduciary to recover assets. In re Niles, 176 N.J. 282, 823 A.2d 1 (2003).

5. In a case somewhat analogous to *Bernhard*, the U.S. Supreme Court has held that attorney's fees and related expenses may not be recovered by a private party under CERCLA as a "response cost." The Court's majority concluded that the Act did not clearly provide for the recovery of attorney's fees expended in litigating a cost recovery action. Justice Scalia's dissent (joined by Justices Blackmun and Thomas) contended that it was sufficient that the Act specifically allowed for the recovery of the costs of "enforcement activities" as part of the definition of the "necessary costs of response" to the release of a hazardous substance. All of the justices agreed that work done by attorneys in identifying other potentially responsible parties was a recoverable "response cost" because such work could be performed by any number of professionals (such as engineers) and benefited the cleanup effort rather than just reallocating the costs. Key Tronic Corp. v. United States, 511 U.S. 809, 114 S.Ct. 1960, 128 L.Ed.2d 797 (1994). Sealy Connecticut, Inc. v. Litton Industries, Inc., 93 F.Supp.2d 177, 189–93 (D.Conn.2000), reviews several cases that have analyzed *Key Tronic* in determining which non-litigation fees paid to attorneys are recoverable. To be recoverable under CERCLA, according to the district court's reading of the cases, "an attorney's work must therefore be closely tied to the actual cleanup, must benefit the entire cleanup and not cost allocation or liability shifting, and cannot be primarily protective of the plaintiff's interests." Id. at 190. See also Note, Key Tronic Corp. v. United States: Ratifying an Inequitable Distribution of Private Party Costs Under Superfund by Refusing to Shift Attorneys' Fees, 4 Geo. Mason L. Rev. 113 (1995) (calling on Congress to permit recovery of fees).

6. Sometimes courts do hold that attorney's fees are included within other legislatively created categories. For example, the Oregon Supreme Court has held that an act limiting the "liability" of a public entity to $100,000

applies to damages, costs and attorney's fees in an employment discrimination action. Griffin v. Tri–County Metropolitan Transportation District, 318 Or. 500, 870 P.2d 808 (1994). The phrase "general and special damages," when used in a revised version of the same statute, does not, however, include attorney's fees. Anglin v. Department of Corrections, 160 Or.App. 463, 982 P.2d 547 (1999).

B. THE PARTIES THAT CONGRESS HAS MADE ELIGIBLE FOR ATTORNEY'S FEES

Congress authorizes the award of fees for a variety of reasons. First, Congress may wish to encourage citizens to bring actions against the government to ensure compliance with congressional directives. Many environmental and civil rights fee awards provisions are designed to foster citizen oversight of government. E.g., Clean Air Act, 42 U.S.C. § 7604(a)(2)(d). Second, Congress sometimes encourages citizens to bring enforcement actions against other private parties because, even though government enforces the law, private attorneys general have the resources, information, or interest needed to get the job done or because the rights involved are sufficiently important that private persons should not have to wait upon government action. E.g., Clayton Act, 15 U.S.C. § 15, False Claims Act, 31 U.S.C. § 3730, Clean Air Act, 42 U.S.C. § 7604(a)(1). Third, Congress may want to make justice more accessible to those who are not rich. E.g., Equal Access to Justice Act, 5 U.S.C. § 504, 28 U.S.C. § 2412. Fourth, Congress may want to deter and punish those who abuse the judicial process. E.g., 28 U.S.C. § 1927; cf. F.R.Civ.P. 11, 16(f), 26(g), 37(a)(4), 56(g). Finally, the Constitution may require it, as in providing counsel for indigents prosecuted for crimes. Criminal Justice Act, 18 U.S.C. § 3006A. (The payment of such fees, unlike most other federal statutes affecting attorney's fees, does not turn on whether the defendant prevails at trial and is not designed to encourage litigation.)

Congress has not seen fit to serve these purposes uniformly. Sometimes statutes that would seem to fit within the pattern of those under which fees are awarded do not authorize fees. E.g., National Environmental Policy Act, 42 U.S.C. § 4331 et seq. It must also be emphasized that statutes that authorize fees do not necessarily allow them for all actions brought under the statute. For instance, fees may be unavailable to certain successful parties. Because there are differences between the fee provisions under many of these statutes, caution must be used in carrying results under one statute over to a case under another. It is necessary to check the specific language, legislative history, and interpretation of each fee provision. It is also important to plead clearly entitlement to relief on the merits under statutes that provide for an award of fees and to request attorney's fees as a specific item in the prayer for relief.

In addition to judgments on the merits, we have held that settlement agreements enforced through a consent decree may serve as the basis for an award of attorney's fees. See Maher v. Gagne, 448 U.S. 122, 100 S.Ct. 2570, 65 L.Ed.2d 653 (1980). Although a consent decree does not always include an admission of liability by the defendant, it nonetheless is a court-ordered "chang[e][in] the legal relationship between [the plaintiff] and the defendant." Texas State Teachers Assn. v. Garland Independent School Dist., 489 U.S. 782, 792, 109 S.Ct. 1486, 103 L.Ed.2d 866 (1989) (citing *Hewitt,* supra, and Rhodes v. Stewart, 488 U.S. 1, 3–4, 109 S.Ct. 202, 102 L.Ed.2d 1 (1988) (per curiam)).[7] These decisions, taken together, establish that enforceable judgments on the merits and court-ordered consent decrees create the "material alteration of the legal relationship of the parties" necessary to permit an award of attorney's fees. [*Garland*]; see also *Hanrahan,* supra ("[I]t seems clearly to have been the intent of Congress to permit . . . an interlocutory award only to a party who has established his entitlement to some relief on the merits of his claims, either in the *trial court* or *on appeal*"(emphasis added)).

We think, however, the "catalyst theory" falls on the other side of the line from these examples. It allows an award where there is no judicially sanctioned change in the legal relationship of the parties. * * * A defendant's voluntary change in conduct, although perhaps accomplishing what the plaintiff sought to achieve by the lawsuit, lacks the necessary judicial *imprimatur* on the change. Our precedents thus counsel against holding that the term "prevailing party" authorizes an award of attorney's fees *without* a corresponding alteration in the legal relationship of the parties.

The dissenters chide us for upsetting "long-prevailing *Circuit* precedent." (emphasis added). But, as Justice Scalia points out in his concurrence, several Courts of Appeals have relied upon dicta in our prior cases in approving the "catalyst theory." Now that the issue is squarely presented, it behooves us to reconcile the plain language of the statutes with our prior *holdings*. We have only awarded attorney's fees where the plaintiff has received a judgment on the merits or obtained a court-ordered consent decree—we have not awarded attorney's fees where the plaintiff has secured the reversal of a directed verdict or acquired a judicial pronouncement that the defendant has violated the Constitution unaccompanied by "*judicial* relief," *Hewitt* (emphasis added). Never have we awarded attorney's fees for a nonjudicial "alteration of actual circumstances." While urging an expansion of our precedents on this front, the dissenters would simultaneously abrogate the "merit" requirement of our prior cases and award attorney's fees where the plaintiff's claim "was at

---

7. We have subsequently characterized the *Maher* opinion as also allowing for an award of attorney's fees for private settlements. But this dicta ignores that *Maher* only "held that fees *may* be assessed . . . after a case has been settled by the entry of a consent decree." Evans v. Jeff D., 475 U.S. 717, 720, 106 S.Ct. 1531, 89 L.Ed.2d 747 (1986). Private settlements do not entail the judicial approval and oversight involved in consent decrees. And federal jurisdiction to enforce a private contractual settlement will often be lacking unless the terms of the agreement are incorporated into the order of dismissal. See Kokkonen v. Guardian Life Ins. Co. of America, 511 U.S. 375, 114 S.Ct. 1673, 128 L.Ed.2d 391 (1994).

least colorable" and "not ... groundless" (internal quotation marks and citation omitted). We cannot agree that the term "prevailing party" authorizes federal courts to award attorney's fees to a plaintiff who, by simply filing a nonfrivolous but nonetheless potentially meritless lawsuit (it will never be determined), has reached the "sought-after destination" without obtaining any judicial relief.

* * *

Petitioners finally assert that the "catalyst theory" is necessary to prevent defendants from unilaterally mooting an action before judgment in an effort to avoid an award of attorney's fees. They also claim that the rejection of the "catalyst theory" will deter plaintiffs with meritorious but expensive cases from bringing suit. We are skeptical of these assertions, which are entirely speculative and unsupported by any empirical evidence (e.g., whether the number of suits brought in the Fourth Circuit has declined, in relation to other Circuits, since the decision in *S–1 and S–2*).

Petitioners discount the disincentive that the "catalyst theory" may have upon a defendant's decision to voluntarily change its conduct, conduct that may not be illegal. "The defendants' potential liability for fees in this kind of litigation can be as significant as, and sometimes even more significant than, their potential liability on the merits," Evans v. Jeff D., 475 U.S. 717, 734, 106 S.Ct. 1531, 89 L.Ed.2d 747 (1986), and the possibility of being assessed attorney's fees may well deter a defendant from altering its conduct.

And petitioners' fear of mischievous defendants only materializes in claims for equitable relief, for so long as the plaintiff has a cause of action for damages, a defendant's change in conduct will not moot the case. Even then, it is not clear how often courts will find a case mooted: "It is well settled that a defendant's voluntary cessation of a challenged practice does not deprive a federal court of its power to determine the legality of the practice" unless it is "absolutely clear that the allegedly wrongful behavior could not reasonably be expected to recur." Friends of Earth, Inc. v. Laidlaw Environmental Services (TOC), Inc., 528 U.S. 167, 189, 120 S.Ct. 693, 145 L.Ed.2d 610 (2000) (internal quotation marks and citations omitted). If a case is not found to be moot, and the plaintiff later procures an enforceable judgment, the court may of course award attorney's fees. Given this possibility, a defendant has a strong incentive to enter a settlement agreement, where it can negotiate attorney's fees and costs.
* * *

We have also stated that "[a] request for attorney's fees should not result in a second major litigation," Hensley v. Eckerhart, 461 U.S. 424, 437, 103 S.Ct. 1933, 76 L.Ed.2d 40 (1983), and have accordingly avoided an interpretation of the fee-shifting statutes that would have "spawn[ed] a second litigation of significant dimension," *Garland*. Among other things, a "catalyst theory" hearing would require analysis of the defendant's subjective motivations in changing its conduct, an analysis that "will likely depend on a highly factbound inquiry and may turn on reasonable inferences from the nature and timing of the defendant's change in conduct." Although we do not doubt the ability of district courts to perform the nuanced "three thresholds" test required by the "catalyst theory"—whether the claim was colorable rather than groundless; whether the lawsuit was a substantial rather than an insubstantial cause of the defendant's change in conduct; whether the defendant's change in conduct was motivated by the plaintiff's threat of victory rather than threat of expense—it is clearly not a formula for "ready administrability." Burlington v. Dague, 505 U.S. 557, 566, 112 S.Ct. 2638, 120 L.Ed.2d 449 (1992).

Given the clear meaning of "prevailing party" in the fee-shifting statutes, we need not determine which way these various policy arguments cut. In *Alyeska,* we said that Congress had not "extended any roving authority to the Judiciary to allow counsel fees as costs or otherwise whenever the courts might deem them warranted." To disregard the clear legislative language and the holdings of our prior cases on the basis of such policy arguments would be a similar assumption of a "roving authority." For the reasons stated above, we hold that the "catalyst theory" is not a permissible basis for the award of attorney's fees under the FHAA and ADA.

The judgment of the Court of Appeals is

Affirmed.

JUSTICE SCALIA, with whom JUSTICE THOMAS joins, concurring.

I join the opinion of the Court in its entirety, and write to respond at greater length to the contentions of the dissent.

I

"Prevailing party" is not some newfangled legal term invented for use in late–20th-century fee-shifting statutes. "[B]y the long established practice and universally recognized rule of the common law, in actions at law, the prevailing party is entitled to recover a judgment for costs...." Mansfield, C. & L.M.R. Co. v. Swan, 111 U.S. 379, 387, 4 S.Ct. 510, 28 L.Ed. 462 (1884).

* * *

It is undoubtedly true, as the dissent points out by quoting a nonlegal dictionary, that the word "prevailing" can have other meanings in other contexts: "prevailing winds" are the winds that predominate, and the "prevailing party" in an election is the party that wins the election. But when "prevailing party" is used by courts or legislatures in the context of a lawsuit, it is a term of art. It has traditionally—and to my knowledge, prior to enactment of the first of the statutes at issue here, *invariably*— meant the party that wins the suit or obtains a finding (or an admission) of liability. * * * Words that have acquired a specialized meaning in the legal context must be accorded their *legal* meaning.

* * *

II

* * *

The dissent points out that petitioners' object in bringing their suit was not to obtain "a judge's approbation," but to "stop enforcement of a [West Virginia] rule;" True enough. But not even the dissent claims that if a petitioner accumulated attorney's fees in preparing a threatened complaint, but *never filed it* prior to the defendant's voluntary cessation of its offending behavior, the wannabe-but-never-was plaintiff could recover fees; that would be countertextual, since the fee-shifting statutes require that there be an "action" or "proceeding,"—which in legal parlance (though not in more general usage) means *a lawsuit*. See [dissent at p. 923] (concluding that a party should be deemed prevailing as a result of a "*postcomplaint* payment or change in conduct"). Does that not leave achievement of the broad congressional purpose identified by the dissent just as unsatisfactorily incomplete as the failure to award fees when there is no decree? Just as the dissent rhetorically asks *why* (never mind the language of the statute) Congress would want to award fees when there is a judgment, but deny fees when the defendant capitulates on the eve of judgment; so also it is fair for us to ask *why* Congress would want to award fees when suit has been filed, but deny fees when the about-to-be defendant capitulates under the threat of filing. Surely, it cannot be because determination of whether suit was actually contemplated and threatened is too difficult. All the proof takes is a threatening letter and a batch of timesheets. Surely *that* obstacle would not deter the Congress that (according to the dissent) was willing to let district judges pursue that much more evasive will-o'-the-wisp called "catalyst." (Is this not why we *have* district courts?, asks the dissent.) My point is not that it would take no more twisting of language to produce prelitigation attorney's fees than to produce the decreeless attorney's fees that the dissent favors (though that may well be true). My point is that the departure from normal usage that the dissent favors cannot be justified on the ground that it establishes a regime of logical even handedness. There *must* be a cutoff of seemingly equivalent entitlements to fees—either the failure to file suit in time or the failure to obtain a judgment in time. The term "prevailing party" suggests the latter rather than the former. One does not prevail in a suit that is never determined.

* * *

III

The dissent points out that the catalyst theory has been accepted by "the clear majority of Federal Circuits." But our disagreeing with a "clear majority" of the Circuits is not at all a rare phenomenon. Indeed, our opinions sometimes contradict the *unanimous* and long-standing interpretation of lower federal courts.

The dissent's insistence that we defer to the "clear majority" of Circuit opinion is particularly peculiar in the present case, since that majority has been nurtured and preserved *by our own misleading dicta* (to which I, unfortunately, contributed). Most of the Circuit Court cases cited by the dissent, as reaffirming the catalyst theory after our decision in Farrar v. Hobby, 506 U.S. 103, 113 S.Ct. 566, 121 L.Ed.2d 494 (1992), relied on our earlier opinion in *Hewitt*. Deferring to our colleagues' own error is bad enough; but enshrining the error that we ourselves have improvidently suggested and blaming it on the near-unanimous judgment of our colleagues would surely be unworthy. Informing the Courts of Appeals that our ill-considered dicta have misled them displays, it seems to me, not "disrespect," but a most becoming (and well-deserved) humility.

* * *

JUSTICE GINSBURG, with whom JUSTICE STEVENS, JUSTICE SOUTER, and JUSTICE BREYER join, dissenting.

The Court today holds that a plaintiff whose suit prompts the precise relief she seeks does not "prevail," and hence cannot obtain an award of attorney's fees, unless she also secures a court entry memorializing her victory. The entry need not be a judgment on the merits. Nor need there be any finding of wrongdoing. A court-approved settlement will do.

The Court's insistence that there be a document filed in court—a litigated judgment or court-endorsed settlement—upsets long-prevailing Circuit precedent applicable to scores of federal fee-shifting statutes. The decision allows a defendant to escape a statutory obligation to pay a plaintiff's counsel fees, even though the suit's merit led the defendant to abandon the fray, to switch rather than fight on, to accord plaintiff sooner rather than later the principal redress sought in the complaint.

* * *

I

* * *

Prior to 1994, every Federal Court of Appeals (except the Federal Circuit, which had not addressed the issue) concluded that plaintiffs in situations like Buckhannon's * * * could obtain a fee award if their suit acted as a "catalyst" for the change they sought, even if they did not obtain a judgment or consent decree.[4] * * *

In 1994, the Fourth Circuit en banc, dividing 6-to-5, broke ranks with its sister courts. The court declared that, in light of Farrar v. Hobby, 506 U.S. 103, 113 S.Ct. 566, 121 L.Ed.2d 494 (1992), a plaintiff could not become a "prevailing party" without "an enforceable judgment, consent

---

4. All *twelve* of these decisions antedate Hewitt v. Helms, 482 U.S. 755, 107 S.Ct. 2672, 96 L.Ed.2d 654 (1987). But cf. (Scalia, J., concurring) (maintaining that this Court's decision in *Hewitt* "improvidently suggested" the catalyst rule, and asserting that only "a few cases adopting the catalyst theory predate *Hewitt*"). *Hewitt* said it was "settled law" that when a lawsuit prompts a defendant's "voluntary action ... that redresses the plaintiff's grievances," the plaintiff "is deemed to have prevailed despite the absence of a formal judgment in his favor." That statement accurately conveyed the unanimous view then held by the Federal Circuits.

decree, or settlement." S–1 and S–2 v. State Bd. of Ed. of N. C., 21 F.3d 49, 51 (1994). * * *

After the Fourth Circuit's en banc ruling, nine Courts of Appeals reaffirmed their own consistently held interpretation of the term "prevail." * * *

The array of federal court decisions applying the catalyst rule suggested three conditions necessary to a party's qualification as "prevailing" short of a favorable final judgment or consent decree. A plaintiff first had to show that the defendant provided "some of the benefit sought" by the lawsuit. Under most Circuits' precedents, a plaintiff had to demonstrate as well that the suit stated a genuine claim, *i.e.*, one that was at least "colorable," not "frivolous, unreasonable, or groundless." Plaintiff finally had to establish that her suit was a "substantial" or "significant" cause of defendant's action providing relief. In some Circuits, to make this causation showing, plaintiff had to satisfy the trial court that the suit achieved results "by threat of victory," not "by dint of nuisance and threat of expense." * * * One who crossed these three thresholds would be recognized as a "prevailing party" to whom the district court, "in its discretion," could award attorney's fees.

Developed over decades and in legions of federal-court decisions, the catalyst rule and these implementing standards deserve this Court's respect and approbation.

II

A

The Court today detects a "clear meaning" of the term prevailing party, that has heretofore eluded the large majority of courts construing those words. "Prevailing party," today's opinion announces, means "one who has been awarded some relief by the court." The Court derives this "clear meaning" principally from Black's Law Dictionary, which defines a "prevailing party," in critical part, as one "in whose favor a judgment is rendered."

One can entirely agree with Black's Law Dictionary that a party "in whose favor a judgment is rendered" prevails, and at the same time resist, as most Courts of Appeals have, any implication that *only* such a party may prevail. * * * Notably, this Court did not refer to Black's Law Dictionary in Maher v. Gagne, 448 U.S. 122, 100 S.Ct. 2570, 65 L.Ed.2d 653 (1980), which held that a consent decree could qualify a plaintiff as "prevailing." The Court explained:

> "The fact that [plaintiff] prevailed through a settlement rather than through litigation does not weaken her claim to fees. Nothing in the language of [42 U.S.C.] § 1988 conditions the District Court's power to award fees on full litigation of the issues or on a judicial determination that the plaintiff's rights have been violated." Id., at 129, 100 S.Ct. 2570.

The spare "prevailing party" language of the fee-shifting provision applicable in *Maher,* and the similar wording of the fee-shifting provisions now before the Court, contrast with prescriptions that so tightly bind fees to judgments as to exclude the application of a catalyst concept. The Prison Litigation Reform Act of 1995, for example, directs that fee awards to prisoners under § 1988 be "proportionately related to the *court ordered relief* for the violation." (Emphasis added). That statute, by its express terms, forecloses an award to a prisoner on a catalyst theory. But the FHAA and ADA fee-shifting prescriptions, modeled on 42 U.S.C. § 1988 unmodified, do not similarly staple fee awards to "court ordered relief." Their very terms do not foreclose a catalyst theory.

B

It is altogether true, as the concurring opinion points out, that litigation costs other than attorney's fees traditionally have been allowed to the "prevailing party," and that a judgment winner ordinarily fits that description. It is not true, however, that precedent on costs calls for the judgment requirement the Court ironly adopts today for attorney's fees.

* * *

IV

* * *

In opposition to the argument that defendants will resist change in order to stave off an award of fees, one could urge that the catalyst rule may lead defendants promptly to comply with the law's requirements: the longer the litigation, the larger the fees. Indeed, one who knows noncompliance will be expensive might be encouraged to conform his conduct to the legal requirements before litigation is threatened. * * * No doubt, a mootness dismissal is unlikely when recurrence of the controversy is under the defendant's control. But * * * why should this Court's fee-shifting rulings drive a plaintiff prepared to accept adequate relief, though out-of-court and unrecorded, to litigate on and on? And if the catalyst rule leads defendants to negotiate not only settlement terms but also allied counsel fees, is that not a consummation to applaud, not deplore?

* * *

The concurring opinion adds another argument against the catalyst rule: That opinion sees the rule as accommodating the "extortionist" who obtains relief because of "greater strength in financial resources, or superiority in media manipulation, rather than *superiority in legal merit.*" This concern overlooks both the character of the rule and the judicial superintendence Congress ordered for all fee allowances. The catalyst rule was auxiliary to fee-shifting statutes whose primary purpose is "to promote the vigorous enforcement" of the civil rights laws. To that end, courts deemed the conduct-altering catalyst that counted to be the substance of the case, not merely the plaintiff's atypically superior financial resources, media ties, or political clout. And Congress assigned responsibility for awarding fees not to automatons unable to recognize extortionists, but to judges expected and instructed to exercise "discretion." So viewed, the catalyst rule provided no berth for nuisance suits, or "thinly disguised forms of extortion."[12]

V

As to our attorney fee precedents, the Court correctly observes, "[w]e have never had occasion to decide whether the term 'prevailing party' allows an award of fees under the 'catalyst theory,'" and "there is language in our cases supporting both petitioners and respondents." It bears emphasis, however, that in determining whether fee shifting is in order, the Court in the past has placed greatest weight not on any "judicial *imprimatur*," but on the practical impact of the lawsuit.[13] In *Maher*, in which the Court held fees could be awarded on the basis of a consent decree, the opinion nowhere relied on the presence of a formal judgment. Some years later, in Hewitt v. Helms, 482 U.S. 755, 107 S.Ct. 2672, 96 L.Ed.2d 654 (1987), the Court suggested that fees might be awarded the plaintiff who "obtain[ed] relief without [the] benefit of a formal judgment." The Court explained: "If the defendant, under the pressure of the lawsuit, pays over a money claim before the judicial judgment is pronounced," or "if the defendant, under pressure of [a suit for declaratory judgment], alters his conduct (or threatened conduct) towards the plaintiff," *i.e.*, conduct "that was the basis for the suit, the plaintiff will have prevailed." I agree, and would apply that analysis to this case.

The Court posits a "'merit' requirement of our prior cases." *Maher*, however, affirmed an award of attorney's fees based on a consent decree that "did not purport to adjudicate [plaintiff's] statutory or constitutional claims." The decree in *Maher* "explicitly stated that 'nothing [therein

---

12. The concurring opinion notes, correctly, that "[t]here *must* be a cut-off of seemingly equivalent entitlements to fees—either the failure to file suit in time or the failure to obtain a judgment in time." The former cutoff, the Court has held, is impelled both by "plain language" requiring a legal "action" or "proceeding" antecedent to a fee award, and by "legislative history ... replete with references to [enforcement] 'in suits,' 'through the courts' and by 'judicial process.'" The latter cut-off, requiring "a judgment in time," is not similarly impelled by text or legislative history.

The concurring opinion also states that a prevailing party must obtain relief "*in the lawsuit*." One can demur to that elaboration of the statutory text and still adhere to the catalyst rule. Under the rule, plaintiff's suit raising genuine issues must trigger the defendant's voluntary action; plaintiff will not prevail under the rule if defendant "ceases ... [his] offensive conduct" by dying or going bankrupt. A behavior-altering event like dying or bankruptcy occurs outside the lawsuit; a change precipitated by the lawsuit's claims and demand for relief is an occurrence brought about "through" or "in" the suit.

13. To qualify for fees in any case, we have held, relief must be real. See Rhodes v. Stewart, 488 U.S. 1, 4, 109 S.Ct. 202, 102 L.Ed.2d 1 (1988) (per curiam) (a plaintiff who obtains a formal declaratory judgment, but gains no real "relief whatsoever," is not a "prevailing party" eligible for fees); *Hewitt* (an interlocutory decision reversing a dismissal for failure to state a claim, although stating that plaintiff's rights were violated, does not entitle plaintiff to fees; to "prevail," plaintiff must gain relief of "substance," i.e., more than a favorable "judicial statement that does not affect the relationship between the plaintiff and the defendant").

was] intended to constitute an admission of fault by either party.'" The catalyst rule, in short, conflicts with none of "our prior *holdings*."[14]

* * *

When this Court rejects the considered judgment prevailing in the Circuits, respect for our colleagues demands a cogent explanation. Today's decision does not provide one. The Court's narrow construction of the words "prevailing party" is unsupported by precedent and unaided by history or logic. Congress prescribed fee-shifting provisions like those included in the FHAA and ADA to encourage private enforcement of laws designed to advance civil rights. Fidelity to that purpose calls for court-awarded fees when a private party's lawsuit, whether or not its settlement is registered in court, vindicates rights Congress sought to secure. I would so hold and therefore dissent from the judgment and opinion of the Court.

NOTES

1. Some commentators assessing the impact of *Buckhannon* have concluded that the decision has limited the quality and quantity of public interest suits, especially those seeking injunctive relief against governmental entities under federal law. E.g., Deborah L. Rhode, Public Interest Law: The Movement at Midlife, 60 Stan.L.Rev. 2027 (2008); Catherine Albiston & Laura Beth Nielsen, The Procedural Attack on Civil Rights: The Empirical Reality of *Buckhannon* for the Private Attorney General, 54 U.C.L.A.L.Rev. 1087 (2007). State courts have continued to decide whether the catalyst theory remains in the interpretation of their respective state fee-shifting statutes. E.g., Mason v. City of Hoboken, 951 A.2d 1017, 196 N.J. 51 (2008) (despite *Buckhannon*, New Jersey law includes the catalyst theory).

---

14. The Court repeatedly quotes passages from *Hanrahan v. Hampton,* stating that to "prevail," plaintiffs must receive relief "on the merits." Nothing in *Hanrahan,* however, declares that relief "on the merits" requires a "judicial *imprimatur.*" As the Court acknowledges, *Hanrahan* concerned an interim award of fees, after plaintiff succeeded in obtaining nothing more than reversal of a directed verdict. At that juncture, plaintiff had obtained no change in defendant's behavior, and the suit's ultimate winner remained undetermined. There is simply no inconsistency between *Hanrahan,* denying fees when a plaintiff might yet obtain no real benefit, and the catalyst rule, allowing fees when a plaintiff obtains the practical result she sought in suing. Indeed, the harmony between the catalyst rule and *Hanrahan* is suggested by *Hanrahan* itself; like *Maher, Hanrahan* quoted the Senate Report recognizing that parties may prevail "through a consent judgment *or* without formally obtaining relief." (quoting S.Rep. No. 94-1011, at 5, U.S.Code Cong. & Admin.News 1976, pp. 5908, 5912) (emphasis added). *Hanrahan* also selected for citation the influential elaboration of the catalyst rule in Nadeau v. Helgemoe, 581 F.2d [275, 279–281 (1st Cir.1978)].

The Court additionally cites Texas State Teachers Assn. v. Garland Independent School Dist., 489 U.S. 782, 109 S.Ct. 1486, 103 L.Ed.2d 866 (1989), which held, unanimously, that a plaintiff could become a "prevailing party" without obtaining relief on the "central issue in the suit." *Texas State Teachers* linked fee awards to a "material alteration of the legal relationship of the parties," but did not say, as the Court does today, that the change must be "court-ordered." The parties' legal relationship does change when the defendant stops engaging in the conduct that furnishes the basis for plaintiff's civil action, and that action, which both parties would otherwise have litigated, is dismissed.

The decision with language most unfavorable to the catalyst rule, Farrar v. Hobby, 506 U.S. 103, 113 S.Ct. 566, 121 L.Ed.2d 494 (1992), does not figure prominently in the Court's opinion—and for good reason, for *Farrar* "involved no catalytic effect." *Farrar* held that a plaintiff who sought damages of $17 million, but received damages of $1, was a "prevailing party" nonetheless not entitled to fees. In reinforcing the link between the right to a fee award and the "degree of success obtained," *Farrar's holding* is consistent with the catalyst rule.

2. As *Buckhannon* indicates, the question of who is "prevailing" is fairly easy to decide if the plaintiff secures a judgment of violation. But how does a court decide whether a party has "prevailed" in other situations?

(a) Is the plaintiff in a position to benefit from relief from the defendant? See, e.g., Rhodes v. Stewart, 488 U.S. 1, 109 S.Ct. 202, 102 L.Ed.2d 1 (1988)(prisoner-plaintiffs were not prevailing parties because their claims were moot: one plaintiff had died and the other had been released from prison when the case was decided in their favor); Hewitt v. Helms, 482 U.S. 755, 107 S.Ct. 2672, 96 L.Ed.2d 654 (1987) (prisoner–plaintiff was not prevailing party despite a change in prison rules that may have been catalyzed by his suit, in part because rule change was not made until after the prisoner was released).

(b) Even if the plaintiff obtained entry of a judgment in court, what degree of success must the plaintiff have achieved to be deemed the prevailing party? In Texas State Teachers Association v. Garland Independent School District, 489 U.S. 782, 791, 109 S.Ct. 1486, 1492–93, 103 L.Ed.2d 866 (1989), the Court determined that a prevailing plaintiff merely had to succeed on " 'any significant issue in litigation which achieve[d] some of the benefit the parties sought in bringing the suit.' " Prior to this case, lower courts had grappled with pinpointing the standard, yielding such tests as success on every claim, success on the central issue, substantial success, some success, or merely the existence of a meritorious claim absent any success. Farrar v. Hobby, 506 U.S. 103, 113, 113 S.Ct. 566, 574, 121 L.Ed.2d 494 (1992), held that a plaintiff who wins an award of even nominal damages is a prevailing party because the award "modifies the defendant's behavior for the plaintiff's benefit by forcing the defendant to pay an amount of money he otherwise would not pay." Under *Farrar*, however, for a plaintiff who does not vindicate important rights and receives only nominal damages because of a failure to prove actual compensable injury, "the only reasonable fee is usually no fee at all." Id. at 115.

(c) What about voluntary dismissal of a case with prejudice? Highway Equipment Co. v. FECO, Ltd., 469 F.3d 1027 (Fed.Cir.2006) (dismissal of case with prejudice following parties' stipulations and covenants not to sue can embody a sufficient "judicial imprimatur" to trigger the judicially sanctioned change in parties' legal relationship required to support a defendants' claim for attorney's fees under federal patent law). However, the Federal Circuit has recognized that there are circuits that disagree with its rule and require some additional benefit on the merits to the plaintiff. E.g., Dean v. Riser, 240 F.3d 505 (5th Cir.2001).

(d) What if the plaintiff accepts an offer of judgment under Rule 68 of the Federal Rules of Civil Procedure (p. 988)? Aynes v. Space Guard Products, Inc., 201 F.R.D. 445 (S.D.Ind.2001) (awarding fees despite *Buckhannon* because an accepted offer of judgment is enforceable by the court). See Symposium: Revitalizing FRCP 68: Can Offers of Judgment Provide Incentives for Fair, Early Settlement of Fee–Recovery Cases?, 57 Mercer L.Rev. 717 (2006). However, one court has held that a routine, private settlement agreement without a court-enforcement mechanism does not have sufficient judicial imprimatur to confer prevailing party status. P.N. v. Seattle School District, 474 F.3d 1165 (9th Cir.2007).

(e) Is obtaining a preliminary injunction sufficient to make the recipient a prevailing party under *Buckhannon*? In Sole v. Wyner, 551 U.S. 74, 127 S.Ct. 2188, 167 L.Ed.2d 1069 (2007), the Supreme Court in an unanimous opinion held that prevailing plaintiff status does not attach to a preliminary injunction that is "reversed, dissolved, or otherwise undone by the final decision in the case." The Court denied section 1988 attorney's fees to a plaintiff who had obtained a preliminary injunction permitting her to stage an antiwar protest at a public beach comprised of nude individuals arranged into the shape of a peace sign. The protest took place, but the plaintiff's further request for a permanent injunction allowing additional nude protests was denied after a full adjudication on the merits. The Court held that such "ephemeral victories" in which the plaintiff wins the battle, but not the war, do not convey prevailing plaintiff status. The Court expressly refrained from deciding whether success in obtaining preliminary relief where there is no subsequent decision on the merits might suffice to confer prevailing party status. For examples of circuit courts addressing this question after *Sole*, compare People Against Police Violence v. City of Pittsburgh, 520 F.3d 226, 232 (3d Cir.2008) (allowing award of attorney's fees for long-lasting preliminary injunction) with Planned Parenthood of Houston and Southeast Texas v. Sanchez, 480 F.3d 734 (5th Cir.2007) (no fees allowed where preliminary injunction was vacated on appeal).

(f) What if the party seeks a fee award as a catalyst under other statutes? Smith v. Fitchburg Public Schools, 401 F.3d 16 (1st Cir.2005) (fee not permitted under catalyst theory for recovery under Individuals with Disabilities Education Act); Brickwood Contractors, Inc. v. United States, 288 F.3d 1371 (Fed.Cir. 2002), cert. denied, 537 U.S. 1106, 123 S.Ct. 871, 154 L.Ed.2d 775 (2003) (*Buckhannon* applies to the Equal Access to Justice Act); New York State Federation of Taxi Drivers, Inc. v. Westchester County Taxi and Limousine Commission, 272 F.3d 154 (2d Cir.2001) (*Buckhannon* applies generally to statutes awarding fees to the "prevailing party," including 42 U.S.C. § 1988). Compare Sierra Club v. EPA, 322 F.3d 718 (D.C.Cir. 2003) (allowing fees under the catalyst theory because the Clean Air Act allows fees "whenever * * * appropriate"), cert. denied, 540 U.S. 1104, 124 S.Ct. 1043, 157 L.Ed.2d 888 (2004); Graham v. DaimlerChrysler Corp., 34 Cal.4th 553, 21 Cal.Rptr.3d 331, 101 P.3d 140 (2004) (*Buckhannon* does not apply to fee awards under state statutes).

(g) What if the prevailing party loses a subsequent appeal? The Eighth Circuit has explained how, despite losing *Jenkins III* (p. 165) in the Supreme Court, the plaintiffs in the Kansas City school desegregation case could still be considered prevailing parties for purposes of awarding fees. Jenkins v. Missouri, 127 F.3d 709 (8th Cir. en banc 1997). The court noted that status as a prevailing party is determined on the outcome of the case as a whole, rather than by piecemeal assessment of how a party fares on each motion along the way. This rule applied to matters decided after judgment on the merits, as well as those decided before.

3. As the post-*Alyeska* decisions repeatedly mention, statutory provisions allowing the court to award fees to the "prevailing party" in its "discretion" have been read to mean that the prevailing *plaintiff* should ordinarily get fees unless special circumstances would render such an award

unjust. E.g., Newman v. Piggie Park Enterprises, Inc., 390 U.S. 400, 88 S.Ct. 964, 19 L.Ed.2d 1263 (1968). What factors should cause a court to *deny* fees to a prevailing party?

(a) Should the prevailing plaintiff get fees even if it is well-heeled and can afford an attorney? E.g., Herrington v. County of Sonoma, 883 F.2d 739 (9th Cir.1989)(wealthy landowners who had strong financial incentive to bring suit awarded fees under section 1988); Jones v. Wilkinson, 800 F.2d 989 (10th Cir.1986)(corporate plaintiffs entitled to fees), aff'd, 480 U.S. 926, 107 S.Ct. 1559, 94 L.Ed.2d 753 (1987). But see 24 U.S.C. § 2412(d)(2)(B) (limiting recovery of fees under the Equal Access to Justice Act to individuals with net worth not exceeding $2 million or to entities with a net worth not exceeding $7 million).

(b) Assume that the defendant, a large, private corporation, prevails against a non-profit citizens group. Should the prevailing defendant get fees? Despite statutes that almost invariably refer to "prevailing parties," the usual rule is that the prevailing defendant does not get fees unless the case is "frivolous, unreasonable, or without foundation." Christiansburg Garment Co. v. EEOC, 434 U.S. 412, 98 S.Ct. 694, 54 L.Ed.2d 648 (1978). What arguments other than "deep pocket" theories can you supply in support of this doctrine? What suppositions do your arguments make about the value of public law litigation? See Thomas D. Rowe, Indemnity or Compensation? The Contract with America, Loser–Pays Attorney Fee Shifting, and a One–Way Alternative, 37 Washburn L.J. 317 (1998); Harold J. Krent, Explaining One–Way Fee Shifting, 79 Va.L.Rev. 2039 (1993).

Under the Copyright Act, however, all "prevailing parties" must be treated alike—i.e., fees are to be awarded to prevailing defendants or prevailing plaintiffs simply as a matter of the court's discretion. Fogerty v. Fantasy, Inc., 510 U.S. 517, 114 S.Ct. 1023, 127 L.Ed.2d 455 (1994). Justice Thomas wrote separately to indicate that while he agreed with the Court's plain language approach in *Fogerty*, he would take the same approach with the virtually identical language contained in Title VII of the Civil Rights Act and, as a result, would reject completely the dual standard created by *Christiansburg Garment*. See also Robert Aloysius Hyde & Lisa M. Sharrock, A Decade Down the Road But Still Running Through the Jungle: A Critical Review of Post-*Fogerty* Fee Awards, 52 U.Kan.L.Rev. 467 (2004).

(c) What if an entity intervenes in a lawsuit brought under Title VII, challenging the plaintiff's legal positions, but the district court rejects the intervenor's contentions and rules in favor of the plaintiffs on the merits? May the prevailing plaintiffs obtain fees from the unsuccessful intervenor for the costs associated with responding to the intervenors? Independent Federation of Flight Attendants v. Zipes, 491 U.S. 754, 109 S.Ct. 2732, 105 L.Ed.2d 639 (1989) (fees awarded only if *Christiansburg Garment* test is met).

(d) Should pro se litigants be awarded fees? In Kay v. Ehrler, 499 U.S. 432, 111 S.Ct. 1435, 113 L.Ed.2d 486 (1991), the Supreme Court unanimously held that a victorious pro se litigant who is also an attorney may not be awarded attorney's fees under 42 U.S.C. § 1988. Although the Court could not find a clear answer to the question in the text or legislative history of section 1988, the Court created a rule serving the policies underlying the statute by making an incentive to retain independent counsel in every case. A lawyer acting in a pro se capacity may be at a disadvantage because he or she may not be able to serve as a witness and would be deprived of the independent and detached judgment of a third party. Although not directly at issue in the case, the Court expressed its satisfaction with the unanimous position of the circuits that pro se litigants who are not lawyers are not entitled to attorney's fees. The *Kay* decision is criticized in Charles Silver, Incoherence and Irrationality in the Law of Attorneys' Fees, 12 Rev. Litigation 301 (1993).

What if a parent who is a lawyer represents her own child in an Individuals with Disabilities Education Act case? Pardini v. Allegheny Intermediate Unit, 524 F.3d 419, 423 (3d Cir.2008) (" '[l]ike attorneys appearing pro se, attorney-parents are generally incapable of exercising sufficient independent judgment on behalf of their children to ensure that reason, rather than emotion will dictate the conduct of the litigation' ") with Matthew V. ex rel. Craig V. v. DeKalb County School System, 244 F.Supp.2d 1331 (N.D.Ga. 2003) (parent-lawyer and child are separate legal entities for purposes of IDEA). See also Winkelman v. Parma City School District, 550 U.S. 516, 127 S.Ct. 1994, 167 L.Ed.2d 904 (2007) (holding that parents have rights of their own to a free appropriate public education for their child, which can be pursued *pro se* in an action under IDEA, but reserving issue of award of fees).

(e) Suppose a plaintiff's lawyer, sensing that her client's case is weak, asks the jury for an award of nominal damages, ostensibly just to vindicate principle. Is it an appropriate response for the court or defense counsel to inform the jury that if it does make an award of nominal damages, the plaintiff may be entitled to attorney's fees? See Brooks v. Cook, 938 F.2d 1048 (9th Cir.1991)(not appropriate). But see Romberg v. Nichols, 48 F.3d 453 (9th Cir.1995), cert. denied, 516 U.S. 943, 116 S.Ct. 379, 133 L.Ed.2d 303 (1995) (after seeking and obtaining only nominal damages at close of trial, prevailing party received no attorney's fee under Farrar v. Hobby, 506 U.S. 103, 113 S.Ct. 566, 121 L.Ed.2d 494 (1992)).

4. When the United States is a party, a private party seeking fees has an additional fee statute available. Under the Equal Access to Justice Act, 28 U.S.C. § 2412(d)(2)(A), fees of up to $125 per hour (which may be adjusted for inflation) may be awarded to a party who has prevailed against the United States (either as plaintiff or defendant), "unless the court finds that the position of the United States was substantially justified * * *."

In Pierce v. Underwood, 487 U.S. 552, 564, 108 S.Ct. 2541, 2550, 101 L.Ed.2d 490 (1988), the Supreme Court interpreted "substantially" to mean "not 'justified to a high degree,' but rather 'justified in substance or in the main'—that is justified to a degree that could satisfy a reasonable person." Three justices, concurring with the majority, disagreed with this definition, arguing that "the Government can avoid fees only where it makes a clear showing that its position had a solid basis (as opposed to a marginal basis or a not unreasonable basis) in both law and fact." Id. at 579, 108 S.Ct. at 2557. See generally Harold J. Krent, Fee-shifting Under the Equal Access to Justice Act—A Qualified Success, 11 Yale L. & Pol'y Rev. 458 (1993); Gregory C. Sisk, The Essentials of the Equal Access to Justice Act: Court Awards of Attorney's

Fees for Unreasonable Government Conduct, 55 La.L.Rev. 217 (1994) (Part One), 56 La.L.Rev. 1 (1995) (Part Two).

5. When should attorney's fees be granted to the plaintiff on remand to state court after the defendant's unsuccessful removal to federal court? Under 28 U.S.C. § 1447(c), a remand order "may require payment of just costs and any actual expenses, including attorney fees," but provides little guidance on when such fees are warranted. Resolving a circuit split, Chief Justice Roberts, for a unanimous Court, held that absent unusual circumstances, attorney's fees should not be awarded when the removing party had an objectively reasonable basis for removal, but normally should be awarded where no objectively reasonable basis for removal existed. The Court expressly rejected the *Piggie Park* presumption in favor of awarding fees as well as the far more narrow test of *Christiansburg Garment* because neither standard fit the policies behind the removal procedure. Martin v. Franklin Capital Corp., 546 U.S. 132, 126 S.Ct. 704, 163 L.Ed.2d 547 (2005).

6. Does the Eleventh Amendment bar the award of attorney's fees against the states? Hutto v. Finney, 437 U.S. 678, 98 S.Ct. 2565, 57 L.Ed.2d 522 (1978), in a divided opinion held that an award may be made against a state under section 1988 because Congress may qualify the Eleventh Amendment in implementing the Fourteenth Amendment and the fees are awarded as an element of costs, which have long been awarded against the states. In Missouri v. Jenkins (*Jenkins I*), 491 U.S. 274, 109 S.Ct. 2463, 105 L.Ed.2d 229 (1989), the Supreme Court reaffirmed that the Eleventh Amendment has no application to an award of attorney's fees which is ancillary to a grant of prospective relief against a State. Because it went on to hold that the same was true for the calculation of the amount of reasonable attorney's fees, the Court concluded that an award against a State of a fee could include an enhancement for delay in payment. (Similarly, Congress has authorized an award against the United States to include interest to compensate for delay in payment. 42 U.S.C. § 2000e–16(d).)

7. May attorney's fees be awarded against state court judges? Supreme Court of Virginia v. Consumers Union, 446 U.S. 719, 100 S.Ct. 1967, 64 L.Ed.2d 641 (1980), held that state court judges could be liable under section 1988 for attorney's fees in their capacity as the enforcement mechanism for state professional responsibility rules but not for acts undertaken in their legislative capacity to promulgate rules for attorneys' professional conduct. Thus the Court reversed an award of attorney's fees against the Virginia Supreme Court and its members that was premised on legislative acts and omissions, specifically the failure to modify a ban on lawyer advertising in the Virginia Code of Professional Responsibility. In Pulliam v. Allen, 466 U.S. 522, 104 S.Ct. 1970, 80 L.Ed.2d 565 (1984), the Court affirmed an attorney's fee award against a state magistrate who was enjoined from unconstitutionally imposing bail on persons arrested for nonjailable offenses and of incarcerating persons who could not meet the bail. Because congressional intent "could hardly be more plain," the Court rejected the contention that attorney's fees were the functional equivalent of monetary damages, which were indisputably prohibited by judicial immunity. Congress overruled *Pulliam* in The Federal Courts Improvement Act of 1996, 110 Stat. 3847, by providing that judicial officers shall not be held liable for costs or fees in any action brought against

such officers unless the challenged action was "clearly in excess of such officer's jurisdiction."

C. THE MEASURE OF THE FEES

Once a court has decided that fees should be awarded in a particular case, it must determine what is a "reasonable" fee under the pertinent statute. Courts have had greater leeway in determining how to calculate fees than even the elastic concept "reasonable" suggests. Prior to the 1970s, many courts awarded attorney's fees as they would a contingency fee, based on a "reasonable" percentage of the recovery. More recently, courts have tended to adopt the "lodestar" formulation, which entails multiplying compensable hours by an hourly rate. In making the calculation, courts have discretion to adjust the lodestar for such factors as risk of losing the case or unusually poor representation by the attorney.

For example, if an attorney spent 2,000 hours on a matter, much of the time may have been spent in administrative proceedings or causes of action that a court would deem uncompensable under a fee statute or insufficiently related to work covered by a fee statute to be reimbursed. Hence, compensable hours might easily be reduced to 500. A court may also exercise wide latitude in calculating the hourly rate. The attorney in this controversy may be ten years out of law school, doing work and carrying responsibilities commensurate to a junior partner at a law firm in a large city who commands $350 per hour, or she may work for a public interest firm where salary plus overhead may amount to only $75 per hour. The higher figures would make the lodestar $700,000 (2000 hours × $350) while the lower would make it $37,500 (500 hours × $75). This variation may be augmented further if the court makes adjustments to the lodestar. If the chance of victory were 1 in 3, the $700,000 lodestar could be increased by a factor of three to $2,100,000. Conversely, if the court disregarded the risk of losing the case and instead elected to penalize the attorney for poor performance, the $37,500 lodestar could be halved to $18,750. Bear in mind that, at the beginning of a case, the attorney has no way of knowing what the fee award will be since a court will make an award determination only after the suit has been resolved on the merits.

In many instances, judges do not have the range of discretion that these numbers suggest. In some statutes, the legislature has imposed limits on fees or otherwise mandated a specific result. For example, the Prison Litigation Reform Act, 42 U.S.C. § 1997e, now limits attorney's fees in prison cases to 150% of the maximum hourly rate paid to appointed counsel in the particular district court. Walker v. Bain, 257 F.3d 660 (6th Cir.2001), cert. denied, 535 U.S. 1095, 122 S.Ct. 2291, 152 L.Ed.2d 1050 (2002) (rejecting equal protection challenge to limit). See also Martin v. Hadix, 527 U.S. 343, 119 S.Ct. 1998, 144 L.Ed.2d 347 (1999) (PLRA limits fees for legal services performed after the Act's effective date, but not for work performed beforehand); Lynn S. Branham, Toothless in Truth? The Ethereal Rational Basis Test and the Prison Litigation Reform Act's

Disparate Restrictions on Attorney's Fees, 89 Cal.L.Rev. 999 (2001). Nonetheless, substantial areas for judicial interpretation remain.

1. WHAT WORK IS COMPENSABLE?

SULLIVAN v. HUDSON
Supreme Court of the United States, 1989
490 U.S. 877, 109 S.Ct. 2248, 104 L.Ed.2d 941

JUSTICE O'CONNOR delivered the opinion of the Court.

The issue before us in this case is whether a Social Security claimant is entitled to an award of attorney's fees under the Equal Access to Justice Act [28 U.S.C. § 2412] for representation provided during administrative proceedings held pursuant to a district court order remanding the action to the Secretary of Health and Human Services. * * *

II

In 1980, Congress passed the EAJA in response to its concern that persons "may be deterred from seeking review of, or defending against, unreasonable governmental action because of the expense involved in securing the vindication of their rights." * * *

The EAJA was designed to rectify this situation by providing for an award of a reasonable attorney's fee to a "prevailing party" in a "civil action" or "adversary adjudication" unless the position taken by the United States in the proceeding at issue "was substantially justified" or "special circumstances make an award unjust." That portion of the Act applicable to "civil actions" provides, as amended, in relevant part that

> [e]xcept as otherwise specifically provided by statute, a court shall award to a prevailing party other than the United States fees and other expenses ... incurred by that party in any civil action ... including proceedings for judicial review of agency action, brought by or against the United States in any court having jurisdiction of that action, unless the court finds that the position of the United States was substantially justified or that special circumstances make an award unjust.

Application of this provision to respondent's situation here requires brief consideration of the structure of administrative proceedings and judicial review under the Social Security Act. [The Court explained that under this Act, the relationship between the reviewing court and the agency was particularly close.] * * *

The detailed provisions for the transfer of proceedings from the courts to the Secretary and for the filing of the Secretary's subsequent findings with the court suggest a degree of direct interaction between a federal court and an administrative agency alien to traditional review of agency action under the Administrative Procedure Act. As one source puts it:

The remand power places the courts, not in their accustomed role as external overseers of the administrative process, making sure that it stays within legal bounds, but virtually as coparticipants in the process, exercising ground-level discretion of the same order as that exercised by ALJs and the Appeals Council when they act upon a request to reopen a decision on the basis of new and material evidence.

J. Mashaw [et al.], Social Security Hearings and Appeals 133 (1978).

Where a court finds that the Secretary has committed a legal or factual error in evaluating a particular claim, the district court's remand order will often include detailed instructions concerning the scope of the remand, the evidence to be adduced, and the legal or factual issues to be addressed. * * * Deviation from the court's remand order in the subsequent administrative proceedings is itself legal error, subject to reversal on further judicial review. In many remand situations, the court will retain jurisdiction over the action pending the Secretary's decision and its filing with the court. The court retains the power in such situations to assure that its prior mandate is effectuated.

Two points important to the application of the EAJA emerge from the interaction of the mechanisms for judicial review of Social Security benefits determinations and the EAJA. First, in a case such as this one, where a court's remand to the agency for further administrative proceedings does not necessarily dictate the receipt of benefits, the claimant will not normally attain "prevailing party" status * * * until after the result of the administrative proceedings is known. * * *

Second, the EAJA provides that an application for fees must be filed with the court "within thirty days of final judgment in the action." * * * The Secretary concedes that a remand order from a district court to the agency is not a final determination of the civil action and that the district court "retains jurisdiction to review any determination rendered on remand."

Thus, for purposes of the EAJA, the Social Security claimant's status as a prevailing party and the final judgment in her "civil action ... for review of agency action" are often completely dependent on the successful completion of the remand proceedings before the Secretary. Moreover, the remanding court continues to retain jurisdiction over the action within the meaning of the EAJA, and may exercise that jurisdiction to determine if its legal instructions on remand have been followed by the Secretary. Our past decisions interpreting other fee-shifting provisions make clear that where administrative proceedings are intimately tied to the resolution of the judicial action and necessary to the attainment of the results Congress sought to promote by providing for fees, they should be considered part and parcel of the action for which fees may be awarded.

In Pennsylvania v. Delaware Valley Citizens' Council, 478 U.S. 546, 106 S.Ct. 3088, 92 L.Ed.2d 439 (1986), we considered whether the costs of representation before federal and state administrative agencies in defense of the provisions of a consent decree entered under the Clean Air Act were compensable under the fee-shifting provision of that statute. Section 304(d) of the Clean Air Act provides for the award of a reasonable attorney fee in conjunction with "any final order in any action brought pursuant to" certain provisions of the Act. In *Delaware Valley,* we rejected the contention that the word "action" in the fee-shifting provision should be read narrowly to exclude all proceedings which could be plausibly characterized as "non-judicial." We indicated that

> [a]lthough it is true that the proceedings [at issue] were not "judicial" in the sense that they did not occur in a courtroom or involve "traditional" legal work such as examination of witnesses or selection of jurors for trial, the work done by counsel in these two phases was as necessary to the attainment of adequate relief for their client as was all of their earlier work in the courtroom which secured Delaware Valley's initial success in obtaining the consent decree.

Similarly, in New York Gaslight Club, Inc. v. Carey, 447 U.S. 54, 100 S.Ct. 2024, 64 L.Ed.2d 723 (1980), we held that under the fee-shifting provision of Title VII, 42 U.S.C. section 2000e–5(k), a federal court could award attorney's fees for services performed in state administrative and judicial enforcement proceedings. We noted that the words of the statute, authorizing "the court" to award attorney's fees "[i]n any action or proceeding under this title," could be read to include only federal administrative or judicial proceedings. Looking to the entire structure of Title VII, we observed that Congress had mandated initial resort to state and local remedies, and that "Congress viewed proceedings before the EEOC and in federal court as supplements to available state remedies for employment discrimination." Given this interlocking system of judicial and administrative avenues to relief, we concluded that the exclusion of state and local administrative proceedings from the fee provisions would clearly clash with the congressional design behind the statutory scheme whose enforcement the fee-shifting provisions was designed to promote. See also, Webb v. Dyer County Board of Education, 471 U.S. 234, 243, 105 S.Ct. 1923, 1928, 85 L.Ed.2d 233 (1985)(work performed in administrative proceedings that is "both useful and of a type ordinarily necessary to advance civil rights litigation" may be compensable under section 1988).

We think the principles we found persuasive in *Delaware Valley* and *Carey* are controlling here. As in *Delaware Valley,* the administrative proceedings on remand in this case were "crucial to the vindication of [respondent's] rights." No fee award at all would have been available to respondent absent successful conclusion of the remand proceedings, and the services of an attorney may be necessary both to ensure compliance with the District Court's order in the administrative proceedings themselves, and to prepare for any further proceedings before the district court to verify such compliance. In addition, as we did in *Carey,* we must endeavor to interpret the fee statute in light of the statutory provisions it was designed to effectuate. Given the "mandatory" nature of the administrative proceedings at issue here, and their close relation in law and fact to the issues before the District Court on judicial review, we find it difficult to ascribe to Congress an intent to throw the Social Security claimant a lifeline that it knew was a foot short. Indeed, the incentive which such a system would create for attorneys to abandon claimants after judicial remand runs directly counter to long established ethical canons of the legal profession. See, American Bar Association, Model Rules of Professional Conduct, Rule 1.16, pp. 53–55 (1984). Given the anomalous nature of this result, and its frustration of the very purposes behind the EAJA itself, Congress cannot lightly be assumed to have intended it. Since the judicial review provisions of the Social Security Act contemplate an ongoing civil action of which the remand proceedings are but a part, and the EAJA allows "any court having jurisdiction of that action" to award fees, 28 U.S.C. § 2412(d)(1)(A), we think the statute, read in light of its purpose "to diminish the deterrent effect of seeking review of, or defending against, governmental action," permits a court to award fees for services performed on remand before the Social Security Administration. Where a court finds that the Secretary's position on judicial review was not substantially justified within the meaning of the EAJA, see, Pierce v. Underwood, 487 U.S. 552, 108 S.Ct. 2541, 101 L.Ed.2d 490 (1988), it is within the court's discretion to conclude that representation on remand was necessary to the effectuation of its mandate and to the ultimate vindication of the claimant's rights, and that an award of fees for work performed in the administrative proceedings is therefore proper.

The Secretary mounts two interrelated challenges to this interpretation of section 2412(d)(1)(A). While the Secretary's contentions are not without some force, neither rises to the level necessary to oust what we think is the most reasonable interpretation of the statute in light of its manifest purpose. First, the Secretary argues that plain meaning of the term "civil action" in section 2412(d)(1)(A) excludes any proceedings outside of a court of law. Of course, if the plain language of the EAJA evinced a congressional intent to preclude the interpretation we reach here, that would be the end of the matter. In support of this proposition, the Secretary points out that the " '[t]erm [action] in its usual legal sense means a suit brought in a court; a formal complaint within the jurisdiction of a court of law.' " Second, the Secretary notes that Congress did authorize EAJA fee awards under 5 U.S.C. section 504(a)(1) where an agency "conducts an adversary adjudication," and that an adversary adjudication is defined in section 504(b)(1)(C) as "an adjudication ... in which the position of the United States is represented by counsel or otherwise." Under 28 U.S.C. section 2412(d)(3) a court is empowered to award fees for representation before an agency to a party who prevails in an action for judicial review to "the same extent authorized in [5 U.S.C. section 504(a)]." Thus, the Secretary concludes that since benefits proceedings before the Secretary and his designates are nonadversarial, and a court is explicitly empowered to award fees for agency proceedings where such proceedings satisfy the requirements of section 504(a)(1), the principle of *expressio unius est exclusio alterius* [the mention of one is the exclusion of another] applies, and a court may never award fees for time spent in nonadversarial administrative proceedings.

We agree with the Secretary that for purposes of the EAJA Social Security benefit proceedings are not "adversarial" within the meaning of section 504(b)(1)(C) either initially or on remand from a court. The plain language of the statute requires that the United States be represented by "counsel or otherwise," and neither is true in this context. Nonetheless, we disagree with the conclusion the Secretary would draw from this fact. First, as *Delaware Valley, Webb,* and *Carey* indicate, administrative proceedings may be so intimately connected with judicial proceedings as to be considered part of the "civil action" for purposes of a fee award. This is particularly so in the Social Security context where "a suit [has been] brought in a court" and "a formal complaint within the jurisdiction of a court of law," remains pending and depends for its resolution upon the outcome of the administrative proceedings. Second, we disagree with the Secretary's submission that a negative implication can be drawn from the power granted a court to award fees based on representation in a prior adversary adjudication before an agency. Section 2412(d)(3) provides that "[i]n awarding fees and other expenses under this subsection to a prevailing party in any action for judicial review of an adversary adjudication" the court may award fees to the same extent that they would have been available before the agency itself under section 504(a)(1). On its face, the provision says nothing about the power of a court to award reasonable fees for representation in a *nonadversarial* adjudication which is wholly ancillary to a civil action for judicial review. That Congress carved the world of EAJA proceedings into "adversary adjudications" and "civil actions" does not necessarily speak to, let alone preclude, a reading of the term "civil action" which includes administrative proceedings necessary to the completion of a civil action.

We conclude that where a court orders a remand to the Secretary in a benefits litigation and retains continuing jurisdiction over the case pending a decision from the Secretary which will determine the claimant's entitlement to benefits, the proceedings on remand are an integral part of the "civil action" for judicial review and thus attorney's fees for representation on remand are available subject to the other limitations in the EAJA. * * *

JUSTICE WHITE, with whom CHIEF JUSTICE [REHNQUIST], JUSTICE SCALIA, and JUSTICE KENNEDY join, dissenting.

* * * [T]he majority looks to § 2412(d)(1)(A), the provision of the EAJA dealing with fees incurred in "civil actions," as the basis for authorizing the award of fees at issue here. The majority reasons that "[s]ince the judicial review provisions of the Social Security Act contemplate an ongoing civil action of which the remand proceedings are but a part, and section 2412(d)(1)(A) of the EAJA allows 'any court having jurisdiction of that action' to award fees, ... the statute ... permits a court to award fees for services performed on remand before the Social

Security Administration." In so construing section 2412, however, the majority * * *—in its effort to reach the result it desires, * * * ignores the plain language of the statute it is construing.

Section 2412(d)(1)(A), by its terms, does not authorize the recovery of fees incurred in proceedings on remand before the Social Security Administration. That section provides in relevant part that "a court shall award to a prevailing party other than the United States fees and other expenses ... *incurred by that party in any civil action* ..., including proceedings for judicial review of agency action, brought by or against the United States in any court having jurisdiction of that action" (Emphasis added). The plain meaning of "civil action" is a proceeding in a court, see, Black's Law Dictionary 26, 222 (5th ed. 1979); Fed.Rules Civ.Proc. 2, 3, and any argument to the contrary is foreclosed by the statute itself—the civil action must be one brought "in any court having jurisdiction." Clearly, the Social Security Administration is not a court, see, 28 U.S.C. section 451 (defining "court of the United States"), and so section 2412 does not apply to fees incurred in proceedings before the Social Security Administration. * * *

Section 504, not section 2412, is the provision of the EAJA that governs the recovery of fees in proceedings before administrative agencies; indeed, Congress was careful to place section 504 in Title 5 of the United States Code, which governs procedures before administrative agencies, while placing section 2412 in Title 28, which governs procedures before the courts. The lack of any authorization in section 504(a)(1) for fees under the present circumstances provides further confirmation of the plain meaning of the EAJA. As the majority holds, the fee authorization in section 504(a)(1) is limited to adversary administrative adjudications, which do not include the nonadversary proceedings before the Social Security Administration. Applying the maxim of statutory construction *expressio unius est exclusio alterius,* the express congressional authorization for recovery of fees in adversary agency adjudications coupled with the lack of authorization for recovery of fees in nonadversary adjudications indicates Congress' intent not to authorize recovery of fees in nonadversary agency adjudications.

The majority's dismissal of these arguments misses the mark. First, the majority takes the position that a "civil action" includes remand proceedings before the Social Security Administration because a formal complaint remains pending in court and depends on the outcome of the administrative proceeding for its resolution. But the mere retention of jurisdiction while the case is on remand before the agency does not transform fees incurred before the agency into fees incurred before the court. It was the Social Security Administration that conducted the proceedings on remand and it was the Social Security Administration that ultimately made the award of benefits in this case, not the District Court. All the District Court did was to dismiss respondent's petition for judicial review once the agency had made its award on remand, which surely is not enough to characterize the agency proceedings as part of an ongoing civil action in court.

In this regard, the majority's reliance on [*Delaware Valley*] and [*Carey*] is misplaced. In *Delaware Valley,* we interpreted section 304(d) of the Clean Air Act, 42 U.S.C. section 7604(d), which allows the "court" to award fees "in issuing any final order in any action brought pursuant to" section 304(a) of the Act, as allowing recovery of fees incurred in enforcing a consent decree in administrative proceedings. But that Act applied to fee awards in "any action" brought under the Act, and did not expressly limit the award to fees "incurred ... in any civil action ... brought ... in any court," as the statute does here. Moreover, the legislative history of the Clean Air Act equated "action" with "proceeding," suggesting a broader meaning to the term, and certainly did not expressly reject the construction we gave to the statute. The same is true of *Carey,* in which this Court construed 42 U.S.C. section 2000e–5(k), authorizing "the court" to award fees "[i]n any action or proceeding under this title," as well as Webb v. Dyer County Bd. of Education, 471 U.S. 234, 243, 105 S.Ct. 1923, 1928, 85 L.Ed.2d 233 (1985)(construing 42 U.S.C. section 1988), and North Carolina Dept. of Transportation v. Crest Street Community Council, Inc., 479 U.S. 6, 15, 107 S.Ct. 336, 342, 93 L.Ed.2d 188 (1986)(same) * * *. In short, these decisions have no application to the EAJA because its plain language indicates otherwise * * *.

I find the statutory language plainly and unambiguously to preclude the construction given the EAJA by the majority. But even if the language of the statute might somehow be seen as ambiguous, its legislative history makes unmistakably clear that Congress did not intend fees to be awarded under the EAJA for work done in proceedings on remand before the Social Security Administration.

Little need be said because the legislative history is so straightforward. That history makes clear that in reenacting the EAJA, Congress considered and rejected a provision that would have extended the EAJA to administrative proceedings before the Social Security Administration, including those on remand from district court. * * * Senator Heflin, an active supporter of the provision extending the EAJA to Social Security proceedings, acknowledged that this effort failed because of "institutional opposition." He stated: "While I believe this is an area ripe for protection, political realities dictate otherwise. And this seems to be a fight which will have to be fought another day." 131 Cong.Rec. 20350 (1985).

There is no suggestion in the legislative history that remand proceedings were somehow included elsewhere in the EAJA. To the contrary, the House Report on the 1985 reenactment expressly states that fees cannot be recovered under the EAJA in precisely the situation facing the Court. The House Report reads as follows:

> The court will usually decline to make an award upon the remand decision because the remand order did not yet make the applicant a "prevailing party" and therefore eligible under the EAJA ... [T]he

remand decision is not a "final judgment," nor is the agency decision after remand. Instead, the District Court should enter an order affirming, modifying, or reversing the final HHS decision, and this will usually be the final judgment that starts the 30 days running.... As ... courts have found the only fees which will be available will be for those activities *undertaken in connection with the initial proceedings and not those associated with the administrative proceeding.*

H.R.Rep. No. 99–120, pt. 1, p. 19–20 (1985)(emphasis added).

This discussion does not, as respondent asserts, refer only to the initial administrative proceeding and not the proceeding on remand. Instead, this language affirms what the language of the EAJA likewise makes plain: that the EAJA does not authorize recovery of fees incurred in remand proceedings before the Social Security Administration.

Our duty is to apply statutes as they were enacted by Congress, not to take it upon ourselves to overcome the "political realities" that blocked what we might consider to be good legislation. However desirable it might be as a matter of policy for Social Security claimants to be able to recover attorney's fees for proceedings on remand before the agency, that is not the statute that Congress enacted. Therefore, I dissent.

NOTES

1. The citizen suit provisions of many statutes allowing fees require that a notice letter be sent so many days in advance of suit warning that the suit will be filed unless the problem is cleared up. Is the time spent in researching and writing the intent-to-sue letter compensable? Public Interest Research Group of New Jersey, Inc. v. Windall, 51 F.3d 1179 (3d Cir.1995) (yes).

2. As *Sullivan* indicates, often an aggrieved party will seek redress in an administrative forum before filing suit in a court. Assume that the party obtains relief in that forum. Should a court have the power to award fees for the work done in that forum? Should it make a difference whether the judicial action is filed before or after the administrative proceeding is completed? Compare New York Gaslight Club, Inc. v. Carey, 447 U.S. 54, 100 S.Ct. 2024, 64 L.Ed.2d 723 (1980)(fees awarded where judicial action filed before the plaintiff prevailed in administrative proceeding) with North Carolina Department of Transportation v. Crest Street Community Council, Inc., 479 U.S. 6, 107 S.Ct. 336, 93 L.Ed.2d 188 (1986)(fees may not be awarded where judicial action not filed until after the plaintiff prevailed in administrative proceeding). Should it make a difference whether aggrieved parties are required to exhaust their administrative remedies before filing a judicial action? Compare New York Gaslight Club, Inc. v. Carey, 447 U.S. 54, 100 S.Ct. 2024, 64 L.Ed.2d 723 (1980)(fees awarded for work performed in administrative forum where administrative remedies had to be exhausted before pursuing judicial remedy) with Webb v. Dyer County Board of Education, 471 U.S. 234, 105 S.Ct. 1923, 85 L.Ed.2d 233 (1985)(no fees awarded for work performed in administrative forum where the plaintiff pursued optional administrative remedy before filing in court). For criticism of having the availability of fees

turn on these distinctions, see Marjorie A. Silver, Evening the Odds: The Case for Attorneys' Fee Awards for Administrative Resolution of Title VI and Title VII Disputes, 67 N.C.L.Rev. 379 (1989).

3. Small distinctions continue to matter in determining whether fees for legal work performed before administrative agencies will be compensable. In Ardestani v. INS, 502 U.S. 129, 112 S.Ct. 515, 116 L.Ed.2d 496 (1991), the Supreme Court rejected a request for fees under the EAJA. The holding was that fees incurred in INS administrative deportation proceedings were not eligible for reimbursement under the EAJA because the proceedings did not occur "under section 554" of the Administrative Procedure Act, even though that section states that it applies to "every case of adjudication required by statute to be determined on the record after opportunity for an agency hearing." Justice O'Connor's majority opinion took a plain language approach to the statutory interpretation question to decide that the EAJA did not reach the INS proceedings. Justices Blackmun and Stevens dissented in *Ardestani* on the basis that once the trial court determined that the government's position was not substantially justified, the specific legislative history and overall purposes of the EAJA strongly favored the availability of attorney's fees in deportation proceedings. They relied heavily on Justice O'Connor's own majority opinion in *Sullivan v. Hudson*.

4. Public officials may seek reimbursement under the Ethics in Government Act, 28 U.S.C. § 593(f), for fees expended to defend themselves when an independent counsel's investigation does not lead to an indictment. However, it can be difficult to meet the Act's requirement that the claimant prove that the fees would not have been expended had there been no independent counsel. Thus, President and Senator Clinton were denied all but $85,000 of a $3.5 million claim for the fees they expended to defend themselves during the independent counsel's investigation of the Whitewater matter. (The Clintons did not seek reimbursement for fees expended in connection with investigation of the President's relations with Monica Lewinsky.) The court held that the Clintons had failed to prove that they would not have incurred certain attorney's fees but for the requirements of the Act. The court believed that the Department of Justice would have conducted an investigation of similar vigor of the Whitewater matter as did Mr. Starr's Office of Independent Counsel. In re Madison Guarantee Savings & Loan (Clinton Fee Application), 334 F.3d 1119 (D.C.Cir.2003).

5. Another series of complications in determining what work is compensable arises when a suit involves more than one claim and:

(a) all the claims have attorney fee shifting provisions, but the plaintiff prevails on only one or a few of them;

(b) only some of the claims litigated provide for counsels' fees, yet the plaintiff prevails on all claims;

(c) only some of the claims allow fee shifting, and the plaintiff prevails only on those claims permitting fee shifting;

(d) only some of the claims allow fee shifting, and the plaintiff prevails only on those claims not permitting fee shifting;

(e) there are multiple claims, some of which authorize fees, yet the court declines to resolve a claim, because it involves constitutional issues or a difficult, novel issue the court prefers to postpone deciding for another time.

Should any fees be awarded in these situations? What work is compensable? For a case sorting out how to award fees in a diversity case involving state law claims, only some of which permit fee-shifting, see Schultz v. Hembree, 975 F.2d 572 (9th Cir.1992). See also Mary F. Derfner & Arthur D. Wolf, 1 Court Awarded Attorney Fees, 12–1—12–30 (2003).

6. Frequently in an institutional reform case, over half the time of the attorneys in a controversy is spent after judgment and relatively little of that time is spent in court or drafting papers for court. Much more time of the attorneys is consumed in determining what the defendants can do, negotiating ways for them to do it and checking that they have done it. What theories can you develop to justify or deny compensation for such time? Assume that the case involves conditions in an institution that will take years or even a decade or more to correct. Does the plaintiff's lawyer have a guarantee of compensation for any time spent acting as a watch dog over that institution as to matters that are somehow connected to the suit? See Ross Sandler & David Schoenbrod, Democracy by Decree 130–31 (2003) (criticizing the practice). Compare, e.g., Halderman v. Pennhurst State School & Hospital, 49 F.3d 939 (3d Cir.1995) (no fees for time spent in public relations efforts in case regarding Pennsylvania's care of mentally retarded citizens) with Johnson v. City of Tulsa, 489 F.3d 1089 (10th Cir.2007) (prevailing party in civil rights class action entitled to attorney's fees for activity related to properly implementing the decree and to "preserve the fruits of the decree;" however, the court cautioned that not all post-decree work is compensable and encouraged the parties to spell out compensable activities in the decree itself).

7. Should the time spent preparing and litigating the fee application be compensable? The Supreme Court has held that once a court determines under the Equal Access to Justice Act that the government's position was not substantially justified, a second finding regarding substantial justification is not necessary to award fees for any litigation over the fee award. INS v. Jean, 496 U.S. 154, 110 S.Ct. 2316, 110 L.Ed.2d 134 (1990). However, the Ninth Circuit has approved reducing the "fees-on-fees" in proportion to the amount actually awarded for work on the underlying merits of the case. Thompson v. Gomez, 45 F.3d 1365 (9th Cir.1995)(awarding 87.2% of fees on fees where the plaintiffs received 87.2% of fees claimed). See also Volk v. Gonzalez, 262 F.3d 528 (5th Cir.2001) (although Prison Litigation Reform Act permits fees on fees, the award is subject to the Act's limitation that total fees awarded may not exceed 150 percent of the judgment).

8. Although fee requests need to be filed in a timely manner, it may not be utterly clear when the time begins to run. For example, in a case like *Sullivan v. Hudson*, where there is a remand to an administrative agency, when must the plaintiff file for fees? In Melkonyan v. Sullivan, 501 U.S. 89, 111 S.Ct. 2157, 115 L.Ed.2d 78 (1991), the Supreme Court held that the filing period for an attorney's fee application under the EAJA commences after expiration of the time to appeal a final judgment rendered by a court that

terminates the action for which EAJA fees may be received. The time period does not commence until after entry of the administrative agency order following remand from the district court, which may well come after the time to appeal the court's final judgment. In Shalala v. Schaefer, 509 U.S. 292, 113 S.Ct. 2625, 125 L.Ed.2d 239 (1993), the Court reiterated that the 30–day time limit is triggered by the entry of judgment rather than final disposition on remand. The Court also eliminated a source of confusion about the application of this rule under the Social Security Act by requiring district courts to enter a judgment whether or not an order of remand is also issued. See also F.R.Civ.P. 54(d)(2)(1993 amendments establish procedures and deadlines for presenting claims for attorney's fees).

2. THE RATE OF COMPENSATION

Ordinarily, less work is compensable than would be billed by an attorney in private practice handling the same matter. In this sense, "reasonable" fees differ from market practices. What about the calculation of the amount of the fees for the work that is compensable? Should the fee be that which an attorney in private practice would bill a prosperous client or what cost the firm actually incurs in providing the legal work? Can the court enhance the award due to factors such as providing an especially high quality of legal work? These questions are vitally important to public interest firms, which may have to rely on court-awarded fees for survival; they also have an influence on the willingness of private firms to take on *pro bono* cases. For an empirical study of the effects of the Supreme Court's decisions interpreting civil rights fee-shifting statutes, see Julie Davies, Federal Civil Rights Practice in the 1990's: The Dichotomy Between Reality and Theory, 48 Hastings L.J. 197 (1997).

In Blum v. Stenson, 465 U.S. 886, 104 S.Ct. 1541, 79 L.Ed.2d 891 (1984), the Supreme Court held that enhancements for quality of work should only rarely be made and only where there is specific evidence of exceptional quality. In addition, the court held that the number of people benefited as a result of the lawsuit was not relevant when the fee was provided for by statute. "Unlike the calculation of attorney's fees under the 'common fund doctrine' where a reasonable fee is based on a percentage of the fund bestowed on the class, a reasonable fee under § 1988 reflects the amount of attorney time reasonably expended on the litigation." See Dan B. Dobbs, Reducing Attorney's Fees for Partial Success: A Comment on *Hensley* and *Blum,* 1986 Wis.L.Rev. 835.

Blum also held that the appropriate hourly rate awarded under the Civil Rights Attorney's Fees Awards Act of 1976, 42 U.S.C. § 1988, should be based on prevailing market rates rather than rates commensurate with the actual cost of providing the service and that these rates should apply to all attorneys, whether they work for a private firm or a public interest group. In a similar vein, the Court has held that a "reasonable attorney's fee" may include separate compensation for paralegals, law clerks, and recent law graduates at prevailing market rates, where the practice in the relevant market is to bill for such work separately. Missouri v. Jenkins (*Jenkins I*), 491 U.S. 274, 109 S.Ct. 2463, 105 L.Ed.2d 229 (1989). Accord, Richlin Security Service Co. v. Chertoff, 553 U.S. ___, 128 S.Ct. 2007, 170 L.Ed.2d 960 (2008) (a prevailing party under the Equal Access to Justice Act may recover its paralegal fees from the U.S. Government at prevailing market rates, not at the lower out-of-pocket cost of the attorney).

In contrast to these decisions, the Supreme Court has consistently held that expert fees are not reimbursable under statutes allowing the recovery of "attorney's fees" or "costs," absent express legislative authority such as 42 U.S.C. § 1988(c). For example, in Arlington Central School District Board of Education v. Murphy, 548 U.S. 291, 126 S.Ct. 2455, 165 L.Ed.2d 526 (2006), the Court held that expenses incurred by parents for expert serving as an educational consultant in an Individuals with Disabilities Education Act case were not recoverable as "costs." See also Crawford Fitting Co. v. J.T. Gibbons, Inc., 482 U.S. 437, 107 S.Ct. 2494, 96 L.Ed.2d 385 (1987) (rejecting fees charged by an expert witness to testify at trial); and West Virginia University Hospitals, Inc. v. Casey, 499 U.S. 83, 111 S.Ct. 1138, 113 L.Ed.2d 68 (1991) (rejecting fees of expert who helped attorney prepare for trial).

The Supreme Court has frequently addressed the propriety of making other upward or downward adjustments:

(A) SUPERIOR PERFORMANCE

In Pennsylvania v. Delaware Valley Citizens' Council for Clean Air, 478 U.S. 546, 565–566, 106 S.Ct. 3088, 3098, 92 L.Ed.2d 439, 456–457 (1986), the Court refined *Blum's* holding:

> A strong presumption that the lodestar figure—the product of reasonable hours times a reasonable rate—represents a "reasonable" fee is wholly consistent with the rationale behind the usual fee-shifting statute, including the one in the present case. These statutes were not designed as a form of economic relief to improve the financial lot of attorneys, nor were they intended to replicate exactly the fee an attorney could earn through a private fee arrangement with his client. Instead, the aim of such statutes was to enable private parties to obtain legal help in seeking redress for injuries resulting from the actual or threatened violation of specific federal laws. Hence, if plaintiffs, such as Delaware Valley, find it possible to engage a lawyer based on the statutory assurance that he will be paid a "reasonable fee," the purpose behind the fee-shifting statute has been satisfied.
>
> Moreover, when an attorney first accepts a case and agrees to represent the client, he obligates himself to perform to the best of his ability and to produce the best possible results commensurate with his skill and his client's interests. Calculating the fee award in a manner that accounts for these factors, either in determining the reasonable

number of hours expended on the litigation or in setting the reasonable hourly rate, thus adequately compensates the attorney, and leaves very little room for enhancing the award based on his post-engagement performance. In short, the lodestar figure includes most, if not all, of the relevant factors comprising a "reasonable" attorney's fee, and it is unnecessary to enhance the fee for superior performance in order to serve the statutory purpose of enabling plaintiffs to secure legal assistance.

(B) RISK OF LOSS CONTINGENCY

In City of Burlington v. Dague, 505 U.S. 557, 112 S.Ct. 2638, 120 L.Ed.2d 449 (1992), the Supreme Court dealt with adjusting the lodestar, under a fee-shifting statute, based on the contingency that there is a risk of losing the case:

> We note at the outset that an enhancement for contingency would likely duplicate in substantial part factors already subsumed in the lodestar. The risk of loss in a particular case (and, therefore, the attorney's contingent risk) is the product of two factors: (1) the legal and factual merits of the claim, and (2) the difficulty of establishing those merits. The second factor, however, is ordinarily reflected in the lodestar—either in the higher number of hours expended to overcome the difficulty, or in the higher hourly rate of the attorney skilled and experienced enough to do so. Taking account of it again through lodestar enhancement amounts to double-counting.
>
> The first factor (relative merits of the claim) is not reflected in the lodestar, but there are good reasons why it should play no part in the calculation of the award. * * * [T]he consequence of awarding contingency enhancement to take account of this "merits" factor would be to provide attorneys with the same incentive to bring relatively meritless claims as relatively meritorious ones. Assume, for example, two claims, one with underlying merit of 20%, the other of 80%. Absent any contingency enhancement, a contingent-fee attorney would prefer to take the latter, since he is four times more likely to be paid. But with a contingency enhancement, this preference will disappear: the enhancement for the 20% claim would be a multiplier of 5 ($^{100}/_{20}$), which is quadruple the 1.25 multiplier ($^{100}/_{80}$) that would attach to the 80% claim. Thus, enhancement for the contingency risk posed by each case would encourage meritorious claims to be brought, but only at the social cost of indiscriminately encouraging nonmeritorious claims to be brought as well. * * *
>
> [W]e perceive no * * * basis, fairly derivable from the fee-shifting statutes, by which contingency enhancement, if adopted, could be restricted to fewer than all contingent-fee cases. And we see a number of reasons for concluding that no contingency enhancement whatever is compatible with the fee-shifting statutes at issue. First, just as the statutory language limiting fees to prevailing (or substantially prevailing) parties bars a prevailing plaintiff from recovering fees relating to

claims on which he lost, so should it bar a prevailing plaintiff from recovering for the risk of loss. An attorney operating on a contingency-fee basis pools the risks presented by his various cases: cases that turn out to be successful pay for the time he gambled on those that did not. To award a contingency enhancement under a fee-shifting statute would in effect pay for the attorney's time (or anticipated time) in cases where his client does not prevail.

Second, * * * "we have generally turned away from the contingent-fee model"—which would make the fee award a percentage of the value of the relief awarded in the primary action—"to the lodestar model." We have done so, it must be noted, even though the lodestar model often (perhaps, generally) results in a larger fee award than the contingent-fee model. * * *

Contingency enhancement is a feature inherent in the contingent-fee model (since attorneys factor in the particular risks of a case in negotiating their fee and in deciding whether to accept the case). To engraft this feature onto the lodestar model would be to concoct a hybrid scheme that resorts to the contingent-fee model to increase a fee award but not to reduce it. Contingency enhancement is therefore not consistent with our general rejection of the contingent-fee model for fee awards, nor is it necessary to the determination of a reasonable fee.

(C) CONTINGENCY FEE CONTRACT

In Blanchard v. Bergeron, 489 U.S. 87, 109 S.Ct. 939, 103 L.Ed.2d 67 (1989), the Court was faced with whether an award of attorney's fees under section 1988 was limited to no more than the amount provided in the plaintiff's contingent-fee arrangement with the attorney. In this case, the 40% contingency contract would have yielded a $4,000 fee on a $10,000 recovery; the district court had calculated the reasonable fee to be $7,500 plus costs. The Court unanimously[a] held:

> As we understand § 1988's provision for allowing a "reasonable attorney's fee," it contemplates reasonable compensation, in light of all of the circumstances, for the time and effort expended by the attorney for the prevailing plaintiff, no more and no less. Should a fee agreement provide less than a reasonable fee calculated in this manner, the defendant should nevertheless be required to pay the higher amount. The defendant is not, however, required to pay the amount called for in a contingent fee contract if it is more than a reasonable fee calculated in the usual way. It is true that the purpose of § 1988 was to make sure that competent counsel was available to civil rights plaintiffs, and it is of course arguable that if a plaintiff is able to secure an attorney on the basis of a contingent or other fee agreement, the purpose of the statute is served if the plaintiff is bound by his contract. On that basis, however, the plaintiff should recover

---

a. Justice Scalia wrote a separate concurring opinion on a point not relevant here.

nothing from the defendant, which would be plainly contrary to the statute. And Congress implemented its purpose by broadly requiring all defendants to pay a reasonable fee to all prevailing plaintiffs, if ordered to do so by the court. Thus it is that a plaintiff's recovery will not be reduced by what he must pay his counsel. Plaintiffs who can afford to hire their own lawyers, as well as impecunious litigants, may take advantage of this provision. And where there are lawyers or organizations that will take a plaintiff's case without compensation, that fact does not bar the award of a reasonable fee. All of this is consistent with and reflects our decisions in cases involving court-awarded attorney's fees. * * *

If a contingent fee agreement were to govern as a strict limitation on the award of attorney's fees, an undesirable emphasis might be placed on the importance of the recovery of damages in civil rights litigation. The intention of Congress was to encourage successful civil rights litigation, not to create a special incentive to prove damages and shortchange efforts to seek effective injunctive or declaratory relief. Affirming the decision below would create an artificial disincentive for an attorney who enters into a contingent fee agreement, unsure of whether his client's claim sounded in state tort law or in federal civil rights, from fully exploring all possible avenues of relief. Section 1988 makes no distinction between actions for damages and suits for equitable relief. Congress has elected to encourage meritorious civil rights claims because of the benefits of such litigation for the named plaintiff and for society at large, irrespective of whether the action seeks monetary damages.

It should also be noted that we have not accepted the contention that fee awards in § 1983 damages cases should be modeled upon the contingent fee arrangements used in personal injury litigation. "[W]e reject the notion that a civil rights action for damages constitutes nothing more than a private tort suit benefiting only the individual plaintiffs whose rights were violated. Unlike most private tort litigants, a civil rights plaintiff seeks to vindicate important civil and constitutional rights that cannot be valued solely in monetary terms." City of Riverside v. Rivera, 477 U.S. 561, 574, 106 S.Ct. 2686, 2694, 91 L.Ed.2d 466 (1986).

Respondent cautions us that refusing to limit recovery to the amount of the contingency agreement will result in a "windfall" to attorneys who accept § 1983 actions. Yet the very nature of recovery under § 1988 is designed to prevent any such "windfall." Fee awards are to be reasonable, reasonable as to billing rates and reasonable as to the number of hours spent in advancing the successful claims. Accordingly, fee awards, properly calculated, by definition will represent the reasonable worth of the services rendered in vindication of a plaintiff's civil rights claim. It is central to the awarding of attorney's fees under § 1988 that the district court judge, in his or her good judgment, make the assessment of what is a reasonable fee under the circumstances of the case. The trial judge should not be limited by the contractual fee agreement between plaintiff and counsel.

489 U.S. at 93–96, 109 S.Ct. at 944–946.

NOTES

1. Some lower courts have read *Dague* as requiring the lodestar to be used in all cases completely unadorned with enhancements. E.g., Newhouse v. McCormick & Co., 110 F.3d 635 (8th Cir.1997). However, other courts have reasoned that *Dague* did not reject all enhancements. Guam Society of Obstetricians & Gynecologists v. Ada, 100 F.3d 691 (9th Cir.1996), cert. denied, 522 U.S. 949, 118 S.Ct. 367, 139 L.Ed.2d 286 (1997), awarded an enhancement to account for the undesirability of the case, which challenged the constitutionality of a highly restrictive abortion statute. Cook v. Niedert, 142 F.3d 1004 (7th Cir.1998), allowed an enhancement for risk in a common fund case because the fee came from the class of plaintiffs and not from the defendants. Ihler v. Chisholm, 298 Mont. 254, 995 P.2d 439 (2000), did not allow an enhancement of the lodestar in light of *Dague*, but permitted out of town counsel to be compensated at their home rates, rather than lower local market rates, where local counsel could not be found to bring a civil rights suit. For discussion of *Dague*, see Peter H. Huang, A New Options Theory for Risk Multipliers of Attorney's Fees in Federal Civil Rights Litigation, 73 N.Y.U.L.Rev.1943 (1998).

2. A court awarding a fee under state law need not follow the Supreme Court's interpretation of the federal attorney's fees statutes. E.g., Schefke v. Reliable Collection Agency, Ltd., 96 Hawai'i 408, 32 P.3d 52 (2001) (enhancements permitted despite *Dague*); Rendine v. Pantzer, 141 N.J. 292, 661 A.2d 1202 (1995) (same); Softsolutions, Inc. v. Brigham Young University, 1 P.3d 1095 (Utah 2000) (despite *Blum*, fees for in-house counsel are limited to consideration actually paid, not market rate).

3. For some time, it was unclear whether there was any per se rule that attorney's fees had to be proportionate to the damages recovered. In City of Riverside v. Rivera, 477 U.S. 561, 106 S.Ct. 2686, 91 L.Ed.2d 466 (1986), the Supreme Court affirmed an attorney's fee award of $245,000 where the jury awarded only $33,350 in compensatory and punitive damages. Only a plurality thought that Congress did not intend to adopt a strict proportionality rule. However, *Blanchard*, pp. 944–946, which on this issue was a unanimous opinion, cited *Rivera* with approval, suggesting that the plurality result is now the law. E.g., Mercer v. Duke University, 401 F.3d 199 (4th Cir.2005) (award of $350,000 in attorney's fees to female college football place kicker, who had prevailed in her Title IX discrimination action against the university but had obtained only $1 nominal damages, was not an abuse of discretion because the case decided an issue of first impression under Title IX, and had served a significant public purpose for female athletes everywhere). But see Farrar v. Hobby, 506 U.S. 103, 113 S.Ct. 566, 121 L.Ed.2d 494 (1992) (when no other relief except nominal damages is awarded, only reasonable fee may be no fee at all).

SEC. C THE MEASURE OF THE FEES 947

4. In *Blanchard*, the fee the court awarded was $7,500 plus costs, rather than the $4,000 called for under the contingency contract. Suppose instead the jury in *Blanchard* awarded $100,000 in damages, making the contingency fee $40,000, but the court still set the "reasonable" statutory fee at $7500. What amount should the attorney receive in each situation? How much should the client net? See Venegas v. Mitchell, 495 U.S. 82, 110 S.Ct. 1679, 109 L.Ed.2d 74 (1990)(the statutory award does not set a ceiling on the contingency fee; it "controls what the losing defendant must pay, not what the prevailing plaintiff must pay his lawyer"). Should there be outside review of the reasonableness of the contingency fee agreement? See Newton v. Cox, 878 S.W.2d 105 (Tenn.1994), cert. denied, 513 U.S. 869, 115 S.Ct. 189, 130 L.Ed.2d 122 (1994) (legislature may set limit on contingency fees in medical malpractice actions). As a practical note, it is well to make written provision between the client and the law firm as to who will receive court-awarded fees. In order to avoid disputes and possible tax problems, it is also prudent for lawyers to make a written assignment to the firm of any fees awarded for their work on the case.

5. The ownership of the fee award comes up in several contexts. For example, in reasoning parallel to *Blanchard*, the Federal Circuit has held that a fee award under the EAJA is made to the prevailing party and not to the party's attorney. FDL Technologies, Inc. v. United States, 967 F.2d 1578 (Fed.Cir.1992). It made a difference because the party had filed for bankruptcy; the award became part of the assets available to all creditors. The attorney was just another unsecured creditor of the debtor. See also Howard v. Mail–Well Envelope Co., 150 F.3d 1227 (10th Cir.), cert. denied, 525 U.S. 1019, 119 S.Ct. 546, 142 L.Ed.2d 454 (1998) ("[T]he attorney remains at the mercy of the client, who can either demand attorney's fees from the defendant, or not, as he chooses. If the client chooses not to ask for the fees, the attorney has no standing to request them.").

The ownership has also been a matter of some controversy because of the tax consequences. The U.S. Supreme Court settled a split in the circuits when it held that the portion of a money judgment or settlement paid to a plaintiff's attorney under a contingent-fee agreement is income attributable to the plaintiff under the Internal Revenue Code. Commissioner of Internal Revenue v. Banks, 543 U.S. 426, 125 S.Ct. 826, 160 L.Ed.2d 859 (2005) (reproduced at pp. 631–636). The significance of the holding concerns the non-deductibility of attorney's fees as miscellaneous itemized deductions under the Alternative Minimum Tax (AMT). If the fees are not deductible, then the plaintiff must pay taxes on the entire amount, even though a substantial portion is immediately paid to the attorney under the contingent-fee agreement. Thus, in years past, a plaintiff like Heather Mercer (Note 3, supra), who received an award of $1, probably would have had to pay a substantial AMT on the $350,000 fee award, even though the fee would have been directed to her attorneys in full. The attorneys also would pay tax on the fee award as earned income. The Court noted that this unfair situation is ameliorated to a degree because Congress enacted the American Jobs Creation Act of 2004, 26 U.S.C. §§ 62(a)(19) and (e). The Act allows future taxpayers, in computing adjusted gross income under the AMT, to deduct "attorney fees and court costs paid by, or on behalf of, the taxpayer," but only in certain categories of employment discrimination and civil rights litigation, such as Heather Mercer's Title IX claim. The Supreme Court's decision on this issue is reviewed and criticized strongly in Robert W. Wood, The Federal Income Taxation of Contingent Attorneys' Fees: Patchwork by Congress and Supreme Court Creates Uncertainty, 67 Mont.L.Rev. 1 (2006) (criticizing the results, which "shriek of inequity and bear no relationship to the fundamentals of a fair system," and noting the limited relief provided by the Jobs Act, which applies only to cases of employment).

6. Other questions concern whether and how a fee award should account for delay in payment. Some courts award fees on the basis of prevailing rates at the time of the award as a means of accounting for delay; others use fees prevailing at the time the work was performed and then add on interest. See, e.g., In re Telesphere International Securities Litigation, 753 F.Supp. 716 (N.D.Ill.1990). In addition, at least six circuits have held that a court also may award post-judgment interest on attorney's fees accruing from the date that the trial court determined that the plaintiff class was entitled to fees, even if the fee award is not quantified until a later point. Two other circuits, however, take the position that interest should run only from the date of quantification of the claim for fees because, before then, the claim is unliquidated and is not a "money judgment" for purposes of the statute. See Boehner v. McDermott, 541 F.Supp.2d 310 (D.D.C.2008) (noting split in circuits, but choosing to follow majority rule in absence of controlling authority from its own circuit court); Russell E. Lovell, Court–Awarded Attorneys' Fees: Examining Issues of Delay, Payment and Risk (1999).

3. APPLYING THE LODESTAR METHOD

The next opinion applies the lodestar approach of awarding fees to prevailing parties in a very well-known public law case, one of the two challenges to the affirmative action policies at the University of Michigan. Consider the choices the district court made as you assess the fairness of the award.

GRATZ v. BOLLINGER

United States District Court, Eastern District of Michigan, 2005
353 F.Supp.2d 929

DUGGAN, DISTRICT JUDGE.

On October 14, 1997, Plaintiffs filed this class-action lawsuit challenging the admissions policy of the University of Michigan's ("University") College of Literature, Science, and the Arts ("LSA"). Presently before the Court is Plaintiffs' motion for an award of attorneys' fees and costs pursuant to 42 U.S.C. § 1988.

FACTUAL AND PROCEDURAL BACKGROUND

Plaintiffs, both of whom are Caucasian, brought this lawsuit alleging that Defendants violated Title VI of the Civil Rights Act of 1964, codified at 42 U.S.C. § 2000d, the Equal Protection Clause of the Fourteenth

Amendment, and 42 U.S.C. § 1981, by considering race as a factor in the LSA's admissions policies. * * *

A group of African–American and Latino students who applied for, or intended to apply for, admission to the University, as well as the Citizens for Affirmative Action's Preservation, a Michigan nonprofit organization, sought to intervene pursuant to Rule 24 of the Federal Rules of Civil Procedure. The Intervenors claimed the resolution of the case directly threatened the access of qualified African–American and Latino students to public higher education and that the University would not adequately represent their interest in educational opportunity. This Court denied the request to intervene, but the Sixth Circuit reversed.

* * *

The parties subsequently filed cross-motions for summary judgment with respect to liability. Plaintiffs asserted that Defendants' use of race as a factor in admissions to the LSA violated Title VI, § 1981, and the Equal Protection Clause of the Fourteenth Amendment. Relying on Justice Powell's opinion in Regents of University of California v. Bakke, 438 U.S. 265, 98 S.Ct. 2733, 57 L.Ed.2d 750 (1978), Defendants responded that the consideration of race as a factor in admissions decisions might serve a compelling government interest in some cases and the LSA had such an interest in the educational benefits that result from having a racially and ethnically diverse student body. Defendants further argued that the LSA's admissions policy was narrowly tailored to serve that interest. The Intervenors argued that the LSA had a compelling interest in remedying the University's past and current discrimination against minorities.

* * *

Because the Court ruled that the current admissions policy was constitutional, it denied Plaintiffs' request for injunctive relief. The Court also issued an opinion and order rejecting the Intervenors' arguments, concluding that the Intervenors "failed to present any evidence that the discrimination alleged by them, or the continuing effects of such discrimination, was the real justification for the LSA's race-conscious admissions programs."

* * *

On June 23, 2003, the Supreme Court issued opinions in both cases. Gratz v. Bollinger, 539 U.S. 244, 123 S.Ct. 2411, 156 L.Ed.2d 257 (2003); Grutter v. Bollinger, 539 U.S. 982, 124 S.Ct. 35, 156 L.Ed.2d 694 (2003) [upholding the admission policy of the Law School at Michigan]. As the Supreme Court set forth in its opinion in this case, Plaintiffs raised two arguments in their challenge to this Court's opinion granting summary judgment to Defendants. The Supreme Court described Plaintiffs' first argument:

> [Plaintiffs] argue[d], first and foremost, that the University's use of race in undergraduate admissions violates the Fourteenth Amend-

ment. Specifically, they contend that this Court has only sanctioned the use of racial classifications to remedy identified discrimination, a justification on which [Defendants] have never relied ... [Plaintiffs] further argue that diversity as a basis for employing racial preferences is simply too open-ended, ill-defined, and indefinite to constitute a compelling interest capable of supporting narrowly-tailored means.

Gratz, 539 U.S. at 268, 123 S.Ct. at 2426. Alternatively, Plaintiffs argued that even if the University's interest in diversity can constitute a compelling state interest, use of race in its admissions policy was not narrowly tailored to achieve such an interest.

The Supreme Court rejected Plaintiffs' first argument, referring to its holding in *Grutter* that a university's interest in a racially and ethnically diverse student body is a compelling interest that may justify its consideration of race in the admissions process. The Supreme Court agreed with Plaintiffs, however, that the LSA's admissions policy was not narrowly tailored to achieve that compelling interest and therefore violates the Equal Protection Clause of the Fourteenth Amendment, Title VI, and 42 U.S.C. § 1981. The Supreme Court therefore reversed this Court's decision granting Defendants' summary judgment motion with respect to liability and remanded the case for proceedings consistent with its opinion.

In a footnote to its decision, the Supreme Court upheld this Court's rejection of the Intervenors' justification for the LSA's race-conscious admissions programs. * * *

On June 30, 2004, Plaintiffs filed the pending motion seeking an interim award of attorneys' fees and costs pursuant to 42 U.S.C. § 1988. Plaintiffs seek an award in the amount of $2,071,352.84. These fees and costs represent expenditures from the Fall of 1997 through the filing of their motion. During that period, Plaintiffs were represented by at least sixteen attorneys from [the Maslon law firm located in Minneapolis, the Center for Individual Rights (CIR) located in Washington, D.C., and local counsel located in Detroit].

Defendants oppose Plaintiffs' motion for an award of attorneys' fees and costs. First, Defendants contend that Plaintiffs are not "prevailing parties" pursuant to § 1988. Alternatively, Defendants argue that the fees and costs Plaintiffs seek are not reasonable. * * *

APPLICABLE LAW AND ANALYSIS

Attorneys' Fees in General and the Meaning of the Term "Prevailing Party"

* * *

Defendants argue that Plaintiffs are not prevailing parties because they have not secured an enforceable judgment against Defendants *that directly benefits* any Plaintiff. In other words, Defendants argue that while the LSA's admissions policies may have been declared unconstitutional by the Supreme Court, "[n]either Gratz, nor Hamacher, nor any class member has shown that they *were not admitted* because of the manner in which the University considered race under its stricken undergraduate policies but *would have been admitted* if the University had considered race in a manner approved by *Grutter.*" This argument, however, ignores one of Congress' primary reasons for enacting § 1988.

Congress specifically enacted § 1988 to encourage "private attorney generals" to further the interests of the general public. * * *

Plaintiffs' civil rights action resulted in a judicial pronouncement that the LSA's admissions policies were unconstitutional and therefore, as a result of their lawsuit, Defendants were required to alter those policies. Regardless of whether this change ever will benefit Gratz, Hamacher, or another specific class member, Plaintiffs achieved a result they pursued for the benefit of the public in general. Thus the Court concludes that Plaintiffs are "prevailing parties" as the Supreme Court has defined that term.

"Reasonable" Attorneys' Fees

Section 1988 only allows a prevailing party to recover its "reasonable" attorneys' fees. * * *

The starting point for calculating a reasonable attorneys' fees award "should be the determination of the fee applicant's 'lodestar,' which is the proven number of hours reasonably expended on the case by an attorney, multiplied by his [or her] court-ascertained reasonable hourly rate." "The party seeking an award of fees should submit evidence supporting the hours worked and rates claimed. Where the documentation of hours is inadequate, the district court may reduce the award accordingly." The Supreme Court has instructed district courts to exclude fees that were not "reasonably expended," such as fees due to overstaffing or redundancy of work.

Once the district court determines the fee applicant's lodestar, the court must consider other factors relevant to the reasonableness of any fee award.[2] One important factor is the "results obtained." As the Supreme Court has explained, there are two situations where the results obtained may affect the fee award:

> In some cases a plaintiff may present in one lawsuit distinctly different claims for relief that are based on different facts and legal theories. In such a suit ... counsel's work on one claim will be unrelated to his work on another claim. Accordingly, work on an

---

2. The factors identified by the Supreme Court are: (1) the time and labor required by a given case; (2) the novelty and difficulty of the questions presented; (3) the skill needed to perform the legal service properly; (4) the preclusion of employment by the attorney due to acceptance of the case; (5) the customary fee; (6) whether the fee is fixed or contingent; (7) time limitations imposed by the client or the circumstances; (8) the amount involved and the results obtained; (9) the experience, reputation, and ability of the attorneys; (10) the "undesirability" of the case; (11) the nature and length of the professional relationship with the client; and (12) awards in similar cases. *Hensley,* 461 U.S. at 430 n. 3, 103 S.Ct. at 1937 n. 3 (citing Johnson v. Georgia Highway Express, Inc., 488 F.2d 714, 717–19 (5th Cir.1974)).

unsuccessful claim cannot be deemed to have been "expended in pursuit of the ultimate result achieved." . . . The congressional intent to limit awards to prevailing parties requires that these unrelated claims be treated as if they had been raised in separate lawsuits, and therefore no fee may be awarded for services on the unsuccessful claim.

[Hensley v. Eckerhart, 461 U.S. 424, 434–35, 103 S.Ct. 1933, 1940, 76 L.Ed.2d 40 (1983).] * * *

As the *Hensley* Court instructed, it is within the district court's discretion to attempt to identify specific hours that should be eliminated or to simply reduce the award to account for the limited success.

Limited Success

Defendants ask the Court to reduce any fee award because Plaintiffs only achieved partial or limited success. Specifically, Defendants argue that Plaintiffs' primary purpose in bringing their lawsuit was to invalidate the consideration of an applicant's race in college admissions decisions. As Defendants point out, this Court and the Supreme Court rejected Plaintiffs' argument that race is never a relevant and legitimate consideration in the admissions process.

* * *

The Court cannot possibly determine from Plaintiffs' billing statements the amount of hours expended on this issue as opposed to the "narrowly tailored" issue on which they prevailed. The Court therefore opts to reduce the hours expended by a percentage amount. In deciding what percentage amount is appropriate, the Court finds it significant that Plaintiffs' lawsuit took on historical significance primarily because they attempted to eliminate race as a permissible factor in undergraduate admissions. Thus the Court concludes that Plaintiffs' failure to prevail on this issue warrants a fifty percent (50%) reduction in the hours expended on this litigation.

Vague Billing Entries and "Block Billing"

Defendants also seek a reduction in the number of hours expended by Plaintiffs' attorneys due to the vagueness of the attorneys' billing records. Defendants argue that vague and general entries such as, "telephone conference," "office conference," "research," and "review article" make it impossible for the Court to evaluate the reasonableness of the hours expended on the litigation. This Court agrees with respect to the billing entries submitted by the Maslon attorneys.

* * *

Additionally, many of the Maslon attorneys' billing entries contain "block billing." For example, Mr. Kolbo's entry for 12/16/97 describes 10 hours of work to: "prepare for and attend pretrial with judge; meet with co-counsel; calls to CIR." Mr. Herr's entry for 4/8/98 describes 10 hours of work for: "conference with Kirk Kolbo; meet with local counsel; review discovery responses and court notes; attend pretrial conference; conferences with Kirk Kolbo." As a result of such "block billing," the Court is not able to determine the number of hours expended on each discrete task. Thus the Court cannot determine whether the number of hours billed are reasonable.

The Court believes that a ten percent (10%) reduction in Maslon's requested fees is appropriate due to its attorneys' block billing and vague entries.

Fees Related to the Intervenors

Defendants object to a fee award that includes the hours Plaintiffs' attorneys expended litigating against the Intervenors. The Supreme Court has held that a prevailing party in a civil rights lawsuit cannot recover attorneys' fees from an intervenor who has not violated the law, unless the intervention is "frivolous, unreasonable or without foundation." Indep. Fed'n of Flight Attendants v. Zipes, 491 U.S. 754, 761, 109 S.Ct. 2732, 2737, 105 L.Ed.2d 639 (1989). The Court, however, has not decided whether a prevailing party can recover such fees and costs from the defendant whose illegal conduct precipitated the intervention.

At least two circuit courts have interpreted *Zipes* as implying that the prevailing plaintiffs should bear the risk of incurring intervention-related costs as a result of filing a lawsuit and therefore have extended *Zipes* to a prevailing parties' request for intervention-related attorneys' fees from the losing defendant. In a case similar to the one now before this Court, the Fifth Circuit upheld the district court's refusal to award intervention-related fees and costs from the defendant's pocket because the plaintiffs "did not 'prevail' on this issue vis-a-vis the defendant." Hopwood v. Texas, 236 F.3d 256, 280 (5th Cir.2000). As the court explained, "the defendant remained neutral on the intervention issue. In addition, the potential intervenors made clear . . . that the purpose of their intervention was to raise arguments and defenses that the defendant itself had no interest in raising." The Fifth Circuit, however, declined to decide whether a prevailing party always should be barred from shifting to the defendant the costs associated with defending against an intervention.

As in *Hopwood,* Defendants in the pending matter remained neutral on the intervention issue and the purpose of the intervention was to raise arguments and defenses that Defendants expressed no interest in raising. The Intervenors argued that the use of race as a factor in LSA's admissions process was necessary to remedy past discrimination by the University a justification the Supreme Court noted in its opinion the University has *never* asserted during this litigation. Because the Intervenors asserted a completely different defense to the University's admissions process, the Court also finds it likely that the intervention delayed the progress of the litigation. At the very least, the intervention resulted in attorneys' fees and costs that Plaintiffs otherwise would not have incurred. The Court therefore concludes that Plaintiffs are not entitled to attorneys' fees and costs related to the Intervenors.

* * *

Fees Related to Public and Media Relations

Defendants ask the Court to exclude as unreasonable any attorneys' fees related to public and media relations efforts. Plaintiffs argue that such fees are reasonable for two reasons. First, Plaintiffs argue that in a highly publicized case such as this, it is important for attorneys to advise their clients in communicating with the media. Second, Plaintiffs argue that in a class action lawsuit involving a large class such as this, the media offers a means of communicating with class members about the progress and status of the case.

Some courts have found fees related to press relations reimbursable to the extent the hours expended "were reasonably necessary for the proper prosecution of the lawsuit." * * *

[H]owever, a number of courts * * * have found time spent communicating with the press and other news media noncompensable. The Third Circuit has held that compensation for work related to "publicity efforts" is not compensable, noting that "[t]he fact that private lawyers may perform tasks other than legal services for their clients, with their consent and approval, does not justify foisting off such expenses on an adversary under the guise of reimbursable fees." This Court is persuaded by the reasoning * * * and concludes that Plaintiffs should not be compensated for the hours their attorneys expended on media and public relations efforts. * * * But even if the Court were to follow [the contrary precedent], the Court finds that Plaintiffs have not met their burden of showing that the hours billed by their attorneys for media and public relations efforts contributed in a meaningful way to the litigation. If the purpose of counsel's efforts was to prevent Plaintiffs from publicly saying something detrimental to their case or image, the Court cannot conclude that such advice was "necessary to the prosecution of the suit." Counsel simply could have advised their clients to avoid speaking to the media altogether. The fact that a plaintiff and/or his or her attorney decide to speak with the media does not mean the opposing party should bear the costs of those efforts. Moreover, the Court finds it more likely in this case that the media and public relations efforts reflect an effort by both sides to sway public opinion in this extremely socially and politically divisive matter.

* * *

Duplication of Efforts

If the prevailing party has not already done so, the Supreme Court has advised district courts to exclude from a fee request hours that are redundant, for example due to overstaffing. In the present matter, Plaintiffs were represented by at least sixteen lawyers in three different cities.

While it appears that the Maslon and CIR attorneys have deleted some duplicative billing (for example, participation by more than one attorney at some hearings and depositions), a significant number of billing entries show multiple attorneys charging for the same tasks or for tasks only made necessary because of the large number of attorneys involved in the litigation. For example, many entries relate to telephone conferences and meetings between the attorneys and to preparation of notes, e-mails, and memoranda for the sole purpose of keeping Plaintiffs' other attorneys apprised of progress in the case. In fact, a significant portion of the work performed by local counsel in this case represents unnecessary, redundant services. * * *

CIR enlisted the Maslon firm to litigate this action as Plaintiffs' primary attorneys. The Court therefore concludes that a reduction of the Maslon attorneys' hours only is appropriate where attorneys within the firm engaged in the same tasks and there is no indication of the specific contribution the various lawyers made with respect to that task beyond simply reviewing another attorney's work. The Court believes that a five percent (5%) reduction in the Maslon attorneys' hours fairly represents such duplicative services.

CIR, on the other hand, describes one of its primary responsibilities as finding talented co-counsel to take the leading role in litigating Plaintiffs' claims. Once CIR accomplished this task, the Court sees no reason why CIR's attorneys expended countless hours reviewing Maslon's work, reviewing documents submitted in the litigation that a Maslon attorney also reviewed and billed, and discussing the course of the litigation with the Maslon attorneys. The Court therefore Court concludes that a ten percent (10%) reduction in CIR's requested fees is appropriate due to duplicative efforts.

Fees Related to Travel

Some courts completely disallow compensation for an attorney's travel time. Other courts allow compensation for such time, although some of those courts reduce the attorney's hourly rate for such time. The Court finds it equitable in this case, particularly because Plaintiffs were represented by two out-of-state law firms, to reimburse Plaintiffs' attorneys for *most* of their travel time but at fifty percent (50%) of their reasonable hourly rate.[5] As discussed below, the Court finds that some of the trips made by the attorneys in this case were unnecessary and it therefore will exclude the travel hours related to those trips completely.

Most of the hours billed for travel relate to the attorneys' trips to Detroit, Michigan for court hearings, meetings with Plaintiffs, and deposi-

---

5. Generally Plaintiffs' attorneys reported their travel time in block billing entries. The Court therefore has determined the time for a direct flight to the attorneys' destination and reduced that amount of time from the total hours billed in the block entry. While this approach does not account for travel time to and from the airport or in the airport terminal, the Court believes this to be a reasonable approach and probably the only possible approach other than reducing the time billed entirely.

tions. Additionally, Plaintiffs' attorneys traveled to San Diego and Sacramento, California and College Station, Texas to complete depositions. * * *

The Maslon attorneys also made several trips to Washington, D.C. to meet with attorneys from CIR. Even if it was necessary for the attorneys from both firms to confer during the progress of the litigation, the Court does not believe that it was necessary for those meetings to take place in person. Moreover, putting aside the issue of whether this litigation required representation by so many well-qualified attorneys from two out-of-state firms, the Court sees no reason why Defendants should bear the additional costs incurred because those firms are located in different and distant cities. The Court also finds unreasonable the multiple trips some of the Maslon attorneys made to Washington, D.C. for moot court arguments prior to their argument before the Supreme Court.[6]

* * *

Miscellaneous Hours and Expenses

The attorneys from CIR additionally billed a number of hours related to "local counsel issues" and "potential plaintiffs." The Court finds these hours unreasonable. As to the first category of hours, the Court does not believe that Defendants should incur the extra costs associated with Plaintiffs' representation by out-of-town counsel (e.g. travel related costs) *and* the fees incurred by out-of-town counsel in order to search for appropriate local counsel. As to the second category of hours, the Court does not believe that § 1988 contemplates an award of fees related to an attorneys' search for clients who will serve as model plaintiffs. * * *

While the Court has not excluded the hours attorneys billed for time spent reading books on affirmative action, the Court finds it unreasonable to bill Defendants for the purchase of those books. Defendants should not bear the costs for Plaintiffs' attorneys to stock their libraries. Similarly, while the Court finds the hours Plaintiffs' attorneys expended preparing for oral argument before the Supreme Court reasonable, the Court does not find it reasonable to bill Defendants for the costs of compact discs containing the Supreme Court's "greatest hits." The Court therefore will exclude $126.94 from the costs sought by CIR * * *.

Next, Plaintiffs' seek reimbursement for $277,858.92 in costs incurred during the course of this litigation. * * * $15,928.54 of this amount is attributable to Westlaw expenses, an amount the Court finds exorbitant. The Court will reduce this latter amount by twenty-five percent (25%) or by $3,982.14. The Court also will deduct the $14,676 the Supreme Court

---

6. Mr. Herr and Mr. Purdy made three trips to Washington, D.C. from mid-April to late March 2003 to engage in "mock arguments" prior to the oral argument before the Supreme Court. While the Court recognizes the value of such mock arguments, the Court finds no reason why the Maslon attorneys could not have conducted some of those arguments in Minneapolis. The Court sees no reason why the Maslon attorneys could not locate well-qualified attorneys in their community capable of helping them prepare. The Court therefore will exclude the costs related to the first and second trips.

already awarded to Plaintiffs for costs which they include in their current request for reimbursement.

Local Counsel

Having reviewed Mr. Wright's and Mr. Morgan's billing entries, the Court finds it difficult to identify what use local counsel served in this case other than to increase the number of duplicative hours expended on this litigation. This is not necessarily the fault of Mr. Wright or Mr. Morgan. More likely it is due to the fact that Plaintiffs were represented by at least fifteen other well-qualified lawyers who primarily handled 100% of the litigation.

Mr. Wright actually expended fewer hours duplicating the work of the Maslon and/or CIR attorneys than Mr. Morgan. The Court finds, however, that a number of tasks completed by Mr. Wright could have been performed by non-legal staff (e.g. calling the University to obtain the names of its officers, president and the various deans of the LS & A and their dates of service). A large percentage of Mr. Wright's billing entries also appear to relate to the filing of "a new complaint," presumably in *Grutter*. Having reviewed Mr. Wright's billing records and deleting such hours, the Court finds 36.8 hours reasonably expended in this litigation. With respect to Mr. Wright's expenses, the Court will exclude $484.20, representing $28.94 billed for purchasing a copy of "Diversity Machine" and the mileage to the bookstore and $455.26 for the purchase of a facsimile machine and attachment cable. These reductions will be reflected in the final fees and costs awarded to Plaintiffs for CIR.

Most of Mr. Morgan's billing entries reflect time spent "receiving and reviewing" materials that also were received and reviewed by the Maslon and CIR attorneys. While Mr. Morgan did attend a handful of depositions, those depositions were taken or defended by other attorneys in the case. Of the 323.50 hours billed by Mr. Morgan, the Court identified only 55 hours where Mr. Morgan did more than review filings, pleadings, documents, drafts, letters etc. The Court finds the costs sought by Mr. Morgan to be reasonable.

Reasonable Hourly Rate[8]

To calculate the "reasonable hourly rate" component of the lodestar calculation, the Supreme Court has instructed district courts to assess the "prevailing market rate in the relevant community." Where a party has selected out-of-town attorneys, the Sixth Circuit has defined the reasonable hourly rate as follows:

> ... when a counselor has voluntarily agreed to represent a plaintiff in an out-of-town lawsuit, thereby necessitating litigation by that lawyer primarily in the alien locale of the court in which the case is pending,

---

8. Rather than seeking interest on their attorneys' fees, Plaintiffs seek reimbursement for all hours at a 2004 hourly rate. The Supreme Court has approved this practice as a method to compensate for any delay in payment. See Missouri v. Jenkins, 491 U.S. 274, 284, 109 S.Ct. 2463, 2469, 105 L.Ed.2d 229 (1989).

the court should deem the "relevant community" for fee purposes to constitute the legal community within that court's territorial jurisdiction; thus the "prevailing market rate" is that rate which lawyers of comparable skill and experience can reasonably expect to command within the venue of the court of record, rather than foreign counsel's typical charge for work performed within a geographical area wherein he maintains his [or her] office and/or normally practices, at least where the lawyer's reasonable "home" rate exceeds the reasonable "local" charge.

Based on the above, the Court rejects Plaintiffs' argument that the rates sought by the CIR attorneys are reasonable based on rates for Washington, D.C. law firms * * *.

Mr. Kolbo is a partner at the Maslon firm who has practiced law principally in the area of civil litigation for approximately twenty years. Mr. Herr, also a Maslon partner, practices in the firm's litigation and appellate practice. Mr. Herr obtained his juris doctorate ("JD") in 1978. Mr. Purdy obtained his JD in 1977 and is a partner focusing on litigation. Mr. McCarthy, who obtained his JD in 1992, is a partner with a general litigation and appellate practice. Mr. Richter worked as a law clerk at the Maslon firm until he obtained his JD in 1999. He now is an associate in Maslon's litigation and appellate practice. Mr. Lien and Ms. Van Tassel obtained their JDs in 1998 and 1999, respectively, and have since practiced in Maslon's litigation practice. Mr. Carlton, who obtained his JD in 1996, was associated with Maslon from August 1998 through June 2000. Ms. Dunbar, Mr. Bazdell, and Ms. Engelstad are paralegals, each with a number of years of experience.

Plaintiffs seek the following hourly rates for the CIR attorneys:

Mr. Rosman = $335

Mr. McDonald = $380

Mr. James Wright = $380

Mr. Casale = $335

Mr. Troy = $335

Mr. Bader = $270

Mr. Krvaric = $220

Student Attorneys = $105

Mr. Rosman graduated Yale University's law school in 1984 and began working at CIR in 1994. Mr. McDonald, one of CIR's founders and the former director of its litigation section, obtained his JD in 1981. Mr. Wright, senior counsel at CIR, obtained his JD in 1972. Mr. Casale, Mr. Troy, and Mr. Bader, each holding the title of associate general counsel for CIR, graduated law school in 1988, 1992, and 1994, respectively. Mr. Krvaric graduated law school in 2000.

CIR has billed local counsel Patrick Wright's time at an hourly rate of $125, with a monthly maximum of $1250. Mr. Morgan seeks reimbursement at an hourly rate of $270. Mr. Morgan obtained his JD in 1980 and has practiced in the area of civil litigation since then.

Plaintiffs claim that the rates sought for their attorneys is in line with the prevailing rates of lawyers of comparable skill, knowledge, qualifications, experience, and reputation in the Detroit metropolitan area. They provide the affidavit of Mark Kowalsky, a partner at the law firm of Hertz, Schram & Saretsky in Bloomfield Hills, Michigan, who states that the rates sought by Plaintiffs' attorneys are reasonable in comparison with prevailing market rates. Plaintiffs seek to further support these rates with records obtained from the University through the Freedom of Information Act ("FOIA") and with the hourly rates charged by some of Defendants' attorneys as published on Butzel Long's website. The FOIA records Plaintiffs offer indicate that the University has spent more than $10 million defending Plaintiffs' lawsuit and the lawsuit in *Grutter*. Additionally, Plaintiffs have sought discovery from Defendants with respect to the rates they were charged by their attorneys' and the attorneys' billing records. Plaintiffs hope to demonstrate through the information sought in their discovery requests that their attorneys' fees and costs are in-line with or less than those incurred by Defendants in this litigation and therefore are reasonable.

Defendants argue that the hourly rates charged by Plaintiffs' attorneys are unreasonable in comparison to civil rights attorneys with comparable skill and experience in the forum market. Defendants rely on the most recent *Economics of Practice* survey issued by the State Bar of Michigan, reporting 2003 hourly rates. According to the survey, attorneys at the largest firms (over 100 lawyers) in the Detroit metropolitan area charge an average hourly rate of $241. The survey further reports a 95th percentile rate of $358. For attorneys, state-wide, with forty or more years of experience, the survey reports an average rate of $188. Defendants note that Plaintiffs seek rates higher than $188 *for all of their Maslon attorneys,* including a 1998 law school graduate. Defendants further note that none of the Maslon attorneys demonstrate any particular expertise in civil rights litigation.

As an initial matter, the Court finds the hourly rates charged by Defendants' attorneys and the hours those attorneys expended defending against Plaintiffs' lawsuit of no particular value to its determination of Plaintiffs' fees award. As Defendants point out, a party seeking attorneys' fees pursuant to § 1988 must support their request with sufficiently detailed records to demonstrate the reasonableness of their fees. If the Court cannot determine the reasonableness of the attorneys' fees based on those billing records without reference to the opposing party's records, the party seeking fees has not met its burden under § 1988. More importantly, § 1988 only guarantees civil rights plaintiffs "competent counsel," whereas a party defending against such a suit may be willing and able to pay top dollar to hire the best lawyers in the country. Similarly, an opposing party's *willingness* to pay its lawyers to perform certain tasks (or perhaps a lawyer's billing for certain tasks which the client may refuse to pay) does not render the same tasks by the prevailing party's attorneys reasonable.

In any event, Defendants provide the following information with respect to the 2003 hourly rate charged by two of their lead attorneys who practice in the prevailing market. Philip Kessler, a shareholder in the law firm of Butzel Long and President of the firm, charged Defendant $230 per hour for his time on this case and the *Grutter* litigation. Mr. Kessler has practiced law since 1972. Att. Leonard Niehoff, also a Butzel Long shareholder, charged Defendant $195 per hour for his time on the two cases. Mr Niehoff has substantial experience in litigation, particularly cases involving civil rights and constitutional issues.

As Defendants note, *all* of the hourly rates Plaintiffs seek to recover for their attorneys exceed Mr. Niehoff's hourly billing rate. This includes the rates sought for five attorneys who only graduated law school *during* this litigation * * * and the rates sought for two attorneys who graduated less than five years before the litigation began * * *. None of the Maslon attorneys demonstrate particular expertise in civil rights or constitutional law issues. The Court therefore does not find Mr. Kessler's or Mr. Niehoff's hourly billing rates helpful to its assessment of the reasonableness of the rates sought by Plaintiffs' attorneys.

Instead, the Court will begin by looking at the rates reported in the State Bar's survey to determine the prevailing market rate applicable to this case. For each of Plaintiffs' attorneys, the Court has determined the prevailing market rate for attorneys with similar legal classifications, years of experience, and fields of law and in comparably-sized practice groups. Because the Bar's survey reports state-wide rates for these categories, for out-of-town counsel the Court has increased those rates by the percentage difference between the average rate for attorneys practicing in Detroit and the average rate for attorneys practicing state-wide (43%). The Court also factored in the average hourly billing rate for attorneys in the Detroit metropolitan area. The Court used the average billing rate set forth in the survey for attorneys in the above categories (rather than a higher percentile) as § 1988 only guarantees Plaintiffs competent counsel, not the best and/or most expensive counsel. With respect to the student attorneys who worked on this case for CIR, the Court found the billing rates of paralegals with five or less years experience and new hires in Detroit with no experience as an equitable basis for determining their appropriate billing rates.

Next, the Court considered the factors set forth in *Johnson*. With respect to CIR's lead attorneys, the Court finds that it is appropriate to increase their rates by approximately 10% to reflect their experience handling civil rights and constitutional law cases. The Court does not believe that an increase in Plaintiffs' fees is warranted by any of the other *Johnson* factors. This was not a particularly complex or novel case. As the Fifth Circuit stated in *Hopwood,* a case involving identical legal issues:

The issues presented by this case may well provide grist for the political and legal mills, but they are "neither novel nor extraordinarily difficult." The underlying arguments about the place of affirmative action in the equal protection paradigm have been percolating since the Supreme Court's decision in *Bakke* if not longer, only the evidence and analysis supporting each side have grown more sophisticated over the past two decades. Stated differently, this is not an issue that demanded a large amount of legal excavation in this instance.

For that reason, the case did not demand unusual skill and while the case required an expenditure of a significant amount of time, because of the number of attorneys representing Plaintiffs, the Court cannot believe the case precluded any attorney from other employment.

Based on the above, the Court finds the following prevailing market rates to be reasonable rates for Plaintiffs' attorneys:

Mr. Kolbo, Mr. Herr, Mr. Purdy = $280[12]

Mr. McCarthy = $275

Mr. Richter, Mr. Lien, Ms. Van Tassel, & Mr. Carlton = $230

Mr. Rosman, Mr. McDonald, & Mr. Wright = $290[13]

Mr. Casale, Mr. Troy, Mr. Bader, & Mr. Krvaric = $200

Mr. Morgan = $188

As the Court has found the prevailing market rate for attorneys comparable to Mr. Richter, Mr. Lien, Ms. Van Tassel, and Mr. Carlton to be higher than the actual rates billed for those attorneys' time, the Court finds the rates sought to be reasonable and will apply those rates in calculating Plaintiffs' award. With respect to Maslon's paralegals, the Court finds an hourly rate of $100 reasonable based on the State Bar of Michigan survey. The survey also indicates that Patrick Wright's $125 hourly rate is reasonable.

Summary as to Fees

* * *

Deducting the above amounts reduces Maslon's fee award to $990,585.25 ($1,398,120.25—$407,535) and CIR's fee award to

---

12. In reaching this amount the Court considered the following:

a) the average rate for partners state-wide = $210 + ($210 x 43%) = $300.30

b) the average rate for attorneys w/20 years of more experience = $188 + ($188 x 43%) = $268.84

c) the average rate for attorneys in firms w/more than 100 attorneys = $241 + ($241 x 43%) = $344.63

d) the average rate for attorneys in the field of litigation (not personal injury) = $176 + ($176 x 43%) = $251.68

e) the average rate for attorneys practicing in downtown Detroit = $238

13. The prevailing market rate for Mr. Rosman and Mr. McDonald is $265 and for Mr. Wright, $262. The Court finds a 10% increase to $290 reasonable in light of their experience in the areas of civil rights and constitutional law.

directed the trial court to review the fee requests again with a more generous hand. 962 F.2d 566 (7th Cir.1992)(Posner, J.)("[I]t is not the function of judges in fee litigation to determine the equivalent of the medieval just price. It is to determine what the lawyer would receive if he were selling his services in the market rather than being paid by court order."). The circuit court was still not satisfied with the district court's work on remand. 985 F.2d 867 (7th Cir.1993). When last heard from, the trial court and plaintiffs' lawyers were litigating yet another mandamus action to determine whether the circuit ordered (or merely suggested) that the trial court award a fee based on a percentage of the common fund. (The trial court preferred to determine a reasonable fee based on the lodestar method while the plaintiffs' attorneys believed they would do better with a percentage.) 813 F.Supp. 633 and 148 F.R.D. 594 (N.D.Ill.1993).

2. One federal judge tried to keep down litigation costs in a securities case by using a novel bidding process to select lead counsel to represent the class of plaintiffs. Judge Vaughn Walker chose the low-bidding law firm, who promised to do the work for a maximum of $325,000 in expenses plus a low contingency fee based on the amount of recovery. In re Oracle Securities Litigation, 132 F.R.D. 538 (N.D.Cal.1990). One losing bidder, who had estimated the costs alone at $1.3 million, later criticized the cap as unethical, arbitrary and unrealistic. This disappointed bidder charged that the winning firm would have to choose between its ethical duty to represent the class zealously and the financial incentive to avoid incurring nonreimbursable expenses. The trial court rejected these contentions. 136 F.R.D. 639 (N.D.Cal. 1991). The case finally settled for $25 million to the plaintiffs, with $5.6 million in fees and expenses for the lead counsel and another $595,000 for other plaintiffs' firms. 852 F.Supp. 1437 (N.D.Cal.1994). See Laura L. Hooper & Marie Leary, Auctioning the Role of Class Counsel in Class Action Cases: A Descriptive Study, 209 F.R.D. 519 (2001) (analyzing practices of many district court judges).

Not all courts have approved the auction method. The Third Circuit has found that district courts may not routinely use the auction method in suits brought under the Private Securities Litigation Reform Act. In re Cendant Corporation Litigation, 264 F.3d 201 (3d Cir.2001), cert. denied sub nom., Mark v. California Public Employees' Retirement System, 535 U.S. 929, 122 S.Ct. 1300, 152 L.Ed.2d 212 (2002). The Third Circuit has also rejected the use of the auction method in a Clean Water Act case, finding the lodestar method to be required. Pennsylvania Environmental Defense Foundation v. Canon–McMillan School District, 152 F.3d 228 (3d Cir.1998). See Jill E. Fisch, Lawyers on the Auction Block: Evaluating the Selection of Class Counsel by Auction, 102 Colum.L.Rev. 650 (2002) (contending that because of concerns about the auction procedure, empowering a lead plaintiff to act is a more effective way to incorporate market forces into selection and compensation of counsel); Third Circuit Task Force on Selection of Class Counsel, 208 F.R.D. 340 (2002) (recommending factors courts should consider in determining whether the case fit the limited circumstances where a class counsel auction might be worthwhile).

3. The general dissatisfaction with the complexities of the lodestar approach have caused some courts to return to compensating on the basis of a

percentage of the recovery, especially in common fund cases. For example, the Second Circuit has joined six other circuits in allowing its district court judges to use either the lodestar or the percentage of the fund methods in calculating attorney's fees in common fund cases. Goldberger v. Integrated Resources, Inc., 209 F.3d 43 (2d Cir.2000). The court noted that because of the problems inherent in either method in attempting to replicate the free market for legal services, no matter which method is selected, judges are to be guided by "the traditional criteria in determining a reasonable common fund fee, including: '(1) the time and labor expended by counsel; (2) the magnitude and complexities of the litigation; (3) the risk of litigation ... ; (4) the quality of representation; (5) the requested fee in relation to the settlement; and (6) public policy considerations.'" Id. at 50.

The Seventh Circuit, however, has criticized *Goldberger's* approach because, "Only ex ante can bargaining occur in the shadow of the litigation's uncertainty; only ex ante can the costs and benefits of particular systems and risk multipliers be assessed intelligently." In re Synthroid Marketing Litigation, 264 F.3d 712, 719 (7th Cir.2001) (adhering to market mimicking even if the district court fails to set the fee structure ex ante), 325 F.3d 974 (7th Cir.2003) (revising fee after remand in further attempt to mimic market). One district court has chosen to follow the Seventh Circuit's minority approach of determining the percentage of fund recovery in common fund cases by "market mimicking," which approximates the rate an attorney would have obtained on the open market at the outset of the case. In re Cabletron Systems Securities Litigation, 239 F.R.D. 30 (D.N.H.2006). The *Cabletron Systems* court did not decide whether the lodestar formula is a required cross-check on the percentage recovery, as some commentators have suggested. See Vaughn R. Walker & Ben Horwich, The Ethical Imperative of a Lodestar Cross–Check: Judicial Misgivings about "Reasonable Percentage" Fees in Common Fund Cases, 18 Geo. J. Legal Ethics 1453 (2005) (written by federal district court judge). In reaching its decision, the *Cabletron Systems* court identified the three existing approaches to determining a reasonable percentage fee in common fund cases: (1) the multi-factored test applying the *Johnson* factors (p. 951 n. 2); (2) the benchmark approach of 25% with case-specific deviations; and (3) the market mimicking approach of replicating market risk factors. The various approaches and permutations of assessing attorney's fees in common fund cases are summarized in the ABA Task Force report. Report on Contingent Fees in Class Action Litigation, 25 Rev.Lit. 459 (2006).

4. It is somewhat unsettled who is entitled to challenge a fee award, if the party who would otherwise have to pay does not object. Compare, e.g., In re Busy Beaver Building Centers, 19 F.3d 833 (3d Cir.1994)(bankruptcy court has power and duty to review fee application even when no interested party objects) with In re First Capital Holdings Corp., 33 F.3d 29 (9th Cir. 1994)(class member who received full recovery on claim lacks standing to object to fee award) and Powers v. Eichen, 229 F.3d 1249 (9th Cir.2000) (unnamed class member who files an objection in district court to the amount of requested attorney's fees in a class action settlement may appeal the award of such fees without intervening in the district court).

D. CONFLICTS OF INTEREST

Negotiations about fees in the context of negotiations over the merits present particular difficulties. Some have charged that in some class action suits, the first item on the agenda of settlement conferences is the fee for the plaintiffs' attorneys. Is it proper in a class action, especially in a public law case, for a negotiated settlement on the merits to include a simultaneously-negotiated fee? Is it proper for the defendants to offer to settle the case on the merits favorably to the plaintiffs only if the plaintiffs waive any fee?

EVANS v. JEFF D.
Supreme Court of the United States, 1986
475 U.S. 717, 106 S.Ct. 1531, 89 L.Ed.2d 747

JUSTICE STEVENS delivered the opinion of the Court.

The Civil Rights Attorney's Fees Awards Act of 1976 (Fees Act), provides that "the court, in its discretion, may allow the prevailing party ... a reasonable attorney's fee" in enumerated civil rights actions. 42 U.S.C. § 1988. In Maher v. Gagne' 448 U.S. 122, 100 S.Ct. 2570, 65 L.Ed.2d 653 (1980), we held that fees *may* be assessed against state officials after a case has been settled by the entry of a consent decree. In this case, we consider the question whether attorney's fees *must* be assessed when the case has been settled by a consent decree granting prospective relief to the plaintiff class but providing that the defendants shall not pay any part of the prevailing party's fees or costs. We hold that the District Court has the power, in its sound discretion, to refuse to award fees.

I

* * * [The petitioners, state officials in Idaho, were sued by a class of handicapped children because of alleged deficiencies in the educational and health care provided. Respondents were represented by Charles Johnson from the Idaho Legal Aid Society.]

In March 1983, one week before trial, petitioners presented respondents with a new settlement proposal. As respondents themselves characterize it, the proposal "offered virtually all of the injunctive relief [they] had sought in their complaint." The Court of Appeals agreed with this characterization, and further noted that the proposed relief was "more than the district court in earlier hearings had indicated it was willing to grant." 743 F.2d 648, 650 (C.A.9 1984). As was true of the earlier partial settlement, however, petitioners' offer included a provision for a waiver by respondents of any claim to fees or costs. Originally, this waiver was unacceptable to the Idaho Legal Aid Society, which had instructed Johnson to reject any settlement offer conditioned upon a waiver of fees, but Johnson ultimately determined that his ethical obligation to his clients mandated acceptance of the proposal. The parties conditioned the waiver on approval by the District Court.

After the stipulation was signed, Johnson filed a written motion requesting the District Court to approve the settlement "except for the provision on costs and attorney's fees," and to allow the respondents to present a bill of costs and fees for consideration by the court. At the oral argument on that motion, Johnson contended that petitioners' offer had exploited his ethical duty to his clients—that he was "forced," by an offer giving his clients "the best result [they] could have gotten in this court or any other court," to waive his attorney's fees.[6] The District Court, however, evaluated the waiver in the context of the entire settlement and rejected the ethical underpinnings of Johnson's argument. Explaining that although petitioners were "not willing to concede that they were obligated to [make the changes in their practices required by the stipulation], . . . they were willing to do them as long as their costs were outlined and they didn't face additional costs," it concluded that "it doesn't violate any ethical considerations for an attorney to give up his attorney fees in the interest of getting a better bargain for his client[s]." Accordingly, the District Court approved the settlement and denied the motion to submit a costs bill.

When respondents appealed from the order denying attorney's fees and costs, petitioners filed a motion requesting the District Court to suspend or stay their obligation to comply with the substantive terms of the settlement. Because the District Court regarded the fee waiver as a material term of the complete settlement, it granted the motion.[7] The Court of Appeals, however, granted two emergency motions for stays requiring enforcement of the substantive terms of the consent decree pending the appeal. More dramatically, after ordering preliminary relief, it invalidated the fee waiver and left standing the remainder of the settlement; it then instructed the District Court to "make its own determination of the fees that are reasonable" and remanded for that limited purpose.

---

6. Johnson's oral presentation to the District Court reads in full as follows:

"In other words, an attorney like myself can be put in the position of either negotiating for his client or negotiating for his attorney's fees, and I think that that is pretty much the situation that occurred in this instance.

"I was forced, because of what I perceived to be a result favorable to the plaintiff class, a result that I didn't want to see jeopardized by a trial or by any other possible problems that might have occurred. And the result is the best result I could have gotten in this court or any other court and it is really a fair and just result in any instance and what should have occurred years earlier and which in fact should have been the case all along. That result I didn't want to see disturbed on the basis that my attorney's fees would cause a problem and cause that result to be jeopardized."

7. The District Court wrote a letter to respondents' counsel explaining the conditional nature of petitioners' settlement offer: "[T]he defendants' signing of the stipulation was dependent upon the Court's approval of the finding that it was appropriate to accept a stipulation where plaintiffs waived attorneys fees. . . . The defendants entered into the stipulation only as a compromise matter with the understanding that they would not pay any attorneys fees, and advised the Court that if there were going to be attorneys fees that they wanted to proceed with trial because they did not think they were required to conform to the stipulation legally. * * * [U]ntil the validity of the stipulation is determined, the Court feels it is entirely unfair to enforce it."

In explaining its holding, the Court of Appeals emphasized that Rule 23(e) of the Federal Rules of Civil Procedure gives the court the power to approve the terms of all settlements of class actions,[8] and that the strong federal policy embodied in the Fees Act normally requires an award of fees to prevailing plaintiffs in civil rights actions, including those who have prevailed through settlement. The court added that "[w]hen attorney's fees are negotiated as part of a class action settlement, a conflict frequently exists between the class lawyers' interest in compensation and the class members' interest in relief." "To avoid this conflict," the Court of Appeals relied on Circuit precedent which had "disapproved simultaneous negotiation of settlements and attorney's fees" absent a showing of "unusual circumstances."[10] In this case, the Court of Appeals found no such "unusual circumstances" and therefore held that an agreement on fees "should not have been a part of the settlement of the claims of the class." It concluded:

> "The historical background of both Rule 23 and section 1988, as well as our experience since their enactment, compel the conclusion that a stipulated waiver of all attorney's fees obtained solely as a condition for obtaining relief for the class should not be accepted by the court."

The importance of the question decided by the Court of Appeals, together with the conflict between its decision and the decisions of other Courts of Appeals, led us to grant certiorari. We now reverse.

II

The disagreement between the parties and *amici* as to what exactly is at issue in this case makes it appropriate to put certain aspects of the case to one side in order to state precisely the question that the case does present.

To begin with, the Court of Appeals' decision rested on an erroneous view of the District Court's power to approve settlements in class actions. Rule 23(e) wisely requires court approval of the terms of any settlement of a class action, but the power to approve or reject a settlement negotiated by the parties before trial does not authorize the court to require the parties to accept a settlement to which they have not agreed. Although changed circumstances may justify a court-ordered modification of a consent decree over the objections of a party after the decree has been entered, and the District Court might have advised petitioners and respondents that it would not approve their proposal unless one or more of its provisions was deleted or modified, Rule 23(e) does not give the court the power, in advance of trial, to modify a proposed consent decree and order

---

8. "Dismissal or Compromise. A class action shall not be dismissed or compromised without the approval of the court, and notice of the proposed dismissal or compromise shall be given to all members of the class in such manner as the court directs." Fed.Rules Civ.Proc. 23(e).

10. [The circuit court cited as precedent, Mendoza v. United States, 623 F.2d 1338 (9th Cir.1980), and Prandini v. National Tea Co., 557 F.2d 1015 (3d Cir.1977). However, in neither case did the courts actually reject a part of a settlement and enforce the remainder.]

its acceptance over either party's objection. The options available to the District Court were essentially the same as those available to respondents: it could have accepted the proposed settlement; it could have rejected the proposal and postponed the trial to see if a different settlement could be achieved; or it could have decided to try the case. The District Court could not enforce the settlement on the merits and award attorney's fees any more than it could, in a situation in which the attorney had negotiated a large fee at the expense of the plaintiff class, preserve the fee award and order greater relief on the merits. The question we must decide, therefore, is whether the District Court had a duty to reject the proposed settlement because it included a waiver of statutorily authorized attorney's fees.

That duty, whether it takes the form of a general prophylactic rule or arises out of the special circumstances of this case, derives ultimately from the Fees Act rather than from the strictures of professional ethics. Although respondents contend that Johnson, as counsel for the class, was faced with an "ethical dilemma" when petitioners offered him relief greater than that which he could reasonably have expected to obtain for his clients at trial (if only he would stipulate to a waiver of the statutory fee award), and although we recognize Johnson's conflicting interests between pursuing relief for the class and a fee for the Idaho Legal Aid Society, we do not believe that the "dilemma" was an "ethical" one in the sense that Johnson had to choose between conflicting duties under the prevailing norms of professional conduct. Plainly, Johnson had no ethical obligation to seek a statutory fee award. His ethical duty was to serve his clients loyally and competently. Since the proposal to settle the merits was more favorable than the probable outcome of the trial, Johnson's decision to recommend acceptance was consistent with the highest standards of our profession. The District Court, therefore, correctly concluded that approval of the settlement involved no breach of ethics in this case.

The defect, if any, in the negotiated fee waiver must be traced not to the rules of ethics but to the Fees Act. Following this tack, respondents argue that the statute must be construed to forbid a fee waiver that is the product of "coercion." They submit that a "coercive waiver" results when the defendant in a civil rights action (1) offers a settlement on the merits of equal or greater value than that which plaintiffs could reasonably expect to achieve at trial but (2) conditions the offer on a waiver of plaintiffs' statutory eligibility for attorney's fees. Such an offer, they claim, exploits the ethical obligation of plaintiffs' counsel to recommend settlement in order to avoid defendant's statutory liability for its opponents' fees and costs.

The question this case presents, then, is whether the Fees Act requires a district court to disapprove a stipulation seeking to settle a civil rights class action under Rule 23 when the offered relief equals or exceeds the probable outcome at trial but is expressly conditioned on waiver of statutory eligibility for attorney's fees. For reasons set out below, we are not persuaded that Congress has commanded that all such settlements must be rejected by the District Court. Moreover, on the facts of record in this case, we are satisfied that the District Court did not abuse its discretion by approving the fee waiver.

III

The text of the Fees Act provides no support for the proposition that Congress intended to ban all fee waivers offered in connection with substantial relief on the merits. * * *

In fact, we believe that a general proscription against negotiated waiver of attorney's fees in exchange for a settlement on the merits would itself impede vindication of civil rights, at least in some cases, by reducing the attractiveness of settlement. * * *

Most defendants are unlikely to settle unless the cost of the predicted judgment, discounted by its probability, plus the transaction costs of further litigation, are greater than the cost of the settlement package. If fee waivers cannot be negotiated, the settlement package must either contain an attorney's fee component of potentially large and typically uncertain magnitude, or else the parties must agree to have the fee fixed by the court. Although either of these alternatives may well be acceptable in many cases, there surely is a significant number in which neither alternative will be as satisfactory as a decision to try the entire case. * * *

The unpredictability of attorney's fees may be just as important as their magnitude when a defendant is striving to fix its liability. Unlike a determination of costs, which ordinarily involve smaller outlays and are more susceptible of calculation, "[t]here is no precise rule or formula" for determining attorney's fees, Hensley v. Eckerhart, 461 U.S. 424, 436, 103 S.Ct. 1933, 1941, 76 L.Ed.2d 40 (1983). Among other considerations, the district court must determine what hours were reasonably expended on what claims, whether that expenditure was reasonable in light of the success obtained, and what is an appropriate hourly rate for the services rendered. Some District Courts have also considered whether a "multiplier" or other adjustment is appropriate. The consequence of this succession of necessarily judgmental decisions for the ultimate fee award is inescapable: a defendant's liability for his opponent's attorney's fees in a civil rights action cannot be fixed with a sufficient degree of confidence to make defendants indifferent to their exclusion from negotiation. It is therefore not implausible to anticipate that parties to a significant number of civil rights cases will refuse to settle if liability for attorney's fees remains open, thereby forcing more cases to trial, unnecessarily burdening the judicial system, and disserving civil rights litigants. Respondents' own waiver of attorney's fees and costs to obtain settlement of their educational claims is eloquent testimony to the utility of fee waivers in vindicating civil rights claims. We conclude, therefore, that it is not necessary to construe the Fees Act as embodying a general rule prohibiting settlements conditioned on the waiver of fees in order to be faithful to the purposes of that Act.

IV

The question remains whether the District Court abused its discretion in this case by approving a settlement which included a complete fee waiver. As noted earlier, Rule 23(e) wisely requires court approval of the terms of any settlement of a class action. The potential conflict among members of the class—in this case, for example, the possible conflict between children primarily interested in better educational programs and those primarily interested in improved health care—fully justifies the requirement of court approval.

The Court of Appeals, respondents, and various *amici* supporting their position, however, suggest that the court's authority to pass on settlements, typically invoked to ensure fair treatment of class members, must be exercised in accordance with the Fees Act to promote the availability of attorneys in civil rights cases. Specifically, respondents assert that the State of Idaho could not pass a valid statute precluding the payment of attorney's fees in settlements of civil rights cases to which the Fees Act applies. From this they reason that the Fees Act must equally preclude the adoption of a uniform state-wide policy that serves the same end, and accordingly contend that a consistent practice of insisting on a fee waiver as a condition of settlement in civil rights litigation is in conflict with the federal statute authorizing fees for prevailing parties, including those who prevail by way of settlement. Remarkably, there seems little disagreement on these points. Petitioners and the *amici* who support them never suggest that the district court is obligated to place its stamp of approval on every settlement in which the plaintiffs' attorneys have agreed to a fee waiver. The Solicitor General, for example, has suggested that a fee waiver need not be approved when the defendant had "no realistic defense on the merits," or if the waiver was part of a "vindictive effort . . . to teach counsel that they had better not bring such cases."

We find it unnecessary to evaluate this argument, however, because the record in this case does not indicate that Idaho has adopted such a statute, policy, or practice. Nor does the record support the narrower proposition that petitioners' request to waive fees was a vindictive effort to deter attorneys from representing plaintiffs in civil rights suits against Idaho. It is true that a fee waiver was requested and obtained as a part of the early settlement of the education claims, but we do not understand respondents to be challenging that waiver, and they have not offered to prove that the petitioners' tactics in this case merely implemented a routine state policy designed to frustrate the objectives of the Fees Act. Our own examination of the record reveals no such policy.

In light of the record, respondents must—to sustain the judgment in their favor—confront the District Court's finding that the extensive structural relief they obtained constituted an adequate quid pro quo for their waiver of attorney's fees. The Court of Appeals did not overturn this finding. Indeed, even that court did not suggest that the option of rejecting the entire settlement and requiring the parties either to try the case or to attempt to negotiate a different settlement would have served the interests of justice. Only by making the unsupported assumption that the respondent class was entitled to retain the favorable portions of the settlement while rejecting the fee waiver could the Court of Appeals conclude that the District Court had acted unwisely.

What the outcome of this settlement illustrates is that the Fees Act has given the victims of civil rights violations a powerful weapon that improves their ability to employ counsel, to obtain access to the courts, and thereafter to vindicate their rights by means of settlement or trial. For aught that appears, it was the "coercive" effect of respondents' statutory right to seek a fee award that motivated petitioners' exceptionally generous offer. Whether this weapon might be even more powerful if fee waivers were prohibited in cases like this is another question, but it is in any event a question that Congress is best equipped to answer. Thus far, the Legislature has not commanded that fees be paid whenever a case is settled. Unless it issues such a command, we shall rely primarily on the sound discretion of the district courts to appraise the reasonableness of particular class-action settlements on a case-by-case basis, in the light of all the relevant circumstances. In this case, the District Court did not abuse its discretion in upholding a fee waiver which secured broad injunctive relief, relief greater than that which plaintiffs could reasonably have expected to achieve at trial.

The judgment of the Court of Appeals is reversed.

It is so ordered.

JUSTICE BRENNAN, with whom JUSTICE MARSHALL and JUSTICE BLACKMUN join, dissenting. [omitted]

NOTES

1. The Supreme Court's decision has been criticized as creating a chilling effect on public interest litigation. The critics contend that attorneys will have less incentive to accept these cases when there is a strong possibility of being faced with the problem in *Evans*. See, e.g., Note, Waive Goodbye to Law in the Public Interest—The Use of Coercive Fee Waivers in Civil Rights Actions, 19 Ariz.St.L.J. 749 (1987).

One response to *Evans* has been to write ethical rules that would prohibit negotiations as to fees, leaving the award of reasonable fees to the court after the parties reach a settlement on the merits. Note, Fee Waivers and Civil Rights Settlement Offers: State Ethics Prohibitions After Evans v. Jeff D., 87 Colum.L.Rev. 1214 (1987). This approach has not succeeded everywhere. For example, in 1989, the California Supreme Court rejected a proposed rule, endorsed by the State Bar, which was intended to nullify *Evans*. Proposed Rule of Professional Conduct 2–400, Bar Misc. 6004, read in part, " 'A member shall not make or present a settlement offer in any case involving a request by the opposing party for attorneys fees pursuant to private attorney general statutes which is conditioned on opposing counsel waiving all or substantially all fees.'" See Comment, Simultaneous Negotiation and the Conditioning of Settlement on the Merits Upon Waiver of Statutory Attorney's Fees: An Ethical and Policy Analysis, 29 Ariz.L.Rev. 517, 526 n.88 (1987)(state bars are divided on the permissibility of fee negotiations and waivers: the District of Columbia, Maine, Maryland, and New York severely restrict them; Michigan and Georgia permit simultaneous negotiations).

Another response has been to make changes when the right to legal representation has in fact been compromised. The Ninth Circuit ordered a case-specific preliminary injunction barring the defendant county from applying its alleged policy of requiring waiver of statutory attorney's fees as a condition of settlement in all federal civil rights suits to the plaintiff's challenge to the policy under section 1983. The plaintiff, proceeding pro se, claimed that she was unable to obtain counsel to help her bring her federal challenges to the policy because of the very policy she was trying to challenge. Bernhardt v. Los Angeles County, 339 F.3d 920 (9th Cir.2003). See also Johnson v. District of Columbia, 190 F.Supp.2d 34, 43 (D.D.C.2002) (in comparison to *Evans*, the "Court should be more inclined to hold that settlement offers conditioned on fee waivers, when part of a consistent policy * * *, or as part of a vindictive effort to undermine the right of parents and children to counsel, violate the IDEA's attorney's fee provision").

2. At least two circuit courts have extended *Evans* from class actions to the context of individual civil rights actions and have concluded that the district court should not allow the plaintiff's attorney to intervene to challenge the propriety of a fee waiver. Willard v. City of Los Angeles, 803 F.2d 526 (9th Cir.1986); Panola Land Buying Association v. Clark, 844 F.2d 1506 (11th Cir.1988). These opinions have been criticized as ignoring the fact that *Evans* merely decided whether a district court was required to disapprove a settlement which included a fee waiver and did not decide whether disapproval was permitted. Note, Fee as the Wind Blows: Waivers of Attorney's Fees in Individual Civil Rights Actions since Evans v. Jeff D., 102 Harv.L.Rev. 1278 (1989).

3. Another tool that defendants can use to their advantage is F.R.Civ.P. 68, reproduced in the Appendix at p. 988, which provides that: "More than 10 days before the trial begins, a party defending against a claim may serve on an opposing party an offer to allow judgment on specified terms, with the costs then accrued." In addition, "[i]f the judgment that the offeree finally obtains is not more favorable than the unaccepted offer, the offeree must pay the costs incurred after the offer was made." F.R.Civ.P. 68(d). Thus, those "costs" accrued after the making and rejection of a valid offer are shifted to the offeree (who is usually the plaintiff) if the latter recovers less than the offer. However, F.R.Civ.P. 68 nowhere defines the term "costs," and is silent on whether attorney's fees are "costs." Plainly, the inclusion of statutorily authorized attorney's fees as "costs" under the rule profoundly affects the availability of a fee award to otherwise entitled plaintiffs or prevailing parties.

In Marek v. Chesny, 473 U.S. 1, 105 S.Ct. 3012, 87 L.Ed.2d 1 (1985), the Supreme Court held that absent congressional expression to the contrary, where the underlying fee shifting statute defined "costs" as including attorney's fees, such fees were to be included as "costs" for purposes of Rule 68.

The Court majority acted over a bitter dissent by Justice Brennan in which he charged that the Court's reasoning was wholly inconsistent with the history and structure of the Federal Rules, that its application would produce absurd variations in Rule 68's operation based on nothing more than minute differences in statutory language, and that the Court's interpretation would seriously undermine the purposes behind the attorney's fees provisions of the civil rights laws. See also Peter Margulies, After *Marek*, the Deluge: Harmonizing the Interaction Under Rule 68 of Statutes That Do and Do Not Classify Attorneys' Fees as "Costs", 73 Iowa L.Rev. 413 (1988)(risk-averse plaintiffs are more likely to accept a low settlement than face paying post-offer costs). Should Rule 68 be amended? If so, how? See, e.g., William W Schwarzer, Fee-shifting Offers of Judgment—An Approach to Reducing the Cost of Litigation, 76 Judicature 147 (1992); David A. Anderson, Improving Settlement Devices: Rule 68 and Beyond, 23 J.Leg.Studies 225 (1994). When the Supreme Court's Advisory Committee on the Civil Rules tried to amend the rule in 1983 and again in 1984, it faced a storm of criticism and abandoned the effort. Other academic and legislative proposals have gone nowhere. See Stephen B. Burbank, Proposals to Amend Rule 68—Time to Abandon Ship, 19 Mich.J.L.Reform 425 (1986); Bruce P. Merenstein, More Proposals to Amend Rule 68: Time to Sink the Ship Once and for All, 184 F.R.D. 145 (1999).

4. *Update on the case.* In November 2007, the district court vacated the consent decree after concluding that the defendants had made significant efforts to substantially comply with the promises first made in 1983. The court found it regrettable that it took so long to resolve the case. It exhorted the defendants to continue to act in good faith in providing appropriate services to the class of Idaho children with severe mental and emotional disabilities. Jeff D. v. Kempthorne, 2007 WL 3256620 (D.Idaho 2007).

Appendix:

Selected Federal Rules of Civil Procedure

■ ■ ■

* * *

TITLE IV. PARTIES

* * *

Rule 19. Required Joinder of Parties

(a) Persons Required to Be Joined if Feasible.

(1) *Required Party.* A person who is subject to service of process and whose joinder will not deprive the court of subject-matter jurisdiction must be joined as a party if:

(A) in that person's absence, the court cannot accord complete relief among existing parties; or

(B) that person claims an interest relating to the subject of the action and is so situated that disposing of the action in the person's absence may:

(i) as a practical matter impair or impede the person's ability to protect the interest; or

(ii) leave an existing party subject to a substantial risk of incurring double, multiple, or otherwise inconsistent obligations because of the interest.

(2) *Joinder by Court Order.* If a person has not been joined as required, the court must order that the person be made a party. A person who refuses to join as a plaintiff may be made either a defendant or, in a proper case, an involuntary plaintiff.

(3) *Venue*. If a joined party objects to venue and the joinder would make venue improper, the court must dismiss that party.

(b) When Joinder Is Not Feasible. If a person who is required to be joined if feasible cannot be joined, the court must determine whether, in equity and good conscience, the action should proceed among the existing parties or should be dismissed. The factors for the court to consider include:

(1) the extent to which a judgment rendered in the person's absence might prejudice that person or the existing parties;

(2) the extent to which any prejudice could be lessened or avoided by:

(A) protective provisions in the judgment;

(B) shaping the relief; or

(C) other measures;

(3) whether a judgment rendered in the person's absence would be adequate; and

(4) whether the plaintiff would have an adequate remedy if the action were dismissed for nonjoinder.

(c) Pleading the Reasons for Nonjoinder. When asserting a claim for relief, a party must state:

(1) the name, if known, of any person who is required to be joined if feasible but is not joined; and

(2) the reasons for not joining that person.

(d) Exception for Class Actions. This rule is subject to Rule 23.

(As amended Feb. 28, 1966, eff. July 1, 1966; Mar. 2, 1987, eff. Aug. 1, 1987; Apr. 30, 2007, effective Dec. 1, 2007.)

* * *

Rule 23. Class Actions

* * *

(a) Prerequisites. One or more members of a class may sue or be sued as representative parties on behalf of all members only if:

(1) the class is so numerous that joinder of all members is impracticable;

(2) there are questions of law or fact common to the class;

(3) the claims or defenses of the representative parties are typical of the claims or defenses of the class; and

(4) the representative parties will fairly and adequately protect the interests of the class.

* * *

(g) Class Counsel.

(1) *Appointing Class Counsel.* Unless a statute provides otherwise, a court that certifies a class must appoint class counsel. In appointing class counsel, the court:

(A) must consider:

(i) the work counsel has done in identifying or investigating potential claims in the action;

(ii) counsel's experience in handling class actions, other complex litigation, and the types of claims asserted in the action;

(iii) counsel's knowledge of the applicable law; and

(iv) the resources that counsel will commit to representing the class;

(B) may consider any other matter pertinent to counsel's ability to fairly and adequately represent the interests of the class;

(C) may order potential class counsel to provide information on any subject pertinent to the appointment and to propose terms for attorney's fees and nontaxable costs;

(D) may include in the appointing order provisions about the award of attorney's fees or nontaxable costs under Rule 23(h); and

(E) may make further orders in connection with the appointment.

(2) *Standard for Appointing Class Counsel.* When one applicant seeks appointment as class counsel, the court may appoint that applicant only if the applicant is adequate under Rule 23(g)(1) and (4). If more than one adequate applicant seeks appointment, the court must appoint the applicant best able to represent the interests of the class.

(3) *Interim Counsel.* The court may designate interim counsel to act on behalf of a putative class before determining whether to certify the action as a class action.

(4) *Duty of Class Counsel.* Class counsel must fairly and adequately represent the interests of the class.

(h) Attorney's Fees and Nontaxable Costs. In a certified class action, the court may award reasonable attorney's fees and nontaxable costs that are authorized by law or by the parties' agreement. The following procedures apply:

(1) A claim for an award must be made by motion under Rule 54(d)(2), subject to the provisions of this subdivision (h), at a time the court sets. Notice of the motion must be served on all parties and, for motions by class counsel, directed to class members in a reasonable manner.

(2) A class member, or a party from whom payment is sought, may object to the motion.

(3) The court may hold a hearing and must find the facts and state its legal conclusions under Rule 52(a).

(4) The court may refer issues related to the amount of the award to a special master or a magistrate judge, as provided in Rule 54(d)(2)(D).

(As amended Feb. 28, 1966, eff. July 1, 1966; Mar. 2, 1987, eff. Aug. 1, 1987; Apr. 24, 1998, eff. Dec. 1, 1998; Mar. 27, 2003, eff. Dec. 1, 2003; Apr. 30, 2007, eff. Dec. 1, 2007.)

Rule 24. Intervention

(a) Intervention of Right. On timely motion, the court must permit anyone to intervene who:

(1) is given an unconditional right to intervene by a federal statute; or

(2) claims an interest relating to the property or transaction that is the subject of the action, and is so situated that disposing of the action may as a practical matter impair or impede the movant's ability to protect its interest, unless existing parties adequately represent that interest.

(b) Permissive Intervention.

(1) *In General.* On timely motion, the court may permit anyone to intervene who:

(A) is given a conditional right to intervene by a federal statute; or

(B) has a claim or defense that shares with the main action a common question of law or fact.

(2) *By a Government Officer or Agency.* On timely motion, the court may permit a federal or state governmental officer or agency to intervene if a party's claim or defense is based on:

(A) a statute or executive order administered by the officer or agency; or

(B) any regulation, order, requirement, or agreement issued or made under the statute or executive order.

(3) *Delay or Prejudice.* In exercising its discretion, the court must consider whether the intervention will unduly delay or prejudice the adjudication of the original parties' rights.

(c) Notice and Pleading Required. A motion to intervene must be served on the parties as provided in Rule 5. The motion must state the grounds for intervention and be accompanied by a pleading that sets out the claim or defense for which intervention is sought.

(As amended Dec. 27, 1946, eff. Mar. 19, 1948; Dec. 29, 1948, eff. Oct. 20, 1949; Jan. 21, 1963, eff. July 1, 1963; Feb. 28, 1966, eff. July 1, 1966; Mar. 2, 1987, eff. Aug. 1, 1987; Apr. 30, 1991, eff. Dec. 1, 1991; Apr. 12, 2006, eff. Dec. 1, 2006; Apr. 30, 2007, eff. Dec. 1, 2007.)

Rule 25. Substitution of Parties

* * *

(d) Public Officers; Death or Separation from Office. An action does not abate when a public officer who is a party in an official capacity dies, resigns, or otherwise ceases to hold office while the action is pending.

The officer's successor is automatically substituted as a party. Later proceedings should be in the substituted party's name, but any misnomer not affecting the parties' substantial rights must be disregarded. The court may order substitution at any time, but the absence of such an order does not affect the substitution.

(As amended Dec. 29, 1948, eff. Oct. 20, 1949; Apr. 17, 1961, eff. July 19, 1961; Jan. 21, 1963, eff. July 1, 1963; Mar. 2, 1987, eff. Aug. 1, 1987; Apr. 30, 2007, eff. Dec. 1, 2007.)

* * *

TITLE VI. TRIALS

Rule 53. Masters

(a) Appointment.

(1) *Scope.* Unless a statute provides otherwise, a court may appoint a master only to:

(A) perform duties consented to by the parties;

(B) hold trial proceedings and make or recommend findings of fact on issues to be decided without a jury if appointment is warranted by:

(i) some exceptional condition; or

(ii) the need to perform an accounting or resolve a difficult computation of damages; or

(C) address pretrial and posttrial matters that cannot be effectively and timely addressed by an available district judge or magistrate judge of the district.

(2) *Disqualification.* A master must not have a relationship to the parties, attorneys, action, or court that would require disqualification of a judge under 28 U.S.C. § 455, unless the parties, with the court's approval, consent to the appointment after the master discloses any potential grounds for disqualification.

(3) *Possible Expense or Delay.* In appointing a master, the court must consider the fairness of imposing the likely expenses on the parties and must protect against unreasonable expense or delay.

(b) Order Appointing a Master.

(1) *Notice.* Before appointing a master, the court must give the parties notice and an opportunity to be heard. Any party may suggest candidates for appointment.

(2) *Contents.* The appointing order must direct the master to proceed with all reasonable diligence and must state:

(A) the master's duties, including any investigation or enforcement duties, and any limits on the master's authority under Rule 53(c);

(B) the circumstances, if any, in which the master may communicate ex parte with the court or a party;

(C) the nature of the materials to be preserved and filed as the record of the master's activities;

(D) the time limits, method of filing the record, other procedures, and standards for reviewing the master's orders, findings, and recommendations; and

(E) the basis, terms, and procedure for fixing the master's compensation under Rule 53(g).

(3) *Issuing.* The court may issue the order only after:

(A) the master files an affidavit disclosing whether there is any ground for disqualification under 28 U.S.C. § 455; and

(B) if a ground is disclosed, the parties, with the court's approval, waive the disqualification.

(4) *Amending.* The order may be amended at any time after notice to the parties and an opportunity to be heard.

(c) Master's Authority.

(1) *In General.* Unless the appointing order directs otherwise, a master may:

(A) regulate all proceedings;

(B) take all appropriate measures to perform the assigned duties fairly and efficiently; and

(C) if conducting an evidentiary hearing, exercise the appointing court's power to compel, take, and record evidence.

(2) *Sanctions.* The master may by order impose on a party any noncontempt sanction provided by Rule 37 or 45, and may recommend a contempt sanction against a party and sanctions against a nonparty.

(d) Master's Orders. A master who issues an order must file it and promptly serve a copy on each party. The clerk must enter the order on the docket.

(e) Master's Reports. A master must report to the court as required by the appointing order. The master must file the report and promptly serve a copy on each party, unless the court orders otherwise.

(f) Action on the Master's Order, Report, or Recommendations.

(1) *Opportunity for a Hearing; Action in General.* In acting on a master's order, report, or recommendations, the court must give the parties notice and an opportunity to be heard; may receive evidence; and may adopt or affirm, modify, wholly or partly reject or reverse, or resubmit to the master with instructions.

(2) *Time to Object or Move to Adopt or Modify.* A party may file objections to—or a motion to adopt or modify—the master's order, report, or recommendations no later than 20 days after a copy is served, unless the court sets a different time.

(3) *Reviewing Factual Findings.* The court must decide de novo all objections to findings of fact made or recommended by a master, unless the parties, with the court's approval, stipulate that:

(A) the findings will be reviewed for clear error; or

(B) the findings of a master appointed under Rule 53(a)(1)(A) or (C) will be final.

(4) *Reviewing Legal Conclusions.* The court must decide de novo all objections to conclusions of law made or recommended by a master.

(5) *Reviewing Procedural Matters.* Unless the appointing order establishes a different standard of review, the court may set aside a master's ruling on a procedural matter only for an abuse of discretion.

(g) **Compensation.**

(1) *Fixing Compensation.* Before or after judgment, the court must fix the master's compensation on the basis and terms stated in the appointing order, but the court may set a new basis and terms after giving notice and an opportunity to be heard.

(2) *Payment.* The compensation must be paid either:

(A) by a party or parties; or

(B) from a fund or subject matter of the action within the court's control.

(3) *Allocating Payment.* The court must allocate payment among the parties after considering the nature and amount of the controversy, the parties' means, and the extent to which any party is more responsible than other parties for the reference to a master. An interim allocation may be amended to reflect a decision on the merits.

(h) **Appointing a Magistrate Judge.** A magistrate judge is subject to this rule only when the order referring a matter to the magistrate judge states that the reference is made under this rule.

(As amended Feb. 28, 1966, eff. July 1, 1966; Apr. 28, 1983, eff. Aug. 1, 1983; Mar. 2, 1987, eff. Aug. 1, 1987; Apr. 30, 1991, eff. Dec. 1, 1991; Apr. 22, 1993, eff. Dec. 1, 1993; Mar. 27, 2003, eff. Dec. 1, 2003; Apr. 30, 2007, eff. Dec. 1, 2007.)

TITLE VII. JUDGMENT

Rule 54. Judgment; Costs

(a) **Definition; Form.** "Judgment" as used in these rules includes a decree and any order from which an appeal lies. A judgment should not include recitals of pleadings, a master's report, or a record of prior proceedings.

(b) **Judgment on Multiple Claims or Involving Multiple Parties.** When an action presents more than one claim for relief—whether as a claim, counterclaim, crossclaim, or third-party claim—or when multiple parties are involved, the court may direct entry of a final judgment as to one or more, but fewer than all, claims or parties only if the court expressly determines that there is no just reason for delay. Otherwise, any order or other decision, however designated, that adjudicates fewer than all the claims or the rights and liabilities of fewer than all the parties does not end the action as to any of the claims or parties and may be revised at any time before the entry of a judgment adjudicating all the claims and all the parties' rights and liabilities.

(c) Demand for Judgment; Relief to Be Granted. A default judgment must not differ in kind from, or exceed in amount, what is demanded in the pleadings. Every other final judgment should grant the relief to which each party is entitled, even if the party has not demanded that relief in its pleadings.

(d) Costs; Attorney's Fees.

(1) *Costs Other Than Attorney's Fees.* Unless a federal statute, these rules, or a court order provides otherwise, costs—other than attorney's fees—should be allowed to the prevailing party. But costs against the United States, its officers, and its agencies may be imposed only to the extent allowed by law. The clerk may tax costs on 1 day's notice. On motion served within the next 5 days, the court may review the clerk's action.

(2) *Attorney's Fees.*

(A) *Claim to Be by Motion.* A claim for attorney's fees and related nontaxable expenses must be made by motion unless the substantive law requires those fees to be proved at trial as an element of damages.

(B) *Timing and Contents of the Motion.* Unless a statute or a court order provides otherwise, the motion must:

(i) be filed no later than 14 days after the entry of judgment;

(ii) specify the judgment and the statute, rule, or other grounds entitling the movant to the award;

(iii) state the amount sought or provide a fair estimate of it; and

(iv) disclose, if the court so orders, the terms of any agreement about fees for the services for which the claim is made.

(C) *Proceedings.* Subject to Rule 23(h), the court must, on a party's request, give an opportunity for adversary submissions on the motion in accordance with Rule 43(c) or 78. The court may decide issues of liability for fees before receiving submissions on the value of services. The court must find the facts and state its conclusions of law as provided in Rule 52(a).

(D) *Special Procedures by Local Rule; Reference to a Master or a Magistrate Judge.* By local rule, the court may establish special procedures to resolve fee-related issues without extensive evidentiary hearings. Also, the court may refer issues concerning the value of services to a special master under Rule 53 without regard to the limitations of Rule 53(a)(1), and may refer a motion for attorney's fees to a magistrate judge under Rule 72(b) as if it were a dispositive pretrial matter.

(E) *Exceptions.* Subparagraphs (A)–(D) do not apply to claims for fees and expenses as sanctions for violating these rules or as sanctions under 28 U.S.C. § 1927.

(As amended Dec. 27, 1946, eff. Mar. 19, 1948; Apr. 17, 1961, eff. July 19, 1961; Mar. 2, 1987, eff. Aug. 1, 1987; Apr. 22, 1993, eff. Dec. 1, 1993; Apr. 29, 2002, eff. Dec. 1, 2002; Mar. 27, 2003, eff. Dec. 1, 2003; Apr. 30, 2007, eff. Dec. 1, 2007.)

* * *

Rule 57. Declaratory Judgment

These rules govern the procedure for obtaining a declaratory judgment under 28 U.S.C. § 2201. Rules 38 and 39 govern a demand for a jury trial. The existence of another adequate remedy does not preclude a declaratory judgment that is otherwise appropriate. The court may order a speedy hearing of a declaratory-judgment action.

(As amended Dec. 29, 1948, eff. Oct. 20, 1949; Apr. 30, 2007, eff. Dec. 1, 2007.)

* * *

Rule 60. Relief from a Judgment or Order

(a) Corrections Based on Clerical Mistakes; Oversights and Omissions. The court may correct a clerical mistake or a mistake arising from oversight or omission whenever one is found in a judgment, order, or other part of the record. The court may do so on motion or on its own, with or without notice. But after an appeal has been docketed in the appellate court and while it is pending, such a mistake may be corrected only with the appellate court's leave.

(b) Grounds for Relief from a Final Judgment, Order, or Proceeding. On motion and just terms, the court may relieve a party or its legal representative from a final judgment, order, or proceeding for the following reasons:

(1) mistake, inadvertence, surprise, or excusable neglect;

(2) newly discovered evidence that, with reasonable diligence, could not have been discovered in time to move for a new trial under Rule 59(b);

(3) fraud (whether previously called intrinsic or extrinsic), misrepresentation, or misconduct by an opposing party;

(4) the judgment is void;

(5) the judgment has been satisfied, released or discharged; it is based on an earlier judgment that has been reversed or vacated; or applying it prospectively is no longer equitable; or

(6) any other reason that justifies relief.

(c) Timing and Effect of the Motion.

(1) *Timing.* A motion under Rule 60(b) must be made within a reasonable time—and for reasons (1), (2), and (3) no more than a year after the entry of the judgment or order or the date of the proceeding.

(2) *Effect on Finality.* The motion does not affect the judgment's finality or suspend its operation.

(d) Other Powers to Grant Relief. This rule does not limit a court's power to:

(1) entertain an independent action to relieve a party from a judgment, order, or proceeding;

(2) grant relief under 28 U.S.C. § 1655 to a defendant who was not personally notified of the action; or

(3) set aside a judgment for fraud on the court.

(e) Bills and Writs Abolished. The following are abolished: bills of review, bills in the nature of bills of review, and writs of coram nobis, coram vobis, and audita querela.

(As amended Dec. 27, 1946, eff. Mar. 19, 1948; Dec. 29, 1948, eff. Oct. 20, 1949; Mar. 2, 1987, eff. Aug. 1, 1987; Apr. 30, 2007, eff. Dec. 1, 2007.)

* * *

Rule 62. Stay of Proceedings to Enforce a Judgment

(a) Automatic Stay; Exceptions for Injunctions, Receiverships, and Patent Accountings. Except as stated in this rule, no execution may issue on a judgment, nor may proceedings be taken to enforce it, until 10 days have passed after its entry. But unless the court orders otherwise, the following are not stayed after being entered, even if an appeal is taken:

(1) an interlocutory or final judgment in an action for an injunction or a receivership; or

(2) a judgment or order that directs an accounting in an action for patent infringement.

(b) Stay Pending the Disposition of a Motion. On appropriate terms for the opposing party's security, the court may stay the execution of a judgment—or any proceedings to enforce it—pending disposition of any of the following motions:

(1) under Rule 50, for judgment as a matter of law;

(2) under Rule 52(b), to amend the findings or for additional findings;

(3) under Rule 59, for a new trial or to alter or amend a judgment; or

(4) under Rule 60, for relief from a judgment or order.

(c) Injunction Pending an Appeal. While an appeal is pending from an interlocutory order or final judgment that grants, dissolves, or denies an injunction, the court may suspend, modify, restore, or grant an injunction on terms for bond or other terms that secure the opposing party's rights. If the judgment appealed from is rendered by a statutory three-judge district court, the order must be made either:

(1) by that court sitting in open session; or

(2) by the assent of all its judges, as evidenced by their signatures.

(d) Stay with Bond on Appeal. If an appeal is taken, the appellant may obtain a stay by supersedeas bond, except in an action described in Rule 62(a)(1) or (2). The bond may be given upon or after filing the notice of appeal or after obtaining the order allowing the appeal. The stay takes effect when the court approves the bond.

(e) Stay Without Bond on an Appeal by the United States, Its Officers, or Its Agencies. The court must not require a bond, obligation, or other security from the appellant when granting a stay on an appeal by the United States, its officers, or its agencies or on an appeal directed by a department of the federal government.

(f) Stay in Favor of a Judgment Debtor Under State Law. If a judgment is a lien on the judgment debtor's property under the law of the state where the court is located, the judgment debtor is entitled to the same stay of execution the state court would give.

(g) Appellate Court's Power Not Limited. This rule does not limit the power of the appellate court or one of its judges or justices:

(1) to stay proceedings—or suspend, modify, restore, or grant an injunction—while an appeal is pending; or

(2) to issue an order to preserve the status quo or the effectiveness of the judgment to be entered.

(h) Stay with Multiple Claims or Parties. A court may stay the enforcement of a final judgment entered under Rule 54(b) until it enters a later judgment or judgments, and may prescribe terms necessary to secure the benefit of the stayed judgment for the party in whose favor it was entered.

(As amended Dec. 27, 1946, eff. Mar. 19, 1948; Dec. 29, 1948, eff. Oct. 20, 1949; Apr. 17, 1961, eff. July 19, 1961; Mar. 2, 1987, eff. Aug. 1, 1987; Apr. 30, 2007, eff. Dec. 1, 2007.)

* * *

TITLE VIII. PROVISIONAL AND FINAL REMEDIES

Rule 64. Seizing a Person or Property

(a) Remedies Under State Law—In General. At the commencement of and throughout an action, every remedy is available that, under the law of the state where the court is located, provides for seizing a person or property to secure satisfaction of the potential judgment. But a federal statute governs to the extent it applies.

(b) Specific Kinds of Remedies. The remedies available under this rule include the following—however designated and regardless of whether state procedure requires an independent action:

- arrest;
- attachment;
- garnishment;
- replevin;
- sequestration; and
- other corresponding or equivalent remedies.

(As amended Apr. 30, 2007, eff. Dec. 1, 2007.)

Rule 65. Injunctions and Restraining Orders

(a) Preliminary Injunction.

(1) *Notice.* The court may issue a preliminary injunction only on notice to the adverse party.

(2) *Consolidating the Hearing with the Trial on the Merits.* Before or after beginning the hearing on a motion for a preliminary injunction, the court may advance the trial on the merits and consolidate it with the hearing. Even when consolidation is not ordered, evidence that is received on the motion and that would be admissible at trial becomes part of the trial record and need not be repeated at trial. But the court must preserve any party's right to a jury trial.

(b) Temporary Restraining Order.

(1) *Issuing Without Notice.* The court may issue a temporary restraining order without written or oral notice to the adverse party or its attorney only if:

(A) specific facts in an affidavit or a verified complaint clearly show that immediate and irreparable injury, loss, or damage will result to the movant before the adverse party can be heard in opposition; and

(B) the movant's attorney certifies in writing any efforts made to give notice and the reasons why it should not be required.

(2) *Contents; Expiration.* Every temporary restraining order issued without notice must state the date and hour it was issued; describe the injury and state why it is irreparable; state why the order was issued without notice; and be promptly filed in the clerk's office and entered in the record. The order expires at the time after entry—not to exceed 10 days—that the court sets, unless before that time the court, for good cause, extends it for a like period or the adverse party consents to a longer extension. The reasons for an extension must be entered in the record.

(3) *Expediting the Preliminary-Injunction Hearing.* If the order is issued without notice, the motion for a preliminary injunction must be set for hearing at the earliest possible time, taking precedence over all other matters except hearings on older matters of the same character. At the hearing, the party who obtained the order must proceed with the motion; if the party does not, the court must dissolve the order.

(4) *Motion to Dissolve.* On 2 days' notice to the party who obtained the order without notice—or on shorter notice set by the court—the adverse party may appear and move to dissolve or modify the order. The court must then hear and decide the motion as promptly as justice requires.

(c) Security. The court may issue a preliminary injunction or a temporary restraining order only if the movant gives security in an amount that the court considers proper to pay the costs and damages sustained by any party found to have been wrongfully enjoined or restrained. The United States, its officers, and its agencies are not required to give security.

(d) Contents and Scope of Every Injunction and Restraining Order.

(1) *Contents.* Every order granting an injunction and every restraining order must:

(A) state the reasons why it issued;

(B) state its terms specifically; and

(C) describe in reasonable detail—and not by referring to the complaint or other document—the act or acts restrained or required.

(2) *Persons Bound.* The order binds only the following who receive actual notice of it by personal service or otherwise:

(A) the parties;

(B) the parties' officers, agents, servants, employees, and attorneys; and

(C) other persons who are in active concert or participation with anyone described in Rule 65(d)(2)(A) or (B).

(e) Other Laws Not Modified. These rules do not modify the following:

(1) any federal statute relating to temporary restraining orders or preliminary injunctions in actions affecting employer and employee;

(2) 28 U.S.C. § 2361, which relates to preliminary injunctions in actions of interpleader or in the nature of interpleader; or

(3) 28 U.S.C. § 2284, which relates to actions that must be heard and decided by a three-judge district court.

(f) Copyright Impoundment. This rule applies to copyright-impoundment proceedings.

(As amended Dec. 27, 1946, eff. Mar. 19, 1948; Dec. 29, 1948, eff. Oct. 20, 1949; Feb. 28, 1966, eff. July 1, 1966; Mar. 2, 1987, eff. Aug. 1, 1987; Apr. 23, 2001, eff. Dec. 1, 2001; Apr. 30, 2007, eff. Dec. 1, 2007.)

Rule 65.1 Proceedings Against a Surety

Whenever these rules (including the Supplemental Rules for Admiralty or Maritime Claims and Asset Forfeiture Actions) require or allow a party to give security, and security is given through a bond or other undertaking with one or more sureties, each surety submits to the court's jurisdiction and irrevocably appoints the court clerk as its agent for receiving service of any papers that affect its liability on the bond or undertaking. The surety's liability may be enforced on motion without an independent action. The motion and any notice that the court orders may be served on the court clerk, who must promptly mail a copy of each to every surety whose address is known.

(Added Feb. 28, 1966, eff. July 1, 1966, and amended Mar. 2, 1987, eff. Aug. 1, 1987; Apr. 12, 2006, eff. Dec. 1, 2006; Apr. 30, 2007, eff. Dec. 1, 2007.)

Rule 66. Receivers

These rules govern an action in which the appointment of a receiver is sought or a receiver sues or is sued. But the practice in administering an estate by a receiver or a similar court-appointed officer must accord with the historical practice in federal courts or with a local rule. An action in which a receiver has been appointed may be dismissed only by court order.

(As amended Dec. 27, 1946, eff. Mar. 19, 1948; Dec. 29, 1948, eff. Oct. 20, 1949; Apr. 30, 2007, eff. Dec. 1, 2007.)

Rule 67. Deposit into Court

(a) Depositing Property. If any part of the relief sought is a money judgment or the disposition of a sum of money or some other deliverable thing, a party—on notice to every other party and by leave of court—may deposit with the court all or part of the money or thing, whether or not that party claims any of it. The depositing party must deliver to the clerk a copy of the order permitting deposit.

(b) Investing and Withdrawing Funds. Money paid into court under this rule must be deposited and withdrawn in accordance with 28 U.S.C. §§ 2041 and 2042 and any like statute. The money must be deposited in an interest-bearing account or invested in a court-approved, interest-bearing instrument.

(As amended Dec. 29, 1948, eff. Oct. 20, 1949; Apr. 28, 1983, eff. Aug. 1, 1983; Apr. 30, 2007, eff. Dec. 1, 2007.)

Rule 68. Offer of Judgment

(a) Making an Offer; Judgment on an Accepted Offer. More than 10 days before the trial begins, a party defending against a claim may serve on an opposing party an offer to allow judgment on specified terms, with the costs then accrued. If, within 10 days after being served, the opposing party serves written notice accepting the offer, either party may then file the offer and notice of acceptance, plus proof of service. The clerk must then enter judgment.

(b) Unaccepted Offer. An unaccepted offer is considered withdrawn, but it does not preclude a later offer. Evidence of an unaccepted offer is not admissible except in a proceeding to determine costs.

(c) Offer After Liability Is Determined. When one party's liability to another has been determined but the extent of liability remains to be determined by further proceedings, the party held liable may make an offer of judgment. It must be served within a reasonable time—but at least 10 days—before a hearing to determine the extent of liability.

(d) Paying Costs After an Unaccepted Offer. If the judgment that the offeree finally obtains is not more favorable than the unaccepted offer, the offeree must pay the costs incurred after the offer was made.

(As amended Dec. 27, 1946, eff. Mar. 19, 1948; Feb. 28, 1966, eff. July 1, 1966; Mar. 2, 1987, eff. Aug. 1, 1987; Apr. 30, 2007, eff. Dec. 1, 2007.)

Rule 69. Execution

(a) In General.

(1) *Money Judgment; Applicable Procedure.* A money judgment is enforced by a writ of execution, unless the court directs otherwise. The procedure on execution—and in proceedings supplementary to and in aid of judgment or execution—must accord with the procedure of the state where the court is located, but a federal statute governs to the extent it applies.

(2) *Obtaining Discovery.* In aid of the judgment or execution, the judgment creditor or a successor in interest whose interest appears of record may obtain discovery from any person—including the judgment debtor—as provided in these rules or by the procedure of the state where the court is located.

(b) Against Certain Public Officers. When a judgment has been entered against a revenue officer in the circumstances stated in 28 U.S.C. § 2006, or against an officer of Congress in the circumstances stated in 2 U.S.C. § 118, the judgment must be satisfied as those statutes provide.

(As amended Dec. 29, 1948, eff. Oct. 20, 1949; Mar. 30, 1970, eff. July 1, 1970; Mar. 2, 1987, eff. Aug. 1, 1987; Apr. 30, 2007, eff. Dec. 1, 2007.)

Rule 70. Enforcing a Judgment for a Specific Act

(a) Party's Failure to Act; Ordering Another to Act. If a judgment requires a party to convey land, to deliver a deed or other document, or to perform any other specific act and the party fails to comply within the time specified, the court may order the act to be done—at the disobedient party's expense—by another person appointed by the court. When done, the act has the same effect as if done by the party.

(b) Vesting Title. If the real or personal property is within the district, the court—instead of ordering a conveyance—may enter a judgment divesting any party's title and vesting it in others. That judgment has the effect of a legally executed conveyance.

(c) Obtaining a Writ of Attachment or Sequestration. On application by a party entitled to performance of an act, the clerk must issue a writ of attachment or sequestration against the disobedient party's property to compel obedience.

(d) Obtaining a Writ of Execution or Assistance. On application by a party who obtains a judgment or order for possession, the clerk must issue a writ of execution or assistance.

(e) Holding in Contempt. The court may also hold the disobedient party in contempt.

(As amended Apr. 30, 2007, eff. Dec. 1, 2007.)

* * *

INDEX

References are to Pages

ACCOUNTING FOR PROFITS
Generally, 738–740, 766–768

ADDITUR
Generally, 461–463

ADEQUACY OF LEGAL REMEDY
    See also Equity
    Generally, 79–90
Constructive trust, 771–772
Crime, injunction against, 80
Irreparable injury, compared, 36
Land contracts, 79
Multiplicity of suits, 79
Personal rights, 79–80
Rescission, 744–745
Restitution, 744–745
Specific performance, generally, 85–88

ADMINISTRATIVE LAW
Balancing the equities, 133–134
Equitable discretion, 133–135
Inadequacy rule, 88–90
Remand as remedy, 43–45, 232
Remedies for illegal actions, 185
Ripeness, 428

ADMINISTRATOR
Generally, 227

ALL WRITS ACT
Injunctions binding non violators, 360

ASSUMPSIT
Generally, 732–735

ATTORNEY'S FEES
    Generally, 373–374, 900–974
Administrative proceedings, 938–941
American rule, generally, 901–904
Auction method, 964
Bad faith, 902–903, 904–913
Civil Rights Attorneys' Fees Awards Act, 903, 966–974
Collateral litigation, 907–908, 911
Common fund, 903, 905
Conflict of interest, 966–974
Contempt, 324
Contingent fees, 944–946
Contingent fees, taxation of, 631–639
Contracts, 747

ATTORNEY'S FEES—Cont'd
Duplication of effort, 954–955
Eleventh amendment, 373–374
Equal Access to Justice Act, 913, 928, 931–932
Intervenors, 953–954
Interest on award, 948
Lodestar, 930, 948–965
Percentage of fund approach, 964–965
Prevailing parties, 901–904, 905, 913–930, 950, 967
Private attorney general, 905, 913
Pro se litigants, 927–928
Publicity efforts, 954
Rate of compensation, 941–948, 961–963
Reasonableness, 928–929, 941–965
Restitution, 748
Rule 68 fees, 973–974
Substantial benefit theory, 903–904
Travel expenses, 955–956

AVOIDABLE CONSEQUENCES
    Generally, 461, 502, 543–550, 608
Contract, 580, 608
Contributory negligence and assumption of risk distinguished, 543
Seat belt rule, 546, 549
Tort, 502, 543–550

BALANCING THE EQUITIES
    See also Injunctions; Preliminary Injunctions
    Generally, 36, 90–134, 850–851
Prejudgment interest, 613–614, 616
Relation to damage caps, 502–504

BIVENS ACTION
Generally, 12–28

CERTAINTY
    Generally, 460–461, 501–502, 538–543
Contract breach, damages, 568–570, 578–580
Difficulty of proof, 501–502
Future harm, 538–543
Specific performance, 182–183
Torts, damages, 490–493, 497–498, 499–500

CHANCELLOR
See Equity

CIVIL CONTEMPT
See Contempt

991

CIVIL ECONOMIC SANCTIONS
See also Punitive Damages
Generally, 529–557
Due process, 803–817
Ex parte seizure, 803–817
Forfeiture, 651–661, 786, 803–817
Forfeiture, first amendment concerns, 557
Jury trial, 538
Recapture standard, 529–539

CIVIL RIGHTS
See also *Bivens* Action; Injunctions
Actions for damages, 12–18, 442–450
Attorney's fees, generally, 913–924, 948–965
Declaratory judgment, 418
Elections and voting, 45–46,137–138, 203, 446, 448
Employment discrimination, 244, 245–254, 361–364
First amendment, 36, 37–43, 137–138, 446, 448
Gang injunctions, 153–155
Housing discrimination, 366–408
Institutions for the developmentally disabled, 8, 233–238, 372–373, 375–376
Nominal damages, 444
Police misconduct, 12–28, 46–52, 62–75, 507–511
Prison conditions, 254–267
School desegregation, 49, 107–112, 155–182, 273–282, 328–336, 372, 376–386, 408–414
Section 1983 actions, 18, 30–31, 46–53, 442–450, 506–511
Value of constitutional rights, 442–450

CLEAN UP DOCTRINE
Generally, 452

COLLATERAL BAR RULE
Generally, 328–336

COLLATERAL SOURCE RULE
Generally, 502–504

COLLECTION OF JUDGMENTS
Attachment, 803, 843–844
Bankruptcy, 820, 829–831, 844
Body execution, 810–814
Bond requirement, 794–797, 817–820
Civil forfeiture, 803–817
Consumer Credit Protection Act, 836–841
Denver boot, 800
Discovery, 819
ERISA, 840
Exempt property, 823, 831, 829–836, 841
Garnishment, 828–829, 836–841
Homesteading, 823, 829–831, 834–835
Judgment lien, 823–828
Lis pendens, 787–799
Prejudgment seizure, 803–817
Replevin, 802–803
Sales and auctions, 308, 828, 830, 841–844, 877–881
Self-help, 801
Sister State Money Judgments Act, 823–825
Use of contempt, 301–309

COLLECTION OF JUDGMENTS—Cont'd
Writ of execution, 823, 828

COMMINGLED FUNDS
Tracing, 779–786

CONSENT DECREE
Defined, 242, 243
Enforcement of, 233–238
Interpretation and modification, 240–271, 968–970
Negotiating, 242, 253–254, 260–262, 267–269
Successors in office, 269–271

CONSTITUTIONAL TORTS
See *Bivens* Action; Civil Rights

CONSTRUCTIVE TRUSTS
See also Accounting for Profits; Equitable Liens; Restitution; Subrogation
Generally, 718, 720, 720–721, 759–769
Accounting for profits, 767
Adequacy of legal remedy, 765–766
Bankruptcy, 769–774
Bona fide purchasers, 776
Breach of fiduciary duty, 759–769
Commingled funds, tracing, 779–786
Embezzled money, 774–776, 786
Express trusts distinguished, 769–771
Fraud, 772–773
Tracing, 777–779, 779–786

CONTEMPT
Generally, 33–34, 239, 301–328, 386–408
Ability to comply, 302–309, 323, 392–393, 402–403, 848
Civil and criminal, distinguished, 33–34, 301–328
Classification of, 309–310, 322–323
Coercive, civil, 34, 310, 309–310, 322–323, 326–327, 386–412
Collateral bar rule, 150, 336–346
Compensatory, civil, 34, 310, 328
Criminal, 33–34, 301–328
Elements of, 323–325
Imprisonment for debt, 302–309, 312–314, 845–849
Intent, 323–324
Jury trial, 327–328
Notice of order, 187, 348, 358–359
Persons subject to, 346–364, 394–402
Procedures, 327–328
Public officials, 328–336, 364–408
Purpose, 33–34, 299–300, 304–306, 313–314
Sanctions, 299–300, 324
Specificity of order requirement,213–216, 217–218
When parties bound, 328–336

CONTRACTS
See also Covenant of Good Faith; Damages; Liquidated Damages
Avoidable consequences rule, 580
Bad faith breach, 585–599
Consequential damages, 567–568, 600–609
Construction contracts, 112, 575

INDEX

References are to Pages

CONTRACTS—Cont'd
Efficient breach theory, 592–593, 596–597
Employment contracts, 112, 760–765
Expectancy recovery, generally, 572–574
Hadley v. Baxendale, see that topic
Incidental damages, 567–568
Measure of damages, 574–576
Measurement at time of breach, 628–629
Mental distress damages, 576
Mitigation, duty of, 580, 608
Profit losses, generally, 580–582
Punitive damages for breach, 585–599
Reliance damages, 572–574, 579–580
Restitutionary recovery, 741–759
Sale of goods, 567–568
Special damages, generally, 459
Specific Performance, see that topic
Uniform Commercial Code, 567–568, 577, 580, 581, 747

CONVERSION
Generally, 732–734

COPYRIGHT
Profit-based recovery, 739–740

COUNTRY LODGE v. MILLER
Balancing the equities, 90
Choice between an injunction and damages, 33
Choice between legal and equitable remedies, 78
Civil or criminal contempt, 301
Collateral bar rule, 336
The damages option, 456–457
Declaratory judgment, 417–418
Defining the rightful position, 37
Determining compliance with an injunction, 220
Drafting and administering an injunction, 213
Injunctions that coerce persons who are not parties, 346
Injunctions that harm persons who are not proven violators, 359
Injunctions that harm persons who are not proven violators and are not parties, 361
Injunctions that require the cooperation of public officials, 364
Obtaining release from an injunction, 271–272
Paying the attorneys, 901
Plaintiff's conduct, 851
Prejudgment interest, 609–610
Prophylactic orders, 134
Remedies in a public law case, 5
Remedies in a traditional private case, 4
Restitution for benefits conferred, 723
A restitution option, 731
Threat of harm, 54
Valuing damages, 467
Violating anticipated order, 329

COVENANT OF GOOD FAITH AND FAIR DEALING
Generally, 587–588, 593–594

CRIMINAL CONTEMPT
See Contempt

CRIMINAL PROSECUTION
Injunction against, 436

CRIMINAL SANCTIONS
Civil sanctions distinguished, 310–328, 640–661
Double jeopardy, 462–647
Eighth amendment, 659–660, 651–660, 705
Proportionality requirement, 660–661

DAMAGES
See also Economic Analysis of Law; Personal Injury; Prejudgment Interest
Additur, 461–463
Avoidable consequences, see that topic
Caps, 502–504
Certainty, see that topic
Civil rights violations, 442–451
Collateral source rule, 502–504
Commodification, 449, 513
Comparability review, 520–523
Compensatory damages, defined, 444, 448–450
Condemnation, 467–484
Consequential damages, 467–484, 567–568, 600–609
See also Special Damages, this topic
Contingent valuation, 472–484, 527
Cost of repair, 473–477
Day-in-the-life films, 519
Diminished value, 482–483
Earning capacity, 528–534, 620–623
Economic waste, 484, 549
Eggshell or thin-skull plaintiff, 501, 536–538
Expert testimony, value of life, 526–527
Foreseeability, see that topic
Future harm, 538–543
General damages, 459, 463–464
Hedonic damages, 506–515
Incidental damages, 567–568, 746–747
Increased risk, 538–543
Jury argument, 519–520
Lesser-of rule, contract, 483–484
Lesser-of rule, tort, 482–483
Liquidated damages, 461, 582–585
Loss of a chance, 542–543
Loss of consortium, 520–524, 549
Loss of life, 506–515
Market value, 460–461, 467–471
Measurement, 460–461, 515–535, 576
Medical surveillance, 490–496, 498–499
Mental distress, see that topic
Mitigation, duty of, see Avoidable Consequences
Nominal, generally, 445n, 450–452, 485
Non-pecuniary loss, 461, 506–515, 515–523
See also Mental Distress; Loss of Consortium, this topic; Pain and Suffering, this topic
Nuisance, see that topic
Offset, 461, 580
Pain and suffering, 463, 488–490
Pleading, 461–463
Pleading, single controversy rule, 490
Personal injury, see that topic

DAMAGES—Cont'd
Presumed, 446
Property damage, 473–477, 481–484, 486
Punitive, see Punitive Damages
Purpose of, 449–450, 511–514, 520
Redress, 449, 513
Reliance, generally, 572–574
Remittitur, 461–463
Replacement cost, 473–477
Restitution compared, 458–459
Restoration, 473–477
Risk of cancer, 490–493
Section 1983, 442–452
Sentimental value, 471
Single controversy rule, 490
Special damages, 461, 519, 567–568, 603
Survival, 513–515
Taxation, 631–639
Value to owner, 471
Waivers and releases, 461
Wrongful death, 513–515, 543–548

DECLARATORY JUDGMENT
See also Injunctions
Generally, 185, 415–440
Adequacy rule, no requirement, 435
Case or controversy requirement, 418–428
Eleventh amendment, 436
Federal Declaratory Judgment Act, 415–417
Jury trial, 417
Nominal damages compared, 552
Res judicata, 415
Ripeness, 418–429
Subject matter jurisdiction, 436–439
Uniform Declaratory Judgment Act, 415–417, 433

DISCOUNT RATE
See Interest; Present Value

ECONOMIC ANALYSIS OF LAW
Balancing the equities, 92–95
Compensatory damages, purpose, 485
Damages as insurance, 512–513
Efficiency, 84–89, 92–95, 105–106, 476, 596–597, 608–609
Inadequate remedy requirement, 84–89
Internalizing costs, 485
Nonpecuniary harm, 520
Nuisance, 92–95, 105–106
Property rules and liability rules, 34–35, 94–95
Specific performance, 85–89

ECONOMIC HARM
Foreseeability, 498–499, 576–578, 600
Limits on recovery in tort, 607–609
Physical harm and, 499

ELECTIONS
Generally, 45–46, 203

ELECTION OF REMEDIES
Generally, 464–466, 742, 770, 777

ELEVENTH AMENDMENT
See also Immunity, Sovereign

ELEVENTH AMENDMENT—Cont'd
Generally, 369–376, 403, 929
Suit by state, 611

EMOTIONAL DISTRESS
See Mental Distress

EMPLOYMENT
After-acquired evidence, 42
Back pay claims, 454
Discrimination, 42, 245–254, 361–364
Fiduciary duties, 765–766
Wrongful discharge, 589

ENVIRONMENTAL INJURY
CERCLA, 474–484
CERCLA, attorney fees as response cost, 912
Endangered Species Act, 114–121
Federal Water Pollution Control Act, 122–130
Injunction, statutorily mandated, 114–131
Nuisance, injunction against, 92–95
Oil spill, damages, 472–484
Restoration, 473–477

ENVIRONMENTAL PROTECTION AGENCY
Generally, 122–131, 224–225, 230–233

EQUITABLE LIENS
See also Constructive Trusts; Restitution
Generally, 777

EQUITABLE MONETARY RELIEF
Generally, 452–455

EQUITY
Clean up doctrine, 452
Damages contrasted, 452–455
Equitable discretion, 55–59, 155–182
Equitable monetary relief, 452–455
Jurisdiction, 78–79, 351–352, 441, 452
Jury trial, 455–456
Laches, 880–899
Maxims, 79–81
Merger of law and equity, 78–79, 452
Power to tax, 376–386
Rescission, 744–745
Restitution in equity, generally, 720, 727
See also Accounting for Profits; Constructive Trusts; Equitable Liens
Unclean hands, 850–870

ESTOPPEL
Generally, 850, 870–879
Government, against, 870–879

EXEMPLARY DAMAGES
See Punitive Damages

EXEMPTIONS
Generally, 835

EXPECTANCY
See Contracts

FALSE CLAIMS ACT
Generally, 647

INDEX

References are to Pages

FEDERAL RULES OF CIVIL PROCEDURE
See Appendix
Rule 3, p. 649, 849
Rule 13, p. 434
Rule 19, pp. 355, 359, 362, 975–976
Rule 23, pp. 355, 968, 971, 976–978
Rule 24, pp. 359, 363, 978
Rule 25, pp. 356, 978–979
Rule 37, pp. 327–328, 819
Rule 53, pp. 219, 228, 979–981
Rule 54, pp. 71, 981–983
Rule 57, pp. 417, 434, 983
Rule 60, pp. 240, 257–259, 983–984
Rule 62, pp. 819, 984–985
Rule 64, pp. 787, 985–986
Rule 65, pp. 187–188, 210–211, 215, 352–353, 354, 809, 986–987
Rule 65.1, pp. 212, 988
Rule 66, pp. 229, 787, 988
Rule 67, p. 988
Rule 68, pp. 973–974, 988–989
Rule 69, pp. 849, 989
Rule 70, pp. 229, 374, 989–990

FEDERAL RULES OF CRIMINAL PROCEDURE
Rule 6, p. 649
Rule 7, p. 649
Rule 11, p. 316
Rule 15, p. 650
Rule 16, p. 650
Rule 37, p. 316
Rule 46, p. 650

FEDERALISM
Generally, 275, 346–366
Declaratory Relief, 435–436

FORESEEABILITY
See also *Hadley v. Baxendale*
Generally, 460, 499–500, 600–609
Pre-existing condition, eggshell skull, 501
Proximate cause, 500, 608
Tort and contract rules compared, 607–609

FORFEITURE
Generally, 651–661

FRAUD
Generally, 597–598, 741–745, 759–760
Benefit of the bargain, 743–744
Out-of-pocket rule, 743–744

FULL FAITH AND CREDIT CLAUSE
Generally, 113–114, 824–826

GARNISHMENT
Generally, 818–819, 829

HADLEY v. BAXENDALE
Generally, 576–578, 600–609
Contemplation of the parties rule, 577
Proximate cause compared, 608

HAMMURABI, CODE OF
Generally, 1–2, 675

IMMUNITY
See also Eleventh Amendment
Legislative, 390–391, 394–402, 403, 406
Official, 369–376
Sovereign, 369–376

IMPLIED CAUSES OF ACTION
Constitutional, 12–28
Statutory, 28–31

IMPLIED CONTRACT
See Restitution, Assumpsit

IN PARI DELICTO
Generally, 852, 861–870

INADEQUATE REMEDY AT LAW
See Adequacy of Legal Remedy

INCOME TAX
See Taxation of Damage Awards

INFLATION
Generally, 619–631

INJUNCTIONS
Appeals from, 188, 190–204
Balancing the equities, 36, 90–134
Civil Rights, 27
Crimes, injunctions against, 80
Damages actions compared, 34–36
Declaratory judgment compared, 185, 415
Dissolution of, 271–299
Drafting, 213–220
Effect on third parties, 346–364
Elections, 45–46, 203
Endangered Species Act, 114–121
Enforcement, 220, 223–237, 372–386
    See also Contempt
Enforcement against government officials, 328–336, 364–414
Federal Water Pollution Control Act, 122–132
Formulating and administering, 213–240
In rem, 357
Institutional reform, 4–10, 46–53, 233–238, 244, 557
Jury trials, generally, 86
Modification, 240–271
Mootness, 60–62, 71–72
Notice of order, 187–189, 348, 358–359
Out of state activities, 113–115
Parties bound, 346–364, 392
Patent Act, 95–101
Police misconduct, 18–19, 46–53
Power to tax, 376–386
Practicality of enforcement, 36
Preliminary Injunctions, see that topic
Preventive, 52
Prohibitory, 376
Prophylactic injunctions, 36, 134–182, 224, 366
Public interest, 202–203, 208–209
Reparative injunctions, 52
Restricting first amendment rights, 138–155
Rights protected, 75–76, 81–83
Ripeness, 60–62
Schools, integration of, 107–112, 155–182, 273–283, 328–366, 376–386

INJUNCTIONS—Cont'd
Specificity of order, 213–217
Speech, restraint of, 187n, 336–346
Standing, 62–75
Structural, see Institutional reform, this topic
Tax Injunction Act, 88–91
Temporary restraining order, see that topic
Threat of harm, 36, 54–78

INTEREST
Accrual date, 612–617
Compound or simple, 618
Inflation and, 618, 619–631
Legal or market rate, 612, 618
Liquidated and unliquidated claims, 611, 617
Nonpecuniary harm, 617–618
Postjudgment, 619
Prejudgment, 609–619

INTERMEDDLERS
Generally, 727–728

INTERVENTION
Generally, 363, 927

IRREPARABLE HARM
See also Adequacy of Legal Remedy; Equity
Generally, 36, 79, 81–85, 193–195

JUDGMENTS
See also Collection of Judgments
Drafting,
    Aspirational commands, 221–225
    Specificity, 213–220
Enforcement, 452
    See also Contempt
Interest, 609–619
Modification of, 240, 243
Money judgments, 33, 366–369
Periodic payment of, 495–496, 504–505

JURY TRIAL
Generally, 455–456
Contempt cases, 34, 304n, 327–328
Damage awards, 455–456
Declaratory judgment, 417

LACHES
Generally, 850, 874–878, 882–899
Administrative agency, caused by, 874–878
Government as defendant, 874–878
Government as plaintiff, 878–879
Specific performance, 898
Statutes of limitation compared, 880–899
Trademark, 892–899

LIQUIDATED DAMAGES
Generally, 461, 582–585

LOST VOLUME SELLER
Generally, 580–582

MAGNA CARTA
Generally, 843

MAXIMS OF EQUITY
Generally, 79–81, 309

MEASUREMENT
Comparability review, 520–523, 527–528
Contingent valuation, 527
Expert testimony, value of life, 527
Nonpecuniary harm, 515–528

MEDIATORS
Generally, 227

MENTAL DISTRESS
Generally, 515–528
Contract breach, 609
Fear of cancer, 488–490, 499
Loss of consortium, 520–524
Ratio to actual damages, 711
Sentimental value, 471
Wrongful death cases generally, 513–515

MONEY JUDGMENTS
See Judgments, Collection of Judgments

MONITORS
Generally, 226–227, 238–240, 940

MUTUALITY OF REMEDY
Generally, 183

NOMINAL DAMAGES
Generally, 445n, 450–452
Declaratory judgments, compared, 452
Punitive damages, relation, 451–452

NUISANCE
Coming to the nuisance, 103–105
Damages, 488
Indemnity, cost of compliance, 105–106
Injunction, 100–107, 360

OFFICIAL IMMUNITY
See Immunity

PATENT ACT
Generally, 95–101

PERSONAL INJURY
    See also Mental Distress, Damages, Taxation of Damage Awards
Avoidable consequences, 502, 543–550
Collateral source rule, 502–504
Diminished life expectancy, 515
Earning capacity, 528–534, 620–623
Eggshell, or thin-skull plaintiff, 536–538
Golden rule argument, 519
Inflation, 619–631
Loss of future earnings, 528–534
Lost wages, 528–534
Nonpecuniary harm, 515–528
Per diem arguments, 519
Periodic payments, 504–505
Present value, 619–631
Probability of future illness, 501–502, 538–543

PRACTICALITY
See Injunctions

PRELIMINARY INJUNCTIONS
Abuse of discretion, 188
Alternative test, 204–210
Appealability, 188

INDEX 997

References are to Pages

PRELIMINARY INJUNCTIONS—Cont'd
Balancing the hardships, 204–210
Bond, amount of recovery under, 187, 188, 212
Public interest, 202–203
Ripeness of dispute, 60–62
Security requirement, 210–212
Standards for issuance, 189–210
Status quo, preservation of, 189, 201–202
Temporary restraining order, distinguished, 187–189
Traditional requirements for, 187–189
Types of, 52

PRESENT VALUE
Defined, 622–623
Discount rate, 623–627, 630
In contract cases, 628–631
In tort cases, 619–631

PRISON LITIGATION REFORM ACT
Injunctions limited by, 281–299
Damages barred by, 27–28, 448–449

PROBLEMS
See also Country Lodge v. Miller
Moore v. Regents, 759
Racially Biased Election, 45–46
Tracing Problem, 786
Unauthorized Merchants, 188

PROHIBITION, WRIT OF
Injunction, compared, 183–184

PROPORTIONALITY
Criminal sentences, 660–661

PROVISIONAL REMEDIES
See Collection of Judgments; Preliminary Injunctions; Temporary Restraining Order

PUBLIC LAW LITIGATION
Generally, 4–10, 12, 552–564

PUNITIVE DAMAGES
Generally, 661–716
Actual damage requirement, 451–452, 748
Contract breach, 572, 585–599, 662
Disgorgement of profits, 738
Due process, 696–711
Eighth amendment, 659–660
Insurance, 673
Malice defined, 666–667
Mass torts, 663
Nominal damages, sufficiency, 451–452
Products liability, 662–663
Ratio to actual damages, 673–689, 707, 711–717
Remittitur, 708–710
Restitution, 742, 748
Standards for award, 669–670, 673–689
Statutory reforms, 669–670
Statutory violations, 689–690
Theories of punishment, 641
Treble damages, 641–642
Wealth of defendant, 669–670, 708

QUASI-CONTRACT
See Assumpsit; Restitution

RACIAL PROFILING
Generally, 73

RECEIVERS
Generally, 228, 300, 366–367, 405, 787

REFORMATION
Generally, 439–440

REMITTITUR
Generally, 461–463
Punitive damages, 709–710

REPLEVIN
Generally, 184–185, 722

RESCISSION
See Restitution

RESTATEMENT OF RESTITUTION
Section 1, p. 717
Section 2, pp. 727–728
Section 3, p. 737
Section 15, p. 730
Section 112, pp. 728–729
Section 115, p. 729
Section 117, p. 729
Section 151, p. 740
Section 157, p. 740
Section 158, p. 779
Section 160, p. 772
Section 190, p. 766
Section 205, p. 779
Tracing rules, 779–786

RESTATEMENT (SECOND) OF CONFLICT OF LAWS
Section 53, pp. 113–116
Section 102, pp. 113–117

RESTATEMENT (SECOND) OF CONTRACTS
Section 342, p. 662
Section 344, pp. 572, 597
Section 347, pp. 502, 575, 580
Section 349, p. 580
Section 351, p. 578
Section 352, p. 578
Section 355, p. 572
Section 356, p. 580
Section 362, pp. 182–183
Section 366, p. 112

RESTATEMENT (SECOND) OF TORTS
Section 283B, pp. 548–549
Section 461, p. 544
Section 901, p. 485
Section 906, p. 500
Section 908, pp. 661, 667
Section 924, p. 485
Section 928, pp. 481, 486
Section 929, p. 488
Section 945, p. 185
Section 946, p. 185

RESTATEMENT (THIRD) OF RESTITUTION
Section 1, p. 722
Section 9, p. 729
Section 10, p. 728
Section 20, p. 729
Section 21, p. 729

RESTITUTION
　　See also Constructive Trust; Restatement of Restitution
Generally, 717–723
Assumpsit, 732–735
Choice principle, 728
Constructive Trusts, see that topic
Contract breach, 572–574, 576, 741–759, 766
Damages, compared, 458–459
Defendant's profits, 738–740, 748–759, 759–769
Fiduciaries, 759–769
Fraud, 741–744
Gift principle, 728
Implied in fact contract, distinguished, 720–721, 726
Incidental damages, 741–743, 746–747
Loss contracts, 755–756
Market encouragement, 728
Measurement, 732–740, 736–740
Mistake, generally, 723–731
Mistaken payments, 730
Preservation of property, 728–729
Punitive damages, 742, 748
Quasi-contract, 718, 721
Rescission, 741–759
Tortiously acquired benefits, 732–735
Tracing, generally, 779–786
Unenforceable agreements, 745–746
Unrequested services, 729–730
Waiving the tort, 732–736

RIGHTFUL POSITION
　　See also Balancing the Equities
Generally, 3, 375, 458–459
Contract claims, 458–459, 572–574
Defendants', 3. See generally Restitution
Microsoft litigation, 53–54
Plaintiffs', 3, 37–46, 53–54
　　Awarding less than, 90–134
　　Awarding more than, 112, 124–182, 405
Tort claims, 458–459, 499

SATELLITE HOME VIEWER ACT
Generally, 59

SEPARATION OF POWERS
Generally, 364–366, 372–376

SEPTEMBER 11th FUND
　　Generally, 484
Agent Orange litigation and, 552
Collateral source rule, 502–504
Hedonic damages, loss of life, 511–512
Loss of future earnings, 534
Nonpecuniary harm, 528

SOVEREIGN IMMUNITY
See Eleventh Amendment; Immunity

SPECIAL MASTERS
Enforcing injunctions, 226, 228–229, 233–238, 300
Settlement, 553–557

SPECIFIC PERFORMANCE
　　See also Adequacy of Legal Remedy; Equity; Injunctions
Generally, 85–90, 182–183
Land contract, generally, 79
Supervision, 112–114

STANDING
Generally, 62–75

STATUTES OF LIMITATIONS
Generally, 880–892
Equitable tolling, 899

STRUCTURAL INJUNCTION
See Injunctions; Institutional Reform

SUBROGATION
Generally, 777

TAXATION OF DAMAGE AWARDS
Generally, 631–639
Attorney's fees, 631–639
Interest, 638–639
Personal injury, 636–638

TEMPORARY RESTRAINING ORDER
Appealability, 188
Constitutional limitations, 187
Ex parte orders, 187
Irreparable harm, 186
Notice requirements, 187
Prejudgment attachment, compared, 802–803
Preliminary injunction, distinguished, 187–189
Replevin, compared, 802–803
Security requirement, 187, 212
Standards for issuance, 189–211

TORT REFORM
Collateral source rule, 502–504
Constitutionality, 31, 504, 524–525, 691–695
Damage caps, 502–504
Medical malpractice, 503
Pain and suffering, 448, 504–505
Periodic payment of judgments, 504–505
Punitive damages, 689–690

TORT
See Conversion, Constitutional Torts, Damages, Nuisance, Personal Injury, Trespass, Wrongful Death

TRESPASS
Remedies, generally, 37, 104

UNCLEAN HANDS
Generally, 850–870
Collateral matters, 855

UNJUST ENRICHMENT
See Restitution

VALUE
    Generally, 467–484
    Contingent valuation, 472–484
    Cost of repair and market value, 481–482
    Cost-less-depreciation, 467–484
    Discounted cash flow, 471
    Economic waste, 484
    Income approach, 471
    Market data approach, 471
    Market value, 467–484
    Restoration, 472–484
    Sentimental value, 471
    Value to owner, 471

WAIVER
    See also Estoppel

WAIVER—Cont'd
Generally, 870

WAIVER OF TORT
Generally, 732–736

WRITS, JUDICIAL
Attachment, 818–819
Ejectment, 184–186
Execution, 452, 824, 826–827
Habeas Corpus, 183–184, 183–185
Mandamus, 183–185
Prohibition, 183–186
Replevin, 184–187, 452

WRONGFUL DEATH
Generally, 513–515

†